MODERN SOUTHEAST ASIA SERIES

James R. Reckner, *General Editor*

■ Vietnam Chronicles

Vietnam Chronicles

THE ABRAMS TAPES
1968–1972

■

TRANSCRIBED, SELECTED, EDITED,
ANNOTATED, AND WITH AN
INTRODUCTORY ESSAY BY
LEWIS SORLEY

TEXAS TECH UNIVERSITY PRESS

This book is typeset in Times Roman. The acid-free paper used in this book meets the minimum requirements of ANSI/NISO Z39.48-1992 (R1997).

LIBRARY OF CONGRESS CATALOGING-IN-PUBLICATION DATA

Vietnam chronicles : the Abrams tapes, 1968-1972 / transcribed, selected, edited, annotated and with an introductory essay by Lewis Sorley.

    p.   cm. — (Modern Southeast Asia series)

  Includes bibliographical references and index.

  ISBN 0-89672-533-2 (alk. paper)

  1. Vietnamese Conflict, 1961-1975—United States. 2. United States—History—1961-1969.

3. United States—History—1969- 4. Abrams, Creighton W. (Creighton Williams), 1914-1974.

I. Sorley, Lewis, 1934- II. Series.

  DS558.V478 2004

  959.704'3373—dc22

                                   2004002747

Printed in the United States of America

FIRST EDITION

04 05 06 07 08 09 10 11 12 / 9 8 7 6 5 4 3 2 1

Texas Tech University Press
Box 41037
Lubbock, Texas 79409-1037 USA
800.832.4042
www.ttup.ttu.edu

For the people of South Vietnam

CONTENTS

PROLOGUE   xvii

ACKNOWLEDGMENTS   xxiii

READING THE TEXT   xxv

■ 1968   I

■ 1969   89

■ 1970   333

■ 1971   513

■ 1972   737

APPENDIX I   MEETING PARTICIPANTS   881

APPENDIX 2   VIETNAMESE NAMED
    IN MEETINGS   888

GLOSSARY OF SELECTED TERMS,
    ACRONYMS, AND ABBREVIATIONS   891

INDEX   897

ILLUSTRATIONS

(following page 316)

Fig. 1   William Colby, General Abrams, and Ellsworth Bunker.

Fig. 2   Ellsworth Bunker with General Abrams.

Fig. 3   Adm. John S. McCain Jr.

Fig. 4   Maj. Gen. Phillip B. Davidson Jr.

Fig. 5   General Abrams, President Johnson, Vice President Humphrey, and Gen. Earle Wheeler.

Fig. 6   General Abrams with Gen. Andrew Goodpaster.

Fig. 7   Gen. Harold K. Johnson.

Fig. 8   Lt. Col. Donald Marshall.

Fig. 9   Gen. George Brown, Gen. Andrew Goodpaster, General Abrams, William Colby, Lt. Gen. Frank Mildren, and Vice Adm. Elmo Zumwalt.

Fig. 10   Gen. Robert E. Cushman.

Fig. 11   Scene of destruction in Nha Trang after the 1968 Tet Offensive.

Fig. 12   President Nguyen Van Thieu.

Fig. 13   Caskets of some of the 3,000 victims of an enemy massacre at Hue.

Fig. 14   The Ho Chi Minh Trail near the Mu Gia Pass.

Fig. 15   Gen. George S. Brown.

Fig. 16   General Abrams with retired Gen. Bruce C. Clarke, visiting Vietnam.

Fig. 17   Gen. Ralph E. Haines Jr.

Fig. 18   Robert Komer.

Fig. 19   General Abrams with Secretary of Defense Melvin Laird and General Wheeler.

Fig. 20   General Abrams, President Nixon, Secretary of Defense Laird, and General Wheeler.

Fig. 21   Col. Donn A. Starry.

Fig. 22   President Nixon meeting U.S. troops during his July 1969 visit to Saigon.

Fig. 23   Part of Marine redeployment of forces, July 1969.

Fig. 24   U.S. tanks on the move near Khe Sanh, July 1969.

Fig. 25   Gen. Earle Wheeler, Lt. Gen. "Dutch" Kerwin, Secretary of Defense Laird, and General Abrams.

Fig. 26   Gen. William B. Rosson.

Fig. 27   Maj. Gen. George Forsythe with General Abrams.

Fig. 28   Lt. Gen. Julian J. Ewell with ARVN Lt. Gen. Do Cao Tri.

Fig. 29   Vice Adm. Elmo R. Zumwalt.

Fig. 30   Maj. Gen. William E. Potts.

Fig. 31   Secretary of the Army Stanley R. Resor.

Fig. 32   Col. George S. Patton.

(following page 636)

Fig. 33   Lt. Gen. Walter T. Kerwin Jr. with ARVN Lt. Gen. Do Cao Tri and Lt. Gen. Le Nguyen Khang.

Fig. 34   Maj. Gen. Ngo Quang Truong.

Fig. 35   General Abrams and Lt. Gen. Herman Nickerson greet Lt. Gen. Hoang Xuan Lam.

Fig. 36   A 240-mm rocket, part of a huge cache found northwest of Saigon.

Fig. 37   A B-52 bomber delivering its ordnance.

Fig. 38   The legendary John Paul Vann with Lt. Gen. Walter T. Kerwin Jr.

Fig. 39   General Abrams and Gen. Fred Weyand sharing a birthday.

Fig. 40   General Abrams briefing a visiting *Time-Life* group.

Fig. 41   Adm. Thomas H. Moorer.

Fig. 42   The MACV complex at Tan Son Nhut Air Base.

Fig. 43   South Vietnamese troops stacking ammunition captured in Cambodia.

Fig. 44   Helicopters were *the* tactical innovation of the Vietnam War.

Fig. 45   "Miracle rice" gave South Vietnamese farmers better and more crops.

Fig. 46   Abrams presenting the U.S. Legion of Merit to Gen. Cao Van Vien.

Fig. 47   ARVN Col. Hoang Ngoc Lung.

Fig. 48   Adm. John S. McCain Jr. being briefed on riverine operations.

Fig. 49   General Abrams with Col. James H. Leach.

Fig. 50   General Abrams awarding the Presidential Unit Citation.

Fig. 51 Maj. Gen. Edward Bautz Jr.

Fig. 52 Ambassador Ellsworth Bunker.

Fig. 53 Col. George Jacobson with Nguyen Cao Ky and Edward Lansdale.

Fig. 54 Martha Raye with General Abrams.

Fig. 55 Charles Whitehouse with William Colby.

Fig. 56 December 1971 newspaper photograph of a GI reading his mail.

Fig. 57 Shattered remains of a U.S. helicopter.

Fig. 58 Gen. John Lavelle with General Abrams.

Fig. 59 Gen. John W. Vogt.

Fig. 60 Brig. Gen. James F. Hollingsworth.

Fig. 61 President Nguyen Van Thieu, Brig. Gen. Le Van Hung, and Gen. Cao Van Vien.

Fig. 62 Deputy Ambassador Samuel Berger with General Abrams.

Fig. 63 President Nguyen Van Thieu with President Richard Nixon.

Fig. 64 General Abrams greeted by Dezvil, the war dog.

MAPS

MAP 1 SOUTHEAST ASIA   2

MAP 2 SOUTH VIETNAM   5

MAP 3 ENEMY INFILTRATION ROUTES   7

MAP 4 AIR WAR TARGET SECTORS   102

MAP 5 1970 CAMBODIAN INCURSION   409

MAP 6 OPERATION LAM SON 719   526

MAP 7 1972 EASTER OFFENSIVE   802

Long after the war was over, after the fighting had ended, after Bunker was dead, and Abrams too, after the boat people and all the other sad detritus of a lost cause, the eldest of General Abrams's three sons, all Army officers, was on the faculty of the Command & General Staff College at Fort Leavenworth. There someone reminded him of what Robert Shaplen had once said, that his father deserved a better war. "He didn't see it that way," young Creighton responded at once. "He thought the Vietnamese were worth it."

LEWIS SORLEY, *A Better War*

PROLOGUE

THE LONG YEARS of American involvement in the Vietnam War began with an advisory role, supplemented by the provision of logistical, communications, and intelligence assistance to the South Vietnamese. Then, responding to a battle-field crisis and commencing in the spring of 1965, U.S. ground forces in rapidly increasing numbers were introduced into the war. During his tenure, Gen. William C. Westmoreland, who served during 1964–1968 as Commander, U.S. Military Assistance Command, Vietnam, made repeated requests for additional forces, requests that were for several years almost routinely approved and resulted in a buildup to an authorization of 549,500 U.S. troops for South Vietnam and actual deployments there that peaked at 543,400 in April 1969.

A major accomplishment of the earlier years of American involvement was massive upgrading of South Vietnam's infrastructure to enable it to support deployment of forces of such magnitude. Indeed, in many respects the logistical base lagged the troop buildup. In his memoirs General Westmoreland acknowl-edged his "gamble" in bringing in troops before he had developed the logistical system needed to support them. As the base system evolved, however, it was an impressive feat that also contributed to South Vietnam's economic well-being in important ways. Using a combination of military and contractor capabilities, West-moreland recalled, MACV oversaw upgrading of Saigon's deep-draft port and construction of six others, increasing the number of jet-capable airfields from 3 to 8 and adding 84 tactical airstrips and countless helicopter landing pads, building millions of square feet of covered and cold-storage facilities, putting up a nation-wide grid of radio and telephone communications, dredging canals, and building or upgrading innumerable roads and bridges. The construction also included establishment of fairly elaborate "base camps" housing the major units deployed, controversial in that they necessitated use of many troops for their own operation and security. The bulk of what Westmoreland called this "convulsive" construction effort was completed in about two and a half years and constituted, as he justifi-ably described it, "one of the more remarkable accomplishments of American forces in Vietnam."

On the combat front, General Westmoreland, left to devise his own strategic and tactical approaches, chose to fight a war of attrition in which the primary tactic was employment of large formations in "search and destroy" operations designed to find and inflict casualties on the enemy. In this "war of the big battalions" the measure of merit was "body count," meaning simply the number of enemy dead achieved, the premise being that if sufficient casualties were inflicted the enemy would thereby be dissuaded from further aggression against the South Vietnamese.

This approach essentially shouldered South Vietnam's armed forces out of the way, relegating them to secondary roles and greatly impairing their development while U.S. forces were soaking up most of the combat wherewithal—helicopters, air and naval gunfire support, new and improved weaponry, and airlift. At the same time, pacification, including the crucial task of neutralizing enemy infrastructure in South Vietnam's hamlets and villages, was largely ignored. As a consequence, the large numbers of casualties inflicted on the enemy had little impact on the outcome of the war. This reality was underscored by the enemy's 1968 Tet Offensive, a coordinated series of countrywide attacks that cast doubt on the accuracy and candor of recent optimistic forecasts by General Westmoreland and President Lyndon Johnson's administration.

■ ■ ■

Soon after Tet 1968 it was announced that in June of that year General Westmoreland would return to Washington for a new assignment as Army Chief of Staff. He was to be succeeded as U.S. commander in Vietnam by Gen. Creighton W. Abrams.

Abrams had come out to Vietnam in May 1967, assigned as deputy to Westmoreland but expecting to succeed him in the top command within a matter of weeks. As things turned out, however, that succession was delayed for over a year, time during which Abrams occupied himself primarily with working to upgrade South Vietnam's armed forces.

Abrams, a 1936 graduate of West Point—where his classmates included Westmoreland and also Bruce Palmer Jr., another officer who reached four-star rank and played a prominent role during the Vietnam era—first served in the waning days of the horse cavalry, then joined the newly formed 4th Armored Division as World War II approached. During most of that conflict he commanded the 37th Tank Battalion in the fighting across Europe, often as the vanguard of Gen. George S. Patton's Third Army. Abrams led the attack that relieved the 101st Airborne Division when it was encircled at Bastogne during the Battle of the Bulge, and his was the first unit in Third Army to reach the Rhine. In the process Abrams was awarded two Distinguished Service Crosses and a battlefield promotion to colonel.

During the early 1960s, as a major general stationed in the Pentagon, Abrams earned a reputation for coolness and tact when, as personal representative of the Army Chief of Staff, he was on the scene at a number of civil rights crises where army troops were deployed. Back in Europe he commanded the 3rd Armored Division and then V Corps before returning to Washington in 1964 as Army Vice Chief of Staff. His three years in that post gave him a key role in the buildup in Vietnam of the forces he was now to command.

■ ■ ■

Abrams brought to the post a markedly different outlook on the conflict and how it ought to be conducted. Pronouncing it "One War" in which combat operations, improvement of South Vietnamese forces, and pacification were of equal importance and priority, Abrams switched from "search and destroy" to "clear and hold" tactics and from multibattalion assaults into the deep jungle to operations by smaller units mounting a multitude of patrols and ambushes. These operations were designed to protect the people, especially those in South Vietnam's rural hamlets and villages. Under this approach the measure of merit became simply population security.

Some commentators on the war, including even some of the army's official historians, have argued that the changes from Westmoreland to Abrams were evolutionary rather than revolutionary, and that in any event they stemmed largely from failure of the enemy's 1968 Tet Offensive, the heavy losses he incurred at that time, and the changes of strategy and tactics he consequently adopted. But the tapes illustrate conclusively that such an interpretation is not supported by the battlefield realities, for after Tet 1968 the enemy tried repeatedly—in May of 1968, again in August–September 1968, and at Tet 1969—to achieve major military victories through general offensives, even though he continued to suffer very heavy casualties with nothing to show in return. It was not until after Tet 1969, as reflected in COSVN Resolution 9 of July 1969, that the enemy gave up on this approach.

Likewise, it is clear from this material that it was not—as army historians maintain—in response to pressures from Washington that Abrams and MACV begin emphasizing improvement of South Vietnam's military forces. Rather, that thrust was a principal concern of General Abrams during the year he spent as deputy commander, a year he devoted primarily to upgrading South Vietnamese forces. It was when Abrams came to that task, and not before, that South Vietnamese forces, both regular and territorial, began to recover from the effects of long-term neglect and to receive weaponry that was comparable to that issued to U.S. forces, and indeed comparable to that long employed by the enemy.

Complementing these tactical innovations and strenuous efforts to upgrade South Vietnamese armed forces was the equally important effort to advance pacification across the country, both economically and through provision of greater security. An essential aspect was rooting out the Viet Cong infrastructure that had long dominated the rural population through terror and coercion.

The changes in top command, in concept of the nature of the war, in strategy and tactics, and in equal emphasis on all key aspects of the war were dramatic, but they were not the only differences in these latter years of American involvement. The progressive buildup of American forces in the early years was now reversed by a phased withdrawal. The newly elected administration of President Richard Nixon emphasized turning the war back to the South Vietnamese in a program titled "Vietnamization," also enunciating a "Nixon Doctrine" in which allies would bear primary responsibility for providing the manpower for their own defense, while the United States supplied primarily logistics, fire support, and financial assistance.

■ ■ ■

Weekly Intelligence Estimate Update (WIEU) sessions had been inaugurated during General Westmoreland's tenure as a means of periodically taking stock of the situation and what was being done, and should be done, about it. When General Abrams assumed command, he continued the practice but, as is apparent in the transcripts, persistently pushed to broaden both the content and the robustness of the underlying analyses presented. As the staff reacted to this guidance, the actual name of the sessions—"Intelligence Estimate Update"—became less and less descriptive of the wider range of topics and issues addressed.

Often Abrams would direct that a briefing be prepared on some aspect that interested him, then use that briefing as a springboard for wide-ranging discussion of the matter. While the WIEUs were initially concerned primarily with military aspects of the war, under Abrams they evolved into more and more comprehensive considerations of political, economic, and psychological considerations—along with, of course, the military situation—and included relevant material dealing with North Vietnam, the Viet Cong, Laos and Cambodia, the South Vietnamese, and domestic policy and budgetary issues in the United States.

Accordingly, the WIEU agenda underwent substantial modification over the years, both in terms of what was presented and in the order of presentation. Generally speaking, combat operations within South Vietnam got progressively less emphasis, while such topics as pacification and upgrading South Vietnam's armed forces got much more attention. A fairly typical agenda drawn from January 1970 will serve to illustrate: Weather; Out-Country; Seventh Air Force Current Operations Update; In-Country: I CTZ, II CTZ, III CTZ, IV CTZ; NAVFORV Current Operations Update; Combat Operations Summary. Following (for a smaller group): SOG Wrapup.

■ ■ ■

Tape recordings of Weekly Intelligence Estimate Updates constitute the bulk of the material in this compilation. They are from the period June 1968 to June 1972, the years General Abrams was in formal command of U.S. forces in Vietnam. Other sessions covered by the recordings include visits by the secretary of defense; the secretary of the army; the Chairman of the Joint Chiefs of Staff; the Commander in Chief, Pacific; and such others as British counterinsurgency specialist Sir Robert Thompson. All formed part of what I have termed the "Abrams Special Collection."

There are 455 tapes in the collection. Of the old reel-to-reel variety, they constitute more than 2,000 hours of briefings and discussion. These materials were brought back from Vietnam by Abrams when, in June 1972, he returned to Washington for assignment as Army Chief of Staff. When, just over two years later, Abrams died in office, the tapes were sequestered and their existence and location classified top secret. After having published a biography of Abrams, I was told about the tapes by friendly military officers who thought they should be exploited for their historical value.

With help from Brig. Gen. Harold W. Nelson, then Army Chief of Military History, and the approval of Army Chief of Staff Gen. Gordon R. Sullivan, I was granted access to the tapes for research purposes. They were located at Carlisle Barracks, Pennsylvania, under custody of the U.S. Army War College and administered by archivists of the U.S. Army Military History Institute.

It took me exactly a year of weekdays, up to 10 hours a day wearing headphones in a vault, to screen the tapes. In the process I produced almost 3,200 single-spaced pages of handwritten notes and extracts, material that ran to over 835,000 words. After my notes had been cleared by the appropriate government agencies, I used them in preparing my book *A Better War: The Unexamined Victories and Final Tragedy of America's Last Years in Vietnam.*

It was clear, however, that there was more on the tapes—and in the notes—of interest to scholars and historians of the war than could be included in that one book. That realization led to my decision to publish an annotated collection of extensive excerpts. In deciding what material to include, I have been guided by an excellent suggestion I came across somewhere to the effect that a biographer should include everything that is either important or interesting. The tapes offered a rich selection of both, so the only hard part has been deciding what to omit in order to wind up with a publication of reasonable proportions.

There are a number of engrossing stories that run through the tapes and the years they reflect. These include the changes of strategy and tactics for conduct of the war, development of South Vietnam's armed forces, the pacification program and neutralization of the enemy infrastructure among the rural populace, progressive withdrawal of American forces, intelligence breakthroughs in monitoring infiltration down the Ho Chi Minh Trail, interdiction of traffic on that trail, combat incursions into Cambodia and Laos, major battles culminating in the 1972 Easter Offensive, land reform, enemy adaptations to changes in their battlefield fortunes, maturation of South Vietnam's leadership, resumption of the air campaign against North Vietnam, political-military relations in Washington as they spilled over onto American leaders in Saigon, increasingly difficult budget strictures, the impact of negotiations in Paris on conduct of the war, and of course the interplay of colorful and sometimes volatile personalities among both Americans and Vietnamese involved in conduct of the war.

Given that the tapes were made for the most part at MACV, it is not surprising that the most prominent personality represented on them is the commander, Creighton Abrams. But there are many, many other interesting participants in the taped discussions, including Ambassador Ellsworth Bunker, who served a remarkable six years as head of the American embassy in Saigon; William Colby, who directed the pacification program under Abrams with skill and sensitivity; such prominent visitors as Secretary of Defense Melvin Laird; Gen. Earle Wheeler, Chairman of the Joint Chiefs of Staff (1964–1970), and his successor, Adm. Thomas Moorer (1970–1974); Adm. John McCain, Commander in Chief, Pacific; and a collection of usually anonymous and often superb briefers.

Many of the tape boxes contained printed rosters of those present at the session recorded; often an agenda of the meeting was also included. In other cases the names of attendees were read onto the tape by a staff officer (and in yet others no mention was made of who attended). As a result, spelling of the names of some of the less well known people in attendance is sometimes phonetic. The present text includes, besides annotations, a consolidated listing and identification of the people who took part in the sessions recorded, a separate listing of Vietnamese personalities mentioned on the tapes, and a glossary of selected terms, acronyms, and abbreviations to assist those not familiar with the personalities and jargon of the period.

As this publication goes to press, the tapes from which it was drawn are still highly classified. Perhaps they will in due course be declassified and made available to scholars, although the enormous labor that would be involved in screening them and producing complete transcripts may make that infeasible. In the meantime it is hoped that this collection of excerpts will prove useful to researchers of the period and to readers with a general historical interest in the later years of the war in Vietnam.

ACKNOWLEDGMENTS

OVER THE YEARS my work has been assisted by many people, both those with firsthand knowledge of the events of interest and the indispensable community of archivists, librarians, researchers, and historians upon whom so much depends.

In the process of screening the tape recordings on which these volumes are based, then seeing the resulting transcripts through declassification, there is no one to whom I owe more than Mr. Randy Rakers, security manager at the U.S. Army Military History Institute, who assisted me in accessing the materials, reviewed my notes on the army's behalf, performed the laborious tasks of duplicating the notes and forwarding them for review to the other agencies concerned, and helped me get those agencies to respond. This is the fourth book on which I have had his assistance, and my admiration for his energy, good will, and ability has continued to grow over the years of our association.

At the U.S. Army Military History Institute at Carlisle Barracks, I have been assisted by virtually every member of the staff in one way or another. Dr. Richard Sommers, chief archivist, has been a particularly supportive and helpful friend, as has David Keough of his staff.

My work in the Indochina Archive at the University of California, Berkeley, from which a number of the photographs came before the archive relocated to Texas Tech University, was assisted immeasurably by the interest of the late Dr. Douglas Pike, founder and curator of that collection and a valued friend.

While serving as Army Chief of Military History, Brig. Gen. Harold W. Nelson was instrumental in arranging my access to the MACV tapes and in recommending to Gen. Gordon R. Sullivan, then Army Chief of Staff, that he approve that research. Once again Albert D. McJoynt assisted me by preparing excellent maps, for which I am most grateful. My friends Gen. John A. Shaud (USAF), Lt. Gen. Robert D. Beckel (USAF), Rear Adm. Peter A. C. Long (USN), Maj. Gen. Henry M. Hobgood (USAF), Dr. John Carland, and Col. David E. Farnham were very helpful in identifying many of the people who attended the MACV strategy sessions, as was Lt. Gen. William E. Potts, the incomparable impresario of those complex events. Extensive help in identifying the Vietnamese cited in the text was also provided by Col. Viet Mai Ha (ARVN), a valued friend since we were captains together in the Armor Advance Course at Fort Knox in 1961–1962. Another friend, Merle Pribbenow, brought an encyclopedic knowledge derived from his long service in Southeast Asia to helping identify people and places mentioned in the recordings. His help in particular was invaluable.

The staff of Texas Tech University Press have been a delight to work with, and I am grateful to them for bringing this project to completion. I must also record my great respect and admiration for Dr. James Reckner, director of the Vietnam Center at Texas Tech, for his vision, energy, and commitment to preserving and making available to scholars and general readers alike the history of the Vietnam War in all its complex aspects.

Professor Andrew Wiest, University of Southern Mississippi, and Dr. Jeffrey J. Clarke, chief historian of the U.S. Army Center of Military History, read the manuscript in draft and offered many helpful suggestions. I am most grateful to them both.

Finally, and always, I record my profound gratitude to my wife, Virginia Mezey Sorley, who is in her own right a superb professional research librarian.

READING THE TEXT

THE MATERIAL in this volume, even though it comprises about 450,000 words, of course constitutes only a small fraction of the millions of words spoken on the 455 tapes in the Abrams collection that run to more than 2,000 hours of briefings, discussion, and conversation. What has been included, as mentioned earlier, is what seems most important historically and what is most interesting. Much of that is verbatim, but some—especially portions derived from various briefings—is paraphrased. The portions reproduced verbatim are enclosed in quotation marks; paraphrases are not. Given the huge volume of the material, it has not proven feasible to construct a strict transcript of the whole. Rather, what is reproduced has the following characteristics:

■ Closely allied comments by the same speaker are grouped together. If there are omissions within a sentence, they are indicated in the usual manner by ellipses. Subsequent comments on the same topic that closely but not immediately follow are shown as another quoted sentence or group of sentences, as for example:

DAVIDSON: "A very high-powered group from CIA, State Department, DIA, at the Washington level came out, and they now agree with us specifically as to this, that there is high-ranking Cambodian complicity in the movement of arms and ammunition through Cambodia. They're inclined to take a disclaimer that Sihanouk himself is involved, although whether he knows [about] it or not they—I think they're inclined to believe he does, as we are." "There is high-level complicity. It may go as high as Lon Nol, the acting prime minister."

■ Comments are presented in the order in which they were made. The very rare exceptions (one or two instances) are indicated by editorial notes.
■ Comments grouped within the same section are on the same or related topics, but in each section what is presented is simply a selection of material from portions of the discussion. Thus, a comment shown here immediately following another does not necessarily immediately follow that comment in the

original transcripts. It is usually apparent where a comment responds to or picks up on one preceding.

■ General Abrams liked to use briefings as a springboard for discussion. Thus, quite often briefings are interrupted by lengthy dialogue on the topic at hand, sometimes involving the briefer but more often among the senior officers attending. This explains what are frequently fairly lengthy departures from the briefer's presentation.

■ When the proceedings move on to a substantially different topic, that is indicated by the following text separator: ■ ■ ■.

■ Given that the briefings and discussions are taking place at MACV during the years General Abrams was in command, his comments and questions constitute the largest single aspect of the transcripts. Since he knew the other people involved extremely well, and could see by their reactions when they had grasped a point he was making, Abrams often at such times simply stopped speaking in midsentence, which has been indicated by a concluding dash in the text in this manner:

ABRAMS: "It seems to me you can press it to the point—you can never break off communication, and you can't go to a point where you just become a <u>nuisance</u>. Otherwise you've just failed. After that <u>you're</u> not ever going to be effective again. And you can't make that—."

■ Emphatic and unmistakable emphases by speakers, especially but not solely General Abrams, are underlined. In some instances in which the speaker is particularly exercised, this results in multiple words emphasized, even within the same sentence, and not always the words one might expect would have been stressed. This feature has been reproduced on the premise that it provides useful insight into the flavor and emotional temperature of some of the proceedings. For example:

ABRAMS: "I know that these people have struggled with this <u>goddamn</u> war for twenty years. I mean, they really haven't had a hell of a lot of peace around here. And they're tired, and all that. <u>But</u> the truth of the matter is, if they're going to <u>really</u> come out on top of this, <u>goddamn it</u>, they've still got to <u>sacrifice,</u> and <u>they've got to sacrifice a lot!</u> And the <u>alternative</u> to that, the <u>alternative</u> to that, is in the next five or six years, <u>goddamn it</u>, they'll be Communist."

■ Comments by the editor are found in several places, distinguished from the text as follows:
- Editorial comments are found as the prologue and as summary comments at the beginning of each year's section and following the last year.
- Substantive editorial comments within items in the transcript are italicized and set apart.
- Other shorter editorial comments intended to clarify or compress quoted material in the text are included in brackets in the conventional manner and not italicized.

Redactions imposed during declassification review are indicated in the text by [***]. Presumably such redactions were made to protect intelligence data or information regarding friendly governments, or out of consideration for privacy. The bulk of the redactions during initial review of the manuscript were imposed by the National Security Agency; many were subsequently recovered by means of a largely successful reclama. In contrast, parallel review by the Department of the Army and the Central Intelligence Agency produced few redactions.

Comments by all the participants of course have the quality of informal oral communication, and thus do not always track smoothly. There are the usual backing and filling, interpositions, and incomplete statements characteristic of people in groups talking with one another.

Readers should also be aware that all the material presented has been transcribed from tape recordings, which, to begin with, were made under "field" conditions and were not of studio quality. Thus, the audibility and clarity of the material recorded were not of uniform character. Names of people and places presented a particular challenge, especially as they were pronounced (or mispronounced) by Americans. They have been rendered as accurately as possible and researched in connection with the matters under discussion at the time to ensure as much fidelity as possible. It seems inevitable, however, that some inaccuracies remain.

■ 1968

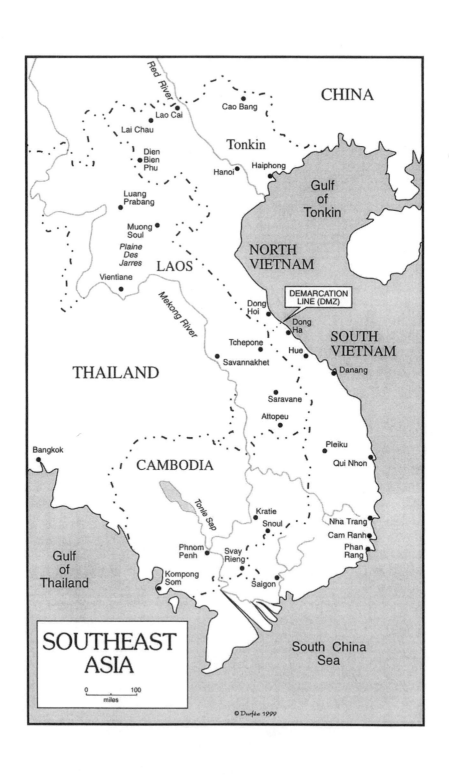

Red River

CHINA

Cao Bang

Lao Cai

Lai Chau

Tonkin

Dien
Bien
Phu

Hanoi   Haiphong

Gulf
of
Tonkin

Luang
Prabang

Muong
Soul

Plaine
Des
Jarres

LAOS

NORTH
VIETNAM

Vientiane

DEMARCATION
LINE (DMZ)

Mekong River

Dong
Hoi

Dong
Ha

SOUTH
VIETNAM

Tchepone

Hue

Savannakhet

Danang

THAILAND

Saravane

Attopeu

Pleiku

Bangkok

Qui Nhon

CAMBODIA

Tonle Sap

Kratie

Snoul

Nha Trang

Cam Ranh

Phnom
Penh

Svay
Rieng

Phan
Rang

Gulf
of
Thailand

Kompong
Som

Saigon

SOUTHEAST
ASIA

South China
Sea

0   100
miles

© Durfee 1999

During 1968 major changes took place in just about every aspect of the war in Vietnam. The enemy's Tet Offensive, commencing in late January, was for him a battlefield disaster in Vietnam but a psychological victory in the United States. Public confidence in Lyndon Johnson's administration and its handling of the war dropped precipitously, while within the administration there developed further widespread dissatisfaction with Gen. William C. Westmoreland's leadership and approach to fighting the war.

Soon after the Tet Offensive it was announced that in June Westmoreland would return to the United States for assignment as Army Chief of Staff, then, a few days later, that Gen. Creighton W. Abrams would succeed him as COMUSMACV—Commander, U.S. Military Assistance Command, Vietnam.

In early May the Communists launched another series of coordinated attacks, subsequently referred to by the allies as "mini-Tet," and in August a further round of attacks that came to be known as the "Third Offensive." In each they suffered additional severe losses.

Under Abrams the strategy, tactics, and concept of the war all changed, with the previous emphasis on body count as the measure of merit now shifting to population security. Large-scale operations conducted primarily in the deep jungles gave way to large numbers of small-unit ambushes and sweeps sited so as to deny the enemy access to the population. A close-knit leadership team headed by Ambassador Ellsworth Bunker, Abrams, and William E. Colby proved to be of one mind on how the war should be conducted, often described by them as "One War" in which combat operations, pacification, and improvement of South Vietnamese forces were of equal importance and received equal attention.

When Colby became Deputy to the COMUSMACV for CORDS (Civil Operations and Revolutionary Development Support), the pacification program, for the first time, began to show real progress, not least because the South Vietnamese, led by President Nguyen Van Thieu himself, got behind the effort.

Late in the year presidential elections in the United States resulted in victory for Richard M. Nixon, who would assume office the following January and take the war in Vietnam as a first order of business for his new administration.

What follows is the earliest tape in the collection. Abrams, who—as is apparent from the message traffic—has been in de facto command since shortly after the Tet Offensive, has now assumed formal command. He continues the practice of assembling the staff principals on Saturdays for a session called the Weekly Intelligence Estimate Update (WIEU). Under Abrams that was really a misnomer, *since, as the transcripts will demonstrate, the sessions constituted increasingly wide-ranging discussions of all aspects of the war, not just intelligence. Once a month these conferences included, in addition to the usual staff, senior tactical commanders from around the country, thus producing a Commanders WIEU.*

29 JUN 1968: WIEU

ATTENDEES: Gen. Abrams, Amb. Komer, Gen. Momyer, MG Kerwin, MG Baker, MG Corcoran, RADM Veth, BG Davidson, BG Frizen, BG McLaughlin, BG Tabor, BG Sidle, BG Bryan, BG Keegan, Col. Avriett, Col. Gleason, Col. Pink, Col. Hinton, Mr. T. D. Morris.

Infiltration refers to movement of enemy personnel south from North Vietnam along the Ho Chi Minh Trail. A recent breakthrough in intelligence, based on interception and decryption of enemy radio message traffic, has provided a valuable predictive mechanism for dealing with impending enemy offensives.

BRIEFER (on infiltration): "Now we're getting even ahead of them getting in the pipeline." This is a new capability based on communications intercepts.

BRIEFER: Infiltration now being observed: "It does not appear that these new groups represent another surge of activity, but rather a planned program to provide a steady flow of replacements and filler personnel."

BRIEFER: "We have seen peaks of infiltration activity in March, April, and May, followed by a lull during the first three weeks of June. Now it appears that a relatively stable flow of replacements is being established."

ABRAMS: Asks (his first question) how many of the groups picked up before entering the pipeline have still not entered it. Answer: 11 of 17. Abrams: "We're going to need to do a little bit more to tie that in for the operational impact down here."

■ ■ ■

BRIEFER: Refers to "the five inner provinces around Saigon." Of 96 U.S./FWMAF/RVNAF battalions conducting operations in III Corps, 77 are in these inner provinces (29 in Gia Dinh Province alone). The U.S. 1st and 25th Infantry Divisions each have a brigade positioned to block the 32nd and 33rd NVA Regiments from infiltrating toward Saigon. U.S. forces are in "the outer ring of III Corps."

BRIEFER: "Last week our indications pointed at mid to late July as the earliest that major offensive activity could be expected in I Corps." Now "the apparent relocation of units out of country from along the DMZ further reduces the threat." Thus it is "difficult to see how a major offensive could be initiated in the northern provinces before late July or early August."

BRIEFER: "Friendly operations have undoubtedly disrupted plans for any large-scale coordinated effort."

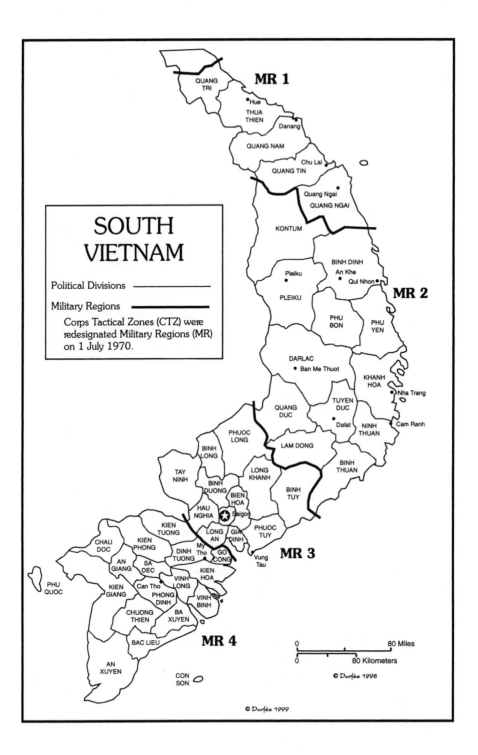

SOUTH VIETNAM

Political Divisions ————————

Military Regions ————————

Corps Tactical Zones (CTZ) were
redesignated Military Regions (MR)
on 1 July 1970.

MR 1

QUANG TRI

•Hue
THUA THIEN

Danang

QUANG NAM

Chu Lai

QUANG TIN

Quang Ngai
QUANG NGAI

KONTUM

BINH DINH

Pleiku
An Khe
Qui Nhon•

PLEIKU

MR 2

PHU BON

PHU YEN

DARLAC
• Ban Me Thuot

KHANH HOA

•Nha Trang

TUYEN DUC

QUANG DUC

Dalat

NINH THUAN

Cam Ranh

PHUOC LONG

LAM DONG

BINH LONG

LONG KHANH

BINH THUAN

TAY NINH

BINH DUONG

BIEN HOA

BINH TUY

HAU NGHIA

☆ Saigon

KIEN TUONG

LONG AN

GIA DINH

PHUOC TUY

CHAU DOC

KIEN PHONG

DINH TUONG

My Tho

GO CONG

Vung Tau

MR 3

AN GIANG

SA DEC

KIEN HOA

PHU QUOC

KIEN GIANG

Can Tho

VINH LONG

PHONG DINH

VINH BINH

CHUONG THIEN

BA XUYEN

BAC LIEU

MR 4

AN XUYEN

CON SON

0 ————————— 80 Miles
0 ————————— 80 Kilometers

© Durfée 1998

© Durfée 1999

© Durfée 1999

ABRAMS: "I'm sitting here watching all this unfold, wondering what it all means."

BRIEFER: "Ongoing intelligence assessments have been dominated by the phrase 'enemy activity throughout the Republic remains at a low level.'" Displays a chart: "Note the drop-off to pre-Tet levels subsequent to the 5 May attacks. Note also the decided decline in the last four weeks, a decline to the lowest level of enemy action we've seen thus far in 1968."

The "5 May attacks" refers to the commencement of "mini-Tet," the enemy's second general offensive of the year.

BRIEFER (analyzing the lull): "If he's not purposely deescalating the war, there are three reasons that could explain this lull: He is preparing for another major offensive, we are preempting him, or he's lost his momentum and effectiveness because his forces are weaker." There "was to have been the late June effort against Saigon." That did not take place.

ABRAMS: "That's an interesting part of the curve out here in June where his [the enemy's] activity goes down, but his KIA go up. That has to mean that ARVN is aggressive. It has to mean that."

SOMEONE: "Plus the elements of the 9th U.S. [Division]."

ABRAMS: "Well, that's right."

ABRAMS: "This is one of the things you can see in this SEER [System for Evaluating the Effectiveness of RVNAF] report. It's true of every ARVN division. The favorable kill ratio goes up when they go on offensive operations. And, with the exception of the 18th ARVN, it goes way down on security and defensive-type things."

BRIEFER: "The concentrated Arc Light strikes started 14 June. In 14 days there have been 124 strikes, 723 sorties, which yielded 153 secondaries." "After the onset of those attacks the pressure on Saigon diminished. On 19 June the last resistance in the Saigon area collapsed with the surrender of 141 remaining members of the Kiep Thang Regiment. Not even a token of his threatened hundred-rocket-a-day attacks ever materialized."

"Secondaries" refers to explosions of matériel on the ground caused by bombing, usually the result of striking petroleum or ammunition.

ABRAMS: "The other day when I was up promoting, pinning another star on, Ray Peers, I was suggesting that the differences between this battle in Kontum and the one last November [1967]—and the possibility that it was because we had different commanders up there. And General Peers hastened to point out [laughing] that the former commander got some 30 B-52 strikes and the current one got—he didn't have that exact figure, but he was very close to it [178]—and he thought that might have made a little difference."

■ ■ ■

Discussion of dealing with the media.

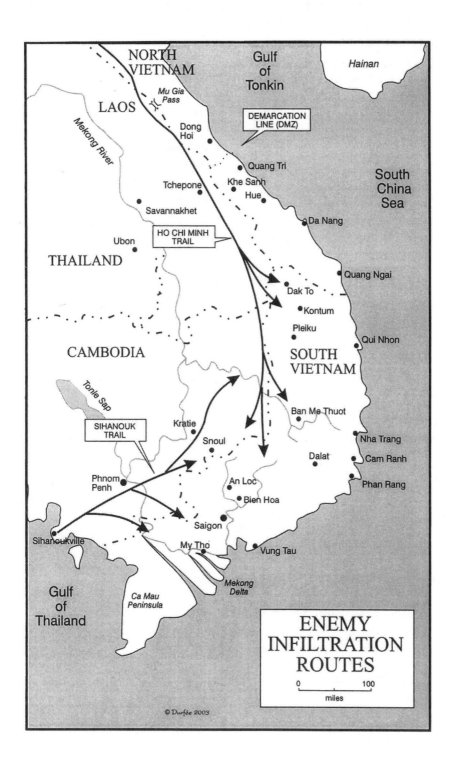

KOMER: "One of the reasons we get such bad press on this Vietnam War is because here we won a campaign and nobody knows it."

ABRAMS: "Yeah, but I must say that, whenever this command goes out to explain how it did something well, they're calling you out before the <u>throw</u> is made to the <u>plate</u>. The <u>umpire</u> out there, the umpire—represented by the bureau chiefs, he's swinging his thumb over the shoulder and, hell, the left fielder still hasn't thrown the <u>ball</u>. It's just that <u>you</u> started for home. And he's calling you out, by god, before the throw is made. That's the game we're in!"

KOMER: "Yeah, but you can do something about choosing the umpire. You get a straight play from Braestrup, Tuohy, Beech, three or four guys."

Peter Braestrup was Saigon bureau chief for the Washington Post, having earlier reported on Southeast Asia for the New York Times. William Tuohy was with the Los Angeles Times, while Keyes Beech represented the Chicago Daily News.

ABRAMS: "Well, I think it's a very serious question. The point you raise is a good one, but the—it's a very serious question, because if we lost <u>out,</u> we run the <u>risk</u> of, with these kind of umpires we've got, they'll just <u>further</u> discredit the <u>command</u>. We don't have a free <u>ride</u> on this thing. It isn't that we just <u>lose</u>— you know, make a good country try and they say, 'Well, you're out,' and that's that. It just further, in the eyes of the American people, in the eyes of observers around the world, it further discredits the command." "There's not an awful lot of human sympathy out there in that crowd."

Opponents of American involvement in the war were arguing that the enemy was showing restraint and deescalating the conflict, and that the United States should take reciprocal action.

BRIEFER: Somewhere in the range of 45–58 enemy maneuver battalions (37 percent of the 155 total) appear to have withdrawn to sanctuaries or into North Vietnam. This lull began approximately four weeks ago. "This of course has tremendous implications in the political context of the current Paris dialogue. However, it's much too early to draw conclusions of political intent, as other evidence indicates no deliberate deescalation."

BRIEFER: "In sum, we believe that the present lull in enemy activity is one that's been forced on the enemy rather than one of his own choosing, a lull that runs counter to his schemes for increasing the intensity and tempo of the war, but one forced upon him by his deteriorating force posture and the overpowering strength of friendly counteraction and firepower."

ABRAMS (re the briefing): "I think what you've got in this thing is very good, all of it. But the question is, if he's hurting, where is he hurting the most? And then, what can we do to aggravate his problem—<u>more</u>?"

ABRAMS (re the enemy): "He's a very resourceful guy. And it hasn't worked out quite the way—. Then what—how did he adjust to it? Which leads you a little closer, then, to the things he <u>really</u> thinks are important in this thing, which then leads you to where you can apply your resources to hurt him the worst."

DAVIDSON: "I think he's been hurt worst in the B-3 Front. Maybe not in sheer casualties, but in what he intended to do versus what he was able to do. That is the most abysmal failure I think we've seen."

The B-3 Front is the enemy's designation for the Central Highlands.

ABRAMS: "Yeah, but what was that—what part did that play in the scheme of things?" "As before, he probably wanted to drag some more forces up there to help him out a little bit in other places, take down the forces somewhat in III Corps, possibly even move forces out of I Corps. That didn't work out, but Saigon certainly is far more important to him than that part of his campaign. And I Corps—Danang, Hue—are certainly more important to him."

ABRAMS: "But it's interesting the way he has just gone ahead and denuded II Corps. And it's even more interesting if we believe that he, as an integral part of his campaign, planned a success in the highlands. See, bringing the 325C down there is no—that's no small thing. And even bringing at least one regiment of the 2nd NVA down there—temporarily. And he has laboriously placed the 32nd and the 33rd down there in Darlac. And with the 3rd NVA in the coastal area, he really sort of set the checkers up to put the—if he could get a good thing going at Ban Me Thuot, get his attack on Kontum, raise hell with Dak Pek, overrun it if he could. And the 3rd NVA doing the best they could down there in the coastal area to tie down the 173rd [Airborne Brigade] or whatever you had down there. And he sort of set the chess game up there—you know, you could make quite a story out of that. Well, now, it hasn't happened like that. There goes the 2nd back. There goes the 3rd—up. He sends the 32nd and the 33rd down. Now you suppose he planned it that way originally?"

ABRAMS: "Spike?"

MOMYER: "I have a real problem, following the Tet Offensive, trying to figure out what his overall strategy is—I mean military strategy, forget about the political strategy."

ABRAMS: "Dutch?"

KERWIN: "There's no doubt he's going for economy of force." "He now realizes that he's got to produce something. There's only two places to do it—I Corps and Saigon." May have seen the last of his offensives in the B-3 Front. "I'm becoming more and more convinced that we're going to see a major confrontation up there in I Corps and down here in Saigon. He just hasn't got the forces to do it at the present time. He's too weak."

ABRAMS: "Charlie?"

CORCORAN: "The moving of our own forces may have some impact on the enemy. Our greatest strength on the ground certainly is in I Corps and around Saigon. If he's having the problems logistically that we think he is, then he's running right into our strongest area."

ABRAMS: "Charlie Stone was on all those peaks out there last November that he [the enemy] had to fight for. That's where all the blood was spilled." "He [Stone] controlled the terrain up there, which did a lot of things. It gave you a lot better intelligence. It's not only that the B-52s were put in there, but they knew a lot more about where they ought to be put. And that derived directly out of being out there in the damn thing. And, as you know, they were—the enemy was around them—you know, they were all out there together. Except Charlie Stone had the B-52s, and they just had some—few mortars, few rockets. It was a mismatch."

ABRAMS: "He's [the enemy] been winning in his terms—psychological impact, political pressures, and so on. What we're talking about is how to prevent that from occurring. I think he has lost a little bit since these talks started. Shelling Saigon didn't do him, really didn't do him any good. It caused some people who were supporting him to criticize this, so in that arena, where he made great progress in Tet, and some of the ground attacks on Saigon—burning buildings here and that sort of thing—he's lost a few of his credits."

4 JUL 1968: Special Brief—COMUS

This is a monthly Commanders Conference.

ATTENDEES: Gen. Abrams, Amb. Komer, Gen. Momyer, LTG Mildren, LTG Weyand, LTG Rosson, LTG Peers, MG Eckhardt, MG Kerwin (Chief of Staff), RADM Veth, MG Corcoran (J-3), MG Baker (J-5) BG Davidson (J-2), BG McLaughlin (COC), BG Bryan (Deputy Chief of Staff). Per tape, also present: BG Flanagan (G-3 III MAF), Col. Beckington (G-2 III MAF), LTC Whitney (G-2 I FFV), Col. Everett (G-3 I FFV), Col. Foulk (G-2 II FFV), Col. Fuller (G-3 II FFV), LTC Carey (G-2 IV Corps), LTC Schofield (G-3 IV Corps), Col. Davis (G-2 USARV), Col. Gibson (G-3 USARV), BG Keegan (DCS Intelligence, Seventh Air Force), BG Sweat (Director of Combat Operations, Seventh Air Force), Capt. Rectanus (N-2, NAVFORV), Capt. Eason (N-3, NAVFORV).

ABRAMS: "We want to kind of wring this out this morning, see what you all think."

Briefer presents an assessment of the enemy situation.

■ "We have concluded that the enemy made a major planning decision, sometime in February when his Tet momentum had waned. This decision probably occurred sometime after his attempt at a countrywide second phase on the 18th of February, and most certainly by the 26th, when his resistance in Hue had collapsed."

■ "This was the situation he faced: He could not afford another countrywide offensive of the Tet magnitude. His permanent losses in less than a month of fighting were nearly 45,000, or one-fifth his total in-country military strength. More than 33,000 of these were KIA alone."

■ "His major objective of smashing the government of Vietnam and causing a general uprising had not been attained. On the other hand, Tet was a psychological success in South Vietnam and the United States, hence a military one that he could continue to exploit. Thus his decision was to sustain the pressure by staggering the main blows of his offensive where and when his capabilities peaked."

■ Evidence: Major unit moves, beginning in early March. Period of very low combat activity. 36,000 men put in the infiltration pipeline in March. Another 31,000 in April. Included the 308th NVA Division, and probably the 312th. "The decision to make this heavy commitment of North Vietnamese replacements and strategic reserves probably occurred in mid to late February." Planned to launch a second general offensive against Saigon and Hue in mid-April, and a major effort in the highlands in mid-May, southern I Corps around Danang in mid-June, and the DMZ area in mid-July. Based on observed activity and troop movements, rallier Colonel Dak, reinforcement flows, [***].

■ Cites "the twice-postponed [from 15 and 27 April] second general offensive, which finally got moving on the 5th of May." "The main effort was Saigon." "By about 11–15 May the assault on Saigon was an obvious failure."

■ "The second general offensive was delayed by two or three weeks. It <u>was</u> countrywide. It was obviously and quickly unsuccessful."

■ "The situation as the enemy must have seen it around 8–9 June: The B-3 Front was a dead loss. Things were comparatively good in the DMZ and near Hue, except for the problem of acquiring rice. Thus things remained quiet."

■ "Basic conclusion of great strategic significance: The enemy has displayed the weakness he inherited from his high-cost failure at Tet. He's been unable to maintain the momentum. He's <u>not</u> been able to execute his offensives at the times planned, nor has he been able to muster the military strength his plans required. The war is not going well for him."

End of this briefing.

■ ■ ■

WEYAND: "The great value of the B-52s to me has been that you've given them to us in advance a couple of days so we could plan ahead and use them in mass."

PEERS (re situation along the border): "He's been hurt, and hurt badly, over there, with those B-52s in particular."

ECKHARDT: "Their great fear is B-52 strikes. They don't know when and where they're going to come. This is bait we use to get the ARVN into the base areas, and we won't use one unless they'll go in after it."

ABRAMS: "What I've really been trying to do is avoid shifting forces, that is maneuver battalions, from one corps to another. I've also been trying to permit the JGS to keep their general reserve, the airborne battalions and four of the marine battalions, here in Saigon. The way I tried to do that is to <u>shift</u> the air effort, which is a fairly <u>painless</u> process compared to moving a brigade from III Corps to II Corps, or I Corps to the B-3 Front, or something like that, and instead try to make up where the real <u>heat</u> is, or other differentials, by the distribution of the air effort—B-52s and the tac air."

ABRAMS: "One thing that shows up here very clearly is the deficit in artillery in

IV Corps [per chart being displayed]." "Also, in another analysis of the performance of ARVN divisions, you'll find that the kill ratio is less favorable in IV Corps than it is in some of the others, and I think that fire support is part of the answer to that."

ABRAMS: "I'm a little frightened by this briefing we've had this morning, because there seems to be so much <u>agreement</u> with it. That's too much agreement to have it real <u>good</u>. You have to be kind of cynical here, I think, about all these things. What I did want to raise with everybody here today is what should we now be doing? <u>Are</u> we doing what we <u>ought</u> to be doing? Yeah, when he comes boiling out, why we all know what to do then, it's just automatic. Everybody's real good at that. There doesn't seem to be any doubt in anybody's mind about what to do. And they're very efficient <u>doing</u> it. They just slaughter them in droves."

ABRAMS: "But he's in another phase there now. He's back there fattening people up and training them. And he's got his psywar people out working them over about getting their spirits up, telling them not to pay any attention to B-52s, tac air, and artillery. 'It's not effective unless it hits you.' You know—pep talk. The planners are hard at work, and so on. And <u>what</u> could <u>we</u> be doing <u>now</u> to—is there a <u>practical</u> way to cause significant <u>attrition</u> on him <u>while</u> he's in this condition? Or while he's <u>doing</u> this kind of thing? Is there any way to get at him, get a <u>hold</u> of him? Because that's—the <u>payoff</u> is getting a hold of this fellow and killing as many of them as you can."

ABRAMS: "I think we've just <u>got</u> to get the ROKs out. The ROKs have just sort of <u>atrophied</u> up there. And not enough enemy to justify what they're doing. We're losing out on the <u>rations</u>. Feeding too many people for what they're doing."

ROKs are the forces of the Republic of Korea (South Korea).

ABRAMS: "So I'd like to hear any ideas you've got. What should we be doing?"

WEYAND (re use of B-52s): "The <u>long</u> view of this thing of working on his ass end [Momyer's plan] and gradually creeping up to his front doesn't charm me at all. My problem here is just the reverse. He's ramming this stuff down, and I'm trying to meet him head on and sop all that stuff <u>up</u> just as fast as we can, because any of it that leaks through, with the psychological or political situation being what it is, is a <u>minus</u>. You get a couple of platoons in Saigon and it's a <u>big</u> minus."

WEYAND: "I couldn't believe more in the truth of what you said about <u>killing</u> people. This is right now what's got to be <u>done</u>—<u>people</u> got to be killed. It isn't so much his supplies and his food, it's just this son of a bitch running around with an AK-47. We've got to <u>find</u> him and <u>kill</u> him—or <u>capture</u> him."

WEYAND: "Now what's been happening in <u>my</u> area is the B-52s have been getting on his <u>head</u>—not his <u>tail</u> at all. These things have been tremendously effective."

WEYAND: "When you talk about what we ought to be doing now that we're not—the thing I can do that'll get the greatest benefit accruing for me is increased

ARVN effectiveness. And there isn't, I don't think, hardly any price I wouldn't pay in terms of trade-offs, whether it's putting U.S. units in direct support of them, or giving them my firepower, or B-52 strikes, that I wouldn't be willing to do. Because if I can get a 10 or 20 percent increase in effectiveness out of these three lousy divisions that I've got, plus RF/PF, I really wouldn't have much to worry about." "That's where I think we've got the opportunity for the greatest gain."

RF/PF refers to the elements of the South Vietnamese Territorial Forces known as Regional Forces and Popular Forces.

WEYAND: "If you hadn't figured all this stuff out and put those B-52s down here when you did, no question in my mind that, while we would have blunted this attack and stopped it, we'd have had a bunch of VC companies and crap such as that milling around the populated area in Saigon right now."

PEERS (re B-52s): "It seems to me the way you've been using them, in mass, is the way they ought to be used."

PEERS: "I'm very concerned about this. . . . ARVN, during the month of June, killed 143 people." Have about 60,000 ARVN in II Corps. "I've got units working with them and so on, and they always come back with, 'Well, they want to train some more.' Hell, they've been training for five and six years. I think they're overtrained."

ABRAMS: "How long has the 3rd Regiment of the 1st Division been out?"

ROSSON: "Since the 19th of May. They're approaching—well, they're into their sixth week, which is an all-time record."

ABRAMS: "Well, it's an all-time record in South Vietnam!"

ROSSON: "In the III MAF area we are blessed with two fine ARVN divisions, one particularly so. The 1st ARVN is aggressive, effective, all the time." "The 2nd ARVN Division is less effective, but it too is on the go most of the time."

ROSSON: "Now as to what we ought to be doing—we've got to use all our assets all the time. There can't be any reserves—we don't have the luxury of that." "I'm a great believer in the mass use of the B-52."

■ ■ ■

ABRAMS: Cites a case of both Saigon English-language daily newspapers headlining a MiG supposedly having shot down a U.S. helicopter 30 kilometers west of Saigon, and another report that the enemy has 51 battalions poised to attack Saigon, both attributed to "informed military spokesmen." "Now, this is doing us a lot of harm. When the enemy can get headlines like that without firing a damn round out of an AK-47, in the great psywar campaign that's going on all over the world these are real blue chips. So I've put out a couple of messages about talking. I just want every one of our people to realize that anything they say can have a real big impact in the great global psywar campaign that's going on. And most of us are not really smart enough to say the things that would result in something good in the psywar campaign. We're pretty pedestrian when it comes to that sophisticated game. To say nothing of—every time we get on this public information thing, we really are out there playing in a hostile court. The umpires are all against us."

WEYAND: "They're not beyond making the damn stuff up. It's going to happen no matter what we do."

ROSSON: "I think the basic problem is we'll take military risks, we'll go out and get people killed, we'll take chances of losing troops, but we don't take any risks in the war of words." "It results in" a situation in which "we leave the field to the other guy." I think we ought to tell the story. "Now it involves a cost. We saw it in the credibility of the previous commanders."

Referring to Generals Paul D. Harkins and William C. Westmoreland.

ABRAMS: "This has been a very beneficial meeting for me here this morning. I understand, I think, what's going on a little better."

■ ■ ■

WEYAND: Disputes contention in the original briefing that at Tet the enemy achieved a psychological victory in South Vietnam. "I think that the reason he's in this fix is that he did not achieve a psychological victory with the people of South Vietnam, or with the military forces, that he expected." "Fatal miscalculation."

ABRAMS: "I think it's a point well taken, because the psychological impact on the Vietnamese armed forces—it's boosted them. It put them ahead of where they were."

WEYAND: "I think it did."

ROSSON: "It certainly improved their motivation."

6 JUL 1968: WIEU

Attendees: Gen. Abrams, Amb. Komer, Gen. Momyer, LTG Mildren, MG Kerwin, MG Baker, MG Corcoran, RADM Veth, BG McLaughlin, MG Rasmussen, BG Sidle, BG Bolton, BG Bryan, BG Davidson, Col. Singlaub.

BRIEFER (re infiltration): Approximately 70 percent of projected infiltration now under way "should arrive during July, giving it potentially an even higher level of infiltration than was observed during January, when two divisions entered the country." Projected: 111,000 into the pipeline since 1 February. Arrivals projected during July–August: DMZ/MR-TTH: 10,000–11,500. MR-5: 12,200–13,700. B-3 Front: 2,200–2,500. COSVN: 10,900–12,400. I Corps expected to get 18,500–21,100 during July–August.

■ ■ ■

BRIEFER: "The enemy maintains a presence around the Khe Sanh combat base as the allied withdrawal continues."

Abrams had directed, as one of his first actions upon assuming command, that U.S. forces be withdrawn from Khe Sanh.

ABRAMS (re low level of enemy-initiated activity, but preparations under way): "One of the things I think about this—for instance, right now he's getting replacements, getting himself organized. But a lot of other fellows are carrying the ammunition up and putting it in caches, and they're getting the radios set up, and getting communications and dispensaries, this sort of thing. And that's going on up in the forward area. I think that's the way he does it. And then, at the last minute, he moves the units in. Well, all this other preparation—CPs set up, the supply setup, and the medical, has all been prepared. Also I think the units, when they move, they probably move pretty light in ammunition, and then they pick it up at the cache. So that sort of activity's probably going on out here now."

An early Abrams articulation of his analysis of the enemy's logistics "nose," logistical support pre-positioned in advance of attacking forces instead of being brought up from the rear as would normally be done from an army's supply train or logistics "tail."

■ ■ ■

DISCUSSION: Speculation on enemy intentions of having another offensive to coincide with U.S. political conventions (Republican to begin 5 August).

ABRAMS: "Xuan Thuy has made a direct appeal to the people of the United States."

ABRAMS: "Any foreigner, any foreigner—with the possible exception of Churchill—that undertakes a direct appeal to the people of the United States, he really solidifies them. And I hope that this turns out to be one of his greatest blunders." "So there are—I think some people are stubbing their toe now and then. It's not all great stuff."

■ ■ ■

ABRAMS: "If that report's right that those 20 civilians were kidnapped because they wouldn't work on the roadblock, it's kind of a sad thing. When the people try to make a little stand in support of their government, we are not able to secure them. I'll always remember this district chief down in Go Cong who said, 'You should never overtly take information from a civilian unless you can guarantee his safety.' Pretty good rule."

■ ■ ■

MOMYER: "It looks like to me we've got two extremes. It looks like his pressure is mounting in the north, mounting in the Saigon [area], and nothing in between." May have need to reposition forces, and thus to plan the airlift needed to do so.

DAVIDSON: "I've looked at this situation from the enemy standpoint." Re

Saigon: "It is without doubt the biggest threat. It is the most imminent threat." "Saigon is the prize. It's the enemy's main objective."

ABRAMS: "I think we probably all agree that in the end what they've got to get done here is control of their own people, and get them secure. The pacification effort is the ultimate effort which has to be made. But right now I think we have to focus on what he's going to do with his major formations."

ABRAMS: "When these commanders were explaining what they were doing, in this meeting we had here—both Rosson and Peers put a lot of emphasis in their discussion on getting out, and the RF and PF, getting on with the security of the people."

■ ■ ■

ABRAMS (re the Koreans): "What you boil down to is what can you get the Koreans doing <u>this</u> month? And that is sort of a sad picture. Anything they do it takes at <u>least</u> a month to plan."

■ ■ ■

ABRAMS: "What we'll do on the B-52s is go ahead and plan between I Corps and III Corps, with an occasional strike down in IV Corps. And I think we should go ahead and submit these B-52 strikes up in Tally Ho and Route Package 1 for approval . . . , and they ought to be arranged in priority, so that we have the—we can get the track clear, and then have the flexibility of moving up there. And in the meantime your tac air program will go ahead."

■ ■ ■

ABRAMS: "Now I will talk with General Chae, and see if we can stimulate some interest there." The ROKs want 20,000 M16s, "and I just don't want to do it."

Gen. Chae Mung Shin commanded the Republic of Korea's forces serving in South Vietnam.

KOMER: "If you want to get rid of me, there's one easy way to do it, and that's not to give the M16 to the RF and PF, because I've just gone around the country with General La promising these guys, and it was the one <u>positive</u> thing we had to say."

ABRAMS: "No, I'm not going to <u>change</u>."

ABRAMS: "And I have got to work around and have a good talk with General Vien about the performance of these divisions. I'll have to figure out how to do that. Certainly can't go at it with these casualty charts and say, 'Now, what we want is to see more Vietnamese killed. We've got to get it up here even.' Somehow that doesn't sound very attractive."

ABRAMS: "Another thing about this is, and you mustn't lose sight of, and that is that the U.S. troops are better equipped and better trained to go out and <u>do</u> these things than the ARVN are. You've got a matériel difference before you start the problem. Part of that has been corrected, but there's still more to be done. They don't have the artillery support."

ABRAMS: "The military—all of us in the military—we have a little <u>problem</u>. We've got an <u>institutional</u> problem, I guess. We recognize <u>trouble</u>, you know, where people are <u>shooting</u> or <u>fighting</u> or <u>punching</u> or <u>rioting</u> or so on. And that's the kind—we know all about that trouble. You know, what it <u>looks</u> like, what it <u>smells</u> like, and what you <u>do</u> about it. But this <u>trouble</u> that nobody can <u>see</u>, and nobody can <u>hear</u>, and so on, but is just <u>meaner</u> than hell—just going around collecting taxes, quietly snatching somebody and taking him off and shooting him, and so on—."

■ ■ ■

KOMER (to the MACV J-4): "Henry, if you're running into any difficulty with the JGS, just let <u>me</u> handle it, and I'll take it up with General <u>La</u>. La is making his reputation as the father of the RF and PF."
ABRAMS: "No, he's talking about equipment for the ARVN."
KOMER: "Oh, the ARVN?"

13 JUL 1968: WIEU

Attendees: Gen. Abrams, Gen. Goodpaster, Amb. Komer, Gen. Momyer, LTG Mildren, MG Kerwin, RADM Veth, MG Corcoran, MG Baker, BG Davidson, BG Rasmussen, BG Sidle, BG Bolton, BG McLaughlin, BG Bryan, Col. Singlaub.

DAVIDSON: Historical level of infiltration about 6,900–7,000 per month.
BRIEFER: Gives new groups identified.
BRIEFER: At Khe Sanh: "Deactivation of the combat base proceeded."

■ ■ ■

ABRAMS: "The ROKs have 4 percent of the friendly strength in-country, and they've accounted for 6 percent of the enemy killed in-country. They've got a kill ratio of 1:11, something like that, which of course is pretty good [compared to] 1:5, the total of everyone else." "Of the population in their area of responsibility, 72 percent of it is in the secure category." This is per HES. "So, if anyone—well, <u>I've</u> pulled in my horns. Last week—." [Someone adds: "They had the highest weapons captured ratio."] "In all the things that <u>count</u>, the ROKs look very good." "You've got to give them <u>credit</u> for the things that really <u>count</u> here—control of the population, establishment of the GVN control over it, that sort of thing, and killing the enemy. They've just done very <u>well</u>."
MILDREN: "The 173rd [Airborne Brigade] recently captured a historical document in the area east of Pleiku [re] operations they had participated in. And they noticed this document kept by the [enemy] unit indicated over 300 percent casualties claimed over what actually occurred. And every unit that I've visited, I notice the same thing comes up about the number of casualties <u>they</u> have inflicted on <u>us</u>. And with all those reports going back to the top command, it must give them—even if they discounted a percentage of it—it must give them a pretty good feeling that they're creating a heavy damage against us

with the type of operations they're conducting." "I cannot understand why they continue to attack our U.S. strong points with such casualties as they're suffering. I don't see <u>why</u> they <u>don't</u> go for major population complexes, why they don't go for some of our big fuel dumps, why they don't go for the big ammunition dumps, where they could really put a dent, I believe—<u>more</u> so than what they're doing." Appears that "it's based on a false assumption."

MILDREN: "I was quite impressed with the fact that many of our commanders right now are taking a real good look at this ammunition expenditure. And I noticed up in 4th Division, and throughout I Field Force, commanders are taking a good look at these so-called H&I fires. I looked at a week's result up there where the H&I fires have practically disappeared in the 4th Division."

ABRAMS: "Charlie's [Stone] been against it from the start. Of course, he has trouble with his subordinates, but he's been philosophically against it from the word go."

CORCORAN: "This is being done throughout I Field Force now, because field force headquarters is getting a report."

ABRAMS: "They've got the <u>best</u> system. <u>Kalergis</u> set that up. <u>First class</u>!"

Brig. Gen. James G. Kalergis was CG, I Field Force, Vietnam, Artillery.

SOMEONE: "We've made somewhat of a pitch to ARVN that they've got to stay within <u>their</u> allocation. And we've made a preliminary analysis of how they're doing, and they're getting pretty well within that, staying within that."

ABRAMS: "This scheme that Ray [Peers] has, where he's paired off a battalion with a regiment, will do a lot to get the ARVN into it in a meaningful way."

■ ■ ■

ABRAMS: "I did recommend B-52s up in Route Package 1. It was turned down at this time. We <u>do</u> have authority to go to 17 degrees 10 minutes. And I'm wondering about that collection of B-52 targets that are over there on [Route] 1036."

ABRAMS: "I suppose what we ought to do is mount up about a two-division effort—the ARVN Airborne Division and the U.S. 1st Division, something like that—and get out here in these base areas and surround them. Trouble is, in this sort of thing they get pretty elusive. You go to monumental effort, and—."

■ ■ ■

ABRAMS: "Now, another thing—meeting in here on Saturday, are we getting the things in here that we really need to get so that we can assess what we ought to be doing? Is the <u>picture</u> we're getting here on Saturdays sufficiently comprehensive so we have some confidence that we know what's going on and what we ought to be doing about it?"

ABRAMS: "What has happened is that [in] the [enemy Base Areas] 101 and 114, the 1st Cavalry, and the 1st Regiment of the 1st ARVN, have taken up <u>residence</u> out there. They've gone—they're combing that goddamn thing back and forth, up and down, up in back of it, and the sides of it, <u>through</u> it. The 3rd

Regiment has been, for about four weeks, located in the <u>middle</u> of 114. That's the <u>base</u> out of which they've been <u>operating</u>." Then the Americal, "out there trying to grapple with the 2nd NVA . . . they're out there <u>deeper</u>, really, than we've <u>ever</u> been before. And they plan to go from <u>there</u> and land on the 3rd NVA."

ABRAMS (re Emerson): "He's almost <u>desperate</u>. He can't get his hooks on the real <u>meat</u>."

ABRAMS: "What we need here on Saturday is a good <u>feel</u> for what they <u>are</u> doing, and what they are <u>planning</u> to do." "The thing we're missing here on Saturday is a good understanding of what they are in <u>fact</u> doing, and what they <u>plan</u> to do."

20 JUL 1968: Commanders WIEU

Attendees: Gen. Abrams. Gen. Goodpaster, Amb. Komer, LTG Mildren, LTG
McMillan, MG Eckhardt, RADM Veth,
pkins, MG Baker, BG Glick,
Rasmussen, BG Sidle, BG
ol. Everett [I FFV], Col. Foulk
[II MAF], Col. Hainey [IV CTZ],
CTZ].

red the pipeline since 1 February
bably arrived at or near their final
l in the pipeline en route to South

[***] "the great victors of Khe
victory celebration for a unit not
tnam.
battles return home and drop by the
d things will leak out. Observers of

304th NVA Division): "Is there any possibility that this <u>could</u> be an element of a grand deception?" "I admit it's far-fetched."

ABRAMS: "Well, I guess I'm too <u>dull</u> to be moved by that. I haven't contemplated any <u>countermove</u>."

■ ■ ■

ABRAMS (re consolidated friendly KIA): "This is a 'One War' chart."

■ ■ ■

In his reference to "One War," Abrams is reflecting his conviction that success requires a comprehensive approach emphasizing not just tactical operations, but also improvement of South Vietnam's armed forces and a vigorous pacification effort, an outlook shared by Ambassadors Bunker and Colby.

ABRAMS: "We just keep milling around here, trying to get a handle on how we've got stuff distributed." Not satisfied with the current chart. Trying battalion equivalents as a way of tabulating forces.

ABRAMS: I've concluded "there is a relationship between kill ratio and firepower. I've never <u>acted</u> on that."

■ ■ ■

ABRAMS: "I asked all of you [the commanders] to come in here this morning because I would like to <u>add</u> to this meeting a note of realism which I was hopeful you would provide. We recognize our limitations in being a little distant from the <u>actual</u> situation. It would be very <u>helpful</u> to us to hear what you feel about your various areas, and what you have in mind doing."

WEYAND: Expect in the next offensive "the 9th Division will be the one that will conduct the main effort. The 7th will be in a support and reinforcing role." Also the 5th. Re the 9th: "General Khang has an agent in that headquarters that he thinks is a good one. Whether or not this guy will give us a clue at the right time, I don't know. They do have a system where they're tapping him weekly."

WEYAND: "We took the Rome plows and cut a 1,000-meter swath from the Michelin [rubber plantation] all the way to the Song Be River." "Before long we're going to have a ring quite a ways out from Saigon."

ECKHARDT: "In the waterways they pick up 1,000, 2,000 craft each day and inspect them." In the process they screen about 5,000 people, and pick up about 20 without identification as suspects.

PEERS: Had a meeting of all the senior planners yesterday, "and I was quite impressed with General Lu Lan."

MCMILLAN: "There's quite a bit of noise associated with our operations, and it provides an alert so the enemy can evade." "Sensors [electronic detection devices] that are beginning to become available have some different properties which might be useful—they're quiet, they work for 24 hours, you don't have to feed them, they don't make any noise."

KOMER: "You know, we've always said in this war that it's not just a big-unit war, although the enemy seems to be becoming more and more conventional in his posture. It's also a political war, or a pacification war, or an other war—we keep using different terms for it. But I think we've got to keep our eye on <u>that</u> aspect of the problem, as well as on the business of the major offensive efforts he's got in mind, or otherwise we may find ourselves in the uncomfortable position where we have defeated his main initiative—as we have, I think, at Tet, and at mini-Tet, and then again, let's say, in late August—but <u>he's</u> come up with something that is very <u>hard</u> for us to cope with, especially in any short term."

WEYAND: "With the RF/PF, I realize that that thing goes slower than most people want, but now that you're giving them weapons, we're seeing a very marked aggressiveness on their part, willingness to get out and mix it up. I think that thing's going to increase by leaps and bounds. I'm very pleased with it."

KOMER: "The HES map . . . it's like a checkerboard. They're all over the place!" "He can say he controls an awful lot, and if I were asked honestly, 'Is he wrong?' and I showed the HES map . . . and you look at our own figures on population control, relative as they are, he looks pretty good. He's got about 45 . . . percent of the rural population that we concede him now. That's under his control, not just in contested areas."

ABRAMS: "My impression is that never have the ARVN been out as much as they are now."

Komer had complained about "static" battalions.

ABRAMS: "Talking with Barsanti last evening, he says the RF and PF up around Hue—they're controlling the thing, night and day."

WEYAND: "I personally think that when this enemy changed the nature of this war, which he did, just like he'd crossed the Yalu, that this very much reflected in the problem that we're talking about. And I think the biggest thing we can do for them now is just to kill VC, and I mean these main units. . . ."

ABRAMS: "This has been a very educational morning for us here in the staff." "It really tones this thing up to have you [the field commanders] here. . . . It makes us feel a little closer to reality." "I don't see, from this meeting here this morning, any necessity to issue any new instructions. It sounds to me like you're doing about what you ought to be doing. Is there anything you think I ought to change?" Nobody suggests anything.

27 JUL 1968: WIEU

ATTENDEES: Gen. Abrams, Gen. Goodpaster, Amb. Komer, LTG Mildren, Dr. McMillan, RADM Veth, MG Corcoran, MG Baker, BG Rasmussen, BG Bolton, BG McLaughlin, BG Davidson, BG Coleman, BG Sidle, BG Bryan, Col. Cunningham, Col. Gleason.

BRIEFER: An estimated 123,000 men have entered the infiltration pipeline since 1 February 1968. Eleven groups have been detected exfiltrating with sick and wounded personnel during June and July. Groups travel at an average rate of 12.2 kilometers per day. But to COSVN they make an average of 10.5 kilometers per day. Countrywide peak occurred in July. COSVN will peak in August. Use the figure of 568 men per group.

Earlier they used 565, and later they will use 570. For arrival strength they use a smaller number, reflecting attrition during the movement down.

These WIEUs early in Abrams's tenure in command do not yet include the extensive political and other nonmilitary aspects of North Vietnam, Laos, and Cambodia that are routinely covered later on.

DAVIDSON: Describes changes in how the combat summary is presented, an experiment. Indications are listed and weighted. For example: "In the DMZ area, we have the following indications of renewed offensive activity—[***] unit moves, political reorientation training, infiltration."

ABRAMS: "You know, this fellow has always— . . . he goes ahead and prepares all of these reserve positions, you know, the position he puts his troops in before he moves out to the attack, in other words, <u>back</u> from the line of departure a little bit. He goes in and gets all these bunkers made. He's <u>always</u> done that." "We don't have too much evidence that that's been done, do we?"

DAVIDSON (re a VC agent that was picked up): "He said without any equivocation the attack is going to come at 2100 hours on the 9th of August."

ABRAMS: "He's got <u>problems</u> right now, and he <u>has</u> had them for several months. He's never really recovered from the Tet thing, never had a <u>chance</u> to. He's been on the—there've been people <u>pushing</u> him ever since then."

BRIEFER: "Evidence continues to mount indicating another attack on Saigon and pointing more clearly to its possible timing." "A mid-August date matches the 45-day enemy planning cycle established by reliable sources and analysis of enemy documents [***]. The COSVN planning meetings were apparently conducted between 1 and 4 July, which would place the subsequent attack time sometime between 15 and 19 August." "The weight of evidence suggests a new Saigon offensive sometime between 10 and 20 August."

ABRAMS: "I wish we could have Saturday every day—it seems like you <u>learn</u> so much."

DAVIDSON: "Sir, the J-2 just couldn't stand it. Most of these men figure their departure dates by how many WIEUs they've got left."

■ ■ ■

ABRAMS (to Veth): "Incidentally, didn't I read in the *Stars & Stripes* about your replacement?"

VETH: "Yes, sir, announced yesterday." Think it will take place about mid-September.

ABRAMS: "I don't know how the navy as a service runs this, but I know in the army when we're making changes like that we always send a wire out to the affected senior commander in the field in advance. And I notice the air force does that, too, because they always notify me by message, official message."

VETH: "I think they should have."

■ ■ ■

ABRAMS: "If you don't know where the enemy is, you shouldn't send a division to find him."

ABRAMS: "Now these spoiling attacks, they can take a lot of different forms. We've been doing—we've been <u>trying</u> to do—quite a bit of spoiling with the air. And a tremendous amount of the long-range patrols—Omega, Sigma, CIDG assets—have been plunged into developing the targets for the air."

CORCORAN: "We go on the basis that <u>we've</u> got what the enemy wants. And by that I don't mean to imply a passive attitude. When we see that he is going after Tay Ninh or Ban Me Thuot, we know that to get to them he has to go through certain areas, far enough out to provide some reasonable degree of security to the city. We beat him there and grab those areas with fire support bases and reaction forces. That way we follow through on what we're trying to do here. We're trying to kill all the Viet Cong and NVA we can. And in that type of an operation we can kill a hell of a lot more than we can out there stewing around in the juice with big forces, in the woods, where the advantage is all his."

ABRAMS: "That's precisely how the battle for Kontum was done. And it's one of the big differences between it and all the previous battles in Kontum. Last October–November we had to go out and wrest those key terrain features away from him, which was a bloody process, because you've got to have them. And this year, as he began his reconnaissance and preparation of positions and so on, Stone began taking those things over—at zero cost."

ABRAMS: Wants "literally hour by hour" monitoring indications of impending attack, both here in the headquarters and in the major subordinate commands. "I'd like to have it so that we can pour everything that we can get our hands on into it on a continuous round-the-clock basis for 36, 48, I don't know—. You can't decide in advance. It's the quality of what you think you've got that determines that. And I would cancel—I would cancel my most hand-on-the-Bible promise to Eckhardt to take advantage of a thing like that." "And if we've got a good clue that he's beginning to put in the starting blocks, or he's on the starting blocks, we should spare no effort, and we should spare no element of power . . . to get behind this thing and really give it to them." "I'm willing to cancel almost anything else—except somebody who's really in deep trouble—to get after it." "August is billed as a great month by the enemy. I want to have everybody accept the challenge of that, that it is a great month."

ABRAMS: Wants a message he can send that night to subordinate commands re monitoring indicators: "I want the message, in tone and direction, to really light up the board from one end to the other." "Night work!"

■ ■ ■

ABRAMS: "The 22nd ARVN's doing about 10 percent of what it ought to be. And I'm mad at the division advisors up there because they haven't brought that up. They've been down there sleeping at the switch, and letting the goddamn thing go, and being content with quarter measures."

ABRAMS: "From this point, throughout the month of August, every advisor is required to bring every unsatisfactory condition to the attention of his next superior, and it's got to pass up the line until the unsatisfactory condition is corrected, if it has to come to me. And units that won't operate, I want to know about it. I want to know about it if the field force commander can't get them operating. In other words, I want to light up the lights and I want to turn on the heat—everywhere! And—you never should threaten people, but I'll tell you one thing, I'll tell you right now—if I become aware of an American who has gone to sleep at the switch, I'm going to <u>ax</u> him, wherever he is, or how many there are. Now, you can't say that in the message, but it ought to be clear to anybody that reads the message. They should be able to deduce that this month is important enough so that anybody that slips is <u>probably</u> going to get that. Also, this will not be the final exertion of the revolution. I anticipate September will be even a higher pitch. We just <u>practice up</u> in August."

1 AUG 1968: Special WIEU for COMUS

ATTENDEES: Gen. Abrams, Gen. Goodpaster, Gen. Brown, LTG Mildren, MG Wetherill, Dr. McMillan, RADM Veth, MG Corcoran, MG Shaefer, MG Rasmussen, BG Sidle, BG Bolton, BG McLaughlin, BG Bryan, Col. Singlaub, BG Cowles, BG Coleman, MG Baker. Others.

BRIEFER: Describes "the decline of the Khe Sanh area front." Consistent "with the withdrawal by the allies from the Khe Sanh combat base."

ABRAMS: Asks whether we lost the ammunition dump at Dong Ha again.

RESPONSE: No, not built back up to an ASP level after it was blown up earlier, when it burned for 10 or 12 days.

ABRAMS: "Well, what was that picture in the *Stars & Stripes?*"

SOMEONE: "Oh, that's the <u>old</u> one."

ABRAMS: "What the hell is *Stars & Stripes* doing <u>that</u> for?"

SIDLE: "It was a Marine Corps picture. Why the Marines even released it—."

ABRAMS: "Well, let's get to the bottom of this. Good god—are they getting <u>sick</u> for bad <u>news</u>?" "I want to know just what the answer is on this, and who put the picture out. And what's *Stars & Stripes* doing with it? What's <u>their</u> politics?"

SOMEONE: "They're supposed to be <u>supporting</u> us."

ABRAMS: "Now I know it's dangerous to get into the business of rapping the knuckles of the *Stars & Stripes,* but by god I'm prepared to do it!"

SIDLE: "We've done it before. No problem."

ABRAMS: "I just took it for granted that somebody had failed to report to me that latest disaster."

■ ■ ■

BRIEFER: On the evidence, "a countrywide offensive, if launched in the next week to 10 days, would not be of the magnitude we saw at Tet or 5 May."

ABRAMS: "Well, it seems to me the gut issue here is whether we've managed to postpone something here—or not. And, as I get the message this morning here, the <u>possibility</u> exists that we <u>may</u> have caused some postponement, but the evidence is not clear that that's the case."

DAVIDSON: "As much credibility as we give to the gold-plated agent's report, we would still like a little confirmatory evidence." But we believe it has happened.

The "gold-plated agent" was a highly regarded human intelligence source in the enemy camp.

■ ■ ■

ECKHARDT: "In all our letters of commendation we've been writing we've been talking about 'Communist insurgency' here in Vietnam, and we've decided to change it and call it 'North Vietnamese/VC Communist aggression.' I think we're dignifying it a little bit by calling it an 'insurgency.'"

ABRAMS: "It's a good point." "I think it's well taken. Stop calling it an insurgency and start calling it an invasion."

■ ■ ■

ABRAMS: "One of the great persuaders in this whole thing is to just hit them more accurately with more B-52s."

ABRAMS: We began in the last two or three days "to get these tales of difficulty and suspicion and postponement from the enemy side. We said he was going to attack, he was going to launch these offensives. We had the timetable and so on. Then we said, 'We're going to do everything we can to <u>stop</u> it, <u>defeat</u> it, <u>anticipate</u> it, and so on. Well, we were on that <u>program</u>, but I just felt we hadn't talked enough—if you get <u>doing</u> it, and you get <u>anticipating</u>, and you get <u>thwarting</u>, get them <u>postponing</u>, then what <u>else</u> should you do?" "There might come a day here when it would be advisable to just abandon the headquarters here, for instance, and everybody take his damn weapon and we'll start marching west, or—." "Of course, that's not such a good idea. There'd be a lot of people shooting themselves in the <u>foot</u>."

3 AUG 1968: WIEU

Attendees: Gen. Abrams, Gen. Goodpaster, Amb. Komer, Gen. Brown, LTG Mildren, Dr. McMillan, RADM Veth, MG Corcoran, MG Shaefer, MG Davidson, MG Rasmussen, MG Baker, BG Sidle, BG Bolton, BG McLaughlin, BG Bryan, BG Coleman, Col. Cavanaugh, Col. Singlaub.

ABRAMS (re a chart with some bars having no identification): "What are those two median bars down there that don't have any <u>entry</u> opposite them?"

DAVIDSON: "They were indicators that we used, sir, and then, after discussion, took out the indicators and failed to take out the bars. Sloppy work, sir."

ABRAMS: "I'm kind of <u>enjoying</u> it."

■ ■ ■

BRIEFER: Describes the arrival of the U.S. 1st Brigade, 5th Infantry Division (Mechanized), in I Corps.

ABRAMS: "Well, I might as well say something now. That really is <u>not</u>—they're going to have to go through training, and haven't got all their equipment yet. So it's <u>not</u> <u>yet</u> a reinforcement." "The same thing applies to the Thais." "And of course at the time this mechanized brigade becomes usable, operational, the 27th RLT will go home. So we're—we haven't got anything there. What we're going to do is have the same amount of battalions up there we've had right along—94. So we're just—it's just <u>kidding</u> ourselves by monkeying with this [chart]. They're not <u>usable,</u> won't be until the first part of September, first of September, and at that time the 27th will depart, and so we'll be at 94, where we were in the beginning. So we're just going through a lot of mathematical juggling here which has not a damn thing to do with our capability."

SOMEONE (re B-52s): "From all causes, weather among them, we've had a history of about 4 percent diverts."

■ ■ ■

ABRAMS: "If you went to a cease-fire, or if you went to a thing of the NVA withdrawing and the U.S. withdrawing, or, you know, some combination of <u>those</u> things, he would have a framework which could absorb an awful lot of people." "This talking in Paris is a part of the whole scheme of how they achieve their objectives."

KOMER: "This <u>could</u> break very quickly. If they run the next big offensive and they don't succeed very well, they could start moving into a new phase fairly fast."

■ ■ ■

ABRAMS: "To me it's really <u>shocking</u> how these politicos in the United States go <u>charging</u> around like a bull in a china shop saying what ought to be done out here <u>politically</u>. God almighty! Trampling on the pansies that are <u>just</u> coming up and so on. <u>God</u>! Absolutely <u>insensitive</u> to the <u>struggle</u>. And it's a <u>real</u> sophisticated <u>struggle</u> that goes on."

■ ■ ■

ABRAMS (re Korea compared to Vietnam): "The war <u>here</u> itself, when you get into . . . the whole infrastructure, and the <u>political</u> structure, this is a <u>far</u> more sophisticated Communist effort than <u>ever</u> got under way in Korea. That was a <u>blunt</u> instrument by comparison. Just <u>caveman</u> tactics!"

ABRAMS: "Now, on the A Shau thing—I've been attracted by the idea of going back in there. There's some evidence that when we went in there before it really shook them up a little bit." "It <u>looks</u> like it <u>disturbed</u> them."

ABRAMS: "I'm <u>convinced</u> that there's <u>no</u> <u>way</u> for us to see here [at MACV] what every platoon is doing in this country. That's your bridges and that's your culverts and that's your highways and that's your ambushes and that's the hamlets and the whole complex, and I just don't believe it can be <u>reviewed</u> here weekly or monthly. It's just too much of a mass of detail. Now, you can <u>get</u> something. You can <u>get</u> something. You can set up a reporting system, but I'll guarantee you it won't be worth the paper it's written on. It's too <u>massive</u>! They've got too many reports to make out already. If you <u>want</u> it bad, you'll <u>get</u> it bad."

ABRAMS: "The only way I know to get a grip on the kind of things you're [Goodpaster] talking about is to just keep spending <u>days</u> out there with divisions and around in their regiments and battalions, and getting into the detail of what they're <u>doing</u>. And then you've <u>some</u> feel, or you can get some feel, for the effectiveness of it and the importance which they attach to it and that sort of thing. But that's the only <u>reliable</u> way that I know of."

17 AUG 1968: WIEU

ATTENDEES: Gen. Abrams, Gen. Goodpaster, Amb. Komer, Gen. Brown, RADM Veth, LTG Mildren, Dr. McMillan, MG Shaefer, MG Corcoran, MG Davidson, BG Bolton, BG Coleman, BG McLaughlin, Col. Cavanaugh, Col. Pink.

BRIEFER: Estimate 128,000 infiltrators have entered the pipeline since 1 February 1968. The enemy put in 36,000 during March.

DAVIDSON: "As far as the infiltration is concerned, he ought to be in pretty good shape."

ABRAMS: "Well, no, that's not necessarily so. He planned the infiltration for July several months ago, in line with what he thought he'd do operationally, and a realistic estimate of his casualties, so on. And that's what's been getting down here. It's <u>really</u> sort of an <u>inflexible</u> system. All that gets here is what he decided five or six months ago, seven months ago, to send."

DAVIDSON: "If not longer. I agree."

ABRAMS: "And that's all he's <u>got</u> here. And, in the meantime, we have <u>not</u> been <u>acting</u> like we've always <u>acted</u>. The way we've hit this fellow with B-52s, the extent to which forces are out here patrolling, ambushing, and so on. The improvements in the ARVN—or at least some of it. And so a possibility <u>exists</u> that he <u>isn't</u> in pretty good shape. But he was going to <u>be</u> in good shape if everything worked out the way he'd planned it. The question is whether it has or not."

■ ■ ■

ABRAMS: "That 54th Regiment—you know, it's a new regiment for the 1st ARVN. All three of its battalions have been operational since the second of August. And in that time they have—the regiment of three battalions—have killed 96, taken 40 prisoners, 45 weapons, and they've had 6 killed and 41 wounded. So it seems to be quite a commendable start for a green regiment." "But it's a mixed bag—another battalion of the 18th got ambushed yesterday."

■ ■ ■

ABRAMS: "You know, Stilwell has that estimate of the enemy, 'Deteriorating Enemy,' paper. And he talks about their leadership and that sort of thing. Now the 1st Cavalry is <u>all</u> over that area. Well, I have to qualify—it's not <u>all</u> over it, <u>but</u> the <u>division</u> is operating in <u>company-size</u> units. And that gives you a feel for the extent to which they're deployed and the extent to which they're covering the area. And they just can't <u>find</u> them."

■ ■ ■

BRIEFER: "In all threat areas, [***] reflects references to impending action." In the DMZ "the deployment of the 320th Division just north of Route 9 constitutes the most immediate threat."

ABRAMS: "All this time he [the enemy] can, by word of mouth, pass the word around that he's, really, he's told them to hold off down here. That's his return for the suspension of the bombing. It's not <u>true</u>. He's got <u>other</u> things—. So the <u>date</u>—I think the <u>date's</u> really a floater. When he—things are just right by his judgment, and he's got the right psychological moment by his judgment and so on, then he'll give them the word and away they'll go. At that time, whether the preparations are complete or not, they're going to go."

■ ■ ■

ABRAMS: "You've <u>always</u> got a special problem with the <u>troops</u>. You get Americans out here somewhere on the battlefield and somebody starts shooting at them. Now they've <u>got</u> to shoot back. And if he hasn't got enough stuff <u>there,</u> <u>you've</u> got to <u>give</u> it to him. You've got to bring air in there—I mean, the simple business of enemy shooting at your <u>soldiers,</u> that just makes a problem there that you've got to respond according to the rule the way the <u>soldier</u> sees the rules. He's functioning out there, he's doing things and so on that, a lot of it, is not really fun, and so on, but he <u>does</u> it. But he's got <u>you</u> by the—well, he's doing it and he expects <u>you</u> to do certain things. And one of them is when he's getting shot at, by god you'll bring <u>everything</u> to bear."

ABRAMS: "And this applies to the guys up there in the DMZ. If guys are shooting artillery at them from over there on the other side, we've got to <u>hit</u> it, or you're going to have a <u>problem</u> with the <u>troops</u> that you're <u>not</u> going to be able to <u>handle,</u> and it's this thing about the <u>rules</u>. It's <u>their</u> rules, but you can't <u>change</u> them. So, if he comes down there with two or three MiG-21s or whatever it is and starts bombing, we've got to go up and take those airfields out. And I don't think the president would be able to <u>stop</u> it. He might <u>delay</u> it for a while, but I'll tell you there'd be a groundswell come out of <u>there</u>. The reporters would be up there talking to those fellows, and we'll <u>all</u> have our feet to the fire."

ABRAMS: "And it's all—I don't know whether I'm oversimplifying this thing, but—you see, sometimes we <u>overlook</u> how powerful the <u>soldier</u> is. I mean marines as well, airmen, and all the rest of it. But the army—for instance, the army really decided against the M16. They bought a few for the airborne, where they could sort of make a case for light weight, but the army really, as an institution, felt that it was not as good a rifle as the M14. And I would say that this, by and large, was also the view of the soldier. <u>Then</u> this thing happened over <u>here</u>. And they got over here and the soldiers said, 'The M16's the best rifle!' That's what—that's where all the procurement—. You talk about testing and the M16—it had adjectives [*sic:* advocates?], there's no question, it's never lacked for them. But they didn't get anywhere, really. But when these soldiers over here started saying, 'We've got to have M16s,' that's what—then that broke the purse strings, the procurement and all this went on. And they do it. Then [laughing], they also threatened to abolish it. You know, they—some of them changed their minds. And all these Congressional investigations, and OSD investigations, and so on, that came from—because men became dissatisfied. And it's just a powerful force, and the country has to respond to it."

■ ■ ■

SOMEONE: "It seems to me that we've jockeyed ourselves into a funny position in Paris vis-à-vis this projected offensive of the enemy that, if everything goes well for the enemy and he's able to mount the offensive, then he gets credit in the headlines for power and so on, like he did at Tet. On the other hand, if, by virtue of our efforts here, we succeed in preempting him and preventing his offensive, then he gets credit for deescalation, which we've given him already. And I just wonder what sort of input we have to Paris, and whether there isn't some way of curtailing that kind of thing."

ABRAMS: "You've described the problem quite well. [Laughter] I think there are some more things that can be done. We had the Fuller thing, first of July, which went above the DMZ pretty heavy with B-52s. And then, after that, that was extended under the air force program up to 17 degrees 10 minutes, also fairly heavy. And in conjunction with that they moved a lot of artillery up to just below the southern boundary. Then you've got this thing that the 2nd ARVN did." "On the 19th they'll go in again with B-52s in the southern DMZ, but troops on the ground and so on."

ABRAMS: "The morning of the 19th is going to be real lively up here—you know, that compression, and then here come the marines and so on, and then just . . . as nightfall comes the light should be real [word unclear] in the TOC there at Hanoi, trying to get more reports about just what's happening down here and so on." "For a while you could make them think."

ABRAMS (re the 19th): "Let's celebrate the anniversary of the uprising in the north!" [Laughter] "I mean, make it a great day up there in the DMZ."

ABRAMS: "I was amazed yesterday to find the degree to which the 1st Cavalry and the 101 are really into the RF/PF, DIOCC, the full gamut of things, and they've just got a lot of damn programs going on, and a lot of work." "The purpose of all this is to get the RF and PF so that they and the district chief can run the district." "To a certain degree the same thing's happening in the Americal."

ABRAMS: "We must work against the whole system!"

24 AUG 1968: WIEU

ATTENDEES: Gen. Abrams, Gen. Haines, Gen. Goodpaster, Amb. Komer, Gen. Brown, LTG Mildren, Dr. McMillan, RADM Veth, MG Corcoran, MG Shaefer, MG Davidson, BG McLaughlin, BG Sidle, BG Coleman, Col. Pink, Col. Cavanaugh, Col. Avriett.

BRIEFER: An estimated 124,000 infiltrators have entered the pipeline since 1 February 1968. No new groups have been picked up in the past week.

Questions have arisen about the accuracy of the infiltration estimates, on which they have been relying heavily.

DAVIDSON: "We've run an operations analysis on the amount of infiltration that we've detected month by month."

ABRAMS: "Well, I have to say that I have put considerable reliance on keeping track of these groups . . . as a measure of the size of the problem we're going to be facing down here in South Vietnam. And, while I have always realized that it—some modest variation there, trail losses and that sort of thing, <u>nevertheless</u> it—for this level, it represented a fairly accurate picture of what was moving into country. Now, if there's—if it's going to be substantially different from that, we're in another ball game."

DAVIDSON: "I don't think it <u>will</u> be substantially different. For our purposes, sir, I think we can treat this with confidence as an order of magnitude of the problem."

ABRAMS (re the issue of "gap groups," although they are not yet using that term): "This would mean something on the order of 75 percent more for that February input." [The problem stems from a skip of maybe 15 numbers in two days, for example—too large to be missed groups.]

Gap groups are numbered infiltration groups whose numbers have not shown up in the communications intercepts, although numbers before and after them have. Thus they are in a "gap" in the numerical sequence. It is presumed they have begun to move south, but no confirmation has yet been received.

DAVIDSON: "This is one of the things, in this recent rundown in trying to develop the estimative method, we found that our time-honored 'it takes six months to determine infiltration' is like a lot of other things that we 'knew' with such great certainty—it wasn't true. At the end of six months you only could find about 80 percent of it. It takes <u>12</u> months to get the 100 percent."

This refers to the methodology employed before the communications intercept capability was achieved. In the earlier period intelligence on infiltration had to be built up laboriously over a period of many months through analysis of captured documents, interrogation of prisoners of war, information from ralliers, and identification of enemy units encountered on the battlefield.

DAVIDSON: Recalls an enemy July 1967 plan for 1968 as "the year of decision."

BRIEFER: Puts up chart "clearly showing that the lull is over and that the Third Offensive has begun. Looking at this data in a different way indicates the nature of his new offensive." Compares incidents countrywide for two six-day periods. "The 5 May attack started out with a large number, then quickly diminished." "The current attacks, particularly attacks by fire, show a trend of increasing in number as time passes." Attacks by fire have not yet reached 5 May totals, but there is some evidence that they are more intense. Average rounds expended: 5 May series—24; current—34. Increase of 40 percent.

BRIEFER: Unlike Tet and 5 May, "the enemy has made no attempt to launch a simultaneous countrywide offensive, yet the attacks in each corps area have been well coordinated." Started 18 August: Attacks throughout the COSVN area in III Corps, and some in the B-3 Front. 19 August: Relatively quiet. Also 20 August. On 21 August: Scene shifted to the delta, continuing there on 22 August, and another flare-up in III Corps. 23 August: Front 4 had numerous attacks by fire and ground probes, principally against MR-5 targets from Danang south to Quang Ngai City. Enemy seems to be purposely staggering his attacks to stretch out his offensive. Has enabled him to keep his casualties proportionately low compared to May figures. And increased intensity and number of attacks with relatively stable KIA.

SOMEONE: "His main objective [Saigon] he hit right off on the night of 4–5 May offensive. His main objective he hasn't hit yet [in this offensive]."

BRIEFER: And "it's been nearly a week now, and—with the exception of the Front 4 area—his principal targets [four of them, as determined from POW interrogation, captured documents, etc.] remain virtually untouched." Supports our prediction that the main effort would occur subsequent to initiation. Pattern emerges consistent with our earlier analysis. Attack outlying areas, draw forces from the cities. "Our agents tell us that a major attack on Saigon will occur after 1 September." "We know that Saigon remains the enemy's main objective in South Vietnam." "The infantry divisions which will have to provide the major punch [for an attack on Saigon] are still at some distance and seemingly occupied with other ventures. The main event is yet to come."

ABRAMS: "At some point in here the question is going to arise, 'Are we doing anything about it?' You know, what we're proving here is that he planned it this way, it's moving along as he planned it, and so on. We're just a bunch of spectators out here reporting the progress of the enemy. You get a little bit of that in this, too. I remember one time [during the Korean War] going down to the Commonwealth Division in Korea. They had a hell of an enemy attack going on down there, and the corps commander could not get any—all he could get was that everything was going according to plan. That's about all the information you could get out of the Commonwealth Division. So he sent me down there to find out what the score was, and that's exactly what it was. They said everything was going according to plan, and it was the enemy's plan!"

ABRAMS: "Well, there's more to it. They were just fascinated, because they'd made an analysis of this, over the weeks preceding, and they felt that he would attack down this ridge on the boundary between them and the marines. And, lo and behold, he was doing exactly that! And it was just—you know, they were really congratulating themselves. But, they also, of course, having figured that out, they had devised a plan to really cream it! And they had a good plan. It was only to be executed when he had reached a certain point of success. And that's what they did. And they did cream him. But what they were reporting— they said everything was going according to plan. They were right. And that's what they were reporting—it was going according to the enemy's plan. And they were just delighted. It was sort of unsettling for the corps commander."

DAVIDSON: "I think we have begun to interfere with them, sir." Two battalions pulled out of Tay Ninh.

KOMER: "I'm frankly baffled by what the enemy's up to. I don't think we've doped it out completely yet by any means what his strategic objective is."

KOMER: "I just have the feeling that another one of his objectives [besides a general uprising and overthrow of the RVN government], which may have assumed greater prominence than the short-term general uprising, is to get the Americans out of here."

Rebutting Davidson.

DAVIDSON: "Well, of course I'm bound by the evidence available, and the evidence available is overwhelming that he's after a general uprising, general offensive."

KOMER: "But that's sort of dogma, you know."

DAVIDSON: "We asked the seven highest-ranking ralliers precisely your question, and only two of them said they thought any of the offensive operations had anything to do with American public opinion."

KOMER: "The big mucks in Hanoi just don't tell the regimental commanders. They may not even tell COSVN what they're operating on."

DAVIDSON: "You know, we made a detailed research of that thesis, Mr. Ambassador, and we could not find one credible document, prisoner of war, or rallier who says that the enemy is interested in territorial acquisition."

ABRAMS: "What all this seems to me—what you're talking about is that the J-2 has unfolded a painting here this morning, and we have said, 'Ha, ha! We now have the painting which was drawn in Hanoi, and it's in the form and the shape and so on as painted and sketched in Hanoi.' In other words, they drew up a scenario, and now it is being carried out. Now—some time ago we thought that there would be a third offensive. We thought that the enemy was prepared for it. So, rather than wait for it to come, the most intensified intelligence effort yet—more patrolling, more focusing—and applying B-52s, tac air, searching and getting caches—caches, probably on a scale which we haven't done before. So this thing that was exposed this morning, I choose to believe, is not his plan. It's what he's been able to do with his plan, with the efforts that we've made against it in all of the days and weeks preceding it. In his plan he's bound to have provided in there for disruption of this and loss of that and some contingencies, but I think he had a <u>better</u> plan than what we have now seen executed, and it's been <u>screwed up</u> on him, and this is the <u>best</u> he could do with what he <u>started out</u> to do—so far."

ABRAMS: "You see, <u>we're</u> the only ones who think he <u>lost</u> on the other two. That's <u>right</u>! He <u>knows</u> what—even the 4–5 May thing, when the TV all over the country had Saigon burning and so on—those were <u>wins</u>! And those are the kinds of wins that he <u>needs</u>. It threatens this government. For the prime minister to stand in the middle of the ashes, down there in Cholon, and say, 'We've defeated them again!' as the refugees pile into the racetrack. That's a—."

ABRAMS (re the leadership in Hanoi): "They've got these <u>problems</u>. They can't tell whether the commanders are lying to them or not. They've got <u>no</u> way of supervising the thing. They <u>depend</u> on the strict discipline of the <u>party</u>. And there's evidence to indicate that they <u>don't</u> know what the truth is."

ABRAMS: "I think he's one of the few guys in the world right now who would try to run a military campaign down here in <u>any</u> kind of shape. He hasn't got the <u>tickets</u> to make it work. And what he's doing right now—it's just an <u>expenditure</u> of men. He's <u>groping</u>."

ABRAMS: "It's because he can't do a goddamn thing militarily, that's why. He hasn't got the <u>tickets</u> to do it. He's caught. He's a prisoner of his own damn strategy, and he can't find a good way <u>out</u>. He can't <u>admit</u> it—that's <u>impossible</u> for him."

ABRAMS: "I think he's got a <u>deteriorating</u> military machine. He's got maybe about three more times, or two more times, that he can <u>somehow</u> lash it forward. And, if we can keep <u>at</u> this, it'll just bust open. I think he's <u>trapped</u>."

ABRAMS: "He's going to lash them right up to the <u>gate</u>. He'll be out there with the whip—'<u>Forward, forward</u>!' It'll be the same thing, hold—like those two battalions up there off of [Route] 14. 'Time to get out.' '<u>No</u>, stand fast!' And they stood fast long enough to put five B-52 strikes on them. Flexibility, that's—why didn't he let them go scampering off through the jungle? No, he made them stand fast. <u>That's</u> not very <u>flexible</u>."

KOMER: "In other words, he's both getting more desperate and more smart, as he sees himself getting cornered militarily."

ABRAMS: "I think that's the thing I stumble over—is when you give him credit for being smart. Look at <u>Khe Sanh</u>. Poor old Giap—and I'm <u>really</u> convinced of this—poor old <u>Giap</u>, I <u>really</u> feel sorry for him. He was a <u>prisoner</u> of his experience. And he <u>kept</u> at that thing, <u>kept</u> at that thing, and <u>chewed</u> those divisions up so there wasn't a <u>damn</u> thing left. And <u>yet</u>, if he'd been the brilliant tactical commander that the U.S. press has—and strategist—that the U.S. press has given him, if he had moved one or both of those divisions down on the coastal plain, I don't know how the hell we'd ever have gotten them out of there! We couldn't put <u>another</u> battalion in northern I Corps! There was a time we couldn't put another <u>company</u> in northern I Corps! And we were having a <u>hell</u> of a time using the ones we <u>had</u> there. And that's why he stayed in Hue for 24 days. And with one or both of those divisions down there, and the marines sitting out there in Khe Sanh with nothing to do, he'd have been in Hue for three months. I don't think Giap's very smart."

ABRAMS: "And this thing they're doing now, this thing they're doing now—why are they having the trouble trying to squeeze the 5th Division through Dau Tieng? It's because they're following the same damn route they came in Tet, and the same route they came in May. Their security isn't any good. We know what their plans are—the ralliers, defectors. And here comes the old 9th back down to Ba Thieu to make it out across Hau Nghia and head for Tan Son Nhut!"

ABRAMS: "Also, I think there's something wrong with his troops. Now that fire support base out there—Ewell—that thing, all that was there was a rifle company, along with the artillery—a rifle company! He had at it, and by god he couldn't take it. It's almost disgraceful. He knew what was there!"

■ ■ ■

SIDLE: "Recent press visitors from the U.S. have been saying to me, 'How in the world are you going to stop this endless series of attacks? How long can this go on?'"

ABRAMS (re the U.S. press): "First they were on a program of underrating the enemy. Now they're on a program of overrating him."

■ ■ ■

GOODPASTER: "All right, let's continue to speculate on what his purposes are, but in the interim I certainly would not prepare for this, or react to it, in the sense that he is going to do less than the full thing he's capable of, and not do it in a wasteful way. Look for him to do that and apply it with as much skill as he can bring to bear—hooked, as I think he is, on the necessity of trying to attack."

■ ■ ■

HAINES (who left Washington 18 July 1968): "In the Department of Defense right now there's a great exercise going on, the so-called 69-3, which is fiscal '69 budget, give up $3 billion for blackmail to Mr. Mills and company. And that impact will be felt even here. Today you can't touch anything that is Vietnam or Vietnam related, but the name of that game has changed a little bit, because there's just not enough in the service budgets." Training base reduction. Sustaining base reduction. Order and ship time to Vietnam, using as an offset the presumed excesses in Vietnam as against reductions in the budget. Holding up the O&M budget worldwide until those excesses are deducted. Relates to hospital support you're getting in Japan. Expenditure limitation. "Right along with that is the gold flow exercise. The president's economists are telling him the country's bleeding to death from this outflow of gold. So there's great thrashing about to reduce here." Construction. "And in the early formulation of the '70 budget, everything says '70 is another austere year just like '69.'" "And I don't think there's going to be an FY '69 supplemental to bail us out, regardless of who is elected."

Gen. Ralph E. Haines Jr. has recently been Army Vice Chief of Staff and is now assigned as Commander in Chief, U.S. Army, Pacific.

The Mills reference is to Congressman Wilbur Mills, longtime chairman of the House Ways and Means Committee.

HAINES: "The thing that is being brought back to Washington by people who are visiting Vietnam—the Commandant of the Marine Corps brought it back to Admiral McCain—was that we have enough forces in Vietnam, we don't need any more forces here. And this is the statement that the secretary of the army brought back in his debriefing. So I think there will be a <u>rigidity</u> on the Program 6 strength figures."

HAINES: "There is a feel here now that we've got to get a handle on the supplies that we have in Vietnam, that we have to introduce a form of financial inventory accounting into Vietnam, and that we have to not only make the most of the excesses, but be sure that what we're now sending in just equals what you're using and doesn't make those excesses greater. All of this, of course, doesn't tie in very well with the imponderables of a combat situation on this end in trying to calculate it this close. But this isn't—."

HAINES: "There is no effort to pare the quantities going to the ARVN, and to the RVNAF, as far as I know. That, of course, also is the feel there that the whole thing has to be shifting of the load, and this has to be perceptible, and you have to be able to sell to the American public, sometime before the second of November, specifically that there is a place we have shifted to the ARVN and you can show graphically that they are carrying a greater percentage of the load."

HAINES: In Japan I met with Alexis Johnson. I said that I hoped that he would lay off a little on the B-52 thing from Okinawa. And he said, "Well, he wasn't making any judgments whether the B-52s were required at the level of 1,800 sorties, but he was just saying that if they are <u>not</u> required absolutely that he would hope that due consideration would be given to pulling the B-52s out of Okinawa." In Washington "Mr. Warnke and others keep thrashing around about it."

Ambassador U. Alexis Johnson served as deputy ambassador in the American Embassy, Saigon (1964–1966) and as undersecretary of state for political affairs (1969–1973).

Paul C. Warnke was assistant secretary of defense for international security affairs (1967–1969).

HAINES: "I'm sure, as General Abrams said, the better you do your job the more difficult it is to prove your credibility."

HAINES: "Well, this is kind of a somber story to bring from home, but I can only say I'm delighted to be in Hawaii rather than Washington."

ABRAMS: "Of course, we must take every economy measure that's practical. But one thing we're going to have to be very careful about is that, through inadvertence or misunderstanding, we don't carve into something that the <u>soldier</u> sees."

ABRAMS: "We've got to be careful what we put out here on saving money and saving expenditures. There—at least there's a <u>part</u> of the people who are over here—that doesn't <u>sound</u> very good to them. Guys at a fire support base, you know, they don't think much about this saving of money. They want to feel they've got <u>full</u> support."

ABRAMS: "I just hope it doesn't get to the point where there's a clear competition between the priority to economize and the priority to support the forces in Vietnam." "I can't see how the army, or the country, can afford to get into <u>that</u> kind of an argument."

■ ■ ■

DISCUSSION: A cavalry squadron being readied for shipment to Vietnam [reserve component, apparently]. Had to be held up because it didn't meet standards. Had one troop added.

HAINES: "That was the troop that started writing letters to Congress." Other outfits were better: Engineer battalion (70 percent Mormon), two artillery battalions. "Actually, your enlisted personnel throughout, because the reserve components have been a haven from the draft, have very, very, very large numbers of college graduates or college-experienced personnel. So you're talking about—many of these units, 70 to 80 percent of them have some college and maybe, of your enlisted personnel, 20 percent are college graduates. And this is even true in a <u>truck</u> company."

ABRAMS: "Should be very high quality units."

SOMEONE: "More capable of writing their congressman." [Laughter]

31 AUG 1968: WIEU and Special Brief on Third Offensive

ATTENDEES: Gen. Abrams, Gen. Goodpaster, Amb. Komer, Gen. Brown, LTG Mildren, Dr. McMillan, RADM Veth, MG Corcoran, MG Shaefer, MG Davidson, BG Bolton, BG Coleman, BG McLaughlin, Col. Avriett, Col. Cavanaugh, Col. Pink, Col. Crooks.

MACV has apparently lost the communications intercept capability on which it has been relying for intelligence on enemy infiltration, a very worrisome development.

BRIEFER: "Nineteen days of almost complete absence of reference to personnel movement in [enemy] communications." Three possibilities: "The most obvious inference is that, for some reason, infiltration has ceased, or at least has been drastically reduced to a minimal level that could escape detection." Or: "North Vietnam Rear Services are observing increased communications security because of frequent public announcements by the U.S. of accurate infiltration figures. Alternate means of communication are readily available, and we believe that wire line is the preferred means of communications in North Vietnam." Or: "We are seeing the results of a combination of events." Shift from radio to wire as the primary means of communication, reduction of infiltration in reaction to recent flooding and the historical pattern, and possible intercept reduction due to heavy rains and tropical storms.

DAVIDSON: We have sent a back-channel message to General Carroll and General Carter asking for help in resolving the cause, because: "If infiltration has really decreased this much, or if they've gone into some sort of secure system, the implications are enormous."

Lt. Gen. Joseph P. Carroll, USAF, served as director, Defense Intelligence Agency (1961–1969). Lt. Gen. Marshall S. Carter was director, National Security Agency (1965–1969).

GOODPASTER: "This will be a form of restraint, the first thing we know."

Meaning it will be interpreted by opponents of the war as evidence of enemy restraint.

■ ■ ■

DAVIDSON (re a three-star NVA commander who was removed): According to an agent, "he has alleged victories in areas under his occupation in monthly reports sent by messenger; he has failed to report casualties, food shortages, etc. So a member of the North Vietnamese defense department and a two-star Chinese general arrived at his command post for a discussion with him on the 14th of August. He said that as of the 16th he had not yet been relieved because he requested permission from the Hanoi government to command a full-scale assault by the North Vietnamese forces in Quang Tri Province. However, [***] the request was not granted and that he has been removed." "And what we see of the area, sir, amply bears out the justification of his removal."

ABRAMS: "Well, I sympathize with him. It's a hazardous business." [Laughter]

■ ■ ■

BRIEFER: Purpose of briefing is "to assess the progress of the enemy's Third Offensive." Eleven days into it. Compare to period 5–15 May 1968. "Thirty-four rounds per attack by fire versus 21 rounds in May, an increase of 62 percent."

BRIEFER: Casualty data demonstrate "once again that the enemy brings on his own high casualties" by the intensity of his ground attacks. Cites "the well established nearly two to one norm" for wounded as compared to KIA for the enemy.

BRIEFER: Re enemy "three divisions plus" that have concentrated in Quang Nam, Quang Tri, and Quang Ngai Provinces: Have had some 12,000 men "knocked out of action" as KIA and WIA in the current offensive. "And he has nothing but failure to show for this high cost."

BRIEFER: "He has yet to launch the attacks against Saigon that cost him so dearly at Tet and 5 May."

BRIEFER: By 15 May, the enemy had launched 121 ground attacks and 171 attacks by fire, totalling 292. But now more emphasis on attacks by fire. Current ground attacks 83 percent of those he launched in May.

BRIEFER (re enemy KIA): "By August 28th he'd sustained nearly 8,700 KIA, or three-quarters of those he suffered during the first 11 days of the May offensive."

BRIEFER: "The enemy's basic problem—he's launched his Third Offensive, this time with new tactics he hoped would give him success—initial attacks on peripheral targets as a diversion, staggered attacks to maintain an extended impression of his initiative and an aura of strength, limited commitment of his forces to hold down casualties and maintain his strength for the subsequent main blow on the major objectives. However, his new tactical plans have failed him. His KIAs are fast approaching those of the 5 May offensive, and he's not scored a single military success."

BRIEFER: "In southern I Corps, where he did try significant military actions, his plans have been badly blunted and his forces severely weakened. He has probably experienced similar difficulties in the southern B-3 Front, where his attempted diversion at Duc Lap only netted him heavy losses—over 640-some right now."

BRIEFER: "We're now receiving good indications that his attack on Saigon may be delayed. While the two-month lull allowed him to build his forces, probably to or even in excess of his pre-Tet strength, his lack of success so far and the heavy KIAs he's sustained to date are probably causing him serious second thoughts."

ABRAMS: "There's a big unknown—what's been accomplished by air and artillery, especially B-52s."

ABRAMS: "My feeling is our intelligence has been better as we approached this August offensive, and consequently our targeting has been better."

DAVIDSON: "You're absolutely right, sir. We'll demonstrate that in just a moment."

BRIEFER (to Abrams): "Last week you requested a comparative assessment of certain operational effects on the enemy for the 30-day periods preceding each of these offensives." Enemy-initiated activity, enemy KIAs sustained, cache discoveries, and secondary explosions and fires resulting from air strikes.

BRIEFER: Indicates enemy-initiated activity cut nearly in half during the 30 days before August (as compared to May), leading to "the now famous lull." "Obviously he was evading contact throughout the country to cut his losses and rebuild his strength."

BRIEFER (re events in May): Mentions "our intercepting his forces as they moved toward Dong Ha and Hue. The 320th [NVA] Division lost more than 600 dead that week [the week <u>before</u> the May offensive began] in the eastern DMZ, and the enemy regiments north and northwest of Hue lost nearly as many. In III Corps, he left a trail of dead as he approached Saigon through Hau Nghia Province and down the Dong Nai River."

BRIEFER: Caches captured 18 July–18 August were nearly 40 percent greater than in the 30-day period before 5 May. In I Corps "nearly doubled," and in IV Corps "tripled."

BRIEFER: From B-52 strikes: "The total number of secondaries has more than doubled, while in III Corps it has quadrupled." Attests to "much greater destruction of his munitions and POL supplies in the later period."

BROWN: "Far more of our strikes are now controlled by forward air controllers, so these claims are <u>not</u> by the guy delivering the ordnance. They're reported by somebody else, so I think you can have greater confidence in them."

BRIEFER: Re the comparison in summary (May versus August): In pre-August he reduced level of activity, and thus losses of personnel. But "his preparations to provide these forces with supplies and munitions appear to have been more severely disrupted countrywide." Uncovered more caches, and air strikes yielded "more than double the number of secondary explosions and fires." Nevertheless, attacks by fire running at 62 percent more rounds on average. "Apparently we've done a much better job against him, but the enemy has vastly improved his logistics system."

DAVIDSON: Per statement from [Ngoc?], "the high-ranking PW": "In III Corps, to the best of his knowledge, of all the caches he <u>knew</u> about we <u>got</u> all but three." For 5 May offensive. He was captured in early July.

ABRAMS: "I suppose it'd be interesting to speculate on this now in connection with the talks, their attitude at the talks, the plans that they had. In other words, they really had planned on a <u>humdinger</u>."

DAVIDSON: "Bigger than <u>ever</u> before, according to their documents."

ABRAMS: "Biggest of all so far. And that would fit <u>so well</u> the Communist as he picks up his suitcase and goes off to the negotiations. And, ah, probably has a lot to do with the intransigence that they have shown. Now, if there's any validity to <u>that</u>, what form is the <u>next</u> shoe going to take that's dropped?"

ABRAMS: "Of course, from our standpoint we can only hope and pray that he will commit the rest of it." "Let's <u>hope</u> that their faith in 'general uprising,' toppling of the government, and so on by just 'another exertion,' maybe 'the final exertion,' will topple it <u>all</u>."

KOMER: "But that takes away his flexibility. Once he's <u>done</u> that, he has no negotiating power—after we kick the hell out of him."

ABRAMS: "Now wait a minute. Now wait a minute. Now wait a minute. Did you see that <u>plank</u> that was defeated by 1,500 to 1,000? <u>I</u> would say that he's got <u>substantial</u> negotiating material. He's got 1,000 Democrats that were at that convention that would have <u>emasculated</u> the position over here."

Abrams is referring to activities at the Democratic party presidential nominating convention in the United States.

KOMER: "But they failed."

ABRAMS: "Ah-ha-ha. The *Stars & Stripes* said it was a 'massive victory.' The thing that bothers the hell out of <u>me</u> is those thousand <u>votes</u>. And that was a <u>horrible</u> plank."

ABRAMS: "I listened to Vice President Humphrey last night. I guess it was his acceptance speech. There was—of course, it should be, I suppose, but—there was something there for every soul that lives in our country." "He's out to be elected. And, in my opinion, this gives them a substantial negotiating position. It isn't these facts here—."

ABRAMS: "What I'm talking about, though, is—at the Wednesday meeting Xuan Thuy sits down there and he starts reading his statement. And he says, 'I've come here today to propose that we have a cease-fire.' And then he has some conditions. And they'd be pretty tough." "But my point is if he drops that at the Wednesday meeting, with things the way they are in the United States, he could get a damn good deal out of it. A lot better than he deserves."

GOODPASTER: "I think he would now have to couple something about the DMZ, and withdrawal of his forces, with that. Or at least not a further buildup through Laos."

ABRAMS: "He wouldn't guarantee anything about the DMZ. He wouldn't guarantee anything about withdrawal. He'd just say, 'Let's have a cease-fire.'"

GOODPASTER: "Well, you may be right there, because that and [word unclear] else would take our forces out of jeopardy, or at least it would appear to."

SOMEONE: "It seems to me if you can convince Washington and the negotiators, Mr. Harriman, that they were in fact going to make an attack but were frustrated in it by our actions that that would put them in at least a fairly strong negotiating position."

GOODPASTER: "There's a good possibility that Hanoi is convinced that the United States is really militarily, economically, and psychologically exhausted, and what they really have in mind is dogging along with the war rather than getting into a major offensive."

ABRAMS: "No, they're not dogging it." "This thing was designed to be the all-out maximum effort that they could make." "It hasn't been frustrated. We've been able to take the first parts of it, but whether he's convinced that it's a no-go, that's something else."

DAVIDSON: "I don't think he is, sir."

ABRAMS: "He may—he may save the day by pushing the balance of it."

DAVIDSON: "Sir, I think he anticipated just about what's happened."

DAVIDSON: "I think a very significant piece of intelligence today was the relief of that commander, because it showed what we have long suspected, that is that they're being misinformed in Hanoi, and possibly COSVN as well, as to what the actual situation is."

DAVIDSON: "One of the things we might want to do here is encourage him to come out and attack." "I think we ought to get some people thinking about the problem. And the psywar guys that I know don't think about that problem. They think about how to get people to surrender and small things."

KOMER: "I think it would be almost impossible for us to stem the response if he came out and just proposed a simple cease-fire before the November election. I don't see how either candidate could oppose it. You know, a cease-fire is like motherhood. How can you be against an armistice? Unconditional. We'd have to negotiate <u>how</u> you cease fire, et cetera, but—. I think that would put us in an <u>extremely</u> difficult position."

KOMER: Further holds forth on tactical matters. Davidson tells him the facts don't support his analysis: "I have to deal with the evidence available." That, says Davidson, contradicts Komer's view that the enemy has committed "less than a quarter of his force." Davidson: "The evidence is overwhelming."

ABRAMS (after letting Davidson and Komer debate for quite some time, stepping in to address Komer's contention that the enemy's May offensive was in effect just Saigon and III Corps): "No, he started down to get <u>Dong Ha</u> in May. He started out to take <u>Kontum</u> in May. He just didn't <u>make</u> it. It <u>wasn't</u> Saigon <u>alone</u>."

KOMER: Repeats his argument of a few days earlier that the enemy has gotten smarter.

ABRAMS: "I would just like to say <u>this</u>—I give him high marks on strategy in terms of psychological and political things, but tactically, down here in South Vietnam, I think he's just <u>stupid</u>. He comes—he's gone to Danang the same damn way he's ever—every <u>time</u> he's gone to Danang. And he's pulled back into [Go Nhong?] Island, where he <u>always</u> pulls back into [Gomoy?] Island. And these things—trying to bring the 5th Division down the Dau Tieng–Saigon River, that corridor between the Saigon and Vam Co Dong and so on. And no military commander in the world deserves the <u>name</u>—to go feeding troops into certain destruction the way <u>he</u> has. So all these—. And it's the <u>only</u> thing he knows how to <u>do</u>. It's the only tactic he really knows—in the end. That's what he did at Khe Sanh. He kept <u>going</u> at Khe Sanh, he had his <u>plan</u>, and they'd come right back up there and get in the same damn place, and the tac air and the B-52s would pour down on them <u>again</u>. And then he'd spend time getting stuff together and coming back in the same damn place to try the same thing <u>over</u> again. So I don't think he's <u>clever</u> at all."

DAVIDSON: "Most of us have forgotten that one time we calculated that the maximum he could put in to the infiltration in one year was somewhere around 110,000. Well, he's put damn near 200,000 in already."

DAVIDSON (re Goodpaster's suggestion that they intensify ground surveillance efforts in North Vietnam and Laos): "I would defer to Cavanaugh, but I think all we have to show for our past efforts is an unbroken string of failures, isn't it?" Cavanaugh more or less agrees, citing the enemy's being on to their pattern of activity.

■ ■ ■

Senior officials in Vietnam had very serious concerns about whether Averell Harriman, heading up the U.S. team negotiating with the North Vietnamese in Paris, understood the situation in Vietnam. Ultimately those concerns extended to his credibility and truthfulness.

SOMEONE: "There have been several press announcements or interviews by Secretary Clifford and by Ambassador Harriman which seem to me to indicate considerable misunderstanding, or at least terrible wishful thinking, on their part vis-à-vis possible NVN escalation—or deescalation. And I'd like to ask Andy [Goodpaster], from his experience in Paris, whether you think that it is understood there that, on the one hand, there's incontrovertible evidence that they were going to mount this Third Offensive, and intended it to be a damn big one, that for our part we've mounted very extensive preemptive actions which have been, at least in some instances, notably successful, so successful that we're, here, a little bit worried that we may have cowed him out of pursuing that third phase, and with these announcements by the secretary and Averell Harriman that—you know, 'Just give us any indication at all that you're going to deescalate and we'll believe it'—it seems to me very important that they not, that our negotiators not be given any chance to misinterpret the fact that we have successfully preempted this guy as in any way a deescalation on his part. I just wonder if that lesson has been driven home to them."

GOODPASTER: "I think the pressures that were mounting during this so-called 'lull' were very, very great, and if it hadn't been for two men, probably, we would have interpreted the lull as this restraint. And those men are Dean Rusk and the president, with of course the advice of General Wheeler. And I don't know who else we would—Rostow you associate with that, but the two principals were surely Rusk and the president."

GOODPASTER: "And the second point I would make is: If the enemy had not started this thing when he did, prior to the Democratic convention, it would be just a damn close thing as to which way that resolution would have gone, whether the president and Rusk would have been rolled, not in the sense of what they were going to do with the remaining months of this government, but what the next government was going to do."

GOODPASTER: "Now, so far as getting this kind of a pattern in the minds of our negotiators, no. The hand on the lever has got to be right there in Washington, right at the very top, because there's no doubt that the whole set and thrust within the top level of our government, and within a lot of political pros—now these were political pros that were there at the Democratic convention, and these are not—it's not biased over on the liberal or radical side, probably otherwise—and you could see that you were down to the very thin red line, and that was these two principal officials."

ABRAMS: "One of the interesting things to me in that—part of that plank was to abolish search and destroy operations, but when you think of a serious proposal in the Democratic platform to prescribe the tactics of the field commander on the battlefield, it's really quite an amazing development."

■ ■ ■

ABRAMS: "You know that they've postponed that squadron of cavalry [a reserve component unit] that was due to come in September." "I'm wondering whether it's possible to go to the GVN and say, 'Can you scrape up the stuff out of the Marine Corps, your Marine Corps, to take over this equipment up here in support of the ROK marines? Can we go to the United States and say, 'Don't send the squadron, send the equipment and we'll man it here'?" "Why can't we push ahead here?" "And I might say, also, that long list of other units that he— we ought to look at <u>that</u>—you know, that Westmoreland said he was sending over, yeah—and see if there are any of those where we just tell them, 'Send the equipment and we'll put Vietnamese on it' and so on." "'Don't send the people. Load the stuff up on the boat and we'll man it here with Vietnamese.'"

■ ■ ■

ABRAMS (re the August offensive): "My <u>impression</u> is that so far in this thing the [South] Vietnamese have done better than they have in <u>any</u> of the three—this is the third. Dak Seang, Duc Lap, this fighting—the 51st has played an important role in the fighting around Danang, as well as the Rangers, the fighting at Tam Ky has been borne largely by the 2nd ARVN, Quang Ngai, and the way Tri has moved these—<u>well</u>, the way Lu Lan has moved battalions around in II Corps, from the coastal plain to the highlands and one thing and another. It's <u>just</u>, it's just—now I'm not trying to say that all that was effective, like Tri moving a battalion of airborne up to Xuan Loc—<u>destitute</u> of <u>virtue</u>, but . . . it certainly is a <u>different</u> frame of mind—on the <u>plus</u> side."

GOODPASTER: "Are we stretching the arrival of M16 rifles to the maximum?"

ABRAMS: "Yeah, yeah. <u>Air</u> shipment from the factory—. If there's any juice left in <u>that</u> turnip—."

GOODPASTER: "They [the South Vietnamese] say that it's [the M16] had a profound psychological effect."

ABRAMS: "Well, this has been a very interesting morning."

UNKNOWN DATE AUG/SEP 1968: Admiral McCain Briefing

Tape box is marked "7 December 1968 WIEU, Tape 2 of 2 Tapes," but the contents sound like they are from much earlier, soon after the August 1968 enemy offensive, a briefing for Admiral McCain.

Adm. John S. McCain Jr. was Commander in Chief, Pacific (1968–1972).

Begins with Davidson: ". . . to look at the enemy's second offensive . . . to see the outlines of it, and to see how this so-called intensification fits in with it."

BRIEFER: COC journals re 5–11 May 1968 Second Offensive. "Amazing similarity, first in ground attacks during the first week of the operation." Dissimilarity: In second, went straight for the major objectives, but this time "he appears to be doing something else."

■ ■ ■

ABRAMS: "There's a lot of evidence to go around of a developing disinterest in body count per se. <u>Weapons</u> are important."

ABRAMS: "The fellows that are running the show up there [in North Vietnam] have been at this a long time. And for them it's been a l-o-n-g, tortuous struggle. And the ones that are left are the ones who never believed for a second that they would lose, or that they would be beaten, in all the time they've been proven right. Giap is alleged to have described Dien Bien Phu— the final phases of Dien Bien Phu—as the last exertion of the revolution. And they'd bet all their cards on that. They had fantastic troubles with supply, with food, all that, but they stuck with it when there wasn't, practically speaking— the odds were all against them. They won it, and with it they got the '54 agree- ment, which to them represented—despite the arrangements and so on—it gave them all of Vietnam. That's the way they saw it. And they've been on that wicket ever since. And so now, if there's anything to what I'm saying, these are the fellows you're up against. They know. They've been down this road before. They've stood right on the precipice and stared hell right straight in the face— and, and, and took it—and took it—and won."

■ ■ ■

ABRAMS (responding to McCain's question about the ARVN desertion rate): "It is a problem for them, but right now I don't read it as a critical problem to the ARVN. The truth of the matter is that their net strength has grown by leaps and bounds. They've replaced all of their losses, combat and desertion, and at the same time have built their structure up."

MCCAIN: "Well, the desertions aren't to the North Vietnamese. They're just desertions going back home into the countryside."

ABRAMS: "That's right."

7 SEP 1968: WIEU

ATTENDEES: Gen. Abrams, Gen. Goodpaster, Amb. Komer, Gen. Brown, LTG Mildren, Dr. McMillan, RADM Veth, MG Corcoran, MG Shaefer, BG Bolton, BG McLaughlin, BG Coleman, Col. Roberts, Col. Cavanaugh, Col. Avriett, Col. Pink, Col. Crooks.

BRIEFER: Twelve new infiltration groups in intercepted messages during the past week. About 129,000 men have entered the pipeline since 1 February 1968. Cites "the newly detected use of rail transport."

■ ■ ■

ABRAMS: "Discipline and revolutionary zeal do not necessarily go hand in hand." Cites "the large number of weapons left on the battlefield at Dak Seang, out- numbering the dead."

■ ■ ■

ABRAMS: Recounts conclusions of a J-2 study of expansion of the Viet Cong force structure: "The VC force structure, countrywide, has been expanded beyond the enemy's capability to fill the ranks by recruitment in South Vietnam. The enemy has greatly increased preparations designed to strengthen his political position in South Vietnam should a coalition government be formed. And the long-range purpose of the VC force structure expansion is to prepare the means by which pressure may be exerted or maintained in a post-cease-fire situation."

■ ■ ■

ABRAMS (following briefing on assessment of the enemy's campaign): "I think, more and more now, we've got to, as we move along here, we've got to think that of all—I'd say at least three things here: The military campaign, which is—that's one thing. And the more successful that is, then the more successful these other two things—the political organization, and fleshing it out, and the more successful this expanded military VC structure can be. There are at least three pieces, it seems clear to me—the political structure, a military structure to support the political structure, and then there's military campaigning to, ah—to create conditions where these other two can advance more rapidly, become more affordable, seem—might even take on an aura of desirability, in other places, and so on."

ABRAMS: "And I think of this in terms of the talks going on, I mean the meetings there in Paris. And it becomes especially sensitive, I think, and it becomes especially important if this [enemy] military campaign is as unsuccessful as it appears to be from this assessment we had this morning. Now we have, this week, polled all the commanders about their feeling on what the enemy is doing and so on. And, although I did ask a leading question, nevertheless without exception it was the feeling of the commanders that the destruction of his forces has been substantially greater than we are able to document. This is a unanimous feeling. And they come out rather strongly on that point." "It's clear to me that, in this particular round of enemy effort, that the performance of the Vietnamese has been better than it has in previous rounds. They've gotten out more, earlier." [Gives examples.]

ABRAMS: "Here in III Corps . . . I can't say anything for the 18th [ARVN Division]—same miserable performance it's put on all year. But the others have been a little better."

ABRAMS: "So I think, realistically, it must be apparent to him [the enemy] that the Vietnamese armed forces are operating somewhat better. It must have been a shocker to him what happened up at Duc Lap. With what he threw in there he had every right to believe that he would take it."

ABRAMS: "The real question is whether this has reached—to him—sort of a bad situation. And if it has, why not shift over to these other things? Now, this expanded VC structure which is more than he can fill—he could fill it with NVA, get it in good shape with NVA, and get it so the 9th, the 5th, the 7th, the 1st, the 2nd and 3rd, and so on, back to Laos and Cambodia and this sort of thing, get this expanded Viet Cong structure in good shape, and then doubling the political structure, and at that juncture call for a cease-fire."

ABRAMS: "And so—I don't say that that's going to <u>happen,</u> <u>but</u> I do think that it's worthwhile for us now to broaden our consideration of this from week to week in the terms of these other two efforts, as well as the military—the results of the military effort, so that the—focusing our attention on the stuff that happened to us, the Vietnamese, it's a [trip sensor?] or something like that." "There's a possibility that, as we begin to get the so-called military situation somewhat more in hand—what else should we be doing with our resources? In other words, could <u>we</u> get sophisticated, instead of 'two up and one back' all the time? Is there somewhere for <u>us</u>, and the Vietnamese, to get in the [word?] game in a <u>big</u> way? I think we've gotten now where we can ambush about as good as <u>he</u> can. Night work's getting to be—even over in the CMD—it's picking up."

Abrams is trying to expand the scope of matters considered in the weekly meetings beyond those primarily military.

ABRAMS: "He's still going to try a few more things in the military campaign, but I think we've got the wherewithal to <u>hinder</u> whatever he does there." "I think about anything can be handled."

ABRAMS: "I think we have to think more about the <u>results.</u>" "What can we do, specifically, to <u>counter</u> these things?" "That infrastructure is just <u>vital,</u> absolutely <u>critical,</u> to the success of either the VC military <u>or</u> this political. They just <u>have</u> to have it."

Here Abrams is talking about the covert Viet Cong infrastructure, which, through terrorism and coercion, was keeping the rural population in South Vietnam's hamlets and villages under domination.

■ ■ ■

ABRAMS (re revising the WIEU): "What I have in mind here, first of all, is to see if we can come to grips with a little bit more comprehension of what the situation is here in South Vietnam with respect to the enemy. In other words, the military campaign—that's one feature. What've they got here in the way of VC? And, also, what have they got in the way of political organization—in addition to the infrastructure? And from this, try to get a better appreciation of 'if he did this' or 'if he did that' and so on, what would be the advantages to him and what would be the bad things for us? To get more specific about it," make Saturday's meeting an assessment incorporating all elements, not just military, "so we try to produce here next Saturday a reasonably comprehensive picture of the whole game Hanoi is playing in South Vietnam." "And it's against <u>that</u> backdrop, this should, from that point on, continue to be the kind of Saturday we spend here."

SOMEONE: "This long-range planning group that you've appointed—will this be a [word unclear] along that line?"

ABRAMS: "No, that's going to have to be another thing. There will come a <u>point</u>

in here in which these can be <u>blended</u>, and probably will, but I want to get this—this is the sort of lead-in."

ABRAMS: "Broaden the assessment of the situation."

14 SEP 1968: WIEU

ATTENDEES: Gen. Abrams, Gen. Goodpaster, Amb. Komer, Gen. Brown, LTG Mildren, Dr. McMillan, RADM Veth, MG Corcoran, BG McLaughlin, BG Clay, BG Keegan, Col. Roberts, Col. Avriett, Col. Crooks, Col. Cavanaugh.

J-2 REPRESENTATIVE (re infiltration): "We feel that he [the enemy] is not allowing us to have the information on which we could make a decent assessment [as to what percentage we're picking up]. We have had, looking in the past—in other words not just the last little while—I would say an 80 to 90 percent confidence factor. We've been able to go back in and check with collateral, and give us a test basis in the months back that we could project forward. The fact that we're receiving information now that they are using rail, instead of coming down through the normal process on foot and by truck. They are reporting logistics, and not reporting personnel movement. This could be an indication that they <u>have</u> decreased. They decreased this time last year, due to the season itself."

■ ■ ■

ABRAMS (questioning why a given contact east of Hue at Vinh Loc Island was not included in the briefing): "Why isn't <u>that</u> in there? What <u>I</u> have is 86 KIA, 175 POW, 181 civilian defendants, 11 Hoi Chanh, 73 weapons, 1 ARVN killed, and 1 PF wounded. Well, it sounds like a good afternoon's <u>work</u>! And while we're reporting other things around here, I don't know why we can't report this. Is it because it's ARVN?"

RESPONSE: "No, sir." "This briefing is cut off at midnight Thursday."

ABRAMS: "Well, now wait a minute. <u>Yesterday</u> is the day we went into the DMZ, and he's briefed on <u>that</u>." [They can't answer.] "Well, let's pull up our socks here and get this thing organized. You've got a cut-off date. You've got a cut-off date. It looks like you're playing it the way you want to. You don't <u>have</u> a cut-off date. Let's know what we're talking about here."

ABRAMS (re enemy morale being affected by artillery and tac air): "It's one of those things that doesn't come out in systems analysis."

BRIEFER: A captured document dated 9 August 1968, signed by the political officer, Dong Nai Regiment, describes "fear of sacrifice, refusal to go on combat missions, and defections." Elements "directed to increase political indoctrination, conduct self-critique sessions, exercise tight thought control, watch unstable persons, improve personal welfare, raise internal solidarity, especially between North Vietnamese and South Vietnamese personnel, highlight heroism, and inculcate deeply an overall proletarian mentality into every member's brain."

ABRAMS: "Incidentally, if there's any question about whether this is doctrinaire Communism that's down here, that sure—."

ABRAMS: "Where he really put in his chips was at Duc Lap."

■ ■ ■

ABRAMS (re why U.S. forces' kill ratio exceeds that of ARVN): "It really ought to be. The ARVN doesn't have the firepower, it doesn't have the mobility, it doesn't have the communications. [Someone: "They don't get the allocation of air support."] That's right."

KOMER: "I was just wondering if this might have some implications when it comes to the modernization of the South Vietnamese forces."

ABRAMS: "Well, of course—that's what it's all about! It's aimed at that very thing!"

ABRAMS: "You've got to face it—the Vietnamese have been given the lowest priority of anybody that's fighting in this country! And that's what we're trying to correct."

STAFF OFFICER (having made quick calculations): Reports kill ratios of roughly 7:1 for U.S. forces, 3:1 for RVNAF, and 25:1 for FWMAF.

ABRAMS: "Which also doesn't mean anything. They're not doing anything! Damn it! They've got a great ratio, but—. The ratio's more impressive than the performance!"

■ ■ ■

BRIEFER: Introduces a presentation responsive to Abrams's request the previous Saturday "for a comprehensive picture of the whole game the enemy's playing in South Vietnam."

BRIEFER: "Significant VC force structure expansion since mid-1967, and especially since Tet." "We see use of NVA personnel for leadership cadre and rank fillers in VC units as necessary." "The VC are trying hard to maintain their guerrilla structure through intensive recruitment." Forty new VC battalions have been formed countrywide since mid-1967. They are in the force structure, but not necessarily at full strength. See the expansion as looking toward a posthostilities situation in which both U.S. and NVA forces are withdrawn, so the VC need it to hold their own.

BRIEFER (re filling out the expanded force structure with NVA personnel): "From North Vietnam's standpoint this is very desirable, for it assures that the VC will remain subordinate to Hanoi's wishes." Captured documents of recent months show stress on the expansion of guerrilla forces and on their role in the enemy's overall strategy. "Essential to his plans."

ABRAMS: "Our problem now is we've got so much information we can't really get all the good out of it." "We're missing it, just because it's so massive. We have documents and prisoners and defectors and all the rest of it."

ABRAMS (re the NLF): "I'm sure that they don't look with joy on filling this thing out with NVA."

20 SEP 1968: Commanders Conference

ABRAMS: Tells commanders about the staff assessment of enemy efforts being presented to them for reaction and discussion: "I would appreciate as wide-ranging a discussion of it—I mean, the sky's the limit. There is <u>nothing</u> set in concrete. It <u>raises</u> the question of whether there is a broader focus that we might take with our efforts." "And that applies—you're all invited. No one here is excluded. Don't worry about where your <u>seat</u> is."

This is apparently the lead-in to the Accelerated Pacification Campaign, and subsequently to implementation of the approach advocated in the PROVN (Program for the Pacification and Long-Term Development of Vietnam) study conducted while Abrams was Army Vice Chief of Staff.

ECKHARDT: "I haven't seen things happen this fast over here." "It's difficult for me to conceive that they [the GVN] would be able to do this in the time frame that we're talking about."

ECKHARDT: "Yesterday I came to you with a recommendation for 24,000 more RF and PF in the next year and a half, which would permit us to put security in these places we're taking."

ECKHARDT: "The plan [APC] is going to require somebody there with a gun on the ground to keep the GVN presence." "With more security forces, and at the same time get the GVN to do <u>their</u> part, we can make a success out of this thing."

ABRAMS: "What has been portrayed here today—for all practical purposes, it's identical with the view that the president [Thieu] holds, and the prime minister—to some extent, and the minister of the interior. General Vien understands this, and I'm going to have a meeting with General Vien on Monday to talk about it. The GVN <u>does</u> recognize this, and they realize that things <u>are</u> going to have to be done. I would say that there is some concern in the GVN as to whether or not their military commanders recognize this <u>and</u> are personally disposed to lend their—not only their good offices, but their <u>muscle</u> to some of the things that have got to be done in here. This <u>can't</u> be done just by governmental representatives." "Corps commanders and division commanders have got to have an appreciation of this, and consequently add their efforts and broaden their own view of the problem." "There is more to the <u>problem</u>, there is more involved <u>in</u> the war, than just that part [military]."

ABRAMS: "And <u>I</u> feel <u>myself</u> that the <u>Americans</u> have got to see, have got to appreciate <u>keenly</u>, that there <u>is</u> more to it, and wherever <u>we</u> are—advisory system, or in the military unit system, commander system—we've got to be preaching this and pressing it and articulating it."

ABRAMS: "So there is fomentation going on—<u>fer</u>mentation, maybe—on the GVN side."

KERWIN: "What I <u>do</u> like about it, it seems to be a very <u>logical</u> approach to the problem which focuses on what we should be doing. I <u>know</u> I could speak for

General Tri. He would be, being the type of person he is—aggressive, he would be enthusiastic on something of this type." "I can say unequivocally that he would be <u>behind</u> anything of this particular type. I'm sure that <u>he</u> would <u>push</u> it."

PEERS: "We certainly agree with what Bill Colby had to say."

Referring to William Colby, architect of the Accelerated Pacification Campaign and apparently the briefer at this session.

PEERS: "Sometimes getting the spaces for the RF and PF is not so easy. One of the things that we are going to try to do is push a little harder on this People's Self-Defense Force, because if some of these people can take over their own villages, the responsibility for their own villages which are now protected by the RF and PF, this will free them so that they can go out and expand further into the countryside to secure more area."

ABRAMS: "Intuitively I feel that we ought to push toward having the forces there belong to the province chief."

PEERS: "We're going to be going full blast on it."

CUSHMAN (CG III MAF): "I'm all for RF and PF <u>up</u>grading, to start with." "Everybody's thinking in terms of main force units, and you have to keep redirecting their sights when it comes to RF and PF and some of these others, redirecting their sights on the necessity for control of the population." On the plan: "I think it's an excellent one to indicate the importance of the political side of this war."

STILWELL (re Truong): "His division likes nothing better than to root VC out of secret holes."

STILWELL: "The more we win, the more troopers we wind up under arms in one form or another, to include at the tail end, presumably thousands and thousands and thousands of armed villagers."

VANN: "I do think we are suggesting a basic policy change in-country. As you know, we have always vacillated between whether we do the job well, and not have to do it again, or whether we go for a quick fix. Right now this suggests a quick fix, to some extent. Particularly the time phasing in Tet."

VANN: "If there is the imminence of a cessation of hostilities here . . . , then this quick fix would seem to be dictated. If, however, this war's going to go on for several years . . . "

VANN: "I think People's Self-Defense is probably the most misunderstood, by we Americans, of any of the concepts that have been advanced by Vietnamese. This is a Vietnamese concept—people's self-defense. It has never been contemplated by the backers on the Vietnamese side that the people are going to <u>fight</u>. When you arm the people, you don't arm them for the expectation of having them fight the enemy—in the Vietnamese concept. You arm them from the standpoint of having them overtly committed to the side of the government. And their key value lies not in the ammunition they throw at the enemy, but in becoming eyes and ears for forces which are trained to <u>fight</u> the enemy. In places where real pacification has taken place, it's been through organization of the population to do two things—willingly cooperate with the government . . . and then secondly, and equally important, is get their overt rejection of the enemy." "With a cooperative population, they inform you where the threat is and a smaller force, centrally located, is able to go out and counter the enemy force."

VANN: "If we're going to go for this basic policy, now, of moving out very rap-idly, this necessarily means a great decentralization—much greater than what we have now, and in the opposite direction from which the government of Vietnam has been moving in the last six months. I wholeheartedly subscribe to the idea that the corps commander has to have the other authority of that of being a government delegate."

VANN: "Just to summarize, sir, I greatly endorse the direction that this presentation suggests that we go, and greatly applaud the effort that's gone into recognizing the basic problems that have got to be countered. I have serious reservations as to the capability of the Vietnamese to be brought aboard and move out on this rapidly. I think something like this would be, should be, programmed over a several-year period of time."

WILBUR WILSON (in IV Corps): "The cheapest thing we Americans can do is to support more rifles in Territorial Forces."

■ ■ ■

KOMER: "We had this fellow Doug Pike out here. . . . He says he thinks the enemy's going through a period of great doctrinal indecision. They've tried several different ways of doing things, and none of them have brought the promised victory."

Douglas Pike served in Saigon for a number of years as a Foreign Service officer, then in retirement wrote extensively about the People's Army of Vietnam and the Viet Cong and founded the Indochina Studies Program and Indochina Archive at the University of California, Berkeley. Subsequently both Pike and his Indochina Archive relocated to Texas Tech University's Vietnam Center.

KOMER: "He [Pike] thinks that three lines of policy are currently being advocated in Hanoi." Foreign Minister [Nguyen Duy] Trinh "favors, sees a way out through negotiated settlement." Truong Chinh: "Protracted war on Maoist lines." Giap: "More of the same." Pike thinks it's questionable how long Giap's views can continue to prevail, given the tremendous losses incurred. Pike also says "he doesn't think the advocates of serious negotiation, i.e., the political solution, will prevail." "Thus he feels in the end the protracted war school will finally prevail."

ABRAMS: "We have to say that every bit of intelligence that we've got says that he's going to continue on with this military effort, even the freshest. What he's telling his people, what he's telling his commanders and his forces, is that, 'Yes, it's been rugged, but this is the right course.'"

■ Cites enemy efforts to establish Liberation Committees with recent "particular sense of urgency." Establishment of revolutionary administrations at village and district levels throughout South Vietnam.

■ HES "imprecise," but analysis "suggests that over 46 percent of the population is under <u>some</u> VC influence." Thus: "In the event of a cease-fire, the enemy might claim political control of about one-half of the population of South Vietnam."

■ "There are few substantial VC-controlled populated areas which are out of the reach of GVN authority or forces."

■ "While effective VC control exists in <u>portions</u> of most provinces, these are widely scattered throughout the nation."

■ "We have developed four campaign concepts." "We believe that they are compatible with the continuation of our current military offensive against VC and NVA forces. In fact, they merge, in effect, into one overall counteroffensive."

  • First: "Spoiling" campaign. Eliminate base areas and command centers of the enemy's <u>political</u> effort. Harass and disrupt. Phoenix is "an essential tool for this action." Plus military counteroffensive.

  • "Preemption" campaign. Against HES-determined areas that are VC controlled, contested, or heavily invested by VC. Plant the GVN flag, saturate with military forces, purge VCI infrastructure.

  • "Pacification" campaign. Population density, lines of communication, governmental and commercial centers as discriminators. Priority areas. Special effort to accelerate the impact of our current pacification program. VCI "one of the most important targets." Phoenix.

  • Territorial security, VCI neutralization, and supporting pacification programs of self-help, self-defense, and self-government.

■ Province elections in October, if possible.

■ "One-third of Vietnam's arable land . . . currently lies fallow because of the war."

■ Time goal of: Tet 1969.

21 SEP 1968: WIEU

ATTENDEES: Gen. Abrams, Gen. Goodpaster, Amb. Komer, Gen. Brown, LTG Mildren, Dr. McMillan, RADM Veth, MG Corcoran, MG Townsend, MG Shaefer, MG Davidson, MG Rasmussen, BG Sidle, BG Bolton, BG Bryan, BG Clay, Col. Davis, Col. Cavanaugh, Col. Pink, Mr. Colby, BG Keegan.

BRIEFER: Infiltration estimate for 1 January–30 September 1968: 191,000. Project an additional 16,000 for arrival during October–December. Total: 207,000.

DAVIDSON: If we "fill in the blanks" by giving the enemy credit for the gap groups, the total reaches 229,000. For 1967, per Davidson, it was 86,843. [Per the 28 September 1968 WIEU: 1966: 89,000. 1965: 36,000. 1964: 12,000.]

DAVIDSON: "His training base has just plain been exhausted, if not his manpower base."

■ ■ ■

DAVIDSON: Quotes an agent nicknamed "Superspook." He reports what a tough target Saigon has become: "ARVN forces are defending Saigon so tightly it is hard to find a weak point to attack." Troops from North Vietnam do not know their way around Saigon. "The majority [of cadre] believe an attack is possible only if defensive forces can be lured from the capital area." "Secret zones are under constant B-52 attack." "Caches are discovered."

■ ■ ■

ABRAMS: "See, he knows—it's crystal clear to him that once some outfit on our side gets in a fight—hell, it's just—every hour the thing mounts and mounts and mounts and mounts, you know, until—throwing in troops, throwing in air, and, if they'll just keep it going long enough, the B-52s'll be there! If they can just hang on for five or six hours, they'll have them in the game. And they know that! And yet here this guy goes fooling around with Duc Lap and—he didn't make a go of it."

■ ■ ■

ABRAMS: "We should work against the system." On the Binh Long–Phuoc Long border, "talking with Tri and Kerwin, what they were concerned about was the movement of the 7th Division down toward Saigon. And they knew that it either came down that corridor on the Binh Long–Phuoc Long border . . . [or] over to the west. So Kerwin put his reconnaissance forces in over to the west, to work on that route, and Tri put his on the Binh Long–Phuoc Long border. And it was these small groups out there—and what they were out there for was to detect the movement of the 7th Division. And instead of that they found the caches for the 7th Division. In other words, they were working against the system—the system he has to use."

23 SEP 1968: Informal Briefing for General Abrams

ABRAMS: Begins by reading (with relish) a long message from Peers about a Chieu Hoi claiming to know the location of the B-3 Front and who rallied by killing six others with a claymore mine so he could get away (confirmed by going to view the corpses, found to be as advertised).

ABRAMS (re possibility of attacking B-3 Front Headquarters): "If we're talking about the B-3 Front here, I don't want anybody monkeying around that thing with a few squads or companies or something. I want the whole B-52 fleet, the whole tac air fleet, and one <u>brigade</u> of the 4th Division! So let's not let this thing fritter away here. Now, we haven't got much <u>time</u>, because they're going to find out that this guy has <u>quit</u>."

ABRAMS (re 320th NVA): "Remember when they came strolling down there the first of May?" Got men killed 300–400 at a whack, about 3,500 total.

SOMEONE: "Over 7,000, sir." [7,300]

ABRAMS: "They just got caught stumbling around."

BRIEFER: "They were taking infiltration groups, as such, and throwing them into battle."

ABRAMS: "Well, that division commander should get a v-e-r-y poor report. The fitness report should be very low on him." Division out of action for almost two months.

28 SEP 1968: WIEU

DAVIDSON: "Our people are right now engaged in a conference at CINCPAC to make sure we all see this infiltration the same way." DIA came out there to take part.

■ ■ ■

DAVIDSON: "We have any number of documents where these people have said this <u>is</u> the year of decision." Abrams inquires as to the lunar year, and is told they think it is the Year of the Monkey. [It is.]

ABRAMS (re chart showing casualties sustained and inflicted by each element of the forces—U.S./RVNAF/FWMAF): "It's getting to where it's not a bad thing to chart. You know, you've got to be careful what you chart. But I think that it tends to support the contention that the Vietnamese forces are shouldering a much greater burden in this war. . . ."

■ ■ ■

BRIEFER: An agent's report that the enemy continues to plan for all-out attack "is borne out by piles of evidence—documents, PWs, Hoi Chanh, and other sources that speak of preparations for major attacks, the coming climactic phases, the imminence of the new Winter–Spring Campaign. Thus we see no hint that the enemy intends at this time to abandon or seriously modify the type of military operations he launched at Tet."

BRIEFER: "Why does he persist in these attacks? Why should he attack again when he's suffered such substantial military defeats at Tet and 5 May and is obviously doing so poorly now? Secretary Clifford asked this question. So has General Wheeler, and many others. The answer lies in three basic enemy imperatives, the dogmatic articles of faith with which he constantly bombards himself and his followers. These three imperatives are his basic doctrine, his view of the situation, and the objective he seeks."

KOMER: "One of the big things that runs through here—we're on the strategic defensive. We're sort of waiting for him to attack <u>our</u> cities."

ABRAMS: "Well—I would say a couple of things about that. From the information that's available to me, every representative of his government, everywhere in the world, is preaching this same thing. It isn't just the COSVN resolution. It's every ambassador, every representative that he's got everywhere in the world."

KOMER (interrupting): "But they're troops. They're propagandists, just like—."

ABRAMS: "All right, all right. Now, ah—that may, that very well may be. But the thing—and this is just the way he's running the war. It's his campaign. Now, the other thing—you talk about a counteroffensive—I think what you're doing there is taking his description of what we're doing and saying that is what we're doing, and then we should change it. And his description of what we're doing is not adequate to what we're doing."

COLBY: Provides analysis of what the enemy says and what he believes. "He's got a wonderful cadre machine, absolutely magnificent cadre machine, but it hasn't turned into mass political support."

ABRAMS: "One of the burning questions of the moment is whether the bombing should be stopped or not. He's [the enemy] pressing to have it stopped. So far, our government hasn't stopped it. Now supposing it did stop it?"

KOMER (speaking bellicosely, pounding the table): "I'll give you a very quick answer. It would prove to him that every damn thing his doctrine has said since 1947 is absolutely right. And he'll keep attacking till the cows come home."

DAVIDSON: Cites 200,000 infiltrators sent this year.

KOMER: "Though they decided, apparently, around June of '67 to launch the general offensive, general uprising, et cetera, we didn't know it until it hit, really, in all of its magnitude and everything else. Now I'm not just talking about the tactical surprise, but they did switch—they went from Phase II to Phase III."

ABRAMS: "That's right."

KOMER: "We caught up with it after the event."

ABRAMS: "Right." "The comfort in the present situation, though, is that their doctrine doesn't have a fourth phase." [Laughter]

ABRAMS: "I think that [Colby's briefing] was a splendid presentation. I think it comes out at a most opportune moment."

5 OCT 1968: WIEU

ATTENDEES: Gen. Abrams, Gen. Goodpaster, Amb. Komer, Gen. Brown, LTG Mildren, Dr. McMillan, VADM Zumwalt, MG Corcoran, MG Townsend, Mr. Colby, MG Shaefer, MG Davidson, MG Rasmussen, BG Frizen, MG Bolton, MG McLaughlin, BG Bryan, BG Keegan, Col. Crooks, Col. Cavanaugh, Col. Pink.

ABRAMS: "Somehow this doesn't sound like the 'Year of Decision.'"

ABRAMS: "I always go back to Tet. Our problem with Tet was that we did not realize that a major switch in strategy had occurred."

■ ■ ■

ABRAMS: Describes a pyramid drawn by Julian Ewell (apparently illustrating his operations). Enemy: Main force, local force, guerrillas, and infrastructure. "What they've got to do," as Ewell explains it to his soldiers, "is get after the whole thing." "The artistry in this is how much you weight each one of these. But the requirement is that you get after all of it. That must be done." "The most important thing is we have got commanders who are looking at this thing in a little broader way and know that there is more to the problem." "The [enemy] units in Long An, according to Ewell, are broken down into squads and half platoons."

ABRAMS (re Tri): "He's really been away from the operating end of the business." Thus "didn't have a feel for the tools that were actually available." They [Kerwin] put on various firepower demonstrations for him. And (to Tri) "logistics is just of no consequence. Convoy operations—'To hell with that, you don't need that.' But he now sees the significance of all that."

KOMER: "It's awfully hard to target U.S. units on the infrastructure."

ABRAMS: "Either the U.S. is going to sit on its ass in Long An and do nothing until the main force units reassemble, or they've got to get out and find some other way to work in the system."

■ ■ ■

ABRAMS: "Because the ARVN does not get the wealth of air support, nor the wealth of artillery support, nor the wealth of gunship support that the U.S. units do, I would say that the proportion in here may be more favorable to the ARVN."

Regarding relative losses imposed on the enemy.

ABRAMS: "We've got several cases where ratings by the advisors are way out of whack with the performance. For instance, for the whole first half of the year the 21st ARVN has been rated very poorly by the advisors, but its performance—in terms of killed and that sort of thing—its performance has been one of the good divisions."

■ ■ ■

BRIEFER: Significant changes in enemy deployments in the last two weeks. 320th NVA Division, MR-TTH, and elements around Duc Lap. Most or all of the 320th has withdrawn from the vicinity of Route 9 to just north of the DMZ. Why? 1. Forced to? Over 1,100 KIA in the past two months. Large caches uncovered. Sweeps, reconnaissance in force. "Falloff in enemy activity during late September." 2. New mission elsewhere? 3. Political move, to give an impression of deescalation?

BRIEFER: Since 23 August the enemy has suffered at least 1,000 KIA at Duc Lap. Enemy elements have withdrawn into Cambodia.

ABRAMS (re enemy in the DMZ area): "They've never been faced with the degree of offensive action that's now been going on up there for a protracted period." It is true that at one time we launched an operation into the southern

DMZ, "but that was the labor pains of an elephant. You know, it was planned and organized for weeks, and finally went moving off. But this—they've just been out there, week after week, short, quick things. It's been a whole series, from the 2nd ARVN Regiment all the way over to that area north of Khe Sanh."

ABRAMS: "I can remember being up there talking with Tompkins in the early days of this thing here where you had Khe Sanh and so on. And the idea—this area up here was regarded at that time as impenetrable." "Now, I don't know whether that was all true. There was a lot of things looked bad then. Khe Sanh looked bad. That looked bad. The Cua Viet looked bad. I mean, the whole damn thing looked bad. It was just sort of a—well, that was the way everybody felt."

DAVIDSON (re infiltration): "Nothing new. No more groups. And we haven't got any better explanation than we had before. We hoped it wouldn't come up." "Tomorrow morning my representative gets back from the joint conference at which they're trying to deduce what is happening."

ABRAMS: "First of all, he [the enemy] has never admitted that there are any NVA in the south. So if he now says, 'We have withdrawn,' it gives him—there's a problem of explanation there. The other thing is he's said—he's really put on a campaign about how they're winning. You know, they've got control and so on."

ABRAMS (re enemy propaganda): "Which I suppose somewhere around 75 or 80 percent of the people in the United States believe. And a 100 percent of the press."

ABRAMS: "It's interesting to contemplate whether we should make a staff study and announce to the world what has happened, and say, 'He's been defeated and withdrawn.'"

ABRAMS: "We've got a public relations problem. He [the enemy] comes marching in there [Paris] to the Wednesday meeting and tells them, 'We've restudied what you've been saying' and so on, 'and we won't attack your forces up there in northern I Corps.' They'll just say that. And the son of a bitch is not going to attack them because he can't right now. So the way to get out of that is for him to take the initiative and say, 'I won't. We'll just be good to you.'"

COLBY: "All his sympathetic press, the Communist press particularly, around the world, made that interpretation of the ceasing of the rocket attacks on Saigon at the end of June."

KOMER (with sarcasm): "Christ, and the American press, too. You know, 'There was a real lull. The enemy signaled us back there a couple of months ago and we just would not listen.'"

ABRAMS: "Even Humphrey is tiptoeing—well, his lieutenants are tiptoeing around with that little thing."

ABRAMS: "We've got to think about this. We've got to think about this."

■ ■ ■

KEEGAN: "We've just finished a five-week exercise of looking at the [***] of logistics flow." Comparing with our interdiction program. "What's becoming more and more clear is that the enemy's having probably extraordinary logistics difficulties." "The five key points north of Mu Gia have been virtually impassable for about seven weeks." [***] for last five weeks an average of 1,600 tons per week of munitions moving south from Vinh. "But in the past five weeks my analysts estimate that the net throughput of trucks . . . into Laos has been less than 30 trucks a day." During the last three weeks net throughput less than 5 trucks.

KEEGAN: "I suspect that he's having to move his units out on those logistic routes to pick up those supplies that are not getting in. He simply has not been able to move munitions, food, and the logistics support that we saw a year ago and that would be necessary to support the operations that have been going on."

KEEGAN: "You have had operated here, for the past two months, a classic logistic situation in which the impedance of flow into the battle area has probably been of a higher order than [at any other time] in the history of the war. And, secondly, you have been attriting so heavily in-country—ground-air operations, the B-52 operations, spoiling attacks—that what you have in effect is the classical situation as airmen we always look for, the situation in which the logistics are being impeded [in their movement] into the battle area and in which they're being consumed, attrited, discovered, spoiled in the battle area. And I think this has caught up with the enemy." "I think he's [the enemy] in one of the most serious logistics situations he's ever been in."

COLBY (re the enemy): "His logistics system is to put the depots ahead, not behind."

ABRAMS: "We're using 90,000 tons a month."

MILDREN: "Remember, the high point was 112,000." [USARV only]

GOODPASTER: "There is an area where his logistics effort is apparently not being impeded—."

ABRAMS: "That's right."

GOODPASTER: "And in that area—."

ABRAMS: "Cambodia, and that's where the fight goes on."

ABRAMS: "I believe that it's urgent to gather this together as a preliminary, tentative view of things, and pass it on to the Chairman [of the Joint Chiefs of Staff]."

ABRAMS (re the enemy): "This guy is a determined man, and he is a bad man. I mean—I sound like him, but by god Christian charity and brotherhood doesn't flow very strong in his veins."

ABRAMS: "For one reason or another the character of things is changing in I Corps. And it is clearly changing in II Corps. We're obviously not going to have our semiannual battle for Dak To."

ABRAMS: Remarks on the outlook that "just screens out" the role of Sihanouk in supplying the enemy.

ABRAMS: "This thing that Keegan's been laying out here this morning is—for all those who have stood for, in favor of, maintaining the bombing, they should get some comfort out of that."

ABRAMS: "Can you imagine Enthoven joining us here for one of these Saturday sessions? Just—!"

Alain Enthoven was the director of Systems Analysis in Robert McNamara's Defense Department.

5 OCT 1968: COMUS Brief to Secretary of the Navy

Paul R. Ignatius was secretary of the navy (1967–1969).

SOMEONE: "Mr. Colby here is the head of our CORDS."

William Colby has replaced Robert Komer as Deputy to the COMUSMACV for CORDS (Civil Operations and Revolutionary Development Support).

DAVIDSON: "I think the intelligence is many times better than what it was six months ago." Due to several factors: "In the first place, the breakthrough that we got on infiltration gave us a great lead on the enemy we never had before." For the first time we have agents placed in the right places, and they are giving invaluable information. "I think our analytic capability has increased immeasurably over the last few months." And benefits of our computer capability are just beginning to be felt.

Davidson served as MACV J-2 for the final year of General Westmoreland's tenure and is now continuing in the position for the first year General Abrams is in command.

ABRAMS: "What's been going on in here is working against the system. And, as a result of that, a lot of caches of weapons, ammunition, medical supplies. . . ."

ABRAMS (re the enemy system): "This thing is pretty rigid tactically. They can't go and fight somewhere else. They've got to follow through pretty much where this thing is laid out, because <u>that's</u> where the supplies are, <u>that's</u> where the sustaining thing is. Any real shift in maneuver is probably not in the cards. They've just got to carry through the way this thing has been set up in advance."

J-3: Describes the B-52s as "the theater commander's artillery." He also speculates on Ho Chi Minh's outlook: "You can kill my soldiers, but if my infrastructure stays here I'm still in pretty good shape."

J-3: "COMUS [Abrams] has just issued instructions that we get this VC [*sic: VCI?*] battle up even with the tactical battle. And he's charging the field force commanders with doing this."

■ ■ ■

ABRAMS (re B-52s): "At Khe Sanh there were 2,600 sorties of B-52s put in there. The affair in Kontum in April and May, we put 1,000 sorties in there. Down here in this latest go for Saigon, we have already put in in excess of 3,600 sorties of B-52s. Where we are convinced that he's ganged up—you know, has really got serious intentions, then we really go after it, around the clock."

SECNAV: "Who releases the B-52s?"

ABRAMS (rapping the table in front of him): "Morning and night." "The whole command structure is zeroed in on this."

GOODPASTER: "Some of the best testimonials on this [the B-52s] come from the enemy."

ABRAMS (re the enemy): "He's got a fair-sized problem. He may not think much about human life, but—."

ABRAMS: "We've got one game to play, and that's straight."

SECNAV: "We're firing many more missions from the naval gunfire support compared with six to eight months ago."

■ ■ ■

COLBY: "We're driving ahead on the political side as energetically as on the military because we want to stop the enemy, but more than that, we want to take the initiative away from him. And we know that, unless we win on the pacification side as well, we really haven't achieved our objective."

COLBY (re HES): Input from district advisors. "Many of them don't speak Vietnamese very well, many of them haven't been there very long, so it's an imperfect system. But it's just an awful lot better than anything we used to use." Six categories of hamlets: A, B, C, D, E, and VC. Relatively secure: A, B, C. Contested: D, E.

COLBY: "By the end of January we'd gotten up to 67.2 percent relatively secure of the total population of South Vietnam. Tet knocked us back quite a ways—59.8. Since then we've been gradually working our way up, and last month, August figures—65.8."

COLBY: "For territorial security, our main focus is on improvement of the Regional and Popular Forces, which are almost half of the army now." "We started last October. General Abrams had a conference here, identified some 30 steps to take. They ranged all the way from improving pay cards to sending out small military advisor teams to work with the RF companies and PF platoons. We now have some 250 of those five-man teams scattered around the country."

COLBY: "This includes some effort to upgrade the weapons. There was quite a shock around here when the AK-47 came in. And there was a problem with morale, as much as anything, with the territorial troops, because they thought they were outgunned." "They now have M2 carbines," upgraded from M1s, "and they are well on the way toward receiving M16s in the RF and PF." In the Capital Military District they all have M16s now.

COLBY: "Over the past eight months, since January, you have enormously increased the total number of troops. There're some 86,000 more of the RF and PF in the country."

COLBY: "We have a program that we have been working on for a bit over a year, called the Phuong Hoang, or Phoenix, program, which is a program of consolidating intelligence and exploitation efforts against these particularly key individuals." The program finally got off the ground really in July when the president signed a decree. Now "it is picking up speed enormously. There was a great deal of confusion and lack of understanding on the part of many of the Vietnamese as to the object of the game, but I think we've gone over that particular hurdle and we're moving into the exploitation. One of the major elements for it is the police force." Built up to 80,000 by adding almost 10,000 this year. The Police Field Force "is targeted specifically at the infrastructure."

COLBY (re infrastructure): "Tet did surface a lot of them. We captured a lot, killed some, and some came in as defectors."

CORCORAN (re pacification): "President Thieu has taken a very strong interest. He ran a meeting just as though it was a class at Leavenworth. He had thought it out and so on."

COLBY: "The thing is that, frankly, six months to a year ago the police were operating in their world and the military were operating in the military, and there was very little attention to the political command structure of the VC."

COLBY (on getting the VCI): "Preferably alive, because obviously he's more valuable alive, but some of them do get killed in the process." "The major effort on our side to date has been organizational, to try to get this accepted as an important target. It wasn't, frankly, for a long time."

ABRAMS: "Several months ago I attended a quarterly review with General Vien. When it was all over he asked if I had any remarks to make, so I got up and gave what I thought was a very stirring speech about eliminating the infrastructure. Then he got up and made a speech about Cambodia. So I realized there really wasn't a meshing of the gears." But that is changed now.

12 OCT 1968: WIEU

Attendees: Gen. Abrams, Gen. Goodpaster, Amb. Komer, Gen. Brown, LTG Mildren, Dr. McMillan, VADM Zumwalt, MG Corcoran, MG Townsend, Mr. Colby, MG Shaefer, MG Davidson, MG Rasmussen, BG Frizen, BG Sidle, BG Bolton, BG McLaughlin, BG Clay, BG Bryan, BG Keegan, Col. Gleason (for Col. Cavanaugh).

MACV 1968 Infiltration Estimate: 246,000.
BRIEFER: On 4 October 1968 the USS *New Jersey* arrived on station.

■ ■ ■

ABRAMS (re reduction in the use of artillery): "I'm almost afraid to talk about it. That September report is—. The August thing I thought, 'Well, the commanders have pulled it off again. They thought they would use up the surplus that was unaccounted for and [make it] possible for Abrams to make good reports.'

Either the surplus was great enough to cover them for two months or they've actually gotten with it."

Abrams had been stressing reduction in excessive use of artillery, largely because of its adverse effect on the rural population they were fighting to protect.

TOWNSEND: "I think they've gotten with it."

■ ■ ■

DISCUSSION: Controlling buildup of surplus. Someone recalls "fire the last round on the last day."

This was allegedly McNamara's objective, that at the end of the war there would be nothing left over, no surplus.

ABRAMS: "There was <u>never</u> anything in Korea that looked like this. I mean, the <u>masses</u>. There was <u>nothing</u> in Korea that would resemble Cam Ranh Bay. I think even if you gathered everything in Korea together you couldn't make it look like Cam Ranh Bay."

■ ■ ■

ABRAMS: "I think one of the most gratifying things on that report of yours [J-3, apparently, re artillery expenditures] is the amount of H&I. They've really gone to work on that."

J-3: "I think every commander I've talked to has gotten behind the program. Peers is convincing the ROKs to join the program."

ABRAMS: "Of course, there's so little enemy left down there it's getting really hard to justify the shooting."

ABRAMS: "The DOD is getting a little concerned that we're doing too much in IV Corps. Apparently they preferred it the way it used to be—nip and tuck."

■ ■ ■

COLBY: "Yesterday the president [Thieu] announced that he was issuing a directive on a program which he calls 'Pacification and Reconstruction' for 1969. However, this includes both the special pacification offensive, running from the first of November until the end of January, and the total of 1969." Plan due by 20 October for the special offensive, followed shortly by national-level seminar. Minimum of 80 percent of the population to be secure by the end of 1969.

ABRAMS: "I think that the picture's clear enough now so that some risks can be taken with respect to large units. I'm saying this in terms of really getting going with the guerrillas, the infrastructure, the local force, all that stuff. Trying to keep track—instead of being out in western Quang Tri with five battalions or whatever it is we've got out there . . . maybe the picture's good enough out there so you can do it with one. And they can afford to go into small-unit operations out there, which is basically reconnaissance teams that shouldn't try to—. Their real purpose would be to keep an eye on the trails and all that kind of stuff out there, and don't get tangled up with too much so that you can tell when the pattern of what the enemy's doing begins to change. Then you're going to have to move forces in there and really start to work on it. But reconnaissance, observation, and so on." "If he's going to move back in there with forces he's going to have to start a logistics effort, he's going to have all this preparation of the support area, and that's the thing we ought to be trying to pick up. And you don't need a lot of force to do that."

ABRAMS: "On the territorial war—the political structure, the administrative structure, the guerrillas, the infrastructure, and territorial security and all that—I think that we could deepen our thinking about that. It's nothing new. For instance, I'm satisfied on this logistics business he's got to have these caches, he's got to have these dispensaries, he's got to have the medical supplies. Like the thing they've been doing out there in the pineapple area. Now we've screwed around with the pineapple area for, oh, a year and a half anyway. But now they're getting out there—you know, they got into this dispensary setup, 4,000 beds, 4,000 wounded, that's what that was designed to take care of. And they've gotten a lot of stuff out of it. It was a fairly sophisticated setup and so on. But the point is he has to have things like that in order to make an attack on Saigon a realistic thing for him to do. He's got to make these kinds of preparations. He's got—like all those caches for the 9th Division. That was the stuff the 9th Division had to have in order to sustain its offensive attacks and so on—the food, the medical supplies, the ammunition and fuzes, and all those things, and he has to position that stuff, he has to have it there, to go ahead and project any combat power. So it's just as important to work at that, and find it and destroy it, as it is to meet his battalions and his regiments and defeat them. Really all you're doing is starting to work on the battle a little earlier, and in geography in a little different place."

ABRAMS: "All right. Just as he needs those caches, and just as he needs ammunition and rifles and medical things, he needs these guerrillas and cadre. They're—if anything, they're more important to him than the caches, or more important to him than the actual strength of his rifle battalions. These are the people that show him where to go. They're the guides. If he wants to get some porters, he gets them from the cadre. And the guerrillas help him and so on. If he wants to get a bunch of people buried, it's the guerrillas and the cadre that can work. They may not do the digging, but they'll get some people that will, places they can do it, and so on. Or where he wants to locate the cadre—."

ABRAMS: "All I'm saying, all I'm trying to make the point here is that this offensive that we've been talking about against the guerrilla, against the infrastructure and so on, I believe is—what we're doing is making an even more advanced step than we ever have made before in licking the autumn–winter, or winter–spring, whatever—no point in getting all mixed up in that—but he's got another one, he's planning something else. Well, in going at this offensive which we've outlined for the command, we're going at that offensive—earlier, and I think in a more vital spot than either caches or the final assault of his assault battalions."

ABRAMS: "We've been working back into the system—his system, the way he has to function. So it's not only, as Bill [Colby] has—that fine briefing he put on here, where he talked about the administrative machinery of government, the political machinery, and things and so on; that's an important feature, too—but in terms of General Kerwin, or anybody that's actually thinking about fighting, 'Where are his divisions now so that I can get at them?'—for guys that, you know, live that game, this is also critical to them. And the way to start to fight, the way to start the winter–spring, or autumn–winter, offensive—the way for us to start working against the autumn–winter offensive is to start now on the guerrillas and the cadre and the local forces, who are going to help and make all these preparations and everything—help them with the dispensary, help them with the [cement?], help them steal stuff off the Americans—you know, all those—all the reconnaissance and so on. So our offensive, our counteroffensive for the autumn–winter or winter–spring, whatever it is, should start now, and it should start against those fellows who have to make the first steps for him. And incidentally, it would be a big help to you, Bill [Colby]. But my point is I think—I don't believe it's any exaggeration, at all, that it helps these combat fellows—you know, the fellows that would like to think about, you know, 'Where is his division?'—it'll be a big boost for them if they can get in there and really work on this thing."

ABRAMS: "What we've been doing, in a way, is sort of on a treadmill. We have focused on these main units, and they're—you know, they're always getting ready to hit Saigon or Tay Ninh, whatever it is, Ban Me Thuot—and so we go after that and we're whacking them with B-52s, tac air, and artillery, and dumping in on them and piling on and that sort of thing. And the history of that is that we go ahead and mash it all up, but then he sends a lot more guys down and builds it back up again and we mash it all up again and just—you know, cause a lot of casualties and so on. Now the way to put a stop to it, the way to get off the treadmill, is to go after this other part which always seems to survive. As long as that's there, his problem's pretty easy. All he's got to do is just feed some more men into it, and it's like putting more gas in the car and keep on driving. And if we'll get in there, into the engine, into the real works, that's the way to start running this thing to ground. You wipe that part out, and then he hasn't got the means. You wipe that part out, and goddamn it, if he's got 50 divisions it's not going to do him any good." "B-52's no good in this thing." "There isn't anything new in what I'm saying." "This is the way to run the war! Our war!"

GOODPASTER: "This thing that Abe was talking about is being worked up as a message [to subordinate commanders] at the present time. And this is big stuff now. And this will involve a real deployment of our forces, everything that can be pulled together that is not really locked onto big operations, to get into the—to get against the local forces, get going against the guerrillas. And that is in itself a step-up of activity."

GOODPASTER: "I would address one other aspect of your point, Bill [Colby], and that—I take it to involve at least some element of taking the press into your confidence as to what your future operations are going to be."

COLBY: "Only a week ahead."

GOODPASTER: "I wouldn't do it 10 seconds ahead. I would just draw an absolute bar against that—never, never anything on future operations. I don't care who they are. There's nothing they can or will do for us that would justify risking the life of one man, and that's what's involved in it. And if they saw something that they could run to get a leg up on their Pulitzer Prize, hell—."

■ ■ ■

BROWN: "May I say a word on Carter's [Townsend] point on this daily cable? That thing had its birth in fear in Washington. The Chairman came out here to General Westy and said, 'Let me have from you daily, personally—.' It started out that way, and then it changed, it got into a routine. But the whole tenor of the thing, the whole—it had its birth in fear. In everything we were on the defensive. The worry was are you going to get kicked out of Khe Sanh? Are you going to lose? And then it went to Con Thien when all that artillery—maybe it was vice versa—but the—. So I really think he's got a very key point. We ought to tear that thing up and look at format, the questions that are addressed, the whole—."

GOODPASTER: "One of these, I think, is the one that I started when I was over in Paris, asking for the—. The one that I asked for was called the trend in the situation, with a daily update on that. That was to serve a specific purpose. It was really to head off this—the conventional wisdom in Washington was that we were being defeated out here, and that time was going against us, and that we were on the losing end of the situation. Well, it just was not so. And the request for this cable was to get a valid commander-level assessment, ongoing assessment, of the situation. And it served that purpose very well. We just had a hell of a row over it in Paris for a matter of a week or 10 days—that this was an inaccurate portrayal of the situation because it was not at all the way people in Washington understood it to be. Well, in other words, it served its purpose, because over a period of time it was found that this was valid, and this thing that had been cooked up in Washington was just a bunch of nightmares. It has served that purpose quite well up until now. Maybe it has completely served it, because that mood has passed to a very considerable degree."

■ ■ ■

TOWNSEND: "It's not a small effort, though, that we're putting into MATs, advisors, and the rest. Right here in this country we have three and a half divisions' worth of company-grade officers and noncommissioned officers in these programs, so it's not small."

BROWN: I wonder "whether there is a quantitative approach which would assist in guiding this allocation [of resources], based upon what our principal objectives are. One can ask the question this way: What could lead the enemy to give up most quickly? I'm not sure that's our objective. Our objective may be, rather: How do we get out of this mess most gracefully while still fulfilling our commitments? The attack that you take in each of these cases is quite different. For example, if you want to get decoupled, then clearly what you want to do is to establish the ARVN capability, the RVNAF, most quickly. And then you can leave the war to them. We back out gracefully, having fulfilled our commitment. Alternatively, if we're trying to make the enemy give up, then that brings in a lot of other factors. What is it that hurts him? Great loss of troops? I'm confused on this question, because we've seen him bring in 250,000 troops and I hear, on one hand, people in Washington say that he can keep that up forever, and other people say, 'Boy, he's about the bottom of the barrel.' And I don't know what the truth of that matter is."

COLBY: "Another question along those same lines is, 'Does great loss of supplies hurt him?' It certainly doesn't help him, but what fraction of the stuff that comes in-country do we actually capture? I don't have a feel for this at all."

GOODPASTER: "We've tested that operationally up in northern I Corps. What happens to him when he loses caches of such and such a size? And this is what happens to him—he finds himself on the other side of the border, he finds his whole structure—his whole system—disintegrating. And this thing is so goddamn complex that you almost have to put it to the test of battle."

GOODPASTER: "Now, to come to your objectives—getting out of here or getting him to surrender and so on—again, you're reading the minds of not just one but many people up in North Vietnam and estimating what the result of their interplay will be, their conniving and intriguing and operating against each other. And that's pretty tough. But I think we can lay out a kind of objective or operational goal, which is that the—whether he decides to give up or not, he's really lost the show here, and he's lost it by virtue of a whole combination of military operations of ourselves and the ARVN. The situation that has been brought about up in northern I Corps, if that were applied throughout this country, the difference between that and some other more formal type of a solution is not very great, not very great."

GOODPASTER: "This is a working objective out here that satisfies every need we have." "Just beat the hell out of this fellow."

GOODPASTER: "A short while back we shifted 250 people into the intelligence support of the Phoenix [program]. And those are the kind of people that it was a hard price to pay. But it was quite obviously the thing to do."

BROWN: "Suppose that it's decided that it really hurts him to kill his troops. Then it's clear that we kill more troops, we kill troops best, when they mass and they're attacking. That's when you can really mow them down. Now if you then adopt an attitude of chase them around in the bush, and keeping them off balance all the time so they never can get massed, and on the other hand you can't find them, you're not killing troops as rapidly as if you did something else for a while, let him mass, and then bashed him."

GOODPASTER: "What was the purpose of killing the troops? It's to win the war in South Vietnam, and you can do it by killing troops and you can do it by going after him out in the bush. Now, yes, there is going to be a little trade-off here, but we don't have too many opportunities and we have to take the opportunities that we get. And we have to go after him <u>all</u> the way, and we <u>can</u>. We've got the resources. We're not resource poor." "We're not using all of our ammunition allowance at the moment."

19 OCT 1968: WIEU

ATTENDEES: Gen. Abrams, Gen. Goodpaster, Amb. Komer, Gen. Brown, LTG Mildren, VADM Zumwalt, MG Corcoran, MG Townsend, Mr. Colby, MG Shaefer, MG Davidson, MG Rasmussen, BG Frizen, BG Sidle, BG McLaughlin, BG Clay, BG Bryan, BG Keegan, Col. Cavanaugh, Col. Pink.

BRIEFER: Last week "we forecast one to two inches of rain in I Corps and we got 36 and 67/100 inches of rain." The maximum rainfall ever reported at Danang for the month of October is 49 inches, "and we're already well over that."

MACV 1968 Infiltration Estimate: 248,000.

ABRAMS (reacting to the staff's inability to respond as to whether U.S. losses KIA for the week are high, low, or what): "That's the kind of a thing—we've got to have a feel for the <u>war,</u> or <u>have</u> a feel for what's going on."

ABRAMS (re the enemy): "Now, what is he doing <u>besides</u> avoiding contact?" "Nobody's doing anything about what he <u>is</u> doing, namely getting ready for more!" "And the character of the operations which are described for the coming week here—more multi-battalion reconnaissance in force and that kind of thing, where they've withdrawn to the base areas somebody should be getting into the base areas . . . keeping the pressure on. Somebody should be out here trying to <u>intercept</u> the supplies, and getting after the guerrillas and the guys that are carrying this stuff, the guys that are leading them, and so on. In other words, if <u>he</u> shifts in what he's doing, it should be reflected that <u>we</u> shift in what <u>we're</u> doing. What we're doing ought to be <u>designed</u> to cripple what <u>he's</u> doing right now!" "What we should be doing is capitalizing on this particular phase of his preparations and operations, and it's <u>not</u> reflected here." What is shown "I don't think is quite the right thing to be doing." "It looks to me like—for the moment, anyway—he's in somewhat of a bad situation. And he's going to try like hell to <u>recover</u> from it. And <u>we</u> should be out here <u>trying</u> to <u>prevent</u> the <u>recovery</u>. And I don't <u>get</u> that from this [J-3] briefing."

ABRAMS: Asks for a message to the commanders "which is an appraisal of what's going on and some guidance about what we ought to be doing about it."

ABRAMS: "The American's not really tied into this thing. They haven't got the same philosophy as the 1st Cav and the 101." "I think that's one of the things we've got to change." "In II Corps, why Ray [Peers] keeps a brigade up there in Kontum I don't know. I guess it's sentimental reasons."

GOODPASTER: "The thesis they use, in one form or another it comes through: 'They might come back.'"

ABRAMS: "What I'm afraid of—we'll lose this three or four weeks going after the wrong thing. In the meantime, he gets done what he <u>wants</u> to get done and then we've got the damn exercise all over again."

21 OCT 1968: Admiral McCain Update Briefing

DAVIDSON: Begins with infiltration, now estimated at 248,000 for the year: "Is this the best he can do, which is in excess of what all the experts thought, a year ago, was within his capability, or is this <u>all</u> he's going to commit?"

DAVIDSON: "He has diverted some of the people coming down the pipeline into logistics activities in Laos and in the area of the two provinces just north of the DMZ." "We're becoming more confident now that the enemy <u>is</u> suffering some serious logistics problems."

ABRAMS: "During all this time, more and more the troop density has—the percentage of personnel down here—has become NVA. Therefore, the replacement requirement—. The <u>structure</u> of NVA is <u>greater</u>. So when you talk about supplying replacements to the structure, it's going to take greater [infiltration] just to have it at the break-even point."

■ ■ ■

ABRAMS: "Sihanouk might be able to take on a wounded squad of Italian motorcyclists, but that's about—."

The reference is to Prince Norodom Sihanouk, the Cambodian head of state.

■ ■ ■

ABRAMS: "General Peers sent me a monograph written on an NVA lieutenant." "This lieutenant . . . says that the NVA can't do a <u>thing</u> down here without the cadre and guerrillas. It's nothing new, and people out here have been saying it all along—<u>forever</u>, I guess—but we ought to get so serious about it that we really get <u>after</u> it."

ABRAMS: "Since you [McCain] were here, the boundary of the XXIV Corps has been moved further south, down to the Hai Van Pass. And this has had a tendency to free up, a little more, the 1st Marine Division in the Quang Nam area. What we need to do, really, is get the circumstances so that in southern I Corps we can get out there with mobile forces further to the west in Quang Nam so that we can start breaking up the base areas out there. Then this will cause this stuff to pull back from Danang."

J-3: "The COMUS has expressed it this way, that while these main forces are out he'd like the areas to be . . . screens along this area, light screens, and get back into this area and work on the VC and the infrastructure. . . ." "This is the way the forces should be used. It won't be spectacular, but you'll be rooting out this VC infrastructure that's the key to the thing."

GOODPASTER: "Admiral, that figure 2,260 over there [enemy KIA], although there've been higher figures—2,260, that's no mean figure, and any notion that, because the enemy is trying to evade, that he is succeeding in evading, his success is only limited. Of course this campaign, this operation, that General Abrams has put into effect of going out <u>after</u> them, <u>after</u> the local forces <u>and</u> the guerrillas <u>and</u> the infrastructure, that's going to keep that figure up. <u>And</u> it'll be clawing out really the <u>structure</u> on which he operates, despite the fact that he's trying to evade contact with his big units. You get—sometimes the impression is created that the enemy can call the shots as to whether, you know, that there's going to be any war, or not going to be any war. Well, he's got a war on his hands, whether he takes his big units back into Cambodia or not."

■ ■ ■

DAVIDSON: "Authority was obtained back in 1967 to start the issue of M16 rifles, and on the first of January they were authorized for all the regular battalions. And by the first of July of 1968 . . . all of these regular elements here had M16s. And now, as of the first of October, they're at 100 percent in those combat elements and already moving into RF and PF."

Until Abrams arrived as Deputy COMUSMACV, the South Vietnamese had been given low priority for modernized weaponry.

ABRAMS: "What we did, we took M2 carbines that were generated by this, and we took M1 carbines that were generated by it. Beefed up, modified, the M1 to an M2. And we went ahead and pushed the M2 into the RF and PF. And <u>that</u>'s been accomplished. Now, as we move along with the M16, <u>it</u> replaces the M2 carbine in the RF and PF. And so we upgunned—the M2 carbine's an automatic thing, and it's light—but we made that interim move of upgunning the RF and PF, plus giving them some more BARs and so on, plus increasing their authorization of M79s."

■ ■ ■

ABRAMS: Describes forays into IV CTZ waterways by Zumwalt's boats "in what had been pure unadulterated VC territory." Began this just in the past few days. Zumwalt's initiative to do so. Navy takes part in this way in the dry season counteroffensive. Working with General Eckhardt. "A pretty good development."

22 OCT 1968: Conference on Intelligence Collection

SOMEONE: "This attack on the infrastructure. . . . It's going to become a greater mission in the future."

■ ■ ■

DAVIDSON: "The Commander is pleased with his intelligence, acts upon it, and has forced the staff to act upon it—that is what has changed in the last four or five months."

DAVIDSON: "I think unquestionably one of the things that's caused success is communications intelligence, perhaps the biggest. Not that it's had tremendous breakthroughs—although that infiltration bit is pretty damn close to one, that's really changed a hell of a lot of things, if you stop to think about it—but the locations, the uses of it, and all of this have continued to improve, not dramatically, but a hell of a lot better than it was a year ago." "I think the most dramatic proof has been the breakthrough in the high-level agents. The COSVN guy, the A-22, Superspook, 23, 24—the guys that are really giving it to you the way it is! You don't have to say, 'Gee, I wonder if this is right or not.' You know that guy's telling you the truth."

SOMEONE: "That's something ARVN's done."

DAVIDSON: "That is an ARVN contribution first rate, you're right."

DAVIDSON: "PWs and documents—that hasn't dramatically improved, but it's sure gotten a hell of a lot better than it was a year ago. We're getting more of them, they're getting translated faster, they're not falling between the cracks like they used to. And that's why all this emphasis we put on the system in PWs and documents has begun to pay off."

DAVIDSON: "But if you took away those factors that I just named without much thought, we wouldn't be much better off than we were sitting around here on our ass eight months ago. And not that that was too damn bad, either."

DAVIDSON: "This is the other thing. Jesus, it used to be the thing to say, whenever anybody came out here, 'The problem we'll never solve is intelligence.' That was the 'in' thing to say. Now all the visitors go back and the 'in' thing to say is, 'My god, that's terrific, that's the best intelligence they ever had.' Now they're both wrong. We weren't as bad as they put us up to be the first time, and we aren't as good as they say this time—although I prefer the latter."

26 OCT 1968: WIEU

ATTENDEES: Gen. Abrams, Gen. Goodpaster, Amb. Komer, Gen. Brown, LTG Mildren, VADM Zumwalt, MG Corcoran, MG Townsend, Mr. Colby, MG Shaefer, MG Davidson, MG Rasmussen, BG Frizen, BG Sidle, BG McLaughlin, BG Clay, BG Bryan, Col. Critchlow, Col. Cavanaugh, Col. Pink.

1968 MACV Infiltration Estimate: 248,000.

BRIEFER: "On 20 October, 9 kilometers north of the Rockpile, U.S. elements received 24 rounds of 130-mm artillery from an enemy position located 19 kilometers north of the Rockpile."

BRIEFER: "Along the coastal plains and in the piedmont, search operations will be continued to locate and destroy the VC infrastructure and matériel." Battalion from the 101st Airborne Division is beginning an operation with an ARVN battalion and the National Police Field Forces on 30 October. Other elements of the 101st Airborne Division "will continue search and clear operations along the coastal plains, giving special attention to the area around Hue." On [5?] October the 1st Marine Division began a combined operation south of

Danang with an amphibious landing force, then the 2/26 Marines joined the 1st Marine Regiment, the 51st ARVN Regiment, and the ROK Marine Brigade in Operation Garrard Bay. This "operation will be targeted against the infrastructure" of the populated area. Interdict enemy LOC to Danang. "Search and clear" and "cordon and search" operations.

ABRAMS: "The way those [operations] have been successful in northern I Corps—you've got a combined Police Field Force, ARVN, RF/PF. There's a very high content of Vietnamese. And that's the people that really can root these fellows [infrastructure] out."

ABRAMS: "By and large those SLF operations have been <u>unproductive</u>. And I think it's because they're largely U.S."

ABRAMS (re enemy activity near the DMZ): "It looks like they had an idea of having some screen or something out there. And those units were put down there in a very <u>ill-prepared</u> way. They apparently weren't tied in with artillery. And I don't believe the units were probably any bigger than a battalion—that was involved altogether in each of those areas. They must not have had any great quantity of RPGs. There's no report of any APCs being hit up there, or tanks. No mines. I think they were just ill prepared for what they got into. And there's no <u>secret</u> about what's up there on our side."

ABRAMS (to briefer): "I would have liked it much better if you had put that together and said something like this: 'The lull in enemy combat unit tactical activity has been matched by an intensification of the logistical, administrative, and reconnaissance efforts.'" Abrams recites the evidence. "That's the <u>picture</u>, or at least [speaking to the J-2] that's what you've <u>painted</u> here this morning. These are not <u>my</u> words. I'm just summing up what you exposed. Combat unit activity, that's one thing. But this other <u>portends</u> what's going to happen a week, or two weeks, or three weeks from <u>now</u>—<u>unless</u> we get <u>at</u> it!"

BRIEFER: "Although the enemy continues to plan for attacks on Saigon, his inactivity and the flooding of the terrain west of Saigon greatly diminish the possibility of any offensive activity in the Saigon area in the near future."

ABRAMS: "Yeah, this weekend!"

BRIEFER: "In summary, the major portion of enemy forces still remain out of country or in remote in-country base areas, where they continue to train and refit while probably preparing for future operations. However, there are no indications the enemy intends to conduct any large-scale coordinated offensive activities in the near future."

ABRAMS (to the J-2): "What do you all think about this—? You know, you recited some rather—in fact, I expected you to break out the <u>champagne</u> here. Those stories of getting out of the delta, Hoi Chanhs pouring in, leaders predicting the loss of the war, the worst condition they've been in in a long time, and so on. What's all that mean?"

J-2: "Sir, that's the subject of a special briefing."

ABRAMS: "Oh, I see." [Laughter]

2 NOV 1968: WIEU

Attendees: Gen. Abrams, Gen. Goodpaster, Amb. Komer, Gen. Brown, LTG Mildren, VADM Zumwalt, MG Corcoran, MG Townsend, Mr. Colby, MG Shaefer, MG Davidson, MG Rasmussen, BG Frizen, BG Sidle, BG Clay, BG Bryan, BG Keegan, Col. Critchlow, Col. Cavanaugh, Col. Pink.

BRIEFER: Reports enemy unit locations based on "civil correspondence" and "letter box numbers" identified with given units. Contents are discussed. Refers to letter box number analysis.

BRIEFER: Infiltration groups 5008 and 9011 identified, filling gaps in the existing number sequence. Also 1068. Some travel by rail.

1968 MACV Infiltration Estimate: 248,000.

ABRAMS (TO J-2): "You know, Phil, the 95 Bravo is an outfit that's had a fairly undistinguished career. Radio discipline has been very poor in that regiment. But it's one that we've watched for a long time. And I was thinking the other day: 'I wonder if it would be worthwhile to—say in 4th Division or I Corps— if they went back and reviewed the whole pattern of [***]. It operates in a fairly small area. And out of that review, and all the other things you could tie in with it, could they cook up a scheme to go ahead and mount an operation to see if they could do away with that regiment? There's an outfit that we've kept very close track of for a long time, and such a pattern analysis conceivably could prove productive."

DAVIDSON: "We certainly could have a go at it, sir." Have machine plotters available here now. "As you say, they do have a patterned activity."

BRIEFER: "The 95 Charlie remains a candidate to join the Headquarters, 1st NVA Division, and its 320th Regiment in III Corps."

ABRAMS: "Getting ready for a historic confrontation between the 1st NVA and the 1st Cavalry. That was the 1st Cavalry's first battle in South Vietnam, one I hope both commanders view as a historic moment."

SOMEONE: "It's a little unequal. He's [the enemy] only got one regiment."

ABRAMS: "Well, the little niceties ignore the issue." [Laughter]

■ ■ ■

KEEGAN: Briefs on interdiction operations. Recalls that enemy buildup for Tet 1968 got under way in September 1967 and peaked in the immediate pre-Tet period, leveled off during the Tet Offensive, then "dipped somewhat. Then there was an immediate resurgence and very steep rise in the traffic [trucks in Laos] for the post-Tet offensive [5 May 1968] . . . which peaked in the month of April and dropped at that time. As the June rise started in preparation for the third general offensive, our interdiction operations got going at this point here [14 July 1968] in an attempt to prevent the traffic buildup which we saw for the first two offensives." Laos and Route Pack 1 [Route Package 1]. Interdiction points. Areas that have been sealed. Six water crossings. Point where "they floated out a pontoon bridge from this cave nightly." "We destroyed that bridge, and since that time he's been confined exclusively to the use of individual ferries, which we've destroyed as we could locate them." Route 101: sought to block. Mines in waterways. Underwater rock causeway, cable bridge, and cable ferry uncovered by B-52 strike and interdicted. Have achieved since September reduction from 125 trucks per week to 20, "and in the last few days shutting entirely, no throughput traffic. Averaging about 15 trucks per week." Increase in interdiction effort: 3,000 sorties in May, 6,500 in July, 8,000 in August, 6,400 in September. Estimates of closure achieved: Route 15 into Mu Gia Pass: 39 percent in August, 74 percent in September, 100 percent in October. Route 137: 53 percent in August, 82 percent in September, about 90 percent in October.

KEEGAN (re the impedance of flow): Monitored truck trends on a daily basis. "On 14 July 1968" the enemy was "putting trucks into Route Pack 1 in Laos at the peak rate he achieved before Tet and for the post-Tet offensive." By 18 or 19 July "he was moving over 1,100 trucks a day. This is the greatest peak of traffic that we've ever noted. By the 20th he was still over 1,000 trucks a day. By the 21st, when the campaign was a week old, the traffic was cut in half. By the 26th the traffic was reduced not quite half again, down to below 340. And, as you recall, in September, when Typhoon Bess hit him very hard—each of these interdiction points had become a sea of mud—the traffic was reduced in half, and down to 19 trucks a day the entire system two days later."

KEEGAN: Results of the interdiction campaign confirmed by visual sightings. "Since the first two weeks in July they have decreased from a daily of 255 to 23 per day. On Route 101 from 736 to 16 per day. [Route] 137 from 298 to 4 trucks per day. The total from 1,289 to 43 trucks per day." Re tonnage throughput: Net in July about 340 tons per day. Now about 35 tons per day.

KEEGAN: Overall, "we believe the net [including cache discovery, etc.] effect has been a very serious, if not disastrous, impact logistically upon the enemy. We believe the forced exodus is related in part to these in-country and out-of-country operations."

KEEGAN: "In contrasting the impedance of flow which might have been achieved by killing trucks, as against the method that we employed in this campaign, namely of keeping known bypasses and points choked to the extent that we could, we compute that the cost using the truck-killing method to impede this much flow might have been on the order of about $13,000 per ton, whereas in the campaign conducted against the non-bypassable points we have achieved a similar impedance of flow at a cost of about $1,000 per ton."

KEEGAN: "The question comes up, 'Can we repeat this in Laos?'" "We have very few non-bypassable points in Laos." We are trying the best we can. "Final net truck throughput into Laos of about 10 trucks per day, a throughput reduction of about 90 percent."

SOMEONE: We're concerned that the enemy's widening and heavy graveling of routes means impending acquisition of the new five-ton-class ZIL truck.

9 NOV 1968: WIEU

ATTENDEES: Gen. Abrams, Gen. Goodpaster, Gen. Brown, LTG Mildren, Dr. McMillan, VADM Zumwalt, MG Corcoran, MG Townsend, Mr. Colby, MG Shaefer, MG Davidson, MG Rasmussen, BG Sidle, BG Bolton, BG Clay, BG Bryan, BG Keegan, Col. Gleason, Col. Pink, Col. Shiflet.

BRIEFER: New WIEU format: Weather followed by briefing on Cambodian matters. Quotes a recently obtained document from the Chief of Staff, Cambodian Army, dated 28 August: "From now on, every chief of post who is located along the border must keep the VC away from the border and Cambodian territory."

BRIEFER: "The Cambodian reactions to expanding Communist activities in the country may indicate that Prince Sihanouk is beginning to suspect that the Communists will not win in South Vietnam."

BRIEFER: Presents intelligence on enemy reinforcement of his antiaircraft capability in Laos. "The bombing halt in North Vietnam will release additional experienced antiaircraft units for employment in the Laotian panhandle."

On 1 November 1968 President Lyndon Johnson suspended all air and naval attacks against targets in North Vietnam. Since 31 March 1968 such attacks had been confined to targets below the 20th parallel.

ABRAMS (catching the briefer up): "Now, just a minute. Are these units that are deploying from North Vietnam into Laos?"

SOMEONE: "No, sir. These are units that have been in Laos. They're just changing their positions right now."

ABRAMS: "Well, this—see, you're sliding—you ought to say what you're <u>talking</u> about. He's redeploying units within Laos. Now what does that mean?"

ABRAMS (to briefer who doubts an impending enemy offensive in Hue): "Oh—I don't agree with you. This is the system. They go out and get bunkers. Now I'm not saying that the attack's going to come. But they go out and get the bunkers built and dug, and the dispensary put in, the supplies brought in, and all that sort of thing. And that's what they—. I <u>believe</u> this guy. And that's the part of the thing we ought to be working against now! <u>Then</u> you'll guarantee that there <u>won't</u> be any offensive. I think they've got guerrillas <u>doing</u> that."

DAVIDSON: "We do, too, sir."

ABRAMS: "I think all the Vietnamese and U.S. and RF and PF and everybody should be out scarfing up these guerrillas so we stop the goddamn bunker building."

SOMEONE: "Like Cu Chi, they build it and might use it five years from now."

ABRAMS: "That's <u>right</u>. Or the pineapple thing out here. Good god, they must have been building that thing for fifteen <u>years</u>!"

■ ■ ■

ABRAMS: "Naturally we're not going to <u>manufacture</u> anything here at this briefing. But more and more the operational <u>side</u> of this at this briefing we've got to bring out what is going on in this thing and so on. Get it out of the sort of FM [field manual] 101-5 ritual and get it into what's being done—and <u>why</u>."

ABRAMS: "Now, while we're talking about I Corps—unless they've got another group of outfits, the 304th, the 308th, the 320th, the 90th [Regiment] is out of the old 324 Bravo, isn't it? The 29th, a regiment, Tri-Thien-Hue, all headed— or <u>in</u>—for North Vietnam, and not only that but <u>upper</u> North Vietnam. So, at least at the moment, the posture of the enemy is certainly not one to create major difficulties in northern I Corps. It's just the contrary. The staff has been concerned about being prepared to go back to northern I Corps with the 1st Cavalry Division. But I think we ought to think about what would cause us to want to <u>do</u> that. And then, how do we start getting the readings on when that might be necessary, if it ever is?"

GOODPASTER: "They'd almost have to start a new war now. That's what it'd amount to."

ABRAMS: "They could always do that, over the next six or seven months."

ABRAMS: "Right now he's [the enemy] given up doing anything up there of any major consequence in the DMZ. He's taken the forces back, he's pulled artillery back, the combat units back. On our side it would be a <u>mistake</u> to devote major forces in there watching something that ain't there." The 2nd ARVN and 3rd Marine Division "could devote their attention to where they've got population out there—Cam Lo area, and also north of Dong Ha." "Really getting that weeded out and under firm control."

ABRAMS: "The 1st ARVN Division has already demonstrated that it knows how to go about this. In fact, I would say it's the most effective program that's going on in the country in terms of pacification, VCI, or whatever."

GOODPASTER: "What they've been doing—they choose a series of, the best terms I can find for it is 'hard points' . . . on which the VC have been struc- tured, out of which they've been operating. They've got a sequence of these lined up. Beyond My Chanh they have . . . three or four more of them planned once they get that far. And that just strikes me as being a hell of an effective way of going about it."

CORCORAN: "Then move the local forces in after, so they don't come back."

GOODPASTER: "Yeah."

ABRAMS: "Or, in some cases, the local forces are there, but they've been ineffec- tive."

■ ■ ■

BRIEFER: Category 1 cities: Saigon, Danang, Hue. Category 2 cities: Major cities and provincial capitals with population over 10,000. Category 3 cities: District and provincial capitals with population over 5,000.

ABRAMS (re enemy attacks by fire): "I want to take these slides and this briefing to the—what is it, Monday?—Mission Council meeting, and I want to give them this. I'll do it myself if Colonel Pink will come and handle the slides for me."

ABRAMS: "What can you say about intensity?" [Number of rounds, caliber, etc.]

DAVIDSON: Points out that by their old criteria only one of these ABFs would have been reported (20 rounds or more).

ABRAMS: "We've escalated. We've escalated the reporting!" [Laughter]

■ ■ ■

SEVENTH AIR FORCE BRIEFER: "The 1 November bombing halt was accompanied by a sharp rise in sensor-detected traffic, which has subsided in the past three days." The enemy has moved AAA and repaired interdiction points in North Vietnam. There has been a dramatic increase in the movement of trucks and watercraft. "Near-capacity transshipment activity."

BRIEFER: Seven interdiction points in Laos: South of the Mu Gia Pass (two points), Ban Laboy ford (closed for 32 days, but reopened 2 November, "putting in 50 to 100 fighter sorties per day to reclose this point"), others.

SOMEONE: "What is the policy about sowing of sensors in North Vietnam?"

BROWN: "No more." [This means that in 90 days or less they will no longer have any sensor coverage there.] "As long as we can continue reconnaissance, really the sensors aren't going to add a hell of a lot." [Since they can't strike anyway.]

DAVIDSON: "They give you more or less continuous coverage, too," whereas reconnaissance shows only what's there at the moment.

BROWN: "That's true."

All this is part of an extended discussion of what has happened since the bombing halt.

■ ■ ■

BRIEFER: Presents a naval operations retrospective:

■ Operation Market Time: Seal 1,200-mile coastline against infiltration. Began March 1965. By July 1965: TF 115. Fast patrol craft. May 1967 the first VNN unit was integrated into coastal surveillance. Now VNN has patrol responsibility in 10 areas, and is expected to man 13 of the 63 stations by the end of 1968. Also gunfire support missions.

■ River Patrol Force: December 1965. First boats March 1966. River patrol boats. Two boat-support landing craft. Now 230 boats in country patrolling all major rivers in the delta. Twenty more boats by end 1968. TF Clearwater [described as "semiautonomous"]: February 1968, with mission of keeping the Cua Viet River open to Dong Ha and the Perfume River open to Hue. Average 2,000 tons of military-essential cargo per day shipped by allied forces via these routes.

■ TF 117: Navy component of the Mobile Riverine Force. June 1967. Doubled in size since July 1968. Afloat base concept.

■ It "became feasible in October 1968 to commence, for the first time, coordinated operations among the three task forces in the delta." Highest priority: interdiction of Viet Cong infiltration routes from Cambodia. Strike operations along the canal system between the Bassac River and the Gulf of Thailand. Intensified upper Mekong River patrols. Securing seaward approaches to the delta canal system. Pacification. Operation Sea Lord.

ABRAMS: "It's a new era."

11 NOV 1968: Briefing for Admiral McCain

ABRAMS: "Washington has been very stubborn about getting on board with all of this that's going on. And, in my viewpoint, this can no longer be tolerated. We're getting a military situation here that's got to be faced up to—and realistically, by our government and by our policies. Now he's got the 9th Division over in here, the 5th Division in here [tapping the map], and the 7th and 1st Divisions around here like this. And these are these same points, base areas and so on, that have been described to you. This is the last really significant military potential that he's got threatening South Vietnam. And I believe it has got to be defeated. And it will be decisive in the outcome of this war. But it does mean that, in order to do it, the policies on Cambodia have got to be changed, in my opinion."

ABRAMS: 1st Cavalry Division closing in III Corps from I Corps. This will permit the U.S. 1st Infantry Division and U.S. 25th Infantry Division "to increase the density of their efforts back here a little further. These are all important base areas." Have to find the caches and destroy them.

ABRAMS: "I think it's criminal to let these enemy outfits park over here, fatten up, reindoctrinate, get their supplies, and so on. Also, we're giving them a cheap way of bringing it in. Up here, to bring it down from North Vietnam through Laos—I don't know what it is, but in order to get one ton into South Vietnam he's got to put nine tons or something like that into the system, maybe even more. Over in this damn place [Cambodia], in order to get one ton into South Vietnam all he's got to do is put one ton into the system, because there's no attrition. And his units are getting a free ride, his supplies are getting a free ride." "We could make this just as impossible for him to do as the other things he's tried to do in the course of this war, and all have been knocked off."

ABRAMS: "So I just want to say that I regard this as an urgent problem and one which we've—. I want to say also we're playing the game straight." Describes an incident of the day before in which an LOH and a gunship on reconnaissance "got over into Cambodia about eight-tenths of a kilometer." Convoy of 25 trucks and some soldiers. "Not realizing that they were in Cambodia, they attacked this, and apparently killed some of the soldiers. At about that time a FAC came along and got a hold of them by radio and told them that they were across the border, so they promptly left and came back. I expect that we're going to get more things like this."

ABRAMS: "The border is very difficult to identify on the ground. You know, it's not marked, and it doesn't follow a clear terrain feature or anything. And our troops, Kerwin's troops and the Vietnamese, are pressing <u>hard</u> in here to <u>prevent</u> the movement of supplies and to prevent the movement of units down in here towards the populated areas. I feel we <u>must</u> do that. We've got the forces to do it. That's why we brought the 1st Cavalry <u>down</u> here. And so some of these <u>mistakes</u>, and they're honest mistakes, are going to occur. But this is a— it never <u>has</u> been a pleasant war, and it isn't <u>now</u>. And I think we've just got to go ahead and <u>do</u> these things and so on, and I <u>hope</u> that the authority we've requested to strike these—we should strike this right here, across here, <u>right</u> now with B-52s, tac air, and artillery, that little piece right in there. We'd get some <u>good</u> out of it in terms of supplies, and there <u>are</u> no civilians in there."

MCCAIN: "Well, I support you."

BRIEFER: "Sir, as you know, SOG operations in North Vietnam have been scaled down considerably, and certain programs have been suspended as a result of the bombing halt. At the same time our operations in Cambodia and Laos have been intensified."

ABRAMS: "I would like to say that, in my opinion, the operations of SOG in Prairie Fire and Daniel Boone have improved tremendously with respect to coordination and the results that they're getting over the last two or three months. The information that they're providing, when put with all the rest— they've been <u>very</u> helpful."

MCLAUGHLIN: "There's not much going on in large-scale operations. The emphasis <u>is</u> on the pacification effort, the effort against the infrastructure."

ABRAMS (re 1st Cavalry Division): "They're going to really move around that area. Wherever the enemy is, they'll play it—play it like an organ." "We won't be able to keep up with it, we'll always be behind. But, if you want to take advantage of it, that's the way it's got to be."

MCLAUGHLIN: "General Ewell indicated that he feels that we've got to keep forces in here, because once you pull them out the enemy comes right back into the vacuum. He feels the same way about the area north of My Tho, and Binh Xuan and Base Area 470. You've got to <u>stay</u> with it in those places to do any <u>lasting</u> good."

BRIEFER: "Graham" is coming out.

Apparently this is James Graham, a CIA analyst who stubbornly resisted the idea that the enemy was using the port of Sihanoukville to bring military supplies into Cambodia. Bills of lading and other documents captured during the 1970 incursion into Cambodia would establish conclusively that he had been profoundly mistaken.

13 NOV 1968: Major General Davidson Discussion

DAVIDSON (as tape begins in midsentence): ". . . <u>vital</u> importance of the Cambodian LOC."

DAVIDSON: Cites the United States, "where the enemy won his greatest victory of 1968." "And there was another factor at play in the United States, a growing awareness on the part of the U.S. news media, and thus the U.S. public, that military victory was in actual fact taking place in Vietnam." "One of the things I'm confident <u>encouraged</u> him to go into the Tet Offensive was the fact that—of the growing dissatisfaction, all the terrible articles about 'ARVN won't fight' and 'the GVN doesn't command anybody's confidence.' Hell, our own newspapers misled the poor son of a bitch."

DAVIDSON (re postulated enemy reassessment about 1 September 1968): "Someplace here <u>his</u> perception of reality and <u>our</u> perception of reality began to come together." Thus he "put the dampers on the Third Offensive." Approached the United States. Decided "to accept our terms and try to move forward politically from there." And came to the "realization that his concept of the general offensive as a means to win the war was a failure." Cites "the critical failure of the proselyting [*sic*]." Enemy positioning himself for a cease-fire?

15 NOV 1968: COMUS Update Briefing

BRIEFER: "What we've seen over the past few weeks leaves little doubt that the enemy has made some fundamental changes in his prosecution of the war, changes possibly as far-reaching and important as his July 1967 decision to escalate to the general offensive and general uprising."

BRIEFER: Cites as root causes infiltration drop-off and casualties (nearly 600,000 since October 1965, of which 250,000 so far this year).

BRIEFER (re enemy northern MR-5): "His forces remain largely in place. This is the only region left in-country where the enemy can seek safety, yet remain close to his objectives near population centers, the only area where a major enemy military headquarters remains in-country. He owns the real estate west of [Kien?] Duc, all the way from the A Shau south to Dak Pek. Unlike our operations in Base Areas 101 and 114, we have never been in Base Area 112 with a sizable force."

BRIEFER: "This morning we have received very valid intelligence, which we believe corroborates this assessment, that a high-level meeting of North Vietnamese diplomats from all over the world is being convened at Hanoi, undoubtedly to receive this new policy change. The only other time we know of such a meeting was during last July when the Hanoi leadership made its decision and announced its intention to launch the general offensive/general uprising."

BRIEFER: Therefore predict enemy efforts to achieve a cease-fire, coalition government, and U.S. withdrawal. "By the end of August the enemy came to the stark realization that his concept of the general offensive was a total failure. With his new perspective of reality, he knew that his military, political, and proselyting efforts had to be radically redirected." "As a result of this fundamental reappraisal, he's changed his tactics. Militarily he will concentrate on small-unit and guerrilla-sized actions. His major targets will be outposts, allied war facilities, and lines of communications, emphasizing standoff and sapper attacks to reduce his casualties. He is shifting the weight of his force from the unpopulated to the populated regions to increase the effectiveness of his infrastructure and expand his control of the people. His political tactics are aimed at the immediate goal of bringing about U.S. withdrawal, while his long-term goal is to so weaken the GVN that it will be unable to survive alone."

COLBY: "On the surface that's a recipe for disaster on their part, but certainly our experience requires a little humility on our part, too. . . ." Cites "fragility on our part" in the United States. But: "If we turn our military strength to the antiguerrilla and anti-infrastructure problem, the likelihood of their being able to carry out this campaign is not very high."

TOWNSEND: "It appears to me that this guy is getting in a position where we could really finish off the war militarily." Enemy now more concentrated. Need to get our government to accept going into the sanctuaries. Suggests keeping up violations (deliberate) "until they become the norm."

Gen. Andrew J. Goodpaster, the Deputy COMUSMACV, reacts very strongly to this suggestion of willful disobedience.

GOODPASTER: "I don't think our government can or will get into the Cambodian business by the by-products, side effects, of a pattern of violations. Matter of fact, I don't think that our policy leaders could possibly permit that to happen. Now, they might make a decision to use that as the technique by which a policy decision on their part to go into Cambodia would be done. I'd be inclined to question that they would use that technique as a means of implementing a policy decision. That's not only impeachable conduct, but it is the kind of thing that would immediately raise that—raise demands of that sort, public demands of that sort. What I think has a better chance, or essentially has the only chance, is that they would step up to the issue, and reach a policy decision on it, after labor pains the likes of which you can't imagine."

TOWNSEND: "My thought is that this is what we would force by getting into accepting this as the norm. In other words, don't back away now, but make them accept this as the norm. That would tend to bring on the policy decision. I think from the commander's point out here, militarily we are practically in an intolerable military situation. Militarily we watch this develop, and we really should do something about it—."

GOODPASTER (interrupting, and in a harder tone): "I think that's going to have to be looked at awfully carefully. I would want to see it spelled out completely. I must say my reaction right now is that that's an improper course on our part, it's an improper thing to do, and we can't be drawn into playing that kind of a game. Yes, I think the time well may come, it may be close at hand, when the military values of going in and really nailing these outfits in Cambodia, in the border areas of Cambodia, would be very, very strong. Those values will be great. But we're just not in the business, I don't <u>believe</u>, of hedging our policy decision makers into something of that kind."

TOWNSEND (persisting): "My thought is we should continue right on up to the limit of what we can do, irrespective of incidents. Let them continue to take place, instead of pulling back and <u>avoiding</u> the incidents."

GOODPASTER: "We've <u>got</u> policy guidance on that. And what does the policy guidance say? It says that unless there are 'extreme or unusual circumstances' we are not to <u>do</u> that. Now if there <u>are</u> what we can validly consider 'extreme or unusual circumstances,' all right, let's do it. Or if we think that that guidance should be changed, let's go in and ask for it to be changed. I don't think we can be in that other—."

TOWNSEND (still persisting): "You've got to have evidence of intolerability. If we stand on the border and consciously <u>avoid</u> the contact, you'll never have evidence of intolerability."

COLBY: "General Goodpaster's right. We can't <u>shove</u>—."

TOWNSEND (interrupting): "That's right. I <u>agree</u> with that. I agree with it. But what I say is don't shy <u>away</u> from contact, or change your modus operandi, within our area on this side of the border."

GOODPASTER: "I don't believe we can permit ourselves to get into a situation where our ability to move on to a satisfactory outcome becomes wholly dependent on what we do about Cambodia. In other words our task, I think, is bound to be to generate a plan of action within South Vietnam itself which is designed to carry to some viable security solution. Now that might involve substantial continued U.S. presence here. I frankly think that it's—in all likelihood it would <u>if</u> the NVA keep any kind of sizable force on the Cambodian border or any kind of sizable force within this country. But that's just the realities of the thing, I think. On the other hand, if we're able to go into Cambodia, or if they withdraw, then this campaign that I'm speaking of would carry us to the point where the residual responsibility could be taken on by the South Vietnamese. Within South Vietnam, then, I think we're left with a real question of how do we—does this that we've seen today, the way it's now formulated, does this suggest any change of emphasis, any change to what we're doing, is there something that we are failing to do that we should concentrate on, either to try to study out or to generate effort against it?"

GOODPASTER: "I was struck by the point that, out of necessity, they may now come to attacks by fire, sapper activity, terrorist and clandestine activity, just to keep insecurity through the whole countryside, and to prevent economic life and so on from going forward. It seems to me that we are confronted with that. I would think that this program that has been laid out—the attack on the local forces, guerrillas, infrastructure—is the <u>right</u> way of going at that." "We're pretty well on target."

■ ■ ■

ABRAMS: Describes how he wants to have covered each Saturday, using the time of the bombing halt as a baseline, enemy efforts north of the DMZ, and those in Laos: "And I hope we can keep it on a purely professional plane, without getting excited and so, just as cold-blooded analysis as we can make it, because we're getting the focus on Cambodia and it would be a shame to have misread the tea leaves that really are pointing to something else."

■ ■ ■

ABRAMS: "I don't think that the JGS is going to influence it [operations by ARVN—in I CTZ, apparently] at all. Lam deals directly with the president on a great many things. Tri has dinner with the president once or twice a week. He gets operational approval, that sort of thing, and Vien's not in on that. In my opinion, Vien's trying to do the best job he can administratively and seeing that the ducks are lined up on things that have got to be done. But direction of the campaign, that sort of thing, is just not coming from him. And his hands are tied on it."

GOODPASTER: "What about the business of moving some of these reserve units? Does he have that kind of authority?"

ABRAMS: "Yes, he does. But what are you going to move? I don't believe in moving airborne out of here up to I Corps—not now, especially if we move three marine battalions down into IV Corps. And that's the only thing he's got."

COLBY: Suggests RF can relieve ARVN to conduct operations farther afield.

ABRAMS: "Let's face it, though, one of the problems we've had in the past is when the corps commander takes battalions out of the province to go off on operations, then the province senior advisor and the province chief really start squawking, and it gets to the president's office. Somebody calls from there, and that's what happened—that specifically happened out here when Tri sailed into the 18th. He made a big effort, but he got his water cut off—from the president's office. And now whether he wants to take that on again probably is—. And it's your [Colby] side of the house that does it to him."

COLBY: "Yeah, 'cause they run right up there."

ABRAMS: "That's right."

SOMEONE: "Same problem with President Diem."

ABRAMS: "Supported by your province senior advisor out there, and John Vann. A lot of this is trying to have your cake and eat it."

ABRAMS: Asks for a paper to be developed on the briefing, expanded a little on the enemy side to include activities ongoing in North Vietnam and Laos, "and then build it up as you have, highlighting the situation that's developed here in Cambodia and III Corps area, and then goes ahead and reviews the policies as they stand with respect to Cambodia, and comes up with some of the long-range alternatives, bearing in mind that you're working toward building the ARVN and the GVN and so on, with the ultimate objective of having them in such a condition that they can handle their own affairs internally, but raising the question of the development of the NLF and COSVN as a Cambodian base in the long pull will maybe—the implication of that is a longer-term deployment of U.S. forces. And <u>then</u> get into the alternative to that, which is making the possibility of selective and decisive military effort in the immediate border areas, and what impact that—some discussion of whether or not that <u>would</u> change the picture, <u>could</u> change the picture, and so on. Now I don't really know how all of that will turn <u>out</u>, but it seems to me that's the kind of a paper that we need now." "What do you think of that?"

GOODPASTER: "I think that's just right. I think it's—."

COLBY: "It fits beautifully with postwar planning."

ABRAMS: "Now, the <u>other</u> thing I want to say is that <u>I</u> think that at least the thrust of the guidance that's out on both sides—the GVN/RVNAF and U.S. and Free World—is <u>right down the line</u> for the strategy that <u>they've</u>—if this is their strategy—<u>just</u> what the doctor ordered. And it only means that—<u>now</u>—that in the execution we should find <u>every</u> conceivable way to improve the effectiveness of this campaign. The direction, the azimuth, is correct. Now it's the execution."

■ ■ ■

ABRAMS: "In talking to Charlie Stone [CG, U.S. 4th Infantry Division], he said a disturbing thing which I will repeat. He feels that there's been a shift in that Special Zone commander—what is it, the 42nd [*sic:* 24th?] Special Zone? They've now got the whole regiment, all four battalions, and they've got the ranger task force—two battalions. And they <u>have</u> been getting up a lot of combined-type operations and so on. And this fellow, according to Charlie, he's not now willing to do that. Instead of that he's got a five-battalion operation going on out there to the east of Kontum, where Charlie Stone says that he's bet him a beer that he will <u>not</u> have any contact. It's just a worthless goddamn operation that's not going to produce anything—<u>east</u> of Kontum, up in the goddamn tundra and so on. This is in the last—since the bombing halt. <u>He</u> suggests that what the Vietnamese are thinking of is that we are going to <u>go home</u>, so until that time just conserve your strength, build your forces, and so on. 'Let the U.S. do the fighting. Then, when they go, we'll be in the best shape.'"

ABRAMS: "I told Charlie Stone categorically that that goddamn attitude didn't exist <u>anywhere</u> that I knew of. <u>I</u> have not come across any of it—other than <u>there</u>. Now, Ray Peers mentioned this to me once before, and he's not so sure it isn't sort of a conflict that's developed between what Charlie Stone thinks ought to be done and what this guy, Colonel Lien, thinks ought to be done, and it's just an honest professional difference. On this staff, we've got to be very careful. <u>If</u>, somewhere, something like that <u>does</u> develop, in fact <u>does</u> develop, then we've got to be able to move on it pretty sharply. <u>But</u> we've also got to use good judgment and make sure that that's the way it is and it isn't some <u>other</u> damn conflict that's going on, as can easily happen. Because <u>that</u> fellow has been doing <u>extremely</u> well up there. And he's the best one we've ever <u>had</u>, at least in the time period <u>I've</u> been here. The <u>other</u> guy was a coward. We've got a good strong province chief up there in Kontum, apparently, and a lot of <u>good</u> things."

30 NOV 1968: WIEU

ATTENDEES: Gen. Abrams, Gen. Goodpaster, Amb. Colby, Gen. Brown, VADM Zumwalt, Dr. McMillan, MG Corcoran, MG Townsend, MG Shaefer, MG Rasmussen, MG Davidson, BG Frizen, BG Clay, BG Keegan, BG Jones, BG Cole, Col. Davis, Col. Gleason, Col. Gorman, Col. Pink.

BRIEFER: "The course of enemy activity since the bombing halt suggests that he is engaged in a major effort to supply the most immediate needs of his forces in Laos and in the North Vietnam panhandle, to reorganize his logistics network in North Vietnam and Laos, and to reconstruct his lines of communication."

ABRAMS: "Saigon <u>is</u> the most important thing." "Saigon is really the <u>plum</u> here."

ABRAMS (re the enemy): "He always has something fairly long range. I mean, he doesn't plan just for Monday."

DAVIDSON: "There's one significant development that hasn't come out here, and that is we've been working on a separate radio net that served the 9th Division. We broke it here about a week or 10 days ago. And you'll probably notice, we're fixing the 9th Division Headquarters and those three regiments almost daily. This is a tremendous accomplishment, as you know, sir, because <u>there's</u> the fellow you've got to watch. And if we can just keep a good tight grip on him, we'll be much more reassured."

■ ■ ■

ABRAMS: "Talking about the prime minister being out there [in III Corps], you've got to add the Tri factor in here. Tri comes down here into Saigon at least twice a week and sees the president, sees the prime minister, and so on. No other corps commander has that. And, as we know, he thwarted the dry season campaign in the delta. He got the president—. I mean, he has <u>not</u> made this enemy any smaller in III Corps than he is. And he just <u>hammers</u> at it every damn time he comes in here. Christ, I don't know, they <u>may</u> have the whole upper and lower <u>house</u> out there for a briefing. Well, I don't know. Anyway, you've got to watch that. It's been <u>highly</u> seasoned."

■ ■ ■

BRIEFER: "In recent weeks Mr. Thuy, the chief North Vietnamese negotiator, has claimed that, with the existence of the National Liberation Committees all throughout South Vietnam, the National Liberation Front now exercises effective administrative control over 10 million people and four-fifths of the countryside." "Using functional village councils as a basis for examination, and the most recent HES population figures, a South Vietnamese claim which can be substantiated might well show that the VC actually exercise control over only 2.5 percent of the total population."

These represent the extremes of competing claims as analyzed by MACCORDS.

■ ■ ■

BRIEFER: "All four corps are reporting that the refugees are moving back into the secured areas."

As a result of the Accelerated Pacification Campaign.

GOODPASTER: "If we get into a statistical war here, that's the kind of thing that the American press just loves, and every soft spot in our figures, they make a feature story out of that."

■ ■ ■

BRIEFER: "In the first seven days after the bombing halt, there were 262 trucks detected by sensors in Route Package 1 and 778 trucks by sensors in the Laotian panhandle. 165 trucks were seen visually." "In the third week the rise was sharp, with 2,220 sensor detections and 1,651 air observations in Laos."

BRIEFER: Tonnage [***] during the past week: 70 percent ammunition. In October 1968: 76 percent ammunition. 1,125 tons of ammunition, and 345 tons of POL amount to over 90 percent of total of 1,535 tons.

BRIEFER: Increased shipment by coastal sea lanes and inland waterways of North Vietnam since the bombing halt. Average 75 ships per day, vice 19 in October. Also heavy tonnage vessels not seen in southern North Vietnam waters since 1965 are back in use.

BRIEFER: North Vietnam is "constructing new POL pipeline in the southern area of the panhandle on a high-priority basis to relieve her dependence on movement of POL by truck."

BROWN: "I think the area north of the DMZ is being rehabilitated after three years of being ravaged. Regiments in the area have got to be fed, they've got to be restructured, refurbished, roads have got to be rebuilt." "I think what you're seeing is a massive building effort. . . . And there will come a point in time, that General Abrams is looking for to project, where the stocks of supplies coming in have brought these units up to the level that they have to be. And there will be a period in which stores are accumulated to sustain heavy action. What do they want to do? At that point they begin to assess the options."

■ ■ ■

BRIEFER: Further reference to "Graham's visit" beginning "next Friday."

DAVIDSON: "We're going to try to approach it objectively. It's not going to do the slightest bit of good, obviously, because Mr. Graham has already written his paper, which says that supplies are not coming through Cambodia." "In our view, they're moving supplies through Cambodia." Have requested additional authorities for intelligence collection in Cambodia (air authorities granted, ground pending).

GOODPASTER: "As I recall back in '64 and early '65 we couldn't prove that he was coming down in strength through Laos, and we just goddamn near lost the war because we couldn't prove it."

DAVIDSON (re Graham): "I think the best we can hope for is to move him in such a direction that he can, with due saving of face, later on come around."

21 DEC 1968: WIEU

BRIEFER (re the Chieu Hoi program): "The weekly rate has continued to go up and still is going up. We now are running well ahead of last year." Trend up in all four corps, but IV Corps more than the other three corps combined. 1968: 16,383 (of which 273 are NVA). Content: 11,342 military, 2,000 VCI, 3,000 other civilian VC elements. Most ralliers are from the local guerrillas.

■ ■ ■

DISCUSSION: Area proposed by the enemy "for 25 December prisoner release discussions." Site is located in a small wooded patch on the south bank of the Vam Co Dong River, five kilometers southwest of Tay Ninh City. Proposed meeting time: 1500 hours. Sunset is at 1842. EENT is at 1932. The site is nine kilometers from the Cambodian border, near the Straight Edge Woods. Liberation Radio offer. Most likely motivation: "To initiate direct contacts between the U.S. and the NLF to achieve de facto recognition of the NLF as a negotiating entity." Re "decision to go through with this": Abrams: "Yeah, it was made in Washington."

■ ■ ■

ABRAMS (re the previous year): "We seemed to be going along pretty well. And then came Tet."

ABRAMS: "This pacification program really bears no resemblance to what was going on last year—as far as results and so on."

■ ■ ■

DAVIDSON (re enemy attacks in Laos): "There's a sort of a tacit agreement, as I understood Ambassador Sullivan explained it at one of these [SEACORD] meetings, between the USSR and the U.S. about just how far these people are going to be permitted to push out . . . to the west."

■ ■ ■

COLBY: "He [the enemy] has to do less this year to have the same political impact as he had last year. In other words, our situation in the Paris talks, and our political situation at home, is a little more finely balanced than it was last year. And a fairly large-scale <u>show,</u> without any real impact at all, could have the kind of political impact he's looking for."

SOMEONE: Suggests using the International Red Cross as an intermediary for the proposed meeting with NLF representatives.

ABRAMS: "Well, let me say this—this ground has been pretty well plowed, and the decision has been <u>made</u>. Now all that remains is <u>how</u>. And the decision's been made it will be done by <u>our</u> military."

■ 1969

Early in 1969, again during the Tet period, the enemy made one final stab at coordinated countrywide attacks. Once again he suffered heavy casualties, apparently leading him at long last to reevaluate his approach and map out a change of direction. The new approach, described in COSVN Resolution 9 of July 1969, involved a shift of emphasis from urban to rural areas and the mission of disrupting pacification. Large units were to be broken down into smaller ones employing sapper tactics so as to preserve strength and protract the war. Meanwhile, large numbers of troops infiltrated from North Vietnam continued to shift the balance of enemy forces in the south from predominantly Viet Cong to more and more NVA.

The policy of "Vietnamization," progressively turning over more and more of the responsibility for conduct of the war to the Vietnamese themselves, was continued. Pacification progressed, aided by major increases in the Regional Forces and Popular Forces and by establishment of an armed People's Self-Defense Force, both contributing to increased local security by providing the "hold" in "clear and hold."

The major development on the U.S. side was redeployment, during July and August, of the first increment—25,000 troops—in what would become a continuing unilateral withdrawal of forces. At year's end the authorized strength was 484,000, down from a peak of 543,400 in April. For the first time fiscal constraints began to impact on the U.S. effort, reflected most notably in reductions in sortie rates for B-52 bombers and tactical air.

In early November President Nixon made an address to the nation in which he asked for support from the "silent majority" for his Vietnam War policies, an appeal that met with considerable success. In Paris, peace talks between the contending parties continued, but without agreement.

11 JAN 1969: Commanders Conference

ABRAMS: Welcomes Ambassador Bunker for a special assessment briefing. They are going to consider three enemy options: a DMZ attack, a Laotian-Military Region Tri-Thien-Hue attack, and a Cambodian option attacking into the Republic of Vietnam from Cambodia.

BRIEFER:

- Now observing accelerated flow of infiltration. Intercepted messages refer to several groups moving by train. By late December the rate of input into the pipeline had only previously been exceeded during the March–April period of 1968. Now more than 37,000 men are moving south.

■ "We have developed a methodology for projection of the COMINT-detected infiltration groups to areas in South Vietnam. [***]. The timing of their arrival is approximate, based on the average rate of travel observed."

■ Tally net gains and losses for the enemy, including gains from infiltration and recruitment. Losses include KIA, died of wounds and disabled, military Hoi Chanh, POW, and nonbattle casualties. During October–December the enemy sustained a net loss of 16,700 due to gains of 36,500 and losses of 53,200. Net losses doubled in each successive month of the period.

■ Re enemy infiltration: "We believe these [***] groups comprise an enemy division, specifically the 304th." Should begin arriving about 25 January 1969. Besides the division, the pipeline is carrying 26,000 replacements. "In summary, we are currently observing a movement of unusual proportions, comparable to that which occurred during the same period in 1968."

ABRAMS: "He [the enemy] is faced, by our estimate, with a 12,000 deficit in his existing structure. And he's adding to structure. He still hasn't made up the deficit, by this thing [the estimate just briefed], in the existing structure. It doesn't—well, it doesn't seem like that's the right way to do it. [Laughter] Of course, he's doing it."

BRIEFER:

■ Describes accelerated logistics buildup by the enemy. Cites "withdrawal of the 320th Division from South Vietnam in September, caused by the inability of the enemy to provide logistics support" due to a successful interdiction campaign.

■ Starting almost immediately after 1 November 1968 [the date on which bombing of North Vietnam was halted] "we began to observe through COMINT and photography the same reconstruction and logistical buildup pattern which we had observed after the April [1968] bombing halt north of 19 degrees. With his newly obtained freedom of movement he has relocated his logistical base from the Thanh Hoa area and the 19th parallel south to the Vinh–Quang Khe–Dong Hoi area." Reconstructed fords, bridges, and ferry crossing sites. Extension of rail segment to Vinh. Roads and railroads, ports. Port facilities at Vinh: Foreign vessels there for the first time in a great many years.

■ "Through the analysis of SLAR imagery, we are able to estimate throughput tonnages moving south from Dong Hoi to the area just north of the" DMZ. Averaging about 300 tons per day. "We estimate that 40 tons per day is the food requirement for the approximately 40,000 NVA combat and support troops in this area." Estimate 100 tons per day going into supply caches and to support enemy troops in I CTZ. Estimate enough now stockpiled in the area between Dong Hoi and the DMZ to support troops already there, plus two more divisions, at minimum levels for four to six months.

■ "In summary, since 1 November the enemy has made extraordinary progress in rebuilding his lines of communication and logistical base in North Vietnam south of the 19th parallel."

■ "In Laos, the enemy has engaged in a tremendous logistical effort since the 1 November bombing halt." "Prior to the bombing halt, the enemy's logistics situation in Laos was becoming critical. Beginning in July, he was forced to withdraw the majority of his units from Military Region Tri-Thien-Hue due to his inability to keep them supplied through Laos."

■ Just prior to the bombing halt, the summer monsoon season had ended and the road conditions were improving rapidly. "The road pattern shows the truck traffic enters Laos from North Vietnam through the Mu Gia Pass or the Ban Karai Pass. The two major interdiction points south of these passes are at Ban Sanat and the Ban Laboy ford. Traffic flows southward from the vicinity of the two interdiction points along an ever-expanding road network into Base Area 604. There is reduced flow south from BA 604."

■ Shows sensor indicators of both southbound and northbound truck traffic north of BA 610. "Traffic flow has increased greatly from 12 November and fluctuated . . . until the 15th of December, when a massive surge of trucks was observed. The increase of trucks moving has continued to a high of 976 on 4 January." "Tonnages being moved into Laos, and into and out of Base Area 604, may be estimated by assuming that each southward-moving truck hauls a cargo of three tons."

■ "During the period 13 November to 3 December an average of 51 tons per day flowed into Laos. Input at Base Area 603 during this period was 63 tons per day, the difference probably being due to local truck activity or transfer southward of stocks located north of the base area. Output moving south from Base Area 604 was 30 tons per day." Daily tonnages then increased throughout the rest of December. "Tonnage moving into Laos has tripled since November, while tonnage moving into BA 604 is more than five times as great."

■ "Based on this methodology, the enemy is estimated to have stockpiled over 4,000 tons in BA 604 since 13 November. Over 2,700 tons have been moved south from BA 604 in the direction of BA 610 and 611." Some may have been destroyed by the interdiction effort or consumed by enemy units in the vicinity of BA 604, which "appears to be the most active logistical storage area in the Laotian panhandle. As far as input is concerned, we do not believe that the enemy met his minimum requirements in South Vietnam and Laos until the last week in December." East of BA 604 is Khe Sanh.

ABRAMS: "I think we should say that this is an area where we just need a lot more work to come to a point of confidence where we know exactly what's happening. The magnitude—one assumption in here is that each one of these trucks is carrying a load of some kind of supplies. Right? ["Yes, sir."] And they might be carrying troops, shuttling tools or—shovels—between work sites. I mean, there's a whole gamut of things that could be going on in there."

ABRAMS: "I'm not trying to be a Pollyanna about it, that there isn't anything going on, but when you come to grips with just what kind of a capability he has created, how <u>much</u> of a capability—that's where this needs to get toughened up. Also, the amount of secondaries [explosions of ammunition or petroleum on the ground caused by bombing] that have come out of storage areas and that sort of thing hasn't been worked into these calculations. We do know that he was in a <u>reasonably</u> desperate situation in Laos—logistically—by the time of the bombing halt—and before. So there was a requirement for a lot of food. There was a requirement for a lot of necessities to get the thing back on just a living basis."

Detailed briefing on enemy use of Sihanoukville to bring supplies in by ship.

BRIEFER:

■ Re the importance of Cambodian base areas: "Sihanoukville is the primary point of entry for supplies, especially arms and ammunition, destined for enemy forces in southern South Vietnam. Since November 1966 34 ships are suspected of having unloaded ordnance at Sihanoukville. Twelve of these instances have been well documented and are probably munitions shipments." These 12 unloaded over 14,000 tons of ordnance during November 1966–October 1968. Adding other ship estimates, this figure may double.

■ "We picked up the flow of munitions into Cambodia approximately six months after Market Time operations had started to choke off enemy shipments of supplies by sea to the coast of the Republic of Vietnam. These shipments are ostensibly made pursuant to Cambodian military aid agreements with Communist China and the Soviet Union and supposedly are for use by the Cambodian armed forces, but the evidence shows otherwise. DIA estimates show that the annual reasonable needs of the Cambodian armed forces, or FARK, are a little over 350 tons of munitions." With the recent 10 percent force expansion, say 400 tons per year are required. While 14,000 tons came in over a two-year period, FARK's reasonable requirements would have been less than 800 tons. Over 12,000 tons of ordnance are thus still unaccounted for during the period, enough to satisfy the enemy's minimum needs in South Vietnam over the same period and permit him to establish sizable reserves.

■ Cites various evidence, including "236 reports from PWs, ralliers, and coded agents, all of which document the flow of ordnance into South Vietnam from Cambodia." "The magnitude of the arms traffic, and its efficient working apparatus, suggest the knowledge, if not active participation, of high-ranking Cambodian military and political figures." Also cites "the employment of FARK trucks in the illicit movement of arms" and reports of enemy personnel unloading munitions from FARK trucks.

■ Re the Hak Ly Trucking Company: Report "described regular Sunday meetings in Phnom Penh between representatives of FARK, the Sihanouk regime, the Hak Ly Trucking Company, and the National Liberation Front. These meetings were held to discuss the movement of supplies through Cambodia to Viet Cong units and to ensure the secrecy of Cambodian involvement. Information concerning incoming cargo was passed during these meetings so that the Royal Khmer Government would not treat it as contraband. It should be noted that the reliability of the sources of this information has been established by a very thorough cross-check of the information and of the sources themselves."

■ Other reports "implicate FARK officers, especially Lieutenant Colonel Um Savoeut, as being involved in the arms traffic from Sihanoukville to Viet Cong bases in the border areas." There is no doubt "of FARK's complicity with the enemy."

■ "After leaving Sihanoukville, the munitions are transported to the Kompong Speu arms depot, 43 kilometers southwest of Phnom Penh, or to warehouses in Phnom Penh itself." Then weekly shipments from there. Trucking firms Machine [Beaufea?] and Hak Ly reportedly involved. Drivers report. Detailed distribution system depicted. "Over 10,000 tons of suspected ordnance in the past year has been delivered to the border regions."

■ "To appreciate the growing importance of Cambodia, we should review the deterioration and collapse of the enemy's other possible logistical routes." Sea infiltration "effectively blocked by Market Time operations since mid-1966." Overland through Laos: "Over the past 12 months, an average of only eight tons per day has been estimated to have moved south of Base Area 610 towards the Cambodian border, 350 kilometers to the south." "Thus the contention by some intelligence analysts at the Washington level that enemy forces in II, III, and IV Corps are receiving the majority of their ordnance via the Laotian overland route fails to be substantiated by the facts." Flow going the other way. "Cambodia has become, and remains, the primary LOC for arms and ammunition reaching enemy forces in III and IV Corps, and possibly II Corps."

BUNKER: "I must say very impressive."

Briefing on interdiction operations against the Ho Chi Minh Trail.

BRIEFER:

■ Re the North Vietnamese "massive buildup after November 1st, particularly in Route Package 1. This buildup continues unabated as of today. The rail yards at Hanoi and the docks at Haiphong have been operating at near capacity levels." Moved south to such points as Nam Loi Island and to Quang Khe by ocean freighter and openly stored. As many as 30 large ships in use (one a 600-ton merchantman) on the Haiphong–Quang Khe route. Also many smaller coastal transshipment points in use, served by hundreds of small ships. And photo of big push after the bombing halt shows trucks moving south two abreast (on 13 November north of the Mu Gia Pass). "The logistics pressure-head is clearly right on the North Vietnamese–Laotian border."

■ "Our campaign in Laos to impede this massive logistics effort is based on the interdiction of lines of communication and the systematic destruction of enemy trucks and supplies as they appear on the roads, and the destruction of truck parks and storage areas as they can be found and targeted. This plan was patterned after the successful interdiction campaign waged in North Vietnam." Northern interdiction area known as "Commando Hunt." Southern end of the panhandle major choke points known as "Steel Tiger South." "Unlike North Vietnam, the terrain and the route structure is against us. There are few non-bypassable choke points, and the further south we proceed the more the route structure expands." Have therefore concentrated efforts in the north, as close to the North Vietnamese border as possible.

■ Two prime access routes to Laos: Mu Gia Pass and Ban Karai Pass. "Interdiction is never static. Each action demands a reaction." But more truck kills achieved in flat open terrain. Road crosses the Nam La Li River in very rugged terrain: "We have had a near perfect record of closures here." Enemy trellis-covered road. Dead foliage discovered by camouflage-detection photography. Enemy moving 85-mm AAA weapons into the pass areas.

■ "Sensor detections are now running at the highest level since the weeks preceding the May offensive." 196 sensors then, however, and 436 now. And new routes are now being monitored. These changes account for about 30 percent of the increase. "During the last two weeks of November truck sightings in Commando Hunt increased more than seven times and the sensor count doubled. The next two weeks saw a dramatic drop in both sensor detections and visual sightings. During this period the B-52 allocation against interdiction points in Laos more than doubled."

■ Trend steadily upward since mid-December. In December 1968: Destroyed or damaged 857 trucks. At the present rate, could kill more than 1,000 trucks in January 1969. Recently brought into play in the Laotian panhandle the AC-123 and AC-130 gunships. The AC-130s began operations on 27 November, the AC-123s on 10 December. "To date the [interdiction] campaign has doubled the truck travel time from Mu Gia to Tchepone. It now takes seven to nine days, thus exposing the trucks to attack for a longer period."

Status of the Accelerated Pacification Campaign.

BRIEFER:

■ "Significant gains continue to be made in all six major elements of that campaign." December 1968 HES Report: Countrywide gain of 3 percent in relatively secure population. Record gain of 3.5 percent in November. By December: 76.3 percent countrywide are relatively secure, based on a combination of security and development scores. December: Contested population decreased by 1.9 percent; VC population dropped 1.1 percent to a two-year low of 12.3 percent. Rural population only. Combined security and development score shows relatively secure population increasing by 4.3 percent over November to 65 percent. The rural population gain constitutes 90 percent of the overall countrywide gain in the relatively secure category.

■ Individual elements of the APC: "The vitally important spoiling campaign has provided the essential umbrella under which pacification forces can function, and has maintained constant pressure on the enemy's entire military and political structure." "1,204 of 1,216 target hamlets have been entered by GVN security forces." "Local security is being primarily provided by 227 RF companies and 710 PF platoons which are now deployed in APC hamlets." Per December 1968 HES: "726 APC hamlets have now been upgraded to the relatively secure category."

ABRAMS: "Now, General Quang told me the other day that the president was going to put out a directive to have an elected government in every village by the end of March. Has that been—do you know?"

SOMEONE (maybe Colby): "The minister has put that order out."

ABRAMS: "They have? I think it's an important move, too."

BUNKER: "When I went with him [President Thieu] to II Corps, one of the things he emphasized to the province chiefs was the need for elected government to offset the 'liberation committees.'" "That's what this APC has done—it has brought government physically into most of these target hamlets. And in many cases they weren't there before. They aren't all elected yet, but that is part of the plan—that they will be elected."

BRIEFER:

■ "If the rate of progress can be maintained in January, about 90 percent of the target hamlet population will be raised to the relatively secure category."

■ "In the Phuong Hoang [Phoenix] campaign, GVN-reported results" are well above target for the 20 October 1968–20 February 1969 campaign period. "Audited results reflecting a strict definition of VCI" are also shown. They give sufficient evidence to conclude "it is unlikely that the goal of 12,000 by 28 February will be met." But "steady progress is being made in this rather complex operation."

■ Re Chieu Hoi program: APC goal of 5,000 ralliers has already been exceeded. There were 713 in the week 29 December–4 January alone. This was the fourth week in a row of more than 700 ralliers. There were 3,146 in December 1968, the second highest monthly total in the history of the program.

■ Re PSDF program: APC goal is 200,000. It does not appear that it will be met.

■ Re Information/Psyops program: Growing confidence reflected in increasing number of refugees returning to their homes, in Chieu Hoi rate, and in rapid expansion of government presence in the target hamlets.

■ "One of the most significant aspects of the APC has been the enthusiasm, hard work, and growing confidence of GVN officials. This psychological breakthrough is reflected in the GVN's improved pacification organization and aggressive planning for 1969."

Ambassador Bunker summing up the past year's accomplishments and current prospects.

BUNKER: "I think—one looks back over this past year, one would certainly have to conclude that it's been a momentous one, perhaps the most momentous we've seen since the decision in 1965 to come in here in force. I recognize there are many problems still ahead of us, but I think that, if we look back over the year to what's happened, one has to conclude, I think, that there has been very great progress this year."

BUNKER: "You go back, starting with the Tet Offensive, which involved—resulted—obviously in a heavy military defeat for the enemy, but also in a very significant psychological victory for him in the United States—I think there isn't any question about that. I went back for three days in April to report to the president, and I said to him and the Cabinet I was <u>shocked</u> to see the effect the Tet Offensive had had at home. There was no panic <u>here</u>. In fact, the government reacted vigorously and strongly and quickly. But I think that, from the Tet Offensive, to two events of the year—external events which had great influence on what happens here—were the Tet Offensive by the enemy and the president's speech of March 31 with the partial cessation of the bombing."

BUNKER: "In the first place, I think the Tet Offensive had <u>constructive</u> effects in giving the Vietnamese confidence—more confidence—in themselves. And the president's speech made them face up to the fact that we're not going to be here forever and that they had, one day, to face up to this fact and to get ready <u>for</u> it. And I think the results which flowed from these two events have been very significant. They brought about full mobilization—something, too, I think, the extent of it and the magnitude of it, which is not appreciated at home. If you take the average of the manpower pool, average population under government control, which is roughly at two-thirds this year, and you calculate that there are a million under arms, it's equivalent to about 18 million in the United States, which would be a tremendous undertaking for us in any terms."

BUNKER: "The installation of the new government, which is much more effective—I think perhaps the most effective, and <u>stable</u>, government that we've ever had here now, as it's developed. The civil defense organization, with over a million in it. The Accelerated Pacification Program which, as Bill [Colby] says, has to be largely a Vietnamese effort, certainly—my observation is that the president here is tremendously interested in it, knows a great deal about it—more than any [other] Vietnamese, I think, and he's determined to press it. He told me only yesterday that he intended to keep on with it. He wants to start <u>another</u> intensive campaign as soon as this one is over. And the attack on the infrastructure, and the Chieu Hoi. All of these are, I think, <u>very</u> favorable developments."

BUNKER: "We've had, on the other hand, as you know, too, a sensitive period here in our relations with the Vietnamese government on the political side which have differed from your relations on the military side, brought about by the decision to stop the bombing, the rest of the bombing, on 1 November, and the refusal of the government here to go to Paris at that time. This was brought about—there were two factors, I think, among the most important which entered into it. One was—no question that I think the government here was playing the election, hoping that Mr. Nixon's election would result in a harder line. Very fortunately, Mr. Nixon disabused them of this idea very quickly after the election. But secondly, too, the action came too fast for them to absorb, and it took time to condition the people here to the fact of going to Paris."

BUNKER: "Their great concern, evident, about the [National Liberation] Front, and the status of the Front. And I think that, while it took nearly a month of difficult and very delicate and patient negotiations to bring them to Paris, the time was well spent. I think it strengthened the hand of the government here—they certainly didn't act like puppets during that period. I think the president obtained wider support from the country in general, and I think that they've gone to Paris, therefore, in a stronger position. And in the long run I think it will turn out to be all to the good. We've also been having another difficult period, you know, on this question of the tables—the shape. I don't think it has been decided yet . . . again, having to do with the Front and their concern about the status of the Front. And it is—it's very difficult for the American public to understand this."

BUNKER: "The result is that, I think it's fair to say, is that the position of the government at home has eroded seriously since 1 November with refusal to go to Paris and now the argument over the shape of the tables. It's difficult, I think, it's difficult for people, Americans, to understand the importance of it. They don't see it as a substantive matter, and they don't understand that procedure can determine substance, and hence can be substantive in itself. And this is one of the problems that makes the relationship difficult. But I'm confident, too, that this will be also overcome and that we'll get on to the talks. I think that once we do, too, that the American people will be more patient with the situation here. And this is the thing that we need. I think they're willing to go on with the fighting, provided the talks also go on at the same time. I think they're unwilling to go on with the fighting when there is an opportunity to negotiate and we're not negotiating. So I think that, as I say, I have confidence that this will be solved, too. We'll get to the talks, and then I think, when we do, that the American people will become more patient."

BUNKER: "My view is that the talks are going to be complex, and difficult, and long, and arduous. And I don't think we're going to reach conclusions easily or quickly. Consequently I think we're going to have time to make more progress here. Just the whole question of a mutual withdrawal is enormously complicated, obviously. But I think that on all of the major elements entering into our objectives here—the military situation, pacification, the development of a government which is strong enough, stable enough, and viable enough to meet the political contest which will follow the military—on all of these fronts I think very substantial progress has been made this year. It's evident, I think, perhaps most clearly in the attitude of the government itself here toward peace and toward negotiations. As the president said to me—what, six months ago?—he could hardly talk about peace or talk about negotiations or anything other than a military victory. Now he can talk about the fact that there has to be a political settlement sometime, and that the context will change from military to political."

BUNKER: "Well, these are all very substantial indicators of progress, not adequately understood at home. But the facts, I think, are catching up, and people are beginning to see, and to recognize—even those who've been more critical—that we <u>are</u> making progress. Even the *New York Times,* and that's saying a good deal. Some of them aren't quite so favorable. Joe Kraft says that my staying on here and Cabot Lodge's appointment are both catastrophes. I don't know, you'll have to take your choice and make your decision. But, anyway, I do think that we have made very, very material progress here. And I think all of you who are here today, all of you gentlemen who had a major hand in this, can take a great deal of satisfaction and a great deal of pride in what's been accomplished. It's been a really great performance, I think."

BUNKER: "My yardstick of success here is what the Vietnamese can do themselves, because that eventually is the ultimate test. They've got to take over someday. It's quite clear that we're not going to be here forever. And what <u>we</u> can get them to do—through instruction, through persuasion, through pressure, in whatever way—to do the job themselves is the ultimate yardstick of success. I think you've come a long way in many aspects here this year. So that, as I say, I think all of you gentlemen here can take great pride in what has been accomplished. I certainly am very proud of what you've done, and I want to express my <u>own</u> appreciation and gratitude for what has been accomplished. I think it's been a remarkable piece of work and someday it will be recognized."

Threat assessments by major field commanders.

CUSHMAN (CG III MAF): Began our assessment by considering that "everything the enemy had would be brought to bear, and at the same time." If two or more possible enemy actions came together, "we would have to adopt essentially a defensive posture." "We would resist at all costs, particularly on the part of the ARVN, pulling back into the provincial and district capitals and setting up static defenses. I think we could probably prevent this. At Tet, they tended to do this, but we managed to get them out in the field in fairly short order, and I think we could do it again."

CUSHMAN (discussing possible reinforcement of I CTZ from the other corps areas): "If the assumptions which we have been given in the originating message for this conference hold true, these units could be used in Laos." "I must admit we request the Delta Force every time we can. . . . They're a very valuable reconnaissance asset." "We can hold, I'm convinced. We may have a little trouble around Danang, but I think we can do it." "If we get help from external sources, we. . . . may be able to attack into Laos if given permission, which would of course be <u>really</u> good. . . ."

STILWELL (CG XXIV Corps): The enemy is now "moving from threshold to threshold of DMZ violations, testing our reaction as he goes." "We achieved a very effective counterbattery posture from 1 July forward last year as a result of our massive firepower exercise the first week of July. Since the first of November we've lost that power. We simply don't know to what extent he has repositioned his artillery to camouflaged, revetted positions."

STILWELL: "My final point, sir, deals with utilization of the planning assumption with regard to ground operations in Laos." Base Areas 604, 610, and 611 are within reach of XXIV Corps. "We would see the 101st [Airborne Division] attacking straight through the A Shau Valley. . . . We would see elements of the 3rd Marine Division coming down the Da Krong Valley toward [Base Area] 611."

ABRAMS: "Now, with respect to both of these [enemy] options, what can be said about <u>preempting</u> them?" "We've done this before. That's what I had to do in Kontum [B-52, tac air, etc.] because I didn't <u>have</u> any reinforcements. I couldn't send a damn <u>battalion</u> up there!"

CUSHMAN: The enemy came down the eastern side of the DMZ in May with not much logistical preparation along the Gio Linh axis. "As far as we could find they didn't have extensive caches as they usually do." This was the 320th NVA Division.

ABRAMS: "Of course they got the <u>hell</u> beat out of them, too. They never <u>got</u> anywhere! And that may be a good—if they use that system, then you don't <u>need</u> reinforcements. All you need to do is just beat the hell out of them again. When he <u>skips</u> this business of constructing his bunkers so that he's got protection from artillery and air, and digging in his caches and so on, he can't <u>run</u> that kind of a war. He isn't <u>capable</u> of it."

SOMEONE (re II CTZ): "Looking at our problem, it becomes one of <u>finding</u> the enemy, and having found him to be able to hold him long enough so you can jump on him and take care of him, so to speak. So this therefore requires that we be able to break down into the smallest common denominator in order to do this so that we can <u>react</u> and we <u>can</u> use our mobility and we <u>can</u> use our firepower to defeat him." "We have a lot of battalion operations going on, but when I say battalion—in many cases it's companies, and the companies are broken down in platoons and so on. But basically putting out many LRRPs or armed equivalents—30 from the 4th Division, 12 from the 173rd Airborne Brigade."

16 JAN 1969: Briefing for Ambassador Johnson

Ambassador U. Alexis Johnson served as deputy ambassador in the American Embassy, Saigon (1964–1966) and as undersecretary of state for political affairs (1969–1973).

DAVIDSON: "As we now know, a key decision—perhaps one of the worst decisions in military history—was made in which the enemy determined to go from Phase II of the classic insurgency into Phase III, in which he called for a general counteroffensive [*sic:* offensive?]. This resulted in the so-called Tet Offensive of 30 January, the second general offensive of 5 May, and the Third Offensive of 18 August. The results of these offensives, militarily, were that the enemy quickly suffered defeat."

ABRAMS (re I Corps): "By our estimate he's got a deficit there in his existing structure of about 12,000." And we see the 304th NVA Division coming in.

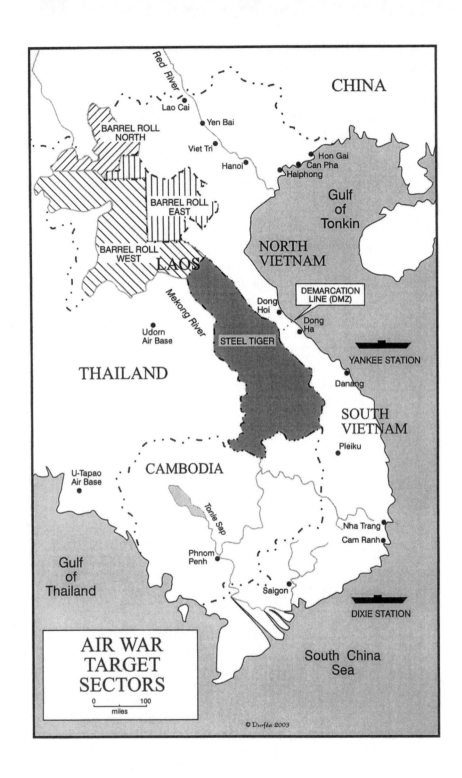

AIR WAR
TARGET
SECTORS

0   100
miles

© Durfée 2003

"So he's adding structure without making up the deficit . . . in the personnel strength of his structure."

DAVIDSON (re 304th NVA): "It's a bloody veteran of Khe Sanh."

ABRAMS: We expect the enemy to make his next primary effort in III Corps, perhaps secondarily in I Corps. "We've got enough forces in III Corps, in our judgment, to handle whatever he may choose to do there. Where we could have a problem is in I Corps, although we're much better off there than we were last year at this time in terms of strength of forces and so on. And the effectiveness of the ARVN has continually increased in I Corps. It's probably, on that score, the best of any of the corps." General Peers is prepared to shift the 173rd Airborne Brigade and one brigade of the 4th Infantry Division to I Corps if necessary, "and I think do that without upsetting the pacification program."

ABRAMS: "Our forces are fragmented in an awful lot of small groups. What we're trying to do is work against the machinery." "The effort is to try [laughing] to have ambushes on every trail, and broken down and out there at night and in the daytime, and try to work against the system. And it's the preparatory thing that he has to go through. I think it has increased his problems."

ABRAMS (re question about both U.S. and ARVN getting out at night): "I think it's improved tremendously." "In fact, in the RF and PF I believe it's been a fairly dramatic improvement."

COLBY: "Associated with the M16 issue, in my judgment."

ABRAMS: "Yeah." But: "We've still got districts . . . where it's very sad."

COLBY: "Back in '67 they estimated that they could put in about 40,000 hectares [of IR-8 rice] during '68. And of course when Tet occurred everybody sort of threw that estimate out the window. But the first crop they put in about 20,000, and the second planting they put in about 24,000, so they exceeded their goal during '68. Next year—200,000." "An Giang, in two years, is going to double its production."

ZUMWALT: Swift boats are the inner coastal surveillance craft. "The Vietnamese sailors are learning very fast." Progressively turning over Swift boats and river craft to them.

BROWN (re air effort in Laos): "It's a frustrating story. In September and October, when we were [bombing] in North Vietnam, we had it pretty well sealed off, between ourselves and the navy. Right now, we've concentrated on the areas of Ban Karai and Mu Gia, but they still get through. They're going around us at Ban Karai. I think there's another pass, and they're not using Ban Karai."

BROWN (re B-52s against this): "We've stepped that up to about 50 percent of the total. We're flying 1,800 Arc Light sorties a month, 60 a day, and about 50 percent of the total so far this month is being applied in Laos. It's most effective, dramatic." "We're averaging about 450 to 500 strike [tac air] sorties a day in Laos, between ourselves and the navy. And he's still pushing trucks through. He's got quite a stockpile now down as far as Tchepone."

ABRAMS: "When the bombing halt came, George [Brown] and the navy and so on, they went to work on these points here to try to stop this flow from coming in here. And for a while, it was going pretty good. It looked like we had the stopper in. But then they started going around it, going around somehow in here and so on, and then it began to build up. And in the first part of January it was really hot. Well, what it looks like is the principal effort was to get it into a massive storage area down here around Tchepone."

BROWN: Last year we had about 150 sensors in place, but now about 400. Two types: seismic and acoustic. "All of this [enemy activity] is under canopy. You're really blind."

BROWN: "Ambassador Sullivan feels that we haven't really got a handle on assessing the effectiveness of our effort. He feels that we really ought to concentrate on many things that we can't measure. One, we can count trucks destroyed and damaged. We can get visual and some photo evidence of truck kills. That's not too accurate. Some crews working at night will claim kills that may not in fact be kills. On the other hand that, I feel, is balanced because the Arc Lights, B-52 strikes against these truck parks through the foliage, we get reactions but we don't claim trucks. We don't see it, or rarely do we see it. So there're trucks probably destroyed there that'll balance the overclaims, or erroneous claims, out on the roads. But there're only two things moving through there that'll burn and explode—that's ammunition and POL, and we're getting a lot of secondary effects."

William H. Sullivan was U.S. ambassador to Laos (1964–1969).

BROWN: "It's the most frustrating experience I've ever had chasing these things [trucks]."

ABRAMS: "He's [the enemy] making a fantastic effort to push stuff down in there. He's not interested in costs. So as far as intent is concerned, he hasn't decided to back away from the problem. That part, I think, is unmistakably clear."

AMBASSADOR JOHNSON: "What happened to the McNamara Line?"

ABRAMS: "Well, ah—basically what we're doing is playing that a little looser. We've backed away from the strong point obstacle system. And we're handling that thing with small forces and sensors and this type of thing."

BROWN: "At least on the air side, and I think probably the ground side too, we've found that the hardware that was a derivative of this program is useful, and there've been certain innovations to further exploit this, and the munitions that went with it, but the concepts that were held by the Jason Group initially—you know, that wrote the report that led to all of this—haven't in all cases panned out."

ABRAMS: "It's given us a degree of intelligence on this that we never had."

ZUMWALT: "And we've used sensors for our river interdiction, so the hardware has really paid off."

ABRAMS: "Since the bombing halt, and we've had this understanding about the DMZ. The truth of the matter is that we've put a little stock in that. We've got relatively light forces in here." Moved the 1st Cavalry Division to III Corps. "Part of being able to do that was taking a little stock in understandings about the DMZ. Now it's true that we have reacted, and have insisted with Washington that we allow no monkey business in the southern half of the DMZ. Well, see—they'll creep up on you if you let them."

■ ■ ■

ABRAMS (re B-52s): "It's an awful mass of power. <u>Nothing</u> can stand up to it."

. . .

DAVIDSON: "A very high powered group from CIA, State Department, DIA at the Washington level came out, and they now agree with us specifically as to this, that there <u>is</u> high-ranking Cambodian complicity in the movement of arms and ammunition through Cambodia. They're inclined to take a disclaimer that Sihanouk himself is involved, although whether he <u>knows</u> [about] it or not they—I <u>think</u> they're inclined to believe he does, as we are." "There is high-level complicity. It may go as high as Lon Nol, the acting prime minister."

JOHNSON: "Is this stuff coming in through Sihanoukville?"

DAVIDSON: "Yes, sir." "Arms and ammunition."

. . .

COLBY: "The main point is, as General Abrams tells us, it's one war. You know, we used to talk about the 'other' war, but he's made it into one war. I think the full strategy here is all of one piece. Pacification is very much a part of the considerations of the regular divisional units. . . . And of course on the pacification side we're trying to build up the support behind the military successes that we had last fall and last summer."

COLBY (re RF and PF): "There're about 91,000 more of them today than there were a year ago." About 100,000 now have M16s, which they didn't have a year ago. Have 350 advisory teams living and working with RF and PF units.

COLBY (re Phoenix): "About a year and a half ago we began worrying about the VC infrastructure," or VCI, and organized Phoenix. In July 1968 "the president [Thieu] issued a decree and it really started to go. We really are putting a lot of emphasis on this." "<u>Most</u> of them are captured." "The emphasis <u>is</u> on capturing and interrogation, follow up and so forth."

COLBY (re PSDF): "There were some people who were worried about whether the weapons would go to the VC. Well, the answer is the VC have their <u>own</u> weapons."

ABRAMS: "They've got <u>better</u> ones."

COLBY: We have about 100,000 weapons out with the PSDF now.

COLBY: "The refugee problem is <u>still</u> an agonizing situation. They've got about 1.3 million refugees in the country. That gets up around 8 percent of the total population—a hell of a lot." About 700,000 are in I Corps. About one million people were displaced during the Tet and May offensives, and about one million received some level of government assistance.

COLBY: Describes the Accelerated Pacification Campaign, which began 1 November 1968 to achieve specific goals during the following three months: Raise 1,000 contested hamlets to relatively secure status. They wound up with 1,330 targeted hamlets, and some force has moved into 1,320 of them. Substance to it. Not complicated. "The philosophy being 'spread out and move into the countryside.'" Pre-Tet 1968: 68 percent secure. Now: 76 percent. In July thought by the end of the year "we <u>might</u> make 70 percent." Now the plan for 1969 has been "signed by every one of the ministers and the prime minister." It begins 1 February, at the end of the special three-month campaign.

Goal: 90 percent of the population secure. And double the PSDF to two million. Resettle 30,000 refugees. And have elected village governments.

ABRAMS: "Mr. Ambassador, there's one cardinal rule here. No program is going to fly unless the president [Thieu] puts his personal stamp on it."

JOHNSON (re Thieu): "He turned out to be a lot stronger fellow than I thought he would."

COLBY: "And organizationally minded."

ABRAMS (re Thieu): "He knows more about pacification than any other Vietnamese."

ABRAMS (re the enemy and pacification): "I feel that he is going to have to react to this. I think this strikes at the real root of his strength. His strength is not in these divisions. His strength is inside this [VCI] program. If that [pacification] moves, he's going to have to do something about it. It's the part he can't let go down the drain."

ABRAMS: "I think the biggest problem the president has on the military side is he has to change the commanders of the 5th and 18th Divisions, and he just can't bring himself to do it." "I've told him it's the principal strategic deficiency that he's got." "I said it's inhibiting me. I had to bring the 1st Cavalry Division down here in a hurry so that I would feel comfortable that Saigon was in no risk. And it's because the two divisions are not earning their rations."

ABRAMS (re the 25th ARVN Division): "It's the best of the three [ARVN divisions in III Corps], which of course is not [words unclear]. The 25th Division is clearly improving. It improved in its performance when it got the M16. The two others declined in performance after issuing the M16. That wasn't the cause, but—."

ABRAMS: "I have no idea, and no one's been able to give me any hint, as to how Giai stays there, what connection there is, or anything else. I don't understand that at all. Vien told me that Giai commanded an airborne battalion for a year and a half, during which time the airborne battalion never had a single contact. That's about the way he's commanded the 18th. They've had contacts, most of them disastrous, but—."

ABRAMS: "Now Thuan is something else. He was chief of staff for Thieu when Thieu commanded the 5th Division. And Thuan comes in and has supper with the president once every week or 10 days. Mrs. Thuan occasionally has lunch with Mrs. Thieu. And so there's a personal bond of friendship there that I'm sure must give the president extreme anguish when he contemplates how to handle this." "But it's his political fate he's monkeying with, and he's just got to do something."

ABRAMS: "Now Vien told me the other day—I raised it again with Vien—I'm almost embarrassed to raise it with anybody—Vien told me, he said, 'Oh, don't worry about it. The president's going to handle this by Tet.' Tet's the 17th of February. But I have a certain amount of impatience here as we fiddle." "It seems to me you can press it to the point—you can never break off communication, and you can't go to a point where you just become a nuisance. Otherwise you've just failed. After that <u>you're</u> not ever going to be effective again. And you can't make that—."

JOHNSON: "Well, this is very much like the confrontation that led up to Quat's getting out and Ky and Thieu coming in in 1965, in the spring. Quat had two ministers that were important to us, interior and economic affairs, who were duds. <u>He</u> knew and <u>we</u> knew it. And, in our do-good sort of way, you know, we kept pushing him to get rid of these fellows. And he said, 'Give me time.' But he moved sooner than he would have because of our pressure on him, and it brought down Quat and a pretty good civilian government. Just being good and doing the right thing isn't always the best answer."

■ ■ ■

JOHNSON: "One thing I'm clear on is that an unconditional cease-fire is a disaster. This worries me more than anything else in the situation."

COLBY: "It's almost impossible to articulate the provisions of a cease-fire that could be sold to the VC and to the government and to us."

JOHNSON: "To me the cease-fire is the end result of the negotiations rather than the beginning."

TOWNSEND: "Wouldn't it be a shame if we were almost ready to win, and then do something like that?"

JOHNSON: "Well, I don't know. Not to pick up Averell [Harriman], but what is winning going to be in this?"

JOHNSON: "The press and TV bear an <u>enormous</u> responsibility for attitudes on this. <u>They're</u> the ones that are determining the attitude of the American people, in a <u>most</u> irresponsible manner."

ABRAMS: "The attitude of the Americans out here continues to be magnificent. The energy, the enthusiasm, the devotion—it's just <u>magnificent</u>. And everybody that comes <u>out</u> here, people of all kinds—entertainers or visitors or clergymen or—. I got a <u>wonderful</u> letter from Billy Graham. He was out here and—he feels <u>he</u> got more out of it than he ever gave."

ABRAMS: "But, <u>now</u>—every month we get 40,000 more Americans [as replacements]. They come from every strata of our society, from every geographic element of it. They're all shapes and kinds. They come right out of <u>Watts</u>. They come out of Detroit. And so on. <u>None</u> of that, none of that <u>attitude</u> has ever been reflected in any significant way here. So I don't know whether the attitude of the American people's being properly <u>reflected</u>. <u>I</u> choose to think that these 40,000 men that come in every month, <u>they</u> represent the attitude of the American people."

JOHNSON: "No university in the United States dares offer Dean Rusk the presidency. No university on the east coast would offer Walt Rostow a job. He said the campuses just wouldn't take him."

18 JAN 1969: WIEU

ATTENDEES: Gen. Abrams, Amb. Colby, Gen. Brown, LTG Mildren, VADM Zumwalt, Dr. Wikner, MG Corcoran, MG Townsend, MG Shaefer, MG Davidson, MG Rasmussen, BG Frizen, BG Long, BG Sidle, BG Galloway, BG Clay, BG Bryan, Col. Gorman, Col. Cavanaugh, Col. Powers.

COLBY: "I think rather interesting are the orders to these people—'Go down there and if things go well maybe we'll do something'—."

ABRAMS: "I noticed that. That's a good point, Bill. And it's not like the orders in May, for instance, and the orders at Tet. Well, they're just advancing the principle of flexibility."

A sarcastic reference to a viewpoint the now departed Robert Komer had advanced concerning the enemy's supposed flexibility.

BROWN: "I can't stop trucks one at a time."

ABRAMS: "I keep saying that it's not what it looks like, and it's so true. You look back over the last three weeks, you know, and you get down to the detail of what he's doing, where we're prognosticating what he has in mind, and it's never like it looks. It's always something else."

COMMANDER BETTS (on his last day at MACV): Briefs on enemy efforts to counter the Accelerated Pacification Campaign: "There is good evidence that the enemy was able to get copies of the plans very shortly after they became available to GVN personnel." "We recently captured a female commo-liaison messenger who was carrying microfilm and copies of the GVN Rural Development Policy for 1969."

ABRAMS: The only good thing is that "maybe the volume exceeds COSVN's capability to correlate it." Unless they've managed to get their hands on a few computers. "We've got so many over here now I doubt if we'd notice it [if they stole some of ours]."

BRIEFER: "On 20 November the enemy started a propaganda campaign against the APC with a broadcast entitled 'What Is the True Nature of the So-Called Urgent Pacification Plan of the U.S. Aggressor and the Treacherous Thieu-Ky-Huong Clique?' This propaganda campaign continues, and has now reached a volume and pitch of hysteria unusual even for Communists. The APC is being equated to the worst 'fascist crimes' of the Diem period, and daily broadcasts list the number of people burned, raped, or buried alive as part of the pacification campaign."

BRIEFER: "We have a copy of the VC counterpacification plan for Sub-Region 5." Dated 12 December 1968. Quoting it: "The present task is that everything must be used in the task of opposing and spoiling the pacification."

BRIEFER: The first objective of the enemy's Winter–Spring Campaign is to "disrupt pacification." "By December the pattern is clear and unmistakable. The enemy has decreased his attacks on our war facilities and concentrated on the rural population and the friendly operations which affect his rural area operations."

COLBY: "Now they talk about destroying it and all that, but they can't quite put their finger on what to destroy."

COLBY: "The pacification team—I suppose that means the RD cadre. They've fixed on that, and of course just at a time when <u>we've</u> put the major emphasis over on the RF and PF."

■ ■ ■

ABRAMS: "Did you see that thing where the Polish ICC guy said that he was never going to go down on an inspection tour in the south of Laos because it was critical to the NLF? Well, no, it's one of those things you can't use."

■ ■ ■

BROWN: "With four airplanes we've gotten 27 percent of the kills," referring to truck kills by two AC-123 and two AC-130 gunships out of a total of some 300 aircraft devoted to the interdiction mission.

SOMEONE: In Washington, we had a hell of a time getting these systems, even though Harold Brown is for it. "Systems Analysis, our good old friends there—."

ABRAMS: "You don't want to just satisfy yourself with numbers. There ought to be some meaningful way of distributing assets that will improve effectiveness."

COLBY: "I spent about a week going around to the different corps and having a one-hour session with each of our province senior advisors. The plan was to discuss the pacification plan before it got locked in concrete."

ABRAMS: "I was kind of proud of old Ray Peers the other day. He came down here to this commanders conference and he offered up a way to take two brigades out of his corps."

■ ■ ■

ABRAMS: "Vien—actually Vien is a good man. He's a reasonably <u>professional</u> man. But it's very difficult for him to exercise the sort of direction which he should, and which I <u>believe</u> he <u>knows</u> he should, because the president is continuously making private arrangements with the corps commanders that box Vien in. And sometimes he doesn't <u>know</u> about it until he bumps into it. And of course <u>no</u> fellow, you know, that's trying to carry on a responsible position, likes to run into that accidentally with one of his senior subordinates. You know, it has a tendency to make you feel <u>inadequate</u>." "I have a great deal of sympathy for General Vien's position."

ABRAMS: "On the other hand, I have to give the president credit for—god knows, <u>nothing</u> would move here if he didn't, actually if he didn't put his shoulder to it. He just does a little more of it, in some places sometimes, than he should."

22 JAN 1969: J-2/J-3 Briefing for Lieutenant General Chesarek

Lt. Gen. Ferdinand J. Chesarek was Army Assistant Vice Chief of Staff (1967–1969) and then, as General, Commanding General, Army Materiel Command (1969–1970).

BRIEFER: In 1968, the second offensive was planned for 27 April, but was delayed to 5 May. The third offensive on 18 August was "rather abortive, preempted mostly by our own friendly forces." Stopped in early September.

BRIEFER: Tet 1968: Enemy losses 42,000. May 1968: Enemy losses 40,000. August 1968: Enemy losses 26,000.

BRIEFER: "But after these huge losses of 1968 we believe he realized he could not win the war militarily." "We feel that he shifted over to prepare for negotiations."

BRIEFER: "He has 11 sanctuaries along the border from the tri-border area down to the Seven Mountains area." "And he does have the LOCs through Cambodia that are free from attack, interdiction, and attrition to supply these bases."

■ ■ ■

ABRAMS: "The policy we follow is to give all the facts to the press every day, and then let them do—. And they, of course, winnow through them and pick the ones they want and so on. But they get them all every day. We make a <u>special</u> effort on <u>bad</u> news to get the facts out as fast as we can, and good news we triple-check it."

■ ■ ■

BRIEFER: "As of 1 November we had no evidence of any infiltration groups moving south within North Vietnam. About 15,000 men were believed to be en route in Laos and Cambodia, all of whom should have arrived in South Vietnam prior to 31 December [1968]."

BRIEFER: But now we are observing an increasing flow of men. During November–December "a rate of input exceeded only during the March–April period of 1968." "More than 37,000 men moving south."

ABRAMS: "I spent all day yesterday up in I Corps." Talked with General Truong, 1st ARVN Division, and Colonel Giai, 2nd ARVN Regiment. "There aren't two finer tactical commanders. And Colonel Giai is a consummate artist in intelligence himself." But, although I talked to numerous U.S. and ARVN commanders, nobody could say with any assurance what the enemy intends to do. "And, you know, this is a business you just don't like to get <u>snookered</u> in. It makes you feel <u>bad</u>."

ABRAMS: "Every so often we get seized with the thought that the slide [rule] guys have figured all this out, and <u>now</u>—they go back and start going over this stuff again." Numbers. Statistics.

ABRAMS: "Davis, who commands the 3rd Mar Div, has this artillery which he used to shoot into the southern half of the DMZ, if there's any enemy activity in there, and he's gone to putting these—he's picked the fire support bases as some real razorback ridge, steep rock formations, or just some crag that sticks up on the top of one of these peaks. He gets his artillery on there, and it only takes a platoon of infantry to protect it. And this has freed up, this has created for him, a lot more mobile forces, and forces that he can put into the pacification area in Cam Lo. He's taken out all of these big bases. Camp Carroll is no more. Ca Lu is about to go."

ABRAMS: "He still uses this Vandegrift out in here."

CHESAREK: "The Rockpile's still there, isn't it?"

ABRAMS: "Yes, but see, that's a crag that sticks up there, and Christ, you can defend it with a squad of Italian motorcyclists—wounded, at that. But this Vandegrift thing, which is a splendid base up on a high point out there, has permitted him, really, to—he can run the whole affair out of there. And that's what he does. So this situation up in the DMZ has <u>freed</u> <u>up</u> an awful lot of forces that have been used, then, on the pacification program and in going all over this." "But, <u>hell</u>—a year ago, if you'd mentioned the 9th Marines being down in here, they'd have run you out of the country as being crazy, get a psychiatrist after you. But this has given us a lot of flexibility up here."

ABRAMS: "And a year ago the, you know, Hanoi's made a big point about how we withdrew from Khe Sanh, all that kind of stuff. Well, this is a <u>whole</u> 'nother ball game now. The forces up here are <u>mobile</u>, so you can concentrate them where the problems are and so on, and you can use them in a variety of ways and so forth. The way they've run this thing up here—he's got a <u>maximum</u> of his rifle strength is in a mobile role. And, you see, <u>last</u> year at this time, when you got these fights in Hue and Quang Tri, all these battalions that were bunkered up in here—not available for the <u>fight</u>! The enemy went and staged it somewhere else. And all the battalions we had at Khe Sanh—bunkered up and so on. Of course there was <u>fighting</u> going on there. But <u>these</u> outfits up here, they just—all <u>they</u> did was listen to AFN to get the daily reports on all the <u>fighting</u> going on other places."

CHESAREK: "That's just a <u>fabulous</u> demonstration of how just a change in the course of action with the same resources can bring about such a change in the military situation."

ABRAMS: "So, if they bring this 304th in here—Mel Zais, he just wants to know where they are, or have they arrived. And Davis, he's complaining now, he says that the troops are getting dispirited, they feel that the war's passed them by, they're not finding any enemy. He says they've just <u>got</u> to have a good fight to keep up the morale and so on." "We're prepared. We can reinforce up here if we really have to, if it gets serious, but my assessment of it right now I <u>don't</u> think it will be <u>required</u> to be reinforced. They're in an <u>excellent</u> posture up here." "If he wants to come out with the big formations and so on, I think he's going to be in trouble."

ABRAMS: "He [the enemy] can't just saddle up north of the Ben Hai and come charging out there with a division or two. He's got to locate his logistics out there ahead, and then they march on the logistics." "That's done ahead of time, and then the troops come in light. And that's why we've been <u>so</u> insistent about keeping patrols in the DMZ, the southern half of the DMZ. As long as we keep doing that, and reconnoitering out there, we'll <u>know</u> when he starts changing the name of the game, starts putting in his caches, starts building his bunkers. And then we'll <u>know</u> that something is in the wind. He <u>has</u> to do it. He has <u>no</u> other system by which he can make these attacks."

ABRAMS: "Last year, up there in Quang Tri, it was being handled by 24 battalions. Right now, it's being handled by 10—<u>far</u> more effectively!" "We brought the 1st Cavalry down to III Corps." "Well, I'll tell you one thing. This fellow Davis is a <u>brilliant</u>, <u>professional</u>, tactician. He is <u>really</u> good. And one of these very quiet, self-effacing, modest men—a tremendous leader, a <u>brilliant</u> tactician."

ABRAMS (re calculation of enemy logistics input and throughput): "We have a <u>very</u> low level of confidence in the figures. But what is, I think, important in here is the comparative—that is, the amount that was being moved in the earlier period versus the amount now." "I <u>attribute</u> it to the fantastic effort that they're making to move logistics through Laos. They've beefed up the engineers in here, beefed up the antiaircraft in here. And they've just gone to extraordinary means to get this through." "We don't feel that there was <u>ever</u> any great tonnage moved across the DMZ."

ABRAMS: "We're <u>convinced</u>, I am convinced, that the 320th was pulled back here, that five regiments out of Tri-Thien-Hue [were pulled] back into Laos, and some up into North Vietnam, was forced on them by the <u>exhaustion</u> of the logistics system. And that was a combination of the interdiction program and the torrential rain in the panhandle of North Vietnam, so virtually nothing—in September and October they weren't getting enough stuff into Laos to <u>feed</u> the service troops that were in there—by our estimates."

ABRAMS: "Down in here, the marines took <u>away</u> from the 320th Division <u>most</u> of the ammunition and food—in caches. The 101st Airborne and the 1st Cav did the same thing to the hospital complexes, ammunition caches, the food caches. These people were subsisting down here on rice gruel—the troops that were left." "That was the situation on the first of November. And these withdrawals had all occurred by that time. And, as I say, I'm convinced that it was not the fighting alone, but the <u>exhaustion</u> of the logistical system. So what is going on in here now is first of all the <u>reestablishment</u> of the logistical backup."

ABRAMS: "The weight of tac air, and the weight of B-52s, is going into [Base Areas] 604 and 611 to try to bust up these supplies on the ground." In one instance "the B-52 crews reported a fire that could be seen for 100 nautical miles." "We're trying to get on the back of this tonnage here and stay with it, on its back, as it goes to these various stages." "We have enough force so we don't need to give them the luxury of <u>any</u> free ride." "Speaking of the 'system' in its most general sense, we try our best to work on the system. It doesn't necessarily mean killing trucks. Once you get the rationale of his system, then you go ahead and work on the best parts of that system, the ones that are most susceptible to destruction."

CHESAREK: "You sent up a briefing to the Joint Chiefs of Staff on this air force—I forget the name of it, the code name for it."

ABRAMS: "Commando Hunt."

CHESAREK: "The general consensus in the Army Staff was it was the air force patting itself on the ass and it was probably considerably inflated. Is that your view, or do you think that was a pretty factual report?"

ABRAMS: "When you're talking about the interdiction program from July through October in the panhandle of North Vietnam, the air force and the navy deserve a <u>real</u> pat on the back."

ABRAMS: Mentions having recently briefed "the president."

CHESAREK: "Is that the old president [LBJ] or the new one [Nixon]?"

ABRAMS: "Thieu—that's the only one I get to see much of." [Laughter]

ABRAMS (re the enemy's requirements for tonnage): "These heavy rockets, automatic weapons—AK-47, RPGs, 120 mortars, antiaircraft—23-mm, 14.7—whatever it is, and so on. All that stuff just burns it up."

TOWNSEND: "Two major changes since last year. The first is the degree of improvement in the maturity of the South Vietnamese armed forces. I was asked the other day by General DePuy's man who was out here if I could give him any exact illustration of how there's been any improvement in the Vietnamese armed forces. The real thing is that they're on the ground, and they're in control of the situation where they are, as opposed to not being in control of it, say, at this time last year, to the same degree."

TOWNSEND: General Abrams "started movement in every TAOR. It's kind of like windshield wipers—he just turned them on. And those people have been running constantly in every TAOR, all the time, except for Christmas day—we had a stand-down for 24 hours Christmas day. But even then the patrols and ambushes were so extensive that practically the contacts that were generated during the stand-down at Christmas were by our local in-close ambushes and patrols bumping into the enemy coming to our place. This constant movement finally broke the enemy and brought about this withdrawal, uncovering of the VC main forces, local forces, his caches, his pulling back to the area of sanctuaries, and enabled us to do what we've been able to do about tearing out the VC infrastructure, going back along his line of communications and tearing it up."

ABRAMS: "I think it's a rate of activity that can be sustained indefinitely."

CHESAREK: "In one of my last sessions with the Secretariat, they were trying to relate the level of activity to ammunition consumption. Bill DePuy and I were trying to tell them that that's not so at all, that the kind of activity you are engaged in out here now, this accelerated search, is probably going to cost more in spare parts consumption, fuel, and all the other things that cost money than is a battalion-size action against something in a given location. And that you may not shoot up a hell of a lot of ammunition in the process, but nevertheless the matériel is being worn out at an accelerated rate."

TOWNSEND: "General Abrams does have a reserve in the strategic sense, the B-52s. This is really his reserve." "With the windshield wipers going, and the tac air and the B-52s and the naval gunfire, this guy [the enemy] is just in a hot position all the time."

TOWNSEND (re the delta): "We've got people into Base Area 470 who've invaded it completely, swept all the way through it several times now. And the first time we did it, here in the fall, is the first time it's ever been done in anybody's recent memory."

ABRAMS: "That Base Area 483—it's the U Minh Forest—the 21st ARVN went in there, two weeks' operation, and the enemy in there had no defensive positions. [Someone: "Never needed them."] That's right. It's a very amazing thing. And they [the enemy] told the <u>people</u> that were in there that the 21st Division had been destroyed and that Saigon was in ruins. And of course the people didn't know anything else."

■ ■ ■

ABRAMS: "The ARVN have been doing real good now for several months. But what they were doing, they were doing the tactics that we taught them two years ago, and doing them real <u>well</u>. In the meantime, we'd found out that those were not the most effective. So we'd <u>changed</u> and we had this problem of [laughing] informing them that it was <u>now</u> time to change. And you run into a little bit of a block there. They say, 'Well, Christ, this is what you—,' you know. 'After all, we're doing what you <u>said</u>' and so on."

ABRAMS: "And of course they don't <u>have</u> the experience and so on. Now <u>they've</u> been getting into this. They've been doing this jitterbugging stuff, and this thing where you get small units, a lot of small units, out—and <u>somebody</u> gets a fight, then you pick up everybody and run over there! And <u>everybody</u> gets in. Anybody that's not in contact gets into <u>that</u> one. And the idea of going out in <u>company</u> strength, or <u>platoon</u> strength— <u>whoot</u>—only <u>battalions</u>! That's the only way they wanted to go. Well, a <u>battalion</u>—it's like trying to sneak up on the enemy with a tank. It's just too damn noisy, everybody talking and so on. If you want to <u>get</u> him, if you want to <u>find</u> him, you've got to do it with these small outfits. And <u>then</u>, once you get him, then everybody jump in! Well, they've been working on it. And I think <u>part</u> of this is because they're beginning to do it on their own."

■ ■ ■

ABRAMS (re the WIEU): "We devote Saturdays to wrestling with this thing. We try to generally have one or two things that have been done in depth over a period of time, trying to challenge what we think. The <u>intelligence</u> is the most <u>important</u> part of this whole damn <u>thing</u>. And if that's good, then you can—. We've got—we keep saying here we've got enough <u>stuff</u>. We can handle <u>any-thing</u>. I think we can handle <u>anything</u> he wants to do—if our intelligence is good. But if we've got resources in the wrong place, if we've plumped them into a—I'm talking about getting a division somewhere, or getting a whole bunch of B-52s or tac air and all that stuff, or moving artillery or throwing the mobile marine force around in the wrong place and so on. You do a lot of <u>that</u>, and <u>then</u> you—that's no <u>good</u>. We haven't got <u>enough</u> to do <u>that</u>."

■ ■ ■

ABRAMS (re Chesarek's question about a rumor that Lam will replace Vien as head of the JGS): "Well, we've lived with Vien departing for 10 months now. And about monthly the rumors seem to start going again. Then they subside, and Vien seems to be happy, and so on. Then it starts over again. There was some thought that General <u>Tri</u> might take his place. Tri is a <u>very</u> close personal friend of the president, sees him two or three evenings a week and that sort of thing. But General Tri is not in good health. He's taking pills and shots and so on. He's been a good tactician, although I had to point out to the president that, while I admire his tactics and so on, he's really fought the war in III Corps with the airborne, the marines, and the rangers, and has done nothing to improve the performance of the—. In fact, I showed the president how the performance of those two divisions has steadily deteriorated. They are worse now, since we issued the M16, than they were before. And that shows clearly in the statistics."

ABRAMS: "On the other hand, the performance of the RF and PF in Gia Dinh has risen <u>dramatically</u> since issuing the M16s. I pointed <u>that</u> out to him."

ABRAMS (re cutting down on some of the advisors): "We have <u>done</u> that. The experiment was conducted on the initiative of Ray Peers and General Lu Lan, and General [Tuan?], in the 22nd ARVN Division. And they have what we call liaison parties, and saved a hundred spaces, something like that. And they're now going ahead and implement it in the 23rd ARVN Division. And in both of those divisions they're quite enthusiastic about it, and General Lu Lan, the corps commander, is enthusiastic about it. We're satisfied now that the enthusiasm is a sincere one." "I have now sent a letter out to each of the other senior advisors—Cushman and Kerwin and Eckhardt—to have them try this on for size."

ABRAMS (re the possibility of trading off a battalion to provide spaces for 120–140 five-man MAT teams requested by Eckhardt): "Maybe now is the time. Maybe we can push this thing along further, <u>faster</u>—. These teams have been eminently successful. They've done a <u>hell</u> of a lot for the RF and PF. You put one of those teams in a district and you've <u>doubled</u> the advisory effort in the district. The district <u>team's</u> five men." "And these people devote their time <u>exclusively</u> to the RF and PF. They live with them, <u>fight</u> with them, <u>patrol</u> with them, <u>ambush</u> with them, and so on. <u>Then</u> you get communications, <u>then</u> you get <u>reaction</u>."

ABRAMS: "Dutch Kerwin out here now—he's got a desk over there in his TOC. And it's got a couple of telephones, and there's two guys, one of whom is <u>always</u> there. And every district advisor has got <u>direct</u> access to that man and that desk, any time of day or night. And if a PF post is under attack, or an RF post is under attack, the district advisor's got to know it, and then he calls this man <u>direct</u>. And that guy has all of General Kerwin's authority—artillery, gunships, light fire teams, the whole damn works, including the U.S. division whose tactical area of interest it is." "We are trying to make the attack of RF and PF one of the most unprofitable exercises that the enemy can engage in. In other words, if you want to really make <u>all</u> of MACV rip-roaring <u>mad</u>, even threaten the B-52s, hit the RF and the PF."

CHESAREK: "The turn-around time [between tours in Vietnam] is beginning to get to our retention and so on." "That has nothing to do with winning the war, but it does give us a lot of concern as far as the future of the army is concerned."

25 JAN 1969: WIEU

ATTENDEES: Gen. Abrams, Amb. Colby, LTG Mildren, VADM Zumwalt, Dr. Wikner, MG Corcoran, MG Townsend, MG Shaefer, MG Davidson, MG Rasmussen, MG Baker, BG Frizen, BG Long, BG Sidle, BG Galloway, BG Clay, BG Bryan, BG Keegan, Col. Cavanaugh, Col. Mahaffey, Col. Powers.

BRIEFER: Since 1 January 1969 7,900 men have entered the infiltration pipeline. "Four large 4000-series groups [totalling 9,700 men] believed to be associated with the 304th NVA Division." Infiltration apparently began again on 23 November 1968.

BRIEFER: "We estimate that 182 tons of supplies were transported each day by truck along Routes 1AC and 101C from Dong Hoi toward the DMZ." Over 500 trucks detected on 19 and 20 January 1969.

ABRAMS (re interdiction): "Whatever effort we put in there last week didn't seem to reduce it over the previous week."

BRIEFER: A computerized program known as TRAP (traffic reporting and analysis program) shows "just about half of this" estimate [on traffic getting through] as was produced by conventional means.

ABRAMS: "Well, I just urge you to get together. I'm getting a little disturbed here. This road watch team, and the evidence that Mr. Shackley is conducting a private intelligence thing. And we've got Ambassador Sullivan, he's got a private intelligence system. Who is responsible? And who's going to get—? For instance, I think I'm responsible for this thing over here, the flow of stuff into South Vietnam. I believe that's very clear. If I am, then I have got to be served by all the intelligence, and the best intelligence, that there is! It's just a sound fundamental principle. And we can't have a lot of goddamn private intelligence games going on! You're not responsible, Shackley's not responsible, and Sullivan's not responsible. I am! That's where the—you don't pass the buck past here. So I want this straightened out, and right now!" "I don't know why that road watch team's down there. Who's it serving?"

Theodore Shackley was CIA's chief of station, Saigon during the period December 1968–February 1972.

DAVIDSON: "Well, it's serving all of us to some extent, sir. It's directed, however, by the chief CIA man in Ambassador Sullivan's office. But, as far as we know, we get all the reports from them, for what they're worth—which incidentally I don't think is very much."

ABRAMS: "Are these more reliable than the sensors?"

DAVIDSON: "No, sir. I think it's a good deal less reliable."

ABRAMS: "You get in the business and you take unreliable stuff and reliable stuff, add it up, and take a mean—see, it's not good. What you should be served by is the best intelligence, and not take a mean of all the crap that's thrown in the system."

ABRAMS: "We've also been prevented from hitting targets [with B-52s] because of the presence of road watch teams."

ABRAMS: "I spoke out about your computer program. I don't mean to indicate that I'm against it, because we've recognized in here every Saturday that we've got trouble estimating this tonnage. There's an awful lot we don't know— about trucks that get knocked off or that sort of thing. But we do—we need to pull together." "And most of all we don't want to kid ourselves."

■ ■ ■

ABRAMS: "All of our people have got to realize what this war is about. It isn't that you, you know, lay around in your base camp waiting for somebody to sight a division marching down the road, and then you sally forth and, you know, take the division on. This war is a far more complex thing than that."

ABRAMS: "We don't want anybody to be—this idea of, 'Well, the people, that's the Vietnamese responsibility, we're just here to take on the 2nd NVA, the 3rd NVA if we can find them.' That's no good. It won't work. And that applies to every U.S. commander."

ABRAMS: "The 3rd Marines are now in it like this, the 101, the 1st ARVN. That's the best example. That's where there's one war, is in northern I Corps. All us on one side and them on the other. Nobody's looking for honors. They're just all for one and one for all. It's just who's nearest." "Now, there's some of that in III Corps, in the 1st Infantry and the 25th." "And that's what we need in southern I Corps, in the lower three provinces. And we don't have that."

■ ■ ■

BRIEFER (re current enemy circumstances): "His most urgent need was to bring about the bombing halt." "It is through negotiations that he seeks to attain his long-range goals." Short term: "Withdrawal of U.S. forces and a coalition government." The enemy has "the capability and intention to continue the war indefinitely."

BRIEFER: Directive No. 34, issued on 12 December 1968 by the VC Current Affairs Committee of Tay Ninh Province: "Obviously an implementation of the undated COSVN directive." Describes four situations that could develop: 1. Coup. 2. Open break Thieu-Ky. 3. Direct U.S. move to replace current GVN leadership. 4. Complete replacement of GVN by popular uprising. "It is significant that he parenthetically states that there is little likelihood of the fourth contingency, our first evidence that he's lost faith in the popular uprising concept."

COLBY: "The period 1962 through about 1963, the government really had a pretty good program going, this pacification—strategic hamlet—thing." The Buddhist uprising "blew the government right out of the water." That was an unforeseen development.

ABRAMS: "You know this thing about 'U.S.-sponsored overthrow.' There's a lot of South Vietnamese that worry about this same thing. So apparently there's at least rumors that times in the distant past the U.S. may have been guilty of tinkering with the machinery and so on. And apparently both sides . . . have this same—at least a suspicion, and so what the COSVN say is very much like what some very patriotic and loyal South Vietnamese suspect."

■ ■ ■

ABRAMS: "What should you do? 'Well, just keep on doing what we're doing.' And the next question is, 'How long is that going to take? What's that going to do? What's the price tag on that? How many lives are you talking about? Another 30,000? I mean, where is this thing going to wind up?' It could be quite a problem."

Giving examples of challenging questions being asked by some in the United States about what is being accomplished in Vietnam.

■ ■ ■

ABRAMS: "This [North Vietnamese scam] isn't going to be so easy to run the second time, because the United States has now had quite a little experience about 'understanding.' And they haven't been good."

A reference to Averell Harriman's insistence that he had an "understanding" with the enemy that, in exchange for cessation of U.S. bombing of North Vietnam, the North Vietnamese would refrain from attacking population centers, would cease violating the demilitarized zone, and would not increase infiltration into the south. Subsequent to the bombing halt, the North Vietnamese did all of those things.

BRIEFER: Shows a photograph of over 50 trucks waiting to cross at one of the two Quang Khe ferries, "one of our key choke points in the summer interdiction campaign. Employment of hard bombs, antimatériel and antipersonnel munitions, plus seeding of the river with Mark 36 mines, bottled up the traffic."

Now, post-bombing halt, it is open.

ABRAMS: "Now we've got these messages in, one very comprehensive one from the JCS, calling for a review of where we stand. I think it's a good thing to do, probably a good time to do it. And it reflects, I think, the deliberate approach of the new administration to the problem at hand and so on. The questions that they've raised drag out every old skeleton in the closet, but I don't think the— our interpretation of that should be at all discouraging. I think what it reflects is that the administration's going to every [word unclear] out there and let every one of these fellows that's had his pet theory and prejudice say his piece, and then they'll proceed to do what they believe is the best and the right thing to do. In other words they'll have made—they'll be able to say, and they will have done, a comprehensive review of it, and then go ahead from there. I'm in hopes that we'll be able to pull together a good piece of professional work and send it in. I'm tentatively hoping to bring all the commanders together before we dispatch this to see if there are any other thoughts that it would be well for us to consider and include in the message. I guess the entire staff is involved in pulling this together. It's a pretty large order, and we don't have an awful lot of time."

Responding to NSSM-1 queries from the newly installed Nixon administration.

ABRAMS: "I also know there are areas in there in which this headquarters has no competence, and that's what I'll report. I am not going to get into anything where we don't have a sound foundation. Somebody else'll have to take that on."

1 FEB 1969: WIEU

ATTENDEES: Gen. Abrams, LTG Mildren, VADM Zumwalt, Dr. Wikner, MG Baker, MG Wetherill, MG Corcoran, MG Townsend, MG Davidson, MG Rasmussen, BG Frizen, BG Long, BG Sidle, BG Galloway, BG Clay, BG Bryan, BG Keegan, Col. Ramsey, Col. Cavanaugh, Col. Powers.

ABRAMS (re estimates of enemy logistical throughput): "We just don't want to kid ourselves on this. He's got a few more cards to play. And what we said before is still right—we've got the tickets, but we've got to play them right—and not, you know, throw them around in the air."

DAVIDSON: "Nobody has any idea what the enemy was able to stockpile previous to this campaign in the A Shau Valley and Laos."

ABRAMS: "It's a <u>little</u> bit unsettling those caches that they got south of the DMZ. It looks like there's more going on there than we thought."

CLAY: "Comparing last season—January—he's about two and one-half months behind the logistics delivery schedule that he achieved for the Tet Offensive. The significance of the campaign this year is that (1) we dried out his stockpiles in I and II Corps, which is why he withdrew. This year, the difference between last year's campaign and the current one is that, in addition to killing about 15 percent of the trucks, in the past two months you have stopped or blocked or checked between 50 and 75 percent of his supply flow. And at this point last season, for the Tet Offensive, his stocks were built up and he was ready to go. And he is roughly about two and a half months behind that schedule this year. And, starting next week, it's going to be very unpleasant around here. The floodgates are opening, and this stuff is going to start coming through in a torrent. We're going to be competing for B-52 sorties, as we predicted we would be, at the point when that logistic wave reaches a crest. And I would guess from the rate of flow that he's now achieving that it will be March before he achieves what he achieved by the 30th of January last season. The essential difference between the campaigns—you're killing the same percentage of trucks killed last season, but you're blocking much more of the traffic."

ABRAMS: "Well, the other thing about last year—you know we've got this theory that it was supposed to go in March, and instead of that he decided he'd kick it off at the end of January. His logistics must have been in such a shape that shoving it up a couple of months, 'no problem at all.' That means it was in damn good shape. And the way he went at it he didn't seem to have any logistics problems. He seemed to have plenty of stuff around."

BRIEFER: "On 29 January, U.S. forces discovered a hospital complex 15 kilometers west of Ninh Thuan in Tay Ninh Province. The hospital, still under construction, consisted of five operating rooms, six wards with a total capacity of approximately 100 patients, two mess halls with a total capacity of 400 men, . . . 12 tunnels, and 100–125 bunkers with overhead cover." Situated to receive casualties evacuated northward along the Saigon River corridor. Estimate that it took about three months to build.

■ ■ ■

ABRAMS: Recalls "that battalion out of the 95 Charlie that came down to ambush the convoy. It was going to be right there in the rubber. Well, between the last reconnaissance and the ambush, all of that had been Rome plowed, and Christ, they were right out in the open. But they went ahead anyway!" "It turned into quite a massacre."

■ ■ ■

ABRAMS: "They need the guerrillas. When they start taking the guerrillas [to fill regular units], they're in a bankrupt position."

■ ■ ■

ABRAMS: "Incidentally, I plan to go up there, spend the day Wednesday, in Quang Ngai and Quang Tin. And I got a call—a call came in from the chief of staff up there yesterday of the Americal wanting to know whether I was interested in the Americal or in the province forces, which serves to emphasize the—this is a very important trip. We've been preaching 'one war.' That's what I'm going up to look into is the 'one war.' And it sounds to me like it ain't. And also I have the impression from what was reported here this morning that what's going on up there is an effort against the Accelerated Pacification Program. That's why they're going in there and killing these civilians and burning their houses down. And it doesn't look like anybody's doing anything about it. They all [have] got to get in bed together up there. They've got enough stuff there to make that an expensive undertaking." "You know, we've put out quite a little guidance on this. This stuff of 'all these on the left are mine and all those on the right are yours' won't hack it."

■ ■ ■

DAVIDSON: Reports on "fuzes that they captured down in the IV Corps cache that had 'Consigned to FARK through Sihanoukville' stamped on the box." "And two sacks said in French 'Through Sihanoukville' in letters about that high. Of course I'm sure Mr. Graham will explain that they used the original contents and then the sack somehow got into [word unclear]."
ABRAMS: "No, he'd say that they did that on purpose."
DAVIDSON: "That we'd planted it is what he'd say!" [Laughter]
ABRAMS: "Yeah! Or that it was a VC ruse—while they were shoving the stuff down through Laos into the delta, they were causing us to think that it was coming through Sihanoukville."
ABRAMS (re sending the sacks to Paris): "And what a wonderful exhibit over in Paris! You know, just keep it over there in the closet, and there may come a day when it would be a real nice exhibit during the coffee break. Or at the press conference." "Send it to the Chairman. He's going to be in meetings, you know." Best time to present it: "At the conclusion of Mr. Graham's presentation."

■ ■ ■

ABRAMS: "Incidentally, last week I went over to U Tapao and visited the operation there. The real purpose was to let them know over there how much their work was appreciated, and also the skill with which we think it's being executed. You know, half of all B-52 strikes are run out of U Tapao. And I suppose I should have known it, but I didn't, that the entire refueling operation for this part of the world is run out of there—the whole tanker thing." Forty KC-135s. "Professionally, I found it quite an exhilarating experience. That is a real professional outfit over there. It's up tight, and it's really impressive." If an aircraft goes down over Laos, for example: "Whatever anybody wants to get these pilots out, they throw it in there. And here comes the refueling to guarantee that it'll be sustained. It's <u>really</u> impressive." 3,300 SAC people there. "The thoroughness and the precision with which it all moves along, and quite a few things have to be done."

8 FEB 1969: WIEU

ATTENDEES: Gen. Abrams, Gen. Haines, Gen. Goodpaster, Amb. Colby, Gen. Brown, LTG Mildren, VADM Zumwalt, Dr. Wikner, MG Wetherill, MG Corcoran, MG Townsend, MG Shaefer, MG Davidson, MG Rasmussen, MG Baker, BG Frizen, BG Long, BG Sidle, BG Galloway, BG Clay, BG Bryant, BG Keegan, Col. Ramsey, Col. Cavanaugh, Col. Powers.

BRIEFER: Commo-liaison station T-10 is part of the enemy's infiltration network. At the present time 19 infiltration groups have entered or reentered the pipeline in January 1969, with a total estimated strength of 11,100. This is a decrease of approximately 66 percent compared to the December 1968 total of 30,000+.

ABRAMS: "That infiltration pattern—it went up after Tet. It went up <u>before</u> Tet, went up again <u>after</u> Tet last year."

DAVIDSON: "It <u>almost</u> coincides with the major offensives, General."

ABRAMS: "I know, but—."

SOMEONE: The 4000 series, which we believe represents the 304th NVA Division, is not yet added in, so the figure will go up.

ABRAMS: "In 1968, a lot of those were replacements. And the 304th is an addition to structure. And replacements are a thermometer of anticipated combat activity. Well, just looking at the ordnance there, it doesn't look like they're planning similar combat activity to last Tet."

ABRAMS (re enemy losses during Tet 1968): "40,000 was countrywide."

DAVIDSON: "They [the enemy] have their units now as close to full strength as probably we'll ever see them." The new 1st VC Regiment has 1,900 men, and "1,200, we've always thought, was a good strong regiment."

ABRAMS: "If we want to go on playing that soft, sweet music that we used to play—you know, we said they were in <u>desperate</u> circumstances down there, had to withdraw troops because they couldn't support them, and that <u>surge</u> in there was to get some <u>food</u> and <u>medicine</u> and so on down there just to get everybody back up off the floor, <u>then</u> build up."

DAVIDSON: "I think what we're seeing now is just around a hundred tons is constantly going to flow into the kitty [building up stockpiles] down there." Cites "initial urge to make sure that something was there in case the bombing halt disappeared." "What we're looking at is gross indicators."

ABRAMS: "I was talking with a battalion commander last week, whose occupation has led him to be a realist. They fired a bunch of artillery one night on SLAR—SLAR readings of trucks. Well, it turned out to be water buffalo."

DAVIDSON: "They're pretty fast water buffalo, then."

ABRAMS: "Well, that's all right, but by god that's what was dead in there. It may be that the trucks were weaving between the water buffalo [laughter], but there weren't any trucks and there were water buffalo. Then he had another one where—these wild pigs—they got—that the PPS-4 [radar] picked up on. And they shot hell out of them, and so on. After a week of that kind of activity, he had to conclude that he hadn't found any VC. You can work yourself up into a condition here where none of this is worth much."

ABRAMS (re Laos): "If he [the enemy] wants to go ahead and turn the heat on over there, there isn't a hell of a lot that can be done about it."

■ ■ ■

DAVIDSON: "From a study of those State Department documents which came in last night, sir, I think I was working on what's at best a questionable premise, and perhaps a false premise, in our discussion yesterday, in that it would occur to me that the North Vietnamese do not understand that a ground attack on Saigon, without 'indiscriminate shelling,' is a violation of the understanding."

GOODPASTER: "Well, that's fairly finespun stuff, Phil—what they understand, what they don't understand, do we understand that they understand, and so on. You get into fairly wispy stuff there."

ABRAMS: "That's right!"

DAVIDSON: "The only thing I'm doing is just quoting from the Paris cable, which spoke of 'indiscriminate ground attack for political purposes.' This distinction was never made clear to the DRV."

ABRAMS: "Yeah, but that thing was put together with great strain. We want to be careful that we don't get so enraptured with this Byzantine calculations, and plots, and counterplots, and so on, that we overlook the fact—the inscrutable oriental and so forth—well, we ought to get back to what can be done, and where things are, what we've got. And what General Goodpaster said, that's—when you get off into what we think that they think, or what we feel that they feel in the understanding that we both have—hah—that's like trying to walk on water."

■ ■ ■

COLBY: "During the past week the president went around the country and had a session in each corps area which was a review of the '68 RD program, a review of the APC, and—in all but the IV Corps area—a review of the '69 planning. We were awash in charts, as you can imagine, a lot of statistics. But I think in general that the '68 RD program met 60–70 percent of its original goals, primarily the construction effort—the schools and so forth. This was the result of the fact that it had been delayed during the first six months by the Tet thing. With respect to the APC, it obviously came out to be a considerable success."

COLBY: Provinces were required to submit plans for 1969 by 15 January. These were reviewed at corps. Then a national staff went to each corps and reviewed each province plan in detail. "And this was followed by the president's meetings." The president said "he wants to maintain the momentum." "He put his major emphasis on the village concept in two respects. First, he urged a rather rapid effort on the business of elections in all the villages in order to meet the VC liberation committee challenge, and actually required that to be done by the end of March in most of the villages. Secondly, he made very clear, and explained in some depth, that he wanted the people of the country involved in the war by being invited to participate in their own decision making. He kept pounding this in on the various province and district chiefs, that they were not just to boss the people around, that they were to <u>let</u> the people make decisions and get involved in the whole problem. So in general it was, I think, a <u>very</u> successful series of meetings. He quite obviously put out the word."

COLBY: "There is a little problem on the statistics thing here, because the president has stated that the GVN will not be in a position of admitting that the VC have control of any part of the country, and therefore <u>he</u> has divided the total category of the country into two general classes: the one, areas in which the government has control; and the second, areas in which the government doesn't quite yet have <u>complete</u> control. That's about all, his point being that the government troops can go anywhere they want to." He has added together A, B, C, D, and E to get the first category, and the VC to get the second. So he says 89 percent under government control, which is the total in A, B, C, D, and E categories. The president said in a press conference yesterday that he was going to establish a deputy prime minister for pacification. "He did emphasize that the enemy <u>would</u> come back and have another try at us. And he made the point that last year the enemy attacked the cities. The government abandoned the country. He said, 'This year I want to make very sure that you stay in the country.'"

ABRAMS: "Well, I haven't detected any tendency to do that—yet."

ABRAMS: "If we believe that pacification is moving ahead, then we've <u>got</u> to believe, it seems to me, that he's [the enemy] going to do something about it. And, while he has attacked the self-defense forces, still getting cadres taking some casualties, terrorism, abduction, some government officials being assassinated, it still hasn't developed into a—there isn't a real cohesive enemy strategy against—or at least I can't, I haven't—it's not clear to me. If it is, it's a very <u>subtle</u> thing that we're not able to identify."

15 FEB 1969: WIEU

ATTENDEES: Gen. Abrams, Gen. Goodpaster, Amb. Colby, Gen. Brown, LTG Mildren, VADM Zumwalt, Dr. Wikner, MG Wetherill, MG Corcoran, MG Townsend, MG Shaefer, MG Davidson, MG Rasmussen, BG Frizen, BG Long, BG Sidle, BG Galloway, BG Clay, BG Bryan, BG Keegan, Col. Cavanaugh, Col. Gleason, Col. Powers.

BRIEFER: Reports the first concrete evidence of infiltration groups being transported by barge. 1968 MACV Infiltration Estimate: There were 247 four-digit groups and 77 probable gaps.

■ ■ ■

BRIEFER: Reports the arrival 9 January 1969 in Sihanoukville "of a CHICOM freighter carrying arms." The *Le Ming.* 4,800 tons of arms, plus foodstuffs. On 11 January 1969 "offloaded by approximately 120 Cambodian Army personnel under the supervision of Cambodian Army Lieutenant Colonel Um Savoeut. Approximately 130 trucks belonging to the Hak Ly and Machine [Beaufe?] trucking firms were used to transport the cargo to FARK munitions depots near

Kompong Speu. A total of 467 truck- and 127 trailerloads of arms were transported to the depot for eventual transfer to frontier regions."

DAVIDSON (re the report): "It just drives another nail in Mr. Graham's coffin."

■ ■ ■

Forecasting a possible major enemy offensive.

BRIEFER:

■ "Sir, the purpose of this briefing is to assess the possibility of a major enemy offensive—its timing, form, and the factors which might influence both. First, to the evidence. Right now we probably have more hard indications of an imminent offensive than we've ever had before." But "many are vague as to the scope of the attack and the date of initiation." "They suggest D-Day's anywhere from mid-January to early April." Ambiguity. "You are familiar with the reports from Paris which indicate that at this time the NLF does not wish to initiate the large-scale attacks which have proven so costly in the past."

■ "An officer rallier from Kien Tuong Province quoted the provincial party secretary as saying that there would be no strong attack like the last general offensive. Otherwise, the allies would not withdraw from South Vietnam and the NLF would lose the opportunity to form a coalition government." Re the reports of a possible enemy offensive, cites "the prominent position III Corps takes in them." And potential attacks on Saigon. "This is quite consistent with the force the enemy has assembled in III Corps, and his longstanding obsession with the capital."

■ Right now notes "the absence of the classic indicators we should see within a week or two prior to a period of major activity." "Movement of units to staging areas, the clustering of UI [***] near target areas, and the increased tactical posture of enemy [***]." "The weight of evidence suggests that . . . any major offensive, if it should occur at all, is probably at least still a week away, and 10 to 20 days would seem more likely."

■ From the evidence "three types of possible enemy activity emerge. First would be a multidivision attack on all major cities and population centers, particularly Saigon." "Taken all together, the reports of this sort of an offensive seem credible. They track with considerable continuity, and they are remarkably similar to the detailed plans the enemy developed for his three major offensives last year. However, other factors make it seem unlikely, at least for the near term. Enemy forces in I Corps are simply incapable of carrying out such a plan." "There's been no move of division or regimental units toward Saigon, and other than the plans themselves we have no signs of preparations for a major assault on the capital." [Tet begins 18 February 1969.] "Some very recent hard evidence tells us there will be no assault on Saigon at this time." "We . . . rule out a major enemy attack on the cities before, during, or in the immediate post-Tet period unless some unforeseen exploitable political circumstance were to occur."

■ Second possible type offensive: "Large-scale attacks against military and peripheral targets." "Seems a great deal more likely." "He has proceeded a great deal further in his actual preparations for this type of attack."

■ Third possibility: Two-phased offensive based on contingencies. The enemy says that: "There will be a Third Force in the near future, after Nixon takes power. This force will consist of the Buddhists and the General Confederation of Labor. It will be antigovernment and anti–Viet Cong, and it will campaign for peace." "Our evidence strongly links the enemy's military offensive plans to the political health of the GVN. He seems confident that the GVN will collapse, and he's deeply involved in political pressures to help bring that collapse about." "We do not foresee a large-scale ground attack on the major cities of South Vietnam before, during, or after Tet. The enemy is not now prepared, nor are his forces suitably deployed."

■ But if the Saigon government were to undergo "an abrupt transformation," then the enemy is prepared to launch a "multidivisional all-out attack on Saigon. He has detailed plans for such an attack and the forces to carry it out. We do not see this possibility at this time. However, an attack conducted under these circumstances could take place at <u>any</u> time . . . , and it would be designed to win the war." "The weight of evidence suggests a two-phase offensive."

■ ■ ■

ABRAMS (re terrorism in Saigon): "I must say, though, driving downtown last night and coming back, it's hard to see that this has had any effect. . . . People are out shopping, coming and going, and the spirit of Tet is in the air. I mean— it's pretty obvious."

SOMEONE: "We're far from the level of violence in Washington, D.C."

■ ■ ■

BRIEFER: This morning the enemy Rear Services in Laos exhorted all troops to the utmost effort because "on the 15th all operations will begin the large general offensive phase."

■ ■ ■

ABRAMS: Cites "the political maneuvering, the political fragmentation, the political jockeying that just goes on <u>incessantly</u> among these Vietnamese. . . ."

■ ■ ■

DAVIDSON: "Lam, who is their [RVN] chief negotiator, told his delegation that the United States is meeting secretly with the DRV and the NLF. He apparently firmly believes it."

ABRAMS: "Bui put out the dope that this had the backing of Bunker. And [chuckles] so the ambassador made a quick trip to the palace. Apparently the president just laughed it off. He said, '<u>I</u> know they're working these things.'"

BERGER: "President Thieu, in a meeting yesterday, asked for and received again very firm assurances from Ambassador Bunker that we were not doing this."

COLBY: "Their [the enemy's] big hope is a conflict between Americans and GVN."

ABRAMS: "The principal target in this whole business is the American people."

BROWN: "I remember both the secretary—both Packard and Laird spoke at some length about the impression that people have at home that the enemy has the initiative. And I really think that we ought to give some thought to how to change that impression."

GOODPASTER: "Nothing we do should interfere with the progress we're making, which is sound progress, it's solid, and it's not going to be taken away from us, in the military sphere."

ABRAMS: "The question . . . is whether we should get out and enter into this arena of the psychological and political warfare on the grand scale. There's no doubt in my mind that, as far as the factual, on the ground, work is concerned, we're doing what we ought to be doing, except for the minor errors that occur out there every day. But the thrust of that is aimed right at his grip on the people."

■　■　■

ABRAMS: Down at IV Corps yesterday, they said that when you put a new PF outpost in a hamlet it gives the people a good feeling. "Well, I challenged that. In my opinion, it doesn't give them the right feeling. It's the same as my attitude on the draft—if the United States ever does away with the draft, what it's doing is turning to purchasing its freedom. And when you try to buy freedom, it's the beginning of the end. And when you put a PF in there, the villagers look on it—it's government. That's another thing, you know. It's paid by the government. It's got a uniform from the government. It's got a rifle from the government. And the thing that we're missing is that those people in that hamlet think that the security's up to somebody else. It's up to the government. And it's a gift—freedom is a gift! Paid for by the government! And they're not involved in it! It's somebody else that's supposed to do that, and if the PF won't do it, then the VC'll do it. But they're not in it! If they were in it, they'd be telling the PF about who was coming, or the kids would be telling them about the VC out looking by the water buffaloes, and so on."

COLBY: "It's no good to send a PF unit out that protects itself. As you say, you've got to somehow get the population both involved in the protection and included in the protection. The answer to that is obviously the self-defense thing."

■　■　■

BROWN (re Paveway): "This is the most cost-effective development that has come along. The fighter bombing system, as it's built, will give you an expected accuracy—average accuracy—of about 230–250 feet. That's with the average guy and a good pattern and all. This thing lets you hit with one bomb. And you put that baby on the front of a 2,000-pound or 750-pound bomb and you'll do the work with one airplane. And before we used to have to send 10 or 12 to have any probability of hitting. It's just great."

■　■　■

ABRAMS (responding to Wetherill pitch on prebriefing the press): "Public information-wise, I think we could say that it has turned out satisfactorily. We haven't gotten really smashed by the press. Now—there may [come] a day when we ought to change, and there's another point of delicate timing. Now, I have backgrounded a few fellows—not a great many. . . . And I've laid it out pretty much to them what's going on—without any predictions, but just kind of the way the thing's going—what we're doing and what they're doing. They know about these options—the press knows that. And I always tell them, 'I don't know whether he's going to exercise them or not. It remains to be seen. But, if he does exercise them, it's within our capacity to handle it.'"

GOODPASTER (re a lot of work left to be done): "It's long and hard and nasty and tough and ugly—<u>if</u> the enemy's going to fight it down to the wire. If he decides to do it, there's no easy or short way of doing that."

ABRAMS: "That's right. And that's why we must <u>constantly</u>—you've got to have the statistics, there's no question about that, absolutely no doubt about it . . . it's the way you get things pointed, and the way you commit assets and that sort of thing—but we've got to fight <u>all the time</u> to look <u>past</u> those, and bear in mind what the <u>real</u> purpose is, and then face the <u>real</u> results in a realistic way. And it's tough." "The thing that remains for us is completely <u>undramatic</u>. It's just a lot of damn <u>drudgery</u>, in a way, in terms of military things and so on. But that's what we've got to do."

ABRAMS: Has the IV Corps map pulled out, and shows (as per his visit there the day before) how they are disestablishing an enemy base area, then going to the next, then the next, examples of the drudgery he is talking about. Base Area 470 "is for all practical purposes gone." Work on the next ones, "and then we start to talk about getting control of the delta."

SIDLE: "Before the May [1968] offensive we adopted this procedure [in dealing with the media], under a different administration, and it doesn't really work as well as you might think. Now we did predict it very accurately, what was going to happen, and I'd say 80 percent of the bureaus went along with us, they didn't overplay it. But those who <u>did</u> overplay it, like UPI and CBS, and those newspaper headline writers back in the States who overplayed it <u>despite</u> what the guy wrote—this is something you can't control."

ABRAMS (re the media): "If these fellows have any confidence in what you tell them, it's only for a day or two. I know of <u>nothing</u> more <u>fragile</u> than our reputation [laughing] with these guys that are reporting out here. If they believe us, it never lasts more than 24 hours."

GOODPASTER: "If they believe us, it's not really through choice. So if they find any opportunity to <u>dis</u>believe us, they don't hesitate to grab it."

ABRAMS: "Yeah, like that so-called favorable article in the *New York Times* which really finally concluded it had been accidental" that we had done any good.

21 FEB 1969: Indications Briefing

BRIEFER: "The enemy has made his plans, and he is completing preparations to carry them out. We are now seeing indications that some offensive activity is imminent. However, it should be noted that the enemy timetable for previous major offensives has repeatedly been delayed, or his plans have been preempted by allied operations. While we see 22 or 23 February as the most likely dates for the start of an enemy offensive, friendly actions could again force a delay."

DAVIDSON: We've talked to Shackley. "He said that he does not see the signs of any coup in the next 72 hours."

ABRAMS: "Well, you've got that other thing, where they've started a rumor of a coup—sponsored by the U.S. I don't mean the <u>rumor's</u> sponsored by the U.S.

[Laughter] And all of that's just designed to pull and tug at the machinery, see if you can weaken it, see if you can start distrust."

ABRAMS: "The only thing that hasn't been covered in the various documents and so on—every possible strategy has now been covered by some PW, some document, or so on, except a couple that this newspaperman posed to me the other day. One was a massive MiG attack out of Cambodia. And I said no, we really hadn't been counting on that. [Laughter] [Someone: "They have 13 total."] I said, 'I don't think the Cambodians can do that.' And he said, 'No, if the North Vietnamese move their MiGs down to Cambodia, and everybody together.' 'Well,' I said, 'I don't believe that has a very high—.' Get all those bombs in there, and all that fuel in there. The other one was a massive tank attack, just pouring down through Tay Ninh, headed right at Saigon. 'Well,' I said, 'they'll have to get through our tanks.' 'Well,' he said, 'they might do it at night.' 'Well, they might, but we don't rate that very high, either.' [Someone: "That takes some doing, too."] You're damn right it does! Be a little refueling going on in that affair. And those tank drivers at night, strange country—."

SOMEONE: "I've never seen a time when the Intelligence Community was in such unanimous agreement."

ABRAMS: "Yeah, that's the dangerous thing about it." [Laughter]

ABRAMS (re possible enemy attack on the cities): "The only thing that makes it intelligent is he may think it's the only damn thing he's got to do. And he's got to do something. He hasn't been able to make a go of tackling the Accelerated Pacification Program. It's down there in the damn machinery. Sure, there's a lot slipping by. There's a lot of VCI we're not getting, a lot of things getting screwed up down there. They've got agents in some parts of the system that are giving them the poop, but in the mess of it they haven't been able to deal with it—despite the exhortations that have gone out."

22 FEB 1969: WIEU

Attendees: Gen. Abrams, Gen. Goodpaster, Gen. Brown, LTG Mildren, VADM Zumwalt, MG Wetherill, MG Corcoran, MG Townsend, MG Shaefer, MG Davidson, MG Rasmussen, BG Frizen, BG Long, BG Sidle, BG Clay, BG Bryan, BG Keegan, Col. Gillert, Col. Hill, Col. Davis, Col. Gleason, Col. Powers.

BRIEFER: There are 41,800 infiltrators projected for the period January–June 1969. Of those, 23,900 are destined for COSVN, which is 57 percent of the total, comparable to the same period of 1968 re COSVN.

ABRAMS (re the combat summary): "One of the things that isn't coming through in this is, well, the combined activities, the integrated activities. I think we've got to press the commanders to report that. The picture should have changed by now in the area of the 2nd ARVN Division. We made some small mention of the 1st ARVN Division. But it's still not coming through. I don't want it reported if it's not happening, but I think the actual picture up there in northern I Corps is far different than is being reported here, and I want the American side to report it." "We're not getting anything about the activities of these troops in support of the '69 pacification program, and I can only presume, then, that there is none. I don't think that's true. I just don't feel that what they're feeding in here is adequate to describe what's happening. I want to emphasize I'm not asking for reports of things that are not happening. If you want it bad enough, you'll get it bad. But I just—comparing it to visiting—it just doesn't give us the picture."

ABRAMS: "I still remember Lang Vei, and I still remember the problems out there at Khe Sanh. And, by god, it was not good! It was not good! As I remember it, the first artillery response from Khe Sanh on Lang Vei was four hours after the initial attack. And that isn't going to hack it!"

1 MAR 1969: WIEU

ATTENDEES: Gen. Abrams, Gen. Goodpaster, Amb. Colby, Gen. Brown, LTG Mildren, VADM Zumwalt, MG Wetherill, MG Corcoran, MG Townsend, MG Shaefer, MG Davidson, MG Rasmussen, BG McLaughlin, BG Long, BG Galloway, BG Clay, BG Bryan, BG Keegan, Col. Gillert, Col. Penuel, Col. Hill, Col. Cavanaugh, Col. Powers.

ABRAMS (as the tape begins in the middle of his reading General Stilwell's message re an apparent cache capture inventory): ". . . 3 each 23-mm AA guns, 30 each light machine guns, and 2 each medium machine guns. Ammunition: 770 122 rockets, 410 122 artillery rounds, 4,000 120-mm mortar rounds, 10,000 82-mm mortar rounds, 950 75-mm recoilless, 19,900 60-mm mortar rounds, 3,160 RPG rounds, 20,000 37-mm AA rounds, 20,000 hand grenades, 6,540 rifle grenades, 11,500 12.7 ammunition, 500 antitank mines, and 800 mines. That, of course, is more ammunition than's been fired in this offensive, and probably the August–September offensive, combined."

SOMEONE: "He wasn't in the Long Binh depot, was he?" [Laughter]

ABRAMS: "Well, apparently not. This 82—I don't think we carry that." [Laughter]

■ ■ ■

Comprehensive recapitulation of the infiltration monitoring breakthrough.

DAVIDSON: "This is Major [Bridener's?] last WIEU, the infiltration expert."

ABRAMS: "What's going to happen here now?" [Laughter]

ABRAMS (re Bridener): "It's really been magnificent—a lot of hard work, and it's one of the really reliable things that we've had."

BRIEFER:

■ "I would like to review the major development during the past year in the area of personnel infiltration." "Although several months were to pass before we were to fully realize it, a new dimension was added to our knowledge of infiltration on 1 November 1967 with the first recorded intercept of the North Vietnamese Rear Services Communications containing references to a numbered infiltration group. [***] By mid-March, 14 four-digit groups had been detected, and we first realized that a large infiltration effort was under way."

■ "During March and April, 114 four-digit groups were reflected in the communications as beginning infiltration, and these contained nearly 66,000 men. By the end of April, [***]. Following the March–April peak, entries into the pipeline declined steadily. Beginning in mid-June, groups with large numbers of sick and wounded were detected in apparent northward movement. Some of these groups, numbered in the 5200 through 5500 series, contained substantial numbers of apparently able-bodied men, and we believe that they represented the withdrawal of the 304th NVA Division."

■ "There were further reductions in infiltration in August and, during September and October, fewer than 6,000 men entered the pipeline. Of note was the first reference to rail transport south of Thanh Hoa, which occurred during this period. There was no immediate reaction to the 1 November bombing halt, but, beginning on 23 November, groups began entering the pipeline at a rate exceeded only by the March–April period last year. By 11 January, the initial surge was completed, but during this period 67 groups totaling 40,000 men began movement south."

■ "It appears that we are currently observing another surge effort. Beginning on 11 February, groups began appearing at a rate of more than two a day, with 34 groups being observed in a 15-day period. A realignment of the infiltration route and way stations in North Vietnam took place during the period September through January, reflecting the use of rail travel south to Vinh and barges from there to southern Ha Tinh Province. In addition, a shift away from the Mu Gia Pass has been noted for groups that are walking, and possibly for those traveling by truck as well."

■ "Combining our knowledge of destinations with observed travel times and attrition factors, we have since May produced continuing estimates of infiltration arriving in South Vietnam. Our current estimate for 1968 contains 504 groups of various types, to include allowance for 55 groups which, although as yet undetected in COMINT or collateral, are believed to have infiltrated. During 1968 an estimated total of 236,200 infiltrators arrived in South Vietnam. The COSVN area received 72,600, or approximately 31 percent of the total. The B-5 Front and Military Region Tri-Thien-Hue received 79,800. . . ." About 34 percent.

■ "In 1969 the emphasis has shifted more heavily to the COSVN area. Of the 52,300 infiltrators currently projected for arrival, 31,400, or approximately 60 percent, are destined for the COSVN area." "We have projected about 80 percent of the groups into the area in which they actually arrive, and 70 percent into the proper arrival month."

ABRAMS: "Wonderful graduation exercise. Thank you very much."

DAVIDSON: "Joe Alsop makes it public with great regularity. I don't know <u>why</u> the enemy hasn't got onto it." "President Johnson used to be a great believer in publicity."

Joseph Alsop was a well-known syndicated columnist, as was his brother Stewart Alsop.

■ ■ ■

ABRAMS (re the cache seizure again): "Well, hell, it's more ammunition than he's fired in this offensive in all of South Vietnam."

SOMEONE: "That's not a cache, that's a depot."

ABRAMS: "You know, we'd really have this thing by the neck if it wound up all being conducted in Laos, fighting over the goddamn caches. That'd be the climax of the interdiction. A lot of it smashed up en route and all that, and then finally when they get down there at the end of the line we move in and scarf it up! It could have quite a—a-a-a-h."

■ ■ ■

ABRAMS: "If they start shooting that artillery up there [DMZ], we have the authority to hit back. I want it laid on. We'll just report it to Washington. But if they open fire with artillery pieces up there, I want the response to be immediate and devastating. I want it—B-52s, tac air, every damn thing we can get, no matter where it's located. And we'll report what we've done. But I want the skids greased. That means we've got to have targeting. And I want it to start with the first round. We won't be able to do that, but [laughing] with a little advance planning we can make it fairly responsive."

ABRAMS: "This whole thing requires a little careful examination. If he does start a lot of force up there out of the DMZ, I don't want to stop this [Operation] Dewey Canyon thing at all. Now whether III MAF has got the forces to contain it at the DMZ and still continue this stuff in western Quang Tri is somewhat of a question. But we should reinforce from II Corps, rather than draw back at all from western Quang Tri. Not only Dewey Canyon, but you know he's [4th Marine Regiment] out there pushing out in the northern, northwestern—. We've got to do all of that. It has to do with that stream, and [Route] 1036, all of that. God, that's the place to fight the war—out there. And we can do it." We have a contingency plan laid on with General Peers to provide two brigades, the 173rd Airborne Brigade and one brigade from the 4th Infantry Division. "If it's necessary, that's what we'll do, because we're not going to take the heat off of western Quang Tri."

■ ■ ■

ABRAMS (re KIA): "Well—in a way that's a very sad chart, because there're so many people killed. But, looking at it dispassionately if you can, that is the most favorable balance of affairs that we have yet seen. Look at III Corps! 31 percent U.S., 67 percent RVNAF. I Corps, where you've got such a heavy U.S. commitment out there—51 percent RVNAF. Ah—you know, there's a story in that chart. Talk about ARVN, whether they're in the game. As I say, it's a sad thing. There's no—it sounds kind of disrespectful to gloat over it, but in the business of who's getting in the war, I think that's an important chart."

■ ■ ■

GOODPASTER: "Have you seen any evidence of this pulling in of the territorials? I haven't seen a bit of it, and the credit for that goes to Thieu."

ABRAMS: "Right. That's right."

■ ■ ■

GOODPASTER: "These border enclaves, that have been detached in all practical purposes from Cambodia—his writ doesn't run—we could do this, just drop the enemy's capability down by some significant amount, and then you've got all kinds of things, all kinds of elbow room. You want to take some of our forces out? We could talk about it."

DAVIDSON: "You've got to offer them something more than just what has been offered them time and time and time again. I remember when General Westmoreland would come in for [authority to attack] some of the base areas. And we just couldn't find a way to sell that. The Chiefs supported him a thousand and one percent, but it was a dull thud on the Third Floor [of the Pentagon] and worse across the river [in the White House and the State Department]. Now if you can show where this might really get you down the road, a change in the balance of power where you might reach the point on force withdrawal, or reduction, this just might do it. You might get somewhere. But without some evidence of a real payoff that those politicians can grab a hold of, I don't think that—."

GOODPASTER: "But there are some things of that kind. It does have that much strategic significance. And out of that, if we can exploit it, do this, get some elbow room here for things that these people are—." "I wouldn't do it out of necessity. I would do it out of an opportunity."

ABRAMS: "That's right. And the thought that he has in fact put himself in a position of great strategic risk [as argued by Goodpaster], and that this could be dramatically unbalanced."

DAVIDSON: "General, I go back to this call you made on the president. You remember he was the only one I saw back there who ever mentioned the force reduction. And he was the one who said, who sent the message, 'If you've got any dirty tricks, use them. I'll back you up.' Of course, Kissinger was almost lost at that point. It really hit him in the gut. But the basic point is if we got some leverage that'll get us through the secretary of defense and the secretary of state, if we ever get this before the president, I think you've got an even money bet that you'll get your way. If the case is presented right, and if the request is a reasonable one . . . the objectives are definite and limited, and the benefits look pretty darn attractive—. And they must be suffering, you know, some chagrin that we didn't retaliate, that we took this, just like we took the *Pueblo*. There's a little national pride involved. We said we would not stop the bombing unless we got these guarantees, and they're violating both of them! I'd just—I'd be embarrassed. I think we all should be a little ashamed of this. So I think maybe we're offering them something that they might find very attractive."

3 MAR 1969: General Abrams Discussion

Contemplating requesting authorization to go into Cambodia.

ABRAMS: "Mearns tells me that they had three rockets at 0456 this morning in Saigon. Eleven civilians were killed, nine from one family. Twenty-one civilians wounded. Thirty-one houses, one- and two-story family dwellings, either destroyed or badly damaged." "The ambassador—Berger—called me about nine o'clock." "And Ambassador Berger felt now was the time to make a retaliation of two or three planes, and wanted to know what I thought about it. So I said, 'I think we ought to think about this. I'd like to mull it over and talk to you later.' See, 'two or three planes' just horrifies me. I'd agree to argue about whether it should be two weeks or three weeks, but that's a 500-a-day—."

ABRAMS: "So far, President Thieu has played this thing very cool. He has not gotten excited about this rocketing. And really his attitude has been exactly the way he expressed it to those *Time-Life* people. He said we should think about this." "He likes the way the Nixon administration is going about things. They think things through."

ABRAMS (re the rocketing of Saigon): "It's related to the whole strategy of the war." "The message has got to make it clear that this is aimed at destroying their strategy of the war." "You've got this whole thing of the talks, and nobody yet sees a way, or has advanced a way, to get these bastards out of Cambodia and Laos. And this kind of—this begins to tackle that point."

COLBY: "Because that's the interminable part of this war."

ABRAMS: "That's right."

COLBY: "Unless you can solve that, you are here forever."

ABRAMS: "No amount of bombing in North Vietnam is going to cause him to rethink his problem. But if we go in those base areas, he's got to rethink the whole damn problem! That's the way I feel about it."

SOMEONE: "It is sort of a one-time shot kind of thing. It has a tremendous payoff initially. What he ought to do in reaction to it is set his bases up deeper in, with all the penalties that that causes him."

ABRAMS: "If we could get into [Base Area] 610—you know, the stuff he's finally gotten down there, at great cost, and just blow it up."

ABRAMS: "And then the other thing is going into these base areas, and this is aimed at his strategy for the conduct of the war. This is in retaliation for his rocketing of Saigon, for his attacks against the people."

ABRAMS: "When the United States does things—you know, act like the United States."

BRIEFER: This offensive began on the morning of 23 February 1969.

3 MAR 1969: COMUS Prebrief for Secretary of Defense

BRIEFER: "The enemy's ultimate goal has never changed. It is the reunification of North and South Vietnam under Communist domination." "To achieve this goal, the enemy seeks to obtain the U.S. withdrawal from South Vietnam and to bring about a coalition government."

BRIEFER: Per a mid-December 1968 COSVN document the enemy sees the United States urgently "trying to find ways for withdrawal of troops from South Vietnam and to de-Americanize the war in South Vietnam." "The document describes the means by which the enemy will attempt to exploit and speed withdrawal."

BRIEFER: COSVN Resolution 8, "which established the enemy's post-bombing halt direction and objectives, states, 'We will have to do our best to set up a coalition government in South Vietnam in which the NLF participates and plays the leading role.'"

BRIEFER (re negotiations): "It is here that he believes he has made his greatest progress—the bombing limitations, then the complete bombing halt; the admission of the NLF to the Paris discussions."

BRIEFER: "To bring about U.S. withdrawal, the enemy is attempting to fan the flames of what he's read as a growing U.S. impatience and discouragement with the war. He's attempting to project an impression of an unending war, of North Vietnamese and Viet Cong intention and resolve to continue indefinitely."

ABRAMS (re the enemy): "I'm not in favor of underestimating him, but if we overestimate him we're going to miss some opportunities."

BRIEFER: "Our earliest dependable strength figures go back to October 1965." Enemy total strength then was about 207,000. "The so-called 'war of liberation' has increasingly become an NVA war." In October 1965, NVA comprised 26 percent of VC/NVA maneuver and combat support strength, while today it is 70 plus.

BRIEFER (re infiltration): Infiltrators move by truck, train, barge, or foot from Vinh to the Laotian border. There is a series of transient camps in North Vietnam known as T-stations. An infiltration group is typically 500–600 men. The cadre accompanies such groups as far as South Vietnam, then returns. From Vinh onward travel is almost always by foot. There are three main routes: through the Mu Gia Pass, the Ban Karai Pass, and just west of the DMZ. Losses en route due to sickness, desertion, and death from attacking aircraft are approximately 12 percent.

BRIEFER: In Laos and Cambodia there are three major border staging areas for infiltration: Base Area 611/A Shau Valley complexes (serving MR-TTH and MR-5, respectively). Base Area 609, farther south in the tri-border area (serving the B-3 Front). Cambodian–Phuoc Long Province border: Base Area 350 (for COSVN).

BRIEFER: "During 1968 approximately 236,000 North Vietnamese infiltrators entered South Vietnam." This movement peaked in March and was sustained until August, "a tremendous effort."

BRIEFER: In 1969 emphasis shifted more heavily to the COSVN area. At this time we project over 52,000 to arrive in South Vietnam in 1969, and we expect more. Although the total is about one-third of that in 1968, the number to COSVN is almost as great. Enemy in-country recruitment difficulties (as GVN control and pacification both progress) are reflected in increasing numbers of NVA in nominally VC units. We estimate they recruited approximately 3,500 per month in 1968, with a generally downward trend which we expect to continue.

BRIEFER: "At least one-third of the VC's in-country replacements last year were between 13 and 17 years of age."

BRIEFER: "During 1968 the enemy lost 289,000 men, or more than 100 percent of his total present military strength."

BRIEFER: "We have seen the recent emergence of female combat units."

BRIEFER: The Hoi Chanh rate has been "climbing steadily since last September." "Significantly, the majority of Hoi Chanhs are from IV Corps, the last holdout of the indigenous war in South Vietnam."

ABRAMS: "Incidentally, they told me this morning at CMAC—you know these assassinations? Took the guy out 300 meters from the village, laid him on the ground, and drove a stake through his heart. It takes some doing to do that. Somebody's got to hold him down, somebody's got to hold the stake, and then swing the hammer. Nasty!"

BRIEFER: Cites "the enemy's economy of force measures, a movement of major units from less profitable areas to his primary target. Throughout last summer, he built a three-plus division force in northern MR-5 targeted against Danang and the populated coastal region there. He's moved seven regiments from II Corps to III Corps, and four battalions from IV Corps to III Corps. To show the magnitude of this trend, at Tet last year there were 49 combat battalions in III Corps or on its Cambodian border. Now there are 88 combat battalions there."

BRIEFER: "In its broadest sense, China and the Soviet Union, and the bloc nations of East Europe, constitute the enemy's rear base. They are the source of virtually all the war matériel with which he stocks his forward supply bases in North Vietnam, Laos, and Cambodia."

BRIEFER: The enemy has "approximately 18 major base areas in South Vietnam itself." "Recently we've made serious inroads in some of the traditional in-country base areas. In I Corps last spring we entered the A Shau Valley for the first time since 1965." Also operations in Base Area 101 and Base Area 114 in the upper two provinces "hurt him badly." Operations in Base Area 112 "have thrown Front 4 forces badly off balance."

BRIEFER: "Almost all the base areas in IV Corps have been entered, particularly 470 and 490. Recent operations in the U Minh Forest were the first friendly penetration ever made there, even as far back as the Viet Minh War. Thus the [in-country] sanctuaries are gradually losing their invulnerability."

BRIEFER: "The most significant aspect of the enemy's in-country system is that he does not have a logistics tail to support him in offensive operations. Instead, we might say he has a logistics 'nose.' He pre-positions supplies in caches along his line of advance, then moves forward on this line. This makes him vulnerable to preemption when we uncover his caches, as we've done with great frequency over the past six months. Also, once he's used up these supplies there is little or no immediate replenishment." In-country movement of supplies is by portering, bicycle, or pack animal.

BRIEFER: "In spite of high truck losses from our air interdiction, the enemy has introduced sufficient additional trucks into the system to increase steadily the level of his effort. But the most significant trend over the past year has been the enemy's increasing reliance on the use of Cambodia. Cambodia has become the prime source of food and munitions for the enemy's forces in III Corps and

IV Corps, and to a great extent II Corps. Our evidence is overwhelming, and it mounts daily. Arms shipments arrive in Sihanoukville in amounts far in excess of the Cambodian armed forces' needs. FARK's direct participation in the growing arms traffic proves beyond any doubt their complicity with the enemy. The Sihanouk regime, if not actively involved, is at least aware of this movement and has given tacit approval to its continuance. In the border regions, the enemy has developed 11 of 15 major out-country base areas into logistical-training complexes. Three of these opposite II Corps grew from regimental to divisional bivouac areas last summer."

BRIEFER: "The Cambodian Fishhook in northern III Corps has long been the principal location for COSVN." "In Ba Thieu, only 36 miles from Saigon, the enemy has established a formidable arsenal, with over 1,750 structures built there during 1968. The enemy simply could not carry out serious military operations in III and IV Corps if he were denied the use of Cambodia."

ABRAMS: "You know, one of the things, I think, about Communist countries—they've got to keep some military forces at home. The Chinese have to, the Soviets—they've got to. And I think these fellows have got to, too. They could never run the risk of—." "Especially with no bombing. That gives the people time to think."

ABRAMS: "Now, I must say—admission against interest—that I'm up in the air here. One of the things here is not losing our cool. In a way, we've already created somewhat of an advantage. I didn't used to see it this way, but he was so sure that we were going to retaliate. Now we didn't. Now, of course, he can say that's because we were weak. That's probably what he will say, publicly. He's trying to say he's doing all this attacking because we were on the offensive. I don't think he can sell it, because what our press has called it was a 'lull.' And they're stuck with that. As much as I disliked it, they—their description of it was a lull. And so he's got the problem now of convincing the U.S. press—. [Somebody: "That wrote it wrong."] Yeah—a pretty rough job. Let him take it on. Wish him good luck, and so on. So maybe if we just continue on here, doing what we're doing—you know, handling things just the way we've been handling it—."

SIDLE: "The press out here keeps asking for some sort of an assessment."

SOMEONE: "He really made his pitch openly that this was in response to our aggressive actions last Thursday in Paris."

GOODPASTER: "We have got more interval room now. We're not pushed right up against the wall."

ABRAMS: "That's right. He hasn't gotten away with anything!" "If we just don't act excited—. See he doesn't—. Behind all the propaganda, I'm sure he does figure these things out pretty carefully. Then he goes ahead with his propaganda and so on. But he knows what's happened down here." "Nothing seems to be happening except beating the shit out of him."

SOMEONE: "These people are compulsive propagandists. Sometimes they dig themselves a hole."

ABRAMS: "And if he is in the process of doing that, we shouldn't do anything that eases his burden. And maybe what we're doing is the best. The other thing is, you know—we have to face it, I think—over the last few months, we've come out pretty—I mean, nobody really likes this, and I'm not trying to say there's been any love feast or anything, but—we've gained a certain <u>minimum</u> degree of respect by the press. They're not lash—they haven't got the cat-o'-nine-tails out, really. So—ah—we've got something in our checking account. We ought to be careful when we spend that, because the minute you start getting out with them [the press], you may win a <u>few</u>, but you're also going to get the <u>hell</u> knocked out of you by a few. You know, they just say, 'W-e-l-l, they've been playing it cozy here, here they come,' the same old <u>stuff</u>. You know, just like wondering when it was going to happen. And they'll let you have it. They'll disagree with your <u>assessment</u>—. And so, I don't know as we really have to <u>spend</u> anything out of that account right now. Let it get a little more interest."

GOODPASTER: "We don't have to go bomb the north. It would be useful if we did, but not necessary. Unless he comes across the DMZ, in which case it will be a different kind of ball game. But the same thing may apply on the press side. You know, our great concern is the effect of his pinging back in the States. But that <u>isn't</u> having too much effect. There's no point in our doing anything about it, and <u>probably</u> if it <u>is</u> having an effect [laughing] there's no point in our trying to do anything about it—other than just laying out and letting the thing cool down to get down to the facts of the thing."

ABRAMS: "Now, another thing—we've been reporting all of this into Washington. We've said it's now a little closer at hand, now the preparations, that substantial forces, massive evidence, offensive planning, you know. And all that's been going in there. <u>But</u> we believe that this can be handled, contained. What's not preempted will be defeated. You know, we've said these things. And, at least <u>so far</u>, that's exactly what's happening."

GOODPASTER: Make the point [in briefing the secretary of defense] that "we find it useful to look at what the enemy is doing as a system, look at the whole Communist system." Main forces, local forces, guerrillas, infrastructure, base areas, line of communications, personnel system, commo-liaison routes, support that he gets from the population, and so on.

GOODPASTER: "This is Mr. Laird's first trip out here, and you may want to say a word on what the terrain is like out here, what the jungle is like, and why he [the enemy] can do these things that he can do. At least lay that down, that here is a particular kind of terrain that he has studied, and he tries to exploit it to the absolute maximum."

GOODPASTER: Quotes Maj. Gen. Orwin C. Talbott, 1st Infantry Division commander, to the effect that "when the enemy gets to Lai Khe he is just about to come out from under the canopy that has protected him all the way from Hanoi."

5 MAR 1969: Brief, Major General Davidson

This is apparently in preparation for briefing Secretary of Defense Laird during his upcoming visit to Vietnam.

DAVIDSON: "Westmoreland used to have a theory—he had a lot of theories which had no basis in fact—and one of them was that there is some standard ratio by which the enemy exaggerates. Now if we researched that once when he was the commander out here, we must have done it four or five times. There isn't! I suspect, if you're going to exaggerate, the first thing you do is take a look at your own casualties and losses, because these have got to be fairly accurately reported, because you've got to get replacements. In other words, if you keep fudging and reporting less casualties than you took, pretty soon you're going to be out of men. So once you say, 'I lost a hundred, and therefore I've got to report a hundred,' the next thing is to say, 'Well, I'd better say I knocked over two hundred of the enemy.' I suspect this, but I don't think there's any figure that they set down."

DAVIDSON: "I've gone through two of these things [secretary of defense visits], and let me give you my reaction to it as an o-l-d hand around here—that's not going to be much older, either, thank goodness. There are varied reasons to come out. We didn't detect what it was last—the first two times. I think we may have detected it this time. Let me illustrate with Mr. McNamara. We had a l-o-n-g list of things to cover, briefings out the kazoo. Fifteen briefings, as I recall. It went all through the first day—no questions until late on the afternoon of the first day. And I mean, when you give a 30-minute intelligence presentation, and not a question in the room, it makes you wonder. And the next presentation. The first five presentations . . . went right through. And then, on a little picky J-1 presentation, it snapped loose. Suddenly the room revived, and you saw what he'd come out here for. N-o-o-o prior indication whatsoever. That visit the theme was, 'What are you doing with your own troops?' And this is the thing, Mr. McNamara bad-mouthing General Westmoreland's manpower conservation and use, I'm confident kept poor General Westmoreland over one more year than he was supposed to have been kept over. And, in effect, led him down the Tet path, et cetera, et cetera. I'm absolutely convinced of it."

DAVIDSON: "Mr. Clifford sat here for a briefing, calm and self-collected, and then just before they terminated the first day, he dropped his anchor, which was, 'What can you do to improve ARVN?' And suddenly he puts his glasses on, deep resonant voice, took a little notebook he had, you know, and said, 'Now I'd like to ask a few questions. What is the desertion rate in ARVN? How many officers were promoted last month?' It's the only time since I've been here that I've seen General Abrams stunned. Because it came right out of a clear blue sky, like a fellow going down and he gets hit from the blind side, and he doesn't know."

DAVIDSON: "All right, now. My guess is that the hidden theme this time, and there's no word of it on the agenda, is, 'When can you start withdrawing troops?' Everybody's gambling, because their view back there is not, 'How can we get on with the war?' It's, 'How can you cut down the cost of the war in either manpower, matériel, or cut down the psychological and political costs?'"

DAVIDSON: "We haven't given—what's all our thought out here?"

SEVERAL VOICES IN UNISON: "Win the war."

DAVIDSON: "What it ought to be is, 'Let's kick the hell out of somebody.' Now that means that you're going to get men killed and hurt. The furtherest thought from our mind is, 'How can you reduce casualties?' That could be the buried—."

SOMEONE (Kraft? Whoever it is has been in Paris): "I can almost guarantee you this exchange was made between Nixon and Lodge in Paris, because he was trying to get General Weyand to pursue the problem of modifying General Abrams's operations here with the view to reduction of casualties. And General Weyand was holding a firm line on that."

DAVIDSON: "Well, how in the hell would you do it and carry out your mission?" "Actually, what you would be forced to do, and it'd never work in the long run, in my opinion, if you follow it to its natural conclusion, you'd have to come back to some such silly scheme as this one that Jim Gavin had of enclaves. You'd have to fall back, try to hold the populated area, and once you lose the— we've lost. The very nature of the war gives them the strategic initiative. There isn't any use arguing about that."

DAVIDSON: "By the very nature, we've got to defend our bases and the cities and the populated areas. And let's say that the enemy had to defend with what he's got—bases, areas, and populace. We'd win the war in a month! We'd kick his tail right out into the ocean. But, nevertheless, we maintain the tactical initiative. As he moves in, we're out there hitting him all the time. But you give up on that, and are forced into inactivity, and you're going to get it."

DAVIDSON: "Any time you get a simple answer in this war, it's probably wrong."

DAVIDSON (re what modification of mission would be needed to reduce casualties): "An expansion of operating authorities into well-defined base areas in Cambodia and Laos."

DAVIDSON (re length of the war): "Under present ground rules, the damn thing is going on indefinitely. And the longer it goes on, in my opinion, the better chance we've got of—I don't like to say losing, but settling for something less than our strength would guarantee us if we could" bring it to bear. "Sooner or later you have got to face those problems. And if you are not going to face them, or won't face them, then you're going to have to settle for something less—a good deal less."

SOMEONE: "The mission has not been formally revised since '62 by the JCS."

SOMEONE ELSE: "Of course the rules of engagement have been changed."

DAVIDSON: "By god, it's a chilling decision to make that one about going into Cambodia and Laos." "It would take a man with absolute selflessness, considering the political aspects. Boy, if the doves have savaged old Johnson—and they did, they drove him out of office—think what they would do with Nixon if he went into Laos and Cambodia!"

SOMEONE: "Do you see any change in Sihanouk's attitude?"

RESPONSE: "Only hourly." "A very sly man, devious."

DAVIDSON (re possible question as to how long the enemy can sustain the effort): "I've got a real wonderful JCS message I'm just going to quote. 'This is beyond our responsibility and competence, however here is what the Joint Chiefs of Staff say.' General Wheeler's sitting in the room; he can defend it. It says that they can continue the input of 1968 for at least five years."

SOMEONE: "That's CIA's manpower base study."

DAVIDSON: "But JCS bought it."

DAVIDSON: "Your Chieu Hoi rate goes up not as a result of sweeps, but as a result of getting in an area and staying in it."

DAVIDSON: "Now I'm not prepared to say that our troops are getting into areas and staying, but with the APC this is what they ought to be doing."

DAVIDSON (re dealing with tough questions): "There's one thing with all these four-star generals and ambassadors, none of them are bashful. They all want to jump in the act. All you have to do is hesitate and one of them will try it, anyway. He may not have a very good answer, but he'll be in there flogging it."

DAVIDSON (in contrast to IV Corps): "The war's largely an NVA war in the other three corps, in fact almost totally in I Corps. And the good old 9th VC, or 5th VC—hell, it's not the VC anymore. It's 70 or 80 or 90 percent NVA."

DAVIDSON (on infiltration): "Until we got onto the present method of calculating, we never were able to calculate input—as far as I know. We never even bothered to do it retroactively, which you could have done."

DAVIDSON (re an enemy recruiting figure of 7,000 a month): "That was one they used way back when. It never had any validity. I inherited the damn thing. I immediately had things run. It just wasn't there—never was. So we're stuck with it." Later used 3,500 a month.

6 MAR–10 MAR 1969: Secretary of Defense Briefing

Discussions take place in the context of the enemy's 1969 Tet Offensive, sometimes also referred to as the Fourth Offensive (following on Tet 1968, mini-Tet in May 1968, and the Third Offensive in August 1968).

This is the first trip to Vietnam for Secretary of Defense Melvin Laird, who served in that post 1969–1973. Accompanying him is Gen. Earle G. Wheeler, Chairman of the Joint Chiefs of Staff, 1964–1970.

LAIRD: "You talk [in a briefing just presented, apparently] about the outcry that's developed in the United States. I think that's true, that there isn't any real consensus that has been developed in the United States to back away from what we're doing over here right now, but I think a lot of that comes about because we've had a change of administration. I think we have to understand that.

They're giving the new administration a little time here. And people aren't raising a lot of hell right now as far as Vietnam is concerned. I think, though, if we'd have had a continuation, if there wouldn't have been a change, there'd be a hell of a lot of hell being raised over there right now. I think we've got some time, and we've got to make the best use of that time that we possibly can. It's important that we <u>have</u> this time, because everything could have been <u>lost</u> without time." "We've got to make the best <u>possible</u> use of the time that we <u>do</u> have."

LAIRD: "I think the overall objective that we've got to try to work for is we've got to develop a national policy that we <u>can</u> go to the people with. I'm going before all these congressional committees, starting the 18th of March, for—I think we have five or six lined up for 22 straight days. If we can develop some sort of a program, and a plan, to show that—first, that we are protecting the safety of our <u>men</u> over here, the Americans that are committed here in Vietnam, and secondly that we are making real progress towards our overall objective, which is the self-determination of South Vietnam. And third, as I pointed out upstairs, we have a program to reduce the United States contribution, not only in the form of men, but in casualties and matériel and in dollars, that will be available to move forward with at the time this time period of ours runs out. I don't know what that time period is, whether it's six months, seven months, nine months, but that program has to be laid out by our president probably within the next three or four months. This is pretty important."

■ ■ ■

BUNKER: "Mr. Secretary, I can give you President Thieu's views on this. He thinks they will continue this type of operation for two, perhaps three, months. I think they can only maintain this kind of attack for a week or so at a time. They'll have to then stop, get their breath again, and go on. I think this may go on for two or three months, four months. I think then . . . having tried this . . . if his objective is political and to influence the United States in opposition doesn't succeed, then I think he will <u>seriously</u> come to negotiations."

■ ■ ■

LAIRD: "I'm going to be asked, I'm sure, a lot about the use of the B-52. And I think one of the important things is what you find out from—as far as intelligence is concerned—the other question we can talk about a little later is its effect in terms of destruction—but I think as far as intelligence is concerned, what do you find out from these people that are coming over and your prisoners? I'd like to get a good picture of its effect as a psychological warfare viewpoint." "This is an expensive thing. It has a very important part in the budget. In the budget that's been currently presented, B-52, the use of it, is scaled down in the months of April, May, and June. It's cut back further in the 1970 budget that's been presented to the Congress. We can talk about it from the military standpoint a little later on, but I'd like to get something from the intelligence."

DAVIDSON: "I can say from interrogation of the PWs, sir, that the B-52 is the most feared weapon in the country."

WHEELER: "In effect General Abrams operates with no reserves, no ground reserves. This is a new situation in warfare so far as I am aware. Now he can pull units and move them from one area to another, but he has no such thing as a division sitting in reserve, or a regiment of a division sitting in reserve. His reserve, basically, is firepower—his strategic reserve. And without those—the B-52s, number one, and the massed artillery number two, is in effect his strategic reserve. Abe may have a different view, but that's the way I look at it from Washington."

ABRAMS: "No, that's right. You have to add tac air. There's nothing really as responsive as the B-52 and tac air. It only takes a couple of hours to change the whole weight and put it where you want it, in whatever quantity you want it."

■ ■ ■

TOWNSEND: "For the first time this year each of these commanders—the COMUSMACV, the Vietnamese commander, the ROK commander, the Thai commander, and the Australian commander—are all signatories to a campaign plan for 1969, so that everybody is going along the same azimuth. This is the first time that this has been done."

■ ■ ■

BRIEFER: During the current offensive the enemy has lost over 10,000 KIA, plus over 1,800 PWs and Hoi Chanh. We estimate for every KIA the enemy suffers two moderately or seriously wounded, and that of the wounded one-sixth will die.

BRIEFER: In Operation Dewey Canyon, north of the A Shau Valley, we uncovered two caches of arms and ammunition in excess of 4,500 tons. "The mortars and rocket rounds alone in these two caches amount to over four times the quantity that he shot at us in this current offensive."

BRIEFER: "We do not expect at this time a major attack across the DMZ, nor do we expect a major attack on Saigon." We believe his strategy to be: "He's trying to improve his negotiating position, he's trying to erode U.S. will, and he's trying to prepare the way for the coalition government."

■ ■ ■

Ambassador Bunker's principal briefing for Secretary Laird.

BUNKER: Refers to "this complex and difficult task that we are all engaged in here—complex and difficult and, I think, in many ways new to American experience, too. And I think that's one reason it's been difficult for the American people to understand it. I think, too, we've had—the nature of the reporting here has made it difficult. It's often been subjective, I think, sometimes tendentious. And I think the fact that this has been the first war fought on television has made it additionally difficult."

BUNKER: "You mentioned this morning, Mr. Secretary, our objectives here, the question of self-determination. I think the objectives, as we have seen it here, we believe are our objectives here, are to achieve, first, a just and durable peace, through negotiations, that will be acceptable to us, to the government here, will of course have to be acceptable to the other side as well. The opportunity, which you mentioned, for the Vietnamese to choose the kind of government under which they want to live, as President Johnson has said on the basis of 'one man, one vote,' which President Thieu has repeated a number of times. To help them build their own political institutions and a viable economy. To make credible our obligations under the United Nations and the SEATO to resist aggression. And eventually, when peace comes, to develop regional organizations through which the Southeast Asian countries can carry out joint undertakings in economic development and mutual cooperation."

BUNKER: "To me this is all one war. General Abrams mentioned that this is all one war on the military side. I think it's one war that everything we do here is an aspect of the total effort to achieve our objectives. And I think, as has been made clear, it isn't our objective to win the war in the conventional sense. When we talk of winning the war, we mean it in the sense of an acceptable political settlement which gives the Vietnamese people the opportunity to choose freely their own government."

BUNKER: "We're engaged in fighting a limited war, for limited objectives, and with limited resources. At the same time we're advising and supporting the Vietnamese in their efforts to carry out—carry through—a social revolution."

BUNKER: "Unless there is progress in these areas of political, economic, and social development, I think a military victory would be meaningless, and in fact I doubt whether it would be possible."

BUNKER: "We can prevent the Vietnamese losing the war, but they in the end have to win it themselves."

BUNKER: Cites "the relatively thin crust of organizational, management, technical talent. Maybe the problem is more acute here, because here is a small country fighting a war for survival, a great strain on its manpower, and at the same time trying to carry through a political and a social transformation. And it requires an effort, too, which is difficult for a westerner, I think, to fathom the subtleties of the Asian mind, because the standards and the yardsticks which are often important to us are not necessarily so to an Asian, and vice versa. So we have to be conscious of, and sensitive to, their aspirations and their motivations if we are in fact to succeed eventually in our objectives."

BUNKER: "We here, because of these problems, these difficulties, complexities, we've felt it important to be selective in assigning priorities to programs and projects that we deem will most effectively achieve our objectives. A number of things which I think I, and all of us here, believe should have received and should continue to receive top priority, and to which we are addressing our programs. These are, first, of course, a vigorous, imaginative, flexible prosecution of the war, within the acceptable limits, with the objective of leaving the enemy no choice but to accept a just and honorable peace. This, I think, is being pursued very imaginatively by General Abrams and his colleagues."

BUNKER: Next: "Through free and honest elections the establishment of a broadly based, stable, and effective constitutional government." And: "An expedited pacification program that will win the allegiance of the Vietnamese people, including the Viet Cong, and which offers them the opportunity to become part of the social and political fabric of the country." And: RVNAF I&M "so they can carry more and more of the burdens of the war without our help." And: "The optimum use of available manpower." And: "Economic stability and development."

BUNKER: "When one realizes that [in South Vietnam] 80 percent of the physically able manpower between the ages of 15 and 35 are in the armed forces, this is quite an undertaking."

BUNKER: "I think it's fair to say that, until the time of the Tet attacks a year ago, steady though not spectacular progress had been made in all these areas. The balance of military power had shifted to our side, pacification had proceeded slowly but steadily, and about two-thirds of the population were considered under government control, or what we call 'relatively secure' category. A Constituent Assembly had been elected, a constitution drafted and promulgated, elections for village and hamlet officials held in the spring of '67, elections for president, vice president, and the National Assembly held in September and October of that year, and the constitutional government established."

BUNKER: "The two events which occurred in 1968 . . . can be viewed as watersheds from which much else flowed. The first was the Tet Offensive, begun just over a year ago, followed by the May–June and the August–September attacks by the enemy. And the second was President Johnson's statement on March 31st ordering the partial cessation of the bombing and announcing that he would not be a candidate for reelection. Despite the setback of Tet, the net result was, I think, to set in motion a whole series of developments which had the effect of greatly stimulating and accelerating progress here. I think it's fair to say, too, that the Tet Offensive had a much greater impact, particularly psychologically, in the United States and in world opinion than it did here in Vietnam. It's true that the enemy gained some matériel and psychological advantage here. There was a heavy loss of lives—<u>civilian</u> and military. Some three-quarters of a million temporary evacuees were created, another 250,000 in the May–June attacks. Upwards of 150,000 homes were, and a number of industrial plants, damaged or destroyed. The economy was set back. There was a distinct loss of confidence in the business community. This, obviously, created both a psychological strain and a heavy drain on resources."

BUNKER: "There was also, as Ambassador Colby mentioned, reduced security in some areas, the relatively secure population going, as he mentioned, from about 67 percent to just under 60, a loss of about a million and a half people from the 'relatively secure' category. But, on the positive side, the Vietnamese forces fought well; as General Abrams remarked once, probably better than they thought they could. There were no uprisings, there were no defections, the government didn't fall apart. On the contrary, it reacted quickly, strongly, vigorously setting about recovery. The people themselves, particularly in the cities, were alienated by the widespread death and destruction caused by the enemy, and by his cruelty and his savagery. And the enemy suffered then the first of a series of heavy military defeats in which he took appalling losses."

BUNKER: "The May–June attacks . . . caused some further damage. But again the cost to the enemy was extreme. In the August–September attacks, they again cost him heavily, with literally nothing to show for it. He never got into a city. And perhaps—well, I think most important of all, the most important effect of these three offensives was the confidence in themselves the Vietnamese acquired the hard way, in their ability to meet and throw back the worst the enemy had to offer."

BUNKER: Also: "President Johnson's statement of March 31st, followed by the partial cessation of the bombing, brought the Vietnamese face to face with the fact that our commitment was not open-ended, and that one day they'd be on their own. This realization I think had an important and subtle impact on the development of Vietnamese attitudes and events. There was initial doubt as to the firmness of our commitment. This subsided, I think, after the meeting in Honolulu between the president and President Thieu. It rose again during the October–November crisis, which I shall describe later. But the net effect, I think, was a further contribution to the feeling of self-reliance and increasing self-confidence."

BUNKER: "Thieu's role throughout this period has been an important element, in fact I think perhaps the crucial one. He has handled problems with a very considerable astuteness and skill. He is an individual of very considerable intellectual capacity. He made the decision in the beginning to follow the constitutional road, not to rule with a clique of generals, which many of them expected he would do. He has been acting more and more like a politician, getting out into the country, following up on the pacification, talking to people, seeing what they want. In these present attacks, I've seen him several times since they started here, and he's been consistently confident and calm and relaxed."

BUNKER: "Under his leadership, a series of measures was undertaken by the government, which I think has very materially advanced the progress here. This is particularly true in the last six or seven months. First there was the full mobilization, now—as you saw—more than a million men, military and paramilitary, under arms. If one compares this, with the manpower pool from which this is drawn, with the population of the United States, it's equivalent to having—our having—between 17 and 18 million men under arms, which would be a very sizable undertaking. Of the 220,000 increase in the armed forces, I think about 160,000 were volunteers. Vietnamese forces, again as I mentioned, have improved steadily in equipment and leadership, morale, performance. Again, as General Abrams has said, they've been paying the price and exacting the toll. I think, General Abrams, you mentioned to me yesterday that in this present offensive 69 percent of the friendly forces killed had been Vietnamese."

BUNKER: "The military command structure was realigned by the president— done, again, skillfully, I think. It's been operating, certainly, more effectively than before. The military command structure of the Capital Military District was also reorganized, and is far more effective than it was. He installed a new government at the end of May, the Tran Van Huong government, and this I think is generally regarded as the strongest and ablest South Vietnam has had in a decade. It is growing in self-confidence and beginning to generate popular support and acquire popular confidence. Huong, I think, is the most respected political leader, probably, in the country today. The legislative and executive branches have their problems from time to time, but I think it's fair to say that they are working fairly well together, particularly when one considers the fact that this is a system that's quite new to people here. Ambassador Colby described the Confucian background. . . . A senator said to me not long ago, 'We have a democratic system, and we have to make it work, although our history goes back 4,000 years and gives us no tradition of democracy.' But this has been—this is something that's come about through <u>our</u> influence. It's pretty much our system, and I think's really working surprisingly well."

BUNKER: "As I said, the government is improving in effectiveness. As Ambassador Colby mentioned, in its attack last year on corruption, for example, 22 province chiefs and 91 district chiefs were removed for corruption or incompetence. Twenty more, I think, are about to be appointed. Police have been cleaned up, or are being cleaned up. Some 800 have been removed or disciplined. And I think, too, that the president has instilled . . . great energy, vigor, and imagination in the pacification program. He has by far the most comprehensive grasp of it of anyone in government. I've been out with him a number of times, and he keeps emphasizing particularly four main points, and that is accelerating the program; the village and hamlet elections to get local government restored; the training and improvement of the village and hamlet selections; and land reform. And he said to me not long ago that he proposed to put through a dramatic land reform program this year, and has made it clear that he wants to do it—not only do it promptly, but see it implemented during the first six months, get it under way."

BUNKER: "He's also been aware, very much aware, of the economic problems. He's introduced a series of revenue measures the effect of which has been to reduce demand pressures significantly. And he has, I think, also been the leader in a very considerable degree of flexibility toward the problems of a political settlement that's taken place here, <u>and</u> has brought the people along with him. This was evident in the situation that developed in October–November when the bombing was stopped on November 1st here and the Vietnamese did <u>not</u> go to Paris with us, which caused concern and pain. I think there's no question that they were playing our elections, but also there was the fact that we tried to push them faster than they could go. We had dealt only with the chief of government, and when they wanted to act almost within the question of hours and he had to consult his security council and others, it was a completely new ball game for them. Obviously they were not ready for it, and it took time. It took nearly a month, but I think the result was that he gained support. The Vietnamese went to Paris stronger, in better shape, than they would have gone otherwise, and with a more unified country behind them. He said to me, not long ago, 'Eight or nine months ago all one could talk about here was a military victory. Now you can talk about peace and negotiations.' He said, 'I said three years ago the time will come when we can take some bacteria into our system, and we're approaching that period.' Now, the fact that people are speaking out loud about the problems of dealing with the [National Liberation] Front, and the problems of the <u>kind</u> of political settlement that may be needed here, is an indication of growing confidence."

BUNKER: "Thieu is fully aware of the importance of <u>our</u> public opinion, and the need, of course, for our support. But he <u>cannot</u> move at the pace that would satisfy our opinion if by doing so he loses the support of his own people, and this was the problem of October–November. And it's a problem we frequently run into—the two time clocks not being synchronized. The question now is, I think, where do we stand now?"

BUNKER: "First, as to the progress of the war, the continuous and heavy pressures that we've kept on the enemy, both in the military aspect of the war and in pacification, have frustrated his objectives and brought him increasing problems. Both our own and ARVN forces are operating deep in enemy base areas. . . . He suffered heavy manpower losses. Even in the lull, so-called lull, here before he started his attacks, his losses were running well over 2,000 a week, not counting Chieu Hoi, not counting the infrastructure neutralized, not counting died of wounds and other losses as well. So they were running at a <u>very</u> heavy rate, even then. He is, therefore, suffering heavy manpower losses. And he has found recruitment in South Vietnam increasingly difficult, which accounts for the fact that this has become more and more a North Vietnamese war. In fact, most Viet Cong units are made up largely of North Vietnamese personnel. The indications of his morale problems are increasing. Again as Ambassador Colby mentioned, the Chieu Hoi rates are up very significantly."

BUNKER: "I don't want to leave the impression that he has no remaining assets. He's still able to infiltrate regular forces, mainly through Laos, supply them through Laos and Cambodia, continues to be supplied by the Soviets and Chinese with a wide range of the most sophisticated weapons and so is still a military force to be reckoned with, and has a variety of options open to him."

"Thieu's view, expressed to me a few days ago, was that he would be unable to sustain the rate of the last week for much more than a week or a little more, but he'd stop to catch his breath and start over again and there'd be a second, third, or fourth phase. And the shelling of Saigon would probably continue. His objective was political. It would have no militarily effective consequences. His view is that this may continue for several months, but that in the end the enemy really has to negotiate seriously. Whether that's so or not, I don't know, but I'm quoting Thieu's view of this."

BUNKER: "As I said, the current offensive has gained nothing for the enemy militarily, and he must, I think, have known this before he started. And the real target of the offensive is political and psychological—psychological effect on American opinion, and on the Paris talks, to prove the bombing halt is unconditional, to raise the morale of his own forces, to convey an impression of strength, and our own ineffectiveness . . . , to try to create divisions between us and the Vietnamese, and I think to test out the new administration."

BUNKER: "My feeling is that Hanoi and the Front have come to Paris for a number of reasons. One, the expectation that they can capitalize on impatience in the United States, and because of that we will put pressure on our allies to make concessions which will put them on the road to an eventual takeover here." Second, they realize "time is now running against them."

BUNKER: "He said he'd accept no conditions for a bombing halt, although that's exactly what he did—even though they were 'understandings,' and even though he's violated them."

BUNKER: "The key word is patience."

■ ■ ■

At another session, the topic of U.S. troop withdrawals is discussed.

WHEELER: "What are you talking about in terms of reductions?"

BRIEFER: "We have not addressed a specific figure in this study." "This was purely to determine the conditions that would or would not permit a reduction."

LAIRD: "If we're going to protect what's been going on here and at least be in a position where we at least accomplish what our objective is, I would think those force levels [for redeployment] would be a matter that we [rather than the Vietnamese] would have to make the determination on."

ABRAMS: "Those figures didn't come from us."

LAIRD (re U.S. withdrawal planning): "This is something we asked the Joint Chiefs to get into last week, so you'll probably be hearing more about it."

WHEELER (to Abrams): "You've already heard about it. We discussed this quietly some time ago."

ABRAMS: "Yeah."

WHEELER: "The point is that, it seems to me, that the only person who's in a position, really, to match the performance of the ARVN—hopefully the improved performance of the ARVN—and the capability for the reduction in U.S. troops presence here, by type of unit, and by number of people, so that there will be no diminution in combat capability, is General Abrams."

WHEELER: "I question, myself, whether it's possible, and I even question whether it's necessary or desirable, that the residual force should be entirely in the spitting image of the American armed forces. Now, we're still not planning on turning out a force here which is going to have the capability to stand up to a sizable attack by North Vietnamese forces. This is for in-country, like a fairly high level of guerrilla-type activity. While all this fancy stuff [sensors, computers] is desirable, the things that are absolutely fundamental are mobility, which they must have, firepower which exceeds that of the enemy, and intelligence. A lot of the intelligence, at least in my judgment, they're not going to get out of sensors and things like that—they're going to get out of in-country human resources."

LAIRD: "Don't you have to plan, though, that you don't get any settlement in Paris?"

GOODPASTER: "That's the assumption this analysis was based on."

WHEELER: "The Chiefs postulated three possibilities. One where you get essentially nothing out of the negotiations. Second, that you get the best of all possible settlements. And the third, which we consider to be probably the most realistic, is in between the two . . . where you achieve a part of your objective. But one of the problems is, if you get nothing out of the peace settlement, you're talking about a really terrific bill in terms of dollars worth of equipment. You're also talking about a great deal of time to train the kinds of units, and to provide the types of sophisticated equipment, that would permit these little fellows to stand up to the North Vietnamese."

LAIRD: "Of course, I think the worst thing you could get out of Paris is an acceptance of Manila, and get out of here in six months. I don't understand why the North Vietnamese don't take that and run."

WHEELER: "Well, we've always been afraid that they might someday wake up to the fact that they've got us in that box and grab it. But they've never been smart enough to yet, and I don't quite understand why, either."

LAIRD: "I would rather have a program that got out of here in 24 [months, as compared to a 6-month deadline for pulling out U.S. forces] or something like that. . . ." "If you showed that kind of orderly progress, you could sell it at home."

■ ■ ■

At another session Ambassador Colby discussed pacification.

COLBY: "The teams have been divided this year so that they can concentrate a bit more on political development work and a bit less on the paramilitary work that they were, for a couple of years, forced to engage in by the situation."

COLBY: "During last year there were some 25 province chiefs who were changed." Intensive effort to upgrade the leadership. "About 22 were changed because they were either inefficient or corrupt. We know it because we helped comment on them. Last year there were about 170 district chiefs changed, and about 90 of those we helped comment on. So the government has a rather intense desire to try to upgrade, and they will accept American advice on the performance of these people."

COLBY: "Over the past several years some 4 million people have gone through refugee status. That's an awful high percentage of a population of 17 million. Last year about a million people were thrown out of their homes, put into a refugee status, as a result of the Tet and May offensives. They were taken care of. They were given some form of temporary care. They were given some form of help to get themselves reestablished." Now: 1.3 million refugees, of whom 680,000 are in I Corps. "The government had no refugee service at all in 1966." In 1967 it developed a ministry. In about May 1968 a new minister took over. Now there is "heavy emphasis on resettlement, and on return to villages." "During the year 1968 about 250,000 people were returned to their own villages." "This is the major thrust of the effort now, to try to get them to return to their own villages where it is secure to do so."

COLBY: In 1968 the government had a goal (before the Tet Offensive) of planting 40,000 hectares of IR-8 ("miracle" rice). After the offensive, although they were pessimistic, they didn't change the goal. At the end of the year, 44,000 hectares had been planted.

A hectare is approximately 2.5 acres.

COLBY: "Their [GVN] contribution to their own military budget has gone up by leaps and bounds over the past few years, so that our percentage to their military budget has gone down considerably."

COLBY: "You can't conduct pacification in the face of a North Vietnamese division. But if you don't conduct pacification after you've knocked that division out, then he resets his 'system'—what General Abrams calls his 'system'—and he comes back. So that behind this success on a military scale you are able to develop a pacification program, and this pacification program—as seen by all the measurements—has been quite successful." The result is that local officials "began to see that maybe this war isn't eternal." Pacification "depends very heavily upon the leadership and effort and energy that the president [Thieu] has put into it."

COLBY (re vulnerabilities): "There is a war weariness, there's no question about it. People are tired of it, and they wish it would be over."

COLBY: "The infrastructure [VCI] is still with us, and there's a lot of work to be done."

COLBY: "We believe that continuation of this kind of an effort can result in a stronger Vietnam that can face the VC, although maybe not the NVA, in the future."

■ ■ ■

Briefing on RVNAF I&M (Republic of Vietnam Armed Forces Improvement & Modernization).

COLONEL GALLOWAY (MACV Assistant Chief of Staff for Military Assistance): "Over the past six months there has been greatly increased emphasis on this task" of preparing RVNAF to assume a greater share of the burden in military operations. Phase I force structure was approved October 1968 and Phase II in December 1968. A Phase II Accelerated Plan, approved 18 December 1968, gives the army additional armor, artillery, and logistics units, and also provides increases for the VNAF and VNN.

GALLOWAY: "The 855,000 figure represents the estimated level of RVNAF that can be sustained over a period of years by the Republic of Vietnam manpower base."

GALLOWAY: "Initially the Phase II plan emphasized fighting strength and was designed with an austere logistics structure. The Accelerated Phase II plan proposed additional logistical units to provide a greater degree of self-sufficiency."

■ ■ ■

Discussion of MACV's approach to conduct of the war.

ABRAMS (on "how we try to run things here"): "The first thing we do here is to set priorities—priorities for the use of resources, resources of units, firepower, that sort of thing. In fact, all of our efforts are governed by this priority system. Our first priority is this area in here [showing on map]—it's around the capital. It's also President Thieu's first priority. It's the seat of government. It's the most important part in terms of stability of the government and that sort of thing. We handle it as a no-risk area. Anything it needs, it <u>gets</u>—in the way of security and that sort of thing."

ABRAMS: "Our second priority has been, and is, the I Corps area. And this has been, for <u>most</u> of the time, the enemy has kept—either <u>in</u> I Corps or in Laos and above the DMZ—major enemy forces. And this has required us to keep major commitments up there in order to assure the security of I Corps. And then the third priority area is the highlands. We've distributed our forces in accordance with this, and as far as the basic ground forces are concerned, both ours and the Vietnamese and the Free World, they pretty much have stayed in the same areas. For the last half of the year that whole Airborne Division has stayed in here in the III Corps area. Three or four of the marine battalions [are there], and two of the marine battalions have been down in the delta."

ABRAMS: "There was a time when the airborne battalions used to be loaned out to the corps for various reasons, but since this has become the enemy's number one priority—it's the president's number one priority, it's <u>my</u> number one priority—the Airborne Division has fought in III Corps, and it's done well. Now we have made some changes. Toward the end of October, because the enemy had withdrawn substantial forces out of I Corps, and because the enemy had reinforced with substantial forces down here in III Corps, we moved the 1st Cavalry Division from northern I Corps down to III Corps. That was an interesting move. We decided to do that one Saturday evening, and we began the movement on Monday morning. And by Thursday the first elements were in combat in contact, out here near the Cambodian border. This is a real team here. Seventh Fleet, MSTS, MAC, Seventh Air Force, everybody pitched in. The job that had to be done took 15 days. We moved everything the 1st Cavalry had down here in 15 days, including their war trophies."

ABRAMS: "The delta has always been a little short on forces. About the first of December we moved five helicopter companies and two air cav troops in there. Before that we had pretty well solidified seven battalions of the 9th Division down there. The purpose of these helicopters was to give the three ARVN divisions down there in the delta a lot more capability of getting out on offensive operations. It meant, by doing this, that every division down there could have helicopters every day, or six out of the seven days a week. It's produced good results, and it <u>has</u> made a lot of difference in the operations of those three divisions that I think has contributed to the progress they've made down in the delta. Other than that, those shifts of forces, everything stays pretty much in the same corps area."

ABRAMS (re allocation of tac air by corps): "That determination is made here. We review it every Saturday, after going over the intelligence, the way the operations have been going, then we come up with the allocation of tac air for the coming week, or a portion of it [the tac air], and the rest of it is retained on sort of an on-call basis. Same thing with the B-52s."

ABRAMS: "About the 20th of December [1968], we thought there was going to be an offensive in III Corps, so the weight of B-52s was switched into III Corps, and it went down [decreased] in Laos. Then we went back up—this is all pressing the interdiction effort, working on the choke points over there in Laos, and on the storage areas." "As General Wheeler has pointed out before, this is my reserve. And that's the way I use it. And really the tac air in-country is used the same way. It's also a part of the reason why I have never felt any lack of confidence in whether or not we had sufficient forces here to handle the problem. As each of these offensives have approached, they've been reported in advance as coming, and we've always given assurance that we can handle it. And part of the assurance is to have a powerful weapon like this. If General Davidson has made some miscalculation in his intelligence—although I don't encourage that—I've still got a couple of tickets to play."

ABRAMS: "General Davidson described the enemy system to you—his logistics system, the VCI, the guerrilla, the whole enemy system. Well, on our side we're trying to work against the system—and the total system. We're trying over there in Laos to work on his logistics as it comes down there. We know we're never going to get it all. In-country—this chart here shows the caches that were discovered in-country in January and February of this year." "He's got a logistics nose and not a logistics tail. So before he brings the 5th Division, or the 7th Division, down here, the initial step is to position the food, the ammunition, the extra weapons, and that sort of thing in caches down to where he's going to finally engage in the fight. This is generally described—while he's doing this—is generally described by the press as a 'lull.' It's not a lull. It's a period of intensive activity on the part of the enemy—bringing it down on the bicycles, oxcarts, and so on, digging bunkers for it and so on. So, if you're going to handle the offensive, you've got to go into a period of intense activity, too. It is no lull. And you've got to get out there and get in his system—find his caches, ambush his parties that are carrying it, get his rice, and so on. The more successful you are at that—. You may not succeed in stopping the attack, but it will influence how long it can be sustained or the strength with which it can be jumped off."

ABRAMS (showing a list of cache contents): "Look at this—1,062 tons of rice! What is that—how many divisions? [Someone: "About five and a half divisions for a month."] That's rice for five and a half divisions for a month. Now these fellows have to eat, and if you get that—now they can get more, but it's going to take them another 10 days, another two weeks, to get that amount of rice back in again. And it means that they can't start moving the troops until they get it back in again."

ABRAMS: "We preach it as 'one war,' just one war. Keep it down to one war. All of the enemy on that side, and all of us on this side. And when we say all of us, we mean all of the army, all of the navy, all the air, all the Vietnamese. We mean the province chief and the district chief, the RF and the PF and the Provincial Reconnaissance Units and the police. Everybody in here has got to work together. And of course, being human beings and belonging to different segments and different strata, this doesn't come easy." "So out here, an American battalion that's operating in one of these districts, he's got to have people permanently with the district chief so that they can talk with the U.S. district advisor, they can talk with the district chief, so the things that the Americans do complement, support, what the district forces or the provincial forces are doing." "The American units shouldn't do anything, really, in the way of operating that the district advisor isn't in on, doesn't know about. If it isn't that way, you're not going to get the most effectiveness out of what you've got." "This is really a complex environment to work in."

ABRAMS: (describing the 9th Marines operating against the enemy system): Twelve 122-mm guns seized from caches. Enemy down Route 922 to Route 548 to BA 611. Over 7,000 artillery rounds, almost 5,000 120-mm mortar rounds. 33,000 60-mm mortar rounds. 23,000 82-mm mortar rounds. "This amount that had run the gauntlet through Mu Gia or Ban Karai, around the interdiction points and through Tchepone down into Base Area 610 and finally got over here . . . then the Marines and the 2nd ARVN came in here and got it. I would just say in passing that's a good way to reduce casualties. This amount of stuff will cause a lot of casualties."

ABRAMS: "In his way of doing things, he [the enemy] really has to have a base area like this if he's going to project military strength, military power, against Danang." "That's where he can store things, that's where he can put up a dispensary, that's a thing that he can withdraw to. It's generally well bunkered, sometimes concrete, and where he's got protection from air and artillery and so on. It's a place he can rest, it's a place he can hide, it's a place he can store the supplies he needs. In his system, it's too long a run to try to do it from Laos all the way to Danang."

ABRAMS (re move of 1st Cavalry Division to III Corps): "And it commenced to work against these divisions that were moving down toward Saigon. The 5th Division, I guess, began its movement about the middle of November—initiated it. They [friendly forces] knew they were coming—got prisoners and this sort of thing. They came down the border between Vinh Long and Phuoc Long. It took them almost three months to get from the Cambodian border down to War Zone D. All that time about five battalions of the 1st Cav were working on them. They got a big hospital out of there, they got caches out of there, they ambushed them, they put B-52s on them, tac air, artillery. But they made it to War Zone D. Then General Kerwin maneuvered a brigade of the Cav around between the 5th Division and Bien Hoa, on the edge of War Zone D. Then one of the things that happened, they—the 174 came across the Dong Nai just where it was supposed to and the 1st Cav brought the artillery in on it. And that scattered them. They never participated in the attack. But what finally wound up, out of the 5th Division—what did they have, five regiments, four regiments?—[Davidson: "They had four, plus the 274th, total of five."] so there was a battalion of the 274 and one battalion of the 275—1st and 3rd—three battalions out of the five regiments ever got into the thing."

WHEELER (responding to a Laird question about measuring the effects of preemption in casualties averted): "You take an attack [Bien Hoa] by three understrength battalions and postulate that it <u>might</u> have been made by five full-strength regiments—we might not only have suffered a severe defeat, rather than <u>them</u> to suffer a severe defeat, it's entirely conceivable that they could have overrun the Bien Hoa airfield and the logistic complex there and given us, I would say, a major disaster."

ABRAMS: "That cost us 178 men. That's the <u>price</u>, that's the <u>real</u> price, of that whole operation. What would it have been if they'd gotten that stuff down to Danang? That's kind of an imponderable."

ABRAMS: "None of this is an easy job, and we can't put out guarantees."

BUNKER: "I think we've <u>had</u> a good measure of success. I believe we're making steady progress, gradually achieving our objectives here, and if we stick with it—I've never looked at this as a short-term proposition—I'm confident that we'll have reasonable success in achieving our objectives."

BUNKER: "I think the most important yardstick by which to measure progress is not so much what <u>we</u> can do, but what the Vietnamese can do for themselves. I think if one applies this standard of measurement, I think it's fair to say that not only has progress been made, but that it is continuing at an accelerated pace. This has been true especially in pacification, which embraces so many aspects of our total effort here. It's been evident in the military situation. The Vietnamese government has reiterated its determination to assume an increasingly larger share of the war effort, and is adjusting to the possibility of reductions in American forces in the future." Refers to "the generally recognized forthcoming political contest with the Communists."

15 MAR 1969: WIEU

Attendees: Gen. Abrams, Gen. Goodpaster, Amb. Colby, Gen. Brown, LTG Mildren, VADM Zumwalt, Dr. Wikner, MG Wetherill, MG Conroy, MG Townsend, MG Shaefer, MG Davidson, MG Rasmussen, BG Frizen, BG Long, BG Wheelock, BG Clay, BG Keegan, BG Potts, Col. Davis, Col. Cavanaugh, Col. Hill, Col. Powers.

ABRAMS: "This is a hell of a note. Somebody's taken the cigars out of my box." [Laughter]

SOMEONE: "A new record at the WIEU."

ABRAMS: "I picked this up [apparently referring to an empty cigar tube] out of a box that just came from Hong Kong yesterday."

ABRAMS (to Davidson re reduction in enemy truck traffic): "Let's be careful that we don't sound some hopeful note in this."

DAVIDSON: "Oh, no, sir. I'm never <u>hopeful</u>, sir."

ABRAMS: "We have to maintain the standards here, Phil."

ABRAMS (re enemy fear of invasion or resumed bombing of North Vietnam): "See, they sit around in <u>their</u> WIEU up there, once a week or so. . . . They laid this on—they knew what was going to happen. Well, it hasn't happened. Kind of being like us. You know, we got the 22–23 February thing sort of tacked down in here. And that's what happened. But suppose it didn't. We'd commence to wonder what kind of dope you [Davidson] had. I wonder if they commence to wonder. I mean, if they take a lot of measures like this—the redeploying aircraft, and hold up on their shipping. These are positive steps. And didn't—turns out it wasn't necessary. Well—we were ready. But somehow I don't think that'll be good enough." "Oh, oh, oh, oh! Actually, it's great!"

ABRAMS: "Someone advanced the idea that the bombing of the north turned out to be the political Achilles' heel of the Johnson administration. And what they wanted to do was get the Nixon administration wrapped around that same axle, as soon as possible. It's kind of heady stuff to be dreaming around here. You see, they knew what they were doing to the understanding. That's what this means, one thing it means—they knew."

■ ■ ■

Discussion of the enemy logistics and infiltration apparatus.

BRIEFER: "Sir, pursuant to your requirement, we've made a study of the entire logistics system of the enemy in an attempt to find the vulnerabilities and how best to get at it."

■ The system is controlled by the General Directorate of Rear Services (GDRS) in Hanoi. It is administered by a Commo-Liaison Bureau through a series of military stations, or *binh trams,* which in turn control T-stations for personnel infiltration and K-facilities for permanent supply warehouses. The 559th Transportation Group, with its own *binh trams,* operates in Laos directly under GDRS. "The system of *binh trams* stretches from Hanoi through North Vietnam and Laos to the tri-border area." The means of transportation include road, rail, pipeline, inland waterway, and ocean transport. Originally the routes ran through the Mu Gia and Ban Karai Passes into Laos. Now they have opened up Na Be, so there are three major access routes. Traffic moves southward by surges, mostly by truck. 559th Headquarters is in Base Area 604. Each *binh tram* has operational control over all antiaircraft, transportation, medical and engineer units operating in its area of responsibility, and the associated commo-liaison stations.

■ Binh Tram 4 serves Base Area 610. BA 611 and BA 607 in the A Shau Valley are served by Binh Tram 42. "There are approximately 40,000 people involved in the 559th's operations." BA 611 feeds MR-TTH. The enemy supplies MR-1 and MR-2 from the north, the rest via Cambodia using Sihanoukville. "Almost the entire Cambodian–South Vietnamese border area is one continuous staging area."

■ "There is no connected and developed road network from north to south of Base Area 609 to Base Area 702 and southward. Instead, the flow of supplies in Cambodia is basically from west to east." "Food can generally be obtained by tactical units from within their areas of operation" in IV Corps.

■ Turning to "examination of those specific areas the destruction of which, or neutralization of which, would most affect the enemy's war effort in South

Vietnam. We have eliminated several of the areas south and west of Base Area 353, including Base Areas 704, 354, and 707, due to sizable concentrations of Cambodian civil or military population." BA 604, centered approximately 45 kilometers from the South Vietnamese border, "is the base area most vital to the enemy's logistical system in the Lao panhandle." "Four major roads and three water routes converge in the area." Estimated stockpiles there are on the order of several thousand tons. At least 19 AA and 3 AW sites currently furnish protection for the area, which includes numerous truck parks and storage areas and is situated among rugged hills and mountains interrupted by several large river valleys. Average annual rainfall there is 80–100."

■ Another vulnerable point is BA 610, centered on the junction of Routes 92 and 922 within 15 kilometers of the South Vietnamese border. It contains an estimated 800 tons of stockpiled supplies. "The recent success of Operation Dewey Canyon in a portion of Base Area 611 indicates the value of this area to the enemy." Hundreds of tons of ammunition were captured, plus heavy artillery pieces. Astride the South Vietnamese border. "Its area hosts more enemy troops for in-country operations than any other within Laos."

■ BA 609 and BA 613 are in the tri-border area. The 40th Artillery Regiment of 1,500 men is in BA 609. Recent attacks including PT-76 tanks against the CIDG camp at Ben Het probably originated in BA 609.

■ "Of all the base areas in Cambodia, the complex formed by Base Areas 352 and 353 is the most important." It houses the largest troop concentration of all the areas considered. Headquarters COSVN is there, and also Headquarters of the National Liberation Front. An estimated 182 tons of ordnance are shipped into BA 353 monthly, and several hospitals are there. "Neutralization of this complex would probably have the most immediate effect upon the conflict, certainly in III Corps."

■ "Ground operations will not be easy in any of them." Weather conditions deteriorate beginning in May. "Neutralization or destruction of the command and control facility, particularly COSVN, in the base areas in Cambodia would have the most immediate effect upon the enemy's operations in South Vietnam." But destruction of logistical facilities in Laos would provide greater long-term effect than similar in Cambodia. In Cambodia "there is no one point, short of Sihanoukville, to stop the flow of arms and ammunition." "Perhaps most importantly, the effective application of friendly power in almost any of these areas would have a profound effect on the enemy's concept of operations. He could no longer feel safe from either ground or air operations. This would undoubtedly provoke a reassessment of his strategy, and cause him enormous efforts in realigning his routes of communication."

■ "Our recommendations for priorities in considering operations against the base areas would be, in Laos, first priority to Base Area 604, and second to Base Area 610; in Cambodia, first priority goes to the Base Area 352/353 complex, followed by Base Area 702, with Base Areas 367 and 706 as possibilities under certain circumstances. One other target, the Base Area 613/609 complex, also merits consideration."

BROWN: "If we can jump to Laos for a minute, 604—the Chairman, when he was here, passed me a note up there at the meeting, asked me why we didn't put Arc Lights in there. I wrote him back that we had when we could get the targets validated through Vientiane. And he said he wanted to talk about it at the lunch. Well, we didn't have the opportunity, so I fixed him up a folder in which we plotted all of the Arc Light boxes in that complex that we had prepared and sent over here and been validated here, gone to Vientiane. Those that were approved, we hit, counting all the sorties that went in, and those we were denied. And it's a pretty revealing picture. Vientiane's got the idea that the 604-Tchepone area is a—is populated by a bunch of good, stout Lao [Someone: "patriots."]—that's right, and we shouldn't be bombing up there." "Our problem here is Vientiane. That gets us back to the basic problem again of responsibility."

ZUMWALT: "If you're going to go into any of those Cambodian areas, I'd sure like to underline the importance of . . . trying at the same time to blockade or quarantine Sihanoukville so you cut the pipeline at both ends."

BRIEFER: "This week a program was initiated which uses F-4 aircraft armed with CBUs to strike along the roads in areas where past experience has indicated the presence of lucrative truck parks and storage depots. This same tactic was used previously in North Vietnam, with very good results." "For the week ending 11 March there were 2,994 secondary explosions and fires in the Laos panhandle."

ABRAMS: "Yeah, but didn't you have one where you got a fire going—?"

SOMEONE: "Yes, a brush fire got going and apparently spread into an ammo storage area."

ABRAMS: "Of course, it's good. I mean, I'm not—." [Laughter]

SOMEONE: "Not very good marksmanship, but still effective."

■ ■ ■

COLBY: "I'm going around with Minister [General] Khiem on another interesting series of visits. He just was named as deputy prime minister for pacification, you know . . . going around to each of the corps. He is a very impatient gentleman, indeed, with the canned briefing—stops it off at about five minutes and throws most of the people out of the room, then sits down with about half a dozen people and just sort of discusses what the problems are." Did III and IV Corps yesterday, and will do I and II Corps on Tuesday. "He's looking for a way to really activate the corps commanders in this area."

ABRAMS: "Of course I know it's a very distasteful thing, but one way to simplify it is put them in command." Colby mentions coordinating authority.

ABRAMS: "Yeah, but somebody's got to sit there and call the balls and strikes, and say 'You're out!' I mean, it takes a lot to pull this thing together. And of course that is no—that doesn't solve everything." "Lam pretty much does this up in I Corps. He's the one that calls it."

GOODPASTER (to Colby): "What's your sense of whether the pacification program is moving, keeping up its momentum?"

COLBY: "Well, it certainly did suffer a pause here during February. The pause was for a variety of reasons. One was that the national budget was held up, and so nobody could get at their '69 money. . . . Secondly, the sense of completion of the APC—the pat on the back, you know, and the feeling, 'Well, the goals now are sort of a long ways ahead.' And thirdly, this reorganization and the appointment of the deputy prime minister, which has been about three weeks in the making . . . and of course Tet itself. That was a time to take a few days off. And the attacks—the enemy attacks have had a very minor effect." Thirty-six provinces respond to query with "no impact at all." One "stalled" and two "set back." Only "23 RD teams withdrawn, so very tiny impact."

ABRAMS (re Khiem): "He's a no-nonsense fellow."

ABRAMS: "Today I think is Hank's [Rasmussen, the J-4] last WIEU."

RASMUSSEN: "Yes, sir. It's the 73rd one I've been to."

ABRAMS: "Well, we're going to miss you, Hank, as we've said before."

RASMUSSEN: "I wouldn't turn my job over to just anybody, but with General Conroy coming in I think it's going to be in good hands."

ABRAMS: "This is also General Potts's and General Conroy's first WIEU, I think. You're probably [to Potts] sitting in the most comfortable chair [you're ever going to occupy here]—. When you get down in that one [the J-2's], the complexion of this whole thing changes." [Laughter]

DAVIDSON: "Drastically!"

ABRAMS: "Good to have you here."

16 MAR 1969: Commanders Conference

There is a problem with dating this item. It is shown on the tape box as recorded 16 March 1970, whereas the material on the tape seems to indicate that it should have been dated 1969. Based on internal evidence it has been given the earlier date.

Ambassador Bunker is present. Abrams tells him that General Nickerson has just returned to Vietnam, scheduled to be General Cushman's replacement, having previously served as Cushman's deputy and as Commander, 1st Marine Division. Since Gen. Herman Nickerson Jr. returned to Vietnam in March 1969, that seems to validate dating the tape in 1969, as does the fact that the session begins with presentation of the same briefing given at the 15 March 1969 WIEU.

ABRAMS: "I might explain a little bit about why we got after this. We've got the talks going on in Paris. We've got the pressures at home of various kinds and degrees on our own government. Out here, we've got our program for '69—pacification, with all of its objectives; the expansion and modernization of the RVNAF, strengthen it so that, between these two programs, the armed forces and the government of South Vietnam will be more capable of handling their own affairs."

ABRAMS: "Now, the enemy has continued his infiltration from North Vietnam, through Laos, into South Vietnam. His infiltration in December was substantial, and it continues at a rate, as we see it through June, that would support the general level of activity that's been going on over the last three or four months.

His logistical efforts in Laos since the bombing halt and the weather change have been <u>prodigious</u>. He has made a <u>fantastic</u> effort to keep his routes open and to move his supplies from North Vietnam, down through Laos, into those base areas we've been talking about."

ABRAMS: "So one comes to the question, then—if he continues like <u>he</u> is, and we continue like <u>we</u> are, what is going to be the <u>picture</u> at the end of '69? And, sort of taking it by the seat of the pants and looking at it, is there anything else that we could add to our program that could substantially change the course of events? General Goodpaster has suggested that the enemy has placed himself in a position of strategic risk by <u>counting</u> on our observance of the borders of Laos and Cambodia. Well, anyway, it's in the context of all of this that this work was initiated. And it's kind of in the context of that that we'd like everyone here today to express their views and thoughts. We have not presented a <u>plan</u> here. This—we're in the exploratory part of this."

BUNKER: "How long can the enemy maintain the current recent level of activity?"

ABRAMS: "You put your finger on a place where I hedged—I said activity over the past <u>several</u> months. It's my impression that the activity we've had since the 22nd of February cannot really be sustained from the infiltration that we've seen."

BUNKER: "I figured out before the secretary's visit the rate of loss, <u>prior</u> to the present activity. If you take the KIA, plus defections, plus infrastructure, his losses average 3,500 a week—approximately. That's 182,000 a year, without died of wounds or disease or anything else. That's a pretty high rate, even at that level of activity everybody considered a 'lull.' It wasn't much of a lull as far as the <u>enemy</u> was concerned, I would say. And then, of course, it more than doubled. So it seems to me that, even at that lower level of activity, he's suffered very heavy losses."

DAVIDSON: "For the year 1968 his total losses ran out at about 289,000. However, his infiltration, and his recruitment, strangely enough seemed to come out just about that way. As a matter of fact, we figured a net gain in 1968 of about 6,000."

BUNKER: "That means that he's <u>depleting</u> his manpower reserve, and this is a pretty heavy rate."

DAVIDSON: "This is a key question, and one that we have no means of obtaining the answer to here, sir. However, the national intelligence agencies have made the forecast that he could continue his infiltration—and his recruitment at a decreasing scale—but his infiltration at the same rate he used last year, at the same rate for several years."

Abrams invites comments.

SOMEONE: "Well, I think it would be a dream come true if we could get over there into [Base Areas] 604 and 610. We'd laid forth the suggestion several times. [Contemplating a U.S. operation.] I realize politically it's probably going to be difficult. There's no question the study has picked out the points most susceptible to damaging the enemy if they are destroyed as far as I Corps is concerned." It is 45 kilometers to Base Area 604 from the border. "It's no—with an LSA at Khe Sanh—it's no farther a reach than we've just accomplished in Dewey Canyon, from Vandegrift down to the border."

ABRAMS: "That's very interesting."

SAME: "And we proved that, without even having an air cav division, you could have that reach—once you have neutralized the air corridor so that you can wheel the choppers down that corridor." "General Davis and I watched that weather on the Khe Sanh Plateau every day since last June."

SOMEONE: How have you "worked over 604 and 610 with B-52s?"

ABRAMS: "Well, 604 is a problem for us. All of these things over there have to be approved by the—ah, Vientiane. And they've been mesmerized over there by the patriotic and loyal Laotian peasantry that's living and habitating in 604. And consequently our use of the B-52 in there has been seriously curtailed. 610 we have hit quite significantly with B-52s. I'm in the process of raising this matter again of 604, because it's clearly of such strategic significance to the whole system in Laos that we've just got to get the authority."

The Vientiane reference is to U.S. Ambassador Sullivan's reluctance to approve air operations in Laos.

DAVIDSON: "If we took out 604, they might attempt to supply the entire country through Cambodia."

BUNKER: "It does seem to me this would have the maximum effect of anything you could do on Paris."

ABRAMS: "That's right, sir, and it's hard to see how they're going to get them out of these places over in Paris."

BUNKER: "Exactly. I think they went to Paris, among other things, because they realized that time is running against them now. Something like this, where you could set them back months, I think might have a very decisive effect on the Paris situation."

ABRAMS (to Kerwin, re BA 367/706): "The only way we can get in there is by helicopter because of that stuff that you put in there—you and George put in there."

KERWIN: "That's right." The Viet Cong maintain a band along the edge of the Parrot's Beak from which Cambodians are excluded. To get the Fishhook, we would get in behind him and sweep outward (toward South Vietnam).

NICKERSON: "I'm a little new to make any offerings, General Abrams, except that if you're going to consider this from an overall viewpoint, it seems to me an amphibious envelopment is much more productive, going into North Vietnam, for results. . . . But I know you're constrained."

ABRAMS: "Well, I don't know. I think that's open to question. The basic thing is that this whole thing is being supported out of Laos and Cambodia. And what we're talking about here is trying to strike a blow of strategic significance to his system, and cause a rethinking of the whole problem. And I don't think the amphibious envelopment would accomplish that. I mean, at <u>least</u> to the same degree."

EWELL: "It's not clear to me whether you're talking about a raid where you scrape out the area and get out or whether you occupy it. The dislocation in time of his system would seem quite different."

ABRAMS: "Well, we really haven't settled on anything like that. I've thought that a month, as a minimum, in one of these areas would be required to really police it up."

BUNKER: "It seems to me the psychological effect could be very material. And, as I say, I think the effect on the Paris talks could be very important. The enemy's present offensive—his objectives are political, essentially, and psychological, more than military. He must realize that he can't succeed militarily, obviously—<u>hasn't</u> been able to, and <u>can't</u>. The objective is, the <u>target</u> is, American opinion, in hopes—and it's already had some result, as you see, Senator Fulbright has already sounded off, despite this six-month truce he was going to give the new administration. So has the *New York Times*—got panicky, the first week's casualties. And this is his objective."

EWELL: "The safest signal is in the Fishhook."

ABRAMS: "You [Ewell] say you don't know what permission we've got. Well, let me clear up that point. We have gotten absolutely no change in any of the rules of engagement—<u>none</u>. This [the study] is an in-house affair. And while I'm talking about that, I might say everyone in this room has just got to be sworn to absolute secrecy on this. You just can't <u>talk</u> about it. The press already is suspicious of things, and you're just not going to be able to let this out to anybody. If that happens, all the other pressures will develop, and then you haven't got a chance. It isn't just a question of observing the rules of security. Anybody that talks about this is putting the whole damn <u>thing</u> in jeopardy, and everything that everybody's trying to do here. So it's a <u>very</u> <u>serious</u> matter."

SOMEONE: "I might say that Mr. Fried called up the day before yesterday—*New York Daily News*—and said that he'd heard we were moving slowly into the Fishhook. Wanted to know if this was true."

ABRAMS: "That's exactly the environment we're working in. My point is, no one can stop the press from speculating, but <u>no</u> <u>one</u> is going to authenticate any of their speculation by <u>any</u> <u>indication</u> <u>whatsoever</u>. Let them run wild on their speculation. They'll do that."

BERGER: "The effect of this would be clear on their side. They'd take very heavy casualties. There'd be very heavy destruction of equipment. They'd be psychologically unbalanced for a time, uncertain as to our future intentions. There would be certain psychological gains in South Vietnam, possibly some shifting over in the feeling that victory's coming. That's <u>one</u> side of it. The other side, we'd get heavier U.S. casualties. We'd get the other side <u>able</u>, if they want to, to reconstruct, if they want to spread it out. We don't really have a strategic success, we don't really knock them out of the war necessarily. And they can come back in 6 months, 8 months, 10 months—they have that capacity."

BERGER: "And then we've got the <u>other</u> thing, which is what is the effect in the United States? Is this going to be the end, or is this just another escalation in a new direction? Will this bring them to the conference table to talk, or will they break off the talks at the conference table? And <u>then</u> where are we? I think we should ask ourselves these questions, because these are the ones that Washington will be asking us. If they, 'Yes, fine, it will be another military success,' is this the end of it? We're as far away from getting what we want as we were before. And we've now increased. In other words, the administration will be asking, 'What can you <u>guarantee</u> us?' or 'What can you <u>assure</u> us of if you do this?' What's our answer to this question?"

COLBY (suggesting a rationale): "You are interested in <u>reducing</u> casualties by limiting the enemy's ability to continue this kind of an action forever. . . . You're engaged in a force of building RVNAF, and that it <u>does</u> look as though it's coming to a stage where they will be able to protect the country with less of an American commitment, provided you reduce the overall threat from the other side by pushing it further away, and that you therefore are doing this in order to give the RVNAF a chance to build up . . . and develop the defenses, to take over some more of the war from us. You have a short-term commitment of going in and cleaning these pirates out of the border bases . . . and just pushing them further away <u>so that</u> the war is not interminable. And if the enemy wants to negotiate, fine. If the enemy wants to continue the war, he will be in a weaker position to continue the war."

ABRAMS: "Right. And you might even go so far as to tie it to troop reductions. In other words, using as a springboard the Dewey Canyon thing where, by accident, and I <u>think</u> this is an honest statement, it was never contemplated that <u>that</u> mess of stuff would be found in the Dewey Canyon operation. It was directed down toward the head of the A Shau Valley, and we were going to get in there and find out <u>what</u> was going on, but—what did it wind up, over 500 tons? But, taking off from there, this was what he was putting in store now for the future. Now, if you're going to turn this over to the Vietnamese on a larger scale, one of the things it's incumbent on us to do is to scarf up those things so the Vietnamese will at least have a chance."

ABRAMS: "Well, I'd never want to be quoted on this, but we did make some calculations on what was gotten out of Dewey Canyon. Now assuming that he went ahead and distributed that, and fired it, then you can say that Dewey Canyon saved us—what? Five [or] six thousand in casualties. That's one of the ways of looking at Dewey Canyon—if you want to be so optimistic as to assume that he would distribute it, it all—and would <u>shoot</u> it all. That would have given us five times the casualties we've had."

GOODPASTER: "There's another point of psychological significance. We've seen that our people do not take very well the posture of Americans taking losses through day after day artillery fire coming in on them. We went through this about a year and a half ago, and I'm convinced to this day that a part of the impact the Tet attacks last year had within the United States came out of that psychology, that had been building up over the weeks ahead, where our people would just take—<u>all</u> the reporting from here was that they were just taking unending artillery fire and casualties—Khe Sanh, that kind of thing. Now this will be one of the by-products of these attacks by fire that they've been conducting here. There'll be a residue of that kind of thing, that Americans are being sent out there and they're just sitting there. The enemy chooses the time and pulls together all this ammunition to fire in on us. It's a <u>psychologically</u> better way to dispose of his ammunition to catch in the base areas and let it be expended that way rather than against us."

SOMEONE: "The country is faced with the problem of doing something. We've made lots of promises, and we've made threats, in retaliation for the border violations and the firing on the cities. And this offers an alternative to bombing."

BUNKER: "I think it's been a very excellent, very interesting morning, as far as I'm concerned. I want to say that I think the handling of this present offensive has been magnificent. As a final personal note I'd like to say that I've always hoped we could do something of this kind. I'd get a <u>personal</u> satisfaction out of it, which is very unimportant. In 1967 I suggested that we ought to go into Laos. General Westmoreland backed me up. I got my ass kicked for the suggestion, so I'd like to see this come through." [Laughter]

ABRAMS: "Now, we'll press ahead with this, and develop it. And try to develop it in the atmosphere of the kind of questions which Ambassador Berger has posed. We've got to face up to it."

22 MAR 1969: WIEU

MACV 1969 Infiltration Estimate: 63,600.

DISCUSSION: Withdrawal of 5th VC Division. Someone: "Phil, why do we call it the 5th <u>VC</u> Division if it's 75 or 80 percent NVA now?"

DAVIDSON: "All the automated intelligence data is under this term. . . . At one time there was a 5th <u>NVA</u> Division that got us all lashed up. Now, this question has arisen, to my certain knowledge, for the last 22 months. We've tried, unsuccessfully, I believe it's three times, to get this thing straightened out." "We're confused enough, generally, in the intelligence field, without confusing <u>ourselves</u> by designations and what not."

ABRAMS: "The 9th [U.S.] Division's still a <u>fantastic</u> performance. Ten killed and 727 enemy. They've sustained that all this month. I think some of that, Frank, as we were talking the other day, is the training they've got down there. Even though he takes people out, and thereby reduces the forces for operations, his <u>results</u> have gone up. His <u>own</u> killed have gone down, and the enemy killed have gone up. And he's got less force operating than he had in January. Of course, the enemy's <u>out</u>, too—that's another thing. That makes a little difference."

DISCUSSION: Increased sapper activity since 22 February: Someone: "The enemy's certainly gotten a lot of mileage out of what he's accomplished with

15 or 20 troops." "A study of these operations indicates that his success is not due entirely to the good training he's had. It's due to the fact that we've been asleep at the switch and really haven't countered in many cases—because we allow him to come back and hit the same damn areas all the time with no real change in tactics or techniques."

COLBY: "Phil [Davidson], is there another way to measure that [enemy effort in this offensive]? Because the measurement against last year, in the public relations sense, I think has had the effect of, in many cases, convincing a lot of people at home, 'My god, can they still do all that, after all that success last year?' You know, 'Are they still that strong, they can do as much as they did last year?' Then they automatically think back to the Tet situation. And I believe it was your assessment they're taking a little bit the cheaper way to do this."

DAVIDSON: "No question."

COLBY: "Whatever the numbers say, it really doesn't represent as much force on his part. Force in the moral sense, almost."

DAVIDSON: "I think we're getting into pretty difficult terrain here. In the first place, he's stronger now—. Let me reverse that—according to our calculations, he was about 6,000 men stronger before this offensive on 22–23 February than he was before Tet [1968]. So I think we could set this out very carefully to a sophisticated and professional audience, but—again, it's like the previous problem, once it gets over in Phil's [Bill's?] area [public affairs] you lose the sophistication."

SOMEONE: "No offense intended." [Laughter]

SOMEONE (Colby?): "Part of the fact is that this year our defensive forces are considerably stronger, also. You have a hundred thousand more RF and PF, and . . . 50,000 or 70,000 more ARVN, M16s all over the place, and all of that stuff."

ABRAMS: "I'm not talking about the public cosmetics of this thing right now. That's something else to be dealt with. But he is making, and has made, a prodigious effort here—greater, in my opinion, greater than Tet [1968] or May [1968]. That's my impression. Now you can say that the ground attacks are less and so on, but what that fails to analyze is what he set out to do, and what got screwed up. The 5th Division, and the—. One of the things he had at Tet last year, he got his—he got a free ride. He came sailing in across the Vam Co Dong without a goddamn glove laid on him. He came down the Saigon River without a glove being laid on him. He came down the Binh Long–Phuoc Long border without a glove laid on him. He got down there in War Zone D in good shape."

ABRAMS: "This year, or this particular offensive, the 1st and the 7th, he hasn't been able to—he took a—getting the 5th into War Zone D was a hell of a tough problem for him, and he took attrition doing it. Then after he got in War Zone D, he was really hit in there. So two or three battalions, at the most, was all that materialized out of that, and it got nailed outside the gate. So—. The other thing is the way he's hanging in here. Now this thing about defending the Michelin. That's a—we didn't have much of that. In other words, he's being pretty stiff about this. In other words, the determination, the preparations, the logistics preparations, the determination to have at it, is certainly as strong as any offensive we've seen, I think." "And the way he's firing rockets at small bases, on a wide scale, hamlets."

ZUMWALT: "He's ended up maintaining these attacks by fire with relatively small increments of rockets here and there. This leads me to raise the question, General Abrams, as to whether or not we really have the right allocation of force between those designed to pounce on him and those designed to interdict him, to keep him from getting those logistics through. I don't know the exact number of navy people I have on the Dong, for example, but it's on the order of 400. They haven't stopped the stuff, but they've taken a pretty good bite out of it. And it's hard to measure such things as these delays, and extra time marching up and down. If there were 2,500 men, instead of 400 or 500, scattered up and down that Dong, I just believe that the attrition would go way up. And I wonder if the same kind of thing is true in the areas where we don't have waterways, and whether some additional increment of force ought not to be devoted to that, to go after this supply line that he has coming in."

ABRAMS: "Well, see—we want to go ahead with the village and hamlet elections. We want to go ahead with the pacification program."

SOMEONE: "We want to keep his big forces out of the populated areas."

ABRAMS: "Right, and—now, we started out, you know, we had the whole 1st Cavalry Division up there doing nothing but working on the system. They weren't involved in pacification, they weren't involved in centers of population, they were just involved in working on the logistics system."

ZUMWALT: "We're entering an era here, in the next several months, where the availability of sensors and that kind of thing really make it possible to get a lot more payoff, to have a much more system approach to some kind of a barrier."

ABRAMS: "Well, I think you've got to be careful about that. We haven't devised a barrier yet that he can't get through or get around. But then, when he does, you've got to shift, and you've got to play this thing kind of loose."

ZUMWALT: "You have to shift, General, if you have 10 percent of your forces [word unintelligible]. Isn't there some percentage that can afford to stay there and catch him both ways, and to keep his attrition high?"

ABRAMS: "Well, we haven't found out how to do that yet."

SOMEONE (Corcoran? Kerwin?): "Plus the fact you can find all the streams very easily. You know, look at a map and you see them all. You go up in that area—western highlands, up southwest of Khe Sanh—you couldn't put half the population of the United States in that area and stop them! They can go anywhere! The most rugged area I've ever seen."

ABRAMS: "I think one of the things you've got to be careful of in here, that you don't get too proud of your screen. You've got to recognize the deficiencies of the screen. Work it, and make it as effective as you can, but recognize that he's going to get through it. And focus your intelligence so that at the point where you think he's gotten enough through to do something with, then you've got to change it, shift it to another place."

ZUMWALT: "Sir, that's [word unintelligible] the question, whether there isn't some finite, reasonably small, percentage that could stay in there, keeping that thing going."

ABRAMS: "Well, it might do some good. We've probably got a lot more of Long Binh and Bien Hoa left because they shifted that brigade of the Cav in there than they would of had they hadn't."

SOMEONE: "I'm sure that's right."

COLBY: "And if you're really going to develop a firm pacification base, and extend it, you really do need the support when he gets in close."

ABRAMS: "You look at the 1st Division, what they've done over the months of January and February and March [1969]. In terms of body count and that sort of thing it probably isn't worth a damn. They're probably one of the—ranks with the 18th [ARVN Infantry Division]."

SOMEONE: "Aw, come on now, General!" [Laughter]

ABRAMS: "No, if you just want to go to body count, but what they—but the 1st Division has stuck with the pacification program out there, and that's what they've largely been doing. And when the Tu Duc Regiment started to filter out in there, into Tu Duc, and that's kind of a classic, they—except for one prose-lyting team—no VC ever got into any of those hamlets, and they scarfed up that proselyting team because the people told them about it, that it was there."

ABRAMS: "And when the advanced elements of the Tu Duc Regiment got out in Tu Duc, the people told them about that, and they went out there and killed about 85 altogether, over a period of five or six days. And that was the end of the Tu Duc! But if that pacification battalion hadn't been there for—what?— two months, or three months, very close to three months, and gotten all this work done, gotten all that established, goddamn it we'd be back on our ass in the pacification program right now because of what the Tu Duc Regiment did to the Tu Duc District!"

COLBY: "And the other example is, if you do do your homework well, like the 101st did, then you do develop the capability of going up and beating them up up there."

ABRAMS: "That's right! But it's not only the 101st, but it's the 1st ARVN. And the whole relationship of province chiefs and district chiefs and the 1st ARVN Division and its regiments and the 101 and its brigades and battalions and so on. And that's a climate of association and cooperation and real working together that we don't have anywhere else in the country. It isn't—well, there's no good to come of trying to sort out who did the best on it. The point is that nobody up there really cares—I think. [Meaning that they're cooperating to get the job done rather than worrying about who gets the credit.] They just don't care. They're all in together, as well as all the advisors up there in the district. There isn't, as far as I can find out, there isn't a grumble coming out of an advisor on the province-district side, nor the advisors with the division—the

1st ARVN Division, or the 101 people. [Someone: "A lot of mutual respect."] That's right."

GOODPASTER (re the chart): "I'm impressed by the part of our casualties that are caused by attacks by fire. It's a considerable part. Our casualties are not so high in operations that we initiate, but the enemy's casualties are high in that. Then, the ground operations that he initiates, our KIA ratio is not as favorable in that case, although it's still quite favorable to us."

COLBY: "There's another set of figures that's revealing about the nature of this attack, and that's the number of civilian casualties, and the number of houses destroyed, which is quite a ways down, because they demonstrate the nature of the enemy's attack. There really haven't been so many of those, comparatively."

GOODPASTER: "Well, he's not in Hue, and he's not in Saigon. That's one reason those numbers are down."

24 MAR 1969: Briefing for Admiral McCain

BRIEFER (re the enemy's current offensive): Began 0200 hours on 23 February 1969. "Within the first 24 hours he struck more than 331 targets throughout the Republic. Most were attacks by fire. Targets included 39 populated areas. Saigon was hit by 10 rockets twice the first day, again by 3 on 2 March, 7 on 6 March, and 4 rockets on the 16th of March, resulting in a total of 45 civilians killed and 96 wounded." Otherwise "heavy concentration on allied military units and facilities. These were fairly evenly divided between U.S. and RVNAF targets." Also "emphasis on Vietnamese self-defense activities," including RF/PF, CIDG, and PSDF.

BRIEFER (re enemy casualties): KIA for four weeks (ending midnight 22 March 1969) are 50 percent greater than for the similar period during the Third Offensive of August 1968. Approximately the same as during the Second Offensive of May 1968. And nearly 72 percent of the 1968 Tet Offensive.

BRIEFER (re incidents): The total so far is greater than in any previous offensive. Three times the Third Offensive, and a third more than either Tet 1968 or the Second Offensive. Ground attacks: a third more than Tet 1968, double the Second Offensive, and four times the Third Offensive. Similar disparity in attacks by fire: Nearly 600 more of these standoff attacks in the current offensive than either Tet 1968 or the Second Offensive, and 1,250 more than the Third Offensive.

BRIEFER: "The current offensive—a well-coordinated and widespread effort, but one designed to be least costly to the enemy. Many small ground attacks, but relatively little significant ground action. Instead, primary reliance on attacks by fire. And these, though numerous, have been comparatively light in munitions expenditures."

BRIEFER: "The enemy did, however, have more serious intentions than he's been so far able to realize. He planned to conduct significant ground attacks on Danang, and on the Bien Hoa–Long Binh complex."

ABRAMS: "A lot of the credit for this goes to the way the police have been operating. They've really gotten with the program. They pick up one of these fellows, and any time they get one they regard it as the end of a piece of yarn, and they try to unravel the whole sweater. And they'll pull that thing—. This is sophisticated work, too."

ABRAMS: "Also the military. The last rocket attack on Saigon, there was supposed to be a patrol out there out of the 6th Ranger Group. And, if he'd gone where he was supposed to, he would have been 50 meters from the launch site. He stopped a kilometer and a half short. He's been court-martialed. The commanding officer of the 6th Ranger Group has been guaranteed 40 days in jail if a single rocket is fired out of his area of responsibility against Saigon. Now, this is new around here. They're getting serious about this. It's a little crude, but I'm sure they'll get the message."

ABRAMS: "I'd like to say this part here, just what he's [the enemy, in the current offensive] set out to do, is very difficult to render judgment on right now. He's had a different problem this time, especially in III Corps. He's had to wrestle with us from the Cambodian border all the way down. They've ridden him, taken his stuff away from him, and he's just had a hell of a time. Then, when he finally got down there, they jumped in front of him again, and the 33rd Regiment got hit with B-52s. The 174th came across the Dong Nai just where they were supposed to, got clobbered with artillery fire, never got to the start line. And so I don't know whether he had all that in his scheme—you know, was counting on all that happening. I think what I'm trying to say is that he had some pretty big plans in mind, and he just hasn't been able to carry them out. So it's hard to render a judgment now on just what all it was that he really planned on doing."

MCCAIN: "The other point, Abe, is on this damn thing with Cambodia. You remember that Mr. Graham came through here from CIA. He came back and was a little bit more amenable in conversation on Sihanoukville. You haven't had occasion to change your thoughts on that subject, have you?"

ABRAMS: "No, it just piles up heavier and heavier with each passing week."

MCCAIN: "Damn fine. Thank you very much."

■ ■ ■

ABRAMS (re ARVN, responding to McCain's question): "They're doing well. Except we've got the problems with the 5th Division. I have to report that the 18th Division last week had a kill ratio of 1:7. I think that last week the 18th Division killed more than they did the entire year of 1968. Now, I don't know why this is happening—the enemy's getting poorer or what."

MCCAIN: "The idea of operating with ARVN is to accelerate this improvement, right?"

ABRAMS: "It's a little more than that. That's one part of it, but out here in these provinces it's just got to get down to one war, with all of us on one side, and all the enemy on the other. That means the RF, the PF, the ARVN, the U.S., the PRUs, the Police Field Forces, the whole damn works, has got to be operating as an entity. Now you can't have command and all that, but you do it by coordination, cooperation."

ABRAMS: "What they've done up there [Americal Division, etc.] is they've divided up the territory and given everybody a piece of it. That's no good. They've got to all be in there together."

ABRAMS: "That's what they've done north of the Hai Van Pass for several months. And that's why you've got the pacification thing going great in the coastal plain where all the people are. They've still, now, got all these forces out in the jungle area and out to the Laotian border. They can do that because they've got it locked on the coastal plain. The VC can't do anything there. They've torn up the infrastructure. The part that's left has gone to the mountains, by and large. And we need it down here in III Corps. I hope the president brings this subject up this afternoon. We'll have a chance to get at it again. Got to do something here in III Corps."

ABRAMS: "The divisions down in the delta are doing very well, I think you can say that of all three of them. We've put a lot more helicopters down there—in December, and it's paid off. Those three divisions down there have been doing damn well in offensive operations, preemptive operations." "I'd have to say the II Corps is satisfactory, too [in ARVN performance]. The best performance of ARVN is up in I Corps. Next, I would say, is IV Corps, with II Corps right in there. The units in II Corps are doing all right. Our problem is in III Corps, and it's limited to the three divisions. The Airborne Division's done well, the marines are doing well, the rangers are doing well everywhere."

ABRAMS: "Right now we shouldn't try to make any changes of any consequence. When you want to change things here with the Vietnamese, everybody's got to stop what they're doing. And everybody's got to sit down and study this and figure out how to reorganize and so on. Now, we can't—we don't want to give anybody any excuse to stop what he's doing. They've just got to go night and day, seven days a week." "Just drive it. If we keep on that track, then someday we're going to get to the point where we can take a day or two to sort of survey the scene, see what else can be done, and readjust to that. In the meantime, we shouldn't take the heat off anybody, and don't give them an excuse to reorganize!"

29 MAR 1969: WIEU

ATTENDEES: Gen. Abrams, Gen. Brown, LTG Mildren, LTG Nickerson, VADM Zumwalt, Dr. Wikner, MG Wetherill, MG Conroy, MG Townsend, MG Shaefer, MG Davidson, BG Frizen, BG Long, BG Wheelock, BG Potts, BG Keegan, BG Galloway, Col. Gibson, Col. Hill, Col. Powers.

Tape begins with discussion already in progress on the apparent topic of Ambassador Sullivan's interference with MACV's employment of B-52 strikes.

ABRAMS: "He's raised this matter of B-52s in anticipation and so on. And at some point in time here I'm going to have to say it, that I'm not going to put up with using the resources that are available to fight <u>this</u> fight over there with a head-quarters that has <u>established</u> and <u>proven</u> incompetence in the conduct of military operations. Their intelligence has been <u>rotten</u>. They have attempted to pussyfoot with the problem. And that's why they're where they're at. [Someone: "I would recommend that you say <u>continuous</u> incompetence, <u>constant</u> incompetence."] So this has got to be raised. [Someone: "You've got to have a single manager."] Well, you mean some kind of a military commander."

■ ■ ■

MACV 1969 Infiltration Estimate: 64,200.

ABRAMS (re a seized cache of enemy rice discovered about 23–25 March): "If I can use the vernacular from the field—I was out in the field yesterday—that 'fucking rice.' I'm having trouble getting that thousand tons in perspective. It seems to me like a lot. Some fellow's got <u>really</u> big ideas. Maybe a thousand tons isn't much rice. I don't know how much rice they eat in Saigon every day. I suppose it's over a thousand tons."

DAVIDSON: "I think, sir, we can look at it in the sense of how long would it support enemy forces in I Corps. The current strength of the main force and local force units is about 47,000 and some. One ton of rice will feed a thousand men for one day, sir. So, applying the mathematics to it, sir, a thousand tons of rice will take care of the main and local force troops in I Corps for about 27 days."

Actually it works out to about 21 days.

ABRAMS: "But, you see, it was all located up there in that one spot. Pretty hard to get it from there to all I Corps."

SOMEONE: This illustrates that "the infiltration has not come up to the general logistics movement." In other words, the enemy was prepared to support more.

ABRAMS: "I just put in a message. The stuff that China and Eastern Europe are piling into North Vietnam and Cambodia is fantastic, and probably exceeds what they're able to use." "And Phil [Davidson] told me yesterday this rice is Chinese."

ABRAMS: "The rice causes problems for the 2s [intelligence officers] and the air force, because they [the enemy] hadn't been credited with getting that much stuff in-country. But it was there." "Hadn't predicted it." "Which, incidentally, emphasizes again that hairy business of predicting."

ABRAMS: "That rice thing is the 'logistics nose' thing." Ties it to the possible movement down of the 304th NVA Division. "Is this time to start moving the 304th, or did they flash back and say, 'They got the fucking rice!'? Or, 'Things are getting hot down there. Should we crank up the old 304th and try to get down there and save the kitchen?'?"

ABRAMS: "They may be having problems up there with <u>excesses</u>. [Laughter] No, this whole goddamn thing. You know, we used to talk, a long time ago, about he knows himself [that] in order to get 5 tons into South Vietnam he's got to start out 80 tons from Hanoi, because he's going to take a 75-ton loss—something like that. Well, all that quit on him [apparently referring to effects of the bombing halt], and he may just have a problem of how to handle the excesses.

We've got a little bit, you know, with herbicide—10-year supply of herbicide, things like that. And of course we've got the GAO and Defense auditors and everybody out here looking into this. . . . And of course our system provides for that—increases the government payroll. But he may have a real problem with excesses up there." "You get the tonnage, but then comes the art of distributing it."

SOMEONE: "It's like McNamara's bomb shortage. He was right, the tonnage was there, but the distribution didn't keep up with the—."

ABRAMS: "Yeah, fins and fuzes, you've got all that kind of stuff."

BRIEFER: "The supply flow into Laos from North Vietnam increased over last week's input as the pattern of activity changed. Truck movements rose to the highest level ever noted, with 8,600 recorded" during the period 19–25 March 1969.

ABRAMS (back on the rice again): "The interesting thing is why the hell all that was there." "Why was he doing that?"

■ ■ ■

BRIEFER (re North Vietnamese propaganda): Based on "analysis that current U.S. policy in Vietnam is to keep U.S. casualties at a minimum while negotiating in Paris and strengthening ARVN forces, and then by countering this policy by repeated violent attacks, U.S. antiwar sentiment would become uncontrollable and force U.S. acceptance of enemy demands. Typical of enemy reasoning on this line was a 22 March Radio Hanoi broadcast which claimed that the attacks of the PLAF forces since 22 February 'are of great military and political significance because what the U.S. is trying to do is keep its casualty lists from lengthening. Its intention is to conduct the war at a lower cost while smoothing [*sic*] the people and avoiding additional economic and political problems at home. PLFA [*sic*] attacks recently have made U.S. casualty figures swell quickly and touched off in the U.S.A. new waves of protest which draws in many congressmen against the Nixon administration for trying to prolong the war.'"

■ ■ ■

BRIEFER: A reconnaissance sergeant from the 5th NVA Regiment captured 20 March 1969 "revealed that Hue and Phu Bai are to be attacked during the period 1–10 April."

ABRAMS: "I was up at Phu Bai yesterday. Four of the 122 rockets—two of them landed by the TOC we built there a year ago, one by the helicopter pad that's just to the rear of the headquarters, and one took off the bar end of General Stilwell's mess, everything north of the fireplace. If they were shooting at the headquarters, that's a degree of accuracy that's pretty tight."

SOMEONE: "First the beer truck and now the bar."

DISCUSSION: Accuracy of the rocket launchers: 150 meters at 9,500. "But we put it through tests, and we've never been able to do better than 500 meters." Have to factor in meteorological data to do better.

BRIEFER: Describes an action of 26 March 1969 north-northwest of Tam Ky where a combined action platoon attacked an estimated enemy platoon. On 27 March 1968, west-northwest of Tam Ky, combined action platoon elements attacked enemy forces on two occasions. "Cumulative results: Friendly none, enemy 53 killed."

ABRAMS: "That was a series of very fine actions."

TOWNSEND: "Those PFs with their M16s are getting taller all the time." "I see a difference. Remember they used to have just carbines and M1s and old BARs. Now they've got this. They figure they can go against an AK now. The only thing they complain about—well, they don't complain, really—they want the M79 [grenade launcher]. They want that and they rate one, every PF platoon rates one. We just haven't gotten around to getting enough together to get it to them."

■ ■ ■

ABRAMS: "That's right. We're pushing them out there as fast as we can get our hands on them."

ABRAMS (re exploiting enemy contacts): "The reaction's got to be quick. You can't wait around studying the goddamn thing. The day we were up there at the change of command, that thing was going on. And I remember talking with Gettys, and he said well, he had another battalion in the oven he could ship in. Well, shit! [Someone: "It's all gone."] That's right! I mean, if somebody's got something, then you grab everything in sight and get it in there, and then study it the next day. [Someone: "While you count the bodies."] Yeah, that's right. And this stuff of waiting for the situation to develop, you know, and commit some more or something, that won't hack it. If there is somebody that's not in contact, they all ought to be rushing to the scene by fastest transportation. The thing to do is to make the mistake that, when it's all over, you say, 'Christ, it could have been handled by a company, and we put four battalions in.' Well, that's the kind of mistake to make."

■ ■ ■

ABRAMS (returning to his favorite topic of the day): "This rice thing bugs me. Another thing about that is that he had all that stuff assembled there, in fact in one place. And the only time he does that is when he's confident it is an area we're not going into. When he's putting out caches where it's dangerous, they're small and there's a lot of them. [Somebody: "He's usually got somebody around there, too."] Yeah, that's right. And this thing is really very puzzling to me. I don't know how he could have misjudged it to that extent. [Someone: "No, I don't think he misjudged the border, General. That's definite terrain in there."] Oh, yeah. But I mean how he misjudged us. [Same someone: "He figured we were tired after Dewey Canyon and wouldn't come in there."] Yeah, but you know, he's been watching. He knows better than that."

■ ■ ■

ABRAMS: "They told me up there yesterday there've been several contacts of the RF and PF around Hue, and not once have they called for any assistance. It's all there, you know. It's available to them. You know, the way that thing's been going up there, they can get it. They can get anything they want. But over the last couple of weeks they haven't called for anything. [Someone: "That province chief—tough cookie."] Yeah. You know, you talk about body count and all that stuff, and it's of course necessary, but things like that—that's the real gauge of whether the war's going ahead or not. That's the sign."

ABRAMS: "Wouldn't it be a great day if the province chief of Thua Thien got a hold of Zais and said, 'I want the goddamn 101 out of this province. Get them out!'?"

SOMEONE: "We know right where we could put them, too." [Laughter]

■ ■ ■

BRIEFER: Reports enemy casualties thus far in the current offensive are greater than in August 1968, about the same as in May 1968, but still significantly below those of Tet 1968.

ABRAMS: "Well, I think if you single out III Corps, and IV Corps, you get a little different picture. One of the big differences here is northern I Corps—between this and Tet [1968]. Khe Sanh, Con Thien, Hue."

SOMEONE: Asks whether for accounting purposes Tet 1968 was considered terminated when Hue was secured.

DAVIDSON: "No, it was terminated on April the 6th." 67 days. Second Offensive in May 1968 "we feel terminated on the 14th of June." 36 days. Third Offensive: 41 days. This current offensive now at 33 days.

BRIEFER: While enemy killed approximate those for the May 1968 attacks, friendly killed are down over 11 percent. "This trend predominates with U.S. killed, despite the fact the enemy is concentrating on U.S. targets in a declared attempt to inflict as many U.S. casualties as possible."

ABRAMS: "I think there's quite a bit in all of this. I think that for this offensive we were far better served by intelligence as we approached it, which meant that we were able to target our own resources against his preparations in a far better way, a far more _effective_ way, than we were in any of the other— although I think in the Third Offensive we had _that_ pretty well knocked. But certainly, in this one, we were able to do a better job _ahead_ than we were for Tet [1968] and the second, the May offensive last year. It's not because anybody's any _smarter_. It's just because the intelligence and the understanding of the problems—. And we have more _forces_, more _resources_, than we had then. So all I'm trying to say is over the past few weeks we've been tangled up with _quite_ an effort, which we worked on during its formative stages _extensively_— caches, casualties, and all of it. And so this is _quite_ a thing."

■ ■ ■

ABRAMS: "Incidentally, you know the _New Jersey_. It just dawned on me, I think yesterday, that that damn thing has to go back to the _United States_. Ah, _well_— this raises a big question in my mind as to its utility. [Someone: "We have a message being prepared right now asking for an extension."] Well, I don't know whether I want to say that, either. I don't know—if we've got some fair weather thing that floats in and out of the theater occasionally, it's not very useful to me. I like that stuff that you can _count_ on, month in and month out."

ZUMWALT: "The trouble is that the decision was made at the beginning. The navy wanted to have two. The SecDef gave them one, and the decision was that it would count like a cruiser, and it would carry on its rotation like the cruisers. Now, it could _be_ kept out here by rotating personnel. At the eleventh hour, _now_ it would be a real mess to try to do it. When we raised this a couple of weeks ago, General, you thought you'd prefer to wait for Admiral McCain to take it up. And I understand he asked a question or two, but we haven't seen any action yet."

ZUMWALT: "But there's one hell of a difference compared to a cruiser, and if you ever had to really do anything up north of the DMZ again, this thing has a tremendous payoff. It got out here at a bad time to show its stuff."

ABRAMS: "Yeah, yeah. Not much to—it's hard to figure it into your plans and so on. It's sort of a fringe benefit that comes and goes. You're lucky when you've got it and so on."

ABRAMS: "How long will it be gone?"

ZUMWALT: "She probably figures to be off the line at least six months."

ABRAMS: "Yeah. I kinda like that stuff that gets out here and kinda sticks with you. Count on it and so on. All right, go ahead!"

■ ■ ■

BRIEFER: "Sir, at your request I took a trip up to have a discussion with the people at Vientiane to try to establish, or reaffirm, an understanding with regard to the impact of the insertion of the road watch teams into the Prairie Fire area, and also to establish a better understanding of our increasing concern about response to the tactical situation in this total area." Problem with Vientiane validating [failing to validate] proposed Arc Light employments. Talked with Hurwitz, the acting ambassador, and key members of his staff. Upshot: As of Monday the road watch team to be extracted and not reinserted. Will immediately revalidate our entire original request. Agree to coordinate in advance any future road watch team insertions into Prairie Fire area. Want to keep a team in on Route 922. Supposedly rendering a daily report that MACV also gets.

ABRAMS: "Let me see the report. The only reason he should be in there is if he's producing something of value to me—me." "Let's come to grips now with the value—to me. I want to know what that is."

ABRAMS: "It sounds to me like the most successful meeting that ever occurred."

SOMEONE: "Well, remember I came back in September full of optimism? I'll believe it when I see it." "We had Hurwitz down. We all gave him the Dutch rub, I fed him lunch, we briefed him, and nothing changed. Maybe you did better. We'll see."

ABRAMS (re some apparent messages relating to use of B-52s in Laos): "What you're talking about are the resources we've got available to run this affair here! We'll loan them the New Jersey. Why is there any confidence that the field headquarters that permitted it to get in this shape is now going to have the intelligence and the so on to solve it! One of the principles that I've followed ever since I've been in the army is never reinforce disaster. And it's stood me in good stead."

SOMEONE (air force): "What's going on now—they've opened up areas that have been denied before. And they were sanctuaries that the Communists could use and store all his stuff in there. Now Souvanna's [Laotian Prince Souvanna Phouma] running scared, so he says, 'Go bomb them.' Well, what we've been doing is systematically, with the FAC control, putting a few strikes—."

ABRAMS: "Well, why don't we raise the thing now about Tchepone? They said, 'Oh, don't bomb the little buddhas out here in'—you know, the loyal and patriotic villagers of Laos. Now, when the fat's in the fire, they say, 'Well, these have been mean bastards. Go after them!' So you go in there and sure, it's secondary explosions and fires going off all over the place. Same thing at Tchepone. And why don't we get a message together saying, 'Why not improve our hindsight, right down to 20-15?' This is the disaster that this policy brought on them. Let's see what we can do about Tchepone."

ABRAMS (re Vientiane): "So that's the kind of real good military planning and so on that's going on over there. And that's what I mean about reinforcing disaster. Disaster is not so much on the ground. The disaster is in the headquarters. They're not thinking these things through. They haven't got a good planning setup. They haven't got good intelligence, and you can't use this stuff unless you have."

SOMEONE (Air Force): "They've certainly been using a double standard about these villages. The Tchepone case is a classic one. One year ago December, sir, through reconnaissance we uncovered the fact that China was building a major road through Dien Bien Phu into the heart of northern Laos. The second thing we discovered was that Tien Quan and Khang Khay, these two great big city centers that they refused to let us attack until a few weeks ago, were being developed as the largest Chinese–North Vietnamese military depots in all of Laos. And they were storing enough for one or two seasons of offensive activity. These photographs were brought to Ambassador Sullivan's attention. We built, very laboriously, large mosaics. This was almost a year and a half ago. And we recommended to him that 60 B-52s be then applied, plus [six?] hundred tac air, and we would remove that entire logistics threat that would affect northern Laos for the next year, or two. And we were treated like we had leprosy."

ABRAMS: "Let's move in on this thing. And let's get all the old skeletons right out of the closet. And I want to get after that [Base Area] 604 in a big way. It's the biggest damn complex. . . . And it should be without any restrictions."

SOMEONE: "A lot of the things we see, the attachés [in Laos] never see. They don't know what's going on."

ABRAMS: "Maybe we should have another meeting and show them the draft for what we want to send to Washington. I mean after all, why should we tiptoe around this fucking thing when—all the men and all the things we've got involved in this thing. And you want to talk about casualties—the way to save casualties is not to retire to Long Binh. The way to save casualties is to get out and blow this goddamn stuff up before it gets in South Vietnam! And now's the time to start laying the money on the table. And if people's feelings are going to get hurt, they're going to get hurt. That's a hell of a lot better than getting guys killed. And I think we've got to move."

■ ■ ■

ABRAMS: "You talk about up in I Corps, where they're out in the A Shau and up along the Laotian border. The only reason that's possible is what was done the six months preceding this. The work of 101, and the 3rd Mar, and the brigade of the 5th Mech, down in there cleaning out that damn coastal area. The only VCI left are up in the hills. They had a guy turn in the other day up there. He was the last member of the proselyting team. No, there were two—he came in with his bodyguard. That's all that was left. And he'd seen them get ground up. And he looked around, and—you and me. Me and thou! [Laughter] And in he came. But that's what has—. The only reason that they can get out in the A Shau, and way out in Quang Tri, is because they've got this thing under control back there in the coastal area. That's what's made it possible. And hell, here's the 2nd ARVN way out there on the Laotian border. Two batteries of their artillery out there. It's tremendous! But it's because of what was done." And increased RF/PF activity: "That was part of the process, too, getting them going, getting them out at night. They're about to take over all of the bridges on Route 1 in northern I Corps. That's the kind of building process that's got to go on before you can get tripping the light fantastic out here in the fringes."

■ ■ ■

ABRAMS (at end of meeting): "I want to keep after the significance, and just what does all that rice mean? And what do those weapons? And what's that Dewey Canyon thing? Just what does all that mean?" "And I feel that our explanation of this offensive is oversimplified. You know, 'He wants to overthrow the government of South Vietnam, he wants to influence the talks,' and so on. And look at what the guy's doing now. He's blaming it on us. And goddamn it, he's getting support. [Someone: "From Americans."] Yes! He says we did it. And one or two rather strange messages coming in here from sort of halfway responsible people, wanting to know what it is we did."

SOMEONE: "Aggravating the enemy."

5 APR 1969: WIEU

MACV 1969 Infiltration Estimate: 64,400 (37,700 for COSVN).

BRIEFER: "The 304th [NVA Division] has entered the pipeline, but of course has not [yet] come out the other end." Maybe the 325th as well.

ABRAMS (re infiltration estimate briefing): "What that shows is that the blue chips are in III Corps."

■ ■ ■

ABRAMS: "Most of the solutions that come in here have to do with expanding the forces that are available. Now there's a limit to the manpower in this country. We know already that they're not going to be able to support what's been laid out for the National Police, the RF/PF, the RDPs [?], the ARVN, the navy, the air force, unless there is a drastic reduction in the desertion rate. In all of them. The navy and the air force don't have much of a desertion problem, but the rest of them do. So, instead of looking around for more forces faster, and more equipment, our drive should be on making effective what they've got."

ABRAMS: "Instead of asking for more forces, the first steps should be to carve down the desertion rate, improve the operational performance and effectiveness of what they've got. I see no relief coming from adding more. Every one of their commanders, wherever he is, should be fighting to put us out of business."

ABRAMS (vehemently): "You've got to have mechanics, you've got to have noncoms, you've got to have <u>officers</u>, and you've got to have the <u>equipment</u>, you've [banging the table so hard he's rattling the coffee cups] got to have the <u>training</u>, and <u>goddamn</u> <u>it</u>—otherwise, you're going to put out on the road <u>another</u> ineffective outfit! And they've got enough of that <u>now</u>!"

ABRAMS: "The way this organization and expansion is being <u>run</u>—it's really a PERT system. They meet every week over here and check up on whether the NCO classes have been filled, and whether the specialist classes have been filled, and whether the equipment is in position, and so on—because we <u>don't</u> want to create <u>paper</u> outfits. We want to create <u>fighting</u> outfits. And we're just <u>kidding</u> them, if we work to create anything else."

5 APR 1969: COMUS Special Brief

BRIEFER (re the current offensive in comparison to three previous offensives during the first 36 days of each): "Concentration on U.S. targets during the most recent offensive is obvious." "Throughout the country the enemy targeted much more heavily on U.S. forces than he's ever done before."

BRIEFER (re refugees): "Each time the total was cut by well over one-half from the previous, and during the current offensive they amount to no more than two and a half percent of those the enemy generated last Tet."

ABRAMS: "The U.S. is far more on the offensive in this thing, I believe."

BRIEFER: Enemy casualties are second only to those he sustained during Tet 1968, even though he "sought to carry out this offensive with a minimum cost to his own forces by heavier reliance on attacks by fire. However, he's having increasing difficulties holding his casualties down, difficulties which principally result from a greater allied combat power and our improved ability to preempt him at long range."

■ ■ ■

BRIEFER (re the Accelerated Pacification Campaign launched in late October 1968): A+B up 1,100+ hamlets. C up about the same. D+E down 687. VC-controlled down 800+. A+B = secure. C = relatively secure. D+E = contested. Thus A+B+C up over 2,100 hamlets. Down 1,500 in D+E+VC-controlled. "This numerical success is confirmed by the enemy's growing propaganda virulence directed against our pacification efforts, and by a growing file of intelligence reports which indicate his concern with the APC. Reports from the field reveal that the effect of the current offensive on the pacification program is slight at best."

ABRAMS: "Another interesting thing about that is that the definition of 'C' is probably pretty correct. I mean, he's [the enemy] got the same definition. Huh! <u>Amazing</u>. Which tends to confirm, somewhat, the HES. Now, for the <u>opponents</u> of HES, they've got a handhold here, too. Looking at it realistically, the definition is probably a pretty damn good one. And the categories we've got are probably pretty good, because he <u>agrees</u> with the categories we've got. Those ones [attacks] on D, E, and VC, I would say that that's where we may have been in error in categorizing—at least E and VC. [Someone: "We may be giving him the benefit of the doubt."] That's right. They ought to track those down and incorporate them in the new pacification plan. He wouldn't do that if they were VC. And he <u>probably</u> wouldn't do it if they were E. He's got a better reading than we've got."

■ ■ ■

BRIEFER: Enemy resupply activities through his Cambodian LOC "suffer no attrition."

BRIEFER: "We know that by the end of October the enemy had serious supply problems in I Corps. The flow through Laos had come to a virtual standstill. His forces in MR Tri-Thien-Hue were on the verge of starvation. We were discovering caches of unprecedented magnitude in the DMZ. Because of logistical difficulties and the growing intensity of our own military operations in I Corps, the enemy simply could not support his forces in MR Tri-Thien-Hue or the DMZ. Thus he withdrew them to Laos and North Vietnam."

Then came the bombing halt.

■ ■ ■

BRIEFER: "We believe that the enemy sees time running against him. Each day he sees the GVN and the RVNAF becoming stronger, and as they do they deny him more and more of the population, the essential element of his continuance and survival."

ABRAMS: "If we indulge ourselves in the thought, for a moment, that he misjudged the situation in '68—that is, substantial defections from the ARVN and a popular uprising, could it be that he has again—in this focus on III Corps and all that—misjudged the situation again?"

ABRAMS: "He <u>really</u> made a <u>tremendous</u> effort here in III Corps. The way he stuck with getting that 5th Division down there, the way he stuck with working the 7th and the 1st in there. We were turning up his caches, hounding him on the infiltration routes, knocking off his commo-liaison—you know, all of that. He still <u>poured</u> it on. And he aimed at that Long Binh–Bien Hoa thing. It was <u>possible</u> for him to put five regiments in there. At one time it looked—that's the way he organized, command-wise. And in the end he only got two battalions out there."

DAVIDSON: "We got one document in which he claimed to have inflicted 45,000 U.S. casualties, destroyed hundreds of armored vehicles, and a couple hundred helicopters. If he's getting that kind of reporting, he may think he has succeeded. If he is getting the truth, he will know that he did not."

ABRAMS: "I don't really <u>care</u> how <u>that</u> turns out. If he's believing <u>those</u> reports, it's going to make him <u>far</u> more vulnerable."

DAVIDSON: "I think in one unintentional respect this briefing's inclined to be misleading, because it looks at it totally from the enemy's viewpoint. And I think you could say with equal validity that time is not necessarily on our side, either."

ABRAMS: "No, but one of the things that this thing raises is whether the time isn't <u>ripe</u> to go into the pursuit. [Goodpaster: "Right."] That's the <u>real</u> question that this thing poses. When I say <u>pursuit</u>, I mean pursuit in terms of the ARVN effectiveness, pursuit in terms of the pacification, and pursuit in terms of going into the base areas."

■ ■ ■

ABRAMS: "I want a directive to go out to Eckhardt, Ewell, Seventh Air Force, and navy, and I want special attention paid to not killing Cambodian civilians or military. I'm not going to change any of the rules we've got, but I want an effort made to see that we don't kill any Cambodians. SOG gets this, too." "This has to do with air strikes, it has to do with artillery, it has to do with gunships, and so on. And, by god, they've got to be on the VC-NVA. I don't know whether that's [the Cambodian theater of operations, apparently] going to amount to anything, but at least in this time period, in the kind of situation we're in, I don't want to unwittingly upset some damn thing where an opportunity might come our way. And I don't want to have it jeopardized by indiscriminate [laughing] shooting up—and it's not because I love Cambodians—I'm just thinking of the bigger stakes."

■ ■ ■

ABRAMS: "I turned my old helicopter in, and three days later it crashed and burned over in front of the 3rd Field [Hospital]." "Got a new one." "I guess everybody in their last couple of months should have a brand-new helicopter. I got one with five hours on it. I'm not down to my last two months, but—. At least I'm not aware that I am."

■ ■ ■

ABRAMS: "Another thing—goddamn, we've got to push out to the borders! That's what—that Dewey Canyon thing, this other thing up here on 616—has really saved us grief. That was grief that was on its way. And I mean, you know, a good big basketful of it! And the 101 out there in A Shau."

Meaning operations to find and seize enemy caches.

ABRAMS: "I don't know whether maybe we shouldn't bring the 173rd down here. I don't know if that'd tip the scales enough down here in III Corps. 4th Division would tip 'em! [Pause] Although I must be frank to say I'm not satisfied with the way the 4th has been operating. They haven't got—they haven't been smart, haven't been skillful. Those two miserable [enemy] regiments caused us a lot of trouble up there. It's the smallest force they ever had in there. And goddamn it, we were flying around blind up there, too. We didn't know what the hell we were doing. Ponderous! Really not up on the bit."

ABRAMS: "Also, you know, this business that the way to protect a road is to drive up and down it. I think it's probably the same as a city—the way to protect a damn road is to get out away from it and find his caches and beat up his outfits and stomp 'em in the ground and take his ammunition away from him, take his explosives away from him. Get out there! That's the way to protect a road, instead of sitting on it, waiting for him to get in there with RPGs."

ABRAMS (re his son John, a cavalry lieutenant): "One Montagnard chief presented him with six buffalo. One place—I said, 'Hell, you're probably married. That's a dowry.' I said, 'You're probably in deep Montagnard trouble, and don't even know it.'"

12 APR 1969: WIEU

ATTENDEES: Gen. Abrams, Gen. Goodpaster, Amb. Berger, Gen. Brown,

VADM Zumwalt, Dr. Wikner, MG Wetherill, MG Conroy, MG Townsend, MG Shaefer, MG Jones, BG Bautz, BG Frizen, BG Long, BG Clay, BG Wheelock, BG Bryan, BG Keegan, BG Galloway, Col. Roberts, Col. Cavanaugh, Col. Hill, Col. Powers.

ABRAMS: "Now they've apparently still got this problem on the B-52s. They've got the advance warning on it. And not only that, they know where they're going."

SOMEONE: "We can get the OPSEC people to look at it again. CINCPAC's got their OPSEC group coming out here again shortly."

GOODPASTER: "It would be worth making a check in Laos whether and when we notify Vientiane of the exact time and place of these strikes."

SOMEONE: "Normally 24 hours. And they notify Washington and everybody. Oh, there's a vast network that's notified. You have to do it to even get in-country."

SOMEONE ELSE: "Also Bangkok for permission to launch out of U Tapao."

SOMEONE: "Their last review of this whole procedure was about six months ago, so they're due to have another good look."

GOODPASTER: "I think we ought to make a specific project out of it."

SOMEONE: "They [the enemy] gave them the warning in one case about an hour and a half and in the other case four hours from the strike time."

■ ■ ■

BRIEFER: Quoting the 8 April 1969 issue of a Hanoi newspaper, *Nhan Dan:* "The antiwar movement of the progressive American people constitutes another front in the struggle for an end to U.S. aggression."

BRIEFER: "During a sweep operation along the Cambodian border on 5, 6, and 7 April, ARVN elements contacted unidentified enemy forces, resulting in friendly 5 killed, 15 wounded, enemy 102 killed, one detained. Two caches were discovered in the area totaling approximately 21 tons of assorted munitions. In addition, an extensive bunker and tunnel complex was destroyed, resulting in many secondary explosions. A 360-bed dispensary, along with 3.75 tons of medicine, were captured or destroyed during the operation."

ABRAMS: "Wasn't that a ranger battalion [ARVN] that got in that dispensary? ["Yes, sir."] All these things seem to pass unnoticed. You know, they—'Let's get the ARVN out there. Let's have them do something. Let's have them get in the war.'" "They've been killing the most, too."

13 APR 1969: Special J-2/J-3 Brief to COMUSMACV

ABRAMS: "Basically my feeling right now is . . . General Tri and General Ewell will exact more from the enemy by the improvement of the three ARVN divisions [than by being given more forces]. They won't get another goddamn thing! I'm going to try to stand on that ground—with Vien, with the president, with everybody."

GOODPASTER: "If we're talking about their taking over more of the war, that's the way they take it over—by straightening up."

ABRAMS: "That's what everybody's _talking_. Vice President _Ky's_ talking that way. President _Thieu's_ talking that way. And now's the time to put your money on the table. Let's see the color of the money. I feel that this is as good a move as bringing the 1st Cav down here—the thrust of this. _I'll_ talk with them about reducing _forces_—just as soon as they want them to go."

20 APR 1969: Commanders WIEU

ATTENDEES: Gen. Abrams, Amb. Bunker, Amb. Berger, Gen. Goodpaster, Amb. Colby, Gen. Brown, LTG Rosson, LTG Mildren, LTG Nickerson, LTG Stilwell, LTG Corcoran, LTG Ewell, VADM Zumwalt, MG Wetherill, MG Hollis, MG Shaefer, MG Conroy, MG Townsend, BG Bautz, BG Long, BG Clay, BG Potts, BG McLaughlin, BG Bryan, BG Galloway, Col. Powers, Col. Cavanaugh, Col. Gorman, Col. Penuel, Col. Gilbert, Col. Hill.

ABRAMS: "President Thieu was down in the delta, at the 44th Special Zone Headquarters, and he _instructed_ his people to develop these contacts with the Cambodians." "And it looks like the Cambodians have been authorized to do the same thing." "At one point down there they've provided the Cambodians a radio . . . and they have exchanged information on it."

■ ■ ■

BRIEFER: Describes a PW from the 261B Main Force Battalion who states that in an 11 March 1969 contact with the U.S. 9th Infantry Division near eastern Base Area 470 the battalion lost approximately 100 killed, 20 wounded, 20 by desertion, and most of their heavy weapons. Says unit strength now about 75 men. There were contacts by the U.S. 9th Division in this area on 11 and 12 March that resulted in a reported 97 VC killed. Abrams: "That's pretty good on the body count—good verification. Apparently understated by three."

■ ■ ■

EWELL: "I think it's quite significant, at least in our area, the RF/PF are getting a very high percentage of the ARVN kills."

GOODPASTER: If we broke out the statistics shown on that chart to separate ARVN from RF/PF, "I think that would be rather revealing as to who's fighting the war."

ABRAMS (re improving the effectiveness of ARVN units): "It's one of the few really significant things that are left to do that would dramatically change what's happening in South Vietnam."

ABRAMS: "This particular point has to do with III Corps, where I think the RF and PF are actually better than the divisions. I would be willing to subscribe to disbanding the 18th as a division and creating more RF and PF, and add three marine battalions to the Marine Division. And I think South Vietnam would be strengthened by that move."

ABRAMS: "We're running out of ways to attack this problem. We've tried all the sensible, traditional ways. And I am now in the uncomfortable position of participating in these for almost two years—in another two weeks it will be two years—and a lot of these I've supported personally because I believed that they _would_ do—would accomplish something. And, in all candor, I must say that they have failed. The performance of the 5th and 18th has <u>declined</u> since they've been issued the M16 rifle. That is a novel experience in this country. We've just got to—. The facts are the facts, and we haven't been able to <u>swing</u> it. And some really great guys have tilted that windmill—Fred Weyand, Dutch Kerwin. I climbed right in bed with Fred. I thought he had a <u>great</u> scheme, and I thought it would <u>really</u> do it. And I went <u>months</u> believing that it would happen <u>any day</u>. And, <u>goddamn it</u>, it's only gotten <u>worse</u>. Well, we can't kid ourselves about it."

26 APR 1969: WIEU

Attendees: Gen. Abrams, Gen. Goodpaster, LTG Rosson, Amb. Colby, Gen. Brown, LTG Mildren, VADM Zumwalt, MG Conroy, MG Townsend, MG Shaefer, MG Davidson, Col. Gillert, Mr. Jacobson, BG Bautz, Col. Penuel, BG Long, MG McLaughlin, BG Clay, BG Bryan, BG Potts, BG Keegan, Capt. McNulty, Col. Cavanaugh, Col. Hill, Col. Powers, Col. Kerwin.

BRIEFER: "There have been no groups [with the exception of one re-observance] observed in the infiltration pipeline since 23 March."

ABRAMS: "This is really a <u>very</u> important point. We've just got to keep after it." "Both the president and the vice president, Thieu and Ky, have expressed the view privately that they'll settle down to serious negotiations about June. I <u>believe</u> that this is—well, I don't know <u>how</u> that they arrive at that. I suppose it's some complex summation of a whole lot of things, which I would probably never understand. And, you see, this is a—this <u>fits</u> that. I think you can make a <u>case</u> that it fits it. But it's a very—on the other hand, it's a very <u>dangerous</u> thing to go <u>banking</u> on."

■ ■ ■

GOODPASTER: Asks whether others now accept that arms are flowing through Sihanoukville to the enemy.

DAVIDSON: "Officially they haven't accepted. I understand they're <u>weakening</u>, though." "It's just a question of time, though, before it's got to be accepted." "The last official position by CIA was they still did not believe we had <u>proved</u> it beyond a reasonable doubt. I guess the operative word's 'reasonable.'"

COLBY: "I didn't know that was a requirement in the Intelligence Community." [Laughter]

GOODPASTER: Calls the position of disbelief "moth-eaten."

■ ■ ■

ABRAMS (re J-3 briefing): "We want to keep working toward some way to judge the climate, because we've said that pacification is our number one, and this— on the operational side—tends to <u>judge</u> the climate, or <u>compare</u> it, see how it's going, and so on."

DAVIDSON (re enemy infiltration): "We've been carrying about 15 percent trail loss." Now a captured journal provides a detailed account of a 22 percent loss. That group started with 671 people.

GOODPASTER: Suggests flooding enemy areas with leaflets quoting General Giap's statement that "thus far we've lost half a million killed."

■ ■ ■

DAVIDSON: Gives details: A journalist told Giap the Americans say he has lost 500,000 men. Giap's reply: "That's quite exact."

ABRAMS (commenting on casualty chart): "I think what this shows is the Vietnamese are pulling their weight in I and IV Corps, and they're not in II and III Corps." "Down here in III Corps you've got three ARVN divisions, the Airborne Division, three ranger groups, three marine battalions, plus the RF and the PF—and that produced 159. We're not getting a good return on our rations."

GOODPASTER: "And the place is just crawling with enemy." "Let me have a set of this for my final talk with General Vien."

ABRAMS: "Goddamn it, the three ranger groups, the marine battalions, the Airborne Division, the three ARVN divisions, whacked off 49 last week. And the RF and PF—86. Yeah, this is an excellent chart to take with you—final call. Ummm."

2 MAY 1969: Special Briefing for Ambassador L. E. Walsh

Ambassador Lawrence E. Walsh was at this time deputy head of the U.S. delegation to the Paris peace talks.

ABRAMS: "Beginning with July–August of '68, he began withdrawing units from I Corps, northern I Corps, into Laos and into North Vietnam. We believe here that he did that because he had to. His logistics situation in support of northern I Corps had become very critical. He was not getting the supplies down to them through Laos and through the lower panhandle of North Vietnam—a combination of the effectiveness of the bombing and the weather." "And in South Vietnam, they got into his base areas. They probably took most of the supplies away from the 320th Division that had come down across the DMZ. I believe that the entire hospital system for Military Region Tri-Thien-Hue was captured." Abrams describes a doctor from MR-TTH Headquarters who was captured, and who had a map with plots of facilities: "They went systematically to work, and they got every one that was on that map."

ABRAMS: "We've got a bit of a problem right now. We have not observed an infiltration group entering the system since the 20th of March." Either "there hasn't been any [***] to arrive at the answer to that. The answer we have thus far received from—from the top of the profession—is that what we're reading is correct." "This has come directly from [***]." Discussion of the fact that during this same period "the orbit had been shifted" for aircraft involved in the operation. "So one of the first things to check out was whether it was caused by the change of orbit, the pattern of orbit."

ABRAMS: "The people in Saigon have stood pretty stalwart in all this."

ABRAMS (re General Phu, 44th Special Tactical Zone): "He is an excellent man himself, and apparently has the full personal confidence of the president, and is highly regarded by the military professionals."

ABRAMS (re contacts between South Vietnamese and Cambodian officials along the IV Corps border): "It is <u>our</u> feeling that this sort of contact would never have taken place had it not been blessed by Phnom Penh." "We're trying to play it with understanding and sensitivity so that, if there <u>is</u> anything developing, we're not going to screw it up. I mean, we're going to <u>try</u> hard not to." "And we want to keep the Americans <u>out</u> of it. And President Thieu's attitude on this, I must say, is better than anything else we could have designed."

■ ■ ■

JACOBSON (on pacification): "Our conclusion is that, while we have roughed up and disturbed the VC infrastructure, we have not yet seriously damaged it."

ABRAMS: [Cites difference between existing guidance on the task of Vietnamization and what the newspapers report various U.S. government officials are saying.] "In designing their [the RVNAF's] forces, we've tried to design them to deal with insurgency, and <u>not</u> with an NVA force of the magnitude and kind that is present at the moment in and around South Vietnam. And that's the way this has been designed, that's the way it's been funded, and so on. In other words, the thrust of this whole thing has <u>counted</u> on, I would say, negotiating the North Vietnamese out of South Vietnam. That's the kind of thing that has been visualized here. And this is particularly true if you're talking in terms of all the U.S. forces being out."

ABRAMS: "There's a twilight area in here of how much <u>support</u>, for instance. See, this thing really visualized in the end, when you got all this done, you'd have a MAAG here, you know, an <u>advisory</u> type of effort, and some unilateral U.S. intelligence capability." "And I suppose one possible way of bridging the gap between this thing and whatever else might develop would be the degree of <u>support</u> that could remain."

■ ■ ■

WALSH: Asks how long it would take to develop the RVNAF to fight this kind of war alone if Paris did not succeed.

He seems to have in mind a unilateral U.S. withdrawal.

ABRAMS: "Well, I don't know. What we've got to do—in order to make a recommendation on that, I think you've got to watch for a <u>few</u> months how the pacification program goes, how they go with the improvement of the effectiveness of their own forces, so that you're not entirely betting on the come, so that you've got <u>some</u> substance to make a projection."

ABRAMS: "The basic fact is that this is the way we've gone ahead with the GVN—with the JGS, really, and the minister of defense. See, the units and the equipment and the things that are in this have all been debated, and worked out, and agreement arrived at with the JGS and the minister of defense, and does <u>not</u> contain all of the airplanes, and all of the ships, and all of the <u>things</u> which they presented. When they went to Hawaii, they presented a list which they had worked up unilaterally. They presented that to Secretary Clifford and General Wheeler at that Hawaii meeting. And then we took that and met, and adjusted it, and arbitrated it, and this [guidance] was the foundation on which we did that, and it's <u>why</u>. This was the <u>reason</u>, what it <u>says</u> up there, is the reason why they haven't got—in <u>some</u> cases, or in <u>most</u> cases—why they haven't got in there organizations and equipment which they wanted."

BRIEFER: "The strength level of RVNAF has risen sharply since June of 1967." October 1968 (Phase I): 801,000 authorization/approval obtained. December 1968 (Phase II): 855,000 approval. Up to 875,790 by February 1969 approval. Provides for: Army of 10 infantry divisions, one airborne division, plus combat support and combat service support. More armor, artillery, and logistics. Increased VNAF and VNN to "provide for a balanced RVNAF." "RVNAF will not have a truly combined arms team to meet a residual insurgency threat until the end of fiscal year '72." Expect a total force then of 855,000, the level the RVN can be expected to sustain over a period of years with its manpower base. This is the Accelerated Phase II Plan.

BRIEFER: Before the end of FY 1972, "in the event of a major redeployment of U.S. forces, U.S. units will be required to offset existing deficiencies in the RVNAF force structure." Chart shows RVNAF I&M objectives based on "the level required to cope with the residual insurgency threat only, and not with renewed North Vietnamese aggression." Re offset requirements: "Depending on the time that withdrawal of U.S. forces begins, the size of this package ranges from approximately 21,000 in fiscal year '70 to an estimated phaseout in 1972."

ABRAMS: South Vietnam's army forces will be essentially complete by the end of 1969 (except for three engineer battalions). Then they will need naval forces, air forces, helicopters, and some logistics to complete the overall program. "They've <u>met</u> the requirements of the accelerated program. And also I believe the program is <u>about</u> as tight as we can <u>make</u> it."

WALSH: "The program assumes the elimination of the major threat, and that's in the enemy's hands, not ours."

ABRAMS: "We've developed this T-Day [when a truce or cease-fire might go into effect] planning. I would say it's in pretty solid condition. And that's the <u>foundation</u> for movement of U.S. forces, in any way that—. This has all been laid out. It's all been computer programmed so that you can take out the detail in any form and shape which you might want to do. So we have, I would say, a reasonably comprehensive plan on <u>how</u> to move the U.S. forces out of here if such circumstances—negotiations, the enemy situation, decisions of our government, a whole lot of 'iffies' in there—."

ABRAMS: "In addition to that, there's a requirement to have plans for accomplishing this withdrawal in a variety of ways, or at least under a variety of circumstances. And we're going ahead with that. We turned one in the other day on the assumption of <u>mutual</u> withdrawal—negotiated, tacit, this sort of thing."

ABRAMS: "The equipment has been ordered" that is needed for processing of retrograded matériel to meet U.S. Department of Agriculture standards for entry into the United States.

ABRAMS: T-Day planning "is a logistical and management problem, because you're dealing with a <u>hell</u> of a lot of stuff and a <u>hell</u> of a lot of people here."

ABRAMS: "I think we have at the moment a family of plans which will permit the command to react to whatever opportunities or decisions . . . befall the whole effort."

WALSH: Refers to "what the secretary called 'the other basket,' which is the unilateral reduction of force."

ABRAMS: "We've examined that. Secretary Laird was not very happy with all that it said, but basically we say in there that if the improvements in the effectiveness of the Vietnamese forces move as they have been laid out, if the pacification program moves ahead as it has been laid out, that even with the enemy situation as it is at the moment <u>some</u> reduction of U.S. combat forces becomes practical. This is without changing <u>any</u> of the other things. But <u>I</u> have always—I have consistently avoided a <u>time</u> and an <u>amount</u>. I've kept saying—I don't mean by that that it's any more <u>right</u>, but at least my philosophy has been I've got to see the color of the money. And I've <u>accepted</u>, in all this, the condition that the North Vietnamese would remain about as they are. But at the moment <u>I</u> don't know of anyone who could give you a <u>time</u> and an amount that would have <u>based</u> the thing on facts and cold-blooded analysis of the situation."

WALSH: Puts further questions premised on a unilateral U.S. withdrawal, suggesting under such circumstances the RVNAF I&M program could be accelerated.

ABRAMS: "No, no, I don't say that. In fact, I would <u>always</u> recommend against that. That would be just a case of the United States kidding itself, and [pounding the table] <u>by god</u> you mustn't kid yourself!"

WALSH: "Well, I think that's what's going on to some extent."

ABRAMS: "Well, not from me."

WALSH: "I understand that."

ABRAMS: "In the end, <u>whatever</u> the United States does, it must <u>know</u> and understand it <u>itself</u>. It should <u>not</u> kid <u>itself</u>!"

ABRAMS (re the possibility of further I&M acceleration): "I don't think there's a teaspoon of blood that can be squeezed out of this. If there was, <u>I</u> would do it!"

ABRAMS (re boat turnover to the VNN): I agreed to buy the first half of the boats programmed, and to have Admiral Zumwalt report to me if the buildup was effective. If so, I would authorize the other half. "I think you always have to <u>do</u> something like that so that, as you move ahead, you hold them as hard as you can to the standards. Now these are <u>not</u> the greatest standards in the world to <u>start</u> with, but <u>don't</u> back away from the standards. Have a goddamn boat that's got a crew, but they can't keep it running! A boat with a crew that can keep the motor running, but they can't fire the gun! Or they can fire the gun and keep the motor running, but they can't communicate with anybody! It's no <u>good</u>!"

ABRAMS: "Commodore Chon has been a <u>good</u> man, and they [the VNN] have <u>produced</u> what they <u>said</u> they were going to produce."

ABRAMS (re IV Corps): "It's moving ahead in a <u>very</u> favorable way, and it <u>has</u> been now since, really since June [1968]. They put on a 90-day thing down there that ended on the first of June '68. And what it <u>did</u>, it just got everybody <u>out</u>. It overcame the whole business of hanging around the provincial capitals and certain installations. It just <u>smashed</u> that whole idea up, and it got them <u>moving</u>, the Territorial Forces and the ARVN. Now it wasn't all done well, but it broke up <u>that</u>. And then—they've never stopped since then."

ABRAMS: "The foundation for the Hoi Chanh results <u>now</u> began then. The pressure was put on, and it's never been taken off."

ABRAMS (re U.S. redeployments): "The <u>artistry</u> in this is going to be to determine that the time has come when the move can be made, without—<u>hopefully</u>, the best of all worlds would be that we can see this, and be <u>confident</u> in the judgment, <u>before</u> it becomes a necessity."

ABRAMS: "Oh, we've got to keep <u>quiet</u> publicly. Just keep working <u>hard</u>, you know, knowing that this is what we're after. Keep working hard. Don't say anything."

WALSH: "I'm afraid that's no more real than the things you see—'the enemy will go back.'"

ABRAMS: "Yeah, I know. <u>I</u> realize that."

3 MAY 1969: COMUS Cambodia Brief

ABRAMS (re the inevitability of being criticized): "It's like the 29th Regiment. You fight them in the A Shau and they piss on you for that. You fight them in Hue and they raise hell about that. You can't find a good place to fight them. The <u>places</u> aren't good."

MAJOR MCCARTHY: Briefs on South Vietnamese–Cambodian border meetings, FARK–Viet Cong clashes, and the buildup of FARK elements in northeastern Cambodia. At least 14 border meetings have been recorded during a four-month period. "Problems relating to VC use of Cambodian territory were discussed" and arrangements were made to coordinate operations against them.

ABRAMS (re the U.S. 25th Infantry Division): "They've got a lot of interesting things. It's the most promising visit I've ever made to the 25th Division in over two years." "The analysis they're doing of their own operations, and trying to make improvements—."

4 MAY 1969: WIEU

ATTENDEES: Gen. Abrams, Amb. Colby, Gen. Brown, LTG Mildren, LTG Rosson, VADM Zumwalt, MG Conroy, MG Townsend, MG Shaefer, BG Bautz, BG Frizen, BG Long, BG McLaughlin, BG Clay, BG Bryan, BG Potts, Col. Gorman, BG Galloway, Col. Cavanaugh, Col. Hill, Col. Gillert, Col. Powers.

They are confronting the problem that intercepts about infiltration have dried up. General Potts has now succeeded General Davidson as the MACV J-2.

POTTS: "Let's say infiltration <u>has</u> stopped—it <u>has</u> stopped. We're looking at every other indication that we have, going all the way back to the reports that are coming from some of the Canadians that are up in Hanoi with the teams there and so forth, to see if there's <u>any</u> supporting evidence showing less movement towards the south." "It's our number one collection priority right now." "General Carter's into it, personally." T-12 is back on the air, "but there's nothing about infiltration going through there."

The reference is to Lt. Gen. Marshall S. Carter, director of the National Security Agency at the time.

ABRAMS: "I have been going now, for a year and a half, every Sunday to CMD for a . . . comprehensive briefing on <u>all</u> things going on in the Saigon–Gia Dinh area. And they give a <u>detailed</u>—tubes of medicine, contraband refrigerators, weapons. . . ."

ABRAMS (re Rosson suggestion for improved use of intelligence at the village level): "You ought to do it in a way that fits a Vietnamese village, not go in there with forms from [Fort] Holabird, designed to go on a goddamn computer in Saigon. No—it's got to have the <u>form</u>, the <u>shape</u>, the <u>flavor</u> that is something that <u>can</u> be done, something that is not <u>strange</u> to a Vietnamese <u>village</u>."

COLBY: Mentions "the census grievance program, which is essentially an informant program."

■ ■ ■

ABRAMS: "I must say I don't see any reason to shift in any way the major thrust of what we're trying to do. That is, the azimuth we're on in the <u>major</u> effort, that is the pacification program."

10 MAY 1969: WIEU

ATTENDEES: Gen. Abrams, Gen. Haines, Amb. Colby, Gen. Brown, LTG Rosson, LTG Mildren, VADM Zumwalt, Dr. Wikner, MG Conroy, MG Townsend, Mr. Jacobson, MG Shaefer, BG Bautz, BG Frizen, BG Long, BG McLaughlin, BG Clay, BG Bryan, BG Potts, BG Keegan, BG Galloway, Col. Cavanaugh, Col. Hill, Col. Kerwin, Col. McCarthy.

BRIEFER: During the past week two probable new infiltration groups were observed moving through the infiltration pipeline in North Vietnam. Cites factors that tend to indicate that a suspension of infiltration occurred during the period 20 March–30 April.

ABRAMS: "Now, why did this happen?"

POTTS: "We feel, sir, there's definitely been a stand-down during this period."

ABRAMS "Yeah, but why would Hanoi do <u>that</u>?"

POTTS: "It looks to me like there's been a shortage of personnel, less requirement for personnel, and—."

ABRAMS: "The study that you cited for me the other day—they could go on indefinitely at the 1968 level. That's supposed to be an authoritative study."

POTTS: "We feel, sir, that there are not going to be so many of the large attacks, that there's going to be a conservation of personnel by attacks by fire, harassment, and so forth."

ABRAMS: "How about the attack on Frontier City? I mean, that wasn't a conservation."

POTTS: "Yes, sir."

ABRAMS: "And they started putting heavy artillery fire on those fellows, accurately, <u>while</u> they were forming <u>up</u>. And they made a shambles out of that thing, but it went ahead <u>anyway</u>. Now that is <u>not</u> conserving manpower."

ABRAMS: "Now we've got to <u>think</u> about this. Has it ever stopped for that long?"

POTTS: "No, sir. That's the longest period."

ABRAMS: "<u>Why</u> <u>is</u> <u>that</u>?"

■ ■ ■

BROWN (re Laos, and report thereon): "That's an American-run war. We're [in the report] talking about what the <u>Lao's</u> can't do. <u>Hell</u>, it's what <u>we</u> can't do, under CAS. And <u>all</u> of it is run by <u>us</u>. Vang Pao's campaign, which was so highly successful, was <u>vetoed</u> and drastically cut by Ambassador Sullivan. It could have been <u>more</u> successful, in my judgment. So I think we ought to look at this in the attitude of, you know, we're being critical of ourselves and be very careful of the distribution of this thing."

ABRAMS (agreeing with Brown): "That has been an American design. And it's been orchestrated, note by note, according to a certain philosophy, which has always turned the other cheek." "It looks to me like we've played it over there to see if we can preserve the partition without doing anything <u>overt</u>. How can you expect a thing like that to succeed? The point <u>is</u>, can you ever <u>hope</u>, in dealing with the Communists, in the long haul can you ever hope to play a game like that and have <u>anything</u> <u>except</u> <u>ultimate</u> <u>complete</u> <u>loss</u>?!"

COLBY: This approach stems from decisions made by the United States in 1961. "Meanwhile, they've used the trail. Meanwhile, we've <u>bombed</u> the trail."

ABRAMS: "It's been done under the most <u>extraordinary</u> limitations that anyone's <u>ever</u> seen—and all, <u>all</u> sort of—all <u>managed</u> by the <u>same</u> philosophy that is pissing away <u>Laos</u>."

■ ■ ■

BRIEFER: Quotes a 29 April 1969 *Quan Doi Nhan Dan* article warning that "a summer of active struggle will certainly occur in the United States."

ABRAMS: "They have <u>direct</u> contact with leadership of groups in the United States, and they go ahead and hold meetings on how to step up, <u>in</u> <u>the</u> <u>United States</u>, the summer offensive. And the <u>doctrine</u> and the <u>tactics</u> and all of this goes out and so on. We're <u>involved</u> on a lot of fronts, and so are <u>they</u>. It's no exaggeration to say that they <u>are</u> in the United States."

■ ■ ■

ABRAMS (re the 9th VC Division): "That's their exploitation division." "It's been one of the indicators of how imminent is the assault on Saigon." "I'm not saying we're <u>right</u>, but that's the way we've always looked at it."

ABRAMS: "It may be necessary to hammer at Washington again about our authority in the southern half of the DMZ, the ability to move in there with larger—you know, we're limited now to squads, and a maximum reinforcement of one platoon. And we may need to bring up the subject of B-52s in the southern half of the DMZ. And if that goddamn artillery outfit is going to have a wingding on Ho Chi Minh's birthday . . . maybe the day before Ho Chi Minh's birthday we'll have Teddy Roosevelt Day or something and run B-52s through there to help the 84th or whatever it is get <u>ready</u>."

ABRAMS (re earlier DMZ incident): "They fired two rounds of 155 as counterbattery. I told them to fire <u>600</u> rounds—and then have a look at it to see what more should be done!"

ABRAMS: "Incidentally, up there in that territory where they're tangling with them now—a year ago, a year ago, you couldn't have gotten the 3rd Marine Division to go in there with <u>three</u> regiments. They said that was 'impenetrable.' Massed antiaircraft—37-mm, all kind of stuff. Now of course later on in the <u>year</u> they went in there. That's where they took all that stuff away from the 320th."

ABRAMS: Now getting daily reports on the performance of ARVN in III Corps, so: "I can see what's going to happen on Saturday [WIEU charts]—<u>another</u> miserable performance!" "Maybe we need another conversion program. We're converting CIDG to RF. Now maybe we ought to undertake the conversion of ARVN to CIDG."

ABRAMS (re the enemy): "The time schedule we see being executed now may be a delay brought about by minor administrative difficulties like losing the food [huge rice caches seized earlier], losing the ammunition [seized in Dewey Canyon], having to get more in."

ABRAMS (re caches seized in-country): "Right now they've got about four-fifths of the tonnage in ammunition that was picked up all last year." "Four-fifths or three-fourths, so far this year, of the total picked up last year."

ABRAMS (re seizures in caches this year compared to last): "We've fallen down badly in salt. But everywhere else we're well ahead of program." "I don't think we need to put anything out on it." [Laughter]

■ ■ ■

BROWN: "General, the rules of engagement are quite clear, that if we're fired on we can strike back at the immediately associated facilities and equipment. But it doesn't say anything about <u>time</u>. I think the <u>intent</u> is quite clear, it should be a response in kind that they recognize as a response. But I've been <u>doing</u> it sort of, you know, <u>boom boom</u>!" "But I want to get organized. . . . So if I run in there six or eight hours later, is that going to get us in dutch?" "I'm not going to do it, you know, get shot at Tuesday and go in Thursday." AAA at Mu Gia Pass: "We're really getting hammered" while interdicting. "I'm going to get shot at Tuesday and go in last light Tuesday." "I'm talking like 24 airplanes— go in there and really let them have it."

ABRAMS: "Well, I think we'll have to take that under advisement."

BROWN: "We're trolling all the time."

SOMEONE (Rosson?): Suggests that if they were attacked and kept the attacking elements under continuous surveillance until retaliatory strikes could be organized and brought in that would be legitimate.

BROWN: "You've given me the answer I need."

ABRAMS: "I think so. And the surveillance is a very important feature of this, so that you are hitting not indiscriminately."

18 MAY 1969: WIEU

Per the tape, this is a summation for General Abrams. Per the tape box, this is a "short" WIEU.

DISCUSSION: Indications that elements of the 9th VC Division are in IV Corps (Seven Mountains region), the farthest south it has ever been according to MACV J-2 records.

ABRAMS: "It looks like to me they just declared aces wild." Seems to indicate "that things in the delta are even better than we've been reporting. This is a pretty drastic action that they're taking."

BRIEFER: The enemy began his summer campaign on the night of 11–12 May 1969. "We know from his documents that the enemy intends his campaign to be carried out in a series of phases or 'high points.'"

BRIEFER: Tomorrow (19 May 1969) will be Ho Chi Minh's birthday.

ABRAMS: "It looks like we're on the eve of some sort of increased activity. I don't think there's anything else to do but what we've done. OK, thank you."

19 MAY 1969: COMUS Special Brief

DISCUSSION: Proposed responses to a group of questions, apparently from JCS or CINCPAC.

ABRAMS (disagreeing with a portion of the briefing): "I think that a process is going on in which his tactics and his force levels is inadequate to protect the VCI. For example, April shows Tay Ninh—it's 90 some odd percent under GVN control. And this is with the 9th Division over there lurking at the—on one side, the 1st Division out there in War Zone C, the 7th Division down there in the Saigon River corridor. And the February–March offensive, where they were going to do all these things and so on. That's one example."

ABRAMS (citing progress in operations against the VCI): "That chemistry is just going on. And the foundation is steadily being built. And the effectiveness of the police and the backing of people to the efforts of these DIOCCs and so on—. You see, this is being done. And it's moving ahead. Now I'm not trying to paint a picture of where it's going to sweep the country, but you've got some things working here. As long as faith and confidence that we're on the right road, and the GVN feels that way and the Vietnamese feel that way and we feel that way and we keep at it, he isn't—he's going to lose! What he's got, and the tactics he's using—."

ABRAMS: "Another thing—he has not shaken the confidence. You see? All this stuff he's done—shooting up these places and so on—he has not weakened these people. These efforts are psychological and political and so on, and he only uses the military to <u>foster</u> and <u>encourage</u> distrust and weakness and doubt and so on. And he is not <u>doing</u> that to the Vietnamese."

ABRAMS: "I don't think his tactics, nor the force levels he's got, will get him what he's after." "The GVN control, the pacification program, and so on—it <u>has</u> gone ahead. It <u>has</u> gone ahead. It's <u>real</u>. The prices here in Saigon, the prices of food, have fluctuated very little."

ABRAMS: "What's going on is not so much how many divisions anybody's got, or how many artillery pieces anybody's got. What's going on is whether the South Vietnamese can rise up above this or whether they can't. Whether they can get it in <u>their</u> heads to stop and lick these fellows—you know, and all the things they do, or whether they have to succumb to them. And <u>I</u> think it's moving all—I think it's <u>moving</u> in <u>their</u> favor, the South Vietnamese, clearly and unmistakably. And these things are <u>not</u> having those psychological, those political, effects."

ABRAMS (re situation in South Vietnam): "He's got, <u>today</u>, three or four or five Communists between the upper and the lower house, and by god they've been <u>ineffective</u> in pushing or shoving the position of the government. Even <u>though</u> you get rocket attacks on Saigon. Even <u>though</u> somebody blows up the post office. Even <u>though</u> they terrorize the people. I'm <u>not</u> trying to be a Pollyanna about this, <u>but</u> the truth of the matter <u>is</u> that since 1964 it has <u>never</u> looked so good. There has <u>never</u> been the confidence, there has never <u>been</u> the forward movement in terms of the people <u>themselves</u>, that there is today."

ABRAMS: "I think we have a tough problem in southern I Corps. I <u>don't</u> think we've got a tough problem in III Corps, as long as we can sustain the structure and the program that we've <u>got</u> in III Corps. I don't think—this assault on Saigon, he can't make it. He could <u>try</u>, but he <u>cannot</u> <u>make</u> it. We <u>know</u> too much, we've <u>got</u> too much, we've had <u>too</u> much experience."

ABRAMS: "Now the thing that he can do that'll give us problems is bringing the 304th and the 325th in northern I Corps. Now that's the <u>one</u>—. Southern I Corps is just a <u>tough</u> pacification problem. And by bringing in the 304th and the 325th in northern I Corps, he'll present us with a problem <u>somewhere</u>, either in II Corps or III Corps. But I <u>really</u> believe that that's all he's got <u>left</u>. Ah—that's all he's got left that we can <u>see</u>. His infiltration after June won't even support what he's doing <u>now</u>, to the best of <u>our</u> knowledge. Now of course he can <u>change</u> that—maybe."

ABRAMS: "Anybody that doesn't agree with what I'm saying, I want them to speak up. I don't think <u>I</u> know everything—by a <u>long</u> shot."

ABRAMS: "Now it's true that we have got an Achilles' heel. As he goes killing Americans, the people in the United States, or at least the <u>politicians</u> in the United States, it gets <u>to</u> them. And it's why the secretary of state—he wanted to know, 'Isn't there <u>some</u> way we can do this where we don't get Americans killed?'"

SOMEONE: "He's getting weaker and we're getting stronger."

ABRAMS: "That's <u>right</u>. And that's the whole thrust of the pacification thing. It's not only the <u>program</u> and the <u>azimuth</u>, but <u>goddamn</u> <u>it</u> it <u>has</u> been <u>working</u>!

Now I know that we've been <u>very</u> reluctant to make any claims, which is <u>right</u>. But nevertheless this process <u>has</u> been going <u>on</u>. And what's been <u>done</u> is <u>real</u>." "And this is not an easy thing. All you can point to is a list of the indicators of why you believe what you believe. You can't <u>quantify</u> it!"

ABRAMS: "I want to make a great effort here to bring the intelligence processed by the JGS as close as we can to the intelligence processed by us." Schedule sometime this month a joint meeting of Vien and his J-2, plus our small group here, to go over this intelligence on every region "to see if we have a common understanding. I don't say it all has to be ours. Maybe they have some views that are different." "I would like to shoot for the first of June that we have, between us, a common appreciation of the enemy situation, our situation, and the things that can be done." "I want to thresh this thing out so that <u>either</u> General Vien and I have the <u>same</u> view <u>or</u> each of us understands why our view is different. It doesn't <u>have</u> to be the same."

21 MAY 1969: COMUS Special Brief

ATTENDEES: Gen. Abrams, Gen. Vien, MG Townsend, MG Phong, BG Potts, Col. Thiep.

BRIEFER: Describes the enemy's summer plans as viewed by MACV J-2, then raises questions. "We believe that the enemy plans to conduct another all-out offensive <u>sometime</u> during the summer." This judgment is based on documents and interrogation of PWs and Hoi Chanh. We expect "this large-scale push somewhere between mid-June to July." We believe "the enemy hopes his summer campaign will be more intense than any he has carried out so far." We expect it to "be conducted in a series of phases or high points, climaxing in his all-out offensive."

PHONG (re NVA in IV Corps): "What they have to gain is to control the population. And since the delta is the manpower source, I think that they have to move the troops in."

ABRAMS: "I think my biggest problem is I don't think he should have done it. But he's <u>done</u> it!" [Laughter]

PHONG: "Remember, General Abrams, that the Communists have a different dialectic. It's true—their reasoning is different from us. You cannot say that they will <u>do</u> that, but they <u>will</u> do that."

ABRAMS: "If I had a division commander, an American division commander, who for the last three months had taken the casualties that the division commander of the 9th VC Division has taken, I would be <u>forced</u> to relieve him. No, I <u>would</u>, because this is such a <u>problem</u>." "What do you suppose would happen if I sent in a report that said the 2nd of the 502nd had had 285 killed last night—last night? What do you think would happen? Well, they'd look around for some more <u>talent</u>!"

VIEN: "Maybe they did already."

24 MAY 1969: WIEU

BRIEFER: "Over the past nine weeks only two probable infiltration groups have been observed moving south through North Vietnam." "The Binh Tram 8–T-12 communications link, normally our primary source of information, continues in normal operation."

ABRAMS: "Incidentally, going back to this Hill 937, at one time I got a report that the first battalion up on the top was an ARVN battalion. I don't really know how that thing finally turned out. But anyway, the way it was shown on TV here was the 101. I don't know _what_ the _facts_ are."

Referring to the battle at what came to be known as Hamburger Hill.

ABRAMS (re the Citadel at Hue during Tet 1968): "It was really the Black Panthers company. The company commander took that Communist flag and ran back to the headquarters with it and gave it to General Truong in his office, and he made him a captain right on the spot—and then called up the president to get it authorized."

SOMEONE (re Hamburger Hill): "They got up to the crest of the hill, as a matter of fact ahead of the artillery preparation that was going in. The resistance was on the west slope—the 3rd of the—3/187. And they then had to back Dinh's battalion off the top of the hill so they could put the artillery in on the reverse slope. So then he—it was an hour and a half later when he got _back_ on top of the hill and _met_ them. He was there to meet the 3rd of the 187th. So the facts are the first people to the crest was the ARVN."

■ ■ ■

ABRAMS: "In the great fishbowl that we're doing everything in it's kind of unfortunate, but the _cosmetics_ of the thing are more important than what's _accomplished_—in a great many ways. And I think we've got to be _sensitive_ to that. We've _still_ got to get the job _done_. I'm not—we must _never_ lose sight of _that_. But _now_ the _cosmetics_ of it, as long as you can stay with the _facts_, and it's very _important_ in the world fishbowl that we're in—we're just like—we're like a half a dozen goldfish, all of us together, swimming around in a goddamn crystal bowl. And _everybody_ in the world's looking at us. Christ, you can't even take a shower that somebody isn't _seeing_ it. I mean, it's _really_—that's the way it _is_. And, as long as it _is_ that way, we ought to see what the whole thing is. Don't let any of these goldfish get in front of another one—you know, so they can't see the second one—they think they're all females, because they can't see any males. It's all U.S., because you can't see any ARVN."

ABRAMS: "Another thing, you can't say, 'Well, piss on it, we've got our TV and they've got their TV. They can cover their side on their TV and we'll cover our side on ours—our TV.' Well, that's no way to _do_ it. We've got to see that our TV covers _both_ sides. That means what you—what's said to the reporters—. I know everybody's proud of their unit." "I never did it when _I_ had a unit, I didn't brag about anybody else's outfit. But that was another _war_. That's not the _same_ as this one. But, ah—. Now, I must say that when people go visiting up there—well, _anywhere_—this is made very clear to the visitors. But the problem is it's not getting on the TV and it's not getting in the news." "Now, mind you, I'm not talking about building up something that isn't there, not for one second. But where there is good performance, by god it's got to be shown, and we've got to see to it that it's done."

■ ■ ■

ABRAMS (re a chart showing an estimate of VCI neutralized during the month): "That's a very difficult calculation, because you've got to know how many there are, and that's what we don't have too good a handle on."

ABRAMS: Cites "that sort of inexorable axiom that the more statistics you assemble the greater your appetite becomes for even more statistics. Somehow—somehow you feel that, in the end, you can solve the whole god-damn problem if you just had enough statistics!" "But [re the array of statistics displayed at the WIEU] this has gotten better every week. It doesn't mean we should stop. We're portraying a relative environment. We're getting a little nearer."

COLBY: "That HES—limiting it to the security, and limiting it to the rural popu-lation, I think is a very good figure, because you see how that does transpose against the contacts per operation and so forth."

■ ■ ■

ABRAMS: "Incidentally, I was out at one of the fire support bases of the 1st Cav-alry yesterday." "They'd just been there a short time—two days. But I found the development of the position was really quite impressive. It has a lot to do with the effectiveness when the thing gets under attack. It looked to me like it was pretty stout." "Actually, one of the things I was thinking of as I got into the helicopter to leave—I wouldn't mind spending a night out there myself, even if it was going to be attacked. I think it's pretty good."

■ ■ ■

ABRAMS (re the enemy versus ARVN): "Incidentally, the mission of that unit to draw units away from Xuan Loc coincides with our own. We've been trying to get them out of Xuan Loc, too." [Laughter] [The mission of the 174th NVA Regiment had been briefed as "to ambush allied force along Route 20 and draw troops away from Xuan Loc."] "Maybe between the two of us we'll suc-ceed."

EWELL: "Considering the past history of the 18th ARVN, they've done a pretty good job the past couple of weeks. They've killed 300 or 400." "That's not bad for government work."

ABRAMS: "I would like nothing better than to be proven wrong about the 18th [ARVN Division]."

ABRAMS (re enemy KIA summary): "I must say that, in the many weeks that we've been looking at this chart, the RVNAF in III Corps looks better than it ever has—in the whole history of this chart." "This has been a most irritating thing to look at, Saturday after Saturday. And I suppose the 18th [ARVN Divi-sion] has influenced this week as much as anybody else."

ABRAMS: "By golly, that RF and PF down there in IV Corps—they certainly are in the war."

30 MAY 1969: COMUS Brief on VC Strategy

ATTENDEES: Gen. Abrams, MG Townsend, BG Potts. Briefer: LTC Criton.

BRIEFER:

■ "We have strong evidence that the enemy is once again in the process of changing his strategy, perhaps a far-reaching change. The most outward sign is the recent meeting of North Vietnamese ambassadors in Hanoi." It included at least nine envoys to East European bloc nations. They arrived in Hanoi on 4 May 1969, probably, aboard an IL-14 from Peking. "Two previously known meetings of this type occurred at major turning points in the enemy's strategy, one in July 1967 after he decided to escalate to the general offensive/general uprising, the other during late November and early December 1968 after the enemy developed his post-bombing halt plans."

■ "Coincidental was Le Duc Tho's 3 May return from Hanoi to Paris. He'd been absent from Paris since 10 February [1969], the longest single absence since the talks began. He was in Hanoi throughout the enemy's post-Tet 1969 offensive, the subsequent reappraisal of it, and any resultant decisions made by the Hanoi leadership. The meeting of the ambassadors was possibly called in late March."

■ "Also during late March there were some significant shifts in enemy activity. First, we saw the start of what appears to be a major suspension of infiltration groups entering the pipeline. Not a single group was detected entering the pipeline for six weeks between 20 March and 1 May. With the reappearance of an infiltration group on 1 May, and another on May 3rd, it is probable that infiltration had both stopped during the intervening period and has stopped again subsequent to those two groups." Those [***] were "headed for the B-3 Front."

■ Re infiltration during the period September 1968–20 March 1969: "May have been the major part of what the enemy intended to send to South Vietnam for a full year. The 72,000 total is between two-thirds and three-quarters of what he sent to South Vietnam in 1966 and 1967. His surge effort may have been to take advantage of the dry season and what he may have viewed as a short-lived bombing halt." Other possibility: Limitation of his training base. We estimate that capacity at 78,000 to 96,000 per year. Or it may have been the "result of the enemy's reappraisal of the successes and failures of his 1969 post-Tet offensive." Maybe they changed training to provide "more emphasis on small unit, guerrilla, and sapper tactics, or techniques of standoff attacks." Maybe there is "a manpower shortage in North Vietnam."

■ But a recent CIA/DIA study credits North Vietnam with being able to sustain "its forces in the south at the 1968 loss rate for at least several more years."

■ "Unless we see a surge equal to or exceeding his early 1968 effort, the number of North Vietnamese soldiers being pumped into South Vietnam after July will be far less than that required to support the enemy's current level and intensity of warfare and the resultant losses he's taking from it. On the same day that infiltration was suspended, the 20th of March, we saw the start of a possibly seasonally premature decline in enemy logistical movement within the Laotian panhandle. For two months now, truck movements in Laos reported by sensors have continued their downward spiral. By 22 April traffic had dropped to approximately half its late March peak, and by now is only a small fraction of that earlier level."

■ "The third significant trend which began during the latter part of March is the redeployment of some important enemy units. [***] to the 304th Division, [***] started the southward movement of the 57th Regiment. At approximately the same time, the 2nd NVA Division started its southerly shift." "In III Corps during this general time period there was yet another important enemy redeployment." According to PWs, advance elements of the 273rd Regiment departed Hau Nghia Province in early April for Chau Doc Province. This is "the first sizable deployment of NVA to IV Corps."

■ "Half of his in-country recruitment comes from IV Corps, which contains only a third of the population."

■ Another trend appearing in documents in late March "was the initial note of doubt by the Communist hierarchy and a recognition that victory may still be a long way off." Cites a "19 March message from Ho Chi Minh to soldiers and cadre in South Vietnam which hints at a long period of fighting ahead." Also cites a "Sub-Region 2 document which received so much public attention. It clearly sees the need for the longer haul when it points out that 'we do not intend to obtain the victory overnight or in a single phase, nor do we plan to obtain the victory in any predetermined phase after conducting many phases. The victory will not come to us in such an easy way. It will come in a difficult and complicated way.' And a key closing phrase: 'It will be a limited victory.'" Also cites a Sub-Region 3 document that states that "the all-out offensive and uprising is not the [strategy?]. It will consist of many phases intended to gradually compel the Americans to accept their defeat.' The operative word is 'gradually.' Both these documents are probably the result of new guidance set forth by COSVN in late March." A PW refers to a "new COSVN resolution dated 26 March [1969]."

■ But, per a Sub-Region 6 report about a meeting attended by General Nguyen Huu Xuyen, deputy commander, Liberation Army, Xuyen reportedly stated in a private conversation "that if the military attack plan for the summer should fail, the VC military forces will have to fall back on the defensive and will not be able to launch further offensives. He even left the door open by saying progress in the Paris peace talks could cause cancellation of the summer offensive." "General Xuyen is not the only one who suggests the possibility of one final offensive." At an early April meeting in II Corps an NVA captain read a message from Ho Chi Minh that stated, according to a Hoi Chanh, "that allied defensive positions would be vital targets in the coming final offensive to be waged during the monsoon season."

■ The enemy has good reasons for changing his strategy. "His numerical strength is fast diminishing. His losses so far in 1969 have way outpaced his gains." "Total net loss for the seven-month period is over 52,000."

■ "There is an ambivalence in the enemy's current plans and outlook. All our evidence points to yet another offensive this summer." "Yet there is also evidence of the enemy's recognition that he must be prepared psychologically and militarily to stretch out the war for the long pull."

■ "His current logistical and manpower assets are adequate to support another all-out offensive, particularly in III Corps. We expect his next offensive to be similar to the one he launched in February of this year." This will cost him heavy losses, however, and from what we see so far "he has not planned and possibly is not capable of replacing them." "If his next offensive should fail, as it surely will, his alternative to defeat will be a severe reduction of the intensity of his fighting and the amount of force he can commit to South Vietnam." "There are signs, though tenuous ones, that he's recognized this and already started his long-range readjustment." "He must soon, or perhaps already has, abandon the general offensive/general uprising and revert to a type of warfare we saw before Tet of 1968. As Ho Chi Minh said in a letter of November 1968, . . . 'a stable must be constructed according to the size of the cow.'"

ABRAMS: "Well, Carter [Townsend]?"
TOWNSEND: "This is not the time to relax."
ABRAMS: "No, it sure isn't."

31 MAY 1969: WIEU

ATTENDEES: Gen. Abrams, Gen. Rosson, Gen. Brown, Amb. Colby, LTG Mildren, VADM Zumwalt, Dr. Wikner, MG Wetherill, MG Conroy, MG Townsend, Mr. Jacobson, MG Shaefer, BG Frizen, BG Bautz, BG Long, BG McLaughlin, BG Clay, BG Bryan, BG Potts, Capt. McNulty, Col. Gorman, Col. Cavanaugh Col. Hill, Col. Powers.

BRIEFER: "Sensors in Laos are used primarily to detect truck movement, while sensors in-country are used to detect personnel movement."

■ ■ ■

BROWN: "We can always entice them into shooting at us."

■ ■ ■

SOMEONE: Recalls a point made by the president (Nixon, presumably) in a speech or broadcast "that he wouldn't insist that they acknowledge that they [North Vietnam] have forces in South Vietnam, because the case could be made prima facie in other ways anyway."

■ ■ ■

ABRAMS (re effective operations against enemy forces threatening Saigon): "But I think it also had something to do with all this crap about 'the way to save casualties is to stay in your base camp.' Well, nothing like the Vam Co Dong and the Vam Co Tay and out there in that goddamn swamp and fire bases and patrols and Frontier City and [Fire Support Base] Diamond and so on. Just sit back there and give the son of a bitch a <u>free</u> ride! And let him get <u>all</u> his stuff hauled in, and <u>all</u> his troops ready, and then <u>clobber</u> the <u>hell</u> out of you!"

"Christ, we haven't had Saigon burning [knocks on wood] for over a year!"

ABRAMS: "Like I told Fred Weyand out there to give his summary of what happened in the May 5th offensive. He got all through what a great success it had been. I said, 'Well, I agree with you. But,' I said, 'you know I came out here frequently, several times a week, and as I rode back in my helicopter after hearing how well we were doing smoke was billowing up in Saigon, flames shooting up in the air, and,' I said, 'I have estimated that we can successfully defend Saigon seven more times, and then we're going to be faced with the embarrassment that there's no city left. And I don't know how the hell we're going to explain these nine successful defenses of Saigon, but no goddamn city.'"

ABRAMS (re Hamburger Hill): "After all, you know, the 29th that they tangled with up there, the 29th was in Hue last year. And this year the 29th fought out there on Hamburger Hill. They weren't within—Christ, they weren't within V-2 range of Hue." "So I don't know whether it's better—. Well, I do know [laughing]. I think it's better to fight the 29th in the A Shau. We wouldn't get any less casualties fighting them in Hue. We took a lot of casualties in Hue. S-o-o-o—. I don't know why these people can't—. Of course, Senator Kennedy does have military experience. He was a guard at Norstad's headquarters. I think he got to be a Speedy Four. [Someone: "No, sir, PFC."] PFC?" "Yeah, but hell, it's serious business."

"Speedy Four" is slang for specialist four, one rank higher than private first class.

7 JUN 1969: WIEU

ATTENDEES: Gen. Abrams, Gen. Rosson, Gen. Brown, Amb. Colby, LTG Mildren, VADM Zumwalt, Dr. Wikner, MG Conroy, MG Townsend, Mr. Jacobson, BG Potts, BG Bautz, BG Frizen, BG Bryan, BG Vande Hey, BG Galloway, BG McLaughlin, Col. Gorman. Col. Sykes, Col. Cavanaugh, Col. Ramsey, Col. [Timora?], Col. Powers.

BRIEFER: No new infiltration groups during the past week. "The Binh Tram 8–T–12 communications link, normally our primary source of infiltration information, continues in operation, passing both administrative and logistics traffic."

∎ ∎ ∎

BROWN: "I had a conversation in Vientiane with Devlin, who's the CAS fellow, and the attachés, army and air force, who were the three operators up there on this Base Area 604, and told them that I just didn't think we could continue to live with two standards." "[Words unclear], while up north someone pulled things down to six clicks [kilometers], 250 meter restrictions when they got panicky. And that this area'd been in the hands of the Communists for about four or five years, the good people'd been driven out or [words unclear] slaves, and we ought to go in there and clean it up—and unrestricted access to it. And they agreed. And I said, 'Well, why hasn't it been approved when we talked about it before?' And they said, 'Well, that was Ambassador Sullivan.' And they made it sound as though he personally—now that he'd left town we had a fighting chance. 'Well,' I said, 'what do you need?' And they said, 'We'll work up a package.'" "When Godley gets there it will be right on his desk."

Ambassador William H. Sullivan was being replaced by Ambassador G. McMurtrie Godley at the U.S. Embassy in Vientiane.

BROWN: "I also talked to them about the great disparity between the road watch team reports and sensors and VR—you know, FACs and all that. We've got a concentrated effort going to try to find some correlation. If they were off by a factor of about 20 percent you wouldn't be too concerned, but it sometimes runs 60 percent. He told me of all the work they go to to try to catch their guys cheating. . . . They're working the problem."

POTTS: "Here in our evaluation we take sensors first. . . . And we fall back on road watch teams only if we don't have anything else."

■ ■ ■

ABRAMS: "One of the reasons they [the enemy] go there is that's the tactical area of responsibility of the 7th Regiment of the 5th Division. It's one of the safest places that the VC can assemble. God, that—won't get out. They told me out there the other day the regimental commander's never been out of his CP—except to go to Saigon."

BRIEFER: There is evidence that the enemy is planning further high points similar to the coordinated indirect fire and sapper attacks conducted on the night of 11–12 May 1969. We believe the events of the night of 5–6 June were another such. Each month during May, June, and July is expected to have "its brief surge of activity."

BRIEFER (re the 5–6 June 1969 upsurge of enemy activity): Attacks by fire are "still the primary, now almost exclusive means of attack." "Notable is the continued reduction in the number of rounds expended per attack, now only 13." "A reliable agent has described a meeting in Tay Ninh Province, conducted 14–16 May, concerning VC plans during the 1969 Summer Campaign. Describing military activity, he quotes the VC leadership as saying, 'It is our experience that shelling need not be intensive. Three to 15 rounds will be adequate for surprise shelling. Any more will be useless.'"

ABRAMS: "How about those 113 rockets that were—in [place name unclear] up there? That guy hasn't got the word." [Laughter]

BRIEFER: Notes a "sharp reversal of a trend which has been building since the Tet attacks of 1968—U.S. forces and installations are not his primary target this time."

BRIEFER: Per agent report of the new COSVN guidance for the 1969 Summer Campaign: "We must understand clearly that attacks on and elimination of Americans, though very important, fulfill our immediate objective only, that of forcing the Americans to settle the war. The important long-range objective is elimination of the puppet army and other forces of opposition which are being nurtured by the Americans to replace them as they withdraw."

BRIEFER: "Apparently the enemy has again shifted his emphasis, this time to attack the ARVN and RD security forces whose growing viability and effectiveness is a correspondingly growing threat to his long-term survival."

■ ■ ■

ABRAMS: "President Thieu has told his people there are two objectives. One is pacification and the other is replacement of the U.S. by ARVN—or by RVNAF. In other words, both of these things have got to be done. And it means that, over time here, more and more the Vietnamese have got to take on the task. Now, one of the problems they have, the Vietnamese—of course we all have it, but it's just the ponderous nature of bureaucracy. And we're going to have to, more and more, keep after this machinery and get it to do the things that it must do." "It's getting in there and pointing out these goddamn things that anybody with any common sense knows has got to be done."

ABRAMS: "I think we're doing very well on administrative and logistical support of combat troops." "But we need to have this attitude of the logistics offensive spread out into the whole damn thing." "And we need to develop this in the Vietnamese, too. If a fellow wants to get discouraged, I've often thought that this is about the easiest place in the world to do it, if that's what you want to do—the opportunities are legion, but in this thing now, we've got to pick it up. There's an awful lot to be done here."

COLBY: At a II Corps meeting, a province chief stood up and said, "'General, I'd pacify those 10 hamlets if I could find them, but I can't find them.' And nobody laughed."

JACOBSON: "This was really a high point of my time in Vietnam."

ABRAMS: "Well, I'll leave this afternoon and go to Honolulu for the meeting, and on to Midway for another one. And we'll just have to see how things work out. I want to thank the staff. There's been a lot of poop pulled together, stuff that will be very valuable to me. I think I ought to be, with what I have, prepared to address just about anything they want to talk about in connection with this thing over here. All right, thank you."

12 JUN 1969: Commanders Conference

Attendees: Gen. Abrams, Gen. Rosson, Gen. Brown, Amb. Colby, LTG Mildren, LTG Nickerson, LTG Stilwell, VADM Zumwalt, LTG Ewell, Dr. Wikner, MG Russ, MG Wetherill, MG Conroy, MG Townsend, Mr. Jacobson, BG Frizen, BG Bautz, BG Potts, BG Galloway, Col. [Stiner?], Col. Ramsey, BG Vande Hey, Col. Hill, BG Wheelock, Col. Starry, LTC Walker.

Briefing by Lt. Col. Donald Marshall on area security. Abrams has brought Marshall, who worked on the PROVN Study, out as his long-range planner to facilitate implementation of PROVN (Program for the Pacification and Long-Term Development of Vietnam). This is a crucial session in delineating Abrams's approach to conduct of the war.

MARSHALL: The purpose of the briefing is "to provide you with details of the principles for area security. This is a fundamental concept of the MACV

Strategic Objectives Plan presented to you at the 5 April [1969] Commanders meeting."

■ "For the enemy to achieve his ultimate objective of political control of South Vietnam, it's necessary for him to demonstrate to the populace that the GVN is not capable of providing its citizens with personal security, even with U.S. assistance. And too often the enemy is successful in demonstrating the GVN inability to provide security, by either threatening GVN-controlled areas himself or by provoking an exceptionally destructive response by allied forces."

■ "There can be considered to be essentially two military approaches to defeat the enemy ambitions and accomplish U.S. objectives in Vietnam. The first approach focuses on destruction of the enemy main forces in the belief that, by destroying the enemy's <u>combat</u> units, the ultimate security of the people is assured. In practice, however, U.S. policy denies friendly operations to cross the borders, which precludes total destruction of the enemy forces. A second limitation can be the tendency to slight those aspects of local security that <u>could</u> provide protection for the Vietnamese people. Finally, critics argue that some of the allied counteroperations frequently constitute as great a threat to Vietnamese people themselves as that posed by the enemy."

■ "What is perceived to be a threat is a variable. A military commander's definition of threat, for example, may differ from that of a villager. The rural Vietnamese farmer, even one leaning toward the government of Vietnam, who is in a military commander's tactical area of responsibility may regard <u>both</u> the enemy forces <u>and</u> the friendly forces as a threat to his security, that is to his safety, his well-being and that of his family." "While a PF soldier and a U.S. commander normally would fear artillery fire only from the <u>enemy</u>, a <u>villager</u> fears our artillery and air strikes as much as he fears the enemy rockets or mortars. Thus actions taken by one element to ensure security may constitute a threat to <u>another</u> element in whose name the action is taken."

■ "The second approach is to focus on providing security for the people. If the people are secure, the government will be able to expand its authority and strengthen itself. Thus operations should be focused on destruction of the VC infrastructure and local forces while preventing main forces from reaching the population centers. The enemy main forces are blind without the VC infrastructure. They cannot obtain intelligence, they cannot obtain food, and they cannot prepare the battlefield."

■ "<u>Neither</u> approach in itself is appropriate at all times countrywide. Neither is exclusive of the other. But a careful mixture of the two strategic approaches is appropriate. This briefing focuses upon the second approach and the relationship between the two."

■ "The first strategic approach . . . best describes many of the allied operations in Vietnam until recently, focused upon . . . the destruction of the main forces."

■ "Advocates of [the second strategic] approach favor the creation of more effective territorial forces and express their doubt as to whether the ultimate product of the RVNAF Improvement & Modernization Program, by itself, is sufficient for the job to be done."

■ "The MACV Strategic Objectives Plan . . . provides for area security at the present level of hostilities while at the same time takes into account the requirements of a posthostilities system." Cites the "vital mission of controlling and protecting the people, which is the principal objective of both sides in this revolutionary warfare."

■ "The key to an effective security system is assignment of responsibility for security in each area to a single individual who has control of all the necessary military, police, and paramilitary assets located within his own clearly defined area of responsibility."

■ "The ultimate objective is security up to the borders of South Vietnam which is not dependent on the continued presence of U.S. combat forces. The enemy will be more vulnerable, and the enemy strategy of winning by weakening the resolve of the United States will be less relevant, since the security will be provided ultimately by Vietnamese forces, which could weaken the enemy's resolve to continue the war, something that's not been done up until now."

■ "A third principal feature of the system is provision of clear support for a progressive movement from military to civilian rule within the government of Vietnam. That is, as security progressively is established, and then retained, the citizen increasingly will be protected by police, People's Self-Defense Forces, and territorial rather than regular forces, leaving the regular forces a more mobile role. The citizen will be governed by elected civil officials rather than appointed military officers. Increasing security will mean increasing government service, with civilian officials rather than military activities and the presence of soldiers."

■ "The term 'area security,' used to identify the concept, refers to a delineation of authority and responsibility for providing security for the populace in the area concerned, not to the defense of the geographic area itself."

■ "The populated area is considered secure when the normal functions of an effective local government are conducted and there is freedom of movement within the area, both day and night, except for GVN administrative controls. There is no imminent threat of attack by enemy formations at the organized squad level or above, and terrorist activity is reduced to a level characterized by only occasional acts of violence. Indirect fire attacks constitute only a remote threat and most urban precincts and rural hamlets in the area have an A or B security rating under the Hamlet Evaluation System, or HES."

■ "In the transitional zone between the secure area and the clearing zone, hamlets predominantly will have C ratings under the HES. There is an ever-increasing degree of GVN security here, and this zone provides a security screen for the secure area and it is undergoing intensive pacification operations. Security within this consolidation zone is provided primarily by the Territorial Forces. The contested area, the clearing zone, contains outlying friendly operational bases and includes unpopulated as well as VC-controlled areas broken into tactical areas of responsibility assigned to ARVN divisions, although separate U.S./Free World TAORs that exist now may continue to be necessary until ARVN can take over."

■ "The border surveillance zone is contiguous to the national borders of South Vietnam. Border surveillance and interdiction activities within this zone detect the enemy approach and prevent his buildup and reinforcement capability."

■ "Where operations are focused on the enemy main forces and base areas, that is in the clearing zone, the ARVN division or other mobile field unit commander is responsible for security operations."

■ "In areas where operations are focused on increasing the level of security and expanding the functions of government, that is in the secure and the consolidation zones, the province chief has the security responsibility."

■ "Initially, due to the specific criteria of security, the secure areas . . . will be very limited in size and few in number. At the completion of this 1969 pacification campaign, for example, most of the areas which might be designated 'secure' then will be part of what now would have to be classed as the consolidation zone."

■ "The principal task within the secure area is to maintain and increase the quality of security. National Police and National Police Field Force operations will concentrate upon the provision of law and order, populace and resources control, and preventing the regeneration of the VC infrastructure through surveillance, checkpoints, patrol operations, and other standard police techniques."

■ "Popular Forces, assisted by People's Self-Defense Forces, will constitute the basic defense of the villages, hamlets, and precincts within the secure area. Popular Force units will continue patrolling among the hamlets, will assist the National Police in manning checkpoints, and will deploy ambushes to pick up any infiltrators that might have slipped through the consolidation zone."

■ "There are two principal tasks within the consolidation zone. First, to protect the secure area, and second, to raise the level of security within the consolidation zone itself. As in the secure area, friendly operations are focused primarily on protection of the population in the zone rather than chasing the enemy outside the zone."

■ "Territorial Forces will protect the police, as well as other government agents, provide hamlet and village defense, make extensive use of small-unit and night ambush to detect enemy units and prevent the movement of enemy commo-liaison personnel and carrying parties."

■ "By saturating an area with ambushes, enemy movement can be reduced substantially. Defense of hamlets and villages will be facilitated by the fact that the enemy will find it difficult to assemble for an attack. Police working in the villages to neutralize the VC infrastructure also will be protected. The enemy infiltrators will find it extremely difficult to get to the secure area, and the inability of the enemy to move about freely will disrupt his recruiting and proselyting activities, his communications network, and his logistics system."

■ "Military activity in the consolidation zone is characterized by continuous day and night patrolling to seek out and destroy enemy units, the VC infrastructure, caches, and indirect fire weapons positions. This procedure should assure that nothing larger than an enemy platoon will be able to operate in the area without immediate detection. Populace and resources control is intensive. The movement of personnel and commodities is limited and subject to continuous checks and controls during daylight, and a curfew is strictly enforced during darkness."

■ "To ensure achievement of the purposes of the consolidation zone, the zone that is critical to this concept, we must provide a means for more rapidly upgrading the Territorial Forces which will carry out most of the task here. To accomplish this within the time we can realistically expect to have at our disposal requires employment of some U.S. manpower. From the experience of the CAPs and the MATs, the Mobile Strike Forces and the PRUs, we've learned what relatively small numbers of properly selected, properly motivated U.S. personnel can accomplish with Vietnamese paramilitary personnel, and we should build upon that experience."

■ "The consolidation zone thus serves a dual purpose. It's the area where active, detailed, in-depth pacification is conducted. It's also the buffer between the secure area and the clearing operation zone. Military operations, particularly the massive use of the night ambush in-depth system, are designed to provide a very high degree of probability of detection and engagement of hostile units moving toward the objectives therein and keeping them outside of the secure area."

■ "In the clearing zone, friendly operations focus on the enemy main forces and base areas. ARVN should be free to concentrate on mobile operations against the enemy. In the past, the overwhelming mobility and firepower of U.S. forces, as well as the aggressiveness of U.S. commanders, and/or the reluctance of ARVN commanders, often has led to U.S. domination of the TAOR, with ARVN being squeezed, or permitting themselves to remain in, a subsidiary role. This problem must be overcome."

■ In Hau Nghia Province "there were several commanders taking responsibility for the area but orienting on, in each case, seeking out and destroying the Viet Cong, but . . . even the province chief was not oriented upon the protection of the populace of the area."

■ "The HES C security category upon which the 1969 effort is based simply does not provide for sufficient security for the populace to ensure their cooperation with the GVN, nor does it adequately deny the resources of the populace to the VC, particularly to the VC infrastructure. In our view the C category goal of the pacification campaign does not provide security for the population from the threat of VC infrastructure terrorism." "Stated another way, the HES category C simply is too porous to provide for the success in a conflict in which the population is the primary object for both sides."

ABRAMS: "Questions or comments?"
1ST QUESTION (Wetherill): "One thing that puzzles me a little bit about this—

and I think practically this is a very worthy concept and ought to be furthered—but take the Hau Nghia example. How much reshuffling of RF and PF are required within the province to get this arrangement within the secure area and consolidation zone?"

MARSHALL: "This presumes that there will be a steady movement of RF, very much less so of PF, although it also presumes that PF will be moved in the secure areas individually to a different category." Police and PSDF will take over.

2ND QUESTION (Ewell): "Is this just an intellectual exercise or is this a serious proposal?" [Laughter] "If the latter I would like to comment to it. If it's just an intellectual drill I'd as soon not comment."

ABRAMS: "No, go ahead and comment."

EWELL: "Well, this really is reinventing the wheel by another name. This is an oil spot theory from Malaya—Malaysia. And there's nothing wrong with that. I suppose it's hard to dream up anything new. I detect, particularly in this area, I would imagine in parts of I Corps you could make this fit very nicely, but I think it would be a very bad mistake at this juncture, or in the foreseeable future, to give the ARVN division commander an excuse to go after nothing but main force units, because that's what they're trying to do now. And that's part of why we're in jail. They look for main force units 10 clicks down the road, and can have local guerrillas running around right outside the compound terrorizing the people."

EWELL: "But I—I think this concept, at least in the Saigon area, requires a high degree of cooperation on the part of the enemy. He has to react according to the way you conceive the operation, and I think his whole process is to upset balanced situations. Where you get a balanced situation, his whole tactic is to stick something in there to upset that situation. I think you need a much more mobile concept than this would—ah—ah—envisage."

EWELL: "Oh, I don't basically resist the methodology. What I resist is that the ARVN do what you tell them, and if you told them to do this, they'd do that and nothing else. And I think it would be very difficult to apply in an area where the security—the real security—situation is quite edgy." "And the way you maximize effectiveness is you take the PF, RF, the PRU, the ARVN, and U.S., and they're all cutting across everything in sight. And each one takes a piece out. And the ultimate result becomes very painful to the enemy."

EWELL: "I'd be very uneasy about this except in maybe the Saigon area itself as you draw it out."

3RD QUESTION (Colby): "I think the problem is that conceptually, as stated, it really has a great deal to commend it as logic. But when you then go to look on the map of where the D hamlets are, and where the B ones and the C ones and so forth, and then consider cutting your command channels different for those different ones, I get a little lost as to whether I can find a place which is properly a division commander's in zone D and a place which is properly only a province chief's without the ARVN—because they're so mixed up, I think, in the real world. And of course they change from month to month, because the

VC moves around or because something else happens. As a concept, as a basic approach to the problem, <u>sure</u>—but when you tinker with the command lines, I get a little unsure there."

4TH QUESTION (Ewell): "I'd be a little unclear as to where to <u>start</u> on this to lay it out in all III Corps."

5TH QUESTION (Jacobson): "I don't think you could <u>start</u> on it. I think it's an <u>objective</u>. For example, there are very few secure areas in Vietnam right now, very few areas in the middle of Saigon where the government would be comfortable if there were only the police on the beat and, let's say, a PF squad. Also, the concept envisages everybody doing their job the way they're supposed to do it. If the RF and the PF in the consolidation area <u>actually</u> put out <u>meaningful</u> ambushes in every place where they <u>could</u>, and where a driving U.S. commander <u>would</u> do it, it would be a very different situation, and it would work—probably. I view this as something to work <u>toward</u>, not something to go <u>into</u> on a specific date."

6TH QUESTION (Nickerson): "Well, I'd like to interpose an objection to all this. I think that's the most outstanding review I've seen on how to win this war."

ABRAMS: "The difficulty with Hue is that they can still occasionally shoot a rocket in there." "I'm quibbling over stuff, but Hue has that <u>one</u> deficiency." "It has nothing to do with the effectiveness [of RF and PF], <u>fucking</u> geography and jungle and that stuff."

SOMEONE: "If you could move the hills back."

ABRAMS: "Yeah, that's right. Well, you could get Herman Kahn to work on that." [Laughter]

Kahn, a defense theorist who headed the Hudson Institute, had recommended building a moat around Saigon.

ABRAMS: "If you got from this the idea that we're <u>proposing</u>, or <u>thinking</u> of saying, that by 1 August, or 1 November, or something like that, or 1 <u>January</u>, a-a-a-l-l-l provinces in South Vietnam will be configured into this philosophy, it's not the case at all. But as a philosophy, and as a method, Marshall's descriptions of—for instance, the political necessities of the moment—are really quite realistic." "In the long term of getting the kind of a South Vietnam that they've got to have here in order to <u>live</u>, in order to <u>really</u> make it, they've got to go to some—this—when you're talking about B minus and that sort of thing, that's where you've got to <u>get</u>. Then you have the political strength. Then you'll be on the way to getting a hold of things."

COLBY: "I think Rod Wetherill may have said the point, but really what this does is give you a tool to set <u>goals</u> [Abrams: "<u>Yeah</u>."] for planning. In other words, your <u>goal</u> is that by the end of October you'd be in a situation where a certain area—."

NICKERSON: "Why don't you put it another way, that it is a <u>method</u> by which you <u>attain</u> your goals? Because this is really what it is. It's a blueprint for you to follow in order to <u>get</u> there."

ABRAMS: "The other thing about this is that it's <u>realistic</u>. The only way most

Vietnamese can see advancing right now is that they have to have more PF, they have to have more police, they have to have more RF, and they've got to increase the size of ARVN. This, this—they cling to this in the face of the reality of a lack of manpower to support any such damn thing! And sustain it! You might be able to assemble the structure, let's say for the first of November. You'd have it one day, and the minute somebody started a fight the fucking thing would start going down. They haven't got the manpower to do all this, not under the circumstances. And this . . . realistically looks out in the future and sees that you've got to have a system and a concept that will permit you to accomplish what you've got to accomplish for this government within the realistic manpower resources that are available to them."

ABRAMS: Invites Marshall to comment.

EWELL (before Marshall has a chance to respond): "Have you still got a copy of AB/138 around? It would be interesting to compare your charts with the formulation of Colonel Nguyen Duc Thang."

MARSHALL: "We're very sensitive to the charge that this is a revival of the oil spot theory. I've never been able to find a good explanation of the oil spot theory. However, whether it is or is not what was originally contemplated, we think the principles involved are the significant thing, and not the good or bad connotations of the term 'oil spot.'" Reemphasizes crucial night ambushes; key role of RF and PF being advised by the United States "on an austere basis, on a sequential basis, on a temporary basis." "I think, General Ewell, you are quite right when you say there isn't very much new here, if anything. We hope that these are tested principles, because we feel that they must work. This is not something we can try and not have work." Next step: test provinces.

EWELL: "Well, I apologize for brass knuckling you for inventing the wheel. That was a low blow."

ABRAMS: "We're all trained to it, Julian." [Laughter]

EWELL: "I would be willing to predict, if we don't get a massive drawdown, that in the Saigon area in between 6 to 12 months that you will begin to develop a core area which is manageable in what I call the Malaysian approach, where you're beginning to make the turnover from the military to a civilian-type approach. But it's going to take lots of work. It's going to be real tough. It's complicated by the fact that you have six divisions sitting not too far down the road. You have to control the six divisions [in border sanctuaries], the local main force regiment, the local battalions, the local companies, and the guerrillas, all at the same time. Sort of an octopus is required to keep his finger on all these people."

EWELL: "And I'm afraid if you go into too formalized a structure you aren't going to be able to keep the pressure on all these people at the time, because it takes a highly sensitive and mobile type of operation. Once you get out where you have this manageable area, then I think you can start making this work." "The one thing which really bothers me, which the Communists haven't done—if they go to a pure guerrilla war with their main forces, boy that's going to be tough." "The only thing that saves us is that COSVN is a bunch of militaristic goddamn army officers who want to win the war in big battles. If they ever flip it over, for six months that thing's just going to be hanging in the balance."

ABRAMS: "Well, I don't know. I know it could create problems, but so much of their military manpower is now North Vietnamese that they're not the—."

EWELL: "They may have lost the option."

NICKERSON: "Eighty-seven percent, Ewell, is NVA."

ABRAMS: "Thank you, Marshall."

Apparently Marshall departs.

SOMEONE: "Quite independently, we've been looking at how you could make force reductions, and where." "Unfortunately, every time we get to the point the terrain and the enemy foul us up."

ABRAMS: "Well of course that's been the problem right along, the enemy." [Laughter]

ABRAMS: Asks how long Marshall and company have been working on their study.

Abrams already knows the answer, since he brought Marshall out to MACV and has had him reporting directly to himself.

SOMEONE: "It started last September, sir."

ABRAMS: "There's been a hell of a lot of—. And it isn't just an ivory tower thing. A tremendous amount of fieldwork went into it."

■ ■ ■

ABRAMS: "There is one thing I wanted to ask the commanders about, and it has to do with racial problems. Of course you know this is at a very intense level in the United States. And there's always the possibility that people are at work trying to get it going over here. And I'm wondering what you all feel about it."

EWELL: "We had a slight ripple at Bien Hoa Army Base a few weeks ago, and we haven't been able to find anything really hard in there." Others report scattered incidents involving two or three soldiers or marines.

SOMEONE (maybe Mildren): "We have a Watch Committee, as you know, that keeps an eye on this, and we also have a series of agents that we've brought into country to keep an eye on it. We have had some problems at Pleiku. There've been a couple of racial incidents up there. Another area is Qui Nhon. One at Cam Ranh, and at Long Binh. In all cases we've spread these people out, and sent some out of the country if we can't try them under disciplinary measures." "Long Binh and Pleiku have been the worst."

SOMEONE (maybe Nickerson): "In Danang we had rumors of a meeting or two." Couldn't pin it down under investigation.

SOMEONE: "There's the potential any time."

SOMEONE: "You have the sensing that there's some background noise."

ABRAMS: "You think we've got enough antennae out?" "The real thing we've got going for us over here, in my opinion, has been the attitude of the Americans. Good god, it's been magnificent. I sometimes say, if a fellow's really interested in being discouraged, this is probably one of the easiest places in the world to take it aboard in large quantities. But the attitude has been great. It's the strongest thing, I think, we've got going for us. It's more important than B-52s. It's more important than divisions. If you contemplate what it would be if you didn't have it, god it would—well, it would be unmanageable."

ABRAMS: "It's hard to have a feel for all the sort of chemistry that's going on as a result of this announcement and so on. There's a lot of human chemistry involved here that is a little hard to predict. And I think we should all be quite alert to it, keeping hard at the job and watching for—."

Apparently Abrams is referring to an announcement of impending U.S. troop withdrawals and their potential impact on troop attitudes and conduct.

ABRAMS: "Conyers dispatched from Bangkok his preliminary report for release at the same time" as the NLF announcement of a united front organization. "And this is the report of the repression of political dissidents, the repression of the religious sector, all these—all bad—about the existing government here. Now, you can say, 'Well, that's just a coincidence.' There's just a lot of evidence that this thing is really being orchestrated on an international basis. They've got groups that positively are working for them in the United States, and having these congresses and so on to whip up the antiwar spirit in the United States." "So we've got a—our country's got quite a problem. Actually I think President Thieu is freer to move around in his country than President Nixon is in his. You know, the places he can go and so on without having a goddamn riot. Now it may be because it's an oppressive government, but anyway it does have the advantage of a little more security." "But all of this is part of the problem. And that's the environment in which we perform our labors of love."

14 JUN 1969: WIEU

Attendees: Gen. Abrams, Gen. Rosson, Gen. Brown, Amb. Colby, LTG Mildren, VADM Zumwalt, Dr. Wikner, MG Conroy, MG Townsend, Mr. Jacobson, BG McLaughlin, BG Vande Hey, BG Frizen, BG Bautz, BG Potts, BG Galloway, Col. Hill, Col. Sykes, Col. Cavanaugh, Col. Ramsey, Col. [Timura?], Col. Powers.

BRIEFER: Still no new infiltration groups detected.

BROWN: "You remember [Ambassador] Sullivan used to talk about he and the Russians had sort of a quiet agreement they wouldn't let this war get too big in either direction."

ABRAMS: "Souvanna Phouma—I don't like what he's saying. He's saying, roughly, if the North Vietnamese will leave Laos then he'll stop the bombing."

BROWN: "I thought he said it the other way, that he wouldn't stop the bombing with the North Vietnamese running around in the north."

ABRAMS (re Vang Pao): "On the other hand, if there's a guy in all of Laos to support, he's the guy. To hell with all the rest of them. That fellow's got spirit."

BROWN: "Oh, he's a warrior."

ABRAMS: "We could use him here."

18 JUN 1969: Special Brief for Admiral McCain

ATTENDEES: Gen. Abrams, Adm. McCain, MG Peterson, Mr. Jacobson, BG Bautz, RADM Flanagan, BG Potts, Capt. Butts, Capt. [Begler or Zegler?], LTC [Hoydra?].

POTTS: The enemy plans a three-month spring–summer offensive, May–July, with at least one high point, a "brief surge of enemy activity," per month. The first occurred the night of 11–12 May 1969. The second was the night of 5–6 June 1969. Attacks by fire continue to be the enemy's primary method of attack. Continues the downward trend in number of rounds per ABF to an all-time low of 11 rounds average, "perhaps showing the great difficulty he's having in resupply."

ABRAMS: "He's [the enemy] put out the word on these attacks by fire that it wasn't necessary to fire a lot—3 to 15 rounds. That's clearly not a military solution. You accomplish no <u>military</u> results firing three rounds of <u>anything</u>. Well, I don't know—maybe three <u>B-52s</u> will do something. [McCain: "Or three nuclear tactical weapons."] But, the stuff he's <u>using</u>, you're not going to do anything militarily with three rounds. So the whole <u>purpose</u> of it—it <u>has</u> a purpose—isn't military. It's going to have to be political and psychological. Whether that is because of his limitations on his capabilities . . . or just what, that's kind of hard to deal with. But the thrust of this—. For instance, that's not a way to cause U.S. casualties, keeping it to 3 to 15. If that's your real objective, to cause U.S. casualties, then you ought to <u>up</u> it!"

POTTS: "We think, sir, he's having trouble with his resupply, [***]." "This 5–6 June high point reveals to us the enemy's declining effectiveness on the battlefield." "Widening gap between his intentions and his capabilities." Expect next high point tomorrow night.

POTTS: "Looking to the near future, we can expect a surge of enemy activity during July. This is almost certain. And we feel there is definitely going to be another high point during the next several days."

ABRAMS: Notes that, despite enemy reliance on attacks by fire, he mounted a two-battalion attack by the 88th Regiment in Tay Ninh on Fire Support Base Crook, taking terrible losses. He also tried to get to An Loc, but was preempted in some good fights out in the jungle. "There has to be some explanation for the very substantial losses he's taken trying to do these things. He's had a lot of <u>experience</u> attacking these—Diamond, Frontier City, and Crook."

ABRAMS: "Between the effort in Laos, between the secondaries accomplished in-country, between the caches and the necessity for him to fight, you're working on every part of the logistics system to try to cripple it."

BAUTZ: In cache seizures alone for the first five months of 1969 we have taken enough food to feed 10 NVA divisions for a month, more than enough ammunition to supply all the enemy forces for a month, and weapons enough to equip 28 NVA battalions.

ABRAMS: "That southern I Corps is one of the toughest pacification problems we've got in the whole damn country. It's worse than Long An. It's worse than Hau Nghia."

JACOBSON (agreeing): "The best place in the world to hide from your draft board would be out in those mountains."

■ ■ ■

JACOBSON: "Since Admiral Zumwalt and Admiral Flanagan have been here, the navy support to pacification, and the operations that they have done, is about five light years better than anything that we've seen before. It's been of great, great assistance."

JACOBSON: "These flurries that the VC have been into have not significantly affected pacification." "We now stand at 84.2 percent of the population [secure]."

21 JUN 1969: Commanders WIEU

Attendees: Gen. Abrams, Gen. Rosson, Gen. Brown, Amb. Colby, LTG Mildren, LTG Nickerson, LTG Corcoran, LTG Ewell, Dr. Wikner, MG Wetherill, MG Conroy, Mr. Megellas, Mr. Firfer, MG Townsend, Mr. Jacobson, Mr. Vann, MG Wheeler, BG Frizen, BG Bautz, BG McLaughlin, BG Vande Hey, BG Potts, BG Galloway, RADM Flanagan, Col. Sykes, Col. Cavanaugh, Col. Ramsey, Col. Hill, Col. [Tenori?], Col. [Reholt?], Col. Kerwin, Col. Stiner.

BRIEFER: Reports on the countrywide refugee situation: 69.5 refugees per 1,000 population. Total of 1.2 million refugees out of a population of 17 million. Almost half are from I Corps.

■ ■ ■

ABRAMS (reacting to a report that in Qui Nhon things are so slow that PF have taken additional jobs working as local hires in the American depot): "And of course I wonder what the advisors are doing up in Qui Nhon—PF working in the depots in the daytime and manning the ramparts at night—why somebody wouldn't have noticed that."

ABRAMS: "What'd we get, 43,000 M16s in the month of May? That we gave them—43,000!"

DISCUSSION: Pilfering from an in-country POL pipeline. They are pumping only water from Qui Nhon to An Khe "just for this reason." On the line north to Phu Cat "the loss there in April reached about 600,000 gallons." Abrams wants to send a letter to the GVN minister of defense.

SOMEONE: "This is pretty shocking, but these are common criminals."

MILDREN: "Well, we're getting it solved. We're burying the Tuy Hoa line completely. We're now working on the Phu Cat. And we're going to work on this line from Qui Nhon to An Khe. There's your three big pilferage areas—about four and a half million gallons a month, right now." Someone suggests ambushing the people responsible.

ABRAMS: "I'd like to try this other thing first [the letter] before you go ambushing. . . ."

EWELL: "I really feel that [Bill? or Hill?] has the right idea. Anybody stealing gas is a VC sympathizer. You knock off about five and the rate of stealing in that general area will go down precipitously."

MILDREN: "Yeah, but you can't shoot people for petty larceny."

EWELL: "B-u-l-l-shit."

ABRAMS: "Now wait a minute, wait a minute, wait a minute."

EWELL: "If you have a pipeline, you put out rules that people aren't supposed to steal gas . . . and that we're going to get these VC that are doing it and just go shoot them."

ABRAMS: "You've got to think about these people here. Shooting them—'Well, that'll stop it.' Christ, these people have been shot at for the last twenty years! I don't—going out there and killing a few of them is not, in my opinion, going to have the effect. I think they're all sort of fatalists."

EWELL: "Well, I don't agree with you, General. You can get a sapper unit mining the road, and you kill two or three and they'll knock it off. It may be that a month later they'll come back. These people can count. And, boy, when you line them up [bodies] and they count one, two, three, four, their enthusiasm is highly reduced. That's the way we opened up Highway 4—just killing them. It doesn't take many."

ABRAMS: "All right, we'll study it." [Laughter]

EWELL: "I think you ought to—." [Interrupted by others.]

ABRAMS: "One last thing you ought to consider when you handle this is how it's going to look when the *New York Times* and *Newsweek* and some of those describe it to the American people. I'm not quite ready to take that one on. They might flavor it. They might lose their objectivity."

■ ■ ■

ABRAMS (re chart showing terrorism way down): "Incidentally, that's a sign that we want to be a little careful what we do with these civilians. We don't want to get a U.S. terrorism rate that's higher than the VC. I keep going back to that chart of Marshall's that gives you the villager's view of who's the enemy, who's going to hurt him—or what's going to hurt him."

28 JUN 1969: WIEU

ATTENDEES: Gen. Abrams, Gen. Rosson, Gen. Brown, Amb. Colby, LTG Mildren, VADM Zumwalt, Dr. Wikner, MG Conroy, MG Townsend, Mr. Jacobson, BG Frizen, BG Bautz, BG McLaughlin, BG Vande Hey, BG Smith, BG Potts, Col. Sykes, Capt. McNulty, Col. Cavanaugh, Col. Ramsey, Col. Hill, Col. [Timori?], Col. Kerwin.

POTTS: "We're at an all-time low [of four tons per day]" of enemy movement of supplies south.

ABRAMS: "Well, I don't know about all that. They're sure as hell firing a lot of artillery and mortar up there."

POTTS: "That's the approach we're using, that it is coming up from Cambodia."

■ ■ ■

BRIEFER: In-country enemy recruitment is estimated to have averaged about 5,850 per month during January–June 1969.

BRIEFER: We are using as a rule of thumb 35 percent of KIA totals to estimate the number who died of wounds or were permanently disabled. Enemy non-battle losses estimated at 2,000 per month.

BRIEFER: "Countrywide, we see net losses for each month [during the first half of 1969], and a total net loss of almost 75,000." This estimate does not reflect unit movements outside the infiltration pipeline.

POTTS: We are using an 85 percent arrival figure for groups put into the pipeline, but some are down as low as 50 percent.

■ ■ ■

SOMEONE (re apparent pause in infiltration): "This same thing could be happening, though, without any deal, and these people are just taking advantage of the situation to eventually fade back into the woodwork."

ABRAMS: "Now that's the one I'm inclined to think, because they are really stonewalling over there in Paris. Absolutely rock! And the way the Communists are, the tougher the situation they're in, the tougher they are at the table. That's why I think there's no deal."

ABRAMS: "The trouble with this is, it tends to make you feel good. And that's about the worst condition you can get in here."

SOMEONE: "The question it raises in my mind is whether or not a deal hasn't been arrived at."

ABRAMS: "I've got no answer to that. I've been traveling on the basis that the government's been—our government—has been honest with me. That gets fairly hairy, and if I got thinking about that I would really get confused. That throws another—. I don't believe it [that there is a deal]. The reason I don't believe it is our own government is under such pressure at home . . . that they—at the very highest level it would be almost impossible for them to withhold something that appeared to be a favorable development."

ABRAMS: "Joe Alsop has got two articles [on the drop in infiltration]. . . . I wonder who in the hell is feeding this to Joe."

POTTS: "This has been checked back through the Pentagon, and the approach they gave us there was that this is coming from the same old source, indicating the basement of the White House."

SOMEONE: "The better you're doing, the more you'll hear from Harriman, I think."

ABRAMS (re Harriman on Laos): "No, his view would be that we screwed it up by going in and supporting them. Goddamn it, 'If we'd left it alone, and let them work it out themselves, they would have come to an amicable settlement. But the . . . military and the fucking hawks got in there and screwed up what was otherwise a damn fine solution.' Irritated the hell out of the Soviets, pissed off the North Vietnamese, and so on."

■ ■ ■

ABRAMS: "I had dinner last night with the bureau chiefs, and Colonel Hill. They were really quite pleasant. I went there with my steel helmet and flak vest—at least mentally—on. But it was a very relaxed group, and the temperature never rose. And the questions they asked were pretty intelligent, I thought. They certainly know it isn't black and white. They all know that."

■ ■ ■

ABRAMS: "Well, there's one 'irreversible' path we're on right now—in most places we're beating the shit out of them! That's kind of irreversible, too. And there's a lot of that going on, although I'm a little sorry to see their killed in action dropped below 3,000. That's the first week that's happened in a long time."

POTTS: Since 1 January 1969 there have been only two infiltration groups identified by PWs that had not previously been picked up in GRDS messages [sic: GDRS?]. And no groups identified that have entered the pipeline since 20 March 1969.

BROWN: "General Jones, who just got back from Washington, tells of the concerted effort by Mr. Kissinger to pull together this Cambodian story [of enemy matériel coming in through Sihanoukville]. Contributions from all of the normal activities resulted in a fragmented effort that he didn't like. Nobody could agree. So he sent them back to the drawing boards, and apparently now there is a major intergovernmental look at the problem."

ABRAMS: "It's because of that that I started them to working on this when I got back from Midway."

POTTS: "OSA [referring to CIA's Saigon station] cannot speak, because they've got people that differ with them a little bit back home."

ABRAMS: "What happened on this, Kissinger talked to Wheeler on it while we were en route from Honolulu to Midway. We were seated there together, and Kissinger felt that it would be a good thing if I sent one or two that were really experts on this so that they could pull the thing together. Well, the Chairman intervened at that point. He felt that he could provide that. So I said, 'Well, I'll keep it on tap.'"

POTTS: "It's ready, sir, and we've taken the Graham Report that was done out here, long before my arrival—we've gone through that, point by point. . . . We really have pretty good archival materials."

SOMEONE: "One of the problems they have is the reliability of some of the sources. That's to be charitable."

ABRAMS: "Of course, we have a problem, too, and that's accounting for this goddamn rain of rocket and mortar rounds. It's a little hard to figure out where the hell they come from!"

■ ■ ■

ABRAMS (re South Vietnamese governmental deficiencies): "And as a government, and as planners, they are not doing fair work. It's like this goddamn submission they made at Midway—completely and totally unrealistic! They've got to get to work now and start running an organization that really tries to do the best thing for the country. I told him [General Vien], 'It's our job to support everything and every way that we can, and we'll do it. We want to! That's the name of the game. That's our job. But,' I said, 'we're not going to support these things that are out of balance or going to be harmful to the security of the people, to the management of the war effort, to other aspects of pacification and military operations.'"

ABRAMS: "I think one of the problems is there's nobody who will argue with the president." "And also I don't think the president is getting reported the facts." "Well, anyway, it's not a very sophisticated outfit. They're great people, but—.

You know, by comparison there's quite a lot of initiative here. You know, related to—say—a couple of years ago. And there's—Jesus, there was a time when you couldn't interest anybody in the goddamn <u>government</u> in the PF, <u>or</u> the police. And the interest in the RF was certainly not overwhelming. So I suppose we really should be running around having a dance or something over what's happened, but they've still got quite a bit to do."

ROSSON: "I had the same kind of discussion with General Phong yesterday afternoon. I took up all the points that you had taken up with General Vien, right along the same vein. And when we finally finished, he came back to this thing, 'But the president has told us to go, and we've just got to do the best we can.' He comes back to that each time."

ABRAMS: "Well, I can understand that." [Laughter]

3 JUL 1969: COMUS Update

Attendees: Gen. Abrams, Amb. Bunker, Amb. Berger, Amb. Colby, MG Townsend, BG Bautz, BG McLaughlin, BG Vande Hey, BG Potts, Col. Kerwin.

POTTS: "Terrorism in Saigon is way down low now, sir."

BRIEFER: Discusses reports that the enemy may be considering a cease-fire proposal. "Even though certain late documents state that the enemy is engaged in his final campaign, others mention plans for an autumn campaign." "The enemy has told his people that only by achieving victories on the battlefield can they expect to win at the peace table." "The enemy sees time running out for the Nixon administration, and he may be willing to play a waiting game."

BRIEFER: "A late May [1969] statement by Tran Buu Kiem in Paris implied that the basic Communist objection to allied proposals for mutual withdrawal or cease-fire is that they do not provide adequate security to ensure even the survival of the Communist apparatus, much less its right to establish a legitimate political power base." He said that "U.S. proposals would leave Communist forces at the mercy of South Vietnamese military operations."

BRIEFER: Conclusion: "It appears that the enemy will <u>not</u> propose a cease-fire in the immediate future." But "the enemy may be changing his strategic direction of the war. We believe it is significant that enemy documents seldom refer to future offensives. After the disastrous post-Tet offensive of 1969 the enemy appears to have settled for a succession of 'high points' or action phases in the framework of his season campaigns. Evidence suggests that the enemy may abandon his so-called general offensive, general uprising stage."

BRIEFER: "The enemy has become increasingly defensive about his July 1967 decision to advance to the general offensive stage. A COSVN document claims that the party made a correct decision, but the people let it down."

BRIEFER: "For three months no CHICOM or Soviet munitions ships have arrived in Sihanoukville. Previously large amounts of munitions were delivered to this port before each period of heightened enemy activity." The enemy "is possibly prepared for an eventual lowering of the war's intensity. . . . The enemy, more than ever, seems plagued with doubts about achieving a meaningful near-term victory in South Vietnam. He has already told his cadre, in high-level meetings and by COSVN directives, that they must prepare themselves for something less."

BUNKER: Comments on the fact that there has been more ammunition seized in the first five and a half months of 1969 than in all of 1968: "More than we got all last year. I must say that's a very encouraging table."

BUNKER: "Is better intelligence contributing to this?"

ABRAMS: "Mr. Ambassador, I think that all of this is this whole business of trying to work on his system. And his system—it's the VCI, the guerrillas, it's the commo-liaison, it's getting out on the trails, it's patrolling, ambushing, and out in the things that he's using to move the supplies in and make the liaison and that sort of thing. And I think that's why it occurs. Well, and the other thing, of course, is that he's moving it in. Of course the way we try to tackle this is to take the caches that we get, take the secondaries in-country, take the secondaries in Laos, because the whole thing works against his total logistics system—trying to get stuff in here."

ABRAMS (skeptical of Potts's answer to Bunker that they are getting more information volunteered by the people): "We were saying that before Tet '68."

BUNKER: "I'll tell you what Air Marshal Dawee said to me in Bangkok. He said he's been over here, and he's urging his people to get into the villages, his troops. He said not just for civic action. He said, 'I want you to have love affairs.' He said that's how you get your intelligence." [Laughter]

ABRAMS: "We've got all of that we need." [Laughter]

5 JUL 1969: WIEU

Attendees: Gen. Rosson, Amb. Colby, VADM Zumwalt, Dr. Wikner, MG Mabry, MG Townsend, MG Conroy, MG Jones, Mr. Jacobson, BG Bautz, BG McLaughlin, BG Vande Hey, BG Smith, BG Potts, BG Galloway, Col. Sykes, Col. Cavanaugh, Col. Ramsey, Col. Hill, Col. [Rennull?], Col. [Dimori?], Col. Kerwin.

BRIEFER: "In Cambodia a report from a frequent and reliable source cites the statement of former Cambodian Minister of Defense Ok Khiem Ong. Ong stated that 'every time Communist China sent military aid to Cambodia a portion was to be sent to the Viet Cong.' In late 1966, as minister of defense under Prime Minister Lon Nol, Ong asked Nol for an explanation of this diversion of arms and ammunition from Cambodian stocks. After a short delay, Nol showed him an order written by Prince Sihanouk which stipulated that whenever Cambodia received military aid from Communist China a portion had to be sent to the Viet Cong."

10 JUL 1969: Admiral McCain Brief

ATTENDEES: Gen. Rosson, Adm. McCain, VADM Curtis, BG Bautz, BG Long, BG Potts, Col. Lynn, Mr. Rogers.

MCCAIN: Complains of Washington's unwillingness to accept that the enemy is being supplied through Cambodia, "particularly this damn CIA, the opinion they have of it."

POTTS: "And here in-country we have had the State Department and CAS officials working on our paper before it goes forward—unofficially."

In rebuttal of the CIA position, with CIA's Saigon station taking MACV's side in the dispute.

MCCAIN: "That's goddamn good. I don't know what the hell the CIA's reluctance to accept this thing is, unless it's due to some stand they took a year or two ago on which they're afraid to go ahead now and admit a mistake."

ROSSON: "I think it boils down mostly to how one evaluates the validity of the source."

POTTS: "This is right."

SOMEONE: "Except that the one man responsible for the position three years ago, and the position a year ago, is the man who authored the current CIA paper."

MCCAIN: "Who is that, Graham?"

SOMEONE: "Graham."

ROSSON: "My impression is that the Graham Report has eroded quite a bit back in Washington now."

SOMEONE: "The concern to me is that what finally gets to the president will be handled through and by CIA."

14 JUL 1969: COMUS Update

ATTENDEES: Gen. Abrams, MG Townsend, BG Potts.

BRIEFER: Since 22 March 1969 only two new infiltration groups revealed by COMINT. Mentions Binh Tram 8, "which has been our primary source on the southward flow of infiltration groups." "Headquarters Binh Tram 8 is believed to be located at Vinh." "Collateral intelligence [document exploitation and PW interrogation] now provides evidence that infiltration from North Vietnam has in fact continued."

ABRAMS: "The Chairman has it?"

POTTS: "Yes, and Admiral McCain."

ABRAMS: "The real question here is whether COMINT any longer gives us a hold on this."

DISCUSSION: Exfiltration of people going back north on the trail. These are believed to be sick and wounded, returning cadres, and "travelers."

POTTS: Based on our analysis, "we can't say infiltration appears to have stopped. It's been greatly reduced, and it doesn't affect anything significant as far as the overall [word unclear]."

ABRAMS: "Well, I'm not anxious to cling to anything. If our estimates have been off, then we will say that our estimates have been off. There's nothing sacred in this. The only thing that's sacred is try to know the truth. That's the thing that's sacred. We've got to—we've got to put our best work into this! And we've got to look at it, because our own government is just going haywire on the dreams that they're manufacturing out of no infiltration. We've said all along, we've said from the very beginning, that this was one of the most critical things in this whole business. It's of strategic impact. Now this crap of negotiating two provinces in each corps—four in one and two in each of the rest and so on—by our government and the NLF, or the PLG, or whatever the hell it is, I don't believe it. That's just a wonderful thing for them to push to split us apart. It's a natural. And there'll be others like it. [Someone: "And it's from the French."] Yeah—just about the stinkingest bunch of people that you could get anything from at this stage of the game."

POTTS (re supposed lull in infiltration): "They're [Washington, or Paris] trying to read into it what they want."

ABRAMS: "It shows you what weak men will do—what weak men will do!"

17 JUL 1969: General Wheeler Brief

ATTENDEES: Gen. Wheeler, Adm. McCain, Gen. Abrams, Gen. Rosson, Amb. Colby, VADM Zumwalt, MG Mabry, MG Peterson, MG Townsend, MG Jones, RADM Lemos, BG Bautz, BG McLaughlin, BG Potts, BG Keegan, Capt. McNulty, Col. Kerwin, Capt. Butts, Col. Jackson, Col. Smith.

Gen. Earle G. Wheeler, Chairman of the Joint Chiefs of Staff, is visiting Vietnam.

BRIEFER (re the reasons for current low level of enemy activity): "First, a reduction in his capability as a result of friendly combat operations. Second, that it is part of the normal cycle of operations which is a withdrawal to refit, retrain, and receive replacements, and then return to the attack. The third is that he has deliberately lowered the level of activity, perhaps to encourage withdrawal of allied forces, after which he would again initiate operations against RVNAF with the expectation that U.S. forces would not return." Re enemy: "He apparently realizes he has no chance of winning a military victory as long as U.S. presence is maintained at its current level."

WHEELER: I had DIA analyze Giap's recent speech and compare it with ones he made earlier in September 1967 and December 1968. "They told me that they could find no substantial change in the basic theses General Giap enunciated, that he'd been completely consistent, which led them to the belief that the Tet Offensive was probably conducted over his objection."

KEEGAN: "My personal view is that the loss projection is an exceedingly conservative one." "I happen to think they're excessively conservative."

POTTS: "We think so, too, sir. We're using the national estimate where you put your hand on a man and he's dead, and then they take 35 percent of that total and make that the number that die or loses an arm—they can't come back to fight. We know that total's higher because we get this report from officers that we've interrogated. Instead of it being 30 percent, sometimes it's one and a half more."

KEEGAN: "Which leads me to speculate as to whether or not the manpower problems in the north are not considerably more serious than generally accepted as a result of the damage and the harm we've inflicted on them."

WHEELER: We've had DIA and CIA assess that a number of times, and invariably they come up with the finding that the gross manpower "can sustain this kind of attrition." "Whether Ho Chi Minh and his buddies recognize that they have mortgaged the future . . . for the chance of making a coup in the present—."

■ ■ ■

COLBY: "One of the points we'd like to make in this assessment is that pacification is now <u>organized</u>. We recall the problems we had in the American government in getting it organized under one command structure. I believe on the Vietnamese side they've gone through the same agony, but I think they've come into some sort of a harbor."

ABRAMS (re police operations in Saigon): "<u>Very</u> high quality. It's not without blemish, but it's been high-quality police work nevertheless."

COLBY: "You know our special program on the VCI, General. This, frankly, we can't report any great success on." "We have a fairly soft estimate of the total strength of the VCI. If you take a percentage of that as eliminated each month, you get about 1 1/2–2 percent." Therefore maybe 20 percent projected to the end of the year. "And they can probably replace a good part of that." "We have tightened up on the definitions here, rather deliberately, to try to point them toward people of somewhat more prominence."

COLBY (re five-month campaign ending 30 June 1969): A little over goal of 83 percent secure. "What this amounts to is an additional million people brought into the A/B/C category." Goal by year end: 90 percent secure. "Or a little over a thousand hamlets." During the APC added 1.5 million. "I think this is the major accomplishment of this period."

COLBY: Along with 90 percent A/B/C goal, a 50 percent A/B goal. "The president very clearly says that the purpose of that is to get it so the government can absolutely count on at least 50 percent of the population to vote for them in a challenge with the Communists. And they'll <u>probably</u> get a good portion of the rest, but he wants to be absolutely sure of the 50 percent." "Our major problem area in pacification is still in IV Corps."

COLBY: "They conducted almost 800 village elections, and 4,500 hamlet elections, during this past few months. They had a very high rate of participation." "The promise of the country [economically], there's no question about it. It will go like a shot if they stop shooting at one another." "We have the problem of the infrastructure, which hasn't been hurt that much." "A certain element, let's admit it, of fragility."

SOMEONE (re VNAF): Setting records in practically every category the past few months. "Their accident rates are lower."

WHEELER: "That's a very interesting observation, because I recall the VNAF as pretty much a 9 to 4, 9 to 5, five-and-a-half-day air force."

. . .

WHEELER: When I visited in 1967, I had a long talk with General Truong, CG of the 1st ARVN Division, who said his biggest problem was lack of replacements, with some battalions under 400 men. Then I talked with General Vien, who was pushing for an increase in structure. I told him that, "as far as I could make out, the quickest way to increase the effectiveness of the ARVN was not to create more structure, but to put more heroes in the units he had, particularly ones like the 1st Division which were operating effectively."

WHEELER (re RVNAF strength): "We were talking about this in the Chiefs the other day. Westmoreland said that he had been surprised that they were able to get to this figure of 876 [876,000], if that's the proper figure. Apparently in '66 he had a study run which came up with a gross supportable figure of 802,000."

21 JUL 1969: Strengths Brief

BRIEFER: Estimates show an enemy net loss of 24,000 over the period January–May 1969.

BRIEFER: "CIA has estimated a quarter of a million enemy personnel which we do not carry as part of the enemy force structure."

POTTS: "Someday we'll get into this thing with CIA and DIA. But that's not bothering us right now."

POTTS: "I don't think we want to get into that hassle with him [General Abrams] in this brief. We're trying to solve one of the two big problems, and that's the in-country part." "We just want to show him the strength in-country that he has to fight. That's what he's asked for."

POTTS: "These are the self-defense forces, assault youth, commo-liaison personnel, VCI, and impressed laborers. Undoubtedly these personnel suffer losses and are included in our KIA statistics."

POTTS: Estimate the enemy at 225,000–255,000 and use single figure of 241,000. (As of last day of May 1969.) June: 234,500.

POTTS: "The objective of the brief is very simple. The objective of the brief is to show the current enemy strength in South Vietnam." Potts talks the briefer through exactly how the briefing should unfold, chart by chart and flip by flip. "The last thing is we explain away where the minus 72,000 went." "The only thing that gets hard is down here at the end where you have to explain that away." "General Abrams wants to know, 'How do we account for these?' See, that's what started this whole thing."

POTTS apparently leaves. One of the briefers, remaining, to another: "Too big to cry, and it hurts too much to laugh." Another: "If he changes the rules one more time, I'm cutting my goddamn throat." Someone: "I still think you've got a goddamn good brief." Another: "So do I, and I'll bet <u>that's</u> what COMUS <u>really</u> wants."

24 JUL 1969: Briefing for COMUS and General Vy

ABRAMS: What we have for you [Vy] is an "assessment at this time relative to a further reduction of U.S. forces." I hope the presentation "will encourage discussion among us so that we can arrive at our best judgment on what can and could be done." "The presentation will be in French." Potts introduces Lieutenant Jones, who briefs in French. Abrams also makes some comments in French.

INTERPRETER: "Minister Vy says that he finds the presentation very well made, very well taken, and as he has been discussing these subjects with General Abrams recently, he has come up with virtually the same conclusions."

ABRAMS: "The difficulty, to me, at this point is there are some things that make him [the enemy] look weak. There are preparations that make him look strong for some time, some point, in the future. And now to <u>weigh</u> carefully what he can do."

INTERPRETER: "Minister Vy believes that the Communists have learned some lessons from past offensives and, as a result of this, Minister Vy does not think that the enemy in the future is going to waste his time by launching large offensive operations against areas which are too much in the interior of our territory. And in any case they are no longer capable of launching large operations in the center of our territory, because allied troops and allied operations have managed to in large part destroy his logistical organization in the central part of Vietnam. Although they are not in a position to launch large-scale offensives, they <u>are</u> in a position to continue harassing attacks, artillery attacks, and mortar attacks."

INTERPRETER: "On the other hand, as concerns the provinces which are near the borders of Cambodia and Laos, Minister Vy believes the enemy still has largely intact units which are hiding out in safe zones either on the borders themselves or inside Laos and inside Cambodia. And, as one of our slides showed, we have seen very important logistical movement through Sihanoukville and through eastern Laos. Which leads Minister Vy to the conclusion that, if the enemy is going to attack in the near future, launch offensives in the near future, it will be against objectives which are reasonably near the Laotian and Cambodian frontiers." "So Minister Vy does not think the enemy has the capability to launch another general offensive such as the 1968 Tet Offensive. . . ."

ABRAMS: "The question is, what political importance to GVN are the <u>border</u> areas? Specifically Kontum, Pleiku, Tuan Duc, Phuoc Long, Binh Long, and Tay Ninh. I think that it is important that we all understand the political importance of this to GVN, because it then determines the amount of military effort you are willing to expend to achieve the security, the protection. How <u>impor-</u>

tant is Song Be? How _important_ is Loc Ninh? An Loc? How _important_ is Tay Ninh? How important is Kontum City and the villages north of Kontum to Dak To along Route 14? It's the _political_ importance of these, as seen by _your_ government, that then determines how much effort, how much _military_ effort, we are willing to put to assure it. If it's of no consequence politically, then it's not worth the military effort. But if it _is_ important politically _to_ GVN, then we must make the effort."

INTERPRETER: "The Minister states that the GVN regards these border provinces, these border areas, as _extremely_ important and would regard the loss of one or any of them as an extremely serious political setback. And that is why the GVN is asking for continued military pressure to defend these areas."

POTTS: Provides comparative infiltration figures requested by Abrams. Through July in each case: In 1967: 73,000. 1968: 133,000. 1969: 80,000.

ABRAMS: "What we've had to do for the last year is to maintain the infantry strength _assigned_ at 102 percent because casualties are the things that affect the strength, and most of the casualties are in the infantrymen. So that one or two hard fights in a division, the infantry companies can still be sustained. You don't have to wait for somebody from the _States_. You've got an adequate strength of infantry so that the division can make adjustments . . . and can keep the rifle companies going in combat. Everybody has the problem of casualties, and if the fighting strength of the infantry is to be maintained special measures have to be taken on replacements."

ABRAMS: "We think it's a very bad thing if one of our rifle companies is below 100. It really should be at 125 when it goes in the field. If you don't, your casualties will go up—the casualties in the company. It's just not strong enough."

ABRAMS: "I am required to turn this [redeployment plan] in by the 3rd of August to CINCPAC, Admiral McCain. And from there it will go to the Joint Chiefs of Staff, I suppose in two or three days. The 10th of August it has to be to the Joint Chiefs of Staff." "I have discussed this with General Wheeler, and he knows what this contains. And he agrees with the number. He agrees with the rationale. I've been anxious to pull it together and to start discussions with you, and the staff, so that if some pressure develops to know sooner—which I don't know of, but if it does, then we have at least _begun_ to talk about it." "That's the agreement that President Nixon and President Thieu have now, that this will be reviewed and they make their decision sometime in the early part of August. I think that's what they agreed to at Okinawa—I mean _Midway_."

ABRAMS: "I think it would be well, for the moment, to hold it closely, so that not too many—. It would be good to keep it from the newspaper reporters."

ABRAMS (this said very politely but seriously): "The documents which the representatives of the GVN presented to Secretary Laird at Midway contained a great many requirements. It's not only the personnel and so on, but a lot of equipment requirements and many other things. So I would appreciate from Minister Vy a paper which explains the priorities and the time frame so that I may have it as a basis of discussion with Ambassador Bunker. While I am anxious to support the programs of the GVN, I also have a duty to my <u>own</u> government to render a judgment on the attainability of these. And, as I indicated earlier, I've been very concerned as I have watched it. I'm as anxious that—<u>almost</u> as anxious—that all of this in Vietnam turn out <u>your</u> way as <u>you</u> are. But I have been concerned, and my concern has continued to grow, that too much is being attempted so that it all won't get done."

ABRAMS: "I fully appreciate the priority which the president and his cabinet and everyone else has placed on the PF. I understand that. But I would be so bold as to offer the opinion that the security for the people is <u>more</u> than PF. It's the PF, it's the RF, it's the police, it's the PSDF, and it's the ARVN. And they all have a <u>role</u>, depending somewhat on the city or the village or the province or the district. Not all are quite the same. But it takes them <u>all</u>. And if one is very <u>good</u>, and very <u>strong</u>, but the others don't have enough people, don't have enough leadership, it won't <u>work</u>."

24 JUL 1969: COMUS Special Brief

BRIEFER (re infiltration): The last two groups detected were on 3 and 5 May. "Since then a period of approximately 13 weeks has elapsed with no additional infiltration groups being observed in the pipeline within North Vietnam. The Binh Tram 8 communications complex, which has been our primary source of information on the southward flow of infiltration groups, has remained active, passing both administrative and logistical traffic, as well as information on the northward movement of personnel. This nonobservance of infiltration in COMINT has caused MACV to begin an aggressive program of captured document exploitation and PW interrogation to determine the possible trends in infiltration. Collateral information obtained over the past few weeks has provided evidence that infiltration from North Vietnam has continued subsequent to 22 March." Group 1089 arrived 8 June in Quang Nam Province, per captured notebook. Other evidence is cited.

POTTS: Typically 3 percent cadre return north from an infiltration group.

■ ■ ■

MACV 1969 Infiltration Estimate: 83,100.

■ ■ ■

BRIEFER (re a typical infiltration pattern): Groups commence movement from the general Hanoi area with a one-day train trip to Vinh. Then on barges down rivers to commo-liaison station T-12, believed located in the vicinity of [words unclear] railroad bridge, 35 kilometers south of Vinh. About 55 kilometers in five to six hours by barge. From T-12 some move by truck to Quang Tin Province, but most go by foot from there (T-12). The entire trip from Hanoi to the western DMZ area takes some 20–25 days. Then through Laos. Approximate travel times range from 73 to 92 days, depending on destination.

ABRAMS: Directs that a message be prepared from him to CJCS providing the substance of the briefing. "It's kind of important. Over there in Paris they get into the talking about, 'Well, you wait and see. We understand. We'll do things in good faith,' and so on. Well, if we've got a window that can look at some of this, we might be able to tell when the bastards are lying as usual or whether they <u>are</u> doing some <u>small</u>—." Re the collateral developed: "I tell you, that's been very, very important." "The prisoner used to be worth his weight in gold. Now I guess he's worth double his weight in gold." "This matter of infiltration has tremendous political implications to our government and so on." "We've grown unsure now that we <u>know</u> a reasonably good picture. We're <u>unsure</u> of that. And it's been brought out by this prisoner and document effort that we <u>had</u> missed something." "If we read this wrong, or our <u>government</u> winds up reading it wrong, it's possible to make <u>quite</u> a tragic mistake. That's what we don't want to do."

BRIEFER: Current estimate of enemy strength in and adjacent to the RVN: 234,500 as of 30 June 1969. A drop of 32,500 since 1 January 1969.

ABRAMS: "Sihanouk said in one of his talks, 'If the Americans bomb where the VC are, that's none of my business, just as long as there're no Cambodians there, then there're no Cambodians to report it. I wouldn't even know.' And, you know, went on in <u>that</u> line. Then he said, 'I can't <u>imagine</u> the Hanoi representative coming to my minister of foreign affairs and saying, 'I have the honor to inform you that the Americans have bombed my forces who are in your country without authority.' Remember that quote of Sihanouk?"

■ ■ ■

The next refers to an upcoming visit to Southeast Asia by President Nixon.

ABRAMS: "Quite frankly, when the president's in Bangkok he might call me over there. And I might have 10 minutes, or 15 minutes, to cover the whole <u>goddamn</u> situation in South Vietnam. This would be the condition of the ARVN, and the condition of the pacification, all that. What <u>I</u> want to do is tell him about the <u>enemy</u>. So I need—this is the <u>most</u> difficult thing that you can have, where you've got a <u>short</u> time, you've got a <u>busy</u> man, a man with a tremendous responsibility, and to give him the essence, the <u>essence</u>, of what the enemy has done and what he's capable of doing, being <u>very</u> careful not to make him any taller, or any shorter, than he actually is. And what would be the three, five, ten points? Now you can say, right at the beginning, that that's <u>inadequate</u>. Well, that's not my <u>problem</u>. [Laughter] It's what I've <u>got</u> to do there."

POTTS: "We can do that, sir."

ABRAMS: Suggests as items infiltration, trend in enemy strength, logistics system.

26 JUL 1969: Commanders WIEU

Tracking enemy infiltration through COMINT.

ABRAMS: "For some time now our best intelligence on the quantity of infiltration has been through [***]. We've had this window in the system that kept track of this quite well for us, and even strengths, the areas that they were going to in South Vietnam, and all of that. And this, over time, has been confirmed by collateral—later—in-country to give a very high degree of reliability to the intelligence that we are getting in COMINT. Well, as has been explained, we've stopped picking it up. We've just stopped—at the end of March, except for two groups in May, it's gone on to this date without any more being picked up in COMINT except the 11,500 and the five groups, which is a sort of a spurious thing. It's true, I'm sure, but it's not in the context of the way we've been watching the system."

ABRAMS: "Well, of course all of this has been reported. So everybody in Washington knows this, including Joe Alsop. So great—over time, a great—although we've caveated it, and tried to point out some of the cautions about it, tremendous political significance has been attached to it. Well, some time back we, when it was foreseen that this was going to present—and it had rather grave stakes here as far as the policies of our government and so on were going to be—so it was important that we know whether this was true or not. And so we desperately needed something—. I will say this, the whole Intelligence Community focused on this as a problem. All kind of things have been done technically to try to revamp and make sure that this COMINT coverage was reliable, was comprehensive, and so on. So from a technical standpoint everything has been done in the COMINT field that anyone in the community—. And Washington, NSA, has worked on this itself very hard. It's been a priority matter for them. I have personally informed them that it's of absolutely critical significance to this command. And they responded to that."

ABRAMS: "Well, anyway, we just needed more. We needed more efforts of other kinds to see if a—. So there has been an intensified and special effort on PWs and documents to see if we can pick up in-country groups that had not been—. Now, I just sent a message to all commanders—I approved it last night, and I don't know whether you've seen it—focusing on this. And that's the significance of it." "It's really quite important." "See, there's a large body of people that think that these fellows are really pretty nice guys, honorable chaps, and they're trying to show us that they really want to call this thing off. But they have so much pride and so on that they can't afford to announce it publicly. They're just sending discreet—ah—signals. Well, we don't want to get screwed on that. I must say that group is not too widespread here, but that's not all that is involved in the problem. So that's why this is important, and anything you can do to help it along has quite a bit of importance."

BRIEFER: "Beginning in April an increase in the number of people moving north through the Binh Tram 8 area has been observed." About 3,763 in April 1969, 4,800 in May, 8,979 in June, 3,260 as of 24 July reflected in COMINT. "Of the total 20,802 personnel [sic]: 7,583 were sick and wounded, 8,353 were 'travellers.'" About 2,200 were associated with the 559th Transportation Group (about 5.5 percent of its total strength). Per NSA re-analysis, this is a programmed move based on anticipated reduction in operations during the rainy season.

ABRAMS (re the new data on returnees): "I have reported it, heavily—almost suffocatingly—caveated. But I am responsible to report it. You see, in some quarters this is such an overwhelming demonstration of good will that we'd have trouble hanging on to an advisory detachment. You see, all this stuff lands in a different kind of waters back there. We can sit here and talk about it, and give it kind of a hard-nosed look—'good will' and 'good faith' are not in the lexicon of verbiage used out here, but—."

■ ■ ■

Ambassador Averell Harriman and "The Understandings."

EWELL: "Can I ask a question? I notice a recent *Time* quoted Harriman that three divisions had withdrawn north. Was that a correct quote?"

ABRAMS: "Well, Harriman, of course, is not being briefed on the intelligence that occurred since he left the government service, so he's not alluding to any of this current thing. I think what they're talking about is what Harriman said about what they did as a result of the bombing halt. And Harriman has—either consciously or unconsciously—has distorted the facts that were given to him when he was the negotiator over there. And all of that withdrawal occurred before—not all of it, there was one, I think one regiment [Potts: "That's right, sir."] that withdrew after the bombing halt, but the whole mess of it, which includes three divisions, or the equivalent of three divisions, did withdraw before the bombing halt."

ABRAMS (re Harriman): "You see, he's—it's been a most unfortunate thing—he has used it to indicate it was their response to the bombing halt, and the facts are that it started in the summer and was virtually completed, except for one regiment, before the bombing halt. In fact, the combination—. See, what was happening up there on Route Package 1 and 2—shit, they weren't getting six trucks a day into Laos—combination of the interdiction program and the weather, they just weren't moving. And they weren't getting the stuff down to the DMZ and so on. And then, in-country, the heat was on them all over. They're out there in the base areas, they're in the A Shau Valley gathering up these caches and so on. I've been convinced all along that the reason that those outfits were withdrawing was because they could no longer be supported. They couldn't get any food out of the coastal area. This is all northern I Corps we're talking about. And this is one of the factors that was considered in making the bombing halt."

EWELL: "As I understand Mr. Harriman's point, he's saying that each side made a move, and then because we were maliciously and deliberately aggressive in-country they had to kind of undo that gesture."

ABRAMS: "Yeah, in a way you're right, but he's twisted the facts in order to support his thesis. He says that they came out after the bombing halt. That was their gesture. And then we turned on the heat. Well, balls."

■ ■ ■

ABRAMS: Mentions "this executive officer of the 814th [who] committed suicide—not enough food for his men, not enough ammunition, weapons, requirements for constant attacks, B-52s and tac air chasing them around, moving all the time, so he just cashed in his chips. They investigated it, and somebody captured the report. Apparently he did it while he was in the hospital. Malaria—just a lot of problems. Wish we could get that program going."

■ ■ ■

BRIEFER: "With Lon Nol's appointment as Commander in Chief of Cambodia's armed forces, he is now in a position of almost unprecedented power." No one in Cambodian history has previously held the posts of CINC FARK, defense minister, and acting prime minister simultaneously.

ABRAMS (re Lon Nol): "Hasn't he been involved in this trucking?"

POTTS: "Yes, sir. He's been into it."

ABRAMS: "It'd been a great day if they'd stop moving that stuff from Sihanoukville up there." "It's a fairly lucrative business so, the Cambodians being what they are, it'd be pretty hard to pass that up."

■ ■ ■

ABRAMS (re action west of Dong Ha): "That's [RF outpost] what the attack was against, and they beat that thing off with their own resources. Apparently sappers were involved in it, too, and they got creamed. The other interesting thing is that thing was in charge of an officer, and he was either killed or wounded [Potts: "He was killed, sir."]—killed, and the sergeant took over the thing. Remember, this is all RF. No gunships, no spookies, no artillery, so on. And apparently General Truong went up the next day and promoted this sergeant to the 1st sergeant. And then the story goes that they wanted to move another outfit in there to give these some rest and the 1st sergeant wouldn't leave. And he stayed there. Mel [Zais] gave him a Bronze Star. It's quite a thing. The RF and PF up here have taken on quite a damn aggressive posture."

BRIEFER: "In western Quang Tri Province on 19 July, 13 kilometers south-southeast of Vandegrift combat base, ARVN elements found 15 bunkers containing a cache of ordnance weighing approximately 36.2 tons."

ABRAMS: "Probably intended for use by the 24 Bravo. It makes a lot of sense. If they're going to move to the east, then they—just as it always happens—they've got to position this stuff out there. It's a good thing to do [to scarf up the cache]. They have to now go and redo it. I think it's kind of a classic example of how to—instead of hunkering down there around Quang Tri, building the fences and so on for the 24 Bravo's arrival—get out there and work in his system a bit, because this is the way he has to do it. He hasn't got another method."

ABRAMS: "Another thing is, that's what the bastards are doing. When it looks like they're just kind of hanging back there and posing no threat, they've been pretty nice, and they've decided to stay out there in the jungles with the malaria and everything, and it looks pretty good. You know, week after week fixing them [determining their position by radio intercepts] and so on. You say, 'Well, those bastards, they don't dare come down here.' All that time the little guys are carrying a round apiece and so on, just like a bunch of goddamn ants. And then they get it all built up there, then he pushes them past that. Then you see it's getting pretty well done there. So the next thing you know, 'Well, how the hell did this happen?' There he is screwing around Quang Tri, when we've had all this—. 'They must have gotten new orders.' No, they haven't got new orders! It's the way they do it. And they've been working on it, all these little bastards going back and forth, bicycles, and carrying that damn stuff. So when it's peace and quiet, that's just before the goddamn tornado. And he needs the time, and he will make the effort, no matter how painstaking it has to be, how long it takes, and all that. He's going to <u>make</u> it. And <u>that's</u> the sign of good will! You see. That's what good will means."

ABRAMS: "Incidentally, quite a remarkable thing—that 1st [ARVN] Regiment, for the month of July, all four of its battalions have been in the jungle, and they've got a kill ratio of 1:20." "They got in a hospital down there . . . got a capacity of about 900." "This stage of the game, things like that hospital, those caches, and so on I think are <u>real</u> important. Screwing up the system."

ABRAMS (re capture of some enemy 85-mm artillery near FSB Veigle): "We all flew out there yesterday, to the 5/47th. The staggering thing is, how in the <u>hell</u> did they get those 85-mm's in there? <u>God damn</u>! [Said in an appreciative whisper.] [Somebody: "Last time I was there they had to push the <u>jeep</u>!"] [Laughter] About the only way you can figure it out is they <u>disassembled</u> the goddamn things." "It wasn't <u>easy</u>, but it's an example of the lengths that they are prepared to go to get this stuff where they want it. It's an <u>extraordinary</u> effort."

■ ■ ■

BRIEFER: "Sensor-detected truck movement in southern Laos continues to decline." "It has been at a virtual standstill for the past month, reaching an all-time low for the year with 58 movers this week." "There are more sensors deployed, covering a wider geographical area in Laos, this year than there were last year." "As a result of this continuing decrease, we have been able to reduce the number of sorties fragged in Steel Tiger."

ABRAMS: "Things like the 7th Division down there—not up to strength, and here it's one of the damn <u>test</u> areas of whether ARVN's going to be able to <u>hack</u> it when you take the U.S. out. And as much as I've talked about it with the JGS, and Minister Vy, and so on, they have not responded to it. The 42nd is a good example, and I told them here, the other day, I said, 'Here's the [enemy] 28th and the 66th and the 24th over there close order drilling, cleaning their goddamn weapons, marksmanship training, the psywar political officer's in there telling them about how we'll be in Kontum by September, and it'll all be ours, and so on, getting replacements in—they're sending them down from North Vietnam, through the goddamn Laotian panhandle, trudging along in the mud and the rain, and no rations and all that kind of stuff, but they're getting them up to strength! And the [friendly] 42nd, and this ranger battalion, for instance, I cited at Duc Me—<u>preparing</u> them for what's coming up, 'cause they're coming <u>back</u>. And, <u>goddamn</u> it, they're not getting them ready."

ABRAMS: "W-e-l-l, a-a-a-h-h, these are things that the senior—JGS, corps commander, and so on—that's what they're supposed to <u>rise</u> to." "I'll tell you, I've gotten so goddamn many stories about the 42nd, and it's never been <u>right</u>. A lot of hopes and dreams, but no <u>reality</u>. So—it's not good."

ABRAMS: Tells the commanders about how the 1st Regiment, 1st ARVN Division, uses prisoners [its own apprehended deserters and so on] to work in the fire bases instead of being in prison. Also: "That fire support base is immaculate." "It's <u>tight</u>." "And of course they all act like they own Vietnam. Great!" "I'll tell you <u>one</u> thing, you'll <u>never</u> see an American unit, from the <u>finest</u> battalion we've got, that's got a fire support base in that condition in three days. Never!"

· · ·

A key briefing on planning for continued redeployment of U.S. forces from Vietnam. The first increment of 25,000 is being withdrawn during July–August 1969. Col. Donn A. Starry was Abrams's close-hold planner.

BRIEFER (Colonel Starry) on redeployment planning:

■ "Using our original 50,000 plan as a basis, here is the composition of the forces identified for the second increment. The major combat elements would be the 3rd Marine Division with its two remaining regimental landing teams; one fighter squadron, two medium helicopter squadrons, one heavy helicopter squadron, and an observation airplane squadron of the 1st Marine Air Wing would accompany the division. There would also be two Army National Guard 155-mm artillery battalions." "Three air force squadrons: one F-100 squadron . . . , one special operations squadron from Pleiku and another from Nha Trang."

■ Re why the 3rd Marine Division was selected as the major combat unit to redeploy: "It has an excellent combat record, its withdrawal would be evidence to everyone that the Vietnamese are really taking over more of the war—that we are not just sending home service support troops and claiming to have given over more of the war to Vietnamese forces. The division would be withdrawn from an area where we have been making progress in military operations—the enemy threat in I Corps, while still formidable, appears to be in a state of change and there are also signs the enemy is having difficulty there. There is progress in securing the population—in Quang Tri Province now 85 percent of the people live in A or B or C category hamlets, and in Thua Thien 95 percent of the people live in hamlets in these categories." "The ARVN unit in the area, the 1st ARVN Division, is one of the best, if not the best, in the ARVN."

ABRAMS: "I'll entertain arguments if anybody's got a candidate to counter that. It's so clear to me now that it is, looking at all of them and what they do and how they run their affairs. There just isn't anything that can compare with them [the 1st ARVN Division]. The leadership is solid." "There isn't anybody that can challenge their supremacy. Part of it's because they've been fighting the NVA for over a year."

STARRY:

■ "The redeployment of the first increment is barely under way, and a sound assessment of the impact of redeploying the first 25,000 troops is not possible at this time."

■ "The South Vietnamese seem to have accepted redeployment of the first 25,000 in a positive fashion. Except for the time interval felt to be necessary for a thoroughgoing assessment, all the criteria we initially set forth before the 8th of June as requisite to the success of U.S. redeployments have been met.

These criteria were: no significant increase in enemy strength, activity or infiltration levels, or in his logistics capability; no new enemy weapons systems introduced into or capable of reaching South Vietnam; continued identifiable progress in pacification; improvement and modernization of RVNAF continues on schedule, with concomitant improvement in RVNAF effectiveness; an adequate level of U.S. tac air, B-52, helicopter, and nondivisional artillery support; and a capability for rapid reentry of at least part of the redeployed force."

■ "Our assessment of the factors and conditions we have just outlined leads us to conclude that, unless conditions change significantly between now and then, we should propose on the 3rd of August that we go ahead with redeployment of the second increment of 25,000 troops." That announcement to be made about 15 August, with redeployments to begin on 30 September and be completed by the end of November.

■ "Two general approaches to post–Phase 2 redeployments appear to us to be appropriate. One involves thinning out by brigade forces. This avoids leaving large division-size gaps which would be more difficult for ARVN to fill and into which the enemy could move should ARVN prove incapable of organizing and expanding operations rapidly. Two significant factors, however, argue against this course of action. First, the requirement to redeploy an arbitrary number of troops—say 50,000—makes it difficult to structure the redeploying force without taking out a large combat increment. For example, five separate brigades would have to redeploy in order to meet a 50,000 redeployment package ceiling. If, on the other hand, a division were redeployed, four brigades would be required, the division base and nondivisional support making up for the other brigade. Thinning out does not get spaces, and spaces are the goal of these redeployments—at least as Washington sees it. Also arguing against thinning out is that it tends to spread the risk evenly across a wide area. Instead of reassessing priorities and focusing on where the risk is least undesirable, it apportions a degree of risk to everyone, everywhere."

■ "The second general approach to additional redeployments is to take out division-size forces and an appropriate service support slice. This makes it easier to get to the ceiling required at a minimum cost in combat forces. On the other hand, it leaves a sizable gap to be filled by the forces remaining. Here is a brief of some of the considerations we applied in selecting units for redeployment beyond the 50,000 level. First, we felt it would be desirable to avoid taking more troops from I Corps until there has been time to fully evaluate the effects of the initial redeployments on pacification, on RVNAF, and on the enemy. Second, we felt it would be imprudent to take too much too fast out of II Corps. Security of the large number of U.S. bases in the vast land area of II Corps could become critical if the ARVN is not able to expand operationally. The ongoing I Force V [I Field Force, Vietnam] plan to Vietnamize the highlands war needs time for testing. The ARVN units available to take over the 4th Division missions are largely untried in larger-scale operations. Pacification is progressing in most areas, however, and with time the possibility of withdrawing significant numbers of U.S. troops may become more apparent. Third, in III Corps the enemy concentration on Tay Ninh and his intrusions into the border area require the presence of U.S. forces there. The weakness of ARVN divisions in III Corps militates against redeployment of significant U.S. forces. There are advances in pacification which the continued presence of U.S. troops could sustain."

■ "Recognizing the risks involved, our planning settled finally on taking a division out of III Corps and a brigade out of II Corps. The division would tentatively be the 1st Infantry Division, and the brigade either a brigade of the 4th [Infantry Division] or the 173rd Airborne [Brigade]. This force would total about 50,000. Hopefully it could be divided into two increments, with the division-size force in the first increment of about 25,000 and the brigade and its support from II Corps, and the service support units from III Corps, in the second increment. The military risks of this course of action are apparent to us all. Especially is this true when one recognizes that we are <u>probably</u> forcing the 5th ARVN Division into a 'fish or cut bait' situation. We run the danger of increased opportunity for enemy infiltration on the northern approaches to Saigon. Pacification is bound to be retarded, if not regressed, in some areas."

■ "Next we addressed ourselves to the problem of <u>when</u> additional U.S. redeployments could be made if the current lull in enemy activity continues. There will in all probability be no recognizable indicators of enemy reaction on the basis of which one might make a recommendation about timing. If, as has been alleged, the enemy is trying to 'signal' us with the lull, his diminished activity can be expected to continue, at least until he has encouraged sufficient U.S. redeployments that another course of action becomes more attractive to him. Assuming this 'worst case,' that is, no identifiable enemy reaction for some time to come, how then should we approach the timing of additional redeployments? Our initial criteria about the enemy, the RVNAF, pacification, and friendly combat support resources still obtain. But additionally, and more critical from the standpoint of the possible success of Vietnamizing the war, is the matter of time. There must be time for combined planning with the Vietnamese, for the orderly and progressive transfer of responsibilities for operational areas, for bases and facilities, for participation in pacification programs, and for all resources of the government of Vietnam to be brought to bear in a realistic manner on the problem with which they are about to be confronted."

■ "Psychologically the Vietnamese seem to have accepted the prospect of about 50,000 U.S. troops being redeployed in calendar 1969. The judgment has been made that, unless there is some favorable development not now in evidence, the withdrawal of 100,000 troops by the end of this year would have the most serious political repercussions. No matter <u>how</u> we explained it, it would be regarded by the Vietnamese as the beginning of a precipitous withdrawal, unrelated to the criteria of President Nixon, and would involve the risk of incurring an irreversible political and psychological chain reaction. The military risks, combined with the adverse political and psychological potential of calendar '69 redeployments on the order of 100,000 U.S. troops, lead inevitably to the conclusion that a withdrawal of this magnitude in 1969 represents a course of action it would not be prudent to pursue. Again, however, should the lull continue, either as a signal or for some other reason, and if there are no adverse indications to the contrary with regard to other criteria, then we should probably begin to plan in earnest for the subsequent redeployment of about 50,000 U.S. troops in the first half of 1970, and additional increments in the last half of that year. Here again, however, if all goes well the ultimate criteria will be how fast the Vietnamese can get themselves organized for the progressive and orderly transfer of functions and responsibilities, to include continued progress in all aspects of pacification. We should, in fact, take advantage of this lull, if it extends, to exert extra effort on pacification and RVNAF improvement."

ABRAMS: "I've got a few comments to make. First of all, this little nugget that's been dropped out here in the last few minutes is, of course, extremely sensitive, and I debated—we've had to proceed, especially under the guidance we've had, on a very close-hold basis with all of this sort of planning. The question was would it be appropriate to give it to this group today. Well, the way I looked at it is this: you've been coming in here, privy to really the most sensitive things that we <u>have</u>, and if you can't discuss this sort of thing with this group, then I've really <u>had</u> it. This is sensitive for a variety of reasons. It's sensitive because it has not yet been submitted to CINCPAC. It has not yet been submitted to the JCS. It has not yet been submitted to the secretary of defense or the president. And of course we cannot be in the game of preempting any of those authorities."

ABRAMS: "Now the <u>status</u> of this is, as Colonel Starry said, that we have to submit it to CINCPAC by the 3rd, and by the 10th it will be submitted to the JCS—10th of August. Now, further than that, when General Wheeler and Admiral McCain were here—earlier—General Rosson and I conferred with them. And they had all of the assessments and so on [that] you've heard. And while neither of them went into the detail of how many artillery battalions, they know it's the 3rd Marine—they know the <u>form</u> of the <u>package</u>. And the four of us were in agreement that this is what should be done. <u>Now</u>, Admiral McCain's staff has not had an opportunity to examine this at this point, and neither has the Joint Staff. And of course neither has the staff of the secretary of defense."

ABRAMS: "Then, on Wednesday, we had Minister Vy and General La and General Phong and General Dzu here, in this room, and we gave our—we gave a complete assessment of—pacification-wise, the enemy situation—we went over North Vietnam, Laos, Cambodia, in-country, . . . the only thing we left out were the specifics of COMINT. . . . Other than that, they got it just the way we've given it today, really. And then the RVNAF expansion and modernization, pacification, and then this proposal. It was all done in French, ably assisted by Ambassador Colby, who turns out to be quite an <u>accomplished</u> linguist, and with the rank of ambassador made it very helpful." [Laughter]

ABRAMS: "Then we gave Minister Vy, at the time, a copy of this nugget, the rationale of why this should be it, what it consisted of, and so on. We were able to give him that <u>at</u> the meeting. Subsequent to that we gave him four copies of the _entire_ briefing with all of its—the whole thing, in French, all of the evaluations and assessments and all that stuff. General Potts delivered those to him, and Minister Vy has reported to General Potts that he has gone over the entire matter with President Thieu, and he and President Thieu are in agreement that this is—_can_ be done, and the specifics of the areas involved they concur in. And Minister Vy has asked General Potts to convey to me that that _is_ the position of GVN."

ABRAMS: "Ambassador Bunker knows, and Ambassador Berger, all this. Now I might say that the four of us—General Rosson, Admiral McCain, General Wheeler, and myself—discussed also whether this should be a larger thing than 25,000—say 30,000, or 35,000, and so on. And we were all in agreement that this was just about the right size. We also discussed 100,000 by the end of '69, and we're all in agreement, and the Chairman has reported to the secretary of defense, and to the president, that the implications of a greater than 50,000 thing would have the most _serious_ effects in South Vietnam. There's great doubt in _our_ mind that the morale and fiber of the—not only the military, but the government itself—could survive really something which they have not contemplated."

ABRAMS: "And I should tell you one other thing. I received today authority to go ahead on a joint planning basis, with representatives of the GVN and JGS, joint planning on how to go about this over the next few years. So we'll be able to get down to brass tacks on planning—say out through FY '72, which is a good point because that—FY '72—we're now programmed to complete the modernization of the navy and the air force and the army and the marines and the whole thing. So how we approach that day, including residuals and so on, and we can get into how you do it, different rates of Vietnamizing, doing it in 24 months or doing it in 48 months, you know, play the thing in there. So— now that doesn't mean too much, _except_ that will be sort of laying the cards on the table with them, and we'll be able to work _jointly_. This is a _hell_ of a complicated _thing_. I mean, what's _practical_ to do and _impractical_ to do is _one_ subject. But even after you agree on _that_, the complexities of all of this—the facilities, and changes, and so on—_really_ something. So that's where we stand on that."

ABRAMS: "Now, I would like to say something _about_ this. We're talking about doing this in—really in October and November, which would start 28 September. And of course they always screw me a little bit on it. We set up for 30 September, and something's happening in Arizona or somewhere, and they think, 'Well, the 25th,' and then it gets to the 15th. I get screwed a little bit there, but it generally turns out to be manageable. You can do it with a battalion. I mean, you're going to get _that_. But this is October–November. Now _none_ of us can predict what the hell the enemy is going to be doing in October, or at least _I_ don't have any advisors around here who are—who satisfy _me_ that they can predict with _confidence_ what the enemy's going to do in October or November."

ABRAMS: "So while this particular composition is related to the situation as we know it right now, it may turn out to be unrelated to the situation in October or November. But my answer to that is we'll never be able to—on any of this, no matter how you try to do it, can you guess, or forecast, what that situation's going to be. But there is such a necessity to settle on what you're going to do in terms of getting bases, the facilities and the arrangements with the troops and the equipment, and all of the things the services have to do, that what I've decided, or what I've come down on, and I'm going—you'll all have a chance in a minute to express your views on this—is settle on that so that the planning can be good and we can go ahead and march down the road on that basis."

ABRAMS: "Now, when October comes and November comes, what this bastard does, I mean what the enemy does, we'll then shift our deployments and our arrangements and so on to meet that with the things we've got and so on and let this other thing go moving on down the pike like it—and that will practically guarantee that that part will be well done and efficient. There's all this stuff about personnel—you know, you've got to rearrange personnel and officers and all that, and that should get in good, hard—you know, fairly decent shape, and let it go on, because we know that it's not easy to do this, and you can get a lot of things screwed up if you keep shifting it. Now—JGS and ourselves are going to have to go ahead and develop contingencies against different postures that the enemy can take when October and November come. And we'll all have to be privy to that—on the assumption that he does this or that or some other thing. So that's about the situation in a nutshell, and I'm ready for comments."

SOMEONE: "I'd like to say the Vietnamese have not been privy to anything about an additional 50,000 we've talked about here."

ABRAMS: "That's right. And of course we have examined it to get a sensing of what the—in the staff here, we've examined it to get the sensing of what it amounts to if you had to do something like that. But you should know that we are—and, I must say, Ambassador Bunker, Ambassador Berger, General Rosson, myself, and Ambassador Colby—we are locked arm-in-arm on this thing of no more past 50,000 for '69. Now, we don't have a final decision on this yet and the Chairman, and Admiral McCain—that's about the array we've got at the moment."

ABRAMS: "We'd have a lot more flexibility around here if the 5th and the 18th [ARVN Divisions] were just a mass of tigers out there looking for raw meat. We'd have more flexibility if the 22nd was a rip-snorting ripping and tearing outfit. But you're just going to have to keep working on that and see what happens."

NICKERSON: "My only concern" is "the mobility that I'll have left" and resultant "ability to react." "That's my only concern."

ABRAMS: "What we're trying to do on this is move it along so there is movement, but not create panic."

■ ■ ■

COLBY: "From the pacification point of view one of the, I think, most important elements of the program this past whole year, really, has been momentum, the feeling of going ahead, and this has been as much a psychological factor as it has been a physical one, this moving into additional hamlets and so on. But the fact is they moved in with a certain amount of <u>confidence</u>. They felt that they were on the forward end of a wave. I think the important thing for the pacification program is to keep that kind of a spirit, because underneath the pacification program you can take these reductions without too much difficulty."

ABRAMS (reacting heatedly to Zumwalt's asking, "Why would a corps commander turn down troops?" re Vietnamese CG IV Corps not accepting two VNMC battalions to go in where the U.S. 9th Division had pulled out): "<u>Wait</u> a minute, <u>Bud</u>—now <u>wait</u> a minute! We <u>cannot</u> jam down—part of Vietnamization is that they—the <u>solution</u> has got to be <u>their</u> solution. Now we can advise them and so on, but in the <u>end</u> there's no point in us trying to jam two marine battalions down the corps commander's throat when he doesn't <u>want</u> them!"

ZUMWALT: "I sure understand that, but shouldn't there therefore be time for him to find out he's wrong?" [Zumwalt earlier had argued for a longer "hiatus" between redeployment increments.]

ABRAMS: "Well, you're convinced he's wrong. <u>He's</u> convinced he's <u>right</u>. [Laughter] And what <u>we've</u> got to do is back <u>him</u>."

EWELL: "In III Corps, the first two increments really don't touch it. Essentially it's unharmed. They've gotten enough enthusiasm and—luck, I guess—to where it looks like they might shift some high-ranking commanders. They might knock off two or three regimental commanders. They might knock off 25 percent of the battalion commanders in an effort to rejuvenate the leadership. Pacification, I think, is going to be the most difficult part, because we essentially have the <u>easy</u> part done. Now we're getting into the <u>real</u>—we're adjusting the watch, and I can predict we're going to have to can about two to four province chiefs. Now this is going to come real tough, because it won't be a visible failure, it will just be inability to meet the demands of a sophisticated program."

ABRAMS: "My recommendation for the first increment was 22,629." [Laughter]

■ ■ ■

COLBY: "One thing we're trying to do on this VCI thing, which is really going nowhere at the moment—nothing much is happening—I think we've picked up about one percent a month of the estimated strength . . . is to set up some record systems and goals so it becomes pretty obvious that Colonel So-and-So is falling flat on his face and Colonel So-and-So is doing a pretty good job." "But the VCI thing . . . we're trying to figure out something that will stop them from lying to us, as they are now, and make it so that they really <u>have</u> to pick up some of these guys."

■ ■ ■

ABRAMS: "The situation in the United States, I mean—all these fine words of yours [Zumwalt, arguing for more time between increments] just doesn't make a <u>dent</u> in it. If we can manage somehow to keep this thing moving along, and putting out a few sops to the pressures that exist <u>there</u>—keep the <u>goddamn</u> thing from falling <u>apart</u>—then we will have done a <u>magnificent</u> job. The <u>pressures</u> are <u>fantastic</u>! And what you've got is a small group of about six advisors pitted against <u>thousands</u>. Don't underestimate the thousands. That has to do with elections, and it has to do with a lot of things. You've got the <u>entire</u> press against you!

The public information media in the United States are <u>massed</u> against us!"

ZUMWALT: "Understood. My point is that I think you have a better chance of getting the time after this next phase if you start asking for it now."

ABRAMS: "I am under no such illusions! It'll be a <u>fight</u>, every goddamn <u>week</u> 'til the <u>end</u>! And it's going to be <u>nasty</u>!"

EWELL: "It seems to me that when Santa Claus comes around on Christmas Day, if he doesn't pull that 100,000 figure out of his pack they're going to shoot him. The president has no choice. He might have some flexibility on stretching the actual redeployments—."

ABRAMS: "Everybody's grown up and over 21, and they've got to stand for what they believe's right. And <u>piss</u> on Santa Claus. He just isn't <u>coming</u> this year." [Laughter]

■ ■ ■

ABRAMS: "It's [the 22nd ARVN Division] like the 173rd Airborne [Brigade]. They've [the 173rd] got <u>rigging</u> equipment, and they've got TO&Es for air dropping wherever in the world the United States wants to put them, and they're all airborne trained and they're all 'All the way, sir!' and all that kind of stuff. We don't <u>need</u> it! We don't <u>need</u> it! Instead what they've got to do is get out there and cream the <u>VCI</u>, get out there in little units muckering around at night, helping the goddamn villagers, seeing that the goddamn rice stays in the warehouse and so on, and—Christ, there isn't room for a <u>parachute</u>! The only thing you can do is use it for a picnic with the villagers or something."

ABRAMS: "And, unfortunately, the 22nd [ARVN] Division can't <u>see</u> that. It isn't being a great division, going out battling with <u>regiments</u> and <u>battalions</u> and so on! <u>Goddamn it</u>, the name of the game that's got to be done is this <u>other</u> thing! And that's what <u>needs</u> to be done in Binh Dinh! And that's what [banging table] the 22nd Division can't <u>see</u>! And that's what the division commander is psychologically indisposed to do! And what <u>everybody's</u> got to do, instead of talking about going off to war and <u>battling</u> with the—Christ, they've been down there licking their chops waiting for the 3rd NVA to come back! Well, of course if the 3rd NVA came back they'd clean their clock. [Laughter] But that's the day they're waiting for—when the 3rd NVA comes back! W-e-l-l, <u>bullshit</u>! [Laughter] The thing—you <u>can't</u> do what you're <u>organized</u> for, you <u>can't</u> do what you're <u>trained</u> for. You've got to go out to do what has to be done right now in this country! <u>Everybody's</u> got to do it!"

CORCORAN: "Looking at this in the long haul, and looking at what the enemy has done in the past, what he is doing now, you have to get more ARVN strength into the highlands."

ABRAMS: "<u>Concur</u>! <u>Concur</u>! We've started to broach [laughing] that with the JGS, and I'll tell you it's got them on the rafters. [Laughter] But—you're right. And we agree in principle to proceed, trying to work this thing out. And I <u>agree</u>. I'm not arguing with you about that. But when the 22nd Division gets up <u>there</u>—if the 20th, the 66th, the 24th, and so on, all of that stuff, doesn't come <u>boiling</u> out of <u>Cambodia</u>, they shouldn't sit around on their ass waiting for that to <u>happen</u>. But <u>that's</u> what they'll <u>do</u> if you send them up there this weekend! They <u>won't</u> work with the Montagnards, they <u>won't</u> cooperate with the province chiefs and the district chiefs!"

■ ■ ■

ROSSON (re a problem he encounters): "I leave my helicopter and I move over toward the province chief and his advisor. The advisor charges out, salutes, reports, begins talking. Finally we get around to meeting the province chief. Commentary begins. The advisor is at my side, doing all the talking, answering all the questions, and so on. We go into a briefing room, for example. There are three or four seats lined up in front of a board. The visitors sit down. We look around to find the province chief. If he's <u>lucky</u> he may get up in the second row. Chances are he's probably back down the line a ways. . . . All too often I wind up, initially at least, in a dialogue with the advisor, with his counterpart playing no really effective part in it at all. So I've had to resort to just telling the advisor to shut up, on a few occasions, and let the Vietnamese speak for themselves. Either that or I start addressing the Vietnamese, moving them up, and so forth." "I think the lesson is that we've got to start giving the impression, from the top to the bottom, that all elements of the RVNAF, all of the administrative echelons—province, district, and the like, stand on their own as far as officialdom is concerned. Our questions should be addressed to them, in the main, and they should be given a chance to respond, to develop their own data, and to in effect <u>know</u> that we're down there to visit <u>that</u> unit and to hear from <u>those</u> people."

2 AUG 1969: WIEU

ATTENDEES: Gen. Abrams, Gen. Rosson, LTG Mildren, MG Townsend, VADM Zumwalt, BG Vande Hey, BG Smith, Amb. Colby, BG Potts, [LTG?] Jones, BG Bautz, MG Dixon, BG McLaughlin, MG Conroy, MG Shaefer, BG Cheadle, BG Galloway, BG Long, Col. Stemen, Col. Gibson, BG Sykes, Col. Hill, Col. Doody.

BRIEFER (re northbound traffic on the Ho Chi Minh Trail): "We believe that the term 'travelers' is a general term that probably applies to a broad range of personnel, including military personnel, returning to North Vietnam from Laos and the Republic [of Vietnam] for rest, reassignment, or administrative reasons."

BRIEFER (re the Lao panhandle): "Truck movement as detected by sensors during the period 23–29 July declined to less than 50, the lowest weekly total <u>ever</u> recorded." Cites "the total absence of sensor detected and visually observed truck traffic on 28 July. This is the first time since the emplacement of the sensor field in December 1967 that no movement was recorded." Air interdiction, heavy rainfall, flooding.

■ ■ ■

BRIEFER: Cites a captured letter from the People's Revolutionary Committee, Phu My District, urging "all elements to increase attacks in order to disrupt the Accelerated Pacification plan, and to counter the psywar effort and Chieu Hoi program."

ROSSON: "They're going pretty strong. I notice that Hanoi said they'd done away with 330,000 of us since the beginning of the year."

ABRAMS: "That's pretty good."

ABRAMS: "I wonder if we could arrange a swap of division commanders—we'd take two of theirs and give them two of ours [ARVN]."

SOMEONE: "Who would win on that?"

ABRAMS: "Well, I know who wouldn't <u>lose</u>." [Laughter]

■ ■ ■

BRIEFER: "The source reports that, in accordance with a new COSVN directive, the enemy planned military high points in Tay Ninh Province on 19 August, 12 September, and 23 September."

POTTS: "This has been our fine source in the past."

POTTS: "During the month of July alone, an all-time high for us. 780,000 pages of captured documents were brought into this center here in town." Divisions in III and IV Corps fly this material in in the afternoon. "We work on it all night, and the next morning reports are flown right back to them." "Of course they don't translate all of that, but they scan it quickly, pull out the significant ones," and then work with them intensively.

■ ■ ■

ABRAMS (re report of military operations in Laos per the embassy): "I tell you, we're just going to have <u>trouble</u>. They've never known how to run the damn thing over there. They've always got some screwy cloak and dagger stuff that they, you know—. And that's what has let the whole fucking thing <u>collapse</u> over there. They want to go ahead and get after this fellow now—well, there's a tried and true way of doing <u>that</u>. And that's to move in there and <u>really</u> open up a campaign that'll cut his damn jugular vein. And you've got rain and all kinds of things that will help you. It makes it harder bombing, but the combination of water and bombs and mines and so on gives those fellows <u>fits</u>. But if they get <u>tiptoeing</u> around with this—." "If you don't <u>do</u> this right, you're just <u>wasting</u> the air assets. Picking around here and there between the goddamned <u>agents</u>, and <u>stopping</u> and <u>starting</u> and <u>shifting</u> and so on. They [CAS] don't have any <u>concept</u> of how to get at it and <u>really</u> create pain for this fellow."

ABRAMS: "A lot of other characters can talk about whether the interdiction program is successful or not successful and so on. And I don't <u>care</u>. They can talk about it all they want to. <u>We</u> know what it does. And when it comes to the serious business of getting on with the war, wherever it's going on, by god— they use that, but we <u>know</u>. You've got a <u>system</u>, and you apply it against <u>his</u> system, and that's what you've been doing. When I say system, it's a combination of the photography, the intelligence—all-source intelligence, it's the studying of his system, and so on. It isn't any flying around in an airplane looking for something to <u>hit</u>. They've got to <u>appreciate</u> that."

ABRAMS: "Now today has been the first time that we've had specifics of further offensive action. This is vis-à-vis the debate of whether this lull is a signal, or how long will the lull go on. . . ."

ABRAMS: "I don't think they can <u>do</u> that [maintain a lull for much longer, he apparently means]. I think they've <u>got</u> to take action, because—although there's no point in getting out of hand on it—the pacification program, and all it means in terms of security, in terms of working somewhat against the infrastructure, in terms of the RF and PF, working on the guerrillas, that thing just continues to move. And you leave it alone, virtually, for seven or eight months, and by god I think you're going to have trouble—I mean he is. That's the way I feel."

■ ■ ■

ABRAMS: "I'd just like to say I thought the visit of the president was a very successful—. The real thrust of his visit was political and psychological. That's what it was really about. He had a fine meeting with President Thieu, I would say, and this time Ambassador Bunker was present. It was very reassuring. And then he came in for a few minutes with the cabinet and some of [our?] officers. I thought the president was quite forceful. I mean unequivocal—just real strong, and said simply and directly, so it would be impossible, in my judgment, it would be impossible to misinterpret what he said. It was firm—. His visit with the troops was really very good for him. I rode back on the airplane and got a chance to talk with him for part time, and it really gave the president quite a lift. It was obvious. He was bubbling over with that experience. These men—they turned him on." "They were all around him. Newspaper men couldn't get near him because he was surrounded by soldiers."

5 AUG 1969: Ambassador Godley Briefing

ATTENDEES: Gen. Abrams, Gen. Rosson, Amb. Colby, Col. Dessert, BG Bautz, BG McLaughlin, Col. Hill, Col. Hanifen, Amb. George M. Godley, LTC Duskin, LTC Lowrey, Mr. Cutter, Gen. Brown, MG Dixon, MG [Kirkendahl?], BG Sykes.

BRIEFER: The enemy has divided I CTZ into three military areas: In the north the B-5 Front, in the center section MR-TTH, and MR-5 for the southern three provinces and south into II CTZ. The B-5 Front includes the DMZ and extends south to the Cua Viet River and Highway 9.

ABRAMS: "His problem here in northern I Corps is he has really become ineffective in the coastal—in the populated areas. His intelligence is poor, and he can't get enough food out of it to really support his forces in the vicinity. Well, he's had to bring them in. Those people who come across the DMZ—they have to bring their food with them. It's because of what's been happening in the pacification effort—security, efforts against the local forces, guerrillas, and the infrastructure. So this right now is kind of a tough problem for him."

ABRAMS: "His main means of supply and infiltration for southern I Corps has come through A Shau out of Base Areas 604, 610, 611—into the A Shau, and then down into Base Area 112." "Now he hasn't been able to use A Shau for some months. We've been there—the ARVN and U.S.—and we're going to stay there."

BRIEFER: Most of II CTZ is part of the enemy's COSVN area, including MR-6 and, below that, MR-10, which extends down into III CTZ. The B-3 Front is the Highlands Front. III CTZ's 11 provinces and the Capital Military District are all under COSVN. Enemy MR-10 contains Binh Long and Phuoc Long Provinces, plus a portion of II CTZ. MR-7 is most of the southeastern quadrant of III CTZ. Saigon is designated Sub-Region 6. Enemy MR-2 is the northern part of IV CTZ, and MR-3 the rest.

■ ■ ■

ABRAMS: "Some newspaperman, talking about Saigon—I don't know if he was complaining about security, but he said, 'You can't drive out to Long Binh and Bien Hoa at night.' Well, the problem is this: When you try to take the night away from the enemy, you get out there with a hell of a lot of ambushes and so on. We went through a period here around Saigon, and the provinces immediately bordering Saigon, where the only reaction force you could use at night was either—on the ground, it had to be mechanized, or it would get ambushed by your own ambush! I mean, there's such a density of ambushes out there that you couldn't move ground troops at night without running the risk of running them into your own people. You know, it gets to be quite a conglomeration of RF, PF, ARVN, U.S., and so on."

ABRAMS: "I'd hate like hell to drive down Route 4 at night—not for any fear of getting picked off by the VC, I don't think there's a chance of that, but you run an excellent chance of getting shot up by your own people out there."

■ ■ ■

ABRAMS: "The Australians and the New Zealanders are really first-class people. We put American units under command of the Australians . . . you just do, where the Australians are, what needs to be done, and nobody cares—either way."

ABRAMS: "The Koreans, of course, are very professional in the fighting that they do, but they're the kind—the state that they're in, it takes a couple of months for them to lay on an operation—that's to get all the planning. It all has to be approved down here in Saigon, in detail. It's generally very expensive in support—the demands run fairly high on that. So flexibility in the use and employment of Korean forces is limited. Now, this shouldn't detract one bit from— when they've laid the plan, and they've set the thing to go, it is executed in a very professional way. They're excellent fighters. Their troops are in splendid condition. First class. They're well led. They've got excellent company officers, NCOs. Graduates of their military academy down there commanding those companies. Highly motivated and all that sort of thing. But razooing them around the country where the situation demands it at the moment—you know, as the thing shifts—you can't do that."

ABRAMS: "Now the Thais—when they get here, it takes a little time for them to really get a feel for the problem and get out. But they've been excellent fighters—I mean excellent defensive fighters. They've done a good job at it. Their performance there I would say is very good. Their artillery, for the standard artillery work, is as good as any artillery."

ABRAMS (re the Thais): "I visited one of their fire support bases out here a few weeks ago, and I felt that it was the best fire support base I had visited in South Vietnam. [Godley: "Including ours?"] Oh, yes. The standard of excellence there—and they put on some firing demonstrations around there—and god! I don't give a damn if they practiced it for two days before I got there, which I'm inclined to think they didn't, but if they had it was still spectacular. It was precision, and it was fast, and god, the way that thing was constructed and laid out and so on—and <u>clean</u>, sanitation and all that stuff, fire prevention, all the little things you could look into about whether it had been lacking—nah, it wasn't there, it <u>wasn't</u> there." "I can tell you that, in the great Order of Saint Barbara, they are rather deeply steeped in artillery doctrine as it is known all over the world."

■ ■ ■

ABRAMS (re artillery): "We do an awful lot of—and in the delta the ARVN do, too—moving artillery around by helicopter. It changes the range of artillery to the range of the helicopter."

ABRAMS (re Thai artillery): "Firing techniques, fire control, fire distribution, accuracy, precision, those things—at least what's been over here has been <u>damn</u> good." "I asked this battery commander out there, I said, 'When did you go to Fort Sill?' He said, 'I've never been there.' Heh, heh, heh! So they've got an artillery school of their own."

■ ■ ■

ABRAMS (re the South Vietnamese): "One of the things this means, Mr. Ambassador, is that these fellows, when they make up their minds to do something, by god there isn't <u>anything</u> they can't <u>do</u>. They've <u>got</u> the talent. They've just got to decide to get <u>with</u> it! And when they've decided—you know, the whole structure's decided to get with it, by golly it'll go."

■ ■ ■

BRIEFER: "This is our concept. We call it the 'one war' concept. It has three principal objectives: the achievement of pacification, the improvement of the RVNAF (not only in modernization of their equipment, but effectively employing it), and combat operations itself. We consider all three of these of equal priority, although at any given time and under any given circumstances one might take <u>temporary</u> priority over the others."

J-3: "In the southern three provinces of I Corps we are <u>not</u> out on the border, and never <u>have</u> been, really. <u>It's</u> the only place in-country where we're in that position." "Very rugged, very heavily VC-infrastructured, and it's been that way for many years."

■ ■ ■

ABRAMS: Desertions in ARVN about 25 per 1,000 per month. In the overall structure stabilized at about 12–13 per 1,000 per month.

GODLEY: "That's way down!"

ABRAMS: "Yeah, that's right. But in our rather tenuous estimate of manpower that they've got that's usable, they cannot support the structure that we're aiming at over time and accept that kind of losses through desertion. It's got to be cut in half—at <u>least</u>."

■ ■ ■

ABRAMS: "Very clearly . . . ARVN effectiveness has improved significantly. The RF and PF have contributed an important part of that 102,000 [enemy KIA]." "And that's the improvement in the RF and PF—it's the M16s, it's the M79s, it's more PRC-25 radios and this sort of thing."

ABRAMS (re Arc Light): "We're getting more good out of 1,600 sorties per month than we were getting out of 1,800 sorties per month a year ago, because—and <u>only</u> because—of the targeting and intelligence."

GODLEY: "Have you attributed that to sensors?"

ABRAMS: "No. Mr. Ambassador, it's so much more complicated than that. It's the all-source [intelligence]. And the real secret on targeting is all the sources of intelligence and the capacity to pull them all together so that then you get a good picture."

ABRAMS: "The cache thing—the part that intelligence has played here is studying his system, and then the design of the operations to work against the system. These caches are predominantly not brought in—it doesn't come from informants and so on. It comes from operations, the operations that are based on the study of the design of his system to support his forces."

ABRAMS: "We look at this—you've got to work against the whole system—his whole system. When it starts out of North Vietnam, when it starts down the trail, you've got to hammer away at it there. You've got to hammer away at it in-country with tac air and B-52s. And then you've got to go after it on the ground in-country. And this—the sum of the whole thing—is the effect that you're producing on him and his capability in South Vietnam."

ABRAMS: "It was very difficult for us to understand why we didn't get high points in July. His documents showed that we would. They've always been reliable. There may be some postponement—the day may shift from the 15th to the 25th or something like that, but it's gone. In July, we didn't have it. And either he cancelled it, or he couldn't do it, or something. Or he thinks he did it and we haven't been able to read it from the results."

ABRAMS: "The B-41 RPG-7 is the best handheld antitank gun in the world."

ABRAMS: "You've got the 1st ARVN Division up here. It's got 17 maneuver battalions. It's a first-class division. It's clearly the best troops they've got in-country. They're well led, from battalion commander right up to the top. The division commander—I don't think there's a division commander like him in the Vietnamese armed forces. He's a skilled tactician, he's a leader, and he is apolitical. So it's a solid outfit."

ABRAMS: "The delicate thing in all of this [is to build South Vietnamese] confidence so they know they can handle [the enemy], and you can take your companies or battalions out of there. And that, sir, is the real trick. Americans—mostly—try to help people too much. They take either one of two positions—don't help them at all, or [laughing] help them too much. And this operation is a delicate one so that you do in fact build their pride and their confidence and so on."

ABRAMS (re Colby): "Bill's our expert. Bill's got more experience over here than any of the rest of us."

ABRAMS: "We're doing these things with the 18th and the 5th and the 25th [ARVN Divisions], and in other places. And I think it's useful. We'd feel badly—I would feel badly if we weren't doing it, if we weren't making that try. But in the end they're not going to be any better, no matter what we do, no matter what we give them in the way of equipment, and no matter what we do with them in the way of training, unless they've got the kind of leadership that'll take a hold of it and carry it. That's been the history of it."

GODLEY: "General, I've learned a lot this afternoon. But I'm worried, too, because the successes that you're having here, and the progress, and everything that you've told me is known to Hanoi just as well. Their losses have [word indistinct], and this gets back to our stage of the war up there in northern Laos. I'm beginning to see that one in a fuller way. The push he's making there, which is nickel and dime compared to the losses he's taking here. . . . If I were Hanoi, and if I knew what I just learned here this afternoon, I'd beat the loving bejesus out of northern Laos. And what does that mean? Heretofore, before this briefing . . . I thought the enemy was trying to convert Laos into another Cambodia where he could have [word unclear] and unimpeded access down the panhandle. But it looks to me quite clearly that he must feel like he's lost— not the war, but he's well on the way to losing it down here. And, what with the Paris negotiations and everything else, if I were Ho, or his staff, I'd recommend actions there for getting the best he can out of the area, the region. And I'd really push hard in Laos."

J-3: What's new is "the single hope of breaking American will. And that's his major factor now."

6 AUG 1969: Briefing for General Chapman

Gen. Leonard F. Chapman Jr. is Commandant of the Marine Corps.

ATTENDEES: Gen. Chapman, Gen. Rosson, BG Bautz, BG McLaughlin, Col. Anglen, Col. Dessert, LTC Truesdale.

CHAPMAN: "Well, do you feel in general that they're hurting?"

BRIEFER: "Yes, sir."

ROSSON: "It's hard to see how they couldn't be hurting."

BRIEFER: Re enemy KIA: 182,000 during 1968. 102,000 during the first half of 1969.

CHAPMAN: "Whose side is time on?"

MCLAUGHLIN: "We've got these two or three major variables working: improvement of the RVNAF, attrition of the VCI, combat effectiveness of the NVA. In that respect, I would say time is on our side in that the longer we can maintain what we're doing the better we're going to get—if we keep on doing what we're doing.

CHAPMAN: "That his doom is inevitable?"

MCLAUGHLIN: "Inevitable."

ROSSON: "As viewed from the standpoint of in-country operations."

MCLAUGHLIN: "Yes."

ROSSON: "When you couple those to domestic pressures at home, the attitude in Paris—it's hard to treat these things in isolation—I think our position is that developments are such that time is on our side under the present—."

MCLAUGHLIN: "I'd hate to take a guess—I've only been back about four months this time, but things look so much better this time than when I was here before—I just have the feeling—like in Binh Dinh—if we can hang in there for about another six months maybe that will be secure enough so it can be turned over to the Territorial Forces, with maybe one or two regular ARVN battalions working around there."

CHAPMAN: "Now if time is on our side, and if we keep at it, and as a result in time his total defeat, military and political, is inevitable, what's he going to do about it?"

MCLAUGHLIN: "Well, I would think that the best thing he could do right now is to get us out of here. He can just deny contact. He can get into sanctuaries, he can lie low, he can build up, he can wait and turn into a small guerrilla harassment-type thing. But even here I think time is on our side because it's my feeling that, for the most part, the RVNAF is moving ahead. I sense a cohesion among the people, too, that didn't exist before. I'm not saying that that could not be destroyed, but I think it's better than it's ever been in recent years."

ROSSON: "Well, if he's unable—or elects to conduct this diminished level of activity, this is going to cost him dearly with respect to pacification. It means a greater opportunity, it means control of the people, and he'll suffer in terms of cohesion of his guerrilla apparatus, his infrastructure."

JACOBSON: "Yes, he will."

8 AUG 1969: Briefing for General Bonesteel

Gen. Charles H. Bonesteel III is Commander in Chief, United Nations Command; Commander, U.S. Forces, Korea; and Commanding General, Eighth U.S. Army in Korea.

ATTENDEES: Gen. Abrams, Gen. Bonesteel, BG Bautz, Col. Dessert, Mr. Jacobson.

BONESTEEL (re intelligence): "Which is—what—half the game over here?"

ABRAMS: "W-e-e-l-l-l, sometimes I get it up around 90 percent. But I've never gotten below 50! This is your life blood. It's your life blood! When I think of—when I look back on my service, and especially my times in the Pentagon, I wish I had seen this as clearly. And I regret it."

ABRAMS: "However, Tick [Bonesteel], I think the intelligence corps, the branch, and the quality . . . has really been functioning. We're getting some fine talent." "Another place that I think they're strong—there're some warrant officers in these radio research units that are really first-class professionals. Been at it a long time, and they're dedicated to it."

■ ■ ■

ABRAMS (re the "understandings"): "As you know, one of the understandings in the bombing halt was that everyone would observe the DMZ. And these characters in their—when pressed on this, they always said, 'You will see. You will see. We will understand and we will do appropriate things,' and so on. So this sort of bullshit developed into an 'understanding.' Well, it turns out that the understanding was quite different. Now, we wanted to have freedom to the Ben Hai—in other words, to the demarcation line. And I can tell you that at the meeting in Washington when this decision was made, I <u>lost</u> that, because <u>they</u> said that our—the understanding was that we would <u>both</u> keep out of the demilitarized zone. Well, this handicaps—. We've stood against this <u>forever</u>, because it <u>handicaps</u> us. I didn't want to go into the southern half of the DMZ, <u>except</u> when it served the good purposes of the command and so on. Well, what he has done since the bombing halt has just made it crystal clear that the goddamn DMZ is <u>not</u> respected by him, this <u>isn't</u> a demarcation line, and so on. And the other thing about it is that he has—he has <u>never</u>, although we give him the <u>capability</u> of doing it—he has never mounted any kind of an <u>offensive</u>. It's been, I think, purely and simply designed to show that the goddamn DMZ doesn't mean anything to <u>him</u>, and it's just part of the war."

■ ■ ■

ABRAMS (re Harriman): "And of course last year, despite what Mr. Harriman says, <u>Governor</u> Harriman, an awful lot of units withdrew out of here into North Vietnam prior to the bombing halt. And the <u>reason</u>, <u>we</u> think, that it occurred was that they were <u>not</u> able to support them. They weren't getting the supplies down to the DMZ, they weren't getting them through Laos. There weren't a half a dozen trucks a day ever got in Laos during this concentrated interdiction program in North Vietnam."

■ ■ ■

ABRAMS (re the A Shau Valley): "I <u>believe</u> we're going to stay in the A Shau. I think they're going to keep a couple of battalions in there. They're fixing up a pretty good base for them. We've got the road open into A Shau, and a lot of it's pretty damn good road—comes out of Hue here. Because A Shau <u>was</u> probably the principal supply route for the other three, as well as Thua Thien. And they haven't been able to use that now for several months."

ABRAMS: "The Vietnamese have now gotten where they're pretty damn good at what we were trying to get them to do two years ago. But that's <u>not</u> what to do <u>now</u>. <u>We've</u> learned a lot in the meantime, and going around and telling them that <u>that's</u> a crock of you know what, and <u>this</u> is the thing to do, really doesn't say—they <u>wonder</u> about the Americans."

ABRAMS: "On this keeping things secret, we have a problem with the Americans on this, too . . . and we all know that there's a lot of things that are infiltrated. I don't know <u>how</u> many VC are working out at Long Binh, but it's some. You've got them in ARVN units . . . and I suppose in the province headquarters, and maybe in some cases district headquarters. So there's <u>always</u> danger. However, I think we really have to <u>accept</u> that and <u>go ahead</u>. We've <u>got</u> to talk with the district chiefs, we've <u>got</u> to talk with the province chiefs, and the ARVN commanders, and develop in them ways of doing these things. . . . And there <u>are</u> ways of doing it, and <u>that's</u> what's got to be developed, rather than keep them out of the—. That's a <u>no-win</u> policy. How the hell are people going to develop confidence in themselves if nobody, <u>nobody</u> will trust them? So that's just a dead-end street."

■ ■ ■

ABRAMS (re new tactics): "Now what's going on out here at the present time [vicinity Tay Ninh and so on] is that the 1st Cavalry, the 25th Division, the 1st Infantry Division, the ARVN to a lesser degree, they're all operating out here in about platoon-size and smaller forces. You see, they're really deployed on <u>top</u> of all this. And what they've been killing in here are rear services types, no—very little—of combat types. Well, now they sense that this is changing. They've begun to pick up caches of rice and ammunition—not great stuff." "So what's going on in here now is a very intensive reconnaissance, trying to sense the movement of the combat units, and also looking for supplies and this sort of thing, which will give you a key to <u>where</u> the effort's going to be and a little sense of the timing." "So what's happened this year is, from what he [enemy] started out with—I mean the plans and schemes and objectives he had, he's had to continuously re-cut the cloth to bring his objectives more in line with his capabilities."

■ ■ ■

ABRAMS: "I'm not aware of any supplies at all that come from North Vietnam into III Corps, unless you want to count that that is carried on the individuals that arrive. It <u>all</u> comes through Sihanoukville." "I would say that somewhere between 60 and 75 percent of <u>all</u> the supply that comes into South Vietnam comes from Sihanoukville—or Cambodia."

■ ■ ■

BONESTEEL: "You have to work hard to stay ahead of General Abrams."

9 AUG 1969: WIEU

BRIEFER: On the Pleiku Plateau during the past week 14 inches of rain fell at Pleiku in a six-day period, compared to a normal 19 inches for the entire month of August. Most fell on Saturday and Sunday in heavy early evening thundershowers. The six and a half inches on Sunday recorded a record 24-hour rainfall for Pleiku.

■ ■ ■

BRIEFER: Headquarters 559th Transportation Group has relocated from the Tchepone area to North Vietnam. But a forward headquarters has been reactivated.

BRIEFER (re enemy sickness): "[***] personnel of the 37th Engineer Battalion and the 45th Anti-Aircraft Battalion, both subordinate to Binh Tram 42, located in Base Area 611, were experiencing serious health problems. Since both the numbers of personnel and percentages given exceed the listed strengths of the units, it is evident that many personnel are suffering from more than one illness." 37th Engineer Battalion: Of 241 personnel assigned, 183 (76 percent) have malaria, 70 (29 percent) are suffering from exhaustion, 29 (12 percent) have various other illnesses. 45th Anti-Aircraft Battalion: Of 261 personnel assigned, 135 (66 percent) have malaria, 67 (33 percent) exhaustion, and 81 (39 percent) other.

■ ■ ■

ABRAMS (re some enemy unit): "They won't have much to brag about when they get to Base Area 483. It hardly will be the arrival of the conquering heroes." "I don't know—it may be getting a little euphoric about this, but Christ, it's been the RF out there, tangling with these NVA. I mean, if anybody thought they were going to spread terror and horror in the minds of the local inhabitants as they came marching in, the territorials got out there <u>mixing</u> it with them."

COLBY: "I think that's part of the return on the investment in the M16."

ABRAMS: "Yeah."

13 AUG 1969: General Vien Briefing

BRIEFER: "The enemy's total strength appears to be declining." "We believe that . . . the enemy is still short of replacing his losses for 1969." Estimate about 90,000 infiltration for January–July 1969, compared to 174,000 for the same period in 1968. Estimate current enemy strength in and adjacent to South Vietnam at about 240,000 (131,000 maneuver and combat support, 55,000 administrative support, 54,000 guerrillas) (includes an estimated 93,000 NVA troops).

BRIEFER: Average trucks per day entering the panhandle in June 1969 were 74 percent below May 1969. Averages per day were, in May: 34, June: 9, July: 4. Per Seventh Air Force estimates, enemy stockpiles in Laos had a net decrease of 1,200 tons in June and 330 tons more in July. Estimate 51 tons per day moving through the panhandle being destroyed by air action. Overall therefore estimated that only 6.1 tons per day arrived in South Vietnam from Laos during June, and only 2 tons daily during July.

BRIEFER (re in-country caches): "Crew-served weapons ammunition captured from the enemy during the first half of 1969 equalled three times the rate captured for the entire year in 1968." "Small-arms ammunition was captured at nearly twice the 1968 rate."

ABRAMS: "We had a very bad sapper action up in southern I Corps. They got into C Troop of the 1st Squadron, 1st Cavalry—U.S., and destroyed eight APCs . . . 12 killed, something like that. Very bad! Now, we've put out a lot of instruction about this sapper thing, and emphasizing it with everybody. And they should—they're [the enemy] not that smart. Where the trouble comes is people are not alert enough, they're not awake enough, and that's how it happens. I refuse to accept any excuse for a successful sapper attack, I don't care how they do it. We've just got to be smarter, and we've got to be more alert. . . . That's what we have to do!"

ABRAMS (re 1st ARVN Division): "They have a very good system up there on the deserters. They're all out on those fire bases. I don't think they've got anybody in the stockade." "They're out there working every day on the fire bases in the jungle, fixing the wire, clearing the fields of fire, and so on. No place to escape because . . . if you go, then you're going to have to walk through the jungle, by yourself. Not very good. They keep in good health, because they're working out in the fresh air, and keeping strong. It's a very good system. Now, everyone can't do that. Well, for instance, he can't do it with the battalions that are working in the coastal plain."

POTTS: Tells Vien he just got back from a week at CINCPAC, where his family is located. While there he went to Tripler Hospital and visited Vietnamese patients. "My wife goes there once a week to see these wounded men." Major Phan Ngoc Luan is one she has visited. He was CO, 1st Battalion, 3rd Regiment, 1st ARVN Division.

VIEN: "He has only one leg. I remember."

POTTS: He won the DSC during Tet 1968. Also the Bronze Star. Wounded four times. Will arrive here 27 August. General Pixton is there on leave and will bring him back with him.

ABRAMS: "From the very beginning General Stilwell had a lot of interest in him. He wanted him sent back to the States." Got an artificial leg at Tripler. "Every American that's ever met him thinks he's really great."

16 AUG 1969: WIEU

ATTENDEES: Gen. Abrams, Gen. Rosson, Gen. Brown, Amb. Colby, LTG Mildren, VADM Zumwalt, MG Conroy, MG Townsend, Mr. Jacobson, MG Shaefer, BG Bautz, BG Long, BG McLaughlin, BG Vande Hey, BG Smith, BG Potts, BG Galloway, BG Sykes, Col. Gibson, Col. Hanifen, Col. Penuel, Col. Doody.

ABRAMS (re infiltration): "In doing backgrounders with the press, talking with the press, you'd be well advised not to get into figures over these summer and fall months. We should say as background for the press that, what we know of the infiltration for July and so far this month, it does appear to us that it's down. And leave it that way. But don't get muckering around with percentages or numbers. Now, in the end they'll get mad about that and start saying that 'informed officials in Saigon say that infiltration is way down, 10 percent of what it used to be, but they don't want to let it out because it'll hasten the withdrawal of U.S. troops.' That'll be the next go round. And then we'll have to decide whether or not to deny that. Anyway, for the present let's not get mixed up in figures. My main reason is that I'm getting a little chary on just how tight a grip we've got on what the hell's happening in the infiltration thing." Earlier: "Frankly, I felt fairly confident that we had it, numbers-wise and about the timing. We had a good firm hold on it—in advance."

POTTS: "Destination, too."

ABRAMS: "Yeah, all that. Well, I'm telling you, I don't have that feeling right now."

BRIEFER: Apparent merging of missions by Binh Tram 8 and Binh Tram 10. This includes "changes in communications structures." New *binh tram* complex. "It appears that the North Vietnamese no longer are using Thanh Khanh Hoa as their base for the control of the flow of men and matériel and are consolidating their control farther to the south at Vinh. Vinh is the present terminus of the heavy-duty rail line. It is the beginning of a major inland water route south, and sits astride major land lines of communications moving south and west. Its port is open to oceangoing vessels. With the cessation of the bombing, the North Vietnamese have rebuilt the rail line, thereby facilitating movement from Thanh Hoa south at least as far as Vinh. They can bypass many of the once heavily used personnel way stations and supply storage areas. This realignment reflects a further streamlining of the General Directorate of Rear Services system within North Vietnam and provides a faster, more efficient processing of men and matériel."

■ ■ ■

ABRAMS (re allocating medical treatment to wounded Americans and PWs): "There's nothing better for saving American lives than the best goddamn intelligence. [Someone: "It's long-range view versus short-range view."] Well, no, it's <u>balanced</u> view versus <u>parochial</u> view. Most nonmilitary people think that <u>really</u> the thing to do is get in these bases and hunker down and <u>that's</u> the way to save American—." "Another thing they say, 'What are you doing out <u>there</u>?' Well, who wants to take on the political implications of turning over Vinh Long to the enemy? Or fighting them in Saigon, while they use Vinh Long and Phuoc Long for R&R? It's the same thing with the A Shau. 'Why are you out in the A Shau?' Well, it's better than fighting in Hue. And that's where the fight for Hue has to come from."

■ ■ ■

More on Ambassador Averell Harriman and "The Understandings."

SOMEONE: "Have any of the press come to you to follow up on any of Harriman's utterances that, you know, we really didn't respond to that seven-week lull? If we had, it would have led to a cease-fire?"

ABRAMS: "No, but this citizens' group that's here, they raised that last night. And it's a v-e-r-y—you have to—<u>I</u> feel, anyway, you have to be rather <u>careful</u> about it. First of all, there are several in that group that <u>admire</u> Mr. Harriman tremendously. You know, 'He's devoted a lifetime to this kind of thing—service and that sort of thing.' So I <u>joined</u> them in that. And they went and <u>saw</u> him before they came out here, spent five or six hours with him, at least some of them did. And one that I was talking to, a skilled mathematician—that fellow, I want to tell you, that man is <u>sharp</u>. And the kind of fellow you've got to recognize right away and don't go sailing into <u>him</u>, because if he <u>wants</u> to he'll just wrap you around and tie you up and ship you out as refuse. [Laughter] That guy's got a—with figures, his mind just goes like a goddamn computer. You can almost hear it whirring. And we just haven't <u>got</u> anybody around here that can deal with that. Well, <u>I</u> haven't <u>seen</u> him. <u>Well</u>, and <u>so</u> I told him that the thing that really puzzled me was that, first of all I had the same identical high view of Ambassador Harriman, Governor Harriman, and his service, and I respected him just as much as all the other Americans respected him. And I said that's why it made it so difficult for me to understand why he said these movements out of South Vietnam occurred after the bombing halt. I said maybe it's because of his age, his memory. I said how I <u>know</u> he at one time <u>knew</u> better than that, because <u>I</u> was the one that was <u>reporting</u> it to him. And this all occurred—. And I said, it's just a—it's given me quite a <u>problem</u>, sort of a <u>personal</u> problem, because of the <u>regard</u> that I hold for him, and then <u>this</u> thing. Well, as we walked back in [laughing] after getting through with <u>that</u> explanation, this guy was walking along with me, and he said, 'Well, I'll tell you,' he said, 'I love him, but,' he said, 'he has—this came, the whole thing came as a tremendous personal disappointment, that he hadn't wound up that negotiation. It would have been his last service and so on. So,' he said, 'that has eaten on him. It has had a tendency to disturb the objective view that he usually—that used to be the <u>hallmark</u> of his service.' Well, I was kind of happy to hear it from this man, who is obviously a staunch—. But he sees it, apparently, himself. He just got a little too personally involved in it."

21 AUG 1969: Secretary of the Army Resor Briefing

ATTENDEES: Gen. Abrams, Mr. Resor, Gen. Haines, Mr. [Siena?], MG Townsend, MG Conroy, Mr. Jacobson, BG Bautz, BG Yates, BG Potts, BG Long, BG Galloway, Col. Hill, Col. Hanifen, LTC Harris, LTC Schweitzer, Col. [Faza-coli?].

Stanley R. Resor served as secretary of the army 1965–1971.

BRIEFER: Enemy strength: July 1968: 288,000. August 1969: 232,500. "The war continues to be fought primarily by NVA troops."

ABRAMS: "He started out—the beginning of this year, Saigon was his target. It was in his documents, it was in his prisoners. Every week we picked up recon people out of the 9th Division out there in Hau Nghia or Gia Dinh, reconnoitering routes for the 9th Division into Saigon and to Tan Son Nhut. Later on—that never got off, and then later on it was Tay Ninh, Long Binh/Bien Hoa, and that didn't work out. Then one time, the one high point, they went after the 'Holy See' up there in Tay Ninh City. That didn't work out. They never got near it. Now they're up there in Loc Ninh, An Loc, Quan Loi, Bo Duc, and Song Be. In other words, I really think that . . . as time has moved along this year, he's had to continuously re-cut the cloth to fit what he's capable of doing, or what he thinks he's capable of doing. This thing he's going after now is really small potatoes compared to the sort of thing he had his eye on. Now, of course, I say it's small potatoes, but politically you can't stand that, either. We certainly can't give him Loc Ninh—although there's more people in this compound than there are in Loc Ninh."

ABRAMS: "Let's be frank about it—the 5th Division could not go backwards. It was as far back as it could go except for just disbanding."

ABRAMS: "I think the real problem here is personnel and training. It's not equipment."

23 AUG 1969: Commanders WIEU

ATTENDEES: Gen. Abrams, Gen. Rosson, Gen. Brown, LTG Mildren, LTG Nickerson, VADM Zumwalt, LTG Corcoran, LTG Ewell, LTG Zais, MG Wetherill, MG Conroy, Mr. Megellas, Mr. Firfer, MG Townsend, Mr. Jacobson, Mr. Vann, MG Shaefer, Mr. Whitehouse, BG Bautz, BG Long, BG Kraft, BG McLaughlin, BG Vande Hey, BG Potts, BG Jaskilka, BG Cheadle, BG Sykes, Capt. McNulty, Col. Hanifen, Col. Hill, Col. Gibson, Col. Church, Col. Doody.

BRIEFER: Shows a chart depicting rural security.

ABRAMS: "W-e-l-l, look at that—that's 93 [percent] rural security. We shouldn't have all those people getting wounded and getting killed and abducted and so on if that damn thing _means_ anything. Something's—some one of these charts is wrong." [Terrorism chart had been shown before this one.] "A lot of this is psychological, and that's all those characters have got left to work with. And they just keep doing that, week after week, and they'll change all those damn people _around_!" "That's the kind of _war_ it is."

ABRAMS: "In Saigon the only thing that's really effective is the police. Everybody else is too ham-handed. You get a couple of VCI, but the goddamn _house_ is gone."

ABRAMS (re the district chiefs who are the safest): "They're so incompetent that assassination would be counterproductive." [Laughter]

ABRAMS (re CMD): "This whole area around Saigon really ought to be handled by the police, and the RF and the PF, and the PSDF." "It's _not_ a good place for these troops—those [ARVN] rangers and so on, and the airborne." "It's _not_ a good place for troops—too many temptations, too many opportunities for screwing up, of getting in a lot of bad things."

ABRAMS: "The RF and PF, a year ago, received the highest priority of anybody. That's where the first M16s went, _before_ ARVN. I mean, we fixed them up with the weapons." "They've been given, for over a year, the very _highest_ priority. And, to be perfectly frank, it's like anything else. I mean, you put your money in soldiers' deposits, you get 10 percent [interest] and so on. Goddamn it, we made an investment _here_, and there ought to—. That's _priority_, above anybody else in the _country_, over a _year_ ago!"

28 AUG 1969: SEACOORDS Briefing

BUNKER: SEACOORDS was initiated about five years ago.

The acronym stands for "Southeast Asia Coordinating Committee for U.S. Missions," which brings together the U.S. ambassadors to countries in the region for periodic consultation and discussions.

POTTS (re Cambodia): "Our reports, and the fine support we receive from Mr. Shackley here, indicated that the ships come into Sihanoukville, and there the supplies are unloaded onto Cambodian armed force vehicles and onto vehicles of private firms. They take them into the Lovek area, and then some of those supplies are processed out to these—one or more of these—13 base areas, running from 609 there to 704 in the south." Fourteen such ships since October 1966.

BUNKER: "Interesting that in Senator Mansfield's report of his talk with Sihanouk two days ago, Sihanouk commented that there are no supplies coming into Sihanoukville going to the other side. He admitted they were getting them, but said he didn't know how they were coming in." [Laughter]

POTTS: "The majority of supplies for II Corps, and we feel _all_ of them for III and IV Corps, are coming through Cambodia."

■ ■ ■

ABRAMS: "In the whole picture of the war, the _battles_ don't really mean much."

BRIEFER: "With respect to combat operations, the ultimate objective in the Republic of South Vietnam [*sic*] is to provide security for the population so that pacification can progress."

BRIEFER: "Strategically we're conducting a mobile defense within the political boundaries of South Vietnam, supported by an interdiction campaign where we're permitted to do so. Tactically, we conduct extensive reconnaissance to detect enemy units and react to prevent them from approaching and operating in the populated areas. We attempt to preempt the enemy by promptly engaging his forces and seizing, or destroying, his supply caches. And in so doing we make extensive use of our flexible, concentrated firepower, particularly our tactical air and our B-52s."

BERGER: "Fears exist . . . that the program of reductions [meaning U.S. troop withdrawals] or redeployments might be proceeding on a mechanical basis, that a timetable is established, and that in fact it is perhaps a cloak for outright withdrawal." "If they [the enemy] feel that we're going to pull out anyway, obviously they don't have to make any concessions in Paris."

BRIEFER: Most Hoi Chanhs "are southerners who have something to come to."

6 SEP 1969: WIEU

ATTENDEES: Gen. Abrams, Gen. Rosson, Gen. Brown, LTG Mildren, VADM Zumwalt, MG Shaefer, MG Bautz, BG Long, BG Vande Hey, BG Potts, BG Jaskilka, BG Cheadle, BG Sykes, Capt. McNulty, Col. Cavanaugh, Col. Hanifen, Col. Hill, Col. Cutrona, Col. Church, Col. Doody, Col. Black.

SOMEONE (re Prime Minister Khiem): "He's stood for the village philosophy all along. In fact, he's been the prime innovator, according to his reputation."

■ ■ ■

ABRAMS (re an inconclusive report on Cambodia just briefed): "Well, I would say that that report is noteworthy for the lack of light that it has shed on the whole situation. And also, it starts out bad, reporting a conversation between Sihanouk and an Indian journalist! Christ, that's about like a wounded battalion motor sergeant."

BRIEFER (reporting speculation on the impact of Ho Chi Minh's death on the lineup of senior leadership in Hanoi): "The Politburo is split in three ways. There is an ideological split between those who are pro-Peking and those pro-Moscow. Another dispute between moderates and militants in policy matters has had greater relevance to governmental affairs. A third cleavage centers on conflicting military strategies to be followed in the south."

BRIEFER (re the three factions in Hanoi): "The first, and dominant, group included Ho, Le Duan, and General Giap, and advocates a firm pursuit of the war, with only minor interest in domestic problems. The second faction, led by Truong Chinh, favors the Peking notion of protracted war with small-scale units and without conventional attacks. The third group, led by Foreign Minister Nguyen Duy Trinh, weakened as a result of the arrest of 200 cadre, favors victory at the negotiating table, using only limited guerrilla forces." The first group is likely to control, with little change in approach in the near future.

■ ■ ■

ABRAMS: "The one I liked the best was that reporter's report on—he was standing out where some GIs were, trying to get their reaction [regarding enemy leadership]. He found it difficult to get them on the subject. Finally there was a lull in the World Series talk, and one of them said, 'Oh, some other bastard will take charge.'" [Laughter] "I think that's good enough for me as an assessment. It cuts through all that party squabbling." "I choose to believe that that's one of the most accurate reports—it sounds so typical of a bunch of soldiers standing around . . . and batting the breeze about this momentous event."

■ ■ ■

ABRAMS: "Now, there's two things, I think, that we should put together—at least so far—going back to the Chairman. One of them is this business about the return of the 559th [Transportation Group], and the other one is this pipeline development west of the DMZ. They're always looking for 'signals' back there in Washington, but they have a tendency to put on blinders and they're selective about the signals. I think this is a pretty good signal, too. What we're probably seeing is the initial preparations for Tet 1970."

■ ■ ■

ABRAMS: "I went down to dinner at Ambassador Berger's the other night. Mr. Alsop was there. Mr. Alsop has been out visiting some of his favorite haunts in Hau Nghia and Gia Dinh down at the district level. He told me that what they're telling him out there is guerrillas have been reduced by 75 percent, or 80 percent, this sort of thing. There just aren't—local forces and the guerrillas." "Well, I don't know. Of course, I told him, when the evening was drawing to a close, I said, 'Well, maybe that's so, but Hau Nghia and Long An still show up on the reports that I have as 2 of the 10 worst provinces in all South Vietnam. Why these fellows don't report to me what they've reported to you I have no way of explaining.'" "Well, of course he has quite a credibility gap himself."

8 SEP 1969: COMUS Update

BRIEFER: "In North Vietnam, more than 3,100 trucks were unloaded [delivered] in Haiphong during the period January through July." Slightly higher than for the same period in 1968. Hanoi has requested from the USSR 38 tons of POL for September and 40 tons for October. "The enemy's large stated requirements suggest that he intends to continue his logistic activity in support of combat operations."

BRIEFER: "In the directive for his 1969 Summer Campaign, the enemy ordered his forces to inflict losses on American troops, hoping to force the U.S. to grant concessions at Paris." That constituted about half his total effort. In instructions for the Autumn Campaign, the enemy directed efforts also be exerted against the pacification campaign. In instructions now being issued for the 1969–1970 Winter–Spring Campaign, "the enemy has told his cadre that they must 'defeat the de-Americanization' of the war by inflicting casualties on U.S. forces and step up attacks to 'control the population and increase liberated areas.'"

BRIEFER: We are carrying enemy strength now at 230,000.

ABRAMS: "What was it in January '68?"

POTTS: "January '68 was about 270,000."

ABRAMS: "Well, how the hell do you get 270,000 in a structure of 250 battalions and 230,000 in a structure of 344 battalions—a <u>hundred</u> more battalions?"

SOMEONE: "Many of these <u>are</u> understrength. Some of them do retain their command and control elements and, were they to be filled out, they would represent significant increases in strength. At the present time they do not because of the understrength status."

ABRAMS: "Yeah, but still—<u>Jesus</u>. Of the 270,000, what was the combat strength?"

SOMEONE (they look it up): "170,000?"

POTTS: "Total maneuver and combat support strength was 156,000."

ABRAMS: "What is it now?"

POTTS: "At the present time it's about 123,000."

ABRAMS: "This really <u>boggles</u> credibility." Invites Rosson to comment: "Do you find any problem with this?"

ROSSON: "Not when I heard it this <u>morning</u>, but I begin to now. Well, I'm just trying to think what the devil this could be. It's 94 additional battalions—."

ABRAMS: "Just in rough order of magnitude it means that the average strength per battalion was somewhere around 600 in January '68, and now it's somewhere around 300."

ABRAMS: "The other thing—January of '68, god, they got into Hue, they had Khe Sanh surrounded with two divisions, fighting in the DMZ, they had quite a few troops in II Corps, the 9th Division got into the edge of Tan Son Nhut in Saigon, and so on. Now they've got—this month they've got 94 more battalions and, <u>Christ</u>, they're not able to do <u>any</u> of that. My god—<u>we</u> haven't gotten <u>that</u> good!"

ABRAMS: "It's kind of a <u>staggering</u> thing."

ABRAMS: "I don't even think my question is very <u>smart</u>. I'm not <u>saying</u> that. But, you know, it raises these other things, then you commence to wonder what the hell is it that we're—what <u>is</u> the order of battle? Does it have anything to do with the <u>enemy</u>? Jesus, if I'd known we were kicking the shit out of 94 more battalions than we had there in January—Christ. I think I'd have been making a public <u>speech</u> or something, I'd have been so carried away with it. You know—it looks like we're doing a hell of a lot <u>better</u>. Jeez—we were on our—. I tell you, end of January '68 we were on our <u>knockers</u> around here. We were in <u>trouble</u>! We were in trouble everywhere in the damn <u>country</u>! Hell, they were in Ban Me Thuot. They got into Pleiku. They were in Qui Nhon—they knocked off the radio station. They took Hue and <u>held</u> it for 27 days, or 26 days, something like that. Either they were a <u>hell</u> of a lot better or some—. I mean, something's happening here. God, we were <u>bleeding</u> and <u>dying</u> over Khe Sanh and—. General Westmoreland had to stay here in the CP because it wasn't <u>safe</u> for him to try to get <u>home</u>. Remember that? Hell, he <u>lived</u> here for <u>months</u>. Of course, <u>I</u> do now, <u>too</u>, but—."

ABRAMS: "But I mean 94 battalions is nothing to sneeze at!" "Well, anyway, I don't know what it means. It's just kind of puzzling to me." "Christ, that's faster than we've been able to expand the ARVN! It looks like he's winning the race on Vietnamization."

■ ■ ■

BRIEFER: "If you were to improve the ARVN divisions to the utmost, with all of their strength problems, firepower problems, desertion problems, and so forth solved, you would probably get them up to the place where they're about 60 percent of the effectiveness of a U.S. division." "In the first place they're smaller, they have less firepower, they have less combat support and so on."

■ ■ ■

Redeployment Briefing by Col. Donn A. Starry.

STARRY: Cites Phase I on 1 September 1969: 9th Infantry Division and one RLT of the 3rd Marine Division having been redeployed. Phase II in current planning: Remainder of 3rd Marine Division and a separate brigade. "When we get to Phase III we've reached the point where we no longer have parity with the enemy as far as total maneuver battalions are concerned. The situation deteriorates after that. This points out, of course, that we produced this plan on the assumption that the enemy strength remains the same."

STARRY: Cites "the average daily sortie rate [for tac air support]. . . . We have now lost 104 of those sorties by fiscal '70 budget reductions, without ever Vietnamizing the war." "This budget reduction took out more sorties from our current capability than we were planning to lose in the first five phases of Vietnamization."

STARRY: "The critical phase is Phase III. We no longer have parity with the enemy in maneuver battalions, and we begin to see a degradation in helicopters, artillery tubes, and—again, after Phase IV—in tactical air sorties."

STARRY: "When we started planning this, the crossover point was in Phase IV. As Phase II got bigger—first of all, with the necessity for making up the spaces between 25,000 and, actually, 34,500, and then we go to 38,500, and we had to go with 40.5 [40,500 withdrawn]—we had to drag things up from succeeding phases so that when we got to the 38,500 level we had to pull another brigade into Phase II, which meant we had to pull everything up through here, and it moved the crossover point up into Phase III from Phase IV."

ROSSON: "I think it's important to raise this . . . the shifting base of criteria on which this planning is accomplished. Until very recently, you know, the guidelines that governed this called for developing a force that would be capable of handling the VC threat. Now this, of course, shows the threat constant on the basis of VC and NVA maneuver battalions. Now more recently, of course, the guidance has come out that that is, in fact, the threat. But we really proceeded with Vietnamization planning on this basis, even though we were talking about coping only with the [Abrams: "Yeah."] VC threat. There's some inconsistency here."

ROSSON (re the enemy): "He's said that he's going to gear up for 1970—the hardest, bloodiest year so far."

STARRY: "If you look at it from the systems analysis side of the house, and assume that we had to give up 40,500 spaces to get to the end of Phase II, there are 224,000 spaces left between here and Phase VI." To the "residual level." "That's 112,000 in the first six months of next year, and 112,000 in the last six months of next year, and that's the . . . timetable. If we hold out for 100,000 next year, all year, and 100,000 in 1971 all year, that brings you to the [39,000?] number."

ROSSON: Keeps pushing for taking a position based on the original criteria. Nobody opposes him, but nobody supports him, either. [They know it's not going to happen that way.] Except someone, maybe Townsend: "There's no sound substitute for this 'cut and try.'"

ABRAMS: "I'd say, after last night, just about anything is feasible as viewed from Washington. Actually, as viewed by systems analysis, it requires no analysis. Actually, I would say that last night's activities were destitute of analysis. Not a scrap of evidence got mixed up in the problem. [Laughing] They didn't even have systems analysis there! Obviously it was an intuitive analysis—the shakiest of them all."

ABRAMS (re the crossover chart): "Of course, this gets to be rather an interesting chart. One of the initial impressions you get from that chart is that somewhere in here you've got to prepare for defeat, or accept that you can't go any further [with redeployments]. So then we'll come up—what are we going to do? Of course, the obvious answer that we'd have is probably not going to, you know, sound too good. Then there'll be a lot of exploration of what else we can do. Then out will come the flags and so on. You'll have to be prepared to handle that."

ABRAMS (re the structure chart they had up before): "One of the things about it in terms of 'chartography,' or 'the manual of the chart,' or whatever you want to call it—it has a tendency to, those additional 94 battalions have a tendency to push that crossover toward the left [meaning earlier]. That's one of the variables in here, and shows that we should have started this Vietnamization last year. Then we would have been able to do it faster. If we'd started a year and a half ago, at the time of Tet, the crossover point would have been much further to the right. Well, this is leading me astray."

ROSSON: "Well, of course we have gone on record as saying that this is not the way to do it."

ABRAMS: "Yes, and [laughing] that's been disapproved."

ROSSON: "We have just recently looked at how do you overcome this by enhancing the progress in modernization and improvement. Well, we went back and said that really we can't do very much, and that if you have this kind of a threat then the only way you can compensate for that is to have more U.S. forces on the scene." "We've gone about as far as we think we can go, and as fast as we can go, on this M&I [sic]."

TOWNSEND: "You're coming down to too thin an edge in a combat situation."

ROSSON: "If a decision has been made, regardless of all these considerations, that we are going down, then [long pause] this leaves you out in very, very—."

ABRAMS: "If that's the case, then how's the best way to do it?"

STARRY: "The best way to do it is what we wanted to do in the first place—thin out, a brigade at a time here and there and test the thing for gas before you take the thing out, see if the Vietnamese can take it over. But you're forced off of that by this business of putting a ceiling on the redeployment package. It forces you out of that. You can't make what would appear to us, at any rate, to make a tactically sound redeployment in the face of these ceilings that they put on the redeployment."

STARRY: "What they've done is—we come down every time and don't take the squadrons out, so they say, 'Well, we'll fix 'em, we'll just cut the sortie rate.'"

STARRY: "We plotted this here on the basis of providing each U.S. maneuver battalion with the same number of sorties a day it's getting now. We increased the sorties available to RVNAF—or to ARVN—by 50 percent. This will reduce that by a factor of about 25 percent."

ABRAMS: "All right, now, I think we've spent enough time on this."

ABRAMS: "Well, so that we know where we stand, I know of no one back there who's going to say a good word except the Chairman—no one."

ABRAMS (re disparity between enemy strength and structure): "It's a development that's really very difficult to sort of associate with what you know about the general condition of things throughout the country."

9 SEP 1969: COMUS Update

POTTS: Tells Abrams they will brief on COSVN fixed locations, a special briefing he has asked for, and "then after that, sir, working last night, we've taken these 94 battalions that we had in question and got that all tied down and we'll show you how it comes out."

BRIEFER: "The enemy has, at the present time, approximately 230,000 troops in or adjacent to South Vietnam. Approximately 106,000 are North Vietnamese. In spite of a decline from approximately 250,500 at the beginning of 1969, he is making determined efforts to maintain this strength in South Vietnam and improve his military capability."

POTTS: The estimate through September of infiltration is 96,400, "but for the whole year 110,000 is what we're carrying."

ABRAMS: "Incidentally, talking with General Vien the other day, I was advancing the view that possibly the 2nd ARVN Division had shown some advance in effectiveness this year over last. And he said, 'Well,' he said, 'General Toan, he doesn't supervise things the way General Truong does.' He said, 'General Truong puts out his instructions, then he goes everywhere and sees what is carried out—everywhere.' He said, 'General Toan doesn't do that.' Well, I went on to another subject. This is a very keen and, I think, a very correct observation. He admits—he agrees—that there has been improvement in the performance of the 2nd ARVN, but he's issuing a warning that one should not get it in the same league with the 1st ARVN."

20 SEP 1969: WIEU

ATTENDEES: Gen. Abrams, Gen. Rosson, Gen. Brown, Amb. Colby, LTG Mildren, VADM Zumwalt, Mr. Kirk, MG Conroy, MG Townsend, Mr. Jacobson, MG Shaefer, MG Bautz, BG Gunn, BG Long, BG Kraft, BG Potts, BG Jaskilka, BG Sykes, Col. Cavanaugh, Col. Hanifen, Col. Penuel, Col. Cutrona, Col. Church.

BROWN (re the war in Laos): "He's had more air support than any infantry commander in the history of <u>warfare</u>." "He's had about 200 sorties a day there at peak in late July and early August. It's dropped off a little now because of the weather. We still <u>plan</u> about 180, 190. We don't get them all <u>in</u> there. <u>Plus</u> the Lao efforts. And he's never had more than six battalions."

ABRAMS (re Laos): "<u>I</u> don't know what the situation is over there, but Christ— putting <u>armored cars</u> in! I mean—mechanics and spare parts and tires and points and spark plugs and somebody that knows when you're supposed to put them in and you're not, all of that kind of—. Goddamn it, <u>armored cars</u>—yeah, it's a great thing, but how about all that—? I mean, you can't, you just can't <u>run</u> armored cars unless you've got all that other sh—stuff—in there, and the same with the M-41 tanks."

BROWN: "Their strength, the thing that's kept the place alive over the years, has been the marriage between the guerrilla and the airplane. <u>That's</u> what they need—lots and lots of that."

ABRAMS: "That's right."

■ ■ ■

ABRAMS: "Incidentally, I just—I noticed a book review yesterday where this famous Englishman who masterminded the Malaysian victory—[Someone: "Bob Thompson."] Thompson, Sir Robert Thompson, has published a book on Vietnam. And, as I understand it from this book review, <u>no one</u> comes out unscathed. <u>Everyone</u> is—. Apparently he lights on the <u>helicopter</u>, also, as one of the mistakes we made—one of the most grievous."

JACOBSON: "Sir Robert has never really accepted the fact that this was an aggression rather than an insurgency. He still considers it to be totally—almost totally—a police problem rather than a war. And he never has figured out the difference. It's a book worth reading, though, as all his stuff is. He's a bright guy."

ABRAMS: "I—in fact, I <u>agree</u> with that. I agree with it as far as it goes. Now when you—when they get down here with the 9th, the 5th and 7th and the 1st Divisions, <u>goddamn</u> it, there isn't any way to handle that with administration and police! I mean, I don't care <u>what</u> kind of a damn genius you are, you can't get out here and give them tickets or arrest them or what the hell ever you do with police. I mean, these are just mean bastards with a lot of firepower and a lot of strength. . . ." "One of the things, apparently, in this book too is we <u>never</u> should have made any investment in ARVN. We should have put it into police, the administrative structure, that sort of thing."

■ ■ ■

JACOBSON: "Well, Joe Alsop, you can expect him to ask you a question about how you can afford to thin out the forces in I Corps, and then you'll get an hour's answer." "That will be his prime theme."

ABRAMS: "Yeah, I know, I know. I think that's the only reason he's coming to lunch is to try to convince me that that should be changed."

JACOBSON: "He's got two objectives. That is the first one. And the second one is to get on a first-name basis with you, which bothers him very much that he is not. He said, 'I still call him General Abrams. Goddamn, I'm older than he is and everything else, but I still feel constrained—I can't call him Abe.' He gave me about a half hour on that." [Laughter]

ABRAMS: "And I call him—never fail—Mr. Alsop." [Laughter] "It takes two to tango."

ABRAMS: "However, he does—as everybody knows—he's been for the commitment over here, and he's taken a hell of a beating, a source of journalistic pummeling."

JACOBSON: "Well, what he reported in 1967 is actually true today, so maybe he's a prophet with no honor at all. I mean, generally speaking. He was reporting the situation as good in '67 as it is right now, so god knows what he's going to say now."

SOMEONE: "It seems to me he's certainly earned being called 'Joe' by our general."

ABRAMS: "W-e-l-l, it's an individual's choice." [Laughter]

■ ■ ■

ABRAMS: "It's the people, in the end—that's the critical thing of the whole business."

ABRAMS: "When we've forces in there working on pacification, the 173rd as a case in point, he's going after the guerrillas, the local forces, and so on, because that's the enemy apparatus for controlling the people, on the one hand, and it's the way he gets taxes collected and food and so on, and it's the way he can bring regular units in if and when he decides to do it. They're the guides and all that stuff, and his source of intelligence. So . . . when we've got forces working hot on pacification, then they try to work on all of these pieces that he has that represent his control and his influence over the people."

BRIEFER: "A 7 July [captured] document from Binh Long Province concerns the development of better unity between NVA and VC troops. Apparently directed at VC troops and cadre, it opens with quotations from Ho Chi Minh and states that 'the youth from the north have left comparative comfort to come here to help us liberate our homeland, and they should be welcomed as comrades and be treated as guests who are strange to the ways of the south.'"

ABRAMS: "This [bringing in NVA] must have been a very difficult decision for COSVN to make. So there must have been some extraordinary circumstances. They know this, of course, better than we do."

JACOBSON: "It could have been rammed down their throats."

ABRAMS: "Oh, boy, that would make it even better."

BRIEFER: "A 10 September Hoi Chanh, the former commander of the 303rd Battalion, Z-1 Regiment, stated during initial interrogation that the NVA forces are coming into the delta because the VC are too weak and are tired of war."

ABRAMS: "Now, we're going to have a Commanders WIEU on the 27th, a week from today. I hope by that time, Bill [Potts], we can have struggled with an intelligence estimate that goes far past order of battle and so on and tries to take some perspective of what he's been doing over the last many months, and what it now appears that he _is_ doing." "I have an uneasy feeling at the moment that things—he may be planning a way of doing things which we haven't quite got a good hard _hold_ on. We want to make _sure_ that what we're doing is really what we _ought_ to be doing."

ABRAMS (re friction between northern and southern Vietnamese): "Christ, you can't get them together at a free beer party, really."

21 SEP 1969: I & II CTZ Updates

NICKERSON: "On the VCI, I think our targets are much too low. I've told General Lam and all of his people that we're going to have to target more of these, not just 2 percent or 3 percent or 4 percent of the total, or we're going to be here a thousand years, to get them off." "We accept your point of view, too, that it's better to capture them than it is to kill them."

23 SEP 1969: III & IV Corps Intelligence Update

EWELL: "Starting next month we're going to divide up the local force companies and start at the top of what we consider the most dangerous local force companies and try to break them down to about 50 percent of TO&E over a period of about three months. . . . And in my opinion, which I don't have anything to base on, an intuitive feel, once we really get going on this—and it's the most difficult job there is—I think it will tend to expose more VCI than any other single thing, because you sort of take the protective mantle off the VCI." "I'm not sure we can _do_ it, but at _least_ it's worth a try." "I have a hunch if you clobber the local force unit the local guerrilla will Chieu Hoi."

BRIEFER: In III Corps, the enemy is 82 percent NVA. In I Corps: 92 percent.

EWELL: We are trying to "drop the level of tactical operations down to company level, both U.S. and ARVN." We are seeking "a reconnaissance-oriented tactical operation as opposed to an attack-type operation." We're looking for "a highly flexible type operation. I'd say we're about halfway home on this. They're making progress. Of course, I'm perfectly willing to admit pacification's my primary mission."

EWELL: A good sign is that the Vietnamese now are "insisting on the validity of their point of view militarily."

27 SEP 1969: Commanders WIEU

ATTENDEES: Gen. Abrams, Amb. Berger, Gen. Rosson, Gen. Brown, Amb. Colby, LTG Mildren, LTG Nickerson, VADM Zumwalt, LTG Corcoran, LTG Ewell, MG Richardson, LTG Zais, MG Wetherill, MG Conroy, Mr. Megellas, Mr.

Firfer, MG Townsend, Mr. Jacobson, Mr. Vann, MG Shaefer, Mr. Whitehouse, MG Bautz, MG Russ, BG Gunn, BG Long, BG Smith, BG Potts, BG Jaskilka, BG Sykes, Col. Cavanaugh, Col. Hanifen, Col. Penuel, Col. Doody, Col. Stoker, Col. Healy, Mr. Kirk.

BRIEFER: MACV 1969 Infiltration Estimate: 96,700 (47,700 destined for COSVN). Also, not included in these totals, 11,200 in five groups referred to in an 8 July message.

ABRAMS (re an infiltration group that, per intercepts, took 25 percent loss en route due to illness and desertions): "Among the military, that would be considered a poor performance."

■ ■ ■

Consequences of the Bombing Halt.

COLONEL JOHNSON (Seventh Air Force briefer): "The North Vietnamese have engaged in extensive reconstruction since the bombing halt last November." They have rehabilitated and improved lines of communication in the Route Package 1 area. The enemy has established "an extensive system of transshipment points and storage areas." Vinh is "the logistics hub in the panhandle." The entry corridor goes south from Quang Khe, restored from its previous bombed-out condition. Ferry slip. Rail-mounted trucks are "often substituted for locomotives due to the weakened condition of the rail bridges." "The rail system in North Vietnam was one of the first items of restoration following the bombing halt." Now there is under way new construction to extend the rail net to the south.

JOHNSON: "The entries into Laos most used in the past have been the Keo Nua, Mu Gia, and Ban Karai Passes." "A fourth entry corridor has been under extensive development, for a year now, the 1036/1039 complex that skirts the DMZ and affords the enemy a longer route of safe passage before being exposed to our strikes in Laos."

JOHNSON: Antiaircraft defenses have been increased. Fuel caches have been established along the major routes. And we have recently discovered a POL pipeline west of the DMZ in Laos.

JOHNSON: We estimate that North Vietnam has emplaced four million gallons of POL storage in 5,000-gallon tankers, 55-gallon drums, etc. Offshore discharge from tanker ships to Quang Khe. In Quang Binh Province alone, 736 5,000-gallon tanks and 16,915 55-gallon drums provide 4,610,325 gallons of POL storage capacity.

■ ■ ■

BRIEFER: The 559th Transportation Group is experiencing a severe outbreak of cholera, described as an epidemic.

ABRAMS (re government forces in Laos): "They're going to run into a hornet's nest if they try to get into Tchepone. Christ, that's a—."

BRIEFER: The GVN draft, the Accelerated Pacification Campaign, and growing Viet Cong hardships contribute to [enemy] problems. By the end of August the enemy had lost over 126,000 killed this year. That far exceeds the entire combat losses for any other previous year except 1968. Also, by the end of September about 33,000 enemy will have become Hoi Chanhs, which already exceeds the total for any single previous year. Enemy strength has thus been reduced from 267,000 on 1 January 1969 to 230,000 on 31 August 1969.

BRIEFER: The enemy also is experiencing logistics problems due to allied air interdiction and abnormally heavy monsoon rains, and to the capture of caches in South Vietnam. During 1 January 1969–1 September 1969 a total of 1,989 caches were captured. These included 10,408 weapons, 1,483 tons of ammunition, 3,841 tons of rice, and 314 tons of salt.

BRIEFER: A POL pipeline running from north of Vinh through the Mu Gia Pass can pump an estimated 1,130 metric tons of fuel per day, the equivalent capacity of over 400 trucks. Another pipeline is situated in Laos about 12 kilometers west of the DMZ.

BRIEFER: A total of 3,782 tons of explosives was shipped by rail from the Soviet Union to North Vietnam via the PRC during January–June 1969, compared to about 1,200 tons in 1968. Other enemy actions include creation of new sapper units, conversion of some infantry to sappers, and increased sapper training. The enemy has the capability of reinforcing with up to three divisions in two days. His overall military structure is still intact, including sanctuaries and effective command and control. His most likely course of action will be to continue a level of combat activity consistent with his reduced capabilities for the remainder of 1969 and early 1970, relying primarily on attacks by fire and small-unit ground attacks, along with increased guerrilla, sapper, terrorist, political, and propaganda activities.

ABRAMS: "The intelligence that we have today, I think it is fair to say, is far more—far deeper, and far more comprehensive, than we had in this period in '67."

ABRAMS: 40,000 is our estimate of enemy forces involved in running the infiltration network in Laos. They are separate from the combat units in northern Laos.

■ ■ ■

COSVN Resolution 9 Briefing.

BRIEFER: Reviews COSVN Resolution 9. Also a comparison with Resolution 8 of a year ago. This is from "a recently captured lesson plan." The document states that "the U.S. is anxious to settle the Vietnam War, but is unwilling to accept a coalition government for fear of eventual VC control. The U.S. is prolonging its withdrawal to give RVNAF adequate time to become self-sufficient."

BRIEFER: Objectives of the enemy campaign: 1. Force rapid and complete withdrawal of U.S. forces from South Vietnam. 2. Disrupt RVNAF improvement. 3. Roll back the pacification program. 4. Lay groundwork for exploitation of a negotiated peace settlement.

BRIEFER: Resolution No. 8 was issued about August 1968 for the 1968–1969 Winter–Spring Offensive. It called for an ultimate military victory similar to that contemplated in the 1968 Tet Offensive.

BRIEFER: Resolution No. 9 appears to be a direct continuation of the high-point strategy. Significant changes from No. 8: References to a complete military victory have been dropped. There is a shift of emphasis from urban to rural areas (to expand the political base in preparation for a coalition government). More emphasis is placed on disruption of pacification. There is stress on producing American casualties to increase pressures in the United States for more rapid troop withdrawals. "It formalizes the strategic modifications already forced upon him by RVNAF and allied operations and demonstrates his recognition that he cannot win as long as significant U.S. forces remain in Vietnam."

ABRAMS: "One of the thoughts that has occurred to me is that, in the resolutions preceding 9, he felt that he had the strategic initiative. This is what brought on Tet—the surprise element, the mass element, all these things. And it was he who would set the pace and call the shots. That continued in Resolution 8, and the effort made in the Tet period of '69. Now this seems to me—well, let me explain. While all of that was being executed—Resolution 8, and what preceded it in Tet '68—everybody on both sides were really struggling with this thing and trying to get their hands on it. He trying to get what he wanted and us trying to—. And so we kind of milled around and wrestled and fought here during '68."

ABRAMS: "And then, about this time in '68, or a little earlier—I think it was in September, maybe August—we got talking about this Accelerated Pacification Program. And the GVN grabbed a hold of it and so on. 1 November of '68 you launched the Accelerated Pacification Program. Well, Christ, he's still in the—he's still, in his Resolution 8, is in the belief that he is exercising the strategic initiative, he's calling the shots. The Accelerated Pacification Program went on. We started it—we were deep in the modernization of Territorial Forces. All of this—I don't mean that there was any great—ha—any great deep philosophical thinking and all that. It just kind of—it looked like you ought to do this, and it looked like you ought to do that, and everybody started believing in the RF/PF. The GVN started believing in them, and we put M16s there and this kind of stuff."

ABRAMS: "And then they kind of got a half-assed Phoenix program going and, you know, all of those. There were a lot of things that looked like they were good and ought to be backed. And the PSDF! I mean, there were a bunch of kind of disjointed things, which I think—. . . . And then, as the year went along . . . it all got sort of formalized, and everybody pulled up their britches and . . . that whole thing energized and went at the Accelerated Pacification Program, which to, frankly, everyone's amazement actually moved out a lot better."

ABRAMS: "And probably one of the reasons it did—he was playing hardball and we all were playing volleyball, and it wasn't any goddamn match. We were after something that he—I mean, he had another idea in mind, and we had another idea in mind." "What I read in this [new directive] is that every one of those things—disruption of pacification—that's defensive. He's reacting to an initiative which has now, in his own estimate, begun to create a problem for him. Vietnamization . . . when he wrote Resolution 8, he just wasn't worried about this."

ABRAMS: "So it seems to me that—I don't necessarily like the term 'forced.' He is a resourceful fellow, and he is an intelligent fellow. And just as he changed from what he'd been doing before to another level when—'67 to '68, or from '64 to '65—he's doing the same thing again. But maybe, maybe for the first time his response, his guidance here, is—in terms of where the initiatives are—he's responding to the initiatives that have been exercised over almost the last year by our side, which no small part of is the GVN itself."

EWELL: "I do think he has several areas for initiative which are quite favorable to him. I think any form of negotiation will tend to improve his position. The only way a negotiation would go would be detrimental to the U.S. and the South Vietnamese and favorable to the North Vietnamese in terms of making inroads into South Vietnam." "I think he probably thinks he can accelerate the U.S. withdrawal, although I don't know how you can accelerate something that's up against the firewall already."

COLBY: "You have a time line. . . . The North Vietnamese WIEU that developed this particular plan probably took place two or three months ago." "It states as one of the premises of his problem the key relationship of the public opinion war in the United States, which he is fairly confident of winning. He really thinks he can win that."

ABRAMS: "This is his problem." [Whether U.S. public opinion will pull the United States out before Vietnamization and pacification are sufficiently advanced to enable South Vietnam to survive.]

EWELL (contemplating the effect of further U.S. troop withdrawals): "You've got about six to nine months to really make hay, and then you're going to have to start buttoning up all over the place."

NICKERSON: "I don't really sense that he shouldn't attack now, because I sense the country is not going to let us do anything with any forces that we don't already have. So if he were smart, I think he'd come right through the Z [the DMZ]."

ABRAMS: "Frankly, I think the situation is a little different here in South Vietnam than it was at the beginning of '68." "I don't mean that they're all gone. I understand that. And Christ, they'll never be all gone. But there's confidence, there's strength, there's capability in the countryside that just wasn't there."

ABRAMS: "And also, if we've got another—five months, three months, four months, whatever it is, while he prepares himself and so on—and, as Julian [Ewell] has said, if in that time we're pounding away at this, at the VCI, the locals, the guerrillas, getting the goddamn government where it's effective—I mean effective in doing things, the ministries and that kind of stuff at the village and—out there, really get them out there and get that thing going, and get the police, everything we can to strengthen the police, expand them a little bit and really harden up the government's presence, control, and—hopefully—the people's good will towards them, out there, then what kind of a problem has he got?"

ABRAMS: "Also, every passing month the content of his structure down here that's North Vietnamese is going up." "So the demands for manpower from North Vietnam are somewhat different than they used to be."

ABRAMS: "I think one of these days . . . even if all of the U.S. has gone, it's going to be a problem for him whether he really has got the moxie to take it over."

ABRAMS: "If somebody doesn't really screw it up somewhere, they're going to have a thing here which is quite different." Cites Vung Tau training of local officials as an example of what is being done.

ABRAMS: "For instance, down there the 273rd—a vaunted regiment, 80 percent NVA, out of the great, the famous 9th Division—unfortunately stumbled into some RFs down there, was part of it, and got the shit kicked out of them. Well, this is not a great thing, it's not going to change the war, but it's something."

NICKERSON: "I just don't think we should delude ourselves with the president and the country backing us if he does come, because I get the distinct feeling nothing's going to escalate this war—not even complete military disaster." "I just get the feeling that they're tired of it and they wouldn't back us."

SOMEONE (maybe Berger): "I agree with Nick. Everything I read—."

SOMEONE ELSE: "I sure don't argue with that."

ABRAMS: "Well, first place, I believe that what we've got here in South Vietnam, and what we'll have here in South Vietnam when we get through with this current withdrawal, is enough to handle any fucking thing he designs! There's no doubt in my mind about it. So where are we there?"

NICKERSON: "No, I'm with you on that."

JACOBSON: "Every single day goes by in the things he's [the enemy] trying to do there, he's got a tougher job to do it than he had the day before. While you can make a good argument that he's been winning a lot in Paris, and all he's got to do is sit back and wait and it'll fall into his lap like a ripe plum, that isn't necessarily true, because he's got troubles in the delta, he's unpopular politically, he hasn't disrupted pacification, he is worried about Vietnamization, and he may just say, 'By god, we can't afford to wait for Paris. We've got to do something right now in order to upset this applecart.'"

ABRAMS: "I don't think it makes any difference how many losses he takes. I don't think that makes any difference."

EWELL: "The press and Senator Kennedy don't have the responsibility—shit, they can say anything, and do."

SOMEONE (re civilians in the delta reporting on the enemy): "Everyone tells you where they are, all the time."

VANN: Four years ago Vu Van Thai, the Vietnamese representative to the UN, "said there would be two major indications of whether or not we were going to be successful in South Vietnam. The first . . . would be whether or not we could achieve a stable government in South Vietnam. The second would be the extent to which the North Vietnamese had to take over the war."

■ ■ ■

BRIEFER: The FY 1970 budget reduction cut down tac air to a point that it had been thought would not be reached until after several more phases. Since then "another budget exercise known as 703." Thus more proposed budget reductions. Ordnance and POL limitations. Someone: "It's going to take an auditor to keep us out of jail." Effective 1 September: Reductions in both tac air and B-52 sorties (B-52s cut to 1,400 a month).

BROWN: "On this sortie thing, this is a _gross_ way to do business, because dollars aren't directly associated." B-52 sorties from Andersen at Guam cost almost twice as much as sorties from U Tapao. "It's a _screwy_ way to do business." Fighter sortie costs are a function of duration, ordnance load, and other variables.

ABRAMS: "After all, George, this was _done_ in the _Pentagon_—"

BROWN: "On the _third_ _floor_ of the Pentagon."

ABRAMS: "—where quality control is rather loose."

BROWN: "Very active, though."

ABRAMS: "And they move down the year, watching expenditures, and it turns out that this goddamn method is not producing the expenditure reductions—o-o-o-h-h, let's not _think_ of _that_!"

■ ■ ■

ABRAMS: "Take the air control—there _isn't_ any air control. There are more damn people flying around over here—the VNAF—we're all using the same system. The VNAF, the Air America people, Americans bringing the nurses back home, unauthorized flying things going on, illegal flying's going on, and it's like when we got up there with the radars, [and] were going to shoot down enemy helicopters in II Corps. Jesus, every intercept we ever _ran_ it turned out to be some American, Air America or so on, cleared with nobody, or mixed up in the intelligence business, and of course [this said with irony] they can't let _anybody_ know what they're doing. And there they are, all flying around up there _at_ _night_! Plus battles going on and people flying in _that_!"

■ ■ ■

ABRAMS: "I don't have all the facts and figures, but I think we're getting some upswing, some modest upswing, in incidents among our own troops, either based on racial problems or some other kind of friction. And I just want—every commander has got to pay attention to this and try to keep on top of it." Cites a _Time_ magazine article on the matter. Then his own view: "The most powerful thing we've got here is the attitude of the Americans who are assigned here, military and civilian. And I tell you if that ever deteriorates substantially, that'll be worse than _any_ goddamn thing that Giap or any of the rest of them can think of. This is _important_. It's _critical_." "I don't believe you do it with _poop_ _sheets_. The commander's got to be sensitive to it. He's got to be intelligent about it. They've got to _talk_ with their men."

■ ■ ■

ABRAMS: "Help the PF and the RF in every way—." "It seems to me that in every imaginative and intelligent and sensitive way that we, and all the people down the line, can find to help _this_ part of the thing along now. I don't think it's really anything that—it doesn't need any _directive_ from _me_, from _MACV_, because when you try to put something together _here_, it loses all of the artistry that's needed. It's got to be done in each area like it's best to do it in _that_ area. I think it's _enough_ if we agree here today that this is kind of the way we should be shoving, pushing, pulling, persuading, and influencing or what over the next three or four months."

ABRAMS: "I read a report somewhere recently that President Thieu was quite impressed with President Nixon, and one of the reasons was that when they were talking President Nixon kept his hands folded, and this is proof of a man who is not arrogant."

4 OCT 1969: Briefing for General Wheeler

Gen. Earle G. Wheeler, Chairman of the Joint Chiefs of Staff, is visiting Vietnam.

ATTENDEES: Gen. Wheeler, Gen. Abrams, Gen. Rosson, Gen. Brown, Amb. Colby, VADM Zumwalt, MG Townsend, BG Potts, BG Kraft, BG Gunn, Col. Pauley, Col. Jones, Col. Hanifen, Mr. Kerney.

BRIEFER: In the past week in North Vietnam we have detected six new infiltration groups totalling about 3,700 personnel. That brings to 10,470 the number on the move toward Laos since 29 August.

■ ■ ■

BRIEFER (re COSVN Resolution 9): "It calls for continued military operations with more modest aims, preparation of his political cadre, establishment of the delta as a priority area, disruption of the pacification program, and defeat of the policy for Vietnamization of the war."

WHEELER: "I must say that's an admirable encapsulation. I think you could summarize by saying this guy's in deep trouble and knows it."

■ ■ ■

ABRAMS (re pacification after Tet): "As we came staggering out of the corner, struggling up from the stool, if you will, to get back into the game, on our side the programs were redesigned—the thrust of them, anyway. And we've sort of doggedly—there's no brilliance involved in any of this, it's just doggedly struggling back against it, trying to make it fit the circumstances—and that's moved along well enough. And he hung around too long before he redesigned his program."

ABRAMS: "You take the strength of the existing government here, with all its— 'strength' of it, with all its weaknesses, and the delicate nature of a lot of it, nevertheless it's marching on." Cites training of village and hamlet leadership.

ABRAMS: "While I don't think he [the enemy] cares too much about casualties, they may have gotten to the point where they've become a problem for him."

■ ■ ■

WHEELER: "The problem that I have—and when I say 'I,' I guess I mean the Joint Chiefs of Staff—is attempting to get the political leadership, past and present, to understand, really comprehend, what this military situation is in Vietnam the way it's developed over the past couple of years, and comprehend—I guess even more important—to comprehend what this really means as regards our own continuing actions, and the actions which are available to us. This failure in communications has plagued us. I think George [Brown] knows this from his happier days back in the Office of the Chairman. Bill [Potts? Colby?] remembers it, I know. You were there briefing the Joint Staff. And then again this was reflected in the fact that for some reason or other, the administration in turn has always—has been for the past several years practically apologizing for our position, or the situation in Vietnam. It's a very, very curious, almost a phenomenal, situation."

WHEELER: "Now I think probably it's too late to correct. The efforts of the American press, the attitude of a considerable segment of the Congress who are always shooting off their mouths about things they know nothing about, just have created a public impression, I gather, that we're hanging on over here by our teeth, barely able to stay in the stadium. . . . Well, I'll be goddamned if I've ever—I haven't been able to figure out any way to solve the problem. It seems almost impossible to get the secretary of state, the secretary of defense, equally or more important the president, to realize that they are dealing from a position of military strength. And I really mean military strength. Not just a marginal position of strength, but a very substantial position of strength. Christ, they act and talk, on many occasions, the Commander in Chief . . . [and] particularly the secretary of state, as though the damned peace talks, or peace negotiations or whatever terminology you want to use, in Paris, [as though] we're the guys that are doing the suing."

■ ■ ■

DISCUSSION: Contents of huge caches seized in the Plaine des Jarres.

ABRAMS: "This is not the stuff you take to a family homecoming. This is real. Shows you what those bastards have in mind." The take included 12 tanks. "That typewriter they captured there is probably going to screw things up more than anything else."

■ ■ ■

BRIEFER: We are contemplating a reduction in our currently authorized strength "on the order of 50,000." "A reduction of this size, which would have to include a division and two brigades, would bring us below parity."

ABRAMS: "I think that we have to say that the reduction in B-52s and tactical air support has been entirely a budgetary motivated thing and has not considered the tactical situation in South Vietnam."

WHEELER: "Oh, yes."

ABRAMS: "In these troop withdrawal exercises, the way these have occurred, we go into a sort of elaborate analysis of the enemy and friendly, and how much the RVNAF has improved and, you know, that sort of a thing. I'm not saying that that's all done with great precision, it's not a precise exercise, but anyway you get involved in all of that. This other, the reduction of the B-52s, and the reduction of tac air, is—that's a nonprofessional exercise. It's a magician's work. This is 'doing it with mirrors' stuff. In other words, there's quite a difference, at least philosophically, the way each of those things has been approached. It's been quite different."

ABRAMS: You calculate "what you think is a manageable troop reduction. Then this other exercise is conducted in Washington, and it's unrelated. It raises a question of how much of each of these programs—the 'mirror' program and the sort of 'tactical analytical' program—how much of each of this that the command will have to bear. For instance, had I, at the time—pondering over taking out the 3rd Marines, 3rd [Brigade] of the 82nd [Airborne Division], that sort of thing—at that _time_ when I had acquiesced and accepted the addition of the 3rd of the 82nd, had I at the same time had on my plate the B-52 and tac air reductions—. _Eventually_, you see—. I'm not trying to make any federal case out of it, but _eventually_, as a responsible commander in the field, I have to begin to worry about getting the job done under a two-program attack, one of which I know very little about and was not consulted on at all, <u>although</u> they are <u>critical</u> and <u>integral</u> parts of the forces that are available to me to do the <u>job</u>."

■ ■ ■

WHEELER: "The $3 billion reduction which was imposed in FY '70 <u>is</u> unrelated to the Vietnamization program in a very real sense. What it stems from is an effort by the Congress, or some portions of the Congress, to do two things. One, to impose an expenditure limitation on the government, which they have already done by legislation—$198 billion. Then, within this limitation, disregarding the president's budget, they have voted add-on programs. For example, they added $1.2 billion to the president's program in the health, education, and welfare area, and there're going to be other add-ons by the Congress in different areas. To get the <u>money</u> to finance the programs, these social programs . . . , many of the younger elements on the Senate and House Armed Services Committees voted for this measure. Now this was the younger, more liberal, types."

WHEELER: "Now, Defense is faced with a very real problem. Here four months of FY '70 have elapsed, and we still don't have a budget. We're operating on what they call a 'continuing resolution' or something like that, which means you can spend not <u>over</u> the same level of money that you expended the year before." "The only problem is you can't start any <u>new</u> programs. You're inhibited. You have no authorization, you have no funding. The longer you delay in taking certain cuts, the more of an effect you impose on yourself for the later parts of the year." "The Chiefs . . . have had to walk a very narrow line, more like a tightrope, between current capabilities and the future. We simply can't afford to cut back on programs such as the Minuteman III, Poseidon MIRV, other highly classified, very esoteric programs, because if you do you're going to hand to the enemy a strategic superiority, not parity, in the future. At the same time, if you don't retain sufficient capability <u>today</u>, you may never survive to <u>benefit</u> from your ongoing programs. It's simply <u>one</u> <u>hell</u> <u>of</u> <u>a</u> <u>problem</u>." "We briefed the Highest Authority [the president] on what the effect was going to be, what it <u>had</u> to be, in order to get the kind of money they're <u>talking</u> about."

WHEELER: "We figured out . . . that the services had been forced to accommodate to a reduction of over $14.5 billion in obligational authority in less than one year, which is one <u>hell</u> of a cut. And the effect of it is going to be felt worldwide, politically as well as militarily. It will be felt in Europe, in NATO. I was at a NATO Military Committee meeting in London, about two weeks ago, I guess, and these guys were as nervous as cats on a hot tin roof. It's going to be felt in the Far East. It's going to be felt <u>here</u>. There's a—very frankly, I'm not wise enough, I wish I were, to forecast exactly what the impact is going to be, except I know it's going to be extremely serious. It's precisely—I mean, people deal in signals, and you know what I think of signals as far as the signaling of Hanoi and the Soviets and so on. If we're dealing in signals, we're giving exactly the wrong kind of signal."

WHEELER: "That's the reason I sent you that message the other day to—don't think I've gone crazy, or any crazier than I've been in the past, for telling you two different things in two different messages. But you've got this bunch of softheads who—things like this Senator Aiken shooting off his mouth; he's one of the least obnoxious ones—a bunch of young Democrats in the House are just as bad as this older group in the Senate. . . ." [Next part inaudible.]

ABRAMS: "We haven't really come to grips with what all the implications of this tac air reduction are, but the thing I wonder about on this—you know, at one time out here there was some rumbling that the troops weren't getting the tac air support that they needed. We went through a time when we didn't have enough jungle boots, or enough M16s, ammunition was rationed, and so on. And those things develop pressures of their own. They start writing letters and so on, and that starts a whole new bunch of things going. Now, I don't mean that this, what's been done thus far, is going to create precisely that, but if it gathers momentum and support, that's what they're going to get into. And then you're going to have a whole new set of problems. You can't have soldiers out here, even in this sort of war, who begin to complain about not getting the kind of support they need when they get into battle. And this is what they approach dickering with in this budget thing. Also, the way this has to be done, they've taken sort of rough-cut measures that are designed to produce certain savings in expenditures. The services have really never been very expert in financial management from an expenditure standpoint. The whole financial management system has really been designed around an obligational—management of obligations. As the year goes along, I would say that it would be accidental if the measures that have been prescribed in fact produce the expenditure savings sought."

WHEELER: "Plans that were being considered by the United States Army would inactivate the 1st and 2nd Armored Divisions and drastically reduce the 5th Mech, even though they are earmarked for NATO in 30 days. Well, you can't conceal something like this. This was politically unacceptable, so the army had to go into other things. The navy had to go into reductions in operations, the air force O&M reductions, which led to your reduction in B-52 sorties." "Of course we all know this about discharging men early—it costs you two months' pay to discharge a guy from the service by the time you pay him off for all the various benefits he's entitled to, which means that if you wait until the first of June to discharge the guy it costs you money instead of saving money—in a given fiscal year." "This is the kind of a bind we're in." "As far as expenditure money is concerned, the surest way to save the money lies in the field of personnel. That's the reason why we inactivated the 9th Infantry Division. It's the reason we're going to inactivate the 3rd Brigade of the 82nd. It's the reason the marines are going to inactivate the 5th Marine Division. It's the reason that the navy is laying up ships and discharging people."

BROWN: "You can probably fly the max sorties that U Tapao can support at about one-third the costs you can fly them from Guam—flying time, ground-to-air, engine consumption. And the same way with tac air. The sortie is a real crude measure. You've got weapons loading, the duration of sortie, POL." "It's a very crude clamp they've got on."

WHEELER: "_Damn_ crude. We all recognize it, George."

WHEELER: "Hell, you take the 3rd Marine Division out of Vietnam and plunk them down in Okie [Okinawa] or CONUS, and the cost of the division is cut in half— bang! Just like that. That we know. As I say, this is not the best way of doing it. But, as you say, Abe, we're just not that expert. We can't calculate that closely."

WHEELER: "You _know_ it costs you money to close a base. You don't save a _dime_ until the following year. Christ, they're even talking about inactivating Fort Polk again. Can you imagine that? If I were a resident of Leesville, I think I'd get out my Confederate flag and print some Confederate money and start a _secession_ movement. That place is like a revolving door. I closed it out in 1959 the last time when I commanded Fort Hood. They did me the favor of putting me in command of both posts and told me to close out Polk. Well, the mayor of Leesville—. I don't know whether I've told you this story or not. I was flying over the place one day to oversee the dissolution of the place and moth-balling and so on. The mayor of Leesville sent word he'd like to come down and see me. And I said, 'Oh, _god_!' I expected to get the usual tirade. The only thing he said to me was, 'General, I wish you would recommend to your superior authorities that they _never, never, never_ reopen Camp Polk again. Just leave us alone!'" "Jesus, they'd just gotten through floating a bond issue to improve the public school system so it could take care of the military kids."

WHEELER: "The only thing I can say is I think—in fact, I _know_—that the services are doing their level best to swallow this with the least impairment of present capabilities, and of future capabilities. I know they've made mistakes. There's no question about it." "But they've put an honest effort into it, and I've gone over the program line by line. _I_ can't think of a better way to _do_ it." "But, hell, the navy's laying up the whole damn fleet. The navy can't meet their NATO commitment—_period_. It just can't be done. We're short a CVA, a couple of ASW carriers, god knows _how_ many escorts."

WHEELER: "As I informed you, Abe, and I hope what I've got to say won't go outside this room, we briefed the president on this the other day, chapter and verse. We spent two hours telling him _exactly_, line by line—$3 billion. Then we went into the additional $2 billion."

■ ■ ■

COLBY (re pacification): "You'll recall that our goal for October was 90 percent. We were just a little bit away from it at the end of August."

COLBY: The program was aimed at creating more C hamlets, "but the thing that's really grown [over the past year] is B's. I think that what's happened is that as they went out further, the center became safer."

ABRAMS: "Julian Ewell, in this review in here area by area, he made the statement that by sometime in the spring he thought III Corps would have achieved the 1970 goals. This is a rather amazing statement. . . ." [Goals "of 90 percent A/B and 100 percent C."]

COLBY: "They're not far from 100 percent right now."

COLBY: "If you look at the terrorist situation, you'll find that the enemy has kept up, very distinctly. As a matter of fact, by this time this year he's not too far away from his total last year in terms of incidents—9,400 last year, 8,600 already." "It gives you an idea of the cost of the war from the civilian's point of view." 1968: 5,400 killed. 1969: 5,100 already.

COLBY: "Self-Defense—here they're already over their 2,000,000 goal for the end of the year." "About two or three months ago they launched an energetic program to get women, children, and old men." Now organized in two blocs: Self-Defense combat and Self-Defense support. "There have been something over 2,000 Self-Defense people killed this year."

COLBY: "The Chieu Hois are very high indeed. I just learned this afternoon that we had last week something like 1,097, which is the highest week we've ever had."

COLBY (re Phoenix): "This has been kind of a wormy program." "The government started an information program in which they brought this program out from behind the curtain. It's not a secret program, but protection of the people against terrorism. They are trying to make it something not vague and menacing and threatening, but actually something that is a normal part of life and will engage a lot of people as a process of improving the basic security."

COLBY (re police): Authorized 92,000, but understrength. Army told to give them 13,000; have provided about 1,000 to date. "They are getting out to the villages—1,500 of the 2,200 villages have police in them."

COLBY (re Revolutionary Development cadres): Reduced from 59-man to 30-man teams. "A lot of them feel sorry for themselves not having M16s." RD: "They have a new minister, the former Chief of Staff of the Joint General Staff, General Phong, who is a first-class officer."

COLBY: "If '68 was a year of military contest, and if '69 was a year of expansion of security, '70 is going to be a process of economic and political and security consolidation. It's beginning to really solidify."

COLBY: "The president's still the number one case officer" for pacification.

WHEELER (re pacification): "This area . . . I guess is really the proof of the pudding."

ABRAMS: "A week ago yesterday we had a meeting here of all the commanders and the DEPCORDS." "And when we got all through, I think it was the unanimous opinion of everyone who was here that the place to put your money now, in terms of energy, effort, imagination, and all the rest of it is into this pacification program—enhancing the security, enhancing the effectiveness of government out among the people. This is not the B-52 league, and it's not the tac air league. It's really not the maneuver battalion league so much. It's all of the little things that you can do in there to push this along."

ABRAMS: "As implied . . . in the assessment, '70 can be a troublesome time." "In the meantime, the thing to do is go all out in this area, everything that anyone can think of to help this, to stimulate, and that sort of thing. It might be a truck here or a helicopter there, a two-man liaison detachment somewhere else. All the things that you can do in there to shove this along and make the effectiveness of the government—their government—clearer and—out there among the people. That was kind of the note we broke up on a week ago Saturday."

ABRAMS (re the people): "That's what both sides are struggling for."

■ ■ ■

ABRAMS: "Minister Khiem—he is far more, at least in my opinion, he is far more civilian than he is a general." [Said approvingly.] "It isn't one of those staid old military guys talking. He's giving them a philosophy, the philosophy of the democratic process, the philosophy of the village. Politics is no stranger to General Khiem."

ABRAMS: "They got into real problems rushing into that PF thing." "But, once the president tells them to do something, no advisor's going to stand in the way. It's just going to get done. It may not be well done, but the number on the chart will show on the terminal date that it was done."

WHEELER: "At least we're making progress. This [RVNAF I&M] plus pacification, it seems to me, are really our only way out." "If there's any progress in Paris, it certainly isn't visible to the keenest eye." "All you get is the same old crap."

■ ■ ■

WHEELER: "Speeches and television interviews by politicians—really tremendous pressures that the president is under. In my more cynical moments I even suspect that some of these expenditure limitations are designed basically to force a reduction in our efforts here in Vietnam. Nobody'll ever admit that. It's all based on far more high-minded humanitarian reasons. But these people who are behind all this—this is at least one of the objectives that these people have. And of course the Congress . . . holds the purse strings. They meter out the money in such a way that you're just forced to choose the least of a series of unattractive alternatives—or else compromise, which is what we usually end up doing. We end up sort of allocating deficiencies . . . while trying to preserve to the degree we can a viable military posture to meet our multitudinous commitments, none of which the military's ever made. In fact, the goddamn commitments have been made by successive administrations and validated by successive Congresses. If I sound bitter, why—I am!"

WHEELER: "But there is progress. I remember so many years, going back to '64 and '65, when hell, there wasn't any progress."

6 OCT 1969: Briefing for General Wheeler

WHEELER: "I can tell you, which you already know, that there is this terrific squeeze on money."

ABRAMS: "They had some rainfall yesterday up in I Corps. Hue got 14 1/2 inches." "A new all-time record high." Dong Ha: 7.2 inches.

WHEELER: "Practically a drought at Dong Ha."

BROWN (re interdiction last year): "It was the first time that, the first season, that the whole organization, the whole system, could be brought to bear on the problem."

ABRAMS: "I don't really think much of organization, but integrated intelligence—I mean, <u>integrated</u>, <u>every</u> goddamn—. It's a <u>powerful</u> thing. And it's a <u>key</u> thing."

SOMEONE (re recent action at Fire Support Base Crook) (where all the intelligence came together, and the 25th Division reacted in a pre-planned and coordinated attack, resulting in 323 enemy KIA and U.S. 2 WIA): "That's probably going to go down as one of the greatest offensive actions of this war. And they never left their bunkers."

ABRAMS (admiring this automatic pre-planned reaction): "The first key in it was <u>integrated</u> intelligence." "And then they had an <u>integrated</u> operational response that was <u>executed</u> without change. That was the way it <u>had</u> to be done. Once the intelligence said, 'There they are,' then the execution was <u>rigid</u>. The tac air went in this way and the gunships had this, the artillery had this, and it had all been designed so it could all go at the same time without interfering with each other. And you can't take any <u>readings</u> on it while that's going on. That just goes on. And after an hour you stop it and look around and see if there's anything more."

■ ■ ■

WHEELER: "The more background information I have, the better off I am back there, because I get asked the <u>damnedest</u> questions."

WHEELER: "You know the sensitivities back there, and the difficulty of getting these guys to understand what the hell you're talking about. If you were talking to the Chiefs, this [interdiction plan] is pretty simple. But you've got to sit down here and really write sort of a <u>thesis</u> on the subject—."

ABRAMS: "The way Seventh Air Force is functioning with this in-country, out of country, Barrel Roll, Steel Tiger, and so on, you—as long as George [Brown] has got his hands on the thing, it <u>slips</u> and <u>slides</u> with the—. And it doesn't—. I mean, you don't have to staff it. It goes with the—."

ABRAMS (now to the navy): "And <u>this</u> thing is the same way. Bud's [Zumwalt] got his hands on his <u>boats</u>. And he talks to me, or I talk to him, and it <u>slid</u> with the way the enemy's doing things. And we don't get all snarled up in somebody with dedicated forces disapproving, you know—."

ABRAMS (and the logisticians): "And it's the same thing with the 1st Log [Logistics] Command. If you want a—. Ewell doesn't own anything in the 1st Log Command, and neither does Corcoran, neither does Zais. So when you want to <u>move</u>, all you have to do is talk to Joe Heiser, or Frank Noble, and all of that in the background—they <u>know</u> what they're doing. They've got the responsibility for the total thing, like <u>George</u> has got the total responsibility, Bud <u>Zumwalt's</u> got the total responsibility. And in a command, the kind of thing we've got here, this is a great, I just think it's <u>great</u>. These fellows <u>accept</u> their responsibility, so I don't have <u>any</u> worry about <u>that</u>. None of these fellows are going to, you know, let something go to hell. <u>They</u> know that can't be done. They just slide it with the—. And if your intelligence is good enough, and you keep after it daily and so on, then you can <u>do</u> these things." "Of course, I didn't use to <u>think</u> that. You know, when I was down there like one of these fellows I had to <u>own</u> everything. Well, it's not a good system. Some of these things are much better if they're—."

■ ■ ■

ZUMWALT: "Overriding all of our <u>apparent</u> success with the Vietnamese Navy, I have one great fear. And that is if anything should ever happen, either physically or politically, to Commodore Chon, I would be in terrible trouble. He is a <u>really</u> outstanding professional, a man of great wisdom. He's the <u>only</u> one, of all the senior officers, who's interested in getting with it, breaking the tradition and the bureaucracy, and getting things done."

■ ■ ■

ABRAMS: "As confidence develops, and some improvement is <u>clear</u>, the Vietnamese just have problems handling success. <u>Adversity</u> has a tendency to pull them together, and they <u>subordinate</u> some of their sensitivities, but as success comes along and they're not under the gun so much, then these other damn personality things come out, and they get feeling their oats, and they're much freer about criticizing their superiors and the different views that they've got and this sort of thing. That was a <u>horrible</u> report that Charlie Whitehouse turned in—his conversation with General Tri. That's <u>really</u> about the <u>last</u> thing they <u>need</u>—the goddamn <u>bickering</u> and <u>backbiting</u> among the <u>seniors</u>. This country just can't <u>stand</u> it. But Tri is feeling his oats—that's what I chalk it down to. Everybody knows that the situation is a hell of a lot better in III Corps, and the longer Tri contemplates that the more clearly he sees that it's been his personal handiwork that's <u>done</u> it.

WHEELER: "And he really ought to be [as he sees it] sitting in General Vien's seat."

ABRAMS: "Yeah. That's right. Then you could put into practice <u>everywhere</u> in South Vietnam those great programs which he has initiated and executed so successfully in III Corps." "Goddamn it, if they unloaded a thousand rockets on his CP out there we'd get back to business." [Laughter] "And put that off for another year." "When we come down to getting it done, it's these <u>other</u> things that you have to wrestle with. I'm not trying to be a prophet of gloom [<i>sic</i>] here at all, but you've just got to get in there and hand wrestle it and try to move ahead."

ABRAMS: In IV Corps "all of a sudden, in one day, the corps commander decided he <u>did</u> want to use [boats], so he ordered the boats and the marines, one morning, to assault that afternoon. Christ, they had no plan, they didn't have maps, their communications weren't set, no logistics. It was a <u>debacle</u>! It reminded me of my first regimental commander. I was his communications officer. I had these four pack radios on horses. And I was never allowed to be near the regimental headquarters with them. He was <u>opposed</u> to radios, and he used mounted messengers for all of his communications. So one day we were out on a maneuver, and I was about 10 miles back. They sent somebody back to get me, and I galloped up, reported to the regimental commander, and he said, 'Can you send a message to the brigade commander?' I said, 'Yes, sir.' 'All right,' he said, 'send this message: "<u>Compliments</u> of Colonel Herr. I have

<u>no</u> communications <u>left</u>. Send back my messengers.""[Laughter]

WHEELER (speaking very slowly and haltingly): "This ought to be a very interesting experiment, because when you come right down to it what you were briefing [the area security plan], it seemed to me what I was listening to was a distillation of the successful efforts in many areas that we had made over the past four or five years. In other words, what I've said very badly is that we have tried <u>innumerable</u> programs, variations of programs, concepts, devices, stratagems, with differing success—some of them flat failures, some have shown some success, some have shown a great deal. As I say, what you came up with here and presented, <u>conceptually</u>, it seems to me, represents the fruits of experience. Maybe it won't work when you try to put the whole damn thing together as a package, but I certainly think it's worth a try. You can't cavil with the objective, security for the people, defend the nation. I mean, this is what the war is all about. It certainly breaks out the utilization of assets. If we could just get that many human beings to settle down and actually use what they've got."

11 OCT 1969: WIEU

BRIEFER: Since 1 October "the monsoonal trough which separates southwesterlies from northeasterlies made steady progress southward from I Corps." Surge of poor weather into I Corps and the Lao panhandle. Now northeast monsoon in its early stages covers all of Southeast Asia. During 1–9 October, rainfall at Hue–Phu Bai totalled 59 inches, "greater than any <u>monthly</u> total ever recorded over the past 30 years at any station in Vietnam." On one day alone (5 October) 22 inches of rain fell during the 24-hour period. Elsewhere during the nine-day period: Dong Ha 22 inches, Danang 31 inches, Chu Lai 29 inches, Duc Pho 18 inches. Cites "arrival of the northeast monsoon yesterday." "In sharp contrast to the southwest monsoon, the air streams which comprise the northeast monsoon originate over the cold expanses of Siberia and over the northwest Pacific Ocean." Loses much of its moisture on the eastern side of the Annam Mountains. Longer of our two seasons. Generally lasts through April.

BRIEFER: Reports enemy efforts to put the runway at Dien Bien Phu back into serviceable condition.

ABRAMS: "A little runway like that—Christ, you can't even supply them with <u>cigars</u> with that!"

ABRAMS: "Did you hear the secretary of defense's press conference? Oh, damn—<u>why</u> they keep talking, if they didn't have to. He was talking about new instructions that had been issued out here."

SOMEONE: "Well, he used this term 'protective reaction.' That really has caught on. Jesus, they <u>love</u> that!" [Laughter]

ABRAMS: "I would like to say, also, I don't think it's a term Julian Ewell would have thought of." [More laughter] "<u>Nor</u> Zais, <u>nor</u> Nickerson, <u>nor</u> Charlie Corcoran. Well, of course, the reason for that is they've got these military minds with very limited vocabulary."

■ ■ ■

BRIEFER: "Interrogation of a prisoner captured on 12 August [in the southern subregion, Military Region 5] near Tuy Hoa reveals that she is a member of a special action unit in Tuy Hoa District, Phu Yen Province. She states that in early July she attended a three-day study session on COSVN Resolution No. 9. The resolution directs the VC to preserve their strength in order to protract the war. It also directs that large NVA units are to be broken down into smaller units and that they, along with main force units, are to employ sapper tactics and target themselves against U.S. troops and installations. All provincial local force units are to be divided into small cells and target themselves against Revolutionary Development teams and GVN cadre at hamlet and village level to break the GVN's control of the population."

ABRAMS: "They're [the enemy] going to this sapper and small unit, and it's where the NVA are going to be. The NVA are <u>screwed</u> if you can get in there, get the guerrillas, and get the local people out. The NVA then are <u>lost</u>, really. They don't <u>know</u> the country that well. This is <u>really</u> the name of the game here for the next few months."

■ ■ ■

ABRAMS (considering all the friendly forces in the 22nd Division Tactical Area): "Christ, a guerrilla shouldn't be able to go to the <u>latrine</u>!"

ABRAMS: "It's like I told Wright one day. He's got all this stuff about the <u>doctrine</u> of the airmobile and so on. And I told him about the 173rd—<u>airborne</u>, so it's one of the permanent airborne outfits, we've got parachutes and air drop stuff and god only knows what so we can parachute them in anywhere in the world. And I said, 'We're not using a goddamn bit of it. It's just rotting. Because it's not what we've got to <u>do</u>. We don't <u>need</u> any of that. We've got to use the 173rd for something <u>else</u>. It's got to <u>fit</u>. I mean, <u>this</u> is the <u>problem</u>. The <u>hell</u> with <u>other</u> things, and doctrine, and so on. We've got this <u>other</u> thing."

■ ■ ■

BROWN (re close air support in the Plaine des Jarres): "When I was up there I asked the CAS about that figure [apparently Lao reports of results]—how far off was it? Was 10 percent of it a reasonable figure to swallow, or 50 percent? And they couldn't guess. So I talked to Vang Pao, and he said, 'Well, you know, Americans <u>like</u> BDA, [laughter] and we like <u>Americans</u>, and they come back when they get good BDA.' And he said his forward air guys, they don't give BDA to the Thai pilots, because Thai Buddhists don't like to kill people. So that's the way the whole thing works. But at least he admits it."

ABRAMS: "All right—I must say I think the only thing is to keep <u>boring in</u> on this pacification side, and all that stuff that <u>pertains</u> to it and <u>associated</u> with it."

16 OCT 1969: Ambassador Bunker Briefing

BRIEFER: MACV 1969 Infiltration Estimate: 97,000 to date. Plus 8 July intercept from Binh Tram 35 re 11,200 plus five groups to move through its area before the end of the year. Not yet accepted into the estimate. Would bring the total to about 111,000.

■ ■ ■

BRIEFER: Summarizing Resolution 9: "It calls for continued military operations with more modest aims, preparation of his political cadre, establishment of the delta as a priority area, disruption of the pacification program, and defeat of the policy for Vietnamization of the war." "It demonstrates his recognition he cannot win as long as significant U.S. forces remain in Vietnam."

ABRAMS: "One of the things that I think about this is that 6, 7, and 8 were strategy, tactics, and policy where he felt that he had the initiative. In other words, he was making moves not expected by us. . . . Resolution 9 seems to me to be just the opposite. Now he is responding to initiatives undertaken by the GVN."

BUNKER: "Right."

ABRAMS: "The pacification program is no longer a laughing matter from his viewpoint. It's after people, and that's what he's after—that's what the whole thing's about."

ABRAMS: "And Vietnamization—he's ridiculed the armed forces. He really—I don't think he's really thought that they were worth much. Now he stuck with this all through '68, and through February–March of '69. And in the meantime the GVN, after spending the better part of the year getting them out of the cities, and getting them pushed back a little bit—the GVN then came up with this Accelerated Pacification Program, and all those things, last November, while he was still on this wicket. And he stayed on that wicket, and the GVN went on on their wicket. So I think a little bit of a case could be made, at least in this small way, [that] the GVN's assessment of what had to be done was a little more accurate than his assessment. He would have been wiser to change earlier."

BUNKER (re enemy interference with pacification): "It seems to me he hasn't been able to do very much."

ABRAMS: "No, they haven't jarred it."

■ ■ ■

ABRAMS: "I think one of the reasons that the U.S. casualties are down—I was out the other day visiting several of these fire support bases in III Corps, and the quality of bunkers, the quality of fortifications, bear no resemblance to what they were a year ago. In other words, you get attacks by fire and the chances of high casualties has really gone down because of the quality."

ABRAMS: "Other things, like the—well, I felt a little uneasy one place we landed. The helicopter pad was surrounded by must have been 75 claymore mines, all hooked up. The thought occurred to me, 'I wonder whether those things can be set off by the down blast of a helicopter.' But apparently not. No, but—wire, and warning devices, and claymores—this is against the sappers. A lot of improvement's been made there."

BRIEFER: In the delta: 34 percent of the RVN population. VCI infrastructure: 41 percent of the total are in IV CTZ. Seven of the 10 worst provinces by HES standards are in the delta. Also the delta is where the Viet Minh revolution began. "COSVN became concerned over its waning influence in the delta as early as February 1968, when a nine-man leadership team was dispatched there to solve problems with personnel shortages, primarily due to recruiting difficulties and a high desertion rate."

ABRAMS: "I must say, when you take the whole thing, I mean the whole thing—the progress in pacification, even though you don't have to—no one has to buy the 90 percent, or 86 percent, but the fact that security of the people is improving every month, I think, is clear." "I feel that he has to do something, because the march of events seems to me to be inexorable."

BUNKER: "That's the way it seems to me. If he only keeps at his present level of activity, what he's been doing this year—it seems to me if you go back to January 1, quite clearly his position is steadily deteriorating. The big improvement in pacification, and all the other [words unclear]. One indication, it seems to me, of the security situation is the refugees [who are returning to their homes]. I think that's one of the best indications that you could have, a feeling of assurance on the part of the people."

SHACKLEY: "If we go back to the deployment in III Corps alone—he does have the possibility of creating a situation where eventually the GVN will have 90 percent of the terrain, and somewhere around 88 to 90 percent of the population. But he will come down to that hard core where we will not be able to make much more of a dent in it, because of the way he's deployed, and the way he's got access to the sanctuaries, and his logistics system, and so forth. And then, when we get into that bottom platform, there we have a dimension which is a pleasant one to consider, and something that we haven't had to deal with before. But we have got the problem of containing that."

ABRAMS (re eight caches just seized in II Corps): "Well, I would say that losing that amount of stuff, the NVA losing that amount of stuff, is just plain disaster. No one could take that, especially the kind of forces and fighting and that sort of thing they do up there, without it being a disaster. Now the job they've got, of course, is to replace it, which they're working hard to do. But that's one hell of a blow."

■ ■ ■

SHACKLEY (re Laos): "I think we have to expect, Mr. Ambassador, that most of these gains, however, will be gone as the dry season starts in Laos. And take a look at that panhandle area in Laos—most of the gains will be given back to the enemy." "So all of this has to be viewed in the context of what it's been, a very successful diversionary operation, but the odds of this being consolidated are very slim."

SHACKLEY: "Where we'll end up is back on the outer perimeter of the Plaine des Jarres." "The Meo are not good in static defense. The whole sociological structure is really geared to having no respect for terrain. The slash and burn people, terrain has no value to them. They move on after you exhaust the soil after two or three years. And when they have to stand and fight over terrain, it's a concept that they don't understand."

■ ■ ■

COLBY: "The training at Vung Tau is going ahead. There's another course in there now, and the president has gone to every one. About 9,000 have been in the course this year, including the class there now. And 1,400 village chiefs . . . that's three-quarters of the villages in the country."

COLBY: "They have this new minister [of revolutionary development] who really looks very good, and I think he's taking hold of it—former chief of staff of JGS, Major General Phong, a first-class officer."

ABRAMS: "At the end of September we had a meeting here with the commanders and the DEPCORDS. We reviewed much the same material that's been reviewed here today and, sitting here together, we concluded that the best thing we could do for the rest of this year is really what we're doing now. And that is to put every bit of imagination and energy and resources into the pacification program, try to move that—security of the people, trying to grind the mechanism down inside—in every way that we can. And that's the best thing we can do. And it's the most important thing we can do."

BUNKER: "Yes."

ABRAMS: "I think that right now sort of the easy part of the war has been gotten in hand. What we've got now is the hard part that's always been there, and we haven't until—. Well, beginning last November—we haven't been able to get to it."

BUNKER: "Yes."

ABRAMS: "And that's what we're getting to now, the thing we eventually had to get to. So, while there're some things here that sound pretty good, and very hopeful, there's still an awful lot of hard work to be done in this other thing. And at the same time we can't let that other part get out of hand. We have to keep an eye on it."

ABRAMS: "So this is not intended to be an optimistic view of the thing. It's meant to see the problem a little more clearly."

BUNKER: "Yeah."

18 OCT 1969: WIEU

BRIEFER: "Yesterday the Soviet ELINT trawler *Guidrifon* was hit by .50-caliber machine gun and possibly M79 fire from a Republic of Vietnam Navy motor gunboat." Off the RVN coast east of Danang. "When ordered to stand to the vessel altered course. A warning shot was fired across her bow, but *Guidrifon* commenced evasive tactics."

ZUMWALT: "I'm full of admiration for the skipper of the *Guidrifon*. I wish the commanding officer of the *Pueblo* had behaved half so well." [Long silence]

■ ■ ■

ABRAMS: "There's a requirement, you know, all the time to take the long view. I think this is important." "There's a tendency to get kind of happy when these divisions get pushed back. The 803rd is moving out, or the 24 Bravo. But that's not the war. That's just one part of the war. It's these other—it's this goddamn infrastructure, and it's the goddamn guerrillas, it's the political machinery. And that's the long haul thing that has—politically—this country has got to be able to defeat."

ABRAMS: "We're getting now to where the real hard work, the real tough part of the war, is coming up. And it's the part that you can't solve with B-52s, or tac air, or artillery."

BROWN: "But you can't let the security thing go, or the weeds are going to come up in the garden again."

ABRAMS: "Oh, yeah, yeah, yeah. I'm not wafting off into that yet."

■ ■ ■

POTTS: "You know in our COSVN Resolution 9, sir, we were working from a lesson plan, and also the interrogation of a prisoner. And all units had been alerted to be trying to get a hold of this thing. Well, we were lucky and it turned up here a day or two ago. It's 41 pages long. We translated it last night, and of course the first thing we looked for was the date on it—it was July of 1969. The 199th Brigade got it in an ambush they'd set up."

■ ■ ■

ABRAMS: "One thing I've been chafing under—when we brief visitors, the role of the RF and PF in this war is substantially submerged. There's a tendency to talk about the ARVN, and for some time now the RF and PF have borne the brunt of casualties and this sort of thing, and the toll that they're exacting from the enemy is substantial—I mean, if you just want to deal in that sort of thing. But if we get talking about the security of the people this is a big part of this whole thing. This is where it is."

ABRAMS: "Another thing—I don't know how long it's gone on, whether three, four, or five weeks, where the Vietnamese have contributed more than half of the enemy casualties. Here again, I think that these are important things to bring out in briefings to visitors. Now, we've got to be a little careful about it, because we don't want people to get the idea that this is the way you figure out how the war's going. But the Vietnamese are paying the biggest price. The Vietnamese are exacting the biggest price. That's the way it's been going here for a little while."

BRIEFER: By 15 December 1969 "allied combat capability will have been reduced by about 18 percent in maneuver battalions as a result of the redeployment of U.S. combat elements in Phases I and II." "In addition, budget reductions—imposed quite aside from any redeployment considerations—will have reduced our B-52 sortie rates by over 22 percent and our tac air sortie availability by about 25 percent. Thus the total combat power reductions, on the order of 20–25 percent, will have been made in the very forces which have in the past produced more than two-thirds of our operational results."

BRIEFER: "The Phuong Hoang program against the VC infrastructure has barely scratched the surface. Police, despite successes in the populated centers, have not really found a role in rural law and order."

BRIEFER: The president's (Thieu's) "emphasis on decentralization of decision making to local governments is designed to create a sense of community so long absent from Vietnam."

BRIEFER (re pacification): "Statistics with regard to these programs may impart an appearance of greater success than may be the actual case. However, skepticism about the numbers must not be permitted to conceal the very real strength the programs are producing among the Vietnamese people and their communities." "The enemy has recognized this momentum as a major threat."

BRIEFER: "The key factor in eliminating the VCI, uncovering caches, ferreting out guerrillas, and disrupting larger unit operations is continued progress in pacification, for without the support of the people the enemy chances of success are severely limited."

BRIEFER: "The rapid expansion of RVNAF has impeded efforts to improve the effectiveness of existing units." "A serious lack of qualified leaders, and a series of manpower problems, from desertion to a high proportion of noneffectives, prevents more rapid improvement in RVNAF combat effectiveness."

BRIEFER: Cites "changes in leadership in the 5th and 18th [ARVN] Divisions."

BRIEFER: "The inability to maintain satisfactory strength in ARVN combat units is a serious weakness." "In ARVN divisions the desertion rate for the 14-month period ending August 1969 was almost 32 per 1,000." For the RVNAF as a whole it was about 12 per 1,000.

BRIEFER: "The currently approved program to add quantitatively to the ground combat power of ARVN is virtually complete." "From this time forward, then, qualitative improvement must provide the basis for significant advances in ARVN."

BRIEFER: "The most attractive means for improving the overall effectiveness of RVNAF—except for solving the obvious problems in manpower management, leadership, and operational effectiveness—is to expand security to the point that the Territorial Forces can take over that function, freeing regular forces to project operations into areas vacated by redeploying U.S. forces."

BRIEFER: "Conclusions: As in the past, the key to what happens next in South Vietnam is the enemy." "Unless North Vietnamese forces return to North Vietnam, there is little chance that any improvement in RVNAF or any degree of progress in pacification, no matter how significant, could justify significant reductions in U.S. forces from their present level."

BRIEFER: "In light of this analysis it is concluded that, from a military standpoint, the redeployment of major U.S. forces from South Vietnam before late spring of 1970 cannot be recommended, and that should major redeployments before that time be directed they represent military risks which it is considered imprudent to accept at this time."

ABRAMS: "At some point down the road—let's say after you've taken out two or three more divisions—the amount of combat support that will then be available for the support of ARVN and Territorial Forces will be somewhat greater than it is at present."

ABRAMS: "I don't know if I would really favor any more rifle companies in the ARVN. If the manpower was available, I think the investment in Territorial Forces would be of greater value."

ABRAMS: "If you get where the security of the population—that is, right where the population is and the immediate environs of that—is in the hands of the Territorial Forces and the police and the Popular Self-Defense Force and that whole conglomeration of stuff, so that ARVN can interpose itself between the borders and where these others are—effectively, then you got a pretty good—probably the way it ought to be."

ABRAMS (re further redeployments): "The point is that you can't recommend it now. That's the point. Now this is not to say that in January, or because of some other thing, possibly even in December, something will occur that will justify a recommendation along these lines. That's the point of trying to make an assessment at this time. In making an assessment at this time you just can't bring yourself to recommend on a sound basis major troop withdrawals during some time frame in early '70. The justification for it just isn't there—now."

ABRAMS: The important thing that the enemy has done is that he has retained a structure—a structure of battalions, regiments, divisions, and so on, and his command and control structure. Now, unless he fleshes that thing out with a lot more people than he has so far indicated, it's not going to have a great capability. And with each passing week its capability is really declining—under the present circumstances. But the point is he's retained it. And if he wants to saddle up and move 150,000 people down here, he's got the structure to absorb them and use them." "Then [in making the point that way] you're not digging any hole for yourself. I think you're being honest and straightforward."

24 OCT 1969: Briefings for Sir General Wilton and Lieutenant General Lavelle

ABRAMS (re Thieu talking to village chief courses): "We've got feedback where these fellows go back and they tell the villagers back there what the president said about their village—to them. They heard it. They were right there." "I mean, this isn't going to—no one's taken a picture of a great parade with 'See It Through with President Thieu' or anything like that, but it can't help but be a stimulant in a modest way, in a mild way, to the electorate."

ABRAMS: "Prime Minister Khiem has been dragging these ministers out, and he's getting a reputation as the most traveled prime minister they've ever had. That's good, too. And he can say it, too. He knows what to say. He's very articulate. When these province chiefs balk at the idea of giving authority down there in the village and so on, he tells them about who's important—and those people are all in the village. They're not in the provincial capital."

25 OCT 1969: Commanders WIEU

Anticipating a visit by Sir Robert Thompson on behalf of President Nixon.

ABRAMS: "On the 28th Sir Robert Thompson will arrive here in Saigon. And he will have one man with him—Desmond Palmer. And he'll be here for about a month. I think he'll be under RAND auspices. He's going to make an assessment of the situation and render a report. What's the title of his book? *No Exit from Vietnam,* his latest work. In spots it's somewhat critical. He was in Malaysia, or at least he was there for the mop-up phases, and gained quite a reputation from that. He's a skillful writer, and a student—[a] scholar."

ABRAMS: "We'll discuss with him a program. We want to do what he wants to do—that's the thrust of this whole thing. And instead of laying out now a schedule for him, we'll talk the whole thing over and see what it is that he wants to do, and then we'll do that. He should be supported, and anything he wants to see, and any<u>one</u> he wants to see, talk with, and however much time, that sort of thing."

ABRAMS: "Don't bulldoze him around. Let him at least leave here with a feeling that he's had a free hand in talking and seeing and looking, this kind of thing, just everywhere he wants to go." We have no plans to brief him here. "I <u>hope</u> that what he decides to do is really get out and go and see for himself."

ABRAMS (re *No Exit*): "In the initial part of it he's got an <u>excellent</u> dissertation on the character of insurgency. So you're talking with a fellow that knows something about it."

ABRAMS: "Here we're going to try to keep the tone nonargumentative, but <u>explaining</u> and so on. I think he gathered the material—well, he wound up out here in the latter part of '68. His last glimpse before he put this thing [the book] together was last fall." "I had the impression, from reading the book, that he really isn't familiar with what's happened in the last year or so."

JACOBSON (responding to Abrams's comment, "You know him."): "He's not a boorish guy. He's a nice man. Everybody will enjoy talking to him. He's a policeman is what he is."

■ ■ ■

ROSSON: "My visit to Paris proved to me that all the work we're all doing to keep General Weyand informed is work very well done. He has the <u>highest</u> credibility with both Ambassador Lodge and Mr. Habib."

ABRAMS: "I think this Cambodian LOC is a factor, because in the overall Communist strategy the development of Cambodia to support the III and IV Corps is an important step." "And it's the only thing, I think, that <u>really</u> made <u>practical</u> the substantial effort in III Corps. It's just too far to bring it <u>all</u>—all those munitions and that stuff—down through Laos and Cambodia, support the whole thing, over the Ho Chi Minh Trail. It's too <u>far</u>, the attrition on it and so on, and this way you get—except for what the Cambodians steal—you get—."

ABRAMS: "When did Sihanouk start saying that the VC were in his territory?"

BRIEFER: Fall of 1968. We believe they had an oral agreement that the VC would stay in designated areas, would not interact with or subvert the populace. But up in the northeast they began to violate this.

ABRAMS: Then Sihanouk went public with a map showing VC dispositions.

POTTS: "That was one of the maps that we provided to him."

ABRAMS: "To hell with what <u>we</u> did. I mean, it's trying to understand what he's doing, which is a Herculean task." "In the northeast . . . an insurgency was blossoming there. And he said they were furnishing the Khmer Rouge with <u>weapons</u>."

■ ■ ■

ABRAMS: "That was the essence of what I said the other day up in I Corps—it's what <u>every</u> man in uniform—policeman, RF/PF, PSDF with an armband on, Korean, American, ARVN, <u>whatever</u> they may be—<u>he</u> represents the government. Even <u>we</u> represent the government because we're helping it. And it means that every last man, to the <u>villager</u>, that's the government. And if he takes away their goddamn chickens, if he throws beer cans at them out of a truck, if he forces them off the <u>road</u> with his truck, every damn <u>one</u> of those things is—you can say, 'We're not VC, we don't kill them, or we <u>try</u> not to,' and so on, but every damn <u>one</u> of these things—. So you know that thing—we could expand that chart of Marshall's, you know, that has the villager's view of the war. Well, goddamn it, throwing <u>beer</u> cans out of <u>trucks</u>, that <u>ought</u> to be on there. What does the villager think of <u>that</u>? And how does he think of that compared to what the <u>VC</u> do? Or running some old guy off the road with his bicycle? I'm just saying—there's <u>no</u> point in getting too <u>excited</u> about it, but <u>that's</u> what's up for <u>grabs</u>."

ABRAMS: "Now whether <u>we</u>—<u>all</u> of us, I mean everybody that's mixed up in the damn thing—what the villager, the peasant, all these guys out there, what <u>they</u> think—<u>that's</u> what's <u>important</u>. And <u>every</u> damn thing we <u>do</u> is cumulatively, all of these little things—I mean, none of them, no single one really is important, but down there in the <u>village</u> <u>it's</u> <u>all</u> <u>piling</u> <u>up</u>! It's <u>added</u> up. To us it's nothing. They jerk their hats off and go by and so on, but it <u>all</u> adds up, as they sit around there at night, before going to bed, talking. And there's always some son of a bitch who we don't know about, part of the infrastructure, not surfaced, but he— as they talk and visit and so on—he can keep adding the total for them—you know, in a mild way." "So this part of it is up for grabs. And this is the part of the war that, certainly for the next few months, this is what we're <u>in</u>." "And we shouldn't automatically think that everybody sees the VC the same way that <u>we</u> do. Down there in the village they're looking over the whole array of <u>bastards</u>." "And to get <u>commitment</u>, to get real <u>commitment</u>, they've got to think, 'This is a pretty damn good bunch. They'll treat us halfway decent.'"

JACOBSON: "This is the <u>single</u> area in which—Professor Popkins from Harvard came over here after an absence of two years—and he found vast improvement in every single area except that, the manhandling and discourtesy and improper conduct of all troops, including American troops. Other than that, <u>everything</u> had improved. <u>That</u> had not."

ABRAMS: "And also, in this game, the good works of a thousand can be negated by the bad works of ten."

■ ■ ■

BRIEFER: Key aspects of the Combined Campaign Plan for 1970, AB/145:

■ Prepared jointly by JGS and MACV. "We did everything possible in this effort to make it one by the Vietnamese. The size of the plan and a good bit of repetition attest to the success of that endeavor." To be issued at the end of October 1969.

■ "The major thrust of AB/145 places emphasis on assuring protection of the Vietnamese people, on pacification and development, and on improving the combat effectiveness of RVNAF. The principles of area security have been incorporated."

■ "The mission statement has been reworded to reflect the importance of providing security to the people."

■ "It is significant that this year's plan, in contrast to AB/144, calls for participation <u>in</u>, rather than support <u>of</u>, pacification and development."

■ Incorporates goals of the GVN Pacification and Development Plan. Includes:

Provide B level of security to 90 percent of the people and at least a C level to 100 percent.

- "The Free World and RVNAF regular forces, including CIDG, will conduct operations primarily to locate and neutralize enemy main forces, base areas, and logistics systems in RVN; deter enemy incursions into RVN along the DMZ, the Laotian and Cambodian borders, and in coastal waters; and prevent enemy main forces incursions into consolidation zones and secure areas."

- "The Territorial Forces, consisting of RF and PF, supported by National Police and People's Self-Defense Forces, and by regular forces when the situation requires, will conduct operations primarily to participate in GVN pacification and development, and to prevent enemy infiltration, attacks, and harassment in secure areas and pacification areas."

ABRAMS: "And it's a great struggle to get everybody to work together. The ministries are jealous of their own empires. The regular forces look down on the Territorial Forces, and the Territorial Forces look down on the Popular Self-Defense Forces, and everybody looks down on the police. And the province thinks they're giving too much to the village, the village thinks the district is monkeying in their affairs, nobody's interested in the people. I mean, you've got all of these things. And the thing in it is how to keep the whole thing together. The cement that holds it together is a very poor grade. The natural tendency of practically every South Vietnamese is to fly off into his own goddamn pursuits. It's just unnatural, especially when they commence to feel a little prosperous, or a little safe—Jesus, that's the time to abandon the government and get out for yourself and build your own political party, starting with two—you and your wife, and with some vision of becoming prime minister." [Laughter]

ABRAMS: "This thing is held together under great tension. The tension [*sic:* tendency?] is for it to all blow apart." "You've got to see beyond the charts, and think beyond the charts. There's no way to portray the whole thing. It's not even possible to portray adequately. The important thing's in the whole thing."

SOMEONE: "We've got some real problems." At Nha Trang we turned over the responsibility for firefighting to the VNAF, but there was a little difficulty with driving the fire truck. "Goddamn—the guy can reach the wheel, but he can't touch the pedals!" [Laughter]

SOMEONE: "I took the day before yesterday morning to go over Highway 20. And the change that's occurred there, even within six months, over Highway 20 from QL-1 up beyond the II Corps boundary, is little short of remarkable. You see people out cultivating, even in the areas that were burned over and desolate six months ago. You see little plots of vegetables, farms, lumbering of course out the kazoo, and traffic up on QL-20 with the dry season coming up—if we can just get in there and tar it and iron it out—General, that's a fabulous transformation."

■ ■ ■

ABRAMS: "The input to HES—as we get down here in A/B/C, and A/B gets where it's covering most of the country, most of the population, I think we should see if we can't toughen up our view of what's A and what's B. I mean, filling out the thing about the conditions that finally wind up that <u>mean</u> that it's A or B or C. Because it may be that, under the pressure of <u>goals</u> and <u>targets</u> and so on that everyone—<u>not</u> everyone, but some have leaned a little bit over backwards to look at the better side of things, which—god knows we <u>need</u> a positive attitude and so on, but now's the time when you've got to look past the chart and it mustn't be only A/B/C on the chart and A/B in the HES report, but this government's <u>life</u> depends on it being what it <u>says</u>!'"

COLBY: We are now running old and modified new HES systems in parallel. The new features a revised set of questions. "I think all your district advisors have almost unanimously testified that they feel that the new one would be more accurate than the old one, because it's more objective in terms of counting <u>things</u> rather than giving a subjective answer to questions."

ABRAMS: "All of this <u>other</u>, this other <u>part</u>, has got to go, or you've got <u>nothing</u>—except, except, a national disgrace for the United States. <u>We're</u> the advisors, <u>we're</u> the ones that pass on it, <u>we're</u> the ones that recommend it, <u>we're</u> the ones that urge our government to buy it and provide it, take the taxpayers' money, and so on. We're supposed to be <u>pros</u>. We <u>know</u> all of this. And that capability has got to be built in <u>or</u> you're not going to <u>have</u> anything."

26 OCT 1969: Lieutenant General Weyand Brief

Lt. Gen. Frederick C. Weyand, previously in Vietnam as a division and then field force commander, is now in Paris as Joint Chief of Staffs representative to the U.S. negotiating team.

POTTS: We've been sending you our "'Weydergram' [Wee-der gram], we refer to it, every day." We sent you our latest assessment about 10 days ago.

WEYAND: "I briefed the ambassador and Phil Habib just before they went back to meet with the president, so they were—not that they passed it on to the president, but just got them up to the level of the other guys so they weren't in for any surprises."

POTTS: "We looked at January '68, when we had 250 [enemy] battalions in-country. Then we ran a check just the other day, and there's 344 in-country, an increase of 94. As we go through, you'll see they're all at about half strength."

POTTS: "Prior to November 1968, 13 regiments relocated out of the northern two provinces and into North Vietnam. Since that time, excluding the 812th Regiment, the equivalent 13 regiments have relocated back <u>into</u> the northern two provinces. And at present, of those 13, 7 still remain in South Vietnam."

POTTS: "Let's pause here a minute. Now this is significant because Mr. Harriman was mentioning [Weyand, laughing, "Yeah."] those in some comments. He said, 'Because of the bombing halt . . . in '68, they pulled out all of this.' All of that was done <u>before</u> the bombing halt. <u>Since</u> the bombing halt they've put it back in."

POTTS: "Let's move right ahead with out of country, because this will give you some of the indications that have come down as to whether they're going to continue or not. It's a very important thing."

POTTS: "In North Vietnam, since 22 March only three new infiltration groups have been detected moving south through the infiltration pipeline within North Vietnam. However, since 8 August 12 additional infiltration groups have been detected through message intercepts of General Directorate of Rear Services communications originating from the Binh Tram 34 area in Laos."

POTTS: "We saw the truck traffic jump to 144 trucks last week, compared to one the week before." And the 559th Transportation Group is moving back into position.

POTTS (re a cryptographic officer rallier): "He brought in what we think is going to be the most significant break in the collection effort during this war." 3,500 pieces of information.

BRIEFER (J-3 type): As of 4 October 1969 we had a total friendly force of 300 infantry battalions, 1,477 RF companies, and almost 5,000 PF platoons. Equivalency ratio: 1 U.S. infantry battalion = 2 ARVN or VNMC infantry battalions = 10 RF companies = 50 PF platoons.

27 OCT 1969: General Vien Brief

Gen. Cao Van Vien is Chief of the South Vietnamese Joint General Staff.

ABRAMS (to Vien): "There's just a lot of activity in Laos. It's building up." Vien suggests it would be good to let Washington know about this.

ABRAMS: "Have no fear. Have no fear. I understand very well the importance of keeping Washington fully informed so that—. You know, there are some that say, 'Well, there's a lull.' Well, some places there's a lull and some places there's great effort. And so, to get the balance, consider it all. Yeah, very important."

VIEN (re the enemy): "I don't think they are ready to do something in Saigon, but Saigon is still the objective."

■ ■ ■

ABRAMS: "I think the targeting keeps improving. That's very important. If the targeting is of good quality, then it lands on the enemy or his supplies. No good to land in the jungle, you know—nothing but monkeys or elephants." "That's all intelligence—it's the only way."

■ ■ ■

ABRAMS: "I was up at Pine Camp in 1941, in a tank regiment. And two American officers who had been to visit the British army in the desert . . . came to give us a talk about the war. None of us had ever been in the war. So we were all in the theater, all the officers. And this officer got up, and he said, 'The Germans have a new antitank shell.' He said, 'Anywhere it hits the tank, in one-half a second the entire tank is raised to 10,000 degrees Fahrenheit. Everything is burned instantly!' Well, I was in tanks, and this sounded very bad. [Laughter] But you had to believe him, because here he was—none of us had ever been, and he'd been to the battlefield. Well, as we now know, the Germans never had any such thing. And of course I don't know why that man said that, but he didn't know what he was talking about. Isn't that something? I was there. This is a true story. I heard him say it, because I remember how I felt—very bad. So I said, 'We've just got to keep moving! Make it hard to hit!'"

29 OCT 1969: Sir Robert Thompson Briefing

Sir Robert Thompson, a British counterinsurgency specialist, has been sent out to Vietnam by President Nixon as his personal representative to make an assessment of the current state of affairs.

COLBY: Briefs the state of pacification, very low key. Cites the essentiality of involving the people, making them feel that "it's their effort, it's their war, it's their security."

COLBY: "The big thing that's different this year from what you saw before is that they have organized for pacification, and very seriously." Describes the council, chaired by President Thieu, and the plan.

COLBY: "Pacification used to be largely RD, and when you talked about it it was almost exclusively these teams. These are a very minor part of the total effort at this point. The real thrust is on the security." Re RD: "These fellows are helpful. They do a halfway good job. They've reached their peak in terms of numbers. They provide an ad interim government and organizational effort in the village."

ABRAMS: "It's like RF and PF—what, two, three years ago? Nobody gave—. Nobody, nobody. Now it's a—Christ, it's just great. I mean, you can't be anybody unless you're for them. Same thing with the Popular Self-Defense. My god, I don't believe there were five province chiefs in Vietnam who thought that was a good idea—or even an acceptable idea. Now there's probably no more than five that are dragging their feet."

ABRAMS: Points out that for terrorist incident statistics "the base has changed." The government extends into more areas. And some are in effect combat losses, as where the enemy targets the PSDF or elected officials.

1 NOV 1969: WIEU

Attendees: Adm. McCain, Gen. Abrams, Gen. Rosson, Gen. Brown, Amb. Colby, LTG Mildren, VADM Zumwalt, MG Peterson, MG Conroy, MG Townsend, Mr. Jacobson, MG Shaefer, MG Bautz, RADM Butts, BG Gunn, BG Long, BG Kraft, BG Vande Hey, BG Smith, BG Potts, BG Jaskilka, BG Sykes, Col. Cavanaugh, Col. Penuel, Col. Cutrona, Col. Dewey, Col. Hanifen.

ABRAMS: "In most of these things where we've screwed up on the border, and we have, in the end our people have been fairly honest about it. They've admitted it and so on, even though some of it's been inexcusable. So I think we've got a fairly reliable base. And if they're [the enemy] reporting that they shot one down and by god we don't know anything about it, you commence to wonder just exactly what it is that's going on."

ABRAMS: "This war is getting simpler and simpler as we all [we and the enemy] focus on the same thing. We were talking the other day, Admiral [McCain], about a few fleeting examples of where the enemy has been instructing his people to be <u>nice</u> to the local people. And of course we've been trying to push that a little bit, too. And if this war ever got into a shape where <u>both</u> sides were busting their ass to be nice to the people the thing might get over in a <u>hurry</u>." [Laughter]

ABRAMS: "The South Vietnamese aren't the pushovers that they once were. And you [the enemy] go out there and you start muckering around with them and a lot of people get hurt. Or you try to keep away from them and they come out and pop you off. If these VC types ever get the idea that the Vietnamese are <u>tough</u>, it's going to make a big difference."

ABRAMS: Re "General Tam over here in Free World Forces. I'd like to tack his you-know-what on a stump and push him over backwards." "<u>He's</u> the guy that says the VC control most of the country."

SOMEONE: "He's never been out of Saigon, has he?"

ABRAMS: "No, you're wrong. He's visited out at the headquarters of the Thai Division—by helicopter. And he's also, within the last year, visited the Filipinos for lunch out there at Tay Ninh."

POTTS: "He doesn't even go to the briefings over at the JGS, sir."

ABRAMS: "I don't know how much <u>effect</u> it has, but it <u>certainly</u> is irritating."

JACOBSON: "That was an interesting party Tran Van Don gave the other day, he and Big Minh and some 300 guests. Made some helpful remarks."

ABRAMS: Yeah, he's another one. And Big <u>Minh</u>—I don't know whether he's really <u>smart</u> or—."

JACOBSON: "You can be sure—he's a lot of <u>things</u>, but he's not smart."

ABRAMS: "He says he's saving himself for the <u>people</u>. Well, any of these fellows that are thinking about the people, I don't know why the hell they don't put their shoulder to the wheel and get in here and <u>do</u> something, goddamn it! Instead of <u>hanging</u> <u>around</u> like that. He said, 'Well, the thing to do is at the right moment go into exile.' What a wonderful bunch of chaps! And it shows you the size of the problem that the president's got. <u>He</u> knows all this crap's going on. He knows all these characters."

■ ■ ■

Re problems with expanding force structure.

ABRAMS: "They're just taking hellacious <u>blows</u> here in the <u>quality</u> of their armed forces and paramilitary forces. These PF platoons are coming out of those goddamn training centers, and they couldn't fight their way out of a paper <u>sack</u>! They've been overcrowded, they haven't been properly equipped, and—goddamn it, they're mesmerized with <u>numbers</u>. And they keep spreading the leadership thinner and thinner and, goddamn it, it's already reported as being inadequate."

ABRAMS: "But no one seems to be able to <u>prevail</u> in this area. If they were studying it, or if they had looked into it, and made that judgment—you know, that by god they could afford, in terms of further quality sacrifice and so on, they could afford it and still have effective forces. But, goddamn it, they haven't done that! They haven't [bangs table] made that kind of an explanation."

ABRAMS: "And, frankly, I think we've been pushing them, some of our people have been pushing them to do this. And then the same guys will turn around and piss and moan about the weak leadership! And the lack of training! And the lack of discipline! And that's when—. And then they want U.S. rifle companies to come in there and stay with them for six months until they get trained and get functioning and get their confidence up and this. Well, that's all right. More MAT teams! Trying to make up with MAT teams, goddamn it, for what has [bangs table] failed to be done basically."

ABRAMS: "We've got our work cut out for us, trying to get something done, in these goddamn areas that they won't do anything about—or they won't have anything. You can't have effective forces unless you have these other things."

JACOBSON (rising to the challenge): "I've got to say, because I've got a paper floating around the staff recommending these platoons that they have unilaterally decided be activated now. I have recommended pushing that up until the first of January, so I've got to speak to that now that this comes up. The reason is, particularly for PF, when you go into a new area with RF and start the pacification moving, it is possible to recruit PF. Admittedly they're not well trained. They're not well anything. [But] we've never had them turn the guns the wrong way. And what we're really doing is recruiting, by god, the local VC squad. And they want to stay home so bad that they'll join the—the—the PF to do it. So I guess, in defense of what I have done, I've got to say that I think that, that the increase in PF can be justified on the basis that it's a damn cheap way to get some government forces into places where there aren't any now."

COLBY: "I was all for doing it the first of January myself." "By then the training centers would begin emptying out."

ABRAMS: "I'll bet you they've ordered this without finding out whether they've got any goddamn boots for them, whether they've got any uniforms for them, whether they've got a goddamn thing for them, whether there's room in the training centers, whether there will be room in the training centers, or any other thing. And, despite all you say, George, goddamn it, that just isn't the way to run the business. [Pause] If they're just recruiting the local VC squad, then maybe you don't need to send them to the training center at all." [Laughter]

ABRAMS: "I'll tell you one thing about training, though. General Truong has had a policy which he has never—which he has consistently followed. And that is the rotation of his battalions through his training center. And he's got the best division over here, goddamn it, and I think training has something to do with it."

■ ■ ■

ABRAMS (later): "Can't seem to get this off my mind, but that's what Patton meant when he said that it's not the purpose for you to go out and give your life for your country. The purpose is to go out and make some <u>other</u> son of a bitch give <u>his</u> life for <u>his</u> country. [Laughter] Well, now the way you <u>do</u> that's by <u>training</u>. If you want to just go out and give your life for your <u>country</u>, see that's the way to do it, just stumble along. Say, 'All right, forward, men. Here's some rifles. We'll hand them out as you pass the gate.' And that's the way you go out and give your life for your <u>country</u>. But if there's any validity in this theory of making some other son of a bitch give <u>his</u> life for <u>his</u> country, <u>then</u> you've got to <u>train</u> them. A-n-d, I like to hear all these—. I mean, we should have a good discussion and everything, but—. And I like to be open-minded, but I'm not—I don't think I'll <u>budge</u> on this." [Laughter]

4 NOV 1969: General Michaelis and Major General Ryan

Gen. John H. Michaelis, Commander in Chief of U.S. Forces in Korea, is visiting MACV. He is also a 1936 classmate of Abrams's from West Point.

ABRAMS: "This determination is made by me—what percentage of the air effort is applied in South Vietnam, what percentage is applied in Laos. We do this on the basis of the intelligence. And we make the determination on the weight of effort that goes into northern Laos." "All the targeting of the B-52s, and the application of that effort, is all determined here." "Back in the days when they were bombing around Hanoi and Haiphong, that was run from CINCPAC." When they reduced the bombing, "in the process the Route Packages 1 and 2 were turned over to MACV. So when you got to south of the 20th parallel, CINCPAC was then out of the air war and it was all run from here." Re when they could bomb up to the 20th parallel: "You're damn <u>right</u> it was good. It covered all of the passes."

ABRAMS: "In the summer and early fall of '68, during the northeast monsoon season in North Vietnam, the interdiction program from the 20th parallel down was <u>so</u> effective he was not getting six trucks a week into Laos—a combination of the interdiction program and the weather. And that's the situation you had when the bombing halt occurred."

MICHAELIS: "I'm having this problem . . . on the command and control of out-of-country operations. CINCPAC, or PACAF really, say they're going to run it completely. You've had this before, I suppose."

ABRAMS: "Well, I only want to say that when I sat there and listened to the briefing over there in your headquarters I was absolutely <u>aghast</u>. In fact, sitting over there in the quarters one night with the Chairman, I told him. I said, 'That's—I couldn't <u>believe</u> it.' I said, 'That's the goddamnedest arrangement I've <u>ever</u> heard of.'"

MICHAELIS: "Well, I have <u>zero</u> flexibility, you see."

ABRAMS: "Huh! What you've got is a lot of implied responsibility and absolutely no authority. Just a <u>horrible</u> mess! And the other day I told Admiral McCain, I said, 'That'll never happen here.' I mean, I know what you're talking about."

ABRAMS (complaining about a briefing chart): "We've just got to get this straightened out. We're still thinking in terms of Tet '68." "When you get on that thing and start talking about it, you've got your U.S. hat on. The charts are U.S., it's what you're talking about, and then the little bit that you mention about the Vietnamese has to do with the ARVN, and nothing about the RF and PF. I mean, if you want to really talk about what's at work in these areas, and what's keeping the damn thing together, it isn't the ARVN."

ABRAMS: "The plan in each of these areas is Vietnamese—the pacification plan, the campaign plan, the whole goddamn thing. And we're in there to support that! That's the way the thing works."

ABRAMS: "The dominant military force in the delta, in terms of numerical strength, is the RF/PF. Half of all the tactical air sorties applied in the delta are VNAF—Vietnamese. The tactical air control system in the delta is run entirely by the Vietnamese. The bulk of the coastal surveillance and interdiction in the delta is done by the Vietnamese Navy."

ABRAMS (re ARVN divisions): "I would say that the 1st Division is just as good as most U.S. divisions. It's not as good as the best, but it's a very good division. Next in line would come the 2nd. And after that they kind of string out. I suppose that the third one is the 21st Division, down here in the delta. It's [given] a very fine performance."

ABRAMS: "Leadership—where that's good, they're good. Where it's mediocre, they're mediocre. Where it's piss poor, they're piss poor. It's just that simple. We've had some very dramatic examples here of where one man has changed—one man, just the commander, and in a month and a half time you've got an entirely new outfit. Used to be flat on its ass, wouldn't go anywhere, couldn't fight. Only changed one man—transformed the whole thing."

MICHAELIS: "How do you effect a change? Do you have to do it by persuasion?"

ABRAMS: "Yes, that's the simplest way to describe it. It's just tough. They've got to do it. All general officer assignments are made by the president. There is nobody else can change that."

BRIEFER: "General Abrams, I think it's interesting that there are only 54 generals for a million-man force. They really don't have a lot of flexibility in their general officer corps."

ABRAMS: "And even that is understrength. They've set up their own authorization for generals. They're way below that. The 23rd Division has been commanded now for about a year by a colonel."

BRIEFER: "So has the 9th."

ABRAMS: "They haven't got a good legal system for retiring them or getting rid of them once they've decided that they're not any good. They still are on the rolls, and they still have to find some job for them to do. You can say, 'Well, shoot them or something.' Well, they still try to—. They'd like to have a— some legality. I mean, that's what they'd prefer to do." "So it's quite a step for them to make one of these guys a general, because they're really committed."

MICHAELIS: "I just discovered we have a system in our army whereby you can reduce a temporary brigadier back to colonel."

ABRAMS: "Oh, yes. [Pause] We don't <u>use</u> it enough."

■ ■ ■

ABRAMS: "I have taken a very firm position, and Westy too, that the <u>air</u> will be in the VNAF. They haven't got enough <u>talent</u>—they haven't got enough talent logistically, in terms of pilots—they're <u>pilot</u>-limited, they're <u>logistically</u> limited, they're <u>skill</u>-limited—and goddamn it this country cannot afford having four or five air forces!"

ABRAMS: "And so we've taken all the <u>ills</u> of having the helicopters in—the <u>best</u> place, if you're a real wealthy outfit, you know, and money doesn't mean a hell of a lot, like with the U.S., you give everybody their air force. It gets you away from the uncomfortable decisions of who has it and that sort of thing. Just give <u>everybody</u> some."

ABRAMS: "And the same thing with boats—give <u>everybody</u> some boats. I mean, the air force has got boats, the army's got more boats than the navy's got. The army's got more airplanes than the air force has got. <u>That's</u> the way <u>we</u> run it. But <u>everybody's</u> got what they want, and their <u>private</u> air forces, their <u>private</u> navies, their <u>private</u> armies. The air force has got a pretty good army now, that's developed during this war in the guise of base security and so on. <u>Well</u>!"

ABRAMS: "But, with these people, you shouldn't <u>do</u> that. I don't know what the staff is studying at the present time, but it's certainly not at <u>my</u> initiative. <u>This</u> country can't afford, at this time, putting air forces in the army and air forces in the navy, and air forces with the marines and so on. They haven't <u>got</u> it."

■ ■ ■

BRIEFER: Displays chart on "the results" depicting KIA and cites "the crossover point occurring back last March [1969]."

ABRAMS (re some group that has called about a visit to Vietnam): "<u>No</u>, I'm saying <u>they</u> <u>can't</u> <u>come</u> <u>here</u> unless they get below five! These damn general and flag officers that can't get their business done unless they've got 15 or 20 assistants with them are just <u>nonprofessional</u>." "This is the <u>navy</u>—U.S."

■ ■ ■

ABRAMS (re provinces and pacification): "One of the interesting things about that is that 4 of the 10 worst are 80 percent. The way that thing used to look a year ago, if you got in the—if you were in the 10 worst you were down there in that 50 and low 60, that's the way you got in the 10 worst. We won't hang our hat on any of these figures, but General Long is so right—it's <u>trends</u>. And that's very—you can see it yourself if you go out and fly around, drive around, visiting the country. It's clearly—something's happening. It's <u>better</u>. Whether it's 98.5 or 86.2, it really—we don't know."

ABRAMS (re An Xuyen, the lowest province): "It used to be down around 20, or 15, percent."

■ ■ ■

BROADCAST: At 10:30 A.M. local time they monitor a live radio broadcast by President Nixon. Per the introduction, White House Press Secretary Ronald Zeigler "said this speech will bear Mr. Nixon's personal stamp more than any other major address he's given. Zeigler said the president wrote it himself, and his speech writers had little to do with the final text." Nixon has just returned from Camp David, where he spent the weekend working on the speech and conferring with Kissinger. It is also stated that the GVN "has been fully advised of the contents of the speech and agrees with what Mr. Nixon will say."

They listen to the broadcast at MACV.

NIXON: Speak on "a subject of great concern . . . , the war in Vietnam." Nixon rehearses the situation he inherited, including: "540,000 Americans were in Vietnam, and with no plans to reduce the number." ". . . and many others, I among them, have been strongly critical of the way the war has been conducted [under LBJ]." Cites "3,000 civilians . . . shot to death" by the enemy last year in Hue. "A nation cannot remain great if it betrays its allies and lets down its friends."

NIXON: Discloses the previously secret attempts to negotiate. "Hanoi's replies called in effect for our surrender before negotiations." Describes his letter to Ho Chi Minh, and quotes from it. Received Ho Chi Minh's reply on 30 August, "three days before his death. It simply reiterated the [word unclear] position North Vietnam had taken in Paris and flatly rejected my initiative."

NIXON: Cites 11 secret Lodge meetings in Paris, says others still secret continue. Describes Nixon Doctrine as it was enunciated at Guam. "In the previous administration, we Americanized the war in South Vietnam. In this administration, we are Vietnamizing the search for peace." "The policy of the previous administration not only resulted in our assuming the primary responsibility for fighting the war, but even more significant did not adequately stress the goal of strengthening the South Vietnamese so that they could defend themselves when we left."

NIXON: "The Vietnamization plan was launched following Secretary Laird's visit to Vietnam in March [1969]." "In July, on my visit to Vietnam, I changed General Abrams's orders so that they were consistent with the objectives of our new policy. Under the new orders, the primary mission of our troops is to enable the South Vietnamese forces to assume the full responsibility for the security of South Vietnam."

NIXON: "Our air operations have been reduced by over 20 percent." "After five years of Americans going into Vietnam we are finally bringing American men home. By December 15th, over 60,000 men will have been withdrawn from South Vietnam, including 20 percent of all of our combat forces." "Enemy infiltration over the past three months is less than 20 percent of what it was over the same period last year." "United States casualties have declined during the last two months to the lowest point in three years."

NIXON: "We have adopted a plan, which we have worked out in cooperation with the South Vietnamese, for the complete withdrawal of all U.S. combat ground forces, and their replacement by South Vietnamese forces, on an orderly, scheduled timetable." Reiterates the pacing factors: Progress in Paris talks, level of enemy activity, progress of South Vietnamese forces. Made our first estimates in June 1969.

NIXON: "At the time of the bombing halt, just a year ago, there was some confusion as to whether there was an 'understanding' on the part of the enemy that if we stopped the bombing of North Vietnam they would stop the shelling of cities in South Vietnam. I want to be sure that there is no misunderstanding on the part of the enemy with regard to our withdrawal program. We have noted the reduced level of infiltration, the reduction of our casualties, and are basing our withdrawal decisions partially on those factors. If the level of infiltration, or our casualties, increase while we are trying to scale down the fighting, it will be the result of a conscious decision by the enemy. Hanoi could make no greater mistake than to assume that an increase in violence would be to its advantage."

NIXON: Appeals to "the great silent majority of my fellow Americans." "Goal of a just and lasting peace."

End of speech broadcast.

■ ■ ■

At MACV they return immediately to the briefing, without discussion of the president's talk.

BRIEFER: Arming the PSDF began "last summer" [1969]. 350,000 weapons have been issued to date.

ABRAMS: "My feeling, since they've gone into general mobilization . . . I don't think that avoidance of the draft is very widespread." "They're awful tight on manpower here. Manpower is a tough problem for them."

8 NOV 1969: WIEU

ATTENDEES: Gen. Abrams, Gen. Rosson, Gen. Brown, Amb. Colby, LTG Mildren, MG Conroy, MG Townsend, Mr. Jacobson, MG Shaefer, MG Bautz, BG Gunn, BG Long, BG Vande Hey, BG Smith, BG Potts, BG Jaskilka, RADM Flanagan, BG Cheadle, BG Sykes, Col. Cavanaugh, Col. Hanifen, Col. Cutrona, Col. Doody.

MACV 1969 Infiltration Estimate: 100,400. MACV 1970 Infiltration Estimate: 900.

BRIEFER: "With the detection of Groups 2151 and 2152, the probability exists that only one infiltration group destined for COSVN, Group 2150, moved south through the infiltration pipeline within North Vietnam during the past seven months." "Group 2150 has never been detected in COMINT," but it is considered a gap group and accepted for September 1969 arrival at COSVN.

ABRAMS: Refers to a cable he received last evening from a Mr. Hertz containing a lot of questions from the NSC about infiltration reporting. "Now we're going to have to be very careful with this, because it has a lot of political significance. And there's going to be a tendency to get it to the press. And you can't do it. And our people, some of the commanders, are going to feel like saying, 'I told you so.' And they can't do that. We're going to have to watch this very carefully."

ABRAMS: "There's been so much said about how the infiltration is down. That's the problem. And a lot of people have attached significance to it—political signals being made, deescalation, all that kind of stuff. And a great many people have hung their ass out the window on this where everybody can see it. Now the ball game's changed. And it's going to be a great mixture. There'll be those who—heh, heh—those who didn't agree with them and are just going to be so anxious to point out what they did."

ABRAMS: "What's the president say? 'It's 20 percent of what it was.'"

POTTS (re infiltration): "We have detected in our study this past week a reduction in time for these men to come down. You know, we used to say 120 days to COSVN. We've detected that up in the north they're moving between the BTs [*binh trams*] a little faster. Sometime in the new few days we'll shave a few days off of that time and present it to you."

■ ■ ■

ABRAMS: Re an attack on a navy/marine task force: "That was a planned disaster [for the enemy]. I told Admiral Zumwalt that a squad of wounded Italian motorcyclists couldn't have put up with that insult. They'd have rose up out of the jungle and attacked the goddamn thing. That's one of the clearest cases I've seen in a long time of—instead of—. You know, if you just go ahead and work hard and try to do your best, you're going to have some disasters. Those are disasters by chance. And they'll happen even to the best of fellows. But the thing you should never do is organize disaster. And that's what they did down there."

■ ■ ■

BRIEFER: Re enemy propaganda on President Nixon's 3 November 1969 speech: "Radio Hanoi . . . claimed that it 'clearly evades two fundamental issues, namely the United States must withdraw completely and unconditionally its troops from South Vietnam, and give up clinging to the Saigon puppet administration.' The broadcast terminated with the claim that, 'supported by the progressive peoples of the world, including the American people, we will certainly win total victory.'"

■ ■ ■

ABRAMS: "I notice that the army strength [U.S. Army strength in the units in Vietnam] is down. It's actually, I think, below what it's supposed to be on the 15th of December."

MILDREN: "That's right. We were shorted approximately 7,000 out of the 25,000 we should have received last month." "This is the wrong time for this to occur. And I received a promise they'll try to make this up in November." "That's the furthest short we've been in the last year."

15 NOV 1969: WIEU

Briefer says on tape this is 15 October 1969 WIEU, but the tape box says 15 November 1969. 15 November is a Saturday, the normal day for a WIEU, whereas

15 October would be a Wednesday. Therefore the probable correct date is 15 November 1969.

ATTENDEES: Gen. Abrams, Gen. Rosson, Gen. Brown, LTG Mildren, Amb. Colby, MG Conroy, MG Townsend, Mr. Jacobson, MG Shaefer, VADM Zumwalt, BG Potts, BG Smith, BG Cheadle, BG Vande Hey, BG Jaskilka, BG Long, MG Bautz, Col. Cutrona, BG Sykes, Col. Cavanaugh, Col. Hanifen.

BRIEFER: No new infiltration groups have been detected, but we have included five 4000-series gap groups that "met ICG [Intelligence Coordination Group] methodology requirements established for gap groups."

MACV 1969 Infiltration Estimate: 102,900. MACV 1970 Infiltration Estimate: 900.

■ ■ ■

ABRAMS: "The other day I was out, and I got a good briefing by General Hieu, 5th ARVN." "That's the first time I've been to the 5th since he's been the division commander. And I must say it was—this doesn't have too much to do with how the division <u>performs</u>, but the <u>quality</u> of the briefing was very high, including a very frank and, I would guess, honest discussion of personnel strengths, desertions, desertions by regiment, and all this kind of stuff, including the fact that desertions are <u>up</u>, which—that's not a good <u>sign</u>, of course, but I must say it's a change of pace out there in the 5th Division to be <u>leveling</u> on things like <u>that</u>."

16 NOV 1969: Deputy Secretary of Defense Packard Briefing

David Packard served as deputy secretary of defense 1969–1971.

ABRAMS: Begins the briefing himself. Shows a slide that is "a schematic of the problem as we see it." Includes the external support of Hanoi. Mentions shipments through Sihanoukville. "North Vietnam—what they supply it's really not much in the way of matériel, but it's the leadership and the motivation and the manpower, and the political structure and strength." Describes impact of the sanctuaries. "And also part of the problem is the part of U.S. domestic opinion which is against the war." "Then the competence and effectiveness of the armed forces, regular and paramilitary forces, of South Vietnam—to the extent that they're lacking in leadership, in training, in motivation, that's also a part of the internal problem."

ABRAMS: Briefs personnel infiltration. Now figuring about 15 percent loss en route. Re the current level: "Now, it's true that this is far <u>below</u> anything they've done before. And I think to come down hard on why this is you've just got to wait a little longer."

PACKARD: "It seems to me that it comes down lower than the figures we've had back in Washington." They tell him they're together with DIA. "Well," [remarks Packard] "we've got some other inputs." [Laughter]

ABRAMS: "His strength in South Vietnam was quite adequately sustained through all of 1968. In other words, although he took substantial losses, his estimating of it in terms of the campaign he intended to run appeared to be quite realistic."

■ ■ ■

ABRAMS: "These are the three thrusts of what we're trying to do—the improvement of the capability of their armed forces and their paramilitary forces. Equipment is one thing, but as you know it's so much more. It's the leadership, it's the training, and it's the development of communications systems, capabilities in communications, development of their intelligence structure and organization—military intelligence—and so on."

ABRAMS: "And along with that the pacification program. . . . We've got a lot of assets committed to that. It's the thing that's got to go. It's the government presence with its people, all over the country, reasonable security, and so on. You mentioned General Barnes. That's all it did, his whole brigade, was pacification. I don't mean that's all it did in terms that it wasn't much. I mean that that was his job."

ABRAMS: "And then the combat operations, which basically are designed to keep the bad men away from where the pacification's going on."

ABRAMS: Describes friendly or "blue" aspects of the threat as seen by the villager. "During this year we've tried to stress this point so that all of our people would have a tendency more to understand why the villager would look at it this way, and why you should go about your business in such a way that—. All of us here, regardless of what country we come from, to the villager we represent the GVN government, the government of South Vietnam. And the battle, in a sense, is who are those people going to vote for? I mean, who are they going to commit themselves to, the other side or this side?" "If he does bad things, or is insensitive to the villager, you're helping to make him go the other way. And the war is in a phase where real effort should be made to" influence people to go our way.

ABRAMS: In redeployments, we are down to 489,000 on the way to a goal of 484,000 by 15 December.

This is from a high-water mark of U.S. forces in South Vietnam of 543,400 at the end of April 1969.

COLBY: M16s for the PF "will not be available until" the fourth quarter of FY 1970.

20 NOV 1969: Infiltration Briefing for General Abrams

ATTENDEES: Gen. Abrams, MG Bautz, MG Townsend, BG Potts.

ABRAMS (to briefer): "Are you the infiltration man?"
BRIEFER: "Yes, sir."
ABRAMS: "How long have you been here?"
BRIEFER: "Three months now, sir." [Pause] "I have a very good feel for this subject, sir."

BRIEFER: Last numbered group: 2149 in March. Then (in new bunch) 2151. Only missing one number (2150) in the 2100 series, and estimate it arrived in September.

BRIEFER (re the missing unnumbered elements): "I feel this was a schedule that was never executed. DIA thinks probably it . . . was <u>northward</u> movers."

ABRAMS: "You want to remember that we went through the <u>trauma</u> of when this went down—stopped picking them up—we went through the trauma of something was wrong with the system, we reoriented our mission, and then we thought they'd gotten wise to what we were doing [***]. You know, we went through all that. And it was in that—while all that was going on—it was in that process that <u>this</u> was picked up. So there was a little bit of a tendency—I won't <u>accuse</u> anyone else of it—but <u>I</u> had a tendency to think that, 'Well, they've got another thing going,' and they're acting more like Communists <u>now</u>—you know, sending more down."

BRIEFER: "Since 31 October 11 groups have been detected." MACV 1970 Infiltration Estimate: 4,400.

BRIEFER: 20 November message said two groups a day headed south. When there was a similar message in December 1968, 30,000 came south in the period 4 December–1 January.

ABRAMS: "You know, we've been v-e-r-y—we've held a very conservative position. Everybody got overjoyed about this drop-off in infiltration, 'signals' coming from—and all that kind of stuff. And we kept talking about the cyclic nature of this. We never crossed paths with those fellows. I'm almost <u>happy</u> to see them doing this." "He's done it about in time to save us."

ABRAMS: "This is going to be a bitter pill for some people to digest. O-o-h, they're going to have trouble with it. I won't say that it's always been good [the intelligence]. I'm not prepared to make <u>that</u> statement. I'll never forget '67. That's why so much time has been spent on intelligence, so much effort. It wasn't good. Well, it was—the <u>machinery</u> was getting formed and all that sort of thing. The <u>field</u> is far more up on the step on intelligence than they were then—<u>far</u> more."

ABRAMS: "Another thing—it would be kind of interesting to speculate here as to when they inducted these men that are coming down here now, and from that when was the decision made?"

TOWNSEND: "There's a side that will say they're just doing this now because we took a tough stand."

ABRAMS: "Yeah, in response to the president's speech. Bullshit!"

ABRAMS: "And the October 15th moratorium. See, that's all—Christ, that stuff's all orchestrated."

ABRAMS: "All these fellows, you know, talking about how to save lives. <u>My god</u>! The best way to save lives is keep attacking. Not the way <u>he</u> does it, but he doesn't <u>have</u> that program of saving lives."

ABRAMS (re including holiday truce as topic in a message): "When you talk about withdrawals and so on, see we're going to have to be <u>unpleasant</u> about <u>that</u> subject. That's what this <u>all</u> shows. We're going to have to be unpleasant.

And this is kind of the basic thing I'm going to have to lay on the table, or lay on the sofa, or wherever we lay it, with the secretary of defense, deputy secretary of defense, tomorrow."

ABRAMS: "The way the thing should read is just the cold logic of developments now as they have been—. 'Here's the situation.' And don't want to get any words in there that are argumentative or anything. Just lay the problem right out, and the recommendations, so that they're clear."

22 NOV 1969: Commanders WIEU

ATTENDEES: Amb. Bunker, Gen. Abrams, Gen. Rosson, Gen. Brown, Amb. Colby, LTG Mildren, LTG Nickerson, VADM Zumwalt, LTG Corcoran, LTG Ewell, LTG Zais, MG Wetherill, MG Conroy, Mr. Megellas, MG Townsend, Mr. Jacobson, Mr. Vann, MG Shaefer, Mr. Whitehouse, Mr. Pickering, MG Bautz, BG Gunn, BG Clement, BG Long, BG Vande Hey, BG Smith, BG Potts, BG Jaskilka, Mr. Fritz, BG Cheadle, BG Sykes, Col. Cavanaugh, Col. Hanifen, Col. Cutrona, Col. Healy, Col. Doody.

This very important commanders conference features an extended and somewhat agonized discussion of potential withdrawal increments.
Somebody apparently has a "Beat Navy" sign.

BUNKER: "That's all right, but I understand that's next Saturday. Today the slogan is 'Beat Harvard!'" [Laughter]

MACV 1969 Infiltration Estimate: 102,900 (47,800 destined for COSVN).

BRIEFER: On 29 October a Chinese Communist vessel unloaded 10,000 tons of rice at Sihanoukville.

ABRAMS: "What? That's really bringing coals to Newcastle. What would rice be coming into Cambodia for?"

SOMEONE: "Sir, we will explain that in a moment." [Laughter] According to a PRG–Royal Cambodian Government trade agreement, rice is one of the commodities to be sold to the Viet Cong for hard currency.

■ ■ ■

BRIEFER (re NVA/VC propaganda after the November moratorium): "Statements by national figures such as Senators McCarthy, McGovern, and Goodell and the major demonstrations in Washington, San Francisco, and New York were highlighted."

■ ■ ■

NICKERSON: "Twelve through six o'clock in the morning on the 22nd, in that area of Hoi An and Tam Ky there were 529 KIA, 159 PWs, 53 Hoi Chanh. They collected up 11 crew-served and 185 individual weapons and 22 1/2 tons of rice." "I think it's breaking up a little. I don't want to get overenthusiastic about it, but I really do." "If this keeps up, we can all go home—huh?" [Laughter]

ABRAMS: "I'm just staggered by the thought of my latest extension being curtailed." [Laughter]

ABRAMS (to the briefer): "Let's have some bad news so we can get back to reality."

ABRAMS: President Thieu is "talking about the People's Army," referring to the PSDF, "and he wants 500,000 more weapons for them next year." "Like John Vann finally got us squared away on the RF and PF, somebody's got to get us squared away on the contribution of the PSDF."

BUNKER: "The president's [Thieu] very keen on that."

VANN: "I believe if you'll check you'll find the RF and PF casualties as a valid indicator of pacification in that, before—when we controlled over all of the country about 60 percent of the population, their ratio of casualties vis-à-vis ARVN was much higher, and as we've gotten control has gone much down."

■ ■ ■

BROWN: "It sounds silly, when you've got 14,000 [tac air sorties] a month, to say you're allocating the shortages, but that's really what we're doing." "Now if we could get this fellow Vang Pao to quit having a war up there, that would free up about 900 a week to get down here where we're fighting. On the other hand, we've got to try to not let him lose, at least too fast, because that could have a very dire impact on what we're doing in southern Laos."

■ ■ ■

ABRAMS: "I remember that ranger group we had up in II Corps. They changed one man, and in four weeks it changed the whole thing. Just one man! He just transformed it into a bunch of tigers."

BUNKER: "The Turks say it's always the head of the fish that stinks first." [Laughter]

■ ■ ■

BRIEFER: VCI neutralization is "one of the highest priority objectives of the pacification plan." Monthly objective: 1,800. Results: August 1,839, September 2,005, October 1,906. Met Phase II goal of 7,200.

BRIEFER: Ninety-two percent of the villages and 91 percent of hamlets now have elected officials as of 30 September 1969. The National Training Center at Vung Tau has trained over 9,300 local officials.

BRIEFER: 147,000 hectares of government-owned land to be distributed in 1969. Slow start. Appears that fewer than 100,000 will be transferred by the end of the year. This is French-appropriated land, much of it in insecure areas.

BRIEFER: Goal of a 20 percent increase in rice production during 1969. About 125,000 hectares of IR-5 and IR-8 rice have been planted (out of a Phase II goal of 200,000 hectares). Fall harvest looks very good. It appears the goal will be met.

■ ■ ■

ABRAMS (re personnel requirements): "You've got to be very humble when you think you're going to outsmart the system." [Laughter]

SOMEONE (J-1): "We have to place some average people somewhere." [Laughter]

ABRAMS: "That is a very profound remark."

■ ■ ■

J-2 ASSESSMENT: "Our study of the enemy situation indicates a number of trends favorable to friendly forces." Strength reduced from about 267,000 on 1 January 1969 to about 226,000 on 31 October 1969. High combat losses throughout the year. By mid-November the enemy had lost over 153,800 KIA (plus died of wounds, permanently disabled, and nonbattle losses due to disease and desertion). Already exceeds combat losses for any previous year except 1968. Also high Hoi Chanh rate. By 15 November 1969 approximately 41,327 (of which 319 were NVA) had rallied, already exceeding the total for any previous year. Reasons most often stated for rallying: increasing allied military pressures, shortages of food and medical supplies, war weariness, fear of being killed.

BRIEFER: During the period 1 January–31 October 1969, more cached weapons, ammunition, and foodstuffs were captured than in all of 1968, to include: 11,862 weapons, 1,825 tons of ammunition, and 4,157 tons of rice. Per captured documents: Logistical problems are more severe due to allied incursions into in-country base areas.

BRIEFER: "Pessimism and illusions of peace" are said by the enemy to have developed in the 3rd NVA Division. "Planned and directed July high point was never launched, nor has the enemy initiated a coordinated countrywide high point since early September." He has employed the high-point system since he shifted to it in May 1969. "The number of battalion-size attacks has fallen sharply." There were 36 during the 36-day post-Tet offensive in February–March 1969. During the three-month 1969 Summer Campaign there were 24. During the three-month 1969 Autumn Campaign: 14. Current Winter–Spring Campaign initiated the first week of November 1969. Stepping up: Between 4 and 12 November the enemy launched 10 battalion-size attacks.

BRIEFER: Infiltration has shown a marked increase during the past four weeks. The total of 102,900 is lower than 1968, but higher than 1966 and 1967 (and the enemy now requires more to maintain his strength in South Vietnam due to the infusion of NVA personnel).

ABRAMS: "You take the body count and the prisoners and the Hoi Chanh and add that all up, and then the estimate of the recruiting capability and what we know of infiltration and subtract that, and take the net effect and his strength would be substantially lower than that that we carry. I think that's true in every corps. But what we _use_ as the strength is the estimate turned in by each of the commands, extrapolated from that that they know to—I don't know what the whole process is—and that's the strength we use. I've had a lot of _difficulty_ with this. If you take the body count reported, the Hoi Chanhs reported—the _military_ Hoi Chanhs—and the prisoners of war, and compare that with the infiltration, you just can't come up with the 225,000 or whatever we're carrying now."

NICKERSON: "I think where the guerrillas are located is important, too, General Abrams. We may _have_ an increase in guerrillas in northern I Corps. I'm not sure we do. But _if_ we do, it would have to be out in the jungles. It's really a _decrease_ in the hamlets and villages, and what guerrillas were in the villages and hamlets have gone out to the jungles. So the numbers can be deceptive."

ABRAMS: "The guerrillas have stayed around 50,000, I think, for _months_. Despite _all_ of the pacification, despite _all_ of the body count by RF and PF, despite the PSDF, despite the Hoi Chanh, and so on, the guerrilla strength has stayed at about 50,000 [in our estimates]."

VANN: "I think without question we're the victims of _underestimates_ for _years_ over here before."

ABRAMS: "Maybe it is too strong to say that he's going to launch an offensive, but the 4,900 trucks, fuel storage, multiple pipelines, two infiltration groups a day. We shouldn't be misled. We gave the example of what happened in '68, I mean '67 and '68, and we took the period from 4 December to 1 January. I remind you that he said this starts on the 20th of November. He didn't say when it would stop. There's nothing in there to indicate—. And we shouldn't assume that it'll run for 27 days—at two a day. But all of those things far exceed the requirement for a subsistence level of his structure here in South Vietnam."

ABRAMS: "We're off kind of a deep end, because we don't know what body count really means. Because, as I said before, you can't match body count, Hoi Chanhs, and PWs with infiltration and recruitment and make any sense out of what we carry as strength."

ABRAMS: "On the other hand, if it's at a subsistence level, I would say that it's safe to proceed with the withdrawal of American forces. If that's the way you interpret the intelligence that's been reported, it's reasonable to do that. And that's the critical point."

BUNKER: "I think COSVN Resolution 9 makes sense from his point of view, because I think he's afraid of Vietnamization. Because he sees the long-range results, very possibly—. Our casualties are down, we're not going to be impatient about getting out of here, he won't get a quick settlement—at least they're hoping for, and the only way he can get it is to raise our casualties. This is what COSVN Resolution 9 says, really—beat us up out here. Two ways he can do it, maybe. One, by keeping it at such a low level that we get out faster than we'd planned. And the other way is to increase casualties. I think the COSVN Resolution 9 makes it fairly clear that he feels the only way to do it is to raise casualties."

EWELL: "He's been trying to raise casualties for six months, and they've kept going down."

■ ■ ■

EWELL: "You inferred that the purpose of this estimate was rather narrow—to determine the extent and timing of U.S. withdrawal and to guide it, is that right?"

ABRAMS: "No, no, no, no. The purpose of the estimate is to make the best estimate you can of what he's up to, where his efforts are going to be, and the magnitude of it. And after you clear that up, then you address yourself, with this as a foundation, to what you can do on withdrawals. It doesn't have the sole purpose of—and if that's what it's for, then it's missed the ballpark. But whatever you do on withdrawals certainly ought to be based on what this estimate comes up with."

■ ■ ■

Current Situation and Redeployment Proposals

BRIEFER: "The purpose of this part of the briefing is to obtain approval of a message to the Chairman and the CINCPAC which is in two parts. The first forwards the MACV estimate of the situation, updated as of 20 November, and the second provides comments on two proposals for Phase III redeployments which were contained in the Chairman's message of 19 November."

■ "The 1970 Pacification and Development Plan, aimed at consolidating 1969 gains, has now been approved and distributed." "Security is still tenuous in many areas."

■ "Personnel strengths in ARVN combat units continue to decline in competition with other segments of the GVN program." "The adequacy of GVN manpower is a matter of continuing concern." May be approaching the upper limit of manpower availability. "ARVN desertion rates remain high."

■ "From early October to date 591 new PF platoons completed training and were deployed." During the same period the number of ARVN combat battalions supporting pacification decreased by over one-third. "The JGS had directed that all ARVN units will be released from pacification support by 30 June 1970."

■ Pacification and RVNAF Improvement & Modernization are progressing satisfactorily. "However, the key to what happens next in the Republic of Vietnam still lies with the enemy."

■ "The situation at this time precludes recommendations for further U.S. troop redeployments."

■ Re new topic of a CJCS 19 November 1969 message: "He requested comments soonest on two concepts." 1. Phase III redeployment of 100,000 during the period 15 December 1969 to mid-July or mid-August 1970, with redeployments during the first quarter permitted to be as low as 5,000 per month. 2. Phase III redeployment of 50,000 in the period 15 December 1969 to mid-March or mid-April 1970.

■ "By 15 December we'll have drawn down 15,500 more spaces than contemplated or recommended in our original redeployment planning."

■ Re 100,000 proposal: MACV's NSSM-36 planning for redeployments contemplates Phases III, IV, and V primarily army troops, then marine units in Phases V and VI. Chairman's message outlines an "accelerated pace" of redeployment. Two broad alternatives: 1. Follow the scheme laid out in our original plan for Vietnamizing the war: redeploy additional army troops until the army support level that remains after Phase VI is reached, then take out the rest of the marines. "This would mean, in the next 100,000, three army divisions and three brigades, a total of 12 brigade forces with three division bases." 2. "Virtually reverse the process by redeploying some army forces and all the marines in the next 100,000. If we do this, the next 100,000 package would contain one army and one marine division, the 26th Marine RLT and one army brigade, a total of eight brigade forces and two division bases." Also a MAW, including nine attack fighter squadrons. "Marine-heavy option." "It would seem highly imprudent to redeploy 12 brigades when we can defer four by taking out the marines first."

■ This approach would reduce available sorties by 116 per day. "A trade-off of 116 sorties per day for the retention of four brigades appears to be a manageable risk. Therefore the marine-heavy option is recommended and preferred."

■ Re the 100,000 proposal: "It abandons the concept of 'cut and try' by fixing U.S. redeployments for the first half of next year in the face of increasing enemy threat." "It adversely affects the morale of troops who deploy late in the package, who must stay and fight until stand-down."

ABRAMS: "Let me ask a question about this—'adversely affects morale.' I've thought that, too. But, at least what's been happening in some cases, a unit that's going to be deactivated or redeployed, men in it who have six or eight months left, they're moved out, and they're put in another unit. In other words, prevailing philosophy here is that everyone has come to serve 12 months, or whatever the tour is. And it seems to me, as this thing has gone along, that's been accepted. And this movement of people has been accomplished apparently without any <u>substantial</u> ill effects. His <u>unit</u> may go home, but he accepts the fact that he has to stay and finish his tour."

SOMEONE: So far we have handled it as described, because we have not redeployed any baseline units. But in the case of baseline units we must send that unit home at 80 percent strength. "I think we have to consider what happens to other units in the theater if we start pulling people out and putting others in in their place."

Baseline units were those scheduled to be retained in the active army structure after redeploying from Vietnam rather than being deactivated.

BRIEFER:

■ "In light of all prior occurrences, once numbers and dates are set the plan will soon become public knowledge, by accident or design. . . ."

■ "It passes the initiative to the enemy by announcing U.S. intentions for the next six to eight months."

■ "It jeopardizes RVN confidence by creating tactical holes faster than they can fill them." "In our best judgment the RVNAF could not cover a redeployment of this magnitude in the time allowed."

■ Re the 50,000 proposal: "Reduces . . . by six brigade equivalents at the very time when, by past performance, the enemy threat will be at its peak." "No further reduction of U.S. forces in northern I Corps is feasible during early 1970."

■ "The Vietnamese would be unable, in our best judgment, to cover a 50,000 redeployment within the compressed time period suggested and still retain the flexibility to respond to enemy initiatives countrywide."

■ "The 100,000 proposal is clearly unacceptable."

ABRAMS: "In the time frame."

BRIEFER: "—in the time frame." "The 50,000 redeployment proposal contains risks which would be imprudent to accept. If directed by higher authority to redeploy additional forces, a 35,000 package, with a ceiling to be reached about 1 April, minimizes the risk. Based on the situation, further redeployments cannot be recommended at this time."

■ ■ ■

BRIEFER (on new topic of longer-range planning requirement): "On 10 November the secretary of defense tasked the Joint Chiefs of Staff to prepare a plan for Phase III RVNAF Modernization & Improvement." Designated the "Consolidation Phase."

BRIEFER: "The key feature of this objective is that it does not provide for a continuing U.S. support force. In effect, it calls for an RVNAF capable by 1 July 1973 of handling the total threat, both internal and external."

A very significant change in that, to this point, plans had always contemplated a residual U.S. force of some magnitude, perhaps similar to that in Korea. And now the South Vietnamese are going to be expected to handle both the internal Viet Cong threat and the external North Vietnamese Army threat, rather than just the Viet Cong as previously contemplated.

BRIEFER: The secretary of defense has asked that: "The plan include a comprehensive review of RVNAF missions, force structure, and force mix, as well as equipment requirements appropriate to the objective. The plan is also to cover ways to overcome deficiencies in less tangible areas such as training, leadership, and morale." Also it is "to include an updated reexamination of U.S. force redeployment." The secretary of defense states that he is hopeful of reaching by 1 July 1971 "a lower level than contemplated in our original planning." Thus to "about 260,000 by that date, or to 190,000 by that same date, and then to an advisory force by 1 July 1973." The secretary of defense wants such a plan not later than 31 January 1970.

ABRAMS: "Now, the other thing I wanted to raise here, too—without <u>abandoning</u> any of the things that we've held to and so on, but <u>has</u> the character and the nature of this war changed somewhat, so that some of the risks that we saw in other times are not the same kinds or types of risks that they are <u>now</u>? For example, in Tet of '68 they were able to bring some battalions right here to the outskirts of Saigon—right on the edge. They rested up during the daytime before the jump-off. Then that night they jumped off into the outlying precincts. We didn't know they were there. <u>No one</u> knew they were there. We had RF/PF— there was RF/PF and so on. And all of this was done. They were right there, on the doorstep, <u>and</u> in some cases <u>in</u> the <u>city</u>. Probably the people that attacked the embassy were <u>billeted</u> in the city. And, you remember, some of them who were in the city went off and celebrated—had dinner and saw a show and had some wine and so on—and <u>celebrated</u>. And then at midnight started out for the naval installation, for instance, down there—oh, a couple of Lambrettas of them. They were a little drunk and in Saigon got <u>nailed</u> down there."

ABRAMS: "But, anyway, that's what they <u>did</u>. And the same with Hue and Can Tho and so on. And they'd come through Hau Nghia, they'd come through Long An. They came down the Saigon corridor and into Bien Hoa. You know, all that." "But there was a structure in place that facilitated all that—furnished the guides—. And a-l-l of that was there—boxes of supplies positioned, weapons positioned, and so on. They came into Saigon in buses, and after the celebration they went down and drew their weapons, drew the ammunition, drew the explosives, and so on, and sallied forth in pedicabs and one thing and another, to do their job. Ah—now, I don't think he's got all that. I don't mean it's gone, but its effectiveness in getting the intelligence, its effectiveness in positioning the supplies, its effectiveness in furnishing the guides, keeping the liaison stations functioning, and so on—I think that that capability has deteriorated, at least to some degree."

ABRAMS: "So—has this gotten in a shape where you can, in trying to predict where we're going to stand by June of 1970—pacification program going on, more Popular Self-Defense, more PF, some more RF, some modest improvements in the ARVN performance and so on—what is going to be the situation by June of '70? And then, what are you going to be able to do in the last six months of '70?"

ABRAMS: "What I'm really raising—is it possible to say that 100,000, or 150,000, is a practical goal for withdrawal in the calendar year of 1970? You've heard what is happening on the infiltration, some view that it may be a subsistence level."

COLBY: "The real question in my mind is whether ARVN is really cranking up to meet the challenges." "I think that's the heart of it."

ABRAMS: "Let's look at it the other way. Supposing the ARVN doesn't. Then where are we?"

COLBY: "Then we're in a hell of a state. The national policy—."

ABRAMS: "No, I think we're in a hell of a state as far as the war's concerned, aside from any consideration in the United States. It just means that we've shown that we have not been able to do the job. That's what it shows!"

ABRAMS: "I think if I sent a message in tonight and said that, in our judgment, the president can announce on the 15th of December 1969 that the United States will withdraw 150,000 troops in calendar year 1970, it would be accepted by return message. And they would leave the schedule of getting that done entirely in our hands. I think you put that caveat on it. And so—there's the job—150,000, 12 months to do it in, and we go through and we don't move a damn thing until May. Then, of course, you've got the job to do. But by May—. The trouble is, though, when you say that—.

SOMEONE: "It's imprudent to try and reach that judgment before we let this threat develop to the point where we can make it in good conscience. That's what I'm saying. And I think we may do this country a disservice by trying to make it on the evidence we have at hand today." Of course, if the redeployment is too compressed: "Nobody's going to be able to do anything. We're all going to be packing and crating."

ABRAMS: "What we did this year was roughly 10,000 a month. That's what it averaged. 224,000 over an 18-month period is somewhere around 12,000 a month. If, then, you cut that 18 down to 14, your rate is—I don't think you—see, you go ahead and plan all this—the rate is not exhausting."

ROSSON: "Under T-Day planning, the most extreme case, we were going to take the whole half million out of here in six months." [None of them believe it could have been done.]

T-Day refers to the time of a possible truce, following which U.S. forces would presumably be withdrawn by some specified date or over some specified period of time.

ABRAMS: "If you went for something like 150,000, the only way it could be done is if you leave the rate, and the scheduling, right here. I mean, done in accordance with the situation here. This would give us a chance to get over January, February, March, and so on, and as we saw it."

ABRAMS: "There's no question in my mind that we've got the tickets now, and the organization and arrangements, to take on whatever it is they want to send down. It's just going to get the hell beat out of it. And then, I mean, you start the problem all over again. So the point, then, would be when you began. And if that could be governed entirely by the circumstances and the situation here—you know, and flavor it that way, then you—."

ABRAMS: "Now of course this gets to be a horrendous problem for the services. You know, the people who have to clean up the mess you've created—personnel and money, equipment and supplies, all that kind of stuff. The way to run that business is to program everything neatly for the year and then don't let it get off of program. So it creates a horrendous problem for them."

ABRAMS: "But of course the thing is that, once this has been announced, then that's what has got to be done."

COLBY: "There's almost a demand that something be announced by Christmas time, something." Suggests that at that time they're either going to announce 35,000 or the whole 150,000.

ABRAMS: "No. No. [Long pause] There aren't very many people that are in favor of announcing 35,000—outside of here. I can tell you that. So it isn't going to be that. It's going to be something larger than that, if they choose this course. And then, when it's going to be done. And they may say it'll be done in the—done in the first quarter. Or by April 1st or something like that. Certainly the thrust of a good many government officials back there is to do something like that. Well, I think they feel it's compelling."

ABRAMS: "Now, I really don't like the idea of taking 50,000 out of here under the circumstances in January, February, and March. I just don't like that." "Snaking the 1st Division out in January and February—it lacks that real appeal. And, to avoid that kind of thing, offer the year package, which then lets you—. Then, of course, you don't [laughing] know what other problems are going to arise later in the year. So, we're—that's kind of the way it is."

ABRAMS (re Thieu): "He's said 100,000 is acceptable, 150,000 is the maximum, in calendar year '70. He has told this to Ambassador Bunker, and Ambassador Bunker has of course reported this to the president."

SOMEONE: Points out that senators would be questioning the rate of withdrawal if it weren't constant.

ABRAMS: "That's right. But I want to tell you, I want to tell you, it doesn't make any difference what we do. Not one—. It won't make any difference what we do. Goddamn it, if we took 200,000 out by February 28th—. We will be criticized by the same fellows you're talking about. Only some of them would have switched and say, 'Now you're abandoning the honor of the United States. We never were for that.' It would split them a little bit." [Laughter] "I'm just saying we're not going to win in that league—any way."

SOMEONE: "By 15 December our strength is supposed to be 484[000]. In all probability it'll be about 475[000]." "With the controls we have on the manpower, we're always short."

ABRAMS: "I just wrote a letter to some congressman, wanted to get his constituent's son home—instead of in January, get him home before Christmas. And I wrote him back and said I was sure that every mother whose son was over here would like to have that, but we really can't do it."

SOMEONE: "It was going to be his first Christmas away from home ever."

ABRAMS: "God, I really bled over that!" [Laughter]

SOMEONE ELSE: "That really tears me up!" [Laughter]

ABRAMS: "I wouldn't want to propose 100,000—or 150,000, either one—unless I was convinced it could be carried out, no matter how many caveats you put on it. I've been through this before, and they—they just don't apply."

SOMEONE: Suggests replying that "we don't see how there can be any announcement, period."

ABRAMS: "Well, first of all, this is a serious matter for the president. Also, so far in this whole thing—the ambassador knows this better than I do, but so far in this thing the president has really been the strongest man in the whole United States."

BUNKER: "No question about it."

ABRAMS: "I mean, he has really faced the tough and stood there. He's been like a rock. And we—we want to—. It's not a question of trying to help the president. I mean, that's not the point, or trying to ease his burden. But what we recommend to him should be the soundest, and the most honest, judgment that we can give him at this time. And we shouldn't put too many bogeymen in the closet, you know, you think are going to jump out, or any of those things. It should be the most honest and straightforward recommendation we can make. And it's on that basis that, see, here today, in the light of everything—that's why Bill's [Colby] here, and it's why Jake's [Jacobson] here, as well as the rest of us—in the light of the strength or fragility of the government as it's functioning out there in the provinces and so on, in the light of how the ARVN and the rest of them are performing, and what we know about the enemy, what can we say?"

ROSSON: "My judgment is that we should continue to anchor our case on the 'cut and try' philosophy. That's what we've said in the past. It's what we're saying here. On that basis we would say we don't believe we can come forth with a realistic estimate until—ah, say along about March, possibly, of next year. And on that basis we do not agree an announcement in December should be made. I feel pretty strongly about that."

ABRAMS: Asks how long it would take to read "that speech by the secretary of defense." Someone estimates about eight minutes.

ABRAMS: "Let's read it, because you want to hear this, too."

ROSSON: "He has to consider input from various sources. So ours would be one that might make it a little more difficult for him, I suppose. I think we have a difficult situation here."

ABRAMS: "My feeling is the president is really quite accustomed to facing very bad things. I mean, that's the job."

Laird Senate Foreign Relations Committee Statement

BRIEFER: "Sir, Mr. Laird requested that the following statement, which he made before the Senate Foreign Relations Committee in executive session on 19 November, be passed on to you." Items:

■ "The problem that, above all others, absorbs the attention, time, and energy of the president and the Department of Defense, the restoration of peace in Vietnam."

■ "Discuss not 'why Vietnam?' but 'why Vietnamization?'"

■ Cites Nixon talks of 14 May and 3 November, plus at Guam. Nixon Doctrine for Asia.

■ "In a sense Vietnamization is both a complement and an alternative to the Paris talks."

■ "Our single objective: the right of self-determination for the people of Vietnam."

■ Vietnamization "an end to the American combat role in Vietnam."

■ Reviews "the unproductive record of negotiations."

■ Nixon 14 May 1969 proposal: Cease-fire, withdrawal of outside troops, free elections, prompt release of prisoners of war, and observance of the Geneva Agreements of 1954 and 1962.

■ "The war in Vietnam continues because Hanoi and its suppliers will it to continue."

■ "When the present administration took office, a program of upgrading the training and equipment of South Vietnamese forces had begun. The goal of this program, however, was limited to increasing the combat capability of the forces of the Republic of Vietnam to the level needed to defeat the Viet Cong once all North Vietnamese forces had been withdrawn from the south. The Nixon administration early this year worked out a new objective with the government of South Vietnam for the training and equipping of the armed forces of South Vietnam. The objective we set was attainment by the South Vietnamese of a level of combat capability which would be adequate to defeat not only the Viet Cong, but the invading North Vietnamese forces as well."

ABRAMS: "Just a minute. We, we—I don't think—have discussed that with South

Vietnam. I have not been authorized to do that. Remember I raised—?"

BUNKER: "Yes."

ABRAMS: "Read that part over again."

SOMEONE: "That's not true in my case."

BRIEFER (continuing with Laird's statement):

■ Cites three factors regulating the size and frequency of U.S. troop reductions in Vietnam: progress in Vietnamization, level of enemy activity, and progress toward a negotiated peace.

■ "The threat to a sturdy, free, and independent South Vietnam is more than a military threat."

■ U.S. forces in Vietnam will have been reduced by more than 60,000 by 15 December 1969. "Further reductions are planned."

■ Cites evidence of progress, including reduction of refugees "by well over 50 percent, from 1,450,000 to 537,000 as of October 31st." Returned to homes or resettled in secure areas.

■ "Past policy envisioned a continued massive American military presence in South Vietnam until a satisfactory settlement was achieved by negotiation, or until North Vietnamese troops withdrew from South Vietnam. Present policy entails the replacement of American troops by South Vietnamese troops."

■ "Late last year the previous administration was still increasing U.S. forces. On September 25, 1968, my predecessor as secretary of defense said, 'We have not yet reached the level of 549,500 American troops in South Vietnam. We intend to continue to build toward that level. We have no intention of lowering that level at any time in the foreseeable future.'"

■ "There is an obvious difference between maintaining a massive American force in Vietnam until the North Vietnamese withdraw and reducing the size of the American force as South Vietnamese forces assume greater responsibility for the conduct of the war."

■ "There is an obvious difference between using American troops in Vietnam for the primary purpose of engaging enemy forces and using them in a supporting role for the primary purpose of assisting the South Vietnamese forces to achieve the capability to defend themselves."

■ "I can say to you that we are on the path that has the best chance of minimizing U.S. casualties while resolving the war in the shortest possible time without abandoning our basic objective."

■ "The success of Vietnamization depends primarily on the South Vietnamese."

■ "In my view the greatest obstacle to peace in Vietnam is the belief of the leaders in Hanoi, conditioned by the outcome of their war with France, that public opinion in this country will force the president to capitulate in order to end the war."

End of Laird remarks.

SOMEONE: Suggest "you get more mileage out of a big announcement in March than you do out of a smaller one in December."

ABRAMS: "Well, that kind of judgment I think really has to be made back there."

BUNKER: "I think—yes, only the president can make that."

SOMEONE: "You might be able to make 150,000 [in 1970], but you wouldn't want to say it publicly at this time."

ROSSON: "We don't feel that the situation is clear enough to permit us to do it now, but when <u>do</u> we make a recommendation?"

ABRAMS: "<u>Yeah</u>—if anybody <u>knows</u> when that is, <u>I'd</u> like to know."

ABRAMS: "We have told them what we <u>thought</u> could be done. I did that at the meeting in Honolulu before Midway, and again for the second increment. Now it's true that they haven't come out <u>precisely</u> that way—some 15,500 <u>more</u>—but it's close enough for government work. So that's the way it has gone along. I must say, too, that, certainly in retrospect, I think that it was a very smart move, because it <u>has</u> stimulated the Vietnamese, in my opinion, in a very substantial way."

BUNKER: "Sure."

ABRAMS: "And their reaction has been quite a good one. It's been serious, and they've gotten with it."

SOMEONE: "Is there anything magic about 150,000, sir? Isn't 100,000 a good round number?"

ABRAMS: "Let me say what's happened so far. A few weeks ago, not long ago, the ambassador and I sent in a message and said that, under the circumstances and so on, we didn't feel that either a time or number—or quantity—could be recommended and so on. And then yesterday, in my exit interview with Secretary Packard, I . . . reviewed this intelligence and brought up the pluses and so on, and that over the last six months, or since the . . . withdrawals, and pacification has continued to progress, ARVN has . . . expanded, and they've got more things operational, and although the leadership and the technical skills have been thinned out more to cover more structure, nevertheless you have to say that over this period . . . on the whole, even when you take into account those that have not improved at all—their overall performance has gone up."

ABRAMS: "And we took out 60,000—65,000—of structure, we reduced—B-52s have been reduced 50 percent, tac air 20 percent, and naval gunfire 22 percent, and so on. And the thing has continued to move ahead. But it's also been in a time when infiltration has been down, the enemy's <u>intensity</u> of his activities has been at a lower level, and so on. Then . . . I told him . . . my <u>tentative</u> conclusion was that, at this time, in the light of <u>all</u> of these developments, that I could not recommend a <u>date</u>, <u>a</u> <u>time</u> frame, or a <u>quantity</u>. On all this business of 100,000, 150,000, or any of those over a longer period of time, I urged that we stick with the 'cut and try.'"

SOMEONE: "Did he make any observation on that comment?"

ABRAMS: "Yes, yes, he did. He felt that the president was going to probably feel the need to make some announcement in December." "And then he got into the choices of the 50,000 or 100,000." "He said that, 'I appreciate'—he used <u>40,000</u>, actually—somewhere between 35 and 50, but he used 40,000 . . . he said, 'I can . . . see why it would be very painful for you if it occurred before April.'"

ABRAMS: "The first problem is to get Vien thinking of reinforcing in the delta, which he's not now thinking of."

ABRAMS: "Now these things we've talked about here this afternoon are extremely sensitive, and I think everybody here knows it. We can't talk about it and so on. I appreciate the small staff that you had working with us today, and I hope that they've been selected with the greatest of care."

NICKERSON: "Well, I selected mine to cover my ass. I don't know what the rest of you—." [Laughter]

ABRAMS: "But we can handle these things as long as we keep it that way. We have got, I think, one or two things left around here that haven't been published in the press—I mean so far."

BUNKER: "A very useful day as far as I'm concerned. I must say—as you know I was back [in the United States] in September–October. And General Abrams and I met with the president, and I again in October. And I think he is determined, and more determined than anyone I've talked to, to see this come out right. And I think he feels that the long-range effect of failure here could be much more serious than any other outcome of failure. So I think he's very strong and, as General Abrams said, I think the strongest man we've had in government in his determination to see it through. I must say, it's a bit depressing at home. I remember I said when I came back I was glad to be back where some constructive work was going on."

ABRAMS: "My feeling out of all this discussion that's occurred here this afternoon is that the 'cut and try' and—is the thing, and we're really not ready to come down on a time period and a quantity. Now, having said that—and that will be the thrust of our report—I think we should all appreciate what they're after. We listened to Secretary Laird's speech. No one's going to bug out on this thing. But we've got to take seriously, in every way we can find out how to do it, what they're after—this Vietnamization . . . developing of the Vietnamese. . . . I don't mean just getting them forward in the attack, but getting them up there and it's their plan and their command."

■ ■ ■

ABRAMS: "Now the other thing—now I know the fighting's important. I know they've got to, if the 324 Bravo comes chugging down [Route] 547 into Hue you've got to get out there and really lick them. But all of these things in the pacification, where the machinery of government had the philosophy that President Thieu is—building the village and the hamlet, and really building a base there and so on. I really think that, of all the things, that's the most important. That's where the battle ultimately is won."

ABRAMS: "These other things are kind of—you know, they're kind of campaigns that are necessary and so on, but the real thing is where those people are and the effectiveness of everything that goes on there. And that brings me down to the thing we've mentioned so many times, and I was reminded of it again when General Nickerson spoke about personal response. I think you all know what that program is, but I kind of wish we'd all been on that, you know, back at the <u>beginning</u>. But we've got to go from where we are. But the <u>attitude</u>, the <u>deportment</u>, the <u>conduct</u> of <u>every</u> one of our people, in uniform or civilian, is—just his demeanor toward—. A fellow that can't respect the Vietnamese has got to get into some kind of a job where they won't see him."

ABRAMS: "I mean, it's kind of that—. Because this guy, or some battalion commander who calls them 'dinks' or things like that—well, jeez, in the process of building pride and confidence and, you know, and national spirit and all that kind of stuff, this is—he does a lot of damage. Even talking about the <u>VC</u>, you know—there's really no point in calling <u>them</u> little yellow bastards, because <u>they're</u> Vietnamese, <u>too</u>. Now it may be that the <u>Vietnamese</u> here get mad at them, but that's the <u>good</u> thing if <u>they're</u> mad at them. But when <u>we</u> call them bad things we're calling the <u>Vietnamese</u> bad. Well, anyway—and all this truck driving and all that stuff, and pulling the girls' pigtails or—there's a lot of little things like that, and so on. And it just—we can't do, we can't <u>overdo</u> it in getting the right deportment and right conduct, or <u>reasonable</u>. Our people are, really, the vast majority of them, are really great fellows, and they do a great job. But they <u>have</u> got to—you've got to keep after them. Really a great part of the whole thing here is to <u>respect</u> these people and develop their pride and their confidence. I've often said the day that General Vien calls me on the telephone and <u>really gives me hell</u> is going to be the happiest day of my life. He won't <u>do</u> it—he's too much of a gentleman, but I wish he would."

24 NOV 1969: MACV Assessment Presented to General Vien

ATTENDEES: Gen. Vien, Gen. Abrams, MG Townsend, BG Potts, Col. Thiep.

ABRAMS: Points out how, unlike at this time the previous year, many of the enemy's units are understrength: "I think this is true out here in III Corps."

Laying the groundwork for discussion of moving some ARVN forces out of III Corps.

■ ■ ■

ABRAMS: "You know, they are anxious to release this COSVN Resolution 9 to the public. But they were telling me this morning they have a great deal of difficulty translating it. They've got the two or three very best men that they have, but in the Communist jargon they are using words and thoughts not common to the Vietnamese."

VIEN: "Yes, you are right."

ABRAMS: "So to get what it <u>really</u> says apparently is a very difficult translation job."

VIEN: "And sometimes the dialect is different."

POTTS: "Colonel Thiep and I had our very best translators on this over at the Document Center—42 pages. There's <u>so</u> much propaganda in there, too, that it's hard to get the meat out."

William Colby, Creighton Abrams, and
Ellsworth Bunker formed a triumvirate of
like-minded leaders who conceived and
prosecuted a better war. *Bunker Family
Collection*

Ambassador Ellsworth Bunker with Gen.
Creighton Abrams. South Vietnamese
Ambassador Bui Diem remarked on the
shared confidence of the two men, "walking
together." *U.S. Army Center of Military History*

Adm. John S. McCain Jr. served during 1968–1972 as Commander in Chief, Pacific. Said Abrams gratefully of his nominal boss, "He's supported every damn thing I've wanted to do." *U.S. Army Military History Institute*

Maj. Gen. Phillip B. Davidson Jr. had the interesting experience of serving as MACV J-2 Intelligence Officer for the last year General Westmoreland was in command and the first year under General Abrams. What changed under Abrams, Davidson told a theaterwide intelligence conference, "is that the commander is pleased with his intelligence, acts upon it, and has forced the staff to act upon it." *U.S. Army Military History Institute*

Before being named COMUSMACV, General Abrams was called home from Vietnam for consultations with President Lyndon Johnson, along with Vice President Hubert Humphrey and Gen. Earle Wheeler. Later in 1968, having taken command, Abrams was instructed by LBJ to "follow the enemy in relentless pursuit." *LBJ Library*

General Abrams with Gen. Andrew Goodpaster, his deputy during 1968–1969. Goodpaster spent part of the year helping Dr. Henry Kissinger set up a National Security Council system for President Nixon similar to that President Eisenhower had used during his tenure. *U.S. Army Military History Institute*

While serving as Army Chief of Staff (1964–1968) Gen. Harold K. Johnson sponsored the PROVN Study (Program for the Pacification and Long-Term Development of Vietnam), which provided the blueprint for General Abrams's approach to conduct of the war. *Frank X. Kaiser Collection*

Lt. Col. Donald Marshall played an important part in the PROVN Study, which stressed population security as the essential aspect of the war. When Abrams took command, he brought Marshall out to be his long-range planner for implementing PROVN's approach. *Marshall Family Collection*

Gen. George Brown, Gen. Andrew Goodpaster, General Abrams, William Colby, Lt. Gen. Frank Mildren, and Vice Adm. Elmo Zumwalt, members of the talented team that prosecuted a better war. Brown was later Air Force Chief of Staff and then Chairman of the Joint Chiefs of Staff; Goodpaster served as Supreme Allied Commander, Europe; Abrams became Army Chief of Staff; Colby was director of Central Intelligence; Mildren took a four-star NATO command; and Zumwalt became Chief of Naval Operations. *Colby Family Collection*

Gen. Robert E. Cushman, shown here as Commandant of the Marine Corps, commanded III Marine Amphibious Force in Vietnam during 1967–1969.
U.S. Army Military History Institute

Scenes of destruction such as this in Nha Trang were common in the wake of the 1968 Tet Offensive. The battlefield defeat suffered by the enemy was offset by a psychological victory in the United States. *Indochina Archive, University of California at Berkeley*

President Nguyen Van Thieu touring a center in the Mekong Delta set up to shelter refugees created by the enemy's Tet Offensive in 1968. *Indochina Archive, University of California at Berkeley*

An elder of Phu Thu village watches as caskets are aligned for burial of some of the 3,000 victims of an enemy massacre at Hue during the 1968 Tet Offensive. Calculated acts of murder, kidnapping, impressment, and terror were a key part of the enemy's way of waging war. *National Archives*

After President Lyndon Johnson stopped the bombing of North Vietnam on 1 November 1968, interdiction of the Ho Chi Minh Trail—shown here sinuously coursing south near the Mu Gia Pass—became the primary means of stemming enemy infiltration of men and matériel.
U.S. Air Force

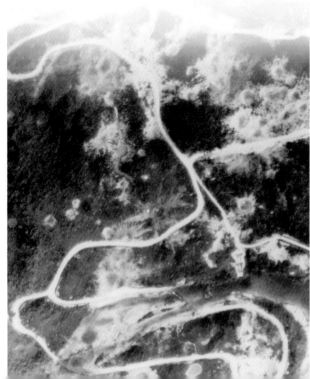

Gen. George S. Brown, shown here as Air Force Chief of Staff, commanded Seventh Air Force during 1968–1970. Regarding the attempt to destroy enemy trucks coming down the Ho Chi Minh Trail, Brown lamented: "It's the most frustrating experience I've ever had chasing these things!" Self-imposed rules of engagement prohibited wiping the equipment out en masse in North Vietnamese truck parks.

U.S. Army Military History Institute

General Abrams with retired Gen. Bruce C. Clarke, visiting Vietnam. Abrams had served under Clarke in the 4th Armored Division during World War II, then later at the Armor School at Fort Knox. When Clarke returned to Washington he urged President Lyndon Johnson to give M-16 rifles to the South Vietnamese, who were outgunned by enemy forces armed with AK-47s provided by the Chinese and Soviets. Secretary of Defense McNamara had refused to procure the better weapons for the South Vietnamese.

4th Armored Division Association

Gen. Ralph E. Haines Jr. visited Vietnam in August 1968 from his new post as Commander in Chief, U.S. Army, Pacific, and reported a severe budget crunch in Washington and urgency there about MACV's shifting the load to ARVN and being able to "show graphically that they are carrying a greater percentage of the load" before the November elections. *U.S. Army Military History Institute*

Robert Komer served as Deputy to the COMUSMACV for CORDS (Civil Operations and Revolutionary Development Support) under General Westmoreland (1967–1968). Shortly after General Abrams took command, Komer was replaced by William Colby. *Colby Family Collection*

General Abrams with Secretary of Defense Melvin Laird (left) and Gen. Earle G. Wheeler (right), Chairman of the Joint Chiefs of Staff, during their 1969 visit to Saigon. Laird's primary concern was to get U.S. forces out of Vietnam as rapidly as possible. *U.S. Army Military History Institute*

In May 1969 General Abrams conferred with President Richard Nixon at the White House, along with Secretary of Defense Melvin Laird and Gen. Earle G. Wheeler, Chairman of the Joint Chiefs of Staff. The first increment of U.S. withdrawals from Vietnam began two months later. *Nixon Presidential Materials Project, National Archives*

Col. Donn A. Starry served as Abrams's close-hold planner for the initial redeployment of U.S. forces, then took command of the 11th Armored Cavalry Regiment. In later years he reached four-star rank and headed the army's Training and Doctrine Command. *General Donn A. Starry Collection*

President Nixon meeting U.S. troops during his July 1969 visit to Saigon. During this same month unilateral U.S. troop withdrawals began with an initial increment of 25,000. *Nixon Presidential Materials Project, National Archives*

Marines board troopship at Danang as part of first increment of U.S. redeployment of forces from Vietnam in July 1969. By year's end 65,500 had been withdrawn from a peak strength of 543,400. *Indochina Archive, University of California at Berkeley*

U.S. tanks on the move near Khe Sanh in July 1969. Tanks, mechanized infantry, and armored cavalry made such an important contribution that General Abrams held them as long as he could during the progressive redeployment of U.S. forces. *National Archives*

Gen. Earle Wheeler, Lt. Gen. "Dutch" Kerwin, Secretary of Defense Melvin Laird, and General Abrams being briefed at Bien Hoa village in March 1969. During an autumn visit Wheeler lamented the difficulty of getting civilian leaders to understand they were dealing from a position of military strength in Vietnam under the new U.S. leadership. "If I sound bitter," he concluded, "well, I am!" *U.S. Army Center of Military History*

Gen. William B. Rosson, Deputy COMUSMACV during 1969–1970, tries out a bicycle captured from the enemy in the II Corps Tactical Zone. *Col. Paul F. Braim Collection*

Maj. Gen. George Forsythe, Commanding General, 1st Air Cavalry Division, with General Abrams at Phuoc Van in January 1969. A reporter once described Abrams as looking like "an unmade bed smoking a cigar," a characterization that delighted Abrams. *U.S. Army Center of Military History*

Lt. Gen. Julian J. Ewell commanded successively the 9th Infantry Division and II Field Force, Vietnam. Here he signs a joint artillery plan with ARVN Lt. Gen. Do Cao Tri, commanding III Corps. Ewell was widely known for his interest in body count, but by September 1969 would say openly, "I'm perfectly willing to admit that pacification's my primary mission." *National Archives*

Vice Adm. Elmo R. Zumwalt headed the "brown water navy" in Vietnam, then the entire navy as Chief of Naval Operations.
U.S. Army Military History Institute

Maj. Gen. William E. Potts served for three years as MACV's J-2 Intelligence Officer and the brilliant impresario of the Weekly Intelligence Estimate Updates. *U.S. Army Military History Institute*

Secretary of the Army Stanley R. Resor visited elements of the 1st Infantry Division during a trip to Vietnam. Resor told General Abrams in June 1970 that the U.S. was locked into further redeployments because of budget constraints and programmed lower draft calls. *National Archives*

General Abrams assigned Colonel George S. Patton to command the 11th Armored Cavalry Regiment, one of the lead outfits demonstrating that armored forces could operate effectively in the Vietnamese environment. *Patton Family Collection*

VIEN (after discussion in Vietnamese with Colonel Thiep): "Do you think it's proper to publish it?"

ABRAMS: "Oh, yes. I see no reason why we shouldn't. Do you?"

VIEN: "No."

ABRAMS: "And it may have some propaganda value."

VIEN: "All our people are ready." This morning sent a letter to President Thieu to get his approval.

29 NOV 1969: WIEU

ATTENDEES: Gen. Abrams, Gen. Rosson, Gen. Brown, LTG Mildren, MG Townsend, MG Conroy, MG Shaefer, MG Bautz, BG Gunn, BG Clement, BG Long, BG Vande Hey, BG Smith, BG Potts, BG Jaskilka, RADM Flanagan, BG Sykes, Col. Hanifen, Col. Gibson, Col. Penuel, Col. Cutrona, Col. Doody.

BROWN (re Barrel Roll): "Two significant things have occurred. One is that he's moved the main flow of his traffic westward. And we think—we don't know, but we think this is for two reasons. One is we think the packages are having some effect and pushing him back. But the other thing is we think he's going out there probably mainly because the main route structure's now so damn defoliated he doesn't have anywhere to hide. And he's over there where it's harder for us to find him and he can get under the trees and canopy if he's attacked."

BROWN: "The second significant feature is defenses. This month has been the most costly month of the war to us in Laos. Our losses are higher, our rate, computed yesterday, was 1.2 per 1,000, and the navy's rate is 1.0 per 1,000, which—the highest the navy has ever experienced is 0.6, and the highest we've ever experienced was 1.0. To be specific, we've lost 12 aircraft, and the navy has lost 3. We haven't lost a lot of crews. We've picked up most of the crews. But what we're doing about it—we really haven't been going after this AA the way we've got to. We're changing the plan and we're doubling, effective today, the number of aircraft that attack flak as a primary objective with special ordnance—Paveway and guided stuff that can hit." "They got [to] a point last year where it was reported [they were] chaining crews to guns."

■ ■ ■

ABRAMS: "Apparently what's coming up is they're going to make an effort in northern I Corps in early 1970." Stresses scarfing up stuff throughout December so "you've interfered a lot with the mechanism that makes that thing go."

■ ■ ■

ABRAMS: "What is the status of the publication of Resolution 9? Have they finished the translation?"

POTTS: "No, sir, they're still working on it, going over it very carefully. I've talked to the translators who've worked on it over at our Documents Center. These are all college professors who teach English, and know the dialects up north also, and they feel they've got a pretty good one. The only place that they may not be sure of is in some of the propaganda and political aspects. That part they weren't so sure of. But from a military point of view, what the objectives are, they're positive they have it airtight. Mr. Shackley says they'll work on it for about two weeks, he thinks. Then he'll let me know how they stand over there."

ABRAMS (impatient): "They've been muckering around with this thing for a long time. But it's one of those things I guess you can't do anything about."

6 DEC 1969: WIEU

ATTENDEES: Gen. Abrams, Amb. Colby, LTG Mildren, VADM Zumwalt, Mr. Kirk, MG Conroy, MG Dixon, Mr. Jacobson, MG Shaefer, MG Bautz, BG Gunn, BG Clement, BG Long, BG Vande Hey, BG Smith, BG Potts, BG Jaskilka, BG Cheadle, Col. Cavanaugh, Col. Hanifen, Col. Cutrona, Col. [Stewart? Stuart?].

BRIEFER: Two new infiltration groups detected in COMINT. At T-44 in BA 611 in Laos: Group 2165 (630 men) and Group 2168 (540 men). Projected for February 1970 arrival in COSVN.

MACV 1969 Infiltration Estimate: 102,900. MACV 1970 Infiltration Estimate: 5,700. 485 is the accepted strength for gap groups.

ABRAMS: "At least so far, there's nothing to get very excited about this rate of infiltration." Even if all gap groups accepted, only about 12,000 for 1970 thus far.

■ ■ ■

ABRAMS: "The 1st Cavalry's knowledge today is far more extensive than it was. And also they've done an awful lot in the training of their men. Well, the results show—they're much more skillful in the jungle."

ABRAMS: "But I'll tell you one thing, that 25th Division—woo, that's a cold-blooded outfit! They're really sharp—the U.S. 25th. There's no bullshit there. That's a very professional thing. I got no dancing girls in the briefing or any of that. Really tight."

SOMEONE: "Well, they're taking on a pretty good challenge right now in trying to upgrade the ARVN 25th Division, particularly that cavalry outfit."

ABRAMS: "I went up the other day, and I wound up at the 23rd ARVN, and was briefed by Colonel Canh, I guess it is. And when it was all over I told him that that was the most professional briefing by an ARVN division commander that I'd received since I'd been in Vietnam. His briefing not only covered all of the intelligence and operations and his organization for combat and so on. He went into considerable detail in the logistics—requirements, flow, amounts, and then into the personnel thing. And he's got a task force on replacements in the system, he's got a division replacement thing, and rotating battalions out and bringing replacements in, a short training program. And what they've done up there, I think has been really something. So one thing we've gotten out of Duc Lap and Bu Prang, we've now got a division. We know we've got a division that'll function as a division."

ABRAMS: Colonel Canh "removed the 47th Regiment, according to what the advisor told me up there. He went to Bu Prang himself and he told the—in the presence of about 50 people—he told the regimental commander of the 47th that he was a dirty yellow bastard, and forthwith removed him and his regiment from Bu Prang."

ABRAMS: "And then he put in the 53rd. They've changed regimental commanders in the 53rd in the last six weeks, and it's done very well."

JACOBSON: "Is the 'dirty yellow bastard' still in charge of the 47th?"

ABRAMS: "Yes, he is. Of course, that 47th, you know, belongs to the 22nd, so what Colonel Canh has done, he's turned that whole problem over to the corps commander and the division commander of the 22nd, and has canceled any invitation to return to the 23rd. [Laughing] So it's their problem."

ABRAMS: "The other interesting turn of events there . . . the 53rd's never been in Bu Prang. They've been out, in company size, which is quite hairy. But that's what they've been doing, and they've been quite successful at it." Re Canh: "He's really a pretty sound tactical thinker."

■ ■ ■

JACOBSON: "As you know, we've always carried Saigon in the C category, more for psychological reasons than anything else. But apparently General Minh gave Mayor Nhieu hell about his lousy security in Saigon—'the Americans rate you as C! By god, get with it here!' We're going to have to do something about that."

■ ■ ■

ABRAMS: "Troops that are supposed to fight—it's an unfortunate thing, but if they don't have any fighting, god they get in awful shape. Their senses get dulled. It's like in peacetime no one gives a damn who's in the medical detachment. But come the war, and god everybody commences, 'Here's a place where we need some quality here,' and so on. And 'Hell, get them up there at the head of the mess line! Stop pushing that medic—he's got to get his beer!' Well, the attitude—a whole lot of things change."

ABRAMS (re Mrs. Vien, who had owned a villa in Vung Tau leased to the Americans, but which had been turned back to her): "She doesn't have a lease or a contract with us anywhere. I'm quite certain she doesn't. And I must say it was at her initiative. She just wanted to terminate all dealings she had with the U.S. government in that regard."

7 DEC 1969: General Rosson Update

ROSSON: Begins by complaining about "those three books of cables that were dumped on my desk this morning. There're over 200 of them." Wants to be briefed so he doesn't have to wade through them.

13 DEC 1969: WIEU

ATTENDEES: Gen. Abrams, Gen. Rosson, Gen. Brown, Amb. Colby, LTG Mildren, VADM Zumwalt, Mr. Kirk, MG Townsend, MG Conroy, Mr. Jacobson, MG Shaefer, MG Bautz, BG Gunn, BG Clement, BG Long, BG Kraft, BG Vande Hey, BG Smith, BG Jaskilka, BG Cheadle, BG Sykes, Col. Cavanaugh, Col. Cutrona, Col. Hanifen, Col. Dessert.

BRIEFER: Two new infiltration groups (4048, 4049) identified during the week (were gap groups predicted for March 1969 arrival) (apparently held up) (now projected for December 1969 arrival). Derived from COMINT.

ABRAMS: "Well, I don't know what to think about this. This is quite an unusual development. See, I've been going along kind of on the basis that after a while, after a few months, this estimate was pretty hard. What's the total number of gap groups we had in '69? This is not going to drop gently into Washington."

BRIEFER: CINCPAC wants to drop gap groups 4050 and 4051. Bravely volunteered by the briefer: "We have gone back with a message suggesting that the whole gap group methodology for the 4000 series be reviewed, and that they hold before dropping—because of the implications. Many of the gap groups . . . have been confirmed in collateral. The gap group methodology has merit."

ABRAMS: "<u>Well</u>—I think I could agree with that if you were posing it as an alternate to '<u>destitute</u> of merit.' But <u>now</u>—you know, there are some things that you think you can lean on fairly—with some [confidence?] and not wind up in the cesspool. Well, I'm going to want to know more about this whole gap thing in '69 and so on in the . . . next couple of days, three days."

MACV 1969 Infiltration Estimate: 102,900. MACV 1970 Infiltration Estimate: 740.

ABRAMS: "Well, at this stage of the game I must say that this [what's been briefed] doesn't add up to a hell of a lot of infiltration."

SOMEONE: "The press has done its best to tell them where we're getting the information."

ABRAMS: "Well, they've been, of course, ably assisted by senior officials in the government."

■ ■ ■

BROWN: "Why are people so timid about that damn road building [by Chinese in Laos]? Why can't we go photograph it or bomb it or something?"

ABRAMS: "The <u>traffic</u> on this subject has just been about the most <u>disgusting</u> and <u>disgraceful</u>—! I get <u>nauseous</u> reading it! It's <u>absolutely</u> unbelievable!"

BROWN: "I thought there was some understandable reason that's been escaping me."

ABRAMS: "Well, all I can say is I've been unable to detect it. It's just <u>crap</u>. I don't see <u>how</u> they can—<u>eeeww</u>!"

SOMEONE: "Souvanna's all set to go do it. He said to hell with them. He doesn't want the road."

ABRAMS: "What Washington is standing on [laughing] is that the <u>king</u> should write a letter to Chou En Lai, Mao Tse Tung, and so on." [Saying thanks, the road is finished.] "This thing—well, let's get on with the other problems." "No, sincerely, it is <u>difficult</u> to see the line of reasoning—well, <u>I</u> haven't been able to."

COLBY: "The reasoning is, 'Don't stir up the nasty Chinese. They might get dangerous.'"

ABRAMS: "Which is what they're <u>proceeding</u> to <u>do</u>."

COLBY: "They're now proceeding to get dangerous on their own."

ABRAMS: "On the <u>Mekong</u>—they're going to be on the <u>Mekong</u>."

COLBY: "But it keeps it out of the headlines."

ABRAMS (re President Nixon's press conference answers to questions on Laos): "The guidance on that is that 'no comment' or 'the president's response speaks for itself, I have nothing to add.' Well, I think of the choices that the 'no comment' is by far the most <u>powerful</u>."

■ ■ ■

BRIEFER: "In Cambodia, an extremely sensitive CAS report has been received providing information on the shipment of Chinese military supplies for the VC through Cambodia. [***]. Information provided in the report closely parallels that which has been developed by U.S. intelligence. According to the source, Communist China commenced supplying the VC with military supplies through Cambodia in October 1966. He states that between October 1966 and April 1967, an estimated 15,000 tons of munitions arrived in Sihanoukville. The supplies destined for the VC were stored in Kompong Speu. MACV holds three arms carriers having arrived in Sihanoukville during this period, but holds only 740 tons of probable and possible munitions being delivered."

BRIEFER: "The source stated that between April 1967 and March 1969 an additional 5,000 tons of munitions, plus 3,000 tons of canned foods of various kinds, were delivered to the VC via Cambodia. In March 1969, 5,000 tons of munitions destined for the VC remained in Kompong Speu depot, according to the source. This was substantiated by other CAS reports. The source claims that a large portion of munitions destined for the VC was stored near the South Vietnamese frontier on the Cambodian side of the border. He states that only immediate tactical requirements were actually taken across the border."

BRIEFER: "VC representatives in Phnom Penh explained that they were deliberately stockpiled against the day when, for political reasons, supply through Cambodia might cease. Moreover, according to the source, they might still have requirements for arms after peace had officially been declared in the Republic. The source said that no Soviet supplies had passed through Cambodia to the VC. He explained that, because of Chinese insistence, Soviet aid to the VC consisted of an annual contribution of nine tons of gold which was sold on the London market. According to the report, between October 1966 and March 1969 20,000 tons of munitions were brought into Sihanoukville. For the time period, MACV carries 17,540 tons of munitions. This is only about 2,500 tons short of the total stated by the source. He also alleged that 10 percent of this total went to FARK. This would mean about 2,000 tons of munitions. This correlates well with MACV holdings, as we estimated approximately 1,800 tons were required by FARK for the same period."

ABRAMS: "What was the name of that CIA chap that came out here?"

POTTS: [***].

SOMEONE: "Fortunately he changed his mind before this report, sir. He's a believer now."

ABRAMS: "He is?"

SAME SOMEONE: "Yeah. But he was <u>hard</u> to convince."

ABRAMS: "Yeah, but he's the one that said out here—remember he told Davidson that 'there are political reasons why you should not arrive at the conclusion.' Remember? Davidson told us that here one morning, right here at this table."

■ ■ ■

ABRAMS: "I was up there the other day in the 1st [ARVN] Division, and that division just looks <u>better</u> every time you <u>go</u> there." "That Camp Carroll out there is probably the <u>finest</u> constructed fire base in <u>all</u> of South Vietnam. Another thing that's happened in the 1st Division that's <u>quite</u> noticeable—any one of their fire bases you go to, there's <u>no</u> garbage, there's <u>no</u> crap, it's <u>neat</u>. The preparations they've got for sappers out there at Camp Carroll, that goddamn tanglefoot, they must have a hundred, maybe over a hundred, meters. And it's in <u>good</u>. Christ, it's been <u>surveyed</u> in. And then inside the base, you know, it's all compartmented, with interwoven wire, and the bunkers are <u>real</u> stout. It's <u>all</u> business, it's <u>all</u> business."

ROSSON: "Another thing that's always impressed me about that outfit—their commanders."

ABRAMS: "Yeah, yeah. They don't allow <u>any</u> staff officers to talk. That's right. You go up there to their attack CP, and the briefing's given by Colonel Giai. He doesn't—I don't mean by this that they—they don't <u>underrate</u> the enemy. They give him his due. It's really impressive. As I say, I think that Camp Carroll's the strongest fire base we've got in South Vietnam—of <u>anybody</u>, U.S. or anything else. It's safer than the <u>Pentagon</u>."

■ ■ ■

ABRAMS: "Up in Thua Thien, there's a district where there's a battalion of the 101 working exclusively for the district chief. They've got a combined TOC. And they've got the DIOCC right in there adjacent to it."

SOMEONE: "They really are working that VCI."

ABRAMS: "What he did, he took the two best officers he had in his battalion—the sharpest—and put them in his 2 [intelligence] section. And apparently they've got a pretty good district 2." "But the climax up there was a sergeant, an American sergeant, a platoon leader. And they brought him in to explain what he'd been doing. His platoon had been put in this village to help train the PSDF and PF, work on whatever things that the villagers were interested in working on—had a small dam they were trying to get built. This sergeant had a total of 17 months' service, and of course he doesn't have any briefing, he doesn't have any charts, anything. He just explains what he and his men have been doing. And I'll tell you, you can have all the goddamn theories, and you can put out all the guidance and the directives and so on, but the <u>truth</u> of the matter is if this moves ahead it's because of guys like him. <u>Clearly</u> sensitive. You know, he really <u>understands</u> the thing."

ABRAMS: "For instance, he says, 'We got working there in the village—.' Well, he described about training the PF—going out with them on ambushes. Christ, he says they were smoking, talking, and didn't really have any plan. 'And,' he said, 'we talked about it among ourselves.' He said, 'We decided that the problem was whether we were going to have the <u>patience</u> to change them.' Isn't that something? 'So,' he said, 'we'—talking about his platoon, see?— 'kept at it. Now, they're really good.' He says now he sends one American and, he says, <u>they</u> lay it all out. 'When they've finished it, we don't tell them anything. <u>They</u> lay it out. Then we go around and <u>check</u> it.' And he says they do real good—no more smoking, no more talking."

ABRAMS: "Then they got—there's a small river, not far away. They went down there to bathe, a few of them at a time. Then, he says, 'we got taking the kids down there. And,' he said, 'we took all the kids down there. And,' he said, 'we'd get them in there, teaching them to swim, and the medic tells me it's done a lot of good. He says all these skin sores are pretty much all gone. It's been good hygiene.' Then they got them—water sports. Found a hell of a lot of them could swim. And he said, 'I don't know <u>why</u> they didn't wash down there—lots of water.' Then, on [these] work things that the villagers were trying to do—repair this, fix up a small road there, and so on, he said, 'We talked about that, and we thought it best if we let two or three of our guys just work along <u>with</u> them—just kind of help carry the sand, that kind of thing.' He says, 'so that when it was done it would <u>really</u> be theirs. We just kind of helped them.' <u>God</u> <u>damn</u>! And he says, 'You know this—.' He says they had to bring the sand and the rock up from the river for this dam. He says, 'You know, they've got a system where they have a stick and you've got a basket on each end.' And he says, 'General, there's a trick to that.' He says, 'You've got to have just the right kind of step, or that damn thing just sways back and forth and it'll throw you down.' He says, 'I guess the villagers had <u>more</u> fun watching us try to master that than anything we did.'" "He comes <u>through</u> <u>so</u> <u>sincere</u>. He's <u>really</u> <u>credible</u>."

ABRAMS: "I ran into a captain down in the delta who's the same kind of a guy. Now this sergeant was drafted. He was in a pre-med course, and he was working as a ward boy to help pay his way, and that's when he was drafted. And I said, 'Are you going back and take that up again?' 'Yes, sir,' he said, 'in due time, in due time.'"

ABRAMS: "Oh, yeah, one other thing the sergeant—I'll go back to the sergeant for just a minute. Telling about the training program—well, he had machine-gun instruction. He said, 'We skipped that. They're really better machine gunners than we are.' [Laughs] He said, 'We skipped that after the first try.'"

14 DEC 1969: Commanders Briefing

ATTENDEES: Gen. Abrams, Gen. Rosson, Gen. Brown, Amb. Colby, LTG Mildren, VADM Zumwalt, LTG Corcoran, LTG Zais, LTG Nickerson, MG Wetherill, MG Conroy, MG Townsend, MG McCown, Mr. Jacobson, MG Shaefer, MG Bautz, BG Gunn, BG Vande Hey, BG Smith, Col. Cavanaugh, Col. Healy, Col. Dessert, Col. Hanifen.

BRIEFER (re Phase III troop deployments): "On 15 December in Washington President Nixon will announce a new U.S. troop ceiling of 434,000 to be reached by 15 April 1970. This will mean a redeployment of 50,000 within the next four months."

ABRAMS: "In the meantime, the ambassador <u>has</u> received a message from the secretary of state on the same subject. In General <u>Wheeler's</u> <u>message</u>, with considerable precision, he pointed out that the announcement would be a new troop ceiling of 434,000 to be reached by April 15th. The secretary of state's message says that the president would announce a reduction of 50,000. Now, in the arithmetic game—now I have not gone back to the <u>Chairman</u>. I'm just sitting here quivering about <u>how</u> this is really going to turn <u>out</u>. As the Chairman has reported it to <u>me</u>, it's the way we've been fighting to have it <u>done</u>. See, we're going to be—we're about 10,000 understrength, I think, right now. We're at 474,000. And if the president says we've got to cut 50,000, we're apt to be snarled up in 424,000. Of course, I'd ask you all to consult with your chaplains. Anything, any pressure we can bring to bear—."

SOMEONE: "In the vernacular of the planner that's called being double dipped."

ABRAMS: "There is an element of uncertainty here. We just have to await the speech."

BRIEFER: "As you were briefed on 22 November, the next 100,000 reduction was reviewed and the marine-heavy option was recommended to the Chairman and to CINCPAC for planning further redeployments." "It delays redeployment of four brigades and one division base when compared to the army-heavy option. CINCPAC supports this plan, but as yet no comment on the troop composition has been received from the Joint Chiefs of Staff."

BRIEFER: "Due to the enemy threat and the upcoming Tet period, it is planned to withdraw the bulk of the forces as late in Phase III as possible."

ABRAMS: "The president's speech, I think, will occur Tuesday morning our time. It will be Monday evening Washington time." "It's very important that this not be leaked here before the president speaks." "This has been stressed with President Thieu, and he probably will not discuss it with members of his cabinet or the vice president. He leaked it the last time—the vice president."

ABRAMS: "The way things stand today, I think that tactically we can go ahead with the 1st Division." "We're not placing anything in jeopardy, I don't believe. However, the I Corps thing is a little different nature, and I talked with General Vien about that. And I think both he and we are going to have to consider some adjustments in our dispositions, because the situation right now is just not that good in Quang Nam to take that amount of force out." Vien will use either marines or airborne to reinforce there.

ABRAMS: "So III Corps, I think, is going to wind up losing <u>more</u> than the 1st Division. At least you ought to be considering that possibility."

ABRAMS (re choosing the marine-heavy option, thereby retaining the four combat brigades): "Under the circumstances, . . . I don't think there's a hell of a lot of choice. There's just one route to go—that makes sense."

BROWN: "There's one other item of resistance to this scheduled optimum of redeployment, in addition to the transportation guys, and it's going to be the services. For any units they want to lay up, like some of our stuff in the air force, they're going to want to get that out as early in the fiscal year as they can so they'll <u>save</u> a buck."

ABRAMS: "Yeah, that's right. The services, under the financial pressures that they're under—." "For instance, the army is really fighting this marine-heavy thing. It's financial. And that's all right. That doesn't make me mad or anything. I understand the kind of thing they're—." "But we've got to support what we honestly believe is the best thing, the best stand for us to take in the overall picture. You're quite right, the services are going to have their problems. But [laughing] we've got a few here, too."

MILDREN: Two weeks' stand-down was adequate for the 9th Division and the 3rd Brigade of the 82nd (because they transferred their equipment here in-country). But the 1st Division is listed as a baseline unit. If we have to ship all that equipment, and meet Department of Agriculture standards (for sanitizing the equipment for reentry into the United States), we'll need more time.

ABRAMS: "AMC is controlling the disposition of this equipment. Some of it will go to Europe, some of it will go back to the States, some will stay here, some of it will go to Korea."

■ ■ ■

ABRAMS: "I was talking to Bill Colby this morning. I want to do what I can to try to improve the kind of advisors we've got. But I think we're kind of hung up on what's quality. We have a tendency to look and see if he's been to the Command & General Staff College, to the War College, whether he's been promoted out of zone. And what we need are guys that can lead in this kind of a thing. For instance, that sergeant we heard up there the other day. If there were some way to put lieutenant colonel's leaves on him, I'd back him as a province senior advisor. It's human relations. It's a respect for the Vietnamese. It's a sensitivity, a sensitivity to humans. These are the qualities that are important."

ABRAMS: "Well, for instance, say that the guy that should be the advisor to an ARVN infantry regiment is a guy that commanded a U.S. infantry battalion. Nope. If that's what you use, I think you're making a mistake, because there are some guys who have commanded, and maybe commanded quite well, a U.S. infantry battalion that just haven't got the sensitivity, the understanding of human relations, a natural human respect for other humans, just because they're human. And it's these kind of guys—and you don't get in and tell them, 'You do this' and 'You do that,' you know. Somehow it's the fellows who know how to pull them out, so that it's theirs—. It's true that he's influencing it, but he's influencing it in a very sophisticated way, so the fellow that's being influenced winds up thinking that he did it all himself. And those are the guys who are worth their weight in gold in Vietnam at this time."

SOMEONE: "I had a perfect example of that. I had a new brigade commander. I won't name him. He comes with a brilliant record. Commanded a battalion over here in 1966. I stood with him in the Ia Drang Valley. He's a crackerjack. He's big, strong, square-jawed, Popeye arms. Soldiers love him. I went down to get his first briefing after he'd taken over the brigade. The first thing he tells me is 'Captain [Viet?] in [Nam La?] is no good. We've got to move him.' Well, Captain Viet in Nam La [or Hoa?] is just a little guy. But, Christ, he's been through it for two years. He's been wounded twice. He's had a jeep shot up under him. He's been right out there on the western fringes, just . . . served his country well, and he's got a pair of balls. Now this guy says we've got to move him. He says we've got to stop the goddamn <u>woodcutters</u> from going out there, too." "Then he says to me he's going to put some CS [high-powered tear gas] in on them. God, I was only there five minutes and I filed right through that dugout. I <u>just</u>—<u>goddamn</u>! Well, we had about a 30-minute one-sided conversation, right after that."

ABRAMS: "I'll tell you, the guy is dangerous because you're probably <u>not</u> going to be able to change him. That's the unfortunate part. And you're <u>certainly</u> not going to change him into the kind of a guy <u>I'm</u> talking about."

■ ■ ■

ABRAMS: "Now, I want to tell you something else. I sat there and listened to that briefing in the 101. Oh, I <u>really</u> was <u>cringing</u>. Now by their standards it was absolutely faultless. But it's the mouthing of a lot of <u>goddamn</u> <u>sterile</u> <u>doctrine</u>, plus a lot of bragging and so on. And one of the things—see, they've sort of discovered Christmas. And I remembered being up there one day—I'm not trying to pat you [Zais?] on the back, but I was up there one day when <u>you</u> had the division and your assistant G-5 got up there. Really an unimpressive-looking character. Anybody that had his photograph would never accept him."

ABRAMS: "But this guy went on and told what the division was doing, and how it was doing it, in these districts and so on. The guy was <u>really</u> terrific. He <u>understood</u>. And he understood how to get things done <u>with</u> them and so on, without ever causing the system to tremble and shake and get horrified and so on—but <u>still</u> getting <u>results</u>. In fact, I was so impressed with that later on—Dick Stilwell was temporarily—Cushman, I think, was on leave—and Dick was holding the sack up there. And we went down and visited the Americal. And they gave their briefing and wanted to know if there were any questions afterward. 'No. I want to meet with General Gettys and General Stilwell in General Gettys's office.' Went over there, and I said, 'This <u>shit's</u> got to stop. You're <u>not</u> in the <u>ball</u> <u>game</u>. You don't—. You're not <u>talking</u> about this <u>problem</u>. It's <u>horrible</u>!' And I told him, I said, 'I want the principal staff taken up to the 101. I want them briefed up there on what they're doing and how they're doing it.' And I said, 'One of the guys that's got to be in this briefing is that assistant G-5.' And I said, 'I know you don't like it, but that's what you've got to do. And I want it <u>done</u>! You've got to get in bed with the 2nd ARVN,' and so on. Well—."

■ ■ ■

ABRAMS: "The other thing I wanted to mention here is these atrocities. This is a r-e-a-l—this is a <u>real</u> problem. It's captivated—I'm told it's captivated the whole press in the United States, <u>TV</u>. And of course it's got a lot of guys talking on hearsay and rumors and gossip that they heard. And all of these things are having to be traced down. So we can't do <u>enough</u>, we can't do <u>too</u> <u>much</u> in getting after the way our commanders go about their business, and the way our units, the way our men, handle themselves. <u>I</u> think <u>I</u> understand how difficult the problem is, but we've <u>really</u> got to stand for the <u>right</u> way to do it. And cutting off the woodcutters, or the fishermen—I'm <u>preaching</u> to the <u>choir</u>, but—and I <u>know</u> that, that everybody in <u>this</u> <u>room</u>—but I just tell you, we <u>can't</u> make <u>too</u> much effort on that."

. . .

ABRAMS (re U.S. troop unit newspapers): "It's the newspapers that I don't think give a—. You can't get the fighting out of them, but it's so <u>blatantly</u> the main subject of the whole goddamn thing. How Charlie Troop slaughtered 85. And, you know, it's got—that's <u>really</u> the thing. To whatever extent newspapers could begin to get some balance in there and try to—. I know that it's <u>still</u> important to beat the enemy, and when you catch him to really work him over. I'm doing the best <u>I</u> can with the B-52s and all the rest. I <u>know</u> that that's still part of the <u>war</u>."

ABRAMS: "But this other is <u>now</u>—it just keeps growing <u>every</u> day in its criticality and its <u>importance</u>. And it has to do with the political strength that this government can muster. It has to do with the commitment of these <u>people</u> to the government. And all of us, we <u>represent</u> it. And, incidentally, that ought to come out in our <u>briefing</u>—when visitors come around and so on. It isn't just the goddamn <u>kill ratio</u>. That's <u>something</u>, but there's a lot of other parts of this. And a visitor who comes and spends an hour with you—he ought to sense that. I'm not talking in terms of <u>hiding</u> the other, or trying, you know, to submerge it and say, 'Oh, no, we never <u>kill</u> anybody. I mean, we're just all—.' I'm not saying <u>that</u>. But <u>they</u>, and <u>we</u>—they should realize that we see more, there's <u>more</u> involved in this than just killing the enemy. There's a building on the other side."

ABRAMS: "You know, if we could have had the candid camera hidden up there the other day, and recorded that sergeant. He's got <u>no</u> doctrine, <u>no</u> theory. And he likes <u>people</u>."

. . .

ABRAMS: "This country <u>is</u> fighting for its life."

20 DEC 1969: WIEU

ATTENDEES: Gen. Rosson, Adm. McCain, Gen. Brown, Amb. Colby, LTG Mildren, VADM Zumwalt, MG Townsend, MG Conroy, Mr. Jacobson, MG Shaefer, MG Bautz, RADM Butts, BG Gunn, BG Clement, BG Kraft, BG Vande Hey, BG Smith, "and after a long vacation BG Potts," BG Cheadle, BG Sykes, Col. [Steman?], Col. Hanifen, Col. Gibson, Col. Hofmann, Col. Cutrona, Col. Doody.

BROWN (re attacking enemy SAM launchers): "What we'll do, Admiral, if we— obviously if we find those things in Laos, no problem, we'll destroy them. If we determine that they're just across the border, which is a possibility, I think, we can't rule out, or <u>additional</u> ones just across the border, I think our options are two. One, we lay this out and come forward for specific authority to attack SAMs that are deployed that now pose a threat. The other is to go ahead with our normal reconnaissance program in the likelihood we'll be fired on. In this case we then are authorized to go, and we sort of clean these up while we're [words unclear]. That's—you know, I think that's sort of fudging on our normal authority . . . unless they fire a SAM. If they fire a SAM, we've got authorization to go in and clean up the SAM site and associated facilities."

ROSSON: "Frankly, I think that's the way to do it. I would tend to <u>bend</u> the authority a little bit."

Deputy COMUSMACV Rosson taking this position in the absence of General Abrams.

BROWN: "I don't want to pose this as a problem for solution at the moment. I only want to flag the thing, because—we've got two specific requests for authorization in now that haven't even been <u>responded</u> to. You remember the one was to permit us to overfly the border with a passive aircraft to illuminate a target for a laser strike, a strike in Laos. They haven't ever told us yes or no. They haven't answered the mail on that one. That's been up there now for two months. The other one was your cable asking for authority to get in there and clean out the stuff immediately across the border, and <u>I</u> didn't see a response to that."

BROWN: "But that's—you know, if somebody wants to attack in North Vietnam, that's the place to do it, because there're no civilians involved, no communities, no hamlets or villages. It's out there in the mountains, and there's not a damn thing out there that isn't military. And there're supplies out there by the ton. Trucks—they don't even bother to camouflage them or revet them. We could have a field day there for a couple of days."

MCCAIN: "I'm a firm believer in this goddamn thing of bending the rules, see."

BROWN: "We can get fired at any time we want to get fired at."

MCCAIN: "Right, right."

BROWN: "And then, once fired on, we can attack. And of course you can parlay this into an attack on <u>Hanoi</u> if you want to carry it to the extreme, which is obviously far beyond anything we're thinking about." "You know, from time to time we've waited until they've—we're ready, and we've got the thing planned, and then we've gone across there with [words unclear] artillery, as the Chairman says, and really laid on an attack. It's led to many queries. You know, we get questions. But nobody says don't ever do it again. And nobody's ever slapped us on the wrist for it. Maybe it's about time to, you know, try another one."

27 DEC 1969: Commanders WIEU

ATTENDEES: Gen. Abrams, Gen. Rosson, Amb. Colby, VADM Zumwalt, LTG Corcoran, LTG Ewell, LTG Zais, VADM Weisner, MG Wetherill, MG Mabry (for LTG Mildren), Mr. Firfer, MG Townsend, MG McCown, MG Dixon (for Gen. Brown), Mr. Jacobson, MG Bautz, BG Gunn, BG Clement, BG Kraft, BG Vande Hey, BG Smith, BG Potts, BG Sykes, Mr. Wilson (for Mr. Vann), Mr. Cruikshank (for Mr. Whitehouse), Col. Jackson (for MG Shaefer), Col. Black (for MG Conroy), Col. Steman, Col. Hanifen, Col. Cavanaugh, Col. Hofmann (for BG Jaskilka), Col. Cutrona, Col. Martin (for BG Cheadle), Col. Doody (for Mr. Kirk).

ABRAMS: "One of the things that puzzled me in the secretary of defense's office— he had a pencil-written tabulation of infiltration arriving in South Vietnam in '68 and '69 through November 30th. And his total through November 30th of '69 was 67,000. And I don't know <u>where</u> he got that."

BRIEFER: "Sir, that's approximately the strength that the ARVN carry."

ABRAMS: "Uh-huh."

POTTS: "See, the ARVN does not have access to anything really but collateral."

BRIEFER: "But it is higher than our collateral. Our collateral figure for 1969's approximately 35,000."

ABRAMS: "Well, that explains that."

ABRAMS: "On that infiltration—even for, even taking all the gap groups and adding them in, and even for III Corps, I don't see it as much more than a subsistence level. In other words, what we know of infiltration now just doesn't add up to any major enemy effort—in terms of the kind of efforts he's put on in the past. Not yet."

■ ■ ■

NNNABRAMS (to Corcoran): "I just worry about the 42nd [ARVN Regiment]. Christ, they haven't killed five enemy in the last six months. And it just worries me that the 28th Regiment at 15 percent strength will come boiling out of Cambodia, headed for Dak To, and the 42nd Regiment just won't be able to find their ass with both hands to get out there, you know, and—. I worry about it."

CORCORAN: "Well, I am, too."

■ ■ ■

EWELL: "What I'm afraid of is the North Vietnamese will propose cease-fire and we'll, Christ, we'll empty out our billfold, say, 'OK, right now, sign right here.'"

ABRAMS: "O-h-h—let me just say one thing. . . . Our Commander in Chief doesn't see the problem that way. See, this is a hell of an important thing for our country. And he of all people is looking way down the road. I don't think anybody is going to come up and sell him anything cheap."

EWELL: "Where the hell did Secretary Rogers get this crap he's putting out about infiltration being down?"

SOMEONE: "The ARVN figures."

ABRAMS: "All I've got to say about that is he's not the Commander-in-Chief."

EWELL: "Good."

ABRAMS: "Anyway, for better or worse, that's where my chips are. And I'm probably like you—I don't listen to staff." [Laughter]

■ ■ ■

ABRAMS (re "the trend in what's happened the last three or four months in who's making a contribution—weapons, KIA"): "It's kind of interesting. In terms of results, which is enemy killed, weapons captured, caches, and so on, the ARVN contribution stayed at about the same—26 percent, 27 percent. And U.S. and Free World percent has gone down. And, at least percentage-wise, that slack has been taken up by the Territorial Forces. And this has happened since August."

SOMEONE: "It's the nature of the war."

ABRAMS: "Yes, that's right. But it's also—you know, I was always wondering about what the hell would we get for that investment in those 300,000 M16s— you know, all that? Well, it's commencing to show."

■ ■ ■

BRIEFER: JCS approved redeploying only one RLT in Phase III instead of two as proposed by MACV. Substituting a brigade of the 4th Infantry Division. "During the exchange of messages exploring the marine-heavy versus army-heavy alternatives with the Chairman, it became clear that the JCS considered it desirable to retain appropriate combat representation from all services in the Republic of Vietnam until the support transitional level was reached. The support transitional level was formerly called the residual force level."

BRIEFER: Rationale for MACV's having recommended the marine-heavy option (not approved by JCS): "We retained 3 brigades with 11 infantry battalions for a number of months longer in 1970, which reduces the risks to achieving our goals. The price we pay will be the loss of approximately 116 marine air sorties per day."

ABRAMS: "You know, we don't _have_ any pool of spaces. And everybody wants to add something on, and nobody wants to give up anything. We've got to come off of _that_ crap, too! Incidentally, too, when they—when the Vietnamese make up their minds to do something, it doesn't make any goddamn difference whether we agree with it or not _here_—in case anybody doesn't _know_ that. When they want to _do_ something, they _do_ it! Whether we've funded it, whether we'll support it—mox nix. They _do_ it! And this running and saying somehow MACV should _intervene,_ it's just—that's so much crap. If they want to do it, they're going to do it. And if they don't want to do it, they ain't gonna do it."

■ ■ ■

BRIEFER: Cites "the real purpose of the area security concept, to get the regular forces out of the populated areas and into the field, where they can focus on the main force enemy."

BRIEFER: End November 1969: 92.5 percent of the population in A/B/C category. In A/B: 56.7 percent with Saigon included; 64.9 percent excluding Saigon. Estimated 500,000 people under VC control, about 3 percent of the national total. Twenty-nine provinces have A/B/C of 90 percent or better.

BRIEFER: "The division of the PSDF into combat and support categories has been completed. There are now more than 1,300,000 men and women in the combat arm, and approximately 1,750,000 elderly men, women, and children in the support arm." Four-day PSDF training sessions are scheduled nationwide during December 1969.

BRIEFER: "The Phuong Hoang program against the VC infrastructure remains a problem area in the GVN's pacification effort, although there are indications it is beginning to take hold. November was the fourth month in a row in which the monthly goal of 1,800 VCI neutralized was exceeded." "Since the beginning of the year about 18,000 have been neutralized."

BRIEFER: Chieu Hoi for the year are at about 44,000, or about twice the 1968 total. "The insertion of RF/PF outposts is an important factor in the high returnee rate."

BRIEFER: Refugee population at 30 November 1969: 416,000. Over 1,000,000 less than at the peak of nearly 1.5 million in March 1969. Includes: 175,000 temporary refugees, 145,000 in resettlement projects, and about 100,000 out-of-camp refugees.

BRIEFER: Describes a November 1969 nationwide campaign to publicize the Phuong Hoang program. Posters and photos of VCI put up, leading to their capture. "Information obtained from them has led to subsequent arrests."

ABRAMS (skeptical): "The facts are that it went <u>down</u> in November." [Compared to October.] "<u>Right</u>? Well, let's not get <u>cheering</u> the new program until we've got some positive evidence. Let's not <u>mesmerize</u> ourselves. I mean, I <u>agree</u> with you. <u>I've</u> been entranced by some of these examples, <u>too</u>. They even told a story about one fellow, turned himself in to <u>complain</u> because they'd published a photo of some <u>other</u> guy and said <u>he</u> was the district chief, and [really] he was the <u>deputy</u>. And this guy turned himself in and said <u>he</u> was the <u>chief</u>. They'd made a bad mistake! Well, I enjoy those, too, war stories and all that. But let's not get the eye off the ball."

■ ■ ■

COLBY: New Hamlet Evaluation System briefed to General Abrams yesterday. Have his approval to brief it to the Mission Council and the GVN. "Cannot be implemented without the GVN's acceptance and approval." The revised system is called HES 70.

BRIEFER: "It has been under development since mid-1968." Operating in parallel with the current HES since July 1969. The current HES gets district advisor graded input on 18 pacification indicators, plus 10 questions on matters at hamlet level. Among problems: "Each advisor is required to make subjective assessments of several complex criteria within each category." Need training and experience to produce reliable results. Also does not monitor several significant elements related to pacification. Does not monitor private sector economic activity or political activity.

BRIEFER: Goals of HES 70 include reducing "the degree of subjectivity to obtain a more uniform evaluation system." To be put into operation in July 1970. Advantages: "Question set is objective. Advisors report observed conditions rather than assign hamlet ratings." Elected officials? Night reaction forces? Organized PSDF? "Total amount of information has been expanded. One hundred thirty-nine questions cover 19 areas at village and hamlet level. Some are monthly, some quarterly. Three major areas: security, political, development. Scoring not done by advisor on the ground.

BRIEFER: Running old and new systems in parallel. Maximum difference about 6 percent. On average HES 70 the percent of the population secured comes out about 5 percent lower than HES (for A/B/C countrywide, apparently).

ABRAMS: Points out that "the same fellow filled out HES and HES 70."

BRIEFER: "Fifty-eight percent of all hamlets maintained their same rating." "Ninety-seven percent were rated within one letter category of their original HES score."

■1970

In 1970 redeployment of U.S. forces from Vietnam continued, with another 140,000 troops departing during the year. Fiscal constraints compounded the effects of the drawdown, especially in reducing available sorties by B-52 bombers and tactical aircraft.

In Paris, Henry Kissinger began secret talks with the North Vietnamese, supplementing the conspicuously unproductive open sessions. Enemy forces maintained a low level of combat operations in South Vietnam, relying heavily on terrorism, attacks by fire, and low-level harassing and sapper attacks.

In mid-March Cambodia's Prince Norodom Sihanouk was overthrown by General Lon Nol, who promptly closed the port of Sihanoukville to enemy logistics traffic and issued an ultimatum telling Communist forces to leave the country. In late April, in a surprising and somewhat controversial development, ARVN and U.S. forces conducted limited incursions into Cambodia to seize or destroy enemy supplies stockpiled in sanctuaries in the border region. The two-month operation achieved considerable success in clearing out base areas and setting the enemy back logistically. Later in the year further operations by ARVN acting alone further disrupted enemy logistical activities and denied him easy access to the Republic of Vietnam.

President Thieu implemented the Land to the Tiller program of land reform, resulting in a million hectares of land being designated for distribution to some 500,000 families. Most villages and hamlets conducted elections to choose their governing officials, a large number of whom then received training at national centers. Expansion and upgrading the armament of the Territorial Forces (Regional Forces and Popular Forces) continued, with these elements being made part of the regular armed forces, of which they by then constituted fully half.

Near year's end the U.S. Congress enacted a statute prohibiting U.S. combat forces or advisors from taking part in operations in Laos and Cambodia.

8 JAN 1970: Blue Ribbon Defense Panel Briefing

ATTENDEES: Gen. Rosson, Mr. Fitzhugh, Mr. Jackson, Mr. Buzhardt, Mr. Powell, MG Shaefer (J-5), Mr. Howard, MG Bautz (J-3), BG Potts (J-2), BG Cheadle.

POTTS: Explains that current intercepts reveal what is taking place in Binh Trams 18 and 34. "A *binh tram* is a station that provides coordination, support, and rest for these infiltration groups coming down from North Vietnam." "Last year we read only Binh Tram 18, called Binh Tram 8 at that time."

SOMEONE: Asks why we "leave them alone." It is explained that they are in North Vietnam, currently off-limits.

POTTS: "And it is to our advantage not to interfere at all. The fact that we are reading this traffic and getting this advance information makes them very valuable to us."

POTTS (re intelligence): "We started out pretty much on a shoestring. But this thing has been developed through an evolutionary approach to reach what we think is optimum now. It is very solid and very good. We did not have this, sir, at the beginning, or even at the end of the first year." "General Rosson was here when it started, and I was here, and General Bautz." "The direct support concept is something we created here." "We fought hard for it."

■ ■ ■

ROSSON: "One of the problems we face is jurisdictional disputes."

SOMEONE: "That's what we're looking for."

ROSSON: "Between CIA and NSA and DIA . . . and that type of thing, and hassles between the service intelligence agencies and the Joint Staff. Now I can say I'm not aware of a single problem of any consequence to us out here."

POTTS: "There is no conflict in any way here in Vietnam between the coordination and cooperation of CAS, NSA, and the military."

SOMEONE: Asks about CAS.

POTTS: "The CIA. Controlled American Source is their terminology overseas." "Mr. Shackley, who is the senior CAS representative in-country, I see his people weekly." [***] Shackley gives them to this man, he makes his trip up there, he checks out my material, and it comes back to me. Three of these high points that we discussed this morning CAS has called me early in the evening to give me the latest information they had on these before they broke shortly after midnight. I had it through [***]. They had it through one of their agents that was reporting in to them. It was that tight. I take my briefings to General Abrams and we go to the ambassador and present them, along with a CAS representative and members of the State Department. They come here and attend our meetings. Our estimates look very similar. We have no trouble within country. It works very well. The best I have ever seen is right here."

9 JAN 1970: Brief for Gen. Leonard F. Chapman Jr., Commandant of the Marine Corps

ATTENDEES: Gen. Rosson, Gen. Chapman, MG Bautz, BG Potts, others.

BRIEFER: The COSVN area contains 14 million people (78 percent of South Vietnam's total of 17.5 million). Fifty-three percent of the land mass. Also the majority of the wealth: rice (83 percent) (in 1968).

BRIEFER: 1969 infiltration has gone 47 percent to the COSVN area. In 1968 it was about 33 percent. Emphasis continues in early 1970.

CHAPMAN: Could the enemy launch a coordinated countrywide attack on the scale of Tet 1968?

POTTS: "No, sir."

12 JAN 1970: COMUS Update

ATTENDEES: Gen. Abrams, Gen. Rosson, MG Townsend, MG Bautz, BG Potts.

BRIEFER: 1969 Infiltration Estimate remains at 103,600. 1970 Infiltration Estimate: 12,900.

BRIEFER: Reconnaissance photo shows occupied SAM sites in the vicinity of the Ban Karai and Mu Gia Passes. First time this has been sighted.

POTTS: "We think that this is probably the most significant thing that's happened here recently."

ABRAMS: "Now, this amount of infiltration—from what we know now, it's not even up to a subsistence level. I mean, Christ, he had 2,600 killed last week—10,000 a month. 10,000 a month, and goddamn it, you're not getting that many [coming in as infiltrators]."

POTTS: "Those numbers are falling right in line."

ABRAMS: "I know it. I know it."

ABRAMS: "If he's really struggling at the present time to get a hold of the countryside, I wonder how he's making out with it. You see, when you start talking that business you're talking effectiveness of cadre, effectiveness of guerrillas and the local forces. Now I found it quite surprising in that I Corps thing that he's goddamn putting in these aid stations and picking up these people out there in the coastal area, and they're talking about using that same goddamn route of logistics and so on down there, across the Cua Viet, down the coastal plain, down the Street without Joy, that same thing they used in Tet of '68. But out in the countryside, I don't know how much of that iceberg we're seeing. You know, how good is GVN control? Are these guys making any headway? It isn't just a question of attacking outposts. That's part of it. But are these bastards [word unclear]? What the hell is that—in Quang Dien or whoever's district committee out there farting around, making arrangements for aid stations and all that sort of thing out there in eastern Thua Thien. They're not supposed to be doing that. We're supposed to be HES-ing them right out of business."

■ ■ ■

POTTS (re Luong): "Wounded four times. He has our DSC. He has our Bronze Star. And he's been recommended for the Silver Star, but it hasn't come through. And I think we ought to . . . it would be a very good opportunity . . . send him home so he can enjoy the Tet holiday." "From all the stories he must have been a real tiger and a real fine leader."

ROSSON: Cites "the rather extravagant proposal the Vietnamese have made for food and financial support in connection with Vietnamization. I feel, myself, that the supplemental food program has become fairly well established as an element of our effort over here, but that it ought to be modest. . . ."

ABRAMS: "The trouble with these things is that we don't know too much about what really happens. They can get it, then turn around and sell it."

15 JAN 1970: General Abrams—Blue Ribbon Defense Panel

The Blue Ribbon Defense Panel, visiting from Washington, is looking at governmental organization.

POTTS: "In this war, the intelligence function is much more important than it used to be."

POTTS: "General Truong, the 1st Division commander, is very impressive. He's by far the best division commander."

■ ■ ■

ABRAMS: "I spent a year here as the deputy and . . . I'd have to say personally I found it a rather frustrating experience, . . . and I sympathize with deputies wherever they are." Cites "the psychological frame of mind that you are in," then a change when you take command. As the deputy, "you know it's not your judgment that's going to prevail."

ABRAMS: As the new COMUSMACV, "I wanted to look seriously at what my job was, what my mission was, what they wanted me to do, what they expected me to get done. So I immediately put some people to work gathering me official documents so I could study it and get myself oriented on the chain of command and so on. That is a very frustrating story. I knew quite well what was going on here. I'd been all over this country, what was going on day to day, and what was going to happen, and who was going to do it and all these kinds of things—I think I knew that."

ABRAMS: I studied the documents, and I had the staff explain them. "And it was so unreal, what was going on, compared to that—that I then organized a study group to determine what my mission should be."

ABRAMS: "What I finally concluded out of that was the best thing I could do was to leave the thing [the convoluted structure of command relationships] alone and try to operate as it stood, and try to keep all the things moving forward." "It's easy enough, I think, to understand what our government wants to do. I've never had any trouble with that. I've never been confused as to what the government, in terms of the president and so on, wants."

ABRAMS: "But, then, trying to make it work—it's absolutely critical that I know all that Bunker knows, and Bunker knows all that I know, and that we see the problem together. And I've said from the beginning that if the day ever comes when that splits, then I've failed in my job."

ABRAMS: "If we can't be together here, the fragmentation that will occur from there on multiplies in a sort of geometric." "Here you've got to have a course, you've got to have an azimuth, because all this stuff has got to move down that thing. Under the best of circumstances it's a tough job to keep everything moving in the same direction here in South Vietnam."

ABRAMS: "We've got a lot of commanders who are strong men, who are individuals, who've got a lot of experience, and none of the senior ones are 'yes men.' They're strong men in their own right, and that's what you've got to have. You can't get anything done with any other kind."

ABRAMS (re other allies): "That we pay for much of what they use doesn't change the fact that they are proud and sensitive entities." The Koreans "actually like Americans." Re the South Vietnamese: "I think, as time goes on, and we achieve a satisfactory outcome, we may well enjoy the same position."

ABRAMS: "I was in Korea for 16 months, and I think we're probably in about the same position here vis-à-vis the South Vietnamese as we were at that time vis-à-vis the South Koreans."

ABRAMS: "With the exception of the Australians and the New Zealanders, these people are just different. The rest of them will take Uncle Sam for anything they can, any day, and any hour of the day."

ABRAMS (re advisors): "In this business of preserving relationships [at the expense of producing results]—see, I can't let them do that. They mustn't. You have to be constant, and you have to be absolutely unyielding, and when you say no it has to be absolutely crystal clear."

ABRAMS: "All we have to work with, in terms of men, money, or things, is what the [military] services provide. That's where everything here comes from."

ABRAMS: "Over time, as this thing has gone along—. In the beginning, I really wasn't getting much advice on how to do it. The summer of '68 was really not a very good one—bad public relations problems, we had some real problems here in South Vietnam. At that time, I wasn't getting much advice on how to do it. But as things have begun to improve, and as we have taken on officially, governmentally, the Vietnamization program, and I think the situation has improved—the armed forces of the Vietnamese have become more effective, and their security has improved, and the councils of government have begun to come alive out in the country, and a feeling of movement has even begun to leak into the press here—the volume of advice has grown."

ABRAMS: "I've put my time and attention into learning how to live best with the system that we have and make this thing work here. If you start trying to wrench the machinery from here, the sort of thing that that would generate I will confess has overawed me."

ABRAMS (re CINCPAC): "It's too late to change it now, but a more effective system would be dealing directly with CONUS on personnel, logistics, financial aspects, asset shipment—some central point or points, you might wind up having five—but you deal from a point here with a point there." "Requirements, financial control, and the shipment of assets" especially.

ABRAMS (re CINCPAC): "Take the extreme of the Horatio Hornblower stories—but you know who was the commander, and who had sent him out . . . we've come a long way from that day, and that's <u>not</u> the way to do things. Washington is the <u>hub</u>, and that's where the direction <u>has</u> to come from, and that's where it <u>does</u> come from, and I think as nearly as it can be in direct communication with the [field commander?] the more you're getting to the optimum."

ABRAMS: "I've always been satisfied with the degree of control we have here in Saigon over the application of air. I realize that they don't belong to me, but the system has operated in such a way that from day to day air assets that are based in Thailand . . . where we want the effort, that's where the effort goes."

ABRAMS: "When the Communists moved into the Plaine des Jarres, we shifted more than half of the air effort involved into the Plaine des Jarres. That has nothing to do with the Ho Chi Minh Trail. But what I saw in the Plaine des Jarres—that's the way to turn off our interdiction program in Laos. Put [those areas] under pressure, and get Souvanna Phouma to ask the United States as a price to turn off the bombing in Laos. From my viewpoint, I can't stand that. While Ambassador Godley may look at it in a different way, which is all right, that action that was going on in the Plaine des Jarres was critical to me. I saw my problem. So whatever was needed, or whatever could be used effectively, that's what they got." "CINCPAC and JCS know what's been done, so what's been done is entirely agreeable to them."

ABRAMS: "In the beginning, when Admiral McCain first took over, I talked to him about this [channels of communication], and what I did for a long time—every message I sent out, I sent from Abrams to Wheeler/McCain. The only difference was when they received them, the difference in transmission time if there is any. I tried to get them out at six o'clock or so in the evening here, between six and seven, and that means that the Chairman will have them at breakfast. That gives him a head start on the day."

ABRAMS: "The Chairman, in the beginning, was sending his messages McCain and Abrams. In the last few months the Chairman would send McCain and Abrams, then McCain would come out and set a deadline, and request that my answer go to him so that our views could be coordinated and a common position set. Well, after that happened a few times, then the Chairman started the practice of sending it to McCain, Info Abrams. Then the other day I got one from the Chairman that was to Abrams, Info McCain. From my viewpoint, this is <u>really</u> unimportant."

SOMEONE: "Does that mean that CINCPAC doesn't contribute too much to the dialogue?"

ABRAMS: "I think on most things that's probably true. What generally happens is the message that I send to him would be the message that goes forward. See, he's supported every damn thing I've wanted to do. Psychologically, that's the way McCain's disposed. Now, if you had a fellow there who was really intent on being [president?] or something, it would really be tough."

ABRAMS: "The present system is cumbersome, but it's working."

16 JAN 1970: IV Corps Assessment Given to General Abrams

BRIEFER: Elements of five ARVN regiments have been shifted to IV CTZ from III CTZ since 1 May 1969.

ABRAMS: "What we're doing here is trying to read these tea leaves. I'm with you—that's what we've got to do. But I don't quite see the distinctive pattern that you've been able to detect."

ABRAMS: "Three-fourths, over 80 percent, of your armed strength in the delta is RF and PF. This is quite a different picture than in any other corps area."

ABRAMS: "There are so many people in the delta—if there weren't any people, this would be a simple damn war."

ABRAMS: "They had that action [at Kien Tuong] with the 88th the other day. The whole battle was decided on sampan security. They really don't know how to handle the sampans. Before the battle really got started, most of the enemy drowned." The NVA will in time adapt to the unfamiliar operating environment. "These are ham and eggers, not the tough bastards. I may be getting carried away." "The province chief said, 'You know, we did that with RF and PF.'"

ABRAMS: "The attitude of the commanders down there is—I'm not saying they're right—it's easier to fight these guys [the NVA] than those stinking VC—you know, they're so damn clever."

ABRAMS (re booby traps and the NVA): "They're just as bad as we are at it. It's only the VC who are the real artists."

17 JAN 1970: WIEU

ATTENDEES: Gen. Abrams, Gen. Rosson, Gen. Brown, Amb. Colby, LTG Mildren, Mr. Kirk, MG Townsend, MG Dixon, Mr. Jacobson, MG Shaefer, MG Bautz, RADM Flanagan (for VADM Zumwalt), BG Gunn, BG Clement, BG Kraft, BG Vande Hey, BG Potts, BG Henderson, BG Jaskilka, BG Sykes, BG Cheadle, Col. Cavanaugh, Col. Black (for MG Conroy), Col. Hanifen, Col. Church (for BG Smith), Col. Cutrona.

Agenda (typical of this period): Weather; Out-Country; Seventh Air Force Current Operations Update; In-Country: I CTZ, II CTZ, III CTZ, IV CTZ; NAVFORV Current Operations Update; Combat Operations Summary. Following (for a smaller group): SOG Wrap-up.

BRIEFER: "Since 20 November [1969] when COMINT revealed that two groups per day were to move south through Binh Tram 18, 41 groups may have passed through the Vinh area. This represents less than one group per day." Travel time for infiltrators to COSVN: 120 days. To the B-3 Front: 60 days.

POTTS: "Except those arriving in January, every single man currently projected for arrival is destined for COSVN."

BRIEFER: Quoting Binh Tram 32 in January 1970: "In order to carry out the stipulations of [the 559th Transportation] Group, the *binh tram* will open a war of deception during the months of the crash program from today and for three months of 1970." The deception included AAA setting up in areas away from troop concentrations and warehouses. They were instructed to fire so as to attract attacks in areas where no damage would be done. Troops were instructed to start fires throughout areas. Apparently this was intended to hamper reconnaissance and confuse attacking aircraft.

■ ■ ■

BRIEFER: We have a report that on 23 December 1969 [Cambodian] First Deputy Prime Minister Matak stated that he had issued personal orders to FARK units to "attack VC/NVA units located within the borders of Cambodia." Says the VC/NVA units possess certificates signed by former FARK Chief of Staff Lieutenant General [Tu Long?]. Matak says that Lon Nol has refused to recognize the validity of such certificates and "has urged that the VC/NVA troops be opposed by Cambodian units."

BRIEFER: "He's running the government while Lon Nol and Sihanouk are out of the country." Sihanouk is convalescing in Moscow (or plans to in March). Lon Nol is in Paris for medical treatment.

■ ■ ■

ABRAMS: "Everybody's got the problem—how the hell do you keep the momentum up? How do you keep people interested in the <u>problem</u>? And keep their <u>spirits</u> up? A lot of times you have to organize campaigns just for <u>that</u>. You know, just so people won't be sitting on their ass wondering about when <u>furlough's</u> coming. Back home my mother used to put on a mustard plaster in the spring. We'd get that every year. You know, she placed a lot of faith in that. Christ, nobody could ever figure out—you know, it wasn't a very comfortable thing. But you just <u>did</u> that—you <u>did</u> that, damn it. There wasn't anything going wrong, you just <u>did</u> it."

■ ■ ■

ABRAMS (re activities in Binh Dinh): "What this really is is an enemy drive against the pacification program. That's the <u>character</u> of it, and the <u>purpose</u> of it. I think it would be <u>helpful</u> to talk about it that way, because on the other side of the thing, ours should be to consolidate, to protect. In other words, the type of things you do, the <u>arrangements</u> you make, are not for an enemy <u>military</u> offensive. The character of the whole thing is the pacification program. So what <u>we</u> do, the way <u>we</u> look at it, the way <u>we</u> pick the important things that we don't want to get clobbered, the <u>concerns</u> <u>that</u> <u>we</u> <u>have</u>—you might think about that."

ABRAMS: "In terms of pushing the guerrillas and the local forces away from the people, quite a bit of that's been <u>done</u>. Now the thing to do is make sure it isn't temporary. And that's their purpose—to show that it was temporary. That's the character of what that whole damn thing is about up there!" "They [the enemy] haven't been able to get the rice out of there. You know, now Cunningham's helicoptering rice out to market, and such stuff as that. And I guess helicoptering the p's [piasters, in payment] back. Yeah. Use a Chinook to bring it out and an LOH to bring the p's back." [Laughter]

ABRAMS: "The war has an awful lot of faces, and it's not the same face showing in every area. I think it is kind of important to describe as accurately as we can what kind of a face is really showing."

■ ■ ■

ABRAMS: "Incidentally, somebody—I think it was Congressman Marsh—raised with me the other day—he has discovered to his—it's been rather a shocking discovery to him, and he's wondering how soon it could be corrected—he found that the Vietnamese marines are not a part of the Vietnamese Department of the Navy." [Laughs] "He discovered this. In the first place it's amazed him that they've apparently gotten on quite well—despite the rather tragic error." "Well, I thought I'd think about it for a while before we really got anything going." [Laughter]

SOMEONE: "He didn't listen to anybody."

ABRAMS: "I should have warned everybody. He's an old friend of General Loc's."

JACOBSON: "Just call me 'Jack.'"

SOMEONE: "He was supposed to be in there for 15 minutes, and Bill [Potts] held him for two hours and a half."

POTTS: "I had to hold him that long in order to get in a couple of points I wanted to get in!" [Laughter]

■ ■ ■

JACOBSON: "I thought those three we had lunch with the other day and later briefed—Bray, Burns, and Wilson—were about as typical politicians as I have ever seen in my whole life."

ABRAMS: "Yeah, that's right. And another thing that impressed me—I guess it's the first time I ever paid any attention to it, but Burns—well, he's cut out of the—he could have been one of the key characters in *The Last Hurrah*. But Wilson—he comes from—that's another kind of environment. There isn't any machine like that, and he has to—of course, his whole life, his blood, his everything is politics. But he has to play it another way.

JACOBSON: "And Bray still another way."

ABRAMS: "That's right!" "Burns probably goes to every wake in his district. And Wilson has probably never been to one. And I know Bray hasn't."

ABRAMS (re Allis-Chalmers Corporation): "In the conference between the Senate and the House, their defense contract survived. So they had a blowout back in Indianapolis. Bray had to delay his trip to attend that. And he explained it. Absolutely [mandatory for him]." "Incidentally, Jake, I think what they wanted to do was just stay there. They'd spent the afternoon sitting around smoking cigars and so on. That would have been about what they wanted."

JACOBSON: "Wilson went down to meet a constituent and give him a flag that had flown over the Capitol, and the other two sat around dissecting the briefings to find out what they could pull out of them to take back and impress their colleagues and the folks back home. And what I liked about them was they said, 'That's what we want it for, that's what we need it for.' There was no shilly-shallying at all. 'We don't much give a shit about this, but we've got some folks back home who might be able to play with it a little.'" [Laughter]

■ ■ ■

BRIEFER: "The enemy has an extensive and effective COMINT effort in III Corps."

ABRAMS: Asks about leak of this [capture of an enemy COMINT team] to the press from General Ewell's headquarters.

POTTS: Two staff officers talked to the press, and investigation by J-2 revealed no policy on such matters in II Field Force, Vietnam. Ewell has a mea culpa message in.

ABRAMS: "We took all the wraps off of this. We told the soldiers and the commanders and all that. But, goddamn it, why you have to get up at a press briefing and start telling them how smart you were and caught this stuff and all that—! God damn it! We got too many guys around here, all over the lot, that just can't keep from bragging. That's the whole motivation! Christ, they're not trying to advance the war! It's bragging! And that's the thing that gets them to do this. Just like—you've got somebody up in your headquarters that's so fucking proud of what's going on up in Laos that he just can't keep his mouth shut. This latest one this morning—Jesus Christ! Afraid somehow they won't get credit. Afraid somehow the next promotion board won't know what they did. Or some other damn thing, I don't know. Well, it's just a whole mess of stuff that you just have to live with every day. The trouble is it keeps piling up! You don't ever get rid of any of it. They're just always hanging around, chopping away, making you feel bad. And you just have to—. And it doesn't—I mean, it doesn't—even though it's there, it doesn't make it any nicer. It's irritating."

■ ■ ■

ABRAMS: "Some time ago, if you . . . visited a field force headquarters and asked them to bring you up to date on what was happening, what you got was a report of what the U.S. combat units had done over the last six months. That's what you got. There wasn't another fucking thing mentioned! And one thing that this [firepower equivalents chart] . . . does do is show you that there's more involved in this war, goddamn it, than U.S. brigades and battalions and divisions. It says something about the nature of the war. And it says something about some of the things that have got to be paid attention to if the war is going to turn out right—with the Vietnamese on top and the VC underneath."

ABRAMS: "I know that these people have struggled with this goddamn war for twenty years. I mean, they really haven't had a hell of a lot of peace around here. And they're tired, and all that. But the truth of the matter is, if they're going to really come out on top of this, goddamn it, they've still got to sacrifice, and they've got to sacrifice a lot! And the alternative to that, the alternative to that, is in the next five or six years, goddamn it, they'll be Communist. Interfere with their fucking work? Yes! Interfere with whether they're going to give a day off to visit their relatives or something? Yes! It's like Mrs. Kittihara telling about how 'the poor people here, drug down by the war.' I don't know about that. I go around here in Saigon. I know that they're poor, but they're all eating, cooking their rice, and so on. I remember in Tokyo. 'My family had nothing to eat but grass. We cooked it, we boiled it, we steamed.' She said, 'I think that's hardship.' I don't mean all the Vietnamese should be eating grass. There isn't enough of it, actually. But—.'"

ABRAMS: "Well, I got rambling around, but—. But the point is—on our side, instead of talking about offensives, we've got to get into that RF/PF, PSDF, NP/NPFF, you know, all that stuff, and we've got to put a lot of effort up there so that pacification continues to march and continues to consolidate. That's the nature of the beast! Instead of toying around about whether you ought to move another brigade of the 4th Division, something like that. That's not the real answer!"

BROWN: "But you know how these guys that come out here from Washington are. They're looking for things to help them do what they think has to be done back there."

■ ■ ■

COLBY (re Territorial Forces): "You can almost draw a line somewhere—I don't think you can physically—but you can draw a line somewhere with the object of these troops is not to go out and kill people. It's just to sit at home and keep people out of their backyard if they come."

ABRAMS: "I'd be a little careful about that, Bill. This RF and PF up in I Corps— they're not doing too much of that waiting. And in fact I think it's why they're successful." Ambushing, patrolling, small operations. "It's watchful waiting where they move out a kilometer or two and bushwhack the bastards."

JACOBSON: "All good things come to him who waiteth, provided he knows just where to waiteth."

■ ■ ■

JACOBSON: "The president has said this is the year of consolidation, and we all agree that some of these 'C' hamlets do need, by god, a little upgrading before they can be called relatively secure. But the problem is 'consolidation' for the Vietnamese is just the finest excuse for sitting on their ass that anybody's ever seen."

JACOBSON: "'68 we were fighting people off the gate. '69 we were moving out in every direction. And we've lost some momentum now, because this 'consolidation' is a damn good excuse not to do anything."

ABRAMS: "We're coming <u>full</u> circle. We used to sit here and John Vann would let us have it right in the <u>butt</u> that we'd neglected to say anything about the RF/PF. Well, now we're trying to <u>do</u> that, and we're saying <u>too</u> <u>much</u>!" [Laughter]

19 JAN 1970: IV CTZ Assessment Presented to General Vien

ATTENDEES: Gen. Abrams, BG Vande Hey, BG Potts, Gen. Vien, LTG Manh, Col. Thiep.

BRIEFER: "The single most important development in the enemy situation has been the shift of five new regiments from III Corps to IV Corps since 1 May 1969." This began with the movement of the 273rd VC Regiment in May and the 18B NVA Regiment in August. (The 273rd VC is about 80 percent NVA personnel.) 273rd is now in the U Minh Forest. The 18B is in the Seven Mountains in Base Area 400. The 88th NVA Regiment is on the Cambodian border. The 101D NVA Regiment arrived in the IV Corps area in December, and is now in the Seven Mountains area. The 95th NVA Regiment is also deploying to IV Corps, and is now in Base Area 704 in Chau Doc Province. Thus main force enemy battalions in IV Corps are up from 19 in May 1969 to 36 on 31 December 1969. Total strength up 67 percent in main force.

ABRAMS: "I still don't feel too confident about how well we understand what he is really trying to do."

■ ■ ■

ABRAMS (re captured enemy COMINT team): All the messages were from the U.S. 1st Infantry Division. "This has had quite an impact on the commanders. It's the first time we have been able to make them stand still and see for themselves what is happening." Putting out information on air strikes two and a half hours in advance: "Very bad." "I know, many of the commanders felt that their plans were being given away." They felt that this was happening because of agents. "I suppose there's <u>some</u> of that, but when you've got <u>this</u> kind of thing going on, they're getting an awful lot of information from that. We're giving it to them <u>free</u>."

22 JAN 1970: Senator Javits Briefing

ATTENDEES: Gen. Abrams, MG Bautz, BG Potts, Sen. Javits, Mr. "Pete" Lakeman. [Colby is also present, although not mentioned, and Jacobson.]

JAVITS: "I have no a priori-ized ideas in coming here. I think the world of our people and our command. There's not the remotest question in my mind about that, notwithstanding My Lai or anything else." Last here in 1966.

JAVITS: "I hope you can give me somebody who can brief me on the My Lai thing, because I'll be asked about that when I get back."

ABRAMS: "That should be Colonel Williams. He's my staff judge advocate, and he's my lawyer . . . and a fine gentleman."

ABRAMS: "It's [domestic opposition to the war in the United States] something we have to think about. It exerts pressures on our own government. In the environment, so many of the things you do—this My Lai thing, it <u>increases</u> the domestic opposition and free world opposition."

■ ■ ■

ABRAMS: "Prince Sihanouk really, if you can separate yourself from our own problems and so on, has rather a difficult and complex task himself. The one thing he is for <u>really</u> is Cambodia. There's a lot of VC and NVA in Cambodia. To get down to the facts, he has not got the <u>strength</u> to keep them out."

■ ■ ■

ABRAMS (re the makeup of enemy forces in South Vietnam): In 1965: 74 percent VC/26 percent NVA. In 1970 about the reciprocal. "If you graphed it month by month, you'd find it would be about a straight-line function."

POTTS: "We carry 226,900. When we first started looking at our figures consistently, back in October 1965, it was 230,000." Basically steady state, but with changing composition.

■ ■ ■

ABRAMS: Total South Vietnamese force: ARVN 40 percent, RF 28 percent, PF 24 percent, VNAF/VNN the rest [8 percent]. "The Territorial Forces are an important and significant part of their whole military structure."

■ ■ ■

JAVITS (re artillery): "Is it still useful in this kind of a war?"

ABRAMS: "It's an absolute <u>must</u>."

JAVITS: "I had a 4.2 battalion in World War II." (But only in training. Chemical Corps?) They mention that almost every part of every province is covered by a fan. Javits asks what a fan is.

ABRAMS: "In the area of support the U.S. plays a much more dominant role" than in combat forces. So as the drawdown continues the support has to go on much longer than the combat elements.

ABRAMS: "The man we're interested in is the villager. And if a mortar shell lands on his house, it makes no difference to him whether it's an enemy mortar shell or one of ours—it's a disaster."

■ ■ ■

ABRAMS (re what has been done for the South Vietnamese armed forces): "In the last half of 1969 it began to <u>show</u>."

JAVITS (re U.S. withdrawals): "The president said on November 3rd that he has agreed on a timetable with them [the South Vietnamese], but he wouldn't disclose the timetable."

ABRAMS: "What we have tried to do so far is—I think we have taken out as much, and as rapidly, as we could and <u>not</u> put the thing in jeopardy. And a big thing in this is not what the South Vietnamese can do—it's what the South Vietnamese <u>believe</u> they can do."

ABRAMS: Before redeployments began "you would have gotten very few votes for taking anything out" from the South Vietnamese. But: "Among the senior military, they had been conditioned and prepared . . . by their president that this was going to be done. When that started, when the announcement came and then the troops withdrew and so on, the reaction was a good one. You know, there is such a thing as helping someone too much."

ABRAMS: "It isn't all—it isn't all in how many rifles they've got or how many artillery tubes they've got or how many battalions they've got, or how many helicopters or airplanes or anything <u>else</u> that they've got. It's the development in here also of their will and determination and pride—<u>pride</u> as <u>Vietnamese</u>. I can say quite frankly that this has influenced the recommendations that I make to <u>my</u> superiors, because I believe the psychology of this is an <u>important</u> factor in moving them down the road to independence."

ABRAMS: "Anything we do to get U.S. personnel out of here is heartily endorsed by North Vietnam. They like <u>that</u>. Their only complaint is that we don't do it rapidly enough."

COLBY: "They [the enemy] hope to see a collapse—a collapse in the United States which would be followed by a collapse here."

ABRAMS: "Or a collapse here which would be followed by a collapse in the United States."

COLBY: "If you add up your balance on both sides, I think you come to a conclusion that a successful outcome is possible, but not inevitable."

24 JAN 1970: Commanders WIEU

ATTENDEES: Gen. Abrams, Adm. Hyland, Gen. Brown, Amb. Colby, LTG Mildren, LTG Nickerson, VADM Zumwalt, LTG Corcoran, LTG Ewell, LTG Zais, Mr. Kirk, Mr. Megellas, Mr. Firfer, MG Townsend, MG McCown, Mr. Jacobson, Mr. Vann, MG Shaefer, Mr. Whitehouse, MG Bautz, BG Gunn, BG Clement, BG Kraft, BG Vande Hey, BG Smith, BG Potts, BG Henderson, BG Jaskilka, BG Sykes, BG Cheadle, Col. Cavanaugh, Col. Black (for MG Conroy), Col. Hanifen, Col. Healy, Col. Cutrona.

ABRAMS: "Have you seen Ambassador Godley's message on B-52s?" "I don't think we should be miserly if we get authority [from Washington] to respond. Those fellows should <u>know</u> we're responding."

ABRAMS (re successes of enemy forces in Laos): "<u>We</u>—Ambassador Godley's got other reasons—but <u>we</u> don't want this to happen, either." "All those moves I look on as jeopardizing the interdiction program of the Ho Chi Minh Trail. I think it's the only reason they <u>do</u> it."

· · ·

BRIEFER: MACV 1969 Infiltration Estimate: 103,100 (adjusted). MACV 1970 Infiltration Estimate: 18,600 (15,300 to COSVN).

ABRAMS: "We've talked about many times, there's some kind of a—. He's just not <u>doing</u> it the same way. Then, of course, we wonder why. And that's <u>embarrassing</u>, because we can't answer it."

POTTS: "Yesterday was the highest day we've ever recorded. We just got the report from the air force this morning—1,629 [trucks, per sensor activations] in one day."

BROWN: "And our kills are up. We're destroying and damaging more than we ever have."

· · ·

ABRAMS: "We had a message in here this morning on Thieu and his ideas on military reorganization—from <u>State</u>! We're in a time period where it's the goddamnedest ball game—outfielders are running around in the infield, infielders are out, and people are shoving the pitcher and trying to get a chance at it. [Someone: "The sportswriters are down on the field, too."] [Laughter] That's right. Not only that, but some of the <u>fans</u> and so on. It's really—if Pete Gorman or somebody could fly around and look down on it this thing now, it's a <u>mess</u>. <u>Jesus</u>, <u>everybody's</u> in the act and, as I say, they've completely abandoned the territory that they're supposed to be covering and they're just <u>roaming</u>. Somebody ought to move in there and really jerk the government into <u>shape</u>. One other thing—the <u>officials</u> have abandoned the field. The umpires are in the locker room."

· · ·

BRIEFER: "In I Corps, there have been increasing indications of impending offensive activity, particularly during the Tet period." Expect heavy attacks by fire and intensive sapper activity.

NICKERSON: Look for enemy offensive on 27 January because of the lunar calendar, "and also because that's when General Lam thinks it's going to hit. I don't know where he gets it."

ABRAMS: "Well, they visit these astrologers. And who's to say that the other guy isn't doing the same goddamn thing?"

ABRAMS (re COMSEC problems): "I'm really getting gun shy on this goddamn security. We don't <u>have</u> any. The only thing that saves us is that there's so goddamn much of it that their own intelligence officers aren't able to handle it. We're just flooding the system. Not enough people in the J-2 section to handle it—sort it out." "And those little bastards writing it all down."

ABRAMS: "So—what is the <u>nature</u> of what he is really up to? And, on the other side, what should <u>we</u> be doing? Are we <u>really</u> doing—and I'm talking about <u>all</u>

the assets that we've got—are we doing the <u>right</u> thing, the <u>best</u> thing, for our side, in light of what he is really trying to get done?" "One of the things that gets very important is how effective are the RF and PF? How effective are the DIOCCs? How effective is the whole goddamn advisory effort in the district, and in the province? While I'm not <u>saying</u> that we should make some great upheaval of things, is there any merit in taking . . . a <u>look</u>? Have we got any 'ugly Americans' working down there with RF and PF? Have we got any 'ugly Americans' working in the advisory detachment? Have we got some bastard who's <u>drinking</u> too much? Or have we got some guy down there that doesn't <u>fit</u> with Vietnamese, doesn't really <u>like</u> them in the first place? This <u>thing</u> of pacification, security for the people, moving things along down there among the <u>people</u>—wrenching the VCI, knocking off the guerrillas, chasing them back into the hills, getting them off the people's backs, getting the goddamn tax collectors out, so people can do some of the things <u>they</u> want to do—are we <u>in</u> there?" "Should we take some good personnel and <u>swap</u> them—internally? One guy that really doesn't think much of the Vietnamese, a guy like that floundering around down there in a small community, can really fuck things up for everybody. On the other hand a guy like that—what was that sergeant's name—Greenschmidt? Doesn't know anything about doctrine, doesn't know anything about insurgency, counterinsurgency. All he knows is <u>people</u>. Worth a <u>truckload</u> of gold—a guy like that. Of course he's just one guy in his one little spot, but—and that isn't the whole war, and it isn't the whole country, <u>I</u> know that—."

ABRAMS: "If they're going to start their move, then you've got to get out and tangle with them before they <u>get</u> where the people are."

ABRAMS: "I'd like to encourage everybody to kind of throw off what I'll call the 'VC offensive syndrome.' You talk about the offensive, and right away you think about 'what do military people do when there's an offensive in the wind?'" "And <u>maybe</u> that isn't quite the <u>nature</u> of what this guy's <u>really</u> doing."

ABRAMS (re slide, shown for first time, depicting distribution of ground firepower): "I guess I'd have to say most of it is not favorable. What that is is sort of pounds of lead per minute. So it skips blithely over a lot of other quality factors, capability factors, that sort of thing. <u>But</u>, as Ambassador Colby frequently describes it, the enemy conducts this war at a series of levels. And one of the things that has to be done on our side is we have to meet him, and lick him, at each of the levels he has set up for running his system."

■ ■ ■

ABRAMS (re the PSDF): "President Thieu has got it in the front rank of his total political-governmental effort. Well, it <u>is</u> a lot of people. Now it's true they're not going to go out and take on the 9th VC, but there's a <u>job</u> that's got to be done, and <u>these</u> fellows are the best <u>for</u> it. The job that they're doing they can do better than an ARVN battalion can do. I don't think there's any <u>question</u> about it. It's the same thing with the Territorial Forces—the RF and the PF.

And those guys that are in the National Police, and so on. Recognizing that they all have different capabilities, you still have to keep in mind that they all are <u>important</u>. And the job they're doing is an <u>essential</u> job to this thing finally turning out right. There isn't anything on there that can be neglected."

ABRAMS: "Sometimes I think about it in terms of how much murdering and robbing and crap goes on in Detroit. You know, down here in Saigon that's at a very low level."

ABRAMS: "They got excited <u>here</u> about putting a wall around Saigon. At one time the president and the minister of defense and so on were <u>really</u>—god, they were <u>driving</u> on that. I think the thing that killed it was asking the question, 'Are the people inside the thing better than the people <u>outside</u>?' And how are the <u>people</u> going to look at it—the ones the government has decided will be <u>outside,</u> and the ones the government has decided will be inside? Does it mean that the government doesn't <u>need</u> the people who are outside? Anyway, they never did it. . . . There are just a hell of a lot of ideas that have been tried on over here that haven't been worth a shit—even though we've <u>pushed</u> them [laughter] aggressively and all that."

■ ■ ■

ABRAMS (re problems of getting North Vietnamese fishermen whose boats have capsized in storms, not even involved in the war, back home): "See, you're dealing with a bunch of <u>shits</u> on the other side!" [Laughter] "There are 62 seriously wounded [NVA] that out of purely humanitarian concerns they want to get them back with their families, the GVN does. We haven't gotten anywhere with that—<u>zero</u>." Two hundred NVA have been treated in U.S. military facilities. "Those fellows are <u>grateful</u>. It's very clear."

■ ■ ■

BRIEFER: "The enemy strength declined throughout 1969." The enemy suffered a reduction from about 267,000 on 1 January to about 226,000 at year's end. "He sustained high combat losses, with approximately 172,000 killed in action during the year." That does not include those who died of wounds, were permanently disabled, or were nonbattle losses due to disease and desertion.

BRIEFER: "Although lower than his losses for 1968, they are considerably greater than his combat losses for any other previous year. The enemy also sustained a high Hoi Chanh rate in 1969. A total of 47,023 enemy personnel rallied to the GVN. Of this total, 368 were NVA. This number exceeds the total for 1968 by 150 percent."

ABRAMS: "Let me interrupt there for just a minute. I'm not quarrelling with the Hoi Chanh thing, but I think you have to be careful. I think the important thing about it is not so much what it's done to his <u>military</u> strength, because there's an awful lot of funny fellows in that thing. But I think, first of all, that it is manpower that is not readily available to him. You know, it's gotten over into another thing where they can't work for him, or help him, or something like that. But maybe the most <u>important</u> thing is that there's some kind of psychological symmetry going on, at least in <u>little</u> fellows—you know, kind of like a pedicab driver or something. He senses that his chance is a little better if he's on the other side, <u>or</u> if it <u>looks</u> like he's on the other side. . . . The <u>combat</u> losses, a lot of them, have probably been real losses. . . ."

VANN (re the III Corps experience): "It is very dangerous to deduct <u>all</u> of these from the military order of battle."

■ ■ ■

BRIEFER: "There are also indications that the enemy is experiencing logistics problems. Known truck kills in Laos were 6,932 destroyed and 3,256 damaged, for a total of 10,188 in 1969. Just since 1 December, 2,158 have been destroyed or damaged."

BRIEFER: In 1969 allied forces captured within the RVN 2,689 enemy caches, a 30 percent increase over 1968 (and they contained more weapons, ammunition, and foodstuffs than in 1968).

SOMEONE (re caches): "But we're just not getting it—the last three months, anyway."

SOMEONE: "You can't <u>find</u> a cache in the highlands, in these places you could always get them. They've moved it to Cambodia."

SOMEONE ELSE: They've also broken down into many smaller caches, as evidenced by the rarity of getting the many secondary explosions in one place that used to be common.

BRIEFER: Captured in 1969: 12,524 weapons. 1,855 tons of ammunition. 5,325 tons of rice. 682 tons of salt. Rice enough to feed 380,000 enemy soldiers for one month at minimum rations.

BRIEFER: 100-mm AAA weapons were recently introduced in Laos by the enemy, and in the vicinity of the passes.

■ ■ ■

BRIEFER: "The enemy's most probable course of action will be to step up military activity during the remainder of his current Winter–Spring Campaign in hopes of inflicting maximum allied casualties, disrupting RVNAF modernization, discrediting the RVNAF, and impeding pacification."

ABRAMS: "This kind of assessment seems to me to be heavily weighted on his pure military capabilities. Now, earlier we had a presentation on the way Giap looks at things. He's got a whole—. The military part is one of the features— that's right. But he <u>himself</u>, as a military leader, lays great store on the functioning of the cadre, the political, the psychological, and so on, the guerrilla, and their functioning in the system, and the play between guerrillas and main force. . . . I think one way of saying it is that he looks for that whole construct to be functional. I mean, you can't <u>do</u> it with just one <u>piece</u> of it. You've got to have the <u>whole</u> thing going."

ABRAMS: "There's no denying the POL shipments and the truck shipments and the pipeline and the truck traffic in Laos and the prodigious efforts and so on, but in the <u>meantime</u>, down <u>here</u> in South Vietnam, if the Territorial Forces, PSDF, Phuong Hoang, police, the ARVN themselves, and all that keep marching down the road, just what kind of a thing are you going to have? And this thing right <u>now</u>—. Maybe it's just <u>temporary</u> and so on, but I think one of the reasons that he's not—well, one of the reasons we're not finding caches in III Corps is because he's not putting them <u>out</u> there." "You know, I'm not trying to preach <u>victory</u> here or anything, but . . . I think all of these things. . . . It's in the <u>system</u>."

ABRAMS: "And it's true the Phuong Hoang program hasn't produced the results that everybody wants, but what it <u>has</u> gotten out—it's again working away at the <u>system</u>—where they knock off guerrillas, and where they take down guerrilla strength and so on—<u>it's</u> working against that <u>system</u>. And in Giap's whole concept, and <u>whole</u>—. There's nobody in the world more <u>doctrinal</u> than Giap. <u>I</u> think that something's happening to a piece of his <u>concept</u>. And he may get up to a <u>dozen</u> goddamn pipelines in <u>Laos</u>, but if he hasn't got that <u>system</u> in South Vietnam—the political, intelligence, that organizational thing in there, he's got to run the war in a different goddamn way."

■ ■ ■

SOMEONE: "The Pentagon has got one problem right now, and that's dollars. And the big accounts are out here."

ABRAMS: "There's no better place to spend it."

SAME SOMEONE: "All you need is one suggestion that things are really going well, and you don't need something, and they'll cut it off."

ABRAMS: "I'm talking about <u>us</u>—right here. We went quite a while where I think, in <u>general</u>, we understood what he was up to. The general form of what he did sort of turned out the way it looked like it was <u>going</u> to. And then there's been counteraction." "I think it's [pacification] turned out to be a good initiative. And probably targeted better than just about any major thing that's been undertaken. With all its faults, and people falling on their butts, and so on and so on, but probably was really good for this war. Now the problem is trying to assess with some real accuracy where <u>that</u> kind of thing, and <u>his</u> kind of thing, now really stand in their ability to move forward—either <u>he</u> to move forward or the <u>GVN</u> to move forward. You know, <u>better</u>."

VANN: "He [the enemy] tries to get all the mileage he can out of a modest personnel commitment. And at the same time he tries to attack pacification and turn the war over, where he established legal cadre and tries to rebuild his infrastructure for political struggle if you have a cease-fire or a truce. And the two are somewhat complementary. So we're getting demilitarization of the war to a certain extent, with a stronger emphasis on political action than we've seen, or been able to detect, in the past."

SOMEONE: "He's [the enemy] losing every day that goes by if we play all the strings on this."

VANN: "Well, I don't know. Our chances of getting out of this alive are about

50-50, or 49-51. Now I agree if we're doing better all the time maybe our chances are 60-40, but there's so many things can go <u>wrong</u>."

VANN: "He's trying to gain time, for one thing, because his judgment is the ARVN can't keep it up."

JACOBSON: "It's his <u>option</u>. It's his <u>move</u>. If he doesn't come in-country in big numbers, we can't go out of country and get him. And he <u>hasn't</u> been <u>doing</u> that."

ABRAMS: "Then you get into—without getting in there and to U.S. run it, how the hell can the U.S. help? It's like the Mets—how the hell are you going to get them through the next season? It's not good for the U.S. to be out in front. That's the thing you have to say right at the start. But how can you help?"

ABRAMS: "The best example I like to use is the 173rd. It's probably the most permanent airborne unit in the American army. I think it's been fairly well settled that it will stay forever. And it's got all kinds of parachutes and rigging—you know, it's an expensive proposition. And they've <u>got</u> all that stuff. What are they doing? It's <u>never</u> going to be used here—<u>none</u> of it! And the reason is that that's not what you need. Really, in order to help this thing along, you've got to do something <u>else</u>. <u>That's</u> no good, that parachuting around the country. It isn't going to advance the cause by a nickel." "And I think <u>everyone</u>, especially the military officers, has got to realize—. I mean, you can say, 'Jeez, it's nonmilitary, I mean that's not what the military is supposed to be doing.' No shit. <u>Too</u> <u>bad</u>! That's not what we've got. We've got something <u>else</u>! And we've got to do what this thing needs, and the problem is to understand what is best and what it does most need, and then go ahead and do it. Whether you have to put on knickers or some other thing—I mean, all right, that's what we've got to do. Do what's <u>needed</u> in <u>this</u> <u>thing</u>! And to <u>hell</u> with the rest of it!"

■ ■ ■

BRIEFER: Refers to "the unarmed VCI who manage and in effect command the armed VC terrorists."

BRIEFER (re land reform): More land was distributed in 1969 than in the previous seven years.

■ ■ ■

ABRAMS: "I'm going to have to stop you here. I have an appointment with the ambassador, and I want to make a few remarks before I have to leave here."

ABRAMS: "I've often said that, for a fellow who likes to get discouraged, this is a great place for him to come. The opportunities for that are just almost without compare anywhere else. But of course that's not what's going to happen. The thing moves along because the people predominate who are not easily discouraged."

ABRAMS: "Both CAS and the political section of the embassy have deployed field investigators, or field observers, I guess, to sit down in private talks and so on with the ARVN leadership and get their views of how Vietnamization is going, what they see as their capabilities in the future, their confidence, and that sort of thing. Some of these reports show, at least what they <u>tell</u> these observers is that in some cases they out and out don't believe they can hack it. Now one of the surprising ones to me is Colonel Canh, who really, as a division commander, I thought had done rather a magnificent job under very trying circumstances."

ABRAMS: "Now as we go down the road, the development of attitudes and so on is really part of the job. Instilling confidence, independence, that sort of thing is part of what we have to keep working on. The Vietnamese, really, can do anything that they make up their minds to do. I think the sky's the limit. It's not so much a question of what they can do as what they <u>believe</u> they can do. And we just have to keep after it, and it's <u>part</u> of the <u>problem</u>. There are a good many other problems. This is just another one of them."

ABRAMS: "The other thing I wanted to talk about—I guess it's a matter of human relations and leadership. I think, a lot of times, we forget—or <u>some</u> people forget—how much offense they can <u>give</u> to others who have pride in themselves. The term 'dink' or 'slope' or that sort of thing starts out calling the enemy that, and he's Vietnamese, the same as these, so then the next thing is <u>all</u> Vietnamese, call them that. It's just a <u>bad</u> thing. And I'm <u>sure</u> a great many who use it don't use it intentionally to offend, but there's no question but what it does. They're all <u>people</u>, they're all human beings, they do things—they live a little differently than we do, do things a little differently than we do. Oh, you could say there's a <u>lot</u> of differences, but they <u>are</u> human beings, they <u>are</u>, in the main, they're proud people, and we're not doing ourselves any good, and we're not doing the GVN any good, by letting the use of these names continue. And I think that we should, without making a federal case out of it, and having the whole—press backgrounders and so on on it—we ought to move to <u>eliminate</u> that in our—just get it out of the damn vocabulary and so on."

ABRAMS: "The same thing applies to <u>Americans</u>. I put out a little thing about, you know, about leadership and trying to emphasize that, and I agree with some of these observers on the racial strife thing. But we've got some human chemistry going on here which old attitudes are <u>just</u> <u>not</u> going to be <u>adequate</u> to. There's a sense of pride, an awful lot of it justified by what's been done here. It's developing in the Negro, and there again we find all the bad words, all the insensitivity. We have a tendency to—sometimes we just don't think about it. We're the victims of our own experience and so on, and it <u>isn't</u>—I don't think it's <u>entirely</u> or purely a question of maintaining proper discipline. I think there's a human relations thing here. I think that we've got to <u>realize</u> that human chemistry is at <u>work</u> and so on, and we've got to be <u>sensitive</u> to it. And I found during that presentation by this Colonel Price—<u>White</u>, Colonel <u>White</u> . . .—I found a lot of sense in that. And he's quite a disciplinarian himself. But what he says makes sense."

ABRAMS: "We've had a few things happen that don't involve race, and don't involve Vietnamese, but the real root cause is just plain not being a satisfactory leader—not communicating with the men, not communicating with your subordinates. You know, it's never changed, it's always been that way. It's different times, but it's <u>still</u> necessary, and there isn't a substitute for it. That's what brings men—it brings the <u>best</u> out of them. Most <u>every</u> one of them would <u>like</u> to be with the right. And if the show's run right, that's what you're going to get. You'll get that kind of response. Of course, we've got an awful lot here that, a lot of units and things where you're not going to be able to improve it much. It's just <u>good</u> right now. But we need to get around into the backwater areas where this is—."

ABRAMS: "I think this has been a fine meeting today. I've enjoyed the exchanges here. I hope we can all nudge this thing on the path here a little bit more. I think the azimuth is still about right. We just need some refinements."

28 JAN 1970: COMUS Brief: Commando Hunt

BRIEFER: Purpose is to compare the enemy logistical situation in the Laotian panhandle during the last three months of 1968 and the same period of time in 1969 in order to see if we can assess the impact of Commando Hunt, the air interdiction effort in the panhandle, on enemy-initiated activities in I Corps and northern II Corps.

BRIEFER: Shows plots of sensor string activations by movers (<u>not</u> = trucks, since one truck can cause multiple activations in a given day). Up from around 20,000 activations in the last quarter of 1968 to about 30,000 during the same period in 1969.

BRIEFER: Effort expended:

4Q 1968	28,569 tac air sorties	1,750 B-52 sorties
4Q 1969	19,281 tac air sorties	1,388 B-52 sorties

BRIEFER: "The reduction was primarily due to the ceiling placed on tac air and Arc Light sorties because of budgetary reasons." But truck kills still rose significantly because of more trucks on the road, refined Commando Hunt target acquisition and operational expertise, and the introduction of AC-123, AC-130, and AC-119 gunships "which proved to be extremely effective in this environment."

ABRAMS: "I'm tempted to interrupt. <u>Movement</u> between '68 and '69 was up 50 percent—a little more than 50 percent. And fires and secondary explosions were up a 100 percent—6,000 versus 3,000. You're comparing it with the <u>effort</u> made. Another <u>reason</u> for increased results would be that there were <u>more</u> of <u>them</u>. You've got quite a few things working here. In a sense, he was more <u>exposed</u>—by having more movement. We made less of an effort, <u>but</u> we did have better things in terms of the gunships, and we did have, probably, better techniques."

BRIEFER: In October 1968 the 559th Transportation Group had 1,200–1,400 trucks available for use in the panhandle. During October–December 1,427 trucks were reported damaged or destroyed. Movers continued to be detected.

Therefore continuous truck replacements apparently were phased into the system. And "some of the trucks damaged were undoubtedly rehabilitated."

BRIEFER: In 1969 there was a similar situation. Therefore "it must be assumed that truck replacement was adequate to maintain the enemy's truck inventory in Laos."

ABRAMS: Doubt estimate that the enemy had (only) the same number of trucks in 1969 as in 1968. "That would be quite an achievement to get 50 percent more movement out of the same inventory of trucks. You're getting down into the truckmaster's business now, and that means he's maintaining and all that kind of stuff—. Well, OK."

ABRAMS: "I think we can conclude that it's not a problem for him [to maintain his truck inventory], because far more trucks than that have been inputted and so on. And as a matter of fact it may help him with his maintenance—none of the trucks are getting old!"

BRIEFER: In 1969 40 percent more input was noted moving into the panhandle. Air effort damaged or destroyed 50 percent more trucks. Throughput was reduced by about 50 percent. "Thus, although the enemy increased his effort significantly in 1969, he was less successful in achieving his objectives."

ABRAMS (re use of B-52s): "There's no point in outrunning the intelligence. You just don't know whether you're doing anything or not."

1 FEB 1970: WIEU

ATTENDEES: Gen. Abrams, Gen. Rosson, LTG Mildren, VADM Zumwalt, Mr. Kirk, MG Townsend, MG Conroy, MG Dixon, Mr. Jacobson, MG Shaefer, BG Gunn, BG Clement, BG Kraft, BG Smith, BG Potts, BG Henderson, BG Jaskilka, BG Sykes, Col. Cavanaugh, Col. Cutrona, Col. Martin, Col. Kerwin.

MACV 1969 Infiltration Estimate: 103,100.

ABRAMS (re infiltration data shown): "The most that that says to me is he wants to keep the thing going about the way he's got it going now—as far as the forces in-country." "By the time the rainy season comes he should have stock-piled for whatever he has in mind—whatever that may be."

BRIEFER: Compares what was presented on infiltration distribution at the 1 February 1969 WIEU with the current estimate:

	1 FEB 1969	1 FEB 1970
DMZ/MR-TTH	35%	13%
MR-5	12%	8%
B-3 Front	5%	2%
COSVN	48%	77%

ABRAMS: "This infiltration last year was applied predominantly to III Corps." "This year, it's going to have to be spread between MR-6, III Corps, and IV Corps." "The structure hasn't changed much, but the manpower's got to be spread more."

ABRAMS: "The statement of the president bothered me. We're—not so much what will happen right now, but later on we'll be talking—end of February, March, we'll be able to talk about infiltration and [input?] in December and January— you know, in sort of unclassified thing, because it'll be after the fact. And so we'll be dealing in this 2,300, which is 1,700 came in we think in December. Because I think in the past we have given what has infiltrated—you know, as history. And somebody is going to say, 'The president said it was up in January.' And how you skate—slide—through that—."

Apparently the issue is that input into the pipeline was up, knowledge of which is based on highly classified sources, whereas arrivals were not yet up.

ABRAMS: "How are you going to explain how you know about the 36th Regiment?"

SOMEONE: A recent *New York Times* article specifically stated that "more were entering the pipeline."

SOMEONE: "He [the president] really stumbled on his words. He started out calling 'infiltration' 'inflation.'"

ABRAMS: "Well, that's a Freudian slip." "He's got several problems running through his head, you can be sure of that."

ABRAMS (re indications the 325th NVA Division is moving to the DMZ): "That may be the answer to all this goddamn logistics effort."

ABRAMS: "I think we'd better zero in on this. If he's sending two or three divisions in there, the pucker factor's going to go up here. We have always thought when something like this develops we really have to turn to with air—and B-52s. We can't do that effectively unless we've got all these preparations up there—targeting, intelligence, coordination, all that stuff."

■ ■ ■

BRIEFER: "Sir, the Chief of Staff has requested that this be read at this time: 'COMUSMACV has received a message from the secretary of defense in which concern was expressed over recent articles which have appeared in the U.S. press concerning air operations in Laos. One article discussed B-52s bombing the Ho Chi Minh Trail despite the increased SAM threat in the Lao–North Vietnamese border area. Other articles related USAF sortie rates and AC-130 aircraft losses and B-52 activity. The stories, while having some inaccuracies, were sufficiently correct to indicate the provision of some accurate information to reporters by knowledgeable personnel. Such stories are politically damaging, both internationally and domestically. In order to stop such publicity harmful to the U.S. effort, request that all personnel take prompt action to preclude further loose talk and other unauthorized disclosures to the press.'"

ABRAMS: "I think we really have a problem here. You know, the press has really been raising hell about these alleged agents with press credentials. I think it's because they've got people that they deal with regularly that supply them with the information—Americans, probably some of them on my staff, probably some of them on Dixon's staff, some of them on your staff. I always remember the fellow at the change of command of the 1st Division who came up talking to me about the Green Beret case. He said it's the damnedest thing he'd ever seen in 23 years of reporting. He said, 'Friends of mine that have been showing me top secret documents just clam up on this subject.' Well, the whole thing—I was <u>uninterested</u> in the Green Beret thing. This 'friends of mine' that had been showing him top secret documents—. And I just feel that we've <u>got</u> some of that. There's no question about it that some of the information they're being provided is factual. It comes out of the operations that we're conducting. There's a lot of <u>specifics</u> in it. The <u>timing</u> is right, some of it damn near as fast as we get it—<u>I</u> get it. And I think their reaction to this shows that [words not clear]. And incidentally, I might say to all of you on that—what we have, in a very compressed area of time, we had several people who achieved the Peter Principle. That is, they arrived simultaneously at <u>their</u> level of incompetence. Just the most . . . it's <u>true</u> that they had press credentials, but it really had nothing to do with the press—except that."

■ ■ ■

BRIEFER: "It is difficult to determine what the real throughput is." "A prediction of enemy activity . . . based on Commando Hunt data alone would be extremely tenuous." Cites "recent all-source indications that large amounts of matériel are moving through the system." "The enemy is quite capable of moving large quantities of matériel by means not detectable by sensors, such as man pack."

ABRAMS: "In a way, it's the same thing that's happened on the ground here in South Vietnam. Actually, the enemy casualties have continued quite high. But it's picking it off one, two, three, here and there. Keep after it every goddamn night and every day—patrols and ambushes and small units and LOHs and every other goddamn thing. It's like a bunch of ants." "They're resourceful little bastards."

ABRAMS: "We've really got to have our hands on this whole thing in a big way by the 10th of February. I exhort the J-2 to, first of all, challenge everything you've ever said. And do it yourself <u>to</u> yourself, to try to harden, try to find things that we maybe have overlooked, to really get at the picture of what this fellow is doing and what we can expect."

Secretary of Defense Laird is due out on 10 February 1970, apparently.

■ ■ ■

ABRAMS (re a French Communist journalist sent over by some newspaper): "The <u>community</u>—that's all <u>right</u>! Let a fucking Commun—I mean, let a Communist come in the thing, and give <u>him</u> credentials, and ride him all over the country in your helicopters and C-130s and so on, give him a camera and let him in—that's <u>all</u> <u>right</u>! But let a couple of these poor misguided investigators go flying around and the whole—aah. It's a great world. Interesting, though. I just say this lake is really full of sharks. It's a hell of a place to swim, but it's the only place we've got." [Laughter] [Someone: "It's polluted, too."] "Yeah, hell yes. You can catch bad things."

■ ■ ■

ABRAMS: "I really think the whole crux of this visit that starts on the 10th of February is going to be around the further withdrawal of American forces, and whether or not we can at this time [inaudible] [from context, probably something like "speed it up"]."

7 FEB 1970: WIEU

ATTENDEES: Gen. Abrams, Gen. Haines, Gen. Rosson, Amb. Colby, LTG Mildren, VADM Zumwalt, Mr. Kirk, MG Townsend, MG Dolvin, MG Conroy, MG Dixon (for Gen. Brown), Mr. Jacobson, MG Shaefer, BG Gunn, BG Kraft, BG Vande Hey, BG Smith, BG Potts, BG Henderson, BG Jaskilka, BG Sykes, BG Cheadle, Col. Cavanaugh, Col. Hanifen, Col. Cutrona.

WEATHER BRIEFER: Reports that the month of January "had slightly more than twice the average monthly rainfall."
ABRAMS: "All I've got to say is I've been here too long. I thought it was the best January we've ever had."
BRIEFER: First report of an infiltration group composed entirely of 78 female "civil administrators."
BRIEFER: Reports intercept of enemy message saying "the final victory will take place during February 1970."

■ ■ ■

BRIEFER (re Cambodia): "According to a recent report, in mid-January Acting Prime Minister Sirik Matak and Provisional Revolutionary Government Minister Nguyen Van Tien had private talks in Phnom Penh. . . . The source reported that Matak threatened to take military action against the VC/NVA forces in Cambodia. Matak bluntly accused the Communists of killing many Cambodians, even though Cambodia was aiding the VC. Matak presumably was referring to the logistical support Phnom Penh gives to Communist troops in Laos and South Vietnam. Tien warned Matak that any military operation on the part of the Cambodians against the VC would result in 'tough fighting.' Tien claimed that the Vietnamese Communists had paid Sihanouk 'an enormous amount of money' for the right to use Cambodian territory."
BRIEFER: Describes the impact of progress in pacification, including reduction in VC taxes collected, decrease in food supplies acquired by the enemy, decrease in enemy recruiting.
ABRAMS: "If you ever needed any proof that it's just one war, after all—pacifica-

tion, combat operations, Vietnamization—it's all one thing, it's the effect it has on the infrastructure. It makes it tougher for them. The more that advances, the more—."

The preceding comment was precipitated by a report of interrogation of a Tay Ninh Province prisoner captured 28 December. He identified himself as the chief of the Finance and Economy Section of [Lelaton?] District and revealed that "the government's pacification program is seriously affecting Communist influence" in the district. "The source feels that during the past year both ARVN and Regional Forces have improved significantly and states that the resultant expansion of government-controlled areas has inhibited Communist activities by reducing their mobility and access to the population." There has been a 30 percent decrease in tax collection compared to the prior year.

BRIEFER: On 5–6 February, Mobile Strike Force elements in III CTZ captured three enemy munitions caches with a total weight of 54.7 tons, 12 kilometers northeast of Rang Rang in War Zone D.

ABRAMS: "The people of Long Binh and Bien Hoa are grateful."

POTTS: "Now what you see there, sir, is just the initial report. So yesterday we dispatched a go team out there to help get into it, to see what was actually there. It may go well over a hundred tons. Major Tipton has just returned, and I have pictures and a little update for you."

TIPTON: Briefs and shows photos of the captured matériel. "This is developing into something more than just a series of caches. The area is several acres in size and the entire area is very heavily booby-trapped. In taking the inventory alone we lost four killed and six wounded due to booby traps."

ABRAMS: "How would you feel if you broke your back carrying it that far, and now somebody's picked it up?"

ABRAMS: "I knew all about this, but I wanted to give the staff [in briefing it] its moment of glory." "It's kind of significant. We haven't found anything down there in a long time. It's a famous supply area." "It's all tied up with what they think they might do in the future."

POTTS: Tells Abrams it may take seven days or more to inventory the munitions, and that they'll be giving him daily updates.

ABRAMS: "Well, Christ, if it's all booby-trapped I don't <u>want</u> to know."

Meaning he doesn't want to lose people just to count the stuff.

ABRAMS (re the enemy logistics effort): "You've got to give them credit."

■ ■ ■

ABRAMS: "Every time we win, we lose. And if you lose, you take a double loss. The extent to which they're [Washington] getting into everything out here is just fantastic."

ABRAMS: "You know, the big thing on Thieu [what his critics claim] is that he is isolated from the people, doesn't know what's going on, and that people don't know him at all. He has religiously attended every one of those classes down there." [At the training center at Vung Tau.]

9 FEB 1970: Practice for SecDef/CJCS Given to General Abrams and Staff

ATTENDEES: Gen. Abrams, Gen. Rosson, Amb. Colby, VADM Zumwalt, MG Townsend, MG Conroy, MG Dixon, MG Shaefer, Mr. Jacobson, BG Gunn, BG Kraft, BG Vande Hey, BG Potts, BG Henderson, BG Jaskilka, BG Bevan, Col. Jackson, Col. Hanket, Col. Gerrity, Col. Seaman, LTC Payson, LTC Cardinalli, Col. Hamilton.

ABRAMS: "I think I said in here also one day—and I want to face up to this thing—what's happening to us in the interdiction program. And if the Communists have suffered from the interdiction program, I want to say so. Now I feel they wound up the dry season in Laos and have concluded that they didn't meet the subsistence requirements, let alone any buildup for the rainy season. That was the final review and conclusion of the whole goddamn thing. They all bought in on that [in 1969]."

ABRAMS: "What it looks to me like is that this year they've found a way to buck the interdiction program. And that's what they've been doing in January, and it's what they're going to start doing again on the 10th or 12th of February. And that's what I'm anxious to know. That's what I want MACV to face up to. I think that's what they've done."

ABRAMS: "We took a 25 percent reduction in B-52s and tac air. And now they've gone on the board [more planned reductions?]. I'd just like to know how in the hell anybody expects us to play this ball game out here if they're going to continue to do that kind of thing."

ABRAMS: "I'm not now, and I never <u>have</u> been, against the interdiction program. You know that. I know that. But they're gonna be <u>out</u> here—tomorrow night, and I want to be armed—I don't want to try to establish anything more than we can with confidence. I'm basically willing to say this is only the beginning, and maybe something more will happen. But—."

ABRAMS: "There wasn't any mistake made in the message. It's the goddamn intentional stuff that those kind of fellows back there do!" [This said heatedly.] "I want to put this on the dining room table with the secretary of defense, or the coffee table, or wherever the hell I have the opportunity."

■ ■ ■

ABRAMS: "I've been trying to figure out why I have an upset stomach, and I think it's these congressmen." Congressman Morrissey is mentioned. "Either that, or eating too goddamn many pickles." "All right, let's go."

ABRAMS: "I want anybody to speak up—this is a free-for-all. Anything you don't like—if you don't like the <u>color</u>, don't be afraid to say so. [They are reviewing graphics for the SecDef briefing.] Whatever you think, say so."

SOMEONE: Suggests that if you were preparing the briefing for the Chairman you should show trend lines, but for a politician "with his ability to remember numbers" you should show the absolute figures.

ABRAMS: "Take all those symbols off there. See, they don't know what any of those goddamn symbols mean. It took me until I'd been two years as director of tactics down at Knox until I finally got those damn things memorized—platoon, company, so on—division. Then I had to go to Leavenworth to get the corps and army." [Laughter] "Then when I got it all in hand I felt better. I knew it, but jeez, I couldn't really see where it had done me much good."

ABRAMS: "All I gotta say is that the first time while I was here that McNamara came, McNamara never cared any goddamn thing about RVNAF in IV Corps or RF and PF in IV Corps and so on. This is the war!"

ABRAMS (re somebody who was in 4.2-inch mortars, chemical warfare, who came out as a visitor): "Depth of ignorance!"

ABRAMS: "One of the things that set the game back—if I were a senator, I would never start with body count. I'd start with rice required for one man for one day. Ammunition required for one man for one day. Ralliers, prisoners, and finally enemy killed in action. One of the things about this is trying to get away from the idea that the only way MACV looks at things is, 'How many enemy have been killed?' Base your whole goddamn strategy out here on body count!"

ABRAMS: "We should say that rice for one man for one month is equal to a rallier. That's a _hell_ of a lot better than getting into a long, involved argument here about the reliability of body count. I can deal with, 'How come you say that one rallier is worth 30 kilos of rice?'"

ABRAMS (re body count): "I'd like to get the argument started on some other basis. Christ, we've been saying this for the last four years. Body count! At least they won't be able to go back and say _that_. They'll have a whole new thing about this [the way it's been presented]. They probably won't like _it_ any better, but it'll be _changed_."

ABRAMS: "We're getting more political [in conduct of the war] than we are military."

ABRAMS: "There are a lot of things in there [the calculus of factors affecting progress of the war] there's no way we know of yet to deal with [to measure] it. Medicine's a good example. Hospitals is a good example. I just _know_ that's hurting. They can't run any big show without that. At _least_ they have to be able to take care of their officers and senior NCOs."

ABRAMS: "Another thing you can say about this—of the RF and PF, somewhere around 50 percent of them are effective."

ABRAMS: "We say terrorism is still high and so on, and that is right. But there's a lot of terrorism going on that we had no way of finding out it was happening—and now we do. In other words, if you take the terrorism we knew about in May of '68, how it appears on there [briefing chart] is against a much smaller group of people than the terrorism that you've got in January [of 1970]."

STAFFER: "The target for terrorism is greater now that more people are under government control and therefore fewer are under enemy control." "They're not going to terrorize their own. Therefore the more they have the fewer terrorist incidents are likely to occur in their own areas."

■ ■ ■

DIXON: "The other campaign we talked about, and that you have preferred, and that the Chairman has preferred, is to take a whack at these missile sites. Now, we used the rules which now exist—and I'll plead the Fifth Amendment if anybody wants to go into exactly how we used them—to get that one site. Nothing succeeds like success. . . . But if we get the authorization that we've been requesting, we can make that SAM problem really unbearable for that guy. We are almost able to do it the way it is now, with the rules we've got. If we can calmly, coolly, and scientifically go in there and hack away at those, we can move them back off the edge. . . . It's clear to me that what they intend to do is they want to get a B-52 with a MiG or with a SAM, and they want to move us back. . . ."

■ ■ ■

BRIEFER (re the situation as now seen by Sihanouk): "The VC/NVA are not winning, and the war has become a much longer struggle than initially anticipated." The earlier "policy of complicity with the VC/NVA was seemingly based on the assumption that the VC/NVA would triumph in the Republic of Vietnam in a relatively short time. Personal gain was possible by cooperating with the VC/NVA, and placating their aggressive nature seemed sensible." Now, in some areas "Cambodia is experiencing a de facto occupation of her territory" by the VC/NVA.

BRIEFER: An estimated "4,000 tons of munitions delivered to Cambodia in 1969." "[***] analysis indicates that the enemy is meeting his goals for the shipment of supplies in spite of our interdiction efforts." "The increased deployment of antiaircraft artillery and SAM missiles reflects the enemy's determination to protect his improved lines of communication against allied air strikes." Cites a recent report of receipt by Binh Tram 34 of 400 tons of 122-mm rockets.

ABRAMS (heatedly): "He's [the enemy] in a situation where he's pouring more resources in, and we're pulling resources out. Now, this kind of a goddamn program is—I mean, with just that basic fact he's bound to do better and we're bound to do worse."

10 FEB 1970: Rehearsal for SecDef/CJCS Brief

DISCUSSION: Proposed slides are shown depicting the cost of various types of munitions delivered by aircraft.

ABRAMS: "I don't know whether we need to talk to this subject at all."

POTTS: "We might get a cut in B-52s out of it. You know, 'I can save a hundred million dollars a month by cutting these back and using less air munitions.' Bang!"

ABRAMS: "Knock those out!"

■ ■ ■

BRIEFER: Discusses phasedown of forces "eventually to a MAAG." Shows a slide of what they visualize "the ultimate MAAG level" to be.

BRIEFER: "Considering future redeployment phases, it is much too soon to say how many troops and when. Phases IV, V, and VI are wholly conjectural at this time, and the exact composition of each, as well as the timing, would be heavily dependent on local conditions in the areas from which the troops would be withdrawn, and on the five critical conditions shown on this slide."

BRIEFER: "On a purely conjectural basis only, we foresee a Phase IV redeployment of 50,000 as including the 1st Marine Division (minus one RLT), the Marine Air Wing (minus), navy support forces, and one army brigade plus support. Forces remaining in country would total 384,000. In Phase V, again at a 50,000 level, six army brigades with two division bases might redeploy, leaving the in-country force at 334,000. Phase VI could look like this, the redeploying forces again totalling 50,000. If 74,000 could be redeployed in Phase VI, the remaining in-country force would then be at the 260,000 level. If only 50,000 could redeploy, a seventh phase would be required."

At this point, then, they are apparently contemplating a 260,000 end state or residual force.

BRIEFER: RVNAF increase in FY '69 was more than 110,000, bringing the total to 875,790. In FY '70 more increases, primarily in RF/PF. For planning purposes, FY '71 increases in logistical support.

11 FEB 1970: SecDef Laird and CJCS Wheeler Brief

ATTENDEES: Amb. Bunker, Sec. Laird, Gen. Wheeler, Asst. Sec. Nutter, Mr. Henkin, Amb. Berger, Gen. Abrams, Gen. Rosson, Gen. Brown, Amb. Colby, VADM Zumwalt, Mr. Herz, Mr. Newman, MG Conroy, MG Townsend, Mr. Shackley, BG Gunn, BG Blanchard, BG Clement, BG Kraft, BG Potts, BG Pursley, Mr. Pickering, Col. Cutrona, Col. Hanifen.

Agenda: Pacification by Amb. Colby; Intelligence, Operations, and Vietnamization by Gen. Abrams; Status of RVNAF I&M (Phases I & II) and GVN Phase III Requests by LTC Payson.

ABRAMS: Introduces Ambassador Colby, "who is leaving today to be the senior witness from here before the Fulbright Committee."

LAIRD (re Colby): "He's going back to a rather fine experience. I can assure him he'll be having a pleasant few days. Ought to be great fun."

COLBY: "We have our questions as to the absolute veracity of the HES figures . . . , but I think the key thing is the change. Approximately three million people, and 2,600 hamlets, last year moved from the something less than 'C' category up to the C or above. What the absolute level of security is is another question, but the fact they moved is really not [in] much doubt." "Security did expand during 1969."

COLBY: "In 1970 we're looking ahead to some changes in the basic strategy, and I think the key to it was set by the president, President Thieu, last summer, when he first said that he wanted to go beyond raising hamlets up to C, and he wanted to think of the next stage to raise them up to B." "He set a goal of 50 percent A/B for 1969, which they made." "When he came up to the end of the year, he chose the figure of 90 percent A/B for next year. He also said a hundred percent A/B/C. Probably you'll never make a hundred percent. . . ." "The 90 percent will be hard to make, there's no question about it." "There's strong emphasis on the People's Self-Defense as a base point on which to build the rest of the security structure. It's both a paramilitary and a political force for the future." Major emphasis on the Phoenix program.

COLBY (re November 1968): "'People's Mobilization' is a very grand name for an effort to activate the whole government mechanism here to use it as a transmission belt out to the people. This was tried once before . . . in November 1968 . . . when the Vietnamese government had a little trouble with our effort to get them to go to Paris, and they stood fast there for a bit. At that time the president really activated the government machinery he had. He went down through the command levels, all the different services—the civil services, the military services—and they got the word out to the country in a very few days as to exactly what the government's position was. They weren't having any basic disagreement with the United States, but they were having a little argument. And they got exactly what they wanted out of it. They got a great deal of support, but understanding support, and they avoided a panic."

COLBY: "Almost 40 percent of the population now lives in urban areas." "Change from about 20 percent 8 or 10 years ago." "The urban areas are kind of a mess in a lot of ways." "And they are a fragmented, atomized population which is politically quite dangerous for the future." This year they will try to mobilize the urban population as was previously done in rural areas.

COLBY: "The thrust of 1970 will be a consolidation of the security, because you've expanded about as far as you're going in most areas."

COLBY: "The force levels of the Territorial Forces have rather sharply grown in the last two years, and will continue to grow during the next six months." That is the greatest reason for expanded security. Effectiveness: "A little over half of being fairly good troops." In combat self-defense: "About 100,000 women who have volunteered to carry arms."

COLBY: "The police have gotten out into the countryside, a function that the police in this country really never had done. The police here were—their tradition was a colonial police whose function was to protect the administration. It is gradually turning to a police whose function is to give the <u>population</u> some protection in terms of law and order."

LAIRD (coaching Colby for his congressional appearances, especially re Symington): "One of the points we've got to make is that there is an effort to get the National Police involved in this program [Phoenix]."

COLBY: Former 59-man Revolutionary Development cadres have been reduced to 30 men each, and will probably be further reduced, a change made possible by the improved security provided by Territorial Forces.

COLBY (re HES): "We've been using it, and defending it, over the years. We've emphasized that we don't think it's a precise thermometer for the situation, but it's been a <u>very</u> handy tool. It's given us an idea of differences over time and it's given us an idea of differences over space." We started a study in June 1968 of how it might be improved. We ran a test session for three months last winter. Began a new system in July 1969 in parallel with the existing system. Results of the new system were slightly below those rendered by the old system. We have sent a recent message to Washington proposing to implement the new system.

■ ■ ■

ABRAMS (beginning with infiltration): "The president's news conference gives us a <u>little</u> problem. He indicated there that infiltration was <u>up</u> in January. And of course all that <u>we</u> know is that it wasn't. What was <u>up</u> in January—he was talking about <u>input</u>."

LAIRD: "We ought to stay away from those things anyway. It gives us trouble. We should have learned the last time."

ABRAMS (re January 1970): "This is the biggest logistical effort he's ever made in Laos." "It far exceeds what he did in January of 1969."

ABRAMS: "The way the fight was run in III Corps was on munitions that were brought in from Sihanoukville to the units and the base areas in III Corps. That's the way that military effort was supported, was by the shipments through Sihanoukville."

SHACKLEY: "The arms and munitions that come in through Sihanoukville are distributed to the VC by a FARK-controlled mechanism. It is controlled by the Cambodian army, using trucking companies and so forth that they have set up in conjunction with the North Vietnamese to move this matériel. It's an integral part of their total logistics system. And on that they've been having political difficulties, because the Cambodians have held up on portions of it since Matak has been running the government. This has been an on again–off again proposition. The North Vietnamese in Cambodia are concerned because they feel that they've paid for a service and that service is not being delivered at the moment. Now the trickle is on again. Hanoi must be concerned about the reliability of that system. Rice and pharmaceuticals are moved by a purchasing commission that the North Vietnamese actually have in Phnom Penh, where they make their own deals and transactions with the Cambodians or Sino-Cambodians in Phnom Penh for the movement of that kind of matériel through a different pipeline. It's not really FARK-associated. That's the distinction between the two systems."

■ ■ ■

ABRAMS: "III Corps, for some time now, we've tried to run it as a no-risk area. It's the capital. It's the seat of government. You can't have the capital under threat and all that, so an awful lot in assets—ours and theirs—have gone into III Corps."

ABRAMS (re IV Corps situation, where the United States has engineers and advisors and signal and aviation): "This question comes up about, 'Who's going to protect the U.S.'s that are left when everybody pulls out?' Well, there's 20,000 down there getting along pretty good. The only thing they've got around them—and their helicopters and their trucks and signal vans and so on—the only thing they've got down there is Vietnamese. That's their security."

ABRAMS: "There's no question about it, that the RF and PF, and the PSDF, those are the people who can—when you've got them up where they're performing well—there isn't <u>anybody</u> in this country can work as well with the people and get along as well with the people, enjoy the <u>confidence</u> of the people, the way those people can." "The RF and PF don't have that, if you will, the military mind. They're really kind of home folks. It just works better."

ABRAMS (re RF/PF/PSDF): "That's where we've <u>really</u> got to make some yardage in 1970. So we've gone into <u>actively</u> shifting talent from U.S. units into the advisory thing." "We've got to dig in there and get some blue chips out of the one bag and stick them in the other." "What <u>one</u> good sergeant, what <u>one</u> good sergeant can do in three or four months, it's just not for <u>sale</u>, you can't <u>buy</u> it."

ABRAMS: "We had a fellow up here in Thua Thien, he's just a genius. Trouble is, <u>he</u> doesn't know it. Maybe that's his greatest strength. No, he <u>is</u>. He went in there from the A Shau Valley. He scarcely had even <u>seen</u> a Vietnamese, let alone <u>know</u> anything about them. But he understood them from the <u>beginning—completely</u>."

ABRAMS: "For instance, this sergeant—I asked him—he was a pre-med student when he was drafted. I said, 'When do you think you're going to be able to take <u>that</u> back up?' He said, 'That'll come in due time. That'll come in due time. Right now I've got this to do.' So <u>he</u> knew what he was doing was worthwhile."

■ ■ ■

BRIEFER: In RVNAF I&M there was an FY 1969 increase of 110,000+ for a new total of 875,790. More will occur during FY 1970, primarily RF/PF.

LAIRD (re the $575 million required for the recommended Phase III I&M): "We've got available in the 1971 budget a total of $300 million." "Now there're only two ways to finance that. One way is to go to Congress for more money in supplementals, which really isn't much of a possibility this year. The second is to accelerate your force reduction—or else establish priorities within the approvals [of I&M]." "We've got a problem here, don't we, Bus [Wheeler]?"

WHEELER: "We've got a real problem. In the first place I don't see how anyone, lacking an operable crystal ball, can sit here and say with any degree of confidence that we can reach 260,000 by 30 June 1971. Hopefully we can, but there are several unknowns in this equation, including what the enemy may do. I myself would be most reluctant to hang my hat on that case."

LAIRD (re the possibility of a supplemental appropriation): "I think we'll be doing well if we get our budget approved the way we submitted it."

ABRAMS: The GVN has set a 1.1 million manpower limitation. "It's their figure, and not ours."

ABRAMS: "When my staff works with them [the Vietnamese], that's one of the things that they have to look at—how this structure of theirs is going to fit with the ultimate structure we're going to have."

Obviously at this point they still contemplate a residual U.S. military presence.

ABRAMS: "Up in I Corps, northern I Corps, it's now the 1st ARVN Division who largely is in contact along the DMZ. We still have a brigade of the 5th Mech up there, part of it. In the piedmont, further south from the DMZ, it's the 1st ARVN Division that's out in the piedmont and out in the jungle. And they're doing most of the jungle work out there. This all used to be done by the 1st Cavalry and the 101st Airmobile and the 3rd Marine. The same thing in II Corps. The battles of Ben Het, Dak To, Bu Prang and Duc Lap—those were fought this year by the Vietnamese. This is a thing you just can't—you can't say, 'Well, this is going to start 1 March, and from 1 March on that's the way it's going to be.' It's got to be a development of their confidence and pride, and you use the American units in the best way you can to develop that."

ABRAMS: "I only say that in all this time what we've tried to do is put the effort into Vietnamization. That is in the sense that more and more of the problem is the Vietnamese's, and less and less it's ours. More and more it's their capability and their confidence running the thing, and less and less it's Americans carrying the ball."

■ ■ ■

ABRAMS: "I'll tell you one thing—if you're going to have American infantry sitting around in base camps over here, I don't want to do it. I think they're better off home, because all they're doing is preparing themselves to be killed. The only way this infantry over here of ours—and you've got to keep it that way, otherwise you ought to take it home—you've got to keep it out there where it's sharp, it's tough, it's disciplined, and it's well trained for a dangerous job. When you're no longer going to do that with it, no longer going to use it that way, don't call it infantry, or don't leave it here. The casualties that we have here, a lot of it, are the people who are just not up on the stick. Now I'm not criticizing anybody that gets killed, but that's why."

ABRAMS: "Well, anyway, as I say—the American infantry that's here, that's the kind of shape it's got to be kept in, and that's the way you keep them alive. That's the way you guarantee that most all of them will go home on one of the 707s with the wine and dinner and [inaudible]."

■ ■ ■

ABRAMS (to Laird): "Now, can I ask you a question? [Laird: "You bet."] I want to see if I understand what you have told us. Now, you said that what has been approved so far had established the requirement for $575 million for FY '71. And what's in the budget, and if it all passes and so on, is $300 million. So you've got a $275 million deficit there. Then the next thing are these reductions in tac air and B-52s required. And if that weren't done, then this would be another deficit, I mean another shortfall."

LAIRD: "I don't think we'll be able to go the supplemental route. What we'd like to be able to do is make the case on how, for a much cheaper investment from the standpoint of dollars, we can get a lot more and do a better job from the Vietnamization program than we can if American forces have the responsibility." Cites "the $9 billion that we lost in the tax bill."

ABRAMS: "First of all, let me say I don't think that we can devise tactics that will get the job done and save money. Our big savings on tactics has been [wise?]. And frankly, we've played hard ball on that. We took the course that no one would ever approve, and I think it's paid off. And I don't want to do anything to change that picture." "Where the Vietnamese are susceptible to advice and counsel on tactics, the same thing has paid off for them."

ABRAMS: "The [South Vietnamese] Airborne Division now for about five weeks has been fighting in the jungle at a kill ratio of about 1:20. This is awfully good, and not all American units can do that."

WHEELER (on redeployment, apparently meaning more or faster): "You do save money there that you have available, we have in our budget. But the risk involved with that, if the threat—should the threat increase, it could jeopardize the whole Vietnamization program if we're not careful."

ABRAMS: "Our basic problems right now are—first of all, in southern I Corps pacification just hasn't moved far enough ahead to make any further substantial withdrawals over that already planned. We've got to make more progress in pacification there. In II Corps we've also gone, for the moment, as far as we can because . . . we're changing the whole concept around so that they'll have an advance of the 22nd Division up in the highlands . . . which has also not been tested as a division. . . . In III Corps, you got two ARVN divisions that have been hothouse grown, and nobody has really felt free to get them out where they can get some rain on them or something. . . . And those two divisions are not confident themselves. The delta—how is that going to come out down there with those five regiments?"

ABRAMS: "I don't know what percentage, but there's some of the Vietnamese who, despite anything we say, believe what we're really going to do is cut and run. And, no matter what you say, you can't change it. And then there are some Vietnamese—military—who just feel uncertain whether they can handle any kind of—you know, whether they can handle the problem, no matter what you gave them. So one of the big things that has to be done this year is try in every way we can to build their confidence and their willingness—sincere and heart-felt willingness—to take on the task."

ABRAMS: "So when you get into the priority system, or how much of this are you going to be able to do, how much are you going to continue to be able to do, you're not playing it against a whole bunch of real tigers. Some of these hot-house plants which we hope, with careful work, we'll get into fairly rugged trees—you know, can stand out here in the monsoon and all that—. You can say, 'Well, that's a hell of a state of affairs,' and I agree, but that's what it is. And that's what we must build up, and build on, and so on."

LAIRD: "Everyone's talking at home about restructuring our priorities and so forth. Well, the number one national priority is to make Vietnamization work."

ABRAMS (re planned reductions in sortie rates): "We're just getting around to giving them [the enemy] a free ride through Laos."

WHEELER: Asked if he has any ideas. He doesn't.

■ ■ ■

SOMEONE: "Do you think the Vietnamese can hack it as far as what leadership they have?"

ABRAMS: "Yes, sir, I think they can." They have expanded their forces greatly, and also continued to take casualties. "In the first few days of the Ben Het thing, they lost 14 company commanders out of the 32nd Regiment. Fourteen company commanders. I tell you any U.S. regiment is going to have a problem with that." "They've expanded, and they've had to spread what they have." But they have kept officer and NCO training centers open at full capacity. "So what they've done, while you can fault the quality and all of that, nevertheless it's quite a remarkable job." "By god, they've been out there fighting, and they're doing a good job. And they're sticking with it. And finally I'd like to say as long as I've been in the army we've always cursed the small-unit leadership we've had. It's never been adequate, never been good enough, and never will be. So the first thing you say about any army is that one of its defects is small-unit leadership. Any American will report that without even looking around, because he knows it's an inescapable fact."

14 FEB 1970: WIEU

ATTENDEES: Gen. Abrams, Gen. Rosson, Gen. Brown, LTG Mildren, VADM Zumwalt, MG Townsend, MG Dolvin, MG Conroy, Mr. Jacobson, MG Shaefer, BG Gunn, BG Kraft, BG Vande Hey, BG Smith, BG Potts, BG Henderson, BG Jaskilka, BG Sykes, BG Cheadle, Col. Cavanaugh, Col. Hanifen, Col. Cutrona, Col. Doody (for Mr. Kirk).

ABRAMS (re Godley requests for air strikes): "As we've talked about here many times, yeah, there's a lot of power. But it's no good, you really can't use it, unless you've got the intelligence and the targeting and so on. And those poor fellows up there—."

BROWN: Suggests using the existing system insofar as possible to deal with Godley's requirements.

ABRAMS: "Well, that's right, but here's the way the thing gets going. The other night over there at the house, here comes the secretary of defense for dinner. And he gets General Wheeler and I in the private office. He's got this goddamn thing direct from the ambassador, which neither you nor I are info addressees on. And he's talking about Arc Light. Well, really, at that point I was unaware that the fire had broken out in the Plaine des Jarres. But—really, it's not upsetting to me, because this whole—actually, the way it's been operating, a lot of times I know these things after the fact. The system is automatic, it's all set up there to respond to whatever, and the people do it—there's initiative and all this kind of stuff. But here's the secretary of defense and B-52s and—aah— and the imminent collapse of Laos and so on. Well, it's fairly heady wine. Anyway, I told them one thing. I've told them over and over again about the system. And then the next morning he's got another message from Godley which, among other things, implores the secretary of defense to use his good offices to put in the maximum tactical air effort. Frankly, quite frankly, it's not even a thing for me and Ambassador Godley to arrange. The system's got to do it. And the system will do it. And it will do it better than anything else we've got. But this thing of solving it all between Ambassador Godley and Secretary Laird—B-52s and tac air and 105s and F-4s—it's getting too big of men involved in too little of a problem."

BROWN: "We got it back on track." "The only regrettable thing is that I think the ambassador wound up looking like a guy who was sort of panicking and didn't know what he was doing."

ABRAMS: "Well, it's regrettable, but true!"

ABRAMS (re Laos): "I told the secretary of defense we regard that as an integral part of this war." "The efforts there are really designed to shut off the interdiction program in Laos."

TOWNSEND: "Mr. Nutter said that that was the first time a reasonable appraisal and explanation of this action had ever reached the secretary."

ABRAMS: "There's a message in from the SSO DIA to the SSO CINCPAC or some kind of thing like that. And DIA has been charged with providing the Chairman with an assessment of bombing. Then following that's a message from the SSO CINCPAC to the SSO MACV wanting to provide the—huh, huh, huh—aah—the material for the assessment of the bombing. Now what I want to do . . . is send a back channel to the Chairman, and to the admiral, pointing out our—. You know, we just got through turning in the third or fourth one of these things. And the independent assessment he seeks has come back around the corner and we're just going to feed into it the same damn thing we fed into it for him. I mean, the point is, is this trip necessary?" "This is the third or fourth time in three months that we've done this." "It doesn't sound like good work."

ABRAMS (re initiation of the APC): "When it was launched the president was at the helm. And he was up there briefing. I remember him—god, he got so he knew this whole thing by <u>heart</u>. He needed no briefing. The whole concept was clear to him. He'd brief the cabinet. He'd brief the Americans. He'd brief <u>everybody</u>. Now, it's true that a good bit of it was generated and fed in from the American side, many of the ideas in it and that sort of thing, <u>but</u> the truth of the matter is, and why it <u>went</u>, because the Vietnamese <u>believed</u> it—at least the <u>top</u>—believed that this was the program for Vietnam, to hell with who thought of it. See, a lot of the programs that we advance, they never get anywhere, although we get enthusiastic about them, and it's because the Vietnamese, god-damn it, just don't see that that's the thing that's going to really pull the chips out of the fire."

■ ■ ■

ABRAMS: "I think realistically—aside from the goddamn border command and the concrete forts—it's just—just another thing, it's like when they wanted to build a wall around Saigon. And of course we've still got those characters. But, aside from that, and realistically, it seems to me that the enemy <u>does</u> face a more complicated problem than he ever has had before. You go back into the early days of Diem and coming on down—the strategic hamlet thing. But <u>now</u> in this country, accepting all of its faults, and . . . the level of ineptness that runs through the whole thing, this PSDF, the amount and the equipment of the PF and the RF, and all of this . . . adds up to a kind of problem for the enemy which he has not yet had to really face up to."

ABRAMS: "Take the situation in '65. You just didn't <u>have</u> anything like this in '65. I certainly don't want to go off into dreamland about what the American contribution is worth, but in this kind of a war, quite frankly, that's just not enough. If we'd brought the whole fucking Army and Marine Corps over here, taken it all out of Europe, and taken it all out of Korea, and brought it over here—that wouldn't have done it. You've got to have this <u>other</u> thing. So I think the problem <u>he's</u> up against <u>is</u> a more difficult problem <u>because</u> of these things—because of the PSDF, because of the Territorial Forces, and some <u>modest</u> improvement in the police, especially in the Police Special Branch."

JACOBSON: "In '65 he was at his <u>best</u> and we were at our <u>absolute</u> worst. He had his best leaders, he had his local forces that were good and the main forces that were good, and his infrastructure that was totally intact. And we didn't have much of anything at all. We're a hell of a lot better on the Vietnamese side across the board than we were in '65, and he's got to be a hell of a lot worse. You just can't take that kind of losses without having your capabilities go down."

■ ■ ■

ABRAMS (responding to Brown's recollection of some contingency plan on which they "had a <u>hell</u> of a time"): "You remember what that came out of? That came out of SecDef's visit last March [1969]. And we sat over there in the damn palace. And Vice President Ky—God bless him, he's basically a patriot [laughing], but he really blew his ass that day. [Laughter] And [laughing] he made this impassioned and entirely emotional speech. And he said, 'Mr. Secretary, you let <u>us</u> go north!' He said, 'Let <u>my</u> pilots be captured! Let <u>them</u> be the prisoners of war! Let <u>us</u> do this!' So the secretary of defense, of course, immediately took me aside afterwards, and he said, 'Now, god, why are we holding them back?' [Uproarious laughter] What can you say? I just said, 'No excuse, sir.'" [More laughter]

ABRAMS: "I remember when that thing finally boiled down. Remember when he had to draw up a contingency plan? It had to be presented to the president and General Vien and all of that. And so, as I recall the rough figures, to make this one-time attack on the bastions of the north by the VNAF, there were 16 A-1s total involved, and 225 aircraft of all types out of the [U.S.] air force, navy, and marines."

BROWN: "And their targets were way off just north of the western end of the DMZ, just barely in there, and we had to fly cover for them. There were no known [air] defenses, but they wanted us to—."

■ ■ ■

ABRAMS: "This statement by the secretary of defense about protective reaction— we've got to do <u>everything</u> we can to keep from going past that. I want to emphasize it. We've <u>never</u> discussed the rules of engagement [with the press], the details of the rules of engagement, and we're not going to <u>now</u>. So I don't want <u>any</u>body—I don't want some captain somewhere—explaining to these newspapermen what this really means. And as a matter of fact nobody can anyway, because all of these situations are a little different."

ABRAMS (re a report that a U.S. O-1 was crossing back and forth across the border): "Now, I want to really get after—I want to go after this again, especially in III Corps and IV Corps. <u>I just don't want our people going over into Cambodia</u>! And shooting up the goddamn <u>Cambodians</u>! I agree a hundred percent when we're getting fire out of Cambodia into South Vietnam we've got to hit it. I accept <u>that</u>. And we <u>do</u> that. But I'm beginning to get suspicious now that a lot of these bastards are out roaming around <u>looking</u> for trouble. Or that they're not well enough oriented, where the border is and so on, and that they're getting over there. And I tell you, in the light of all that's going <u>on</u>, it is counterproductive for us to be killing <u>Cambodians</u>! Or the goddamn buffalo, or knocking over their bulldozer, or some <u>other</u> damn thing. And <u>I just don't want it done</u>!"

■ ■ ■

ABRAMS (re prioritizing Phase III RVNAF I&M proposals): "I heard all that discussion about money [when Laird was here]. It appears to me that they probably <u>do</u> have somewhat of a problem. And I think that, understanding that, we should do our utmost to improve and refine the quality of our submission. Not only the quality in terms of justification and supporting reasons and that sort of thing, but also quality in terms of what really is needed here. That is, that we won't support—I think we have to be a little careful about supporting for emotional reasons, or supporting for psychological reasons, although I know that enters into it. And I think that should be the influence that those discussions here have on us. Or, another way of saying it, I don't think that we should put on a drive here to find ways and means of solving the financial problems of the Department of Defense. Actually, we're in no position—we don't know enough to indulge in that."

ABRAMS: "The other thing about trade-off—piss on it! See, they've got their own problem, and we just get little flashes and glimpses and pieces of it. I think it would be a mistake for us to think that we could trade something that costs $100 million for something else that costs $100 million. We'd wind up minus $200 million."

ABRAMS (re the Department of Defense): "Now, I think that we do have, in sort of a general way, their support. They have these grievous problems, which are hard for them. On the other hand, they don't want this to fall on its ass. As a matter of fact, they can't stand it. They can't take it. And I think that the secretary of defense is in a far better position now than he was a year ago to decide things in this arena—not so much because of his visit here, but because he knows an awful lot more." "And he's—good god, if there ever was a man wedded to Vietnamization and its defense—his whole political future is tied to that!"

ABRAMS (re Laird): "I think the main purpose of his visit out here . . . is the form. He's going up to Congress, and the president publicly stated that he was sending him for a reassessment. He's been out here, and he's consulted with all of us, with the embassy, the economic advisors, financial experts, and so on. He's consulted and conferred with Thieu and Ky and the prime minister, the minister of defense, and so on. Those are all facts. And, as I say, for what's coming up over the next three or four months that form is of tremendous importance to the secretary of defense. Because, regardless of what he does, this visit provides a credible—well, almost invincible—backdrop for whatever his proposals may be—some of which you and I may know absolutely nothing about at this time. So I think that was the real reason for it."

ABRAMS (re last Wednesday's meetings with Laird): "You enter that thing, putting it in the crudest terms, with a stacked deck. The important thing—if there is, as a matter of fact, any importance to it—is somehow, in that stacked deck environment, to insert a few credible thoughts. Nothing in the way of argumentation. I think that's pointless and useless."

17 FEB 1970: Under SecArmy Beal Briefing

Thaddeus R. Beal was under secretary of the army, 1969–1971.

ATTENDEES: Gen. Abrams, Mr. Beal, MG Baldwin, MG Conroy, BG Potts, BG Gunn, BG Kraft, Mr. Jacobson, Col. Borders.

JACOBSON: "There's no question that pacification is either 90 percent or 10 percent security, depending on which expert you talk to. But there isn't any expert that will doubt that it's the <u>first</u> 10 percent or the <u>first</u> 90 percent. You just can't conduct pacification in the face of an NVA division." "Organization is the second most important thing . . . after security."

ABRAMS: "Since the Accelerated Pacification Program began on 1 November 1968, it's been President Thieu's <u>personal</u> involvement, it's been his critiquing of province chiefs and corps commanders and that sort of thing—that's <u>really</u> why this thing goes. <u>Without</u> it, without his personal involvement on a continuing basis, this thing would have folded a good many times. That's what makes it work." "Quarterly he went from one end of the country to the other, critiquing, encouraging here and cracking the whip there." "PSDF—there wasn't <u>anybody</u> in favor of it—except the president, and the people." "It would be difficult to overstate the role that the president has played in this." "He knew the program better than <u>anybody</u> in the government here in Saigon. There's no question of it."

JACOBSON: "We're going into a new HES system this month." Old one: Based on 18 questions. New one: 137 questions. Have been testing it since July 1969. "They base their plans on this. They've accepted this as <u>their</u> management tool." New report "will cause generally about a 5 percent drop in the A/B/C category." The new system is called HES 70.

20 FEB 1970: Briefing for General Abrams, Sir Robert Thompson, Ambassador J. O. Moreton (British Ambassador to the RVN), and Brigadier General Potts

ABRAMS: "We've captured North Vietnamese women." "They were just awful, absolutely incorrigible. I can't tell you how bad they were. Any group of men are easier to handle."

ABRAMS: "Several individual soldiers' packs have been captured on the battlefield. They are really first class, mostly of Chinese manufacture, containing extra uniforms—high quality—comparable in quality to our own—double stitching and so on, sleeping bags, first aid, and so on. They don't bring all that stuff down the trail. They travel light from station to station. They are then equipped in those base areas over in Cambodia."

BRIEFER: "The enemy is continuing to meet his goals for supplies despite our interdiction effort."

BRIEFER: "The enemy must be credited with having developed a relatively sophisticated logistical system which, in spite of our interdiction efforts, is providing support not only to his forces in South Vietnam, but to his forces in northern Laos, while concurrently supporting his personnel infiltration system."

ABRAMS: "He's working very hard at it."

BRIEFER: "Portions of Cambodia are under de facto occupation by the enemy."

21 FEB 1970: Commanders WIEU

ATTENDEES: Gen. Abrams, Gen. Rosson, Gen. Brown, LTG Mildren, LTG Collins, LTG Nickerson, VADM Zumwalt, LTG Corcoran, LTG Ewell, LTG Zais, MG Townsend, MG Dolvin, MG Conroy, Mr. Megellas, Mr. Firfer, MG McCown, Mr. Jacobson, MG Shaefer, Mr. Whitehouse, BG Gunn, BG Kraft, BG Vande Hey, BG Smith, BG Potts, BG Henderson, BG Jaskilka, BG Sykes, BG Cheadle, Mr. Wilson (for Mr. Vann), Col. Hanifen, Col. Healy, Col. Cutrona, Col. Doody, Col. Marriott (for Col. Cavanaugh).

ABRAMS: Describes situation in which Thailand, apparently seeking concessions on where Thai International airline could fly, has blocked Pan Am [effective 25 February 1970] from coming into Bangkok (maybe just from Vietnam). So Abrams quietly shut down the R&R program to Bangkok, shifting it to Taipei. Consulted with Ambassador Unger. "Along with this is that we're unable to take any Thai troops to Bangkok for R&R. The R&R program is completely open to them at other sites. We'll transport them—take them to Hong Kong or Taipei or. . . ."

SOMEONE: "You've got $22 million revenue that's going to dry up in five days."

ABRAMS: "What we're doing here is taking our cue from Ambassador Unger." "He's on a good course."

■ ■ ■

BRIEFER: On 18 February 1970 Prime Minister Lon Nol returned to Phnom Penh from Paris. Meanwhile Sihanouk apparently is visiting a succession of Communist capitals: Prague and Moscow. Briefer cites "recently noted Royal Khmer Government measures to limit resupply of munitions to the VC/NVA and control VC/NVA activities in the border regions."

BRIEFER: Reviews the past nine months in Cambodian politics. Economy is in serious trouble. Rice exports dropped to practically nothing in 1969. Cause: Sihanouk's policy of nationalizing the commercial sector of the economy. Reopened diplomatic relations with the United States on 15 August 1969, three days after the Lon Nol government was formed. Prince Sirik Matak "has been serving, for all practical purposes, as prime minister since the government was formed because of Lon Nol's almost continuous absence." "The previous policy of complicity with the VC/NVA was seemingly based on the assumption that the VC/NVA would triumph in the Republic of Vietnam in a relatively short time." That didn't turn out to be the case. Cites a "growing possibility that the ARVN will engage the VC/NVA on Cambodian soil" per Cambodian outlook.

■ ■ ■

BRIEFER: Describes press accounts containing classified information, including one that specified "the locations of the bases and carriers from which the air attacks were launched" into the Plaine des Jarres and against the Ho Chi Minh Trail, "and also reported that B-52s struck NVA supply depots in eastern Laos." On 20 February 1970 an AP item in the *Saigon Post:* "American B-52 bombing strikes in South Vietnam were halted for 36 hours while the Strategic Air Command force was diverted to North Vietnamese targets in Laos. . . ."

EWELL: "We had a story break that wasn't sensitive, but I would say it was awkward. And, after digging around for about three weeks, we found that a news agency had a soldier stringer in the headquarters who was directly relaying them reports."

ABRAMS: The "timeliness and the accuracy" of the news reports shows that "some individual in the system, where this all is put together quickly, . . . is passing it on." "I'm convinced now we've got guys in the system who are doing this." "The unfortunate fact has been, for well over a year and a half, that if there's something which has to be secure and cannot—just cannot, just cannot—be in the hands of the press, then you <u>cannot</u> use the regular staff organization. I don't care <u>what</u> you classify it, you cannot use your regular staff organization. There can be <u>no</u> messengers, there can be <u>no</u> message center, there can be <u>no</u> normal handling of super-classified material. It's got to be done by <u>only</u> the individuals directly concerned. They are the <u>only</u> ones who can handle the papers. They must keep them in their own safes themselves. And when there has to be coordination in meetings and so on, they have to <u>go</u> and they have to carry their papers with them. And it all has to be handled verbally and orally among that close-knit group. Otherwise, you have a high degree of probability, a high degree of probability, that it will be in the *Washington Post,* the *New York Times,* and on the AP and UPI wires and so on. And that's the plain, hard, cold <u>fact</u>!"

ABRAMS: "And I'm talking now about the <u>military</u> system, and the <u>military</u> people. And that's what we've <u>got</u>. You've got to recognize that there are people in the system who are against the war. There are <u>military</u> people in the system who are against the war. It's not a great number. It doesn't <u>have</u> to be a great number. And then, you've got the other kind. You see, some men just can't <u>live</u>, they just can't <u>exist</u>, unless what they're doing receives credit. They've just <u>got</u> to have it, or they just can't carry on in their work. So <u>those</u> guys are there. Now they're not against the war. They're not against anybody. But goddamn it their department has got to get the public recognition for the <u>sacrifice</u> and the <u>fantastic effort</u> that they're making! <u>All</u>, up until now, going absolutely unheralded and unknown. Promotion boards won't know it, the higher authorities won't know it, the people handling budgets won't know it— all of this."

BRIEFER (on enemy logistics): During 1969 imports into North Vietnam "total almost 1.9 million tons by sea and over 200,000 tons by rail." Bringing in about 500 trucks per month. About 4,137 trucks in the major parks in North Vietnam now. During 1969 an estimated 4,000 tons of arms and munitions were delivered to Cambodia. During 1969 the allies captured almost 300 in-country caches. In early February 1970 a large munitions cache was discovered in III CTZ, at this point totaling over 153 tons.

BRIEFER: The enemy system, despite our interdiction efforts, is providing support to his forces in South Vietnam, northern Laos, and in the personnel infiltration system.

■ ■ ■

ABRAMS: "It's very clear to me that we are not going to be able to have everything that we want. Every part of the program has got to be justified not only in terms that it's useful, but it's more useful than other parts of the program. I don't want anything going on here just because we've always had it and gotten used to it. And every one of these projects has its own parochial protagonist who rates it above anything else. But that's not going to do us any good. We've got to be cold-blooded about it, and we've got to put our money where we're going to get the most good out of it."

ABRAMS: "It's true we're now getting more out of 1,400 [B-52 sorties] a month than we were getting out of 1,800 a month. Of course also the problem is bigger. Their effort's greater, and there's more there. But anyway, the quality of targeting has gone up a little over 100 percent—which is good."

ABRAMS (re chart displaying alleged Cambodian border incidents): "Old Uncle Sam is the only goddamn one in the world that will wince with every goddamn one of these reports—the only one. And he'll get serious about it and he'll go to work and he'll try to get the truth, shoulder the blame where he's been wrong and apologize, pay off."

■ ■ ■

MILDREN (on safety): "Last fall we had a case of two warrant officers—pilots—practicing quick draw. They were both equally as fast, and they shot one another. I didn't think that I'd ever run into that again, but last week we had the same thing but only one of them got shot—the other one was faster. Well, now, why would people do that?"

ABRAMS (re problems in Hong Kong created by MACV personnel on R&R): "This is commanders' business. This thing with the Negroes is symptomatic—it's symptomatic of our lack of success thus far in South Vietnam of dealing effectively with the friction and the problem between the races. As we talked here once before, it's not only between the blacks and the whites, it's the whites and the Vietnamese, and the older whites and the younger whites, and the older blacks and the younger blacks—I mean, there's all kinds of things involved. And these are the times we're living in, and it does no good to sit around and piss about the good old days, because they aren't here—if they ever were." "In terms of total people, it's insignificant. Except that . . . the impact is far—."

NICKERSON: Says the senior sergeant of III MAF was in Hong Kong and told of seeing three American blacks dressed in suits they had had made there—one tan, one light green, and one pink. One had an orange comb in his hair. "Maybe I'm an old fart, but I would think a PX-type coat would get you on the airplane." And later: "Have you seen these white lace shirts they wear with it?" Wants to control this. Others laugh, ask where they can get such a shirt.

ABRAMS: "I'll tell you one thing, I think any program that we might consider getting launched on that has to do with regulation dress should be examined in some depth before really getting serious with it, because it will not pass unnoticed. And then you have to figure out whether you can really win when the flak goes up—you know, it gets fairly dense."

■ ■ ■

BRIEFER (on herbicide operations): All are initiated at province level (U.S. or SVN). Both the American Embassy and MACV sign off on the RVN plan. The process takes four to six months and "generally reflects President Thieu's desire to limit herbicide operations to areas of low population density and enemy infiltration routes." The air force FY 1971 budget for herbicides is $3 million. To cover the stated requirements would cost $27 million.

ABRAMS: "There's not going to be a supplemental. The secretary of defense seemed to be quite firm on that. So it has to come out of the service budgets elsewhere." "I raise the question whether we should insist on this $24 million for herbicides—in the environment that I've described to you." "I'm trying to push in the direction of taking a hard stand on those things that are most critical. I doubt, quite frankly, I doubt that this is in that category." "I want to make it clear I'm not trying to help out with the budget. I'm not trying to accept the problems with DOD's budget here. What I'm trying to do is be realistic in the environment that they're trying to resolve our problems in, and just hang on like a bulldog to those things which are the most critical to us."

EWELL: "There's no doubt in my mind herbicides are going out of style."

■ ■ ■

ABRAMS: "This thing about shifting some of our assets over from the more or less regular U.S. forces into the advisory—I just want to tell you we're real serious about it. I'm prepared to listen to a considerable amount of screaming. I just want to tell you that I probably will be unsympathetic to most of it, even though it becomes rather strident, because I'm set. I believe absolutely that this is right."

■ ■ ■

NICKERSON: "I'd like to say sayonara to the WIEU. I'd like to make a speech thanking everyone for a liberal education this past year. General Abrams—I've enjoyed serving under General Abrams. And everyone, I can't think of a better way to leave the service after 35 years in the Marine Corps than to be told today by the ROK president—he honored me with the Ulchi—'To Lieutenant General Herman Nickerson, United States <u>Army</u>.'" [Uproarious laughter, applause]

ABRAMS: "Nick, no matter what banner you're flying, you are a welcome addition to the community, anywhere, anytime."

25 FEB 1970: Admiral McCain Briefing

macv 1970 Infiltration Estimate: 27,500 (75 percent to COSVN).

POTTS (re enemy strength "in-country and adjacent"): "We find that the 227,000–228,000 that we account for right now is about 40,000 less than it was just one year ago at this time. About three-quarters of the combat strength is NVA."

POTTS: "At the time of the last SEACORDS meeting on 28 August [1969]—for that whole week there were 20 sensor detections of vehicle activity—<u>20</u>. Last week: 13,692."

BRIEFER: Describes the major cache discovered in III Corps: Total weight 169 tons. 3,700,000 rounds of small-arms ammunition. 122-mm rockets. Rocket launchers from Romania, shovels from India, tires from Cambodia, rifle grenades from North Vietnam. But 95 percent of the total was from the PRC. Cache was fortified, with overhead cover. Dugouts with steps, ammo above-ground on pallets, covered with plastic sheeting, leaves and vine cover. Been there not longer than nine months. Telephones from Czechoslovakia. Some packed as late as December 1969. They refer to it as "the Rang Rang cache."

■ ■ ■

COLBY: "The main effort of the Phoenix program is the identification, by name and position, of the members of the Viet Cong infrastructure." "Then our main effort . . . is the <u>capture</u> of those people, through the means of either inducing them to rally or capturing those people in order to get additional information on the rest of the people within this wiring diagram. Unfortunately the program, through the good offices of our press friends, has gotten the label of 'assassination.' Our major objective is the opposite of assassination. The main effort is on inducement to rally or capture in order to obtain additional information."

BRIEFER: In 1969, 19,534 class A and B infrastructure members were neutralized. Also 28,316 class C. Monthly goal in 1969 and 1970: 1,800 per month. At the beginning of 1969: Estimated 82,000 VCI. At end 1969: Estimated 74,000 VCI. Not much confidence in the numbers.

JACOBSON (re the VCI): "Without these people, the other side cannot win."

28 FEB 1970: WIEU

ATTENDEES: Gen. Abrams, Gen. Rosson, LTG Mildren, Mr. Kirk, MG Townsend, MG Dolvin, MG Conroy, MG Dixon (for Gen. Brown), Mr. Jacobson, MG Shaefer, MG Bautz, MG Dettre, RADM Suerstedt (for VADM Zumwalt), BG Gunn, BG Kraft, BG Vande Hey, BG Smith, BG Potts, BG Henderson, BG Jaskilka, BG Sykes, BG Cheadle, Col. Cavanaugh, Col. Hanifen, Col. Cutrona.

ABRAMS: "I'm not saying that the Cambodians are friends of ours, or friends of the Vietnamese, but some of the little things they're doing in their own self-interest are helpful. And we ought to look at it that way and not go promiscuously killing Cambodians."

ABRAMS (re capture and exploitation of VCI roster for Binh Thuan): "One of the fellows they snatched up right away was the mimeograph operator in the province headquarters. That little bastard was in there taking a copy of everything." "The thing that we have to work harder and harder on in 1970 is an understanding of this part of it. You can go out here and beat the shit out of the 9th Division—I mean reduce it so all they've got left is 150 men in the whole division, but if you haven't advanced on this other front it's all for naught. You haven't gotten anywhere! You just think you have. I know body count, you know—it has something about it, but it's really a l-o-n-g way from what's involved in this war. Yeah, you have to do that, I know that, but the mistake is to think that that's the central issue."

ABRAMS: "It's like the PSDF or the PF. You can brag about how you've got almost double the artillery in ARVN, you've got four Huey squadrons flying around in VNAF, you've got all these boats turned over and the crews are functioning well and they're aggressive and so on, almost 400,000 M16s distributed, and so on. But when you come to the end of '70 and you've still got half of the PF that are really unsatisfactory, and three-fourths of the PSDF couldn't find their way to the outhouse—I'll tell you, all that other stuff, the boats and the helicopters and the M16s and the artillery, is for nothing."

■ ■ ■

ABRAMS: "Charlie Corcoran told me a story about Bu Prang . . . the Americans . . . realized that morale in there was shaken up. Well, they thought it was from the shelling and so on. Well, it turns out that wasn't the reason at all. The camp is part Cambodians and part Montagnards. And outside the camp, near the camp, lived a large python which the Montagnards worshipped, and occasionally took offerings to the python. Well, the Cambodians went out one day and they killed the python and ate him. And this was just not acceptable to the Montagnards. Well, and that's where the Special Forces types . . . understand these things. So they conferred with the Montagnards, and it was decided this could all be resolved by an appropriate sacrifice. Well, it turned out an appropriate sacrifice would be a white water buffalo. So then they searched the highlands to locate a white water buffalo. They eventually did [find one] and bought the thing, and got it to an airfield and tried to get it in a C-7. I guess there weren't any real expert livestock handlers, because they couldn't get the damn thing in the C-7. So then they got a rig—a sling and a hook—and hoisted this water buffalo up with the hook [cargo helicopter] and took off for Bu Prang. Well, as they later reconstructed it, somehow the rather sizable male organs of the water buffalo had gotten entangled in the sling and the resulting frantic gyrations of the buffalo broke his neck. So he arrived at Bu Prang dead. Well, that wouldn't fill the bill. To end this thing up, what they finally settled on were two hundred chickens. So they went out and bought two hundred chickens and flew them into Bu Prang, and then had a great feast of the chickens <u>and</u> the water buffalo. The chickens filled the bill for the sacrifice, and the water buffalo—they just dressed him out and threw that in the pot, too. And peace and quiet then reigned over Bu Prang. Morale was back and restored, and the Cambodians and the Montagnards were able to go on peacefully together."

7 MAR 1970: WIEU

ATTENDEES: Gen. Abrams, Gen. Rosson, Gen. Brown, Amb. Colby, LTG Mildren, VADM Zumwalt, Mr. Kirk, MG Townsend, MG Dolvin, MG Conroy, Mr. Jacobson, MG Shaefer, MG Bautz, MG Dettre, BG Gunn, BG Kraft, BG Vande Hey, BG Potts, BG Henderson, BG Jaskilka, BG Sykes, Col. Cavanaugh, Col. Hanifen, Col. Cutrona, Col. Church (for BG Smith), Col. Martin (for BG Cheadle).

ABRAMS: "I'm not guaranteeing a big battle in May, but some of the evidence, some of the indicators, are there." "And I don't want to get misled by the goddamn preparations for it the way I was last year. I had *Good Housekeeping* stamps of approval—everything—on the arrangements up there. And, Christ, they couldn't have stood a Sunday outing by a mass of Boy Scouts. They just came apart at the seams."

CUTRONA: "We received guidance from Defense to the effect that we will report air activities in Vietnam, the Republic of Vietnam. We have nothing to add to what the president has said on the subject of Laos. Any further information on Laos will come from Washington, and they underlined Washington, and not Department of Defense, or the embassy in Vientiane. The Department of Defense intends to refer queries to the White House, and possibly eventually to the Department of State. We don't know what State's position is going to be as yet."

■ ■ ■

BRIEFER (quoting from Royal Cambodian Government cabinet council debate broadcast by Phnom Penh domestic service on 5 February 1970): "At this meeting Matak urged all Cambodian officials to make more determined efforts to control the smuggling of rice and cattle beyond the Cambodian border.

Matak related incidents of military and civilian officials who are tolerating and providing support for smuggling activities and stated that this lack of integrity was seriously hurting the antismuggling effort and the national economy. Matak then went on to divulge the government's involvement with the VC and stated, 'I have something to say about the story that the fact that we transport rice and other products for the VC constitutes smuggling. I must state that the Royal government has concluded a trade agreement with the Provisional Revolutionary Government, an agreement as official as those we have signed with France and other countries and according to which we have sold our product against payment of currencies. Recently I have heard that we have transported a lot of products for the VC. This is true, but it is in accordance with the agreement. The other day we actually transported 1,500 tons of rice for the VC because they wanted to buy from us. From now on we must stop smuggling for them, because we already have an agreement with them. If they want to buy something, they have only to buy directly.'" "'The government is now legally transporting rice for the Viet Cong. I want the public to know this.'"

ABRAMS: "The other amazing thing is that he was able to discover the term 'integrity.' He probably had some help on that."

BRIEFER: "This statement represents the first conclusive evidence of the degree of Matak's complicity as acting prime minister with the VC/NVA." The agreement was concluded in September 1969.

■ ■ ■

BRIEFER: "On 28 February, F-105s targeted against an interdiction point on Route 7, 11 miles from the border and 7 miles west of the previous 4-mile restricted area, were fired upon by four surface-to-air missiles." They "took evasive action, and no damage to the aircraft occurred. As a result of this incident, MACV has prohibited operations within the SAM envelope. This restriction precludes strikes against the best interdiction point on Route 7 east of Ban Ban."

ABRAMS: "Well, just a minute. I think you need one more word in there, and that is that the air force does not have the authority to attack that site, even when it's fired at. Right?"

BROWN: "No, sir, we can't attack that."

ABRAMS: "So, under those circumstances, I just don't see how you can call on people to go up there to work. That's the whole point in this thing, the lack of authority to attack that damn site, or any other site up there in that area that opens up on you. Of course, we've tried to get the authority, and I'll be goddamned if I understand why we can't, because the photo recon guys that go in North Vietnam—of course, they're limited, too, but they can attack anybody that shoots at them from North Vietnam."

BROWN: "We're south of 19 degrees."

ABRAMS: "Yes, I know, but all this crap about we can take whatever action's required to protect our own forces, protective reaction—all kind of great patriotic speeches have been made about that! And if the principle doesn't apply here, I'll be damned—. Of course, I suppose there are policy questions that I don't know about. Anyway, I <u>must</u> say, from a rigid parochial position, this is <u>very</u> difficult to understand."

BROWN: "We're not taking a hell of a risk with fighters. You know, they've all got warning gear and all that stuff. I wouldn't under any circumstances put 130 [C-130] gunships in there, or heavy stuff that can't outmaneuver the missiles."

ABRAMS: "I know, George, but if we accept it for this, what the hell is the <u>next</u> one we're going to have to accept it for?"

SOMEONE: Authorities run out at the end of next month. We have a message coming in for General Abrams to send asking for an extension.

BROWN: "I don't want to overstate this thing. This isn't going to win or lose the war. On the other hand, you do sort of hate to give the enemy a piece of Laos, a piece of territory that we ought to be able to work in."

ABRAMS: "I don't quarrel with any of that. I just think there're other things involved here."

ABRAMS: "I don't know whether it was Mu Gia or Ban Karai—you know, they went back the next day? And after the—basically, after antiaircraft—and the damn fools fired the missile. And they really clobbered that position—<u>good</u>. That's the kind of thing—you know, giving 'signals' and 'sending messages' and all that, that's the kind they <u>r-e-a-l-l-y</u> understand." Same with the photo missions after the bombing halt. They were "pretty gay" shooting at our aircraft until we started retaliating with those 1,000-pound bombs. "Some things they understand, and some things they don't."

BROWN: "We used 3,000-pound bombs."

ABRAMS: "I knew you upped the ante. Let's not quibble over a couple thousand pounds." [Laughter]

ABRAMS: "<u>But</u>—it's just so <u>true</u>! Christ, sending notes—you know. They <u>love</u> that. They can do that, everybody. All it costs is the paper."

■ ■ ■

ABRAMS (re the DMZ): "Since the bombing halt we have been limited to staying below the southern demarcation line, except for patrols, and except for the authority to return fire." Therefore we are not in a position to establish a corridor in the DMZ for potential return of prisoners to North Vietnam, as proposed in a State Department message. "<u>We</u> [the U.S. and the GVN] don't have <u>control</u> of that. The North Vietnamese have control of that. We <u>gave</u> it to them in the understanding accompanying the bombing halt." The fellow in State who wrote the message apparently doesn't understand that. "He's probably still living in this dream world that the North Vietnamese are north of the river and the South Vietnamese are south of the river." "Are we going to go out there and engage in a bunch of goddamn battles, that sort of thing, in order to open up a fucking road for a half a day to move—and take a bunch of casualties—you know, open it by force? <u>No</u>, we're <u>not</u>!"

■ ■ ■

ABRAMS (re current J-2 assessment): "It's not <u>complete</u> enough to describe the purely military situation." "Government effectiveness, government control, security, terrorism, RF/PF, PSDF" are all important parts of the situation. Re assessment of the enemy: "We talk about what are the capabilities of his military program. All right, what are the capabilities of his cadre, his guerrillas, his local forces? You know, we've been preaching the doctrine that this thing is conducted at several levels and we've got to push all these levels along. Well, by god, you haven't solved the problem. And <u>that</u> means reduction in the effectiveness of this other critical part of the <u>doctrine</u> by which they conduct <u>this</u> kind of a war. Giap never neglected the political cadre, the infrastr—, the cadre, and the guerrillas, and the local forces. And he's said many times this is intelligence, it's guides, it's labor, it's revenue, it's food, and so on. And also, if you're talking in terms of political contests, or political confrontation, or even if you're talking about the development of political force, it's <u>critical</u>. It's absolutely <u>essential</u> to that that cadres be functional and so on. I guess I'm only saying that this is one part that the J-2 is presenting here, and it is by no means the whole war. And it's by no means what has got to be <u>done</u> by the Vietnamese. It's one thing to try to have a look at these outfits and what—the damn things that they're doing and so on, but the other part has got to be done, <u>too</u>."

■ ■ ■

ABRAMS (re Cambodian outposts): "The amount of interference [with enemy activity] that that causes is really insignificant. It's quite like our border camps for CIDG. <u>Christ</u>, what they do . . . in infiltration, the flow of logistics, and all that kind of stuff is virtually <u>zero</u>. <u>Bo Duc</u>! What the hell has that ever done about the highway down the Song Be?" "For instance, I just got the IG report on Dak Pek—the joint IG report on Dak Pek. In that particular field this goddamn thing is <u>anti</u>government—in a way. The way they <u>exploit</u> the strikers, the way they <u>exploit</u> the people, and so on. Jeez, it's not [pounding the table] advancing the cause of the GVN <u>at all</u>! It's sending it the other way!" "<u>God damn</u>, it's just pure exploitation!"

14 MAR 1970: Commanders WIEU

ATTENDEES: Gen. Abrams, Gen. Rosson, Gen. Brown, Amb. Colby, LTG Mildren, LTG Collins, LTG Zais, LTG McCutcheon, Mr. Kirk, MG Townsend, MG Dolvin, MG Conroy, Mr. Firfer, MG McCown, Mr. Jacobson, Mr. Vann, Mr. Whitehouse, MG Milloy (for LTG Ewell), MG Bautz, MG Dettre, BG Gunn, BG Kraft, BG Vande Hey, BG Greene, BG Potts, BG Henderson, BG Jaskilka, RADM Suerstedt (for VADM Zumwalt), BG Sykes, BG Cheadle, Mr. Chambers (for Mr. Megellas), Col. Cavanaugh, Col. Hanifen, Col. Healy, Col. Cutrona.

macv 1970 Infiltration Estimate: 34,100 (68 percent to COSVN).

ABRAMS (re infiltration statistics): "It just isn't the way the ball game is played—

on averages. What he has been doing is peaking for certain things."

BROWN: On Routes 1039 and 92 just west of the DMZ we're seeing "a tremendous road-building activity, and river development, to include damming to permit controlled water levels, chutes to vector supplies down. . . . It flows right into [Base Area] 604."

■ ■ ■

BRIEFER: "Our general interpretation is, sir, that Lon Nol and Sirik Matak are getting involved in forcing a policy change from Sihanouk's idea of covert complicity with the VC/NVA to overt neutralism." "This policy has been evolving since last March [1969], at least that was the first public announcement. On March 14th Sihanouk admitted that the VC/NVA were in the country."

■ ■ ■

BRIEFER: Strike by 30 fighters on Route 914B on 7 March 1970 three miles southwest of Tchepone against a large ammunition and supply storage area produced over 1,700 secondary explosions and fires.

■ ■ ■

SOMEONE: Suggests discrediting an AP report by giving the correct story to a competitor.

ABRAMS: "This is kind of like helicopter sightings—it's such a <u>tempting</u> thing. [Laughter] But I want to just say again the old adage about pigs: 'Don't wrestle with pigs—they <u>love</u> it, and you get <u>dirty</u>!'" [Laughter]

■ ■ ■

BRIEFER: Enemy strength declined from about 267,000 on 1 January 1969 to about 228,200 at the end of February 1970. About 172,000 KIA during 1969. In January–February 1970: 19,210 more KIA. And during 1969, 47,023 Hoi Chanhs (28,045 of them military). Total 1969 losses due to KIA, Hoi Chanh, died of wounds, permanently disabled, and nonbattle losses exceeded those for 1968 by 2,010.

BRIEFER: "The progress of the Accelerated Pacification Program, and the enemy's resultant loss of control of the population in large areas, account for much of his difficulty in recruiting."

BRIEFER: "The capture of enemy caches in-country continues to compound the enemy's logistical problems. As of 28 February, allied forces have captured 560 enemy caches, including the 169-ton munitions cache and a 135-ton rice cache in III Corps, a 62-ton rice cache in I Corps, and numerous smaller caches countrywide."

BRIEFER: "The VCI remains a viable organization."

ABRAMS: Cites "the increase in the capability of the Vietnamese [reacting to briefer's statement that the principal obstacle to VC/NVA is the presence of large American forces]. This applies—it's not really just the regular forces, it applies to the Territorial Forces, it applies to the government, actually—getting out and doing a little more, police, operation of the Phoenix program, the whole gamut of things that's happening on the <u>Vietnamese</u> side.'"

ABRAMS (re the enemy): "They say that Vietnamization is not going to work. However, they're concerned that it <u>might</u>. And, in the long pull, this is really a greater concern to them than the presence of U.S. forces. See, if that gambit works out, they've <u>really</u> got a problem. Encouraging the antiwar element in the United States is not going to do them a hell of a lot of good if the South Vietnamese have turned into a bunch of tigers. That's kind of a wasted effort then."

■ ■ ■

ABRAMS (re the short-term importance of U.S. forces): "It's not so much—you get into this—it's not so much our infantry battalions, or rifle battalions. We've had a discussion here in the last few days about, 'What if they propose a cease-fire, and out of that comes regroupment, regroupment of all non–South Vietnamese?' Well, that would mean regroupment of all U.S. Well, for instance, we regroup the medical evacuation helicopters—companies, right now evacuating 95 percent, 98 percent, of all Vietnamese military and civilian casualties. What's that going to do when you regroup the medical helicopter companies, or you regroup the tactical airlift? You know, you <u>regroup</u>. All the NVA regroups to War Zone C, Seven Mountains, the U Minh, A Shau, and so on. Or you regroup all the <u>artillery</u>. Regroup the U.S. <u>signal</u> companies, battalions, groups, and brigades. I mean, I don't know how they define what's regrouped and that sort of thing, but if you insist on regroupment—you know, of all non–South Vietnamese, this presence of U.S. forces—it isn't just the U.S. rifle battalions. That's enough of a problem, but it's a lot of these other things. There's quite a lot of helicopters in the country every day that are dedicated to the pacification program."

ABRAMS (re possible regroupment or the like): "One of the things that you're up against when you start talking about the possibility of this kind of thing occurring—the real Boy Scout attitude among, the natural national instinct for being Boy Scouts. Of course, nationally, we're not a bunch of Boy Scouts, but somehow that's the image we always like to push out. And so the whole conversation gets all confused about 'being fair with the North Vietnamese and being fair with the VC,' you know, this kind of—. And 'what we demand, or insist, that the North Vietnamese do, then we must do the same thing, we must be meticulous about it, if we want them to be meticulous about it.'"

ABRAMS: "And it's very hard to get into that discussion, or exchange, any talk about what <u>bastards</u> they've really been for the last—well, I mean, the Communists are Communists, as they always have been the same. They've never stood by an agreement anywhere in the world. In fact, their energies are <u>devoted</u> to getting around <u>every</u> agreement, and still posing as the great people and all that kind of stuff. Well, again, it's not what the facts are, it's what people <u>believe</u> the facts are. And the U.S. types that mucker around in this and advance these kind of ideas are just that kind of people—insisting on fairness and equality for all and this sort of thing. Of course, it's terrible, but that's the way they are."

ABRAMS: "See, that's what happened to <u>Laos</u>. Why should we stick our head in the sand like an ostrich? I mean, that was sold as a pretty damn good thing at the time by the <u>same</u> kind of people." But the enemy: "These are just bad <u>people</u>." "It's just the plain facts of history, and why should they change now? But you've still got these U.S. characters that float around in a world of—<u>completely</u> separated from reality. And that's what fri—well, concerns, me—about how definitions finally are drawn—. And then plus—<u>plus</u>, I might say—they'll gather in that whole other bunch of guys that are wrestling with the budget. And boy, I'll tell you, you stand down 3,000 helicopters and 1,500 tactical aircraft, and no bombs being consumed, and <u>Jesus</u>—what that does! I mean, you're talking hundreds of millions as a Christmas present. All you've got to do is follow this story. Sixty-one helicopters we've got to do nothing but medical evac, every day—for the Vietnamese."

BROWN: "There's no question in my mind but what we'll make work the thing that most people understand Vietnamization to be—that is, we'll form the units, equip them, train them. But, in the time remaining, we're not going to create a force that will take the place of the force that's here now at the present. So what you've got to do is trim the security problem to a dimension that that force you create can handle. That's pacification and that means continuing our presence over here until that pacification reaches the point of" filling the bill.

■ ■ ■

COLBY: "The only two things that the Fulbright Committee was interested in, and most of Washington, <u>really</u>—I mean, they were polite about all the rest, but the only two things that were listened to were Phoenix and the Chau case. The Chau case is a problem that we have to solve in other ways, but the Phoenix—I went out very flatly on the point that the United States government is not associated with a program of assassination, and that the government of South Vietnam is <u>trying</u> to make this a decent program, a normal internal security program conducted under decent standards. I was very fortunate because the press had been sent out to dig and obviously see what they could find. Two articles came out the day I testified about this thing, and <u>if</u> this program had been a program of assassination and brutality and so forth then we would have had a lot of trouble. Those reporters did not find that kind of a thing. The Walter Cronkite show put the testimony on first and then showed a water treatment interrogation of an old man someplace. I have no idea where it came from. I think the key to it is the extent to which we can <u>police</u> this program, make our advisors aware of our <u>insistence</u> that it be carried on in decent standards, improve the mechanisms— the legal procedures, interrogation procedures, and so forth."

The "Chau case" involved Tran Ngoc Chau, who had served as a Viet Minh battalion commander during the war against the French. Later he joined the ARVN and rose to become a colonel and a province chief. In the late 1960s he was elected to the Vietnamese National Assembly, where he opposed many of the policies of President Thieu. In 1969 his brother, Tran Ngoc Hien, who was a North Vietnamese intelligence officer, was captured by South Vietnamese police. During interrogation Hien told the police that he had been in regular contact with his brother Chau. Chau had apparently told one or two American officials about those contacts, but had not informed the South Vietnamese government. Chau was arrested and prosecuted for espionage. He denied the charges, but was convicted and imprisoned until the fall of South Vietnam. After the Communists took over, Chau was placed in a "re-education" camp. He emigrated to the United States in the late 1980s.

■ ■ ■

ABRAMS: "I'm almost hesitant to raise the matter of budget in this group, but at some risk I'm going to do it. It's gradually beginning to unfold, but it's pretty clear now that the Defense budget for '71 is going to be quite restricted, and South Vietnam has not been excluded from the effects of this. And, as the experts in budget matters are capable of doing, if you're going to make savings in FY '71, then you've got to take some actions in FY '70 in terms of production and contracts, cancellations and slowdowns, that sort of thing. Well, anyway, without going into the specifics, that's the <u>climate</u> that we're clearly going into. I'm a little hesitant to raise it here, as I said, because any good field commander with that prospect in view is going to prepare himself for the days of austerity by—well, by getting the things that would tide him over the lean times."

ABRAMS: "What I want to tell you is that, from the evidence at hand, it really isn't necessary for you to <u>do</u> that. If you'll just inventory the mountains of excess which you now have, I think you'll find that you have adequate provision to carry you through the <u>slimmest</u> kind of period. The experience so far in units leaving South Vietnam, redeploying or being deactivated—the amount of excess that finally starts pouring in by convoys and so on is really extraordinary. It reminds me of the day that Ray Peers told me he turned in 1,200 CONEX containers that had never been opened out at Camp Enari. He said, 'Just leave me alone a little while longer. I'll get the <u>rest</u> of them out.'"

ABRAMS: "And that's the trouble with excess—excess, ordinarily, there isn't a soul in the outfit that knows what's there. And so they just keep ordering more. None of this stuff is any good unless you know what you've got, and where it is." "I just tell you, there's an awful lot that's got to be done on this. A lot <u>has</u> been done, but the surface really hasn't been scratched." "And of course, I guess two cases that we know of, in order to expedite getting rid of this stuff they've taken advantage of a hole already existing or they've dug one, then gone ahead and buried it."

ABRAMS: "We are <u>fighting</u> for some of the things that we <u>really</u> need. You know, really think that we've got to have in this budget squeeze, and we'll continue to do that. But if a few, just a few, handful of stories like that about burying ammunition when we're fighting for ammunition and so on. Here some bastard goes out here and buries a truckload of ammunition in order to get rid of it. It works against you. They want to know how that goes on when you say you need so much. And, while Washington is seldom very practical, you have to admit they have a point."

■ ■ ■

ABRAMS: "I want to touch on the same thing that Ambassador Colby talked about, and that is the enemy system. And I want to raise it because I'm not satisfied that everywhere there is an understanding or comprehension, first of all, of what his system is and, secondly, the essentiality of working against his system. Now when I talk about the system it's the same as Ambassador Colby mentioned. It's his cadres, the political structure that he's got, his intelligence structure, his guerrillas, his local forces, the whole system of logistics and administration and communications. I'm not talking about radio communication now, I'm not talking about telephone communication. I'm talking about the communication of either officers or officials in his system going forward and back to pass on instructions, to give guidance. It goes into the smaller [word unclear], noncoms, even the messengers who are carrying stuff back and forth. He needs all of these things to conduct the kind of war which he's been conducting here for 20-odd years. He needs that! They are essential and critical to the operation of his system!"

As the years go by and people rotate home from a tour in Vietnam, Abrams finds it necessary repeatedly to school their replacements in such matters.

ABRAMS: "This whole system—it's his hospital system, it's his administrative system, and the communications system, the logistics system, the cadres, the guerrillas, the local forces—they're all critical parts. It's just like a damn watch or something. There aren't any spare gears in a watch, and he hasn't got any spare ones in his system. And they've got to work or, by god, the system's not going to work."

ABRAMS: "I think in some places, either knowingly or just in the natural progression of events, that some quite satisfactory effort has been made against the total system. It's not enough to work on one part of it. That won't hack it. There's got to be something continuous."

■ ■ ■

ABRAMS: "When I was at the Americal [the other day] I got talking about this, and I never felt that I got in communication. And I was convinced of it when they got up to give that last minute or two about the 4th and 6th Regiments. See, I realized that if one of those 2nd Division battalions, or two of them, got down there in the outskirts of Quang Ngai, there isn't anything to do but get out there and really wrestle them to the ground. Or, you know, put enough heat on them so they get the hell out of there. You've got to <u>do</u> that."

ABRAMS: "But the <u>suspicion</u> that some battalion is somewhere in the jungle is <u>not</u>, in my opinion, justification to go ahead and try to find them and do battle with them. If they don't want to do it, you're not either. But what <u>is</u> important is to work against his <u>system</u> out there in the jungle, and that's his trails, his base areas, his caches, all of those. And we're not <u>necessarily</u> talking about big operations. It's operations that are tailored and designed to reduce the effectiveness of that system. And if those <u>succeed</u>, the <u>battalions</u> will go further back, because they need the system to <u>exist</u>! And if the food's taken away from them, and they're having trouble getting people through and so on, then they've <u>got</u> to—they are <u>forced</u> to move."

ABRAMS: "I think a lot has happened in III Corps that has <u>seriously</u> affected the efficiency with which <u>his</u> system can operate. It doesn't mean—for instance, with the cadre—that they have been reduced in numbers by all that [great an] amount, but if they've even temporarily been forced to go into the jungle, or go back out there away from the population, they're not doing their job. They're existing, that's right. And they can come back, <u>that's</u> right. But, while they're out there, they're not doing the job which they're set up to do. Revenue collecting, manpower recruiting, and all that sort of thing, just doesn't go on with the effectiveness that they need."

ABRAMS: "Then his supply system has been, I think, seriously damaged, including the people who work in it. So I'm just offering up here now to encourage more thinking, and then maybe some <u>application</u>, in terms of his total system. I don't want to go back to what's hackneyed—'one war' and all that sort of thing—but it is still the kind of a thing. And it's why, if this thing does move along the way it's supposed to, then <u>what</u> the Phoenix program does, what the <u>police</u> do, what the <u>PSDF</u> do, what the <u>Territorial Forces</u> do—see, this is <u>all</u> counter." "There may be a better way to design it, but we haven't got the time. And if you tried to go ahead with a real big redesign of the whole thing, <u>Christ</u>, it would set us back a <u>year</u>. . . . There may be better ways to organize it, but we've got to go from where we are. But all of these pieces are designed to fulfill a function in working against his system. They may not be all <u>attack</u> types against his system. Some of it is <u>defense</u> against his system getting started again where it's been brought down to a certain level."

■ ■ ■

ABRAMS: "Over the last few months I've had the, I can honestly say, the pleasure of talking with individuals, either visiting out here or some of them have been here for some time. These fellows—they're all guys that have had a year and a half or two years as a minimum here, some of them longer. Some of them speak Vietnamese. They're all—the ones <u>I'm</u> talking about—they're <u>deeply</u> involved with what's being done out here. They're <u>personally</u>, and even <u>emotionally</u>, attached to what basically our government started out to do and is still trying to do here in South Vietnam. In other words, as far as our national objectives, as far as the national objectives of the Vietnamese are concerned, these men are by no means hostile but in fact <u>want</u> to see it done, and done right."

ABRAMS: "Well, as I say, these are <u>experienced</u> people. And <u>all</u> of them make a real plea for longer tours, for language training, for deeper understanding of the Vietnamese people themselves and the Vietnamese culture and so on. There's not an argument <u>against</u> that. I think that's <u>right</u>. The <u>problem</u> is that we can't <u>do</u> it. Now I don't mean by that that we cannot <u>increase</u> the numbers of people who <u>have</u> the language training, who get the necessary schooling, and that sort of thing. That can be done. But I think even the best effort that's made on that is not going to turn up in the end with sufficient people to do the whole job. So while there's no <u>question</u>, in theory, that they're right in pressing this, and that that <u>is</u>, in the end, the most effective kind, it's <u>not</u> what we're going to have to get the total job done."

ABRAMS: "I hope this business of transfer and so on has started enough to begin to make at least a small degree of improvement there on the advisory side. We'll <u>press</u> that as much as we can, and we'll just have to take some lumps elsewhere."

Referring to a program of transferring people from U.S. troop units to the advisory role.

18 MAR 1970: Laos Update

J-3 (probably): "Godley wired me yesterday asking for all kinds of air support. I wired him back asking for target recommendations. I wanted to put the ball back in his court. I didn't want the record to show he asked for air support and we didn't respond."

ABRAMS: "In order to do anything you've got to have targets, you've got to have intelligence. They haven't got enough influence anywhere on the battlefield up there to get any intelligence."

ABRAMS: "Quite frankly, there's more to it than just wasting the goddamn B-52s. Back there in Washington, you fight to get this decision so that you can use them and so on and save the day, and it <u>doesn't</u> save the day. You know, that's the basis—'All right, we'll do it to save Laos.' And shit, they sleep on. All right, 'What has it done, the B-52s?' You talk about the budget, you talk about wanting 1,400 or 1,800 a month out here and so on, 'Well, piss on it. You couldn't do any good in Laos. I don't know why the hell you think it will do any good in South Vietnam. When we were in real trouble in Laos it wouldn't do it.' And it's just done on that basis. The fact that [slams table] there's no goddamn intelligence that's worth a shit, the fact that the thing has never been tactically run on a sound basis up there, just by a bunch of guys playing soldier—none of that's taken into account."

ABRAMS: "When all this damn thing is over [laughing], I don't want somebody up there in Systems Analysis to wipe the whole thing out on the basis that we couldn't do a damn thing in Laos—'This proves the case in Vietnam!'"

21 MAR 1970: WIEU

ATTENDEES: Gen. Abrams, Gen. Rosson, Gen. Brown, Amb. Colby, LTG Mildren, Mr. Kirk, VADM Zumwalt, MG Dolvin, MG Conroy, Mr. Jacobson, MG Bautz, MG Dettre, BG Gunn, BG Vande Hey, BG Greene, BG Henderson, BG Jaskilka, BG Sykes, BG Cheadle, Col. Cavanaugh, Col. Dessert (for BG Potts), Col. Hanifen, Col. Cutrona.

macv 1970 Infiltration Estimate: 36,500 (24,000 to COSVN).

ABRAMS: "Regardless of whatever logic you can develop for whatever position you want, the guys who are going to <u>decide</u> what the logic is are the <u>press</u>. So far, they haven't really come out with an overabundance of helpful solutions."

BRIEFER: "A letter captured on 25 February from a member of the 22nd NVA Regiment states that in the near future he would be transferred from the 3rd NVA Division to the Binh Dinh provincial unit to fight as a local force member. Possibly related are the statements of former members of the XCII Local Force Battalion, who stated that the battalion had been deactivated to provide replacements to district units in Binh Dinh Province. The transfer of NVA personnel to local force units, and the deactivation of local force battalions to provide replacements to districts, provide continuing indications of the effectiveness of the government pacification program."

ABRAMS: "I was out in the [U.S.] 4th Division and they were briefing me and they got into the <u>tactics</u>. They feel some frustration at not being able to <u>locate</u> the enemy and get into these big—well, you know, tackle a battalion or two and really chop them up. They went on to say they'd been quite impressed with the Korean operations. And—I must say somewhat to my <u>horror</u>—they found these multibattalion things quite impressive. So they had run one themselves. Now they said you have to have good intelligence for these things to be successful, and said they didn't think they had very good intelligence because I think they found one or two enemy in the five-battalion affair. But they thought that was probably intelligence and—anyway, they're planning another one."

ABRAMS: "I don't like to—first place, I have a tremendous respect for Walker, a really thorough professional—and I don't like to get into directing the tactics some division has conjured up. But I did undertake to explain to them that I <u>really</u> hadn't found these—in fact, had been <u>trying</u> to nudge the Koreans <u>out</u> of that sort of thing."

ABRAMS: "Then I got talking with them about this matter of working against the <u>system</u>. I've sort of become wedded to preaching about the system. And even going so far as to say, 'You can go out here and cut one of these battalions down to 60 men, but in three or four months, five months, they'll build it back again—as long as their <u>system</u> is functioning—supply, medical, infiltration, recruits—you know, all of those things. So the way to—one of the things—if you can get at that <u>system</u> and start putting inefficiency, failures, into the <u>system</u>, they're just going to have to move back.'"

ABRAMS: "And I assured them I wasn't trying to tell them what to do. And I told them I'd come back after they get through with this operation and have a chance to study it, assess it, and so on. I'd like to hear what they think of it, because the way the enemy's operating, I don't think, I <u>really</u> don't think that's the way to do it. Or—it's one way, there's no question about that. But is it the most effective thing you can do now?"

28 MAR 1970: WIEU

ATTENDEES: Gen. Rosson, Gen. Brown, LTG Mildren, VADM Zumwalt, MG Dolvin, MG Conroy, Mr. Jacobson, MG Dettre, BG Gunn, BG Clement, BG Kraft, BG Vande Hey, BG Greene, BG Henderson, BG Jaskilka, BG Sykes, RADM Rapp, BG Cheadle, Col. Dessert (for BG Potts), Col. Franklin, Col. Doody.

macv 1969 Infiltration Estimate: 106,000.
MACV 1970 Infiltration Estimate: 36,400 (23,500 to COSVN).

ROSSON: "Are any of you scheduled to see Joe Alsop while he's still in-country?"
JACOBSON: "Good lord, yes."
ROSSON: "Well, he's seen General Abrams and myself, and the discussion I had with him he got to nosing around in <u>this</u> business [infiltration]. And it's obvious that somebody—in Washington, I would judge—gave him the <u>input</u> figures to the pipeline, and he's talking about a monthly rate of about 9,000. Remember—in January, I think it was—the president made a rather unfortunate statement which had to be brought back in a graceful way. Without going through that whole story again, I just caution everyone that runs into Joe to be very, very careful of this. What <u>I</u> told him was that our information on infiltration is based on what we can pick up down here, which runs around 4,000 to 5,000 a month. That's our view of what's happened up into March, and our projection through the midyear, from documentation, defectors, PWs, and so on. But somebody can really get <u>burned</u> if they're ever caught up in talking about some of this [***] with somebody like Alsop. Although he's getting it someplace."

30 MAR 1970: COMUS Update, Cambodia Military and Political

BRIEFER: Speaks of the situation "as of the time of the coup." Lon Nol's brother was killed by demonstrators on 27 March. Prince Sihanouk remains in Peking.
ABRAMS: "I know that I'm recognized as generally being critical of assault by parachute, so there's no use in my trying to placate that reputation. But the point is that this is just—by Jesus, I'll tell you that any battalion you parachute

into 353 [as apparently advocated by General Vien in a discussion that afternoon], you can just scrub it from the books—unless you've already put four or five battalions in there to surround the LZ."

ABRAMS: "You know that LZ up above Tay Ninh? The 173rd made an airborne assault into that. It lost some of its truly combat quality when it was learned that *Life* photographers had been pre-positioned in the LZ so they'd get good shots of the parachutes coming down and be there on the ground to talk to some of the parachutists. It lacked some of the elements of a truly combat assault."

31 MAR 1970: COMUS Cambodian Assessment

ATTENDEES: Gen. Abrams, MG Dolvin, MG Bautz, MG Jaskilka, Col. Dessert. [Gen. Rosson is also present.]

ABRAMS: "Julian's [Ewell] in with a proposal to bus people from his area out there into Saigon so they'll have an opportunity to see the Vietnamese culture."

ROSSON: "He came in with this request and talked with me for about an hour and then had lunch with me. He's got quite a few things that he's thinking of sending in. I told him that on that one there was no point in sending it in. It was contrary to the thrust of everything we were attempting to do here with regard to the U.S. presence in Saigon."

ABRAMS: "I would scarcely call it 'culture' that they—I think it causes quite a b-r-o-a-d spectrum of activity, none of which is designed to enhance the image of American forces in Vietnam."

ROSSON: General Ewell thought "there should be sort of free intercourse" between U.S. and Vietnamese.

ABRAMS: "I don't think it's free."

1 APR 1970: Hon. Fraser, Minister of Defence, Australia, Briefing

ABRAMS: "When the bombing halt came, he wasn't getting six trucks a week into Laos. We went into that phase where bombing was restricted to below 20 degrees, and the navy and the air force went to work on that piece of North Vietnam south of 20 degrees. And, between the air and the weather—they had a lot of rain—that was turned into a morass. You just couldn't—you couldn't work it, you couldn't repair it. And virtually nothing was getting into Laos. I believe that, I've satisfied myself, that the reason during this period leading up to the bombing halt units were withdrawn from South Vietnam into North Vietnam was that he could not supply them. There wasn't enough getting through to sustain those forces. Now, since that stop, he's completely repaired all the roads, and he's got a free ride, and in anticipation of the dry season he goes and stockpiles stuff right up against the Mu Gia Pass or the Ban Karai

Pass and so on, getting everything ready so, when the roads are open, it starts in a big rush."

BRIEFER: "Back during Tet 1968, and in two other offensives that he conducted in 1968, and a post-Tet offensive of last year, he was going on the 'grand scale, win the war in a hurry' concept, mass uprisings, the general offensive-type campaign. He lost <u>heavily</u> in this type of activity during these four offensives—over 100,000 personnel."

ABRAMS: "Everybody knew that this was coming last night. There was quite a mass of intelligence on it, and everybody was warned."

ABRAMS: "COSVN Resolution 9 was their reaction to what happened at Tet '68. I think the GVN reaction was not only earlier, but it was more <u>accurate</u>. It was more accurately targeted on what had to be done from <u>their</u> viewpoint than the Communists were. They were <u>late</u>, and didn't have <u>their</u> effort organized. So I think at that point, first of November 1968—although no one would have heralded it as such at the time—it was a turning point in where the <u>GVN</u> took the initiative in South Vietnam—the initiative in the larger sense of the total war."

ABRAMS: "It's nothing dramatic, there isn't anything spectacular, just a whole lot of small units ambushing, patrolling, and working. And it's all to keep that system from getting back into a functioning state."

ABRAMS (re VCI): "It's not entirely how many you have eliminated or caught or jailed. What's happened to some of this infrastructure is it's out in the jungle where it can [gain] the security of its forces, which means that it's <u>not</u> functioning in the population. Now, it's true they'll survive in the jungle. And it's always something that can come out again if the Territorial Forces, the police, the PSDF, and so on aren't up to snuff. But, in terms of getting the job done, the only thing they're doing is surviving. They're <u>not</u> collecting taxes, they're <u>not</u> getting intelligence, they're <u>not</u> propagandizing the people, they're <u>not</u> twisting their arm, and this sort of thing. They're <u>dormant</u> where that situation exists."

ABRAMS: "What we've been preaching to the command goes something like this: This war, if you're really going to understand it and really get with it—<u>he</u> runs it, the enemy runs it, at about five or six levels. The levels are his infrastructure, guerrilla structure, local force structure, main force structure, his political effort, his propaganda effort. In order to play in that game effectively, <u>you've</u> got to operate at all those levels <u>yourself</u>. Or, to put it in other terms, if we've got the 5th and the 7th and the 9th backed up out in the jungle, backed up against the border, they can't do anything, well that's great. The 1st Cavalry's proud of that, and the ARVN Airborne's proud of it, and so on."

ABRAMS: "But what we're telling the commanders is you want to sort out priorities. The PSDF—huh! Everybody knows it's a civilian outfit, not that much training, not much firepower, weapons modest—in a way a kind of a half-assed outfit if you compare it with <u>regulars</u>. Can't hold a candle to the ARVN Airborne or the 1st ARVN Division. And the <u>PF</u>, little local chaps, that sort of thing. <u>But</u>, if right now the PSDF is about 50 percent effective, when we come to the end of 1970 if that hasn't been boosted to 80 or 90, it doesn't make any difference that the whole year we've held the 5th, 7th, and 9th right there on the border! We've failed for 1970 if we haven't done any more than that with the PSDF! You can be proud of the 1st Cavalry, you can be proud of the ARVN Airborne, you can be proud of the 25th ARVN and all of that, but if this hasn't come up we've failed!"

ABRAMS: "And we've got to face it now! Because that will be the day of accounting on the 31st of December of what we've done with the PSDF, with the PF, with the RF, with even the VIS and the police and all the rest of these. And every commander, I don't care if he's a brigade commander in the Big Red One or the 199th, he's got to look at this and understand this the same way. Yes, they've got to hold them out, I know that, and it's important. We mustn't let them come in. But we've got to realize that that's not the whole war. It may not even be the most important thing in the war. And we've got to be prepared to accept that."

ABRAMS: "It's this other that's got to move out. It's more difficult—the command and control, the chain of command, all of these things, you know, is not all that clear and positive and tight when you get over into these fields. And you mustn't look down on the PSDF because he's out there with an M1 carbine, and a limited amount of ammunition, and his clothes are a little worn, and he doesn't have any boots—he's just got sandals, and so on. He's got to be recognized as a key man, just the same as a platoon leader in A Company. He's important, too. And so we can't have priorities where the regulars are in priority 1 and the PSDF are in priority 12 if this thing is going to go right in 1970. For the job they do—and it's a limited one—but for the job they do they've got to have the same priority as the regulars, because that job has got to be done, and it's got to be done well."

■ ■ ■

ABRAMS (re VNAF): "General Brown tells me that their accuracy and so on is comparable to the Seventh Air Force. He says there is no practical difference between what his pilots are able to do and what they do." Accuracy, responsiveness, operationally ready rate.

ABRAMS (on VNAF): "They had a little trouble with maintenance on helicopters. Well, what they did, they overflew the flying hour program by a hundred percent for about three months, and they now have learned that you can't do that. You can do that, but you pay a price."

ABRAMS: "I was briefing Senator Javits in here one day and we were in this same general area. And I said to him, one of the examples, I said, 'We've practically doubled their artillery.' 'Oh,' he says, 'they don't need that, do they?' I said, 'Well, sir,' I said, 'tomorrow you're going down in the delta, and you'll talk with district chiefs and RF people—you'll see those fellows.' I said, 'I think it would be best to ask them. Give them the same thing. They'll give you an answer. You don't need an answer from me.'"

BRIEFER (re rice captured in-country): "In February, which is a record in itself, 303 tons. For March, 486 tons, and this is not all in yet [more to be reported]."

ABRAMS: "I am particularly happy about the rice that has been captured here in III Corps, and in IV Corps. That in III Corps is all rice that came out of Cambodia. And in the present environment of things, I think this is very timely."

BRIEFER: "I think it's quite significant, too, that last night, for instance, in Long An and Dinh Tuong Provinces, the attacks were very light. I think there were no attacks in Long An and I think 15 rounds on Dong Tam. But just a month and a half ago a large ammunition cache was found on the Long An–Dinh Tuong border. To my mind, this is the preemptive action. That cache, getting that ammunition—they just couldn't get off the ground."

ABRAMS: "There has been a significant downward trend in the casualties, the killed in action, on the friendly side." But (re the enemy): "His killed in action has stayed at roughly the same level over the past several months. So the cost to him has been fairly constant, while ours has declined substantially. In other words, I don't think that the policy of attacks by fire, standoff attacks, and sappers has really produced in concrete terms. He sees it as a way of saving his own manpower and increasing our losses, and I don't think—take the whole thing, it hasn't quite worked out that way."

BRIEFER: A Popular Force platoon is 35 men. "Under the operational control of the village chiefs, which is something new for 1969." "No longer the supply points for the Viet Cong which they used to be." "Engaged in defending their own mothers."

JACOBSON (re PSDF organization): "There is an organization. It's loose, and fluid, but it hasn't been contaminated by very much Western advice, so it's doing quite well in its own fashion." "It's a very Vietnamese solution to a very Vietnamese problem, and it's working very well. We're trying to stay out of it as much as we can."

■ ■ ■

JACOBSON (re the situation in 1961–1964 compared to 1970): "I believe that the people had regard for the VC, and I believe that—had free elections been possible—they would have won by a very considerable percentage. I now believe that, in those areas that they do not control, the Viet Cong exert their influence by sheer naked terror, and by little else. But that is their method of operation—exactly." "I think if a free election could be held now, the VC would lose." "You can't get popular throwing grenades into marketplaces and blowing up school buses."

4 APR 1970: WIEU

ATTENDEES: Gen. Abrams, Gen. Rosson, Gen. Brown, LTG Mildren, VADM Zumwalt, Mr. Kirk, MG Dolvin, MG Conroy, MG Cowles, Mr. Jacobson, MG Dettre, BG Gunn, BG Clement, BG Kraft, BG Vande Hey, BG Greene, BG Jaskilka, BG Sykes, Col. Dessert (for BG Potts), Col. Cutrona, Col. Franklin (for Col. Cavanaugh), Col. Martin (for BG Cheadle), Col. Steman (for BG Henderson).

BRIEFER: "DIA reports that, according to an East European correspondent in Hanoi, the North Vietnamese consider the overthrow of Sihanouk a grave crisis for the Communists in Southeast Asia. The correspondent claims that the sacking of the Communist embassies in Phnom Penh and the ouster of Sihanouk produced near panic among the government officials in Hanoi. Although they did not directly accuse the U.S. of being involved, the European said the Soviet diplomatic community in Hanoi viewed Sihanouk's ouster as a victory for the U.S. The Soviets believe the events in Cambodia have completely changed the war in the Republic. They did not think the Cambodians could stand up to a determined North Vietnamese challenge, but did not consider that North Vietnam would try for military overthrow of the government. The Soviets did not think the U.S. would commit ground forces in support of Cambodia."

■ ■ ■

BRIEFER: A 31 March 1970 message regarding Binh Tram 33 indicated that two subordinate transportation battalions had a total of 133 vehicles, of which only 58 were operable. If this report is true, the enemy vehicle deadline rate in at least these two battalions could be as high as 56 percent."

ABRAMS: "That's overflying the flying hour program."

MILDREN: "Well, you know, we have a hell of a time maintaining better than 70 percent in hard surface [motor]pools, lighted conditions, sheds to work under—goddamn, all the support they get. And these poor guys are out in the woods getting bombed, driving over lousy roads in the dark. I'm surprised if they keep 50 or 60 percent running. That would be pretty good under those conditions."

BRIEFER: Sihanouk's overthrow took place 18 March 1970.

ABRAMS (re Camp Carroll): "That makes a wonderful training ground for sappers. If they can successfully traverse that, they can be given a certificate. It's probably the best defensive position in the country." "Goddamn—that wire they've got out there for sappers, you can plink it and it sounds like a violin! It's all just tight as hell! In fact, I don't think you need any noise devices. If you cut one of those—t-w-a-n-g!"

Abrams is a connoisseur of barbed wire.

11 APR 1970: WIEU

ATTENDEES: Gen. Abrams, Gen. Haines, Gen. Rosson, Gen. Brown, LTG Mildren, VADM Baumberger, VADM Zumwalt, Mr. Kirk, MG Dolvin, MG Conroy, MG Cowles, MG Dettre, BG Clement, BG Camp, BG Kraft, BG Vande Hey, BG Greene, BG Henderson, BG Jaskilka, BG Sykes, BG Cramer, Col.

Dessert (for BG Potts), Col. Cutrona, Col. Martin (for BG Cheadle), Col. Cavanaugh, Col. Holt.

MACV 1970 Infiltration Estimate: 42,300. Destinations: COSVN: 27,100. MR-5: 9,000. B-3 Front: 3,400. DMZ/MR-TTH: 2,800.

ABRAMS: "You've just got to look past body count. I always remember the rallier that came in out of the 24th Regiment. I think he was out of the 5th Battalion. . . . The 4th Battalion had been hit by B-52 strikes, and had a strength of 440. And 40 men were all that were left in that battalion. It wasn't enough to bury the dead. So he had been part of a detail out of the 5th Battalion that went to the 4th Battalion to help them in burying the dead. And it was as a result of this experience that he turned himself in. Two days later—if this report was correct—the remaining 40 men of the 4th Battalion ran an ambush—it was an abortive affair—but they ran an ambush on a convoy on Route 14, out of which a prisoner also—one or two—were taken. And <u>he</u> largely confirmed what the rallier had said. But you stop and think about that, a battalion that gets whacked like that, and the remainder—the 10 percent remaining—go out two days later and set up a goddamn ambush and have a go at it. Body count—it has a place, I <u>suppose</u>, but you've got to look at <u>quite</u> a few other things."

ABRAMS (re failure of the enemy to mount a major spring campaign): "This is not the way it's gone in the past. And we have not yet put the <u>effort</u> into it that we've had to put in the past just to hang on. Of course, it's always possible to be a prisoner of your own experience. It's the only way you can <u>see</u> things. But this is <u>not</u> the way the battles in western Kontum have gone, that they slack off at this stage of the game. Those <u>bastards</u> hang on in there. It's been almost two months. And with the kind of logistics that's been pouring into [Base Area] 609—I just have a gut feeling we're just in the first, we haven't even finished the first chapter of the annual battle for western Kontum."

ABRAMS: "I remember that [Dak To] so well. And that was <u>tough</u>. <u>Westy</u> was in Washington and—heh, heh—I was going up there every couple of days and coming back and firing in another comprehensive [laughing] in-depth review. One of the things they wanted to know, and I remember—I will never forget it—they wanted to know what the hell we were doing out on these <u>hills</u>. Well, all you've got to do is stand there on the air strip at Dak To and—heh, heh, heh—you can see the importance of the hills. That's all there <u>is</u>—to the front and the rear, and the right and the left—is <u>hills</u> looking down on Dak To. Ha-ha-ha-ha-ha! Yeah, they said, 'What are you doing out on those hills?'"

18 APR 1970: Commanders WIEU

ATTENDEES: Gen. Abrams, Gen. Rosson, Gen. Brown, Amb. Colby, LTG Mildren, LTG Collins, LTG Davison, LTG Zais, Mr. Kirk, LTG McCutcheon, MG Dolvin, MG Sutherland, MG Conroy, MG Brown, MG McCown, MG Cowles, Mr. Jacobson, Mr. Vann, Mr. Whitehouse, MG Dettre, BG Clement, BG Camp,

BG Kraft, BG Vande Hey, BG Henderson, BG Jaskilka, BG Sykes, BG Cheadle, Mr. Chambers (for Mr. Megellas), Mr. Fritz (for Mr. Firfer), Col. Cavanaugh, Col. Dessert (for BG Potts), Col. Healy, Col. Cutrona, Col. Church (for BG Greene), Col. Todd, Capt. Tidd (for VADM Zumwalt).

macv 1970 Infiltration Estimate: 42,400 (64 percent for COSVN).

VANN: "All along the border within IV Corps the NVA and VC have largely taken over control of the border."

VANN: "East of the Mekong is where they picked up, the day before yesterday, 233 SKSs and a large number of crew-served weapons and about 15 tons of ammunition."

VANN: "All this suggests within the IV Corps area—and naturally it would be a matter of very high-level decision—that some Vietnamese offensives in this area could be very lucrative in this period of time. It would also quite possibly take the pressure off these operations going to the north. These areas, which I had personal knowledge of going back to '62, have long been developed as base areas with complete sanctuary and by paying off local Cambodian officials." "It just seems to me there's a great opportunity for the Republic of Vietnam to help itself by removing long-held sanctuaries and bases and weapons caches and ammo caches."

■ ■ ■

BRIEFER: Describes RVNAF operations on and across the Cambodian border during the period 15 March–17 April. Characterized by "FARK cooperation in many instances and strict avoidance of U.S. involvement."

ABRAMS (re Cambodia): "As I'm sure you're all aware, this whole thing has had to be played with great delicacy. The remarks you made, John [Vann], I think are fully appreciated here—the situation and so on. I really am quite grateful for the discipline that has been apparent on the part of the U.S. It would just be bad for us to get publicly involved over there in Cambodia. The Vietnamese—that's a different, somewhat different, story. Even then it has to be done with some care, or it <u>has</u> had to be done with some care."

ABRAMS: "It's a pretty fluid situation now. It may be that we'll get some additional guidance. A lot of these things don't make first-class military sense. I won't <u>argue</u> about that. If you've got any statements about that, I'll accept it and agree with you. But that's not exactly what we can <u>do</u>. So it requires a <u>high</u> order of understanding by the Americans that are mixed up in this thing one way or another—close to it. And we've got to continue with that. And any time there's a possibility of change I will be personally in touch with the responsible commanders about it. We've got to be zigging and zagging at the right points and time."

ABRAMS: "It's interesting. Last night I was down at the British observance of the Queen's birthday. And the ambassadors that were there—they just don't <u>believe</u> that we aren't over there, especially in the air, just really raising hell.

But, as you know, I was able to give them a flat, absolute no. We're not doing it. But I don't know if they even believed that."

■ ■ ■

ABRAMS: "The other day when I was over talking to General Vien . . . , he spent a considerable amount of time trying to elicit from me how in the hell our government ever went and launched this damn moon thing on the 13th. [An inauspicious date.] Christ, everybody knows about that! Incredible! I said, 'I understand, but you see they're all scientific people. They're unaware of all these other things that go on.'"

COLBY: "And then when it's the 13th there, it's the 14th out here."

ABRAMS: "He goes by what it was where it started."

■ ■ ■

ABRAMS: "I'll tell you frankly I don't think much of [the claimed] 29,000 night operations in III Corps. If there were half of those the rockets in Saigon would have been reduced from seven to at least about two. It's just a crock of shit! I don't believe it. And furthermore, what this alludes to is something that's got to get done this year, and it just—it isn't. This is security, it's working on what he's working on, and I think where his major effort is, and by god we're—the Vietnamese—are not hacking it. It's really got to be changed."

ABRAMS: "We can say, 'Well, rockets in Saigon—well, so what? They ought to get a taste of it, too.' Something like that. Not right. That's another thing the ambassadors are all buzzing about—rockets in Saigon. I don't mean that the ambassadors—I'm not trying to berate them. But they're all reporting to their own governments, and when they fill out their weekly poop sheet, whatever system they've got, and all of them are here in Saigon—.'" "That whole part of the thing is really pretty damn important—the whole psychological part, the opinion part, what people think. It isn't so much what the realities of damage, or the realities of killed, the realities of that sort of thing, it's what's in people's minds. And that's the stage we're in."

■ ■ ■

VANN: "General Abrams, for the first time that I know of in Vietnam the corps commander has directed a test wherein one district—it's going to begin on 1 May—we're putting nine Australian advisors in to help them—to do all their operations at night and not conduct these useless walks in the sun to comply with mandatory requirements. The second month of the test he's going to add a second district. The first district's going to be Ben Tranh in Dinh Tuong. The second district's going to be Cho Gao. The third month of the test he's going to throw in all of Go Cong Province." "Right now we largely waste most of our RF and PF by meeting the mandatory requirements to go on about five daytime operations a week. And naturally when the troops go out and walk 10 or 15 kilometers during the day, they're going to sleep at night, even though they're going to report that they are complying with the JGS directive for two-thirds being out at night. I really believe that, if this thing works and we can convince them to go more widespread, that for the first time we'll really get on top of this thing from the standpoint of small-unit night activities."

COLBY: "I think the critical thing in that chart is the small number of contacts for this astronomical [number of] claimed operations. What you actually have here—the chart shows the fakery of the numbers of operations. If that's all the contacts you have, you really aren't out there."

JACOBSON (re terrorism): "For the week ending 9 April the total number of victims was 1,427, which was the highest we've ever had since Tet of '68, when they were so high we couldn't even keep track of them."

BRIEFER (re PSDF): "The first class of 7,834 key interteam leaders graduated on 31 March. A second class of 5,840 leaders is now in session."

BRIEFER (re National Police): "The total strength as of the end of March is 88,398."

BRIEFER (re Phuong Hoang): "The national goal is 1,800 neutralizations per month. The apparent decline in 1970 is due to a change in accounting procedures. In 1969, killed, rallied, and captured were counted as neutralized, while in 1970 only killed, rallied, and sentenced are counted." President Thieu has recently announced that the program will be integrated into the National Police.

Briefing on "The Changing Nature of the War."

BRIEFER: "The nature of the military conflict in South Vietnam has been under change since Tet of 1968. Although shifts in the level of violence, type of military operations, and size and location of forces involved are characteristics of this change, the allied realization that the war was basically a political contest has, thus far, been decisive. The most significant development in this shift of allied policy has been the enemy's increasing loss of control over the population. The Accelerated Pacification Campaign, the allied clear and hold strategy, and programs such as Phoenix and Chieu Hoi have contributed to the progress achieved to date."

BRIEFER: "The enemy still retains a viable military and political apparatus throughout the Republic, although sustained allied efforts are causing a gradual erosion of this capability. To counter this situation the Communists undertook a basic reappraisal of their own strategy of how best to achieve unification of Vietnam. Party resolutions of 1969 set forth a new strategy that dismissed the possibility of an immediate military victory. Current enemy strategy seeks to parlay limited military victory into withdrawal of U.S. troops, establishment of a neutralist coalition government, and an ultimate Communist political victory. The basic change has been to reemphasize protracted warfare rather than an all-out military general offensive campaign. A greater effort is to be made in political activity, such as proselyting and development of revolutionary committees, and a greater flexibility introduced into military operations."

BRIEFER: "A review of COSVN Resolution No. 14, captured in early March [1970] in IV Corps, substantiates the emphasis on guerrilla warfare." Cites "the three strategic areas of the urban, delta, and mountains." "The mission of the guerrillas is to serve as a hard-core element to guide the revolutionary movement."

ABRAMS: "The requirement for North Vietnamese forces is far greater now than it was in these earlier days." And they also need forces in Laos and Cambodia, as well as filling VC units in South Vietnam with NVA. "His requirements for North Vietnamese fillers or replacements here in South Vietnam are fantastically greater than they were in '66, where you've gone from the 25-75 to 75-25 [percentages, respectively, of NVA and VC in enemy units in the south], plus a bigger structure. And in that light, in that light, this infiltration that we know so far [for 1970] is really very small—against the need."

ZAIS: "Well, Christ, I don't think he's staying active to protect his supply line in Base Area 611. I think he's staying active to impose his will on the populated area by pushing forward as far as he can and, from those positions there, trying to work on the infrastructure which he'd lost before and is going to try to rebuild."

J-2 (or his representative): Seeks to argue "we're saying the same thing."

ABRAMS: "No–no–no. His point is quite different."

ZAIS: "My point changes my reaction. That is, if I believed that he was just sitting out there trying to protect his supplies in 611, we'd stand off and we'd just keep pounding him and cause him as much damage as we could with artillery and firepower. But as long as I interpret his efforts to continue to encroach further and further to the east, then it's incumbent on me to go after him before he gets too far east. And so that affects my course of action in terms of response."

Extended discussion follows.

ABRAMS: "I favor General Zais's view on that particular point. I think we ought to change this thing [the briefing and assessment] to reflect it."

BRIEFER: Over the past year enemy sapper strength has increased, whereas guerrilla strength has declined.

BRIEFER: "On fragmentation of main force units . . . during September of 1969 the headquarters of the 10th NVA Regiment was disbanded and its battalions were resubordinated to provincial control in Phu Yen and Khanh Hoa Provinces. Additionally, the XT-11 Main Force Infantry Battalion in Binh Dinh Province was disbanded in June [1969] and its companies were placed under local force control. There are indications today that elements of the 22nd NVA Regiment are in the process of being subordinated to local force or provincial control in Binh Dinh Province."

JACOBSON: "The VC is going to do what he's been told to do—get at pacification, get back among the people, scare hell out of them, make them realize they're not secure, show up these lousy Territorial Forces for what they are— nothing. They're not doing their job, and the people are being proved that they're not doing their job. In certain areas he's doing it with abductions, in other areas he's doing it by knocking out posts where everybody's asleep. But he's doing what he's been told to do, and what we know he's going to do, and that's carrying out Resolution 9. He <u>always</u> does what he's told to do."

SOMEONE: "If Sihanouk comes back and makes a flat-out alliance, almost, with the VC, and you don't have the NVA pussyfooting down the edge of the border, but rather the establishment of depots and replacement centers and the movement of troops by ship to Sihanoukville instead of walking down the Trail, we can have a whole new picture in III and IV Corps."

ABRAMS: "Agreed."

VANN (re IV Corps): Cites "the changing nature of the war there, where it was going from almost totally an insurgency war with all South Vietnamese to, now, more of a main force war, despite the enemy's intention to reinforce the guerrilla effort—in which he's thus far not being successful."

VANN: "The other interesting thing that I find is that—the NVA units began coming in last May [1969], as units. With the exception of the attack on the Chi Lang Training Center, which was largely an indirect fire attack, there hasn't been a military success in the delta that was attributed to the NVA units. There have been about eight major <u>defeats</u> that they have suffered, three of these being at the hands of Territorial Forces. They seem to have reached the point now where not only can they not build up further because of the drag of logistics, but they're having a hell of a time just keeping up with the attrition in the NVA units that they have already put down, let alone getting these units out to reinforce and build up the guerrilla effort."

VANN: "I see a distinctly better situation today in the delta than existed last May, before the NVA units came in. A lot of that is an intangible, the attitude of the population in that it seems to make this war down there much more black and white, where it had been a very gray thing in the past because so many of the VC and the guerrilla are relatives or friends of the family."

VANN (re the NVA): "They don't mix too well in the delta. They have a <u>problem</u> there. I think they can get away with it up-country a little better."

JACOBSON: "They're having a hell of a time with it in Long An. I went into two districts there where they refused to bury the NVA forces. When our side kills them, the VC walk away and let them lie there. And <u>nothing</u> is worse than that to the Vietnamese. That's the worst thing that can happen—much worse than getting killed."

ABRAMS: "Incidentally, I think John Vann's point's a good one. It has something to do with the character of things. That's what we're <u>searching</u> for here."

BRIEFER: "There has . . . been a substantial change in the nature of the conflict in one regard. For the first time in the war the enemy's traditional bases of power are being directly challenged—his political organization and his control of the population. While this task has only just begun, it appears that the outcome of the war will be decided here. Presently, at least, both sides are finally fighting the same war."

JACOBSON: "I've just got a gut feeling that I can't prove, but I've just got a feeling that pacification . . . has lost its momentum, that it's <u>not</u> moving forward. And if it's not moving <u>forward</u>, it <u>will</u> move backward."

VANN: "I think we're moving forward, but with a hell of a lot less momentum than before. The thing damn near came to a halt in January and February, and did finally get going in March, but not with very much speed." "There has just been a distinct loss of command interest by the president and the prime minister . . . and all of them in coming down and kicking ass. They were doing it on a regular basis before. And when they don't do that, people get into a rut and just kind of stop."

COLLINS: "I would support that observation. It's inching forward, but it's a matter of time. When we look at the time we have to accomplish these things, at the rate it's going it's not going to get there."

VANN: "The change in the HES system had a certain depressing effect upon the morale of province and district chiefs. You know, it went down an average of about 6 percent."

ABRAMS: "Yeah, and that comes out of another sickness, and that is the worship of <u>charts</u>. . . . It finally gets to the point where that's really the whole war—fucking <u>charts</u>, and where they're supposed to go up if you can make them rise, and where they're supposed to go down if you can push them down, and I would by just about any means whatsoever, instead of really thinking about what the whole thing's about, and what really has to be done. Yeah, all these guidelines and objectives and so on—you can't fault them, and that ought to be <u>part</u> of it. But then we get wrapped around the axle watching these charts, and it becomes—somehow the chart <u>itself</u> becomes the whole damn war, instead of the <u>people</u> and the <u>real</u> things."

ABRAMS: "I don't think there's anything <u>wrong</u> with the whole <u>theory</u> of Territorial Forces and the Popular Self-Defense Force and that sort of thing. I think that's what they've got to have. The point is it's got to be better than <u>Hanoi's</u> got. <u>They</u> run the same <u>system</u>."

ABRAMS: "As one of the briefers said earlier, now everybody's fighting the war on the same basis. The objectives are the same—of course, they're <u>opposed</u>—but everybody's finally gotten down to working at the same thing. And that makes it a good clean game. It's a question of who's the <u>best</u>."

ABRAMS (re the enemy): "The 'high points' and the main force and so on—the way he's using that, that's the piece of the iceberg he wants us to see. He wants the press to see it, he wants the public at home to see it, he wants <u>us</u> to see it. . . . <u>That's</u> the big <u>thing</u>. But what he is <u>really</u> working at is down there in the people—getting some of his people on the village council, provincial committee, and getting back there with that control over the people. . . ."

ABRAMS: "It's down in <u>here</u>, and in that whole thing, and which, on the side we're on, it involves the territorials, the effectiveness of district and province, the effectiveness of the villages, the PSDF, the police, and so on. And I think <u>this</u> part of the problem—one of the briefers said, 'This is where the war is won or lost.' I <u>believe</u> that! It's <u>not</u> with the high points. And <u>this</u> part of it is, in terms of the effort and the attention and direction that he's given it, I think is as <u>10</u> is to <u>1</u>—between the effort on <u>this</u> and the effort on the high points—something like that."

25 APR 1970: WIEU

ATTENDEES: Gen. Abrams, Amb. Colby, LTG Mildren, VADM Zumwalt, Mr. Kirk, MG Dolvin, MG Conroy, MG Hardin (new Seventh Air Force DCS/Ops), MG Cowles, MG Dixon (for Gen. Brown), MG Dettre, BG Camp, BG Kraft, BG Vande Hey, BG Greene, BG Henderson, BG Jaskilka, BG Sykes, BG Cheadle, BG Potts, Col. Cutrona, Col. Cavanaugh, Col. Todd.

POTTS (re Indochina People's United Front formed by the enemy: Vietnamese, Lao, and Khmer): "Lieutenant Wynn will stay on top of this for you."

ABRAMS (after Lieutenant Wynn finishes his briefing and departs): "How much time does he have left here?"

POTTS: "Sir, he leaves in August of this year. He was an associate editor of the *Michigan Law Review,* associate with a San Francisco law firm. He was inducted as an enlisted man, served for a year, direct commission one year ago about this time. And he's our North Vietnamese expert as far as politics . . . are concerned."

ABRAMS: "I must say the services have really become enlightened. They directly commissioned him, and he also wound up doing work like this. It's really amazing—amazing."

BRIEFER: "On 27 March COSVN sent its subordinate elements a directive concerning the current situation in Cambodia. . . . The analysis determined that the U.S. was behind the overthrow of Sihanouk. The U.S. would not send troops into Cambodia, but would provide finances, advisors, weapons, and war matériel."

This message, per an earlier briefer, was able to be read retroactively after recent capture of a number of enemy codebooks and one-time pads.

ABRAMS (re the enemy): "The Indochina Front—that's the way for the Communists to play it. You know, we've always accepted that when they wanted to march into Vientiane they could do it. And I think we'd also say if they want to march into Phnom Penh they could probably do it. But that's not the way to do it, not in their—."

ABRAMS (re Sihanouk): "Apparently he did get mad as hell when he found out he'd been thrown out of office. He didn't realize it until he got off the plane in Moscow. That's the first word he had."

1 MAY 1970: COMUS Cambodia Update

BRIEFER: "The world and domestic U.S. reaction to American support for ARVN cross-border operations, as reported by AP and UPI, has for the most part ranged from polite support to outright denunciation." "On the U.S. domestic political scene criticism has emanated from expected sources. Members of the Senate Foreign Relations Committee have criticized the American support, along with bipartisan political elements favoring a U.S. withdrawal

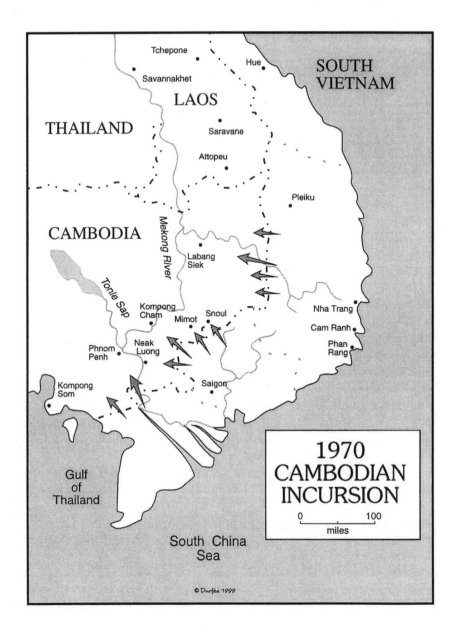

1970
CAMBODIAN
INCURSION

0   100
miles

© Durfee 1999

from Southeast Asia. Even where approval has been voiced, it seemingly has been caveated." Cites "this general critical tone in the body politic in the United States and the Congress." In the United States "the byword was disengagement, with little respect for changing circumstances."

BRIEFER: "Forty ARVN wounded by U.S. gunships. Reportedly this was due to improper marking of the ground by friendly troops."

ABRAMS: "Ah—just <u>unprofessional</u>, <u>just</u> unprofessional. I'm not going to <u>accept</u> any of that excuses. It's a <u>poor</u> performance."

. . .

ABRAMS: "Jesus, what a switcheroo they've made on public information. They even want _me_ to hold a _press_ conference. I've _never_ held a press conference since I've been in command."

. . .

President Nixon on the Cambodian Incursion.

Next on the tape: President Nixon's speech on the Cambodian incursion, via AFRS. Cites his "report to the nation on Vietnam" of 10 days earlier, at which he announced that another 150,000 U.S. troops were to be withdrawn over the next year. "To protect our men who are in Vietnam, and to guarantee the continued success of our withdrawal and the Vietnamization program, I have concluded that the time has come for action." American policy has been "to scrupulously respect" the neutrality of Cambodia. "The major responsibility for the ground operations is being assumed by South Vietnamese forces."

NIXON: "Tonight, American and South Vietnamese units will attack the headquarters for the _entire_ Communist military operation in South Vietnam. This key control center has been occupied by the North Vietnamese and Viet Cong for five years, in blatant violation of Cambodia's neutrality." "This is _not_ an invasion of Cambodia. The areas in which these attacks will be launched and conducted are completely occupied by North Vietnamese forces." "A majority of the American people . . . are for the withdrawal of our forces from Vietnam." "A majority of the American people want to end this war, rather than have it drag on interminably." In Vietnam: "We stopped the bombing of North Vietnam. We have cut air operations by over 20 percent. We've announced the withdrawal of over 250,000 of our men. We've offered to withdraw _all_ of our men if they will withdraw theirs." "We will not be defeated." Re negotiations: "We've made major efforts, many of which must remain secret."

2 MAY 1970: WIEU

ATTENDEES: Gen. Abrams, Gen. Brown, Amb. Colby, LTG Mildren, VADM Zumwalt, Mr. Kirk, MG Dolvin, MG Conroy, MG Cowles, MG Dixon, MG Dettre, BG Clement, BG Camp, BG Kraft, BG Vande Hey, BG Greene, BG Henderson, BG Jaskilka, BG Sykes, BG Potts, Col. Cavanaugh, Col. Cutrona, Col. Martin (for BG Cheadle), Col. Todd.

ABRAMS (describing someone): "I talked to him yesterday. You've gotta remember, this fellow is a Harvard graduate—he's got a-l-l of that. He's an intellectual as a person." Quoting whoever this was, commenting on demonstrators tearing down the American flag in Washington: "I certainly _hope_ that the _police_ don't brutalize these people." [Laughter]

ABRAMS (looking at enemy logistical activity): "I don't know what it <u>means</u> or anything, but the <u>pattern's</u> different from other years. You've got a steady decline in previous years. You've got the same kind of weather pattern that you had in other years." Discusses with Potts. "I think it could be the realization that Sihanoukville is not open."

BRIEFER: States that in Laos, north of the Plaine des Jarres, the enemy is digging trenches and tunnels toward friendly positions, "a technique that was also used as an offensive measure at Dien Bien Phu to infiltrate the French defensive perimeter."

ABRAMS (interrupting): "Well, it was also used during the Civil War. We're kind of hung up on Dien Bien Phu."

■ ■ ■

BRIEFER: "In Binh Thuan Province, further interrogation of six prisoners captured in the vicinity of Sang Mao on 1 April reveals serious problems affecting enemy units in the province. The prisoners state that the combat efficiency of units . . . had been reduced considerably over the past four years. The primary factors contributing to this . . . are poorly trained NVA replacements, malaria, lack of food, denial of access to hamlets and villages, insecure sanctuary areas, and the increased effectiveness of RF and PF forces." Substantiated by reduced level of enemy-initiated actions in the province.

3 MAY 1970: Intelligence Update

BRIEFER: Operation Thuan Tang 43 continued in the Fishhook area. "At 1409 hours yesterday the Strategic Intelligence Bureau, COSVN, was [***] north-northwest of Base Area 352."

BRIEFER: Cumulative results of Thuan Tang 43 to date: Friendly: 13 KIA, 71 WIA. Enemy: 554 KIA, 4 POW, 126 detainees, 37 IW, 4 CSW, 72 tons of rice, 2 tons medical supplies, 1,100 gas masks, ammunition.

BRIEFER: Cumulative results of Operation Rockcrusher in III Corps to date: Friendly: 57 KIA, 371 WIA. Enemy: 606 KIA, 64 detained, 12 POW, 32 Hoi Chanh, 185 IW, 27 CSW, 76 tons rice, 1 ton weapons and munitions, and a 100-bed hospital captured.

BRIEFER: Cumulative results of Operation Rockcrusher in IV Corps to date: Friendly: 36 KIA, 154 WIA. Enemy: 443 KIA, 46 detained, 288 IW, 36 CSW, 1 ton munitions and mortar rounds.

BRIEFER: Cumulative results of Operation Rockcrusher in Parrot's Beak area to date: Friendly: 93 KIA, 525 WIA. Enemy: 1,049 KIA, 110 detained, 12 POW, 32 Hoi Chanh, 473 IW, 63 CSW, a 100-bed hospital, 76 tons rice, 2 tons weapons and ammunition.

BRIEFER: "COSVN [***] in the Fishhook area." Last on 22 March. Next: 26 March in BA 353. Next: In Cambodia west of BA 353. Last: 2 May north-northwest of BA 353.

Fixing the changing locations of COSVN.

ABRAMS: "What we need right now is another division—go in deep. We need to go west from where we are, we need to go north and east from where we are. And we need to do it now. It's <u>moving</u>, and—<u>goddamn</u>, <u>god</u>damn [said with great sorrow and regret]."

SOMEONE: "Time to exploit."

ABRAMS: "<u>Christ</u>—it's so clear. Don't let them pick up the <u>pieces</u>. Don't let them pick up the pieces [said very softly]. Just like the Germans—you give them 36 hours and, goddamn it, you've got to start the war all over again."

ABRAMS (giving instructions for drafting an update message to CJCS): "Don't conclude, don't conclude anything. Report the <u>facts</u> that we know."

POTTS: Besides photos sent via Compass Link to CJCS, the night before last we sent a packet of 35 photos, and last night 20 more.

ABRAMS: "I understand there's a lot of pictures of Tri in there."

POTTS: "Sir, he's in just about every picture."

ABRAMS: "He needs it."

ABRAMS: "Aside from the tactical, and maybe even strategical, effects of these things, this is a <u>tremendous</u> opportunity for the Vietnamese armed forces to do themselves a joint operation—the VNAF and the navy and the army and so on, all working together. It would be a good time for General Dzu to go down and take command of it."

6 MAY 1970: COMUS Update for General Vien, Major General Manh, and Colonel Thiep

ABRAMS: "Ambassador Colby was telling me this morning he went up and spent the night with Colonel [Than?], the province chief of Thua Thien. And so about ten o'clock last night—and Ambassador Colby had a visiting ambassador with him, forgotten who that is, an American ambassador from somewhere—about ten o'clock last night Colonel Than said, 'Would you like to drive around?' So they went out, Ambassador Colby and the other ambassador and Colonel Than in one jeep, and the province senior advisor and a couple of others in the <u>other</u> jeep. And they drove around for about two hours, out 12, 15 kilometers from Hue. This was really quite impressive. It must mean <u>something</u> about security. They got back a little after midnight. No escorts, nothing. I don't think anyone would <u>do</u> that last year. Of course that's not all of South Vietnam, but it's interesting."

9 MAY 1970: WIEU

ATTENDEES: Gen. Abrams, Amb. Berger, Gen. Rosson, Gen. Brown, Amb. Colby, LTG Mildren, VADM Zumwalt, MG Dolvin, MG Conroy, MG Cowles, MG Dettre, BG Clement, BG Camp, BG Kraft, BG Vande Hey, BG Greene, BG

Henderson, BG Jaskilka, BG Sykes, BG Potts, Col. Cavanaugh, Col. Cutrona, Col. Martin (for BG Cheadle), Col. Phillips (for Mr. Kirk), Col. Todd.

BRIEFER: MACV 1970 Infiltration Estimate: 42,800. Dealing in groups as small as five people. QL2073 with 10 personnel forecast for August arrival in COSVN. Now an estimated 23,500 in the pipeline for May–August arrival. But will be disrupted by allied operations.

POTTS: "Sir, we've had a very significant development here in the past few days. Getting into the documents that were captured out in the Fishhook by the 1st Cav, we have found a 78-page notebook that reveals the plan for infiltration for 1970. . . . We checked very quickly to see if it compared favorably with the estimate we have here, and it does, almost to a group."

BRIEFER: "No guerrilla war has ever been able to reach a 'victorious' end without sanctuary." Fourteen enemy sanctuaries along the border, 10 of them contiguous to III and IV Corps (7 to III Corps). Cambodia thus provided "the LOC for munitions, the LOC for food, the basic infiltration route, and the base areas."

ABRAMS: "The war is about the control of people."

ABRAMS (after briefer describes logbook with captured Chinese weapon): "Just a bunch of guerrillas, you know, in a civil war—grabbing up what's handy. Manufacturing their own, making little bullets."

■ ■ ■

BRIEFER: "It appears that the enemy will attempt to avoid costly large-scale contact with allied forces operating in and adjacent to his base areas by withdrawing as necessary."

ABRAMS (re enemy defense of a portion of his supplies): "So far, that has not occurred. In fact, just the opposite. What they do is move out. That's true in [Base Area] 702, it's true in 351, 350, 352, 353, 354, the whole action of the 9th Division—9th VC. In the Parrot's Beak."

BROWN: "He can't even feed them up there [in southern Laos]. He's got a hell of a problem."

ABRAMS: "Well, that's right, George. But, you see, he's used to a hell of a problem. He lives in an environment where he's got a hell of a problem. I get a certain amount of enjoyment, I must say, out of seeing the problem get complicated. But it isn't worth much. He's a pretty determined chap, when you get right down to it."

12 MAY 1970: COMUS: ROK Generals' Brief on Cambodia

BRIEFER: "Hanoi has never admitted to its people that its troops are stationed in Cambodia."

BRIEFER: On 12 March 1970, Lon Nol issued a proclamation requiring all VC/NVA to be out of Cambodia by 15 March. Intervention began 29 April. Enemy strategic variables: munitions, rice supply, sanctuaries, infiltration route.

BRIEFER: Rule of thumb: One and a half pounds of rice per day to feed an enemy soldier. So far have captured 6,500 man-years of rice. Two weeks into it and, per General Potts, have captured more matériel than from caches discovered in all of 1968; expect in next few days to exceed all that discovered in 1969 in captured caches.

ABRAMS: "I would like to say that the performance of the South Vietnamese forces has really been quite extraordinary. After all, they had not engaged in this kind of operation, in this magnitude, with this much movement, and the requirement of this much coordination in the whole history of their armed forces. And they have done an <u>excellent</u> job."

ABRAMS: Cites an operation in which three ARVN airborne battalions were helilifted into battle. All hit their landing zones on time except for one battalion that was five minutes late. Reason: It came under attack in its loading zone, and took about ten minutes to deal with that, then assaulted and arrived only five minutes late.

16 MAY 1970: WIEU

ATTENDEES: Gen. Abrams, Gen. Nazzaro, Gen. Rosson, Gen. Brown, Amb. Colby, LTG Mildren, Mr. Kirk, VADM King, MG Dolvin, MG Conroy, MG Cowles, MG Dettre, BG Clement, BG Camp, BG Kraft, BG Vande Hey, BG Greene, BG Potts, BG Jaskilka, BG Sykes, BG Henion, Col. Cavanaugh, Col. Cutrona, Col. Martin (for BG Cheadle), Col. Weeks (for Mr. Jacobson), Col. Holt. Briefer adds: Amb. Berger.

General Potts is identified by the briefer in the introduction to the tape as major general-selectee.

BRIEFER: "VC forces in the Parrot's Beak area had received orders to move their supplies away from the border area, but did not have time prior to the arrival of allied forces in the area."

POTTS: Thirty-two boxes of crypto material just obtained (shows codebooks and one-time pads).

ABRAMS: "Well, of course, this stuff—they don't have to code it for me." [Laughter]

Meaning he doesn't read Vietnamese.

ABRAMS: "I went out yesterday for a few minutes to Di An, and I'm gonna have to see a lot more out there before I believe any of these goddamn results [of enemy matériel captured in Cambodia] that have been reported. It may be. But the weapons I saw out there are a lot of <u>junk</u>. And I'd been led to believe that the— you know, some of the weapons that we've seen in here—that we were capturing first-line weapons."

POTTS: "They were, sir, and I actually saw them in the caches."

ABRAMS: "All right, then, what's happening to them?"

SOMEONE ELSE: "There were a lot of SKSs, brand new ones, and I'm afraid those are being funneled off by individuals and museums."

ABRAMS: "Where can we fire a shot here that's going to get some action? Because it's just not being done. There's been adequate instruction, as far as I'm concerned, to get this done. And it's not being done. They've got a hell of a lot of troops out there. III Corps has got over a thousand helicopters. Why can't this thing move?"

Referring to evacuation and collection of captured matériel.

ABRAMS: "The word's been put around that we're gonna bring this up so the press can all go out there and so on. Now I don't want any goddamn press out there until I give the word. Because what you're building up is a big fraud, and that's what they'll tag you with."

ABRAMS: "Incidentally, with this kind of thing going on, I can't help but—I just have to say that these charts that show results and tonnage and all that kind of stuff—I just have to tell you that I don't believe 'em! I don't believe the reporting system. And I don't know where the hell you're going to stand when it comes down here to making an estimate of just what the situation is and what's been the impact of these operations. And it goes even further. Where the hell are all these weapons and so on that—you know, we had the weapons ratio and all that kind of stuff over the last two years. You get out here and try to find these things and goddamn it they're not there. It's really very sickening to sit around here and contemplate the fact that we've been sitting around talking about a basketful of fog."

BRIEFER: Shows a series of slides depicting captured ammunition on the ground, in trucks being moved out, and being segregated and stored in yards back in South Vietnam. Shows three CHICOM copies of a Soviet twin-barrel 14.5-mm heavy machine gun [weighing 1,400 pounds each] captured in the Fishhook area.

ABRAMS: "I'll tell you, that thing there makes that troop in a helicopter feel a little thin."

SOMEONE: "They sit on their flak vests."

SOMEONE ELSE: "You need more than that with that thing."

ABRAMS: "Yeah, you do, with that damn thing. That's a vicious round, and most of that stuff is a hundred percent armor-piercing."

POTTS (probably speaking as the tape runs during a break): "I myself have been in four of these major areas. I know they're reporting it, they've shown me lists that they're compiling, it's there for everybody to see, I've seen the vehicles going into the place, choppers going in and out, so the goddamn stuff is going someplace. I do know that the SKSs may not make it."

■ ■ ■

ABRAMS: "To get on a pleasanter subject, the chief has just handed me the new major general's list. I know you'll all be interested in it. I'll just read off a few:

Butch, has the brigade up in 5th Mech; Kraft [Hey! clapping]; [Wicks?]; John Wheelock, he used to be here; Bill Potts [Hey! clapping]. One that interests— Marshall Garth. . . . A great [policeman?]. Garth had a brigade in the 4th Division, and I went out to Fort Lewis three times while the 4th Division was mobilizing and training out there . . . and he had a brigade that had a cadre, and then they brought the fresh ex-civilians in there, and that's what that brigade was built of. And 11 months after they received the recruits—straight from civilian life, so all the basic training, advanced individual training, and so on was done right in the brigade—but 11 months after they got those men at Fort Lewis they were in this big battle up in War Zone C, that brigade, where they were attacked one morning about five or six o'clock by one of these regiments out of the 9th Division. And a tremendous battle. And this brigade really performed in a first-class way. And Garth was the commander from the start, and he was the commander in that battle. Very rare that a fellow gets to see the results of his training effort, you know." Reads some more names.

■ ■ ■

BRIEFER: COSVN Headquarters has moved deeper into Cambodia. 8,509 individual weapons captured to date. 1,098 crew-served weapons captured to date. 9,607 total, compared to 12,673 weapons captured in caches during 1969. During May–September 1969 rainy season in the COSVN area the enemy lost 18,780 individual weapons and 1,244 crew-served weapons on the battlefield. And 3,046 tons of rice have been seized so far.

■ ■ ■

ABRAMS: "Now, the temporary suspension of these infiltration groups—I believe the way we've understood it in the past is that they come down fairly light. They don't have the weapons—just a few for their local security." "We can tell from the weapons and equipment captured on the battlefield, brand new gear, that it had been issued to them in the border base areas."

ABRAMS: (after all this, two and a half hours into the session, out of the blue): "Well, I see the name of Joseph F. Cutrona here on the BGs [brigadier generals promotion] list. [Cheers and applause] The information types are really moving up."

ABRAMS: "A year from now, maybe the U.S. forces that are here should be in I and II Corps, partly because that's where he [the enemy] has the greatest capability. I Corps is the corps where we've really never been out on the border, so they've got a substantial infrastructure in terms of logistics and all that inside South Vietnam." "It's been 10 years, I guess, since anyone's been in the Do Xa."

19 MAY 1970: Commanders Conference

ATTENDEES: Gen. Abrams, Gen. Rosson, Gen. Brown, LTG Mildren, LTG Davison, VADM King, MG Dolvin, MG Conroy, MG McGown, MG Cowles, BG

Potts, BG Kraft, BG Jaskilka, BG Vande Hey, SJS Rep (Col. Todd).

DAVISON: Presents overview of II Field Force operations: "We did not achieve tactical surprise in the Parrot's Beak. It would appear that we took him by surprise in the north." "I think it's clear to everybody that COSVN displaced before we went across the border." "A prisoner told us they had a seven-hour notice before the B-52 strike in there. When that notice came, the high-level cadre immediately departed." Enemy forces have protected base areas north of 351 with a "very persistent delaying. We've had real difficulty getting in." "His losses, if we're anywhere close to the mark, are approaching his infiltration rate."

DAVISON: In the ARVN Airborne Division AO: An area they've tried to get into for five days, and every time they've been repulsed. We are preparing to hit it with a B-52 strike and have given them an 11th ACR tank company to support a further attempt.

Enemy not just withdrawing here, but fighting hard.

ABRAMS: "On the weapons—my concern now is not with the cosmetics. Out of this whole operation we need to come to grips with just what has it done to the enemy. The number of weapons which he has in fact been deprived of—the number of serviceable weapons—as a result of these operations is one of the factors. If what we think we've gotten is substantially more than we've actually gotten, then we're only misleading ourselves. This has nothing to do with the cosmetics or photographs or anything else. This is just the cold-blooded business of trying to evaluate the current and future effects of these operations on his military capability. And that's what I'm now concerned about. There's nothing worse than basing your analysis on what turns out to be a basketful of fog."

POTTS: "By and large contact throughout the entire area has been extremely minor. Extremely light casualties." "At one point they found a factory with 50 Singer sewing machines making NVA uniforms." "The enemy is extremely hard to find." "I do not think the enemy is hurt seriously in his personnel strength."

ABRAMS (re giving captured VC/NVA weapons to the Cambodian armed forces): "It's the most inexpensive MAP program we've ever run."

ABRAMS: "I'm sure you all understand when we get down to the 30th [of June] there should not be one single American anywhere in Cambodia—above it, in the water, or on the ground. The press will be looking for slips on that, salivating to report it."

POTTS (re the ARVN forces involved): "The professionalism of those three divisions and five armored cav squadrons has increased a hundred percent." "The 21st Division couldn't believe how the [?] had performed. They've actually moved toward the enemy." [Laughter]

ABRAMS (re what to do after the 30th of June): "It seems to me that what we should do now is take as much stuff away from him as we can . . . and try to impart as much stiffening as we can to at least selected parts of the Cambodian [forces]." "It seems to me the other thing we have to do is really get going on the pacification program—the Territorial Forces and the PSDF—and really get this thing cranked up before he can marshal his efforts again. It may be difficult for the corps commanders to see that. This is pretty heady wine that they've been drinking here."

ABRAMS (re ARVN units): "The 25th looks real good in there. The 9th does. 1st of the 2nd. The rangers in the delta and the rangers in I Corps have come up. The rangers in III Corps don't look like much, and that's because they're weighted down by the CMD [Capital Military District]—'How many have you killed and how many have you captured?' The cavalry squadrons in I Corps and in IV Corps look a little better. In the 25th Division their recon elements, their cavalry squadrons, and their infantry regiments look pretty good. They've attained some kind of balance, I guess."

ABRAMS: "I just want to encourage you, in talking with the corps commanders— not only on the problems of the moment, but what they've really got to get at after the great tide of this thing has subsided."

ABRAMS: "The 25th [Division] is an interesting thing. Two years ago—although the competition was very stiff—the 25th won that hands down, month after month after month, and it was unanimous [for worst unit in the ARVN?]" "Now it's showing up as a very solid division. I must say it's hard for me to see the signs of that developing in the 5th."

20 MAY 1970: Admiral McCain Update

ATTENDEES: Adm. McCain, Amb. Koren, RADM Butts, Gen. Abrams, MG Baldwin, Col. Todd, BG Potts, MG Cowles, MG Conroy.

ABRAMS: "There have been some damn good doctors either rally or captured. Now these are professional men. I remember one rallier up there in the highlands. The reason he came in was that, by god, he could not do what a doctor should be able to do for his men. A man, I would say, of great ethical standards, and discipline within his profession."

ABRAMS: "And the enemy has some of the finest medical equipment, such that it would take men of great skill to use it. I remember, up in the 25th Division, they uncovered a cache including medical instruments. A doctor up there had had on requisition for about nine months a particular surgical instrument. And in the captured matériel they discovered this very instrument, from the exact medical supply company, that this American doctor had been waiting for. He was quite delighted to have his requisition filled from this cache."

■ ■ ■

ABRAMS: "The handling of the forces and the tactics by all the forces in IV Corps can only be described as brilliant. . . . General Thanh, the corps commander—

his plan for the assault in the Parrot's Beak was really brilliantly conceived. In fact, it made a lot of the rest of them look like elephants."

ABRAMS: "Another thing about this—he [Thanh] drew up the plan himself. No member of his staff knew anything about it. His deputy was completely ignorant of it. He kept it in his pocket. Eventually he did show it to General McCown. And the day before the operation was to begin he went up and briefed the division commander of the 9th Division on what he was to do, and forbid him to discuss it with his staff, and turned the operation over to him to execute. It was really beautifully done."

ABRAMS: "That 4th Regiment is really something. They've got probably one of the finest tactical commanders in the whole country. He is really skillful. When he goes into these VC areas, the first thing they've got to do is get a prisoner. He's got to be healthy, and he's got to be a VC, and they must get him immediately. Every company and every platoon is charged with that, and he says that's what takes care of the booby traps. They get out there and start telling them where the booby traps are. Of course, if they don't tell them [laughing], their status may change." "He's the only commander I've run into who specializes in that. He's a young and vigorous lieutenant colonel. There's been quite a transformation in that division."

ABRAMS: "They took the province chief of Hau Nghia over into the Parrot's Beak yesterday to show him what had been done. He went home and said he didn't want regular forces back in Hau Nghia—he could handle it with RF and PF. We don't think he can, but we like his spirit."

21 MAY 1970: Brigadier General Haig

Brig. Gen. Alexander M. Haig Jr. is assigned as deputy to National Security Advisor Henry A. Kissinger.

BRIEFER: Covers a COSVN document directing cadre into Cambodia "far prior to our Cambodia operation." Haig picks up on this as counter to claims of "some of the nitpickers" that it was the cross-border operation that precipitated North Vietnamese moves into Cambodia. Briefer also cites a 23 March 1970 Sihanouk speech calling for overthrow of the Lon Nol government and formation of a front.

HAIG: "The president made a speech on the 20th of April, at which time he felt, and our assessments back there were, it was still somewhat ambiguous what the NVA/VC were up to. We suspected they may be going for a much enlarged control, and may have wanted to move that way, but we weren't sure at that time. I think this is important."

POTTS: Observes they've had the time now to analyze after the fact.

HAIG: "But hang on now, General Potts. There're going to be a lot of nitpickers coming out here to see you. We have to convey this thing as it was, but all I'm trying to get across to you is, the way the picture came to the president from the Intelligence Community. It wasn't—. When he made his speech on the 20th, he felt in his own mind that there was still some hope of pulling these people back in a little bit, and therefore he (a) offered to withdraw 150,000, which was a sign, an expression, of desire to move out here ultimately, (b) he reaffirmed his three warnings with respect to Laos, Cambodia, and South Vietnam. And four [*sic*], he offered to negotiate. Now it was nearly 24 hours after that before we got a picture in the White House that these guys were really moving in a <u>very</u> decisive way towards the sea to get a band which would permit lateral movement and permit them debouch out in a threatening way which we'd never had been faced with before. But what I'm afraid of is that we to be—if we're wrong back there, it's because of a drag in—."

POTTS (talking over Haig): "Well, this is not a drag. This was just put together the other day." "So we must be very careful, when this is presented, to say that this analysis of events that have happened. . . ."

HAIG: "Very much so, because I think it will make the president look like a dumbbell, or something."

HAIG: "I'd hate like hell to think that the president was justifying his actions on faulty information, or lagging information." "He maintains, and frankly this is what he was <u>getting</u> from his cabinet and from the briefings we were getting, that it was ambiguous."

BRIEFER: "It was ambiguous at the time."

HAIG: "I can see now, where I <u>do</u> remember these things happening, and they fit into the patterns you're talking about, but at that <u>time</u> they weren't that <u>clear</u>." "That's very fine. That's very helpful to me." "What the president really wrestled with was we were pressuring, 'For god's sake don't announce another troop withdrawal in the midst of this mess <u>here</u>.' And he said, 'Well, it's still ambiguous. I'll go all out with 150,000, and if Hanoi really means they want to settle there's <u>some</u> signal in that announcement.' Well, <u>god</u>, it was two days later that—then we really got this <u>rush</u> of things, the roads are cut, the province capitals are being attacked, and he said, 'Goddamn it, they didn't listen to me.'"

HAIG: "I watched the map on penetration of the Fishhook, and they were just nibbling at the fringes." Re the amount of caches seized: "This is the thing the president is so damn anxious about." "I'll tell you what we're doing. <u>Every day</u> they go over to the Hill and the Congress. <u>Every day</u> they go to the press. And while they're not <u>publishing</u> a goddamn thing, they're making it <u>very</u> hot on them." Potts describes sending pictures back to the CJCS every night.

SOMEONE (to Haig): "We have two of your messages. One of them says 'go get 'em' and the other one says 'hurry up and get out.'"

HAIG: "Well, it's 'go get 'em' until the end of the period."

POTTS (re enemy KIA reported): "It's based on a body count. Remember a few years ago it was an <u>estimate</u> and the thing got inflated out of all <u>proportion</u>. In fact, in one year we killed more enemy than there was in the country. Then they went back and got very hard on body count, and even that you have to keep purifying."

POTTS: To date out of the base areas "we have picked up 1.2 million pages of documents." Thirty-two cases of crypto material.

POTTS (re the intelligence take, apart from matériel seizures): "What's coming out of that <u>really</u> gives us a much better handle on the enemy's intentions, and what he's done in the past, and what he thinks he can do in the future. So it's a very, very healthy thing."

HAIG (referring to tabulations of the take in Cambodia): "You might be interested in knowing that <u>twice</u> a day, in my office, we have a guy full-time and that's the <u>first</u> goddamn thing that goes to the president. And it's in there on the moment."

SOMEONE (apparently in Haig's party): "And when you drop your mortar rounds by 50 percent from one day to the next he really wants to know what the hell happened!"

HAIG: "I know it must drive you up the wall to get plugged on the stuff [captured] this way, but it's important."

POTTS: "<u>But</u> the objective is to get the true story out to everybody, because for us this has been a very wonderful thing. And a very courageous decision by the president. And it's going to have a major effect on the future of III and IV Corps. The ARVN can almost handle it by themselves when you take all this away from the enemy."

HAIG: "If you had air authority to move in and strike targets east of the Mekong, could you do it right now? Could you start hitting targets, or do you feel you'd have to have more reconnaissance and more control? We're having some <u>problems</u>."

POTTS: "Yes, I know this."

HAIG: "They're asking you, from JCS, whether or not you <u>have</u> any targets. Now if you go back and you say 'yes,' you have targets, and then they say 'all right, you can strike them'—or 'what are they?' Then you're losing 12 hours, 24 hours. These <u>fixes</u> you get are time sensitive. Does it make any sense, as a conceptual process, to have to tell Washington that you <u>have</u> a target, and then request permission to <u>hit</u> it?"

ANSWER: "No, it doesn't."

HAIG: "Well, why the hell don't we get authority to hit the targets when you <u>fix</u> them?"

ANSWER: "Well, that's what we're trying to get."

HAIG: "What's your estimate of time? If you had authority <u>now</u> to strike targets, do you have some targets that you can strike, that you are reasonably sure are not going to result in civilian casualties, and will be renumerative [*sic*] targets?"

ANSWER: "Yes, we do."

HAIG: "It's been a wonderland. It's been a goddamn week since the president put out the word he wanted these targets hit."

SOMEONE: "Well, we came out with a plan, and they came back and told us, Christ, that we were too bold, going far beyond the guidelines that they had in mind, and all that kind of stuff."

HAIG: "And this is the time when we can be doing the damage."

SOMEONE: "When we got that answer back from the JCS saying we were being a little bit too bold—. We don't think the guy who wrote the first message is the same fellow who answered our response."

■ ■ ■

SOMEONE: "General McCown briefed General Abrams a few days ago, telling him it was interesting to hear the Cambodians speak with awe of the power of the Vietnamese, the fact that they're so well organized and they come charging across the border—three divisions, helicopters, APCs, the whole schmear."

SOMEONE: "Two days ago we had a day where we didn't lose one man in-country—in combat. Goddamn!"

HAIG: "I've seen the yellow report every morning from the NMCC, and I get the distinct impression that the RF/PF are coming along exceptionally well."

BRIEFER: "During these offensive operations in Cambodia, and the significant results attained, average U.S. KIA have been almost 50 percent lower than the nine-month period [July 1969–March 1970: 15.8 compared to 9.2], with this lower result despite increased activity in I and II Corps."

SOMEONE: "We've always maintained—you know they've been yelling back home to cut out your offensive operations because it causes casualties? Well, the fact is it doesn't."

HAIG: "Of course it doesn't. That's a myth."

SAME SOMEONE: "Only the doves think that way. But this is evidence—go on the offensive, your casualties go down."

HAIG: "This has been damn good. That air business just leaves me astonished."

23 MAY 1970: Commanders WIEU

ATTENDEES: Amb. Bunker, Amb. Berger, Gen. Abrams, Gen. Rosson, Gen. Brown, Amb. Colby, LTG Mildren, LTG Collins, LTG Davison, LTG Zais, Mr. Kirk, LTG McCutcheon, VADM King, MG Dolvin, MG Brown, MG Conroy, Mr. Firfer, MG McCown, MG Cowles, Mr. Jacobson, Mr. Vann, MG Dettre, BG Clement, BG Camp, BG Kraft, BG Vande Hey, BG Greene, BG Potts, BG Jaskilka, BG Sykes, BG Henion, Mr. Chambers (for Mr. Megellas), Mr. Cruikshank (for Mr. Whitehouse), Col. Cavanaugh, Col. Cutrona, Col. Martin (for BG Cheadle), Col. Healy, Col. Todd, Col. Weeks (for BG Henderson).

BRIEFER (re the Cambodian armed forces): "Armed with a mixture of CHICOM, Soviet, and U.S. weapons. There is no support structure for any of these weapon systems. Troop transportation is by civilian truck or bus. Few military vehicles are usable due to lack of maintenance support." "Lack of individual arms, communications equipment, crew-served weapons, and artillery for FANK brigades and battalions." Only 50,000 troops are currently armed (and poorly).

■ ■ ■

DAVISON: "As I understood the discussion of the cross-border operation, the briefer said that they [the enemy] withdrew behind the 30-click [kilometer] line. We saw it in a little different light than that. I think there's clear evidence in the Parrot's Beak that SR-2 and SR-3 and their units attempted to defend in place, for which we were duly thankful, because I think the ARVN cut both of them up pretty badly. The regiment of the 9th Division that was down in that area attempted on at least two occasions to defend against the ARVN and suffered moderately heavy casualties."

DAVISON: In the Fishhook area: "They've been very stubborn, they've fought very effective delaying actions, and they've really kept us out of what we think is another cache area for about six days." "I really wouldn't characterize it as a withdrawal."

SOMEONE: "In IV Corps, they most definitely withdrew on all fronts."

COLLINS: "Those that were in [Base Area] 702 hung in there and fought very effectively."

■ ■ ■

BRIEFER: "There have been some criticisms in terms of U.S. cross-border operations causing VC/NVA penetrations of Cambodia. Many of these penetrations began before the 29th. There was obviously a movement in the area to reestablish the strategic position in Cambodia prior to any U.S. or ARVN cross-border operations, and that can be documented."

BRIEFER: On 9 May 1970: Highest U.S. troop density in Cambodia: 19,300. The highest ARVN density occurred on 20 May: 29,000+.

BRIEFER: Shows items of ordnance captured and discusses them. 107-mm "over caliber" rocket equivalent to 240-mm. 14.5-mm heavy machine gun from the Fishhook area, a dual-barrel version.

DAVISON: "Even in the Cambodian sanctuaries they still follow the same secretive pattern that you see inside Vietnam. They bury things—in the Parrot's Beak there's not a thing above ground, everything is underground." "Very difficult to locate unless you come right up on it." These weapons were found in an area where they'd already been operating for two weeks. A patrol came across a piece of commo wire and followed it to the cache bunker. Some caches are buried in streambeds.

BRIEFER: In Base Area 702 the enemy even had X-ray machines.

■ ■ ■

DAVISON: "The deputy commander of SR-2 Chieu Hoi'd. He's been taking people back into the Parrot's Beak and showing them things." Wrote a letter, which Davison gives to Abrams (in translation) and Abrams reads aloud: "To all the comrades in arms belonging to SR-2: Dear My Friends. . . . I have just cooperated with the government of South Vietnam on 20 May 1970. The reason which I have done this is that I saw that most of NVA leaders treated you, the wounded soldiers, miserably. In part of cadres who have some deficiencies they have not been satisfied that they have to suffer, scold, and curse. When I came back to cooperate with the GVN, I saw that they have ways to operate which corresponded with the people's aspirations, and for that reason I rallied to the GVN." Invites them to do likewise. "I am awaiting for your decision."

■ ■ ■

ABRAMS: "All the Vietnamese have really been inspired by this chance to get into Cambodia and tear around in the base areas and—it's been very heady wine for them. They've got the enemy off balance. He's out of position. He hasn't had time to run things the way he ordinarily runs them. They're practically drunk with power. And they've gotten over there and they see the Cambodians—and the Cambodians see them. Always before, they'd been comparing themselves to the U.S. forces, the Korean forces, and the VC/NVA, and they've gotten over here and they've got a chance to compare themselves to the Cambodians. Well, good god, it has an effect on them. And at the same time the VC and NVA are running—they know they're running, they're trying to get away—it's not everywhere, but it's certainly true opposite IV Corps and so on. And it's reflected in some of these things—'On to Kratie,' 'On to Kompong Cham,' 'On to Phnom Penh.' Wow! But the main problem is still South Vietnam. If they can come back into South Vietnam and apply all this enthusiasm and vigor and initiative and aggressiveness and high spirits and so on to the drudgery of pacification, the drudgery of the jungle and the base areas, then we've got something. But that isn't going to automatically happen."

■ ■ ■

BRIEFER: Helicopter losses in April 1970: 95. Highest ever in one month were 110 in 1968.

Responding to Abrams's question.

SOMEONE: "We're flying the wings off 'em, General." Of the 95, 65 are combat losses.
ABRAMS: "What about the engine problem—the Lycoming strike?"
SOMEONE: "If it goes another 30 days it could be bad."
COLLINS: "We're beginning to notice more .50-caliber AA fire in the highlands, and that makes a difference."

■ ■ ■

CORDS BRIEFER: "Generally the overall momentum of the pacification program has slowed." Country overall per HES reports a "slight regression" during April 1970. Total A/B/C down from 89.7 to 88.9. In II Corps all provinces regressed.
ABRAMS: "We ought to be able to change this stuff from here on out—next couple of months."
BRIEFER: On 26 March 1970 a land reform bill was promulgated. It will involve some one million hectares, or one-third of the land currently under cultivation. Some 500,000 families could become landowners. Three hectares each.
COMMENT: Terrorist incidents have held relatively steady while (as pacification

progresses) the number of people subject to terrorism has increased substantially.

SOMEONE (Brown?): "We think we see a way to provide for the early activation of three additional fighter squadrons for the VNAF. I put this forward to the air force."

ABRAMS: "I would say, in the climate now existing in Washington, that that would be snatched up without review. In the existing climate, which doesn't care about what you can't see. . . ."

■ ■ ■

ABRAMS (turning to Bunker, who has apparently recently returned after having been away): "Mr. Ambassador?"

BUNKER: "Well, I'm glad to get back to a place where one has a sense of some purpose and commitment, I may say. Sometimes at home you get the sense that the commitment is against the orderly processes of government and the institutions on which it's based. I must say, too, that the increased polarization that I sensed there, and observed there, is rather disturbing. I think it was heightened, too—not only by the president's statement, but by that tragedy at Kent State University, and this touched off these demonstrations in a big way."

BUNKER: "When I was there in Washington we had some 75,000 students on May 9th. I talked to some of them. I talked to a great many of them while I was there. It was quite an orderly performance, but—and this of course stirred up counterdemonstrations. You've probably heard about the hard hats in New York, the construction workers who turned out and beat up the students; then some 5,000 of them then went after Mayor Lindsay, I'm glad to say. [Laughter] Two days later, some 10,000 turned out and marched up Broadway to City Hall, and I think a couple of days ago some 150,000 turned out."

BUNKER: "But the disturbing thing, I thought, was that some of the people who have been pretty strong supporters say, 'Well, if this is going to tear the country apart it isn't worth it.' One example: Dean Acheson, who's been a strong supporter of what we've been doing here, of the policies. I had lunch with him and the secretary and asked him what he thought about the president's decision. He said, 'I think it's a mistake,' very strong and firm on that. Well, I argued with him about it."

BUNKER: "And another disturbing feature, I think, is the dissent within the government and the disclosure of classified documents that's gone on. On the other hand, certainly the coolest man in Washington is the president. He is determined and strong and cool."

BUNKER: "I don't mean to say, or to give the impression, that the country's going to hell in a hat. When you go up to West Point, as I did, and see 4,000 of those young fellows there, you have hope for the young generation."

BUNKER: "But the president is very firm and very strong and very cool. And the polls show that he has the majority with him. He's convinced that he has done the right thing, and he's very pleased, I may say, with this operation in Cambodia, and pleased with your reports, General Abrams, about the performance of the Vietnamese forces. This, I think, is extremely useful there, too, in replying to the critics who have said that the Vietnamese wouldn't fight and couldn't develop a good force. As Kissinger said in a press backgrounder, 'You fellows were saying six months ago, a year ago, the Vietnamese wouldn't fight. Now you're saying they're too aggressive.'"

BUNKER: "I think with this progress . . . proof that Vietnamization is working, and I think they continue to make progress, not only on the military aspect of it, but pacification, consolidation, economic development, handling economic problems, stability in the country, I think we can confound the prophets of doom. And as a matter of fact I think it's a great opportunity for us, really, to show that the country has the patience and the will to accept the responsibility of the power."

BUNKER: "I think that you all have been doing a great job here. It's certainly appreciated by the president, I can tell you that. And there are a lot of stalwart people with him. This has been a very encouraging report today." "I congratulate you all."

ABRAMS: "I hope we can, as soon as possible, return the interest of the Vietnamese to Vietnam. It needs it. It still is the most important thing in the whole business. We have got to get back after it. This terrorism thing is not good. And everywhere there are still some problems to get at. There's enough work to be done. Thank you very much."

29 MAY 1970: Briefing for General Abrams, Ambassador Bunker, and Ambassador Berger

ATTENDEES: Gen. Abrams, Amb. Bunker, Amb. Berger, MG Dolvin, MG Cowles, BG Potts.

macv Infiltration Estimate now 43,500. Regular size infiltration group: 570. K group: 70–90.

BRIEFER: COSVN has two important elements: Political Headquarters and Headquarters South Vietnam. On 20 April 1970 COSVN began relocating from its secondary base area to its secondary alternate base area. On the night of 9–10 May 1970 it relocated northeast to an area south of the Cho Long River. On 11 May 1970: During the early morning 35 B-52s struck the secondary alternate base area. Results: 151 bodies, 64 secondary explosions. We learned that they got a seven-hour advance warning.

BUNKER: "They've been kept on the road, I'd say."

ABRAMS: "How useful is all this [infiltration] manpower going to be [if we've scarfed up the wherewithal that would have been used to equip them when they arrived]?" "It's no good putting soldiers in if you don't have stuff for 'em. All they do is eat."

2 JUN 1970: COMUS Update: Cambodia, North Vietnam, In-Country

BRIEFER: On 30 May 1970 Lon Nol declared martial law. Among offenses warranting 5–20 years imprisonment is listening to Radio Peking.

ABRAMS (re enemy pipeline to the west of the DMZ into Base Area 604): "If they get the goddamn pipeline in, and tested, and operating—that's what they did, despite all the air effort!"

BRIEFER (noting Abrams's having departed on 29 May 1970): "Sir, as you know, the air interdiction operations in northeast Cambodia were planned prior to your departure." On 30 May six targets were hit of eight planned. One was not hit "because it was too close to a populated area."

6 JUN 1970: WIEU

ATTENDEES: Gen. Abrams, Gen. Rosson, Gen. Brown, Amb. Colby, LTG Mildren, Mr. Kirk, VADM King, MG Dolvin, MG Conroy, MG Cowles, Mr. Jacobson, MG Dettre, BG Camp, BG Kraft, BG Greene, BG Potts, BG Jaskilka, Col. Cutrona, Col. Stewart (for BG Sykes), Col. Franklin (for Col. Cavanaugh), Col. Martin (for BG Cheadle), Col. Weeks (for BG Henderson), Col. Todd.

Tape opens with discussion of some recent briefing, apparently for a visiting congressional delegation.

ABRAMS: "He must have had his tape recorder going. [Chuckles] See, that won't be good without a tape."

SOMEONE: "Well, I think little jewels like, you know, when you turned on Senator McIntyre would be <u>very</u> useful."

ABRAMS: "Senator Tower thought it was—he spoke to me last night down there at dinner—<u>he</u> thought that was very good. But of course they don't see eye to eye. He spends most of his days trying to do the same thing."

SOMEONE: "I thought I'd just made a pleasant greeting to Senator McIntyre when I met him at lunch and said how fine it was he could come on the trip. He said, 'Goddamn, I didn't <u>want</u> to come!'"

SOMEONE: "He was quoted in the *Stars & Stripes* that he came along only to keep the rest of them honest."

SOMEONE: "It must have made the others very happy to hear that."

ABRAMS: "I think this is going to be worthwhile for them. Maybe not for this other guy. The ones that are in support—see, they get a lot of tough questions and so on, and they really are trying to fill up their baskets so they will have a little more to come back on. So that part is probably useful to them."

■ ■ ■

BRIEFER: "The southwest monsoon has been very weak. We don't have the support in the higher levels of the atmosphere that we need to get the monsoon here in full strength."

ABRAMS: "I was about to make a remark that somewhere up there somebody stepped into this thing and it <u>is</u> helping us."

BRIEFER: "But at any rate—." [Laughter]

ABRAMS: "You want to be sure you understand what that <u>laughter</u> is about. It's with <u>you</u>. Don't misunderstand it."

■ ■ ■

BRIEFER: MACV 1970 Infiltration Estimate: 43,600 (61 percent to COSVN).

BRIEFER (re infiltration): Document captured in the Fishhook area revealed group K2058 with unknown strength, the sixth K group discovered in documents captured during the Cambodian border operation that was not detected in COMINT. K groups in the 2050 series were first detected in COMINT in December 1969. Average strength: 20.

■ ■ ■

BRIEFER: On 31 May 1970 the Soviet tanker [*Havagor*?] arrived in Haiphong carrying 4,030 metric tons of POL. This was the 10th delivery in May, bringing to 32,775 metric tons the total for the month. This represents 83 percent of the requested 39,500 metric tons.

POTTS: For the year to date, about 75 percent of the amount requested, "about the same as last year."

ABRAMS: "I let it go, but Admiral Moorer—at the meeting with the president and so on—he pulled out, at some point in the thing, he pulled out this message he had and gave the same report on this tanker, and I think the same total. But he classified it as an extraordinary shipment of POL, drawing some inference from it. Well, I didn't have a POL chart, so I just had to let it go, but I knew damn well that about 40,000 metric tons a month is what they've been asking for, and actually it goes back long before this chart to last year as well."

POTTS: "Nothing unusual there, sir."

■ ■ ■

BRIEFER: Describes enemy messages alerting *binh trams* in Laos to be prepared to defend themselves.

ABRAMS: "What was going through my mind was, 'What triggered that?'" "It's one of the things that sort of—the <u>press</u> talks about it. The other night when I had dinner down there they brought this up and so on. It's hard to believe that they [the press, apparently] perform some useful service, but that may be the whole foundation of the goddamn thing." [Laughter]

ABRAMS: "Last night I was reading these two articles in *Newsweek* and *Time* magazine, both on General Tri. One of them is captioned 'The Patton of the Parrot's Beak.' [Laughter, and "<u>Oh</u>, god!"] No, these are described as 'the spunky little commander of the rejuvenated ARVN forces' or some such a thing as that. Got a picture of him lolling peacefully under a palm tree, 'somewhere in Cambodia' it says. [Laughter] <u>Well</u>—we can laugh about it, but in the <u>other</u> game I think this other fellow watches very carefully this is quite a <u>thing</u>. Somebody up there's got a few gas pains over—Christ almighty, the heroes that will be coming out of this thing."

POTTS: "Three or four weeks ago he was a corrupt son of a gun."

ABRAMS: "And one of the articles mentions that, but passes it off—obviously an erroneous report! And this is the <u>U.S.</u> <u>press</u> writing stuff like this. I suppose, from <u>their</u> standpoint, this is not a good kind of publicity to be floating around. Always a possibility, I suppose, that these corps commanders could get <u>competing</u> for this sort of thing. Maybe they understand Lam better than <u>we</u> do. In fact, he <u>is</u> cooking such a thing. Want to be known as 'the Patton of the Ho Chi Minh Trail'!"

JACOBSON: "Kind of interesting, because the last time we went to see the prime minister there was conversation about <u>moving</u> Tri. The question was what in hell to <u>do</u> with him, so senior and all. But they didn't talk like he was the Patton of <u>anything</u>. We suggested he might become the Patton of the RF and PF. There's no lengths to which we wouldn't go to get rid of that goddamn La, of course."

ABRAMS: "I think that's a fair statement."

■ ■ ■

DISCUSSION: Possibility of reopening rail traffic from Thailand to Phnom Penh, last run in 1962.

BRIEFER: "The railroad itself is quite vulnerable to sabotage in the sense that there are 173 bridges between the Thai border and Phnom Penh."

■ ■ ■

DISCUSSION: The 275th NVA Regiment in Cambodia.

ABRAMS: "I must say several things puzzle me about this. The way the 275th has operated in the past, tied tightly to a base area and so on. As far as I know the VC/NVA never had any setup out in that territory ["near Kompong Thom"] to—for resupply ammunition, care of the wounded, any of those things. It's just a hell of a distance. Well, it's <u>extraordinary</u> in terms of what they did before. Such basic things as where the hell did they get the maps for it, or—. I suppose you can assume that they confiscated transportation, but what kind of a system is there to refuel the trucks? What do they do with their wounded, or their sick? Where do they <u>get</u> their ammunition? Assume that they pick up <u>food</u> from the peasantry and live that way, live off the country. There aren't any guerrillas out there, and the thing isn't well organized, I don't believe, in terms of guerrillas. There may be some Khmer Rouge. It's just a hell of a lot <u>different</u> than anything that those fellows have been <u>accustomed</u> to. Does this mean they're just super-adaptable?"

■ ■ ■

ABRAMS: "It seems to me that this <u>part</u> of the thing, while we've got to keep track of it and report it, and we've got to finish it up the best we can, as thoroughly as we can by the 30th of June, now at this <u>level</u> I'd say that that part is <u>over</u>. We've got to start grappling here with what happens, the things to be done, after the 30th of June on our side. And we haven't got a handle on the <u>enemy</u>—what he's up to, how he's conducting his business. You know, I look back to the good old days when—of course, they're <u>gone</u>, I know that, but we were reading his mail, picking up his recon men, getting a few Hoi Chanhs, and 'the plan for Binh Hoa is developing, it's going to come off in five more days,' and 'the plan for Tay Ninh City, and it's going to be this regiment and this regiment,' you know—we just kind of <u>understood</u> the thing. And then we could do a little something about it and so on."

ABRAMS: "Well, <u>goddamn</u>, in <u>this</u> thing all that—well, I just feel very uncomfortable. I don't <u>know</u> anything like that. Here this guy is, wandering around all over <u>Indochina</u> practically, apparently at will, everything in good shape, and it's—I don't <u>understand</u> it. Is he getting out there and waiting till the 30th of June, and then he's going to do something else? Or has he decided—has the decision been made—to just take over? You know, they began saying, from Hanoi, talking <u>eastern</u> Cambodia. Is he <u>now</u> going to work and organize this whole <u>glob</u> up here? I don't know just where you'd draw the boundary or anything, but—. We got this interdiction program that's been authorized, and so on. If that's going to be worth a goddamn we ought to have some idea of what we <u>target</u> against. And if you're going to have some idea of what you target it against, you ought to have some idea of what the hell <u>he's</u> about doing. Just don't have any <u>feel</u> for that."

WEYAND (re the enemy): "Even <u>Napoleon</u> couldn't do what the Cambodians say <u>this</u> guy's doing. They've got him aiming further west than they showed on their <u>map</u>."

ABRAMS: "Oh, Christ, we've got him over there fishing in the damn <u>race</u>!" "And it's not only that, but here he is ambushing the poor television fellows down here to the southwest of Phnom Penh, and so on. Far as <u>I</u> know, these are the same forces that—well, you know, early in '69 they still were trying to get into Saigon. Then they cut the cloth little different and they started working on Tay Ninh City, Binh Hoa, and so on, and then they finally wound up screwing around with Loc Ninh. Even got where there weren't any warning flags going up in Loc Ninh. They were all screwing around on the <u>border</u>. These are the same fellows. And every once in a while, a shortage of food . . . shortage of medicine. These reports—well, about <u>malaria</u>. They've been getting <u>cases</u> and <u>cases</u> of malaria pills. Maybe it's like some supply that we have, that keep the goddamn stuff in the warehouse or they won't have any reserve—I don't know. And here's this same outfit—hah! Well, they're taking over another <u>country</u>!"

JACOBSON: Easier country to take over. Just ride around.

ABRAMS: "Well, you know, that isn't really the way they like to do business. You know, they've got—well, at least I <u>thought</u>, anyway—that these fellows are really quite doctrinaire. And you've got—the way you run these wars—you've got your cadres and tax collectors and control of the people and all this sort of thing, and you <u>build</u> on that. It's like when they took over North Vietnam. You either ship all the crud out—as <u>they</u> view it, I mean the contraries, the people that don't like this stuff—you ship them out, or you kill them. And then you go ahead—you've got your people, and they're all over everywhere, and you've got <u>control</u>. After a while you can even have <u>voting</u>—one candidate, one ballot, but you can have all the accouterments of democracy. It just is no son of a bitch is going to put in a 'no'! And if he does, he's <u>shot</u>. And then you just <u>run</u> it that way. That's the way you <u>run</u> things. And that's the <u>only</u> way the <u>Communists</u> feel <u>good</u> about things. That's why they go into Czechoslovakia. The people, some bastard over there, started thinking a little—well, he was thinking a little screwy—you know, by the <u>doctrine</u>, by the doctrine, which is control, and absolute control, of all the people. Well, <u>he</u> doesn't have <u>that</u>."

BRIEFER: Reports on caches in Cambodia. Brings out a weapon.

ABRAMS: "I hope, in keeping with your normal practice, you're not going to fire that." It's a flamethrower.

ABRAMS: "What's the Seventh Air Force evaluation of the quality of these officers [five Cambodian air force officers on duty with the Seventh Air Force for target validation purposes]?"

ANSWER: "They got airsick on their first flight." [Laughter]

WEYAND: "Could happen to anybody."

ABRAMS: "That's right, that's right—shouldn't draw any hasty conclusions." [Laughter]

■ ■ ■

ABRAMS (re mundane problems of allied cooperation): Recalls an operation when "Tri couldn't start on Monday 'cause Tuesday, according to his astrologer—[Somebody: "an inauspicious day"] one of the worst in the whole year. And so he couldn't start till Wednesday. And he didn't. <u>Crazy</u>!"

■ ■ ■

ABRAMS: "The general theme of this interdiction program that's been authorized is to do those things in Cambodia which will be helpful to <u>us</u> in South Vietnam. So all the things that can create more and more problems for the enemy—after taking due account for civilians and, you know, not hitting, not doing that—but anything we can do to complicate <u>his</u> problems for reestablishing himself on the borders and in South Vietnam, that's what we should be doing and that's the <u>purpose</u> of the whole thing. That's the general attitude, and that's what they <u>want</u> done. As a matter of fact, they're really quite <u>insistent</u> that we do <u>everything</u> we can in this area to complicate <u>his</u> problems. Now this is <u>his</u> problem with respect to South Vietnam. That's the <u>context</u> in which this is all done. So bulldozers and steamrollers [as targets] give me no pain."

■ ■ ■

ABRAMS (apparently in reference to visiting congressional delegations and Congressman Schwengle, coming for a visit): "They should operate on the prin-

cipal that MACV will not try to <u>impose</u> itself on anybody. If there's some bastard that doesn't want briefings, he's come to the <u>right</u> place!"

JACOBSON: "He used Peter Arnett's articles for his interrogation of all of us
when he was out here a couple of years ago."

ABRAMS: "Some of these fellows who <u>read</u> something that has come out, they
vaguely and dimly recall that either they <u>thought</u> of the same thing, or mentioned it to a friend some years ago. And they <u>now</u> are delighted to see it being
implemented." Cites "that little speech by Mr. Bray. Incidentally, I've never
seen a man more <u>aptly</u> named. [Laughter] I've had quite a long acquaintance
with him. He was on the House Armed Services Committee, and I was three
years and three months in the reserve components business in the Pentagon.
And of course he <u>is</u> the <u>great</u> spokesman for the National Guard on the House
Armed Services Committee, having been a tank battalion commander at one
time—in the National Guard. But you notice yesterday he found that recommendation which he had <u>urged</u>, on one of his other trips, had somewhat haltingly, but nevertheless been put into effect. [Chuckling] 'Of course,' he said,
[making his voice pompous as he repeats this] 'any experience has been completely with the tactical end.'" [Laughs]

13 JUN 1970: WIEU

ATTENDEES: Amb. Bunker, Gen. Abrams, Gen. Rosson, Gen. Brown, Amb.
Colby, LTG Mildren, Mr. Kirk, VADM King, MG Dolvin, MG Conroy, MG
Cowles, Mr. Jacobson, MG Dettre, BG Camp, BG Kraft, BG Greene, BG Potts,
BG Cheadle, BG Henion, Col. Cavanaugh, Col. Cutrona, Col. Stewart (for BG
Sykes), Col. Weeks (for BG Henderson), Col. Greer, Col. Todd.

macv 1970 Infiltration Estimate: 43,800 (61 percent for COSVN).

POTTS: From Binh Tram 18 it would take infiltrators about 120 days to reach
COSVN.

ABRAMS: "We annually have turned in an assessment of what we did in the interdiction program over there in the dry season. And I remember one year it said
he didn't even meet the subsistence level, let alone build up the stocks for the
rainy season. And later on we thought that that had an <u>effect</u> on the low level of
activity in I Corps. Well, if that had been right, if that was a correct assessment, I should have thought he would have known it too and continued on in
the rainy season, like he's doing now, because he was in bad shape. Or he just
decided not to do it. Well, why is he—? I mean, I don't know as I quite understand why this is happening."

BROWN: "Last year we made the estimate that he didn't get down the levels of
stocks that he needed currently and to see him through the next rainy season.
This year we've estimated that he's gotten through better than 19,000 tons.
We've destroyed a bunch of that coming down. He put in to the campaign
about 25 percent more effort than last year—in numbers of trucks and numbers
of people. And <u>we</u> put in about 25 percent <u>less</u> in airpower. It's not <u>here</u>. It's

gone <u>home</u>. So he <u>should</u> have done better. <u>I</u> don't know why he didn't push in the rainy season last year. I don't remember that he <u>tried</u>, as a matter of fact. But this year he's <u>said</u> that he's going to <u>try</u>. And <u>I</u> don't think he'll be able to <u>do</u> it."

ABRAMS: "Yeah, but just listen to all the contradictions that are in that. See, last year we thought we did pretty well preventing him from doing everything he wanted to. So the rainy season comes along—he doesn't do anything. This year <u>we</u> think <u>he</u> did pretty well, and here comes the rainy season—I'll be damned, he's going at it <u>again</u>."

BROWN: "And there's another <u>greater</u> contradiction which is all these supplies when there's less infiltration to support. He's pushing harder, greater [word indistinct], and less troops. <u>I</u> don't understand it."

ABRAMS (to Potts): "You've got a story going around that he's opted for a protracted war. You don't need all this tonnage for a protracted war." "We've got a lot of things here that just don't add <u>up</u>! Either we've been kidding ourselves <u>before</u>, or <u>something</u>. How 'bout this protracted war, and then here's all this damn tonnage?"

POTTS: Induced by operations in Cambodia. "We think it's a desperation effort."

ABRAMS: "The infiltration pattern doesn't support that. It's because we've always—and we may not be right about <u>this</u>—before, when he's planned some military campaigning, he has put personnel into the infiltration system to support it. Maybe <u>that's</u> been changed, too."

ABRAMS (re Vietnamese operating in the rainy season): "I can understand how the Americans get over here and say, 'Well, it's the rainy season, can't do anything now. In the dry season we can do something.' Americans haven't <u>been</u> here very long compared to these people. . . . I mean, their grandfather and the great-grandfather and all the way back . . . they've been <u>living</u> in this rainy season, dry season thing, so they're not the same as us."

BROWN: "But they haven't been driving trucks and using bulldozers and all that jazz they've got wrapped around their neck now. They used to just take an elephant and <u>go</u>."

ABRAMS: "What is the reason for this rather extraordinary logistical effort compared to any other year that we know about? Even—you talk about '68—he left the 559th [Transportation Group] in, but his truck traffic went <u>down</u>. What the 559 was doing was moving <u>people</u>, not logistics."

ABRAMS (re the enemy's shuttle system for supplies): "It's like a python eating a pig. He gets it in his mouth, and it moves a foot. Some digestive process goes on, then it moves another foot, and so on. And that's <u>kind</u> of the way the supplies move down here."

■ ■ ■

BRIEFER: Enemy reports that the "101st American Division and 200 tanks had started moving north. [***] overreacting to [***] guerrilla incursions into its area of operations."

ABRAMS: "No, no—they and Ambassador Kittihara have the same source, apparently. They've latched onto <u>somebody</u> who doesn't know what's going on. What do you fellows call the agent that is most reliable—A-1? They think they've got an A-1, and what they've got's about an X. <u>F-6</u>!" "Well, if some way we could get Peter Arnett to write this stuff, that'll put them in an absolute <u>frenzy</u>. As a matter of fact, if you could publicize this enough you might get that Cooper-Church amendment modified to prohibit taking U.S. forces into Tchepone. Then I think we'd—they're a step <u>behind</u>. I think we'd really have something then. Might even get specific and say the <u>101</u> won't go to Tchepone. Then I could issue a public statement <u>denying</u> that we had planned to do that. [Laughter] That would start an investigative committee."

■ ■ ■

ABRAMS (re operations in Laos): "We're sort of victims of our own experience. . . . When we talk about something <u>falling</u> we had some kind of a tremendous defense, you know, and everybody's trying to <u>save</u> the farm, and great heroics being performed and all that, and finally it's <u>lost</u>. And you generally have some fairly decent feel of what it was that was attacking—whether it was a company or a platoon or a battalion, or even occasionally two battalions. What happens over here—as a matter of fact, what happens in <u>Cambodia</u>—you just don't <u>know</u> what happened! It <u>isn't</u> that kind of a picture. You know, they've even got stories going around now that the VC/NVA have stopped <u>using</u> ammunition—they've got records and loudspeakers. They've recorded battle sounds from South Vietnam—and they probably [laughing] recorded some <u>B-52s</u>! When they invest one of these posts they just get that out and <u>play</u> it. Then you can walk in and have lunch the next day."

BRIEFER: Notes that North Vietnam's National Assembly was convened last week for only the fourth time in the past five years, and suggests that each time it was in conjunction with a major turning point in Hanoi's conduct of the war. Abrams asks for a study to lay that all out.

BUNKER: (re Vietnamese living in Cambodia): "President Thieu said to General Abrams and me—most of them had gone there to avoid the war <u>here</u>."

■ ■ ■

BRIEFER: Since the cross-border operation began there have been a total of 35 captures of cryptographic documents, including the 14 May capture of over 1,000 pounds in BA 701 ("deemed to be of major significance"). Sealed in 32 metal boxes, and included over 3,000 one-time pads and about 1,500 codebooks, all new. Enough keying material for the encryption of over 500,000 messages." Never distributed, so no help in deciphering.

■ ■ ■

BRIEFER: "A usually reliable medium-level VC agent reported that the Tay Ninh province committee held a meeting on 29 May to set the guidelines for the summer campaign. He said these guidelines were based on guidance from COSVN. . . . He stated that cadre were cautioned that, although III Corps and

Cambodia operations were currently in focus, they were to remember that the Central Highlands in II Corps and northern I Corps remained the major battle-field."

ABRAMS: "Baloney! That defies a-l-l facts that are available. Why have they got 61 percent of all infiltration coming into COSVN? Is that a ruse, while they make the major effort in the highlands? That fellow's getting less reliable." [Laughter]

16 JUN 1970: Briefing for Admiral McCain

BRIEFER (Lieutenant Wynn, the star briefer]: Summarizes political developments in Southeast Asia. Sihanouk and his entourage departed Hanoi for Peking last week after a two-week state visit in North Vietnam. After less than a week they have moved on by train for North Korea for another state visit. They previously had spent five weeks in the USSR and left without fanfare.

BRIEFER: "The war in the Republic of Vietnam can be broadly divided into two related conflicts, the in-country political and military struggle for control of the population and the out-country logistical campaign. While in the past the military-political conflagration has been fairly well confined to the Republic of Vietnam and a thin strip along its borders, the logistical struggle has always been an Indochina war involving all countries of the peninsula. Success of either side depends on victory in both conflicts."

BRIEFER: Cites "the 30-kilometer restraint placed on American forces and their eventual total withdrawal by 30 June" from Cambodia.

BRIEFER: The enemy is facing four actual or potential problem areas: 1. Significant expansion of the area of operations, complicating command and control, logistical support, and personnel replacement. 2. Problem of Khmer-Vietnamese antipathy. 3. Diversion of troops formerly operating in South Vietnam. 4. Closing of the Kompong Son [Sihanoukville] line of communication.

BRIEFER: "Captured documents indicate that COSVN did forewarn its units about possible allied operations, allowing some supplies to be moved."

BRIEFER: "There is no evidence to confirm or deny that the enemy is experiencing personnel replacement problems."

ABRAMS (to McCain, apparently re Washington): "As you know, they've been seized again with the idea that we won't comply with the orders. [Long pause] It gets habit-forming after 30 years. I don't know what the hell they're worried about."

POTTS: "We now have the equivalent of 16,562 attacks by fire that have been pulled out of these base areas."

Referring to captured ammunition, based on an average of about eight rounds per attack by fire.

MCCAIN (re continuation of the drawdown of U.S. forces): "Everybody in this room knows it's going to be rough. I don't have any recourse. One—not beyond this goddamn room—one ray of light, if they <u>fritz</u> up this thing in the Middle East far enough, why it may reverse the trend of events."

17 JUN 1970: Cambodian Update

Presented to General Abrams by NAVFORV, Seventh Air Force, J-2, J-3, J-4, and MACMA/MACT.

BRIEFER: Discusses authorities, rules of engagement, and restrictions on U.S. forces <u>after</u> 30 June 1970. "All air authorities expire 1 July." Until that time, "a special authority permits air operations to a depth of 60 kilometers from the South Vietnam border against clearly identified elements of COSVN Headquarters."

They have prepared for Abrams's signature a message requesting extension of air authorities to 30 September. Abrams (re the proposed message): "Part of getting it approved the way we want it is to <u>assure</u> them that arrangements worked out will have integrally [sic] approval by the Cambodians. Otherwise they'll just be suspicious that we're going to go bombing any goddamn thing we want to over there, including monuments—probably <u>especially</u> monuments."

■ ■ ■

ROSSON: "I noticed in the message traffic this morning that a high-powered group has been established in Washington to take control of the psyops effort—develop themes and arrange for master coordination and the like."
ABRAMS: "I must have missed that. <u>That'll</u> <u>solve</u> <u>it</u>." [Laughter]
ABRAMS: "On the leaflet thing—I got a letter one time from some chap who went on at great length that, instead of shooting all these shells, he said you should fill some of them with <u>leaflets</u>, messages of hope and that sort of thing, for the enemy. So—I never sent that to the staff. I sat down and wrote an answer myself. And—he wanted to introduce the <u>leaflet</u> business to this war. [Laughter] I said, 'Over the'—I've forgotten the exact figures—'over the last nine months we have delivered ten and a half <u>billion</u> leaflets to the enemy, by every means—aircraft and all this kind of thing.' I said, 'At the same time he's been delivering a modest number of leaflets to our own forces.' I said, 'My estimate is that <u>our</u> effect on <u>him</u> has been just about the same as <u>his</u> effect on <u>our</u> forces, and I know the effect on our forces has been <u>zero</u>.' [Laughter] See, I could have never gotten that out of the psywarriors. [More laughter] I couldn't send that down to the staff."

■ ■ ■

SOMEONE: "The <u>pressure</u> to get weapons in there [Cambodia] comes from Washington. We have put 25,000 in there."
ABRAMS: "This same rule, incidentally, applies to that whole goddamn <u>flood</u> of messages that we got today. Now I want to go back—I am <u>not</u> going to be—I

don't care what happens, I am not going to be a party to doing things which we know in our own experience and judgment are absolutely unsound. And I don't care _how_ much the pressure is. We should _tell_ them what the facts are."

■ ■ ■

ABRAMS: "Now this supply business—somebody over there has got to have the ABC of supply. A: You must know _what_ you've got, the name, and what it's for. B: You've got to know how _much_ you've got—600, two dozen, whatever it is. And C: You've got to know where it is, specifically—stack number two, row number three, and so on. I don't care, even if you're just a little Cambodian army, or whether you're a great big Vietnamese army, if you don't have A, B, and C you _cannot_ use what you've _got_! It is _impossible_ to use what you've got. You'll just keep _asking_ for the same fucking stuff. [Someone: "That's their situation there."] They don't need a computer. [Laughter] All they need is the stub pencil system. But they've got to know _what_ it is, how _much_ it is, and _where_ it is. And you never can _lose_ that."

ABRAMS: "What Washington is screaming for is a push system. And when you get a push system, you wind up with these three things _unknown_—_unknown_!"

SOMEONE: "And you don't know where the stuff is that you've given them. That's what we've got right now on 15,000 rifles. They couldn't tell you where they are."

ABRAMS: "Right. And Rives has always answered that he's practically certain that they're being gainfully employed. The need is so great."

All of this has to do with MAP-type assistance to Cambodia.

ABRAMS (re aid to the Cambodians from Thailand): "The _attitude_ of those _bastards_ is—it _really_ is _awful_!"

ABRAMS: "Every _bastard_ that's trying to do anything in this is trying to do it for his own _good_. And in this league I must say, by god the Vietnamese look like real heroes. I mean, they've _paid_—they've paid in blood to do a lot of these things. You can say, 'Well, it's in their own self-interest,' but by god nobody else is out there _dying_ in their own self-interest. Every damn one of them wants Uncle Sam to foot the whole bill for everything—at the inflated rates."

■ ■ ■

Discussion of instructions, often conflicting, from Washington, and the frustrations engendered by them.

BROWN (re bombing in northern Laos): "If they ask, 'What have you _done_ in this interdiction program that I directed?' in number of sorties it isn't very dramatic, it isn't very impressive, in contrast to what we continue to do in Barrel Roll, in Steel Tiger, and in-country. But on the other hand it's what we think has been right based on the targets and what reconnaissance has developed, et cetera. But I think we ought to _know_ that, and _recognize_ it—we haven't been putting sorties in there just to put _sorties_ in. And there haven't been any targets go unstruck."

ABRAMS: "Well, you know how it's been described—'unimaginative.'"

BROWN: "I know. And I've been in Washington and had to go up to the third floor to the secretary and say, 'This is what we're doing out here.' And he didn't _like_ it. But by god it was what made _sense_. And I don't know whether we're apt to get an order to _double_ it or something. I guess we'll _comply_. But so far we haven't gotten that sort of order."

ABRAMS: "I've contemplated sort of trying to take them on. See, this has—it's really gotten quite _bad_. I would say—well, I would say it's really very _unprofessional_. And, in a way, they really ought to be _told_ so. But I don't know whether that really winds up _getting_ you anywhere. Maybe if we just keep hold, ah, patience, and keep sending back what we _believe_ is the right thing to do, and _why_ we think it's the right thing to do—."

ABRAMS: "Now this thing—for instance, they've got a thing in there about increasing the RF and PF and expanding the forces and so on. Well, I don't know . . . the comptroller was over there the other day . . . the critique they had of Chuck Cooper's report. And they've got a hell of an economic crisis here, and how they're going to be able to handle the military forces—it's costing them about 80 percent of their GNP, the way it is now. And they cannot, according to Cooper, no matter how they tighten up the system, and no matter what realistic tax increases that they impose, they still cannot solve their problem. And somewhere there's got to be found somewhere around $150 million to—some figure like that—to bail this situation _out_. And _how_—and they've got a whole _group_ back there in Washington, of which Cooper's one of the representatives, who are trying to face up to this economic thing. One of the things is that their military force is too large, but they all seem to agree that, for political and psychological reasons, you can't _do_ anything about it— plus the realities of the fighting itself. So why they came out with _that_ message about expanding the force and so on—. It's _not_ only the economic situation, but it's simply the manpower situation in this country anyway."

SOMEONE: "Were they talking about a conversion?"

ABRAMS: "_No_—_expansion_, above the 1.1 [million manpower ceiling in] Phase III that's been approved." "That's why it's very difficult to understand how _that_ goddamn thing would come out—you know? Then there's another one in there—they want to ensure that Colonel Cavanaugh's work [SOG] will be utilized in your [Brown's] work. What the _shit_ do they think we've been _doing_?! I mean, what _were_ we doing it for? Just to give Cavanaugh a _job_? Then we got another one—they want a plan for the attack of the base areas—in South Vietnam. And Jesus, it's been an integral part of [the annual campaign plans for the past three years,] _AB/143_, _144_, _145_ [pounding the table as he names each one]—it's been going on for _three_ goddamn years! It's _recorded_ in every quarterly review. I mean—_why_?"

SOMEONE: "We just got back the I&M program, too, with a lot of caveats in it— be sure and save money." [Laughter]

ABRAMS: "That's right. Along with it we've got the requirement to come up with a plan for _reducing_ the forces 100,000. This is another plan which is required for _expanding_ the force. It places no _limit_ on how _much_ they'll be expanded."

SOMEONE: "I saw one the other day where it said they weren't going to spend any more on Cavanaugh's business for the ARVN. That was wasting all that resources."

ABRAMS: "See, nothing is to be gained out of _that_ $13 million. Then this message—'Be _sure_ that General Brown's using it.'"

Much laughing all through this.

ABRAMS: "I must say, a little earlier in the day I was _depressed_ by all this, but now I'm beginning to—." "Then last night at ten o'clock the acting chairman [Moorer] called me on the telephone and wanted to know _immediately_ the situation in Kompong Speu."

SOMEONE: "If you'd complied with the _other_ admiral's request he'd have had an hourly appraisal there. _He_ [McCain] could have answered the question."

ABRAMS: "I called him back in about 10 minutes. I—fortunately the communications all working pretty good—and I got a hold of McCown, and as luck would have it he had only recently been through a session with General Dzu, who had been there that afternoon, yesterday afternoon, apparently up until quite late. So the whole thing was right there, fresh in McCown's notebook, and I must say in some detail. So it only took about 10 minutes and I had the acting chairman back on the phone and gave him the situation. And at the end I asked him—oh, yeah, he wanted to know about another town. The truth of the matter was none of us knew where that was—McCown didn't, neither did—you know, it required getting the map and so on. At the end I asked him what I was responding to. Was it some reports that had been submitted by my headquarters, or was it newspaper reports? He said 'newspaper reports.' _Goddamn!_"

SOMEONE: "Of course responding in such a complete and timely manner is only going to encourage this frequently."

ABRAMS: "Well, let's leave it that I haven't given you the _entire_ conversation. [Laughter] I'm not worried about that."

■ ■ ■

ABRAMS: "One of the _strangest_ things that ever happened—well, no, I can't say that—a great many strange things in this whole thing over here, but they established _contact_ with the VC, out there in the vicinity of Tay Ninh, and on two or three occasions, in agreement with the VC, dispatched a _liaison_ officer—a major of the Philippine army, and he went and met with these chaps at their CP—had tea and talked over the situation and so on. This was a long time ago. And this was done at the direction of Marcos." "Isn't that strange? Without consultation, I might say, with another damn soul involved in the fracas over here." "The first one was before Westmoreland left. I remember that. And the other two were afterwards. I remember that, too."

■ ■ ■

ABRAMS (re Mr. Fred Ladd in Cambodia): "He is employed and paid by the State

Department. He has the same grade as Rives." "The basic idea was to provide someone, working in his part of things, who was, first of all, familiar with this kind of war and so on. Also, somebody who has a fairly solid military background and so on. And by that sort of help the total situation. And he's <u>apparently</u> going to be the principal guy as far as this MAP program is concerned. I mean, that's the fellow to <u>deal</u> with on MAP."

Col. Jonathan F. Ladd commanded 5th Special Forces Group in Vietnam during 1967–1968. Now retired from the army, he was assigned as politico-military counselor at the embassy in Phnom Penh.

SOMEONE: "If Rives is smart enough to use him, he's got a winner. If Rives is a little bit of Bill Sullivan, we're still in trouble."

Lloyd Rives was U.S. chargé d'affaires in Phnom Penh.

ABRAMS: "I remember spending a couple of evenings with Pony [Scherrer] after he had returned from completion of that mission to Cambodia. At that time he was a <u>powerful</u> supporter of the prince. All of these things that were alleged to be occurring by the VC, that sort of thing, he said, '<u>Not</u> a <u>one</u> of them!' He said, 'He lets me take his plane and go out and see for myself.'" "The point was he [Sihanouk] was over the deep end." "So, as happens to us all, he [Scherrer] made a bit of a misjudgment. He couldn't <u>believe</u> that he was tangled up with the miserable shit that he was—'Fine gentleman of the royal family, honest, devoted to his country and his people, a <u>servant</u> of the common man.' He said, 'Very unusual, very unusual for a man of royal blood, to have such a feeling.'"
SOMEONE: "And playing saxophone in his own orchestra."
ABRAMS: "Plus writing the music for it!"

Much laughter throughout.

20 JUN 1970: WIEU

ATTENDEES: Gen. Abrams, Amb. Berger, Gen. Rosson, Gen. Brown, Amb. Colby, LTG Mildren, LTG McCaffrey, Mr. Kirk, VADM King, MG Dolvin, MG Conroy, MG Dettre, BG Camp, BG Kraft, BG Greene, BG Henderson, BG Potts, BG Jaskilka, BG Cheadle, BG Henion, Col. Cavanaugh, Col. Cutrona, Col. Stewart (for BG Sykes), Col. Todd.

1970 Infiltration Estimate: 44,300 (60 percent to COSVN).

BRIEFER: During the reporting period an estimated daily average of 67 tons of cargo entered the Lao panhandle through the established entry gates. An estimated 188 tons were transported to border base areas daily. Rice, gasoline, ordnance.
BRIEFER: A Binh Tram 33 message of 13 June indicates that "the cadre seemed to be tired at the end of the season and are hoping to quickly conclude the

transportation program." Instructed the battalion commanders to "instill determination in your troops to transport during the rainy season."

ABRAMS (re the J-2 briefing): "Like the statement that 'reliable agent reports indicate they will continue to have tactical activity.' Well, yeah, that's right. I think you could guess that even if you hadn't heard it from a reliable agent. He can't afford not to have some kind of stuff going on. But what's he got to go off and do it with? And that's changed—what he's got to do it with."

ABRAMS: "What we've got to have here [in the WIEU] is what the hell's going on—in fact! And what we are up against, and what are the Cambodians up against?"

ABRAMS: "You see, with all these messages that call for us to do more in Cambodia—. Now see we—all we've got is what we've had before. We haven't got any more. Now when you go rendering judgments about where you—how much air, how much of this, and so on, you're applying to the total problem, you ought to have some—some fairly decent understanding of what the enemy has done, and what he can do."

■ ■ ■

SOMEONE: "In his order of the day for yesterday he [President Thieu] mentioned—it was sort of obscurely worded—the reorganization of the regional administration."

SOMEONE ELSE: "I can give you something on that. . . . He said from the first of July they're going to rename the corps, the corps tactical areas, corps and military regions. The main difference would be to abolish [the position occupied by] General La and the separate RF/PF establishment which ran under him would be incorporated under the army staff. And the powers of corps commanders over RF and PF will be increased."

JACOBSON: "Quite an improvement—god, I wonder how they ever swung that?!"

ABRAMS: "It's so good that there must be—." [Laughter]

27 JUN 1970: Commanders WIEU

ATTENDEES: Amb. Berger, Gen. Abrams, Gen. Rosson, Gen. Brown, Amb. Colby, LTG Mildren, LTG Collins, LTG Davison, Mr. Kirk, LTG McCaffrey, LTG Sutherland, LTG McCutcheon, MG Dolvin, MG Conroy, Mr. Firfer, MG McCown, MG Cowles, Mr. Jacobson, Mr. Whitehouse, MG Dettre, BG Camp, BG Kraft, BG Greene, BG Potts, BG Henderson, BG Jaskilka, BG Cheadle, BG Henion, RADM Matthews, Mr. Chambers, Mr. Wilson (for Mr. Vann), Col. Cavanaugh, Col. Sadler, Col. Cutrona, Col. Stewart (for BG Sykes), Col. Healy, Col. Todd.

1970 Infiltration Estimate: 44,700 (60 percent to COSVN).

BRIEFER: Documents captured in Cambodia reveal composition of six K-designated groups (of infiltrators), all of which were previously detected in COMINT. Specialized personnel. The attrition rate is very high: 116 reportedly began, and only 39 reached their destination with the original groups. "The remainder fell victim to malaria and other illnesses and have stopped along the trail to recover."

POTTS: The special groups "are getting about 34 percent of their personnel down, [of] the ones that start. This compares to 85 percent of the regular infiltration groups." Some were female, some were civilians—civil administrators.

BRIEFER (re six two-digit designated infiltration groups totalling about 3,311 personnel): These are believed to be primarily infantry of two regimental-type units. Believed to have originated from the 338th or 320B Training Divisions. Destination not now known.

ABRAMS: "I was talking to this fellow yesterday, a newspaperman, and he's spent some time over in Phnom Penh. And he has looked with a jaundiced eye on this intelligence that they've got over there. There's apparently a Cercle Sportif over there in Phnom Penh, or the equivalent of it, and he says that's where the whole goddamn intelligence picture is developed, out there around the pool. [Laughter] That damn French delegation and so on, they sit around out there and drink their gin and tonics and speculate and so on. He says that's where the attacks on Phnom Penh came from. You know, they've had four or five real hot alerts over there, everybody at the barricades and so on, and Christ, not a— nothing. He says it comes out of the Cercle Sportif." "Pernod—I suppose four or five of those under your belt. . . ." [Laughter]

■ ■ ■

ABRAMS: "If somebody throws a grenade and two or three kids are killed, it's a disaster." No matter whether the overall number of incidents is reduced, that's still the case. "Whether his overall effectiveness in Saigon or Washington, per effort, has somehow gone down doesn't change the fact of the human disaster that occurs at that point. So I don't think we ought to compromise. If it's bad, then we ought to face it, try to do something about it. All of this represents his activity, and it's not good."

BRIEFER (re Consolidated RVNAF Improvement & Modernization Program, CRIMP, approved 5 June 1970): New units added are 175-mm howitzer battalions, AAA battalions, and 105-mm howitzer platoons.

ABRAMS: You've all heard the directives issued by JGS for RVNAF operations in Cambodia. "I think these are quite reasonable—it has to be based on intelligence, it has to be in response to a request from the Cambodians, and it has to be within their capabilities. I think they've been doing that. Anything beyond that is going to have to have, in each case, the president's personal approval."

ABRAMS: "On this, in your work with the corps commanders, try to keep them in this ballpark. Here and there, one of them may get a little frustrated with his government, that it's moving too slowly or ineptly, but that's by god what they're going to do, is what their government wants them to do. The president, and the JGS, have got a fairly firm grip on this, and I don't want anything done by Americans to loosen that. That's the way this country <u>needs</u> to be, and we should just encourage it, and don't get trapped into some son of a bitch that's trying to make an end run around his own government—even though his motives may be of the best."

■ ■ ■

ABRAMS: "Now I do think we will in the eleventh hour here get the authority to continue the air operations in Cambodia. That's just going to take a little time. Most of what we get is fairly short fuze anyway. I know [laughing] you're entirely familiar with that [laughter], with that <u>art</u>, but that's the way it is. Actually our own government, I think, is anxious to do everything it can to help the Cambodians. And their constraints are the difficulties they've got with the Senate and the political atmosphere in the United States. That's what inhibits the number of dollars in the MAP program, the amount of weapons, and the things that you can do. And I know it sounds a little silly and so on, but we cannot use the term 'close air support' with respect to Cambodia—certainly after the 30th of June. And we can't use it outside—<u>until</u> the 30th of June—we can't use that term about what the air is doing outside the 21.7 miles. Don't ask me to explain it. It's just that we're not going to use that term. 'Interdiction,' yes. The position of the government is that we're going to do the things—the way our government's explaining it, we're going to do all the things that will assure the safety and security of the allied forces here in South Vietnam. In <u>practice</u>, they expect us to make the most <u>liberal</u> interpretation of that—always paying attention to the cultural objects, the monuments, and the civilian noncombatant population, and those things. We can't mucker them up."

■ ■ ■

ABRAMS: "I'm not in any disagreement with the assessment that was made here today, but I think the enemy also has a rather full plate. He's trying to do all these things with the forces and the organization which he once used only on South Vietnam. Now he's got these other things to do in areas where his system has not really been established, if you will—the guerrillas, the cadre, the base areas, the bunkers—the storage bunkers and that sort of thing. So <u>he</u> has <u>his</u> problems. With the limited authorities we have, and trying to get on with it, it's going to be sort of a nip and tuck <u>thing</u>. Trying to strengthen the Cambodians, on the one hand, and trying to interfere with the enemy as much as we can, and always bearing in mind that South Vietnam comes first."

ABRAMS: "I hope that with the president's [Thieu] approval of this new program, beginning the first of July, that everybody can get behind it and whip up some enthusiasm. They'll never have a better time to try to go ahead and consolidate their hold on the population and the territory in South Vietnam than they've got right now. This is not <u>entirely</u> true in I Corps, but it's certainly true in the rest of the country. So, as always, it just isn't that nice neat package of things that would satisfy the meticulous leader. It's [laughing] still squashy, and the guidance has a tendency to shift rather quickly and so on, but that's <u>really</u> the way it's always <u>been</u>. So we need <u>patience</u> and <u>understanding</u>, and just keep working hard on the basic things that have <u>got</u> to be done. And I think that, on that basis, it's a fairly decent road ahead."

ABRAMS: "The president [Thieu] has got a firm hand on the tiller here, and I think we should applaud that."

29 JUN 1970: Secretary of the Army Resor

SOMEONE: "Well, we're down to 1,700 1st Cav people in Cambodia. . . ." "The 25th is all out." "As George Casey reported last night, his 17 companies and 3 platoons are, with one exception, in the walk-out position right now."

Resor arrives. Among those present: Conroy, Potts, Tarbox.

RESOR (re the situation in Washington): "There's nothing very tranquil about it. We're going through the '72 budget drill for about the third or fourth time. We're trying to come in with—in fact they have to submit it . . . Monday, Washington time—we have to come in with the kind of program we'd have if we were to reduce army outlays by another billion four [$1.4 billion] in '72 over the figure we'd originally been given."

RESOR: Plus Mahon expects to take about $1 billion out of '71 expenditures, army share $300 million. "Difficult." "The effect here and in Korea is that to reduce expenditures in '71 we really have to reduce—have a lower manpower program, less people. And that's, of course, directly related to what your redeployment schedule is after October 15."

RESOR: "The problem's much simpler if we can make withdrawals between October 15 and the end of the year. If you try to get a layoff and then bunch it all in the next calendar year, it becomes quite a serious problem, both money-wise and trained strength-wise, because we've really already set the draft on the assumption that there would be redeployments in that period—in other words, based on the old schedule. And of course now it's too late to go back and—any change in the draft now doesn't produce trained men until, say, next February. So that's <u>one</u> problem."

RESOR: "At least as far as the army is concerned, there isn't any money in non–Southeast Asia accounts that can be, any significant amount, that can be reprogrammed." "There will have to be trade-offs, paid for within the army by, say, reduced ground ammunition consumption, or if we can possibly reduce O&M consumption further." "Or, going outside the army, reduce sortie levels."

RESOR: "I think we're really now in a position where the operation here has to be managed from a point of view of the number of resources that are budgeted for it. One really has to look at the trade-offs. In other words, you've got a limited amount of dollars to spend on the war here, and if you need them in one area—say to slip your deployment schedule, you'll have to watch immediately the dollar cost of that and be ready to fund it yourself out of a saving of some other program. That shouldn't—if you look ahead and manage it, that shouldn't really hamper you too much, because there's still a lot of money in the budget for the war in '71. I think it's about $11 billion."

DISCUSSION: Increment 5 redeployment to take place during the period October–December 1970.

RESOR: "When you took out the marines instead of the army, and left the army forces here, it caused us to go short in trained strength." "You got General Westmoreland's message about the problem of delivering people for these three months." "When you shifted to the so-called marine-heavy withdrawal, it cost the army $298 million more than we'd budgeted, because you kept army people here, where they're more expensive than in the CONUS." "Now we've gone to OSD and asked them to transfer marine funds to us, because we believe that the marines should save . . . $274 million." "The marines won't admit it, so we've got a problem."

ROSSON: "As you know, Mr. Secretary, we don't approach the problem this way out here. We're still using this 'cut and try' approach wherein we have to look at the enemy, we have to look at the progress of improvement and modernization on the RVNAF side, our own posture, and keep an eye out on the state of the economy and pacification, all of these factors, and come in with what we consider our best professional judgment on the military pros and cons, and then we come down on a solution. Our present recommendation is we come out between 15 October and the end of the year with only 10,000.

Earlier Resor had used a figure of 30,000, which astounded the MACV people, who had not heard that before.

RESOR: "How many of those would be army?"

ROSSON: "Well, probably a minor number."

RESOR: "There's another factor, of course, and that is—and this is something, of course, that Mr. Laird is, will be the final, the best judge of—and that is the, whether from a point of view of domestic support for the war it isn't almost essential to keep a sort of steady withdrawal. In other words, I think one thing that became very clear from the severe domestic reaction to the Cambodian operation was that—or rather, looking at the situation we were in before Cambodia, we were going right along on a steady basis, and the casualties had come down, and the troops were coming back on a steady basis, and the thing had gone off the front page of the papers, and everybody was pretty quiescent—the opposition was. Even though they thought we weren't withdrawing as fast as they'd like, they couldn't get any real public interest in the problem that was pretty much on the back burner. And the Mobilization Committee to End the War had just disbanded, as a good example of where we were."

RESOR: "And unfortunately the effect of the Cambodian operation has sort of catalyzed bringing together all the opposition, resulting in the Cooper-Church amendment and the McGovern-Goodell amendment. I personally think that it will begin to simmer down some now, but we've got to avoid any other event that catalyzes, brings them all together again and they all come down to Washington. I mean that's what—after Cambodia there were just great delegations of people, some very substantial people, coming down to call on their congressmen to do something about getting out faster. I would think there would be a very <u>serious</u> problem if it looked like we were not going to withdraw anybody between October—any significant number—between October and the end of the year. In other words, I would think that Mr. Laird would feel that one has to announce some significant withdrawal, something like 30,000, because of—to ensure the credibility of the president's commitment to get 150,000 out by May 1. A lot of people no longer believe, you know, what you say. It's only what you do. And they see people coming out gradually. Then they believe it, and they can't generate all this opposition."

RESOR: "There's the money problem, and then there's the problem of how you calculate domestic support."

ROSSON (re redeployment): "Why doesn't the administration make a frank and persuasive presentation as to why it's being done this way? I think the people would understand it, because there are very good reasons why we have held combat strength intact here as long as we could." "We have never yet failed to meet a deadline."

RESOR: "As I said, Mr. Laird would be the best judge of this—this other aspect of this. My <u>own</u> feeling is that one would do well here to see how close you could come to something like 30,000 between now and the end of the year."

SOMEONE: "If I understand <u>you</u>, sir, <u>your</u> schedule would <u>exceed</u> the monthly average."

ROSSON: "Six weeks ago we felt, for very good reasons, that 10,000 would be the max, and we were <u>upheld</u> in that in military channels in Washington. Our guidance, as we have it, is 50,000-10,000-90,000 [increments to make up the 150,000 total to be withdrawn by 1 May 1971]."

RESOR: "You really ought to look pretty carefully at this answer he [Laird] came back with."

ROSSON: "It's true we have no directive beyond 15 October—."

RESOR: "<u>Other</u> than to stay within the budget."

SOMEONE: "But, see, we don't know what that is. That's where we get <u>trapped</u>. The JCS doesn't send us the budget."

RESOR: "Mr. Laird has a very real world problem—he can't <u>get</u> any more money. In fact, he's going to get a billion dollars less than he asked for." "I think the JCS really ought to send you the numbers, because I think from now on one has to really manage it out here with the resources in mind. Up to now it's been, whatever was needed out here we somehow got the money from Congress and you got it. But the climate in Congress is <u>so</u> different now that it's just—it would be putting our heads in the sand, really, to make that assumption any more."

ROSSON: "We know generally the parameters as this game is unfolding, but I think a very strong case can be made for requiring <u>us</u> to come in with a <u>military</u> estimate, a <u>military</u> assessment, as the commander has to look at it out here, with the responsibility for the lives of the people, which don't equate to money."

RESOR: You know better than Laird where to take the cuts.

ROSSON: Give us the options and let us choose.

RESOR: "It has to be done by Systems Analysis essentially."

All this has been ad hoc discussion before they even get to the briefings for Resor.

POTTS: Last year infiltration amounted to 106,000 total. So far for 1970: 45,200. "Out of the prisoners and the documents that we've gotten in the cross-border operations we've actually confirmed 90 percent of the groups we detected through COMINT coming into the COSVN area from January through May."

RESOR: "I think that's an amazing achievement."

POTTS: In Cambodia allied forces seized enough weapons to equip 55 full-strength VC infantry battalions. "Of course, all of them are less than 50 percent strength, so that would be well over 100." Also enough rice to feed 25,100 enemy soldiers for a whole year. In six or seven weeks scarfed up more than in a whole year in-country.

ROSSON: 44,000 SVN and 32,000 U.S. in Cambodia. "This is a process of shift in, shift out." Maximum of 19,000 at one time over there for U.S., and SVN 31,000. "Despite the importance of these operations, and the publicity they've received, they have not constituted a major commitment of our resources." "There's been a very high payoff from this rather modest commitment."

■ ■ ■

RESOR: "There's another way of looking at it [adequacy of funding for the war]. What do we figure, General Potts, the war costs the enemy annually?"

POTTS: "We have no positive figures on the exact cost, but we know that it is much less, of course, than we're putting in." No air effort.

RESOR: "We've been spending—in '69 it was $22 billion, in '70 it's $17 billion, and we've got in '71 about $11 billion budgeted now. I'm sure we can't do all the bombing that everybody asks for, but one would hope that with that ratio of overall contribution of resources, we would have enough to do an adequate job."

DOLVIN (implying that this is a function of the disparate investments in the war): "They've lost over a half a million men, and we've lost 42,000."

RESOR: "How long we can continue here, how many man-years we can put in from here on out, is a function, in large measure, of two things. One, our casualty rates. And secondly, our costs. And higher casualties and higher costs are counterproductive. And in the end they will reduce the resources we'll have, the man-years and the dollars, over the years ahead, so that there's a trade-off there. That's a judgment that, of course, you can't really make here—except to know that that is a consideration."

4 JUL 1970: WIEU

ATTENDEES: Gen. Rosson, Gen. Brown, Amb. Colby, LTG McCaffrey, Mr. Kirk, VADM King, MG Dolvin, MG Conroy, MG Cowles, Mr. Jacobson, MG

Dettre, BG Camp, BG Kraft, BG Greene, BG Henderson, BG Potts, BG Jaskilka, BG Cheadle, BG Henion, Col. Cavanaugh, Col. Cutrona, Col. Stewart (for BG Sykes), Col. Todd. [Per briefer on tape, also attending: BG Vande Hey and Col. Sadler.]

SOMEONE (probably Rosson): "The latest report on General Abrams is very favorable. We hope to get some kind of reading from the hospital each day, and there'll be an announcement with some frequency so everyone can follow his progress."

Abrams has gone to a U.S. military medical facility in Japan for surgery to remove his gall bladder.

BRIEFER: MACV 1970 Infiltration Estimate: 45,200 (59 percent to COSVN).

BRIEFER: Refers to the "90th and 92nd Straggler Recovery and Replacement Regiments, South Vietnam Liberation Army. Per intercept, they processed (12 January–9 May) 19,870 members of various infiltration groups destined for COSVN."

BRIEFER: Mentions enemy 162nd Barge Battalion as responsible for cargo being floated down the Sekong River. Also a report that the enemy is constructing a fleet of 45 river boats at [Ben Bhai?] in Base Area 612 for use on the Sekong during the rainy season.

SOMEONE: M16 rifles cost $164.

BRIEFER: Today the minister of defense is expected to sign a document reorganizing JGS. President Thieu, in a guidance letter to JGS of 22 June 1970, directed that the armed forces are to consist of three services (army, air force, navy). RF and PF no longer are separate services, but become part of the army (and are kept intact, with RF the main force at province and district level, and the PF being the armed people's force at village and hamlet level).

BRIEFER (re JGS reorganization): Also directed a territorial reorganization "to stress the importance of territorial security and pacification and development." The CTZ [corps tactical zone] is to become a military region, with no change in boundaries or corps organization. Corps commanders are also the military region commanders.

■ ■ ■

BROWN: "I just want to make an observation for those of you who have not read the CINCPAC message on psywarfare and bombarding North Vietnam with leaflets. It's a goddamn book! On our teletype paper, which is about yea long and single-spaced, it's nine goddamn pages. They turn those psywarriors loose up there and they've gone wild. And they've demanded we have to put in a plan. And the stuff they ask us for is a goddamn bunch of nonsense. We've been wind-drifting messages for years. We just don't need this goddamn thing. The one way to handle it that I know of is to find that guy and suggest he come out here and maybe we can wind-drift him." [Laughter]

7 JUL 1970: PFIAB Briefing

General Rosson chaired. General Potts briefed.

PFIAB CHAIRMAN (apparently) (re Phnom Penh): "We've got an army attaché over there that doesn't speak French. We've got a naval attaché over there who's never been in the intelligence business before except as a pilot in a reconnaissance squadron. He's had a short course. This is an important area. We've got to get it—."

PFIAB (re Mr. Ladd in Phnom Penh): "He doesn't even have a secretary. He doesn't have an assistant to do any of the accounting. He's carrying his papers around in his briefcase. You can't do a job that way."

PFIAB (very assertive and self-important): "The other day I was in Dr. Kissinger's office, and he was very upset, because at that particular date the number of individual weapons . . . was 17,000. And the National Estimate was that we'd gotten 10 percent of the individual weapons that were in Cambodia. And he did some mental arithmetic and said, 'Well, first of all, do you believe that they have 170,000 individual weapons there? And, if so, how did they <u>know</u> that there were any such number there?' He said it didn't seem reasonable. I agreed. Nothing of that sort came out of <u>here</u>, did it?"

POTTS: "No, sir. That report was not released from here, sir."

PFIAB: "Then they finally came up, and I think it was in the president's speech that he used the figure that we got 60 percent of their ammunition and weapons that they had in Cambodia. Was there any basis? Was that just a shotgun estimate?"

POTTS: "We here, in our business, were able to estimate, because of line-crossers, intelligence that we had, and so forth, what we <u>thought</u> actually was in these base areas. Then we <u>know</u> what was reported having been taken out. So we could actually come up with a very rough percentage only. But we must realize that what we had to start with was an estimate."

POTTS: Example: We thought there were 20 hospitals, and "we came up with 14 in our cross-border operations." We got 116 or 120 percent of the rice that we thought was there. But ammunition and so on only 60+ percent, "realizing some of it might have been moved back."

PFIAB: "I assume a large part of this matériel [Chinese arms and ammunition] came through Sihanoukville?"

POTTS: "That's right, sir."

PFIAB: "Do you feel that the North Vietnamese and the Viet Cong are really strapped for people now?"

POTTS: "In the people field . . . we feel that they have personnel in the lower age group and in the senior citizens, that they can still supply adequate personnel, not only for South Vietnam, but limited extent in Cambodia and Laos. However, they must go to the protracted-type war. They cannot meet the demands like they did in '68 and one offensive in '69. It is <u>one</u> of the things that they have to consider in making their plans for the future throughout Southeast

Asia. They are <u>reduced</u> in manpower, but they still have <u>adequate</u> manpower for this protracted war."

11 JUL 1970: General Westmoreland Briefing

Gen. William C. Westmoreland, Army Chief of Staff, is visiting from Washington.

POTTS: "Out of the six and a half tons of documents that we brought out of Cambodia, thus far we've been able to identify 93 percent of the units that we detected through SIGINT in the infiltration pipeline."

POTTS: After the four offensives in 1968–1969: "We also have the documents that show that they had a critique of all of these and found out it wasn't best to continue with this. They were just suffering too heavily. So, they had to go to the high-point system. And in the documents we have, and the prisoners since then that we've talked to, they said that there would be at least one per month. And they said that each of these would be of longer duration and greater intensity than the one preceding it. And of course this has not been true. On each one of these, we knew the date that they would occur, and through the human intelligence . . . we actually had these down just about to the hour. The one in July was preempted, was actually preempted out in the III Corps area. Then . . . we came to the Winter–Spring Campaign, and again that's documented. And they did away with the countrywide high-point coordinated effort and went to isolated MRs, or by corps in some cases."

POTTS: "Along with this evolution we saw this change in tactics—relying on the attacks by fire (hoping to increase our casualties and hold theirs down)." Reduction in number of rounds per ABF: 7.7 rounds during the past month. Used to routinely be over 20. Battalion-size attacks "almost a thing of the past" by enemy: one in May, two in June. "More emphasis on terrorism, harassment, and sapper attacks."

POTTS (re cache recoveries during cross-border operations in Cambodia): Almost, in these two months, the equivalent of in-country seizures during the two years 1968 and 1969. Enough individual weapons to equip 55 Viet Cong battalions. Enough rice to feed 25,200 enemy soldiers for a year. Enough mortar and rocket ammunition to conduct 18,600 attacks by fire.

POTTS: We got COSVN Resolution 9 in October 1969: "One of our real finds." Went back to Resolutions 6, 7, and 8 to see the trend in thinking: "complete military victory." They backed off from that. Concentration on cities, and hardly any mention of Vietnamization or pacification in the earlier documents, but these are given strong emphasis in Resolution 9.

ROSSON: The 5th and 18th ARVN Divisions are "mediocre," "second rate." "The 25th is excellent—one of the most improved units in the country."

WESTMORELAND (re the current CG 25th ARVN Division): "I remember when he had the 23rd Division. He got axed. I axed him. It was in 1964, when he came down and cut Highway 9—Kontum, Ban Me Thuot, Pleiku were all isolated. We had no troops at that time. But he fell completely apart, just completely. He just gave up."

SOMEONE (correcting Westmoreland): That officer had the 22nd Division.

COLBY (re Territorial Forces): "There're about 200,000 more of them now than in early '68." "<u>Excellent</u> program that the mobile advisory teams have conducted." Working particularly now on "the village defense plan" as an integrated plan involving local security forces, etc. Re RF/PF performance: "We think they really are doing pretty well, frankly, in terms of being able to stand up to the enemy forces." "The program this year is to try to get 30 provinces into a state where they depend only on Territorial Forces, and no need for an ARVN."

JACOBSON: "Another thing, that General Abrams feels strongly about, is what the Vietnamese <u>think</u> they can do. He attaches a great deal of importance to that. And, as you know only too well, once they make up their minds that they're in the game for high stakes, they can do some remarkable things."

WESTMORELAND: "The battle is going to be decided by Hanoi or Saigon, depending upon who has the greater staying power. And there's no reason at all why South Vietnam, the Saigon government, should not have greater staying power than North Vietnam, because they've got so much going for them."

COLBY: "There's no reason why 17 million South Vietnamese can't hold off 18 million North Vietnamese."

SOMEONE (re RVNAF logistics): "They showed remarkable action when they got ready to move into Cambodia. They moved their forward supply points up . . . forward, without anybody staying behind. They got out there, they had the stuff moving . . . and they really performed <u>well</u>."

SAME SOMEONE (re Cambodian forces): "We've got some problems up ahead as far as supporting the Cambodians." "We've gone very strongly for the light infantry." Some 80 companies being trained in South Vietnam. "We're equipping them here on the ground and delivering them by air to Can Tho and by LST into Phnom Penh." Re $8.9 million program: "We put this together in about three days at the request of DOD." Moved by VNAF aircraft and VNN sealift. "The Vietnamese have absolutely been <u>remarkable</u> in this. They've done a <u>wonderful</u> job."

WESTMORELAND: "Is ARVN capable of supporting operations itself in the Khe Sanh plateau, the A Shau, Dak To, Dak Pek?"

ANSWER: "In every respect except airlift. That's the 130s [C-130 aircraft]. We take care of about 75 percent of the airlift in this country."

WESTMORELAND: "It seems to me very important that we tailor a logistics organization that will give them [ARVN] their own organic capability of operating along the border, almost on a continuous basis." "This capability is awfully important."

18 JUL 1970: WIEU

ATTENDEES: Amb. Berger, Gen. Rosson, Gen. Brown, Amb. Colby, LTG McCaffrey, VADM King, MG Dolvin, MG Conroy, MG Cowles, MG Dettre, BG Camp, BG Vande Hey, BG Greene, BG Potts, BG Henderson (for Mr. Jacobson), BG Jaskilka, BG Sykes, BG Cheadle, BG Henion, BG Heiser, BG Doehler, Col. Cutrona, Col. Sadler, Col. Todd, Col. Phillips (for Mr. Kirk), Col. Weeks.

BRIEFER: Quotes comments made by Prince Sihanouk during a recent interview with Agence France-Presse: "It is true that there are Vietnamese in Cambodia. Why should anyone be astonished that the Indochinese people unite? The Americans have erased the line of demarcation and have turned the Vietnam War into an Indochina War."

BRIEFER: "Hanoi will certainly be disconcerted with this statement by Sihanouk, for North Vietnam continues to claim that it has no troops in Cambodia and that the Cambodian Liberation Army is doing the fighting there."

BRIEFER: "It is interesting to note that Sihanouk told his press interviewers that he would not allow the Vietnamese to liberate his country. He said, 'I shall not let the Vietnamese liberate my country. I shall liberate it when we are ready to do so. We will be liberated by Cambodians, and Phnom Penh will be taken by Cambodians.' Some intelligence analysts feel that it is for this very reason that Hanoi has not yet sent its forces into Phnom Penh. The political cost of having North Vietnamese assaulting and even capturing Phnom Penh would be too great for Hanoi. In addition, the notion of waiting for a Cambodian insurgent force to attempt to take the city is more consistent with the theory of protracted warfare."

BRIEFER: "In his interview Sihanouk repeated his claim that he is not a Communist, and that after the liberation he will resign as head of state and retire to southern France."

25 JUL 1970: Commanders WIEU

ATTENDEES: Gen. Rosson, Amb. Colby, LTG Collins, LTG Davison, LTG McCaffrey, LTG Sutherland, LTG McCutcheon, MG Dolvin, MG Conroy, Mr. Firfer, MG Hardin (for Gen. Brown), MG Cowles, Mr. Jacobson, Mr. Vann, Mr. Whitehouse, MG Dettre, Mr. Chambers, BG Camp, BG Vande Hey, BG Greene, BG Potts, BG Cushman (for MG McCown), BG Sykes, BG Cheadle, BG Henion, BG Heiser, BG Doehler, RADM Matthews (for VADM King), Col. Cutrona, Col. Sadler, Col. Healy, Col. Todd, Col. Phillips (for Mr. Kirk), Col. Weeks (for BG Henderson).

Infiltration Estimate for 1970: 48,400 (57 percent to COSVN).

BRIEFER: "In order to replace the tremendous losses to its forces in the Republic of Vietnam, it is estimated that North Vietnam has infiltrated into the Republic of Vietnam over 700,000 persons since 1960."

BRIEFER: "A manpower shortage does not appear to constitute a critically limiting factor for Hanoi's leadership in the formulation of strategic plans."

BRIEFER: In North Vietnam there are "approximately 110,000 physically fit youths reaching draft age annually." Also North Vietnam is "able to augment its manpower pool by recalling former service personnel, lowering induction and training standards, and extending terms of service."

ROSSON: "How many of them are in the military now?"

BRIEFER: "340,000, sir, in North Vietnam in the army. 3,000 in the navy, perhaps 10,000 in the air force."

ROSSON: "What is the population of North Vietnam held to be?"

BRIEFER: "As of January of this year, sir, it was 19,920,000."

BRIEFER: "Thus it is apparent that North Vietnam has the capability to continue its present rate of infiltration, or even to increase it."

■ ■ ■

Assessment of Effect of Allied Cross-Border Operations on Enemy Planning and Operations

BRIEFER:

■ Closing of Kompong Son line of communications.

■ "Manpower is Hanoi's major economic resource and is at present its main contribution to the war in the south."

■ "Communist China and the Soviet Union supply the bulk of war matériel, while North Vietnam supplies the men that move them and, in growing percentages, the men that use them."

■ "Hanoi's adoption of a protracted war strategy and the tactic of indirect fire attacks reflects an attempt to economize on all resources, but especially manpower."

■ "The closing of Kompong Son means that the major portion of supplies bound for Third and Fourth Military Regions must be transported from Laos. The Kompong Son LOC, when active, needed only a bare minimum of NVA manpower. Supplies were hauled by truck over an all-weather road system, free from interdiction, up to the border. The NVA provided only supervisory personnel. Now this matériel must be transported through the Laotian system and then south by land and water to the using units in Cambodia and in the Republic [of Vietnam]. This effort will demand an expanded manpower commitment."

■ In Cambodia, instead of a secure rear area as before, the enemy now has an exposed western flank.

VANN: "Even the government officials will concede that the commercial interests will sell rice to the VC when the price is right. And I concluded a long time ago, never having seen a dead VC that was skinny, that it's an effort that is just wasted when you try to [word indistinct] food."

ROSSON: This assessment "points up the opportunity that we have now, and will have for a minimum of six months, to get behind pacification and drive it forward under circumstances in which the enemy will be hard pressed to interfere with it." "And this without question is our most serious mission today, to use every resource at our disposal to drive pacification forward during the period."

26 JUL 1970: Ambassador Bruce Briefing

Ambassador David K. E. Bruce headed the U.S. delegation to the Paris peace talks in 1970–1971.

ATTENDEES: Gen. Rosson, Amb. Bunker, Amb. Colby, MG Dolvin, MG Cowles, MG Dettre, BG Potts, Col. Jones, Capt. Packer.

ROSSON: 44 provinces, 257 districts, 2,464 villages, 11,729 hamlets. 1,500 miles of coast from the DMZ to the border with Cambodia in the Gulf of Siam. 935 miles of interior border with Laos and Cambodia.

ROSSON: 246,000 enemy (and, including the infrastructure, a grand total of 317,600). In maneuver elements: 100,700. In combat support (artillery, air defense, sappers, recon): 19,100. Total (maneuver and combat support): c. 120,000. Administrative services and logistics: 85,900. Guerrillas: 40,300.

POTTS: In 1968 enemy infiltration got up to 19,600 per month average. In 1969: About 8,800 per month average. "The average so far for this year would run about 4,800, a very definite drop-off in infiltration." In 1969: 106,000 total. In 1968: 235,000.

POTTS: "Through communications intercepts we are able to pick up enemy infiltration groups as they come down through a pipeline through Laos and toward the Republic of Vietnam. They have a four-digit number assigned to them, and by experience now we can tell where those infiltration groups are going to go into the Republic [of Vietnam]." Last year 47 percent went to COSVN, and 57 percent so far this year.

POTTS: "If we go back to October 1965, about the first time we had a good feel on enemy composition and strength, at that time we noticed that only 26 percent of these combat troops were the North Vietnamese Army personnel. The Viet Cong—VC—74 [percent]. But today this has almost been reversed, showing that the so-called 'war of liberation' here in the south is being fought by North Vietnamese Army personnel coming down. . . ."

POTTS: Enemy losses are calculated as total of killed in action; died of wounds or disabled, never to return again to an enemy unit; prisoners of war; Hoi Chanhs; and nonbattle losses. From the beginning of 1965 the enemy has lost over 600,000 KIA. Total enemy losses: 1,000,000+ over five and a half years. "Recruiting in-country to fill his [the enemy's] ranks has dropped off very definitely." "The delta has always been a source of personnel for the enemy."

POTTS: In the Laotian panhandle, the rainy season runs from the middle of May through the middle of October. During that period the enemy logistical activity along the trail is almost at a stop. This year he is making a very deliberate effort to continue his logistical effort into the rainy season.

POTTS: Four general offensives that lasted about 36 days each: Tet 1968, May 1968, August 1968, 23 February 1969. Then the enemy critiqued his performance, changed his strategy from this type of general offensive to "what he calls the 'high point,' and he was going to have one of these, at least, every month. Each one would last three or four days."

POTTS: "We had information, through our intelligence resources, of the date— and almost the hour—that each one of these would be conducted." "This was a countrywide coordinated effort." "Starting in the Winter–Spring Campaign on 3 November 1969, he departed from his countrywide efforts and started having these offensives widely scattered." Not coordinated.

POTTS: "His tactics have changed as follows. We see increased reliance on attacks by fire." "He does this because he hopes to get allied casualties and hold down his own. There is no combat."

POTTS: "We hardly ever see any battalion-size attacks—none this month, two last month, and one the month before. This is where he loses very heavily—when he commits battalions." "We see more emphasis on terrorism, harassment, and sapper attacks."

POTTS: A VC battalion at full strength numbers 500 men. But now they are mostly at 35–40 percent strength. NVA battalions average about 80 percent of the 600 authorized. An NVA division is about 12,500 men.

POTTS: We expect enemy "ground attacks on selected targets. And that is going to come, we feel, up in the northern area, the 1st Military Region, because in the south he has been very definitely limited by the cross-border operations."

POTTS: On 29 April 1970 ARVN forces began cross-border operations into Cambodia, followed 1 May 1970 by U.S. forces. "The enemy withdrew" using delaying actions. He lost his supplies along the border.

COWLES: "We ended operations in Cambodia 30 June 1970." "A very minimum of forces participated" in the cross-border operations. The United States attacked three base areas unilaterally, there were two combined U.S.-SVN operations, and "by far the largest number, nine separate operations, were conducted by the Vietnamese unilaterally with some logistics and air support from the United States."

COWLES: "These operations did several things. They certainly reduced the enemy threat. . . . More than that, they really enhanced the morale of the Vietnamese forces and gave them increased confidence that they can in fact secure their own country."

COWLES: And these operations dealt the enemy a hard blow logistically. Enough individual weapons were captured to equip 55 VC battalions. Enough crew-served weapons for 33 battalions. Rice tonnage sufficient to feed 25,200 men for one year on full rations. "During the short two-month period in Cambodia we captured almost as many weapons as during the full year of either 1968 or

1969 in-country." And far more rice and ammunition than captured in any year in South Vietnam.

COWLES: The navy: Market Time operations involving 40 U.S. and 350 VNN craft. Also riverine operations, primarily in IV CTZ, involving 75 U.S. and 510 VNN craft in combined operations.

COWLES: Now 48 U.S. tac air squadrons: 32 USAF in RVN and Thailand, 10 navy at sea, 6 USMC in MR-1. 44 percent out of country, 56 percent in-country. Strategic: 67 percent out of country and 33 percent in-country. Supported by elements of five B-52 squadrons based in Guam, Thailand, and Okinawa, a total of 80 aircraft.

COWLES: 15 October 1970 deadline for redeployment of 50,000 troops.

COWLES: Operationally, "what we do next will of course be determined largely by the changing nature of the war, to include the outcome in Cambodia. It also will be determined, of course, by the additional 100,000 General Rosson mentioned must be redeployed by 1 May [1971], and lastly—but not leastly—by the growing Vietnamese capabilities."

PACKER: Re RVNAF I&M [CRIMP]: "The ultimate goal is to provide a force of sufficient size and capability to be self-sufficient and permit the total withdrawal of U.S. combat forces." Ultimate planned strength: 1,100,000. Territorial Forces make up about 50 percent of the total armed forces. "Within the army, the major ground units are now complete. The army units still remaining to be activated are primarily artillery." Shows planned completion of the force (all services) in July 1973.

PACKER: "Today the ARVN has 100 percent of the M16 rifle." Territorial Forces have 95 percent of their M16s. All units will have complete rifle authorizations by 1 July 1972.

ROSSON: "I think the U.S. has spent over $3 million already buying AK-47 ammunition. And we've had to go to this ARMCO outfit in Alexandria, Virginia, to buy foreign-make ammunition. I mean, the greatest country in the world, and that's what we're up against when we're trying to support this program [MAP for Cambodia] using these non-U.S. weapons. I think we're doing pretty well."

SOMEONE (re Cambodia): "Mr. Ambassador, you've got a situation where you're trying to run a war on a MAP program."

COLBY: "I think what we've been learning here, and what pacification now represents, is the allied answer to the Communist tactics of the people's war."

COLBY: Enemy stages: 1957 sent cadres south for political preparation, 1959 guerrilla warfare, 1964 larger-scale warfare (third stage) (first NVA troop units south in early 1965) (probably would have won the war by 1966, but for U.S. intervention).

COLBY: "Guerrillas can erode a government in the countryside, but they can't take power in the centers of government, particularly if that government is supported by outside forces."

COLBY: The four general offensives of 1968–1969 were the enemy's response to his assessment of the pacification program. "You got to the rather strange situation of the enemy, which had started this war as a people's war, in 1968 is fighting almost exclusively a military-level war. The government [GVN], on the other hand, was accelerating . . . into strengthening its operation at the other levels of the war."

COLBY: The key is that the government has developed an approach combining security and development. "What you're really dealing with here, fundamentally, is a political process."

COLBY: "What was necessary was to put the various programs together to fight what General Abrams calls 'One War' instead of fighting a whole lot of separate ones." "The program was articulated into national plan in late 1968, and essentially followed in 1969 and 1970." "It all depends on successful military operations, because military security is vital." "Some of it is security, and some is development, and I think that's the key."

COLBY: Territorial Forces increased from early 1968 by about 200,000 men, now totaling over 500,000. Weapons gained/lost ratio is now about three enemy weapons taken for every one friendly weapon lost; five years ago just the opposite.

COLBY: Also "in mid-1968 the government began the program of the People's Self-Defense Force." "The government decided in 1968 to go out and essentially arm the people to participate in their defense. There were a lot of people who had faint hearts about this and disagreed with it as being dangerous, politically dangerous, confusing, all the rest of it. The president and the prime minister said, 'No, do it.' They went out and made this a major program of enlisting the population in its own defense." Support even involved children down to the age of seven. "The important figure here is the 357,000 weapons actually out in the countryside." Another 100,000 weapons are in the system to be given out. Re PSDF: "Sometimes they fight well, sometimes they fight badly and run away. They're not an effective force yet by any means, but they are contributing to the security of their community."

COLBY: "The internal security force, the National Police, has a very checkered history here." "When the national mobilization took place the police were not included in it, because they're not a favored group here by any means, and they actually lost strength. But the government today is making a thrust to try to improve the police in performance and in numbers." Fifteen thousand people have been taken out of the armed forces to put into the police. And "they have changed the basic policy role, which in the past was basically that of a colonial police force designed to protect that administration against all comers. They are being thrust out into the villages with the mission of providing law and order support in the countryside."

COLBY: "One of the key elements . . . is the Phoenix program that I'm sure you've read about in the newspapers. This is designed to get at the organizational level of the Communist apparatus, the command and control structure, if you will, of the enemy." "This means identifying them, and intelligence can, arresting them, or going out and catching them in a base area, having the firefight, and going in and getting them there, or getting them to turn over and come to the government side. It means a decent <u>legal</u> system whereby they can be held and prosecuted. It means a decent detention system. We've had a little trouble with <u>that</u>. And it means a reeducation system, which we've <u>barely</u> started on, frankly. And it means a process of controlling them after their release." "Now we've changed the rules on this, the definitions of what constitutes success, so often that we've succeeded in keeping them below their goal line for a little while, but I'm delighted to see, Mr. Ambassador [Bunker], that this past month they've gotten above the goal line for the first time, even under tighter rules."

BUNKER: "That shows, I think, that we're pretty honest about it."

COLBY: "During 1968 there was a lot of firing, shooting, and so forth around the country. During 1969 the enemy, as General Potts said, changed to the high-point strategy, but essentially was continuing the attack on the military forces. And he was trying to exploit the <u>very substantial</u> strategic-psychological victory he had achieved at Tet. . . . But in the process he was ignoring the other parts of the war. Now the government, as I said, in 1968 decided to put together this program—and it really put it together and enforced it <u>very</u> strongly, the president being a leading element—and pushed it out into the country throughout the country."

COLBY: "The enemy ignored it. A friend of mine says they just thought, 'Oh, hell, another one of these pacification programs. They've had so many around here in the past, and they've never amounted to anything. This won't, either.' But this one did. And about halfway through, [word indistinct] woke up again and made another assessment. And this is what came up in COSVN Resolution 9 that General Potts was talking about. In this they said, 'No, let's go out and get this thing. Let's go out and stop it. Let's destroy the self-defense. Let's suppress these local administrations and so forth that are popping up around here.'"

COLBY: "Well, nothing happened for a long time, but in March of this year [1970] we began to see a [trend?], and it went up to very high levels, comparatively, in terrorism. This is only one of the indicator programs, but it's very revealing, I think. Essentially the same thing happened in the small-scale attacks and incidents. Went up to a very high level in April, dropped off in May, dropped off further in June, and is dropping off further in July." One explanation: Due to the Cambodian operation he wasn't able to sustain this. Better explanation: The government's actions in 1969 "got the government relatively so far ahead of the enemy that this phase could not be sustained against" the forces in place.

COLBY: "Terrorism is still a <u>substantial</u> problem in this country, and a lot of people get killed every day."

COLBY: "The development side of this program [of pacification] was particularly a political effort, and it was particularly a matter of decentralization of authority to the local governments and local communities, the process of developing community relations. And in a Confucian society, in which the basic relationship is with your family only, this is a tough job. The government here—traditionally all power had been in the palace, and it went out to the population—under the emperor, under the French, under Diem, under the military. But this government has decided on the strategy of decentralizing, of trying to revive local government for local communities." At the beginning of 1969 about half of the hamlets and villages had elected officials. "During 1969 they built that up to about 90-odd percent." "Now they have mostly elected officials."

COLBY: Also have begun a program of bringing hamlet and village chiefs to a national center for training "with essentially two messages. The first message was the one which is handed out by the very brilliant officer [Colonel Be] who runs this program down there, and has been running it for several years. His basic theme is, 'You live in a corrupt and antiquated society, and you've got to go out and change it—and make it a better one.' The other basic message in that training is given by the president to the village chiefs, saying, 'You are important. You are a little president in your community. You are responsible both to lead and protect and help your people. And our job is to help you.'"

COLBY: "Another part of the political program is getting people away from the enemy, inviting them to return to the government side. This went very well during 1969, largely as a result of this expansion into new areas that, frankly, had been under Communist control. This did not mean a great intellectual conversion of these people, but it does mean they were quite happy to join the government side when the government was there to join. And they did so in droves. This figure has dropped off this year, largely as a result of the fact that there isn't very much further to go in terms of new areas." "One disappointing aspect is that we've only had a very small percentage of North Vietnamese who've joined this program."

COLBY: Cites "the enormous war victim problem we've had in this country. We estimate something between three and four million people have been in refugee status in this country sometime in the past three years." In early 1969 active cases numbered a million and a half. "They [the government] did a magnificent job during 1969," putting some 600,000 people back into their own villages. And they paid benefits to the others.

COLBY (re still unresolved problems of disabled veterans): "When you're combing battalions out of your hair, you really drop off some of these other programs that you just can't get to. And that's what happened."

COLBY: The government is stressing self-sufficiency. "It is looking for a new base for its authority, which in the past was to rest on the administration, on the military. They're now looking to try to form a new base for power in this country." Revival of rural economy is a part. "They have just passed a very revolutionary land reform bill." Village self-development program. "I think the government is sincere."

COLBY (re HES): Useful for trends. "It has a certain validity as a trend indicator." Points out that A hamlets average 3,000 people, B about 2,000, C about 1,800, D about 1,000, and E about 500. "So that where you have the security, where the government is in control, people move toward it and participate in it." "The trend can also be shown not only by looking at a chart, but also in a number of ways—by looking in the countryside, by riding on the roads, and so on."

COLBY: "We do have, unfortunately, a tradition of conspiratorial politics here, and the business of building a new political form, particularly political parties, has not gone on very fast."

COLBY: "We still have the heritage of the French class structure that they left here, where they educated the elite away from their cultural heritage, really, making them into quasi-Frenchmen. And this is related to the political problems. It's still a problem. There is still a gap between the peasantry and the elite. It's being put together by these various programs. . . ."

ROSSON: "It's a shame that General Abrams couldn't be here, because he has an extraordinarily sensitive feel for all of this and is able to portray portions of it in a way that none of us is able to do."

General Abrams is recuperating from the gallbladder surgery.

BRUCE: Asks "why in the world the [media] reporting . . . on the existing situation is erroneous?"

SOMEONE: "That's been a source of acute frustration and mystery to us for many years. One almost gains the impression that there are forces at work to make it that way."

SOMEONE: "The journalists don't know what's going on on the other side. They don't really care any more."

1 AUG 1970: WIEU

ATTENDEES: Gen. Haines, Amb. Berger, Gen. Rosson, Amb. Colby, LTG McCaffrey, VADM King, MG Dolvin, MG Conroy, MG Hardin (for Gen. Brown), MG Cowles, Mr. Jacobson, MG Dettre, BG Camp, BG Vande Hey, BG Potts, BG Sykes, BG Cheadle, BG Henion, BG Doehler, Col. Cutrona, Col. Sadler, Col. Todd (also for BG Greene), Col. Phillips (for Mr. Kirk), Col. Weeks (for BG Henderson).

Gen. Ralph E. Haines Jr., Commander in Chief, U.S. Army, Pacific, is visiting Saigon.

BRIEFER: Groups 1128–1133 projected for October arrival in MR-5 (1131 had been a gap group). Infiltration estimate now: 50,800 (12 percent to DMZ/MR-TTH, 23 percent to MR-5, 11 percent to B-3 Front, 54 percent to COSVN).

BRIEFER: Six and a half tons of documents were uncovered in the course of the Cambodian cross-border operation. Show enemy objectives from that period. "All pro-Sihanouk very strongly."

POTTS: These documents show "there were plans then to attack the Lon Nol government, even before we crossed the border."

ROSSON: "We've been discussing with JGS at the staff level, and I have discussed with General Vien, the matter of reinforcing northern I Corps." "General Vien is not to be moved on this. Apparently he discussed it with the president and says that he is not in a position to move any elements of the general reserve, the primary reason being his heavy commitment in Cambodia. That's taking up more of their forces down here in the south than they may have anticipated—apparently. And he's also pointing out that there are going to be substantial U.S. troop withdrawals—redeployments—in the near future in the 3rd Region, and that that is a matter that disturbs him a little bit, in the sense of any further thinning out of their forces."

8 AUG 1970: WIEU

ATTENDEES: Gen. Rosson, Amb. Colby, LTG McCaffrey, Mr. Kirk, MG Dolvin, MG Conroy, MG Hardin, MG Cowles, Mr. Jacobson, MG Dettre, BG Vande Hey, BG Greene, BG Henderson, BG Potts, BG Sykes, BG Heiser, BG Doehler, RADM Matthews, Col. Cutrona, Col. Sadler, Col. Martin, Capt. Packer, Col. Todd.

ROSSON (re large volume of ammunition used in attacks by fire): "A similar thing has taken place up in the Krek area. They've expended over 2,000 rounds. I think the first of those large-scale attacks occurred the 27th of July, when Task Force 333 was coming out. I wonder where the hell they're getting this stuff? I can't figure it out. You know, we've raised in here from time to time this matter of where these people get their supplies. And we never have pinned it down yet. It's a very, very elusive matter. Some say, you know, they're getting it by sea. But the weight of evidence is that that's just not so. It's an unknown to me. I just don't see where they're getting it. They must have stores that we're essentially not aware of—still rather plentiful."

■ ■ ■

SOMEONE (re repeated requests for emergency resupply airdrops to Cambodian forces): "You can't run anything unless you [we] have competent people on the ground, and this we don't have."

■ ■ ■

ROSSON (re training Cambodian personnel to operate and maintain T-28s and so on): "SecDef addressed himself to CINCPAC yesterday . . . and this statement is made—it has considerable meaning, and this is the SecDef speaking now: 'While we recognize the need for technically trained personnel to be on the scene, the prohibition against increasing U.S. presence in Cambodia and of providing U.S. advisory personnel in-country is overriding.'" We can't get four qualified MAP people in there. "I notice in the file this morning that approval has been given for one individual to go over, one officer, and they may give him an enlisted assistant." "This is indicative of what we're up against in dealing with this Cambodian thing." "We're [the United States?] just unprofessional as hell in the way we're carrying out our affairs with regard to this thing.

We get these unsubstantiated requirements, reports of all kinds that we can't verify, we're hamstrung in moving people back and forth from here to Phnom Penh to check on the situation, the chargé keeps popping off about low visibility, and I'm getting a little uneasy about the whole thing."

SOMEONE: "We work with Ladd. I must say he's probably the most reliable. When we get a hold of him and we ask him something, when we get an answer from him it's usually pretty solid."

SAME SOMEONE: "What is really serious about this is that I think, whether we have the responsibility here or not, I think Washington thinks we have, because when something goes wrong, they come right to the Chief and say, 'What is the situation?' They'll get you up at two o'clock in the morning about something you have nothing to do with." "We had a query here the other day from San Clemente, at four o'clock in the morning, through CINCPAC, asking us the situation on these 23,000 M1 rifles, which is something that's being negotiated between Ladd and Lon Nol. They expect us to know that. So I think that, by indirection, we're being pulled into the position of being responsible for a pretty poor operation."

SOMEONE (also re Cambodia): "We know what we've shipped in there, but I'll be damned if I believe they know what's happened to it."

ROSSON: "We have guidance—from the Highest Authority, as I understand it— that none of us is to discuss or make any public statements with respect to coalition government in Vietnam, redeployment of U.S. forces, and cease-fire. If we're asked any questions about it, the answer is to be, 'Washington announcements on this subject speak for themselves.'"

15 AUG 1970: WIEU

ATTENDEES: Amb. Bunker, Gen. Abrams (first time back after surgery), Gen. Rosson, LTG McCaffrey, Mr. Kirk, VADM King, MG Dolvin, MG Conroy, MG Hardin (for Gen. Brown), MG Cowles, Mr. Jacobson, MG Dettre, BG Vande Hey, BG Greene, BG Henderson, BG Potts, BG Cheadle, BG Henion, BG Heiser, BG Doehler, Col. Cutrona, Col. Sadler, Col. Stewart (for BG Sykes), Capt. Packer (for BG Camp), Col. Todd.

POTTS: "Most important to mention this morning is that, first, we have really tightened up on the ARDF activity in the Cambodian area, and with the air force working deep and with us working with army aircraft along the border, you notice all these fixes of these old units are very current. We're staying right on top of it. And that's probably our best indication of the movement of units."

POTTS: "We have worked an agreement now with the Cambodians so that when NVA prisoners are taken, they are immediately processed, real quickly they are flown here and they go into one of our combined centers. All documents that are captured are immediately flown over here and put into our combined center. And matériel the same way. We translate it and give it back to the

ARVN, and they get it back over, working with the Cambodians. So it's tightened up considerably."

ROSSON (re operations, particularly air operations, in Cambodia): "As you know, Admiral McCain has been trying to get some MAP people over there. They've finally authorized him <u>one man</u>. He's been trying to install communications. He can't send any military people in there. He's got to use civilian contractor individuals. The 228th Maintenance has to be run by third-country hired personnel. So the really <u>professional</u>, first-class way of doing this is not the way it's to be done. There has to be some other system which, frankly, is adopted because of other overriding considerations. The political stake in the whole thing, the question of Cambodian neutrality—those appear to be overriding with regard to how we go about this."

SOMEONE: "This is all kind of dependent on the forward air controller, though. He's the key. We cover the area pretty thoroughly. We fly French-speaking people with them. And we're working them awfully hard to <u>try</u> to know what's going on. But it's on the verge of disaster all the time."

ABRAMS (putting the Cambodian problems in perspective by comparing with the situation in South Vietnam): "I just think about what's gone on here in Vietnam and the system for air. Good god! The <u>clearances</u>, and <u>even then</u> we've erred, we've hit our own troops, we've hit civilians, we've attacked targets that we didn't want to attack, and that sort of thing. <u>Now</u>, over <u>here</u> [Cambodia], there's none of that basic control—<u>none</u> of it! Cambodians flying around, Thais flying around. Now they're proposing sheep-dipped Thais, and the U.S. Air Force and so on. Then the newspaper over there in Bangkok came out and said that the Thai air force had bombed Angkor Wat. And someone in the government said, 'Well, they were under U.S. air control.' Now I want to tell you we're not going to get mixed up in Angkor Wat—not at all."

HARDIN: "I'm not saying we've hit everything we've aimed at, but what we're aiming at there's an enemy in it. I've assured General Rosson that's so, and that <u>is</u> so."

SOMEONE: "We have a tremendous off-limits area around Angkor Wat, and a thousand-meter radius <u>around</u> any temple."

SOMEONE: "The only people who don't know what they're doing are the Cambodians."

■ ■ ■

BRIEFER: Hoi Chanh who rallied at Plei Djereng CIDG camp on 29 July 1970 said he was chief of staff, 28th Reconnaissance Battalion, B-3 Front. "He states that he was once assigned to a B-3 Front comms unit which had the mission of intercepting allied communications. He states that the interception of allied communications is fairly easy, and that elements of the B-3 Front had three days' prior knowledge of the allied cross-border operation."

ABRAMS (re whether the traffic intercepted by the enemy was U.S. or ARVN): "It's <u>both</u>. There's no question about that."

JACOBSON: Shows chart depicting change of 10 province chiefs since 10 June. One ("the most important") is Binh Dinh. "All in all, it's better."

ABRAMS: "You mean the algebraic <u>sum</u> is a <u>plus</u>?"

JACOBSON: "That's correct. Well, just getting rid of that fellow in Binh Dinh—if nothing else had happened. And Bac Lieu."

ABRAMS: "I wondered how you left Bac Lieu out."

JACOBSON: Reads these figures since 1 January 1970:

	Assassinations	Abductions	Wounded
I CTZ	1,031	443	2,250
II CTZ	1,132	3,369	1,930
III CTZ	492	353	1,177
IV CTZ	995	573	2,224

JACOBSON: HES for July 1970 showed an increase countrywide of 1.3 percent of the population in A/B/C hamlets.

■ ■ ■

ABRAMS: "Earlier in the year . . . there was a memorandum from the secretary of defense about the changing situation in South Vietnam, and reexamination of our strategy, how the new mission assigned by the secretary of defense shortly after he took office was working out, and so on. Well, <u>since then</u> there's been all this Cambodian thing, quite a bit of air effort—B-52s, 19 or 20 ARVN battalions going around over there, weapons being—just about everything that's gone to help Cambodia has come out of Vietnam—a little bit from Thailand." "I know before I left they hadn't changed the mission in a formal statement. And I was wondering if there'd been anything done—." [Apparently not.] "It's sort of an ad hoc—."

■ ■ ■

ROSSON: "Before too much longer, we're going to have to be authorized to level with the JGS on the matter of redeployment planning, because it's been hypothetical beyond this next year, really beyond this next 150,000. And they really don't know that we are in the process of phasing down at a rather rapid rate. And this has a bearing on the way they react."

ABRAMS: "I don't know how they couldn't understand that. I have no idea what they—. I think it's rather significant they've gone on sustaining these rather sizable forces in Cambodia. You'd think they'd take them out. It's no small feat."

15 AUG 1970: COMUS Update

BRIEFER: Cites 14,000 enemy KIA/POW during the Cambodian operation.

POTTS (to Abrams): Only about 5,000 enemy infiltrators have come down since your last briefing, so "that infiltration's way behind schedule. I noticed in *Stars*

& *Stripes* today a release from Washington, and they actually gave the accurate figure for infiltration last year. They say between 100,000 and 102,000. It was actually 106,000. They said 250,000 for 1968. We said 235,000." "And they also said 5,000 average per month this year. We say 5,200." Somebody back in the Washington area "is putting accurate data out on infiltration."

POTTS: "The big thing on Cambodia is development of the infrastructure, and they're [the enemy] really working on that."

ABRAMS: "It's hard for me to believe they couldn't take Kompong Son if they wanted to. Maybe—I don't know how much damage has been done up there." [Answer: A great deal. Up to 90 percent in some areas.] "It's always a little confusing to me. You take some of the battles we've had at Dak Tieng and Dak To and Duc Lap and that sort of thing where—goddamn! They just kept at it, and we've had to support it with artillery and tac air. And pretty decent intelligence." "They expended men like they were going out of style."

ABRAMS: "It looks like to me that they recognize they can't, at this stage of the game, mount a military campaign of any significance." "It's not the military campaign that's their big effort, it's the political and the psychological and the organizational and all the groundwork. And they're not looking at '70. They're looking at '71 and '72—or [laughing] '75, I don't know."

■ ■ ■

ABRAMS: "A month after Tet was over, and we'd had a chance to sort out the documents and all the things we'd learned about what really happened, I think the best picture was here in III Corps. The logistical system was pretty well laid out . . . and the role of the cadre and the role of the guerrilla . . . and all this sort of thing. So we said if we could do away with that—find his caches, he has to push his caches out, knock off his guerrillas, work on the cadre, drive them out in the woods, capture them, get them, then he can't bring these units in. Those are the people—they get the labor, they get the people to help carry off the wounded and the dead, they help build bunkers and so on. And you just drive them out. Well, what's happened in III Corps over the last couple of years—it looks like that is right."

ABRAMS (continuing): "Remember he gave up—he still talked about Saigon, but early in '69 he really quit. And then he was talking about Binh Hoa and Tay Ninh, and still working caches, guerrillas, locals—you know, just working in the system, what you call working in the system. Tear up his system, and then he can't—and he finally wound up there in the goddamn jungles of Binh Long, Phuoc Long, and Tay Ninh. So it seemed like that, as a proposition, was sound."

■ ■ ■

ABRAMS: In May 1968 "I had the staff draw a line around Saigon and nobody could use artillery, gunships, tac air, or anything inside that line unless for each specific individual mission I personally approved it. Of course, that's impossible, but that was the rule. All I'm saying is that this beating these places up [referring to recent air strikes in defense of Phnom Penh, or maybe Kompong Son] in this game it is not good." Example: "Five VC would get in the corner of a factory out here, and by the time the fight was over there wasn't anything left of the factory. Air strikes, gunships, artillery—and when you got all through, what did you have? The most anybody could locate was five dead VC. It's just—there's other ways to do this."

19 AUG 1970: COMUS Update

ATTENDEES: Gen. Abrams, MG Dolvin, BG Potts.

BRIEFER (Captain McClure): "It's apparent that North Vietnam has the capacity to continue its present annual rate of infiltration, and even to increase it."

ABRAMS: "See, infiltration is not the only demand. You're talking about infiltration into South Vietnam. But extensive manpower requirements in Laos—first to run the war in Laos, second to run the logistics system and air defenses and engineer effort and all that sort of thing, and then their logistics system in Cambodia, as represented by the base areas. So the total demand outside of North Vietnam is greater than the one you're postulating as infiltration into South Vietnam, and you're comparing that with his total availability."

BRIEFER: Total serving in the North Vietnamese armed forces, in and out of country, we estimate at approximately 477,000.

ABRAMS: "What do we know about [enemy] recruiting in South Vietnam?"

POTTS: "On the first of January last year [1969] it was 7,000. On the first of January this year [1970] it had dropped down to around 4,000, and at the end of June this year 2,900." "And the quality of personnel has very, very definitely dropped off. And many of that 2,900 immediately defect or get away as soon as they can."

22 AUG 1970: WIEU

MACV 1970 Infiltration Estimate: 50,800 (54 percent to COSVN).

SOMEONE (re Cambodia): "It's a long way from being a coordinated effort." Re the system: "It leaves a lot to be desired, but we think it's about all the [***] will bear at this point."

ABRAMS: "Well, I don't think the traffic will bear it." "The ambassador [in Phnom Penh?]—I'm kind of waiting to see what his attitude's going to be. Right now I think that the greatest effort—. You know, there's a lot of things about Cambodia, but the thing he's focused on is keeping Americans out of Cambodia. Every message on that subject is handwritten by him. It looks to me like he's just sort of organized himself—he's selected that as the one thing, by god, that he can contribute to this whole [matter?]. No, I'm not being facetious about this."

SOMEONE: "Mortar fire within hearing distance might change his attitude some-what."

ABRAMS: "The only exception to this, the only exception on Americans, is when they themselves want something—over there. And that goes just like that—same day! But every one of these things are just sticky, and the mere launching of an idea that could possibly lead to one more American, and Christ, the antenna are up—."

■ ■ ■

ABRAMS: "Incidentally, I was really gratified with the [results?] of the B-52s up there that come out of the 1st ARVN Division and its B-52 targeting." "Nowhere over here have you got this kind of stuff going on in the ARVN. And of course nowhere over here have you got the quality of work in [***] that's going on up there. God, that's a—. It's not only that they're using it, but they've got this thing tuned up so that reaction is instantaneous. I was up there yesterday. While I was there, [***] the 324 Bravo [***]. And Christ, they got more artillery, tac air started coming in and so on, and when I left up there they were trying to divert a B-52!" [Laughter] "No, but [***] on where this bastard was." "Well, goddamn it, he [the enemy who [***] position] had a great day yesterday! But the point is, it's one thing to have it and have it working and every week or so have a guy come in and tell you what they heard, you know, that kind of stuff. But they have got this—when something like that, it just grabs the whole system! The division commander was immediately informed, and one of them briefed him on what they were doing to keep him from—to keep him calm." [Laughter] This was in Tay Ninh, just before we left Evans. General Truong. "It's really quite gratifying. It's really professional."

POTTS: "That's that special technical detachment. General Truong was very pleased when that unit intercepted the fire commands, about three weeks ago, of the enemy getting ready to fire on one of his units. He moved that unit 250 meters before the rounds fell, exactly where they had been."

ABRAMS (re Truong): "He puts his policies out. Then he goes around to every last unit, it takes him about four or five days, to see if his policies are being effected. Well, it just has to be!"

■ ■ ■

ABRAMS: Reports talking to Lieutenant General Lam about how the two enemy battalions penetrated I Corps without being reported. They came to the edge of the area, got under triple canopy in an unpopulated place, delayed for a day and a night, then made their move at eight o'clock at night, avoiding populated areas, "and took up their position outside of their target hamlet." Got there about four in the morning, then at five-thirty or six they moved into the hamlet. "There isn't the evidence that infrastructure and guerrillas and that sort of thing were able to lay this on. The unit just studied this and made their move." Think 350 of 500 enemy KIA. "So if that was sort of an experimental thing, a trial tactic, it was fairly costly."

Origin of the Study "Where Do We Let Peace Come to Vietnam?"

ABRAMS: "Now another thing I want to start thinking about here—I want to raise this with the commanders—I think that there're areas around here in Vietnam right now where the question should be asked whether artillery, gunships, tac air, and all that kind of stuff, whether it ought to be used at all. Out here to try to get four guerrillas—three air strikes, and 155s and 105s, and two helicopter gunship runs—."

BROWN: Demurs, says you need to keep the system viable.

ABRAMS: "All right, but this has got to be examined. We've got to find out—. I don't want to be just out here banging up the goddamn country in order to keep the system going."

ABRAMS: "Maybe there's a way to keep the system without these guys banging away at they don't know what's there, or whether there's anything there, and so on. I don't think it's too soon to start thinking of some places around here where you just don't do any of that stuff. And you go ahead and solve the problem, whatever the problems are around there, by other means." "I sometimes wonder, sitting over there at the quarters, I hear these explosions out there. Christ! Then I look at the book and see nothing happened in Saigon. What the hell are they doing, exercising their recoil systems? Well, goddamn it, you can't use it against terrorism."

SOMEONE: "I talked to General Truong about this. He is not a keen supporter of the ammo conservation program."

ABRAMS: "I think when you've got these units out there in the jungle and that sort of thing—that's not the kind of situation I'm talking about. Take Gia Dinh. Why should we shoot any more artillery in Gia Dinh?"

ABRAMS: "Now I didn't bring this up on the basis of saving ammunition. As a matter of fact, that's only—that's gotten in here later. And I can tell you, that's not why I brought it up. I'm thinking about the Vietnamese people, the whole atmosphere of political and economic and a healthy attitude toward the government and all that kind of stuff! I don't know too much about it, but Christ! What the hell do the villages think out here—this stuff just keeps going off, banging around out there, and so on. The most charitable thing, I suppose, is that they think somebody's coming. And probably what they do think is, 'Goddamn it, why are they doing that? There hasn't been anybody—there hasn't been a VC around here in a month.'" "That's what I'm talking about." "No, men that are fighting, and fighting the enemy, they've got to be supported by everything we can do."

ABRAMS (returning to the topic later in the discussion): "I want to get more into this idea about the artillery and the gunships and the tac air and so on, with the idea of making some kind of presentation of this Saturday at the Commanders WIEU." "I think that's just what we have to do. But I, especially now with respect to Regions 2 and 3, I just feel that there may be going on there things that are not necessary. And only some sort of blind faith would lead you to believe that they were productive."

■ ■ ■

ABRAMS (to Gen. Frederick C. Weyand, newly arrived as Deputy COMUS-MACV): "Fred, welcome back! Like the good old days!"

29 AUG 1970: Commanders WIEU

ATTENDEES: Gen. Abrams, Gen. Rosson, Gen. Brown, Mr. Kirk, LTG Collins, LTG Weyand, LTG Davison, LTG McCaffrey, LTG Sutherland, LTG McCutcheon, VADM King, MG Dolvin, MG Conroy, MG McCown, MG Cowles, Mr. Jacobson, MG Dettre, Mr. Vann, Mr. Whitehouse, MG Wagstaff, BG Vande Hey, BG Greene, BG Henderson, Mr. Long (for Mr. Chambers), Mr. Fritz, BG Cheadle, BG Henion, BG Heiser, BG Doehler, Col. Mahl (for BG Potts), Col. Cutrona, Col. Leonard, Col. Sadler, Col. Stewart (for BG Sykes), Capt. Packer (for BG Camp), Col. Jones, Col. Todd, LTC Veasey (for Col. Healy).

ABRAMS (in discussion of Vice President Agnew visit): "Another thing he did—he was down in Australia, and in some idle conversation down there agreed to buy fifteen million bucks' worth of mutton." [Laughter] "And got back and said the army would use it." "And the interesting thing about that is . . . there's a continuing program of surveying the troops to see what it is they like to eat. And mutton is down there somewhere close to brussel sprouts!" [Laughter] "It's damn near in the basement!"

■ ■ ■

Enemy COMINT in South Vietnam

BRIEFER: The enemy organization devoted to this is "an organization so secret that its members are billeted separately from all other troops and instructed never to acknowledge the existence of their activity." Under control of CRD (Central Research Directorate) Hanoi. Have detachments with maneuver elements down to company level with the mission of "satisfying the real-time, immediate-value intelligence requirements of supported commanders."

BRIEFER: "The enemy command structure has changed substantially since the 1965–1966 period." Also some elements are directly subordinate to COSVN. Technical Reconnaissance and Intelligence Department. Have acquired large numbers of captured U.S. radios. Also possess a variety of commercial radios. Small battery-operated tape recorders for use in exploitation of voice communications. Estimated over 4,000 in direct support of tactical units and COSVN. May be over 5,000 performing such functions throughout South Vietnam. "The enemy knows that the communications of the artillery warning control centers are productive sources of information concerning imminent B-52 strikes."

BRIEFER: A captured unit commander stated that "the unit worked against both U.S. and ARVN communications and copied both voice and manual Morse code transmissions. The effort is targeted against those [word unintelligible] giving . . . locations and plans, particularly ambush plans. He said that a normal day would yield about 10 significant intercepts, and that the ambush locations were frequently compromised as much as 24 hours prior to positioning."

BRIEFER: Gives specific examples of prior knowledge of impending B-52 strikes. Also other examples of compromised locations and operations from each CTZ. "One of the prime targets being exploited by the enemy in Vietnam is our telephone system. In addition to wiretapping, the radio links in the telephone system are being intercepted." "Homemade codes are <u>extremely</u> vulnerable, and there is <u>indisputable</u> evidence that . . . point of origin [codes] are being written in plain text as they are intercepted by the NVA/VC operators."

BRIEFER: "In summary, ralliers and prisoners state that the information received from their COMINT units is highly valued. They characterize COMINT as the easiest, safest, and most accurate means of obtaining targets, and a continuous source of information on the movement, operations, and overall missions of opposing forces." "In conclusion, the enemy COMINT effort is large, well organized, well managed, well trained, well equipped, and successful."

ABRAMS: "Anyone have any questions?" [None.] "If we could make any substantial improvement in our own communications security, it would <u>really</u> be a leap forward. I don't think that we've succeeded in impressing all of our people with how <u>good</u> <u>these</u> fellows are in this area, and how <u>damaging</u> it is to a lot of things that we set out to do. So we've got to get more and more activist. We're taking <u>casualties</u> for—just because of poor communications security. Guys are getting killed out here and guys are getting wounded out here just because we haven't got it, to say nothing of missions that have been thwarted or made more difficult. We start out by having some hot poop— [***], and goddamn it, it's <u>thwarted</u> because they know what our reaction is."

ABRAMS: "It's part of the <u>price</u> for communications security—is doing less, or doing it later, or delay—you know, in order to <u>guarantee</u> security—you know, absolutely <u>guarantee</u> it. It either takes more <u>time</u> to put it together, or it takes more <u>people</u>, or some other thing. I think the <u>price</u> is <u>worth</u> it! It's an <u>illusion</u> that—. I mean, we're deluded in a lot of things that we do by not understanding this particular <u>part</u>. And out of it has grown this great thing about how these little bastards, once you've got them surrounded, you know, how they just manage to—. Everybody's looking, and all that, and then these bastards have all slipped between us and <u>gone</u>! Not so. They knew this was coming ahead of time and they all <u>went</u>. And what you've surrounded is the place they used to be before they were informed that you were coming there. You haven't surrounded <u>anybody</u>."

ABRAMS: "I think you've got a cultural problem here. An awful lot of Americans just can't <u>believe</u> that one of these <u>runts</u>, wearing shower shoes and so on, could just be that goddamn <u>smart</u>. And that <u>quick</u>. I guess <u>all</u> people have some kind of hang-ups of one kind or another. And we've got people that are hung up on <u>that</u>. And that's why they—well, you know, 'slopes' and 'dinks' and that sort of thing—just can't believe that these little bastards are that <u>clever</u>."

■ ■ ■

ABRAMS: "The thing that's kind of interesting there is the price that the RF/PF is paying. In every military region except the 1st, they're paying the <u>heaviest</u> costs." Observes that in MR-4 the RF/PF is 80 percent of the total military strength. In MR-2 around 50–60 percent. MR-3 a little under 50 percent.

COLLINS: "There are places [in MR-2] where the RF/PF can get in a fight any day, and they <u>do</u>. The ARVN battalions that go out in that area, they thrash around for a week, and they come back in with no results. They're [RF/PF] carrying the load there."

4 SEP 1970: Sir Robert Thompson Briefing

BRIEFER (re infiltration): "Arrivals projected through October amount to only 51,800, less than half of the total infiltration last year." "Losses have not been offset by infiltration."

ABRAMS (re MR-1): "There's not much respectable weather left, maybe another two or three weeks. And I think that's why the battalions south of the Ben Hai have started to go down, because you know the rain will begin to come up there late this month, and certainly October and November. They're really torrential. You just get an awful lot of water. And it's difficult for <u>them</u>, as well as anybody else. In other words, it's not a thing that just messes us up, but they historically have not been able to function effectively in it, either. Annually, in anticipation of this, they have pulled back across the Ben Hai."

ABRAMS: "Infiltration is really way down. If they're going to do anything in the <u>military</u> way—well, at least each time in the past when they have decided to do something serious in the military way they've backed it up with a replacement flow that would be adequate. And <u>that</u> sign isn't there yet. That again tends to indicate, along with the good weather in Laos and so on, if you're talking purely military activity, it <u>must</u> be something like four or five months away."

ABRAMS: Re COSVN Resolution 9 and follow-on documents: "It really doesn't contemplate any recognizable <u>military</u> campaign, as has occurred at some times in the past." "Also, they're not all playing it the same way."

ABRAMS: "That thing up there in Quang Nam where they hit the orphanage and the hospital and so on up there—a <u>perfectly</u> <u>senseless</u>—. I mean, even trying to look at it from <u>their</u> view, it was just a <u>senseless</u> thing. And apparently they also executed a <u>monk</u>." "It's very difficult for <u>me</u> to see how this is <u>helpful</u> to <u>them</u>."

ABRAMS (re resettlement): "Montagnards are just not <u>amenable</u>. I mean, there's no logic that you can provide to persuade a Montagnard to leave his land. There <u>isn't</u> any."

ABRAMS: "I might mention the 25th Division, U.S., and the 101st. They've each got 300 people [assigned to help pacification], and they're in every DIOCC and PIOCC, and they're resident. They link the intelligence and operations types with communications. And when you link that with liaison with the ARVN divisions, and with the MR-3 headquarters, it's all designed for a <u>daily</u> exchange of intelligence." Also training teams and support teams that work with the Territorial Forces. "There are substantial human assets out of each of these divisions that are really over there working in the system that improves the effectiveness of the intelligence, improves the effectiveness of the territorials, and an interchange of information. And in the process I think they're going to do a respectable job also on using sanitation and all this sort of thing. So the kind of things that could affect them in a district, if there's anybody that knows it, that district's going to know it. There's always exceptions. I'm not claiming that it's been gripped by perfection. But I think this is helpful. As a matter of fact, it may even be more important than some of the other things we're doing."

ABRAMS: "I don't think there's any question that the attitude, the spirit, whatever you want to call it, of the Cambodian forces has started to go up. It reached a pretty low ebb, where they expected to take a licking every time they turned around. But, I must say, entirely trainable. They weren't trained for this, you know, all of the things—they just weren't <u>up</u> to it. And, as you know, well— the first time you get into combat it's pretty noisy. But they are sticking in there a lot better. They've actually thrown off some of these attacks. And then every once in a while you get a little break on intelligence and really <u>cream</u> them. It's been mostly air support, but they've had a couple of pretty good ones."

ABRAMS: "The only entrepreneur that I know of that's tried to play it straight is 'Coke' [Coca-Cola]. I guess they want to make money, but they <u>have</u> played it straight."

ABRAMS (re 175-mm guns): "It's for use up in the DMZ area. And we just couldn't <u>bring</u> ourselves to walk out of here and not give them <u>something</u> that they had a chance of doing counterbattery with if they had to. And nothing else has got the range, so that's <u>really</u> what that's about."

ABRAMS (re turnover of coastal and riverine craft to the VNN): "If anybody wanted to get down in and look what actually happened here, and what's been involved, this is a <u>fairly</u> remarkable performance. After all, it takes a little doing to keep those boats running, and the communications equipment, and the weapons and so on. The only time we've had a delay in that was we were supposed to complete the last turnover by the 1st of June, or the 30th of June. Well, every damn thing was committed in Cambodia and so on, and frankly there wasn't time—. I mean, you had to have a ceremony, you always have to have that, and there wasn't time to set this up for the ceremony, and so we decided to do it a little later. <u>But</u> the performance of the Vietnamese Navy, and I must take my hat off to our own navy the way they've worked with them, it's been a team effort, and it's been really quite remarkable."

ABRAMS (re VNMC): "Earlier this year, and towards the end of last year, its performance really got pretty seedy. It wasn't their fault. We got the JGS fellows looking at it. They were being improperly handled. You have to watch that with a general reserve. You know, the corps commander, he's just a human being, and he looks on certain things as they're his. He owns them, they belong to him, and all that. Well, you give him something out of the general reserve and it's not in that category at all. And it's no skin off of him if he gets them worn out. Then he'll ship it back to JGS and so on. That's what was happening to the marines. I think that's all squared away."

ABRAMS (re the RVNAF): "What we've tried to do is keep them with one air force. You can't afford to have—. Not like us—the army has its air force, the navy has its air force, the marines have its air force, and the air force has one— it's one of the smaller ones, but—. [Laughter] The biggest air force we've got is the one in the army, if you add up the number of vehicles."

BRIEFER: When I&M is completed, RVNAF will have a force of 12 ground combat divisions, 50 air force squadrons, 1,232 craft in naval operations, 1,679 RF companies, 7,335 PF platoons. "The plan for expansion and equipping of this force is on schedule."

THOMPSON: "It's still a long-term thing you're talking about for Vietnam here."

5 SEP 1970: WIEU

ATTENDEES: Gen. Abrams, Amb. Colby, Gen. Clay, LTG Weyand, LTG McCaffrey, VADM King, MG Dolvin, MG Conroy, MG Cowles, Mr. Jacobson, MG Dettre, BG Vande Hey, BG Greene, BG Potts, BG Sykes, BG Cheadle, BG Henion, BG Heiser, BG Doehler, Col. Ahern (for BG Henderson), Col. Sadler, Capt. Packer (for BG Camp), Col. Leonard, Col. Jones, Col. Todd, Col. Phillips (for Mr. Kirk).

ABRAMS (re confrontation between National Police and veterans): "It looks like maybe the veterans are trying to work around and get into a thing where we get mixed up in it, and just kind of push it and push it until you've got a fight or some damn thing between Americans and veterans. And I'll tell you, we don't want that." "This isn't a good, nice veterans movement to take care of the poor veterans who lost their legs and—. It isn't that kind of a thing at all. It's a nasty thing. They're looting shops, they're coercing—taking money, and there have been some fights between factions in the veterans thing. But what worries me now is that they may be working around to get the U.S. personnel involved in this—opening up on them with a machine gun, some damn thing like that. And I'll tell you, even though this is a nasty outfit, that term 'veterans' has got some real cosmetics. Well, just what'll happen at the next American Legion convention if they've got photographs there of the U.S. beating the shit out of veterans—veterans—in Saigon? And the American Legion, they don't know what it's about. All they need is that veterans. That's what they are. 'What's become of our country, now that we're out—?'"

JACOBSON: "This veterans thing is insidious as hell, because there's a lot of money behind it. All of these chaps have the same outfit, made out of the same kind of material—they're kind of prefab, so that they can—. And the same thing in Danang. And the same thing in Nha Trang. How the hell they—. And with this new bill, which is really quite good for veterans, this is just definitely a political ploy that is as dangerous as anything that's happened here since I know of. And they're a very determined group of people."

BRIEFER: Ninety-five ralliers "stated hunger and fear of aircraft as reasons for returning to GVN control. All had heard psyops broadcasts and seen leaflets dropped. They further stated that the VC had taken the leaflets away from them and banged on large tin cans to prevent them from hearing the broadcasts."

■ ■ ■

ABRAMS: "I'm getting a little uneasy now that [meaning "whether"] some of the format of this Saturday meeting shouldn't be changed." "What this meeting ought to do in here is give us a sensitive description of how the war, in all its features, is kind of going on."

ABRAMS: Concerned "whether we're reading the whole thing right and whether we're really sensitive to what is important, and whether we can get talking and discussing about what's important and so on. Because I think some things in some places are now far more important than other things used to be."

ABRAMS: "You see, there's now a tendency that the thing that gets recognized is where somebody got some KIAs, or he finds a cache, and so on. Well, take one of these fellows milling around in this other [support for pacification], like the 173rd, you see." "All this [the briefing chart] shows is that they've been sitting on their ass doing nothing. They haven't qualified for nothing at our meeting here [meaning they haven't made the charts as they are now constituted]. You wouldn't even think they were here. Well, I think they're doing better than that. But the thing that does get mentioned is those goddamn battalions and brigades of the 4th Division and so on that haven't done anything, either, except been out, and then they, you know—comes up zero. Now, even that may—I would be prepared, depending on, you know, a detailed briefing of precisely what they were doing and what it was aimed at and so on, and maybe it did do good. And the way the reporting system goes, it looks like they didn't do anything—except be out. So—I'm not being critical of the 4th! But the way the reporting system is, it doesn't give me any—. Well, of course, maybe at this level you're not supposed to have any feel for things. I don't know." [Laughter]

ABRAMS: Recalls chart in IV CTZ he discussed yesterday with Sir Robert Thompson. Concerned a group of provinces. In them, about a million people. In 1967, per the chart, only about 100,000 under government control. "Now, you can argue that our view of this thing in '67 may have exaggerated what in fact was controlled by the VC. They may not have had all of that."

JACOBSON: "We didn't have it, for sure."

ABRAMS: "No, and by god we weren't going out and find out, either! And, you know, that's one of the things that happened in the Accelerated Pacification Program. Christ, they got out there with a PF platoon and found there weren't any VC there at all! I mean armed. And these people had been waiting all the time, and then you got a lot of ralliers out of it because they'd made Ho Chi Minh sandals or something like that, and so they came in and said, 'We won't work for them any more.' They probably hadn't worked for them for two or three months anyway. Well! And then you can also say what we call government control now, they—there's a lot of degrees in that. However, government presence, without getting into an argument about the effectiveness in each and every, you know, thing—the change in government presence is really dramatic! You know, it isn't the same ball game."

JACOBSON: "For example, in '68 An Giang Province, as I recall, was 36 percent of the people [secure]. Now it's still in the bottom 10, but it's up in the 80s."

ABRAMS: "Yeah. And then, of course, you go around and the amount of boats on the canals, and things on the road, and the amount of roads that are being used. And then, well, up in I Corps—the one place in the country that I'm always reminded of Tet '68 is when I get up in I Corps. It's always—that's what I think of, right away. No other place has that effect on me. Wow! For instance, going over the Hai Van Pass the other day. Jeez! That's a damn good highway. It's all paved, you know, and they've got the turns all—. Christ, it's a first-class highway. And of course now you can't go out there and plant mines in it with the ease that you once could, and so on. So that's a—. Well. And you get up there and ride over the 'Street without Joy' now. By god, there are people living and working there. You know, there's a lot of resettlement been done up there."

ABRAMS: "And people come over here and visit. Now these two drug guys—. [Someone: "Crow and Tim?"] Yeah. Now they had their work to do, finding out about drugs and all that, but they were really—. I think what impressed them the most was the way the thing looked over here and the way they got around. Christ, they were out riding around and, you know, all that kind of stuff. And they just didn't think it was that way. And those economists that came over here from OSD to look into the economy, you know, and all that. The most impressive thing to them [laughing]—. They know there's economic problems and they're serious. They've got a lot to say about that. But they went all over the country, and—'Why, people—people don't understand this.'"

ABRAMS: "Sometimes I even wonder—now, of course, the highway of our experience in Vietnam [laughing] is littered with the skeletons of the optimists, you know, in bygone—, and predictors and so on. So almost everyone [laughing] would rather quit than be forced into an optimistic statement. [Laughter] Dishonorable as quitting might be, it's preferable to becoming one of those skeletons. So I wonder sometimes whether even we are prepared to accept that it has moved as much as it's moved. And how you ease up on that, in a sort of a cold-blooded and realistic way, without getting into that dreamy world of, 'My god, we've got the answer.' We don't [want] that, but—."

JACOBSON: "The best thing that could happen is to have somebody come over that was here before. I talked to an AP guy yesterday who last was here in '68. And he came back from the delta. And, you know, he's not supposed to write about that kind of thing. He's in trouble—got to find something wrong. He just talked about it. He said, 'I can't believe it that you can drive to Ca Mau like I did.' He was appalled. And he apparently didn't have a damn thing to write about, because his chain would never accept that kind of stuff."

■ ■ ■

BRIEFER: MACV Infiltration Estimate: 51,800 (53 percent to COSVN).

ABRAMS: "I view it that, manpower-wise, they're [the enemy] kind of in a weakened position. And I think even that applies in northern I Corps and in southern I Corps." "They've just been roughed up." "To really get something going, I don't think their manpower situation is very good. Now they can—I think they've got enough manpower to keep working away at the basic stuff in Resolution 9 and the things that followed after that, nipping away at pacification, trying to gang up on outposts, assassination, abduction, and so on."

ABRAMS: "COSVN Resolution 9 results from some policy decision in Hanoi. And it looks like that's the course they are continuing on. They've had to adapt to the Cambodian thing. When they change their mind up there, if they do—if they change their mind, one of the—. It depends on what they change to, but one of the things that reflect, one of the thermometers for change, will be this thing [infiltration], kind of the rate at which you start picking them up, you know, that sort of thing. Because if they're going to do anything bad that's different, they've got to do something about the manpower. I don't think—the manpower situation isn't such that it would support even a localized campaign."

ABRAMS (re enemy in Laos and Cambodia): "I think we need to lay this all out. Then you get down into when COSVN and the B-3 Front and so on began getting over onto the Mekong and—. So you've got a more comprehensive picture of what Hanoi's decided to do when the government changed—the change of government in Cambodia."

ABRAMS: "Let's see what kind of a comprehensive picture we can get of what Hanoi decided to do once this occurred. That's what we're interested in. What are they deciding to do up there in Hanoi? You see, we've made—we've actually made a lot of assumptions."

ABRAMS (to Potts): "You might try to reproduce the op order that came out of Hanoi on the 19th of March, or whenever it was." [Laughter]

ABRAMS (to someone): It is necessary in analysis not to rely on the teachings of "your alma mater, [Fort] Leavenworth, but to be a better Asian."

12 SEP 1970: Briefing for Ambassador Swank

Emory C. Swank was U.S. ambassador to Cambodia 1970–1973.

ABRAMS: Introduces General Clay, Commander Seventh Air Force, and others to Ambassador Swank, including Maples, Potts, COMNAVFORV Admiral King, and others. Potts leads off. Begins very basic: RVN is divided into four corps and 44 provinces. "Until the 2nd of July these military regions were called corps tactical zones. President Thieu redesignated them on that date."

POTTS: Describes enemy area designators: B-5 Front (which runs about 20 kilometers south of the DMZ and 20 kilometers north). MR-TTH (named after two provinces and the city of Hue). MR-5 (six coastal provinces). B-3 Front (the highlands). COSVN (area including 32 of South Vietnam's 44 provinces, 69 percent of the population, the capital city of Saigon, and the rich rice-producing delta region). High Command Hanoi (commands and controls these five geographical area commands).

POTTS (re *binh trams*): "We have one numbered 44, but we only know of the existence of 38."

BRIEFER: Infiltration groups: 4000 series destined for COSVN (the journey takes 120 days).

POTTS: "We've had a development this year—we're reading three other *binh trams*—32, 33, and 14." Last year reading only BT 18.

ABRAMS: The enemy stayed on the general offensive/general uprising wicket until February 1969. He came off it beginning in May 1969. In the meantime, the RVN was going ahead with one campaign after another with Accelerated Pacification, beginning 1 November 1968. "And it went quite well, probably better than anyone would have expected. And in terms of government presence, and in terms of the degree of control that each side can exercise over the people, the South Vietnamese really made substantial strides, and the Viet Cong took substantial losses in the degree of control over the people. So you see reflected, then, in COSVN Resolution 9, which is a policy directive that came out July or August last year [Potts: "We captured it on the ninth of October."], and in that they had finally faced up to what the South Vietnamese had been doing. So, from that point on, they've made a principal effort against the pacification program. That's been their <u>intention</u>. But I think it's fair to say, without getting too smart about it, that the <u>machinery</u> . . . wasn't very good, although the <u>policy</u> was there. The <u>effectiveness</u> of it . . . was not good."

JACOBSON: "You couldn't even notice it until March."

ABRAMS: "There was a period here when we were wondering why—here was this policy directive. It was clear and authentic. There was no question about <u>that</u>. But you couldn't see that it was being carried out."

ABRAMS: "And what you've got now is them [the enemy] reacting to the total program of the South Vietnamese government. And before November of '68 what you had was all of us down here reacting to the Hanoi program." "I don't, as I say, want to get too worked up about this. It's still a hell of a struggle. And <u>now</u>, where you can say maybe that the <u>military</u> situation, if you can separate something out like that—it's sort of dangerous, and oversimplifies things—but that particular facet of the thing is more or less under control. And now these <u>other</u> things—the operation of the infrastructure, the state of the economy and inflation, and political strength of the government, all of those, those are the—instead of trying to chase the 9th VC Division out of the 9th Precinct down here, which <u>used</u> to be the daily assignment, <u>now</u> that's—<u>they're</u> gone, and now these <u>other</u> things, and they're pretty vexious, and of course you can't solve them with B-52s. The name of the game and the tools and all that are changing."

ABRAMS: "The other thing about it—the Vietnamese—if you want to look around for faults, they're easy to find. <u>But</u> when the Vietnamese make up their mind to do something . . . they <u>do</u> it."

ABRAMS: "Of course, Mr. Ambassador, they could have <u>always</u> taken Phnom Penh, anytime they wanted to." That was true for a time, certainly for several weeks. "But as of today I wouldn't go lunging off making that statement."

12 SEP 1970: WIEU

Tape box is marked 13 September 1970, but a printed agenda in the tape box reads 12 September, and a staffer on the tape also says 12 September 1970. In addition, 12 September is a Saturday, the date on which the WIEU is normally conducted. <u>But</u> Abrams refers to talks with Ambassador Swank "yesterday." Possibly they had talks with him the day before his 12 September briefing session.

ATTENDEES: Gen. Abrams, Amb. Colby, Gen. Clay, LTG Weyand, LTG McCaffrey, VADM King, MG Cowles, Mr. Jacobson, MG Maples, MG Dettre, BG Camp, BG Vande Hey, BG Potts, BG Henderson, BG Sykes, BG Heiser, BG Doehler, Col. Franklin (for Col. Sadler), Col. Martin (for BG Cheadle), Col. Leonard, Col. Jones (also for BG Greene), Col. Phillips (for Mr. Kirk).

macv 1970 Infiltration Estimate: 52,300 (53 percent destined for COSVN).

BRIEFER (who has just made a visit to Phnom Penh): Mr. Rives's view re "personnel coming into the country" and "his great fear" is that "there is a large press corps in Phnom Penh with very little to report. And they watch the American Embassy activities <u>very</u> closely. And they are definitely afraid of any large growth in the American contingent that would be [in] any way misinterpreted by the press and bring out the doves on the Washington side."

■ ■ ■

On the VCI Threat

BRIEFER: As of August 1970 the estimated VCI strength is about 65,000 cadre, not including guerrilla or low-level supporters. Over 37,000 have been identified by name and position. Remaining estimated. "The most important function of the infrastructure is to organize the people so that they have no alternative but to support the insurgency. In order to organize the people, the VCI must have access to the population."

BRIEFER: "The success of the GVN, on the other hand, depends on its ability to separate the VCI from the people." "The key to measuring the threat of the VCI is access." "Analysis of the most recent data shows that the VCI have access to three-fifths of the population of Vietnam." "What is surprising is that in B hamlets the VCI have access to 56 percent of the population. And even in A hamlets the VCI have contact with 25 percent of the people." "As long as this access exists, the people know the Viet Cong can come in the night, if they choose, and settle any score."

BRIEFER (re the vulnerability of pacification gains): Phu Yen is an example. Twelfth best rating in the country. And 12th in RF/PF. But due to "the Phu Yen abduction campaign" in the five-month period February–June 1970 over 1,400 people were kidnapped in the province. When U.S. and FWMAF forces leave, large numbers of additional people will be newly exposed to VCI access. Now 14 provinces have at least brigade strength of U.S./FWMAF battalions.

■ ■ ■

ABRAMS (re emphasis in the WIEU): "The way that part of it's going right now [the military part]—yeah, you ought to tell what the 5th seems to be doing— about what they were doing last week, the 7th's the same, the 9th's the same, and so on. There hasn't been any shift. But just kind of breeze right on through that as long as there hasn't been any—. We <u>don't</u> want to lose track of them. I don't want to say they're no longer of any importance. But, in terms of <u>time</u> that we spend in here, and things that we <u>talk</u> about and discuss and so on—." "Rather liked" the officer's briefing on enemy counterpacification efforts. "This is kind of the gutty part of the thing right now. It's the biggest thing that's going—. Well, anyway, it's the biggest thing that's going on in Vietnam that you can <u>see</u>." And: "The police program, what they're doing—kind of get that out here every Saturday." "The way things are right now, and maybe for the next two or three or four months this <u>is</u> going to be the major <u>business</u>. So we need to thrash it out more and see if we can understand a little better all of what he's doing, <u>and</u> what <u>we're</u> doing. The military activity by region could be covered with a lot bigger brush."

WEYAND (re the enemy): "This meeting is starting to get broader than focusing on the B-52 program and on the main force, where he was and what the hell was he up to. The poor son of a bitch <u>now</u> is just kind of fumbling around. I don't even know if <u>he</u> knows what he's up to, so for us trying to figure it out is pretty hard."

ABRAMS: "Our own capabilities are diminishing. And you'd have to get a micrometer to measure the amount of flexibility there is, but one should not be disturbed by <u>that</u>, even if it has to be measured by a micrometer, if you've got some it would be well to <u>apply</u> it—I mean to do things intelligently in the light of <u>all</u> of this, in the light of <u>all</u> of it, not just where the goddamn 7th Division is."

ABRAMS: "I worry whether we <u>look</u> at it right. I'm not so worried about whether it will come <u>out</u> right as—that's not it. I think there's really <u>enough</u> if—of everything—if you go ahead and <u>do</u> it, and focus on the things that really ought to be done, the things that are important at this stage of the game."

ABRAMS (re the enemy): "Everybody knows that he's tough, that he's—carry on. Adversity does nothing but strengthen him. But this fellow has—has really taken a lot of punishment. And some places it's showing. He isn't—the situation isn't the same it was this time in '67. It just isn't. He hasn't got those tickets."

ABRAMS: "I guess we had ought to change the name, but you see that'll—. Secret as the meeting is, you abandon the term 'WIEU,' it's going—. I mean, the building will shake a little bit and so on. You know, it's become quite a thing. And the press will have it. And the next thing, some guy in UPI is going to call up Leonard and say, 'Report is that MACV has abandoned the WIEU. Now what do you have to say about that?'" "You're right, though, Fred [Weyand]. I think what we're really talking about is broadening the considerations that go into this meeting on Saturdays."

13 SEP 1970: Lieutenant General Weyand Update

WEYAND: "I want to ask a question, because it's something that bothers me. They always say that Kompong Son—Sihanoukville—is vital to him, and yet the last ship that stopped there was July or something of last year." [Potts: July 11th.]

POTTS: "What happened is that that was arms and ammunition only. So we list 15 ships, going back to October of '66." "But even after that ships came in with other types of military equipment—signal, medical, a lot of things like that. And the depots at [Luba?] and Kompong Speu were pretty well stocked. And traffic continued to go out of those depots into the base areas as late as March." "CIA finally agreed with us that the IV Corps, the III Corps, and most of II Corps were being primarily resupplied through Sihanoukville."

POTTS: "Base Area 609 was never gotten in the cross-border operation. Never got that. And, incidentally, the 702, just below was" not really gotten. "You heard our [***] with two-day notice." The attackers "had to withdraw." That gave them another day's rest that they could come in. "So it just didn't go well."

WEYAND (re assessment that the enemy's objective continues to be domination of all Vietnam and of Indochina): "I think the most significant aspect of that is that he continues to seek it through the use of force. I don't think he's ever going to change his objective of the domination. The important thing, to us, and to the world, is how the hell is he planning on doing that?" "I don't think that's ever going to change a hell of a lot, but it may in degree. Which is, of course, why he won't negotiate, because he's convinced that the way to get us out of here is by force. It's not that he can eject us, . . . but he believes the American people will force us out through a sense of futility that he creates through his military tactics."

19 SEP 1970: WIEU

ATTENDEES: Gen. Abrams, Amb. Colby, Gen. Clay, LTG Weyand, LTG McCaffrey, Mr. Kirk, VADM King, MG Dolvin, MG Cowles, Mr. Jacobson, MG Maples, MG Dettre, BG Camp, BG Vande Hey, BG Potts, BG Henderson, BG Sykes, BG Henion, BG Heiser, BG Doehler, Col. Sadler, Col. Martin (for BG Cheadle), Col. Leonard, Col. Jones (for BG Greene).

General Weyand is not included in list read on the tape, but he is on printed list in the tape box. Printed list also shows as visitors General Haines and Colonel Hoffman, but they are not mentioned on the tape.

MACV 1970 Infiltration Estimate: 52,300 (of which 53 percent are destined for COSVN).

POTTS: "This is the fourth week in a row we've reported the 5000 series groups coming to southern Laos, showing the emphasis that's been placed there. We ran a survey of last year. Seven groups came down, primarily specialist groups, totaling 750. This year, so far, 48 groups, mostly specialist types, 5,700 personnel, an increase of seven to eight times. Now the significant thing is that 5,500 out of the 5,700 will arrive after 15 July. 4,100 are still en route. So these decisions were made well after the cross-border operations, and a lot of them after the cross-border operations had terminated."

ABRAMS: "You go back to the infiltration charts, and there isn't any in October, November, December for COSVN, right?"

POTTS: "Yes, sir." "The last significant arrival was July—4,900. And since then only 400 people, total."

ABRAMS: "Well, they're not in that good a shape. See, on balance, they're doing the southern Laos thing."

Long pause.

POTTS: "Shortage of personnel and supplies we'll hit real hard in our in-country this morning. We'll show you."

ABRAMS: "But you know, Bill [Potts], if there was _ever_ a time, if there was _ever_ a time to _really_ move out—pacification, territorials, police, government, of course three months out of 25 years isn't much, but it's—there's a—in MR-3 and 4 there's a _three months'_ free _ride_, and it could even be longer. I mean, it's _really_—it's one of the best opportunities _we've_ been able to see."

ABRAMS: "I'll tell you, though, flying back from Bangkok the other day, the weather was clear, and that's really just one great _lake_. _God_, there's water! Well, it isn't even _that_ bad in the _delta_." "Phnom Penh is kind of a _tiny_ island in the Tonle Sap." "It's the only time I've _seen_ Phnom Penh, and, gee whiz, it's really pretty _small_. I was kind of surprised, at least looking at Saigon."

ABRAMS: "You see, the cosmetics of the thing—you've got the press reporting a raging battle, preparations for the assault on Phnom Penh. Christ, even these young chaps, they've got to get it into sort of a World War II context. Otherwise, you can't report it. And that's _not_ what's going on over there. It just _isn't_." "The only way they can explain it. Christ, talk about the _traditionalists_. They're not among _us_, it's these young chaps _reporting_. And this movie on Patton, you see—it comes at the wrong time. It just _reinforces_ all that. You've got a war on, that's about the only way you can run it [supposedly]. OK."

ABRAMS (re trying to correlate assessments of truck kills with reports in documents captured from the 559th Transportation Group): "There's a _few_ people scattered around the world that don't think the interdiction program's worthwhile—expensive and so on. Anything we can do there, being _factual_—. I mean, we're got to be _honest_ and so on."

ABRAMS: "Any time you get in that situation where you feel that resources are somewhat limited, that's the time you've got to _reject_ any idea of doing a little bit for everybody. That's the time you've got to do it, and focus on what is _critical_ and put the money there. It's just a time when you don't _cover_ all bets, and you make some hard choices and _stick_ by them. Put the blue chips out there, by god, and—put them on 23 and _spin_ _the_ _wheel_. We're a little better off than that. We _know_ more than that." "And it means that some fellows are going to be disappointed. Well, I think some are going to have to be."

BRIEFER (re debriefing of Nguyen Luong Nhan, VCI rallier of 29 June 1970 from VC Soc Trang Province): He was formerly deputy chief of the administrative staff office of the provincial current affairs committee. He says there has been attrition since January 1968 of 1,500 party members in the province, and that they have only been able to recruit some 100 in the last two years. He stated that tax collections were cut in half from 1967 to 1969 due to "increasing GVN control of the population and the embezzlement of party funds by VC cadre."

BRIEFER (re key COSVN documents): "COSVN Resolution 14 deals generally with the importance to the VC of intensifying guerrilla warfare." "It argues that guerrilla warfare is the only practical means of coping with an enemy who is stronger both in available forces and war matériel." Also "states that a strong guerrilla force is a necessary condition for success in larger-scale main force operations." It is also required "in order to be able to defeat the GVN pacification program." Also per 20 September 1969 pamphlet: "VC headquarters had recently called for the dispersion of all troop units into small elements." Resolution 14 was issued six weeks after the pamphlet, on about 1 November 1969.

26 SEP 1970: Special Brief for Mr. Shultz

ATTENDEES: Gen. Abrams, Mr. Shultz, Amb. Bunker, Amb. Colby, Mr. Erlichmann, Mr. Cooper, Gen. Weyand, Mr. [Humman?], Mr. [Lawfer?], BG Potts, MG Dolvin, MG Maples, MG Cowles, Mr. Jacobson, MG Dettre, MG Doehler, BG Greene, BG Camp, BG Vande Hey, Mr. Mills, BG Heiser, Col. Jones.

Possibly the visitor is Secretary of Labor George Shultz.

SCHULTZ: "I thought these people [the enemy] didn't have any administration."

ABRAMS: <u>O-o-o-h</u>, no. <u>O-o-o-h</u>, dear."

SHULTZ: "Low overhead—like Robert Hall [a well-known discount clothier of the day]."

ABRAMS: "Oh, no. This is a very sophisticated organizational setup." Intelligence, logistics, personnel, medical. "The myth that this is a bunch of fellows running around in black pajamas and that's about all you've got to deal with just ain't so." "His total administrative and logistical support strength is about the same as ours."

ABRAMS: "<u>Everything</u> they shoot, and transportation, all that sort of thing—that all comes from the Soviet Union or China. And they have to <u>have</u> that. They have no capability to support <u>themselves</u> in carrying on the war. A lot of their <u>food</u> is imported. We've captured rice down in Military Region 1 that came from China."

Shultz had asked if the enemy was self-sufficient.

COLBY: The strategic hamlet program "collapsed in the political collapse of the Diem regime." "In late 1964 . . . the first ethnic North Vietnamese units—battalions, regiments, and so forth—began to come down the Trail to join the fight." "I think most of us feel that it would have ended about 1966, with a victory on the Communist side, if it had not been for the arrival of United States combat forces. Our forces met the attack at the third level, the military level of war. But during the ensuing years, couple of years, we began to learn about the need to conduct the war at the <u>other</u> level of effort. We developed a political structure and a constitution which was adopted in '67."

COLBY: "General Abrams led a committee, with the Vietnamese, in '67 to refurbish and strengthen the <u>Territorial</u> Forces—not just the regular army, but the local forces."

COLBY: "Well, the enemy took a reassessment of the situation in '67 and then girded himself up for the big attacks, big offensives, of '68. He was probably grossly misled as to the situation, because he <u>did</u> expect the people to rise and support him. The fact is that they <u>didn't</u>. The fact is that the government <u>held</u>. And the <u>big</u> thing that happened was that this stimulated the government into an acceleration of this process of learning how to fight this 'people's war.'" "At that point, as General Abrams said, they picked up the initiative, and picked it up by beginning an offensive at the other levels of the people's war. Instead of just fighting on the military level, they developed the other."

COLBY: "Territorial security starts it. You cannot conduct any kind of a program in the face of a North Vietnamese division." Also need local forces that are there all the time and protect against the guerrillas. Now the RF/PF have over 500,000 men all armed with M16s and specially trained.

COLBY: The PSDF was begun in 1968. 450,000 weapons out for distribution. "1,200,000 people engaged in the combat element <u>are</u> contributing very much to the security of their local communities."

COLBY: "The war used to be about North Vietnamese divisions. Now it's about terrorists, and it's about economics. And it's about politics. That's where the fight is."

27 SEP 1970: Commanders WIEU

ATTENDEES: Gen. Abrams, Amb. Colby, Gen. Clay, Mr. Kirk, LTG Collins, Gen. Weyand, LTG Davison, LTG McCaffrey, LTG Sutherland, LTG McCutcheon, VADM King, LTG Dolvin, MG McCown, MG Cowles, Mr. Jacobson, [MG?] Buckner, Mr. Whitehouse, Mr. Funkhouser, BG Long, BG Wilson, BG Dean, BG Camp, BG Vande Hey, BG Greene, BG Potts, BG Henderson, BG Sykes, BG Cheadle, BG Henion, BG Heiser, Col. Doyle, Col. Jones, Capt. Burke, Col. Sadler, Col. Franklin, Col. Leonard, Col. Jones, Col. Healy.

BRIEFER: "On 5 October 1969 Hue/Phu Bai recorded 21.65 inches of rain in a 24-hour period. Wound up with 75.06 inches of rain for the month. And it didn't rain on 14 days of the month." [Laughter]

ABRAMS: "I think that's [the enemy's moving guerrillas up to bring local and main force units to full strength] an unfortunate choice from his viewpoint. That's one of the faults they critiqued on Tet in '68—put a lot of guerrillas in there and lost them. And this thing, this kind of a thing, depends on the guerrillas. You've got to have them. You can't get along without them."

ABRAMS: "Incidentally, I got a message the last thing yesterday . . . from the Chairman authorizing me to go and talk to Vien . . . about the thing that we talked about in that commanders meeting a week or so ago." "Also this message said that Ambassador Bunker—they'd give him authority to go and talk to the president. And that'll happen in the next couple of days."

Redeployment, apparently.

SOMEONE (anticipating working on whatever it is, and eager to get going on it): "I just get nervous."

ABRAMS: "On that subject, that is not difficult to do over here."

ABRAMS (re good news not getting on television): "It's like that reporter out in Jim Anderson's battalion. He grabs this Speedy Four [specialist four] with a peace medal on him, over in Cambodia, and wants to know, 'What do you think about the United States inv—,' tape recorder going, camera—'invading Cambodia?' And he says, 'Shit, it should have been done two years ago!' [Laughter] Then he says, 'Well, how can you say things like that and there you are wearing a peace medal?' And this guy says, 'I'm for peace, but you've got to fight for it!' [Laughter] Well, there went that." Not broadcast.

DAVISON: "I was talking to this NBC news guy who's just gotten over here, his first assignment. I said, 'What was the biggest surprise you've found since you've been here?' He'd only been here about four weeks. He said, 'General, all those beads and peace symbols those soldiers are wearing don't mean a damn thing!'"

BRIEFER: "The herbicide program has been drastically curtailed during the past year." Budgetary cutbacks and "a suspension on the use of Herbicide Orange. Orange had been the most commonly used agent in Vietnam, and comprised over 90 percent of in-country stocks." Also cites "the MACV policy terminating fixed-wing defoliation and directing the effort toward destruction of enemy-grown crops." "Ground and helicopter defoliation continues, primarily to clear foliage around the perimeters of bases and installations." Crop destruction is "an integral part of the resource denial program."

Where Do We Let Peace Come to Vietnam?

SEVENTH AIR FORCE BRIEFER (Captain Horton): Address the question, "where do we let peace come to Vietnam?" As relates to the utilization of air power. Looked at conditions under which the application of air power produces undesirable consequences, and where that application may be unproductive. Investigated the effects of air strikes on pacification under various conditions. Describes a causal model for analysis, including enemy presence and activity, perceptions (of the people) of enemy and friendly activity (air, artillery, and ground). "We envision the final product of our study to be rules of engagement that are tied to the Hamlet Evaluation System pacification security scores." Study to be done.

CLAY: "General Abrams, this is an attempt we've tried to make when you had suggested that we take a look at how we could bring peace to Vietnam."

DAVISON: "After the last Commanders WIEU we took a look at our tac air strikes. And I recognize what I'm saying is peculiar to the situation in MR-3. We've been running, following Cambodia, 25 to 35 pre-planneds a day, and maybe, depending on the situation, 10, 15, 20 immediates a day. And then we looked at the sort of targets they were—the pre-planneds were going against, whether they were confirmed targets or suspected targets. And then we took a look at the—what the FAC's BDA was, whether he thought it was a good strike or a fair strike or a poor strike. And then we just sort of came to some gross conclusions that we had too many pre-planned strikes. And, after looking over the results . . . and looking at what the situation was, we came to the conclusion we could cut the pre-planneds down to 12 a day, which is the level we're at now. We've been running about 12 a day, and maybe 10, 13, immediates. However, and I think this is one of the real problems in this business of the application of air strikes within Vietnam, in MR-3 the VNAF is running, oh, hell, 60–65 pre-planneds a day, which is an awful lot, given the level of activity. Now some of those do go into Cambodia, into the Parrot's Beak and so on. But, given the level of activity, that's an awful lot of strikes, an awful lot of bombs."

ABRAMS: "I think you ought to start interesting them in it, too."

DAVISON: Working on it.

ABRAMS: "I think it's a worthwhile thing to go ahead and grapple with this, see what happens."

■ ■ ■

BRIEFER: "Our intelligence indicators lead us to expect an all-out enemy logistics effort in Laos." "During the height of the 1968–1969 dry season the enemy had 1,600 trucks in his logistics system in Steel Tiger. At the peak of the last dry season he had 2,400 trucks." Expect he will use more trucks this year.

BRIEFER: In 1966: 750 kilometers of roads in the route network. In 1970: 3,700 kilometers. More work continues.

BRIEFER: Problem is how to counter a stronger enemy effort with a reduced force. Considered three alternatives of sortie allocation. Preferred alternative gives the biggest increase to AAA suppression. "Most sorties will be applied to trucks, a category we plan to attack whenever and wherever found." Plan 9,800 fighter sorties (70 percent of the sortie authorization) for that purpose. "We recognize that fewer U.S. sorties will be available on a regular basis in South Vietnam." So recommend.

ABRAMS: "Comments?" There are none.

ABRAMS: "One day I talked with Spike Momyer. I said, 'These B-52s—we've always got an hour and a half or two hours between strikes. I've been wondering what in the hell that fellow's doing. He now <u>knows</u> that, and what's he <u>doing</u>? And is there any way you could cut that out and just kind of line them all up and, you know, have them come one right after another, just keep it <u>up</u>?' Well, he came back a while later and they'd worked out a thing with SAC and had this <u>compression</u> thing. At that time you could do 48—I think we worked out you could do 48 in the morning and 48 at night, and then the next day—you see, 60 was the sortie rate. Then the next day you got, because of the recycling problem, the maintenance, all that sort of thing, you dropped down to 36. But you could do it once in the morning and once at night, and compress it in about an hour and thirty, forty minutes."

ABRAMS: "Well, we had problems down in III Corps and up in the highlands. They were giving us <u>hell</u> up there in the DMZ. They knocked out a hell of a lot of fuel out of Cua Viet. We lost a big ammunition dump, 10,000 tons or so up in Dong Ha. And all this is artillery and rockets out of the goddamn DMZ. They really were giving us a <u>fit</u>. But we had so many problems down here we just had to kind of <u>take</u> it. But in the meantime all the photography and the intelligence and so on—we finally got set for the first of July 1968. And about seven o'clock in the morning the B-52s came in up there in the DMZ. In an hour and forty minutes 48 of them—[thumps table], like that. And then the artillery, the tac air, the naval gunfire . . . they took up and had a great time all day. And then, about 1600 in the afternoon, here came 48 more and did it. We did that for seven days. It costs you sorties—you lose them. It's <u>expensive</u>. We did it for seven days. I want to tell you, it was 45 days before there was ever a fucking <u>round</u> fired out of the DMZ! [Laughter] <u>Forty-five days</u>! And Xuan Thuy told Ambassador Harriman, he said, 'This bombing is <u>insane</u>!' Best BDA we ever had! [Laughter] I'll tell you—heh, heh—they got in <u>among</u> them!" "And it's kind of what happened up at Khe Sanh in the end. The amount of <u>power</u> that was thrown in <u>there</u> . . . well, you know, it was pretty <u>tremendous</u>. Hell, it made that thing over there in Normandy, when they came in with the

Flying Forts, the St. Lo breakout—oh, Christ, that was sort of an <u>experimental</u> thing."

ABRAMS: "There are times when it's really better to zero in with everything you've got. I don't know whether this is one of those. I <u>really</u> don't know. As a matter of fact, I'm not <u>advocating</u> it. I'm just raising the <u>question</u>." "Instead of running it all the way down to Attopeu and all that, and up to Mu Gia and so on, just settle for so many square kilometers over there, and anybody that wants to go through that is going to have a hell of a time, no matter <u>when</u> he wants to go. Put his bulldozers in there, they just get ground up. Put his trucks in there—. And make it into a thing where a <u>crow</u> flying over it has got to carry his own rations." [Laughter]

WEYAND: "You know, considering the results of the Cambodian operation and the way he's been having to operate for the last two, three months, I think when you're looking for decisive impact on the enemy we're probably, if we only knew it—he's in greater jeopardy today than he's ever been."

ABRAMS: "That's <u>right</u>. If we could <u>really</u> knock this thing in the <u>head</u> . . . I think he would have some <u>real</u> troubles. He's <u>got</u> to <u>have</u> it! And we <u>know</u> he's got to have it! This—you know, in this kind of business this really <u>simplifies</u> the <u>problem</u>. We <u>know</u> what he <u>has</u> to have! He can't get along without it. He's <u>got</u> to do it! Whether it's even good judgment or not, he's <u>got</u> to do it. You know, you don't <u>get</u> one of these chaps in that shape too often. He's got no <u>alterna-tive</u>."

ABRAMS (to Clay): "Mull that thing over and let me know how you feel about it."

CLAY: "We can certainly always mass at any given time."

ABRAMS: "Yeah, but I'm talking about <u>60</u> <u>days</u>. Sixty days, goddamn it! [Whis-pering] Twenty-four hours a day! Just raining [thumps table], and every damn thing. I mean—one of the things you <u>shouldn't</u> do with this kind of stuff is piddle around with it." "Now I'll have to qualify that. I'm also in favor of using the scalpel. But if you want to turn it on, <u>then</u> [shouting] <u>you</u> <u>should</u> <u>turn</u> <u>it</u> <u>on</u>! I mean so that every son of a bitch in the whole business <u>knows</u> it! If you could get Xuan Thuy in there talking to Bruce about the '<u>insanity</u>' again, we'd be in good shape. A <u>week's</u> no good! A <u>month's</u> no good! Because you know how he is—he's a <u>dogged</u>, <u>resourceful</u> [pounding], <u>determined</u> [pound]—that's what you're up against! Hell, he'll get people killed and stuff torn up and that sort of thing—he'll just <u>keep</u> at it! Like a <u>bulldog</u>! But give him 60 days of it and then let's see how he—. I don't know. Don't be misled by apparent enthusiasm on my part. It's still got to be a cold-blooded evaluation. [Laughter] No, I <u>accept</u> that, I accept it."

ABRAMS: "Yeah, they've cut us back. 12–14,000 sorties a month, it's a big <u>reduction</u>. <u>But</u>—that's a hell of a lot of—it's a <u>lot</u> of <u>stuff</u>, as long as you don't spread it all over kingdom come, where, Christ, nobody—only get bombed once a week, or once every 10 days. Ought to be there at every <u>meal</u>, [laughter] every <u>meeting</u>, every <u>conference</u>."

COLBY: The GVN is thinking of simplifying objectives under "self-defense, self-government, and self-development." Also a possible name change to substitute some other term for "pacification" in the security element of the 1971 plan.

COLLINS: "I sense a growing hostility in the attitude of the people, of the Vietnamese, with respect to our troops in certain occasions. Now, as far as I'm concerned, sir, this is what I would call a justifiable hostility, because you take the accidents that we have, the number of heavy vehicles we had on the road, and when we get in an accident it's a _bad_ one. And also we have these cute tricks that some of our soldiers dream up. _Very_ small number, but—oh, they're going along and they'll try to grab someone's hat—they're on a motorbike—and. . . ."

COLLINS (on a new but related point): "It's the type of thing that, anytime we start pulling out of a country, we always run into this. I think we can _expect_ increased hostility, because there's _bound_ to be some feeling, 'Yeah, they were with us, but now they're going to _leave_ us.'"

COLLINS: "We've got something going for us in General Dzu. He's been up there a month now, and I don't think you could ask more of a man. I can say I've never seen before a Vietnamese that works harder than Americans. He works a lot harder than _I_ do. I've never _seen_ anyone work like this man. He starts early in the morning and he's going till late at night. He's already visited _all_ of the provinces, he's visited _all_ of the regiments, he's visited _all_ of the border camps. He's now starting a round of all of the districts. He says the district chief, that's where the war is going to be won. I've found him to be very perceptive. . . . He's decisive." After two days he moved his pacification people to Nha Trang from Pleiku to co-locate with my people, and the _next morning_ they went. "I've just been tremendously impressed with the man."

ABRAMS (re Resolutions 9, 14, etc.): "I think it's gotten to the point where you can say with some confidence what he's _up_ to. He hasn't got the capability to do some of the things that he did in '68, or '67, and even in the beginning of '69. He hasn't _got_ it, and so he's redesigned his effort and so on. And I think we've got to pay _attention_ to that. And the Vietnamese. . . . So what state are we _at_? I think we're somewhere around '64. It may be—I don't know—it may be you go back a little further, I won't argue about that. It's _somewhere_ back in there where he—probably a little earlier—where his effort now is on his guerrillas, his cadre, and his local force. Now, he's _got_ to have that. It's the administrative machinery, it's the intelligence machinery, it's the political machinery. And he's got to have that or he can't run this _show_. It's more important than _any_ of these divisions, _any_ of these regiments. He has to _have_ it. And _some_ of it has gotten into a little _trouble_. It's not as effective and so on. And so the _thrust_ of all this—if he's going to bring the 9th Division back here, he's got to have _them_. He can't _do_ it without them."

ABRAMS (speculating on how enemy assassinations affect the outlook of the populace on the GVN): "This damn assassination and terrorism and . . . abduction and so on—this problem here, it's giving it _fits_. Well, _body_ _count_—that's no good in this. But that's the thing they're _after_ now, and it's psychological impact and it's an emotional impact on the people. And I think that somehow this is _most_ of what he is now capable of _doing_."

ABRAMS: "In January '69 some of these loyal Vietnamese citizens down here in Saigon began writing me about generators making too much noise or black smoke coming out of the diesel generators and all that. It was <u>great</u>! Before that, of course, they were yelling about the <u>rockets</u>."

ABRAMS: "There's a lot of conflicting <u>stuff</u>, and always has been, about the Vietnamese over in Cambodia. And it depends on what office is putting it out on what day back there in Washington. First they want them doing <u>less</u>. And then they don't want them doing <u>anything</u>. And then they're causing <u>trouble</u>. Then they've got some idea of mounting a <u>division</u> operation. So we've had a little trouble—it hasn't always been too clear or consistent. <u>However</u>, however, I <u>do</u> believe that in all of these things that this <u>country</u>—we have to have the kind of a—yeah, I know, we don't want the government over there to fall, but while we're all rampaging around over in Cambodia we don't—turn around and say, 'My god, they've got <u>Saigon</u>!'" [Laughter]

ABRAMS (re the terrorism): "It's now come time where that's not good. It's a <u>bad</u> thing to have happen. Again, '68—when they're hammering at the gates and so on, well <u>that's</u> the problem. But—I think you said one time, Bill [Colby], this thing—the whole thing is kind of in layers. You peel back one layer and, you know, you feel pretty good and so on, but my god, you look under <u>there</u> and here's a whole lot of other things now that, well, you weren't too concerned about because of the <u>original</u> layer and its problems."

ABRAMS: "Now, I think—it looks like to me—there's some <u>time</u>, maybe even quite a bit of time, before they can change what they're now doing, certainly in MR-3 and MR-4. There're several <u>months</u>—. I don't know how many, I'm not going to speculate. But the logistics has got to get going, the personnel and all that, before they can make a basic <u>shift</u> in what they're trying to do. And <u>maybe</u>, maybe, they don't even intend to <u>do</u> that—make a basic shift. They'll play this string <u>out</u> just the way they're <u>going</u> at it. And we'll sit around here and—you know, we've all been watching the HES chart, and <u>I</u> like it and <u>I</u> know it's a good system and it helps us have a little handle on everything, but that 92 percent—I don't <u>believe</u> that. Because <u>in</u> that 92 percent there are guys out there—every week <u>somebody's</u> getting <u>shot</u>. It works on the village. Yeah, maybe it comes up blue, but—."

ABRAMS (re villages with a VC platoon in the vicinity): "I'll tell you, come election time—you know, say Madame Binh was running for president and President Thieu was running for president, well—where that VC platoon is that village is going for Madame <u>Binh</u>!"

ABRAMS (summing up): "It's <u>really</u> a case of sensitive, intelligent understanding of what's important in the particular area that you're working in or talking in—all <u>different</u>. And the Vietnamese you have to work with, <u>they're</u> different. Even the <u>good</u> ones are different. The <u>good</u> ones don't do things the same. And the <u>enemy's</u> different. Some of these guys are <u>smarter</u> than others. They've got some really first-class chaps that are just smarter than <u>hell</u>. And other places they're kind of ham-handed. So, as we go down the road here, I think <u>all</u> of us need to keep thinking and keep trying to see for ourselves what's important, what's critical, where <u>are</u> we in the thing? And, I don't want to roll out the champagne here, but you know, if we could be <u>fairly</u> successful on this dry season thing, and if we could really get this VCI and the guerrillas mobile forces tamped down to a <u>relative</u>—they're <u>always</u> going to be here, some number, but get them down to where they really aren't effective, where by god they wouldn't have a <u>chance</u> in an election, <u>then</u> we—if all <u>that</u> happens, we'd say, 'Christ, we can all go home and give lectures on how you fight the people's war, write books, theorize about it.' It would be a wonderful thing. But, anyway, there's a lot of <u>hard</u> and <u>sensitive</u> kind of <u>thinking</u> and <u>work</u> that needs to be done."

ABRAMS: "And your best guys are the ones that <u>are</u> sensitive. Like that Sergeant Greenschmidt—just solid gold. Heh—knew nothing about Vietnamese, or no language training, but he just understands people, and he thinks people are great, and it doesn't make any difference whether they're big or small or bow-legged or yellow or black or white or any of that stuff. He just thinks people are great. <u>And</u> he thinks they're all <u>equal</u>. So he gets out there muckering around with the Vietnamese and they think <u>he's</u> great. They told me the other day he's extended and went home on 30 days' leave and he's going to rejoin that district team up there, same district. Yeah. He's done that <u>himself</u>. And, hell, nobody's offered him more <u>pay</u>, more promotions, and so on. That's the thing they don't <u>understand</u>. His greatest reward is his satisfaction. You can't <u>touch</u> it. Jake doesn't believe that. [Laughter] Well, it's been a good meeting."

28 SEP 1970: SEACORDS Briefing

Attendees include the American ambassadors to the various countries in the region.

BUNKER: "A good deal's happened since our last meeting in February." "The developments in Cambodia obviously have added a new dimension to the whole Indochina conflict. They have presented us, and the enemy, too, with an entirely new situation—new problems and, I think, also new opportunities. What happens in Laos and Cambodia obviously will have very far-reaching implications for our objectives in Vietnam, and for all of this area."

SHACKLEY (on North Vietnamese intentions, per Bunker): "Hanoi-watching is no more of a precise science than is China-watching." But: "An understanding of Hanoi's intentions can be developed in an intelligence manner from NVA/VC prisoner interrogations, captured documents, [***], photography, reporting from friendly missions in Hanoi, access to North Vietnamese domestic radio broadcasts, an analysis of Hanoi's press, and the product of clandestine agent operations."

SHACKLEY: "The North Vietnamese economy is <u>not</u> on the verge of collapse as British Hanoi-watcher Professor P. J. Honey suggests. . . ." Support to North Vietnam from the USSR and the PRC is estimated at $1 billion during FY 1970. "Our best estimate suggests that, without outside assistance by countries like Japan, none of Hanoi's key industries can begin operating at capacity in less than 5, or even 10, years."

SHACKLEY: "Party control over the populace is far less effective than Hanoi would like." "Moreover, the full human costs of the war are becoming increasingly apparent to the population at home."

SHACKLEY: "One million men are draft age in North Vietnam, but only half of these are serving in the army and probably no more than 300,000 are assigned to duty outside North Vietnam. Hence there are enough men on call in North Vietnam to facilitate a considerable step-up in current levels of infiltration to the south if this were required in the pursuit of Hanoi's national policy goals."

SHACKLEY: "The available intelligence indicates that Hanoi will continue to view the Paris peace talks as primarily a way of manipulating public opinion in the United States and elsewhere."

SHACKLEY: Laos "is where Hanoi will probably be most actively engaged over the next six months." "With the loss of Sihanoukville, Laos is now the terrain through which all logistics must flow to feed Hanoi's military apparatus in both South Vietnam and Cambodia."

SHACKLEY: "The attrition rate among North Vietnamese Army personnel infiltrating through Laos is, from all causes, probably at least 15 percent. The loss of supplies is also substantial, although there is no way of determining the price values or quantities involved."

10 OCT 1970: WIEU

ATTENDEES: Gen. Abrams, Amb. Colby, Gen. Clay, LTG Weyand, LTG McCaffrey, Mr. Kirk, VADM King, MG Dolvin, MG Maples, MG Dettre, BG Camp, BG Greene, BG Potts, BG Henderson (for Mr. Jacobson), BG Sykes, BG Cheadle, BG Henion, BG Heiser (for MG Cowles), BG Doehler, Col. Sadler, Col. Leonard, Col. Jones.

ABRAMS: "Yesterday was—I found it sort of a disgusting sort of a day, anyway. These messages aren't too bad if you can take them in daily doses. You know, you're calloused a certain amount. But, by god, when you read a collection of three or four or five days of that crap it gets to you. By four o'clock in the afternoon I've gotten pretty damn mad. [Laughter] So, in the midst of all that yesterday, Bill Potts sends up that article. 'Reliable sources at the Embassy.' And they've got the whole damn thing spelled out, three days in advance, on the MPC conversion—chapter and verse. [Someone: "There's only two people down there that know about it—other than the truck drivers and people like that."] [Laughter] Well, I suppose it's really all right. It's just—they let some of their friends know so that they won't get caught—you know, lose a lot of money. So I guess that's probably all right. Gee whiz!"

WEYAND: "I've only been here a short time, but the more I see of General Vien and that JGS, just compared to what it was when I left here two years ago, it's pretty damn good. It really is."

ABRAMS: "One of the—Christ, one of the real <u>secrets</u> out here is that they've got, actually, a damn good military set-up. It's <u>functioning</u>, it knows what the hell it's doing, it's gotten so logistics gets ground into the thing and all that, and hell—they can handle airplanes and helicopters and ships and all the rest of it. It's a pretty <u>damn</u> good outfit. And compared to these other characters out here, it's <u>really</u> first class. You've got this absurd situation here now where the Cambodians and the Vietnamese are trying like hell to beat up on the enemy over there in Cambodia while the goddamn Thais are over there checking photographs and ID cards." [Laughter]

12 OCT 1970: General Vien Briefing

Gen. Cao Van Vien is Chief of the South Vietnamese Joint General Staff.

BRIEFER: "Infiltration has been declining since 1968, and so far in 1970 the monthly average has been only about 60 percent of the 1969 rate."

ABRAMS: "The B-52s are going about 85 percent into the Laos interdiction program." "We're <u>trying</u> to make the most powerful effort that we can possibly make." "Because we feel that although Laos has always been very important to him, that <u>this</u> year—<u>this</u> year he doesn't have <u>any</u> other choice. He's <u>got</u> to make that work." "Now, you know, we don't often <u>have</u> him like that." "<u>We</u> think it's different this year. He's <u>got</u> to make that work. And if he <u>doesn't</u>, he's going to be in <u>trouble</u> next year." "So he's just got to do it, and that's <u>where</u> he's got to do it. He can't <u>go</u> anywhere else." "So we think we should get in there <u>with</u> him." "But of course he's very resourceful—."

BRIEFER: "In Binh Dinh Province during the spring of 1970 the 22nd NVA Regiment was broken down, with its eight battalions subordinated to local provincial units, who continue to conduct assassinations, abductions, and other terrorist activities focused upon the Binh Dinh pacification effort."

ABRAMS: "That's kind of the way this <u>war</u> is. It really <u>isn't</u> a war. It's just not like—you say 'war,' and everybody has some—they saw a movie somewhere, something about war, so they've got kind of a picture of what war is. Well, that's not what this is. It's a <u>different</u> kind of <u>thing</u>."

ABRAMS (re Tet 1968): "A couple of things went <u>wrong</u>. It didn't do what it was <u>supposed</u> to do. They didn't have it—they didn't <u>calculate</u> that quite right. The people didn't rise up like they thought they were going to, and they kind of made a mistake then, too, about this guerrilla thing."

ABRAMS: "You've got all this talk about cease-fire. Nobody knows what's going to come of all that. But, as I started out saying, calling it a war—well, you've got to be careful about calling it a war, because that'll mislead you into thinking that it is, and—you know—that it ought to <u>look</u> like a war. Well, it <u>doesn't</u> look like a war. You've got <u>these</u> kind of things happening [student and veterans uprisings manipulated by the enemy]. And the <u>important</u> thing is that <u>that's</u> what's got to be <u>beat</u>. I mean, one year it's chasing them away from Saigon, and trying to stop the rockets and so on, and next year you're out there and you've got to lick these guys at their game of trying to organize the peasants, or infiltrating the PSDF, or infiltrating the territorials. You know, that's the way—that's the game, that year."

ABRAMS: "Well, a lot of things you've got here—the B-52s are no good for that, you know. And then tanks—they're no good for that, either. And so on. So you've got a lot of stuff that's sort of peripheral for this kind of thing. It just takes other techniques, and it takes understanding, and all that."

ABRAMS: "But, I don't know, General Vien. I've gotten where I kind of feel pretty good about it. Simply because, you kind of stand around here and watch what's happened over the years, and the South Vietnamese have always wound up figuring these damn things out."

ABRAMS: "You know, General Vien, when President Thieu decided to have the PSDF—you know, in the beginning—just about everybody, just about every province chief and nearly every division commander, they worried about that. Giving weapons out like this to all the people and so on and so on. There was always that apprehension, there was always the concern, that you'd do that and then one day these people would just turn around on it and they'd turn against you." "You remember in the beginning. I don't believe there was a province chief in the whole country who really believed that this was a good thing to do. You know—sincerely, personally believed. But then it got going. You know, it kind of got rolling, and everybody got behind it."

ABRAMS: When they get the hamlet and village chiefs in training down at Vung Tau, President Thieu goes down to address the group. "And he can talk to them, because his father was a village chief for a long time."

ABRAMS: "It doesn't get any easier. It just gets kind of different. And here's all this—us poor soldiers. You know, we've been to Leavenworth or something, and had all those lessons and books. And I don't ever remember anybody talking about this kind of stuff you and I are talking about today. [Vien laughs appreciatively.] They didn't have any lectures on that—anything! And they don't have any FMs [field manuals] about that. And here we are, we're all mixed up in it, supposed to be helping." "I don't think any of us could graduate now. They'd probably have to expose us—too dumb. Can't understand it."

ABRAMS: "We've been talking around here a lot about how this looks. I think we're getting closer all the time. This has been helpful here today, helps us to understand it a little better."

18 OCT 1970: Special Brief for Mr. Helms

Richard Helms was director of Central Intelligence.

WEYAND: "I know General Abrams is tremendously heartened by the appointment of Truong and Dzu to those two positions [as corps commanders], and the way he looks at it is that, for the first time since he's been here, there are four corps commanders who are all professionally fully qualified, clean—certainly by their standards if not by ours—natural leaders, and fully aware . . . of the problems before them and of the relative priorities of things. Lam is a known quantity, of course. Dzu is known from the days when—I knew him when he was in JGS as an extremely competent young officer." "He's a very ambitious young officer, and I give him a lot of credit. It's not just an ambition that's reflected in brownnosing and that sort of thing. He got in and really produced results down there with John Vann and General McCown. [They] thought [he] had pushed IV Corps ahead in the time that he was there further than any other time, at a faster rate, than [meaning "since"?] they'd been there. And for a man to come in that's new and do that, I think gave <u>some</u> measure of his ability."

WEYAND: "So far, up in the 2nd Military Region, it's sort of been like Cassius Clay at his best. Every move he's made has been applauded by everybody, and you begin to wonder. <u>Something</u> must be wrong." The day after he got there he moved his deputy for pacification to Nha Trang, where he'd be co-located with his U.S. counterpart. "He went to see the ROK commander, who's been a great problem to us simply because of their complete immobility." "And they <u>really</u> are not providing the kind of security to the populated areas, under the new thrust of the enemy, that they <u>should</u>." "Well, Dzu did a much better job than we've done of convincing the ROK commanders that the enemy <u>had</u> changed, so we had to change <u>with</u> him, and got some very specific commitments out of them for redeployment and so forth." "He has two weak regimental commanders in the 23rd Division." Dzu gave the division commander (who supported the two regimental commanders) 60 days for them to show positive results or they'd be relieved. "He <u>is</u> from Binh Dinh." Now "each commander is from his own military region."

WEYAND: "Truong . . . I don't have to say much about him, because he's another known quantity, having commanded that 1st Division—which was really, in terms of the troops available to him, he had to coordinate two-plus divisions." "He has demonstrated over a long period of time his outstanding leadership. He's absolutely incorruptible. Likewise, since he's gone down to IV Corps the priorities he's set for things to be done down there, his own dynamism—he's got both John Vann and McCown just so high on him it's hard to believe." "It looks like we've got an awful good situation."

WEYAND: "Tri is probably—if we've got a problem, it's him. He's a <u>hell</u> of a professional soldier, but he's not a team player. And we don't think he has the breadth to, say, take over Vien's job. Yet as a field commander he's really something, as he proved in the Cambodian thing." "I think [General Abrams] is, as I am, heartened by the fact that backing Tri up is this General Minh, a young lieutenant general that put together the defense of Saigon and is very much President Thieu's man." "He's just a tremendously loyal officer. I think he'd be this way to whomever was president. And a tremendously effective officer."

■ ■ ■

POTTS (re infiltration): "<u>All</u> of 1971 so far is going into the COSVN area."
POTTS (on gap groups): "The methodology calls for, if we don't pick them up,

and they're within a series of five, a spread of five, we pick them up anyway eventually."

POTTS: "They talk of high points, but those high points have been just slight increases in activity. We are seeing some of our main force units, old historic main force units, being pushed down, dissolved, put into sapper teams, that type of activity."

■ ■ ■

CLAY: "I think probably the best way to describe my job at the moment is the one that General Abrams gave here the other day, which was that he wants that Ho Chi Minh Trail in such a shape that a crow has to carry his rations to fly over it."

CLAY: "About two years ago we were able to mount something on the order of 28,000 to 30,000 sorties a month across the spectrum of Southeast Asia. . . . But this year, when we go into the problem, I am sortie-constrained. Specifically, we're authorized, under the budget guidance that we have right now, to fly 14,000 sorties a month."

CLAY: "The interdiction problem itself has increased." "Over the past year we've seen a continual increase in the road network, the trails, the alternate route structure, and things of that nature, which give the enemy many, many more options in terms of moving his equipment and supplies down there. And we also see a continual increase . . . in the intensity of the AAA defenses in the area."

CLAY: "It's very clear, from General Abrams's instruction to us, [that] the priority must go against the LOC problem associated with the trails in Laos. And to that end he has directed, for planning purposes anyway, that we're going to put 70 percent of our air effort into the LOC campaign for the forthcoming dry season." About 9,800 tac air sorties. "Plus also his decision to utilize the B-52s almost exclusively, for the first time, in the Laos interdiction campaign." "Now we do this because, as General Potts has pointed out, in-country we're seeing an entirely different pattern of war. We're not seeing main force confrontations and things of that nature."

CLAY: "As we look to the future, we don't expect to see a great return in terms of trying to chase B-52s after crossroads. We think the dispersal pattern has been so good, and developed so highly, that it's going to be quite difficult to find a given target that's going to produce several hundred secondary explosions and trucks flying in the air and things of that nature. They're just not there. The dispersal factor has been accomplished beautifully, they move at night, they move at regular predetermined times, they move to one place, stay and hide, unload, pick up another truck and move on down, hiding in the canopy, so it's just an extremely difficult problem."

CLAY: "To overcome that we have picked for this coming dry season four areas that we're going to try to block." Target Boxes A, B, C, and D. Associated with the prime input areas in our projection. Mu Gia Pass area, Ban Karai Pass, and two associated with the Ban Raving [Pass] just west of the DMZ."

CLAY: Attacking the boxes, putting 27 B-52 sorties per day in there; plus 125–150 [tac air] sorties, day and night. Thus will have ordnance falling in those boxes every 20 minutes, 24 hours a day, for the next 60 days. "I have high hopes that this will . . . have a tremendous impact on the input capacity." Risk involved: "We're putting the B-52s right up in the SAM envelope."

CLAY: "With respect to the rest of the activities, we're going to place most of our faith on the introduction of the gunships. This year we have the B-57Gs coming in. It's an old airplane, but it's been updated significantly with the introduction of all kinds of sensor capability." Also have the Gunship II; the gunship surprise package last year was our most effective truck killer "primarily because of the ordnance." 40-mm cannon "that can really hammer trucks." Bringing 12 back this year, versus one last year. Statistics credit Gunship II with seven trucks destroyed per sortie. For the AC-130 gunship: 4. And for fighters (with 500-pound bombs): 0.

■ ■ ■

COLBY: "The base is the PSDF. . . . They are now forming what they call hard-core key teams. In other words, this guerrilla movement is going through the same process which guerrilla movements go through everywhere in the world. They start as a rabble in arms, and five years later they've got artillery."

COLBY: "Next level is the PF and RF." "The whole effort during '68 and '69 has given them better weapons and training and that sort of thing." "The PF was the real key to the expansion program. The way you did it is you recruited people, signed them up, put a little fort in. Then people began to assemble, people came back from the countryside, gathered around that little security, sort of like in the Middle Ages clustered around the castle kind of thing."

COLBY: "They've got to free ARVN, because out of your total force here of 500,000, roughly, PSDF weapons; 500,000 RF/PF; 500,000 ARVN; and 500,000 Americans, you're going to drop out the last one. You're going to cut your force by a quarter, and it's the strongest quarter and the quarter that's been contributing most. ARVN's got to be freed of everything else so it can replace that. That's your real gap."

COLBY: "The Phuong Hoang program . . . this highly sophisticated program is attriting the enemy. Now, not alone. This program isn't doing that alone. The whole program is doing that, the whole pressure against the enemy. But the infrastructure is having trouble. There's no question about it. Defectors say so and so forth. And they are coming under some pressure. Now, as you know, we change the rules on them all the time, so we make it harder and harder to get the brownie points—the goals and so forth. The first year it was all VCI. The second year we left out the C category. It was only A's and B's. This year we put in the rule that it wasn't 'captured,' it was 'sentenced,' in order to put some heat on the sentencing process and make it work properly. And we'll invent something else next year to make it more effective."

COLBY: "The campaign next year, he's [Thieu] changing the name, and I think it's a good thing to do. It started out as the pacification program, then became pacification and reconstruction, then became pacification and development. Next year it's going to be called community defense and local development, and eliminate the word 'pacification.'" "Three major goals: self-defense, self-government, and self-development."

COLBY (showing HES data): The bottom province is 74 percent secure. It used to be An Xuyen, which used to be about 35 percent secure a year and a half ago or so. "And that trend line I think is basically accurate."

COLBY: "This HES has been the foundation stone of most of the pacification planning around here. We all know it's not accurate by specifics, but every province and village chief knows what his ratings are. And he works on it in order to get them up. For that purpose, it's really done a good job."

COLBY: "I think there's no question about it, that in the earlier stages of this our staffs were doing a great deal of the work, and the Vietnamese were translating a large part of it. That's changed. The Vietnamese are picking up and doing a great deal of the work. And we are commenting, and putting ideas in. Some they take and some they don't. So it's becoming something in the governmental structure, and the boss of it [Thieu] really runs it very tightly."

■ ■ ■

WEYAND (re withdrawal of U.S. forces): "Abe would probably tell you that the flexibility is starting to be sucked out of this thing. So everything's sort of got to work." "He's losing now, at a steady rate, 15,000 troops a month." "And we cannot deviate from that. So we're starting to build up some problems which are purely budget-driven." To leave a brigade in the highlands for even an additional month "we'd have to go in for a supplemental." But: "These essential things are moving. If they weren't, we'd be in deep trouble."

24 OCT 1970: Commanders WIEU

MACV 1970 Infiltration Estimate: 53,400 (52 percent to COSVN).

MACV 1971 Infiltration Estimate: 4,200 (100 percent to COSVN).

BRIEFER: "COMUSMACV has directed that a comprehensive review be initiated by the J-3 interagency 303 Committee of the crop destruction program." "Pending completion of the review, and COMUS approval thereof, no herbicide operations will be processed by this headquarters."

BRIEFER: In Cambodia, three ARVN cross-border operations continue, with over 12,000 troops participating.

ABRAMS: "If it's true that the nature of the war and the character of the war is shifting, and it is getting on kind of a—. The COSVN 27, and the political-military-diplomatic and so on, then it seems to me that these things are more germane to what is happening [results of population attitudinal survey: outlook on government, the economy, security] than those other things we saw about

KIA and WIA and all that. Apologies to the J-3, but if it's true that the character and nature of things is changing, then these things . . . I assume that they're more of what we ought to be thinking and talking and doing something with."

■ ■ ■

ABRAMS (to General Watson): "I've been sitting down there for over two years at the Mission Council, practically every week, hearing explanations about this rice, and why it's being held, why it's being put, and so on. The thing I've become convinced of is there isn't a goddamn soul in this country that knows why rice does what it does." [Laughter]

JACOBSON: "Now, that's an analysis I'll buy!"

ABRAMS: "It never seems to do what it's supposed to" in the analysis. "Rice is kind of a big subject here. A lot of people use it." [Laughter]

■ ■ ■

ABRAMS: Re "some of the realities. We'll be down to 284,000 by the first of May [1971]. But all that is is what's been announced so far. And what happens after the first of May? I don't think there's any question that our government is on a course of continuing a withdrawal of American forces. If somebody—say you're sitting over there in President Thieu's chair—you've got to face that as something that's going to occur." "When are you going to start telling them they've got to start thinking about this?"

SOMEONE: "You ought to tell them right now."

ABRAMS: "Yeah. You tell them now and maybe in a year's time they'll be able to do something. But they've kind of got to get used to the idea. And . . . in the beginning it's obnoxious and impossible."

ABRAMS: "I was out there the day the Koreans had a review for General Rosson the day he left. And these Korean soldiers came marching down there—I guess they must have had 700–800 of them out there—they came marching down there past the reviewing stand. And I tell you that was just about the damnedest sight you ever saw. Heads up, walking like they owned the whole damned thing, arms swinging, and just moving on down there! In 1950, the Korean army, for all practical purposes, was destroyed—destroyed. Not so. That's just what the statistics said. And after a while they didn't believe it. And then after a while [laughing] they knew it was a myth."

ABRAMS: "I don't want to get euphoric about these things, and I don't know—I suppose there's a million problems left and so on—there's just a hell of a lot. But there's also been quite a bit done. There's been quite a bit done by the Vietnamese. And they—they've come along quite a ways."

■ ■ ■

BRIEFER (re LOC Program): "Since 1968 the U.S. has been working with the Vietnamese to restore a basic highway system for the country. The LOC Program has been a high priority part of our Vietnamization program." About

10,000 U.S. troops have been directly involved in construction of roads and bridges during the past year, plus 2,200 locally hired Vietnamese employees, about 4,000 civilian contractor employees, and about 4,000 ARVN engineer troops.

■ ■ ■

ABRAMS: "In September we put out a message to encourage the careful management of flying hours for helicopters so that we really are taking care of the essentials and so on. Now the response to that has really been quite gratifying. There's been a substantial reduction in flying hours." "See, the whole thing comes from the amount of money that's been allocated for support—by the army—for the support of these helicopters." "You've got to do the operations, essential operations, you know you <u>must</u> do. Be <u>really</u> severe on anything else. If <u>you</u> handle it, and <u>you</u> do it, you're going to do a lot better job of it than if we finally have to come out with a <u>directed</u> flying hour program in order to meet the funds that are available."

■ ■ ■

ABRAMS: "When President Johnson lost his strength as political leader and president, <u>it was really hell</u>. That's when you find out that you don't—. I mean, you can't get a <u>decision</u>, you can't get anything <u>processed</u>. And I tell you, out <u>here</u>, it was <u>really rough</u>! And it all has to do with how much strength, <u>political</u> strength, really, that the president of the United States has."

ABRAMS: "Well, <u>we're in that</u>—<u>all of us</u>! That's the league, that's the pool we're swimming around in, every last one of us! And so—I'll come here to some specifics. It's like this—we had a case here where some fellows went out and used this Orange herbicide. They knew that it had been suspended. And they knew that the instructions were that they weren't to use it. But they went ahead and used it <u>anyway</u>, because they—I don't know what they—I haven't talked with them. But they decided to use it, and they thought they needed to, and so on. And then some fellow in the press went up there."

ABRAMS: "And on that, <u>if</u> we're wrong, <u>if</u> we've made a mistake somewhere, done something, or something's happened that shouldn't have happened, as <u>quickly</u> as you can you've got to get the facts, and you've got to <u>say</u> that it was wrong. And the guys that did it wrong, they've got to know from you, or an appropriate person, that they <u>did</u> do wrong, and so on. I think forthrightness— I don't think there really is much <u>alternative</u> in <u>this</u> climate to forthrightness and candor and cleaning up the debris."

ABRAMS: "Along with this, I want to mention two other things, and that's drug abuse and racial confrontation. I want to encourage every commander everywhere in the command to look at this as hard and as realistically as he can. I don't want <u>anybody</u> taking these things for granted—about those two subjects. They've <u>got</u> to get in there. They've <u>got</u> to know their men. They've <u>got</u> to know what they're doing. They've <u>got</u> to know about the drugs and about the friction between people and that sort of thing. And they've <u>got</u> to work at it. I believe that we have these problems. Probably in some places they're quite severe. I can't put my finger on the spots and so on, but they—. Now we've got a—we've had a group working on this drug business. They're about to firm up this thing and so on. So we ought to wait a little while longer. But—well, we are having men die over here from drugs. And it appears that it's possible that it's increasing and so on. We're going to track all this out and get it out to everybody so they know about it."

ABRAMS: "So this whole collection of things I've been talking about here. . . . The fighting spirit and the forces in the field, all of them—the navy, the air, the marines, the army, and all of that—yeah. I'm just telling you that, in addition to that, these things are also critical to the outcome here in Vietnam. It's not a question of trying to spur the good old horse on that's been running so well over the years—in terms of the whole U.S. effort out here—but times are changing, and the character of things is changing, and we've got to be professional enough, and alert enough, and sensitive enough to see the significance and the importance of these things to the whole damn mission! It's asking for a little bit more, and so on. But we've got the horses to do this with. I know that. And we've just got to get at it."

ABRAMS: "I couldn't feel better about the commanders that we've got, and especially the ones that are here today, in terms of confidence and so on. I think it's great and so on. But we've all got to think about these things, and look at them."

31 OCT 1970: WIEU

ATTENDEES: Gen. Abrams, Amb. Colby, Gen. Clay, LTG Weyand, LTG McCaffrey, VADM King, MG Cowles, MG Maples, MG Dettre, BG Camp, BG Vande Hey, BG Potts, BG Watkins, BG Sykes, BG Cheadle, BG Henion, BG Heiser, BG Doehler, BG Forrester (for Mr. Jacobson), Col. Franklin (for Col. Sadler), Col. Leonard, Col. Jones (for BG Greene), Col. Phillips (for Mr. Kirk).

MACV 1970 Infiltration Estimate: 53,500.

MACV 1971 Infiltration Estimate: 7,700.

POTTS (re February 1971 projected infiltration): "The most important thing, sir, is that out of those COSVN groups coming in in February, we have 19 detected now, but there's 17 that are gaps. When we fill in the gap groups, and we're picking them up very quickly—we got six last week—when all of them come in, that comes up to 14,450 moving into the COSVN area in one month. This is an all-time high since back in 1968." "Averaging 299 men per group."

■ ■ ■

BRIEFER: There is evidence that the 320th NVA Division is deploying southward. Forward elements are 13 nautical miles southwest of Tchepone, Laos. The

88th Regiment (308th NVA Division) was located in the Vinh area on 20 October 1970.

BRIEFER: NVA forces in the Lao panhandle are reportedly experiencing high rates of disease, and have been instructed to clean up sanitation throughout the area to reduce the spread of disease.

ABRAMS: "I think that's been ongoing. We hear about that every year. I want to say this about it—your assessment's probably correct, they're having trouble with it and so on. But goddamn it—either they've got enough that are well or something. But they seem to be able to work on the roads, keep the trucks going, still fire the antiaircraft, still move the supplies, and unload it and load it, backpack it and all that. So I'd say they're right on schedule—you know, with the sickness they've had every year. I don't think it means that somehow they're going to screw it up." It may mean the commanders out there have quotas and are trying to get some slack.

BRIEFER: Rallier reports VC Sub-Region 1 directive to all units directing self-sufficiency during 1 October 1970–1 January 1971. "According to the source, the directive stated that because of considerable disruption caused by allied operations during recent months, effective 1 October Sub-Region 1 units and staff elements would no longer be able to rely on the subregion's rear service staff for rice supplies, military equipment, and financial allowances." Recommended hiring themselves out as daily agricultural workers (thereby getting daily issue of food) and trying to catch fish.

■ ■ ■

The Enemy Shadow Supply System

BRIEFER: Discussion of "the enemy's method of supporting military units and political organizations throughout the Republic of Vietnam with funds and supplies." "Although most enemy war matériel comes from Communist bloc countries, the VC/NVA are primarily dependent upon the people and land of the south for other assistance." Money from external financing and in-country taxation. "The use of American banknotes has increased during 1970." Agricultural taxes exacted in kind, up to 40 percent. (Such as rice in Quang Ngai. Failure to pay tax: three-month sentence in a thought reform camp.) "The magnitude of this system is revealed by the ability of the enemy to acquire imported U.S. supplies from urban sources." United States captured 66 tons of wheat flour in Binh Tuy Province in July 1970. All shipped to RVN by USAID. Major vulnerability: "Access to the population remains the key."

■ ■ ■

CLAY (on interdiction): "As far as I can determine, it's the first time we've gone for four weeks without any throughput. I don't want to say that it's all a function of the box system. On the other hand, it is interesting to note, at least, at this time that this is the fourth week in a row that there's been no throughput calculated."

SOMEONE (re enemy claim of "insane bombing"): "We bit old Xuan Thuy right in the ass. He lost that diplomatic savoir faire." [Laughter]

CLAY: "I think we're going to see a determined effort to fight their way through those passes."

ABRAMS: "That's right. In terms of what they've got to do, the trawlers can only meet local emergencies. But for the whole program that they've got, you know, in mind for South Vietnam and Laos, they've got to pour through those passes." "I don't see anything to change [in the way we are operating]."

7 NOV 1970: WIEU

MACV 1970 Infiltration Estimate: 53,600 (52 percent to COSVN).

MACV 1971 Infiltration Estimate: 9,600.

ABRAMS: "Whenever Mr. Xuan Thuy comes out with something . . . they [U.S. diplomats] all get out and—hell, they look at it upside down, and read it back and forth and so on, thinking that somehow in here he may in some devious oriental way be passing a signal."

WEYAND: "You're a dirty son of a bitch" is probably the signal. "Probably a translation error" say the hopeful.

■ ■ ■

BRIEFER: "In a press conference on Tuesday, Souvanna said he had no intention of changing his bargaining position on peace talks. He said, 'I have no intention of making any new proposal. Everything depends on the move of the other party.' Souvanna reiterated his long-held position that settlement of the Ho Chi Minh Trail controversy, including negotiations for a bombing halt, will be left to the United States and North Vietnam. He added, however, that in saying this he meant only the old Ho Chi Minh Trail before it was expanded. He said, 'The new trail, including Attopeu and Saravane, is out of the question. I will never permit any foreign power to use it freely.' The press conference transcript adds that, after saying this, the prime minister cried 'No!' loudly."

ABRAMS: "Now what [laughing] was the significance of that?!" [Laughter] "Cries 'No!' loudly. What's that mean?"

BRIEFER: "On other matters, Souvanna told the press that he was adamantly opposed to any South Vietnamese or American incursions onto Laotian soil. He also predicted that hostilities would not intensify in the coming dry season and that the enemy would not launch a major offensive."

■ ■ ■

BRIEFER: Binh Tram 14 revealed in COMINT that its two subordinate battalions had a total of 188 trucks. Half 5 ton, half 2 1/2 ton. "They also stated that all but seven of these were operational at this time."

ABRAMS: "Damn good!"

SOMEONE: "Probably from not using them."

ABRAMS: "Well—no, don't talk like that. It's just damn good."

■ ■ ■

ABRAMS: "Now, the French—I think the Americans ought to understand a little about <u>them</u>. They just aren't—they have not been <u>helpful</u>. Well, it's like—. I know you can't <u>say</u> it, but you get <u>consorting</u> with <u>them</u> and you're consorting with some dangerous <u>folk</u>. Now, of course, I suppose in the <u>diplomatic</u> world, why that's all right. You get <u>used</u> to that and so on. But—I don't <u>know</u>— they're not trying to help <u>solve</u> some things here."

BERGER (re the French business community): "Individually they all pay off the local VC, there's no question about that, whether they pay off in Paris or pay off here. The French government position has been <u>stinking</u> for years, ever since de Gaulle said, 'Well, since the French lost the place, why you Americans have to lose it, too.' He sort of gave us several pushes in that direction."

ABRAMS: "Yeah."

BERGER (re the French diplomatic representative): "They try to send one out who <u>talks</u> sympathetically so he can maintain some contact."

■ ■ ■

COLBY (on flood relief): "The president went up there the other day . . . and conducted what amounts to a barnstorming tour." He said he would provide relief, including getting 25 million piasters worth of replacement seed up there. "Various advisors commented on two main points. First, the helicopters obviously saved an <u>awful</u> lot of people. And really absolutely magnificent sort of flying at 100-foot ceiling, quarter of a mile visibility, and just going around and putting a Chinook down in three feet of water, picking people up and putting them on it and so forth. But, aside from that, the Americans really didn't <u>do</u> very much—didn't <u>have</u> to do very much. The Vietnamese machinery kind of took over. They managed the thing, took the leadership, and all the rest of it. And there's a <u>very</u> sharp difference, in the eyes of various people there, from the '64 flood. The president was, yesterday, checking on the rice, biting the rice to see whether it was wet, and so forth."

■ ■ ■

BRIEFER: "The saturation bombing of the air interdiction boxes continues." Target Box B south of the Ban Karai Pass: "Our major effort." 1,242 sorties flown in support of the interdiction program. "Seventy percent of total sorties were flown against the entry route boxes, expending 18,735 bombs. The combination of craters and heavy rains rendered the four areas impassable, and all boxes remain closed to vehicular traffic."

■ ■ ■

ABRAMS: "I would report that, well—if this is seven days, General Weyand's been wearing those four stars, and it looks like he's settling in all right. He seems to be comfortable and so on."

WEYAND: "I'm giving the maids hell over there at the house. I'm working gradually up to—." [Laughter]

21 NOV 1970: Commanders WIEU

ABRAMS: "You know that Admiral Gayler? He's worried about whether we're doing anything over in Laos. I don't know why these people don't stick to their own subjects." [Laughter] [This comment out of the blue.]

BRIEFER: Currently in the process of redeploying Increment 5 forces, which will result in a 31 December 1970 space ceiling of 344,000. During the period 1 January–30 April 1971: Increment 6 forces will be redeployed, reducing the authorized in-country strength to 284,000. Between 1 May and 30 June 1971 additional redeployment will be prepared to reach a transitional support force level. The current authorized TSF level is 260,000. "There are indicators that service contributions may fall short of the JCS-approved goal." "Within these spaces we are trying to maintain a nine-brigade TSF structure." Must therefore redeploy nonessential army spaces.

BRIEFER: Cites "the continuing need to reduce the size of Headquarters MACV and component command headquarters." "Current planning is that I Field Force, II Field Force, and DMAC will reorganize to a similar military assistance command headquarters configuration with a target date of about 1 July 1971. Headquarters XXIV Corps will do likewise by 1 July 1972. Integrate in each case the field command, advisory, and CORDS elements into a single headquarters. One commander in charge of all. Phased reduction of advisory effort also contemplated.

ABRAMS: "I'd just like to say about this—we'll get these proposals out to you. And let's postpone the emotional stage of this until a little later. [Laughter] I'm really seeking advice, and I would appreciate some good professional and objective and realistic judgment on how best to do this. We really haven't— well, I can speak for myself. I haven't settled on how this rather complex thing is best to be handled." "Ambassador Colby and General Weyand and some members of the staff and I have talked this over, and we realize that a good clear solution is not immediately apparent. And the more you think about it the more complex it gets."

■ ■ ■

COLLINS: "I'm certain a number of those from the 4th Military Region, and also those on the staff, who know General Dzu will be interested in how he's doing. Sir, you just couldn't ask for more from anyone. I think this operation into Base Areas 701 and 704 are indicative of the scope of the man. Tactically, I think it was superb the way he developed it. He thought of things like the light of the moon, and he related this to a period when the enemy wouldn't be so active, and when his RF/PF could do better along the line of communications that he would have to keep open along Highway 19. The movement of the elements—this was good and very encouraging in the professional way the division went about it. But as an indication of the man, on Sunday afternoon he came in from a reconnaissance over Cambodia, over the area. He'd been out to Duc Co to check on the supplies in the forward area, Plei Djereng. You know, all the things that a good commander could do." "Again, he's just <u>very</u> dynamic. He has a good mind. He thinks ahead." "He just follows up on <u>everything</u> and is a superb commander. And god, if he can just get a few commanders up there that have one-tenth the <u>energy</u> and the <u>force</u> and the <u>drive</u> that he has, it will be great. All I worry now is that something might happen to him, because he's tremendous as far as I'm concerned. Really doing a good job."

■ ■ ■

ABRAMS: "I'll tell you one thing—they've reduced our strength in many ways out here, but my god, the" onslaught of visitors and advice from Washington continues unabated.
WEYAND: "Yeah, Bob Komer showed you how your friends are really helpful."
ABRAMS: "Actually, my aide just took my pistol away. Otherwise—." [Laughter]
WEYAND: "That's why I came down here early. I figured the first guy you saw was going to catch it."
JACOBSON (worried): "Komer's not coming <u>back</u>, is he?"
ABRAMS: "I'd say it would be a very unhealthy thing for him to do." [Laughter]

■ ■ ■

Indochina Assessment

BRIEFER: "Sir, this is an assessment of North Vietnam's total strategy for the war in Indochina." North Vietnam after 1954 was left "as a deficit agricultural producer. Consequently, even with substantial foreign aid, its possibilities of achieving its desired economic objectives are limited. Conversely, the Geneva agreements gave the South the rich agricultural areas of Vietnam. Using and instigating political dissidence aimed at the Diem regime, the North launched a rural-based revolution in the south committed to achieving its end of economic and political domination of the RVN. The consolidation of the revolution in the north, therefore, became tied to the liberation of the south and the unification of the country. Hanoi has chosen, though, to cloak her support of the war in the RVN as anti-imperialistic and nationalistic rather than in the harsh realities of political and economic power seeking. This deception also serves to cover the fundamental political question in the conflict—what institutional system shall prevail in South Vietnam? The turmoil in Vietnamese society over the last half century has been, to a great degree, the result of the replacement of the Confucian mandarin system of social organization and government administration with new institutional structures. The ideological struggle being waged in South

Vietnam has added the dimension of social revolution to the war. The conflict over institutions stands at the vortex of the war between the North and the South."

BRIEFER: About 1965 "Hanoi made two significant decisions. Both decisions broke with theoretical conceptions of a war of liberation. First, Hanoi dispatched large numbers of North Vietnamese troops to the RVN." "Secondly . . . Hanoi adopted a strategy of general offensives based on main force units from the north. Not only did the main force units fail in their objective, but their formation committed Hanoi to the support of units that were not internally self-sufficient."

BRIEFER: Cites another significant external factor, initiation in 1968 of the Accelerated Pacification Program, which "has succeeded in halting the erosion of the central government's resource base in rural areas while reasserting government control over what once were insurgent domains and resources. The program took the strategic initiative away from the VC/NVA in the rural areas."

BRIEFER: "The failure of the general offensive, the manpower drain from the north, the effectiveness of pacification in cutting the resource base in the south, and the need to rebuild the economy of the north to at least its prewar level were all factors in influencing Hanoi to change its national priorities. The first public announcement of this change was made in Le Duan's 2 February 1970 speech to the party cadre on the occasion of the party's 40th anniversary celebration."

BRIEFER: There are seven interrelated conflicts: 1: War in northern Laos. 2: Logistics war in southern Laos and northeastern Cambodia. 3: Cambodian conflict. 4: COSVN area of the RVN. 5: VC MR-5 conflict. 6: B-5 Front and MR-TTH. 7: B-3 Front.

BRIEFER: "The logistics war . . . now stands as the critical conflict for the VC/NVA." The enemy "has opted for a protracted war." "In North Vietnam approximately 209,000 men become of draft age each year, of which 110,000 are physically fit under present standards. North Vietnam is probably capable of sustaining an infiltration rate of 100,000–120,000 per year for a <u>long</u> period, or of dispatching over 235,000 in a single year, as it did in 1968."

■ ■ ■

ABRAMS: "Everything <u>good</u> that happens seems to come from good intelligence. A lot of this galloping around produces nothing because the intelligence—."

VANN (looking at HES results): "We've come a long way when one of the 10 low provinces can have 90 percent A/B/C control."

ABRAMS: "One thing came out on PSDF up in the I Corps quarterly review that's kind of interesting. They killed more enemy than they had killed. They captured more weapons than they lost. And they took more prisoners than they had missing in action. That's the only military region where that kind of situation exists."

ABRAMS: "How long have we been equipping the PSDF with M16s?"

SOMEONE: "They're equipping themselves."

ABRAMS (re enemy infiltrating PSDF/RF/PF/ARVN): "With a resourceful and clever enemy like this, I think it's part of what's got to be expected to happen. I mean, not that you want it to happen, and we do everything we can so it won't—. I think the PSDF's a better bet than some of these damn officials, just ordinary citizens, who are buying penicillin down here and carting it out and turning it over to COSVN. I mean, in the whole thing of what's being—. If you want to get excited about a dozen PSDF here or another dozen somewhere else and that sort of thing, and try to manufacture that into some goddamn country-wide movement, better look at some of this other stuff that's going on, too! Politically, for this government, and so on, this program—there's a lot in it. That's one of the reasons why they're [the enemy] trying so hard against it, because it is a threat, a political threat."

1 DEC 1970: COMUS Update

POTTS: "In preparation for your meeting this afternoon with General Vien, we'll lead off with truck traffic and interdiction."

BRIEFER: In Laos "a sharp increase in sensor string activations." 2,860 activations during the last reporting period versus 865 in the prior period. And the increase is holding up: 2,734 during the five days since the reporting period ended.

SOMEONE: "The air force is having some difficulty with the computers on the gunships." "They're seeing the trucks, but they're not getting results." "They've got some real trouble with the equipment. Where they should be getting 200 trucks they're getting 10, or—. They're just not hitting."

ABRAMS: "Y-e-a-a-h. Yeah. It's kind of like one evening I told my aide I wanted to talk to General Ewell on the phone. He came back in a few minutes, and he said, 'General Ewell's in Manila.' I said, 'Goddamn it, I didn't ask where he is. I said I want to talk to him on the telephone.' [Laughs] It's kind of a sad story about this, but how long are we all going to gather around crying about it before somebody gets it repaired and functioning?"

RESPONSE: They say tech reps are due from the States shortly. Planned B-52 surge on Target Box B tomorrow for 24 hours. Later surge planned on Box C.

■ ■ ■

WEYAND: "General Tri is giving General La a reprimand."

WEYAND (to Abrams, re Vien): "You and he have been so frank with one another. . . ."

■ ■ ■

ABRAMS: "Gee, that's a wonderful paper Bill Colby's put together about the three levels and so on." "That's a good paper." "It's true you've got to use military forces, but that ain't gonna buy you anything unless you've got this other moving!"

ABRAMS: "Yesterday I spent the afternoon with the 2nd Division, the Quang Nhai province chief, and a district, and 4th Regiment. I must say, in relating this back, I've never seen the Vietnamese more confident."

ABRAMS: "I'm just talking about the level of confidence. Certainly, go back a couple of years, or a year, that wasn't the way you'd—you wouldn't come away from a visit up there with . . . that kind of a feeling. They're under no illusions that the war is over. They're not like that. They all know that there's a lot of hard work still to be done. But the thing is that they believe they can do it."

ABRAMS: "You've just got to go through [in Cambodia] all the heartaches, and all of the disappointments, and all the sacrifices and so on we've gone through in Vietnam, hopefully not committing any of the obvious errors that were committed here—save yourself that. But all this development of territorials, or whatever they want to call it, but somebody to perform that function, and political organization of the people . . . the marshaling of the people in support of the government . . . so that they're not prey to the Communists, and his military forces, regular forces, they've got to be brought along, too."

ABRAMS: 2nd ARVN Division is operating with companies and platoons. "Now, a year ago, they wouldn't go anywhere with less than a battalion. Now part of it is because the enemy is not so effective. He hasn't got the strength, and he can't mass against them like he could. But it also means that the company commanders have come along, and the battalion commander can see his way clear for that company to be out there alone." "Well, there isn't any shortcut to it." "At least four years that we know have been invested in getting to that point. And really a lot longer."

5 DEC 1970: WIEU

BRIEFER: Comrade Van captured. Staff assistant for military affairs, Binh Thuan Provincial Unit. He states that the enemy has two criteria for degree of control: "Complete control if he could collect taxes freely and proselyte the people, even if only during periods of darkness." "Limited control when the population of a village or hamlet was completely dominated by GVN military presence, but the VC still had access to them." "Source stated that during period January 1969 to the present, percentages of VC complete control in rural areas declined from 70 to 25 percent and limited control from 10 to 3 percent." "During the same period in city and capital district areas complete control declined from 33 to 20 percent."

■ ■ ■

ABRAMS: "The way this RF and PF is in the war is something."

DISCUSSION: Planned use that day of a C-130. Delivers a 15,000-pound "Commando Vault" bomb. Someone: "The pictures at Eglin [Air Force Base in Florida] show a hole about 30 or 40 feet deep and 60 feet around. It might make them think. I don't know whether it will slow them down, but we're going to try it."

ABRAMS (re use of the C-130): "A four-engine bomber." [Laughter]

17 DEC 1970: SEACORDS Brief

BUNKER: This meeting is one in a series begun in 1964 by Ambassador Taylor. In September 1970, we agreed to get together again early in the dry season to examine collectively what we are faced with in military terms, plus political and economic factors.

BUNKER: "We all recognize how critical the period immediately ahead is, and how necessary it is for us to make the maximum use of our limited resources."

SHACKLEY: "There is evidence, from COSVN Directive 28, which has recently been reported out, that the enemy thinks that we're going to make a major move in the tri-border area of Laos, Cambodia, and South Vietnam during this particular dry season, and that's having an impact on his planning over the near term."

Apparent enemy anticipation of Lam Son 719, the incursion into Laos launched by South Vietnamese forces in late January 1971, as early as mid-December 1970, although the anticipated strike point cited here is considerably south of the actual point of entry when the operation is implemented.

BRIEFER: On 10 October 1970 we began the Commando Hunt 5 interdiction program. Four choke points: Box Alpha: the Mu Gia Pass. Box Bravo: the Ban Karai Pass. Box Charlie: the Ban Raving Pass. Box Delta: west edge of the DMZ. "Currently 30 Arc Light and 140–150 tac air sorties per day are programmed against the four boxes." About 1,300 tons of bombs per day.

BRIEFER: "The RVNAF cross-border operations since 30 June of '70 continue to deny the enemy his former border sanctuaries and disrupt his once immune lines of communication. Without the use of the old sanctuaries and free movement into South Vietnam along these lines of communication, the enemy main force threat has been significantly reduced in the southern part of Vietnam. This reduced threat has enhanced security, provided a greater chance for pacification to succeed, and provided the environment for the orderly Vietnamization of the war and U.S. troop withdrawals. As a side benefit, the Cambodian operations have resulted in improved effectiveness in the Republic of Vietnam Armed Forces and their ability to conduct large-scale independent operations which have included the employment of integrated ground, air, and naval resources."

BRIEFER: In South Vietnam "the general level of enemy activity has decreased from large-scale operations to an increase in terrorism and small-unit harassing actions." "Our in-country strategy is designed to counter COSVN Resolutions 9 and 14. Allied military operations have concentrated on providing security in the densely populated areas and are targeted against enemy base areas in the Republic of Vietnam." "We are now promoting military operations to secure areas vital to the economic development of the Republic." These include agriculture, logging, and land lines of communications.

BRIEFER: "This region adjacent to the DMZ and Laos is the area of highest enemy main force threat. . . . A major trend during recent months has been the operation of ARVN forces in the rugged areas in the western portion. These units have produced <u>outstanding</u> results."

BRIEFER: MR-2: Largest, covering half the Republic. In MR-3: "All four ARVN divisions have participated in cross-border operations." In MR-4: Also cross-border, but also assaults on long-standing enemy base areas in Kien Hoa, Seven Mountains/Three Sisters, etc.

BRIEFER: ARVN: Ten infantry and one airborne divisions, which is the planned level and now achieved. Territorial Forces about 50 percent of the total armed forces.

BRIEFER: RF/PF: Armed with M16 rifles, M60 machine guns, PRC-25 radios.

MR. LADD: "FANK alone should not be expected to perform independent spectacular or dramatic military miracles, now or in the foreseeable future. Seven months ago FANK was a 35,000-man semimilitary force, loosely organized, inadequately equipped, poorly trained, uninspiredly led, and dedicated principally to civic-action-type missions. In the past eight months FANK has expanded to a strength of about 180,000." About one-third now are "reasonably well armed" light infantry capable of performing in a "semiprofessional military manner." "We feel confident that the Cambodians are, under the circumstances, doing the best they can with what they have in both men and matériel. FANK is far from being an effective military force in our concept, but it does have determination, high morale, personal courage, and is learning the art of warfare . . . on the hard road of knocks."

19 DEC 1970: WIEU

BRIEFER (re Paris peace talks): "Xuan Thuy, the chief negotiator for the DRV in Paris, suggested on Thursday [95th session] that if the U.S. cannot accept the PRG 30 June 1971 withdrawal date that it should suggest its own alternate date within a reasonable time frame. Ambassador David Bruce replied that withdrawals will only be discussed in connection with similar NVA withdrawals from South Vietnam, Laos, and Cambodia."

MACV 1970 Infiltration Estimate: 53,600.
MACV 1971 Infiltration Estimate: 22,000.

ABRAMS: "That's a very strong RF/PF in I Corps. The kill ratio, the ratio of <u>their</u> initiated contacts versus enemy-initiated, all those things are <u>better</u>." "I remember when . . . we went into this district headquarters, and the district chief got up there, a fellow about four feet seven, weighed maybe 75 pounds. He jumped up there in the front, and he saluted and yelled, 'All the way, sir!' [Laughter] And so on. And then he started this briefing. Now this is in '68, probably April of '68. And he got up there, and he got talking about his RF and PF, and he said he will not conduct <u>any</u> operations in the daytime unless specifically directed in each instance by the province chief. <u>All</u> <u>of</u> <u>it's</u> <u>at</u> <u>night</u>! And they were just having rather remarkable results."

ABRAMS: "Christ, the command arrangements were—well, there <u>weren't</u> any. Just everybody get in the <u>fight</u>! And then they'd kind of straighten it out as the night went on. For that whole thing, after Tet, that whole thing was quite a psychological stimulus. And, as I say, Barsanti was <u>devoted</u> to this."

ABRAMS: "Well, as has been for the last several weeks, where the war is really at fever pitch is in the delta. That's where <u>he's</u> taking losses, that's where <u>our</u> side's taking losses. More than all the rest of the country."

■ ■ ■

ABRAMS (to Clay): "Looks like you're doing good over there in Cambodia." "I think the interdiction program's probably as close in as any interdiction program's ever been. [Laughter] But, hell, if it gets results—. We want to stop them way out, but if we stop them close in I guess it's—."

CLAY: "It's just as effective."

ABRAMS: "Yeah, it makes no difference where you do it if you hit them. It probably will bring up <u>doctrinal</u> problems later on [laughter], in the historical review. But you and I will be gone."

CLAY: "The war colleges will discuss this for years."

ABRAMS: "Yeah, and how it was screwed up. But, anyway, it looks like it's going pretty good right now."

■ 1971

During 1971 redeployment of U.S. forces from Vietnam continued, with an additional 160,000 taken out in four increments. In Paris the peace talks, both public and secret, also continued but without visible progress.

In early February South Vietnamese forces launched a three-division raid, designated Lam Son 719, into Laos for the purpose of temporarily disrupting operation of the Ho Chi Minh Trail and seizing or destroying stockpiled enemy armaments and matériel. Both sides fought fiercely, inflicting and suffering substantial losses, before the South Vietnamese withdrew after six weeks. U.S. forces, prohibited by Congress from entering Laos to take part in the ground operation, provided helicopter and other air support in Laos and, from across the border in South Vietnam, artillery, logistical, and other kinds of assistance. Media assessment of the operation was generally critical of the South Vietnamese and their performance, but, as the tapes document, at MACV and among the South Vietnamese themselves the results were viewed as far more favorable. Meanwhile other South Vietnamese forces continued extensive operations in Cambodia for most of the year.

In October the Republic of Vietnam conducted presidential elections. President Thieu ran unopposed for reelection after two other candidates, Gen. Duong Van Minh and Vice President Nguyen Cao Ky, withdrew during the campaign.

2 JAN 1971: WIEU

ABRAMS: "We commence another year's activities with this group. Must be a full year, with what's going on—elections coming up. There's a real frantic effort going on to see how that's gonna wind up. The opinion takers down there in the mission are really going wild. Anyone who's got an opinion, it gets recorded. I guess it's a Gallup poll. Apparently they believe that Ky's gonna run."

SOMEONE: "As time goes by, it becomes less sure that Thieu is a shoo-in."

ABRAMS: "I would say right now it's their opinion that he isn't."

■ ■ ■

SOMEONE: (from Seventh Air Force, re the MiG threat): "It's a damn dismal picture. We just don't pick 'em up. We don't have the radar coverage." "He's got GCI, and we don't know he's coming."

ABRAMS: Asks for a complete briefing: "You fix it up, and I'll come there." Very concerned about possibly losing a B-52.

BRIEFER: 1970 infiltration total: 53,600.

POTTS: "Sir, Lieutenant [Paziar?], who's been our briefer here for Saturday morning off and on now for the past year, and handled many of our distinguished visitors, is leaving this week. He's an accountant with Price and Waterhouse in Boston, Massachusetts, and he's returning to that firm."

ABRAMS: "Well, we wish you the very best and thank you for the fine job you've done. And I must say you're privileged to be returning to God's country, the seat of American civilization."

Abrams is from Massachusetts.

SOMEONE: "And 40 inches of snow!"

∎ ∎ ∎

BRIEFER: "The enemy has decided Lon Nol's heavy reliance on the destructiveness of air power makes him vulnerable to charges of callousness and heavy-handedness toward the Khmer people. This vulnerability is currently being heavily exploited in enemy propaganda."

ABRAMS: "South Vietnam all over again."

ABRAMS: "I remember at the time we were battling for Hue, Vice President Ky came up there. I was talking with Ky and General Lam, and I told them that we had concrete evidence that they'd [the enemy] taken up positions in these Buddhist temples and the grounds right around them. Vice President Ky said, 'Those things were made by men. They can be rebuilt by men. Hit 'em.' Of course, that was in an hour of great need, and bleeding pretty badly."

ABRAMS: "I'm sure that when he [the enemy] lays on his plan, he cranks in a factor—I don't know what it is—that his effort will be enough, will be adequate, so that he can take 25 percent or 30 percent losses and still meet his basic logistics requirements—something like that. We don't know what that is, of course. An unknown there is kind of important."

DISCUSSION: The assessment has stated that the enemy has been "forced" to fragment some units to shore up others. Someone objects to use of the term, suggesting the enemy chose to do that rather than having been forced to do so.

ABRAMS: Agreed. "It's more the way he wants to do it under the circumstances he has."

ABRAMS: "I must say that sort of in front of me is the imminent arrival of the secretary of defense and the Chairman. And here the cosmetics of verbiage begin to be—I think there are ways to say this. You don't know what switch you turn on. Around here, where we're all working together all the time, we've gotten kinda used to one another and we know what switches—Bill Potts and his people probably work here Saturday and say, 'Oh, don't say that. You'll get him going!' [Laughter] Well, that's 'cause they've found out what all my switches are, and they only want to turn 'em on selectively, or not turn 'em on at all. But, no—there's a lot in this. When these fellows come here, these distinguished leaders from Washington, we don't know all that. Three or four things like that—it's <u>possible</u> it could turn that withdrawal switch all the way over to full speed ahead. I don't think any of us <u>believe</u> that. I'm not talking about being dishonest, or not laying out the facts, but we have to lay 'em out with due care to all the implications and so on. I just—."

WEYAND: "This secretary of defense, who obviously is interested in continuing Vietnamization at a good clip, and maybe increasing it. . . ."

ABRAMS: After the 1968–1969 dry season, a group assessed the results of Commando Hunt. "And they eventually worked themselves into a fervor about the conclusions." "And then what happened in South Vietnam supported the conclusions that had been reached." [Those were that the enemy had not met his objectives of getting through enough tonnage to support the current operation and to build up a stockpile to see him through to the next season of replenishment.]

SOMEONE: "The only argument that the Systems Analysis people could make to that was, 'No, he got through what he needed to get through.' In other words, the pace of the war was the way he wanted it, which I think was completely fallacious. But that was their counter to that study you're talking about."

ABRAMS: "And that particular one was also supported by pressure on our part inside Vietnam—capture of caches and this sort of thing. So you were going at his system both ways—at the consumption end inside South Vietnam, and at the resupply part. So you're working the problem both ways."

■ ■ ■

BRIEFER: Quotes from a captured letter written by the deputy leader of Hoa Da District Unit, Binh Thuan Province, re shirking by cadre members: "If we are sweet and soft on them, few people will do work. But if we are strict and hard on them, no one will do anything."

BRIEFER: Cites various evidence of enemy shortages of medical supplies, food (cadre having to work the fields, with consequent loss of combat effectiveness and morale). Also an account of buying food from corrupt South Vietnamese officials. "Legal" cadre buy in cities, deliver by truck through GVN National Police checkpoints (driver had documentation). Revealed by Hoi Chanh. Done with relative ease.

■ ■ ■

ABRAMS: "We had an awful lot of uncontrolled firing on New Year's Eve."
SOMEONE: "There'll be less of us here to shoot next year."
SOMEONE ELSE: "We had several rounds in the general's trailer. I <u>hope</u> that was an accident."

■ ■ ■

BRIEFER: "The Popular Forces continue to make the greatest number of significant contacts." The PF in Quang Tri Province captured 22, including at least 16 who were members of the 126th NVA Naval Sapper Regiment, many of them wearing wet suits, including two women. One prisoner claims that a 2,000-pound sophisticated mine of Soviet manufacture, detected offshore by allied forces, had been towed into place from north of the DMZ by swimmers. [Abrams: "God, what a task!"] The prisoner says three such mines were emplaced; to date the allies have recovered only two.

■ ■ ■

ABRAMS: "Guys in the squads regard company headquarters as a goddamned Long Binh installation—never in the war. It just depends on where you're located what perspective you have."

■ ■ ■

BRIEFER: Reports November Pacification Attitude Analysis Survey results. They show a chart depicting attitudes toward the Phuong Hoang [Phoenix] program.

COLBY: It was pointed out to me in Washington that the ratio of those who opposed the program to those who supported it was about the same in November as it had been in March, but that "we've moved a lot out of the undecided column." "That's what systems analysis contributes."

ABRAMS: "That's right. You take a chart like that, and the first task taken on by the systems analysts is to negate that big black stuff, if that's positive. You've gotta get at that, and get it torn down, and if possible emphasize how the red has tripled."

SOMEONE: "They have trouble with the blue, though. Not much they can say about that."

ABRAMS: "Except that in the end what you're talking about is opinion, anyway, and what's that worth? Throw away the whole thing!"

WEYAND (reflecting on what he observed in Paris): "I know there's going to be a lot of talk about [Duong Van] Minh, in particular [with respect to the upcoming presidential election], and the idea that the enemy says that you've got to get rid of the Thieu-Ky-Khiem clique, and then that they'll talk with these people. And that's a popular notion. It hasn't been—people haven't been disabused on that score very much, either, in recent times, but what the guys there in Paris said very clearly was that, first of all, you get rid of those people. But that didn't bring them to the point where they'd talk. Let's say that Minh gets in there. They then insist that this group, whoever it is, other than Thieu-Ky-Khiem, they constitute a peace cabinet. But, before they'll talk with them, they've got to prove their allegiance to the principles of peace, democracy, independence, and neutrality." "This outfit then will have to prove their allegiance to these principles by freeing all political prisoners, by stopping censorship of the press, by permitting freedom of assembly and all of that, and by declaring firmly on the Geneva Accords, which involves, on the neutrality side, the withdrawal of all foreign forces, and no military alliances. Now all this is before they—"

SOMEONE: "Then they talk."

WEYAND: "Yeah, maybe. That gets you to the point of maybe. So there're just—they've really sold a hell of a good bill of goods on this business, really. I suppose if you asked most of the American people if they thought that if you got rid of Thieu, and particularly Ky, these guys would talk to you, the answer would be yes. And you wouldn't be any further down the road than you are right now, actually. But I think it's a good thing to keep in mind that they're not talking about personalities. They're talking about the whole system. In fact, the next steps are to abolish the National Assembly and call for a new Constituent Assembly, which then draws up a whole new gut system of government. It's clear and simple: what they're saying is they'd take over by political means, which they haven't been able to do by a combination of military and political means. But still the *New York Times,* in fact, hell, a lot of senators on our side, they all—[Someone: "Harriman!"] and I think—. About Harriman, I know goddamn good and well he can't believe this. But we have a lot of honest people that believe it—that there's some one personality, or two, that's standing in the way."

WEYAND: "I think in talking to people—not that we have a hell of a lot of influence—that there's one thing to keep in mind. What the enemy's seeking to destroy is a system."

■ ■ ■

BRIEFER: Describes several instances of swimmer-emplaced mines and demolitions in various waterways, then use of trained dolphins to interdict enemy swimmers. Five U.S. Navy-trained Atlantic bottle-nosed dolphins arrived at Cam Ranh Bay on 19 December 1970 in Project Shoretime. Shows film clip made in Hawaii of "swimmer defense system." Dolphin takes a "nullification device" to attack swimmer with barb and strobe light from the rear. Tried them out in the vicinity of the ammunition pier at Cam Ranh Bay. "The enemy has been led to believe that the dolphin is trained to attack a male swimmer's privates. Our latest information has it that the enemy plans to counteract this by employing female swimmer-sappers in the future. In light of this information, the navy has a contingency plan to respond with male dolphins."

ABRAMS: I've seen dolphins at a park in Hawaii. "Remarkable animals."

SOMEONE: "I have to report, sir, that as of yesterday we have one AWOL [dolphin]."

■ ■ ■

BRIEFER: "The U Minh campaign continues." One result: 11,000+ refugees moved out and are being resettled.

ABRAMS: "What it's designed to do is tear up that base area and put a permanent presence in there, in time, so that it just isn't a foundation for MR-3."

SOMEONE: "It sure is costing us."

ABRAMS: "Yeah, I know it." Thieu spent overnight in the base camp at Christmas, with a retinue consisting of 174 people.

BRIEFER: Two ARVN cross-border operations continue with over 10,000 troops involved. VNAF extensive resupply by air effort.

ABRAMS: "They're [SecDef party] probably going to be kind of mean when they get here—further withdrawals and that sort of thing."

ABRAMS: "Regarding these elections—I suppose in a theoretical sense it has great value, but it's a very divisive thing going on at a time when you need a lot of strength in the political side of things. And, hell, this will have a tendency to—. And it's a time when saviors have a tendency to materialize. And the way those polls go, all a savior's got to do to pack a wallop is get out there with some of those motherhood positions about peace, working for the people, helping the peasants, against corruption and inflation. I mean, you could put a good platform together pretty easily. The problems are fairly well identified, the things that bother the people, and all you've got to do is stand for that and promise that you are in fact the only savior that can carry this program through. And avoid getting into the details of your program of execution."

ABRAMS: "Well, happy new year."

15 JAN 1971: COMUS Special Brief

VISITOR: "You've gotta give those little bastards credit for perseverance. They're dedicated."

ABRAMS: "That's right."

ABRAMS (re efforts to pacify mountain tribal areas on both sides of the border): "Those people up there aren't for Cambodia, or for Vietnam. They don't know all that stuff about these governments and all that. They're hill people. But they're good people. If you could just get it working so at least it wasn't a damn labor force and crop-growing outfit for the enemy, it'd be worthwhile."

ABRAMS: "It's really been going along pretty well inside South Vietnam. There's a good government effort on the VCI. They've made it a Vietnamese program. When they do that, that's the beginning of getting something done. Nothing works here that's a U.S. program. When they take a hold of it, then we're in."

ABRAMS: Describes how he has gone the day before to the National Police Academy graduation. The new commander of the National Police, General Phong, was there. "He's a good man." President Thieu was there, and made "a very fine address." He said he wants "a new spirit to the police—training, discipline. It's a critical part of the whole community for security of the country and the people." "It's the launching of what they're going to do with their police force."

ABRAMS: "I talked with the chief justice out there yesterday, and he told me they're now getting in the police graduates of law school, and he thinks that's a good thing." "The kind of consolidation and work that's going on inside South Vietnam" doesn't show up in the military briefing, "to stabilize the situation, get it under better control, improve the effectiveness of government, and all of its tentacles out there among the people and so on."

ABRAMS: "The other day, when we were down in Long An Province—about September of 1970, in terms of kilometers of road open and in use, and bridges functioning and serviceable, they passed the mark of 1963. They've got a very interesting chart there. You could kind of trace the war. You start at the 1963 level, which is when things were in pretty good shape, bustling and all that. Then as you go 1964, 1965, 1966, 1967, 1968, the kilometers of road and the number of bridges just keeps going down and down and down. <u>Then</u> it starts back up, and in September of 1970 they passed the 1963 level, and are considerably above it now."

ABRAMS: "But then they got talking about terrorism. Over the last eight or nine months terrorism has stayed at about the same level. It's at a <u>fairly</u> low level in Long An. So they wanted to know about that. The way they responded was to say, 'Well, what's happened now, the National Police are functioning out in the villages, and a lot of these things have been investigated by the police and it's not the VC at all. It's ordinary crime.'" "It's not that we're in favor of crime. We're not. But it does indicate that things have moved far enough so that some of the ordinary things that take place within a society can go on—like the police investigating and things like that."

ABRAMS: "And they've just moved the province chief from Long An to Gia Dinh. That's his fifth province. He's really a terrific province chief. The day he took over Go Cong Province, they were having sort of a change of command ceremony at the province capital—this in the afternoon, right after lunch—and the VC started shelling it with an 82-mm mortar. So the new province chief, this Colonel [Thu?], disbanded the ceremony, gathered up some RFs and PFs who were there as part of the honor guard, and took off with them. Before it got dark he was back, and he had the mortar, the bipod, the base plate, and a dozen rounds of ammunition. That was the day he took command. I must say he also had a little luck, but that's the kind of a fellow he is."

ABRAMS: In a meeting one day the issue came up of giving Colonel Thu a division. "President Thieu said, 'Why, yes, he's capable of commanding a division any day. But it's more important that he continue as a province chief. When it's all over, then he can have a division.' Now that's the kind of priorities he's got."

16 JAN 1971: WIEU

ATTENDEES: Gen. Abrams, Gen. Weyand, Amb. Colby, Gen. Clay, Mr. Kirk, LTG McCaffrey, VADM King, MG Dolvin, MG Cowles, MG Maples, MG Wilson, MG Young, MG Potts, BG Camp, BG Vande Hey, BG Greene, BG Watkin, Mr. Chambers, BG John, BG Cheadle, BG Henion, BG Doehler, BG Forrester (for Mr. Jacobson), Capt. Birdt (for MG Dettre), Col. Sadler, Col. Leonard, Col. Jones.

SOMEONE: "Did you hear the rumor of Lowenstein's disgrace . . . ?"
ABRAMS: "I think I'm qualified to elevate that above the level of rumor. I was

there in the 23rd Division yesterday, and received what might be termed an eyewitness account. Mr. Lowenstein . . . needed to relieve himself, so they directed him to one of those little outside affairs with a little screen around it. And this one was a 55-gallon drum sunk in the ground, with chicken wire over the top. Apparently he was unfamiliar with the device, because what he did was stand on it—and plummeted to the bottom. Well, as you know, it's the rainy season up there, and so this 55-gallon drum was virtually full of a mixture of you know what. Fortunately, he was not injured in any way, and they took him over to a trailer, where he disrobed and showered and so on, and got some fresh clothes on him, and then he went off and so on. Well, that was the last that was thought of it until, I guess it was after dinner, the division commander came back to his trailer. When he opened the door they remembered they had done nothing to police it. So they had to open that up and air it out for two or three hours."

SOMEONE: "That's done more for morale in USARV than anything since the two-week leave."

Much laughter throughout this account. James G. Lowenstein was a staff member for the Senate Foreign Relations Committee who made periodic visits to Vietnam.

■ ■ ■

BRIEFER: "ENEMY ACTIONS REMAINED AT A LOW LEVEL THROUGHOUT ALL OF SOUTH VIET-NAM."

BRIEFER: Describes re the 88th NVA Regiment a captured document dated 21 October 1970 that states that "a number of combatants had thrown away, hidden, or lost their weapons when they fled the battlefield."

ABRAMS: "If *Newsweek* wanted to do a balanced article on troops—now that thing about throwing their weapons away as they fled the battlefield. They haven't been able to dig one of those up on us yet. That makes pretty good— he's got problems."

ABRAMS (re the progressing situation in Long An): "People are not going to support the government because of any choice between Communism and democracy, but because this is a better way to live. By god, you're going along and you're making a little money, and you say, 'Well, to hell with that.'"

ABRAMS: "Did Jake tell you about that RF lieutenant he met down in Vinh Long? Nineteen Gallantry Crosses; four Bronze Stars, U.S., with 'V'; three Commendation Medals, U.S., with 'V'; six wound—. A lieutenant. And what he wants, his lifelong ambition, is to command a battalion."

SOMEONE: "How long's he been a lieutenant?"

ABRAMS: "Oh, I suppose eight, nine years."

SAME SOMEONE: "He's going to come into the zone of consideration pretty soon."

ABRAMS: "Of course, I suppose locally they've been keeping that a secret. They don't want to see him leave."

SOMEONE: "We've got a battalion."

Meaning one that he could have.

SOMEONE ELSE: "If he speaks English, we could give him the 3rd of the 22nd."

ABRAMS: "We've got these English language schools here. Maybe it's time we started getting some advisors from the Vietnamese. Help our units out."

ABRAMS (re what is going on in the U Minh): "It's bloody, there's no question about that, but it does seem to have a dampening effect."

DISCUSSION: C-rated hamlets as viewed by the inhabitants: "Which means our HES rating is optimistic—in the view of the people."

POTTS: An impending change in grading of the HES is going to take about 75 percent of 1,500 or so A hamlets to B, and of about 7,000 B hamlets a quarter are going down to C.

BRIEFER: Four ARVN cross-border operations continue, with over 14,000 troops participating.

BRIEFER: Introduces Major Wynn to narrate a short film showing a C-130 with low-light-level television for spotting the enemy at night. He is said to have been on "a mission the other night that destroyed 58 trucks and damaged 7." He shows film from that strike. "We did find a huge truck park," despite no moon and the television set not the best. Has infrared illuminator on. Firing 20-mm. In order to classify a truck as destroyed, need a fire. If using 40-mm, if hit, then considered destroyed. Film from BDA recorder, running while shooting. Firing at 7,500 feet for 20-mm. Higher for 40-mm. IR operator searches for next target while he's shooting the current one. On a recent mission, the crew reported 19 trucks destroyed; postmission review of the film revealed 31 destroyed. Briefer turns on the sound: "<u>Oh</u>, <u>yes</u>, you got him!" [Laughter]

BRIEFER: Night truck killing reached a record level this week.

23 JAN 1971: Commanders WIEU

BRIEFER: MACV 1971 Infiltration Estimate to date: 27,900 (20,500 destined for COSVN). Total includes 51 COSVN groups and 6 gap groups. QL prefix: probably specialists such as technicians, sappers, and engineers.

BRIEFER: There are indications that the enemy is planning a major dry season offensive in Laos in the area west of the Plaine des Jarres. Two regiments of the 316th Division are in the area. Maybe also elements of the 312th Division.

ABRAMS: "We've just got to keep close tabs here on this thing all the way from the Plaine des Jarres down to the Pich Nil Pass. And that includes the interdiction, and what we're doing in Freedom Deal—that whole gamut of things. We've got to play the air assets here in the best way we can—and we've got to look at the whole thing, because it's going to take it all. Well, it's going to take more than all of it—that's the problem. So we've really got to do a balancing act in here." "We need to apply the air, including the B-52s, in the best way we know how."

SOMEONE (re ARVN operations in the Seven Mountains and Three Sisters areas): "Those are the hardest kills I've ever seen. Individual caves. If you get one for one you're doing good." The U Minh campaign continues. And Truong's corps-wide saturation operation. "A lot of these casualties were inflicted by PF soldiers who have never before killed an enemy."

BRIEFER: Three ARVN cross-border operations in progress, with over 12,000 troops participating.

BRIEFER: The enemy continues his logistics surge in Laos begun two weeks earlier. MACV devoted 89 percent of B-52 strikes to the anti-infiltration boxes. The enemy got 44 percent through or around the box areas. A box is one kilometer by two kilometers.

BRIEFER: Record high truck kills achieved this week, beating last year's record high of 636.

POTTS: "That's mighty heartening."

BRIEFER (re the Phuong Hoang campaign): 1970 was the first year that neutralizations have exceeded the national goal. Nationally there are 3.4 VCI per 1,000 SVN population.

■ ■ ■

ABRAMS: "I did want to say a word while we're all here today. You know some months ago we began looking into the organization of MACV, CORDS, and each of the regions as we began the phasedown. You've all commented. I've been over each of those comments—Ambassador Colby, General Weyand, and myself." In the months ahead there is "quite a bit to be done."

ABRAMS: "If we could get to the end of 1971, and the bulk of the population in every district in this country was all in the hands of the police, the PSDF, the RF/PF, and you had an information program where people knew about their government and knew about everything that was going on and that sort of thing—. And the closer you can get to that sort of condition by the third of October, the better off this whole thing is going to be. The election [that] is going to occur here on the third of October is a very important event. I don't think it can be pulled off by so-called stuffing the ballot boxes. It has to wind up with credibility. In order to do that, the VCI and the guerrillas and all of his apparatus needs to have been shoved down as far as it can go. The more that can be done by this conglomerate of police, PSDF, the territorials, and the information service, the better off it's going to be, the solider the results, and the better in South Vietnam. That's what it kind of looks like to me."

ABRAMS: "What we also have to pay a lot of attention to is balancing our air, from Barrel Roll down to the interdiction program, and what we have to do in Laos, what we have to do in Cambodia, and what we must do in South Vietnam. We've just got to play that with great sensitivity and artistry."

ABRAMS (re pending MACV reorganization): "I think the most important thing we Americans need to have during this period is peace with ourselves. All Americans have got to be pulling in the same direction, and all together. And that's always a neat trick to do under the most ideal circumstances. Americans are all different. They're individualists and enthusiasts, optimists and pessimists, then a slight sprinkling of just screwups."

ABRAMS (on reorganization): "I don't think it's time to get out the crowbars and really get at the timbers." Maintain working relationships. "I want you to know that I've postponed any further serious examination into our organizational structure."

30 JAN 1971: WIEU

BRIEFER: Weather: Northeast monsoon. Socked down everything east of the ridgeline, all the way up to the Red River delta.

BRIEFER: 325th and 308th NVA Divisions remain in place. Also the 304th and 312th. Arrived in Laos: 165th and 209th NVA Regiment Headquarters elements. The 320th Division remains in northern Quang Binh Province. Headquarters of the 64th NVA Regiment is south-southeast of the Ban Karai Pass, near the North Vietnam–Laos border, moving south.

BRIEFER: COMINT reveals the enemy's concern over anticipated friendly operations in northern MR-1 and the contiguous areas of Laos. In messages intercepted beginning on 24 January 1971 Binh Trams 9, 27, 33, and 34 reflect concern that friendly forces in MR-1 "were planning operations in the RVN and might strike across the border in an effort to interdict the enemy's logistic corridor system." One message indicated the enemy believed friendly forces would use Routes 9 and 616/926 to cross the border and strike into northern Laos. "They have directed all units in the area to increase their vigilance and to prepare for combat activities in the immediate future."

Briefing is halted while something is apparently whispered to Abrams. Possibly he is shown a message just received. Pause of about two or three minutes. During this time, absolute silence is maintained by all others present. As subsequent discussion seems to indicate, it was a proposed response to Washington regarding partial lifting of the press embargo imposed in anticipation of commencement of Lam Son 719.

ABRAMS: "Well, the answer to this is no. The sole purpose of this is military security. He hasn't figured out what's going on. This briefing . . . about the unrest over there—that's incomplete, because he's also suspecting invasion by sea, invasion by air from the carriers into Laos, all these things. He hasn't figured this thing out. And the movement of the 141, in my opinion, reflects that. Now it also reflects his sensitivity to those operations [Silver Buckle, southern portion of BA 611?] down there. And we just cannot—and send it flash."

WEYAND: "That's what the [press] embargo's all about."

ABRAMS: "That's right. And lift it a little bit—that's more of that being a little bit pregnant. Lift it a little bit! Huh! You either got to have the guts to stand and take the pummeling or, goddamn it, you shouldn't be in the business. That's about the way it is. Get out of the kitchen—you get too hot in the kitchen, get out!"

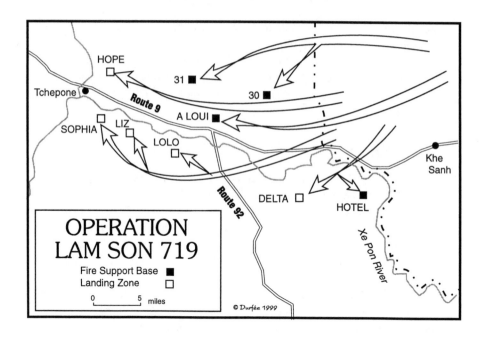

OPERATION
LAM SON 719

Fire Support Base ■
Landing Zone □

0   5   miles

© Durfée 1999

WEYAND: "It really doesn't make any sense."

ABRAMS: "It says 'lift it a little.' All you've got to have is a crack of light coming through there. It's like a little crack in a dam. The next thing you've got's a flood—the dam's gone, the houses are swept down the valley, people are dead. That's what this is—people are dead. <u>Pressure</u>! How about the pressure in the first platoon? How about the pressure there? Or A Company?"

WEYAND: "If we told them yes, we'd have the shortest embargo on record."

ABRAMS: "Dispatch it. And make sure it's clear." [Laughter]

WEYAND: "You could say it in three different languages—nyet, no, non."

■ ■ ■

BRIEFER: In the Parrot's Beak ARVN forces made several contacts along Route 1. On 22 January: 2 friendly KIA, enemy 26 KIA. Then on 27 January several contacts: 0 friendly KIA, enemy 46 KIA, 2 crew-served and 23 individual weapons captured.

ABRAMS: "I find that a very heart-warming sort of a thing. That's the 49th Regiment. That's a lot of small-unit action. They did <u>find</u> the enemy, and they did a rather skillful job of knocking him off. I guess the most remarkable part of all—there are no advisors with them. I mean, you're really commencing to <u>get</u> something here. It's a lot better than <u>HES</u>. We don't have anything for that. It's just something that's kind of <u>results</u>."

BRIEFER: There are reports that an enemy agent operation in I Corps Headquarters, which so far "has not produced any useful information, will be expanded."

ABRAMS: "An operation that has not produced any useful information is being expanded?"

BRIEFER: "That's what it says."

ABRAMS: "We've got 'em licked!" [Laughter] "They're reinforcing disaster. That's one of those handler guys, you see. If he can show that he's tripled the number that he's got, he's really doing good. And he'll get away with it because there's some guy above him that believes the same way. And neither one of them will look at what they've produced. That's the way our own system operates." [Laughter]

■ ■ ■

BRIEFER: Cites rallier reports on the effectiveness of the Phuong Hoang program and countermeasures adopted: VCI have less contact with their families, those suspected of GVN sympathies are transferred frequently, death threats are made against civilians who cooperated, those who were suspected "were sent away for six months of thought reform and indoctrination." As a result of fear of the Phuong Hoang program, district and hamlet cadre are forbidden to live together, and are not allowed to know where one another live. Daily contact with higher-level cadre, which was common before 1968, is now permitted only once or twice monthly, and then only at the initiative of the higher level. "The stringent nature of these directives indicates the great fear of GVN penetration into the VC infrastructure and the improved effectiveness of the GVN counterinfrastructure program."

ABRAMS: "The one thing that's good about it is it's causing them to pay attention to the program. . . . No matter what their physical losses have been, that operates to constrain the effectiveness of the system."

ABRAMS: "I think that going into Cambodia, and that our government was willing to take the political heat to do that, means you [enemy] gotta watch out. 'What are these crazy fellas gonna do?' Then that Son Tay thing, small as it was and so on, but to come in and go out without even getting your hair parted—. And the only thing they had to latch on to was the helicopter that the fellows blew up themselves in accordance with the plan. They crowed about how they destroyed that."

ABRAMS (re enemy high points): "In the past the way we've studied them, and graphed them, and related them to the moon, and Ho Chi Minh's birthday, anniversary of the revolution, and all those things so we can be better on predicting the high points—well, I mentioned to Ambassador Colby, the VC province chief up there in Quang Tin has gotta be figuring how is Colonel Ta deciding on his high points?' Because every one of them is just causing a hell of a lot of damage to their system, and they've got to pay attention to it. I suppose they're trying to find out who his astrologer is, and get it related to the moon. As far as I've been able to determine, Ta is an unusual Vietnamese who doesn't use an astrologer."

CORDS briefer *begins, then long pause for whispered conference on some matter. It is apparently the finished message brought for Abrams's approval.*

ABRAMS (quietly, to someone): "Take this—these first two sentences—."

■ ■ ■

ABRAMS (in discussion) (about someone, middle of conversation, beginning side two of the tape): "We used to think that he didn't believe that, that he put a Jesus factor on his reports. Apparently not. That's what makes a guy so valuable that tells you what he thinks instead of what he believes you want to hear."

ABRAMS: "Incidentally, I was kinda proud of the way they were able to put a clamp on, for Tet, the shooting—. In fact, Vien, who is really a very—well, he's just <u>never</u> going to get his <u>light</u> <u>out</u> [meaning he is not going to boost himself], you know, and so on, but he asked me if I noted that. He's <u>really</u> intensely proud of it. And not only that, but of those who violated it, they incarcerated a substantial number of them. And he's even prouder of that. The ones that wanted to violate it, they caught 'em! Well, not all of them, but a substantial—." "And the president mentioned the other day he was very proud about what the civilians had done about firecrackers. He said there was practically nothing." "That was one of the worst features of Tet '68. At the height of the battle [laughing], most people thought, 'I guess they got bigger fireworks this year or something,' and hell, it was the VC!"

JACOBSON: "They had a prime minister named Loc who gave Ambassador Bunker a string of firecrackers that much in diameter and 16 meters long. And we hung it up on one of those tall trees in front of the embassy and lit that thing. And it went for 21 minutes. And they were all over town like that."

SOMEONE: "Bill, when was the last time we had a battalion-sized attack against anything?"

POTTS (without an instant's hesitation): "You've had 11 since the first of July. One this past week was reported as battalion-size, but after the reports all got in it was a company-size."

BRIEFER: Damaged or destroyed 774 trucks, as compared to the record 1,207 last week. Bad weather a factor in "the truck-killing effort." "The cumulative total of trucks damaged or destroyed this dry season is 4,425."

Discussion of press embargo and impending cross-border operation.

ABRAMS: "Today both the JGS and ourselves are administering a reinforcement of MR-1. This is because of a certain amount of buildup there—some movement of enemy units. The bulk of the input into South Vietnam has been coming into the A Shau over 922. . . . Now, last night we put an embargo on all reporting pertaining to this activity. And that affects all accredited U.S. and Third Country National accredited correspondents."

ABRAMS: "The announcement of the embargo was also embargoed, so that you can't even announce that it was embargoed. This evening at 1800—. See, embargo is the name of the game here, and it's done for military security purposes. They can't report these things, or they lose their accreditation. And it's to protect the security of what it is you're doing. There are a lot of significant movements we've got to make before all of this is really in action. We've been watching this intelligence pretty carefully, and I don't believe—or at least I'm convinced—that he [the enemy] hasn't figured all this out. He suspects many things, and that's about where he stands."

ABRAMS: "Now, on the other hand, the application of an embargo puts certain requirements on us. We have to tell them what's going on, and that's the purpose of this briefing at 1800 this afternoon. And each day—it'll be done out here. It's not part of what's come to be called the 'Five O'Clock Follies.' We'll tell them all that's happened. Within the limits of available transportation we'll permit pools of reporters, TV, and photographers to go into the operational area. Their film will also be embargoed. In other words, you can embargo it and they can't break it. I mean, that's the rule. But when you do, you're also—we're required to keep them abreast. In other words, you pay a price for it. It does mean that they—by the time you lift the embargo they probably will know more about the operation than they ordinarily would in the routine. I think that's the way it really works out."

ABRAMS: "I want everyone to understand that, because the only place the rules on the embargo can be changed is here, by my headquarters. And the only place the briefing will be done is here. So I don't want anybody else passing on what they know. You shouldn't do it. The embargo still applies, but it runs the risk of only confusing the picture. And that's what that message was a little earlier. They, of course, don't like it, and they've tried very hard ever since last night when it was put on—they've invoked all the home offices and everything to try to get it changed. I guess Washington was feeling the heat enough they thought we could let it up 'a little bit.' Well, this kind of thing, there isn't any such thing as letting it up a little bit."

ABRAMS: "This handling of it was endorsed with enthusiasm—I would certainly say was vigorously endorsed—by the Department of Defense before we undertook it. And now we just need to stick with it."

ABRAMS: "Fulbright's in full cry." "As I indicated earlier, the pressure may be pretty great. But every time I consider that it may be getting too bad, I'm going to think of the 1st Platoon. I think the pressure's worse there, and they're doing their job." "When you think of all the guys doing things like that—hell, this stuff looks pretty easy."

6 FEB 1971: WIEU

ATTENDEES: Amb. Berger, Mr. Shackley, Gen. Abrams, Gen. Weyand, Amb. Colby, Gen. Clay, LTG McCaffrey, VADM King, MG Dolvin, MG Cowles, Mr. Jacobson, MG Maples, MG Bowley, MG Dettre, MG Wilson, MG Young, MG Potts, BG Camp, BG Greene, BG Watkin, Mr. Chambers, BG John, BG Cheadle,

BG Henion, BG Heiser, BG Doehler, BG Forrester, Col. Franklin (for Col. Sadler), Col. Leonard, Col. Phillips (for Mr. Kirk), LTC Dodds.

BRIEFER: Intercepts: "Alert Phase One." 2 February 1971: Quang Binh referenced "an allied troop buildup along Route 9, to include a paratroop division, a brigade of marines, and armor elements." Another: Unit prepared to strike the allied forces "when allied units strike the coast." "Analysis of all these messages indicates that the enemy in North Vietnam is uncertain of allied intentions."

BRIEFER: "Rumors of an impending invasion by South Vietnamese troops and American aircraft led to considerable concern and consternation in Laos last week." Pathet Lao propaganda called U.S. forces "a dying tiger with a spear through its neck." Radio Hanoi reported that the Lao government had made a secret agreement allowing two South Vietnamese divisions to penetrate 20 miles into Laos.

BRIEFER: Intercept: Expect enemy forces to execute parachute assault on Route 9 vicinity of Ban Dong.

BRIEFER: Intercepts of 1–4 February: First indications of enemy reaction to anticipated invasion by moving units that had been in RVN back into Laos. AAA battalions, engineers, heavy weapons. "Our analysis indicates that the enemy is improving his defensive positions and is currently increasing his alert status in preparation for anticipated allied operations into his LOC. However, the widespread area of his preparations and the general nature of his communications indicate that he is still uncertain as to the time and location of friendly operations."

ABRAMS (re dispersed enemy preparations): "If there's any comfort in it at all, it's that—for once—he doesn't have the OPLAN two or three days after it was put out. He hasn't got it. That represents quite an advance."

■ ■ ■

BRIEFER: Rallier in Kien Phong Province states that in mid-1968 COSVN directed VC MR-2 to implement a program of purchasing weapons and ammunition from GVN military personnel in order to supplement supplies sent from North Vietnam. After the overthrow of Sihanouk, VC elements were ordered to increase their efforts to procure weapons and ammunition, as resupply from North Vietnam was expected to be delayed indefinitely. The source stated that the program had been very successful, and that the principal sources had been ARVN soldiers, particularly supply personnel, and GVN officials having access to the distribution of military supplies. Also stated that the VC encouraged young children to sift through rubbish dumps near U.S. installations for metal scrap to be used in making mines, grenades, and booby traps.

■ ■ ■

ABRAMS: "We've got that message in where JCS wants a whole lot of detail. When we respond to that—. I'm a little worried. You see, that fellow [Cobb?] that got those figures—remember that? Those figures were correct, and he got those. He's a State Department reporter. In other words, they ask for all this detail, and they get it in there, and then, goddamn it, it gets in the press. And we just don't want that happening. I think they get it back there, and then they just mimeograph it and give it to everybody and his brother. Goddamn it! And then out here we're doing it all by hand, so there won't even be any electrical transmissions of it. I think we've got to tell them we're disturbed by that. And we can give that example."

ABRAMS: "The thing they [Washington] don't seem to understand is the whole thing is in the hands of Lam and Sutherland and their subordinates, and the hourly and minute-to-minute decisions that are being made by them. That's the way the whole—you can't change it. That's just the way it is. There isn't anything I can tell them, or anybody else."

BRIEFER: Operation Dewey Canyon II was initiated in Quang Tri Province during the reporting period. An attack was launched at 0001 hours on 30 January 1971 from FSB Vandegrift by elements of 1st Brigade, 5th Mechanized Division. During day three, infantry task forces combat assaulted into the Khe Sanh area. During the week Task Forces 4/3 Infantry, 3/187 Airborne Infantry, and 1/77 Armor conducted search and clear and route security operations along QL-9 with no significant contact. 3rd Squadron, 5th Cavalry, is attacking south with the mission of opening a pioneer road from the Rockpile to Khe Sanh. TF 1/11 Infantry has been securing the Khe Sanh area since 2 February 1971. 1/1 Cavalry is conducting reconnaissance in force west of Khe Sanh along QL-9. Artillery units are being phased into the Khe Sanh area. The 1st ARVN Ranger Group combat assaults on 4 February to provide flank security on the north. The Airborne Division Headquarters and 3rd Brigade, and 1st ARVN Division Headquarters, have displaced to Khe Sanh. The route is open past Khe Sanh. The airstrip at Khe Sanh is under repair, and a combat assault strip is being constructed there. It is estimated that the airstrip will be ready on 14 February, and the air assault strip on 9 February.

BRIEFER: A special airlift of troops, matériel, and supplies into MR-1 began on 1 February 1971 in support of Operation Dewey Canyon II. To date: 459 sorties have been flown by C-130s, airlifting over 8,800 passengers and 3,400 tons of cargo.

ABRAMS: "Busy!"

■ ■ ■

BRIEFER: During the reporting period 641 trucks from North Vietnam entered the Laotian LOC system. Eighty-one percent of Arc Lights were devoted to the interdiction effort, plus 32 percent of tac air sorties. 581 truckload equivalents passed through or around the box areas. Enemy throughput to RVN was 83 truckloads.

SEVENTH AIR FORCE: "We have done everything we can, General Abrams, to try to interdict that Route 922. It's flat as a pancake, there are multiple routes to go around. We have seeded, we have CBUed, we have bombed, we've done every damn thing we can do. . . . But they sure want to come through there."

"And the weather's stinking most of the time. It's discouraging." Trucks damaged or destroyed totaled 1,072, the second highest total this dry season. This makes 5,475 cumulative trucks damaged or destroyed this dry season, counting from 10 October 1970.

POTTS: "Four hundred trucks a month come into Haiphong."

SEVENTH AIR FORCE: Estimated that 9,000 trucks are operating throughout the system: 3,000 in Laos, 3,000 in Route Pack 1, and 3,000 farther north. PACAF says they estimate the total to be 12,000.

ABRAMS: "I would think that eventually, if you keep this up, it would have some effect."

POTTS: "They had 6,000 in the truck parks up there [NVN] when the dry season started. That's held up pretty well for about three months."

JACOBSON: "It builds character to drive a truck."

13 FEB 1971: WIEU

ATTENDEES: Amb. Berger, Mr. Shackley, Gen. Abrams, Gen. Weyand, Amb. Colby, Gen. Clay, Mr. Kirk, LTG McCaffrey, MG Dolvin, MG Cowles, MG Maples, MG Dettre, MG Wilson, MG Potts, BG Camp, BG Greene, Mr. Chambers, BG John, RADM McManus (for VADM King), BG Cheadle, BG Henion, BG Heiser, BG Doehler, BG Forrester (for Mr. Jacobson), Col. Sadler, Col. Zerbe, Col. Leonard, Col. Jones.

BRIEFER: Weather: By Monday the full force of the monsoon had developed to the point where it was now affecting the greater portion of Southeast Asia to the east of the Annam ridgeline. In the Lam Son area conditions go to rather poor until noontime, zero-zero, then burns off fairly rapidly until about 6:00 P.M. when cloudiness builds up. Expect it to deteriorate through the week. Marginal. Low fog and stratus. In the Tchepone–Route 9 area, morning fog will initially be the only problem. Increased cloudiness later in the week, but generally good in the Tchepone area, less good on the ridgeline.

■ ■ ■

MACV 1971 Infiltration Estimate for Cambodia and SVN: 28,400 (21,000 destined for COSVN).

BRIEFER: Intercepts "continue to indicate a high state of alert in the southern provinces of North Vietnam." On 5 February a Quang Binh provincial unit disclosed "extensive preparations were being made against anticipated allied attacks in North Vietnam."

BRIEFER: "Political developments in Laos this week centered on the ARVN operations in the Tchepone area. After President Thieu's statement on 8 February, Prime Minister Souvanna Phouma issued a formal statement of protest." The language of the statement suggests that it was merely a pro forma protest couched in the mildest terms that would permit Souvanna to claim the position of a neutralist. Quoting: "Certainly the primary responsibility rests with the Democratic Republic of Vietnam which, scornful of international law . . . , began and continues to violate the neutrality and territorial integrity of the Kingdom of Laos."

BRIEFER: Allied forces entered Laos on 8 February 1971. First significant caches located by ARVN forces, including one containing over 600 individual weapons, on 12 February 1971.

ABRAMS: "I talked with the S-3 of the 2/17th yesterday, and they feel that they stopped a T-34. It was clearly a tank. They showed the pilot an identification book, and what he picked out was a T-34."

ABRAMS (re enemy dispositions in the Lam Son 719 area): "It gets more and more realistic with each passing day."

ABRAMS: "Jock [Sutherland] told me yesterday that on that Route 9 some of those weather cuts that were in that road, across it, were 20 feet deep. That's what slowed the engineer work on it. They missed that in the readout of the aerial photography. It was good—they had good photography of it. I guess the assumption was they were two feet deep. There's quite a difference."

BRIEFER: On 8 February 1971 Lon Nol suffered what was described as a mild stroke. Deputy Prime Minister Matak has taken over the dual role of prime minister and defense minister.

BRIEFER: Reports an NVA Hoi Chanh who says the morale of the 95C Regiment is low.

ABRAMS: "What he means is his morale is low."

COLBY: "When we start to have 250-odd North Vietnamese Hoi Chanh a week, instead of per year, then I'll believe in low morale."

ABRAMS: "Right! Right! Right!"

■ ■ ■

BRIEFER: Describes VC efforts to emplace agents (pretending to be ralliers) under legal cover.

CORDS OFFICIAL (responding to Abrams's question): "What we don't know is how many of them will be willing to respond after they've been corrupted by the women, the Hondas, the TV sets."

ABRAMS: "That's all part of the struggle."

■ ■ ■

ABRAMS (talking during a break, and apparently referring to Colonel Mike Healy, CO of 5th Special Forces Group): "I don't know where we could have found a guy that has on the one hand the charisma, and on the other the judgment and the loyalty of [***]."

SOMEONE: "He's a colorful guy."

ABRAMS: "Oh, you're right. But what he's done, in a very difficult—."

SOMEONE: "His two predecessors [Rheault and Lemberes] were disasters."

ABRAMS: "Yeah, you're right."

SOMEONE: "He's a winner."

SOMEONE ELSE: "I want you to know that Al Lemberes is standing in the door, ready to come back." [Laughter]

ABRAMS: "Well, I'm relieved to hear that! It's just too bad, the way we're going down, that the opportunities just aren't—. We better let [***] know about that. Strengthen his hand."

■ ■ ■

ABRAMS (re the Khe Sanh area): "I was out there yesterday, and it's hard to believe—the helicopters, the trucks, the artillery, the amount of equipment that is in that whole thing up there. I'll tell you, I've never seen anything like it in the time I've been here. It's quite remarkable." "Fifty-three Chinooks, really something."

BRIEFER (re Lam Son 719): "After moving into positions in the vicinity of Khe Sanh and Lang Vei during the period 3–7 February, the attack into Laos was launched at 1000 hours on 8 February when units of the 1st ARVN Armored Brigade Task Force crossed the border. At 1045 hours the Headquarters of the 3rd ARVN Airborne Brigade, along with one battalion, combat assaulted." A second airborne brigade combat assaulted into another location, followed by the 21st Ranger Battalion. Other units followed.

BRIEFER: On 10 February the 9th ARVN Airborne Battalion combat assaulted after initially being delayed by antiaircraft fire, then linked up with elements of the armored task force. The 1st Infantry regimental CP, plus one battalion, helilifted in on the 10th. The 39th Ranger Battalion closed in the AO on the 11th. Lead elements of the armored brigade task force have advanced five kilometers west of Objective Aloui. Two significant contacts have been reported: 21st ARVN Ranger Battalion at 1820 on 11 February engaged an estimated enemy platoon, killing 11 without any friendly casualties. On 12 February at 0900 the 2nd ARVN Airborne Battalion had contact resulting in enemy 32 KIA, 20 individual weapons, and three crew-served weapons. ARVN took three KIA.

BRIEFER: Two ARVN cross-border operations (other than Lam Son 719) continue, with over 19,000 troops involved.

■ ■ ■

BRIEFER: Enemy throughput to the Republic was 30 truckloads (vice 83 the previous week). Also four trucks entered Cambodia. Damaged or destroyed 1,122, a new second high for the dry season. Strike-to-kill ratio: 64 percent. Cumulative damaged or destroyed: 7,434.

BRIEFER: Authorized sortie rate is 14,000 per month (those that expend ordnance).

CLAY: "I'm flying roughly 12,000 support sorties a month in addition to this. I'm flying 21,000 sorties a month in airlift. I'm flying roughly 850–900 sorties a month in recce [reconnaissance]. The point I'm making, of course, is that's all maintenance capability, whether you expend ordnance or not. There's a limit to what you can do in generating sorties."

16 FEB 1971: COMUS Update: NVN, Laos, Cambodia

ABRAMS: "With what's happened so far, it appears—so far—that he's going to handle Route 9 with what he had in the B-5 Front, and his reinforcement is going into Laos. Is that right?"

POTTS: "This is right, with the exception that some of the artillery in the DMZ has been moved down some so it can fire further into Front 5."

BRIEFER: We believe the 141st NVA Regiment has disengaged from Silver Buckle [elsewhere in Laos] and may be responsible for some ABFs in the Lam Son 719 AO.

BRIEFER: In the Lam Son 719 AO, an estimated 300 tons of ammunition were destroyed by tac air at one cache site. Also 300 cases of 37-mm ammo have been seized. On 15 February, ARVN forces entered what appeared to be a large training area—over 400 buildings, including bleachers.

BRIEFER: While Lam Son 719 is under way, operations continue in the Plaine des Jarres in western Laos and in Cambodia, as well as in the Republic of Vietnam.

BRIEFER (re Lam Son 719 since the WIEU of 13 February): The first C-130 landed at 1545 on 15 February at Khe Sanh. ARVN forces in Laos continued operations in the eastern half of the AO. 1st Infantry Division, airborne, armor task force, rangers, marines. Effective 0600 on 14 February, General Lam expanded the AO to the south. Some scheduled combat assaults were delayed due to adverse weather conditions. A total of 10,621 ARVN are in Laos now. Two helicopters lost during the period. To date 16 U.S. and 2 VN helicopters have been lost total. Averaging 107 tac air sorties per day in support. Meanwhile, ARVN has 31 battalions in Cambodia, totalling 17,822 men.

WEYAND: "Obviously Lam, and I guess probably President Thieu, too, are looking at [Routes] 92 and 1032 as the major portion, or if not that then certainly half of the problem, and their tactical moves are obviously designed to get a solid footing there before they go on further. They've apparently divided this thing into two pieces. One is that [road] complex, and the next one is Tchepone and west."

BRIEFER: When the ARVN assault cut off Route 92, the traffic shifted to Route 914 southeast out of Tchepone. If that is successfully interdicted, and I believe General Lam is reinforcing the southern portion of this operation for that purpose, it will cut off the traffic out of Tchepone southeast.

19 FEB 1971: COMUS Briefing with Admiral McCain

ABRAMS: "The one thing here, Admiral—in South Vietnam, so far, they've [the enemy] decided to run this thing with the troops that were in the B-5 Front. That is, there's been no cross-the-DMZ reinforcement effort. They've taken the troops that they had, and that's the thing that they're using to raise the level of violence along Route 9 in South Vietnam. And the reinforcement has all occurred over in Laos. It looks like that's the way he's playing the hand now. He's putting his money in the Laos pot."

BRIEFER: "In Laos, the ground contacts have remained at a relatively light level, with company-size and smaller contacts reported throughout the AO. Also, attacks by fire have remained at a relatively low level."

BRIEFER: "Yesterday, air cav units sighted two segments of the POL pipeline." They attacked them, and the pipeline burst into flames.

BRIEFER: "Route 914 has become the primary route for the movement of trucks out of Base Area 604 since the ARVN forces interdicted Route 1032 and Route 92."

BRIEFER: Reportedly Binh Tram 33 rear service element troops have been issued individual weapons and told to be prepared to fight.

BRIEFER: We now carry six enemy regiments committed against ARVN forces in the Lam Son AO: 24B, 102 (of the 308th Division), 1 VC (2nd Div), 64 (320th), 88 (308th), and 141 (2nd NVA). We believe the enemy can reinforce with three additional regiments from the west and north within two days: 48 (320th), 36, and 66. We believe there are three additional regiments in the south that could reinforce immediately into our AO: 812 (324B), 29 (324B), 803 (324B).

■ ■ ■

MCCAIN: "Got any distinguished members of the press up there?"

ABRAMS: "Yeah, they're all over the place. Of course you know we're supporting them, Admiral. They're colleagues of ours, friends. We're doing everything we can for them. And of course they're doing everything they can for us."

MCCAIN: "They've got to keep the great American public informed at the proper level."

SOMEONE: "They're pretty anxious to ride in U.S. helicopters, too, not ARVN." [Laughter]

■ ■ ■

ABRAMS: "Lam told me the other day when I was up there that those prisoners from the 88th were out of companies at a strength of 50 men. That's the way they came into Laos."

ABRAMS: "The Vietnamese—as they see it, to do these things in Cambodia and Laos, you have to take a lot of risks in South Vietnam, but now's the time to take them. The JGS put out to all the sector people, in the course of this they've got to up the operations of the territorials and that sort of thing because of this VC reaction [to try to take advantage in South Vietnam of the out-of-country ARVN deployments]. Police Special Branch has got a thing going on all over the country. They're trying to stimulate the Police Special Branch in picking up sappers and guerrillas and VCI and that sort of thing. So the South Vietnamese have got a program going on themselves, inside South Vietnam, to try to peak it. They expected this, back when it was first discussed, these operations in Cambodia and Laos, and so they've been trying to meet it with increased activity by their own people internally."

BRIEFER: The Lam Son 719 objective is to destroy the enemy system within Base Areas 604 and 611.

BRIEFER: To date 980 enemy KIA, 9 detained, 1,046 individual and 106 crew-served weapons captured. ARVN: 135 KIA, 513 WIA. U.S.: 31 KIA, 163 WIA, 12 MIA. Twenty-one helicopters lost (of close to 7,000 sorties).

ABRAMS: "Tri's got that old-fashioned idea that his job is to destroy the enemy." "I think it's [his operations in Cambodia against the 5th, 7th, and 9th Divisions] pretty good."

WEYAND: "I agree."

ABRAMS: "We've never seen a gathering [of enemy forces] like this since I've been here, both in Laos and this thing here [Cambodia]."

WEYAND: "And what this is doing to take the heat off of Cambodia while they get squared away is beyond calculation—three of those divisions tied down."

ABRAMS: "And it's a good way to welcome those replacements arriving this month."

ABRAMS: "Well, I'll tell you, if what Lam told me the other day up there is correct, if those companies of the 88th had 50 men in them, something's wrong in North Vietnam. That regiment's been up there for months."

POTTS: "Just hasn't filled it up."

ABRAMS: "That's right."

POTTS: "The real significance of that Lam Son operation is the enemy has everything committed, or en route, that he has, with the exception of the 325th Division and the 9th Regiment out of the 304th. So if they're hurt, he's really going to be beat for a long time."

ABRAMS: "And of course we're trying to welcome them all, best we can."

■ ■ ■

MCCAIN: "I think when this <u>damn</u> thing comes out in clear writing sometime, maybe 5 or 10 years from now, you're going to find out that we were a goddamn sight closer to some sort of a successful conclusion to this <u>damn</u> thing than the politicians and newspapers in the United States won't [sic] admit, and a few other things."

ABRAMS: "I thought we'd read that in your memoirs."

MCCAIN: "I'm not going to write any goddamn memoirs. I decided that a long time ago." "Sure going to be interesting to see what some other people say about me in their memoirs, though. I hope I'm around long enough to read some of them."

ABRAMS (serious, not joking): "Well, I think on that score, Admiral, none of us can hope for any of that to be good."

MCCAIN: "Memoirs won't be read if they're good. That's a fact. I can tell you that right now."

■ ■ ■

MCCAIN: "One thing I wanted to ask you about is this, which comes up all the time. Are there any indications, remote or otherwise, that Red China is beginning to move, or even taking a cursory interest in what the frig is going on down here?"

POTTS: "We have nothing at all, and we're watching that carefully."

ABRAMS (re attacking North Vietnam with ground forces): "If they get all this stuff in there, and it gets in the meat grinder and gets chewed up, then you can commence to talk realistically about going into Vinh or Quang Khe or someplace like that. Because they won't have a pot to piss in or a window to throw it out. And the fellows down here are going to get a little bellicose. I noticed yesterday, flying down to the embassy, their LSTs were all painted up, looked pretty good. So—just load them up—.Well, a fellow can dream."

ABRAMS (re Nixon): "That news conference that we got yesterday—really magnificent, magnificent! When you think of the way he's done his homework, stand up there and do all that thing, no script. It's really good. The depth of it. And they give him one of these damn questions—it's got about four questions in it—and he'd take it all and he'd say, 'Now, let me put that in two parts.' And then he'd just—ah, just a masterful performance. And you can't get a handhold to tear it up. It's just too good."

20 FEB 1971: Commanders WIEU

ATTENDEES: Amb. Bunker, Amb. Berger, Gen. Abrams, Gen. Weyand, Amb. Colby, Gen. Clay, Mr. Kirk, LTG Davison, LTG Sutherland, LTG Robertson, MG Dolvin, MG Brown, MG McCown, MG Cowles, MG Gettys (for LTG McCaffrey), Mr. Jacobson, MG Maples, MG Bowley, MG Dettre, MG Young, MG Potts, MG Wilson, Mr. Funkhouser, Mr. Lazar, Mr. Vann, Mr. Long, BG Camp, BG L. Greene, BG Watkin, Mr. Chambers, BG John, RADM McManus (for VADM King), BG Cheadle, BG Henion, BG Heiser, BG Doehler, BG Forrester, Col. Sadler, Col. Leonard, Col. Jones, Col. Healy.

Operation Lam Son 719, ongoing in Laos, is the central issue at the moment.

BRIEFER: During the past week there have been major moves by NVA forces to reinforce the AO in Laos.

POTTS: "All units that were in North Vietnam are en route or committed now, with the exception of the 325th Division and the 9th of the 304th."

BRIEFER: Elements of five enemy divisions are in or near the Lam Son 719 AO: 308th Division (102nd and 88th Regiments), 2 (1 VC, 141), 304 (24B), 320 (64), 324B (812, 29). Six NVA regiments are committed now against ARVN in the AO.

BRIEFER: The first significant enemy counterattack occurred on the night of 18 February. Two NVA battalions attacked the ARVN 39th Ranger Battalion northeast of Ban Dong.

BRIEFER: The pipeline has now been interdicted in four locations. At one place a fire started at 1115 and went until 1700. Two rice caches found yesterday totaled 110 tons and 20 tons.

ABRAMS: "Get a hatful of that rice and find out where it came from."

ABRAMS: "The situation you've got up there is that, each 24 hours, they've got between five and eight hours of helicopter time. There's 18 battalions over there, and 10 batteries of artillery—and all the resupply and everything that's got to be done for those 18 battalions and 10 batteries in the 5 to 8 hours every 24. Well, there isn't a lot of sightseeing going on."

BRIEFER: U.S. artillery supporting Lam Son 719: 18 155-mm howitzers, 16 175-mm, and 8 8-inch artillery pieces positioned along the border.

BRIEFER: In Laos (Lam Son 719) 18 battalion-sized task forces continue search and clear operations. The westernmost task force is approximately the same location as last week, five kilometers west of the junction of Highways 9 and 92.

SUTHERLAND (re extraction of the 6th ARVN Airborne Battalion from Objective 31 area): "Practically one whole company was put in the wrong place, and they never got it together." "Lam and Dong decided to pull it out, and I think it was a wise choice—get it out and get it back together. Go with another battalion. By the way, that extraction—I thought that was going to be a hairy operation, because we've had a hell of a time supplying that Objective 31 a few days this week, getting all kinds of fire. But that went off like clockwork. Started about 9:30 and had them out by 12:30—over 400 people."

BRIEFER: "Numerous significant cache discoveries." Plots them: red dots = munitions and weapons; blue squares = foodstuffs; black stars = equipment (other than weapons and ammo); green diamonds = medical supplies.

SUTHERLAND: Since 8 February 1971 we've had over 1,600 troop lift sorties into Laos. Have over the whole period to date only lost 21 helicopters (19 to enemy action, 2 to accidents) (plus one marine H-53 to accident). "I think that's very, very low, considering the AA we're going up against." Re marine helicopters: "They're doing a tremendous job." The briefer had omitted the USMC H-53 from his tabulation on the grounds he did not think it was part of Lam Son 719. Sutherland: "It sure was."

ABRAMS: "The marines are back in Khe Sanh, and doing a hell of a job."

BRIEFER: During the reporting period three battalions of infantry, three ranger battalions, and two armored cavalry squadrons moved from the central and southern portions of MR-1 to participate in or support operation Lam Son 719.

■ ■ ■

ABRAMS: "I spent a little time out with the 1st Cav yesterday. It's really kind of amazing what's happened up there in Phuoc Long. Roads open, the civilian traffic up there, timber cutting, out there in that Indian country."

DAVISON: "You can take a Lambretta from Song Be to Bo Duc."

JACOBSON: "I think that province ranks second in the nation on the HES."

ABRAMS: "In terms of economic development—a hundred lumber vehicles operating up there."

SOMEONE: "We had to supply them by air for three years."

COLBY: When we established as a goal each province to become self-sufficient in producing rice and other necessities, some people questioned that, saying that specialization would be more efficient. "Of course, you look back about two years—the reason those goals were put was that it was a matter of supplying them by air or something like that when they got in trouble. So I think the self-sufficiency for each province has a certain long-term value around here, even if it costs you a little in economic terms."

BUNKER: "I remember the high HES ratings they had when they had to be supplied by air all the time." [Laughter]

DAVISON: "I think Colonel Lu Yen deserves a great deal of credit." Province chief of Phuoc Long. "Very energetic, smart, and apparently honest."

BRIEFER (re Hoi Chanh): "This week we had the highest weekly total since August of 1969." Three of the top four provinces were in the U Minh. Outposts are being built, and they "realize there's a permanent presence going in." Over 500 Hoi Chanh over the past three weeks from the U Minh.

■ ■ ■

ABRAMS: "General Putnam told me yesterday that the platoon leader of one of the recon platoons that was standing down came to him and said the entire platoon volunteered to extend if they could go as a platoon to one of the battalions that was staying in Vietnam." [Sarcastically]: "That's another one of those torn apart by racial problems, sick with drugs and rebellion and insubordination, and so on. But they're doing pretty good." "I think in that platoon there are something like 10 men who are college graduates—have their degrees. . . . I guess some of the college students are all right."

ABRAMS: "I went over to the hospital and pinned a DSC on this young man. One of those citations that just about make you weep—you couldn't believe what he'd done. He was wounded day before yesterday. When he was wounded he had 10 days left to do. I asked him where he was from. 'New Jersey.' I asked him, 'What are you going to do when you get home?' He said, 'I'm going to be a cop. I'll have to wait a little while. I'm not old enough yet.' He's 19. New Jersey may not understand it, but he is old enough. He's quite a young fellow. Very well liked in his own outfit."

ABRAMS (re operational—not due to enemy action—helicopter losses): "That's guys sticking the tail rotor in a tree and hooking the skids in the wires and all that kind of stuff. The sort of thing we're ordinarily against—we have a policy of that." [Laughter]

■ ■ ■

BRIEFER: New record in truck kills reached this week. 1,299 reported destroyed or damaged. Previous high: 1,207. Last week: 1,122. "The Plaine of Jarres and the area west of Ban Ban again produced most of the successful strikes."

ABRAMS: "Well, in Barrel Roll."

BRIEFER: "Yes, sir. In Steel Tiger the strikes continued to be distributed throughout the full route structure." Overall strike-to-kill ratio: 67 percent, the highest of the dry season.

■ ■ ■

BRIEFER: The RLAF flew 978 sorties in support of ground operations during the week.

CLAY: "The Royal Lao Air Force, General Abrams. They're doing a hell of a job. The guys are out there. They're flying hard. They're short sorties, so they can maintain this kind of a rate, but there's a real fine little bunch of guys trying to work a tough problem."

■ ■ ■

BRIEFER: Suggests future tactical planning include consideration of providing security to important economic installations as well as to the people. Examples: rubber plantations, sugarcane and other agricultural pursuits, fishing grounds, logging areas, farm-to-market roads. Elsewhere military operations have long inhibited the planting of economically important crops such as pineapples, sugarcane, coconut, rubber. Need to lift these restrictions as early as the military situation will permit.

ABRAMS: "We've got to be conscious of these things that General Watkin has just talked about. Because it's true—at least I'm convinced —that we can do things inadvertently that will hurt them economically." "We didn't have to think about this when we were trying to get the rockets stopped in Saigon, or get them back away from the Danang airport. None of these things then—hell, you didn't even have to put them in the equation. There were other things then that were more pressing. Well, now it's come their day. It isn't just some ivory tower economic theorist. This is a plain fact of life coming out of Vietnam as a viable country. We have to understand that—at least understand it enough not to go busting up the china. There are places here where we've got to go kind of soft, and don't go rotating your turret."

ABRAMS: "The other things I'm going to be advancing with all of you involves our human relations with the Vietnamese—our relations with their officials, our relations with their people. We've got to get into this more and get organized things going where we're meeting with them, where we're discussing problems with them and getting them out on the table. And recognize that it is their country. In these kinds of meetings they'll be chaired by them. We'll be there. And we're not all right! We're going to have to do this even where you think it's all going swell, because it won't be going swell in July. Some of these activist groups will get going, and they'll start stimulating things on you. You've got to have this mutual trust and confidence down there, facing up to the problems, working solutions out that will meet our needs and theirs. That's going to be a vital part, and if we can't swing it then we're going to screw up everything that's been accomplished. The nature of the thing changes, and we've got to change with it. We've got to be sensitive, and have a little more faith where it's kind of weak now."

ABRAMS: "Having said all that, I do want to point out—earlier in the meeting here today, we saw this Chup thing, that Military Region 3 thing, and we've seen the Lam Son 719 thing. Now what we're headed into here, the way he's gathering in Chup and the way they're gathering up there in Laos, is one hell of a battle. Now both of those have got to be won, and they are going to be won. They're going to go on for about two months. I want to ask all the commanders—General Clay, General Gettys representing USARV, and members of the staff—let's not let priorities, or policies, that have been appropriate over the last six months now gum us up where we're not giving the support. We'll give these two things anything it takes that we've got! And I want it done. And if there's some policy we've got, some procedure we've got, that's standing in the way of that, call me or Weyand or the Chief, but let's find a way to see that the Vietnamese have got everything we can give them and help them to get this job done and these two battles won! I think they're of critical importance to the rest of '71 and '72. It's an opportunity to deal the enemy a blow which probably hasn't existed before as clearly cut in the war. Those are military operations, and I'm not pushing this now as sort of a parochial love of a great battle. It's not that at all. I think it's critical. I think it's time for it. The risks in getting it done were all known and understood in the beginning, and it was felt that it was time to take the risks. Now we cover those by every effort that we can make—equipment-wise, supply-wise, anything we've got, and see the thing through."

BUNKER: "This past week I was in Washington, and went through this whole decision-making process there. One of the things I think was of great concern is the point that General Abrams has just made—the risk involved if this didn't succeed. And what we'd do, through our policy here—how it would affect the elections, Thieu's position, and the whole situation in Vietnam. There were a good many other things that were taken into consideration—what the effect would be in the northern part of Laos, what the effect would be on the Chinese, and on Souvanna's position. The principal thing was the risk involved in getting into Laos and, as I said, the South Vietnamese getting chewed up. But these were all weighed very carefully. And the president, of course, made the decision. Obviously I'm glad the way it turned out."

BUNKER: "I think one interesting thing, and significant thing, [was] the skill in which—the way in which the president handled the political aspect of this at home. There was great apprehension, too, that there would be reaction to this. Not to the extent there was in the Cambodian operation last May, but nevertheless very substantial. But the whole scenario was very carefully worked out. The first thing the president insisted was that our part of this should be played in low key. It should be put forward primarily as a Vietnamese operation. And it was handled in that way. Great care was taken, also, in briefing the Congress, the chairmen of the committees, and the whole scenario—the statements which President Thieu made, and which Souvanna made, were excellent. In fact, when they came into Washington the reaction was they were perfect from our point, too. And the reaction at home, as you know, has been very modest, very moderate. Even Senator Cooper said on television that our going into Laos did not contravene the Cooper-Church amendment. Senator Church agreed with him. And, to my great surprise, Averell Harriman said to me that the Laos thing didn't bother him very much because they've been violating Laotian neutrality for 10 years. So that was quite a plus."

BUNKER: "But, I think, as General Abrams said, this is going to be a critical year for the test of our policy here. With the elections coming up, it is clearly in our interest, I think, to see that this administration continues. And how these operations in Cambodia and Laos turn out obviously is going to have a very direct bearing on it. It's also going to be a test of the whole political situation, to see whether a Western-type constitution grafted onto an authoritarian, family-oriented heritage will survive the political contest and a war. I think we just have to see that it's done. And I think we can. Stay with it."

24 FEB 1971: COMUS Update

BRIEFER: No change in enemy dispositions in North Vietnam. Intercepts still reflect concern about allied ship deployments off the coast. 812th Regiment (324B Division) is preparing attacks in the Lang Vei area, viewed by the enemy as "a good opportunity to gain a victory."

BRIEFER: A rallier from 24B Regiment revealed the location and identity of a new front-level headquarters controlling three NVA divisions in the Lam Son AO. 70B Front: 320, 304, 308 NVA Divisions.

BRIEFER: We are carrying six NVA regiments committed against ARVN forces in the Lam Son 719 AO. Three additional regiments are positioned where they could be committed: 29, 812, 36. Also 48 and 66 from NVN could be within 48 hours.

BRIEFER: We assess significant casualties having been inflicted at this time on three enemy regiments: 102, 24B, 88. We believe two battalions of the 102 and one battalion each of the 24B and 88 have been rendered combat ineffective. Thus, of 18 battalions subordinate to the six enemy regiments committed, the equivalent of four battalions may be ineffective at this time.

BRIEFER: Binh Tram 41 is making a major effort to withdraw the bulk of its ammunition stocks back into the Binh Tram 33 area. Meanwhile Binh Tram 33 is trying to shift as much of its stocks as possible south into BA 611.

BRIEFER (re the current AA threat in the Lam Son AO): Elements of 282 and 591 AAA Regiments displaced west into reinforcing positions along Route 9 east of Tchepone. Some elements have moved back across the Se Bang Hieng River. Overlapping concentrations develop in the Tchepone area, especially to the west along the river. Estimate 96 AAA weapons of 23-mm or larger in the AO. Represents a reduction of about 34 since the beginning of the operation, "probably reflecting the results of the intensified air campaign against these weapons."

BRIEFER: Cumulative results to date: Enemy: 2,191 KIA. ARVN: 276 KIA, 842 WIA, 101 MIA. U.S.: 54 KIA, 235 WIA, 15 MIA. Twenty-six helicopters lost in the operation so far.

■ ■ ■

An ARVN catastrophe. Lt. Gen. Do Cao Tri is killed in action.

BRIEFER: At 0920 hours yesterday the VNAF helicopter carrying the CG of III Corps and his assistant G-3 for Operations crashed and burned at Tay Ninh. Both were killed. CG 18th ARVN Division, Major General Thinh, has assumed command of III Corps and is directing operations in Cambodia.

ABRAMS: "It's General Minh. He's taken command."

■ ■ ■

An unexpected and serious crisis in aviation support for Lam Son 719.

ABRAMS: "Now, has anybody got any comments on this message?"

J-3: "Yes, sir. We were with General Sutherland from four to six last evening. A Brigadier General Smith, who is apparently acting as his aviation expert, raised this issue in a meeting that we had with them. I suggested to General Sutherland at that time that if this was the situation he ought to get a personal message in to you. The problem as I got it up there, sir, is of course not the combat loss but it's primarily the dust that's beginning to kill them. That, coupled with the fact that part of Route 9 he cannot move his 5,000-gallon tankers over has required him to use more lift to move fuel than he had anticipated."

J-3: "He raised the issue of the UH-1C being inadequate—Smith did—for the task. I suggested if that were the case he put the UH-1Cs in the 23rd, and take the 10 out of there, the 10 Cobras that he claims he needs, and put them up front. But Smith didn't want the UH-1Cs anywhere up there. I don't know how he can get away from that. As far as the additional Chinook company he needs, although I don't have a definite recommendation yet, it looks feasible to me that if you elect to give him one we can do it without degradation of Tuan Thang 71."

J-3: "The aerial weapons company is a different problem. You only have three others available to you, one in each of your other MRs, and the one in MR [number unclear] is of course a relatively small unit supporting primarily SOG. His Cobra problem is the one that's of concern to him, primarily from a maintenance point of view. General Sutherland told me his maintenance was really working full-time getting this stuff up. But until we got into this with Smith last night up there, I think it's fair to say we had no feel that his helicopter situation was quite as acute."

J-3: "We also went over with him the Arc Light situation, and he is seeing General Lam first thing this morning with a view to letting Bill Doehler stage the Arc Lights in along Route 9 against the antiair—start saturating the route—and Tchepone. What they have been doing—Lam has been picking the targets, and our targeteers up there—both Potts and J-3 each have a man up there—have been trying to scrub down the intelligence and adapt the boxes as appropriate. We suggested to General Sutherland he may want to divert it into a different type of mission. He's for it, and he's going to discuss that with General Lam today. Bill is prepared—what is it, starting tomorrow morning?—putting an Arc Light cell of three ships in every one hour and 50 minutes. General Sutherland is in favor of that. He's going to discuss that with General Lam."

J-3: "General Lam also has a plan—he's going to move the 3rd and 2nd Regiments forward, first to Fire Support Base Brown and another a few clicks farther to the west, south of the highway preliminary to going into Tchepone. Then he plans to airlift one brigade a day into Tchepone for two days to start building that up. [Someone: "He indicated he did have the airlift to do that."] That's right. The only other Cobras available at the moment in the north are a total of 16, sir, 6 of which are reserved to SOG—to support SOG operations. I have not been able to reach Sadler to discuss that with him. And then there are 10 others in XXIV Corps."

J-3: "It does appear, based on our discussions with General Sutherland, that he could use another hook [cargo helicopter] company because of the lift requirements. In the message he requested another Cobra company, of course, or two ARA [aerial rocket artillery] units. ARA you're short on, too. We have one battalion, actually, in the 1st Cav, and that's been supporting III Corps. I told General Sutherland if he has a requirement that he ought to get it in to you, and that we would take a look and make a recommendation to you on what we had available, that you had accorded him first priority, but it looked to me at the moment, and particularly in view of Tri's death, you might not want to degrade anything in III Corps. So unless he had something pretty serious, it looked like we had to pull it from either II Corps or IV Corps."

J-3: "The problem, I honestly believe, sir, is one of maintenance, and the Chief has talked to General McCaffrey on the entire issue this morning. Whether they need more direct support I'm not in a position to say. Their Cobras _are_ down. They don't have too many flyable. In the other lift he's not in bad shape, and the hooks are intended to augment his current lift capability, primarily because he can't use Route 9 to the extent he wanted. He's having trouble building up JP-4 forward. He's never gotten it up to the 200,000 gallons he wants. There's one section of that route, as I mentioned, that his 5,000-gallon tankers can't take. It just rips the guts out of them, because of the gradient."

ABRAMS: "What did General McCaffrey say?"

SOMEONE: "He said that he wasn't aware of the acuteness of this problem at all when he got this message." "He indicated no great shortage. He said he was only short six Cobras theaterwide."

ABRAMS: "The way this thing is supposed to work is that, once I said _what_ the priorities were and _what_ was going to be done around here, goddamn it then these—USARV's responsible for the support of helicopters. Now, goddamn it, they're supposed to have maintenance people up there, keeping track of this, goddamn it! And they should _know_ what's happening! That's their job! That's

McCaffrey's responsibility! And that's what hasn't been done. You got any views on this, Fred?"

WEYAND: "Well, I guess I'm not too forgiving on Jock [Sutherland]. I recognize the truth of what you're saying, but goddamn it, you've got a corps commander up there who's supposed to be keeping track of every fucking bird in the place every hour of the day. And there ought to be night briefings in which—. If this thing happened in an hour or two, I could understand it. I just don't. There's something wrong there. You've got an organizational problem of some kind. He just doesn't know what the hell's going on. A battalion on 914 for two days before he knew about it—we knew about it —tells me that the coordination and tie-in between his headquarters and Lam's is not fully effective. I think we've got an organizational problem, just as you say. USARV better have some sort of a section up there where you've got the kind of experts—. They're just too far away from it down here." And re UH-1C: "It sounds to me like General Smith has just gone completely ape. Those aircraft can't be totally ineffective. To a certain extent we've got to rely on Jock and those people of his up there running the show."

ABRAMS: "I believe we've got the tickets to straighten this out. I just want to get a new game plan."

Long pause—several minutes.

ABRAMS: "I guess I'd better go up and talk with General McCaffrey now." "I just feel we've got to get some people up there today who can be feeding the facts back." "Move the goddamn men and the tools and the stuff and get with it."

27 FEB 1971: WIEU

Attendees: Gen. Abrams, Gen. Weyand, Amb. Colby, Gen. Clay, Mr. Kirk, LTG McCaffrey, MG Dolvin, MG Cowles, Mr. Jacobson, MG Maples, MG Bowley, MG Dettre, MG Wilson, MG Young, MG Potts, BG Camp, MG Watkin, Mr. Chambers, RADM McManus (for VADM King), BG Cheadle, BG Henion, BG Brown, BG Doehler, BG Forrester, Col. Zerbe (for Col. Sadler), Col. Leonard, Col. DeBruler, Col. Jones. Discussion shows Amb. Bunker or Amb. Berger also present.

POTTS (re infiltration): "There have been only four gap groups that had not previously been detected by COMINT or eventually confirmed by collateral. 1971 MACV estimate now at 31,300 (76 percent to COSVN).

BRIEFER (reflecting, as of this date, little enemy reaction to the incursion into Laos): 325th NVA Division (101, 95, 18 Regiments) remains in its normal AO. 312th NVA Division (141 Regiment) probably remains in the Thanh Hoa and Vinh areas. 29 and 165 Regiments are in northern Laos per COMINT. The 308th NVA Division (88, 102 Regiments) is east of Tchepone and in contact in the Lam Son 719 AO. The 36th Regiment may also be in the AO. 304th Division (9 Regiment) in Dong Hoi. 66th Regiment made a southwest move of 16 nautical miles to northwest DMZ and may move to the AO. 24B Regiment is 30 kilometers east of Tchepone and in contact. 320th Division is in the Dong Hoi area, but a forward element of it was fixed in Laos with the 48th Regiment 65 kilometers west of Tchepone. 64th Regiment in contact approximately 30 kilometers east of Tchepone. 52nd Regiment is in Cambodia.

BRIEFER: COMINT reveals NVA units in the southern provinces of NVN are still concerned about allied ships off the coast, including reported embarked troops: "Continuing buildup of allied forces in the coastal waters of southern North Vietnam." "Preparing to attack." "Prepare for battle." In North Vietnam an exercise rehearsing a defensive counteraction against an enemy assault was conducted by the 271st Independent Infantry Regiment and other elements in the area north of Vinh.

BRIEFER: Laos is in a declared state of emergency, with curfews in effect in all major cities except Vientiane, and rumors of on-the-spot conscription of draft-age males (resulting in "a marked decrease in the number of young men observed on the streets of Laotian towns").

BRIEFER: Official French reaction to Lam Son 719 has been unfavorable. This week the Quai d'Orsay's director of Asian Affairs, Messr. Promo Maurice, complained that "military considerations always seem to prevail in U.S. decision making," saying also that "the U.S. always seemed to prefer taking military rather than political risks."

BRIEFER: A new NVA headquarters appears to be controlling tactical units north of Route 9. The 559th Group (Binh Trams 41 and 33) seems to have retained control of the tactical units operating south of Route 9 (and the considerable barrier formed by the escarpment paralleling and south of Route 9).

BRIEFER: We believe elements of the 29th Regiment (324B Division) are now committed in the southern part of the Lam Son 719 AO, bringing to seven the number of enemy NVA regiments committed. We assess 4 (102, 243, 88, 141) as having received significant casualties, 5 of the 21 battalions being rendered combat ineffective. The 812 and 36 are also near the AO and in position to be committed. The 48 and 66 could be.

BRIEFER: There was a major attack against a brigade CP of the 1st ARVN Division at Objective 31, probably by elements of the 64th NVA Regiment, plus tanks, on 25 February. Overrun. Reportedly a brigade commander has been captured by the NVA. At least eight PT-76 tanks involved.

COLONEL DI LORENZO: Provides analysis of captured rice and passes around samples (short, stubby grains from China).

BRIEFER: Border Defense Rangers south of Svay Rieng made contact with enemy forces. Six enemy KIA plus significant cache discovery, including over five tons of ammunition.

ABRAMS: "Territorial Forces?" "Ah, these rabbits are coming along good!"

■ ■ ■

ABRAMS: Asks how many outposts there are in the delta [MR-4].

JACOBSON: "4,465, not counting An Giang and Bac Lieu. I'd say 4,600."

SOMEONE: During the time 21 were overrun, they built almost a couple of hundred.

JACOBSON: Over 1,100 squad-sized. "Of over 500 VC hamlets at the beginning of the year, they've got something like 35 left. And the way they did it was to live dangerously, like this. Results, I think, prove the concept to be a good one."

■ ■ ■

ABRAMS: Recalls when a Soviet ship went into Danang and the VNN fired some shots across its bow: "Washington got very upset."

WEYAND: "Well, after all, the South Vietnamese are at war."

■ ■ ■

DISCUSSION: Intercepting vessels at sea, territorial waters, etc.

JACOBSON: "I don't want to be known as a dove," but this is an area of great potential difficulties.

ABRAMS (after the discussion has rambled for some time): "I guess we're in over our heads."

ABRAMS: "Incidentally, Mr. Ambassador, I'm delighted that you were here on the occasion of the first dove speech by Jake."

SOMEONE: "The house dove in this particular house doesn't have to be very dovish." [Laughter]

■ ■ ■

POTTS: "Sir, Lieutenant Jacobson, your NAVFORV briefer for the past year, is completing his tour this week. This is his last WIEU."

ABRAMS: "W-e-l-l, w-e-l-l! [Laughter] I think you can safely report to Admiral Zumwalt that the navy has retained its sense of humor—which he never was averse to himself. Well, you've done a splendid job here, and we all appreciate it. We wish you well."

■ ■ ■

BRIEFER: During the week 16 RVNAF battalion-sized forces continued search and clear operations in their assigned AOs in Laos. On 20 February the 39th ARVN Ranger Battalion evacuated its position due to enemy pressure and joined the 21st ARVN Ranger Battalion about two kilometers south. Both units have since returned to the RVN.

■ ■ ■

ABRAMS (re B-52s): "They ought to know [be aware that] they're doing some good."

SOMEONE: "SAC seems to have a highly developed sense for finding those things out."

SOMEONE: "I thought tac air got that, myself. Correct our records."

ABRAMS: "Management by conflict."

ABRAMS (re a telephone report received just as the WIEU commenced that an ARVN armor unit had linked up with the forces under attack at FSB 31): "It's important to verify that and see that it's reported to the NMCC."

WEYAND: "That would be very heartening, and show they've still got some determination."

BRIEFER: Three RVNAF cross-border operations continue in Cambodia, with over 21,000 troops participating.

BRIEFER: Helicopter assets decreased by 46 due to turn-in of assets and losses during the period (10 combat and 6 operational losses).

No discussion of U.S. helicopter problems in support of Lam Son 719. Apparently taken care of since the big blowup of 24 February.

■ ■ ■

BRIEFER: Describes an F-4 on a 25 February napalm mission in support of Lam Son 719: Pilot hit by ground fire. Navigator recovers control of the aircraft, flies it to Phu Cat (because their home base of Danang was weathered in) and ejects himself and the pilot. Navigator picked up in good condition, but the pilot was KIA.

ABRAMS: "That's an <u>amazing</u> performance!" "I'm surprised he had room back there [to fly the aircraft]. I thought he had those five or six volumes of rules of engagement." [Laughter]

■ ■ ■

BRIEFER: The JGS proposed accelerating about 8,000 manpower spaces from FY '73 to FY '72, "thereby achieving an RVNAF force of 1.1 million men one year ahead of schedule." MACV and CINCPAC concurred. Forwarded to JCS for consideration.

■ ■ ■

ABRAMS: "What we're in up here, in both Laos and Cambodia, is a real tough fight. We're just going to have to stick with it and <u>win</u> it. We've got the tickets to do it, and that's what's going to be done. We've been in them before. And we've been inundated by the prophets of doom before, as we are now. The one thing that's better about this than any of the rest of them is that some of the units they're fighting with up there in Laos—we used to fight them in Hue. And this is a better place to fight them. And some of those units that they're fighting over there in Cambodia, we used to fight them in the precincts at one time, down here in Saigon. The 9th Division had elements down here in the precincts. This is just a better place to do that. I mean, as long as you're going to have to fight, I think this is a better ring than the one we had."

1 MAR 1971: COMUS Update: NVN, Lam Son 719, Cambodia

BRIEFER: Information has been received that the 36th Regiment has now been committed against ARVN forces. "Based on this, we now have elements of eight infantry regiments committed against ARVN forces in the Lam Son AO." Of 24 enemy battalions committed, we estimate their losses are such that they have lost the effectiveness of an equivalent six battalions. We also estimate the enemy may now have as many as 80 tanks committed to the Lam Son AO.

BRIEFER (re sensor string activations): More north movers than south above the battle area, and more south movers than north below the battle area. In both cases more movement away from the battle area than toward it.

BRIEFER: Total to date 34 helicopters lost in support of Lam Son (23 of them in Laos).

ABRAMS: "It's still a hell of a struggle."

WEYAND: "Up north, I don't think the flavor of this briefing is quite what Jock's reporting on the secure voice. He says the enemy is all over that goddamn area and seems to be getting stronger, if anything. And so there's a real fight going on up there. Particularly that indirect fire thing is worrying."

WEYAND: "I asked Nick and the doc to get organized so that we can give these people the medical support, and keep tied in with them. They're getting a hell of a lot of wounded, and their hospitals are getting filled up. We don't want to start just wholesale bringing them into our hospitals."

4 MAR 1971: COMUS Update: NVN, Lam Son 719, Sensors, J-3

BRIEFER: When ARVN entered Laos on 8 February 1971 the enemy initially assumed a defensive posture. Elements of the 24 Bravo, 64th and 1st VC Regiments, were preparing defensive positions, buying time to get reinforcements into the area and protecting supplies by issuing them from the *binh trams* and removing them to the west.

BRIEFER: On 10 February 1971 the enemy was still in a defensive posture, but up from elements of three to seven regiments in the AO. On 11 February 1971 were the first indications that the enemy was shifting to an offensive posture, but not until 18 February 1971 did the first major counterattack occur (against an ARVN ranger battalion in the northern AO). Counterattacks have continued since that time. Also by 16 February 1971 two additional enemy regiments had been added to the AO (29th and 812th), for a total of nine regiments at this time.

BRIEFER: On 25 February 1971 the enemy apparently detected elements of an ARVN ranger group being airlifted back into RVN, and possibly elements of the Airborne Division also being withdrawn back into RVN. At that time the enemy reported throughout the AO that ARVN forces were being defeated and were attempting to withdraw; their mission was to continue to attack and exploit, attempting to cut off and annihilate withdrawing forces.

BRIEFER: On 1 March 1971 the enemy detected reinforcement of the AO by

ARVN [or armored? word not clear] elements moving on Route 9, and also reinforcement by RVN Marines. From that date, the enemy is reportedly going back to a defensive posture.

BRIEFER: At this time the enemy has elements of eight regiments committed against RVN forces in the AO. Also has the 812th south of Lang Vei, which could be committed immediately. And three additional regiments that could be committed within 48 hours: 48th (now committed against Lao forces), 66th, and 9th (304th Division), both probably moving into the Lam Son AO now.

BRIEFER: In the eight regiments we estimate the enemy has lost the equivalent of seven maneuver battalions in personnel losses.

BRIEFER: We estimate that of 100 tanks the enemy now has 65–70 left (more than half of them medium tanks). T-54s confirmed.

BRIEFER: The entire area is considered high threat for enemy AA weapons: 14.5-mm, 12.7-mm machine guns. Ninety to ninety-five percent of hits sustained by helicopters so far are by these smaller-caliber weapons (including individual automatic weapons).

BRIEFER: Committed enemy strength now estimated at approximately 13,000 combat forces, plus 8,000–10,000 rear service personnel.

BRIEFER: Sixteen ARVN maneuver battalions are currently in Laos. The Airborne Division, organized into two brigades, has seven combat effective battalions, six of which are in Laos. The 2nd Airborne Brigade, with its CP at the border, has three battalions operating along Route 9. 1st ARVN Infantry Division has 13 battalions in Laos. The 1st Armored Task Force is conducting operations along Route 9 and north along Route 92. The 147th VNMC Brigade has one battalion in Laos. Also 12 ARVN artillery batteries are deployed in Laos. Twelve ARVN battalions operating in Quang Tri Province are also considered part of Lam Son 719.

BRIEFER: Action vicinity of Objective 31, also referred to as Fire Support Base 31, 27 February 1971 to date: Enemy: 250 KIA, 12 PT-76, 3 T-34 tanks destroyed. Friendly: 13 KIA, 39 WIA, 3 APCs damaged.

BRIEFER: Today ARVN plans a combat assault by 1st Regiment elements into LZ Lolo.

ABRAMS: "What was your impression of the atmosphere up there yesterday?"

SOMEONE: "Sir, it was very hectic. The senator had been in and out, or was in the process of moving through the area. There were many other people up there. General McCaffrey and his staff were up there supervising the move in of all this comm gear for the FSCC. General Roberts and a few of his people were up there. I was there. And I noted General Sutherland was torn in about 16 different directions by people, so I got out of his hair as soon as I could in my terms of reference."

■ ■ ■

SOMEONE (comes on in midsentence): ". . . retaining a good grip on this thing, even though there may be some problems in the upper echelon of the Airborne Division. The staff that I talked to was full of praise again, and this is a recurring thing, of the 1st ARVN Division. They apparently are doing a bang-up job." In the briefing to me they described how well they are doing both tactically and in Arc Light targeting. Re the Marine Division, "they didn't have a real good grip on how it was going to tie in to the command relationships and the command structure. It would appear that it's probably going to be used as brigades rather than a division."

SAME SOMEONE: "The Fire Support Coordination Center . . . the organization of that is going to be somewhat of a problem. General McCaffrey has been scarfing up communications from all over the country to send up there—from units all over the country. He told me in all candor, he said, 'I'm not sure what kind of shape this stuff is going to be in. It's going to be pretty much chaos until we really get it in here, shake it down, get it set up, and get it running.'" "And his only concern was that we don't have a big flail up there during the period that we're shaking down the FSCC and getting it operational, because he foresees a day or two of utter chaos in setting the thing up and getting it running."

SAME SOMEONE: "General Hemingway I talked to, and he has been tasked with coming up with some new techniques for medevac, and also for this AAA suppression. He told me that he felt that our aviators, our army helicopter operators, had been possibly too aggressive in the beginning. They'd been incountry in a relatively permissive environment. They went over there with the same kind of an approach, and he said they took some pretty significant losses. He said they were backing off now and taking another look at how they should approach this thing."

5 MAR 1971: COMUS Update: Targeting, Lam Son 719, Sensors, Cambodia

BRIEFER: On 3 March 1971 the NVA 66th Regiment was fixed northwest of Ban Dong, making 10 regiments committed against RVNAF in the Lam Son 719 AO. We estimate the enemy has lost the equivalent of 8 of his 30 battalions so far.

ASSESSMENT: The enemy is reacting to ARVN reinforcements in the area of Ban Dong, and to the deployment of forces out to LZ Lolo, Liz, and a new LZ further west. Major enemy strength is astride Route 92 north of Ban Dong, where he has elements of five or six regiments deployed.

ABRAMS: "It does look like he's shifting a little bit."

■ ■ ■

ABRAMS: "See, they know Minh. They know him. When he was a division commander he used to talk on the radio to them. They'd come up on his channel and he'd talk to them. They know him. They don't like him. Well, he lied to them. They found out he's unreliable. And in their terms they probably call him a miserable shit. He'd string along with them, and of course he was trying to find out what they were doing. And of course he doesn't trust them. They know they can't trust him. Then he'd capture one of their radios and he'd come up on their net. The one thing they know is it's not likely he'll retire to Saigon. They wouldn't believe that. In fact, it might be the best way. They'd know that's not right, and they'd say, 'He's coming.'"

6 MAR 1971: WIEU

MACV 1971 Infiltration Estimate: 31,800 (76 percent for COSVN).

BRIEFER: The 36th NVA Regiment was fixed in Laos by ARDF for the first time on 1 March. Hoi Chanh and a prisoner confirm it is now in the Lam Son 719 AO. The 66th Regiment was fixed by ARDF in Laos for the first time on 3 March. 9th NVA Regiment may be preparing to deploy to the AO.

BRIEFER: We are still getting intercepts showing enemy concern with allied naval activity off the southern coast of NVN.

■ ■ ■

BRIEFER: During the past week, eight SAMs were fired in reaction to allied air operations. On 2 March, seven SAMs were fired from an area just north of the DMZ at U.S. aircraft over northern Quang Tri Province operating in support of Lam Son 719. No aircraft damage was sustained from any of these firings.

ABRAMS: "General Clay—those seven, I would have thought they'd have gotten one hit. I used to be a supporter of the Nike Hercules. You know, I find this to be a rather shattering development."

CLAY: "We've never been able to prove just how great ECM is or isn't, depending on whether you're a 'Crow' [an electronic warfare officer] or not a 'Crow'— your evaluation on it, but my estimate is that the fighter airplane, equipped with RHAW gear, getting the signal, can take the maneuver action at the low altitude to pull the hard-G turn [six- or seven-G turn] and go to the deck and get out of the way."

ABRAMS: "Is this view of the commander supported by the scientific community?"

SOMEONE (Kirk, probably): "It is by one member." [Laughter]

BRIEFER: Reports the first photo confirmation of SAM equipment in Laos. Near the Ban Karai Pass. Put 18 sorties on it yesterday, using LORAN (with 100-meter CEP) due to weather.

ABRAMS: "It's necessary to show them that that's a very expensive undertaking."

CLAY: "We're very interested in proving that."

ABRAMS: "It's interesting that he would do that. He certainly knows what's likely to happen. I'm always very careful not to use the word 'desperate,' but this certainly raises the—."

■ ■ ■

ABRAMS: "One of the things that has shown up, as Lam Son 719 has gone along, is that that fuel thing is really a sensitive part of that system. I don't know in the past if we've put the—. Well, you know, going back to World War II, they said the ball bearings! Get the ball bearings out! I think that was disproved afterwards, but the idea was focusing on something that's really critical. Along with that, when Weyand was up there the last time, he talked with Molinelli. And down there right off of 914 was apparently a storage area, [a] terminal point for the pipeline. You could see down in there, and see a pumping station and all that. And it looked like a pretty ideal B-52 target. Do you know if that thing's ever been hit?"

CLAY: "That particular place, I don't believe so. We have never had a specific pumping place target."

ABRAMS: "Well, Molinelli's gone home, and I sure thank God for that. I don't know how he went home alive, the way that fellow's been carrying on. I think his helicopter's had the record of being hit every day. He's a squadron commander."

CLAY: "We have not had any success over a long effort to interdict it [the pipeline] by air alone."

■ ■ ■

ABRAMS: "General Vien asked me if there was any way we could supply more M1 rifles and M2 carbines and so on to the Laotians. I told him . . . that was handled by our embassy with the people in Washington, and I'm not mixed up in that in any way. I closed that off. I had to."

ABRAMS: "I'm going over and see General Vien this afternoon." Want copies of slides on sensor string activations by trucks. The BDA (per Clay) is phenomenal. Gunships are running out of ammo with targets still available.

■ ■ ■

BRIEFER: "With the arrival of the 66th NVA Regiment (304th Division) from North Vietnam, we now have 10 regiments committed against ARVN forces in the [Lam Son 719] AO." Of 30 battalions, the equivalent of 8 have probably been lost due to allied air and ground operations. "The heavy contacts of the last few days indicated that the enemy probably has sustained more than this," but due to task organizing it will take some time to assess which units have been affected.

BRIEFER: On 2 March, over a thousand rounds of indirect fire were reported fired at FSB 30, from which friendly forces withdrew. Knocked out all the friendly artillery. Reported to include 152-mm howitzers by enemy.

BRIEFER: At FSB 31: Contact just south on the night of 1–2 March resulted in 250 enemy killed (probably elements of 36th Regiment). Farther south, friendly elements moving to reinforce engaged a large enemy force and reported killing 383 of them.

BRIEFER: ARVN forces moving into LZ Lolo to the west reported 83 enemy killed by air and ground contacts on 4 March. Moving into LZ Liz found 41 enemy killed, and into LZ Sophia found 124, killed primarily by air. "We believe most of the kills in here are probably coming from elements of the 591st AAA Regiment." Also 282nd AAA Regiment.

BRIEFER: We believe the enemy now has 50–55 tanks still committed in the AO and available for him, especially in the area of Route 92. Most are believed to be T-34 and T-54 medium tanks.

BRIEFER: There were reports on 20 and 21 February that the 105th Rocket Company had entered the AO. Believed to be armed with track-mounted multiple rockets with 16 to 40 tubes.

■ ■ ■

ABRAMS: "Incidentally, General Clay, I noticed that one of your former enthusiastic tac air supporters has apparently revised his philosophy on the efficacy of tac air. He says the strategic air is what's important."

CLAY: "Are you referring to Vice President Ky, sir?"

ABRAMS: "Yes."

CLAY: "I'm going to have to make a call on him, sir. I think he's having some problems."

ABRAMS: "You might have him to lunch."

ABRAMS: "Those ARVN battalions out there are in a really tough environment. But certainly I would think at his [Ky's] level it's necessary to look across the whole spectrum of activity to see what effect it's really having on the enemy. Well, the role of the gunship, and the role of the F-4s. It all adds up, and it's all part of the total. Or you might send Moose over to have a talk with him. I guess [laughing] you better go with him if he goes, Bully [Billy?], to get a little balance in it."

SOMEONE: "The tactical employment of strategic airpower."

CLAY: "We'll let them sort that out back at the Air War College, General Abrams. In the meantime, we'll just press on."

■ ■ ■

ABRAMS: Asks about evaluation of the kills being reported by ARVN.

RESPONSE: "We don't take them at a hundred percent of what they're reported. It's probably a physical impossibility for them to tabulate the bodies, especially after a B-52 strike or something like this. But at the same time, we feel that the number from air and artillery and so forth that are never uncovered probably make up the difference. [Someone: "The order of magnitude is probably coming out about right?"] I feel so."

ABRAMS: "I guess maybe in the battle for Khe Sanh, the siege of Khe Sanh, the firepower was more concentrated than it is now. But other than that I think this is—counting the tac air, the B-52s, the gunships (both tac air and helicopter), and artillery—this may be the heaviest bit of firepower that we've put on during the war in one locale. And while certainly some of it misses the target, or it's striking against where they <u>think</u> it is, the way they're kind of gathered in there around [Route] 92, it would be pretty hard to drop a B-52 strike in there that doesn't get into somebody's company. The <u>basis</u> of these figures is probably questionable, but I think overall it may be an understatement."

ABRAMS (re truck drivers): "It's hard to see how they're now looking forward to the nightly drive down [Route] 914."

ABRAMS (re Lam Son 719): "I had the feeling when the thing began—well, up until the last couple of days, really—that the principal thrust of his effort was that corridor down there. Now the 88th, the move of 24 Bravo, the commitment of the 66th, the move of the 2nd Division Headquarters, then you tie that in with the 141 and the 812th, it's not that picture of a principal, major thrust. And you know he talked of 'the Battle for Route 9,' or 'The Route 9 Battle.' Now the complexion—this may have been what he had in mind all the time, but certainly the complexion of it is somewhat different than I originally visualized it. It's spread more. It still looks like Route 9 is the proper nomenclature for it, but—. What do you think?"

BRIEFER: Agree. The initial drive made it appear like the enemy was making a major effort down in here. That may have been dictated to some extent by a desire to commit his tanks. They were limited somewhat to the routes he had established here. They also had major ARVN forces there, and that's where the major battles took place. Then he got the impression, after what he took to be victories, that ARVN forces were withdrawing and were going to accept defeat. He observed drawback of the ranger units, and some of the airborne units coming out. [***] 'they're withdrawing,' 'exploit,' 'cut them off,' 'destroy their forces,' 'continue the attack.'"

BRIEFER: "Then, I think, he oriented more on the forces in an attempt to cut them off and destroy them. Probably gave renewed emphasis to his attacks down into Route 9 in an attempt to cut off the forces that were already west of here. Since that time he's observed the reinforcement of the AO, the deployment to the west, and is now in the process of reorienting his forces to react to that. And it does give a much more spread out picture of where he is directing his attacks. I have the distinct impression that he is directing some forces against all the ARVN elements he can locate in the AO, and attacking. One of the surprises is that he's attacked during daylight hours with tanks and infantry, and he's continued to do this. He appears to be attempting to maintain continuous pressure (day and night) on all ARVN elements all the time."

POTTS: "He's just about committed everything he has now, with those 10 regiments in."

CLAY (responding to Abrams re XXIV Corps): Have General Wilson up there. Talked to him yesterday. "Thinks we've made a lot of progress in terms of coordinating all the air effort, including helicopter landing zone preps and things like that. And I think it's getting in good shape, General Abrams. And Joe was very optimistic. He's with General Sutherland. The problem is being worked." Wilson returns tomorrow, but I'm sending General Blessé up at the same time. He's moving right in with General Myers, and Sid Berry, and the whole bunch. I told him, "Don't leave until you hear from me."

ABRAMS: "Well, we've got some awful good tickets in there. In fact, we haven't got any better."

ABRAMS (recalling a feat of airmanship in a damaged ship): "He flew that thing back, and controlled its vertical attitude by moving the crew back and forth in the damn airplane. Remember that? Jeez! And they all survived it, as I remember. Whenever you get to feeling arrogant, you think of a thing like that—assuming, you know, that you were a qualified pilot—whether you'd be that cool under those circumstances, or whether you'd just yell, 'Everybody to the chutes!'"

ABRAMS: "I talked with General Vien yesterday." Re these artillery losses, "what it looks like is there's too damn much ammunition on the position, and it's not protected." "It's probably why we lost [Fire Support Base] 31. It wasn't the weight of ammunition he put into it, it was the weight of ours blowing up. That means that the men can't fight then in the position. And the same thing happened, apparently, on [FSB] 30. And this is also the basis of the difficulty up there in the 42nd Regiment in II Corps. And our resupply capability is really much better than that. They don't <u>need</u> to put those quantities of ammunition—. That's where we're taking a licking."

SOMEONE (having analyzed the artillery losses): "If you want to worry, worry about Khe Sanh. It's all over the place up there."

ABRAMS: "Oh, don't—don't bring that up. When I first circled that thing up there, and saw the trucks, helicopters, ammunition, fuel—and I mean it's a <u>vast</u> area, my impulse was to just turn the goddamn helicopter out to sea and try to desert. The JGS themselves became concerned about this. Well! Their concern, in degree, didn't even approach mine. Then I got down on the ground and General Hill briefed me, and I began to feel a little better. Well, I decided not to desert. That was based on his briefing." "Hill—I think he understands the problem."

ABRAMS: "You had Lam up there, jittery. He didn't have enough ammunition. What would he do if he had a fight? Well, they didn't know what they had up there."

9 MAR 1971: COMUS Update: SAM Activity, MR-1, Lam Son 719, Cambodia

BRIEFER: Sappers got into Forward Supply Area 1 near FSB Vandegrift on the morning of 8 March and destroyed 40,000 gallons of JP-4 and 8,000 rounds of 20-mm ammunition. Probably an element of the 15th Sapper Battalion, B-5 Front.

BRIEFER: A prisoner from the 24B Regiment captured 4 March described contacts along Route 92 north of Ban Dong. Based on the heavy casualties he reported, "we are reducing the enemy's effective strength by two more battalions, giving us a total of 10 battalions effectively lost out of the 30 battalions of the 10 regiments committed against ARVN forces in the entire AO."

BRIEFER: In the Lam Son 719 AO at 1500 hours the 5th Airborne Battalion was engaged. Enemy: 78 KIA (of which 58 KBA), 21 IW, 4 CSW, 5,000 rounds 12.7-mm ammunition, 57 rounds 75-mm, 62 rounds 82-mm. Friendly: 12 WIA.

BRIEFER: At 1540 hours the 7th Marine Battalion was engaged. Enemy: 11 KIA, 3 IW, 1 CSW, 4,000 mortar rounds. No friendly casualties.

BRIEFER: At 1600 hours the 4th Battalion, 3rd Infantry Regiment, was engaged. Enemy: 19 KIA, 6 IW, 2 CSW. No friendly losses.

BRIEFER: At 1700 hours the 3rd Battalion, 3rd Infantry Regiment, was engaged. Enemy: 9 KIA, 3 IW. No friendly casualties.

BRIEFER: To date 57 helicopters destroyed in support of Lam Son 719 (46 in Laos).

ABRAMS: "I'm just more and more convinced that what you've got here is maybe the only decisive battle of the war. And they've got a chance to—it'll be hard—a chance to really do it. And the way he's putting—I mean, all he's doing, he's pouring stuff in with his trucks, he's pushing the SAMs down, he's pushing these units in, he's got—well, he's got that 9th Regiment that hasn't been committed. And the power that we can put on it—. There's all kinds of prophets of doom on this thing. But when he elects to commit all of that to try to do battle, and he knows damn well he has never come through—when we've focused firepower on him, he hasn't been able to hack it. That's what happened at Khe Sanh. Christ, he had two divisions there! I mean, he was going to get— he wanted that."

POTTS: "He's lost half of his tanks, half of his AAA, and 10 of his 30 battalions."

ABRAMS: "I mean, you're not going to get the decisiveness out of this if you go fucking around there running up and down 914 and a few other odds and ends. I mean, that's—."

BRIEFER: At 1745 hours yesterday 60 rounds of 82-mm mortar fire fell on the Task Force 9 CP, resulting in friendly losses of 1 KIA, 3 WIA, 1,600 rounds of mortar ammo, 100 rounds of 106-mm recoilless rifle ammo, and over 391,000 rounds of small-arms ammo destroyed.

ABRAMS: "I'd like to pull together a thing—put it in a letter to General Vien— that reviews over the past month the losses we've taken by what apparently is inadequate, or improper, storage of ammunition—not bunkered, not revetted, excess amounts of ammunition, and so on. Now I've talked to him three times about this, and nothing's being done about it. Now this won't be an acrimonious letter, but it'll just recite the facts as we know them."

■ ■ ■

ABRAMS: Recounts with delight an F-4 pilot's press conference and description of getting out of the way of SAMs.

CLAY: "That was Chappie James."

ABRAMS: "I thought he handled himself real well. He really put those bastards down!"

AF GUY: He was Robin Olds's deputy in the 8th Wing. "They used to call them 'Blackman and Robin.'"

10 MAR 1971: COMUS Weather Briefing

BRIEFER: As we go from month to month, we double in precipitation in the A Shau Valley. Two inches this month, four in April, eight, nine in May. "Defining the rainy season is always a problem, because the rainy season depends upon just exactly who wants to use the rain information and for what reason." "We have simply defined it, rather arbitrarily, as late April [the onset, presumably]."

ABRAMS: "I remember talking with Jack Tolson about this. He said rain showers weren't a problem. The helicopters could fly through that. When you've got delays, you're talking 30 minutes, an hour, not being socked in all day. So medevac and resupply and all those things that really drive them up the wall, you don't miss that."

13 MAR 1971: WIEU

Attendees: Gen. Abrams, Amb. Colby, Gen. Clay, Mr. Kirk, LTG McCaffrey, MG Dolvin, MG Cowles, Mr. Jacobson, MG Maples, MG Bowley, MG Dettre, MG Wilson, MG Young, MG Potts, BG Greene, BG Watkin, Mr. Chambers, RADM McManus (for VADM King), BG John, BG Henion, BG Brown, BG Heiser, BG Doehler, BG Forrester, BG Bernstein, Col. Sadler, Col. Miller (for BG Cheadle), Col. Jones, Col. Ludwig (for Col. Leonard).

POTTS: Describes aspects of infiltration estimate methodology: "From Binh Tram 18, up north, we picked them up at [a strength of] 570 [per infiltration group] there, and 15 percent have dropped out as they've come along. But we've lost [communications intercepts from] Binh Tram 18 for a while, and we're picking them up at Binh Tram 35—on down."

BRIEFER: Prince Souvanna Phouma spoke at a youth rally last week and advised his listeners to be prepared for combat duty. "The prince gave the youths a Pathet Lao equivalent of the Boy Scout Law." It included an admonition: "Youth must try not to become sick, and if they do become sick they must get well fast." [Laughter]

BRIEFER: "Another Frenchman had advice for the American military command this week. The French ambassador [to Laos, presumably] suggested that South Vietnamese troops secure Muong Hiem and completely cut off the Ho Chi Minh Trail complex. He guessed that General Giap was trying to create a new Dien Bien Phu, a concept which, because of American airpower, he felt was outdated. The ambassador added that the only reasons Giap won against the French in 1954 were that the French generals feuded too much and Navarre and de Castries, to quote the ambassador, were 'idiots' about Indochina." [Laughter]

BRIEFER: It is estimated that the enemy has 40–45 tanks remaining in the Lam Son 719 AO, deployed along the north of Route 9.

BRIEFER: Reports a Sihanouk message to the Cambodian people in which he quotes extensively from press reports of the statements of Americans who disagree with U.S. policies in Southeast Asia.

ABRAMS: "Even these statements about 'expanding'—I think they really know better than that. For instance, they <u>know</u> that the withdrawals [of U.S. troops from Vietnam] are continuing even during <u>this</u> operation [Lam Son 719]. They know the president's going to announce more in April. However, I think that the war of nerves—maybe this business had to do with the nerves in Hanoi. Going into the Ho Chi Minh Trail is a very sensitive thing."

ABRAMS: "And in the end, even though they've accused us of having troops over there, they know the truth. They know that. They know it's Vietnamese. They've got this other stuff out. See, they've got a damn good COMINT thing. They know with precision what's in fact going on. I think one of the side benefits of this—it may not be much—is that the South Vietnamese military is becoming an effective thing and it's going to be a thing you have to reckon with. I'm not trying to make a big thing out of that."

ABRAMS (after a break, which apparently had been taken when Abrams was called out to take a phone call from Washington): "Just so you'll be at ease that no great new strategic move is on the board, the purpose of that call was to inform me that the messages I received this morning and have read are on the way. [Big laughter] Well, it shows you why you oughta get up before noon. It gives you a chance to read those things before the call comes in."

■ ■ ■

BRIEFER: Describes two enemy medium field guns located in the northern half of the DMZ.

ABRAMS: "Have we gotten any answer to our message?"

SOMEONE: "No, sir. We checked yesterday and it was on the secretary's desk."

ABRAMS: "How many guns have we <u>positively</u> identified there?"

BRIEFER: "There have been four guns positively identified in the northern half of the DMZ."

ABRAMS: "And how late was that photography?"

BRIEFER: "6 March."

ABRAMS: "Are we trying to photograph again?"

BRIEFER: "Yes, sir."

ABRAMS: "Well, as soon as we get another photograph I want to go in <u>again</u>."

BRIEFER: "The 122-mm field gun has a maximum range of 21,900 meters [13 2/3 miles], while the 130-mm field gun has a maximum range of 26,700 meters [16 2/3 miles]." Therefore 130-mm guns positioned in the DMZ can fire along Route 9 from Dong Ha City to a point three kilometers south of the Rock Pile.

ABRAMS: "I tell you, I tell you—they'll give us authority after we've lost one of the damn fuel dumps or ammunition dumps! Goddamn it! Well, gentlemen, just be patient!" [Laughter] "The point, I think, is it doesn't look all that bad the farther you get away from it."

BRIEFER: A fuel storage area at Combat Base Vandegrift has been infiltrated by enemy sappers for the second time. Forty thousand gallons of JP-4 and 8,600 rounds of 20-mm ammunition destroyed.

BRIEFER: "Strikes in support of Lam Son 719 increased to 52 percent of the total U.S. effort flown in Southeast Asia. This compares to 33 percent last week. The trend in force employment for the past six weeks shows the abrupt shift from the interdiction mission to support of Lam Son 719."

BRIEFER: A total of 1,574 trucks destroyed during the reporting period, a new high. Strike-to-kill ratio: 73.7 percent.

ABRAMS: "Of course, they had a lot more out there."

. . .

JACOBSON: "For the first time we've got a head of the National Police who can go to the JGS and get something done."

ABRAMS: "I think that's great."

JACOBSON: "When Phong was the chief of staff out there, he was the greatest goddamn impediment to progress you ever saw in your life. Now that he's on the other side of the fence it's altogether different."

ABRAMS: "I would just like to comment about that, that that is not a peculiarity of General Phong's."

ABRAMS: "When I was a company commander, I realized that where it was screwed up was at battalion. Then, a little later, I got to be a battalion commander and I found out I was wrong—it was regiment. Well, this process kept going, and corps had really become one of my targets until I became the V Corps commander and I could see then, even as old as I was, I'd been wrong about that. Finally, when they sent me into the Pentagon as the Vice Chief I couldn't pass the buck any further. [Laughter] I have great sympathy for General Phong."

. . .

ABRAMS: "You know, back last summer we began trying to beat on the thing that the nature of the war was changing. What used to be good maybe is not gonna be good, and you've gotta think of other things—they're now critical. The things that used to be critical, they're now pushed away. They've been replaced by things that are equally critical to the outcome of the whole thing, but they're not the same. And I think so much of it now—that's really the way it is. And the struggle goes on. Its character is different, but the struggle is going on."

SOMEONE: "The problem I see facing us is explaining to people from Washington that we still have a hell of a security problem here without, at the same time, scaring them to death so that they think the president's Vietnamization program is doomed for failure. We get people out here who say, 'Well, of course now that the war is over, and the security situation is like it is, we can proceed with normal development and all of that kind of thing unimpeded by any of these restrictions.' Well, the trick is to scare them just a little bit, by telling them the facts, without scaring them so damn much that they'll go back and say, 'Well, hell, the Vietnamization program is in danger; they're still up to their knees in blood out there.'" "A lot of people are getting the wrong impression back there. The popular view is that, 'Hell, the war is over.'"

ABRAMS: "I must say that's not my view." "And that's why I say that the struggle continues. The nature of it is different, but it's still a tough struggle. It's still a struggle that has to be won, and in the nature that it's now in. And a-l-l the vigor, and a-l-l the imagination and a-l-l the, you know—'get the pennant up and let's go' stuff that you did in trying to get the 9th out of Saigon and that kind of thing has [now] gotta be applied to this kind of thing."

15 MAR 1971: COMUS Update

ABRAMS: "I think in all these big battles, in the midst of it there's a certain lack of precision, and I think that's what we're dealing with now."

16 MAR 1971: Lieutenant General Ewell Update

BRIEFER: In the last week, as ARVN forces went rapidly from the Ban Dong area out into Tchepone, the enemy was slow to react to this—both due to his severe losses and to the rapidity with which ARVN forces moved out after they had remained in the Route 9 area for so long. We have indications that he is receiving very few replacements. Units are combining to continue operations. We feel the enemy has lost over half the 100 tanks he began the operation with, and may be down to as few as 40.

EWELL: "The air commander up there—whose name escapes me, a brigade deputy commander—told me they'd started an inventory by tail numbers and he felt that in their losses they'd had some double counting and the actual total loss figure might be lower."

EWELL: "By the way, their OR [operational readiness] rate when I was up there Sunday was 79 percent, which I considered astronomical."

BRIEFER: "A number of saturation operations have been conducted since last August. These operations involve maximum use of the Territorial Forces, the National Police, Provincial Reconnaissance Units, Phuong Hoang agencies, and the People's Self-Defense Force in an all-out effort against known and suspected Viet Cong and Viet Cong infrastructure personnel and locations within the area of operations. They may be conducted in a selected district or against an entire province or, if required, they can be conducted throughout a military region."

BRIEFER: The Combined Summer–Fall Campaign Plan has been developed for the period 1 May–31 October 1971. It was sent to the field on 1 March.

EWELL: "This is just the usual bullshit, isn't it—the campaign plan?"

BRIEFER: "Well, yes and no, general. The emphasis General Abrams is putting on it now is almost a hundred percent towards pacification and into this saturation campaign. We're just about out of business in large U.S. force operations."

BRIEFER: In a storage area northwest of Tchepone strikes by Arc Light and tac air produced over 2,000 secondary explosions. There were 1,574 truck kills over the past week (4–10 March 1971), "a new season high." Over 13,000 trucks have been reported damaged or destroyed during the current dry season campaign that began 10 October 1970.

18 MAR 1971: COMUS Update

BRIEFER: "In the Lam Son 719 area of operations, very heavy attacks by fire— 400 rounds or more—were reported in the vicinity of LZ Rollo, the Ban Dong area, and against the marines in the southern part of the AO."

BRIEFER: "The enemy has detected the withdrawal of ARVN units from the Route 9 area, and has directed his forces to surround, annihilate, and destroy those isolated units where they can. The enemy has told his people that some ARVN forces are rebelling against their leaders, that some are running away into the interior, and that based on this he feels the ARVN has been defeated."

BRIEFER: East of FSB Lolo elements of the 1st Infantry Regiment have been in sporadic heavy contact with a large enemy force since 0600 on 14 March 1971. Friendly losses: 66 KIA, 102 WIA. Enemy: well over a thousand reported. 1st Battalion, 1st Regiment, plus the regimental CP and the 3rd Battalion, closed Khe Sanh by air at noon today. The 2nd Battalion, 1st Regiment, is en route there. The 4th Battalion, 1st Regiment, was in contact throughout last night, and the battalion commander and the battalion executive officer were killed. The battalion is down to about 180 men effective fighting strength. Flare ships and gunships supported throughout the night. Three attempts to resupply with food, water, and ammunition during the night had to be aborted.

BRIEFER: Currently there are 16,509 RVNAF troops in Laos. A total of 71 helicopters have been destroyed while in support of Lam Son 719 (57 of them lost in Laos).

ABRAMS: "What do we know about what's happening to the enemy?"

POTTS: We have intercepted messages telling units to follow up [on withdrawing ARVN units]. No reinforcements. No increase in tanks.

Long pause.

ABRAMS: "My interpretation of these message intercepts is that this whole thing is one hell of a bloody battle. And he's now exhorting his people to press on."

SOMEONE: Fills Abrams in informally on a Lam Son 719 briefing he has just given in Thailand. He put the operation in the context of the entire interdiction effort that began last October, explained how it was designed against the enemy system, and described how the ARVN "had performed some pretty doggone professional operations in a complex environment of bad weather, bad terrain, and of course the enemy, and had done a fine soldierly job of it."

19 MAR 1971: DEPCOMUS Update

BRIEFER: ARVN is reporting having inflicted 1,600 casualties on the enemy in the vicinity of LZ Lolo over the last few days. "We are somewhat dubious about these casualty reports." "However, I do feel that the enemy has lost more than a third of his maneuver force capability—to tac air and B-52s primarily." Also estimate the loss of about 3,000 of the 10,000–12,000 rear area service troops in the region.

BRIEFER: Cites the "conflicting nature of operational reports from the ARVN as to what really took place in the vicinity of LZ Lolo." This concerns the sudden return of the 4th Battalion, 1st Infantry Regiment, to the regimental area and the unusual specificity of enemy [***] re 1st Infantry Regiment troops as "frightened," with some running away and some rebelling against their leaders.

The briefer then gives some credence to those characterizations.

20 MAR 1971: Commanders WIEU

Attendees: Visitor: Amb. Bunker. Command group: Gen. Abrams, Gen. Weyand, Amb. Colby, Gen. Clay, MG Bowley, BG Watkin, Col. Jones. Component commanders and staff: LTG McCaffrey, LTG Robertson, RADM McManus (for VADM King), MG Wilson, BG John. Military regions: LTG Davison, Mr. Funkhouser, LTG Sutherland, Mr. Lazar, MG Brown, Mr. Long, MG McCown, Mr. Wilson. MACV Staff: Mr. Kirk, MG Cowles, Mr. Jacobson, MG Maples, MG Dettre, MG Young, MG Potts, BG Greene, Mr. Chambers, BG Henion, BG Brown, BG Heiser, BG Doehler, BG Bernstein, Col. Sadler, Col. Miller (for BG Cheadle), Col. Ludwig (for Col. Leonard).

POTTS: "The enemy's short weapons in MR-4. We average about one weapon for three enemy killed."

■ ■ ■

BUNKER: "Well, I think we've got the same problem we've had for the four years I've been here. That's the kind of reporting you get in the press. Sometimes they seem to have a vested interest in failure. In this situation, particularly in Lam Son [719], they started out with a skeptical view."

BUNKER: "Despite that, I think it's been extremely helpful, this whole operation. It's good to see the president's [Thieu] attitude toward it, apparently the attitude of the Vietnamese. It's given them, I think, pride in what they've been able to do. I do want to say also that I think what we've done, our forces, on the ground and in the air—not only here, not only in Laos and Cambodia—has been magnificent, decisive factor, really, in the whole thing. It's been a great performance. And I think the facts will speak for themselves when we get through with this, despite the press."

ABRAMS: "Well, I certainly join you on that. It's a struggle. It was a hard fight, but its effects for the rest of this year, I think, are going to be substantial. He [the enemy] committed a <u>lot</u> to that Lam Son operation, and it's getting pretty badly hurt.'"

ABRAMS: "One of the things that irritates me a little bit with Washington as an ethnic group [laughter] is that they don't seem to understand the price the Vietnamese are paying doing these things over there. And we haven't always been able to medevac by air the 3,551 wounded there. And, you know, in the RVNAF lexicon those fellows are actually <u>wounded</u>. That's no band-aid proposition there. They've gotta have some kind of medical care. And of course they've been bandied [*sic*] for raping and looting and all that—well, anyway, I think they've done pretty good."

The following material on this tape appears to be from an earlier session, prior to a secretary of defense visit and relating to the progress of Vietnamization.

ABRAMS: "My position on that is that <u>nothing</u> can be accelerated any more. We've <u>hurt</u> ourselves, really, by the amount that we've done. And hurt them. We've bought in on some things I feel kinda bad about. We're pushing then too hard. This ill feeling that's developed, at least temporarily, with Tri and the air force—that's nothing but pushing 'em too hard." "We're just trying too hard—going too far too fast."

ABRAMS: "It's really <u>nobody's</u> fault. Certainly it's not the Vietnamese's fault."

DAVISON: "We got them into that, and then pulled the rug out from under them. I told General Tri, 'I feel like a <u>shit</u>, general.'" [Laughter]

ABRAMS: "Of course I really felt good, marching over—two days in a row." [Laughter]

ABRAMS: "But then I see some of the things that Ambassador Bunker—the sack of crap that he's been directed to carry over to the palace!"

ABRAMS: "But when you get through with all the pluses and minuses, probably the most encouraging thing in the whole business is how in recent months they've been willing to take on this stuff and just go ahead. That's why I've said a number of times that we're dealing with <u>different</u> <u>men</u> now. They're the <u>same</u> men—the names and all that—but they've changed."

ABRAMS (re the mission and any supposed changes in it): "What I'm still doing is going on the basis of the directive I received. I always find it really quite awkward to do things on the basis of the press conferences. So I wait for the directives. I'm sure that this is bound to come up, and I'm prepared to talk about that. He already knows <u>precisely</u> how I feel about that from his last visit out here, the meeting we had down here. I told him then that if somebody had in mind—I said—I made quite a long speech about the infantry, and the thing that brings casualties down, and the biggest guarantee that he'll get on one of those freedom birds and go home is that he be hard, tough, skilled, get used to the jungle, know how to live in the jungle—discipline, training, and so on. And that's the only thing you can do with him. And then you get that going and he's better than the other fellow at it."

ABRAMS: "'And,' I said, 'if somebody has in mind that we're gonna have some infantry over here that's holding guard mount and hanging around Long Binh and so on,' I said, 'I just don't want it. There's more trouble and—.' And then I said, 'You can't do that and then say they're here for an emergency or something happens. They live like that and there's <u>no way</u>, there's <u>no way</u>, to get 'em up for a fight, except that they'd be out there working and developing the skills and so on.' If you take them out of Long Binh and try to thrust them into a fight, the casualties will just be catastrophic. Actually, it's the same with all of these fellows. It's across the board. Same with pilots. The same thing with helicopter crews. And unless they've been doing it, and learned how, and sharpened up—. An awful lot of this is the way their <u>senses</u> are. They get working at it, and then they can <u>smell</u> things. They can smell, they can see— there're all kinds of little things that tell 'em that this is—'Watch out!' If they're not doing that then also you try to take 'em out—they're <u>shooting</u> each other, clips, safeties off. I mean, <u>god</u> almighty, dropping grenades with the pins out. You know, you've got <u>enough</u> of it as it is, despite the best efforts."

23 MAR 1971: COMUS Update (first of two on this date)

BRIEFER: In Laos now we have 11 regiments committed against the ARVN, with the addition of the 803rd Regiment. Nine of these 11 have received heavy casualties. We believe the enemy retains the equivalent of 17 maneuver battalions (of the 33 committed). We also estimate rear service element losses at 3,500.

BRIEFER: In the Lam Son 719 AO currently there are 11,200 RVNAF troops in Laos. A total of 95 helicopters have been lost in the AO (80 in Laos).

23 MAR 1971: COMUS Update (second of two this date)

BRIEFER: Estimated enemy losses in the Lam Son 719 AO are the equivalent of 16 of 33 maneuver battalions organic to the 11 committed regiments. Plus 3,500 rear service force losses.

BRIEFER: Cites "the enemy's reduced logistical capacity. The loss of large quantities of food, equipment, and ammunition in Lam Son 719 has lowered VC/NVA capability to sustain large-scale attacks in the area, while interdiction of southbound routes has seriously delayed movement of supplies to enemy forces throughout the Republic of Vietnam and Cambodia."

BRIEFER (re ARVN armored forces): "They went in with 62 tanks and they brought out 25." A U.S. advisor met them at the border and made a personal count. "They went in with 162 APCs and brought out 64." "They had 60 men killed, and they claim 1,325 enemy killed."

WEYAND: "Part of the problem with the marines is that Lam has apparently pounded on the desk with Khang, the marine commander, who in turn has given explicit directions to brigade commanders and they ignore it. We've had that experience with those lads before, too. This is really the hairiest problem we have out there. We've got a whole bunch of units that, when they want to, they operate independently, and it doesn't make any difference whether it's Lam or who it is. But this still shouldn't keep us from insisting on a unified command out there."

25 MAR 1971: COMUS with Sir Robert Thompson

BRIEFER: "As ARVN forces crossed over into Laos on 8 February, the enemy had elements of three regiments deployed in the [Lam Son 719] AO." "As ARVN forces reached Ban Dong and began to move to the north, and search and clear to the south, the enemy initially was apparently delaying in order to buy time to get his reinforcements into the AO."

BRIEFER: "He did start moving elements of the 70th Front into the AO approximately 11 February." Three divisions were subordinate to the 70th Front: 304th, 308th, and 320th. As the three new divisions came into action, they initiated major counterattacks, initially against ARVN forces deployed north of the AO. That's where the major battles took place—with the 39th ARVN Ranger Battalion at FSB 30 and FSB 31.

BRIEFER: "The ARVN seized the initiative when they moved rapidly out into the Tchepone area. For approximately 10 days the enemy was unable to regain the initiative and mount any major counterattacks against ARVN as they were moving rapidly into the Tchepone area. However, as ARVN forces moved south of Route 9, and began to move down toward Route 914, the 2nd NVA Division moved south in order to protect the road and we had major battles south of Route 9. As ARVN forces started to withdraw from the area west of Ban Dong, the enemy believed that he was in fact routing ARVN forces."

BRIEFER: "As ARVN forces departed Laos, we had elements of 11 NVA regiments committed against these forces. Nine of these regiments have received heavy casualties during this operation."

BRIEFER: The enemy's "total casualties now are over 13,000." We estimate the enemy had 10–15 PT-76 tanks in the AO when the operation began, and that he reinforced with two tank battalions, one of PT-76 light tanks and one of T-34/T-54 medium tanks. It is estimated that a total of 100–110 tanks were committed into the AO, and approximately 75 were destroyed by tac air, artillery, and ground troops.

WEYAND: "This operation has used air cavalry extensively. For example, they were in and around the Tchepone area for 10 days or two weeks before ARVN got in there on the ground, and I mean they were in there at a hundred feet in that whole [Base Area] 604 area. The reason that is significant is because the targeting of the B-52s and the tac air was based upon the information that those guys were bringing back . . . in many ways more effective than even ground patrols—long-range reconnaissance patrols."

WEYAND: Concerning the pipeline, "it was a very significant accomplishment to get in there and whack that up." "Since then, the B-52s have taken into account very detailed information acquired by battalion commanders on the ground. For example, the people who were in Tchepone came back with quite a bit of detailed information on the location of stores that they were unable to destroy in the time that they had. And of course all that's being used for targeting. . . . There's been massive destruction far beyond, I would guess, what was done in Cambodia."

ABRAMS: "The history of the whole thing is that that's [heavy casualties] the critical point in determining what he does. He can lose a whole regiment, and hell, that doesn't—as long as there're five survivors to be able to tell what happened—that's good enough. Policy-wise, he isn't concerned about things like that. Or at least there's no evidence yet that he is concerned by these losses—never has been."

ABRAMS: "If there's a professional outfit in this country, it's the Hac Bao Company [reconnaissance company of the 1st ARVN Division]. They're first-class soldiers. Every man in it's been picked by the division commander himself, and that's been going on for about five years." "They come out of Laos saying the stench of dead bodies is so bad the soldiers can't stand it—they get sick. And we believe the Hac Bao Company—they're proven it so many times." "Recently we had a helicopter shot down with seven Americans on board. We put the Hac Bao Company in to rescue them. It took them two days, during which they killed 67 enemy and got those seven Americans out. It's a little military unit that's first class."

ABRAMS (back to enemy casualties): "But you can't even get swept away by that—of all the damage we do. This fellow is—. These things don't work on him the same way they work on our people."

ABRAMS: "I suppose what you could say in a way—we're betting on Vietnamization, and he's betting on getting that stuff [supplies coming down the Trail] through. It's kind of a liar's dice game. Someday somebody's gonna lift the cup—and instead of four fives it's gonna be garbage."

WEYAND: "What's he gonna do now that he knows this may happen anytime? I think that's one of the great significances of the Laos operation. He just can't be unconcerned about that [the possibility of further cross-border interdiction of his LOC] from now on."

THOMPSON: "Has the large operation made future attacks credible?"

ABRAMS: "I don't have any doubt of that."

THOMPSON: "How far would it still be dependent on very heavy support from the United States?"

ABRAMS: "It'll require air support—that is tac air. They've got, and increasingly will have, a capability of—they're not going to be able to mount anytime—see, you've got over three divisions that were involved in Lam Son, and all of it supplied by air. At the same time you had this thing going on in Cambodia and a couple of other things. Now, the Vietnamese are never going to have the capabilities to do all that simultaneously. But down here in Cambodia the majority of helicopter support, the majority of tac air, is Vietnamese. In other words, the Vietnamese will have the capacity to launch things into Cambodia, or into Laos, selectively. Not on the scale that Lam Son is, but they'll have the capability of getting in on the system. And we're certainly planning on going ahead over the next couple of years with a tac air and B-52 effort that would back that up."

THOMPSON: "I think the other important thing is that ARVN should come out with a high morale on this, and that that should inject into South Vietnam that degree of confidence that to a certain extent has been lacking. . . . I think this sort of psychological area is almost the most important point of all."

ABRAMS: "Yeah, that's right. Now in that connection a survey showed that at least the rural people were substantially in support of operations like this—way up. And it shows a developing pride. . . . Of course they don't know all that's going on, but the Vietnamese radio and TV have reported faithfully, within reason, the casualties that the Vietnamese forces are taking. Apparently it's on radio every hour, and on TV once a night. So the people are aware that it's a big price."

THOMPSON: Asks about the survey. Response: It was recent, in 36 provinces, a pretty good sample, and 92 percent in favor, 3 percent opposed, and the others didn't have an opinion. That was the highest percentage ever recorded on any question on any of these surveys.

ABRAMS: "I talked with Ambassador Bunker this morning. He's got all kinds of feelers out, and his sensing right now is that there's fairly overwhelming support. And that's what President Thieu thinks."

JACOBSON: "I might say that the ever helpful press corps is in for a big surprise—including my good friend Bob Shaplen, I'm sorry to say, a longtime friend—looking forward to these troops coming back from Laos and telling how they were defeated and it was a rout and the casualties were so terrible and all of that. Well, you know, he just doesn't know anything about surviving soldiers, because as every day passes—I don't give a damn if it had been that, it wouldn't be that after the passing days, because it would become an ever more glorious victory no matter what happened. So they're just wrong as hell on that one, and they don't know anything about soldiers. But, by god, you just can't get those people [the press] to thinking anything but negatively. I just wonder what it would take."

Robert Shaplen covered the war in Vietnam for the New Yorker.

ABRAMS: "Well, that 4th Battalion, 1st Regiment, finally came out with about 130 effectives. The battalion commander was killed. The executive officer was killed. This guy who was the battalion commander apparently was just worshipped. Lam was about to move him to a regiment, but this operation came up. I understand he was the highest regarded lieutenant colonel in the division. He and his exec were killed out there, and they were in heavy fighting out there. But that outfit—I think commanded in the end by a lieutenant, a hundred-odd men—kept going and finally worked themselves around to where they could be lifted out. They had four days of night-and-day heavy fighting. Well, you know there were those stories about, 'We wouldn't fight any more, we'd surrendered to the enemy,' and all that. Well, if you're a fellow who's been in that kind of stuff, this really represents quite a bit of character, to hang in there [after losing this charismatic leader]."

ABRAMS: "And then that ranger outfit that came out with a hundred odd. They were in just a hell of a fight, and they carried their wounded—which was more than the effective numbers—and made about two clicks [kilometers] through the jungle at night, fighting their way, and got to this other battalion. You know, Jake's so right—a month from now those are going to be the stories inside that outfit."

ABRAMS: "President Thieu was telling Ambassador Bunker and I this morning that he knows that battalion very well because he once decorated them as a unit for gallantry. And at that time there was one lieutenant and 66 men left in the battalion. And he told them, 'I hope to be able to repeat this.' Well, all I'm saying is—they've got their problems, but there's real guts down in there, and there's expertise down there. And I think their military forces are viable. There's enough of the necessary character to really take it and come back."

THOMPSON: "You were rather cautious in saying that they [the enemy] couldn't mount anything this year. But my impression is that they couldn't mount anything next year either—not that they can sustain. I don't have to be quite so cautious."

ABRAMS: "I think the way we feel is that we've sort of arrived at a crossover point, and you make the assumption that the North Vietnamese are going to continue [onward?]. And the way we feel about it is that that's destined not to be successful. In other words, the Vietnamese have developed, in a whole lot of things—I'm talking about across the spectrum, internal security, they're seriously at work on economic problems, and they face it as a reality, and they're meeting it with reality—not a-l-w-a-y-s with perfection, none of us are—but all those things, and their armed forces. And it's gone over [beyond] the point where I think the North Vietnamese can be successful against them. The war won't stop, but North Vietnam has now got a much tougher problem than they ever had before."

THOMPSON: "What I'm saying is we're going to see the fruits of the Laos operation right through 1972."

ABRAMS: "Of course, that was part of the basis of the operation. I think that that's gonna come true. You can't prove it now. Other than Tet of '68, which was kind of a different thing, that is the bloodiest battle that's been fought in this war—in numbers involved, equipment involved, and so on. It's been a big thing. And I think he's thrown into it everything he—well, I don't think he had any more. If he had, he would have put it in. And he's been badly hurt. And I think, at the moment—realizing all of the uncertainties of prediction and that sort of thing, which as you know you can get in trouble on that—it is going to have the kind of effect it was supposed to have."

ABRAMS: "The other thing we don't really know is what he [the enemy] had in mind for June and July in MR-1. There's a lot of indicators—65 percent of the trucks that got through went into [Base Area] 611—this means something. And most of the enemy units that were involved in Lam Son are former combatants in MR-1. Right now, no one can come down hard on what was afoot for MR-1 in June and July, and then what effect that would have had on the elections. You know, this is kind of a—."

BRIEFER: "Operation Lam Son 719 was designed to disrupt the enemy's LOC at the hub of his road/trail network and to destroy war matériel and supplies in one of his most important base areas, Base Area 604. This operation's objective was to set back the enemy's timetable for the current dry season and disrupt his plans for the war. That extra time would give the Vietnamese forces more opportunity to strengthen defenses and allow U.S. forces to continue redeployment in a safe and orderly manner."

BRIEFER (re the U Minh Forest): The 21st ARVN Division is establishing bases in there, with no intention of leaving.

ABRAMS: "Same thing with Kien Hoa and 470, and Seven Mountains and Three Sisters. The Vietnamese have just made up their minds to stay there. And that's what they're doing."

POTTS: Operations in the U Minh are against the 95th Regiment. "History shows that that was the first NVA regiment to come into the Republic of Vietnam."

■ ■ ■

ABRAMS: "This press business—Admiral McCain called me this morning, and Jack Anderson apparently has an article which discloses a plot developed by General Wheeler, Admiral McCain, and General Abrams, which finally has been brought out into the light of public cognizance. And poor old Jack [McCain] read me his press release. Jesus! I said, 'Jack—the Pig Rule, the Pig Rule!'" [Laughter]

ABRAMS: "And I've been reading this piece of fiction, *Court Martial*. And they've got a Zachary Taylor 'Tanker' Flint, a fictitious character who is in command in Vietnam. Of course I realize it's fiction, and a rebuttal is not really required. I browsed through it and, if you're sensitive, it could get you by the ass." [Laughter]

SOMEONE: "I've gotta ask what's the Pig Rule. I don't know that."

ABRAMS: "Don't wrestle with pigs—you get dirty, and they enjoy it." [Laughter]

WEYAND: "It even applies to arguing with your wife, in slightly different—."

ABRAMS: "W-e-l-l—. I think so much of you that I'm never going to say that you said that. That's how much I think of you."

WEYAND: "If you don't, I think it'll be more than you can stand. I think in a weak moment—." [Laughter]

■ ■ ■

ABRAMS: "Colonel [Tha's?] people got into a VC provincial committee meeting, and they killed the VC deputy province chief. He was a lieutenant colonel. Tha had the man's body brought back to the province capital, with care. He believed that the identification was right, but then they brought in individually some Hoi Chanhs and other people so that he was certain of the identification.

Then he said, 'Now, we must have a proper burial.' They got the monks and the candles and the incense and they prepared the remains and got a nice coffin—a great ceremony—all of this being photographed. Then they went out to the burial ground, and with some monks and people he was laid to rest. Then he took these photographs and he put them into a poster. And it said on there, 'Lieutenant Colonel so-and-so has done some bad things, and he's been very harmful to our people, but now he is dead, and now he is a Vietnamese again, and he must be properly buried like a Vietnamese.' He put that all over the province. I was talking about that with General Lam one day, and I said, 'This is an example. We Americans would <u>never</u> think of something like that. It's <u>pure</u> Vietnamese. It's only the Vietnamese who can understand and do things like this.' And Lam kind of scratched his head and said, "I don't think I'd think of it myself,' which from Lam is just an unbelievable admission."

■ ■ ■

ABRAMS (re pacification): "The way it has to go—it should be a sort of contagious thing. It isn't anything you can put out in a decree and start getting charts on." "Because in the end it's gotta be done with sensitivity and understanding."

ABRAMS: "In Quang Tin they've got everybody but the women and children involved. They've got, by god, postmasters out there." Very short operations. Try to get on top of the enemy's high points. Trigger it three or four days before intelligence says a high point is coming. The enemy starts moving a few days before the planned high point.

WEYAND: "The interesting thing is all this is going on at the same time Lam Son 719 is in progress."

ABRAMS: "President Thieu's made up his mind—no corps commander's ever gonna have their hands on that general reserve again. He's gonna <u>use</u> it. And the corps commanders are gonna get along with the structure they've got. And these two corps commanders down here have three missions. One is to ensure the consolidation within South Vietnam. Two is not let the enemy get back into the sanctuaries. He calls it an offensive defensive. What he's talking about are the sanctuaries, base areas, right next to the border. And three is to help Phnom Penh. And they're gonna do all that with the forces that they have organic. And for <u>trouble</u> in MR-1 or MR-2, that's what the Marine Division and the Airborne Division is for—or for special operations into Laos. When they get it all sorted out, and I would say especially now with the experience that they've had, they are going to be able to do these things."

ABRAMS: "Bob [Thompson], can you imagine ARVN attempting any one of these things in 1963—<u>or</u> in 1966? No. It just wasn't—my g<u>o</u>d, it just wasn't even <u>dreamed</u> about!"

WEYAND: "Try 1968."

ABRAMS: "I think there is one thing about 1968. I think they stood up better than any American would have predicted if he could have predicted all the events that occurred. They had their problems, but they really stood up to the thing."

SOMEONE: "The police did, too."

ABRAMS: "Yeah, they did."

WEYAND: "You read this account of Tet, and we're the ones that didn't stand up too well—we were kinda slow."

WEYAND: "Well, we got a whole new breed of cat coming along. And I don't know how long it's gonna take. I think, and it might be my imagination, I detect a significant difference between the style of leadership, and the real effective leadership, of guys like Truong and Minh, who during this period we're talking about were regimental commanders and division commanders, as opposed to—take the other extreme—your Vinh Locs and Lu Lans. And now even getting down to a man like General Lam, who's somewhere in between. But you're finding these corps commanders are like the corps commanders we'd like to think we had, who understood, for example, development of a fire plan, coordination of fires, precision, and all that, techniques that are so important. We understood those as well as our battalion and regimental commanders, and now—I was up there listening to Minh today, and Minh has educated his division commanders and his regimental commanders. And I think Truong probably does the same thing, because they're at ease with all this. And one of our problems, I think we've found in Lam Son 719, has to do not so much with the strategy and all and the maneuver. It has to do with techniques, for example the coordination of fires."

WEYAND: "You go up there and listen to Minh tell you what the problem is, and it's kind of interesting because he was faced with the same problem, up there, tactically, that we had up in Laos. That is, the fire support base is set up. The enemy's reaction to that is sappers, indirect fire, and their reserve maneuver units outside. The indirect fire comes in, everybody gets their heads down, the sappers come in under that, and unless you get that indirect fire off that fire support base's back, you've just had the schnitzel. There's no way that that outfit is gonna hang in there. It may take a day, it may take three or four days, but our friendly unit's had it. Now, the only way to whip that is you've got to find that indirect artillery and at least harass it and get it off of their backs. And that means that you've got to know how to use tac air, the capabilities of it, gunships, artillery, and the air cav. And Minh can draw a diagram for his battalion commander, fire support base commander, division commander, and tell you how that's gotta be done. He just knows it, 'cause he's lived through it. He goes right to work on that and solves that damn problem. A guy like Vinh Loc—Christ, he couldn't solve it in a thousand years. And we've got a lot of American commanders can't solve it."

WEYAND: "Listening to Minh, and listening to Truong, and these task force commanders, god—you can see what's developing here. Real commanders who know this enemy, and know what he's up to, and know their own capabilities, and how to employ them to counter."

ABRAMS: "I think there's another aspect of that. Some seniors used to be members of that general officer council when Ky was running things and so on. All the things that were done were done on a consultative basis, and they kind of voted or talked over things, which involved those gentlemen in the highest policies—political, military, what have you—in the country. And that was bad for them. Because the ones who are still around feel that—they drank that wine for a while, and it seemed like a hell of a good year. So, having tasted that, they can't divorce themselves from it. Now these fellows, like Truong—Christ, they never even passed him a glass of that. He was down there fighting for his life. And the same thing with Minh—he was never mixed up. They hadn't been exposed. Matter of fact I think our system is very good. By the time you get up into those circles you're very close to retirement and they'll finally be rid of you—you can't do any more damage. 'I remember the last time I talked to the president, and he told me—.' No, this gets to be pretty heady stuff. Somebody asks you, 'Why aren't we backing the new mess kit?' Well, you've been out hobnobbing with the president. What mess kit? You lose the touch because you've been at that monstrous banquet table. That's where Vinh Loc is, that's where Khang is, and so on. I think that's what's happening is this other's pushing up, and the president's really bringing them along. That's the way Dzu is, that's the way Truong is, that's the way Minh is, Phong."

THOMPSON: "Do you know Diem said that to me way back in about 1961 or 1962? He said, 'As soon as I can get rid of all the old French generals and the young Vietnamese come through, we'll be all right.'"

ABRAMS: "Vinh Loc—an order from Saigon! He just picked the ones he thought were appropriate, and the rest of them he ignored."

WEYAND: "Minh says that he's submitted a name, and General Davison's submitted a name, and General Vien submitted a name for a new commander of the [5th?] Division. . . . He says the president wants a colonel. The reason he wants a colonel is he's decided that division commanders should be people who are aggressive and are fighting to get ahead, and therefore he doesn't want to put generals in command of general officer positions. He wants a guy that's on the make. And that's what they're coming up with."

ABRAMS: "Back on the first of May [sic] the president called me up there to talk with him about the cross-border operations. And then he wanted to go over leadership. We got into the matter of Truong. Well, he started in with the corps commanders. He said, 'Start at the DMZ and go down to Ca Mau and tell me about the commanders,' which I did—an evaluation. 'Well,' he said, 'if I have to remove some corps commanders, who do I add?' So I told him then that the one I can recommend, without any reservations at all, and with all the humility of an American who doesn't really know Vietnamese, is General Truong. I think he's proved, over and over and in all the facets—pacification, military operations, whatever it is. I went into some others, and so on. Then he said, 'Who could command the 1st ARVN Division?' So I went over the possibilities there. They have rank problems—some of those are junior colonels and so on. But I told President Thieu then that the only reason a division commander is effective is because he knows himself personally all those little things that have to go on in the fighting. It has to do about how you put the wire, the organization of the staff, the communications, the maneuvering of the men, the welfare of the men—whether they've got their equipment, whether they've got their clothes, whether they're being fed, whether they're being paid, what's happening to their dependents. And I said he must <u>intimately</u> know all that. That's the only way he'll be respected by the regimental commanders, because they're all in it, and they know these things. And if he doesn't have that, he can't do it. I said it's going to be especially hard in the 1st ARVN Division, because General Truong is just that kind of a man. That's what that division has had now for a long time—a man who knows it intimately and knows <u>all</u> aspects of soldiering. And he has the respect of <u>everybody</u>. They respect him for what he is, because he <u>knows</u> more than anybody, and they know he does, about <u>their</u> business. So they wound up with Phu, who was a company commander at Dien Bien Phu. He knows the business, too."

26 MAR 1971: COMUS Update

BRIEFER: "Wednesday afternoon all marines evacuated the [Co Rach?] area under the guise of being members of the battalion scheduled to be extracted. According to General Sutherland, this was done without approval of General Lam. Air strikes and artillery were directed onto the Co Rach area throughout the night in preparation for a reinsertion of marines Thursday."

BRIEFER: Mentions, re B-52s, a "Target Panel" with membership from J-2 MACV, Seventh Air Force, and ARVN. Looking to withdrawal eventually of ARVN forces currently working in enemy base areas in Laos during Lam Son 719, "we initiated an intensive effort to try to develop targets out in that base area," all that logistics structure, to ensure that we had good targets after the troops left there, and to replace the intelligence that would be lost by virtue of the troops on the ground, which was the best we could get of course, being withdrawn. Requested all members of the target panel to help determine lucrative future targets. We're working in terms of not only the collection effort of all the commanders who have been up in that area and have come out and who have been interviewed and interrogated about this to try to develop a model of that entire base area, but also an analysis of our earlier strikes, the ones that got significant BDA: how many times we hit there, where we might go back in again to explore potential lucrative terminals, pumping points, supply points, truck parks, and the rest.

BRIEFER: About three days ago we noticed that the ARVN and XXIV Corps were starting to run out of good targets. So we resumed control of the Arc Light. We put it back on a competitive basis. We told XXIV Corps that any time they needed a divert for troop emergency purposes to let us know and they would get it just as quickly as they could by banking them up there. We are now building a pool of targets. We are getting targets shaping up, some of them, in the vicinity of ten or eleven thousand points. The average seems to be about seven thousand points on that scale, where six weeks ago, before the Lam Son 719 operation, we were averaging about 1,800 points per target.

BRIEFER: In ripping into that system up there, SAC has gone to CICV to get soil analysis of these interdiction points that we've been working on. As a result, recommend that we go back on those target boxes, but do it as soon as the rainy season begins. Conclude that we will "churn that stuff into something that is nothing but silt and mess." Get back on those boxes. The roads have been reconstructed, but with considerable effort. SAC feels that if that is done "those roads will be unusable not only during the rainy season but unrepairable during the rainy season and possibly for a considerable period after that next year."

27 MAR 1971: WIEU

Attendees: Amb. Bunker, Gen. Weyand, Gen. Clay, Mr. Kirk, LTG McCaffrey, MG Dolvin, MG Cowles, Mr. Jacobson, MG Maples, MG Bowley, MG Wilson, MG Young, MG Potts, BG Greene, BG Watkin, Mr. Chambers, BG John, BG Henion, RADM Matthews (for VADM King), BG Heiser, BG Doehler, BG Forrester, BG Bernstein, Capt. Birdt (for MG Dettre), Capt. Bivin (for BG Brown), Col. Leonard, Col. Miller (for BG Cheadle), Col. Zerbe (for Col. Sadler), Col. Jones.

BUNKER (re Land to the Tiller rally at which President Thieu gave a free tractor to the best farmer from each region): President Thieu told the press he only had two things to say: "No press conference" (having one on Tuesday) and "Lam Son 719 is still going on."

WEYAND: "Good for him. Well, I must say he's been doing better with the press and his people than we have back home."

BUNKER: "I've never seen our press worse."

WEYAND: "I had this *New York Times* fellow in yesterday. Before we started out I said, 'Well, how about you telling me what you think of the operation so I'll know what the backdrop of this is?' Well, he thought it was a disaster, so it's kind of hard to pick up the pieces—." [Laughter]

BRIEFER: 1971 MACV Infiltration Estimate: 37,000 (78 percent for COSVN).

WEYAND: "In assessing this Lam Son 719 operation, one of the things you get into is its limited duration and all that. Of course naturally it had to be limited, and was from the outset. President Thieu made that very plain. But the fact that this operation was conducted during a period of enemy intense activity, peak activity [in terms of the annual pattern of infiltration] on the Trail, I think is a point that we add to the list of things of rationale for this operation and so forth. The very fact that throughout the month of February and most of March the ARVN forces were at work on that trail on the ground, or on parts of it, at least, is, I think, important. It's like putting your high point on the enemy's high point."

BRIEFER: "We believe that during the operation the enemy lost the equivalent of 16 of the 33 maneuver battalions they had committed in the AO. In addition, we believe that he's lost at least 3,500 of the 10,000–12,000 rear service personnel that were operating in the area prior to the operation."

POTTS: "That's not just ineffective battalions, sir. That's a complete loss of those battalions."

BRIEFER: "Of the approximately 110 tanks that we believe the enemy brought in in reaction to the Lam Son operation, we believe the enemy has lost at least 75 of these, destroyed primarily by tac air."

POTTS: "Quite a bit of that [infiltration destined for COSVN] got by the area of Lam Son 719 before it started. We're beginning to pick up groups of these individuals down here in Cambodia. We think, sir, that the 5th, 7th, and 9th Divisions, that are so low in strength—the 9th Division 2,800 men, just a little over one regiment for the whole division in strength—we think that those divisions, plus this 32nd Regiment, and the 88th, which is being reconstituted, will be receiving a lot of those. He's just in bad shape."

■ ■ ■

MATTHEWS: Admiral King is being relieved by Admiral Salzer in a couple of weeks. "There are only two admirals in the U.S. Navy who are graduates of Yale, and they're going to relieve each other back to back."

BUNKER: "I think you're going to be all right." [Laughter]

BUNKER: "When we walked into the agricultural exhibit yesterday, the band was playing 'March On Down the Field.'" [Laughter]

■ ■ ■

CLAY (re Route 922): "I'd give my left arm if somebody could put a marine battalion down there sitting on that thing for the rest of the dry season. [A Shau area. Tiger Mountain.] It's been the principal route the whole year. It's a very difficult area to interdict—flat terrain, it's relatively open, and multiple options in terms of where you want to move trucks. We have put navy cutting and seeding, we have bombed in there, we've had gunships in there, and there's just no really good natural interdiction points that aren't easily bypassed, repaired, or moved around. It's just real tough."

WEYAND (re the Vietnamese): "I think, of all the tough times they had in Lam Son 719, the one that—the only one, really—that may get to some of the ARVN troops is the business of having to have left their dead in some [of the places?] back there."

BRIEFER: Shows 81 U.S. and 7 VNAF helicopters destroyed in Laos, and 22 U.S. in RVN, for a total of 103 U.S.

CLAY: "I've got slightly higher figures. It depends on the day, and the time of the day. I've got 108 through the 25th. What date's yours?"

RESPONSE: "26th, at 1800."

SOMEONE: "We're trying to keep one section of USARV Aviation with the exact figures which everybody plays together."

WEYAND: "Let's reconcile these."

BRIEFER: The loss per sortie rate is "down around 0.2, so you've got a damn good chance of coming back." Twenty-one per 100,000. Also 544 damaged.

"They've all been pinged up there. Everybody's got a bullet hole in his aircraft."

BUNKER: "What do we think about the reliability of the enemy loss figures—casualty figures?" "Obviously they've been badly hurt."

POTTS: "We think, sir, that perhaps it's a little conservative, the figures we're using. That'll continue to be modified, and we think we'll have more enemy lost as we get more reports."

WEYAND: "We're putting together now some sort of thing like a commander's evaluation of Lam Son that would be suitable for a background press briefing or to the president or the ambassador or somebody that wants to know what it accomplished and what it was all about. It's very important that we do this, even more so than the Cambodian operation, because we're going to have difficulty quantifying the results of this one, as we did the Cambodian operation. Yet inevitably . . . comparisons are being drawn between Cambodian losses inflicted on the enemy and Lam Son. And I think that we all recognize that we've got a public relations problem or psychological problem, or whatever you want to call it, an information problem which is very, very important. This came home to me yesterday talking with this *New York Times* bureau chief here, and I suppose some of the questions he raised we'll get from other sources or people, too."

WEYAND (re protecting B-52s, which he agrees with): "We've got to keep in mind that this contest is far from over for this season, and in fact what we're going to see here is a real crash effort on the part of the enemy. So there are going to have to be some risks taken to meet that. This is no time to be slacking off on anything. Now I'm particularly concerned about our ineffectiveness in dealing with this indirect fire capability of the enemy's, whether it has to do with SAMs or artillery and mortars. I'm disturbed about it because it is a common theme capability—or deficiency, if you want to look at it from our standpoint—that runs through this whole situation from strategic [has to do with the SAMs] right on down through its impact on infantry divisions and regiments and squads. And you see the enemy's effectiveness in this whether you go out and talk to General Minh on the Chup operation or Lam in Lam Son 719 or artillery in the DMZ hacking away at RF/PF down on the coast and stuff like that. Now what we're going to mount here is a commandwide effort to get at that problem. I want just as much effort put on this tube artillery as we're putting on SAMs and other stuff. I don't want any tube artillery that we can get at left unchallenged."

WEYAND: "Now about Lam Son 719. I think that what we all have to understand . . . was that Lam Son 719 was just a part of, really, an overall campaign to meet, in one part, the enemy's crash program, his determination to continue with this aggression, and on a crash basis, related also to the Cambodian problem and so forth. What we need to do is to lay out the story that starts with what considerations somebody like General Abrams or President Thieu gave to this Lam Son 719. And that means we examine the context in which this operation was conducted. It seems to me that what we had facing us, last early fall, were about three main problems. One of them was the war in-country. And that is central. It should be tacked right up there and kept in view all the time, because it has to do, first of all, with this concept of our effort of defense here, which is providing security for the populated areas, and for South Vietnam. Now that war is . . . killing, week in and week out, resulting in the death of 250 soldiers of this country. And it's a war that goes on and on and on. It's a war that takes . . ." [first side of tape runs out]

WEYAND [picked up in midsentence on side two of the tape]: ". . . always Thieu had limited resources with which to operate. Now, related to that, and as a reflection of the success of Vietnamization, is that Lam Son was conducted because the Vietnamese were able to free three divisions from the war in-country—never been done before. Having freed those three divisions, that was just about all that they could put into this fight, and that was the way their plans were drawn. So always, as number one priority, was the Dong Khoi thing related to it. It's been our concern to maintain the momentum of this war in-country. Secondly, we had the problem of Cambodia. President Thieu very much had that problem—even more so, I think, than the U.S.—on his mind. That problem that faced him of not necessarily supporting Lon Nol's government, but of preventing Cambodia from falling into the hands of the enemy. Now that problem was met . . . by the Kompong Cham operation, by operations on Route 4. The enemy's determined efforts to cut all of the routes leading into Phnom Penh so the security of the Mekong, which [Spence?] worked on and is working on, that was a whole campaign, you might say. And involved in that was this operation of the Chup, Toan Thang 71-1. I think that, looking back on that, that problem was solved, or handled, about as well as it could be. It has achieved, particularly in terms of territorial security, what we hoped it would."

WEYAND: "The Cambodians, going back to the ambassador's question about the enemy hasn't been very active in there, and what's the situation, why is this, we probably don't know the answer to that question why. But we do know we have bought time, which was the purpose of it, for Cambodia. And how the Cambodians used it and all that, well that's all a different problem. Now the third problem that faced us, with which we had to deal, was the crash program of the enemy's to reinforce his effort. Whether it was to rebuild it, or launch new offensives, we're not sure. The people up in I Corps firmly believe that the enemy intended or intends this dry season to launch a major offensive in MR-1. To meet that crash operation, of course the Chup operation was in a sense related to it, sopping up stuff as it came out the bottom of the funnel, of tying down and decimating the three major divisions of the enemy in Cambodia. But it was the air effort, the air interdiction program, that was central to that—B-52 effort of this campaign against the boxes, the gunships, the tac air, mobilizing all that against that enemy threat."

WEYAND: "That's where, it seems to me, Lam Son 719 comes into the picture. Lam Son 719 was simply another piece of our effort to solve that problem we took on that has to do with meeting the enemy's efforts to move south. Now, what this fellow [New York Times] wanted to know was was it worth it. Now how do you measure that? You can't measure it as we did in Cambodian terms. To answer 'Was it worth it?' you have to go back and examine 'Was the rationale for the operation sound?' An operation limited in time. People want to know, 'Why'd you do that?' Well, unless you could sit on the Trail for the whole dry season—. Well, you did it because what's the alternative? The alternative is not go out there at all. The timing of it was related to the enemy, what we expected would be his peak effort. And it was to sit on as much of that trail as we could during that peak effort."

WEYAND: "Another part of the objective was to disrupt and destroy this system of supplies and facilities in there. Now here's one that I find we haven't gotten out to the public at all. Our targeting with the B-52s, and it's still going on, was probably more precise, and based upon better intelligence, than we've ever had before. Because—particularly this is true in the immediate aftermath of Lam Son, where we're targeting based upon ground reconnaissance in detail conducted by battalion commanders, regiments, and all of that. Air cav flying over that area at a hundred feet, all over there. The air cav was in Tchepone 10 days before ground troops were in there, and doing everything short of landing. So our picture of that whole thing, and then the use of air to destroy this guy's facilities, has been, I think we're going to find in retrospect, been more effective than any campaign we've conducted in the past. But I'll admit it's impossible to quantify it, so, like [Spence's?] question about how long does it take to repair the railway, we really don't know all those things, so—. And we can't bank on it, we can't say, 'Well, it takes two weeks so that cuts that business out.'"

WEYAND: "The results are what are going to finally show up and tell us what the effect of Lam Son 719 was. But the cost, in terms of what it cost us, I think you—I don't see how we could say anything other than that that operation was worth it. In fact, how decisive it will be I don't know, but I think it's going to prove to have been terribly decisive. And we've got to continue to work on words that will—in fact will lay that all out. But Lam Son 719 was just a part of the overall plan. The newspeople—and in fact our own officials, I think in some cases—inadvertently look on it as sort of an entirely separate thing, the cost of which should be measured separately. Well, we shouldn't go along with that at all."

BUNKER: "I think that's very important, to get it in perspective, because it's been reported in bits and pieces, and reported by what the press gets from helicopter pilots. President Thieu said the squad leader's view of the war is different from the generals' view of the war. This has been the trouble at home. And all the critics at home have picked on this one operation, claiming that it's not successful. And to an extent, too, this has been the administration's problem. They've had to react to this, you see. I think it's terribly important to get the whole thing [words indistinct], and to work on it and work on it with the press and everybody else. But you can't satisfy the critics, as Henry Kissinger said the last time I was back. A year ago we'd done everything they wanted us to do two years ago. Then we'd done everything they were criticizing a year ago.

Now they want something more, and you can't satisfy them.'"

WEYAND: "It's just as important that we get all that laid out as the operation was itself, really. We're dealing with <u>so</u> much here that's psychological that bears directly on the degree of U.S. support. Apparently the Vietnamese people have—they're satisfied that it was a worthwhile operation, not only worthwhile but necessary."

BUNKER: "As far as we can see, there's very general support among the people here. I've sent a message back on it—to the White House."

BUNKER: "I think there were three phases, really. The first—in the beginning, great enthusiasm. Then, when reports of heavy casualties began to come in, there was apprehension. But then when the reports came in of what the <u>enemy</u> was taking, then I think there was a recurrence of enthusiasm, support, <u>pride</u> in what the ARVN was doing, and confidence. And this, I think, has persisted." "You get reports from the country of more support for the government, and Thieu—a positive result." "As far as the GVN is concerned, it's been a plus."

WEYAND: "You hear Hanoi—they're broadcasting about the great victory and all. I told this fellow from the *New York Times,* 'You know, if it was such a great victory you would sort of expect that, rather than leave the Paris peace talks, they'd kind of want to hold some extra meetings so they could kind of relish all of that, maybe accept our surrender or whatever we were prepared to offer. But instead of that they left.' So I don't think it's been a great victory [for Hanoi]. And I know that last bunch of air strikes up there sure as hell—."

BUNKER: "I want to end on an optimistic note. I want to compliment MACV on its public relations effort. Coming out here I noticed that I passed a jeep named 'Responsive.' I thought that was really a nice touch." [Laughter]

WEYAND: "Well, I think we were all really holding our breath." [Laughter]

30 MAR 1971: COMUS Update

POTTS: "Some of the real values of Lam Son 719 are coming out in the intelligence field. One of them is the work that we've concentrated on and finished last night on this pipeline. We have a pipefitter—PW—who's worked on that pipeline for two and a half years. It's helped us plot the pumping stations and all the tracings along the way."

ABRAMS: "What's our view of how valuable this is to him?"

POTTS: "We've had estimates that this pipeline saves him 400 trucks a day."

■ ■ ■

ABRAMS: "What is it we are really trying to do now in Laos with air? What is it that we're after doing? That's what I wonder. Pull out the map or something. Explain it to me. Here I want to talk about Seventh Air Force has the responsibility of running an interdiction program. And during the height of Lam Son we sacrificed the interdiction program in order to—at least with tac air. Gunships continued to march. There was some gunship assistance to Lam Son 719, but in the main gunships continued to work on their role in the interdiction program. B-52s were largely taken off the interdiction program. And I want to have a feel now of just how—what do we see the problem in Laos? How do we see applying the assets? How do we see Seventh Air Force carrying out their mission? How do we see MACV sticking its pinkie in the thing? Just what are we trying to get done in Laos at this stage of the game? Do you understand my question?"

AIR FORCE BRIEFER: "I feel our mission is as it was before Lam Son, and through Lam Son also—despite the fact we diverted considerable effort into that particular AO—I think our mission is to disrupt and destroy as much of that logistics system throughout the panhandle as we possibly can. There are certain areas where we've got to provide emphasis, and we've got to do it in a hurry because we may lose authorities with regard to B-52s, and I am addressing a priority effort into those areas."

ABRAMS: "That's also Seventh Air Force's mission, isn't it?"

BRIEFER: "Yes, sir, that's correct, and I believe General Clay understands that. He has pulled 120 sorties out of the Lam Son area back into the entire route network, putting them on interdiction points and on trucks throughout the entire Steel Tiger area."

ABRAMS: "Let's see if we can get a little more specific, with a map, just what we ought to be doing in Laos. See, what we really did—I think—was until we started preparation for Lam Son 719, we gave the Seventh Air Force the bulk of the B-52s—there was only an occasional divert out of there for an occasional necessary thing, or at least in our judgment it was necessary. But he had better than 90 percent of the B-52 effort, week in and week out. And he went ahead—he had these choke points, and he had a really integrated system—you know, trying to use the whole thing and play it. Now, Lam Son came along, and the focus had to be put on Lam Son in order to make it go. So that system, and the assignment of responsibilities and that sort of thing, became really fractured. On the one hand, we were guaranteeing that Lam and Sutherland had everything that they needed. And Clay accepted that, and that's what he went ahead and did. And I must say, between he and Wilson and all the rest of them—and who's that guy they had up there? Blessé? They really threw themselves into it. So on the air side, that was extremely well done, or at least I think it was. Now we've got this situation where the troops are out of Laos, for all practical purposes—I guess there's 1,611 left in there, something like that, somewhat less than a normal SOG day had, to get it in perspective. Now, why shouldn't we just turn the thing back to General Clay?"

STAFFER: "With the mission we have now, the destruction of what we know now is a great elaborate system, the information we have that's coming through our side of the house, the ground side of the house, we feel that we should retain the B-52s under our control to complete that destruction."

WEYAND: "Yeah, I agree . . . , sir, I don't think it's quite as complex in the sense that Seventh Air Force was manipulating those B-52s. The way I look at it, we gave them four targets and told them to put all the B-52s in there, and that's what they did. Any stupid jerk could do that. Then we got into a little bit of a hassle when they wanted to, and did, put those down on Box E because they felt the [other] boxes weren't doing it all. . . . Now, the targeting is really complex." The pumping stations "now assume equal importance with the entry boxes."

ABRAMS (re air assets): "We don't <u>have</u> an unlimited amount of it."

ABRAMS: "And also, at this stage of the game, I don't want some hassle to get going on this headquarters versus Seventh Air Force. We got enough hassles going on, and I don't want that. I don't mean by that to give up. We've got to find a way to work together so that everything we've got is doing the best and the most effective thing we know—<u>all</u> of us—Seventh Air Force and ourselves are convinced that this is the best way to use everything we've got, every day, against this fellow. I myself am convinced that he's been badly hurt, and <u>now</u> is the time to turn on the screws tighter and tighter and tighter, but you've got to do it intelligently, so that you're <u>really</u> damaging him."

WEYAND: "I couldn't agree with you more, sir. Our objective is what you laid out to do right at the beginning, beginning 10 October, except <u>now</u> we've got better intelligence. Probably far better than we ever hoped to have, because all we were banking on was trying to keep him from coming out of North Vietnam. Now we're really working that whole system."

3 APR 1971: WIEU

Chaired by Gen. Weyand. Amb. Bunker attends.

1971 Infiltration Estimate to this point: 36,900 (29,200, or 79 percent, destined for COSVN). During the last six months of 1970, per Potts, there was "very little infiltration."

POTTS: "We used to carry recruitment at 5,000 per month, then we dropped that down to 3,200. Now we carry it at 1,700. Most of those are forced recruitment."

WEYAND: Asks about enemy gains versus losses.

POTTS: "We're always doing that, sir, losses versus gains. We have a most difficult time in trying to justify these figures and the methodology used. We've just about quit going on record of saying gains (being recruitment and infiltration) against losses (being kills, wounded—those that are wounded that never come back, and nonbattle casualties). But it has been more losses than gains now for about 18 months—gradually going down."

POTTS: "All the COSVN infiltrators normally get in during the first six months, because they have the 120-day trip to make."

BRIEFER (responding to Weyand question): "Our sensors in the Ban Dong area itself have not revealed any traffic moving through there."

WEYAND: "Yeah, well that sort of disturbs me, because this means that the climate in Washington—they're going back to this, 'Quickly the trail is all restored now.'"

CLAY: "Well, there is a significant change in the truck pattern as you relate it to the previous years of activity. The throughput, or the input, now exceeds what we had last year, and the level of activity that is now going on is far greater than we've had in the whole truck-killing season this year. The fact remains is they are using the route structure associated with the 92 and the Tchepone area and things like that, based on the truck movements we're seeing. They're right back in there again, balls out."

WEYAND: "I agree with that related to last year, but not related to prior to Lam Son 719."

CLAY (re the Ban Dong area): "I'm convinced that the enemy is moving SAMs down there, and I'm convinced they're moving Fire Can [radar] and radar-controlled guns down there, and I'm convinced they have decided they have got to do something to overcome the interdiction effort and get the gunships out of the way and hammer B-52s, and they're going to do it to get some kind of a victory claim to justify their actions. I think we're gonna get one—either one of our gunships or the B-52s are going to be hammered by SAMs down there."

CLAY: "It was something like 78 SAMs to get one airplane, even in the heydays of going north."

■ ■ ■

BRIEFER: On 29 March 1971 between 0157 and 0453 hours 23 122-mm rockets impacted on Danang Air Base, Danang City, and Marble Mountain Air Facility, causing light casualties and damage. Duc Duc district headquarters was overrun at the same time (Quang Nam Province). 91st NVA Sapper Battalion and 8th and 9th Battalions, 38th NVA Regiment. The attack followed a 140-round mortar attack. Friendly: 20 KIA, 46 WIA, 100 civilians KIA, 96 civilians WIA, 1,451 homes destroyed, 101 homes damaged. Enemy losses: 59 KIA, 3 detained, 22 individual weapons, 6 crew-served weapons captured.

SOMEONE: Despite the hundred civilians killed, the attack got very little mention in the American press. "They're not interested in something like that."

WEYAND: "Yeah, the American press, the one I saw said this outfit came roaring down out of the Ho Chi Minh Trail, the clear implication being that all of Lam Son 719 was a failure."

■ ■ ■

BRIEFER: "In Quang Tin Province on 28 March, elements of the 1st Battalion, 46th U.S. Infantry, at Fire Support Base Mary Ann received an attack by fire consisting of an unknown number of 82-mm and CS mortar rounds, followed by a sapper attack which penetrated the perimeter. Results were 33 U.S. killed, 78 U.S. wounded, one 155-mm howitzer destroyed, one 155-mm howitzer damaged, and the battalion tactical operations center heavily damaged. Enemy losses were 12 killed."

■ ■ ■

CLAY: "If you go by the historical trend, the enemy should be coming down. And here he is now really going balls out in terms of pushing things back in. I like to think that this represents the success of Lam Son, that it really did a tremendous amount in terms of destroying matériel, disrupting and confusing the overall logistics situation. So if he's gonna have any recuperability, he's got about a month left to do it. This reflects the tremendous effort he's willing to put in to try to do it." "But there's one heck of a lot of stuff coming into the input area."

WEYAND (re more robust cross-border operations in the future): "I would think maybe our greatest lasting success out of this [Lam Son 719], looking ahead to next year and what the ARVN may be capable of, will be that sort of operation." Interdiction of Route 922 as an example.

CLAY: "I expect to see a very significant [enemy] effort in this year's rainy season to push supplies through." No more five-month vacation (from interdiction) like we've had in the past. Making all-weather roads, bringing in antiaircraft, etc. "And it's going to be tough."

WEYAND: "The enemy throughput is comparable to last year's, but this year he's had added to his problems [requirements] Cambodia and Lam Son."

POTTS: "It should [therefore] be much greater."

WEYAND (re cumulative count of helicopters destroyed in Lam Son 719): "What happened to that 108?"

SOMEONE: "That keeps switching. They've pulled some of them out that we'd counted destroyed and then decided they could repair them. It's by tail number, and it goes back to the first of February. We've got one group that reconciles the count, tail number by tail number."

WEYAND: "For everybody but the press."

BRIEFER: Upon departing the Lam Son 719 AO they put in about 100 separate seedings of air implants with 33-day and 180-day life spans to interdict the route structure (mining). Clay questions the life spans cited. Army briefer says he got that from the navy and air force.

WEYAND: "That means we won't be going back."

BUNKER: President Thieu spent two days up in MR-1, visiting the 1st Division, Airborne, hospitals. He had a very good press conference. "He said he found the morale of the troops excellent, a lot of them saying they wanted to go back again—even among the wounded and in the hospitals." President Thieu said they plan a big victory parade in Hue for the troops that took part in Lam Son 719.

BUNKER: "His [Thieu's] view, of course, as he's said before—he said to General Abrams here—is that the other side has a problem, but we have a victory. He said they had, however, learned some things from the operation. He said, 'We ought to have had six divisions between Cambodia and Laos, but security would only allow us to allocate five divisions to the operations. Next time we'll have to allocate six divisions.' He said, 'We'll have to improve command coordination. We had some problems there. We have to improve that.' And he said, 'We learned a good deal about the enemy combat tactics and operations, and that's going to prove helpful. On the other hand,' he said, 'the enemy now has got to allocate and divert a substantial amount of his forces to protecting the Trail, all the way from Cambodia to Ban Karai, so they're not going to be able to use them in-country here.' So, by and large, I think he feels very satisfied with it. As far as the attitude of the people generally goes, I think, there has been some minor criticism, and some of the opposition has taken the position, preliminarily at least, that the heavy losses are going to work against the president. But I don't think he has any such feeling."

BUNKER: "The most important of the opposition parties, the Progressive Nationalist Force, had its convention here a week ago and passed a resolution in support of Lam Son 719 and the government." "Big Minh feels that he may get some advantage from the heavy losses, but the president's view is that it was something that had to be done, that it came out—despite the numbers of the enemy that they faced—that they did extremely well. It's going to be very useful. My view is that it's going to be a good deal like Cambodia—the facts are going to speak for themselves. When we went into Cambodia there was a great hysteria all over the United States. Three or four months later everyone realized that it was successful. The same thing's going to happen here."

WEYAND: "Well, I'm sure you're right. It's sort of ironic that the same people who were so critical of the body count as a measure of success or failure in the war are now the ones that use the body count as a measure of success here."

BUNKER: "And the big problem at home has been the way this has been reported, obviously. I've been reading the *New York Times*. It's fantastic. Pick out two or three instances where ARVN troops have come out badly hurt or something like this. Then the headline is 'ARVN Morale Is Low,' generalizing from just a few instances. And talking to our helicopter pilots the same thing. This is what builds up the pressure on the president. But this is a situation, I think, we just have to ride it out. We'll come out all right."

CLAY: "Mr. Ambassador, I can't forget a year ago, when I was in the United States, and we'd just gone into Cambodia. On the *Huntley-Brinkley Show* they interviewed four U.S. soldiers under fire. They asked them the question, 'Do you think you really ought to be in Cambodia?' Without exception they said, 'We not only shouldn't be in Cambodia, we shouldn't be in Southeast Asia at all.' Now I don't know how many soldiers they had to ask that question to get four answers like that, but they showed the four like that and that gave 19 million Americans the idea that every American soldier in Cambodia thought this was a waste of time and they shouldn't be there, when heaven knows just the reverse was true."

BUNKER: "You had to let facts speak for themselves. You couldn't convince the press. We had the same kind of reporting. We had it in Cambodia, and now we're getting it again here. But this will come out all right. You'll see a few months from now."

WEYAND: Tad Shultz [*sic:* Szulc?] had an interesting chapter in his book. Sent down to report on some action. He sent in about three pieces, none of which appeared in the *New York Times*. "He couldn't understand this, because he was reporting the action as he saw it, but then copies of the *New York Times* arrived and he read the editorials, and he realized then that what he was reporting was not coinciding with the editorial comment. So he very candidly says he then saw the light and he began writing his stories with—he changed the bad guys to good guys and then his stuff began appearing pretty regularly."

15 APR 1971: COMUS Update Briefing

ABRAMS: "The only thing in psyops that you can prove, in the time while I've been here [is ralliers]—it's where the stuff is put together down there, fitted right to the circumstances of the moment, the environment of the moment, and gotten out there hot and fresh, and in the voice or in the writing of the guy that just came in. And then you get something. And if you can also have a little pressure with it, you know, where they're <u>hurting</u>, that's when you've got something."

BRIEFER: A trawler (an SL-8?) (550 tons) was sighted by a Market Time aircraft on 8 April headed south. On 11 April it penetrated RVN territorial waters and was challenged by U.S. naval surface vessels but failed to heed the challenge. Then taken under fire by U.S. Navy and VNN surface vessels and OV-10 aircraft. Following a large explosion, the trawler sank at 120147H [local time] April 1971. No survivors located. The navy is diving for the trawler. So far it has not been found.

POTTS: "The fireball went 150 feet in the air. It was a very fine explosion." It may have been self-destruction. "We feel frankly that it was."

■ ■ ■

ABRAMS: "Then the helicopter situation in MR-1 is about what it's supposed to be in the transitional support force?"

RESPONSE: "Yes [despite, therefore, the Lam Son 719 losses]."

SOMEONE: Mentions a message just in (from McCain?) urging maximum use of B-52s in Cambodia.

ABRAMS: "<u>Well</u>. As far as I know, we've never had any <u>trouble</u> making maximum use of B-52s."

■ ■ ■

Abrams has apparently been away, and is not happy when he returns with what he finds regarding an ongoing operation.

ABRAMS (re Operation Lam Son 720): "Where the hell is the control headquarters for this whole thing?"

answer: Respondent waffles, but essentially the answer is that there isn't one.

ABRAMS: "Yeah, but where is the decision made as to allocation of resources?"

ANSWER: XXIV Corps and I Corps Headquarters.

ABRAMS: "But <u>where</u>?"

ANSWER: In Danang.

ABRAMS: "Well, it doesn't look like we've learned much."

SOMEONE: "It's really two division operations."

Long silence.

ABRAMS: "Of course, this will work all right as long as there's no serious fighting. All you need is one [real battle]—all you need is one to fuck it up. And when that occurs, there ought to be somebody who's there, right up in that area, who can turn the fire hose on the whole goddamned thing. The thing oughta go on the basis that the reserve is everybody that's not in contact. This thing oughta be set up so that, if the enemy wants to jump on one of those battalions out there, within 45 minutes or something like that he should have cause to <u>regret</u> his decision. That means that air and gunships, and every other goddamn thing, just comes pouring in there from <u>everywhere</u>. This won't permit that. The 101st will be down there reconnoitering by bombing. The marines—they'll feel they aren't being supported. And they may even be right. Aagh! All right, go ahead."

■ ■ ■

ABRAMS (later): Has them put up the map of Lam Son 720, and the artillery support allocation, again. "I don't like the looks of this, Fred [Weyand]. It looks like they're running two separate operations, and apparently out of this they might also have some one-day battalion-type raids into Base Area 611 or somewhere. Well, just like all of these, there needs to be a headquarters up there somewhere in that area that can make the decisions—tac air, B-52s, helicopters, all that sort of thing—vis-à-vis the 101st and 1st ARVN, or vis-à-vis the marines and—and it doesn't look like—that sort of thing [should] be decided in <u>Danang</u>."

WEYAND: "I just don't think—."

ABRAMS: "That general support over there—you don't really <u>know</u> whether that means general support of the whole operation or general support of the 101st."

WEYAND: "Well, that means general support of the whole operation—."

ABRAMS: "And if it is in support of the whole operation, then who makes the decision?"

ABRAMS: "And, as I was saying, this system will work as long as there's no serious fighting. When you don't have any serious fighting you can go out there in the most disorganized goddamn fashion and be successful. I mean, you don't even have to have anybody in command."

WEYAND: "Well, I—."

ABRAMS: "I think the setup oughta be, if the enemy jumps on one of those battalions . . . in about 45 minutes the enemy oughta begin to regret that decision because the system just turns all of the hoses right on that son of a bitch, right now! I mean the air, the artillery, that aerial artillery outfit—the whole damn stuff commences to rain in there, and you do it for about four or five hours, and then everybody stand back and then see what happened."

WEYAND: "Well—."

ABRAMS: "We got a lotta firepower, but in order to use firepower you gotta have a system. The reserves is everybody and everything that's not in contact.

Reconnaissance with bombs—you call that off temporarily while you go where somebody's found some enemy, everybody go there. Now it may be they've got all that and we just don't know it."

WEYAND: "No—well, yeah, they may have it." They don't expect heavy enemy resistance. "This is just sort of a big sweep in which the objective is to look for and destroy enemy supplies, and deliberately are not looking—their mission says they'll not look for a fight with the enemy, they'll avoid it if possible."

ABRAMS: "It's not going to be the big heavy stuff like Laos—I understand that. And they don't really want to get out there and tangle with them in any great infantry battle. I understand that. But for that to work out that way the 324 Bravo's got to have the same philosophy. The elements of the 70th Front have gotta be looking at it the same way. In other words, if you're gonna tango out there, and not get tripping over each other, then everybody's gotta be tangoing. You can't have some son of a bitch doing this rock stuff and some other guy swanning around in the tango. And maybe the thing will all work out that way, but that's not the way to start going out."

ABRAMS: "You can have that as sort of a basic philosophy. That's kind of the way you hope it turns out. You know, you just go ahead and find great stores of ammunition and weapons and medicine and food and all that kind of stuff, and blow it up or burn it up or whatever you do, and then everybody come on home. Well, for one thing this son of a bitch has never played it that way. If he's got any amount of stuff around there under the trees, he isn't gonna give it up for free. He's gonna get in there and start really whanging away. Even though you don't want a fight, a big fight, you must always be prepared for a big fight. The system's gotta be—the ARVN want all this to be successful, and it needs to be successful for a lot of reasons, more reasons than military. That means that you oughta go out there with the idea that no battalion is really gonna get hurt—the whole thing is loaded, locked, and cocked so that if something begins to happen somewhere you don't take two days to figure it out—you know, that somebody's in trouble."

WEYAND: "Well, the 1st Division's running the show to the north and the 101's running it to the south, and that's your command and control. I don't think corps's getting into it at all."

ABRAMS: "Yeah, but then you come down to tac air." It's allocated, but then some battalion gets into a hell of a fight. "That's when you start grabbing off those tac airs and sending them up, helping out that battalion, shove that aerial field artillery outfit, get them going in there, FACs and, you know, just turn the heat on." And within a short time "it should be a'raging. And somebody should now be studying the B-52 train to see if there's anything back there that oughta be pulled off. I don't mean that you do it, but that you've gotta go back and see when the first one could get in there if there was anything worthwhile for it to do, and so on. Well, that takes a mechanism that's fairly close to the scene—closer than Danang. Better communications, intelligence, the whole thing. And there doesn't seem to be much evidence that that's what they've got."

ABRAMS: "The Laos thing—now that was a real tough operation."

Referring to Lam Son 719.

ABRAMS: "I remember the first time we went out to the A Shau—I mean since I've been here; I realize they used to sort of live out there. Well, that's a long time ago—that was considered to be a rather formidable undertaking. And one year we went out there it started out by helicopters falling out of the sky like the goddamn snow. The first day or two—whew! Wham! Bang! They were really knocking them down—1st Cavalry Division. Now of course it's all changed—you can sort of go on in there."

WEYAND: "I don't think this [Lam Son 720] plan's gonna stand up. . . . The enemy's aware of it, so that means right off the bat even with what he had in there there's gonna be some tough fights."

ABRAMS: "All right, let's move on."

WEYAND: "Well, you're going up there in the morning."

ABRAMS: "I think the way to start would be to get a briefing by General Phu, how he sees it. Then go over to the 101st, to Tarpley's people, and wind up at Danang with Manh."

ABRAMS: "Now, I'm not gonna go lumbering off into this. And I'm <u>not</u> gonna be nice about any part of it. I'm not gonna be that compassionate and patient understanding old <u>shit</u>. With all that airborne stuff going in there, this has gotta be signed, sealed, and registered—<u>every</u> inch."

■ ■ ■

WEYAND (re FACs coming back from missions in support of FANK): "Christ, we've been talking to this guy on the ground and he needs help. But he doesn't know where he is and he doesn't know where the target is, and <u>we</u> can't find it."

WEYAND: "These poor Cambodians came in there, and you could tell they'd been up all Saturday night. They were hollow-eyed and [word indistinct] and all of them have been bent over all night long. And they had this map with these big blue arrows. What the thing amounts to is B-52s destroy the enemy, and then they walk on up the road. And you just don't know where to start with trying to tell them that that's not the way it works."

WEYAND (re Cambodians trying to clear Route 4): "Each time the effort gets weaker and the blue arrows get bigger."

■ ■ ■

Anecdote from earlier service as Vice Chief of Staff to Army Chief of Staff Gen. Harold K. Johnson.

ABRAMS: "One evening at seven o'clock General Johnson and I sat down with Secretary Resor and a couple of his able assistants to give a final review to a paper which the secretary intended to sign the following morning and deliver to the secretary of defense. This was on the budget, so it was regarded as a fairly important paper. Well, we started going over that line by line and word by word.

At four o'clock in the morning I requested of the Chief and the secretary that I be excused. I said, 'I have to give a graduation speech at nine o'clock at Syracuse University, and if I don't get home and get cleaned up and change uniforms and so on, I'm not gonna be very presentable.' So they excused me, and I went home. Well, I got up to Syracuse all right, made the speech. And I came on back, and I asked the SGS, 'How'd the paper finally turn out?' He said, 'Well, they all broke up about a half hour after you left. The secretary came back in about ten o'clock and read the paper over again in the cold light of day. Well, they threw it away and started all over again.' But the point is that, after a certain time, you just can't do anything constructive any more. The mind wears out. You're no longer thinking. And the greatest service you can perform is to go to bed. Maybe you'll be late, but Christ—start over again when you can think."

■ ■ ■

WEYAND (back on the Cambodians): "They've [FANK] got Fernandez. Of course, he's no kind of a commander." "When they came in it was Sunday afternoon at five o'clock, and they wanted to kick this thing off the following morning."

ABRAMS: "It's [FANK's operation] kinda like this operation up in MR-1 now. You can't run that from here. The only thing you can do is go up there and satisfy yourself that they're organized to do it right. And if they're not organized to do it right, either they change it or you cancel it."

ABRAMS (re FANK): "There's a high level of incompetence. But you can't improve that by running it from Phnom Penh."

■ ■ ■

Illustrating the complex and constantly changing world of "rules of engagement," including various temporary authorities to undertake certain combat actions, all part of virtually continuous negotiations on the matter between MACV and Washington.

AIR FORCE REPRESENTATIVE (a general officer, probably, re the B-52 effort): "Our air authorities will all expire on the first of May. We sent an officer back to CINCPAC about 10 days ago to attend a conference there to explore all the air authorities that will expire. We sent him back with a MACV position that we had very carefully scrubbed down, and CINCPAC went along with everything that we—Seventh Air Force—had to say. They ginned up a large message that went back to JCS recommending the retention of certain authorities and, for that matter, the expansion of a few. Those few you are already aware of—the SAM strike authority on a sustained basis that we've gone in for time after time but never gotten; another one is the authority to strike any aircraft with hostile intent, any MiG-type aircraft that comes down below 20 degrees north, whether it's in the air or on the ground. These are the two salient points in terms of expansion. We've heard nothing from that to this point."

18 APR 1971: WIEU

ABRAMS: "Well, Jake, I guess you got Mr. McCloskey all squared away."

Apparently a reference to a visiting member of Congress, Rep. Paul "Pete" McCloskey.

JACOBSON: "Yes, sir. He came out here to get information on how best to impeach the president, and we did everything we could to help him in that. God forgive me for lying. He was a miserable man, sir."

SOMEONE: "That's the most polite thing I've heard you say about him."

CLAY: "He had a good visit with the Seventh Air Force. He drove in, said, 'Are you going to release those pictures?' 'No, sir.' Walked out."

SOMEONE: "He must have been pretty [bad?], because I noticed the ambassador's message back was pretty dispirited. It didn't have that lilt to it."

■ ■ ■

ABRAMS: "Well, for those of you who weren't there, South Vietnam had a great day yesterday in Hue. It really was something. It was well done. A couple of things that were really good. Oh, they decorated a lot of people. First place, it was a Vietnamese thing. That's what was up in front at the big reviewing stand, and us allies were back in about the fourth row. There was a little sprinkling of Americans out there getting awards, but it was really very modest. . . . Then they had a promotion thing, and noncoms got promoted. And noncoms to aspirant. And aspirants that had been noncoms going to first lieutenant. And President Thieu said up there that this was just a token—that there were 5,000 promotions involved, down right in the ranks. And these promotions are real battlefield promotions. They're what happened in Laos. And I just don't know of any way to get to a military organization any better than going down and promoting some guys that did a good job." "They haven't done it since I've been here." "General Phu—they made him a major general." "Then they passed in review—huh—all this 'beaten and routed army.' It sure as hell didn't look like that. These are guys who were over in Laos. The whole thing was damn well managed. It was long. It took all day—for me, going up there. They had a box lunch after it was all over, some of that Hue soup with a lot of red peppers in it." "President Thieu was really enjoying it." "The diplomatic corps was there en masse." "The bulk of the press was Vietnamese press. They had some American press—oh, that big <u>horse</u> of a woman. [Someone: "Gloria Emerson?"] Yeah. She was up there."

ABRAMS (to Leonard, his press officer): "They cornered me up there. Did you get anything bad out of that?" [Laughter]

LEONARD: Reads Maggie Kilgore report: "America's top commander in Vietnam said today South Vietnam's Operation Lam Son 720 does not rule out some degree of incursion into Laos, but General Abrams said he didn't know if the operation was going into Laos."

ABRAMS: "Well, you've got to give her good marks. She actually said what I said." [Laughter]

JACOBSON: "Well, the headline will be 'General Abrams Doesn't Know What's Going On.'" [Laughter]

ABRAMS: "Vice President Ky wasn't there. I don't know whether they ran out of seats."

■ ■ ■

MACV 1971 Infiltration Estimate: 44,500 (79 percent to COSVN).

ABRAMS: "COSVN is committed against both South Vietnam and Cambodia."

ABRAMS (re a speech by President Nixon, a tape of which he has just received): "I commend that to everybody. I just don't know how any human being can stand up there off the cuff . . . and answer—the questions were pretty sharp . . .—and that man, extemporaneously—. It's hard for me to believe that a human being could do that."

WEYAND: "Yeah, I agree."

ABRAMS: "I can't see how the American people, listening to that, can't feel pretty good of [*sic*] they've got a damn president that's really working at the business, and he's getting into these things. He isn't leaving anything to <u>staff</u>." The economy. Wiretaps yearly back to 1961 (re "police state" charges). "He's getting into it!" American Society of Newspaper Editors in New York City. "They interrupted him with applause." "And the way he handled this Calley thing—they got into that." "And the way they applauded some of the answers he gave—it was hard to believe that it was editors doing that."

ABRAMS: "You've got to be careful. We've had some leaks out of this room. I'm not pushing the Republicans or anything like that. But by god, I'll tell you, I just <u>admired</u> the way that man handled that thing. When you get to thinking you're pretty smart, you ought to listen to something like that, and how you'd handle it."

ABRAMS (re Nixon on Calley): "What he had to say about that I think is pretty damn good!"

ABRAMS (re Nixon): "He's tremendously candid. At least what I know about the business, he is really straight with them! You know, as far as policy and principle—that's just the way he's been."

JACOBSON (back on McCloskey): "The things [documents] he asked for, my slipstick [slide rule] experts figured out, would take two 6x6s [cargo trucks] to haul."

ABRAMS: "He wanted all the SEACORDS notes and minutes."

JACOBSON: "He was able to take what he got in a very small envelope."

JACOBSON: "The thing that upset him [McCloskey] more than any single other thing was our refusal to talk about Shackley's involvement in anything." "His comment was, over and over and over again, 'Do you mean you're not going to tell me things that I know every last truck driver in this country knows? How can I vote properly?'" "He knows, but he couldn't get anybody to admit it. It drove him up the wall."

ABRAMS (re pictures): "My mother used to have one on the wall of Sir Galahad. 'The strength he has is as the strength of ten because his heart is pure.' I think I'll get that and put it up."

■ ■ ■

ABRAMS: Refers to the court martial of a captain for mistreating prisoners, and an apparent comment of a lieutenant colonel on the board who said it was all right to beat a prisoner up a little bit if you really needed to. "I wonder if maybe there's some other guys like him around. [Someone: "There always are."] We've spent a lot of time and effort trying to teach people that that isn't really the best solution. And I know I'm convinced it isn't, either. [Someone: "The instructions are quite clear."] But the point is it's not smart. Aside from any moral or legal obligations, it isn't the _smart_ way to do it." "Well, I get upset by it. . . . The guy is just professionally deficient." "And the law officer, by god, wouldn't let them throw him off the court!"

■ ■ ■

ABRAMS (re dealing with the press): "I think we ought to stay away from figures and percentages. Hell with them!"

SOMEONE: "The press is trying to change national policy by what they report, not report what's going on. That's the whole name of the game. It [therefore?] doesn't matter what you do to them. You kick them in the balls now—it doesn't matter."

ABRAMS: "Let's proceed on that happy note."

■ ■ ■

BRIEFER: Describes some enemy concerns about Laotian forces.

ABRAMS: "That's a little hard for me to swallow, that they're commencing to worry about what the Laotians might do. Christ, they can't fight their way out of a wet paper sack!"

BRIEFER: Points out how the enemy 48th Regiment drove Laotian forces out of Muang Phalane earlier in the dry season, and how the Laotians later retook the position and have been in almost continuous contact since then. Lao irregulars. [Briefer really stands up to Abrams.] At a minimum, the Lao's have caused the enemy to concentrate and thus present a target for air attack.

■ ■ ■

BRIEFER: Destroyed and damaged trucks during the current season total 18,160, compared to 9,287 for the same period last year. Steel Tiger area.

CLAY: Refers to a "'truck credibility" briefing given to Abrams: "I have always, in my own mind, used my pi factor on any BDA. But even if you go down to 50 percent factor, it's still staggering. We're getting 200 trucks a night. We're going to reach 20,000 trucks. And even if you take it down to 50 percent, I still can't figure out where the hell all the trucks are coming from."

SOMEONE: "Well, sir, we can account for about 3,000 more trucks coming into the Lao panhandle than went out. Best estimates are that it takes from two to three thousand trucks to make the system run." There is a monthly input of trucks into North Vietnam, per our intelligence, of no more than 400–500 trucks.

CLAY: "The best figures I've gotten are about 9,000 trucks in North Vietnam, 3,000 in Laos, and 450 arriving in North Vietnam a month. I've tried all kinds of pluses and minuses, and no matter what I add to that thing, I think, 'Jeez, he ought to be walking barefooted up there.'"

ABRAMS: "Has anybody got any idea of how to grapple with this thing? We've got an internal credibility gap."

CLAY: "No matter how we change the variables, we still come up with, 'Somebody ought to be really hurting on this.'" "The one area that we're weak is on the destroyed area." Criterion: A direct hit with a 40-mm round will destroy a truck. Went to the armament development people at Eglin Air Force Base. They said it was not a very good criterion. So we went to two 40-mm hits to be counted as destroyed. Also we assess RNO (results not observed) in many cases, and that's not even factored into the results we estimate.

ABRAMS: "If this was true, he'd really be screwed up. And he isn't. He's still got a lot of trucks going and all that. Got a big logistic drive going on, telling everybody to get with it." "What's the destroyed, about 20 percent?"

CLAY: "It's about 70 percent destroyed, 30 percent damaged." "Since Lam Son we're still much more photo recce of trucks destroyed just left there on the roads." "It's how much you want to believe about the sensors. I think there's greater input than is shown on the sensors." "We have about 130 strings in right now, and last year at this time they had about 60." Also we have a better sensor now. So the reliability is "higher, much higher," than last year.

WEYAND: "He's a master at hiding his problems from us."

ABRAMS: "Every time you start feeling good about something—you know, kind of getting yourself [word not clear]—that scares me. I don't like it. And I don't believe it." "Our problem is that we don't have any professional way to get to the facts. And when you haven't got any professional way to get to the facts, you're in deep trouble. That's what's bothersome about this. You can say 'cut it in half.' Well, you know, that's very unprofessional. Jesus! You haven't got anything. And here he is—he's expanding, working on [Route] 23 and all that, truck activity's very high—reflected by the sensors. Bearing in mind that the sensor doesn't count trucks, it's representative of a state of activity. Well, the state of activity is high—in a relative sense. Well, that's truck activity. Well, Christ, that sort of means that there's quite a lot of trucks or something. The guy isn't short of trucks. I think I'd kind of conclude that. There's just a hell of a lot about this that we don't know."

WEYAND: It's the same problem as infiltration of people, and we later found out the enemy had lost half a million people.

ABRAMS: "Well, I don't know. People—that's a cottage industry. I was driving through Hue yesterday, and <u>gol-ly</u> the number of kids. I don't know about the rice deficit or what, but by golly they've been turning <u>them</u> out!"

ABRAMS: Asks Clay to go into the computer and get the number that can be confirmed by film. "I don't want to get into extrapolation, or reliability quotients. I have a tendency to believe those films."

Then the poor briefer has to deliver the prepared presentation on claimed truck kills for the reporting period.

24 APR 1971: Commanders WIEU

ATTENDEES: Visitor: Amb. Berger. Command group: Gen. Abrams, Gen. Weyand, Gen. Clay, MG Dolvin, MG Bowley, BG Watkin, Col. Jones. Component commanders and staff: LTG McCaffrey, MG Armstrong, RADM Salzer, BG John, BG Blessé. Military regions: LTG Davison, MG Wagstaff, Mr. Funkhouser, LTG Sutherland, Mr. Lazar, MG Brown, Mr. Long, MG McCown, Mr. Vann. MACV Staff: Mr. Kirk, MG Eckhardt, Mr. Jacobson, MG Maples, MG Dettre, MG Young, BG Greene, BG Cheadle, BG Henion, BG Heiser, BG Doehler, BG Forrester, BG Bernstein, Col. Mahl (for MG Potts), Capt. Bivin (for BG Brown), Col. Leonard, Col. Portaluppi (for Col. Sadler).

WEATHER BRIEFING (a tutorial): Begins with "what a monsoon is. There are people who think a monsoon is a furry animal that chases snakes. A monsoon is a wind. It's also a term used for the season, as the southwest monsoon or the northeast monsoon. But the main thing about it is that it's persistent. It persistently blows from the same direction over a large period of time, and periodically reverses its direction. The term monsoon may or may not have anything to do with rain."

BRIEFER: Northeast monsoon season begins in November and continues generally through the middle of March. It's separated from the southwest monsoon by a spring transition period lasting about six weeks. We get into the southwest monsoon in the middle of May and go into September. A shorter transition period in October brings us back to the northeast monsoon again.

BRIEFER: Cites the "Jelly Sandwich Rule: 'If you sit on a jelly sandwich, the jelly goes away from where the pressure is.'" Weather is the same way—winds go away from areas of high pressure.

BRIEFER: The area west and south of the mountains is dry during the northeast monsoon. In the Republic of Vietnam, the ridgeline of the Annam Mountains provides the break line between the effects of the northeast monsoon and the southwest monsoon. Northeast monsoon: generally low fog and stratus. Southwest monsoon: considerable shower and thunderstorm activity.

BRIEFER: Northeast monsoon: 1–10 inches of rain per month. [Abrams calls them on this. "Well, yes, some months get 20," they admit.]

ABRAMS: "Every year I've been here there's been one hell of a lot of rain up there north of the pass."

BRIEFER: Transition period: 1–10 inches of rain over the entire country. Southwest monsoon: 10–20 inches of rain per month. But all portions receive 1–10 inches during this season.

ABRAMS: "I want to thank you for a very good presentation. In all the time I've been here I've never heard this explained in as much depth. I guess you decided to take us into your confidence." [Laughter]

■ ■ ■

MACV 1971 Infiltration Estimate: 45,900 (76 percent to COSVN).

ABRAMS: "We need to have a wrap-up of all that's transpired in southern Laos since, I guess, about May. The whole package of the way this system is being methodically developed—troop dispositions, security forces, ack-ack [antiaircraft artillery], 470th Group, the Binh Trams 50 series, the whole thing, and the history of truck traffic on [Route] 23. And we oughta have that in pretty good shape by Monday."

■ ■ ■

BRIEFER: As of 31 March 1971: 74.8 percent of the population in A+B hamlets. 93.7 percent are in A+B+C.

■ ■ ■

SOMEONE ("Charlie") (re Lam Son 719): "We never really fought a regiment. He had to fight them as battalions because the regiment really couldn't handle the fight as such."

■ ■ ■

ABRAMS: "There were enough regiments up there to chase those bastards to [place inaudible]. But you didn't have any regimental commanders. From a distance, at least, the brightest spot in the whole thing was the airborne brigade that came down there out of Lam Son—one of those 'destroyed, beaten, and routed' airborne brigades—and they came down there and said something like, 'All those on the right are mine!' No, they did—they sailed into the goddamn thing and told those guys up there, 'Hell, you haven't even <u>been</u> in a fight yet! You oughta see where we've been!'"

■ ■ ■

ABRAMS: "These territorials, it seems to me, they've got to kind of fit the population and the villages and the districts. And you're not going to put any regiment in a district."

ABRAMS: "It's an annual thing, I guess, but the JGS wants to have RF regiments."

ABRAMS: "The real effort needs to be in improving the quality of what you've already got."

SOMEONE: "General, you remember we tried putting ARVN regiments on pacification duty back in 1968, after Tet, and what always happened was that the regimental commander would never take any instruction from the province chief, and vice versa. So finally we had to break it down into battalions to get anything done."

ABRAMS: "You've had some RF battalions in MR-4 that—hell, they went over and operated in Cambodia."

SOMEONE: "General, the Binh Tuy Defense Command is a perfect example of the worthlessness of the regimental system. It took us a year to abolish the thing. It was a draft dodger's haven."

ABRAMS (having asked how others felt about forming RF regiments): "I have a sense of support."

■ ■ ■

ABRAMS: President Thieu "is the biggest pusher of PSDF in the country. And he talks in [terms of] the long pull. And at that meeting up there he said he disagrees with some of the Americans—he doesn't want the PSDF involved, he wants the PSDF to do the war. And he sees that as the replacement for regular forces."

SOMEONE: Chieu Hoi's (ralliers) have dropped off rather suddenly and for no apparent reason, from 550 a week to 200. In the past, such unexplained drops have usually preceded a major enemy-initiated action, either political or military.

SOMEONE ELSE: "But there's no doubt we've pretty well milked the cream out of the U Minh."

ABRAMS (re an opinion survey of the rural population's outlook on Lam Son 719): "If this is any kind of an authentic sampling, it's an amazing percentage that think it's a wise thing to do, aside from the contrast between urban and rural. I don't think you could get that, in our country, on anything the government did—free beer—I don't think you could get it for a repeal of all income taxes. [Pause] Well, I guess I've overstepped myself. But it's still a rather amazing thing."

SOMEONE: "I wonder how much these polls are influenced by the fact that so many Orientals will answer what they think you want them to say."

ABRAMS: "There's no question there's some of that in here. This poll is taken by an indirect method. They don't ask them the question, they talk about the subject. And while I'm sure that that's a factor, we try to factor it out. I'm sure that it's there."

The next chart shows that the government is not rated very high on its handling of economic problems.

ABRAMS (laughing): "They said what they thought on that one."

26 APR 1971: Secretary of the Army Brief

The secretary of the army is Stanley R. Resor, whose long tenure in office covered the period 2 July 1965–20 June 1971.

BRIEFER: On 16 May 1970 elements of the 559th Transportation Group, which controls the enemy logistical setup in Laos, were ordered to stay in Cambodia and continue operations during the wet season (unusual). In September 1970 the main element moved 130 kilometers south to the tri-border area. Nine *binh trams* were realigned southward. Group 470 and Binh Tram 51 were first detected on 23 September 1970. Since then Binh Trams 50–52 and 54 have been detected. They operate the LOC from Laos into Cambodia.

ABRAMS: The advance element of the 559th that moved south became the nucleus of the group that formed 470 [in the tri-border area], which has responsibility in Laos and Cambodia from Base Area 612 on down. Same responsibility as 559 has for the balance of the logistical system. They are coequal. This represents expansion of command and control for the logistical system.

ABRAMS: "We have concluded this is the only supply LOC they've got left" since the closing of Sihanoukville. "In terms of supporting the kind of effort they've got going in Laos and South Vietnam, they can't do it with that trawler system. It doesn't carry enough. What they've got deployed now is a consumer of tonnage—107[-mm] rockets, 122[-mm] rockets, 120-mm mortars. Hell, it used to be 60[-mm] and 82[-mm], now 120[-mm]. And then all this antiaircraft—same thing. They're great weapons and all that, but they're also consumers of tonnage. If you're gonna use them, you have to back it up with tons. Just like some of the stuff we've got—it's great, but it takes quite a bit to keep it going."

BRIEFER (re the pipeline): In February it was observed that the enemy's POL pipeline had been extended into Laos. It now goes as far southward as Base Area 611, and segments (not known whether complete) from there to BA 612. During Lam Son 719 one of the first objectives that was reached was interdiction of the pipeline in the Route 9/92 area. A POW with extensive experience with the pipeline says they keep people and spare pipe all along the pipeline, and repair on average within 2 1/2 to 3 hours any breaks caused by air interdiction.

BRIEFER (re waterways): We have seen the enemy free-floating supplies down the Se Ben Hai all the way from the DMZ to Tchepone.

DISCUSSION: Infiltrators for the logistical system itself (rather than for combat units). Briefer responds to a SecArmy question about how you can tell which ones are so destined.

ABRAMS: "Wait a minute. I don't think I'm happy about that answer." Gives his own more detailed explanation. Then: "The point I was trying to make is that here is a substantial diversion of manpower into the Laos system which we have not seen in other years. In other words, as this has been expanded, and the need for greater security in the lower part of it, he's had to put additional manpower into it. I'm not trying to make the point that maybe this is causing him manpower problems. I'm saying that, as you add all of this up, it's a very clear picture that he's going methodically to work to have a system here that will support whatever political and military effort he intends to carry out over the next several years in South Vietnam and in Cambodia. And he's methodically at work getting this thing in the kind of shape where it will perform that function."

BRIEFER: Suggests expansion of the system west is in anticipation of a repetition of the "Lam Son 719 type thing that might occur from time to time, maybe not in that size, against the system. And the farther west he pushes it, the more difficult it becomes to support something like that. [Improvement of Route] 23 is banking against something that might be done next year—."

BRIEFER: Truck activity this year began about a month earlier than in previous years. Sensor activation trends: remains high even though the rainy season is approaching, again unlike previous years.

ABRAMS: "Actually the sensor coverage over there is far greater than in previous years. As long as he's driving trucks over there, we're just going to get more activations. The trend thing—that's right. But you can't really compare, or at least I don't have any confidence in comparing, the activation rate in 1970–1971 with the activation rate back in 1969–1970. They've fiddled with this so you could try to get a comparison, but nobody's come up with anything you could take some confidence in." In third generation of sensors: "They know the enemy knows all about this, and tries to fool you, to make your own sensor system work against you."

■ ■ ■

BRIEFER: "The Lam Son 719 operation caused him some problems. It disrupted his system. Particularly Binh Tram 53 and 41 were disrupted. We feel it upset his transportation schedules. We estimate he lost killed in action about 3,500 of his 559th Transportation Group people. And undoubtedly he had many additional casualties which we cannot document. He was forced to use less desirable routes to the west, where the terrain is more open and is more vulnerable to both air and ground interdiction—Route 23 and 16. And to establish these routes took additional effort. He had to put in his transshipment points. We notice now the *binh tram* structure is starting to develop down along this route. And of course he has definitely increased consumption for which he may or may not have planned—capture and destruction of sizable amounts of matériel. And of course much of it was destroyed by air strikes. We can't quantify the amount, but we do know that, particularly the B-52 strikes, we got large numbers of secondary explosions. Of course, the support of these forces by the logistical system consumed supplies that were intended for logistical throughput."

BRIEFER: "The input into Laos is running about 114 percent of the 1969–1970 season, again reflecting the tremendous amount of effort that the enemy is putting into this critical requirement. However, his throughput into Cambodia and the Republic [of Vietnam] is only 30 percent of what it was last year, which we think indicates a definite success of the various [interdiction] actions that have taken place."

BRIEFER: "We now have picked up his plans for maintaining a high level of effort in the forthcoming southwest monsoon, where previously he sort of backed off and let things lay."

ABRAMS (re structure): "We have had this [enemy] reduction of regiments to battalions, and turning over personnel to the provincial committees, and their integration into the guerrilla structure and the local force structure. Now that in itself will probably require replacement. I think maybe a satisfactory answer to that, Mr. Secretary, is that the requirements are about the same structure-wise, but the form and shape of the structure is a little different."

BRIEFER: In 1969 "total infiltration a little over 106,000." In 1970, "a little over 53,000. And so far this year, almost 46,000."

ABRAMS: "Over the last two and a half years he [the enemy] has increased the structure in COSVN. He brought seven or eight regiments. This started after Tet of '68—beefing up COSVN." "And of course when you're talking COSVN—when the turn of events took place in Cambodia, he started sorting things out, and there were strong indications that he was organizing in Cambodia—in the lower part of Cambodia, say from Kratie on down to the coast—a headquarters that would be in charge of Cambodia, whatever he was doing in Cambodia. And we had reflection of that for two or three months. Then that has disappeared. And COSVN, we believe now, is responsible for both. In other words, the geographical area of COSVN has been expanded to include his activities in Cambodia, at least from Kratie down. So when we're talking COSVN now, we're not talking about the same mission the outfit had a couple of years ago. Then it had that border area and South Vietnam up to include his Military Region 6 in II Corps, and Military Region 10, which also lopped up into II Corps. And now COSVN includes this whole thing in lower Cambodia. And so far we have been unable to predict or break out how this infiltration is divided within COSVN as between the forces committed in Cambodia and the effort in South Vietnam."

ABRAMS: "That DMZ–MR-TTH area—infiltration there—that's not the important feature, because what he has done over the years up there is he'll take those regiments and divisions and move them back into North Vietnam and refit them. And the ones that fool around in the DMZ, they'll spend four, five, six months below the DMZ, then they'll be replaced by other regiments that have in the meantime been refitting, retraining, and so on in North Vietnam." These include the 324B, 304th, and 66th. Last year the 66th got down in the coastal plain in Quang Tri during the southwest monsoon in "a markedly unsuccessful venture."

ABRAMS: "Elsewhere [other than the DMZ] it's [infiltration] a pretty good reading on what he's doing to try to maintain the capability in that part of the structure."

BRIEFER: "We think that most of the things he [the enemy] does in Cambodia are still keyed to his goal of domination of the Republic of Vietnam. We think his long-term goal is to establish a government in Cambodia which will accept use of territory by the VC and the NVA. Short-term goals are to disrupt the country and to prevent allied operations against his vital LOC area in the Mekong corridor down to the southern terminus."

■ ■ ■

ABRAMS (re a message from "the admiral" that morning about some use of C-141s): "A C-141's a wonderful thing, but you bring it in somewhere there's a couple of infantry battalions and hell, there's no way to unload it [no ground equipment]—unless you get in there with spoons and shovels. I mean, when you get talking that, they're great things, but you gotta have that w-h-o-l-e business there just to get the damn things unloaded. And then when you get a fleet of those things, they're just like all other fleets—they get flat tires, the damn universal joints break. So then, right back of that, is a great big mainte-nance setup, just to keep them going! And then, when you've got all that going, then you've got a whole truck organization. 'Cause, see, you start put-ting 50 C-141 sorties in in a day, you'd be amazed, but in a week's time you won't be able to land a Piper Cub on the damn airfield. It's just terrible the way it'll pile up. So you gotta have a whole truck and transportation organization that's hauling this stuff out, night and day. If you don't, the 141s will bring it in faster than you can distribute it. . . . Plus, the final thing, MAC's gonna land those things where you guarantee the rockets and antiaircraft are not present. That's no battlefield delivery out there. You're not talking about these C-7s that go into some pretty hairy places, and then get shot down. We've just got to give them all the things involved." [Subsides] "You can't do it with wheelbar-rows, I'll tell you that."

■ ■ ■

This briefing leads to an important discussion between Mr. Resor and General Abrams of longer-range prospects in the war.

BRIEFER (re strategy): "Turning now to the request in Mr. Laird's message to attempt to take a look at the enemy strategy, we've looked out to about mid-1972. Certainly we believe that his requirement to reestablish and secure a logistical system is the most critical aspect of all of his requirements. He's faced with major problems. Market Time has interdicted his sea routes. The Commu-nity Defense and Local Development plan is degrading his local procurement capabilities. Lam Son 719 and the air interdiction campaign are disrupting his LOC and reducing the throughput. The Toan Thang operation has disrupted the southern terminus and has caused expenditures of reserve stocks which we think were marginal. We feel that he has no other alternative but to overcome these problems if he's going to remain militarily effective in the Southeast Asia area, particularly the southern confines. Through the end of the 1971–1972 dry period, which would be until about May of 1972, we estimate that he'll maintain pressure on the Royal Lao Government in northern Laos for political purposes in an attempt to get a cessation of the bombing on the Ho Chi Minh Trail."

SECARMY: "Mr. Laird asked specifically—. He [the enemy] seems to get all around—where is it the king lives—Luang Prabang?—but he never seems to go the whole way. Does it make any difference what size friendly force is there? He's apparently inhibited by political considerations. It looks like he has the capability to go in, but he never has."

BRIEFER: "I think he's probably inhibited by political considerations, yes, sir."

SECARMY: "If so, does it make much difference how strong the friendly force is?"

BRIEFER: "I don't believe that he's really interested in taking over the government of Vientiane."

ABRAMS: "I think that's a good question. It's kind of like Phnom Penh. Back in the early days of the change in the attitude of the government, I think he could have gone and taken Phnom Penh with one or two regiments out of the 9th Division. I don't really think it would have been a problem. And he could have done that in military terms. And I think it probably would have been fairly easy. But that's just not the way he wants to do it. It isn't his way. The way he went to work on Phnom Penh was go ahead and cut Route 7, cut Route 4, start interdicting the Mekong and Route 1, so that fuel's not getting in there and they have problems with food itself from out in the countryside. Do a little shelling to get some feeling of apprehension, and so on. If you just squeeze that enough the people will be a mixture of being frightened, and out of that'll come distrust of their own government, that it can't protect its own people or it can't do things and so on. And the whole mixture of things will just cause the government to go down the drain. And out of that, hopefully, would come a government that—."

ABRAMS: "And I think that it's the same way up there with Vientiane and Luang Prabang. You don't go marching in there with your soldiers. After all, there are press and cameras and that kind of stuff in both of these places—or all three of them. He's not after any movies of victorious North Vietnamese troops marching down the Champs-Elysées. He says that these are revolutionary-spirited local inhabitants rising up to throw off oppression and all that. And the cosmetics show that in the end. He wants to change either the policies or the personalities, or both, in those governments. And I think that's the way he plays it. And then you say, 'Well, it doesn't make any difference how strong they are, whether they've got two regiments to defend it or two battalions.' Well, in that same equation I think that it does have some bearing on it. There's, let's say, the king and his advisors, and then the people that are kind of around there—they ought to be able to see a few of their own, you know— in uniform and so on. You get into how much quality there is, or how much quality you ought to try to get, and I think you can discuss a lot of different sides to that. In all of these things there's a limit to what you can get in quality with just equipment. There's <u>some</u> equipment that you <u>have</u> to have. Equipment will help you with quality for at least a short distance, and then the quality is all in terms of experience, motivation, leadership, training, and that sort of thing."

ABRAMS: "And that's the way it really is in Cambodia now, too. I don't mean that we've furnished them all the weapons that they probably need, but when they get talking about some of the more sophisticated things, you have to have some sort of a feel for the quality of the leadership, the experience, the training, the motivation, and that sort of thing. There's a point [where] you can't hang any more equipment on it because it won't do any better, because first it doesn't know how to handle it. O-o-o-h, they'd love to get in there and <u>race</u> the <u>engine</u> and all that, but by golly in terms of getting something done for the country—."

BRIEFER: In RVN: "We think that he'll [the enemy] continue with a protracted warfare strategy, concentrating on guerrilla warfare, proselytizing, and terrorism, with periodic local increases in tactical activity. However, we don't believe any major offensive-type operations will be undertaken. The picture after mid-1972 is less clear. Certainly what he does will depend to a great extent on the success of his logistical campaign. In turn, the success of his logistics campaign will depend to a great extent on our counteractions. Certainly the ultimate objective remains the conquest of South Vietnam and the extension of his sphere of influence throughout Indochina."

SECARMY: "It might be fair to say he's [the enemy] in fact achieved the objective of getting us to withdraw ground troops fairly at a steady and significant rate. He's done that, of course, by the effect he's had in the United States, and that's what's caused it here. Is it possible that his objective will now be to try to get the air effort reduced and to prevent us from having a significant residual force MAAG?" "Those are two problems he's got facing him now, having dealt with the ground forces. . . ." "Perhaps the way he'll go about [dealing with] those is the way he went about the first problem. Make attacks on those issues that would [erode?] domestic support . . . and commit the Democrats to positions which they would be locked in on when they—if they did come to power in '72. Get them to make speeches and so forth so they take public positions so that if they have a change of administration—. And lastly, I suppose his other problem is our economic aid. We're now supporting, in the military assistance program alone, around $2 billion, and I think outside of that is about $800 million, so probably we count $2 billion roughly annually that we're feeding into South Vietnam, so I guess he's got that objective, too, to try to get that shut off. And again, working the same way that he's had success before, in other words to try to get Congress to stop appropriating that kind of funds so that the South Vietnamese would essentially be out of ammunition. They're spending $600 million, shooting up $600 million of ammunition annually."

ABRAMS: "What's happened so far—. Well, one way to describe it is, he got a bombing halt in North Vietnam. Then there was pressure to withdraw American troops, and the administration has gone ahead with the program of doing that, including—I think the president's made it fairly clear that he's got a plan to go all the way."

SECARMY: "That's a little bit subject to the prisoners."

ABRAMS: "Well, that's right."

SECARMY: "But he's left sort of ambiguous what he does if the prisoners aren't returned." Cites "total withdrawal, which is even more ambiguous. That could be more than forces, I suppose."

ABRAMS: "Well, the pressure is kept up that even that program isn't satisfactory. Now there's a mounting effort against the air presence. I think he knows, I think he's satisfied, that sometime in this calendar year our ground forces in South Vietnam are really going to be sort of inconsequential in terms of what really can be done to influence the outcome of events with ground forces of the U.S. And I think he knows that. But that's not enough. Probably the next thing is to get the air. Then he has to think about the elections here. And of course he works hard in that thing [to discredit Thieu]. . . . With all its faults, I would say that it's impossible to put one together here in this country that would equal it [the Thieu government] in effectiveness—with all its faults, which, you know, we could probably fill this room with them, so I'm not trying to paint any great—. But, in relative terms, I doubt that there's any way to assemble any-thing that would be more effective for this country. So he's gotta work on that between now and October. Then you've got all this—in the first place, there's all the equipment. And I don't know whether he wants to work to get that or whether it's the economic aid that would probably be even more destructive if he could get that turned off. That's $750 million a year."

SECARMY: "I would think it would be easier to get the war aid turned off, though. You know, 'The president's killing civilians and refugees, and the U.S. is supporting a terrible thing.' And the way to turn that off is the war aid. The support for economic aid, which people might visualize as taking care of people."

ABRAMS: "All this has gotta be a step at a time, always prepared to take three or four if the opportunity presents itself. And really, I think, it's only—some frac-tion of the war is being done here in Indochina. Then there's another part that's being carried on in the United States, and then there's another piece that's kind of wherever he can make it go in the rest of the world—opinion."

ABRAMS: "All of these things impinge on it—the use of drugs by American forces, race relations within the American forces, anti-Americanism among the Vietnamese. The whole thing is an organ. It's got three or four keyboards on it. It's got a whole mess of stops on it. And each one of these things we've men-tioned is either on one of those keyboards, or there's a stop for it, and so on. I think you have to agree that they're a very skilled player of this thing. Also, in a way, it's a little bit unfair, because some of the pressures that our side is sub-jected to—including this government here—are not available to play on the other side. It's a closed society. You take the relationship of casualties, the impact casualties have. The impact of that is very severe with us. It's severe even with the South Vietnamese. Nobody knows what impact—that doesn't influence him. Another thing is the amount of support China and the Eastern European countries provide him. That sure isn't debated [SecArmy: "Visibly."]. I'm sure among some of the principal leaders they make assessments and evaluations—not in terms of what it cost or what was lost or any of that, but in political terms and the Communist movement and that sort of thing whether this is still a good horse to back. I think on that they're probably realists. You take a thing like what happened to Arabs when the Israelis decided to go out—. The matériel loss there was very high. Plus the incompetence of the Arab leadership was there for everyone to see. You always wonder what happened to the Soviet MAAG chief that was down there sending in his HES reports or whatever it was [laughter] about how this was coming along, and the training and the leadership and so on. But the ruble loss really didn't make much difference to them in the end. The importance to them of maintaining their position in the whole thing was paramount. And even though the Egyptians in terms of skill and training and discipline and that sort of thing looked like a real weak horse to be backing, they still accepted that and started all over again. In this part of this it's really an unfair—I don't know if that's a good term [SecArmy: "Uneven."]—that's right, uneven contest in those terms. Then it goes on to this whole thing has had a lot of effect on the armed forces. For instance, some of the things that Jack Anderson's been printing. It's very difficult—somebody's giving him that—and it's very difficult for me to understand how somebody in our Defense Department is doing that."

SECARMY: "Which one was that? He had the commissary attack."

ABRAMS: "Oh, no, no. I'm not talking about that, or somebody building an extra airfield, or poor old Nick Maples here, who's selling peanut butter. [Laughter] I tried to get him in charge of our peanut butter here, but he's reluctant to do it. I'm not talking about any of those kinds of things. We have things that leak out of this headquarters, or out of the component headquarters—it has to be up—the nature of it has to be up here. So any top secret paper that we have, we have to go over very carefully to make sure that we can accept its publication in the *New York Times*. I don't believe top secret has any meaning. Now, a lot of top secret papers are inoffensive—they're not very good papers, not good substantive things. And of course those don't leak. They have no political value. They can't help guys that want to be helped. This has affected us in ways. I'm sure in the headquarters here that we have people who, first of all, they get concerned, because it's not being told all the good things that are being done. Somebody just isn't getting credit for the wonderful and skillful thing they've got accomplished. Well, they're motivated to get that out, and they don't know what they're doing. That's probably what motivates them."

ABRAMS: "Then there's others that really get mad because the idea or project or concept that they've been advancing got disapproved. I have to say that the motivation there is certainly a sincere one. This is a guy that's worked hard on something and he really believes in it. The trouble is it didn't go that way. So he feels that he has to [leak]. And then you've got some people around who believe that this whole thing is wrong. And they will actively help the opponents if they can. And that condition, I believe, has been brought on us—oh, you know. Then there's always a few unprincipled fellows who just like money. They get attracted by money. In some cases it really doesn't have to be very much. Why somebody would let go of himself for twenty thousand bucks, well you don't really—."

ABRAMS: "So this whole thing, I think, has its effect. Now, of course, you try to work those things out, but it's really as much a part of the problem as anything else. That's there. There's no way to do something someday to just clear the books on that, there'll be no more of that. It's part of the problem, just like drugs. You work hard on drugs, but if anybody, well, would promise you that they'd have that done by Christmas, I wouldn't spend much time with them. I'd get on and talk to somebody else that's been thinking a little deeper, 'cause it's a tough problem. I don't think, and I don't believe, and I think we know even about it that it's not going to overwhelm us. But it's just going to take one hell of a lot of work and a lot of understanding."

BRIEFER (on major strategy developments since the SecArmy's last visit in June 1970): "During August and September the magnitude of the enemy's logistics effort became apparent." "Appreciating the obvious demand on his logistical system, a strategy evolved designed to disrupt his efforts." Three-pronged strategy: intensive tac air effort along the entire system in the Laotian panhandle; coordinated Arc Light, tac air, and fixed-wing gunship campaign against four entry interdiction boxes, or choke points, where the system enters Laos from North Vietnam; and a large-scale ground attack at the heart of the system, which later came to be known as Lam Son 719."

ABRAMS: Those Royal Laotian Air Force "T-28s have kept up quite an effort there." Cambodian air force lost most of its planes. Now doing about 70 sorties (per week?) with only five or six airplanes. "It's not going to change the course of history or anything, but they deserve a hell of a lot of credit for what they've done with what they had left. And I think it is important when you get into this business of the will to do things and the will to continue. And that's pretty important."

■ ■ ■

BRIEFER: Some of the highlights of Lam Son 719 "as we see it from here."

■ "The operation was designed to strike the enemy at the period of his peak activity in Base Area 604."
■ ARVN operated a total of 42 days cross-border.
■ Maps were made and valuable targeting information was acquired; this was used after the operation was over.
■ Air cav was in Tchepone 10 days ahead of the ARVN.
■ Combat support: "Tremendous firepower used in support of the RVNAF."
■ 81 B-52 sorties flown during the first week of the operation. Next week: 77.

Then: 166, 225, 253, 236, 242. Total: 1,280. "Tremendous amount of coordination—and also a lot of firepower."

- "The airmobility concept received a severe test during this operation."
- "Two-thirds of damaged helicopters repaired within 48 hours."
- Summary: "Tested RVNAF against a determined enemy in cross-border operations, and undoubtedly interrupted his [the enemy's] supply schedule. It's really too early to evaluate the full effect, much as it was difficult to evaluate the effect of Cambodia at the time of your last visit, sir."

BRIEFER: "Another area of special interest, sir, is the fallout of Lam Son 719. In an effort to develop techniques and concepts for improving support coordination, we formed a support coordination progress group. We have eight general officers in this group, all of whom have experience in this area and were involved in Lam Son."

SECARMY: "I know Mr. Packard [David Packard, deputy secretary of defense] got the impression that coordination wasn't the best." An air force briefing team came back. At one of the briefings where there wasn't anybody officially from the army monitoring it, they felt they were answering some of the questions about chopper support. (To the army's disadvantage, apparently.) And of course this all comes up at the time of the annual battle in the Congress between the AX and the Cheyenne, and "opponents of the Cheyenne, of course, are trying to maintain that Lam Son 719 proved that helicopters don't survive, won't be useful in Europe, because the losses were heavy in Lam Son 719."

BRIEFER (logistics): "We are shooting to realize this goal [of RVNAF self-sufficiency] by the end of FY '73." They are now rebuilding M-113s and M-41 tanks in-country. Shows a series of "before and after" photos of improved depot facilities. Someone suggests the improvements shown are the result of "better photography."

ABRAMS: Points out to the SecArmy that the "before" pictures were taken in the rainy season and the "after" ones in the dry season. "But it will be interesting to take pictures in this rainy season, which we'll do, and then we'll have a fairer comparison. It's so blatant that I thought I ought to—." [Laughter]

BRIEFER (defensively): "It was the rainy season when we started." [More laughter]

ABRAMS (helping the briefer): "We haven't had a rainy season to take pictures of the improvements yet. It's coming."

BRIEFER: "In 1972, one-half of the 2.2 million able-bodied males 20 to 45 will be serving in the military forces. This leaves us 1.1 million to meet both the RVN military and civilian labor requirements."

ABRAMS: "We used to have U.S. motor pools here in Saigon, and hell, 75 percent of the mechanics in there were women. These women are good!"

MAPLES: "We have some 10-, 11-, and 12-year-old boys working in the depots."

ABRAMS: "I had a talk with Admiral Salzer, who's just come in and taken over. We've got some deep troubles here in the Vietnamese Navy." [In logistical support, apparently.] "My impression is that the operational part has gone along at really a fast clip, and maybe this didn't have quite the attention and the urgency. Because it has to come along with it. I think the air force has got a good program on the logistics side.... It's always been recognized as an absolute must. It <u>had</u> to come along."

MAPLES: "Mr. Secretary, many of our advisors are being advised these days. Many of the youngsters who are coming over here are learning a great deal from the Vietnamese about logistics."

1 MAY 1971: WIEU

MACV 1971 Infiltration Estimate: 45,900 (no change). Last year: 42,800. Last year: 63 percent to COSVN. This year: 76 percent.

■ ■ ■

CLAY: "In line with that, General Abrams, we have over there today our good friends Lowenstein and Moose, from the Senate Committee on Foreign Entanglements or whatever it is. We're probably going to get some complaints again, because I told them not to turn anything over to them. If they want to get information, they request it through the Air Force Secretariat channels and it will be forwarded as appropriate. They'll probably say we're withholding information." [Abrams: "In Vientiane?"] "Yes, sir, then they're going down and General Evans [at Udorn] has them today, And they want to go through the same backup everything we possibly went through and that whole nine yards of ROE and pictures and, 'Give me this, give me that,' routine."

BUNKER: "Unfortunately, they have some unscheduled days on their program. They may show up here."

James G. Lowenstein and Richard M. Moose were staff members of the Senate Foreign Relations Committee.

■ ■ ■

BRIEFER: Binh Tram 33 reports to the 559th Transportation Group that approximately 50 percent of their vehicles are disabled.

ABRAMS: "Well, I guess the interdiction program is having <u>some</u> effect."

CLAY: "It's having an effect on <u>me</u>, general!"

POTTS: "There's no reason for a forward element to be moving south, in my opinion, unless something's going to follow along behind it."

CLAY: We have almost 1,300 sensors in 127 strings on all important routes, including Route 23 (a candidate alternative route to the west). This is the highest we've ever been on sensor coverage.

ABRAMS (re northern Laos): "Well, I must say that thing about, 'Well, if they can afford to put B-52s up there, maybe we'd better look at this B-52 thing again, there's too many, they've got surpluses.' That was the gist of it. [Someone: "A quote of the SecDef memo."] Somebody raised the point that we have occasionally put a B-52 strike up there in response—I must say—in response to the wailing and crying and weeping of Ambassador Godley. And raises the question that, if we can do things like that, we must have surpluses of B-52s. And I think he said he was going to personally review each one of these. [And not approve any more] until we see what is happening with these surpluses. You just wonder how they can [words not clear] things like that."

■ ■ ■

BRIEFER: Two Hoi Chanh say the enemy has low morale in the U Minh. They had been told in North Vietnam by their leaders that most of South Vietnam had already been liberated. "The realities of the situation have led to disillusionment among both VC and NVA." They are also short of food and short of ammunition. There are VC-NVA conflicts.

ABRAMS (re the alleged shortages of food): "You know, I really can't believe it. The ARVN soldiers down there—hell, they've been eating lobster. All you've got to do, about, is reach in the water and scoop these big crabs—well, you can't, of course, reach in with your hand and grab a crab, but they've got a way of getting them out of there. It's really luscious—fruit, bananas. If any of those characters are short of food, they must be pretty unenterprising guys. It's hard for me to believe. That's a very rich place in there."

■ ■ ■

DISCUSSION: Topic is what Abrams calls "a priceless message." [Apparently a naval lieutenant working for Admiral Salzer has complained about hardship due to substitutions for food items on the menu where he is.]

SALZER: "What happened was he's a very eager young supply officer, and somebody released his message without reading it."

ABRAMS: "And it wasn't any sloppy message. I mean, he had the details!" Re the distribution: "I'm on there twice, as the CG of USARV and the commander of MACV. He wanted to be sure wherever I was—."

Abrams asks Weyand to get a copy of the message for the ambassador. But Salzer apparently didn't receive a copy.

WEYAND: "The reason he didn't send it to you [Salzer] was he was going to give General Abrams one more chance!"

ABRAMS: "He also says in there he's going to keep sending these, by golly, until it gets straightened out."

■ ■ ■

BRIEFER: Describes a 26 April 1971 broadcast by Liberation Radio of an order from the People's Liberation Armed Forces Command prescribing treatment of U.S. soldiers who are opposed to the war or who disobey orders or defect. Do not attack them. Assist those who desert. Assist defectors to return to the United States or whatever country they desire.

ABRAMS: "Would you call this a Chieu Hoi program in reverse?"

ABRAMS: "I wanted to say a word in here. You know, we've got this thing about what these American units are going to be doing. What the cavalry brigade is doing out here in MR-3 is working on the headquarters of SR-7 and SR-5. And I visualize that that's what they'll be doing for the next year. If you want to talk about how you provide some measure of security to Long Binh, Bien Hoa, and this sort of thing, and this is what you've got to do it with, I just don't know of any better way to get at it than that. And that means they're out in the jungle, because that's where SR-7 is. And the more they . . . keep the heat on it, take things away from them, and all this . . . some new approach to the shadow supply system . . . possibility you could get after it on Route 1 and Route 20 in a way that, if you got enough sophistication into it, it might be reasonably crippling in terms of what those outfits will be able to do compared to what they <u>want</u> to do." And in MR-1, the 196th Brigade in Quang Nam "is going to have to be out there in the Khe Sanh Valley and all—that's what it's got to be doing, and that has to do with the security of our key installations in Danang. These outfits have all got to be—an awful lot of training, the development of intelligence—they've really got to be skilled, professional, and tough outfits. And I think that's what they're going to be doing. I think that's what they've <u>got</u> to do. And when we respond, I want to be sure we lay out very <u>clearly</u> what they're going to be doing, and why."

SOMEONE: "I might add they have a different kind of backdrop in terms of the local forces and the RVNAF forces in the area. It isn't what it was four or five years ago, where they were almost alone in the area. There is a foundation of local security."

ABRAMS: "You're also going to have, and properly so, some intermingling. The 1st Cav has had as many as seven or eight RF companies involved." "There isn't any U.S. territory and Vietnamese territory. That's all the territory there is."

ABRAMS: "Anything that you do that will help develop the confidence and skill of the territorials, or the People's Self-Defense, or the police—those are all contributing directly—the nature of the thing is such that that is <u>true</u>—[to the security of U.S. installations]."

ABRAMS: "We want to be sure that there doesn't get any fuzzy thinking. You know, 'the war is winding down' or 'the heavy fighting is about over.' This is going to continue to be a nasty business. People are going to get hurt, people are going to get killed. And the best way to keep that at the lowest possible level is skilled, disciplined training, working, and doing all that hard stuff. And then we've got a good chance of doing it right. And these troops—that's the way they've got to be." We've got to take good care of the troops. "But we mustn't get dreaming about it. It's still a tough business. It's going to be that way."

ABRAMS: "He's [the enemy] going to screw us up as much as he can, as bad as he can, and every time he can, and that's what we're in. And it isn't going to change!"

SOMEONE: "If you want another example of where one guy makes a difference, Colonel [Nghia?] down in Binh Thuan is an example. He moved into there, and he just took over the thing, and he's been running it just as hard as he could. And as a result MR-6 just goes down and down."

ABRAMS: "And you know, in the time I've been here that's the first time that trend has really developed in Binh Thuan. Hell, we've had the 1st Cavalry in there, we've had the—. They even moved the cavalry squadron my <u>son</u> was in down there, and <u>that</u> didn't—." [Laughter] They discuss again the former VC leader of MR-6, said (rumored) to have gone to North Vietnam about a year ago. "Used to ride a white horse."

ABRAMS: "There were amazing stories about this guy. Great black cape. Riding through the villages at night. His mother ran the *nuoc mam* business in Phan Thiet. I don't know whether any of it is true."

■ ■ ■

BRIEFER: MACV assumed responsibility for support of the Vung Tau Training Center on 1 July 1969. Since then, over 67,000 have been trained there.

ABRAMS: "This is another part of strategy." Has gone beyond just RD cadre training. Village commissioners for social welfare, etc. Military Academy cadets.

JACOBSON: "The commandant of the school came to me the other day and said he'd like a trip to Israel to see what's going on there. I said, 'Colonel Be, you couldn't possibly be gone during the upcoming election.' He said, 'That's exactly the period I've got to be gone.'"

■ ■ ■

BRIEFER: Route 922 has carried the bulk of the throughput this year. 89 truck-loads entered the RVN, versus last week's season-high 203. Cumulative throughput = 11.5 percent of recorded input. 998 trucks damaged or destroyed. Paveway laser-guided bomb used against a 100-mm gun, which was blown 170 feet and the tube separated from the carriage. MK 82: 500-pounder. MK 84: 2,000-pounder, used here, delivered by a fighter aircraft. Cumulative truck kills: 20,574 for this season.

6 MAY 1971: Update for COMUS on Waterway and Pipeline

BRIEFING: Prepared by General Sutherland's G-2 on the effect of Lam Son 719 on enemy logistics in the Laotian panhandle. Specialist Connors will present the briefing and has been tracking these matters for 21 months. Waterway adjacent to MR-1, the Se Bang Hieng. Apparent loss to the enemy of this route, also designated Waterway 7J, based on multisource intelligence: aerial photography, Hoi Chanhs, PW interrogation, sensors.

CONNORS: Waterway orientation is westward from the western DMZ, then south-ward into BA 604. South of Tchepone, then west, south, and into the Mekong. Crossed by Route 9, fordable at low water. Channel improved by the enemy to make it more navigable during low water. Floating POL drum-type things: free-floating method of moving goods by water. Route 1032A and Route 92A, part of a road-water complex with 7J the connector, became the main route into BA 604. Waterproof bags floated. Also POL drums or barrels. Truck: 16 55-gallon drums. Damage and destruction during Lam Son 719 to transshipment points. Destruction of rock and bamboo channeling devices. In a sense, the waterway has been interdicted. An important portion of the wet season LOC much diminished in utility. Fuel shortage as a result.

ABRAMS: "After that mood valley I arrived in yesterday, deeper than any I've—. I've been trying to fight my way out of it ever since. The therapeutic value of that briefing is really great. And one of the greatest things about it is not entirely the enemy, but that you've done this piece of work. I think that's great."

POTTS: "A very fine piece of work."

9 MAY 1971: Update for Admiral McCain

ATTENDEES: From CINCPAC: Adm. McCain, Mr. Walstrom, Capt. Wilson, Capt. Dwyer, Col. Lynn, LTC Moore, LTC McLanahan, LTC Fuller, Maj. Wheeler. From MACV: Gen. Weyand, MG Dolvin, MG Bowley, MG Cowles, MG Maples, MG Potts, BG Doehler, BG Forrester [CORDS], Col. Jones.

MCCAIN: "Let me ask you a question that's frequently asked of me. What do you think's going to happen in this business in the future—future years?"

POTTS: "We think, sir, that he'll carry on with harassment, terrorism, and so forth in MRs 2, 3, and 4. We think that he's going to continue to try to show strength in the northern MR-1 area. Just in the past four days we've seen indications that the 304th Division is moving back into northern MR-1."

WEYAND: "The answer to whether these people are going to continue a pro-tracted war is, 'Hell, yes.' There isn't any sign to the opposite."

WEYAND: The enemy's apparent plan to bring the 320th Division down into the COSVN area "was frustrated by 719."

WEYAND: "This guy's [the enemy] just not slacking off. I don't think he can. For one thing, the percentage of VC versus NVA has shifted so markedly over on the NVA side, while heartening in that it indicates the internal subversion—his recruiting base—has been pretty well destroyed, still means that there're a hell of a lot of North Vietnamese down here that he can't turn loose of and walk away from it. So he's just got a lot of things that are going to keep him on the field of battle."

WEYAND (re the future): "Our air is going to be the glue that holds all this together. It's the only capability we can't give the South Vietnamese." "If it weren't for that ["air capability, which is driving this guy [enemy] right up the wall"], we'd be in very bad shape, and yet these people back in Washington keep wanting to whack at that, too. Whether the president knows it or not, it's his guarantee of the Nixon Doctrine succeeding. I think we can muck along with a single brigade less or faster out of here, but—."

WEYAND: "Senator Kennedy made quite a bit of the refugees that had been generated by the U Minh campaign. When I was down there the other day, there's been also an influx back into the productive areas of the U Minh, right on the heels of wherever the security's been provided, a lot of people who are coming in there to take advantage of the productivity of the land."

BRIEFER: "In January, the Hamlet Evaluation System scoring system was reaggregated to make the overall rating more sensitive to the political and development aspects. Therefore, the apparent drop in the A/B ratings. . . ." The 1971 Supplemental Pacification and Development Plan sought during November 1970 to February 1971 to eliminate all B hamlets (by upgrading them to A). On 1 March 1971 President Thieu upgraded the National Police to a command and, for the first time, authorized them to recruit draft-age men. National population registration by the police is under way, with almost two-thirds registered by 28 February 1971.

BRIEFER (re Chieu Hoi): "The program is dwindling, primarily because we don't have much left." The big year was 1969: 47,000.

BRIEFER (re Pacification Attitude Analysis System monthly surveys): "A year ago, the survey showed almost all their concern was pointed toward their security. Now most of their concern is pointed toward economics."

WEYAND: Ambassador Berger said he went to a conference of U.S. ambassadors from throughout the region held in Tokyo "and they gave him 10 minutes at the end of the day when everybody was asleep. He said he's not too sure whether Vietnam is going to be very high on the agenda [for the next meeting, upcoming]. He wasn't too happy about that."

WEYAND: "The full impact of this drug thing is starting to hit everybody, including of course us, and there's not much to cheer about in that. We've got some problems all right."

15 MAY 1971: WIEU

Attendees: Amb. Bunker, Gen. Abrams, Gen. Weyand, Amb. Colby, Gen. Clay, Mr. Kirk, LTG McCaffrey, MG Dolvin, MG Eckhardt, MG Cowles, MG Maples, MG Bowley, MG Dettre, MG Young, MG Wilson, MG Potts, BG Watkin, RADM Salzer, BG Cheadle, BG Henion, BG Brown, BG Doehler, BG Forrester, BG Bernstein, Col. Zerbe (for Col. Sadler), Col. DeBruler (for BG John), Col. Ludwig (for Col. Leonard), Col. Jones.

ABRAMS: Raises the question of "whether we can focus the intelligence any more to get at the fuel system, it being kind of the key."

POTTS: "We have the manifests on almost all those ships coming in [to Haiphong] with trucks."

ABRAMS: "Rail imports from China?"

POTTS: "Yes, sir. We have that, too. We don't have manifests on that. These are estimates made by people that are watching the cars go by."

ABRAMS: "I think we have to say, though, Bill, that we don't have a handle on trucks to the extent that we think we have it on POL."

POTTS: "No, that's right."

ABRAMS: "The quality of what we think we have—I think there's quite a difference."

ABRAMS (re MR-4): People get all upset by outposts being overrun, but should focus on the good results of the aggressive policy that puts them in place. Last week there were only 60 victims of terrorist activity, and that in the MR with the most people. "I'll bet you there were more victims of traffic accidents in IV Corps last week than 60."

SOMEONE: "We kill about two a day, countrywide, ourselves [in traffic accidents]."

ABRAMS: "Yeah, but you're just taking the parochial view. They've got quite a program going themselves. That's been Vietnamized!"

■ ■ ■

BRIEFING: Progress of CORDS programs in a given district.

ABRAMS: "Who decided to put this briefing on, anyway?"

SOMEONE: "Probably Bob Komer." [Laughter]

Briefing is on the Saigon Civil Assistance Group.

ABRAMS: Sees it as bureaucratic layering, and tells the J-3 to look at it in terms of his space problem [billets].

■ ■ ■

BRIEFER (re truck kills): Cites "revised BDA criteria" and says "damaged trucks outnumber those destroyed for the first time this dry season. The validity of the new criteria, which require a burner or a blower for a destroyed truck, is still being evaluated." "Even with the new criteria, the weekly percentage of sensor-detected movers reported as destroyed and damaged trucks remains consistent with the season average."

ABRAMS: "There's always the requirement to improve the professional work that you're doing. That's always there! And if you find out, maybe, that you weren't doing it as well as you could, then you ought to change it. We should always do that."

■ ■ ■

ABRAMS: "Then we have that message in from CINCPAC, too, about how come these MiGs are getting away." "It shows that they haven't been over talking to those pilots very much. The one thing a pilot would rather do than any other thing in the world is shoot down a MiG. They'll do anything. I mean, they might even get a little dishonest, if they can just shoot one down. You've got a built-in pressure there that really needs almost no stimulation." [Laughter] "I was over there at Udorn one night, a long time ago, and got really immersed in it. I don't think they've changed."

BRIEFER: Report of a FAC who had 20 trucks in view in Cambodia, brought in a gunship, and then couldn't get clearance to fire.

ABRAMS: They blame that on "the higher-ups." "Remember the one [FAC] you brought in here a while ago? He could <u>barely</u> tolerate us!"

20 MAY 1971: Commanders Conference

Attendees: Gen. Abrams, Amb. Colby, Gen. Weyand, LTG McCaffrey, MG Hardin, RADM Salzer, Mr. Vann, LTG Davison, LTG Sutherland, MG Armstrong, MG Cushman, MG Dettre, MG Maples, MG Cowles, MG Wagstaff, BG Bernstein, MG Doehler, MG Watkin, MG Dolvin, MG Bowley, MG Potts, BG Armstrong, BG Heiser, BG Forrester, LTC Slusar, Col. Borders, Col. Jones, Col. Zerbe.

Impact of future redeployments through November 1971.

BRIEFER: "Last summer the command was faced with redeploying 150,000 spaces by 30 April of this year. It appeared to be a difficult and trying venture." Got it done. "As a result of President Nixon's announcement on 7 April, we are already in the midst of another large redeployment package of 100,000 spaces." This will "without doubt fully tax the commanders, units, and staffs at all levels." "The president stated that Vietnamization has succeeded, whereas previously the general statement had been that Vietnamization was progressing." This increment is to redeploy between 1 May and 1 December 1971. The president also referred to "the U.S. goal as being total withdrawal." This goal was "further amplified by the president" in a 16 April news conference. "He announced that U.S. forces will remain in Vietnam as long as the prisoner of war issue remains unresolved and until the South Vietnamese can defend themselves."

ABRAMS: "Incidentally, that 'total withdrawal' thing always kind of bugged me a little bit, but I note from talking with the undersecretary of state last night—for instance, you know, if we're furnishing equipment and supplies and ammunition, that kind of stuff, there's a legal requirement that you be able to see where it goes and that kind of stuff. So you have to have—the secretary of defense, I think, is the one who's responsible for that. He's got to have people out of the Department of Defense here to keep track of all that kind of stuff, see what it's being used for and that kind of thing. Certainly the undersecretary of state, he understands that. And 'total withdrawal'—it's not so much what do they mean as the press has a tendency to pick up these golden words and say, 'Well, hell, it's not total at all. We counted <u>85</u> just in Saigon. So it's <u>not</u> total!'" "They have to have Americans here, because you're spending American money. But, anyway, they understand all that." "I think what that means is <u>forces</u>. And when you're talking about forces you're talking about fighting types."

BRIEFER: The size and pace of the next withdrawal increment "represents a substantial difference from our initial redeployment planning for this period." Cites a "Transitional Support Force" period beginning 1 July 1971. And completion of the CRIMP program about 1 July 1973. "At that time, our strength here would be approximately 44,000." That is the figure "generally identified with" the "MAAG-level posture."

ABRAMS (re the previously planned rate of withdrawal, now accelerated): "I think the handwriting's on the wall that that's not going to be the solution." "It's an unproductive exercise to dream of anything else." Very difficult to visualize what the U.S. presence in Vietnam is going to look like on 1 October 1972. "The Five O'Clock Follies—is that going to be going on? If it is, what the hell are they going to be talking about—how many short tons were shipped out of port today? Or how many vials of heroin we picked up over the last 24 hours? Just what kind of a thing would that be?" "I'll tell you one thing, it's not going to be a U.S. like it is today, and there are just a whole lot of things that are going to have to change." "We're all victims of our own experience." "When we're there, on 1 October 1972, every last man ought to be gainfully employed in the national interest. And so I said, 'Well, if I don't have the 101st, what the hell—why are we even <u>here</u>?' That's the way Jock looks at it. 'No 101st? Then what the hell are we doing here?' Then Moose, he'll start on this thing, 'What the hell—no advisors with the ground units? Christ, what's the point of having FACs, why have any airplanes?'"

ABRAMS: "Some of the days here are kinda long, but the years go by very quickly."

ABRAMS: "And that thing's [redeployment] going to be on us." "We got no answers [on how to handle accelerated redeployment]."

BRIEFER: Plan to accomplish redeployment of 100,000 between 1 May and 30 November 1971 in three increments. The troop list for Increment 7 was approved by JCS on 15 April 1971, and redeployments are now in progress. Increment 8: July–August 1971. Increment 9: September–November 1971.

ABRAMS: "This redeployment started out with various goals. We were going to be able to do them at a certain rate. And then, hell, almost before you get started, they wanted to accelerate it. Well, not only wanted to—<u>did</u>. That has a <u>hell</u> of an impact on logistics and personnel. Well, in the past we were <u>big</u> enough, and had enough people, so that you could wrench the thing in that way without causing a major disaster. Oh, yes, it caused some problems, but it was not catastrophic—because the whole was big enough . . . to get it done." "I might say here we've had to look down into—I call it the chasm—for several months." "I'm convinced now that we haven't got that flexibility anymore. So we've got to plan quite a ways ahead, in detail, and everybody's got to be in on it. That's the only way we can do anything on personnel that's satisfactory. And on logistics, if we don't do it, I think we'll fail. It's that critical." We are pulled two ways—support what's left and get out what has to get out. "There's an awful lot to be done, and if we're going to do it without <u>scandal</u>, and without the charges of abandonment, we've got to get in it." "And it won't get any better by arguing another week. It just won't. It'll get worse."

Referring to deciding on the composition of Increment 9.

BRIEFER: ROK and Thai forces will also be redeploying, and competing for redeployment assets, especially ports. Closure and turnover of bases can be expected to saturate RVNAF's ability to accept and maintain them. 750 sites, from a five-man team house to a division base camp, to be turned over.

BRIEFER: "The time we thought we had for planning has been considerably shortened. Future redeployment beyond 1 December won't be known until the next presidential announcement, expected in October, but it is possible we'll go through 1 December like a moving train." Level of 184,000 on 1 December 1971 after taking out 100,000 spaces, not people.

ABRAMS: "What's going to happen is that, by 1 December, we'll be looking at another figure that is much smaller than that." "What I hope we can avoid is sending something home that we really need for the remaining part of our mission, while at the same time keeping something that's just going to be taking in their own laundry."

SOMEONE (re a battalion base camp near Danang): "When the Vietnamese in that area saw us start to dismantle this, they swarmed over that place like a bunch of locusts. In just a little over 24 hours there wasn't a stick of anything left in that camp. We had to pull U.S. out of there completely, or we would have had U.S. killing Vietnamese civilians and Vietnamese killing U.S. soldiers." Made the mistake of taking down the perimeter fence first, and not having enough security (only some PF).

ABRAMS (sort of likes the story): "It doesn't fit the nice management thing, but where it wound up is with <u>people</u>." "If you got it together in piles, then you run the risk of bastards selling it—corruption." "While I'm not recommending it, I can also detect that there were in there some benefits."

SOMEONE (who told about this occurrence): "Well, it's one of the cleanest base camps—."

■ ■ ■

VANN: "Right now the advisory effort is just a drop in the bucket. Eventually, down the line, when we are faced with a real requirement to have the minimum strength over here, we can still maximize the advisory effectiveness with a very low level of strength."

VANN: "As far as influencing the direction that the effort goes toward the objective that we're trying to achieve, in a district—when you get beyond the district chief and possibly his police chief, you really don't have anyone to advise."

VANN: "While we have a large number of highly professionally qualified noncoms who are quite capable of advising even battalion commanders, we have almost no Vietnamese officers who are willing to receive one word of advice from an enlisted man of any army. As a result, by and large the enlisted people in the advisory effort represent [only] ration requirements."

■ ■ ■

New MACV Strategy

BRIEFER (Colonel Cannon): "The emphasis is now shifting from the military aspects of the two combined campaign plans toward the more comprehensive aspects involved in the Community Defense and Local Development plan." Strategy: "As a result of improvements in the RVNAF, the success of cross-border operations, and progress in community defense and local development, the level of enemy military activity has diminished considerably and the security of the environment in the RVN has been concomitantly enhanced. This places a lesser demand on military power and emphasizes the other aspects of national strength—political stability, a firm economic base, and a national resolve to survive and grow. This MACV strategy recognizes the diminished level of U.S. combat power, and the dynamic and changing nature of the war, and has adapted to both in order to achieve the U.S. objective of a RVN pursuing its national destiny free of outside interference."

BRIEFER: Purpose of MACV strategy through FY 1972: During 1 May–1 December 1971: Concentrate on improving security and providing for legal functioning of the constitutional process during national elections. Support CDLD. Saturation-type campaigns emphasized. RVNAF will operate against the remaining enemy main force units, base areas, and the logistical system. Cross-border operations into Cambodia continue on a modest scale. Small raid-type RVNAF operations into Laos. Current air interdiction campaign will continue. "As the GVN national elections approach, a point will be reached when U.S. ground combat forces will have redeployed to a level where they will be unable to materially influence the overall situation. At that time the role of U.S. combat forces remaining in the RVN will be dynamic defense in the area of major U.S. installations, security of equipment and supplies to be retrograded, and further assistance in improvement of the RVNAF (to include providing essential CS and CSS). Of U.S. resources available during this period, air power will play an increased role."

BRIEFER: "As redeployments continue, U.S. leverage to influence GVN will decrease due to improved Vietnamese confidence and diminishing U.S. real assets."

BRIEFER: "The confidence of the Government of Vietnam in the sincerity of U.S. intentions must be maintained at a high level."

ABRAMS: "They [RVN] can't support indefinitely the kind of military structure that they've got." JGS is studying how to bring down the regular paid establishment in some modest way and substitute a reserve duty arrangement. "In the long pull they've got to get a more modest structure."

VANN (re these next two or three years): "They [RVN] are somewhat dubious of their own ability to carry it [after U.S. redeployment]."

VANN: "In Go Cong Province we have excess RF and PF. They are not transferable, so the province chief has very wisely put six RF companies to work full-time building roads." This helps the economy, keeps them busy, and improves the image of the government.

DAVISON: "In Tay Ninh there were eight sawmills in operation last May; there are over a hundred now. Fly over War Zone C and you'll see it flourishing—brand new tractors all over the place. The loggers can now go cut trees about anywhere they want to."

■ ■ ■

ABRAMS: "Most of the people, let's say the responsible officials, who have come out here from Washington in recent months raise a lot of questions about whether we should do the bombing. They think that we pay a big political price for bombing. And I suppose they could go and ask, say, the province advisor in Go Cong his view about this bombing program the U.S. has. And I suppose what he'd tell them is, 'Christ, I don't see—I don't know why they've got that damn thing. What's that for? It's not doing any good I can see.' So they'd chalk up one vote there, and so on. That interdiction program over there in Laos is doing a lot to restrict the level of activity that he's able to sustain here in South Vietnam and Cambodia and so on. And I don't think there's any question about it. He's throughput about 15 percent of what he inputted so far. He's going to try to keep her going during the rainy season. Of course we want to stay right with him every way we can in that interdiction program."

ABRAMS: "As this whole process goes on, at least I'm convinced that we're backing a winner. It isn't all done, and the war's not going to stop, but we can't let anything bad—real bad—happen." "W-e-l-l, as this thing goes on, we can't let some big, bad disaster occur. All right, now what can we do about it? Well, yeah, working on the training, and trying to get the skill raised with the advisors and all that. But when it comes right down to the crunch, we need to have this kind of capability [bombing]." "And we've got to have it right on through calendar year '72. I think that's going to be a sensitive year, too."

ABRAMS: "I think one of the things we need to bear in mind here is what our mission is, and what our government's trying to do. It all gets down to what it's up to us to get done here. First of all, we've got to face up realistically to things that need correcting, defects and that sort of thing. The supply discipline in their armed forces is pretty ragged. At least in the army, in ARVN, it's been pretty bad. And you could go on and list other things. It's not our job to list all these and then kind of gather around and support each other by crying over them. That's not what the United States government is trying to get done here! And we're the guys who are supposed to get it done for our government. That's our responsibility, and that's our charge."

ABRAMS: "So we don't—there's no time for crying. It's time for doing. And I hope that 184,000 that we've got here on 1 December—I hope every last one of them is somebody that wants to do something. And he's <u>happy</u> if he's got problems, because that's what he's being paid for—to solve them." "We've got a lot of guys—it's their first time here. And I guess it's pretty shocking. Let's say they came here from Benning—been three years on the faculty down there. Gets out here and sees one of these training centers, and goes through the mess hall, you know. 'Boy, is <u>this</u> what we've got? Jeez, it's bad!'"

ABRAMS: "Well, Bill and I were listening to this young captain the other night, talking, and he was over here advising an ARVN airborne battalion. And they got whacked up there in the DMZ, and nobody could get in to help them and so on. They finally got down to 76 men, and the senior commander told them to break up at night in small units and get out. They had all their dead and all their wounded there. The battalion commander had been killed, so the captain who was the exec had taken over. He said, 'The honor of this battalion is at stake. We'll die here.' Well, the next morning they attacked and, goddamn it, they got some more dead, but they came out with all their dead and all their wounded and all their weapons. That was '66. You go back [to] that '65–'66 period—disasters were commonplace, especially in '65. I mean regimental disasters! And there'd be nothing left! I mean you could gather it together in a saucer."

ABRAMS: "And then you go through that period, to get on another subject, you go through that period after Diem and, Christ, changing governments. Finally they got around and got a constitution, got elections. A lot of people say it's bad, a Western-style democracy is not a good thing here, that these people aren't ready for that kind of stuff. But you can say this for it, the government's stayed there now four years. And before that, the corps commanders did what they wanted to. They picked what directives that came out of Saigon that they thought they'd comply with. The rest of them they just didn't. Yeah, you've got corruption, you've got inefficiency, all that. But it has—we've had four years of reasonable stability in the governmental structure. The Assembly over there, the upper house and the lower house, they cause trouble. They don't pass everything the way some people think they ought to and so on, but goddamn it it's functioning."

ABRAMS: "And now they've got these elections coming up, and I believe they're going to carry those off. If President Thieu's elected, he's going to be in a fairly powerful position. He'll probably even feel he can do some things that he was a little worried about doing before. If he's not elected, I think that the transfer to whoever is elected will occur. I don't think there'll be—. Some of the generals I talk to, they don't want to go back to that system that they had before they had a president. They've tried that. They don't like it. They're not sure this is a good system, but they're willing to let it go [to continue]. They don't want that other one. <u>Well</u>! I just think that even though there's much to be done, and we've got to play our part in getting it done and seeing that it's done, I think we <u>are</u> on the right course. And I think the goal that our president has set out for us is an achievable one."

ABRAMS: "I know that some Vietnamese worry because of U.S. withdrawal. But take what the 2nd Division's doing up there. He's trying to pull off an all-Vietnamese operation. It's their air force, it's their helicopters, it's their troops, and so on. Of course, he's stimulated a little bit because of all the publicity and everything the 1st ARVN got. But the 1st ARVN did it with U.S. support. He's hoping that he's going to be able to show that the 2nd ARVN did it with all Vietnamese. And of course that's what they've got to have, that feeling of national pride or Vietnamese pride, and that it is better, we can do these things better than the Americans can."

ABRAMS: "I think there are Americans up there in I Corps that will tell you that their [the South Vietnamese] battalions, in some cases, are more effective than our own. And that's part of the job of—building that! And that has to be the answer to Vietnam in the end. If it can't get to the point where they can handle it, and run it, then it was a bad deal to start with. And that's the job! It's not going to do us any good, it's not going to help us carry out our responsibility, by badmouthing them. Now, I'm not talking in terms that you and I should blind ourselves to things that need correction, and things that have got to be jacked up! Yeah, and we should take the steps to do that. I'm not talking about kidding ourselves. But also part of this is building their confidence and spirit and determination. It's part of the job! And it's like handling your own people, you know. You don't build your own people by bad-mouthing them."

ABRAMS: "This strategy thing, now—the thing is changing. And all this stuff about the lumber, the beets or rice or sugarcane or rubber or whatever—that's really got to get going. And when people start making money and eating better and dressing better and all of those things, that's going to be the best goddamn Phuong Hoang program that was ever put on in this country! If you've got that stuff started, and beginning to move, you're going to have trouble peddling ideology. Oh, there'll always be some doing it. And you think of a place like Korea, and how that was—talking about the land, the country, and so on—and compare it with this thing, the natural wealth of this place is really quite staggering. All of that has got to help it get turned on. That's the job in here. I hope that when Christmas comes we've succeeded with that bunch we've got left there in convincing them that this is the way we're going, this is our job, and we're going to see that it gets done."

■ ■ ■

Drug Abuse Problem

BRIEFER: "The actual dimensions of the drug abuse problem in Vietnam are impossible to determine." But examine for indications: apprehension of drug users, deaths and hospitalizations, drug survey results, drug confiscations, and admissions to VA hospitals.

BRIEFER: Categories are marijuana, dangerous drugs, narcotics. Trend in narcotics, primarily heroin, "more sharply upward." For first quarter nearly equals total for the previous year. More intensive enforcement effort; availability probably greater.

ABRAMS: "You sure as hell know you've got a problem at 18.8 per thousand" narcotics users.

BRIEFER: Describes new MACV drug abuse reporting system.

SOMEONE: "One air force colonel involved."

SOMEONE ELSE: "Former!"

BRIEFER: MACV racial mix on 8 April 1971: 83 percent Caucasian, 12–13 percent Negro, 4 percent other. In drug abuse, blacks somewhat higher. In hospitals, 91 drug-suspected deaths in the last six months (clinically evaluated). For the quarter, 740 drug-related hospital discharges. For the quarter, 4,041 rehabilitations.

BRIEFER: Survey results indicate that a larger percentage began use in the United States than began in Vietnam.

VANN: A 173rd Airborne Brigade study of about 1,000 men showed that 84 percent of drug users began use in the United States.

BRIEFER: "We can't wait for the troop withdrawal program to reduce the magnitude of this problem."

BRIEFER: "Marijuana is widely available throughout Vietnam. It is grown extensively in the delta as a cash crop." Pack of marijuana cigarettes sells for approximately 250 piasters, or about a dollar. Amphetamines and barbiturates are available in Vietnamese pharmacies without prescription.

BRIEFER: Heroin is brought in by air (Royal Air Laos and Air Vietnam) (also commercial air and military air) to Ban Me Thuot and Saigon, then by truck (civilian or ARVN trucks) or air distributed throughout the country. High-ranking political figures' influence is necessary to permit this to go on. "Currently no confirmed indications that the enemy, either VC or NVA, are or have been involved on a strategic basis with drug trafficking." Heroin available in Vietnam is 94–97 percent pure, whereas in the United States it is 4–12 percent. Low cost.

BRIEFER: "It was recognized in mid-1970 that an urgent need existed to establish a Vietnam-wide" drug education and suppression program. MACV task force was formed in August 1970. Councils down to battalion level. Combined Anti-Narcotics Committee (U.S. and VN). Joint Intelligence. Joint Customs Group. Amnesty/Rehabilitation. Dogs.

ABRAMS: "I think we have a real problem."

ABRAMS: "The president sent Mr. Ingersoll out here with specific instructions to go and see President Thieu. The president of the United States seems to have, you know, kind of gotten into this himself." Thus questions why the postal service bureaucracy has not gotten with it on inspecting mail from Vietnam. "I want a SPECAT, exclusive, personal to McCain, Info Moorer, and lay this thing out, from Abrams."

John E. Ingersoll was director of the U.S. Bureau of Narcotics and Dangerous Drugs.

SOMEONE: "Deliver during nonduty hours." [Laughter]

ABRAMS: "This falls in that category of the damn all left-handed ball gloves, and volleyball nets and no volleyballs, and tennis courts and no rackets—the machinery! Some of these things, it just rips you up!"

ABRAMS: "There are some things that are on my mind, and I want to talk about it. Now, these men of ours come over here, and already quite a significant percentage of them have either tried, experimented, or are on some kind of drug. Also, to some degree, they bring with them the racial tensions that have developed in our country, to include personnel on, I guess, both sides of the black-white thing who have been organizers, militants, activists of one kind or another. To some degree they've been exposed to the antiwar movement in our country. Then they get here."

ABRAMS: "You have to add to that, on the minus side, the sort of human relations between Americans and Vietnamese. There's a cultural chasm there that is pretty big, and some Americans it's just impossible for them to ever bridge it in any workable way. Then you've got all the living conditions and working conditions, that sort of thing. So there's quite a bit there on the negative side, just to start with. On the other hand, we've had some 20,000 go on this two-week leave to the States program, with a desertion rate of [only] about 2 percent. The net loss is really insignificant. Of course those are in all grades and all kinds. I take a little comfort in that. I'm sure that among those who return there are a good many who would prefer not to be here. There're probably some in there, too, who really don't believe that the United States should have been tangled up in this in the first place. But there also must be present among those men at least a sufficient sense of personal responsibility and pride, just in themselves, so that they will go ahead and complete satisfactorily a task which they have to do."

ABRAMS: "The conduct of our men on R&R seems to stay at the same satisfactory standard that it has in the past. I take some comfort from that, because on the negative side—if it really started to rot internally here, you know, men and spirit and all that—I just think when they get in a place like Bangkok or Hong Kong or those places, gee whiz, crime and—. I think they're pretty good men. As we go along here, their attitude, and their spirit, their welfare—. And you know, it's always kind of key. In the darkest hours I think it's probably been the cement, or glue, that kind of held the thing together. It's got to continue that way. And we need them in good spirit and so on."

ABRAMS: "Now, we've got something going for us, too. Really I think we've got two things. We've got organization, and in that organization you've got command and responsibility, you've got staff, you've got all sorts of things to handle administration of justice, medical, you've just got all the things that are required to take care of men, handle men, direct their efforts, supervise, and that sort of thing. That's what makes it different than, say, the city of Chicago. You've got organization. The other thing we've got going for us is that some percentage of our total—I recognize that it's probably not great—but some percentage of the total is very experienced. They've been a lot of places, they've done a lot of things, they've been through adversity in a lot of different places in the world. They've worked with men, and they understand them and they know how to do it. So that's basically what we've got. As we go down the road here, as I see it, it's the components, the services, it's in that chain of command where all these problems are faced up to and dealt with and where we keep the attitude of our force in good shape, get the work done, and our mission accomplished."

ABRAMS: "I think there are some things probably we ought to clarify. First, let me talk about uniform, appearance, standards of dress, and that sort of thing. Now the services are each a little bit different in the standards, or the requirements, that they have in the service. And that's all right. No service should try to impose their standard on men in another service. But each service must assure that the standards prescribed by his chief are met in every instance everywhere in the country. The standards must be met. We must not, anywhere, let someone think that they can make everybody happier if they don't quite meet it. . . . The standard, what your head of service has set, that's just got to be met. If, somewhere, someone begins to accept less, he's started down a terrible slide, and he's going to have a worse thing in a little while. The standards everywhere should meet what the service chiefs have said about dress, appearance, that sort of thing."

ABRAMS: "The next thing I wanted to mention is about marijuana. There's been talk, I know, about whether marijuana's bad and so on. I want to insist, everywhere in this command, that marijuana is illegal and marijuana is bad. Until our government, or our service chiefs, or the secretary of defense changes that by directive, that's where we stand. In doing all this, too, the chain of command—in the components, and the chain of command as a whole—has really got to function a-l-l the way down to the end. At some levels, you're going to have inexperience. That's going to need to be guided, supervised, directed, and supported. The younger officers, they've got to be not only guided and counseled, they've also got to be supported on these basic things. Not only the younger officers, but the senior grade enlisted men—all the chief petty officers, the senior sergeants, and so on. They've got to feel, they've got to know, that every one all the way down there, know that this job can't be done without them. They've got to feel their share of responsibility, and they've got to be supported. And of course where the officer or soldier is inadequate in dealing with the responsibility which is properly his, then some action has to be taken. And that should be part of it. This functioning of organization, functioning of the chain of command, we've just got to make sure that we've got all the— everything working to make that work, because that's what will handle all this. And that's the thing that's capable of taking on one hell of a lot of problems and handling them, and dealing with them and solving them."

ABRAMS: "Now things like administration—if administration, the things like handling the records or processing them, if that's inefficient or cumbersome or insensitive, it builds you frustration among the men, and it really shouldn't be that way. So different layers, in the whole command structure, should be going down to see whether that's in good shape. Or supply—there ought to be somebody getting a mixture of left-hand and right-hand gloves, and rackets matched up with tennis courts, and volleyball nets and volleyballs, all that kind of stuff. And all the guys that work in the chain of command—we've got a good system, except—as we point out today—the goddamn thing sometimes doesn't go right! You haven't pushed the right button in it. Our interest should be in unsnarling those things, uncrossing those wires, and getting done what is supposed to be done, providing what's been authorized and what's there."

ABRAMS: "Now, one of the things I intend to put in practice myself is that I'm going to use my Inspector General's office to visit places in the command. The purpose of that will be to assess the effectiveness of the functioning of command—the supervision, the guidance, getting things done, all of that. Is command functioning effectively? And I'll pass his reports on to the appropriate commanders for their information and so on. I think the effective functioning of the chain of command, and the effective functioning of command itself, is a big part of getting our mission done here, and our job done. And I feel that I have a responsibility, even though I understand I am a joint commander and basically all this functions through the services—that's where the administration of justice belongs and where money comes from. That's where supplies come from and so on. But, overall, I think that, with the tasks that lie ahead, we'll meet them all, we'll do a job that's a credit to our country, we'll see that the Commander in Chief's desires are carried out, by the effective functioning of command."

ABRAMS: "Now my Inspector General—I'm not going to call it an investigation, and this isn't trying to pick places where I think it's really screwed up. I just want to get samplings out of the command structure, and how is it really performing? Then I'll provide them to you as appropriate. I encourage all of you, too, to increase the focus of all of your people on the effective functioning of the command system. That goes [for] all the staff and everything with it. It also means that, in those few cases where you find an inability to handle it, to understand it or make it work, then those people have to be removed, and get somebody that can. I don't want anyone to leave here today with the idea that I'm about to launch one massive 'shake-up' or 'get tough.' No, that's not what I'm talking about. I'm talking about doing what all of us know as professionals ought to be being done, and just insisting that it be done everywhere. Nothing new! It's all old. That's what has always gotten us through in the tight times, and that's what'll do it now. And you know it's got one hell of a lot of history behind it. It isn't anything anybody dreamed up last year. Or they didn't even dream it up this century. A lot of fellows have fooled around with it over a period of—. So that's what we want to do, is make sure that everybody understands that and everybody is going to make it function."

22 MAY 1971: WIEU

Attendees: Gen. Abrams, Gen. Weyand, Amb. Colby, Gen. Clay, Mr. Kirk, LTG McCaffrey, MG Dolvin, MG Eckhardt, MG Cowles, MG Maples, MG Bowley,

MG Dettre, MG Young, MG Wilson, MG Potts, BG Watkin, RADM Salzer, BG Henion, BG Brown, BG Doehler, BG Forrester, BG Bernstein, Col. Zerbe (for Col. Sadler), Col. DeBruler (for BG John), Col. Miller (for BG Cheadle), Col. Ludwig (for Col. Leonard), Col. Jones.

MACV 1971 Infiltration Estimate: 48,900 (72 percent to COSVN).

Enemy Surface-to-Air Missiles

CLAY: "Slowly but surely, General Abrams, they're having an inhibiting effect as far as our air operations are concerned if we stick to the ground rules we've been able to stick to so far, and that is, for example, your B-52s—we just stay out of the 19 nautical mile ring of a confirmed site, and that's how they [have an] impact. . . ." "I think it's sound not to take a B-52 in there to a confirmed site. But we don't have the assets to provide EB-66 coverage and 105 Wild Weasel with all the gunships. We just haven't got that much. . . ."

ABRAMS: "The only thing we're doing to them is every once in a while fire a Shrike or a standard HARM. Otherwise they've got a <u>free</u> ride. By god, for a fellow that's in a war that's not a bad way. Well, hell, it's a tea and crumpets kind of a thing. Let all those people get their nerves calmed down and give them time to think. That's the other thing. Somebody—their IG up there or somebody—is going to bring up the point that they've fired 70 goddamn missiles and they've hit four airplanes. Some Soviet's going to say, 'Well, that's not—all our testing and all our—I guess it's just because you're Asian, or "slopes" or something. We find even the Egyptians are doing better than that.' In other words, they're going to screw that thing down a little bit."

CLAY: "We have a trolling formation that we have working up and down the passes, waiting for them to come up. It takes quite a bit of effort, but we have this Ax Handle project, we call it, that is a trolling mission up there just waiting for something to come up. But we've got to be right there."

■ ■ ■

ABRAMS: "There's a cable in there this morning—the Chinese—about how they're just <u>overjoyed</u>. They say the people, the Americans, are rising up in the revolutionary struggle and all that. Well, look at this damn thing—there's very little comfort in the fact that the Mansfield amendment was defeated. Hell, they had the thing up—I mean, it was in there for a vote. And some of the alternates to it—augh—just awful. 'Tell the Russians if they don't negotiate with us, we're going to withdraw.' No! This is a <u>senator</u>! [Nearly screaming] A <u>United States senator</u>! Why, they must be having champagne parties and celebrations—I don't know, probably even <u>parades</u> over the <u>disarray</u> and the lack of political strength that there is in our country. Jesus! Even the poor Pathet Lao, they're—well, <u>yeah</u>, 'You stop the bombing, we'll do something about prisoners.' Just jumping in that—getting into that pool. I think they just smell victory."

WEYAND: "Well, you might get personally involved in it. Go back and address a joint session of Congress or something." [Laughter]

ABRAMS: "Well, that'd be about the same as parachuting into Hanoi without a parachute." [Laughter]

■ ■ ■

ABRAMS: "I think this is about where I want to interrupt here. This incident we had where they had a whole lot of men killed in one bunker—. [Potts: "Right, sir, 29 killed, 33 wounded."] I saw XXIV Corps has got a message in explaining how this happened and so on. What I want to say is, I'm not satisfied with that, because XXIV Corps had the intelligence about the time this was to occur. As I recall, the attack occurred about an hour or two off of the time that they had. [Potts: "That's right, sir."] Now, I consider this to be inexcusable. When you've got that kind of intelligence, and I don't consider it harassing the troops, they go on a battle station kind of a setup, which may include eating C rations in the bunkers, this sort of thing. You do that from about two hours before to two or three hours afterward. Then, if nothing happens, I think you can relax a little bit."

SOMEONE: "The bunker fell in on them. They were in a bunker."

ABRAMS: "No, but goddamn it, there shouldn't have been all those men in that bunker. And the message explains they were all in the mess hall when the first rounds landed, and so they all ran into the closest bunker. That's what I'm talking about! And it was the fifth or sixth round that hit that bunker. They shouldn't [shouting now] have been in the goddamn mess hall, and that number of men shouldn't have been in that bunker! Now the bunker was going to get hit anyway, but probably what should have happened is that there were 4 men killed, and not 29. That's what I'm talking about! And I want this all explained to General Sutherland, a message put together on it."

ABRAMS: "Now we had a thing like this happened up in [LZ] English, or one of those places. I Field Force had the intelligence. The units had the intelligence. And goddamn it, they were out playing volleyball, and the men had begun to assemble for a movie when the attack by fire came. And we had a lot of people killed and a lot of people wounded, and it was a failure—I'm telling you, it's a failure of command! [Shouting] They had the intelligence, and instead of—I don't know what the hell they're thinking of [sputtering], everybody had— what the hell—don't pay any attention to the intelligence and all of that."

ABRAMS (now much more subdued): "But it's very unprofessional. And I don't want this watered down! It's wrong. I had an experience on this myself. The second night I was up at Phu Bai for General Westmoreland. I'd been in the intelligence up there and so on, and I was convinced that Phu Bai was going to be attacked by fire at 4:30 in the morning, the following morning. So I got everybody in there, the commanders, and told them we would be on a full alert status, everybody in the bunkers and everything loaded and locked and cocked, at three o'clock in the morning. And 4:30 came, and nothing happened. I felt bad. These were all, you know, experienced guys up there, and here was this shit from Saigon. But I didn't change anything, and it came at 5:30. As it would happen, the marine brigadier general who was the commander of troops there, he was down in the TOC—in the bunker. And one 122 rocket landed about eight feet outside of his bedroom, his little cottage he had, and blew that goddamn thing and his bed and everything else just—. So he thought I was a pretty damn good intelligence officer. <u>But</u> the point is you shouldn't fool with this stuff. What you're doing is fooling with men's lives. I'm not satisfied with what they did up there. I think we lost more men than we had to. [Now very subdued.] I want this put together, this personal message to Sutherland."

The incident was at 1738 hours on 21 May 1971, when FSB C2 received an attack by fire of 11 122-mm rockets.

■ ■ ■

ABRAMS: Mentions a State Department message received re a Hanoi broadcast to the North Vietnamese people "indicating that casualties returning to North Vietnam are getting to be a problem, probably aggravated by 719."

■ ■ ■

CLAY: Now the definition is: "A destroyed truck is either a burner or a blower—period."

BRIEFER: Cumulative truck kills in Steel Tiger: 22,650 (damaged or destroyed).

CLAY (re destroyed trucks): "Ever since Lam Son 719, we've seen much more that has been left on the roads than before."

CLAY (re the ground war in Laos): "We've had a hard time in there, General Abrams. We force-fed tac air in there. They didn't even want any, but we made them take it. Then we couldn't get contact with the ground. We sent General [Edmunds?] and a planning team up to Vientiane to try to work out a plan of attack, and they didn't have any. They didn't know where the forces were, who the friendlies were, who the enemy were, nothing. See we've been trying to work with them and try to get some plan of what they're doing, but they don't know what the <u>hell</u> is going on." "It's been sort of a loose as a goose situation there as far as we're concerned. 'Where do you want us to put the ordnance?'"

ABRAMS: "It's interesting. We've found the same thing to be true here and in Cambodia. You have to organize it. You have to have communications, and you have to be able to talk to ground, and the ground's got to be able to talk to the air. I think it probably, sooner or later, ought to be a doctrine. Maybe we haven't had quite enough disasters yet."

25 MAY 1971: COMUS Update: MR-1 and MR-2 Estimates

BRIEFER: Enemy has 11 battalions north of the DMZ, 1 in the northern half of the DMZ, 2 in the southern half, and 8 below the DMZ. There have been indications since 25 April of an enemy buildup for offensive operations.

BRIEFER: Air operations destroyed 27,800 tons of matériel in the Lao panhandle during the 1970–1971 dry season. With a 25 percent reduction in the air effort, 7,000 tons of these supplies would not have been destroyed, and would therefore have been available for throughput to Cambodia and the Republic of Vietnam.

BRIEFER: At the Tet 1968 level of combat intensity, this amount of supplies would sustain an additional 10 days of combat by all enemy forces outside of North Vietnam. If only the forces targeted against the RVN are considered, this could support 17 additional days of combat.

BRIEFER: Fifty percent decrease in air sorties would double these effects. "These are conservative estimates." If a complete bombing halt were directed, the enemy's ability to move supplies south would be "virtually unrestricted." The enemy would be able to "regain the initiative in the Indochina War."

Subsequently General Potts tells the briefer that statement is too strong and he wants it toned down.

29 MAY 1971: Commanders WIEU

ATTENDEES: Visitor: Amb. Bunker. Command group: Gen. Abrams, Gen. Weyand, Amb. Colby, Gen. Clay, MG Dolvin, MG Bowley, Col. Jones. Component commanders and staff: MG Gettys (for LTG McCaffrey), RADM McManus (for RADM Salzer), MG Wilson, BG John. Military regions: MG Wagstaff, Mr. Cruikshank (for Mr. Funkhouser), MG Milloy (for LTG Sutherland), Mr. Lazar, Mr. Vann, BG Armstrong, Mr. Long, MG Cushman, Mr. Wilson. MACV staff: Mr. Kirk, MG Eckhardt, MG Cowles, MG Maples, MG Dettre, MG Young, MG Potts, BG Cheadle, BG Henion, BG Doehler, Mr. Chambers, BG Bernstein, Col. Sadler, Capt. Bivin (for BG Brown), Col. Leonard.

1971 Infiltration Estimate: 49,400 (71 percent for COSVN).

ABRAMS: "We've got to look at southern Laos a little more comprehensively each Saturday. What I'm talking about is looking at the development of the enemy environment in southern Laos. That has not only to do with infiltration, it has to do with the organization of *binh trams* and the 500 group. It has to do with antiaircraft. It has to do with troop units. . . . I just want . . . to be continuingly aware of the enemy environment in southern Laos, because it's <u>changing</u>. When you contemplate, as we will eventually, doing something about it—not only the air interdiction program, which has been going on pretty good, but you talk about incursions and that sort of thing. Bring the JGS J-2—get him doing the same thing. That's a different ball game over there, and they don't want anybody in there. It makes a lot of sense. This whole structure that they've got down here in South Vietnam and Cambodia—that's its lifeline. That's <u>got</u> to work or that whole thing, that military structure, is just going to collapse. And there aren't any alternatives for them. That thing has got to work, or they just can't do what they've set out to do."

ABRAMS: "They know that, and that's why they're moving all those <u>units</u> in there, and it's why this infiltration's going in there that hasn't been before, why the antiaircraft's going in there—37 millimeter and so on. Hell, it's not because they've just got a lot of extra stuff hanging around. They've got to guarantee that that thing'll work, and [that] it'll produce, during the dry season, what they need until the next dry season comes up. And that's why we've got to have 10,000 tac air sorties and 1,000 B-52s [per month]. That's really—the most that we can do against that thing is that effort."

ABRAMS: "Another part of that—there're some guys rattling around wanting to—well, 'The way to do this [is] with irregulars, and small teams, and so on.'" "And you're not going to make a <u>dent</u> in it by screwing around out there with irregular teams and all that kind of stuff. You're just <u>dreaming</u>."

ABRAMS (re the situation in southern Laos): In northern Laos, where some military successes have been achieved against the NVA, "apparently that's all because of one commander. They've got one fellow in charge there, and he just kind of gathered everything up and moved out. That's what they need down in the south. Those damn fellows down there have been politicking, and trafficking and stuff, and internal politics in Laos, and they haven't been paying <u>attention</u> to the military preparations. They [the enemy] got all that stuff down there pretty <u>cheap</u>. All this stuff like you couldn't support with air because you—no communications, no setup to do it and all that sort of thing. Bunch of low-grade politicians in uniform, screwing around down there with internal stuff, and <u>jockeying</u>, and false coups—you know, playing around and having fun with all that stuff, and not paying attention to the business."

■ ■ ■

ABRAMS (re the Vung Tau training center): "That whole chemistry that's going on down there—I keep thinking that's pretty important. And it's now <u>really</u> got the Vietnamese flavor."

ABRAMS: "I hope my colleagues in the military are not going to be offended by this, but for their [Cambodian] military officers who had been trained in the military schools—French or that sort of thing—trying to grasp this kind of a thing is probably pretty well beyond them. It's just foreign. If you can get it down to—o-o-o-h-h, get it back to something like Waterloo, and get the lines, you know, it's got to get a <u>shape</u>. Christ, any military fellow <u>knows</u> that's the way you fight battles. You know, a <u>right</u> wing and a <u>left</u> wing and a center and all that. And <u>this</u> kind of stuff, especially counting on the people and all that— it's a very hard concept."

CUSHMAN: "Down in the countryside, in the districts [in Cambodian border regions] the VC are pretty much in charge. And the Khmer Rouge are getting organized more and more as time goes on. So we're really coming from behind on this." "The main problem is that they are really kidding themselves a lot about what's really going on out there." "When they make these sweeps they make the typical mistake of going in and then coming out. A couple of weeks later you'd never know they were there."

■ ■ ■

ABRAMS (on maintaining secrecy): "One of the things you have to face up to—. I tried to figure it out here one day not long ago. I think it's somewhere around five or six things, in the four years I've been here, that I know of that we tried to keep secret and succeeded. Now the number that we've <u>tried</u> to keep secret is many times that. So our record on that is <u>really</u> very miserable. It just doesn't take it long to be in the press. It's not a question of trying to be anti-press or anything, it's just a question of some things it's best in the interest of all the governments and everything else involved it shouldn't be—. And I don't think there's anything <u>dishonest</u> about that. God, we're not plotting against humanity. But we just can't seem to get it done. And some of these things, when they come out, they don't come out very good, and you find that you've ripped your pants again, and you're a little further behind than you were before."

SOMEONE: Suggests the only consolation is that MACV's record is better than Washington's.

ABRAMS: "It's kind of like the two pitchers arguing about their batting averages. One said he's leading. He had a .055, and the other one had a .042. Well, that's right, he was <u>leading</u>."

■ ■ ■

ABRAMS: "Their basic thinking—talking about Vien and some of those people—is that they'll use the Airborne Division in MR-2 and the Marine Division in MR-1. But that doesn't mean the whole thing. In order to keep the airborne and the marines going on a sustained basis, you should have about two-thirds of them employed. Two-thirds of them can be fighting. You can up that for short periods, three or four weeks maybe. But eventually you've got to come back to that. And I think they <u>have</u> to do it. It's very important that they rotate both the airborne and the marines through their base here in Saigon. It's where their hospital is, it's where their families are. Both of them have got widow and orphan organizations where they're looking after it. It's not <u>paper</u>, either, because they're dealing with their own people and it's got to be real. So those battalions have got to regularly reappear down here and get some training, take on replacements, and that sort of thing."

Looking to future combat operations.

ABRAMS: "My own feeling is that they can play out '71 with this idea of the marines and airborne and handle—and kind of keep II Corps and I Corps, with all the withdrawals that are going to take place by the first of December—they can hack it. Plus the capabilities of the enemy—he's got his problems logistically, and they're a little easier for him to solve in MR-1 than they are a little further south. In III and IV Corps, I think they're kind of up against it. They're not going to be able to exercise that structure for all it's worth. So I think they can play out calendar year '71 probably, on that basis. But '72 I think is a different—'72 has some other potential in it for the enemy, depending a little bit on what he's able to do in the dry season, beginning in October-November-December of '71, and then down the road in '72."

SOMEONE: "As you know the government of Vietnam deliberately, in past years, located ARVN away from their homes. De facto policy shifted about two and a half years ago and they began doing local recruiting and local drafting to the extent of largely becoming indigenous to the area. But there's still a lot of residual carryover from the policy that was in effect the previous 15 years."

■ ■ ■

Abrams on the necessity for U.S. troop withdrawals because of the impact they have on South Vietnamese leadership.

ABRAMS (looking at survey results portraying South Vietnamese views of the reasons): "I don't know if I'll rise to that. [He does.] We had to do this." "There's very clear evidence, at least to me in some things, that we helped too much. And we retarded the Vietnamese by doing it. I know that this is—. I think you get to that by kind of taking the skim off the top of the thing. Fundamentally, you had to do it for the Vietnamese. We can't run this thing. I'm absolutely convinced of that. They've got to run it. The nearer we can get to that the better off they are and the better off we are. It has nothing to do with despair about the disarray at home, just thinking in terms of the Vietnamese themselves."

ABRAMS: "Some Americans are a little dangerous themselves in a thing like this. Basically—the ones I'm talking about—basically they know that nobody in the world can do a thing as well as an American. And it doesn't make any difference where it is that it has to be done. There's nothing wrong with that. That's why our country's gotten where it's gotten—a whole hell of a lot of Americans feel that way. And they have for a long, long time. And so, hell, they'll plow into anything. Nobody's wanted to move the Rockies yet, but if they ever come up with that there'll be somebody tackle it. . . . It's that kind of a thing!"

ABRAMS: "Well. While they may feel that way, that really isn't true. There's a lot of things here in this country that no American could touch a Vietnamese in getting it done, and getting it done right, and getting it done well, and getting it done for the best of this country. And so I say you've got a few Americans that are really kind of dangerous. They're great, they're great fellows! Nothing against them. But they're so convinced of that that they—. It's like the company commander that's just got to do everything. He's sincere and all that, but hell if he hasn't got his first sergeant and noncoms and lieutenants and all doing stuff, and are proud of what they're doing, and he letting them do something, he hasn't got any kind of a company. You always kind of have to admire him for being so interested, devoted, dedicated, and stupid. [Laughter] Hell, it's that kind of a thing."

■ ■ ■

ABRAMS: "We have got a Vietnamization program, and we've got this rather massive effort going on now, with a lot of people involved in it, about how the RVNAF is going to meet its requirements here in South Vietnam. And it's command and control, it's medevac, it's support of the navy, it's support of the army. You know, it's the whole gamut. And we're going to go marching right down the road so that, one day, it is the RVNAF that's doing it. And it's one of those things that we've got to be careful about, that we don't develop in the minds of our counterparts that we're going to fight to the death to keep those things for them forever. Because I can tell you that's not what we're going to do."

ABRAMS: "We've got an agreed structure. It'll get refinements, as it always has, from time to time. But we're marching down the road where that will be the security for South Vietnam. And there won't be any Black Ponies in it. So I'm telling you the way it's going to be. So, yes—in this 184,000 that we have to get to by the first of December, it's a hell of a struggle to make sure that what's in that is what's going to be the most useful for South Vietnam. Well, you've got a couple of things. We've got to get the tonnage out of here, and there's a lot of it. We've got to have a command and control element. We've got to have an advisory element. And we've got to have some kind of support that sees to the mail and rations and hospitals for the Americans. And it's really basically sort of shortfall, at that time, between what they ultimately will have and where they are on that thing [at that time?]. In the end, it will be the RVNAF. We've got to work on the RVNAF, worth with the RVNAF. And also we've got to work out an agreed scheme between ourselves and the JGS that these are the missions that RVNAF is going to have to perform. . . . That's the study that's going on now. I just wanted to clear that point."

5 JUN 1971: Discussion of Preparation of General Abrams–President Thieu Laotian Paper

POTTS: Presides. Reason for the meeting: On Tuesday General Abrams, Ambassador Bunker, and maybe General Vien will meet with President Thieu. General Abrams's part of this is to depict what's happened in Laos since the loss of Sihanoukville. Thus Abrams called last Saturday for a special estimate. Working toward briefing Abrams on Monday.

POTTS: Quoting Abrams re MR-3 and MR-4: "We agree they just have no capability now or during 1971." Also quoting: "His real capability for offensive action in South Vietnam in 1971 is limited. But he's going to be working so that in 1972, and 1973, he has the option for increased activity."

5 JUN 1971: WIEU

Attendees: Amb. Bunker, Amb. Berger, Gen. Abrams, Gen. Weyand, Mr. Kirk, MG Eckhardt, MG Hardin (for Gen. Clay), MG Cowles, MG Gettys (for LTG McCaffrey), MG Bowley, MG Dettre, MG Wilson, MG Potts, MG Kroesen, BG

Watkin, RADM Salzer, BG John, BG Henion, BG Brown, BG Doehler, BG Forrester, BG Bernstein, Col. Horrocks (for MG Maples), Col. Sadler, Col. Miller,
Col. Leonard, Col. Jones.

*MACV 1971 RVN and Cambodia Infiltration Estimate: 50,300. (201 groups so far
and, per Potts, all but nine had been detected through intercepts.) MACV 1971
Southern Laos Infiltration Estimate: 6,800. In 1970: 8,800. In 1969: 750.*

POTTS: "15 March [1970] Sihanoukville closed. He took about 30 to 45 days to
react. Then it takes 60 days' travel time to come to southern Laos. Then you
can see the arrival times start to creep up."

ABRAMS: "Well, that shows you what loss of Sihanoukville meant."

BRIEFER: Describes Soviet POL deliveries to Haiphong by ship. Abrams asks
what the transit times are. If from the Black Sea area, 55–60 days; if from
Vladivostok, 7–9 days.

ABRAMS (after the briefer finishes and departs): Asks Potts how long that briefer
has been working this account. Potts says about nine and a half months.

ABRAMS: "That shows he must be studying his work when he comes up with
those shipping times, both sources, without batting an eye. That tends to cool
you off." [Laughter]

■ ■ ■

BRIEFER: A Polish military advisor to the ICC in Vientiane states that "the North
Vietnamese were both surprised and hurt by the Lam Son [719] operation. He
said that discussions with NVN officials showed that they had lost heavily in
personnel, particularly good reserve units which were chewed up. He further
believed that they had lost heavily in weapons and supplies. He also pointed
out that they suffered a political loss at home because they could not hide their
significant military losses."

BRIEFER: "Soviet and East European sources have almost unanimously reported
that Lam Son [719] caused some serious military problems for the North Vietnamese." Per the Czech military attaché in North Vietnam: The ARVN penetration into Laos created a serious political situation in North Vietnam resulting
from their military losses, which threatened to cause them to turn more to the
Chinese to replace those losses.

BRIEFER: North Vietnamese officials revealed to a source an exact number of
16,224 casualties as a result of Lam Son [719].

BRIEFER (reporting another North Vietnamese view): The ARVN had failed to
win in Laos, despite the massive American air support, and would thus be no
match for the NVA once the United States had departed.

ABRAMS (re the Lam Son 719 reports): "The tough part of this is we know, with
reasonable precision, all the effects on our side—good and bad. And over there
on the other side it's just difficult, it's just difficult. Plus you add to it—and I
agree with that 'sophisticated propaganda.' And we have to say that it's successful. Plus history will show you, about the Communists, it will take <u>years</u> to

find out how bad off they were. So it's pretty tough reading the tea leaves on a week-to-week basis. I think there's something to be gained by grinding into this historical perspective—historical perspective of Communism."

WEYAND: "I think it's important that the South Vietnamese leadership get as good a feel for this [results of Lam Son 719] as we get. They've got a lot at stake, and I suppose they're trying to assess it, too."

■ ■ ■

AMBASSADOR BUNKER: "You know, when we went to that 33rd Regiment base [in the U Minh forest], I asked General Truong if he planned to stay there. He said, 'Yes, forever.'"

ABRAMS: "Incidentally, I went out to Yankee Station [an area in the South China Sea where aircraft carriers operate] the other day, and I can tell you, anybody who gets an invitation to go out there, it's worth it. You can't believe that until you see it. That's an awful small airfield. The whole operation is a controlled crash, whether you're talking about the takeoff or a landing. Or parking. When they get in the scooping them up, they land on that thing at 40-second intervals. You know, that means that one guy lands, and 40 seconds later there's going to be another one hitting the same place. You have to unhook, and then he has to go and park. God, they horse those things around on that deck like they had a hundred acres, turning them and one thing and another. Really it's quite a remarkable thing."

7 JUN 1971: COMUS Update, Laos Assessment

SOMEONE (in prebriefing chitchat): "The morning briefings are getting boring. The war's going to hell!"

BRIEFER: "The change of government in Cambodia on 18 March 1970, loss of the port of Sihanoukville, and the effects of Operation Market Time have left the enemy only one remaining line of communications, the route complex through the Laotian corridor. He must expand and protect this logistical lifeline, and keep it operating, if he is to be militarily effective in southern Indochina."

BRIEFER: The enemy plans to compensate for the loss of Sihanoukville, and to expand, improve, and protect the road system in southern Laos.

BRIEFER: Nine *binh trams* have been realigned, most shifting southward. A new organization has been formed to extend the system into Cambodia, the 470th Transportation Group. 50-series *binh trams* are situated in the vicinity of the Laos-Cambodia border. Additional combat and service units have moved into southern Laos. Development of the route structure itself has proceeded. Since March 1970, the North Vietnamese have developed roads at the western end of the DMZ and have used them to enable goods to move further south within the sanctuary of North Vietnam before being exposed to allied air interdiction. And they have improved roads leading from Laos into Cambodia and westward.

BRIEFER: About 650 kilometers of new roads and bypasses have been put into

Lt. Gen. Walter T. Kerwin Jr. with ARVN Lt. Gen. Do Cao Tri, who commanded III Corps until his death in a helicopter crash during the 1970 Cambodian incursion, and Lt. Gen. Le Nguyen Khang, head of the South Vietnamese Marine Division. *U.S. Army Military History Institute*

Maj. Gen. Ngo Quang Truong, while serving as Commanding General, 1st ARVN Division, presented villagers a tractor donated by American units in Phu Bai. Soon President Thieu's Land to the Tiller program provided some 400,000 farmers title to a million and a half acres of land. "In one fell swoop," said John Paul Vann, the program "eliminated tenancy in Vietnam." *National Archives*

General Abrams and Lt. Gen. Herman Nickerson (USMC), commander of III Marine Amphibious Force, greet South Vietnamese Lt. Gen. Hoang Xuan Lam, commander of I Corps. *U.S. Army Center of Military History*

Abrams stressed the enemy's need to push out a logistics "nose," pre-positioning combat wherewithal in advance of operations, and tasked his units to preempt or diminish enemy offensives by finding and seizing supplies and weapons such as this 240-mm rocket, part of a huge cache found northwest of Saigon.
National Archives

A B-52 bomber delivering its ordnance. Abrams considered the B-52s to be his strategic reserve and employed them in mass to telling effect. *Indochina Archive, University of California at Berkeley*

The legendary John Paul Vann played a key role in U.S. support of pacification until his death in a helicopter crash in June 1972. With him is Lt. Gen. Walter T. Kerwin Jr., who served for a year as MACV Chief of Staff and then took command of II Field Force. *U.S. Army Military History Institute*

General Abrams and Gen. Fred
Weyand shared the same birth-
date, 15 September, which they
celebrated together when Weyand
was serving as Deputy COMUS-
MACV. Weyand succeeded
Abrams as COMUSMACV, then
later as Army Chief of Staff.
Abrams Family Collection

General Abrams, here briefing a
visiting Time-Life group on the
1970 incursion into Cambodia,
emphasized the "one war" of
military operations, pacification,
and improvement of South
Vietnam's forces. Body count, he
concluded, "is really a long way
from what is involved in this
war." *William E. Colby Collection*

Adm. Thomas H. Moorer moved up from Chief of Naval Operations to Chairman of the Joint Chiefs of Staff in July 1970, replacing six-year incumbent Gen. Earle G. Wheeler. By then U.S. troop withdrawal was in high gear, with 140,000 redeploying in that year alone. *U.S. Army Military History Institute*

This large complex at Tan Son Nhut Air Base near Saigon housed the headquarters of U.S. Military Assistance Command, Vietnam. *U.S. Army Military History Institute*

Helicopters were the tactical innovation of the Vietnam War, providing unprecedented mobility to ground troops, logistical support, command and control, and the all-important medical evacuation.
U.S. Army Military History Institute

South Vietnamese troops stacking ammunition captured in the Parrot's Beak area of Cambodia during 1970 incursion. During the 60-day operation U.S. and ARVN troops captured enough weapons to equip 55 enemy infantry battalions. *Indochina Archive, University of California at Berkeley*

Introduction of "miracle rice" gave South Vietnamese farmers better crops and more crops per year. Here one version known as NT 20 is shown next to common rice. Counterintuitively, the miracle version is the shorter crop on the right, better able to withstand monsoons and providing some 600 percent improvement in annual yield.
National Archives

Abrams presented the U.S. Legion of Merit to Gen. Cao Van Vien, Chief of South
Vietnam's Joint General Staff. Vien was an intelligent, professional, and serious officer
who had the respect of Abrams and other Americans who worked with him.
National Archives

ARVN Col. Hoang Ngoc Lung served as J-2 Intelligence
Officer of the Joint General Staff and later wrote an inform-
ative monograph on intelligence in the Vietnam War.
Lt. Gen. William E. Potts Collection

General Abrams with Col. James H. Leach, Commanding Officer, 11th Armored Cavalry Regiment, in Vietnam. During World War II Captain Leach commanded B Company of Lt. Col. Abrams's 37th Tank Battalion. *Brig. Gen. John C. Bahnsen Collection*

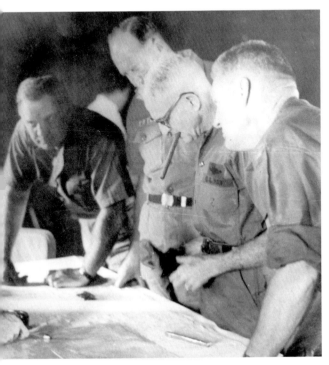

Adm. John S. McCain Jr., Commander in Chief, Pacific, his ever-present cigar well in place, being briefed on riverine operations in Vietnam aboard the USS Benewah. *U.S. Army Military History Institute*

General Abrams awarding the Presidential Unit Citation to 1st Squadron, 11th Armored Cavalry, Maj. John C. Bahnsen commanding. Abrams has inscribed the photo to "a great fighting soldier."
Brig. Gen. John C. Bahnsen Collection

Maj. Gen. Edward Bautz Jr. served in Vietnam as MACV J-3 Operations Officer and then Commanding General, 25th Infantry Division. During World War II Major Bautz had been S-3 Operations Officer of the 37th Tank Battalion commanded by Lt. Col. Creighton Abrams. *U.S. Army Military History Institute*

Ambassador Ellsworth Bunker served for six consecutive years in Saigon, providing stability and continuity that were lacking in prior years when ambassadors shuffled in and out repeatedly. *U.S. Agency for International Development*

Col. George Jacobson with Nguyen Cao Ky (Edward Lansdale at left). Jacobson served in Vietnam as an officer and civilian for nearly two decades, most notably in the pacification program. *Indochina Archive, University of California at Berkeley*

Martha Raye with General Abrams during one of her many visits to the troops in Vietnam.
Abrams Family Collection

Charles Whitehouse (right), shown here with William Colby, served as deputy ambassador late in the war after an earlier tour as a senior pacification official. Whitehouse recalled in his memoirs the "abiding sense of purpose" at senior levels in the American establishment during these later years. *Colby Family Collection*

This December 1971 newspaper photograph of a GI reading his mail on a fire base in Vietnam prompted Army Chief of Staff Gen. William C. Westmoreland to fire off a message to General Abrams complaining that "this soldier is a sorry sight." Meanwhile a survey team from Westmoreland's own headquarters had only recently returned to report its finding that "the American soldier serving in combat arms units in Vietnam is still a responsible, disciplined individual who is proud of having successfully carried out his hazardous combat mission."
United Press International

Shattered remains of a U.S. helicopter mark the site of a successful enemy sapper attack at Khe Sanh during Lam Son 719, the South Vietnamese incursion into Laos. Restricted by congressional action, U.S. forces (except aviation) could not accompany Vietnamese forces, but supported them with artillery and logistics from the other side of the border. Said Abrams, "That was a real tough operation." *U.S. Army*

Gen. John Lavelle, Commander, Seventh Air Force, with General Abrams. Shortly before the 1972 Easter Offensive Lavelle was relieved of his position after it was determined that he had violated the rules of engagement by ordering offensive air strikes in North Vietnam falsely reported as protective reaction strikes. *Patton Museum Library*

General John W. Vogt took command of Seventh Air Force just in time for the 1972 Easter Offensive, when he integrated greatly augmented air forces to help the South Vietnamese prevail. *U.S. Army Military History Institute*

Brig. Gen. James F. Hollingsworth was Assistant Division Commander of the 1st Infantry Division and then later, during the siege of An Loc in the 1972 Easter Offensive, played a key role as senior advisor to the South Vietnamese. On one crucial day Abrams gave him the entire B-52 bombing effort. "By God, it just saved us, that's all!" exulted Hollingsworth. *U.S. Army Military History Institute*

President Nguyen Van Thieu (right) visited An Loc to celebrate the Easter Offensive victory with Brig. Gen. Le Van Hung, valorous commander of the defense. Gen. Cao Van Vien (second from left), Chief of the Joint General Staff, accompanied Thieu.
Indochina Collection, University of California at Berkeley

Deputy Ambassador Samuel Berger with Abrams. The two men formed a close friendship, working together in what Berger later called "this terribly tragic business."
Lon Holmberg Photograph

President Nguyen Van Thieu meets with President Richard Nixon. As an inducement for Thieu to agree to the Paris Accords in January 1973, Nixon promised that the United States would intervene militarily to punish any North Vietnamese violations of the agreement. When the North Vietnamese flagrantly resumed aggression, the U.S. reneged on the commitment, later also drastically scaling back matériel and economic support for the South Vietnamese and ensuring their defeat. *Nixon Presidential Materials Project, National Archives*

General Abrams is greeted by Devil, a war dog that he made a member of his staff. "It was hard to be negative," said Abrams, "in a headquarters that had such a nice dog." *Lon Holmberg Photograph, Abrams Family Collection*

place since the loss of Sihanoukville. POL pipeline system from North Vietnam into Laos has been expanded, including 75 kilometers just in the Laotian panhandle since March 1970. Greater use being made of natural waterways, with rock and wood surfacing. February 1971: SAM sites identified for the first time in Laos. Estimated 665 AA guns, manned by 10,000 troops in 41 AA battalions, currently deployed in Laos.

BRIEFER: "Despite all the efforts expended on LOC expansion and protection, allied interdiction has limited the enemy's ability to move supplies through southern Laos."

BRIEFER: "Although the Communists needed to move more matériel this year than last in order to support forces in the expanded area to the south, now logistically dependent on the sole remaining LOC, total truck activity lagged behind last year's mark until mid-April. It is now about 3 percent ahead, but much of the movement detected during Lam Son 719 was in support of tactical activity."

BRIEFER: An estimated 67,000 short tons of matériel entered southern Laos this year. Only about 14 percent of it, or 9,000 short tons, reached the Republic of Vietnam or Cambodia. Represents only 40 percent of last year's estimated throughput.

BRIEFER: "Analysis of all enemy actions and trends since the loss of Sihanoukville indicates the North Vietnamese probably made an irreversible decision in the spring of 1970. Determined to continue the war in Southeast Asia, and recognizing the requirement for external support of his forces in the Republic of Vietnam and Cambodia, the enemy committed additional resources to southern Laos. Setbacks which his logistical effort has suffered in 1970, and is now sustaining in 1971, will greatly limit his military capability in the Republic of Vietnam throughout the remainder of this year. Meanwhile, it appears the enemy is attempting to develop an option for increased military activity in the RVN in 1972 or 1973, after the majority of U.S. forces have been withdrawn. Development of such a capability will depend primarily on the successful throughput of supplies down the Laotian LOC."

WEYAND: Cites "the disruption of fairly heavy actions that he [the enemy] had in mind before 719."

ABRAMS: "One way of looking at this is that he suffered so badly on Lam Son 719 that he can't afford to let anyone think that. And especially if—he knows we're going to find out eventually that he's moving the 803rd and the 29th back to North Vietnam. And if there wasn't something else going on we could start leaking that and crowing about it as another result of Lam Son 719. So he—. But that doesn't mean that this is going to be any Sunday school picnic, not by any means. They're going to try to work that antiaircraft in there, and get it around Carroll and all that, that's become the tactic now."

CLAY: We've gone in twice in the last six weeks for authority to hit the SAM sites and MiG airfields and GCI in North Vietnam [and been turned down].

ABRAMS: "We've got to pull this together and get it in, for one thing—this developing battle. And then the role of that MiG field up there, the role of these

SAM sites, in this battle—which is about to really get under way here in South Vietnam."

10 JUN 1971: COMUS Update

BRIEFER: "Currently the enemy's greatest capabilities in the Republic of Vietnam are in northern MR-1." There are 30 enemy battalions in the B-5 Front and Quang Tri Province.

BRIEFER: Quotes a late March statement (following Lam Son 719) by North Vietnam's Defense Minister Giap: "On the Route 9 front the U.S. puppets [meaning the South Vietnamese forces] are in an extremely dangerous situation and they will not escape due punishment."

BRIEFER: "GVN elections are scheduled for 29 August and 3 October [1971]. The enemy may hope to influence these elections in his favor by attacks on fire support bases or by inflicting heavy casualties on ARVN units. It would also provide propaganda support for his contention that Lam Son 719 was a Communist victory and that his offensive capabilities remain unchanged."

BRIEFER (re interdiction): In two B-52 boxes, yesterday had one truck move through each.

ABRAMS: "That is a very helpful development."

WEYAND (re a proposed B-52 strike on hold because of a SOG operation in the area): "I'm just a little bit pissed off by this thing being held up by SOG operations, because I just can't believe that those guys mucking around in there are doing a hell of a lot of good."

ABRAMS: "What this needs now is really getting the headquarters going up here and getting the all-source intelligence and really getting to work on targeting. You've got a lot of power, but it isn't any good unless you have intelligence. All you're doing is killing monkeys and stuff out there. Tigers. Just think of a poor goddamn tiger out there, trying to get his supper, and goddamn B-52 strike on him. Sorry damn thing."

ABRAMS: "I kinda like that thing about not very many trucks down there. That's pretty good."

12 JUN 1971: WIEU

Attendees: Gen. Abrams, Gen. Weyand, Gen. Clay, Mr. Kirk, Mr. Duval, MG Eckhardt, MG Cowles, MG Gettys (for LTG McCaffrey), MG Bowley, MG Dettre, MG Wilson, MG Potts, MG Kroesen, BG Watkin, RADM Salzer, BG Henion, BG Brown, BG Heiser, BG Forrester, Col. Horrocks (for MG Maples), Col. Sadler, Col. Miller, Col. DeBruler (for BG John), Col. Leonard, Col. Jones.

ABRAMS: "Chief, these messages from Dolvin about these goddamn camps up there—I don't know what camps they're talking about. Somebody's got to tell me about that—today. It's just a bunch of names—and the implication of disaster, and inaction by this headquarters."

■ ■ ■

MACV 1971 RVN/Cambodia Infiltration Estimate: 50,700 (68 percent to COSVN).
Potts: The emphasis this year is on COSVN. There are 4,600 in September alone,
and they're all going to COSVN.

■ ■ ■

ABRAMS: "General Truong, in my judgment, is the most professionally qualified
   officer that ARVN's got in the field."
ABRAMS: "The other day when I was up there with Ambassador Bunker, seeing
   the president, he talked quite a bit about strengthening the RF battalion so that
   it's got a staff and a commander. He looks at RF battalions in terms of some
   provinces don't need any, but some provinces maybe need five. He's really
   separated from that JGS philosophy [of] everybody gets two, each of the 44
   provinces get two, so you won't have them complaining. He talked about special training, if necessary, so the battalion commander and his staff were professionally up to running the battalion. And then he wants the sector and the
   subsector to have a headquarters that operates 24 hours a day."

■ ■ ■

ABRAMS: "Well, this is going to be <u>bad</u>. Sensor activations are way down, and
   strikes are way down. It's like—some of those fellows in that Dr. Kerr group,
   they think the enemy does some of these things because we make him mad.
   And if we didn't make him mad, he'd stop all that, and we're just <u>goading</u> him
   into doing bad things, and if we'd stop that goading him then he'd be pretty
   nice. And somehow you have to sit here and <u>talk</u> with them about that without,
   without really ruining [laughing]—. Like Fred says, I've got the best training
   aid in the office now, that dog [Devil, a retired war dog "adopted" by Abrams].
   <u>That</u> dog got up off the floor and went over and sat alongside that lady in the
   office. And every once in a while she kind of licked the lady's hand. Pretty
   hard to think bad things—."
WEYAND: "That's right. She knew that dog wouldn't like anybody who's mean."
ABRAMS: "Maybe even the dog copied its personality from me. That's a possibility."

20 JUN 1971: WIEU

MACV 1971 RVN/Cambodia Infiltration Estimate: 53,200 (65 percent to
   COSVN).
BRIEFER: Binh Tram 33 is rationing rice from the normal 24 ounces per day to 6
   1/2 ounces.

■ ■ ■

ABRAMS (during break): "Wait'll you read this fine message in from the
   Chairman telling about the SecDef talked to somebody that told him there

wasn't a goddamn soul awake on any base in this country. How the hell do they think they pulled this parade off yesterday—everybody asleep? My god, old Giap would have given Quang Binh Province to the battalion commander that was able to pull off something like that. We almost had a problem down there yesterday. When they rendered honors to the president, and they played the national anthem, then they fired a salute. And some bastard radioed out 'incoming mortar.' You know, one of those great little cogs down there screwing around in the machinery and using the radio. But that was jumped on by cooler heads before it had a chance to get going. He was promptly taken into custody. It's one of those things there's no point in our following up on. They'd probably want to know if we'd give him civilian counsel."

■ ■ ■

ABRAMS (to Clay): "Lou, I got a message in from Dolvin about his needs for tac air support up there in that Khe Sanh, Ba Long area. And I told the staff this morning we should do that. It's not a—I don't want it to get off the track as being interpreted as critical of what's been done thus far on tac air. That's not it. He went up there yesterday and had a meeting with Dzu and Lam and all of them. That's the way they're talking—they're not getting enough. And this is Tom's solution to it. I think we've got to do it in order to stop that talk." "I think we've got a Vietnamese problem we've got to solve—for a while, at least." "We've just got to be careful during this time. I think a certain amount of hand-holding—. Well, it's a hell of a thing to say, but the hand-holding's sometimes more important than the sorties. It's a question of attitude."

■ ■ ■

BRIEFER: In Saigon, three terrorist attacks during the week.

ABRAMS: "I drove downtown on Friday afternoon. The police and the military were just everywhere in that city. I think I can say that every one I saw had somebody stopped—at least one, sometimes a small group—checking ID cards. And that was going on just everywhere. I went all the way out to Cholon."

ABRAMS: "They pulled off that thing again out there at the National Cemetery. Had all the diplomatic corps and all that out there, attachés and so on. Nothing went wrong out there. . . . I was there last year. After they have the ceremony, the last two years everybody goes down to the graves. This year I noticed that many of them now have a photograph. You know, this process that you can get the photograph put on glass. Well, a lot of these headstones down there have got that, and I asked General Manh about it. It's a practice that they started this year, and if the family has a picture, the army quartermaster will see that that's done."

ABRAMS: "Another interesting thing. I went down to get on my helicopter, but it wasn't there. That's out at the entrance. So I was there about 30 minutes, I guess. Meantime, everybody left. Amazing—it doesn't take long, once the dignitaries have gotten out of the way. That thing really folds up in a hurry—

trucks, and the band, and the troops, flags, and the incense. I mean the whole business is gathered up and away it goes in mighty short order. There just wasn't anybody left except some MPs and myself down at the entrance. And here came walking an ARVN soldier. He was a sergeant. And he had his wife with him. She was pregnant. And they had three little kids. He was carrying one of them. It was so small, you know. <u>Well</u>, it was a long walk. And then there was a little boy. I guess he was probably nine. He was carrying a big bag, plastic bag, a handbag. And it had a big wad of those joss sticks sticking up the top of it, and I suppose a little lunch or something in there. They were on their way—they came in the entrance there, and they were on their way to the graveyard. I suppose, I imagine, some relative or something. All this stuff about, 'The Asians don't care about' or 'don't value life' and all that—I think it's a real myth. I think they feel about these things a lot like our people do. Here are people trudging out there to pay their respects and so on, not a very easy thing for them to do, and they're doing it."

■ ■ ■

ABRAMS: "At the reception yesterday that Indian fellow on the ICC came over and was talking with me. He said, 'You're looking good and confident. Just like when I talk with Giap. He's the same way.'" [Laughter] "And he wanted to know how much of the organization and planning the U.S. did for the Vietnamese on the parade. It showed the guy hasn't found out anything about the Vietnamese. He's ignorant. On something like that, there isn't <u>anything</u> we can do."

SOMEONE: "Does he speak English?"

ABRAMS: "Oh, yes, he's Oxford [doctor?]. It's really magnificent. He recoils a little bit from a cussword now and then. [Laughter] After the first time you see that you have a tendency to throw it in a little more." [Laughter] "I thought I'd ask him about the situation in East Pakistan, but aw, hell—he'd probably think I'm trying to goad him."

■ ■ ■

Abrams compliments the truck killers.

ABRAMS: "Incidentally, I went over with General Clay. We visited those men over at [place name unclear]. You know, we're always talking about the determination of these NVAs to really push that stuff through. I learned a little something about why they're not as successful as they'd like to be, because that is a <u>hell</u> of a determined bunch over there. In fact, just talking determination, I'll stack them up to any [of] Giap's best. They are <u>really</u> in it! You go out and talk with all these B-57G—you know, there's been a case when I've heard harsh words around here about the B-57G. Well, you talk to them. They <u>know</u>—it isn't any point of discussion—they <u>know</u> it's the best truck killer there is! And, of course, you go over to the C-130—well. But, anyway, it's <u>really</u> something. That C-130—it's got 14 people in it. And everything they do, all 14 have got to be working right hand in glove. That's a lot of people to all have doing the right thing, and that's what you've got to have for the whole thing to work—every time. And this is 14. Well, you think a squad, and trying to get a squad doing the right thing. And all this sophisticated stuff in there. It explains a lot. You know, some of these movies we've seen in here, those strikes. Christ, all those viewers in there, they can switch them from infrared and low-light TV, just by pushing the button. And that's what they've now got on there. It's something. We went up and had dinner with them, and standing around talking before dinner and after dinner—well, it just makes you feel good, that's what it does. <u>Really</u> up on the stick. The same thing with those crew chiefs out in the field."

CLAY: "About the only problem I could find over there was if they just didn't have this goddamn Seventh Air Force over their heads they'd have won this war by themselves." [Laughter]

ABRAMS: "Yeah, both General Clay and I got straightened out. We found out we were screwing things up! Especially the FACs. They have quite a feel for that whole damn system. It's true, they do, watching it out there and flying it every day and all that kind of stuff. So they have their own grasp of how his system's functioning. They've noticed, once in a while, a little stupidity getting into the execution. The other thing about it is, it's not arrogance on their part. They're just so <u>consumed</u> in this job, you know, and living it every damn day, they're <u>confident</u> that they've got a good grasp of it, and that's what they want to talk about."

■ ■ ■

BRIEFER: Describes efforts to locate the supply base of enemy units constituting the threat in Quang Tri Province. Intensified effort initiated on the area west of Khe Sanh. Using 26 May 1971 photography, a lucrative area was discovered in a triangle bounded by the border, Route 9, and Route 608. Contained 22 supply areas (some with as many as 15 separate storage sites), truck parks, antiaircraft positions, fortifications, and foxholes. Since 1 June 1971, Arc Light campaign against the complex and the lines of communications leading into it. Targeting Panel working the problem.

■ ■ ■

Security of U.S. elements as the drawdown continues.

ABRAMS: "Two things I want to mention. I know there've been some rumblings about how good our security's going to be when the U.S. ground combat units go down. . . . One thing in this, and it's understandable, one thing the Americans overlook is what the situation has been in the delta now for some time. This is no small matter. What have we got, 10,000 Americans down there? 18,000. Well, we've got 18,000 Americans down there. We've got about 550 helicopters down there. I suppose what you've got to say is they've just gotten used to it. But we're not losing helicopters down there and so on. And we're not getting Americans killed down there and all that. And I just don't want this kind of attitude developing, a sort of desperate, throw your hands up in the air business—'O-o-o-h-h, we got no more 1st Cav, o-o-o-h-h.' That's the time to get working harder on the territorials and the advisory effort in the division, that sort of thing. That's the way it's going to be. That's the <u>problem</u>. And that's what we have to get with. And it can be done!"

Still work left to be done.

ABRAMS: "The other thing I wanted to mention is this business that goes something like this: 'Well, they're going to have to handle it all themselves in the end. They might just as well start now. All of us Americans here, we can sit out on the patio and sip a gin and tonic and let these Vietnamese—. They're going to have to start someday. Might as well start today.' Boy, I'll tell you, if we've got anybody convinced that's what he ought to be doing, I don't want him here. I want him to go home, and with a notation that he's just not acceptable in this kind of work. Because we've got a lot of <u>work</u> left to be done! In advising, and encouraging, and working with them, developing their confidence and developing their skills in those areas that are appropriate for it. In some things, and in some places, they're good enough so that we're not going to contribute anything skill-wise, and we shouldn't be trying to."

ABRAMS: "When our job is done will be sometime after the last small group departs on an airplane. That's when it will be done. The <u>work</u> is there, and it's now, and it's every day, and it's going to continue. We <u>have</u> got a lot of work to do. We've had a good frank discussion with General Vien and his staff. And the ambassador and I went and had a good talk with the president. I think it's all been a very realistic and candid and forthright sort of thing, all the way around, and there's no dreaming in it. I think we've given them a good honest appraisal. Basically, the thing that's needed now is a matter of <u>quality</u>. They've got to correct their manpower situation, which is <u>bad</u>. And they've got to correct the leadership deficiencies. Those are the two main things. Those things cannot be solved by equipment. No way to solve them with equipment! In fact, you just make the problem <u>worse</u> by shoving equipment in."

26 JUN 1971: Commanders WIEU

ATTENDEES: Command group: Gen. Abrams, Gen. Weyand, Amb. Colby, Gen. Clay, MG Cowles, Col. Jones, LTC McDaniel (for BG Watkin). Component commanders and staff: LTG McCaffrey, RADM Salzer, MG Wilson, BG John. Military regions: LTG Dolvin, Mr. Lazar, MG Wagstaff, Mr. Cruikshank (for Mr. Funkhouser), Mr. Vann, BG Armstrong, Mr. James, MG Cushman, Mr. Wilson. MACV staff: Mr. Duval, MG Eckhardt, MG Maples, Mr. Jacobson, MG Dettre, MG Young, MG Potts, MG Kroesen, MG Adamson, BG Trogdon, BG Brown, BG Heiser, BG Doehler, BG Forrester, BG Bernstein, BG McClellan, Col. Zerbe (for Col. Sadler), Col. Leonard.

ABRAMS: "I just want to tell you all—I'm not trying to put in for a Silver Star or anything, but after a few years of coming over to this building in the morning, I want to tell you it's about the same as when the battalion commander calls you in and says, 'Men, we're going to take that hill. They've got a regiment up there, and we've only got two understrength companies. But we're going to take it. And we're going to take it this morning.' And that's what it takes to come out of those damn quarters over there and prepare to receive those messages! [Laughter] It's unbelievable!"

WEYAND: "Over the top!"

ABRAMS: "I have considered, recently, if I shouldn't put together a new B-52 targeting outfit. Hell, we've been using these things out here in Southeast Asia. I've at least got in my mind some excellent targets." [Laughter]

■ ■ ■

ABRAMS: "He's got quite a few more forces in the [Laotian] panhandle this year than he had last year. [Potts: "Three times more, sir."] And he's got, what, a 37 percent increase in ack-ack? And there's all this about he's going to try to work it during the wet season. Well, all those people have got to be fed. They've all got to be supplied with ammunition—ack-ack and—. His supply requirement in Laos must be somewhat greater than it has been before. And if you take that sensor thing—activations—and the movement you see on there, and compare it to last year, if this keeps up I should think the thing would finally get under strain, just trying to take care of the troops he's got there."

■ ■ ■

BRIEFER: "There are some who believe that [North Vietnam's] Defense Minister Giap has suffered an eclipse since failures of the General Offensives of 1965 and 1968." "The shift in Vice Chairman in the NDC [National Defense Committee] appears on the surface to be a demotion for Giap relative to Pham Van Dong, Le Duan, and Truong Chinh."

ABRAMS: "This thing that's happening up in Quang Tri—he [Giap] is without a doubt the architect of that whole thing. It has his fingerprints, footprints, and everything on it. It's out of his personal notebook." "He is still the minister of defense, and there isn't anybody that can do that job better than him."

SOMEONE: "As long as those three guys run it, the war's going to go on."

ABRAMS: "Yeah."

■ ■ ■

BRIEFER: "Now that the U.S. Senate has passed a resolution calling for a troop withdrawal deadline linked to release of American prisoners, it was thought that the Communists might be ready to float a more specific commitment to release prisoners in response to curtailment of U.S. involvement in Vietnam." Le Duc Tho, returning to Paris yesterday, said in a debarkation interview, "I bring nothing new in my pocket for the time being. If Nixon sets a concrete date for withdrawal, we will see what happens."

ABRAMS: "<u>Oh</u>-ho-ho-ho! The <u>same</u> thing he said before. 'You will see.' And we have."

BRIEFER: "Later he added, 'I am convinced that once the date for a pullout is fixed, the problem of release of PWs will be promptly settled.' The effect of Tho's statement will doubtless be to focus additional pressure on the Nixon administration to set a firm date for U.S. withdrawal. Thus Hanoi, while promising nothing concrete in return, baits the U.S. for a firm commitment before the RVN elections."

WEYAND: "The timing of the Mansfield amendment and all of that—just coincidental. Amazing."

SOMEONE: "Well, these words are a little regression from what's his name's comments to the *Washington Post* a couple of weeks ago—interview with Chalmers Roberts, because they were a lot farther out than this statement."

ABRAMS: "Oh, n-o-o-o, don't say regression, Bill [not Potts]. This—see what you've got there is the <u>master</u> has now come to take over the [negotiations?] O-o-o-h-h, yes! And, '<u>You'll</u> <u>see</u>, you'll <u>see</u>. <u>We</u> <u>know</u>. We <u>understand</u>. You'll <u>see</u>.' Duc—and the orchestra he's playing, it's not in Paris—that's just where the <u>podium</u> is. The goddamn <u>orchestra</u> is in Washington! And here is a <u>consummate</u> artist. Christ, he makes Leonard Bernstein look like a five-year-old kid trundling up there for the first time. <u>No</u>, <u>that's</u> what that is—the <u>swells</u>, <u>oh</u>! And that son-of-a-gun standing there—he just <u>knows</u> how to do it."

■ ■ ■

SOMEONE: "I think this [hamlet and village chiefs who remain overnight], plus the tax ability of the VC, are the two most valid indicators of what the real situation is in any hamlet."

VANN: "The advisors who went in with the airborne on 5 June—I talked with one of them the other day when he came down—said that he saw over 400 bodies when his battalion initially made the linkup. This is the most disarray I've seen on a battlefield left by the enemy."

■ ■ ■

ABRAMS: "Now the other thing I want to talk about is the—you know on the 20th I talked with all commanders, May 20th, about the functioning of the chain of command. And I want you to know that that wasn't something I'd thought of that morning on the way walking down to the meeting. When we talk about the functioning of the chain, what we're talking about is that at every layer they take their full measure of responsibility, which includes seeing that the layer below them is doing what it's supposed to be doing, and the layer below that is doing what <u>it's</u> supposed to be doing, and so on. The reason I talked about that was there was quite a bit of evidence at hand—I'm not talking about rumors, I'm talking about evidence—that this just wasn't being done. I think most of the Americans over here really are fine fellows, and they want to do the right thing. And we should be supporting them, wherever they are, by <u>insisting</u> on doing the right thing."

ABRAMS: "And the reason I talked about it on the 20th is that that just isn't the way everything's going out there. And I want it <u>changed</u>. Now this business about winding down the war and so on, and less fighting—the thing you've got to remember is that <u>anybody</u> <u>can</u> <u>still</u> <u>get</u> <u>killed</u> <u>anywhere</u> <u>in</u> <u>this</u> <u>country</u>! This war is still going on! It's true a lot of people have gone home, and I guess they probably feel pretty good back home, but <u>we've</u> got these men <u>here</u>. Even if they don't think so <u>themselves</u>, we've got to see that the measures are taken so that they <u>are</u> properly protected. The security, alertness, discipline—nah, letting the bunkers go to hell, sandbags deteriorate, trenches begin to get filled in, and all these things begin to happen. And then when they get subjected to an attack, and that can occur—you know as well as I do, it can occur just about anywhere—so then you get under pressure, or you get intelligence that it's going to come up. You haven't got the proper place for the men to be protected and so on. Or the whole business of patrols, the sensors, alertness, adequate alert plans, the condition of weapons, the condition of the communications, the internal communications, and all that. Just what's happening out there in some places [is] people aren't paying attention to it."

ABRAMS: "What everybody's got to understand is that the conditions in this country <u>just</u> <u>make</u> <u>that</u> <u>criminal</u> <u>neglect</u>! <u>You</u> <u>can't</u> <u>have</u> <u>it</u>! And commanders that <u>permit</u> it are doing a very bad thing for their men. They're not accepting their responsibility as a commander, and second, they're not accepting their responsibility for the security and well-being of their men. And I just don't know of anything worse a commander can do. That's just—it's <u>bad</u>. They can do some other things—even <u>stealing's</u> not <u>that</u> bad. There just about <u>isn't</u> anything as bad as that. And we're all <u>here</u>, and this is the job to do, and there can be no <u>compromise</u> with it. There just can't! If <u>I</u> don't say these things, and <u>you</u> don't say these things, and then go ahead and insist on it, <u>then</u> <u>we're</u> <u>not</u> <u>doing</u> <u>our</u> <u>job</u>! I don't think I'm doing <u>my</u> job, not living up to the responsibility that's mine."

ABRAMS: "And so I'm going to <u>keep</u> saying it, and I'm going to keep trying to follow up down there and <u>see</u> that this philosophy is seeping down into every last damn unit of two men! And I expect <u>everybody</u> else to be doing the same thing, at their appropriate level, and so on. That's the way we've got to be. And I think the <u>truth</u> of the matter is that if we <u>do</u> it, and get the whole thing pushing, our men are going to be <u>with</u> us! <u>They</u> know that things are wrong, and that we're permitting it. They'd <u>like</u> to be <u>right</u>. And they'd appreciate some other people standing up and being right, too, especially those above them. And I don't want to blame it all on the young officers, either. Hell, we've been blaming it on the young officers for 35 years I know of. Well, the young officers just aren't that bad. And young officers have <u>always</u> needed help and guidance, and they've needed support. And the same thing with the noncoms. Oh, you can—a bad one here or there, you can get rid of him. But that's <u>not</u> the way all of them are. <u>They</u> want it done right, and the <u>men</u> want it done right. And all of us, we've got to see that it is done right. That's what we stand for, and that's the way it's going to <u>be</u>. There's no point in sobbing about the problems—'The press is bad' or 'the people back home are bad'—I mean, to <u>hell</u> with <u>that</u>! That's not your job! You're <u>here</u>! And you're getting <u>paid</u>, and your government <u>expects</u> you, to face the <u>heat</u> and get it done <u>right</u>! And that's what we've got to do. <u>Well</u>, that's what we're <u>going</u> to do."

2 JUL 1971: COMUS Update

BRIEFER: "We have nothing new to report to you in Cambodia or MR-2, 3, or 4."

ABRAMS: "I just want to say you're off to a good start."

BRIEFER: Reports indications the enemy is putting some heavier antiaircraft weapons in storage for the rainy season.

ABRAMS: "I must say, the take they have gotten on all the antiaircraft they've put in there is not very great. Now Lam Son 719, that's something else, but for the Commando Hunt program they haven't gotten much. It's a damn good thing they don't have any of these cost effectiveness guys over there."

BRIEFER: "I think he feels he's capable of defending the LOC with one or two battalions in the rainy season. In the past he's done that."

ABRAMS: "I think he's right."

10 JUL 1971: WIEU

ATTENDEES: Amb. Bunker, Gen. Abrams, Gen. Weyand, Gen. Clay, Mr. Jacobson, LTG McCaffrey, MG Maples, MG Bowley, MG Dettre, MG Wilson, MG Potts, RADM Salzer, MG Adamson, BG Watkin, BG John, BG Trogdon, BG Brown, BG Heiser, BG Doehler, BG Forrester, BG McClellan, Col. Sadler, Col. Leonard, Col. Jones.

JACOBSON (to Potts, during a break): "Damn, Bill, all your geniuses are <u>leaving</u>! You've only got four platoons of them left. Your guys, when they leave here, they go to <u>MIT</u>, go to the <u>Academy</u>. My guys, when they leave here, go to Fort <u>Polk</u> in Louisiana, Camp Baggypants in Montana, or some goddamn place. Just <u>unfair</u>, that's all."

■ ■ ■

ABRAMS (re reported enemy activity in the Long An District): "The way they begin coming back in—they get these intelligence guys and communications guys. They get that started first. Those will be small groups, and they'll be kind of old hands, know their way around. Well, <u>that's</u> the time to really start working on them, before it gets to a big problem. But I'd be willing to bet a cigar or something that everybody's kind of happy out there in Long An and Hau Nghia because there isn't much going on. When there isn't very much going on, especially when you've got the intelligence like this, is the guy's straightening out your collar, getting the noose fitted down, and so on, and in another three weeks you'll feel that knot a little snug, and then in another week they'll trip the goddamn door, and there you are <u>dangling</u> with your neck broken and so on. You wonder, 'How the hell did that happen to me?'"

ABRAMS (re the enemy): "He hasn't <u>changed</u>. He's the same old fellow. The only difference is the Vietnamese have now got the wherewithal to keep this from happening. They've got the territorials, they've got the organization out there, they've got the means, and they can kill this before the darn thing gets blossoming. That's the difference. But it's also necessary they understand him, and understand he's the same bad fellow, and he's going at it in the same bad way, just like he did in '68. That's what it is. I don't mean he's going to be able to mount any Tet '68. He isn't. But he'll do enough out there—if they leave him alone, he'll do something out there in Long An and Hau Nghia that'll really give them a headache. And it'll look bad in the papers, it'll look bad for the government, it'll look bad for everybody."

■ ■ ■

ABRAMS: "Madame Binh came up with these seven points, and the Communists have been pushing this idea quite a few places around the world, pointing out what a wonderful thing it is and so on. One of the easiest things to say about that is that they're taking advantage of the situation in the United States. You know, it's kind of designed to appeal to all the troublemakers in the United States. Well, that probably is about the way it's being done. However, I'd like to look at another aspect of it, and go back to the other time when they came up with what looked like some gift, and that had to do with the bombing halt in '68."

ABRAMS: "I think now probably the reason they came forth at that time trying to dicker with that is that they were in real trouble. They weren't getting anything. There wasn't much being moved below the 20th parallel. I don't think they were getting six trucks a month into Laos. It was <u>really</u> gummed up. Before that, they began taking these regiments back out of northern MR-1—<u>before</u> the bombing halt. And I think they were taking them back because they couldn't support them. Couldn't <u>move</u> anything. When the bombing in North Vietnam became focused on that area south of 19 degrees, that <u>really</u> concentrated the bombing, and made it very bad there."

ABRAMS: "Well, what I'd like to do now is go back and take a look at that thing at Pich Nil Pass. It's always bothered me that, after they had it this last time, they finally gave up on it. The thing out here on the river, with the 271 and 95C. And when the FANK finally moved forward in there they found a certain amount of supplies and so on. It's not like them to give up supplies. And they certainly didn't do it because they were terror-struck by the ferocity of the Khmer Armeé Nationale. And then this thing that's happened up in the Plaine des Jarres. There they are in there finding foodstuffs and ammunition and that sort of thing. And then this thing down in the B-3 Front. They pulled back the 95B, 24th—leaving some, but pulling the main part back. . . . This thing that's going on up in the DMZ at Quang Tri. The 66th, now, looks like it's probably in bad shape. 27th probably is, too. Some movement back of the artillery. . . . And then Lam Son 719—the effect of that. I'm not trying to lay out a conclusion which I'd like to have you gather some information that would support, but I also wonder if a part of why they're willing to come up with another way of saying what they want isn't because they've got some rather severe problems—again."

ABRAMS: "Out there at Pich Nil, and also at Tonle Sap, that just isn't the old NVA. It just isn't. Now they really got hit hard by air, and maybe they were so ill-prepared for that that that's what—. The fact that they left those supplies— that's not <u>like</u> them if they've got things under control. I'm not telling you to put on the rose glasses or anything. Just keep on the usual J-2 dark glasses, but look at this other side of the thing."

■ ■ ■

ABRAMS: "A-a-a-h, a very nice slope to the green line [indicating friendly-initiated contacts]."

■ ■ ■

ABRAMS: "And another thing, Ambassador Edmunds had a sort of a sour attitude about what's going on up here among the territorials." He also reported from a visit with the Khmer defense minister a total lack of Lao-Vietnamese cooperation, and even the possibility of same due to attitudes of hostility.

JACOBSON: "In addition to being a pest, he isn't very bright."

ABRAMS: "I tried to explain to him that it wasn't that way, but of course he's got his sources."

JACOBSON: "Things have got to go bad because he's always predicted that they <u>would</u>. He's got to see to it."

ABRAMS: "Well, one of the sources is Big Minh."

■ ■ ■

ABRAMS (re PSDF having captured two enemy): "That's not a genteel group, the swimmer-sapper outfit. They're just tougher than hell. They're well trained and well disciplined, so you're not out there catching rabbits."

■ ■ ■

DISCUSSION: Ongoing visit by Dr. Jaffe and his party on drug problems.

Dr. Jerome H. Jaffe was at this time President Nixon's special assistant on narcotics and dangerous drugs.

ABRAMS: "What we've got there, I believe, is a level of experience with drug addiction that we don't have <u>anywhere</u> in the military."

ABRAMS: "We need to pay attention to these fellows."

■ ■ ■

JACOBSON: Reports looking into whether it would be feasible to totally declassify the results of the Pacification Attitude Analysis Survey, "primarily to get away from any claims of favoritism during the elections. I've almost come to the conclusion that we either have to declassify it or stop it."

BUNKER: "Yes."

BUNKER: "This is the first WIEU I've attended since returning from Washington. In connection with what Jake has just said, I think the elections are going to be viewed in a highly critical way in the United States. As you know, there are already <u>assumptions</u> that they're not going to be fair and honest. I think we're in for a very difficult period, so I think we've got to be very careful what goes on. I must say, getting back [to the United States] is a fairly depressing experience. It's very nice to get back here where something constructive is going on."

BUNKER: "An interesting sidelight on these *Pentagon Papers*—Henry Kissinger told me that when the *New York Times* June 13th issue came out he just saw the headlines, and he called up General Haig right away. He assumed the leak had come from the Pentagon, so he said, 'Call up the secretary of defense and tell him to cut this out, stop it.' He said Haig telephoned him back (he was out at San Clemente). He said, 'You know (he thought two or three documents had been leaked) how many documents were leaked? Five thousand, two hundred and forty-six.'"

BUNKER: "Well, while you're in front of General Abrams I can give you one good piece of news. That is the Class of 1916 at Yale is solidly behind our Vietnam policy." [Laughter]

ABRAMS: "On that encouraging note, I suggest we adjourn."

17 JUL 1971: WIEU

ATTENDEES: Gen. Abrams, Gen. Clay, Mr. Jacobson, Mr. Duval, LTG McCaffrey, MG Eckhardt, MG Cowles, MG Maples, MG Bowley, MG Dettre, MG Young, MG Wilson, MG Potts, RADM Salzer, MG Adamson, BG Watkin, BG John, BG Trogdon, BG Brown, BG Heiser, BG Doehler, BG Forrester, BG Bernstein, BG McClellan, Col. Sadler, Col. Stevens (for Col. Leonard), LTC Weed (for Col. Jones).

MACV 1971 RVN/Cambodia Infiltration Estimate: 57,500.

ABRAMS: "We have a—it starts out with a SecDef memo about using some imagination about the interdiction program. [Static] Then CINCPAC has come in with a message which outlines an interdiction program against personnel. And this morning I read a message where they're going to hold a <u>conference</u> in Hawaii. And if I read that right, we were information [addressees on the message]. Well, that would mean that the people who are going to put that together are PACAF, PAC Fleet, and USARPAC. Now I know that we've always talked about the changing nature of the war, but I'll tell you one thing—it hasn't changed so goddamn much that those golf players and par shooters back there in Hawaii can now take it over. [No one laughs.] We'd do better to turn it over to my boy's Cub Pack, over in Bangkok. [Laughter] I want to get into, in the first place, that <u>scheme</u> that was outlined."

ABRAMS (to Potts): "It's like that technical fellow of yours coming in here and throwing a five-pound sack of mercury on the floor and asking all us fellows to get up and grab it. That thing's [personnel infiltration] quite a lot different than trucks. Those guys don't need any gasoline, or diesel. They don't need any roads. They don't need any bridges."

ABRAMS (to Clay): "You'll probably be there in time for the final meeting." "In that basic one, of course, they just can't resist throwing a few shovelsful of mud at the air interdiction program. They say, 'Yeah, they've destroyed a lot of trucks, but somehow they seem to have been able to replace them.' Nobody talks about throughput. They'd just like to have a good interdiction program without any cost. That's what they want, and that's what they're thrashing around trying to find. It looks like old Fitzpatrick's about to get in there and show them how you do that."

ABRAMS: "I was up there with the 101st yesterday, out in the A Shau. And they'd found a road out there, all trellised, built over, vines growing, and the goddamn thing's about six meters wide—good road. The thing that really gets you is— see, they went ahead and <u>built</u> the whole damn thing and we didn't know about it."

■ ■ ■

JACOBSON: "What ever happened to that scheme we had to make the mud even muddier?"

ABRAMS: "It went the way of the McNamara Line up on the DMZ. As a matter of fact, as sort of a postscript, I think when we put this answer together it might be well to review the various imaginative proposals that have characterized the history of this war. The McNamara Line. When I think about that damn thing up there—plowing and carrying on, and building bunkers, all that. Then this thing when we just went out there with C-130 loads of Tide or whatever it was. 'That's the answer! Nobody's thought of that!' Then, when it didn't work, it was either too much water or too little water, the soil wasn't just right, you know, the real answer being the whole thing was just a damn farce."

■ ■ ■

ABRAMS: "I guess, the whole time I've been here, I've never seen—had—so many indications that they're going to do something with these elections. You expect this, of course, like Ho Chi Minh's birthday and all that, but by god it's been a ceaseless drumfire of what they're going to do during the elections this time, more than ever."

JACOBSON: "What'll be interesting to watch is whether they back a candidate, and don't try to screw up the elections, but try to get votes out, or whether they really try to disrupt the election."

SOMEONE: "We have reports on both sides. Some of them say, 'Vote for Big Minh,' and the rest of them say, 'Don't go vote at all.'"

ABRAMS: "If they had real control, then they could go ahead and back Big Minh. I just hope Big Minh will be in there on the 3rd of October so somebody can vote for him if they want to."

■ ■ ■

CLAY: "And in spite of everybody's questions—. You know, everybody questions us on going after the interdiction targets—'We're not hitting anything,' 'it's not worth the effort,' you know, 'there's nothing down there,' 'you don't give us any BDA.' And, damn it, I'm convinced that going after these points is good and it's a good return. I can't get anybody that wants to talk to it because you can't say, 'Well, we got 475 secondaries' and 'I got 87 trucks' and all that sort of thing. I'm convinced that selective going after these things [entry points] when they're open and keeping them mucked up is a [logical?] course of action."

ABRAMS: "Well, I don't know—if it's any comfort to you, I'm with you. That's what I believe, too." "We've just got a problem with—they just talk money, and that's what our problem is. You've got a pretty good staff over there. If they could figure out how to do this just as well without money you'd wind up hero of the century—well, at least this month."

ABRAMS: "And then you've got these guys who say the reason they're fighting is we've made them mad, we've irritated them. That's how you solve the money problem—stop being beastly. They'll all go home. Poor little fellows—if we'd leave them alone, they wouldn't bother anybody."

■ ■ ■

ABRAMS: "I spent quite a little time yesterday with the 101st, and I must say when I came back last evening I felt pretty good. I think that's quite a healthy outfit. They have some splendid leadership in it, the kind that gets most everybody going with them. And tough! They've got tough standards, and they're trying to have everybody meet them."

■ ■ ■

ABRAMS: "I might say a thing about this drug business. This urinalysis thing that's now going is another piece of the pie. Everywhere I inquire about this, people are one hundred percent in favor of it. This is going to give us a handle on this thing we never had before." "They're learning every day, and getting a firmer and a better grip on it. And we need this intercommunication between USARV, who's doing all the—who's winding up with all the urine [laughter]—and the medics, and the navy, and the air force."

ABRAMS (to McCaffrey): "Bill, I think the big gap in all this is the cumulative knowledge all over the world on what you do with a man who is using heroin." "I think they can with certainty identify a real, honest to god addict who is really hooked. But then, when you come away from that guy—who is clearly sick, in bad shape, and all that—and come down that train of the casual or infrequent [user] and so on, how those ought to be categorized, or what you can do with them. Even a fellow like Dr. Jaffe . . . hasn't got any pat answers on what you can do. But everybody—well, I won't say everybody, but a good many seem to feel that . . . the educational program, the publicity to it, and knowledge and so on, it's having an effect of causing people to believe that probably this is bad. So there's some self-help going on trying to shake it. These are guys not even getting in the amnesty program or not going to a hospital. So we've just got to really keep after it. This is a long-haul thing. We're not going to—you've got to be long-winded about it. This is no hundred yard dash. This goes cross country. But I think if we stick with it, and keep working harder, and learn more, we've got a chance of turning this thing around."

31 JUL 1971: WIEU

ATTENDEES: Amb. Bunker, Gen. Abrams, Gen. Weyand, Gen. Lavelle, Mr. Jacobson, LTG McCaffrey, MG Eckhardt, MG Cowles, Mr. Duval, MG Maples, MG Bowley, MG Wilson, MG Dettre, MG Jumper, MG Potts, RADM Salzer, MG Adamson, BG Watkin, MG John, BG Trogdon, BG Brown, BG Heiser, BG Doehler, BG Bernstein, BG McClellan, BG Hill, Mr. Christie (for BG Forrester), Col. Portaluppi (for Col. Sadler), Col. Jones, Col. Crockett.

BRIEFER: In Washington the SASC held hearings on proposed amendments to limit U.S. aid to Laos. Symington and Case were the sponsors.

■ ■ ■

ABRAMS: "Some of those Cambodians have funny ideas now. Those officers over here in training got a little upset because they expected them to stay out with their troops at night."
POTTS: "And also to eat the same food."
ABRAMS: "Yeah, when they said they had to eat the same food as the soldiers. Very bad!"

■ ■ ■

ABRAMS: "You know, there have been several articles about how the delta is starting to go to hell in a handbasket. It sure isn't from what we're getting here. Quite the contrary. Look at 11, 11 incidents—12, And how many people are there down there? My golly, there's enough people down there, and there's enough RF and PF down there—. I mean, it's a sorry damn performance! They [the enemy] ought to be able to do more than that."
BUNKER: "It's the way it's slanted in the press. I mean take the *New York Times,* [Patchell's?] article. Somebody just gave him, obviously, one of your reports. Picks out the 8 provinces where there was some retrogression. Says nothing

about the rest of them. Of the 44, there are 36 more where there's progress. There are 8 where there's been some retrogression. This is what you get. And that's the kind of headlines."

ABRAMS: "That was an analysis that John Vann put together for General Truong. That's how you get progress, pointing out what's left to be done."

ABRAMS: "You know, you take all of this—what he's able to do in Cambodia, or what he's <u>doing</u>, what he's doing in Laos, and what he's doing in South Vietnam, what this shows—it doesn't add up to a very powerful thing. Then you compare the territorials, what they're doing, versus what the VC are doing, who's starting these scraps. If he's in good shape, he's sure trying to hide it."

■ ■ ■

JACOBSON (re the upcoming elections): "This is a traumatic experience these days, not only for the enemy, but by god for the Vietnamese people themselves, because for the first time in their whole history they're going to have to back somebody before they know who's going to win. And this is just killing them, just <u>killing</u> them! Very un-Vietnamese."

14 AUG 1971: WIEU

Attendees: Gen. Weyand, Gen. Lavelle, Mr. Jacobson, LTG McCaffrey, MG Eckhardt, Mr. Duval, MG Maples, MG Bowley, MG Jumper, MG Slay (for MG Wilson), RADM Salzer, MG Adamson, MG Carley, BG Watkin, BG John, BG Trogdon, BG Brown, BG Heiser, BG Doehler, BG Bernstein, BG Hill, Mr. Chambers (for BG Forrester), Col. Crego (for MG Potts), Col. Portaluppi (for Col. Sadler), Col. Crockett.

WEYAND: Asks Jacobson how things went with Senator Stevenson.

Adlai E. Stevenson III served as Democratic senator from Illinois 1970–1981.

JACOBSON: "I think they went very well. He's a reasonable man, even when he disagrees with you. He's got a couple of fellows with him that were a little bit difficult. When he left he told me that was the first military briefing he ever had that he could understand." And Congressman Kyros wanted to give the Vietnamese B-52s and everything else.

WEYAND: "Jack's [Lavelle] probably seized with some of these 'try harder' messages from Washington. It's really gotten kind of ridiculous. We keep asking for authorities to do things, and they keep sending them back. And they always end up with, 'What more assistance do you need from us?' From your faithful friends."

17 AUG 1971: COMUS Update

ABRAMS (re three ARVN airborne battalions that have been operating in MR-1 for 15 days with only one very light contact, while the commander has requested another battalion): "Well, you put three battalions out there for 15 days, and you get one light contact—so goddamn light you haven't got any information on it—. It's h-a-r-d to support reinforcing that by putting more battalions to spend two weeks thrashing around. It's not the soldiers. I'm all with them. It's not their fault. It's like this—I don't know what you call these things—put platoons here and platoons there, and companies here and companies there. You start them off early in the morning. If they work three or four hours and can't find anything, pick them up and put them somewhere else until they do find something. And that's kind of what ought to be happening here. And as soon as somebody got contact gather all those platoons and companies together and everybody jump on that."

■ ■ ■

WEYAND: "When you look back on it, President Thieu didn't receive much support [in the elections] from the major cities—Saigon, Danang, Hue."

BRIEFER: Thieu has consistently received his greatest support from the highlands, predominantly Catholic areas, and a variety of rural areas. Least support from urban areas and from areas dominated by opposition religious factions. "In general, enemy strength seems to dominate in those provinces traditionally loyal to Thieu. On the other hand, enemy attacks by fire and terrorist activity thus far this year have tended to be more prevalent in those provinces least loyal to Thieu."

ABRAMS: "Hardly makes sense."

BRIEFER: Mentions "the recently reported COSVN Directive 38, which favors participation in the electoral process, but calls for paramilitary activity to discredit the GVN."

ABRAMS: Asks Weyand if he remembers what the VC had been threatening before the 1967 elections.

WEYAND: "I remember that we expected a lot of enemy activity, but not much happened. And the same has been true of every election since—we always expect a big ruckus, and it doesn't quite come off."

SOMEONE: "The year before [therefore in 1966] we were amazed at the lack of enemy activity. I was up in MR-1 during the political instability that was going on. You remember we had three different MR commanders and governments, and all the soldiers left the field and came into Danang to fight for their warlord up there in MR-1. We didn't know who our enemy was up there for a long time. And yet the VC did not respond to that at all. And ARVN was almost totally debilitated."

ABRAMS: "I notice in the Bangkok municipal elections they had a turnout of 7 percent of the registered voters—7!"

WEYAND: "Well, that shows they weren't stuffing the ballot box."

ABRAMS: "Makes you wonder what these elections really mean."

WEYAND: "If we're going to discuss that [laughing], it probably ought to be in closed session."

18 AUG 1971: COMUSMACV Assessment Briefing: Enemy Peace Initiatives in SEA, Comparisons of Tactical & Terrorist Activities

BRIEFER: Responds to Abrams's comments and questions of about three weeks earlier in the WIEU noting that in several recent instances the NVA had gone off and abandoned supplies. He wondered if they might be hurting more than we thought they were, and also whether this might be connected to the so-called peace initiatives.

ABRAMS: "What got me started on this was prisoners. Everyone seemed to be kind of shocked that, out of 500 prisoners they were going to try to repatriate, only 11 or something agreed to go back. I say people were shocked. Now some people were, despite the fact that both the embassy and ourselves have been telling them, for well over a year, that this is the problem. These guys don't want to go back. And we repeatedly told them about that. But then they just kind of overrode all that and said, 'We want these 500'—."

BRIEFER: Refers to May and June 1969 and September 1970 previous enemy peace initiatives. 150,000 enemy KIA by October 1968. Three major enemy offensives in 1968. February 1969: Fourth general offensive and an additional 30,000 enemy KIA. On 8 June 1969: First U.S. withdrawal announcement.

BRIEFER: "By 1970 the enemy was no longer able to mount countrywide offensive operations."

BRIEFER: "During Lam Son 719 it is estimated that 17 of the 33 VC/NVA infantry battalions involved in the operation were rendered ineffective." Although the enemy needed to move more supplies in 1971 to support an expanded area (to the south) of operations, as a result of Lam Son 719 and air interdiction "only 40 percent of last year's estimated throughput reached RVN and Cambodia this year."

BRIEFER: "Continuing cross-border operations in Cambodia have compounded the enemy's tactical and logistical difficulties."

BRIEFER: "In northern Laos the enemy's military position on the Plaine des Jarres has been increasingly eroded since early June. . . ." We have found sizable quantities of enemy supplies, exposed and under only light guard. "It is unusual for the NVA to leave such quantities of matériel unprotected." Suggests that they were surprised and unprepared for the push from the south.

BRIEFER: On 1 July 1971: PRG seven-point peace proposal.

BRIEFER: "There is little doubt . . . that the atmosphere created by the *Pentagon Papers* release, Clark Clifford's plan for an immediate withdrawal date and a POW release within 30 days, and the succession of draft announcements [by Senators] Cook [*sic*: Cooper?], Stennis, and Mansfield served to prepare a ripe psychological climate for another round of Hanoi's peace offensive."

BRIEFER: "Throughout recent operations the VC/NVA have not shown sufficient staying power to maintain an offensive posture over an extended period. In marked contrast to previous years, they have abandoned sizable amounts of supplies on the battlefield, indicating a lower degree of efficiency."

BRIEFER: "Enemy casualties this year are only approximately 40 percent of the totals for each of the years 1968 and 1969."

BRIEFER: "Because of mounting logistical problems and an expanded area of operations, enemy strength oriented against RVN has declined steadily over the past three years, resulting in a lower tactical profile." Nevertheless, "they [the enemy] continue to demonstrate the will and resolve to continue the conflict."

BRIEFER: Runs through alternatives available to enemy negotiators in Paris. "In conclusion, the enemy has suffered a series of reverses throughout southern Indochina, the cumulative effect of which has been to degrade his tactical capabilities in terms of both personnel and logistics."

■ ■ ■

POTTS: "The next briefing responds to a request by General Weyand to see whether there was any correlation between enemy ground force operations and terrorism, specifically in MR-1. The study has been expanded to include all four corps areas."

BRIEFER: "Tactical activity tends to build up in February, March, and April, and to decline by the September rains." The data show "seasonal fluctuations, a direct phased relationship between tactical and terrorist activity, and a relative shift to terrorist incidents in 1970 or early 1971."

BRIEFER: "Terrorist activities since January 1969 reached their highest intensity during April through June 1970, the period of the first cross-border operation into Cambodia."

BRIEFER: "The 1970 Cambodian cross-border operation, which forced the enemy to withdraw main force units from the RVN in order to protect his one remaining logistics LOC, appeared to have been a turning point, shifting the emphasis from combat activity to a concentration on terrorism and protracted warfare."

ABRAMS: "The other thing—I'm beginning to have a conviction about Lam Son 719 that that was really a death blow."

■ ■ ■

ABRAMS: "Coalition government is capitulation. And the South Vietnamese don't have to do that. As a matter of fact, if the South Vietnamese had a way of getting ammunition, and POL, they're almost in a position where they could tell everybody else to go blow it out their ass. I'm saying that on the basis—look at the damned depots that we've just about finished here—tools, power—and the logistical setup they've got in the air force—overhaul. We're talking now about surviving. No more Santa Claus stuff—now we're talking survive. I mean, I'm not advocating any of this, I'm just saying that—."

POTTS: "We felt the bombing halt was the number one priority as far as the North Vietnamese were concerned, then a cease-fire. As far as survival goes, . . . give these people logistics, like a corollary of Korea. . . ."

ABRAMS: "That's right. Anybody here who was over in Korea at the end of the war—I'll tell you, there weren't very many Americans around." "And you talk about corruption and handling their soldiers—." "You talk about this outfit here [the South Vietnamese]. They're <u>actually</u> in a <u>hell</u> of a lot better shape than Korea was at the end of the war." "But then there are those damn things that are so important, and we can't [do it for them]. What I'm talking about is the determination—god, it's <u>fierce</u>, it is <u>fierce</u>. I was there. Americans didn't see that. Of course there were people like General Van Fleet. He had sort of an emotional faith in the Koreans, so you could say he believed in them all the time. And maybe he sensed that, that kind of determination. But incompetence, and corruption, and bad practice and so on—it just <u>abounded</u> on every side."

ABRAMS: "We talk here in this country about the fact that they don't have any middle managers, and they don't have the technical manpower base, and so on. They're so far ahead of what the Koreans were there's no comparison."

ABRAMS: "A lot of things. In the first place, they [the South Vietnamese] have no 12-month tour. This is forever. This is forever. They don't have any 12-month or 18-month tours."

ABRAMS: "There are, I think, some kinda good signs. Oh, it's not going to be a neat package, but it's kind of on the road to turning out kind of halfway right. Oh, they get all upset about Ky not being able to run. I don't know how you figure all this stuff out. In those mythical elections over in Bangkok, 7 percent of the registered voters turned out [laughs]. There've been reports in the press where they went down and talked to the voters, and Christ—they didn't know any of the candidates. They didn't even recognize their pictures. And Big Minh, you know—as a matter of fact, Ky, too."

ABRAMS: Recalls "the seven points of Madame Binh's last proposal. 'Number 2: U.S. must stop backing Thieu.' Big Minh's playing that fiddle himself. And Ky tried to play it, too. You know, get the U.S. to step in—. I don't mean that either one of those is trying to get together with the PRG, but the effect is they've lined up kind of doing what that second point is. They're on the same wicket."

ABRAMS: "What we've got to do here—just do what's right. We've got to <u>stick</u> to that, and not get excited and go running off at this stage of the game like some kid. It's not a neat package or anything, but the general azimuth that it's been on I think has probably been a good one for this kind of a thing that lacks all the precision and all the orderliness that you'd like to have. But the general direction of it has been almost right, and we've just got to stick with it and not get butterflies at this stage of the game, just kind of keep on."

21 AUG 1971: Commanders WIEU

ATTENDEES: Command group: Gen. Abrams, Gen. Weyand, Gen. Lavelle, Mr. Jacobson, MG Cowles, MG Bowley, MG Watkin, Col. Crockett. Component commanders and staff: LTG McCaffrey, RADM Salzer, MG Slay, BG John. Military regions: LTG Dolvin, MG Eckhardt, MG Maples, MG Young, MG Jumper, MG Adamson, MG Carley, Mr. Chambers, BG Trogdon, BG Brown, BG Heiser, BG

Bernstein, BG McClellan, BG Hill, BG Lanagan, Col. Crego, Col. Zerbe (for Col. Sadler).

ABRAMS: "General Weyand sits on this tripartite deputies information thing—[the Cambodian representative, Paksoman?] and Minh and General Weyand. It was started some time ago to see if, sort of acting as a catalyst, we couldn't get the Cambodians and the Vietnamese kind of working together on strategy and plans and all that kind of stuff. It almost got sunk when the JCS offered to send a 60-man detachment out to help it in its work. That just isn't the way it's done. In time, it's got[ten] a secretariat, so the meetings have taken on a more purposeful and a more substantive sort of thing, and it's progressed to the point where they've got subcommittees made up of staffs from all sides that can work on special problems."

■ ■ ■

BRIEFER: "According to a recently received IR which summarizes an analysis by the French military mission in Hanoi, numerous problems concerning morale have been evidenced in North Vietnam. The report pointed out that since 1968's cessation of large-scale bombing of the north there has been a growing pacifism among the young people and a marked decline in voluntary enlist-ments. The analysis expressed the opinion that Lam Son 719 had a devastating effect upon the morale of the NVA and of the civilian population of North Vietnam. According to the French analysis, the destruction of nearly two North Vietnamese divisions, and increased defections during the same period, caused the morale of all but the NVA officer corps to disintegrate."

SOMEONE: "This report comes from the French military mission in Hanoi. We picked it up in Washington from the French attaché."

ABRAMS: "Kind of a little bit out of character, too."

WEYAND: "Lam Son 719 is still kind of a burning issue in a way. I may be over-stating it, but without—we sure didn't want to color it, but the <u>assessment</u> of Lam Son 719 is still—still isn't in. And somewhere along the line we should be able to come down fairly hard on what we think the results of that are, even though we recognize we aren't going to be able to quantify it as precisely as the Cambodian thing. But still, congressmen always ask about it, and it's always along the line of what about—'How do you explain that disaster?' or some variation on that theme."

ABRAMS: "This is kind of in tune with what the Eastern European attachés were saying not long after Lam Son 719 was over."

ABRAMS: Has talked with Congressman Montgomery, who also visited Hanoi, where he found the First Secretary totally noncommittal about what Vietnam would do concerning U.S. prisoners once U.S. withdrawal from South Vietnam was complete.

ABRAMS: "I think it's safe to assume that they'll just go down their list of things they want to get done. After that, and total U.S. withdrawal . . . what they do with the Americans, first you get everybody out, and that's what they mean—

everybody. It means there wouldn't even be one radio technician. And then the next step is financial support, things like POL and ammunition and some other things. Until those things are achieved I don't think you can expect much on prisoners. Well, at least I think they've probably got it laid out that way. Whether they can carry it all through that way I don't know."

VANN: "It's very interesting to see that in those very difficult provinces [Kontum, Pleiku, Darlac, Phu Bon] that they're [the enemy] at a three-year low, and I think it is also a direct reflection of the Lam Son [719] operation."

VANN: "The picture is much better than this [briefing] reflects, based on a number of factors that may have been considered but were not brought out here in the briefing. Number one, the reporting capability has greatly improved over the period of time that we're looking at, so that much more of what does happen does get reported."

VANN: "Secondly, a large slug, a much higher proportion, of the terrorist incidents are now kidnappings than they ever were before. This reflects, one, the improved reporting capability. Whole villages used to be impressed into service before and we never knew about it. But what it also reflects is that now they have to kidnap them. Three years ago they didn't have to kidnap them, they just went and told them it was their turn to go out and do it, and so the people went, knowing it was their duty, and having had to do that habitually. Now they've got to kind of track them down, and very often bind their wrists in order to take them out. . . ."

VANN: "Three, and this isn't good, but a much higher proportion of what's reported as enemy terrorist incidents are friendly-initiated incidents. This is related to several factors, one which is the inflation and the increased need to supplement income by friendly soldiers, and it gets reported as banditry and is being reported as a terrorist incident. Secondly, it's also related to grenade incidents which are reflected as enemy incidents. As a standard practice I have been following up every time a grenade is exploded in a crowd. It is always reported as VC. At least nine times out of ten, on investigation it is not VC. It is a result of soldiers being drunk, a jealous husband, squabbling over gambling, etc. But it's always reported as VC."

VANN: "There's also an unwritten rule that any time a man is killed accidentally he's [said to be] killed by the VC, because if he's killed accidentally there is no annuity for his family, or if he's killed in a fight, not as a result of enemy action. Finally, there are a couple of other things. We now have a couple million PSDF who are essentially identified with the government, and when anything happens against them—. We didn't have these people before '68, and it's been increasing ever since then, so all these people are now a base on which terrorist incidents and casualties are counted."

VANN: If we plotted the data on a national basis showing friendly deaths and enemy deaths, "what we will see is a very marked decline in friendly deaths, much sharper decline there than the overall decline in enemy-initiated tactical and terrorist incidents." Thus "there is a much lower level of enemy-initiated violence today than is reflected by these trends."

SOMEONE: "Another thing you can say is that many of the problems we have now, that is dealing with the VCI—taxation and the presence of the cadres and so forth that are so difficult to eliminate—are problems because we've eliminated other problems that were more significant." "In a way it's kind of comforting to have these problems."

ABRAMS: "There's also one thing that's not included in this. You've got this, but it sort of looks—well, you could get a favorable trend. But then you tack on Big Minh's withdrawal from the presidential thing here, and I don't know what the hell it does to that chart, but it doesn't help it. It's hard to see any good coming of that. You can get kind of sad about that, saying, 'Why in the hell, when we're where we're at, why do we have to have that?' It's not a good time for it."

WEYAND: If Big Minh had run and lost to Thieu, the same charges of corruption and unrepresentativeness would still have been brought against the Thieu government. "Actually, as far as the support back home for this government, it couldn't get much worse. Well, I guess it could."

ABRAMS: "Oh, yeah, Fred. There's a few things left they could do that they haven't done."

ABRAMS: "For anybody that's in the business, he's [Thieu] really proved [by driving opponents out of the presidential election] that he's not [a U.S. puppet]."

WEYAND: "Senator Stevenson, when he talked with me—Jake was there—well, he started the conversation with about what he thought had to be done, and that is that Big Minh had to run and he had to win. I asked him what if he ran and in a fair race Thieu wins. He said that was unacceptable. It was not going to change anything."

ABRAMS: "Apparently the most knowledgeable people feel that Thieu remained convinced, right up to the night before last, that Minh would not withdraw."

■ ■ ■

BRIEFER: Annual aid by the United States to the RVN now at $3.5 billion.

ABRAMS: "I think Congress comes back to work on the 8th of September. One of the immediate problems is the Mansfield amendment on the draft. What they've done is they've worked out a committee solution which has been agreed to in the conference committee, but they delayed voting on it on the floor until they come back on the 8th of September. Well, that may gin up a lot more."

WEYAND: "You know, our agony over this is a reflection of this briefing we put on, 'The Changing Nature of the War.' We finally, under these pressures—political, diplomatic, and all that—have gotten ourselves to the point where the reason we're here is for self-determination, so these people will have a free choice. So that makes the election of great importance. But still, underneath all this, are the real reasons that we came in here, and that is because we want a non-Communist government. We're here to defeat the external aggression and all that it stands for, which is the use of force to achieve political ends. And those objectives, or reasons, are still with us. We let ourselves get pushed around to where we start dreaming up these very high-flown ideas, and finally got it down to only one."

ABRAMS: "But it will survive *Meet the Press*."

WEYAND: "And the 'domino theory.' That, just by the weight of the news media and the liberal element, that became so if anybody stands for the domino theory, Christ, you're just automatically—something's wrong with you. You're naive, unrealistic, etc., unaware of the changing nature of the world and all that. But the domino theory, in its sophisticated version, for hell's sakes, is still valid. But nobody'd dare say so, except maybe somebody like old Sam Yorty, who's already beyond the pale."

Sam Yorty was mayor of Los Angeles 1961–1973.

ABRAMS: "And the other one—they've drug it out and dusted it off and said, 'Now, by god, in the end the U.S. has finally adopted what Gavin recommended in the first place—that's an enclave [words unclear].' Goddamn!"

SOMEONE: "Hurts, doesn't it?"

ABRAMS: "While we don't have complete unanimity of views, I think most Americans do realize that the whole problem is a far more complex thing than any goddamn simplified enclave theory. I mean, there's no way you can—I mean, anybody that works at this thing for about six months, he'd have a hell of a time trying to jimmy that into how you ought to do things here. There's so much more involved. Just go back three years, to the Saturday WIEU three years ago, and this is really a more hopeful atmosphere, even with Minh out, than the WIEU three years ago."

JACOBSON: Laments the fact that nobody went to Minh and bribed him to stay in the race: "Five million dollars, 10 million dollars, 15 tennis courts," etc.

ABRAMS: "I think that sort of thing was ruled off the course, because the ones that really have worked with him, they've found him to be unreliable. In other words, there wasn't an American left that could talk to him in confidence."

VANN: "President Thieu's career, for the last decade and a half, has never involved a backward step. He's slid sidewise on a few occasions, but he's never lost ground. And I must say [in] at least half of the moves he made disaster was predicted by the U.S. [people] involved. It kind of reflects that he understands Vietnam better than most of us."

ABRAMS: Reports having gotten a letter from Admiral Zumwalt about a new ship that's been named for a SEAL lieutenant who was killed in Vietnam. "That's a pretty good club, that SEAL club." "They've been quite a bunch of performers."

ABRAMS (re a naval task force he had visited): "I went up there once and visited that outfit. Frankly, I was really impressed with them. They're fighters. The discipline and morale there seems to be of a very high level. And I kind of got the feeling they could be trusted. They kind of like it. You know, they get missions and do things. And of course they've done some rather miraculous things—you know, going north. The thing they enjoy the most is to get into one hell of a fight."

■ ■ ■

An F-4 with six or eight 500-pound laser-guided bombs and LORAN plus laser designator is being tested. Three missions scored three direct hits, bull's-eyes, "dropping it in the bucket."

ABRAMS: "If that gets going, it will be interesting to stand at the bar some night and talk to a couple of them. Magic!"

BRIEFER: XXIV Corps has organized an "operational support coordination group," first tested on 3–4 August in a unilateral U.S. CPX. Activated 15 August at Quang Tri combat base. XXIV Corps, 101st Airborne Division, and 1st ARVN Infantry Division represented.

Apparently designed to correct some problems that showed up in Lam Son 719.

■ ■ ■

BRIEFER: In the Boi Loi Woods area of MR-3 on 14 August 1971 a U.S. and an ARVN land clearing company uncovered a regimental-sized tunnel complex of about 70 tunnels in excellent condition.

SOMEONE: "There's no end to them."

ABRAMS: "No, it goes on forever."

BRIEFER: In MR-4, a 12–16 August corps-level Dong Khoi [saturation] campaign was conducted by Territorial Forces, including 392 RF companies, 640 PF platoons, and one ARVN infantry battalion. This is the 12th such operation, totaling 48 days, since February 1971, with over 9,000 enemy killed or detained.

■ ■ ■

ABRAMS: "To go back to something we were talking about a little earlier, Big Minh withdrawing and the reaction to that in the United States, all of that. We're talking about things we don't know how all that's going to work out. Then I suppose there's the uncertainty of the visit to Peking, what all is going on there. All that stuff that—we don't <u>know</u>. And we're going ahead with the withdrawals, get down to the figure set by the first of December, and that's going along. But I don't think we should spend too much time trying to guess all that's happening that we don't know. I don't think we should waste time on that. We've got our job here and, with what we've been told, it's pretty clear to us what we have to do. And I just want everybody trying to do <u>that</u> in the very best professional way we know how."

ABRAMS: "Also, as we go down in strength and so on, I want to be sure that we're trying to set the highest professional standards. In other words, I don't want to look at what we've got as a <u>training</u> ground. What we need now are guys that can carry their share of the load—professionals." "Wherever we have staff, we ought to have people there who can do their work and carry their part. And if they're not, then I think we better send them home. This isn't the place for training guys, or giving guys experience. The job is harder than that."

ABRAMS: "Somewhere here in the headquarters we've got a guy, I don't know who he is, but he doesn't like what's happening. He knows that we refinished the volleyball courts out here, also made a tennis court. And he noticed that we put in a bowling alley over in the annex, and he understands we're doing the same thing out at Long Binh, and he doesn't like this. And of course I don't like him. [Laughter] He says it shows that we don't intend to withdraw. Well, I don't know about <u>that</u>. What it <u>does</u> show is that—I started on this, we took a position on this, in May of '70, that for <u>whatever</u> there was here we were going to try to have some decent facilities, athletic facilities, recreational facilities, all those things that would help us take care of properly what men—. The mess be put in respectable shape, places where they <u>can</u> play volleyball. Christ, I was going home the other time and there were two volleyball teams playing, about six o'clock, raining like hell, and they're hard at it! It was raining pretty hard, and Christ, it had no effect on—. Well, I think that any time you can have things like that going you're at least helping the health part. And <u>that's</u> why they're there. And I believe it's right!"

28 AUG 1971: WIEU

ATTENDEES: Amb. Bunker, Gen. Abrams, Gen. Weyand, Gen. Lavelle, Mr. Jacobson, LTG McCaffrey, MG Eckhardt, MG Cowles, Mr. Duval, MG Bowley, MG Wilson, RADM Salzer, MG Adamson, MG Carley, BG John, BG Trogdon, BG Brown, BG Heiser, BG Bernstein, BG McClellan, BG Hill, BG Lanagan, BG Herbert, Col. Horrocks (for MG Maples), Col. Crego (for MG Potts), Capt. Perez, Col. Zerbe (for Col. Sadler), Col. Crockett.

MACV 1971 RVN/Cambodia Infiltration Estimate: Still stands at 60,800.

WEYAND (re dealing with traditional hostility between Vietnamese and Cambodians): "I've really been impressed with the South Vietnamese leadership and their <u>understanding</u> of this problem."

BRIEFER: The 127th session of the Paris peace talks this week.

■ ■ ■

ABRAMS: "General Phu, the commander of the 1st Division, was one of those Vietnamese 15,759. He was a company commander at Dien Bien Phu. And he's one of those 1,435, or one of the 9.1 percent that survived. He is the only Vietnamese [surviving?] who was a commander at Dien Bien Phu, and he commanded a company. Some Americans have a tendency to look down on these fellows as kind of small, and kind of funny looking. They're also kind of tough. And what'd he say at the end of Lam Son 719? He said, 'Well, Dien Bien Phu was 59 days. This was 45.' A good tough fight at Dien Bien Phu. Then he said the 1st Division was in a good tough fight up there."

ABRAMS: "And I always kind of wind up thinking that General Phu's in this for more than just the pay. I think so."

BRIEFER: Describes information from official French army records made available to Dr. Bernard Fall as to the fate of PWs from the First Indochina War. Only 40.1 percent of the French nationals missing during the period 1945–1954" were eventually returned. Only 9.1 percent of the missing Vietnamese were returned. In addition, of the total of 10,754 PWs returned after the cease-fire in 1954, 6,132 (or about 51 percent) [*sic*] required immediate hospitalization. Of these, 51 died within 90 days. Quoting from Dr. Fall's book *Street without Joy,* "all but 4 of the 51 returnees who died after their return to French custody in 1954 had been in captivity less than four months. It must be emphasized that they were not surgical cases, but simply walking skeletons, men who had been marched to death over 500 miles of jungle paths from points of capture to the PW camps of northern and central Vietnam. In addition, not a single PW with serious injuries of the abdomen, chest, or skull survived Communist captivity."

BRIEFER: The enemy has reportedly issued instructions for cadres (of the 31st NVA Regiment) in the event General Minh withdraws and leaves Thieu to run a one-man race for the presidency in October: "There will be continual demonstrations and strikes by vendors and students, and there will be a mobilization to not go to the polls to vote. The situation is hectic, confused, and contains large internal contradictions. Suggest that you follow and respond to movement in accordance with the requirements and slogans we have issued."

ABRAMS (re VNAF maintenance): "One of the interesting things in that, Mr. Ambassador—you remember after the accident in which General Tri was killed there were a lot of unfavorable remarks made by the press. Well, they got Americans that told them that, that 'these little fellows were not much good at maintenance' and all that. Well, their operationally ready rate—that is, aircraft ready to fly—is really quite high. It's around 80 percent. [Someone: "81 percent."] So the American advisors, and the United States Air Force, got with General Minh and they agreed to an inspection team of experts that would go in and make a surprise inspection of an aircraft that they carried as operationally ready. And the ones that they've checked, they haven't found anything to change the status of OR."

BUNKER: "I remember those articles—*Newsweek.*"

4 SEP 1971: WIEU

ABRAMS: "More and more they've got to look at it the way Seventh Air Force looks at it." "They should look at the whole damn peninsula." "Actually, they've got quite a damn air force." "They should look on dedicated air with the same degree of horror that has characterized Seventh Air Force from the beginning and which I must say, as a non-airman, I fully support. It's just <u>wrong</u>. It should be going where you need it."

ABRAMS: "Probably the most sensitive corps commander on this subject is General Lam. I'm sure he doesn't think for one minute that any of those aircraft belong to General Minh. He's permitted to pay them and that sort of thing, but that's it. So it's a problem. On our side we've got a lot of ground commanders, at least among the seniors, who bought in on this, because they <u>knew</u> when they were in trouble it would <u>be</u> there."

■ ■ ■

ABRAMS: "I want to talk a little bit about—this is Reuters, Mark Meredith: 'A source close to Ky said today that he was determined to stop President Thieu in a one-man election, even if he has to use force. These sources reflect further that Ky threatens to destroy Thieu and that he, Ky, is no longer bound by the constitution. Ky gave Thieu an ultimatum to call off the election within two weeks or face a confrontation by force. In a conference with foreign newsmen the source claimed Ky is confident of control of at least 60 percent of the army, and that Thieu is considered a danger to the country. Ky is reported to feel that the U.S. should cut off aid in order to force an election delay. A spokesman for Ky said if he were planning a coup he would not announce it to the press.'"

ABRAMS: Discusses "political stirrings and all that sort of thing by one faction or another, and probably for a variety of reasons, not very many of them connected with the good of the country and the fate of the Vietnamese people. A lot of personal avarice and that sort of thing. The point is that these stirrings and rumblings and rumors and all that—. I'd like to get a personal message out this afternoon to the principal commanders and—I don't want any alerts or anything—but I want to describe these rumblings, sort of the character of the demonstrations which are likely to occur, and so on, and I want good continuous reporting of things that come to their attention and so on, and possible problems that they foresee, talking to their Vietnamese counterpart and so on. I'd like to have a good flow of reporting coming in here from the responsible people. We have to depend on them to winnow out gossip and trash to some degree, so that we're up on it."

ABRAMS: "And I think that <u>here</u> we should be realistic enough, and up on the stick on this—the operations center around the clock. And we'd better talk with them down there so that they're sensitive to the importance of some of these kinds of reports that come in—it doesn't get, 'Oh, Christ, it's politics.' The atmosphere of that can be very worrisome, and we don't want the Americans to get mixed up in it. If this begins, in some part of Saigon, looks like they're going to get a little uneasy, then we've got to move promptly and see that Americans don't get there. MPs and all that. I don't want anybody to go out of here thinking that I'm <u>alarmed</u> over this. This is just being <u>prudent</u>. I don't expect anything big's going to happen, but the way things are—and the press has got this, you know, they're aquiver. I'll bet you they've got spotters on their buildings down there, looking for the VNAF coming in. They want to get photos of the first bomb run, that's the state of mind they're in."

ABRAMS: "That's the kind of thing we're in, so we don't want to let it run away with us. It's a time to keep your cool, but also being alert to the things that can really be sensitive now. And here in the staff we all should read the messages and reports and so on and be alert to things which could cause us difficulty. What we're trying to do is not have those." "We've got to be very alert, and not look like it, not sound like it."

BUNKER: "All I can say is beware of the press." "The unfortunate thing is that all of this could have been avoided."

11 SEP 1971: WIEU

ATTENDEES: Gen. Abrams, Gen. Weyand, Gen. Lavelle, Mr. Jacobson, LTG McCaffrey, MG Eckhardt, MG Maples, MG Marshall, MG Bowley, MG Wilson, MG Jumper, RADM Salzer, MG Adamson, MG Carley, BG Watkin, BG Bernstein, BG Brown, BG Heiser, BG Herbert, BG Hill, BG Lanagan, Col. Crego (for MG Potts), Col. Sadler, Col. Houseworth (for Mr. Duval), Col. Crockett, Col. Miller (for BG Trogdon), Col. Knepp (for BG McClellan), Col. DeBruler (for BG John).

BRIEFER: On 5 September armor was sighted in Route Pack 1. Five T-54 tanks vicinity [Bac Le?], 17 kilometers northeast of the DMZ.

ABRAMS: "I wonder why they'd have those tanks scattered out like that. It's just odd to have them scattered around like that. Even if it's a training area, you wonder what the hell kind of training is _that_." Not camouflaged. "That gives you the worst refueling problem, the worst maintenance problem. There ought to be some reason for doing it."

ABRAMS: "Those guys that are walking down there [infiltrating], they have to be fed. The system's very _sensitive_ to that. Remember when we had the cross-border operations in Cambodia, they stopped infiltration groups up there and kept them in the _binh trams_ because of the uncertain situation in Cambodia. And they hadn't any more than begun that than the _binh trams_ started raising hell, coming up on the air, because they didn't have food to keep them that long."

BRIEFER: Describes reports that enemy rear service group personnel in the Laotian panhandle have been told there "will be no food at all" sent to them in the coming dry season, and they will need to develop self-sufficiency in food, and reports that "it would be like this everywhere," possibly a result of severe flooding in the rice-growing areas of North Vietnam.

ABRAMS: Recalls that a huge (350-ton) rice cache recently uncovered near the border was rice from China. "There's evidence that they haven't been able to support it [the forces in the south] with food from North Vietnam anyway."

ABRAMS: "If that really is true [food shortages], they're in one <u>hell</u> of a <u>shape</u>. And I don't want to <u>believe</u> that. Because then you start getting soft-headed. Keep looking until you find something that looks good for them."

ABRAMS: "Getting out there and planting potatoes, or rice, and able to start eating it in October's going to be quite a trick. Can't even hydroponics—but gee, that would have worked good during the rainy season."

WEYAND: "Yeah, but you know how higher headquarters are—'Goddamn it, do it! Don't expect any help from us.'"

ABRAMS (re *binh tram* requests for help in moving 212 stretcher cases to the rear): "Isn't that typical, though? He says, 'Christ, we've got to move them to the rear.' They're <u>already</u> in the rear. That's those damn support troops talking, acting like they're at the front."

ABRAMS: "Maybe that's what that self-sufficiency thing is all about—they've got a manpower problem, and they just want to strip down to what they really need."

WEYAND: "There may be a lesson for us in it."

SOMEONE: "You could get rid of the navy in the delta that way—army chow."

■ ■ ■

ABRAMS: "In reading the messages this morning I saw where Johnny Heintges retired, on the list as a lieutenant general. He left here shortly after I arrived in '67. I talked to him quite a bit, and the thing I remember is how <u>good</u> he felt. He spent a lot of time traveling around and so on. He talked about the people were now coming up and feeling good. He just felt <u>good</u>. He was kind of sorry to leave and so on. And, of course, it made <u>me</u> feel good. I didn't <u>know</u> anything about Vietnam. Well, you know all that happened after that. I'm kind of reminded of that this morning."

ABRAMS: "Plus having browsed over a thing last night, one of those that'll really catch you right by the <u>balls</u>. It's one of these 'objective' surveys of the 'real' situation here. It says that the Americans have gone to smoking opium again. They think it's [the situation] pretty good and it is really bad. But they've kidded themselves so long that it's just impossible for them to see it. After you get over being mad, you commence to worry whether he's right. You know, that you've been like the—. You stop and think about it, and the pattern of things in this meeting every Saturday. You know, it's gotten pretty regularized and so on. You wonder whether we are <u>searching</u> enough in our looking at the thing."

JACOBSON: "Funny you never see these 'real' situations as pertains to the other side."

ABRAMS: "The other side is not as fragile as this side is. You've got a political strength on the other side, I guess that's what you'd call it, that is very strong. And it's completely lacking in a lot of the vulnerabilities that the political thing is on this side. Just the simple thing of access by the world press, which makes it tough on the political side here, as well as on the military. And that's a strength that's part of the equation. It's part of the problem."

SOMEONE: Reports a North Vietnamese working on a rice cooperative who defected, made his way all the way down to South Vietnam, and turned himself in as a Hoi Chanh.

ABRAMS: "Yeah, but hell, that doesn't touch the number we've had work their way north into Canada. And they weren't on any goddamn collective farm, either, and their brothers and sisters weren't starving."

WEYAND (re South Vietnam): "The economic situation—hell, that's <u>damn</u> good. This country's done something that <u>no</u> other country in time of war has <u>ever</u> done." But: "How the hell could anybody say the political situation's good?"

JACOBSON: Chuck Cooper told me about a report saying North Vietnam's 1970 exports to the <u>free</u> <u>world</u> totaled $18 million. "All they were able to do here was 12." He said, "I don't understand it." And "some big gob of it was rice."

SOMEONE: "And somebody pointed out that what they do is they get the rice from the Chinese, and then they export it."

ABRAMS: "Kind of like ours. I mean, we get it in here, and then it gets sold to the VC."

JACOBSON: "They're Vietnamese, too."

ABRAMS: "That's one of the things that's happened. The system's gotten screwed up a little bit. For a while there we were feeding both sides. Hell, you can't have anything better than that. <u>Everybody's</u> eating good. Makes it more even."

25 SEP 1971: Commanders WIEU

ATTENDEES: Gen. Abrams, Gen. Weyand, Gen. Rosson, LTG McCaffrey, MG Wagstaff, Mr. Vann, MG Potts. Mr. Jacobson, LTG Dolvin, MG Cushman, RADM Salzer, MG Maples, MG Bowley, MG Marshall, MG Wilson, BG Watkin, Mr. Lazar, MG Carley, MG Cowles, MG Young, MG Jumper, MG Adamson, Mr. Funkhouser, Mr. Duval, BG Hill, BG Herbert, BG Bernstein, BG Brown, BG John, BG Armstrong, BG Trogdon, BG Heiser, BG McClellan, BG Scott, Mr. Wilson, Col. Crockett, BG Lanagan, BG Wickham, Col. Sadler.

WEATHER BRIEFER: States that, while the Route Pack 1 area was unworkable (they're in the transition between monsoons), "the Barrel Roll and northern route packs were good."

ABRAMS: "Well, let me make a correction there. As it turned out, it was unworkable by the old standards . . ."

BRIEFER: "Yes, sir, by normal criteria."

ABRAMS: ". . . but it's a <u>new</u> day."

■ ■ ■

BRIEFER: 1971 Infiltration Estimate shows consistent drop-off that occurs about this time each year.

POTTS: 60,800 projected so far for the year.

BRIEFER: Binh Tram 18 is at Vinh, North Vietnam.

. . .

BRIEFER: Re the Paris peace talks, where Dean has arrived as new U.S. representative: "It appears somewhat logical that the Vietnamese Communists revert to their earlier stonewall tactics and fall back to Hanoi to regroup in the disconcerting barrage of peace feelers from U.S. liberals on the one hand and the arrival of a tough new U.S. chief negotiator on the other."

ABRAMS: "Where do those words come from about 'falling back to regroup' or something?"

BRIEFER: "Those were just analytical comments, sir."

ABRAMS: "I see—authored here?"

BRIEFER: "Yes, sir."

. . .

POTTS: Re the flood situation in North Vietnam and its impact on the rice crop and replanting, foresees no impact on the enemy's transportation offensive or "operations to the south."

ABRAMS: "That comes as sort of a strategic shock, because one of the proposals that's had a rather long life has been the bombing of the dikes, and this apparently was certainly as effective as one could hope for from the bombing of the dikes. It seems [chuckles] that that, too, wouldn't have ended the war."

OTHERS: Report hearing assessments in I and II CTZ of more serious impact of the floods.

ABRAMS: "General Rosson, you were at one time there [in North Vietnam]. Do you have any—?"

ROSSON: "Well, I was there, and I still retain a rather clear picture of what the countryside looks like. I would say that this is precisely what would take place. There's a very extensive system of dikes, and they're massive things, so it's no small matter when one of them gives way. One of them could be a hundred feet thick, and maybe 15 to 30 feet high. And they're centuries old. And I remember when I was Chief of Staff here, in the old headquarters downtown, we had a very influential briefing in connection with the targeting system in North Vietnam. We were bombing in those days. And the consensus of the authorities, who stood behind that briefing and sent it on to Washington, was you couldn't take the dikes out by bombing. And that had quite an impact on decisions with regard to taking that on. There were some who thought it could be done. Most thought it could not. I would say that it would be very, very tough for some of those big dikes—along the Black River, for example, and the lower extension of the Red River, and the White River. These are tremendous things."

ABRAMS: "All right, thank you."

. . .

POTTS: Cites the fifth day after the full moon of the ninth lunar month as the projected date for onset of the enemy logistics offensive. Plotting this preparatory to "getting off a lucky message" to CINCPAC "as we did last year." "Three years in a row they've started exactly on that night." "We have the message ready right now for dispatch to Admiral McCain and Admiral Moorer for us to go on record on this." In 1967, 1968, and 1969 it began then. This will be the night of 9–10 October this year.

■ ■ ■

BRIEFER: As of 31 August 1971, the percentage of the population living in A- or B-rated hamlets fell from 77.3 to 76.3 percent. A-B-C decreased to 94.9 from 95.2. Re pacification: "The enemy can write our report card, no question about that." "Certainly we're not going to make the 95 percent A-B that the president set as a directive."

JACOBSON: "We've been pushing for a more enlightened procedure" for dealing with suspects rounded up under the Phoenix program. New provisions recently ordered include: suspect must be brought before the province security committee; he may have an attorney; the attorney may examine the dossier, "which gives the intelligence people a little pain, but it's in there"; he and his family must be advised as to what the sentence is; voting members of the province security committee have been changed to only three: the province chief, the prosecutor, and the chairman of the province council (the traditional hard hats are thus excluded from voting—the military deputy for security, the MSS chief, and the police chief).

JACOBSON: "Those are all pluses, we think. But something that may be a minus is that in order to extend an An Tri [emergency detention] sentence for an additional two years it requires new evidence. This can be developed in the province, but the way the Vietnamese are interpreting—it has an awful lot to do with his attitude and behavior during the time of imprisonment." "Colonel [Diep?], now the commandant at Con Son, has written many letters to ask for province security committees to give leniency to many prisoners he thinks now are of too low level for that kind of punishment, and asks that leniency be given them." And I'm sure that his conversation with the prime minister resulted in a "2 August message having stated that low-level first offenders will be given very light sentences or released in the custody of a notable of the village." But this "could result in the release of some damn bad people at the end of two years."

■ ■ ■

BRIEFER: RVNAF desertion rates overall have increased since 1969, mostly from combat elements, and are still a problem. There was a spike corresponding to Lam Son 719.

VANN: "Practically every village chief in this country is protecting draft dodgers—protecting them either for money, because of friendship, because of having a relationship with them. The easiest man to recruit in this country is a PF soldier, because he has the opportunity to remain in his home village."

ABRAMS (treating this seriously, coming from Vann): "I won't really argue the logic of your suggestion. But what you've got here right now—this circular really expresses the philosophy which President Thieu has been pushing now for a couple of months. And I've heard him discuss this in his office. He wants to get the responsibility for raising the manpower down in the province, the district and the village. When he describes all this, he counts a lot on the village chief."

ABRAMS: "They've got to increase the military strength in MR-1. That's accepted. They're going to move very little out of any other MR. They're going to do it by authorizing new units, organize another division up in MR-1 and so on, which means that their manpower requirements as far as structure and spaces are concerned are going to go up. We're trying to resist that. They should stay with the 1.1 million, because they're not hacking it, manpower-wise, with the structure they've got. Plus the fact that our withdrawals are going to continue, so their requirements in an operational sense are going to increase."

ABRAMS: "One of the problems, I think, in this whole war—there's a requirement for balance in there between, say, police, PSDF, territorials, and regular forces. There are extremists in the whole philosophical consideration of what that balance ought to be. And you've got, as you always do with a thing like this, extremists at either end. It may be that, 10 years from now, when somebody really has a chance to study it for three or four years—and it probably ought to be somebody that's never been here, so he could escape the constraints of experience—he might find, and be able to show with some degree of certainty, that we didn't have the right balance—or the Vietnamese didn't have the right balance, or [words indistinct] together didn't have the right balance. There should have been a little more of this, a little more of that. But I just feel, for practical operational purposes, for psychological reasons, and probably to some extent for political reasons, they cannot afford at this stage to start reducing their regular structure."

ABRAMS: "I think most people do believe that what they must have in the end is, in fact, a rather small regular force. And as the thing moves along, if it turns out so that you've got a South Vietnam that is independent in its own way, and begins to develop and flourish—it's kind of a rich country, really—it'll be with an excellent police force, it'll be with some kind of—the terms PSDF and territorials may melt away, but it'll be something like that that is the basic element of security. And maybe at that time the regular force could be a very small one. Now we're somewhere on that uncertain path to that day. There will be further withdrawals after 1 December. We know that. That's the program our government's on. The shock of that hasn't all developed yet. And the fellow—it is easy for him to create severe problems in northern MR-1, because it's close to North Vietnam."

ABRAMS: "I think at this stage of the game, and for some period of time—let's say another 9 or 10 months—they've got to lick this manpower problem in their regular forces. In the end, after a-l-l the considerations that they—see, we started out thinking that the—and <u>they</u> did, too, originally—think that you could move substantial regular strength out of MR-3 and 4 in some way, and move it into MR-1. Now, from the beginning they themselves rejected the idea of trying to move a division from down here up there. Their experience with that has been fairly disastrous. So what they always were talking about is just moving the flag, if you will, and then there might be some that would go along with it for reasons of their own. But the combination of the situation in Cambodia, the fact that the delta with all its people and the things it can provide to the nation, they just give it top priority. And that's why they can't see their way clear to taking substantial structure out of the delta, not yet. And it's pretty hard to argue with them about that. In terms of this country, that's right."

ABRAMS: "And then MR-3. The capital's here, and at this time they just can't see putting it at risk. So they're trying to work this thing out in MR-1 in a way where they'll be able to guard the family treasure and yet solve this problem up there. So I think that they must now . . . try to solve this manpower problem in their regular forces. They need to. That's why I'm bringing it up today. I think it's kind of a fundamental problem for them. And I think they <u>can</u> do things about it. They haven't gotten that low in fact in the manpower pool. We've tried to stand strong against increases in structure, because they take comfort in that when really all it does is make everything weaker—you know, by just upping structure. So you've got to force it—force it is not really true, but you've got to encourage it, to get down and tackle what the <u>real</u> problem is. And the real problem is not structure. So that's why I wanted to take this up today, and ask everyone to get it all the way down so that everyone's knowledgeable and do our best to try to make this circular work and begin to show some results."

■ ■ ■

ABRAMS: Asks the air force if the briefing on indicators of the onset of the enemy logistics offensive "did any violence" to their views.
AIR FORCE: "No," they say. They would like to start to operate against it tomorrow, not wait until next week. "As a matter of fact, we are starting." [Laughter]
ABRAMS: "Well, that'll be fine."

■ ■ ■

VANN: Mr. Barnes is the new deputy CORDS advisor in II CTZ. He was in the regular army for six years. "He left the army because they refused to send him to language training. Since that time, in the Foreign Service, he has become fluent in Lao, Thai, Vietnamese, Chinese, Cambod, and French."
ABRAMS: "John, you're making me <u>real</u> <u>proud</u> of the army."

1 OCT 1971: COMUS Update

BRIEFER: Update on "the Saigon situation." Briefed you this morning on the meeting of the People's Congress at the guest house here. Report that Ky arrived at approximately 1100 hours. Stayed about 25 minutes, then left. At 1400 approximately 200 who had attended came out in small groups and dispersed. No parade, no demonstrations. Scattered terrorist incidents. "Two females threw a grenade into an elementary school in Saigon's 11th Precinct. No casualties and no damage. The school is to be used as a polling place for Sunday's election."

ABRAMS: Asks the population of Saigon. About 1.5 million in Saigon proper, he is told, and 3.5 million in the greater Saigon area.

ABRAMS: "Well, a 200-man meeting doesn't represent a ground swell—."

■ ■ ■

ABRAMS: "What we want to start studying in this thing here—. One way to look at this is it was really designed for the election period. Put the government—. See, there's all this thing—the opposition, the fragments of opposition bubbling around in Saigon, little bit of terrorism, it is the capital, it's the seat of government, and the resolution's passed by the Senate against this thing, the An Quang [opposition] tried to take a little more active role. It's just a whole lot of things simmering that have a tendency to put the government under strain."

ABRAMS: "Also we've got that COSVN stuff that says they must stand ready in case of a coup, to take advantage of that, and so on. So I had a tendency to look at this thing happening out there at Krek and Tay Ninh as to just add to the strain in this period and see if they could by doing this nudge some bad thing into happening. But I'm no longer latched onto that. That may be the case, but you can't be confident that the election—. Let's say that the results turn out, and 60 percent of those voted for him. That would meet his stated requirement. I have no confidence that that means everything will then settle down and we can just go on through the rest of October and have a nice ceremony of inauguration, flowers, and all of that, on the first of November."

ABRAMS: "That period may also be a period of unrest, some agitation, opposition, and so on. And he [the enemy] does have quite a few regiments that have not been committed, and you've got to assume have some capability, so he might want to keep that going." "It's going to be important in the next few days to follow that with a great deal of care. Don't get too committed to any one idea. That's bad." "We want to really think hard, and not get too settled with our interpretation of events at the moment. And it's time for General Minh to be thinking in these terms, too. It's going to have to be played pretty carefully. It would be wrong to go lunging around trying to out-think him [the enemy] without any evidence. That's not the way to play this thing, either. There's got to be a little evidence that'll give you confidence that your judgment of what he's doing has some substance to it. So that's what we need to really focus on.

In the meantime, we should continue to be just liberal in the kind of support we provide of all kinds."

1 OCT 1971: Sir Robert Thompson

BRIEFER: Presenting "a J-2 and J-3 update of the enemy and friendly situation in RVN and the enemy situation in North Vietnam, Laos, and Cambodia since the 25 March 1971 visit of Sir Robert."

BRIEFER: Reviews enemy infiltration by year: "The 1971 MACV Infiltration Estimate presently stands at 60,800." Prior years: 1966: 62,000. 1967: 101,000. 1968: 235,000. 1969: 106,000. 1970: 54,000.

BRIEFER: There are 197 prepared SAM sites throughout all of North Vietnam. Of these, 33 are currently occupied. There have been 79 SAM firings this year, and four aircraft lost.

■ ■ ■

ABRAMS: "It's inconceivable that they would break their swords on something like that when, frankly, there were some soft targets up there that would have gotten them the kind of publicity they want to a far greater degree, even, than had they been successful."

Possibly referring to an assault by three NVA Regiments against FSB 6 in the Rocket Ridge area where the enemy sustained 3,500 KIA.

ABRAMS: "But they're obsessed with what they can call a victory over ARVN forces, and they're willing to spend that kind of resources to try to get it. They do it, like going out for football, every year. And they take the goddamnedest losses. The weather breaks and we put that air in there and it's just slaughter."

WEYAND: "It's very encouraging for us . . . to see how the Vietnamese military forces are improving in their staff work and in matters of reinforcement and replacements and all of that. This Lam Son 820, that went on up in I Corps, there wasn't that much U.S. military planning in that. That was fully a Vietnamese thing. And General Abrams was very impressed in an area that was so weak in the past, the command and control of any kind of a complicated operation. But they get the helicopters there and they get the air in, they get replacements, and it was just a far more professional thing."

2 OCT 1971: WIEU

ATTENDEES: Amb. Bunker, Gen. Abrams, Gen. Lavelle, Mr. Jacobson, LTG McCaffrey, MG Eckhardt, MG Cowles, MG Maples, MG Wilson, MG Jumper, MG Adamson, MG Carley, RADM Salzer, Mr. Duval, BG Watkin, BG John, BG Trogdon, BG Brown, BG Bernstein, BG McClellan, BG Heiser, BG Herbert, BG Hill, BG Lanagan, BG Wickham, Col. DeFranco (for MG Potts), Col. Crockett, Col. Zerbe (for Col. Sadler), Capt. Bivin.

ABRAMS (re briefer's report of two terrorist incidents in Saigon): "Terrorist, the way we've been using it, indicates VC. . . . Thugs and robbers and murderers and so on, this is one of the most fertile grounds for them to operate as there probably is in the world, because everything that's done like that is blamed on the VC. It could just as easily be somebody got mad and shot somebody else who was messing around with his wife. But it's chalked up as another VC incident, so he's buried with honors." [Laughter]

JACOBSON: "You know it's damn hard, though, to understand how anybody, knowing the Vietnamese love for children, figure they're going to make any point by throwing something in a schoolyard."

ABRAMS (agreeing): Recalls an incident of about three years earlier in which a 10-year-old boy pushed his bicycle, with an explosive device attached, onto a schoolyard filled with young girls (6 to 9, about). The device went off prematurely, killing the boy and injuring several young girls. "It's very difficult to understand why anybody on either side would feel that it had somehow advanced their cause."

■ ■ ■

BRIEFER: The GVN presidential election will take place tomorrow.

JACOBSON: "And now for the bad news. You just can't do pacification when the manager's eyes are on the election ball."

■ ■ ■

NAVFORV BRIEFER: "On the Cua Viet River, the enemy's water-mining campaign is continuing at a high rate." Three recovered this week by citizen reports. Rewards were provided.

ABRAMS: "Quite cost effective. One of the mistakes the enemy made up there on the Cua Viet was he got [to] hurting people. You know, taking the ferry—needless—and interfering with the fishermen, that sort of thing. So the program up there probably makes a lot of sense to the people."

■ ■ ■

ABRAMS: "Incidentally, I talked with Shaplen, the *New Yorker* guy, yesterday. He said he'd been up in Vientiane, and it is really too bad that Vang Pao couldn't get the air support. And of course he gets that from those bastards up there in Vientiane."

JACOBSON: "Lately he's just been a great quivering mass of the damnedest misinformation I've ever run into about here—."

LAVELLE: "I have a wire, it came in while I was gone last week, from Ambassador Godley, saying that they've had more air support than ever, accomplished more—thanked me personally."

ABRAMS: "Historically, historically, you'll get it from him that way. This other stuff comes out at the same time. That's the way the game's played, and it's just awful."

BRIEFER: Enemy truck traffic and allied air interdiction effort start to pick up as the dry season approaches. "Throughput this week remained at zero."

9 OCT 1971: WIEU

ATTENDEES: Gen. Abrams, Gen. Weyand, Gen. Lavelle, Mr. Jacobson, MG Eckhardt, MG Schweiter (for LTG McCaffrey), MG Bowley, MG Wilson, MG Jumper, MG Potts, MG Carley, Mr. Duval, BG John, RADM Salzer, BG Trogdon, BG Brown, BG Heiser, BG Bernstein, BG Herbert, BG Hill, BG Lanagan, Col. Knepp (for BG McClellan), Col. Sadler, Capt. Bivin, Col. Crockett.

BRIEFER: MiGs have been deployed south, possibly to threaten the B-52s.

ABRAMS: "That means they want to fuck around with [the B-52s?]. Now, isn't there some way to work it so we can shoot a few down? Don't we have the protective reaction—when the MiG comes flying—isn't that the same as turning on the goddamn Spoon Rest [radar being activated]—or something?"

SOMEONE: "Yes, sir."

ABRAMS: "And I know you've got some guys that would love to do that." [Laughter] Describes two navy "rushes" [?] and "their radar picked that up and told those MiGs to come back to Phu Yen. And we know one of them had fuel [low fuel?] and called and asked for permission to bail out—and they declined." [General laughter] "But the navy never saw these MiGs, and the MiGs never saw the navy, but they lost at least one. They can be psyched, too. That's what I'm talking about."

LAVELLE: "We had the F-4s in the air, and the MiGs did go after the B-52s, and the MiGs turned and did run when the F-4s got [words indistinct] the B-52s." "I'm coming to you with a study—it'll probably be ready next week—we've been working and working like hell. We've got people up there at Monkey Mountain to see if we can intercept any of these MiGs. Our conclusion is, and I think we're going to give you a professional job this time, and not motherhood, that when they come down there you're going to have to get 'em on the ground or you're going to give up a B-52 or a C-130, 'cause we can't get them in the air. The distance is too short, the terrain masking our radar with the mountains—they pop up to shoot and get out of there before we can get 'em."

ABRAMS: "Yeah."

LAVELLE: "If you don't let us go get 'em it's going—go get 'em on the ground—you be prepared to give up a 130 or a B-52 or something."

ABRAMS: "OK."

LAVELLE: "I think we've got a professional study this time to prove it."

16 OCT 1971: WIEU

ATTENDEES: Gen. Abrams, Gen. Weyand, Gen. Lavelle, Mr. Jacobson, LTG McCaffrey, MG Cowles, MG Bowley, MG Wilson, MG Jumper, MG Potts, MG Carley, Mr. Duval, BG John, RADM Salzer, BG Trogdon, BG Brown, BG Heiser, BG Bernstein, BG McClellan, BG Herbert, BG Hill, BG Lanagan, BG Wickham, Col. Sadler, Capt. Bivin, Col. Crockett.

BRIEFER: Reports an infiltration group of <u>three</u> personnel.
POTTS: For October, November, and December only six groups totalling 68 people.
BRIEFER: Cites preparations continuing for "the enemy's 1971–1972 dry season campaign."
BRIEFER: Reports two NVA ralliers in Laos.
ABRAMS: Asks why they rallied.
BRIEFER: They were dissatisfied with conditions in their unit, and didn't want to return to South Vietnam. They indicated that most NVA soldiers preferred to remain in Laos rather than go to South Vietnam.
ABRAMS: "We're not doing enough bombing over there. Goddamn place is turning into an R&R center." "Wait'll some psywar guy gets a hold of that. I can see where they'd extrapolate it that, if you stopped all bombing of Laos, everyone would go to Laos. We could support that with troops distributing leaflets, loudspeakers—." "I'll tell you, there haven't been many NVA turn themselves in over there in Laos."

■ ■ ■

BRIEFER: On 3 October 1971 the election of President Thieu took place.
ABRAMS (re reports that the enemy might seek to invalidate and overturn Thieu's election): "After all, however and why ever it happened, that is a massive turnout of votes for any country in the world. Well, I guess Russia does better than that. There's something—<u>something</u>—going on, and after you get through being mad about it being a one-man affair and all that, there's <u>something</u> going on to get that done! Just the <u>mechanics</u> of it. I must say, it's very difficult for me to see where the regime appears to be 'tottering,' the foundations cracking or something. It just isn't there."
SOMEONE ELSE: "It was sure an exhibition of civil obedience."
ABRAMS: "How do you get that? It kind of reminds you of old Dick Russell running for reelection." "Probably the happiest man in all South Vietnam is General Minh."
WEYAND: "At the Mission Council General Abrams said, 'You know, Minh's sitting over in his house, doing nothin'. Just about the same as he'd be doing had he been elected.'" [Laughter]
ABRAMS: "I was down there at lunch yesterday. President Thieu had a lunch for Governor Reagan. And President Thieu is either a greater actor than the Barry-

mores or he's a supremely confident man. He just projected confidence, exchanging political jokes with the governor and so forth. It's funny—the Vietnamese all remember him from movies. And he's a little older, but he can still do it." [Laughter]

ABRAMS: "Governor Reagan asked the president how he thought the war would end. And so the president—first he started out, he said, 'We have to say we don't know. That's the—and we really don't know. But,' he said, 'there are two ways. They could negotiate a solution, or they could just go away.' He said, 'I don't think they would negotiate a solution, because they would have no way to explain that to their people. And,' he said, 'the Communist way—going away, they could explain that. They'd say, "We are now going into a new phase. Everything's the same except now we go to a new phase. All goals remain the same. All victories as reported. . . . But now we go to a new phase."'"

ABRAMS: "Well, the governor was very interested in that. He cited 1947, when the Communists tried to take over the moving picture industry in our country, and he was one of the great leaders of the opposition at that time. He told about the struggles, the meetings, and so on. He said, 'How did it end?' He said, 'One day they weren't there any more. They didn't come to any meetings. And we looked around, and all 17 had gone. We didn't know where.' Then he told about this Japanese-American they put—he's the one that put in that university—college—out there [S. I. Hayikawa]. And he said, 'Jeez, he's just great.' But one day he called the governor up and he said that he was sick and tired, and he asked the governor what he should do. And the governor said, 'You keep doing what you're doing, and one day they just won't be there any more.' He said, 'They'll never come into your office and tell you that you won or that they're going or that they want a compromise.' He says, 'One day they just won't be there any more.' He said, 'That's exactly what happened.'"

ABRAMS: "Now, I think if he has any feeling at all about it, he [Thieu] thinks that will happen here. He thinks that's kind of the way they are. He [Reagan] went on to say, just before he left on this trip, the same fellows that tried to take it over in '47 are back in there now trying to take it over again. And he told the president that 'to show you just what kind of fellows these are, one of the companies is making a film called *1776*. It's quite a patriotic thing. One of the key Communist leaders is playing the part of Benjamin Franklin. So much for that.'"

■ ■ ■

BRIEFER: Land to the Tiller program, per a law of 26 March 1970, will distribute about 1.3 million hectares, half of all the rice lands in the Republic. Permits existing landowners to keep 15 hectares to farm and 5 hectares of "ancestral worship" land. The government pays all the costs. Landlords are to be paid two and a half times the annual crop value.

■ ■ ■

ABRAMS: "Have you ever been in that national cemetery of ours over in Manila? There are 39,000 missing in action—39,000. It's all <u>kinds</u> of things—ships that were sunk, aircraft lost."

23 OCT 1971: Commanders WIEU

ATTENDEES: Amb. Berger, Gen. Abrams, Gen. Weyand, Gen. Lavelle, LTG McCaffrey, LTG Dolvin, Mr. Jacobson, MG Eckhardt, MG Cowles, MG Wagstaff, MG Bowley, MG Wilson, MG Jumper, MG Young, MG Potts, MG Cushman, MG Adamson, MG Carley, RADM Salzer, Mr. Vann, Mr. Lazar, Mr. Duval, Mr. Wilson, BG Armstrong, BG John, BG Trogdon, BG Brown, BG Heiser, BG Bernstein, BG Herbert, BG Hill, BG Lanagan, BG Wickham, Mr. Cruikshank, Col. Knepp, Col. Sadler, Capt. Bivin, Col. Crockett, Mr. Barnes.

ABRAMS: Discusses with Lavelle enemy MiG activity. Lavelle points out that, between MiG CAP and ground alert, being prepared to deal with any MiGs that came up costs 16 strike sorties that could otherwise have been flown.

ABRAMS: "Have you seen the answer we got back?"

LAVELLE: "No, sir. Did we get an answer?"

ABRAMS: "Yeah. It'll make you feel real good."

WEYAND: "Give it to him after lunch so you don't spoil his—."

ABRAMS: "I'd recommend late afternoon."

LAVELLE: "Shall we cancel the briefing for right after lunch? The briefing says if we get permission this is how we're going to do it."

ABRAMS: "I won't need that. [Laughter] I don't know—. When they use their MiGs, don't they have to stand down their, I mean hold passive, their SAM—in other words, you can't in the same cloud up there have both MiGs and SAMs?"

LAVELLE: "In the same cloud, no. But in the same area, yes, because of the IFF system."

ABRAMS: "My memory's very dim on this, but I recall some rather sharp differences in view between the army and the air force, in our own services, having to do with this air defense and missiles and so on. And I certainly had the impression at that time that the flyers were very interested in rather <u>stringent</u> controls—maybe even to the point of, when they took off, they had to have the ignition switch in their pocket until they returned, some kind of a thing like that. Now maybe they've overcome all that."

ABRAMS (to Lavelle): "What we're going to have to do, Jack, is see if there're some other ways of working the problem. And this thing you bring out, what's it costing us? The secretary of defense's solution to this is that—don't send the aircraft where these MiGs can get to. I'm surprised we didn't think of <u>that</u> one. [Laughter] I think that was its trouble—it was too obvious."

LAVELLE: "Well, we've got some eager boys that have got some schemes that we're working on, trying to trap them. We'll [word indistinct] a tanker loaded with fuel, and put an orbit down at about 5,000 feet under the B-52s with a full fuel load, and if they come up after them we'll [blow them out?]. Plus on radio silence and off the radar tube, and you can pop up from there. We're looking at other ways. We want to snooker them into—."

ABRAMS: "Yeah, well, it's—if we're going to be able to do anything, it's going to have to be in this—not that I'm not talking specifics, but it's going to have to be some other kind of a solution."

■ ■ ■

BRIEFER: President Nixon's planned visit to Moscow and his visit to Peking "will doubtless intensify speculation abroad that a war settlement may be eventually reached behind Hanoi's back."

■ ■ ■

BRIEFER: Shows pacification statistics of the 10 low provinces.

ABRAMS: "Kind of interesting on An Xuyen. They're among the 10 low because they've only got 63 percent A-B. Christ, two years ago they didn't have 63 percent <u>C</u>. It's really quite—. In their case, that's sort of a real honor to head that 10 low. There's a hell of a lot of accomplishment there. It's kind of amazing."

BRIEFER (re refugees): "An estimated 6 million Vietnamese have become refugees at some time during the past seven years." About 3.2 million have received government help—1 million to return to their homes, 2.2 million to resettle elsewhere. "Most of Vietnam's displaced people desire only to return to their homes." That has been the major objective of GVN refugee assistance. Another million returned to their homes before the government assistance program began in late 1968. At least another 3 million remain eligible for return; many have taken care of themselves and have never been registered as refugees. About 858,000 now live in resettlement sites.

ABRAMS: "It's hard to find a South Vietnamese who can work effectively with Montagnards in a sensitive and understanding way. . . ." "The chances of those people in Dak Pek being happy, next year and the year after, if they're moved, are really rather remote." "The Vietnamese have not shown, as a general rule, that kind of concern for Montagnards." "I think at this stage of the game it's [resettlement elsewhere] kind of the wrong way to be going. The effort should be the other way."

■ ■ ■

ABRAMS: "PSDF—people <u>armed</u>, and so on. I don't know, there might have been one or two province chiefs out of the 44 that thought PSDF was a good thing, but I don't remember who they were. What I remember is they were all against it. And the <u>military</u> was <u>solidly</u> against it!"

ABRAMS: "One of the things that, and it's been for a long time, the RF and PF are carrying the major burden of the war. Even with all the tremendous battle going on in there in Tay Ninh, still 37—one more—territorial killed than there was ARVN. And they did pretty well against the enemy when you consider there probably weren't any B-52s or tac air supporting the RF and PF. And there was quite a <u>lot</u> supporting those ARVNs."

■ ■ ■

AMBASSADOR BERGER: "Let me say a word about the general situation before the inauguration. Since the election, the developments have been about as we expected. Attempts to form some sort of a front against Thieu came to nothing. The elements were too diverse and too hostile to each other. There was an attempt in the legislature to try to invalidate the election, and that's going to fail. The Supreme Court yesterday found the election valid. . . . The key to this . . . is An Quang, who has refused to go along with any serious attempt to overthrow the government, or to embarrass the government by demonstrations. . . . An Quang did <u>not</u> want to play Ky's game, or into his hands, based on longstanding hostility between the two. And he did not want turmoil in the country because it would play into the hands of the Communists."

BERGER: "I think the lessons of 1963–1966 have been fairly well learned here. They do not want to create a situation which will produce another period of anarchy, and that's one of the most stabilizing factors in the country now. Talk of coup is just talk. It's just nonsense. There's nobody here of any seriousness or of any capability for a coup. Ky's talk of a coup was really talk and did him no good at all. It threw him right up against the grain of the feelings of most people that the country can't stand anything like that. So out of the election has emerged this quite favorable aspect, a strengthening of constitutional processes in the country."

BERGER: "The main thing that President Thieu intends to do right after the inauguration is to address the legislature and to put out a very major and important set of economic reforms. . . ." "We think this thing will pass fairly well, and just as the reforms last year, October 1970, were tremendously successful—they reduced the inflation from 35–40 percent per year to just under 10 percent in the last 12 months—we think these new reforms will have the same effect in terms of the next 12 months." "There will be a major pay increase for the armed forces, and to the civil servants, which will be part of this economic reform package."

BERGER: "The reaction to the election abroad was as we expected, very adverse. At the time, before and since, we thought that the way President Thieu went at this was very unfortunate. He had the election in the bag and could have won it easily against Ky or Minh or both, and he went out of his way to maneuver them out of running. A price is going to be paid for this in the United States in terms of the increased problems we have with the Congress and in terms of general attitude towards this country."

BERGER: "On balance we think the outlook is not unpromising on the political side and quite promising on the economic side."

BERGER: "I don't think Thieu will do anything to Ky. I think he'll just go fishing.

He doesn't really have a lot of support in the country, and whatever support he had he threw away. He talks about creating an opposition, but he won't have any troops. Minh will do nothing. Minh will just raise orchids. He has really no political desire to become important. He's not a political animal at all, and never was."

25 OCT 1971: COMUS Briefing

ABRAMS: "I talked with General Vien today about getting the Vietnamese armed forces more into the problems of interdiction. What we're talking about are adequate command and control arrangements, the integration of navy, air force, and ground people ashore, and this kind of thing. That thing down in the delta is a good start. And then I talked about the interdiction program with respect to the western border—the integration of regular and Territorial Forces, the involvement of province chiefs, chain of command, command and control, the role of the air force—their air force. And I talked to him about the ranger border battalions. And I realize they're the military region commander's and he's got a Ranger Command to supervise and direct them, but I said all the proper authorities are there, but most of those Ranger Commands have been inadequate for the past [word not clear]—something's gotta be done on that. I said this may lead to some equipment changes and so on."

ABRAMS: "I'm really about satisfied now there's almost nothing in the regular Saturday briefings on air operations in Southeast Asia that's worth a god-damn."

SOMEONE: "They're [the Vietnamese] sort of like we were in 1966 or '67. As long as there's booming going on, that's good. They don't want to kill friend-lies, they're not that bad. But you remember the time you had getting [control over] just pre-planneds and artillery H&Is and all that. Well, that psychology—Christ, they haven't even faced up to that."

■ ■ ■

SOMEONE (re requisitioned matériel arriving for the Vietnamese): It takes about three weeks to get to the users, because the depot commanders, being held responsible, are meticulous about opening every box and counting everything inside, even to counting 100 screws if that's what the shipping document says it contains.

ABRAMS: "We had a much better system when we started out over here. We just took it off the ships and moved it right into the yards—the whole business. And we've worked for six years trying to find the goddamn stuff and identify it."

POTTS: Describes how infiltration groups come down in small groups widely sep-arated, and how no northward-bound group ever meets and passes a south-bound group. Thus no substantial targets are ever presented.

ABRAMS: "The difference between a sportsman and a game poacher—the game poacher will get 'em sitting on the water—. And the sportsman, he just won't do that. He takes them on the wing. And that's what we are—we're sportsmen." [Laughter]

The comment relates to dealing with MiGs under the applicable rules of engagement.

ABRAMS: Asks about a comparison of input and throughput for 1970–1971 versus 1969–1970.

POTTS (without a moment's pause): "Put up slide 206, please. We had this updated for you last night, sir." Explains what the data show.

ABRAMS: Notes that it has been about cut in half. Speculates on the reasons, to include Lam Son 719.

POTTS: Cites information from a rallier out of MR-5 that in late January and February of this year their supplies had just completely drawn [*sic:* dried?] up. This correlates to the [word unclear: period?] of Lam Son 719.

ABRAMS: Notes the enemy had a 15 percent increase in input and a 60 percent decrease in throughput.

ABRAMS: "That's kind of an interesting chart, isn't it?"

SOMEONE: "It would be harder to prove that the B-52s, tac air, Lam Son 719, and Cambodia didn't cause that than to prove that they did."

ABRAMS: "Something brought it about."

■ ■ ■

ABRAMS: "Talking with Ambassador Berger the other day. If you take the past three years—and of course that's a self-serving statement on my part—and the mission as a whole, while there's been a tremendous amount of imperfection in execution, and the balance of things may not always have been ideal, nevertheless the general arrangement of priorities and emphasis in this whole effort, Vietnamese and our own, has been, I think, pretty good for this kind of a thing. I'm talking now about bringing up territorials and their role in the thing, and the police, and trying to get something done about the VCI, better quality in province and district and government and land reform and elections and all this stuff."

ABRAMS: "And that thing down there at Vung Tau, the way they've been getting those village and hamlet guys in there, course after course, and we've started indoctrinating and propagandizing 'em and so on. And we've got to train people at the local level so they can handle some of the poop sheets, like on land reform or budgetary—all that kind of stuff. The best proof of it is the pacification scheme. Well, goddamn it, it must have them by the ass. That's why—it's not been good for what they're [the enemy] trying to do, any more than Vietnamization has been good for what they're trying to do. Now they're taking some of the basic elements of the strategy developed by the South Vietnamese—and ourselves to some extent—they're taking some of those basic elements as their target. This means it must have been a pretty goddamn good program."

ABRAMS: "As we sort of get down here to the crunch, and you begin to play around with new and imaginative concepts, there may be some of that that can be effectively used, but it ought to be in the <u>context</u> of this sort of the azimuth and priorities that's been going on now for three years, because it's been <u>good</u> for this country. Oh, yeah, we could sit here and talk for hours about the, again, the imperfections, the miserable <u>shits</u> that were the province chiefs of Bac Lieu and so on. This country's actually big enough to take a couple of province chiefs like that. It's not going to turn the country around. And it isn't going to lose the country to the Communists. He needs to get out. I certainly agree with that. But that's not the most important issue in this country today."

ABRAMS: "Incidentally, I had <u>really</u> a fine talk with General Vien today about chain of command, and responsibility and authority and so on. Hell, you're preaching to the choir. His fundamental beliefs and understanding and so on, it isn't <u>any</u> different, as far as I can find, than any one of us."

■ ■ ■

ABRAMS: "We've never been on the <u>border</u> in MR-1. And that's the only military region that's like that. In terms of this kind of thing, it's important."

BRIEFER: Points out the unlikelihood of the Vietnamese being able "to do without us something we weren't able to do together."

BRIEFER: Interdiction is multifaceted. Interdiction of forces moving through Laos and Cambodia, interdiction across the DMZ, in-country interdiction of the movement of troops and supplies, and interdiction of seaborne elements.

BRIEFER: Displays a map marked to indicate the areas of South Vietnam that need to be protected because they represent the population base, the economic base, the industrial base, the agricultural base.

ABRAMS: "Poor old Duc Lap is left out in the cold." Suggests no one here (except himself) would remember Duc Lap. "We've fought battles for it."

ABRAMS: Mentions the things that General Weyand has been pushing in the Tri-Partite forum. "And General Cushman has become a very intelligent and sensitive lieutenant of yours in that project, and so has General [unclear] and General Di [9th Division commander]."

ABRAMS (describing to his staffers how he wants to respond to McCain messages on the topic of the upcoming SecDef visit): Tell him "what we're going to do is describe the total problem facing the South Vietnamese with our total withdrawal, and then establish priorities and review their forces and then discuss some alternatives and the role that they must play in interdiction."

30 OCT 1971: WIEU

ATTENDEES: Gen. Abrams, Gen. Weyand, Gen. Lavelle, LTG McCaffrey, Mr. Jacobson, MG Eckhardt, MG Cowles, MG Bowley, MG Wilson, MG Jumper, MG Potts, MG Carley, MG Watkins, RADM Salzer, Mr. Duval, BG John, BG Trogdon, BG Brown, BG Heiser, BG McClellan, BG Hill, BG Lanagan, BG Wickham, Col. Sadler, Capt. Bivin, Col. Crockett.

BRIEFER: Typhoon Hester: Winds 100 knots gusting to 120 knots. Directly over Chu Lai base. Rainfall for the week almost 30 inches at Camp Evans. Period 22–24 October 1971.

BRIEFER: Describes Lon Nol's dissolution of the Cambodian National Assembly and the need to adopt a constitution.

ABRAMS: "What you're saying there—that sounds like it comes right out of our State Department. We have a sort of image of how governments oughta be and we get pretty upset when they don't fit that. I don't know whether we ever have figured it out too far about what one of these countries needs for a government. We've got a template we slap on there, and then you wind up with something like a one-man election. And there you are."

■ ■ ■

ABRAMS: "I guess, led by Joe Alsop, there's a feeling that somehow we've shit on the Vietnamese and are not providing them with the kind of a goddamn air force that they need. The truth of the matter is that this thing has been up against the fire wall now for about two years. And goddamn it, you just can't ship airplanes in here and put out a call down in Saigon and say, 'We've got some more airplanes—let's get out and fly.' I don't know what people think has been going on. As I say, old Joe is the most articulate bastard on this of all of them. And he's got some of the good guys in the press—well, no, I take that back—he's got some of the less vicious press people hanging on that thing now. Ordinarily they don't pay any attention to him, 'cause he's too much—establishment. They've become worried about this. Well, I guess I'm worried, too, but the training, and they've gotta be able to repair 'em and they've gotta be able to take care of 'em and they've gotta be able to fly 'em, so—. Within the limits of human appreciation and understanding, wherever the clouds have opened up a little bit and it [the RVNAF program] could be moved forward, I think it's been done."

ABRAMS: "Of course the other thing, in this CRIMP thing, we started out in '68. We were going to get these people by '74 where they could whip hell out of the VC—the VC. Then they changed the goal to lick the VC and the NVA—in South Vietnam. Then they compressed it. They've compressed it about three times, or four times—acceleration. So what we started out with to be over this kind of time is now going to be over this kind of time. And if it's VC, NVA, interdiction, helping Cambodians, and so on—that's what we're working with. And you have to be careful on a thing like this, or you'll get the impression you're being screwed." [Laughter] "You mustn't do that, 'cause it'll get you mad."

WEYAND: "A dynamic program."

ABRAMS: "Dynamic—that's right. Imagination, initiative—that's what's characterized this whole thing. All right—go on." [Laughter] "But I will say—I mean, you just stand back and see what these Vietnamese have done—and it's true in the army, it's true in the navy, it's true in the air force, and it's true in the provinces, and so on. I got mad earlier today about that damn road 22—I don't know why that's screwed up. But there're always a few things like that. But when you see what they've really done, and stepped up to the plate, it's quite remarkable. It's really not a bad bunch of people. They've got a lot of ability."

■ ■ ■

ABRAMS: "[Base Areas] 609, 701, and 702 look like they're up fairly tight. And then they're some other indicators that they're gonna come out of there, maybe next month. If they come in to have a go at Dak To, or Ben Het, that sort of thing, they must be out there now—fixing bunkers and that sort of thing. They don't just come boiling out, scampering about in the field. If they're gonna do that, they're gonna make these preparations. You have carrying parties gettin' ammunition out there—and now's the time to start. We oughta find out—what are they doing about this sort of thing? And I'm not talking about getting out there with a regiment. N-o-o-o-o, that's not what's out there. We oughta find out whether this is going on, and try it in several places—opposite Pleiku, out there along the border, and opposite Dak To, Ben Het, and so on. There should be patrols and all this sort of thing. Maybe the only way that something like that can be done effectively is with Sadler's people [SOG]. Now where those people have been working is farther out than the thing I'm talking about."

ABRAMS: "Like it's been done a lot of times." "The bastards were out there building those bunkers, getting that thing set up, getting the ammunition in there and the food in there and all that. And, when they were ready, they took the troops with it and started beating hell out of everybody. And if they're gonna try for Dak To, one of those places up there, put some pressure on Pleiku, try to raise hell, Kontum City, that preliminary work has to be done." "I'm talking about . . . coming boiling out of Cambodia and trying to raise hell with one of those major centers. And in order to do that they have to—I don't know if they have to, but anyway they do—make these preparations." "You shouldn't let 'em make all those preparations, and then the first thing you know about it is the whole damn thing starts."

4 NOV 1971: Secretary of Defense Laird Briefing

ATTENDEES: Amb. Bunker, Sec. Laird, Adm. Moorer, Amb. Berger, Hon. G. Warren Nutter, Hon. Daniel Henkin, Adm. McCain, Gen. Abrams, Gen. Weyand, MG Cowles, RADM L. R. Vasey, MG Potts, MG Fred Karhohs, MG John T. Carley, Mr. O. V. Armstrong (FSO-1), Mr. R. J. Jantzen (GS-17), BG Robert E. Pursley, BG J. J. Gorman (USAF), BG Thomas W. Brown (USA), Capt. T. Dwyer (USN), Col. A. J. Lynn (USAF), Col. Bennie Davis (USAF), Col. Clyde Clark (USA), Col. E. Markham (USA), Col. P. H. Stevens (USA).

BRIEFER: Begins with the enemy's infiltration system. GDRS. Key stations typically located 30 minutes' walking distance from the trail.

LAIRD: Asks about movement back north on the trail. Potts answers.

LAIRD: "This shows the numbers, for the first time, of people who have been down here for a long time going back north."

RESPONSE: Well, yes and no. Wounded from Lam Son 719.

BRIEFER: Island Tree, a database test program for use in targeting infiltrating personnel, began August 1971. Key data items are location of bivouac areas and schedules for arrival. Sowing sensors by air on probable sites.

ABRAMS: "It's probably going to be December before we have any considerable number of people [coming down as infiltrators] to work with."

BRIEFER: Compares 1970 logistics campaign indicators with 1971. Tri-border areas. The enemy's 1970 "transportation offensive" began in mid-October. Same pattern in 1971. Added feature: air defense elements deploying to protect the LOC. "We believe the start of the 1971 offensive is imminent."

ABRAMS: "We got about a 20 percent increase in input last year, and a 60 percent decrease in throughput. Lam Son 719 had something to do with that. The interdiction program had something to do with it."

ABRAMS (re these enemy logistical preparations): "I would say it's not an indicator of any relaxation of the attitude in Paris."

■ ■ ■

BRIEFER (re redeployment): "During your last visit you [Laird] directed that planning begin to reach an authorized ceiling of 60,000 by 1 September 1972. In March 1971 you were briefed in Washington on the MACV concept to attain that force level. That concept is now contained in MACV Op Plan 208. In response to additional guidance from your office and JCS, an alternative contingency plan, which we refer to as Op Plan 208 Alpha, has been developed to meet an authorized ceiling of approximately 60,000 spaces by 1 July 1972."

BRIEFER: Redeployment Increment 10 covers the period 1 December 1971–30 April 1972. 100,000 spaces to be redeployed under 208A. Thus 84,000 spaces on 1 May 1972, consisting of the authorized 60,000, some security, and a roll-up force.

ABRAMS: "That 60,000 augmentation is actually, Mr. Secretary, reached by 1 May. And what's left above that gets rid of the last of the equipment and supplies and so on not required, so that, when you get to 1 July, all the stuff's gone that should have gone and the people who did it have gone."

BRIEFER: Sixty thousand is referred to as "the sustaining force posture."

ABRAMS: "Whatever men we [still] have here, I think we've got to take good care of. Yeah—they've got to be able to go and see the movies, I stand for 'em bowling, I stand for 'em playin' tennis and volleyball, and they've gotta have a good mess, they've gotta have a good club, and, you know, those kinds of things. And I think if we don't try to—when you get wound down in a thing like this—if you don't try to take care of those men the best you can—I'm not talking about country clubs—no idea of that, and I'm not talking golf courses, but things that the bulk of the men can use—softball diamonds, all this kind of stuff. And that's going to cost us people to do that. That's been surfaced in the course of this thing, and we're going to do that. And I think you really have to in the environment out here."

■ ■ ■

LAIRD (referring to videotapes of NFL games): "How are you coming getting football games out here?"

SOMEONE: "They're just fooling around with it," but we've received at least one.

ABRAMS: "I saw it the other night—the Orioles [*sic*] and the Vikings. And that's the first football game we've had in two and a half weeks."

LAIRD: "Well, Jesus, you can do that—you can see the Washington Redskins—you can get that out here within 48 hours."

Should be able to, he seems to mean.

SOMEONE: "Well, we'll work on that tonight."

SOMEONE ELSE: "Because they're pretty good now." [Laughter]

ABRAMS: "One of the things that I observe is that football has actually become the sport that the men are most interested in. It's not because it's the football season, but they say the interest in football is higher than the interest in baseball. So these films are important to them. They follow it. I hope they don't get interested in that chess competition."

LAIRD: "We better call him [Pete Rozelle] up tonight."

■ ■ ■

SOMEONE: Raises the issue (as per a discussion with General Vien) of whether South Vietnamese forces would need any "permission," apparently from the United States, to make cross-border raids into Laos.

LAIRD: "I wouldn't worry about that, not in the Ho Chi Minh Trail area."

■ ■ ■

BRIEFER: VCI neutralizations are running at about 1,800 a month.

WEYAND (responding to Laird's questions about dealing with the VCI): "Actually, much of the success that's been achieved here since Tet of '68 is due to the fact that this infrastructure was, if not shattered, degraded. Because the enemy did put them out on the table, and many of them were destroyed. They have really not been able to rebuild that. This is what they're desperately trying to do."

WEYAND: "What has happened is that the friendly infrastructure has become stronger and stronger. . . . Now, with the elections, there's just an awful lot—as General Abrams says—chemistry at work which strengthens, day by day, the infrastructure of the government of Vietnam. And I make that point because what we're talking about is a relative balance of power here and the ability of the VCI to influence the people—to tax them, to recruit from them—is in some areas [now] nonexistent. . . . The enemy right now is in a state of . . . confusion, but their cadre really do not know what to do now. So while the attack against the VCI is a very necessary thing, I think the importance of it has relatively become less and less."

WEYAND: "They focused their entire energies on disrupting the election and Thieu's inauguration. When October 31st came and went [successful election and inauguration] they're really adrift, because they had no plans beyond that. So the sense of frustration, the sense of defeat, within these VCI cadres we're talking about is quite deep." "What all the intelligence agencies are now looking for is the enemy's new instructions to the cadres."

ABRAMS (re RF and PF): "It's a mixed bag. I don't know anyplace where it's not improving, and some places it's absolutely outstanding." "A guy like Truong— to him, his bread and butter are the Territorial Forces. That's the way he looks at it."

ABRAMS: "Our big problem in the future is gonna be reallocation—the shifting around of that manpower—the ARVN, the RF, the PF—to the places where it needs to be. And that's coming upon us pretty fast now."

ABRAMS: "The president [Thieu] wants to eliminate the PF in the coming year [here someone interjects "reduce"]—yeah, reduce by 100,000. Well, in the process you reduce it and then you eliminate the rest of it by making it RF."

WEYAND: "What you've got in this country now, unlike a couple of years ago, or say when I was out here before—instead of every place that you dip your finger in having a hell of a massive problem—you now have got problems that you can see, like seeing rocks at low tide, and there are a finite number of them. Some of them are geographical, at a place like Binh Dinh. Others are functional, like the National Police. . . . So it's kind of a management problem. The resources are here, in most cases, to do the job. . . . It's now a problem of getting it all together and focusing on the problem."

ABRAMS: "—he never seems to be able to get anything done on time or very fast. You get something that finally is going, and it's going pretty good—and then all of a sudden it's goin' _real_ good. And then, the next thing you know, there really isn't any _need_ for it anymore, but—hell, nobody'll give it up! It's like Go Cong—they've got 23 RF companies or something down there. Finally they got to the point where there was no VC left, and the VCI had either left or been captured or killed. So there wasn't anything for the RF to do. Of course, they had [a need for?] engineer work down there, so they put the RF to work building roads and so on. Well, hell—that's _good_. I mean, the province can use the roads and all that. It helps the peasants. But you also need more RF up in Quang Nhai. Quang Nhai doesn't _have_ enough RF in it. They've still got a lot of VC and so on. Well, I think somehow what they've gotta do is _give up_ the RF in Go Cong. It's hard to argue with them about it, because 'look at all these fine roads and trails—the farmers are using them' and so on. 'Isn't that wonderful!' Well, hell, it _is_ wonderful. You can't say it isn't. But, goddamn it, you oughta figure out another way to get that done. . . . You don't need any M16s, or M16 ammunition, to build roads. And you don't need any radios to build roads—no PRC-25s or PRC-10s. But they've got to be persuaded, and it finally comes down to the nub of telling the chief, and how are you going to get mad at him? Look at all the wonderful work he's done. And look at the fine condition his province is in. Look how happy his people are. Look at the turnout he had for the election. Look at the number of votes he had—99.9 or something for Thieu. Now, you take that on and go down there and say, 'Goddamn it, there'll be no more RF in this province beginning Monday!' We know it's right. It's gotta be solved . . . and in due time they'll see it themselves."

ABRAMS: "And, maybe more importantly, they'll find a Vietnamese way to get those out of there, keep the province chief happy—supply him with some trucks or graders or something for his highway department, something like that—where he'll be happy, and you can reapply the RF strength to some place where you really need the rifles and the radios and the mortars and the machine guns. But, looking back, there hasn't been an easy step taken here. Every step has been a struggle. And of course a lot of times we've gotten real enthusiastic about something that it turned out, when you got right down to it . . . turned out it wasn't too good an idea anyway—too American. So you have to be a little cautious about that."

ABRAMS: "Fred and I have been talking a lot recently about getting the right balance. This thing of territorials, of how much it ought to be and where it ought to be, and how much you ought to have in the regulars and where it ought to be. And that's why we've started talking to them about this thing of looking at III and IV Corps as an entity . . . and looking at the Vietnamese assets in there as a whole. And I think by summer that that's really going to be a very practical concept, because the delta will have moved along another six months by then. And they're doing very well down there, and they've got the strongest setup they've ever had. They've got the best leadership they've ever had, and it's of uniform excellence. There's only one man that needs to be moved down there. The lower fellows are getting moved by the chain of command, both on the province side and the purely military side."

ABRAMS: "Maybe by the end of next year there will be clearly a surplus of regular units in MR-3 and 4. And if, in the meantime, you've developed in them an attitude of moving about—if you get 'em where they can move 80 kilometers, or 100 kilometers, without thinking that that's about the end of the world, get 'em where they're doing that, then it's not so hard to move 'em 500 [kilometers]. It's all a state of mind. I think actually we may have hoped they would step up to the plate the way they have, but there certainly wasn't anybody that could guarantee it. But I think the truth of the matter is the Vietnamese have stepped up to the plate. There are a lot of things you can get unhappy about from time to time, but—well, it's like [word unclear] up there in the 2nd Division. He always feels he has to fight the reputation of the 1st Division. It's a sort of a cancer that works on him, that the 1st is the best and so on, and of course he doesn't believe that. He's like any division commander, he just won't believe that, whether it's true or not.

ABRAMS: "It's all starting to work together now. There's nothing that's strictly

military. Everything impinges on something else. You can see the thing as a
<u>unit</u> now, and you can see the weaknesses in it in places and you can see the
strengths in it."

ABRAMS: ". . . and they've got confidence in the future. They're not around beg-
ging for much of anything. They all, without exception, look to the strength
that's come from success at building within the community level among the
people. They all philosophically are pointed in that direction. The Chieu Hoi
guy—he wants to release <u>all</u> the VC prisoners. Well, some of them have gone
almost too fast too far, but they really are fine people. And I think they've got
the right idea in mind."

ABRAMS: "Now you take a thing like that Phuong Hoang thing—we can't just
turn loose of that, because it's driving the enemy crazy. But it's not just
Phuong Hoang, it's the RF and the PF out there on these interdiction things at
night, ambushing, and the VCI are just having a hell of a time moving around.
And more and more of them are having to live out in the woods instead of in
the hamlet or the village—the PSDF pick them up and stuff like that. But the
problem—and we'll continue to go full bore on that, all the publicity of identifying and publicizing their identity and all of that, but the damn program is one
that—there's no end to it. We can see now that we'll just go on and on with
this program, and it's not going to improve, and someday the United States
will have to get out of it and there's not going to be anything to take its place.
In other words, it's not building toward something that they'll take over. It's
just that simple."

ABRAMS: "So we've got to now crank into it the national level direction and
interest, the organization that will have the expertise to do this sophisticated
job, and the procedures that will be compatible with what we've learned
through all our investigative experience, and that are compatible with the security that you've gotta have. It's just like the CIA doesn't make a habit of
coming around telling everybody all of the information that they've got on
somebody that they're targeting. And the Vietnamese intelligence agencies are
no different. The police agencies—if they get something that's pretty good on
someone . . . he wants to keep it to himself. He's a little uneasy about telling
somebody from the ARVN or social welfare or something. I didn't want to let
you leave with the feeling that we're kinda—we are backing away from that
Phuong Hoang program, but in a very cautious way, and with the realization
that we've got to keep it going."

13 NOV 1971: WIEU

ATTENDEES: Amb. Bunker, Gen. Abrams, Gen. Weyand, Gen. Lavelle, LTG
McCaffrey, Mr. Jacobson, MG Eckhardt, MG Cowles, MG Bowley, MG Potts,
MG Wilson, MG Jumper, MG Adamson, MG Carley, Mr. Duval, BG John,
RADM Salzer, BG Trogdon, BG Brown, BG Bernstein, BG McClellan, BG Her-
bert, BG Lanagan, BG Wickham, Col. Zerbe, Col. Crockett, Col. Stevens.

POTTS: More people and more equipment, including the first instance of 130-mm guns, are going into the Plaine des Jarres than ever before.

ABRAMS: "It's kinda hard to figure out why they'd bring in 130s to work on those poor little Meos there." And: "They're [the 130-mm guns] hard to find."

BRIEFER: Indications are that the enemy plans to initiate his dry season tactical offensive earlier than he has in previous years, commencing in January or February.

BRIEFER: The DRV representative [Vo Van Sung, delegate general of the DRV to France] in Paris said privately in remarks on 11 and 15 October that "a new military offensive by North Vietnamese forces would occur in 1972 instead of 1973 as had been originally planned." Asked if the DRV had lost confidence in the PRG, Sung replied that "there has been some evidence of PRG loss of influence in certain sectors." He cited the unsuccessful PRG effort to control voting in the 3 October presidential election in areas claimed to be under VC control.

BRIEFER (re comments made mid-October 1971 by "a leftist front correspondent permanently assigned in Hanoi"): The correspondent "expressed deep disappointment that the imperialists were moving ahead at the same time that the socialist camp was weakening. He further stated that the Saigon regime had reinforced its position in the south and can now militarily hold its own, with American matériel support, but without American manpower."

■ ■ ■

ABRAMS: "If you had to order a bale of [word indistinct] for every time Jack Cushman comes out of his lair down there" in IV Corps (to make a pitch for more RF and PF, apparently)—.

SOMEONE: "You're not exposed to Wilbur <u>Wilson</u>!" [Laughter]

ABRAMS: "He was the one I was thinking about the other day when I got to talking with the SecDef about Go Cong. But when the joking's over, they've just hung in there and hung in there—."

ABRAMS: "What these territorials are doing is simply magnificent, but you can't go from there and say, 'Well, hell, the answer then is let's just have territorials.'" In places like the U Minh and Hau Nghia you need regulars to drive out the enemy before the Territorial Forces can move in and establish themselves. "Sometime in '72 I think that it's going to be crystal clear that we don't need some number of those regulars in the delta. Now, one of the effects of that is that it would [word indistinct] you to use in Cambodia [and elsewhere]. . . ."

CORDS BRIEFER: "The field police are extremely effective when properly utilized."

SOMEONE: "We've got a long way to go in the employment of these people."

ABRAMS: "They're like well-trained infantrymen who have also been trained as police. And the important thing is they've got the police power and the authority of police."

18 NOV 1971: Southeast Asia Assessment for COMUS

ATTENDEES: Gen. Abrams, Gen. Weyand, MG Cowles, MG Carley, BG Heiser, MG Potts.

BRIEFER: Forecast of enemy intentions and capabilities through June 1972. "Allied policies of attacking the [enemy's] total system have created difficulty, caused the enemy to continually reassess his situation, reorder priorities, and attempt countermeasures. Currently, the enemy is conducting protracted warfare. He was forced into this phase in 1969 after the failure of his four general offensives, which cost him heavily in men and matériel. Since the spring of 1970, Hanoi's problems have been further compounded by the change of government in Cambodia and the loss of the port of Kompong Som. Cross-border operations, allied air interdiction, great progress in the pacification and Vietnamization programs, and constant development of the Vietnamese armed forces have all continued to weaken the enemy's tactical and logistical posture."

■ ■ ■

ABRAMS (interrupting the briefer, who has just described enemy deployment of 16 130-mm guns in northern Laos): "Stop there. The 122 outshoots the artillery the Laotians have got. I don't know if it does the 155. I guess it does."
POTTS: "Yes, sir."
ABRAMS: "So why the hell would they go to the 130? They already have the Laotian forces outgunned with the 122. Why the hell would they go to the 130? It's more difficult to move up, and the goddamn tonnage when you get into ammunition just goes out—. Unless they've found out the 122 isn't very accurate or something."
POTTS: "We'll check that out."

■ ■ ■

BRIEFER: From Binh Tram 18 to the COSVN area = 120 days' travel time. To MR-TTH is 45 days. B-3 Front: 60 days. Per Potts: Trail attrition is calculated at 15 percent.
ABRAMS: "What they've been doing with that B-3 Front, even this year, that's been a sideshow. And I thought it was done principally to get the general reserve committed in there so they could be more successful in MR-1 [by getting] as much as they can of the general reserve tied down. It hasn't really been a main—it's been used sort of in that role—create as much hob as you can, and—but it's not really a serious effort with some sort of territorial gain in mind."
POTTS: "We've had a number of indicators that the B-3 Front is the next place we'll see increased enemy activity."

The B-3 Front is the enemy's designation for the Central Highlands.

ABRAMS: "That thing about the B-3 Front bothers me because it upsets my view of what they oughta be doing. They're not doing things right."

ABRAMS (bringing back the briefer who began the session by stating the enemy objective and having him read it again): "The enemy goal in Southeast Asia remains complete domination of the Republic of Vietnam and establishment of a sphere of influence throughout Indochina. North Vietnam's designs on South Vietnam continue to be based on the desire to reunite the Vietnamese people under a Communist government."

ABRAMS: "Yep. Well, now! That phrase has been used a long time. But it seems to me—without trying to get, you know, really rolling the rhetoric out and sort of larding it down with adjectives and adverbs—something about, 'The evidence available, the intelligence available, the facts available indicate that Hanoi's intention and plan for Laos, South Vietnam, and Cambodia remain unchanged. In fact, the evidence of their continuing design on Laos, Cambodia, and South Vietnam is supported by an overwhelming mass of evidence.' I think the only problem is I kinda get tired of that. There's nothing wrong with it. It's correct. I can't even argue with it. But I want to give it a little stronger— I guess that's what I'm looking for, something stronger—if anybody that's got any funny ideas about this thing, and about these fellows, this should disabuse them of that. And the tone of the whole thing should be set at the outset. Now the rest of all that follows just supports that. So just try your hand—as I say, nothing wrong. It's right, it's correct, but I wanta give it a little more—I think it can be done with—and you're not exaggerating."

■ ■ ■

POTTS: "The [South] Vietnamese had this theory, for a long time going back to the '60s—they could see the enemy coming into the highlands and going all the way down Route 19 to Qui Nhon, cutting off the northern half of the country."

ABRAMS (re the enemy's four offensives in 1968 and 1969): "One of the things about that that's always been kind of interesting to me—he knew very well that that was gonna be a bloody mess. They had to put those fellows [replacements for the casualties they knew they were going to take] in—given the training, and in those numbers—months ahead."

POTTS: "Six months ahead."

ABRAMS: "So he knew it was—his planning was pretty good. When you talk about the general staff up there, and manpower and so on—Christ, I wish we could get the same kind of interest in manpower here."

■ ■ ■

ABRAMS (on what to do to conclude the assessment briefing): "I think the two things that should be highlighted are the magnitude of the effort in Barrel Roll—the northern Plaine des Jarres exceeds anything in terms of the manpower indications, the 130-mm artillery—and, incidentally, I would like to know why they sent that in when they have 122s already . . . , and the B-3 Front. Those in the near term are the focus of his tactical effort."

20 NOV 1971: Commanders WIEU

BRIEFER: Gives latest infiltration estimates.

POTTS: "Sir, you'll notice that in both these areas [RVN and Cambodia] the [infiltration group numbering] sequence has started over. 2001 here, 2001 over here. Now the sequence in both those areas started in early 1968. And here in the B-3 Front they built up to 3088, in COSVN 2299. And it's starting over after a four-year period. Before 1968 they used a three-digit number, and they were in sequence starting back in 1964." In the B-3 Front they have numbers with suffixes A and B. These may indicate tactical units. The total for the B-3 Front for 1971 is going to equal four times the number for the previous year. December 1971 saw the largest one-month influx into the B-3 Front. Total for 1971 will be about 16,000.

ABRAMS: Recalls the 1965 Battle of the Ia Drang: "In terms of the whole country, that was a rather significant effort. Since that time, there really hasn't been anything with the potential of going deep that that seems to have been designed to do. Regularly you've had these battles in Dak Seang and around Kontum City and so on, but those really, I think, were limited objectives. Although they put a lot into them, nevertheless they had limited objectives."

ABRAMS (re the buildup in the B-3 Front): "We need to think about this quite a bit. I'd be the first to say that I didn't think he was going to play the hand this way, frankly. I think what he's been doing for the last year and a half, certainly the last year, is to try to cause enough mischief up there in the highlands to tie down some of the general reserve—as much of it as he could. Get 'em to commit 'em up there to ease his problem in MR-1, or possibly in MR-2, or some other place. But this portends something more than that. And so . . . this needs a lot of study and a lot of thought. This cross-border thing, that whole idea now needs to be reexamined in the light of this intelligence."

ABRAMS (re Island Tree): "The last time I was briefed on that, although there's a lot of good work going on, it's a hell of a far cry from having a target. We have to know what we're doing, and there has to be more than hope, because it [counterinfiltration] does take away from something else."

Island Tree is an innovative and experimental program of interdicting personnel (as opposed to matériel) coming down the Ho Chi Minh Trail.

ABRAMS: "They're on their way—there's no question about that. The significant thing is the amount of stuff that they've sent into the B-3 Front. Now I don't <u>know</u> whether the B-3 Front has the responsibility to pass through to MR-5, or MR-6—VC MR-5 or MR-6.

POTTS: "They've never had that."

ABRAMS: "So that's another thing you wonder about. The B-3 Front is a separate command from MR-6 or MR-5, and MR-5—normally their replacements come from up above—they don't pass through MR-5."

POTTS: "The B-3 Front has the highest ranking enemy commander."

ABRAMS: "Now, there's another thing about this. I never have really quite understood it. You remember last summer they came out into Pleiku with some of the 24th and some of the 95 Bravo. II Corps went ahead and made some deployments up there, kind of on top of it in a way, and there never really was any real battle. And then finally 95 Bravo and the 24th moved back into Cambodia. This was the second impulse. They never really got up and got going. The Vietnamese—the ARVNs and the rest of them—were out there, but nothing ever came of that. Now that's a little—why that?"

POTTS: Perhaps it was to protect the infiltration stream from any cross-border operations.

ABRAMS: "Do we have any comparisons of the strength there in the highlands with the strength in previous years?"

POTTS: "I'm not sure we have. But it's going to be the most it's ever been."

■ ■ ■

BRIEFER: Quotes recent Premier Pham Van Dong exhortation: "More than ever advance to complete victory, defeat completely Vietnamization and the war, and topple the puppet regime and smash their pacification scheme."

ABRAMS: "One of the interesting things about that—I don't think it means too much, and maybe it doesn't mean anything, but they've been forced to take two of the words that were invented in the south—Vietnamization and pacification—they've been forced to take those two words and start using them. Now that's not the way it was in '65. Hell, they weren't copying anything that was said down here."

ABRAMS: "It doesn't change much, but [it shows that] it's gotten under their skin. Of course, those two words mean not a <u>damn</u> thing to the people of North Vietnam. As far as home consumption is concerned it must be a complete zero. . . . But they must do that because it's sinking in that those two words have taken a hold somehow."

ABRAMS: "It's kind of like this young student who burst into my daughter's room a couple of weeks ago at American University. She announced that she was antiwar, antimilitary, antiviolence, and antigovernment. She was selling subscriptions to a newspaper whose title was *The Militant*." [Laughter]

BRIEFER: Presents the "Southeast Asia Assessment" that Abrams had previewed two days previously. Someone suggests that a summary be added at the end, to include acknowledgment that the enemy is capable of a major offensive operation in the next year.

ABRAMS: Agree. "We should probably look for that in MR-1. We're talking July, August, September. . . . It could be close enough to the election to have an impact." Not later because of the onset of seasonal bad weather. "And I would think it would most likely be MR-1 where that would occur. You have to watch the B-3 Front. . . . I think those are the two principal places."

ABRAMS: "I continue to think, though, that if the GVN continues to maintain the command structure that they've got in MR-1—that's a very capable command structure. It's got a lot of real skills—talking about planning, and the integration of intelligence, and operations. Some of the executions out there, carried out by the Vietnamese, are as good as anybody does it. So you've got that. It may get pretty heavy going up there. And also there seems to be a mutual confidence and respect among those seniors."

ABRAMS: "You clearly don't have that situation in MR-2, nor do you have it in MR-3. I do think you've got it in MR-4. The problem, really, is much different, but I think you've got the same kind of thing down there. . . . Some used to splutter [mutter?] about General [name unclear] and the 21st Division and his relationship with General Truong. That doesn't [now] seem to be a matter of professional significance. The two men, of course, are fighters. Their personal habits are really quite different. But that all seems to be worked out."

SOMEONE: "We have as high a quality of Vietnamese leadership as we have ever had."

■ ■ ■

ABRAMS (re the HES—Hamlet Evaluation System—statistics): "One of the things I sort of wonder about—these percentages have been prominent on the charts since late '68. And they've been described as a management device—specific, but never important, just a trend, a rough line. Among other things that it's been, it's become sort of a report card. I'm satisfied that, even in its role of a report card, it was a good thing. Remember in the beginning, the president himself used to go out. He made all of the corps areas two times in that initial Accelerated Pacification Program. And he—all the province chiefs there—and he critiqued them, he put his finger on where and what was wrong. And he had some kind of a measuring device to go to—'That was supposed to be 60 percent, that was the goal, and you're not at 60 percent, now what's the matter?' You know, that kind of thing."

ABRAMS: "But it seems to me that in a good many [places] the situation has gotten to the point where now the way to get ahead is to throw out the report card and start thinking about what basically and fundamentally this meant. You know, what really does it mean in terms of—well, sociological factors, and how does a country get to be independent, how does it get to be self-sufficient, how does it get to be secure? I'm sure you're always going to need two or three or something divisions if you're going to be up against Communists, but the best security against Communists is their government working down there in some way, and the people are working, and somehow it's gotten together and there's some respect and confidence. And so people, instead of burying their piasters in a wooden box under the bed, will buy a tractor with it. He'll not only pay for the tractor, but he makes more money. You know, that's—and if the people get kind of where they think it's going pretty good, as they see it, it's gonna be hard for another guy to come in there and start peddling something else. You know, 'We've got a better scheme, these are just a bunch of bastards you're fooling around with. We've got a real scheme.'"

ABRAMS: "Well, you can't—it's awful hard, in our country for instance, to defeat an incumbent president if you're in a period of prosperity. I mean, they could say all kinds of bad things about him, say he spends more time playing golf than he does running the country, or he's taken long weekends, or start rumors about he doesn't kiss his wife good-bye in the morning, but you can't touch him if the country's prosperous. <u>But</u> I'm just wondering if, in a lot of places— not only in terms of the kinds of province chiefs that largely exist now in a good many of the provinces—if there's some period down the road where you go to talk or have meetings and this kind of a chart doesn't come up any more, it's not necessary. You still have HES, and you're still getting the reports and so on, but that's not the way the meeting goes. You get into the fundamentals of what really counts for this country, and what are the things now that'll get it—. In other words, you've gotten so far, and you really need something to replace—a new term. I don't even think new charts—I don't even like to <u>think</u> in charts. Something to replace all the impetus of the Accelerated Pacification Program in November of '68. The highway department—instead of checking the guy on how many green hamlets he's got—the number of green [probably he means non-green] hamlets that're left in the country is probably small enough so that they'd probably be eliminated if all the highway departments were good. You don't even need more RF and PF. <u>Somewhere</u> you're getting in that thing where <u>that</u> stuff gets moving. I don't know when that great day will come, but I think some places it's pretty near."

■ ■ ■

BRIEFER: "The years 1968, 1969, and 1970 saw significant advances in the expansion of security throughout South Vietnam." "The improvement in security has been due in great part to increase in both the quality and quantity of Territorial Forces. During this period Territorial Forces were brought into C-rated and D-rated areas and, through their own operations and operations of other friendly forces, the security in these areas was upgraded."

■ ■ ■

SEVENTH AIR FORCE BRIEFER: Shows a slide depicting strikes during the week under review. Long silence while Abrams contemplates it.

ABRAMS: "I'd like to raise a question about [word indistinct]. 750 VNAF strike sorties in South Vietnam. Enemy activity's at really a pretty low level in South Vietnam, and I wonder what they're bombing out there. For instance, we talk about how much fighting's going on in different countries. There's a lot more fighting going on in Cambodia than there is in South Vietnam. 9th Division, 1st Division—those are the only two enemy divisions that are active."

SOMEONE: There are 38 sorties allocated per division per day, and "not being used very well," representing "a substantial waste of assets."

This leads to an extended professional discussion lasting about 30 minutes.

SOMEONE (re RVNAF utilization of air): "The problems go both ways, both to requests for support [from the United States] and use of VNAF assets."

SOMEONE (else?): "We need to get VNAF and ARVN coordinating better. They're just not communicating very well."

SOMEONE: The quality of air support is better in III Corps than in II Corps for two major reasons. There is a much better Vietnamese colonel in charge, and in III Corps the corps headquarters and the air division are located together, whereas in II Corps the corps is in Pleiku and the air division in Nha Trang.

ABRAMS: "You don't have to have those elements co-located. At least thinking of our own setup. That's what makes airmen, air officers, that's what makes the whole damn thing work, except when it gets snarled up, and then somebody from headquarters goes down there and kicks it around. . . . The mechanism down there, that's what makes it work. Isn't that right?"

SOMEONE: "Yes, sir."

ABRAMS: "—the <u>American</u> system."

SOMEONE: "There's nothing wrong with the [VNAF] flying skills. One thing about those pilots—they don't have a DEROS."

SOMEONE: "In Lam Son 719, when I went up and got that briefing—you sent me up to talk to Khang. And you [apparently meaning Abrams] laid on the air to help him. I came back and got General Vien. He tried to get eight A-1s up into I Corps out of II Corps. He has no authority to do that. He's gotta go to JGS, and JGS has gotta get the two MR commanders to agree, one to let 'em go and the other to accept 'em. Never got 'em up there. He tried and tried."

SOMEONE: "From II Corps's standpoint, it isn't as good as it looks. I just wanted you to be aware of the problem. The hours are obviously being flown. My contention is a hell of a lot of the hours that are being flown are not mission oriented and they're not for the purposes which are reflected here."

SOMEONE: "I just have to say that the Vietnamese senior generals don't understand how to use tac air, and they're being educated generally."

SOMEONE: "The reason that the ARVN commanders up in II Corps, the corps commander and the division commanders, don't really get into this more is they have looked [for] so long to the U.S. advisor to take care of the helicopter requirements that they just turn to the U.S. advisors and ask them to solve the problem with the VNAF or in turn cover it with U.S. air."

ABRAMS: "The answer is education and experience, and recrimination has no place in it. Everybody's gotta rise above that, and get down to the <u>serious</u> work of how in time it's solved. And it's solved by education and training. It's not an ethnic hangup, like there are some kind of people who are never going to be able to do it, just because they're Vietnamese—not at all."

SOMEONE: "An essential element is to recognize you have the problem. There has been a use of statistics on a [word indistinct] basis to . . . say we don't have a problem. And we do have a problem." One conclusion "I've come to about statistics in Vietnam is that all of them are false. [Nobody laughs.] And it does tend to obscure getting to the solution. . . ."

SOMEONE: "Over the last eight years, and particularly the last six, with the presence of so many helicopter gunships, the close air support capability of VNAF . . . has really become disused." "The overwhelming majority of our fixed-wing combat support now is dropping of bombs, and it's almost become a lost art [referring, apparently, to close air support]. At one time it was the predominant means of support. This is the decisive element in ground combat."

■ ■ ■

BRIEFER: "The analysis of BDA available indicates that the payoff in terms of damage inflicted on the enemy is low in comparison with the effort expended." This comes from a "special analysis on the employment of VNAF airpower." Period: 15 October–15 November. Fixed wing. In-country. In MR-1: "No clear-cut correlation between the level of ground contacts reported and tac air sorties flown."

ABRAMS: "We should have had Joe Alsop here. He's the one saying we didn't give 'em enough—they didn't have enough air. That's not the problem."

23 NOV 1971: Ambassador Godley Brief

G. McMurtie Godley is the American ambassador to Laos.

ABRAMS: "Up in MR-1, we've taken out all but the last brigade of the 23rd. And in December and January two brigades of the 101 will go out. They're [the South Vietnamese] in the process of organizing the 3rd Division in northern MR-1, a new division. So they'll have quite a full platter in Military Region 1. On the other hand, Military Region 1 and Military Region 4 have got the solidest command setup, in terms of skill and that sort of thing, that the Vietnamese have. And, beginning next year, they should have use of the general reserve. . . ."

ABRAMS: "And Military Region 1 is the easiest for the enemy to mount a military action of any real size. And it's expected that that would occur sometime next year. . . . Of course, it's not dry season in MR-1. Toward the end of next month it starts to get a little better, historically, but it's bad. It's bad weather and so on, and as a matter of fact has historically constrained the enemy until after the first of the year."

ABRAMS: "In '68, in the month of February, we had five days that tac air could be used at all in northern MR-1—five days. . . . We flew a battery of 8-inch self-propelled by C-133 from Chu Lai to Phu Bai because—a fairly extraordinary measure—you needed fire support in there and you just couldn't fly. And—just to go on with war stories—the first C-133—we decided one evening to do that, and the next noon the first C-133 was orbiting over Phu Bai and the goddamn control went out of the tower. I don't know why it is, but the only place those refuel is at Clark [Air Base in the Philippines], so after circling for an hour or something like that, they flew off to Clark and refueled. The 8-inch gun crew walked out of the 133 thinking they were landed at Phu Bai, and they were at Clark—beautiful weather, and of course no war. They refueled and flew back, and it was landed at Phu Bai that evening."

ABRAMS: "So it's a bad weather time right now. In Military Region 2—first of all, the Vietnamese do not have the strength in their command structure in Military Region 2. There's no way—you haven't got the professional skill, and you haven't got the depth in the command structure you've got in Military

Region 1 and 4. And plus right now you've got all kinds of indications. . . ." "Something's in the mill for the B-3 Front. There's bound to be some heavy fighting up there."

ABRAMS: "The way the South Vietnamese are looking at the two southern military regions [MR-3 and MR-4]—the Vietnamese have got three regular divisions in MR-3, and they've got three regular divisions in MR-4. The way they're now approaching this problem is they're looking at that as six divisions—they're not going to dissolve military regions—any of which can be used in either region, or across border, certainly for 60 days or that sort of thing. If they don't get a chance, at least every two months, of being with their families, you just run into a very severe desertion problem. It's just part of the thing."

ABRAMS: "Over on the other side, the enemy's got the 5th, 9th, 7th, and the 1st Divisions. Well, the way to play that is to play it with these six, regard the six as an entity. If all of that works out, and these cooperative arrangements with the Khmer and that sort of thing—we hope that that sort of thing will be adequate so that the two divisions of the general reserve, the airborne and the marines, are freed of any requirement in these two military regions. That means it makes them available for Military Region 1 or 2. But later on, if this gets into solid enough shape, you can then consider significant shifts of military manpower from Military Regions 3 and 4 into Military Regions 1 and 2. And that would be sometime after next summer. And then that opens up opportunities of real serious consideration of what can be done in Laos."

ABRAMS: "I would like to comment on the business of the Vietnamese and what they might do in Laos. There isn't going to be any Lam Son 719 kind of operation. And the big difference is that the American participation in that is really massive. And that's kind of important. Because it was so dependent on us, it was entirely acceptable to work out the relations with the Lao through U.S. government agencies."

ABRAMS: Cites operation recently begun toward Truk rubber plantation over toward Kompong Som, done "largely with Vietnamese resources. Now when you get in that sort of a ball game, they really don't want any advice from us on the tactics, the scheme of maneuver. . . . I mean, they're the ones that are out there doing all the dying, and they're doing all of the work, and so on. So it has to be theirs. And see, in a very real sense, we are trying to work ourselves out of a job. Now we're not going to be completely out, that's for sure, but a year from now we're not going to be in a position of influence with the JGS and the Vietnamese that we have even today."

GODLEY (re Laos): "Even if the prime minister asks for the ARVN to go in to the border area, and the ARVN goes in, he's going to have to protest. He'll do it in a mild way, the way he did in Lam Son 719."

ABRAMS: "Lon Nol has the same problem. He has to ask President Thieu to send troops, and then he has to criticize the Vietnamese troops for depredations and so on. He has an internal political problem that he has to deal with."

ABRAMS: "This country is beginning to get its feet kind of under it, and with that is also a certain amount of pride, a little bit of nationalism occasionally kind of shows through, and President Thieu so far—everything that's been done by his forces in Cambodia is backed up by an official request in writing. So internationally politically he's kept the record clean."

ABRAMS: "This country now—one of the critical things is to get the economy moving. And the circumstances are such that it can move, and it must. They've got to be a little careful about what they do, that they don't put that in jeopardy. The areas for planting sugarcane, the areas for lumber harvesting, and fishing, and all those things now has got to be able to prosper. And this impinges to some at least minor degree on what they can afford to do in their military establishment."

■ ■ ■

ABRAMS: "I think it's fair to say that Island Tree hasn't really produced a hard target yet. Isn't that right?"

POTTS: "That's right."

ABRAMS (re Island Tree): "It all started with sort of an enthusiasm that the key to this would be to start killing people instead of killing trucks. That's the way the whole thing started. The idea was [that] no one's ever paid any attention to people—we've been mesmerized with trucks. So that's what we've been working with. You get in here now and start getting down to brass tacks of really hitting targets that are people and it's a tough problem. That damn system he's got over there—you know, it's so complex, and actually I don't know whether you'd ever really know which key station they're gonna be stopping at. Because sometimes they just arbitrarily change it themselves, and sometimes they just keep moving and won't stop at that one, stop at the next one. It's not one trail, it's a complex of trails. We're not sparing any effort to get at it, but I'm not optimistic at this time that we're going to be able to attrit it by 50 percent."

SOMEONE: "The spokesman was Leonard Sullivan, who came out here about three months ago as the harbinger of tidings of great joy. His last trip here, which was about a month—he went back, not discouraged, but with his tail pretty much between his legs."

ABRAMS: "You notice he gathered momentum as he approached the Mall." [Laughter] "But I think it's getting a little more reasonable. Frankly, Mr. Ambassador, one of the first things I did on that thing was to declare a moratorium on any comments until we could all cool off. There's no point in sending in a [word unclear] prediction."

ABRAMS: "It's kinda like trying to focus in on this personnel infiltration. It's true that we're giving it a lot more attention and a lot more study, and maybe something worthwhile will come out of it. So I don't mind making the intelligence effort. I think that's a good thing. You see, they didn't do that. I mean they just made a quick estimate and then went out and bought some planes—ordered them. W-e-l-l, now, it isn't all that—. There may be some good things. One should never overlook the possibility of a new idea, but there's an awful lot more in that than new ideas. There's just an awful lot of crap in that, too. That's the problem."

4 DEC 1971: WIEU

ATTENDEES: Amb. Bunker, Amb. Berger, Gen. Abrams, Gen. Weyand, MG Eckhardt, MG Cowles, MG Schweiter, MG Maples, MG Jumper, MG Potts, MG Adamson, MG Watkins, MG Slay, RADM Salzer, BG Trogdon, BG Heiser, BG Lanagan, BG Wickham, Mr. Chambers, Col. Knepp, Col. Sadler, Capt. Perez, Col. Houseworth, Col. Crockett, Col. Stevens.

POTTS: "We see the emphasis still on the B-3 Front. 1970: 5,600 total to the B-3 Front. In 1971: 19,000, of which 6,300 come in in December. And now for January 1,800, and for February 1,800. And when four gap groups are filled in it will be 5,600 just for January and February, the same as for all of 1970."

■ ■ ■

ABRAMS: "I was over here, when I was going over there Sunday mornings for the CMD meeting—they had a damn formal ceremony over there and decorated a goose. That's right! They put them in a pen outside the outpost. And there's no way to sneak up on a goose at night. They just start going, just creating a hell of a racket. They're better than a dog. And this goose had alerted the outpost, they'd made a successful defense, and the Vietnamese were decorating the goose. And by god nobody was laughing!" [Laughter]

JACOBSON: "The program fell apart when they started eating them."

ABRAMS: "Meantime, of course, Jack Lavelle was developing all these exotic sensors—flying platforms and so on. And Christ, the cheapest sensor you can get—the goose. And as George points out, it does a good job for a year, then you can eat it on Christmas. You just win all the way around."

SOMEONE: "MR-2 has a program to raise them for just that purpose. Not only that, he's trying to figure out some way to arm them, because they're very aggressive." [Laughter]

■ ■ ■

ABRAMS: "I want to be sure that we're giving all the attention to the B-3 Front— intelligence collection and so on—that we think is appropriate. I think I would have to say right now that I don't believe I quite understand the import of all this infiltration that presumably is going to the B-3 Front. In terms of the structure he's got there, that's a hell of a lot of replacements. And, as you pointed out, he's adding some to the structure, too, with those groups that are lettered."

■ ■ ■

BRIEFER: Cites COSVN Directive 39, "On Conducting a 1971 Reorientation Phase in the Party." COSVN released two training studies in November 1971

to implement portions of the directive. One concerns the VC counterpacification program, and observes that "the GVN has succeeded in relocating people
into GVN-controlled areas, expanded its territorial security forces, and gained
the support of segments of the rural population through the Land to the Tiller
program."

■ ■ ■

ABRAMS: "I think General Minh ought to be thinking about the B-3 Front, too.
Sooner or later they're all going to have to deal with it."

6 DEC 1971: Drug Briefing for COMUSMACV and DEPCOMUSMACV

*MACV is experiencing continuing frustration at not being allowed by the current
rules of engagement to attack hostile fighters and surface-to-air missiles posing a
threat to friendly aircraft.*

ABRAMS and WEYAND: Discuss a press briefing in Washington by Daniel
Henkin and Friedenheim [*sic:* should be "Friedheim"] in which, per Abrams,
"the reporters seemed to be worried about these MiGs that followed some of
our aircraft or something. And finally Dan quieted them all down by telling
them, 'General Abrams has all the authority he needs to protect the lives of the
Americans who are out there. He'll report what he's done.'"

*Henkin was then assistant secretary of defense for public affairs. Jerry Friedheim
was his deputy.*

WEYAND: "'If [laughing] he needs additional authorities, he'll request them!'"
ABRAMS: "Yeah, he did, he said that, too, which showed that I was a member of
the team."
WEYAND: "Maybe they'll start keeping track of those requests like protective
reactions. 'General Abrams has just made the hundred and second request.'"
ABRAMS: "I guess we better start a thing going where we release, prior to its
receipt in Washington, each request. It would just be following up on what Dan
told them about asking for things."
WEYAND: "Well, I'll tell you one thing. I'll bet you there's somebody in Hanoi,
when they read that, started looking for their steel pot. [Laughter all around]
They're not sure just whether or not that might be true. It might have some
ripple effect. I know if I was up there, knowing what kind of a sneaky bastard
you are—." [Laughter]

■ ■ ■

BRIEFER: Progress report on the drug program. On 1 August 1971, COMUS-
MACV tasked J-2 to set up an intelligence effort relating to drugs. Called "Tan
Turtle." It involved establishing a data base.

ABRAMS: "What got us started talking and thinking about this was that the whole drug thing is very important from the standpoint of our government, and when you stood back and looked at what our government was doing out here it was very frightening. If you took the total U.S. government effort, there were certain islands of information that were not really being pulled together—not looking at it from the MACV standpoint, but from the U.S. government's. If some kind of mechanism could be established that would make a coherent and cohesive effort for the U.S., MACV was more than delighted to play whatever role in that they could play."

ABRAMS: "Mr. Mills, in the Mission Council, has admitted that he is the head of the American effort in Vietnam on drugs. And I think we shouldn't argue with him on that. We're playing a part, and we're going to play our part the best way we know how. And it doesn't make too much difference who's in charge of it."

BRIEFER: On 29 September 1971 the Narcotics Working Group at the embassy met for the first time.

ABRAMS (re reported VC involvement in drug distribution): "You know the history of agent reporting. When the agents learn what you're interested in, they begin to furnish what you're interested in."

ABRAMS: "One of the things that sort of puzzles me about this—I don't know how many caches have been found by us and the Vietnamese—all kinds of things, and I don't remember _ever_ hearing of marijuana or heroin being in a cache. Maybe we've just been unlucky, or it follows another system."

ABRAMS (reacting to suggestions that urinalysis and education programs are having some success): "The way for that to come out would be for someone in the press to charge that MACV is withholding information on this matter from the American public, and demand in a fairly dramatic fashion that we tell the whole story. _Oh_, that would be a great day! On down there some day in the cross-examination of the MACV press officer they would be able to report that they had wheedled this information out over the _objections_ of the press officer. Then it would be pretty authentic."

ABRAMS: "I'd be a little careful where this briefing is presented. Right now it's more positive in tone than the intelligence justifies."

8 DEC 1971: B-3 Front Assessment

Attendees: Gen. Abrams, MG Cowles, BG Heiser, BG Lanigan, MG Potts.

BRIEFER: "The VC B-3 Front includes all of four provinces and parts of five others in Military Region 2 of the Republic of Vietnam." "A principal north-south infiltration and logistics corridor is included within the sparsely populated highland region." Three important enemy base areas are located adjacent to the western region of the B-3 Front: BA 609 (in the tri-border area), BA 701, and BA 702 (west of Pleiku, north and south of Route 19).

BRIEFER: "Traditionally, enemy strategy has visualized an attack from the high-lands of the B-3 Front to the east coast designed to separate the northern provinces from the rest of the country."

BRIEFER: In November 1965 "the Ia Drang Valley of the B-3 Front was the scene of the first division-sized VC/NVA attack in the RVN."

BRIEFER: "One of the most significant indicators at this time is [the substantial increase in] the total number of personnel replacements detected in the pipeline for the B-3 Front." The 1971 Infiltration Estimate now stands at approximately 19,000 for the B-3 Front. In 1970 it was 5,600. Of the 1971 total, 6,300 are projected for December arrival (compared to 1968: 0, 1969: 0, 1970: 0). The B-3 Front is getting 27 percent of the total for 1971. It got 10 percent in each of the prior three years. We now project 3,600 for arrival in the B-3 Front during January–February 1972; there are also four gap groups, which could bring that to 5,600, equalling the total for this area for all of 1970.

BRIEFER: Additional indicators: Apparent expansion of B-3 responsibility west-ward into Cambodia, expansion of force structure, efforts to expand and improve supporting base areas, infiltration of such specialists as sappers and political cadre. Road building. "In the past, such changes have preceded an increase in tactical activity." Agent reports, captured documents, and PW inter-rogations. Increased patrolling.

BRIEFER: "The B-3 Front and northern Military Region 1 are the two areas in the Republic of Vietnam where the enemy currently possesses his greatest capability."

POTTS: "It's there, that capability is there."

ABRAMS: "Talking with President Thieu yesterday—he doesn't give all his rea-sons or anything, but the way he sees it, it would break out in the B-3 Front about the 15th of January, something like that. And he thinks that it would probably last a month or so. It might be a little more, the heavy part of it. And then he thinks about 1 April is when MR-1 will be involved. Some of that he— I told him, I said, 'Well,' I thought it would be kind of bad if they had them both at the same time. This has to do with what you do with the general reserve."

ABRAMS: "I talked to Mr. Shackley yesterday about this situation, too, and he's aware of it. And, you know, Mr. Shackley has access in some areas to some penetrations that, you know, can tell what the district committee or the provin-cial committee, what they're having their meetings about. I don't know if there're any assets up there or not. But I asked him if there was anything from there, and he said we ought to press on, because if there—sooner or later, I would think, if they're going to have a campaign, the provincial committee has got to be brought into it, because they assist in some of that. And that ought to be coming out at the 'Saturday WIEU' or something that the VC have."

9 DEC 1971: Briefing, Vietnamization of Intelligence

BRIEFER: "No attempt has been made to develop Vietnamese intelligence capabilities equal to those the U.S. has had in Southeast Asia, particularly concerning out-country collection."

BRIEFER: RVNAF J-2 Colonel Lung "is a dedicated, competent professional supported by an excellent and continually improving staff."

BRIEFER: "The Republic of Vietnam has developed a professional military intelligence organization capable of satisfying virtually all in-country Vietnamese intelligence requirements." But "Vietnamese capability for out-country collection, vital to the defense of South Vietnam, is just in the early stages of development."

■ ■ ■

ABRAMS: "With respect to the last thing that was said, I have eliminated 'residual force' from my vocabulary. I'd appreciate the staff doing the same thing."

ABRAMS: "Actually, in the military lexicon, when you talk 'force' you're talking squadrons of aircraft, flotillas of ships, battalions and brigades—artillery battalions, helicopter battalions—that's 'force.' Or logistics for a support command, that sort of thing, that's 'force.' Five thousand advisors doesn't fit that. Someday we'll say—or I would say—we have no military forces left in South Vietnam, and Senator Fulbright will say, 'Well, what the hell is that 70,000?' Well, we'll both be right, but can't talk to each other."

10 DEC 1971: Special Assessment Briefing

A comprehensive account of the situation as viewed by MACV at this juncture.

ABRAMS: "Last night I was reading President Johnson's book that covers this whole period—a formidable document to digest in one night, but I was thumbing through it, and it has quite a bit in it about affairs out here. What little I glossed over I don't think would be useful to our [analysis?] here. We've got access to a wider range of documents."

BRIEFER: The purpose is to discuss various enemy directives over the past four years, correlate them with developments at the Paris peace talks, and provide a forecast for the near future. Tasked by General Abrams to put this together.

■ "COSVN Resolution 5, adopted in late 1967, and which implemented Resolution 13 of the Lao Dong Party, commented on the failures of the GVN and the U.S. during the 1965–1966 and the 1966–1967 dry seasons. Convinced that the allies were unable to conduct counteroffensives against the Communists, COSVN advocated the initiation of the General Offensive and Uprising to gain a quick and decisive victory."

■ "The 12-month period following the Tet Offensive was characterized generally by a still-firm adherence to the philosophy of the General Offensive.

COSVN Resolutions 6, 7, and 8, released from March to October 1968, emphasized the main objective of a complete military victory through a series of offensive phases in which the control of urban areas was the key to strategic success. The control of rural areas was still viewed as of only secondary importance. Although Directive 58, released in December 1968, drew attention to the necessity of disrupting the newly announced Accelerated Pacification Campaign, VC action during this period generally emphasized offensive action. Similarly, the advent of the Paris peace talks was treated rather lightly by COSVN. In late February 1969 COSVN stated that cadres should not expect to see results from the talks. Rather the struggle in South Vietnam would be won only on the battlefield."

■ "The first indication of a revision in COSVN's strategy for South Vietnam, and a reversion to the tactics of a protracted struggle, appeared in April 1969 with the release of Directive 81. This directive warned cadres of the impossibility of destroying one million ARVN and U.S. forces and called for a limited victory rather than a clear-cut, complete victory. Accordingly, cadre were to struggle for decisive successes to force withdrawal of American troops and establishment of a coalition government."

■ "The reversion to protracted struggle was completed with the promulgation of COSVN Resolutions 9, 10, and 14 during the period July to November 1969. Resolution 9 remains today the basic policy document of the Communists in the south. Resolution 9 represented a departure from the quick and total victory of the General Offensive and a return to limited warfare. It stressed continued limited military operations carried out primarily in rural areas, the delta, and in sparsely populated jungles and highlands. These operations, in conjunction with political moves, would lead to the ultimate victory of the VC. For the first time the allied pacification program took on importance in the Communists' eyes, and the counterpacification and counter-Vietnamization missions received strong emphasis. Thus COSVN Resolution 9 heralded the return of protracted guerrilla war, with its emphasis on small-unit tactics, reliance upon sappers, terrorism, and increased reliance on attacks by fire, as the most efficient means of wearing down the fighting capability of ARVN, heightening demands by the U.S. public for withdrawal of U.S. forces, and eroding the Vietnamese people's faith in their government's ability to maintain their security."

■ "Counterpacification has remained the enemy's primary mission as the GVN has continued to make substantial inroads on VC control of the rural population."

■ "With the destruction of enemy supply lines and capture of enemy stores as a result of the 1970 Cambodian incursion and Lam Son 719 in early 1971, the enemy was forced to break down some of his main force units into smaller elements capable of self-support."

■ "The effects of the enemy's losses in the logistics field were dramatically revealed by COSVN Directive 139, released in the spring of 1970. Discussing transportation difficulties caused by reduced logistical support traffic on the Ho

Chi Minh Trail, COSVN urged its cadres to initiate an austerity program, especially beginning in May 1970, when daily rations would be reduced. The directive even stated that troops should be motivated not to draw clothing items for 1970."

■ "Directives issued this year by COSVN have generally continued to reiterate the themes of COSVN Resolution 9. Directive 01-71, a general guideline for 1971, emphasizes the strategy of continual attacks to achieve piecemeal victories, the predominance of the counterpacification effort, and the necessity to defeat allied efforts to drive the VC into isolated areas and thus away from the rural population on whom they are so dependent."

■ "In November 1971 COSVN issued Directive 39, its most recent policy statement, to subordinate cadre. In a somewhat surprising departure from past Communist pronouncements, COSVN in effect admits to the general success of the GVN pacification program. The most significant change set forth in this document is the apparent decentralization of the rural political and proselyting effort. Cadre are further instructed to remain close to the people, learn their aspirations, and refrain from infringing on their property rights or putting party interests above popular aspirations."

■ In his 17 January 1968 State of the Union address, President Lyndon Johnson "announced that the U.S. was exploring the meaning of a statement from Hanoi that North Vietnam would negotiate if the American bombing were stopped. He emphasized that Hanoi must not take advantage of our restraint. The euphoria of peace hopes was rudely shattered by the Communist Tet Offensive, which began on 30 January 1968. Nevertheless, by the end of March LBJ had decided upon a dramatic peace overture which was calculated to appeal to the VC/NVA in the wake of their severe losses sustained in the abortive Tet Offensive."

■ On 31 March 1968 President Johnson "announced an end to the bombing of North Vietnam above the 20th parallel and promised a complete halt if Hanoi matched the U.S. restraint. He also reiterated a call for peace talks and designated Ambassador Averell Harriman as chief U.S. negotiator for any ensuing talks. On 3 April 1968 North Vietnam offered to send representatives to meet with U.S. representatives and the long preliminary struggle over the site of negotiations, the shape of the room and the negotiating table, and representation began."

■ On 10 May 1968 the U.S. delegation met a North Vietnamese delegation led by Xuan Thuy in Paris. The next eight and a half months were completely monopolized by Communist wrangling over procedural matters.

■ 31 October 1968: Meantime, as an act of good faith LBJ announced a complete bombing halt over North Vietnam "after certain 'understandings' were reached privately with the North Vietnamese representatives."

■ 25 January 1969: The first substantive session of the Paris peace talks was finally held, with Henry Cabot Lodge replacing Harriman as the U.S. chief delegate.

■ 7 April 1969: President Thieu instructed chief South Vietnamese delegate

Lam to present a bold new proposal, the Republic of Vietnam's six-point peace plan. The Vietnamese Communists in Paris quickly repudiated the RVN plan.

■ 8 May 1969: The Communists countered with a ten-point proposal.

■ 14 May 1969: Richard Nixon made his first major speech on the war since being elected president. He hinted at the possibility of unilateral U.S. troop withdrawals. He emphasized that the one indispensable requirement was the right of the South Vietnamese people to determine their own future. He enunciated his new eight-point proposal, subsequently introduced by Ambassador Lodge in Paris.

■ 10 June 1969: The NLF announced formation of the PRG (Provisional Revolutionary Government).

■ 11 July 1969: President Thieu added to his previous 7 April proposal by suggesting elections in which all could participate, including the NLF.

■ 20 November 1969: Ambassador Lodge resigned and left Paris after accusing the Communists of refusing to reciprocate in any kind of meaningful way. Communist intransigence continued throughout 1969. Xuan Thuy thereafter boycotted the talks.

■ 31 July 1970: President Thieu renewed the RVN peace initiative and asked for a cease-fire as a step in leading toward an overall settlement.

■ 17 September 1970: After Ambassador David Bruce, new U.S. chief negotiator, arrived in Paris, Xuan Thuy and Le Duc Tho (a "special advisor") also returned to Paris. The PRG presented an eight-point elaboration of its earlier ten-point proposal. Ambassador Bruce said it contained "unacceptable language" of preconditions and unilateral demands.

■ 7 October 1970: President Nixon put forth a new five-point proposal. Ambassador Bruce presented it subsequently in Paris, where it was immediately denounced by the Communists. Le Duc Tho departed for Hanoi. The remainder of 1970 and the first part of 1971 were uneventful at the Paris talks.

■ Mid-June 1971: Le Duc Tho returned to Paris, and undoubtedly brought with him the terms of a new seven-point peace proposal announced on 1 July 1971.

■ After Tet 1968, U.S. policy began to emphasize that the RVN would shoulder more of the burden of the war. In addition, increased emphasis was placed on attempting to arrange a negotiated settlement to the hostilities.

■ "In March [1968], General Abrams, at that time Deputy COMUSMACV, journeyed to Washington for the first of two meetings with the president in 1968. On 31 March, President Johnson announced an interim bombing halt of North Vietnam that encompassed almost 90 percent of its population."

■ 19–20 July 1968 Honolulu Conference: LBJ and Thieu met and noted that North Vietnam had greatly stepped up its infiltration of men and matériel into the Republic of Vietnam, apparently in the hope that the north could achieve military and psychological victories that could shift the balance of the conflict in its favor. LBJ and Thieu called on the enemy to respond to the 31 March initiatives. The enemy responded on 17 August 1968 by launching his third general offensive of the year.

■ 1 November 1968: LBJ announced a complete bombing halt. In South

Vietnam the Accelerated Pacification Program was launched. This three-month campaign resulted in upgrading the security of a thousand contested hamlets.

■ "In early 1969 General Abrams pointed out the importance of neutralizing the Communist infrastructure, thereby cutting directly into the enemy's military potential by eliminating the elements which facilitated large military operations. He stated that pacification was the gut issue for the Vietnamese. General Abrams also advanced the 'One War' concept, recognizing that no such thing as a separate war of large combat units, pacification, or territorial security existed. Rather, under this newer strategic concept, friendly forces were to carry the battle to the enemy simultaneously in all areas of the conflict and at each echelon of his organization. The major elements of this new concept were pacification, including VCI elimination, RVNAF modernization and improvement, and combat operations, with each element receiving equal emphasis."

■ 8 June 1969 Midway Conference: Nixon, Thieu, Abrams, McCain, Wheeler, others. Joint announcement of initial withdrawal of 25,000 U.S. troops made on 10 June. Further withdrawals were tied to improvement and modernization of the RVNAF, developments in Paris, and the status of enemy capabilities and activities.

■ 25 July 1969: In Guam, President Nixon described the policy that came to be known as the "Nixon Doctrine," which emphasized that the United States intended to maintain its treaty commitments, but that other countries must do more for their own defense, individually and regionally, especially in meeting their military manpower requirements.

■ November 1969: President Nixon made a major policy address asking for domestic support for peace efforts and stressed U.S. resolve to gain a satisfactory negotiated settlement or to complete Vietnamization on an orderly schedule, allowing the GVN to become strong enough to defend its own freedom.

■ 15 March 1970: Prince Sihanouk was overthrown in Cambodia. Lieutenant General Lon Nol took power.

■ 30 April 1970: President Nixon announced U.S./South Vietnamese forces were attacking North Vietnamese sanctuaries in Cambodia, and said that they were doing this to protect the troops the United States still had in South Vietnam and their withdrawal as well as to further Vietnamization.

■ 8 February 1971: President Thieu ordered South Vietnamese forces into Laos to disrupt the supply and infiltration network of the North Vietnamese. The United States was providing full combat air support. Subsequently an estimated 17 of 33 enemy infantry battalions were judged to have been rendered ineffective. An estimated 3,500 rear service troops were KIA. The operation captured enough rice to feed 140 full-strength NVA battalions for a month. Enough weapons to equip more than 14 battalions were captured or destroyed.

■ April 1971: President Nixon announced the planned withdrawal of 100,000 more U.S. troops from Vietnam.

■ 12 November 1971: An additional Nixon withdrawal announcement reduces

U.S. forces in Vietnam from the 1969 high of 524,000 to 139,000 on 1 February 1972.

■ 1954 saw the beginning of protracted war waged by Hanoi for the unification of Vietnam.

■ During 1954–1964: Guerrilla warfare strategy and tactics of the first of the three phases of classic Communist theory of protracted war.

■ In 1964: The war entered the second, or equilibrium, phase, marked by gradual increase in large-unit confrontations and the achievement of Communist military superiority over the Republic of Vietnam.

■ By 1968: COSVN had apparently decided the time was right for advancement to the final, culminating phase of protracted struggle, the General Offensive and Popular Uprising that would result in the victory of Communism. But this was derailed by the failure of the 1968 Tet Offensive.

■ During 1968–1969: Hanoi began gradual reversion to protracted war. This reversion may be said to have culminated in the recent (late 1971) release of COSVN Directive 39, "in which COSVN appears to admit, to some degree, that the war has in fact come full circle, and that the protracted struggle has once again reverted to the guerrilla, or limited, phase."

■ Re Paris peace talks: The "only possible conclusion" at this point re the intentions of the Vietnamese Communists over the past three and a half years "is that they have never had any intention of conducting serious negotiations which could lead to a peaceful settlement of the war—except under conditions which would be tantamount to the total capitulation of the Republic of Vietnam." "Thus the Paris peace talks constitute for the Communists merely a political extension of the confirmed battlefield strategy of protracted warfare."

■ Conclusions: The enemy hopes to take advantage of U.S. troop withdrawals. He will probably increase his activity in the northern part of MR-1 and in the B-3 Front region of MR-2. Also improve and extend his LOC through Laos and Cambodia, rebuild his base areas, and increase available future options.

■ In Question: North Vietnamese capability to continue to sustain a three-front war in South Vietnam, Laos, and Cambodia. Critically dependent on USSR and PRC support.

■ Re the Republic of Vietnam: "Vast improvement in ARVN's military strength and capability; the present rising tide of Vietnamese nationalism, both within ARVN and the public at large; and RVN's gradually improving economic stability." "These factors, coupled with continued substantial U.S. logistical support and military and economic aid, should result in the continued growth and development of the RVN's political, military, and economic strength."

■ ■ ■

ABRAMS (trying to figure out his own government): "Did you read Kissinger's backgrounder? From that it's clear to me, at least in that situation [India-Pakistan], that the policy of our government is to get some measure of peace by fairly sophisticated negotiation and so on. Now it turns out it didn't work.

Although I don't <u>know</u> very much about it, it seems to me that's also what they've been doing in the Middle East. That must be the policy thrust. It looks like they're trying to have enough balance on the military side so that nobody, on either side, will think that they can solve it by military action. Whether they're <u>right</u> or not—I'm not saying that. This probably has to do with the Phantoms for Israel. . . . In terms of <u>policy</u> thrust, it seems to me that that's what this government stands for."

ABRAMS: "Now I turn around and apply it to this thing, the problem here—in a way I think they're trying to get some kind of equilibrium here, where military actions just won't solve it, for either side. Instead of that you've got to go to negotiation—. So [<u>long</u> pause] then they visit Moscow and Peking—have to think that they—I don't know what they—it might never be in so many words to decrease the support . . . to create some state of equilibrium. Now whether that's a successful track to follow or not, I don't know."

SOMEONE: Suggests this parallels what has been done in the strategic nuclear realm, a standoff [mutual assured destruction].

ABRAMS: "Yeah."

SAME SOMEONE: "That is what Kissinger was putting out at Harvard, and it was picked up by John McNaughton, and they kept pushing that same thing."

■ ■ ■

POTTS: We have, and have analyzed, over 115 enemy instructions over a four-year period—resolutions, directives, and pamphlets put out by the enemy.

SOMEONE: My question is whether COSVN is in control of anything now.

POTTS: "They're in control of the COSVN area."

POTTS: "In every case where a COSVN resolution comes out, some of that is reflected up in MR-TTH and in MR-5 and so forth, even though they're not under COSVN."

■ ■ ■

SOMEONE (to Abrams re his point on our government's seeking equilibrium): "That would be consistent with our requests for [easing of] rules and authorities. They've never added an inch. It's almost as though they don't <u>want</u> a military advantage." "It would <u>upset</u> something." "We could do a lot of damage up north."

ABRAMS: "Yeah, that's right."

ABRAMS: "On the other hand, the president's said more than once, 'I don't want them taking advantage of us, or I'll take whatever steps are necessary.' So some of these strikes that we've been permitted to make up there have been— that's <u>him</u> doing it. What he won't buy in on is some 14-day campaign. What <u>I'm</u> saying I think <u>supports</u> what <u>you</u> said. He'll do it enough to show that he isn't being duped by <u>every</u> damn thing that goes on. He doesn't <u>like</u> some of the things that go on, and he wants to let them know it. Now, I don't want anyone to misunderstand me, that for some reason or other I have received the w-o-r-d from the pope—this is nothing but my opinion, just reading these things and trying to, you know, reflect on it a little bit."

■ ■ ■

ABRAMS: "Now, this B-3 Front—the tenuous possibility of the 320th—that gives a little more to it. Now one of the things I got thumbing through that book— what's the title of that book, Tom? ["*Vantage Point.*"] *Vantage Point,* yeah, right. I got into that '67–'68 part there, just thumbing around in it, and the president [LBJ] recalls how they saw this thing building up, and they knew about it, and so on. And I swear—I don't know what the hell I was doing then. I was here. I missed all—I missed the storm clouds, the way they're described. He does have, when he gets all through with it, after Tet, in this book, he's got a thing where he says, 'Although we weren't surprised, nevertheless the extent of it and the strength of it,' and he goes on, 'that was more than had been antic- ipated.' And then, I guess all of us are a little gun-shy on Pearl Harbor. Pearl Harbor had a very lasting effect on the American military. Somehow the Amer- ican military has felt that they probably got sneaked up on, and it's not really a good thing. It's not a comfortable thing."

■ ■ ■

ABRAMS: "They know we're going home anyway. I'm sure, despite all the bull- shit they put out, they know very well that that's being done. I'm talking about the guys that are sitting around like we are—up in Hanoi. I don't think there's any question in their minds. I really don't. They've got this thing figured out."

ABRAMS: "It won't be Tet '68. It'll be limited to the B-3 Front. Now how far they want to go, in Kontum and Pleiku, I just don't know."

POTTS: Confirmation that infiltration group 3002 is going to the B-3 Front.

ABRAMS: "That's not good news."

ABRAMS: "President Thieu looks to about the middle of January when this will all start on the B-3 Front. He never did give all his reasons for that. Of course, he's not the kind of fellow that's very excitable anyway. He's pretty cool. He apparently knew something. He's been talking to General Dzu. In a way he thinks it's also related to Tet—that they would have struck before Tet. I think Tet's about the 15th."

11 DEC 1971: SEACORD Meeting

AMBASSADOR BUNKER: This is a very appropriate time to have this meeting, with the events taking place throughout Indochina, to include the upcoming dry season offensive in Laos, Cambodia, and South Vietnam.

BUNKER: The "major changes on the Asian scene" since the last meeting are the new status of the PRC, contact between the PRC and the United States, and evolution of the Nixon Doctrine.

BUNKER: "I think we can safely discuss these subjects without transgressing the restrictions that have been put on us against speculation on the subject of the president's trip to China."

ADMIRAL MCCAIN: After U.S. forces in Vietnam are drawn down to 139,000 in February 1972, "what happens next is anybody's guess." "Everywhere I go in the world people say the United States is abandoning its obligations in the Pacific." "You just can't get out of the world. And that's it."

ABRAMS: "In the handling of the 10,000 tac air sorties, and the 1,000 B-52 sorties, a month, it's never really quite enough. But we're very conscious that both of those things, northern Laos and Cambodia, do have a direct bearing. From his [the enemy's] standpoint it's one effort, so we have to try to meet the most pressing things on a week-to-week, and sometimes . . . on a day-to-day basis."

AMBASSADOR UNGER (Bangkok): Asian nations meeting in Kuala Lumpur adopted a resolution to make Southeast Asia a zone of "peace, freedom, and neutrality." Long-term trend in U.S. foreign policy is "reducing our presence and reducing our role in this part of the world." Realizes RVNAF cannot in any meaningful sense replace the U.S. air interdiction effort. Wonders whether raids and patrolling can "keep the Trail from becoming an impossible security situation for the South Vietnamese." Countries in the region, watching the U.S. withdrawal from Vietnam, ask what material assistance the U.S. Congress will provide to countries in this region. Cites U.S. air support in the region, "which most of us view as absolutely essential."

AMBASSADOR GODLEY (Vientiane): The leadership in Laos manifests "an intellectual refusal to face up to the future and what it portends." "The Lao always refer to the CIA as 'Sky.' The basis for the name is the fact that someone once asked, 'Well, where are we going to get our rice? Where are we going to get our ammunition? Where are we going to get our support?' And the Lao said, 'Oh, it'll come from the sky.' And since then, 'Sky' is the Lao codeword for CIA." "Ever since the first Ping-Pong match the Lao have followed with great hope and expectation the development of the Washington-Peking relationship."

AMBASSADOR SWANK (Phnom Penh): "The question that seriously preoccupies us is whether the Khmer Republic can survive in the long term." We have no doubt it will survive in the near term—six months or a year. But long-term survival is "not yet assured."

MATAXIS: The MEDT [Military Equipment Delivery Team] was activated in January 1971. "The legislative restraints, particularly those of the Cooper-Church amendment on training, set the stage for our operation."

Brig. Gen. Theodore C. Mataxis heads the MEDT in Cambodia.

AMBASSADOR BERGER (deputy U.S. ambassador, Saigon): "General [Duong Van] Minh is no political leader. He cannot be considered a national leader. Even the people who supported him shuddered at the thought he might someday be elected. He really is not a person in whom anybody can put any confidence. He has a mystical view that there's going to be a great upsurge in the country, a mass demand that he come into office. We see nothing of the kind developing.

At the moment he continues to raise his orchids and play tennis and provide no direction to the opposition—or to anyone else."

BERGER: "Ky is a different order. He has a position. . . . His role in the election was to try to spoil Thieu's chances by drawing off support from Thieu. Thieu could have won the election against Minh hands down, against Minh and Ky without too great difficulty. He miscalculated. He maneuvered to keep Ky out of the race so he could run a straight fight with Minh. He was convinced Minh would run, although we warned him again and again we thought Minh would not run. He found himself in the end confronted by a no-contest election. This hasn't done too much damage, perhaps, inside Vietnam, but it has done a lot of damage in terms of the U.S. feelings and attitudes about Vietnam, and about President Thieu in particular. It had a part in the actions of the Senate, and the frustrations the Senate felt, when they turned down the aid program." Thieu got 98 percent of the vote.

BERGER: "Thieu's main problem, and this is really one of the main problems of the country, is to create a political party to give constitutional support and continuity to the political system here. What you have now is personalized rule without any institutional backing." In November 1970 "some very major economic reforms were instituted in the form of foreign exchange rates, foreign interest rates, things of that kind, which brought the very serious inflation—running about 45 to 50 percent a year of prices—under substantial control. The price rise the following year was under 10 percent, which was quite a record for any country in the world." Major new economic reforms were the only subject of Thieu's November 1971 address to the new parliament. They affect foreign exchange, new tariff systems, more pay for the military and civil service, and legislation to correct some very basic weaknesses in the tax system. "There is a huge rice harvest that starts coming in the end of this month which will give a good underpinning to the economic side during 1972."

BERGER: "We've asked for $550 million in new money for the aid program, and we're not going to get it. We're going to get perhaps something on the order of $245 to $250 million." "The prospects [for aid] beyond FY 1972 could be very serious here."

BERGER: On the military side: "The level of activity inside Vietnam is very substantially diminished. We have terrorism continuing, somewhat lower level, but still substantial, and the country as a whole is girding itself for the dry season campaign." "Australian forces are coming out, Thai forces are coming out, ours are going down, and the first brigade of Korean forces are coming out. That of course is imposing on them [the South Vietnamese] much more substantial responsibilities." "They're meeting that by forming a new division up in MR-1, by more flexible movement of their forces from one military region to another, by better command and control, by more effective leadership—but the main element, as we see it for the future, of air support in this dry season campaign—not only this year, but beyond that, is absolutely fundamental to a very substantial holding of the position as well as it is."

BERGER: "We think the South Vietnamese can handle the situation inside South

Vietnam in this dry season fairly well, although we expect there may be some pretty heavy fighting in MR-1 or the B-3 Front in MR-2. As we see it, Vietnam itself is pretty tough terrain for the NVA and for the very much reduced VC forces. Hanoi's main hope of success in this dry season lies in what they can do in Laos and Cambodia, more so than in here." "They've got some problems in the Vietnamese forces—very high desertion rate, and the percentage of men who are present for active duty in the combat units." November 1971 introduced a very large increase in combat pay for certain units.

BERGER: "Pacification is moving fairly well in most areas. The weakest and most vulnerable areas are in MR-2 and Quang Nam and Quang Nhai provinces in MR-1. The delta is going <u>extremely</u> well, and a good part of MR-3 is moving quite well in pacification. The general picture, then, is not unpromising insofar as South Vietnam is concerned for 1972, with the main apprehensions concerned with what happens in neighboring countries."

BERGER: "The Vietnamese are so preoccupied with their problems and so self-centered that they are only vaguely aware of what's going on in the world." They have been subjected to "some very serious jolts which have shaken them up. The first was the announcement of the president's trip to Peking. The fact that we could do that without any consultation at all, even with the principal countries, such as Japan, who are concerned, suggested to them that we are capable of taking actions without regard to other nations." Reaction was a mixture of hope that something would happen to bring about an end to the war and fear that we would sell them out. "Hanoi itself . . . was shocked by the announcement of the visit."

BERGER: "The second, and even [more] jolting, shock came with the defeat of the U.S. resolution in the UN, the ejection of Taiwan, and the admission of Red China. This had much more impact. . . . Saigon suddenly began to realize that major changes were under way in Asia. And the South Vietnamese, who persist in thinking that the U.S. is capable of doing almost anything we want, or getting almost anything we want, suddenly realized how sharply limited U.S. powers are in such matters." "The biggest, perhaps, longer-term consequence of this was the realization that a change of uncertain character is taking place in the relations between nations, and especially in this part of the world."

BERGER: "The third shock came when President Nixon announced this summer [1971] the emergency economic and financial measures. They suddenly woke up to realize, for the first time, what serious problems we had—in the United States. . . . It drove home to them that the kind of support we gave to them in the past was changing, and that they could not continue to count on us as they had for economic and financial support in the same measure as we had given them in the past."

BERGER: "The next shock came when the Senate rejected the aid bill, although we gave them assurances—and Secretary Laird was here at the time, and Secretary Connally—that we would continue to give them very substantial assistance. They then, here too, realized the feelings developing in the U.S., and that the days of the open checkbook were now really over for them and from now on there was considerable uncertainty as to what levels of aid we would continue to provide them. This had one of the most profound effects, we think, on the semiconscious thinking they go through in relation to the future."

BERGER: "There is very, very great concern as to what may happen in 1973 and beyond." "There's been no panic here, but there is no question about it—there is a growing uneasiness, not yet anxiety, but worry. That there has been nothing more serious than this, we think, is due in large measure to the feeling that the president, the administration, and the American people will not abandon them after all the support and sacrifices that we have made, and all that they have made here." "But there is concern now as to the strength and character of our commitment to this part of the world." "Up to now, they've always taken the view that it'll be all right, the Americans will be there. And now they're beginning to wonder more and more." "The world, and especially the Asian world, appears to be a far more complicated place than it was eight months ago." "There is the feeling that there is a more dangerous time coming for them."

BERGER: "Hanoi continues to draw hope from such things now as the defeat of the U.S. in the UN over Taiwan, the U.S. domestic financial difficulties, opposition to the war in the United States, the trend toward neoisolationism at home, the weakness of Laos and Cambodia, as evidence that if they continue to press they can win the war." "We think 1972 will be a fairly painful year." The enemy "do recognize that Vietnamization is working, and that South Vietnam is a very much tougher proposition now than it has ever been in the past." The enemy "strategy is to continue the war, hope for the best, and look for some break that may bring the war to an end on acceptable terms." "For 1972 we see a lot of tough fighting ahead, and a lot of difficulty, but we think insofar as South Vietnam is concerned that this place will hold together very well."

17 DEC 1971: Enemy Logistics and Interdiction Briefing

BRIEFER: Cites March 1970 as when the enemy lost the use of the port of Kompong Som, "his primary line of communications for arms and ammunition to his forces in Military Regions 2, 3, and 4," and also at least temporarily from Cambodia his sources of food. Twenty tons per day of food before that.

BRIEFER: "We believe the very low level of enemy-initiated activity over the past year is . . . indication of his need to husband his supplies of arms and ammunition."

BRIEFER: There are 30,000 enemy troops estimated to be in northern Laos, and 300,000 in southern Laos, Cambodia, and the Republic of Vietnam.

BRIEFER: "In many areas of the Republic of Vietnam the enemy has been unable to obtain necessary supplies through local procurement because of the loss of control of the population due to pacification successes."

BRIEFER: "One of the most important improvements this year is our ability to deliver laser-guided bombs." Air force and navy.

ABRAMS: "Going back to our weekly Saturday meetings, just thinking of the sense of those, this factor of weather I don't think has really been brought out, the influence of weather. By and large the fellow covering that thing first on Saturday, his pitch has always been about the same, 'The roads are drying out . . . pretty good surface, they're bypassing road cuts.' It always kind of irritated me, because he seemed to be happy about it—the enemy is doing good and so on. So I think we need to look at our Saturday sessions and see if it's deep enough to really give us a feel about what's happening with him and so on."

ABRAMS (re the B-3 Front): "If it gets bad, we've got to do what we can to save it. You know I've hung a fairly heavy hat on this thing myself. . . ."

General Abrams had asked earlier in the briefing to talk with the analyst who follows the enemy 5th, 7th, and 9th Divisions. They bring that officer in at the end of the scheduled briefings.

ABRAMS: "What about the 165th Regiment?"
BRIEFER: Describes in detail when and where it moved from and to.
ABRAMS: "What about the 272?"
BRIEFER: Gives him that location, and dates of fixes, and where he was before.
ABRAMS: "And the 271 and 95 Charlie?"
BRIEFER: Describes that too, including a 15-kilometer move southwest on 14 December.
ABRAMS: "Why moved?"
BRIEFER: In reaction to ARVN forces going into that area, according to an 11 December rallier.

The young officer has it <u>nailed</u>! And he is not the slightest bit intimidated by his high-ranking one-man audience.

BRIEFER: "And further, General, I'd like to add" information that the 141st was hit by an Arc Light and might need some help.
POTTS: "I think General Abrams would be interested in the [***] change between. . . ."

The young briefer has that down, too—gives it in exquisite detail, including:

BRIEFER: Cites "yesterday's [***] pattern." "I would pretty firmly state . . . ," and cites the evidence.
ABRAMS: Ponders all this, speculates on what the enemy may be up to: "I'm sure he doesn't like that, that whole thing. He's just going to have to do something about it. He's never foolhardy. He's learned a lot of lessons about all that." "If the 271 comes back, you'll know goddamned well it's gonna be a stirring Christmas!" "OK, thank you."

19 DEC 1971: Commanders WIEU

MACV 1971 RVN/Cambodia Infiltration Estimate: 67,200 (10 percent to the DMZ/MR-TTH, 13 percent to MR-5, 25 percent to the B-3 Front, 52 percent to COSVN).

MACV 1972 RVN/Cambodia Infiltration Estimate: 15,700 (1 percent to DMZ/MR-TTH, 1 percent to MR-5, 47 percent to the B-3 Front, 51 percent to COSVN).

ABRAMS: "Now, ah, I guess the sum of all that changes that B-3 Front picture as between '71 and '72." "Then this has something to do with the estimated timing of whatever it is the enemy plans to do in the B-3 Front. It might slip a little further into '72."

BRIEFER: "COMINT indicates that the Headquarters 70th Front, which exercised command and control of the 304th [NVA Division] and other elements during Lam Son 719, has issued a warning of a large-scale ARVN operation in the area between northwestern Quang Tri Province and Muang Nong, Laos."

ABRAMS: "Do you remember, when we were getting ready for Lam Son 719, they kind of lost their cool up there in Quang Binh? That had a possibility of landings. When the aircraft carriers went up to two they sent warnings into Laos that they could take people off the carriers, the troops, and land them in Laos in the rear. Then they got concerned that they were coming across the DMZ. Remember that? There was a w-h-o-l-e thing. You can say it is just good smart headquarters work, getting everybody alerted for everything, but I think they go through a period of guessing, and I think they got a little excited. And I wonder if the 70th Front is now, for some reason, or if they're just trying to spoof us, or to raise the morale of their troops by telling them 'they're coming'?"

ABRAMS (re effects of Lam Son 719): "You know, there was a time here where they really didn't pay too much attention to where the ARVN was, except where they had an outfit they wanted to sort of pep it up a little bit, and then they'd find one of the regiments to go ahead and ambush it. The rest of them they didn't pay much attention to where they went, or what they did. Now, that thing kind of got their attention." "Can't disregard it any more."

SOMEONE: "I think they've [the enemy] got every intention of trying them [ARVN] out, too. They're going to draw them out there, come dry weather."

ABRAMS: "I think so, too, but it'll be kind of a Vietnamese way. And old Giai and Phu and Lam and so on, they'll be pondering that. And when it starts, it won't look like anything that ever started before. Or they'll make it look exactly like something and that ain't what it is! I think that's what's going to happen. And they've fooled around with these fellows quite a long time and they know a good bit about them."

■ ■ ■

ABRAMS: Asks about an F-105 shot down earlier.

LAVELLE: Talked to the pilot.

ABRAMS: "And they didn't get any [warning] signal?"

LAVELLE: "No, sir. Apparently the tactics they're using is to home in and get their azimuth, sir, by tracking the aircraft without turning on their Fan Song equipment."

ABRAMS: "This would be by radar?"

LAVELLE: "Yes, sir. As a result of that, they have their azimuth problem all worked out. They can go ahead and fire the missile without turning the Fan Song on until the last minute, the last 20 seconds, before impact—before engagement. So as a result of that the crews getting the signal don't have time to react. The missile's already on them before they can—. So they're using a new tactic is what it amounts to."

Long pause.

ABRAMS: "Well, why haven't they been doing that before?"

LAVELLE: "Good question. I just think it's a new tactic that they're using. Previously, as you know, we'd been getting plenty of warning and reacting to it. The first time this week, as we recall, that they're using this kind of a tactic. And we're only guessing. The F-105 crew did not have any previous warning until practically the time of impact."

Another long pause.

ABRAMS: "Well, that thing's going to require some study."

■ ■ ■

ABRAMS: "Now I expect, certainly by the time the weekend's over, Washington will be up on the air and want an explanation of this <u>extraordinary</u> situation where we've had two planes shot down by SAMs—full and complete explanation of how come that happened. So get moving on that. And they probably won't accept the simple explanation that they got hit. [Laughter] 'How come you authorized that?'"

ABRAMS: "One thing about that, you know, there haven't been a hell of a lot of results out of SAMs for a long time. What I'm about to say wouldn't apply to the F-105s necessarily, but are all these equipments working?"

LAVELLE: "Sir, the requirement is that before anybody ventures into that pass area, they have a self-test feature that's done in the air, and the back seater and the front seater have to make self-tests on the SLAR equipment. If you don't hear the rattlesnake and see the strobe when you press the test button, you divert and go back home and get your RHAW fixed. We do have, I think, a pretty good procedure for ensuring that it does work before we commit them to the passes."

■ ■ ■

BUNKER: "Hanoi has had a degree of success in the Paris talks, and it's been useful to him, because their target has also been public opinion in the United States. And they've zeroed in on this consistently, and with <u>very</u> considerable success."

BUNKER: "They went there originally for two reasons. First, hoping that we would collapse, like the French, and they could come in very quickly. But the Soviets also advised them to go there on the ground that, if we didn't [collapse], we would eventually withdraw, and once the process had been started it would be irreversible and they could then take over. What's thwarted that, of course, is Vietnamization, and the success of it. The success is demonstrated, and the fact they realize they can't take over, walk in and take over, as they were hopeful of doing—that's what the Soviets told—is the <u>violent</u> criticism of it in Paris. . . . It's an acknowledgment, I think, a recognition, of the success of it."

BUNKER (discounting any possibility of reduction in USSR/PRC aid to North Vietnam): "See, one can't take the initiative. If the Chinese take it, the Soviets will take advantage of it, take advantage over the Chinese, and vice versa. I think they're bound to keep up the assistance."

WEYAND: "Our own stance there [in Paris] is markedly different. There's always been these two schools, opposing schools, to simplify it. One who held we didn't want Paris to become another Panmunjon because, as a negotiating forum that rules it out when the negotiators start calling each other sons of bitches instead of your excellency, it just sort of seems that history has shown that the negotiating process is at an end. You've got to move somewhere else, or to some other sort of a situation. <u>Now</u> this is very much like the Panmunjon affair, and mainly because we have shifted our tactic there. You think back to when Ambassador Harriman . . . referred to Xuan Thuy as 'Your Excellency,' and a few pleasantries were exchanged. And now it's like walking into Panmunjon, glaring at each other, and talking about the running dogs and so on, right across the table there."

■ ■ ■

VANN: "In 1970, we put a big emphasis on this village/hamlet security planning. We invested a high percentage of our MAT team effort on that. It's impossible to evaluate exactly how much of a contribution that was to the pacification of the countryside. But . . . I think a fairly high percentage of our current success can be attributed to that." "I might point out that that's the first step toward the security of the countryside, and also the first step toward getting a viable local government." "The 1972 effort is going to have to be directed to the training of village and hamlet officials, and getting the poor villages up to snuff." The range now is from good to "lousy."

BUNKER: "It seems to me that another encouraging thing is the number of initiatives that the RF and PF are taking all the time."

SOMEONE: "That was the result of a concerted training effort, Mr. Ambassador, that we started two or three years ago. I might say that the Australians contributed a great deal to this. And last week they phased out [of MR-4]."

ABRAMS: "I think the major thing that made Lam Son 719 possible was that—well, it has to do a lot with Cambodia. The change in their policy over there in Phnom Penh, and then the cross-border operations. And militarily—militarily, what that did, it freed both divisions of the general reserve, the marines and the airborne, to be applied exclusively in Lam Son 719. And that could be done, at that time, without placing any grave risk on MR-3 or MR-4, and there just wasn't enough there in the B-3 Front to place that thing, really, in jeopardy. So you might say the South Vietnamese had kind of a free ride to use the general reserve somewhere, if they wanted to do that. And he may have—the other fellow may have seen that as sort of basic."

ABRAMS: "So this year, if he can create a situation—. I don't think he [the enemy] wants another Lam Son 719. That sort of foolishness just shouldn't be going on. And right now he probably can't be really positive that they wouldn't try some crazy thing like that again, even though it was crazy. If he can get enough strength there in the B-3 Front to stir that up at will, and he knows that those 22nd and 23rd and so on [are] not very—well, they're certainly not the strongest divisions. And if he can stir up enough there so you've got to be careful where you send the general reserve, that it's not too far away from the B-3 Front, plus these precautionary steps in western Quang Tri to see that you don't get Khe Sanh for free, then kind of play it that way, that might be one of the things about the B-3 Front."

ABRAMS: "The reason we keep talking about this is we can't figure out why he's doing that." [Laughter] "We obviously haven't yet." [More laughter] "It's a sign of deep uncertainty."

22 DEC 1971: Special Intelligence Update for COMUS, DEPCOMUS, Chief of Staff, MG Carley, BG Lanagan, and J-3 Update

ABRAMS: "I worry a little bit, quite frankly—. Well, you heard what I had to say last night, over at the mess. Well, I'll tell you, I'm getting a little worried. I think a whole lot of these things that we've done—going in khakis on Saturday and Sunday, which I did—wanted to have it look a little bit better around here, make people a little more proud as they dressed a little better—but the hell of a price you pay on that is you forget you're still tangled up with a son of a bitch. And he hasn't quit."

ABRAMS: "And that's the way I feel about that air operation last Saturday. God-damn system's deteriorated. It isn't that old sharp, hard thing. And I'm commencing to worry about it. We're not dealing with the same thing we had two years ago—on the American side. Too much thinking about some other thing. And with a damn war going on—that is going on—it hasn't ever stopped. Then a-l-l these senses get sort of dulled, and we're just not up on the step. And he's working at something. The signs are all there. This is very clear. And I don't know to what degree it's infected the Vietnamese. I just don't like the smell of it. And I don't think our apparatus out there is up in that good keen shape. It's not only—we've got to harden up this intelligence, and focus it, and that sort of thing, but it's really got to be impressed everywhere."

ABRAMS: "The sergeant major was up the other day with the advisors of the 3rd Division. They're working like hell getting a MARS station put in, and they're getting a new laundry with laundromats and so on, enough to service the division—161 men there. But no wire, no claymores. And they're out on the edge of the goddamn thing. That's the way everybody's commencing to think about things, and they'll just get their ass creamed. And I just don't like it. So you keep working at this stuff. It's not a question of running scared. God, we got the stuff to do it. But you can't do it if everybody's asleep."

ABRAMS: "I want a meeting in here on the 28th of December—senior commanders, component commanders, the senior staff. And I want to brief it at that time—the intelligence. I just don't like the smell of all this." "I think we better have the DEPCORDS, too."

ABRAMS (explaining why he went along with a CBU B-52 strike in the PDJ): "I don't like it. But in the climate, if any of Ambassador Godley's reasonable demands are not met, the whiplash is going to be bad. I honestly don't believe that it's any better than doing it any other way, with 500s or 750s. The professional judgment over there isn't all that good. It just isn't there. And that's the only thing we're going on. But if we hadn't done it, it's just another thing. So that's why I agreed with you. And even if you hadn't done it and had asked me, I'd have had to do it, too, and [laughing] not liking it any more than I do now."

ABRAMS: "And really, thank god, what the president's [Thieu] thinking of is the B-3 Front and MR-1. And he's got to have his general reserve back in shape for that. And he already knows he's gonna lose it." "Everything's in train. It all stems from the day I went over there. And he's the chief of JGS right now. There's no fooling about that. And he believes in this six division idea, too. In fact it's his. General Truong told him he could do more. Sending a brigade from MR-4 to MR-1, and he told him he could do more."

WEYAND: "Actually, the best job we've ever done on this guy is when he's come out of the woodwork. You can talk all you want, big blue arrows going into the strongholds, but when we look back on it—the son of a bitch, when he's finally got his dander up and has come out, that's when he's gotten [flapped?], and that's probably the way it's going to be this time, except that we've got the drop on him. That's what Minh's doing up there. Minh's not going to get caught. And the guy may just continue to press on him, and if he does he's going to get his ass waxed."

ABRAMS (re promoting a course of action and the changed advisory environment): "We've got to be careful on it. We've got to do it sort of personally, and never get out in any meetings about it or any of that, because there's plenty of signs that they're getting sensitive about—some of these commanders down the line—that they think this is something that the U.S. high command's promoting, and that sort of disqualifies it. And we've got to understand that."

28 DEC 1971: COMUS and Commanders Update

BRIEFER: 1972 RVN/Cambodian MACV Infiltration Estimate: 20,700. DMZ/MR-TTH: 100. MR-5: 200. B-3 Front: 9,400. COSVN: 11,000. Last year at the same time the total was 25,200. This year the B-3 Front is getting a much higher percentage of the total, three times as much as last year. Also there are more groups with a letter suffix.

BRIEFER: On 27 December forward elements were tenuously located in southern Quang Binh Province.

POTTS: "Now, sir, this is the same forward elements that came down in Lam Son 719, the [***]. And you remember that 308th Division was the division that lost five battalions and out of which all three regiments were committed. So it looks like they're about ready to get in shape again where they might be deployed."

POTTS: The 308th Division's 32nd Regiment lost two battalions, the 88th Regiment lost one battalion, and the 102nd Regiment lost two battalions, all in Lam Son 719. Since then "we haven't had anything but training, and then they helped a little bit during that flood."

ABRAMS: "It almost looks like they've got enough structure in the south for just about anything they want to do, and I wonder if this says something about manpower. . . . The 312th and the 316th are gone. They're over there in northern Laos. Now I see the 325th, they've still got that up there."

POTTS: "You've got five divisions up there, sir, and when we finish here in a minute you're going to see that four of those five divisions in a reserve status in North Vietnam, all of the division or part of each of those four, it looks like they're coming south."

ABRAMS: "Well, we should stop talking. It sounds like an exciting story! We should get on with it."

■ ■ ■

BRIEFER: "The North Vietnamese air defense posture has significantly improved since mid-November. MiG activity has increased, and there is no apparent reluctance to engage allied aircraft when conditions are favorable."

BRIEFER: "The surface-to-air missile defense in North Vietnam is also being maintained in a high state of readiness. In the last two weeks, North Vietnam's SAM firing units have expended a minimum of 23 SA-2 against U.S. aircraft operating over North Vietnam or the Laos border area. Fan Song and GCI signals emanating from within North Vietnam have resulted in 21 protective reaction strikes by U.S. aircraft during the same time period."

■ ■ ■

BRIEFER: "In the Republic of Vietnam the enemy's greatest capability will continue to be in northern MR-1 and the B-3 Front." Twenty-three battalions in the DMZ area and five regiments in the B-3 Front. Shorter supply lines, more easily reinforced from North Vietnam. Limited elsewhere by lack of supplies and personnel.

BRIEFER: "It appears that in the near future the enemy will continue the war at the current level, except for increased activity in northern Laos, the B-3 Front, and possibly northern Military Region 1."

ABRAMS: "If we go back to Tet of '68, which represented pretty much of an all-out effort in South Vietnam, did he deploy that percent of his internal reserve for that battle? If he goes ahead with the 308th, the 304th, the 324B, and the 320th, as it now appears that he will, leaving the 325th—one division—in North Vietnam, did he get down to that, one division in North Vietnam, in Tet of '68?"

POTTS: "Yes, sir, and it was the same way with Lam Son 719."

ABRAMS: "No, because you still had some of the 312th."

POTTS: "Yes, sir. You had the 9th of the 304th that he could have committed, but it had moved south. He had the 48th of the 320th still not completely committed. And you remember we had the 66th Regiment over there in the Tchepone area that we thought might have gotten an Arc Light strike on him . . . just looking at divisions, they got down to one division. But they have been very careful to keep one or two or three regiments that were not committed, so they had a reserve a little farther forward with these regiments."

ABRAMS: "Now you've got these infiltration groups with a letter suffix, and as you've pointed out there's quite a lot of them. How does that equate . . . ?"

POTTS: "We've usually found, sir, that one group [***] would represent a battalion, an understrength battalion, meaning that we would get three groups per regiment." Now have detected 13 [***] going into the B-3 Front. Just about equates to the 320th Division.

ABRAMS: "There's a greater effort on <u>units</u> in the infiltration system than there is on individual replacements. Why is that?"

POTTS: "His units, I think, sir, in-country have gotten down to such a strength, and such a status of efficiency, that he's going to come in with these fresh units, and then after that we're going to see the pure infiltration groups come down in more abundance. He's going to get the structure beefed up a little bit with fresh units, and then he'll come in and start trying to increase the strength of those others."

ABRAMS: "Now another thing is moving this additional antiaircraft into Laos, and further south in Laos. Those tanks that are down there just above . . . the Bolovens. All of that means additional tonnage required <u>in</u> Laos before you ever talk about Cambodia or South Vietnam. At least I would <u>think</u> that it does, <u>especially</u> 100-mm, 57-mm. If you're going to go shooting <u>that</u> much, that's tonnage. Now his <u>truck</u> activity, so far this year, has been somewhat less than it was last year, which in a <u>way</u> is related to tonnage. . . . What we would have to conclude so far this year is that the movement of tonnage has been somewhat less than it was last year. And we're still in the phase before 719, so there's no aberration of what all the truck movements were in connection with 719. And his total truck movements last year, for the whole season, were about 20 percent above the season before. But his <u>throughput</u> was about 40 percent <u>below</u>. A-a-h-h, so, ah, would these, ah, with these units moving, or looks like they're moving, the logistics picture doesn't seem to be up to snuff. I don't know, maybe that's not a right way to look at it."

ABRAMS: "After Lam Son 719 I think even the attaché reports up there indicated his losses had been very substantial. Then maybe he had to take the output of his training and use it to rebuild these regiments and battalions. And Lam Son 719, in terms of long-range planning on the training base, and capacity of the training base and this sort of thing—Lam Son 719 was an unexpected event. I don't mean that it gained any real surprise at the moment. But if you go back to their planners, the guy that's running . . . that whole central training command or what the hell ever it is, he didn't have that cranked in, probably, back in say October or September, when he was laying his schemes out for output. In fact, he was probably working on another plan, so maybe that's what he had to do. Now he's gotten them—that's what he elected to do. Now he's got them back in shape, but in the meantime . . . that's where he used up the output of his training establishment."

POTTS: "This 24B Regiment that's coming down—that lost two battalions. Now in our calculations and our work on this when we say 'lost,' we didn't say 'combat ineffective.' They were lost battalions, almost down to a man. Now they went back, and then we had some reports [***] that they were receiving personnel, and then were starting training. It was almost down at the close order drill—."

ABRAMS: "Some of those outfits lost just everything. Remember those? They had those—really suicide attacks, in some cases, where they just got mowed down, officers and NCOs and the whole works."

POTTS: "In the case, sir, of the 100-mm guns you were using as an example, remember this is the unit that turned in, or stored, their weapons in Laos when they went back north, weapons and ammunition that they had left over. So when they came back down and we saw the 100-mm's start to reappear not long ago, they had taken them out of the storage and started to get them ready."

ABRAMS: "Now the timing of this—what do we think about the timing?"

POTTS: "Timing, sir, as far as the 320th Division is concerned, can be in late January in-country, most of it, and ready for activity."

ABRAMS: "I'm talking about something kind of serious, where he really gets with it, brings his lunch and all that."

POTTS: "I think the 320th will make a show in connection with Tet, or perhaps the president's visit to Peking. I think the rest of this, sir, will be closer to U.S. election time."

ABRAMS: "You remember last year, right off on the—sort of on the heels of Lam Son 719, we got into that Fire Support Base 4, 5, and 6 fiasco up there in the B-3 Front, which was a response of his, as I recall it, to Lam Son 719. Well, this kind of thing has all the earmarks of playing that same—in some ways—orchestrating or doing something, playing those two fronts, sort of billiarding them off of each other some way, which screws up what you do with the general reserve—looking at it from the GVN side. It presents some problems about whether they're in the right place at the right time. You know, whether they've overreacted to some thing. And of course if you underreact, that's a little late."

ABRAMS: "But it does seem to me—. I'm just about to finish, but I do want everybody here to really disagree and everything. I'd like to wring this out. But my last feeling is, about this, that with what we've got here now, we can say, after we've related it to how he reacted to 719, the way he went at Tet '68, taking two <u>really</u> substantial efforts that he's made in this war, main force-wise, he's getting ready to do the most that it's possible for him to do. He hasn't <u>got</u> anything more he could, you know—. He's rolling out everything. You put the <u>whole</u> package together—."

ABRAMS: "They don't believe in the blitz. That's not the way they go. It's not in the <u>book</u>—the blitz. Well, at least there comes a stage in the classical doctrine, when I guess they've got everything set about the way they'd like to see it, and that's taken them four, five, six, seven years to get it that way—planning and organization and development of logistics and supply and personnel strength and training and indoctrination and all that—<u>then</u>—but you can hardly call that a <u>blitz</u>."

ABRAMS: "Well, I don't know, I guess the Germans took longer than that to get organized for the blitz, about 20 years or something, in the meantime fighting among themselves about whether they should do it or not, a lot of difference of opinion. But they go at it in a very—they know how to do it their way. And it's all that political administrative machinery, the indoctrination, the dedication, the devotion, the classes, classes, classes, every day talking, and what a stinker these imperialists, and the colonizers, and they don't let people be free, and they're just grinding them under. And <u>every</u> day doing that, and then getting them and giving them some marksmanship, and hand grenade throwing, and drilling, and so on, and away we go, <u>all</u> for god and country—or Buddha and country, something like that. And they've just taken the <u>time</u>."

ABRAMS: "Well, anyway, let's have some discussion. Kroesen, how do you see it?"

KROESEN: "Well, sir, in MR-1 I think there's a general agreement between General Lam and General Dolvin that we are facing a main enemy force threat at Quang Tri that's been pointed out, and we think that this new division in Que Son, [Quan Tien?] Mountains may be exercised against one of the outlying districts, Hiep Duc or Duc Duc. But we are concerned with the main force units in only those two locations. Our biggest concern in MR-1 is the increase in terrorism, increase in sabotage, the harassing attacks on QL-1, the loss of additional bridges. General Lam thinks the Territorial Forces are perfectly capable of coping with this, except they're in for a greater fight than they've had in quite some time."

KROESEN: "Your analysis of the lack of replacements coming down, the fact that they're sending units down instead, I think is reinforced by the fact that we've had an increase in abduction and kidnapping, particularly in Quang Nam

Province." "I think they're doing that to fill the local force units, rather than counting on replacements coming down from the north as they have in the past."

KROESEN: "Within the five provinces of the north, I have been struck by the sense of confidence and optimism, sense of well-being, among both the advisors and government officials in four of those provinces—Quang Tri, Thua Thien, Quang Tin, and Quang Ngai. Everybody seems to think that they have things well in hand, that they're facing a period of increased enemy activity that they're going to have to cope with. Quang Nam is the only exception. Quang Nam you see a completely pessimistic outlook by the advisory staff and, I think, the staff of the province chief. I'm not sure that he shares that pessimism himself. He's a pretty sound individual. But, together, these two staffs seem to indicate the Territorial Forces in Quang Nam are in trouble. Their main concern is that they don't have enough ARVN forces employed in the piedmont area." "So they feel rather naked beyond the coastal plain."

ABRAMS: "Lam's got the new division [3rd ARVN Division]."

ABRAMS: The six regiments of the general reserve cannot all be committed for very long. "We've often felt, if they're handled with reasonable skill, that you can go on fairly indefinitely with a commitment of four regiments," the equivalent in battalions, being rotated periodically.

ABRAMS: "If [General Lam] had the general reserve, is this a manageable problem?"

KROESEN: "I don't think I'm prepared to say, sir."

ABRAMS: "Of course, General Dzu, he'll want the general reserve, too. In his case, it'll be kind of like the way they're used in MR-3. You can't fight with the divisions they've got, so you get the general reserve and let them do the fighting. And that's what General Dzu probably'll want to do. The situation is somewhat different in MR-1. Most everybody up there'll fight."

KROESEN: "I think General Lam, and everybody up there, expects the 3rd Division to be tested by the enemy." "I'm not so sure they would go so far as to say prior to our election. I think they're looking to a little closer in for a test of the 3rd Division."

ABRAMS: "General Wear?"

WEAR: "I wish I could be a lot more optimistic than I really am about the ARVN in II Corps. And I think this time last year I was. They can just about handle the local forces within the boundary. Our experience has been, as you well know, that when the NVA well-trained units come across the border, the ARVN just hasn't stood up against them." "They have just been able to keep the lid on to fill the gaps as the U.S. have moved out, helped by the fact that the VC and NVA south of our northern three provinces have apparently just not been getting the supplies to be able to do very much. Our war is now almost completely limited to Kontum, Pleiku, and Binh Dinh."

WEAR: "We have not had a fall campaign in two years now, '70 and '71, by the enemy." "The Highway 19, of course, is one problem that we have more than we've had in the past, because before we've always had a lot of U.S. artillery within the Task Force 19, an air cav troop pretty much dedicated to that, all of which are now gone. So the supply problem, particularly the POL, it's quite easy to cut." "It sort of surprised me . . . last year that Highway 14 . . . all the way from Pleiku to Dak To, General Dzu was able to move two and three hundred trucks a day back and forth, not even in convoy, and wasn't really bothered. I think any kind of a decent attack and those highways will be bothered."

WEAR: "The two divisions I don't think have really improved in the 17 months I've watched them. Their strength runs about the same, 71 to 76 percent assigned to authorized. His battalions he puts in the field are a little over 300, 320 or something like that." "The leadership problem you know, which is the same." "The airborne brigades were our real fighting force last year in both those battles." "The division commanders commit the corps ranger group, those three battalions, all the time to spare their own battalions." "But of course, when you look at what the enemy's got, and what the ARVN's got, we shouldn't have any trouble up there."

WEAR: "General Dzu spent the whole Christmas holidays up there, visiting around with the troops. And he's making it very clear that there isn't anybody to help. And maybe that could have been one of the problems. We, as advisors, whenever one of their infantry elements was attacked, we brought in gunships and air and so forth. I have noticed that when a unit really got into it, and didn't have a choice, they fought pretty well."

ABRAMS: "General Hollingsworth?"

HOLLINGSWORTH: "The thing that bothers me most is this occupation of Krek and the number of troops it takes to keep that road open from Tay Ninh to Krek. I'd feel pretty good if I could get rid of Krek."

ABRAMS: "Does he [General Minh] feel that he has to hold onto that?"

HOLLINGSWORTH: "Well, he feels that way, sir, and I can't get out of him whether he's been told that or not." Keeps six battalions and one armored cavalry regiment right in Krek, one battalion on the road from Krek to the border, plus a regiment plus below, plus a regiment west of Tay Ninh. Our best regiment and best regimental commander—7th Regiment, 5th ARVN Division. "I'll say this—if we can keep the 9th VC Division tied up, so that he doesn't come down and try to knock off Krek, I think I can handle the 7th Division and the 5th Division. But if that 9th—95 Charles and 271—come back across that river, I know what they're coming for. They're coming down to wipe out Krek, and they're going to—. If we get those two ARVN regiments in there, they're going to know about it. And if they come down, then I've got problems."

HOLLINGSWORTH: "I think [Lam Son] 719 is one of the most devastating blows that they've had. And it just could be that they think you might be going to pull another 719 on them, and they're getting set."

HOLLINGSWORTH: Doubt that the 320th will go to the B-3 Front. The enemy units prefer to work in familiar terrain.

ABRAMS: "It's kind of like sending the marines to II Corps. They get up there—they know damn well that they're bastards at a homecoming, nobody and so on—. And that's just the way they act—the Vietnamese marines. Now that's changed up in MR-1. That was going pretty good towards the end. You know, those marine regiments? Actually accepting orders and carrying them out. It's nothing to go eulogizing them, but it was a hell of an improvement. And then they were working very well down in the delta. I'm talking comparatively, now. But you send them up to MR-2 and they know they've had it. So they just get busy taking in their own laundry, and to hell with the rest of the war."

HOLLINGSWORTH: "General Minh is prepared to lose [give up] all of the general reserve and to try to handle it with what we've got."

WEYAND: "One of the big differences between this year, that is '71, and '72 is probably going to be that it's going to be a hell of a year, I think, because the enemy is going to have the initiative, where we had it last year."

ABRAMS: "Jack?"

CUSHMAN: "It's certainly clear from this presentation that something big is going to happen. I would think that if the JGS looks at it about the same way, and is realistic, the days are short before MR-4 loses a division." "And maybe, if the situation gets desperate, lose two divisions." Meanwhile MR-4 is "working very hard to support the Cambodians," keeping about eight battalions of rangers and a couple of squadrons of armored cavalry over there continually. Working hard on pacification. "The vulnerable sector of their capability is their guerrillas, and these many base-clearing operations and the continual spread out of pacification is eating away at them." "And working on the U Minh, right now with two divisions." "Right now General Truong is redeploying RF forces out of province—bold, even a little bit reckless. He's doing this because he knows that he's got to take advantage of this particular season of the year to move on out."

CUSHMAN: "The thing that worries me in the total picture in the country is the lack on the part of the JGS of what you might call redeployment thinking, that is to say thinking in terms of moving a division out of the delta to someplace else, helping out III Corps with a division. I just don't see any evidence of this." "It's sort of a fixed stationing concept that they get themselves stuck with."

ABRAMS: "We have been trying to peddle the idea that you use the forces that are sort of organic to III and IV Corps to keep III and IV Corps in South Vietnam under control, and then to try to preserve some circle that runs through Kompong Cham and protects Route 7 and Phnom Penh, and then down to Kompong Som, between the Cambodians and the Vietnamese in that thing. We're talking about the total forces organic to MR-3 and MR-4. So the JGS then, the government, has the flexibility of using the general reserve to try to control the situation in MR-1 and MR-2 as it develops and fluctuates over the next six months or so. If we can get a scheme working like that, they'd have a little depth in what they were doing and the way they were planning."

■ ■ ■

ABRAMS (describing an Island Tree mission as per the microphone-type sensors): "They listened to about 25 minutes of these little munitions [CBUs from B-

52s, used to attack a T-station] going pit-pat around in the area, then there's quite a period of secondary explosions, and then you get a period of some screaming, then some more secondaries, then you get a period of a lot of horn blowing, and then you've got sort of all quiet, and you can hear them—some fellow's out there in charge of loading trucks, and he's shouting orders, and sort of typical soldier stuff—somebody tells him to go screw it, we're not ready yet, or we're not going to move out there, it's too far, that gets into it. Well, anyway, it sounds like it got into something." "And I guess one fellow said, 'Don't go over there. There's a lot of them left that haven't gone off.'"

■ ■ ■

ABRAMS: "One thing I wanted to say—I should have mentioned it. One of the purposes of this meeting—last week I got an invitation to the fifth anniversary of 'the light at the end of the tunnel.' It's going to be on New Year's Eve. And I was reminded, Fritz, when you said people were in good humor up there—well, what we're trying to paint here today is you can't see the end of the tunnel. Can't see it. Gotta work at it. That's the only way you're gonna ever open up the end. I'm not trying to exaggerate it, but the handwriting's on the wall, and we've just got to get with it. Oh, I think it will come out if a few things can get done and so on."

31 DEC 1971: General Vien and JGS Brief

MACV 1972 Infiltration Estimate: 25,500 (11,300 for the B-3 Front, 13,400 for COSVN) by April 1972.

ABRAMS: Should also note the December 1971 infiltration figures, which include 6,300 for the B-3 Front. Thus December 1971–April 1972 over 17,000 are going to the B-3 Front, the highest number designated for the B-3 Front since Tet 1968.

ABRAMS: "They've never given that much emphasis to it."

BRIEFER: A fourfold increase over last year.

ABRAMS: "To get down to what we kind of think now, we're pretty well satisfied that the 320th Division is in fact headed for the B-3 Front. The amount of evidence on that . . . I think is pretty substantial. And they oughta be there by the latter part of January, something like that. Now even though we're pretty <u>certain</u> about that, I think we have to give him credit, too—he can change that. He can change it. He's shown the ability to do that before."

ABRAMS: "The only thing you can say for certain right now is that it's very clear that his planners are prepared to move all three of those divisions [308, 304, 324B]. That's what it means. It doesn't mean they will. You can't say that yet." "If he should do that, and this is what I think is kind of important, the only division left in North Vietnam would be the 325th. Now the only time he ever got down to that point was in Tet of 1968, where only one division remained in North Vietnam."

ABRAMS: "There have been some indications that he [the enemy] thinks it's possible that you [General Vien] would do Lam Son 719 again, or something like it." "Though his side said they knew it all along, they were in fact surprised by Lam Son 719. And they reacted to that _after_ it got under way. For a while they themselves were confused as to whether it was coming across the DMZ. Then they even got worried about coming in from the sea. They were counting the carriers all the time and so on. So they reacted _after_—and that's when all those regiments came down."

ABRAMS: "And if there's going to be another one [Lam Son 719], he wants to handle his part different than he did the last time. He'd like to have more of these units in position rather than trying to push them in after the fight and the bombing and all that gets started." "The important point is we know that he has already decided, in his own mind, that he is prepared to commit the remaining divisions in North Vietnam except for the 325th." "I think it's _important_ that his attitude would be that way."

ABRAMS: "In the newspapers, and in a-l-l the Intelligence Community and everything, everybody's got fastened on the idea of protracted war, and then that gets translated into guerrillas and sappers, and so you really don't need to get prepared for big fights, just lots of little tiny fights. And he's put out a lot, there's a justification for that—instructions from COSVN and so on, 'protracted war' and so on. But if he moves the 304th, the 308th, and the 324 Bravo into Quang Tri and Thua Thien, that ain't protracted war. That's main force. That's a big battle."

ABRAMS: "So I wind it all up by saying we don't know _when_, or _where_, these would move. The only thing we know is that he has decided in his thinking, and in his planning, he has decided that at an appropriate time, or under certain circumstances, or what have you, when he sees it's propitious he's willing to commit the whole damn thing. That's all."

ABRAMS: "Now we've been, urged on by our own Department of Defense, studying the personnel infiltration system over here, and trying to get all the intelligence together that we can get to see if there's some way to attack the personnel when they're moving." T-stations and bivouacs along the way. Putting in microphone-like sensors. And CBUs on B-52s. Tape recording of three B-52s dropping their bombs at commo-liaison station T-31 in the early morning of 23 December 1971. BLU-23 and BLU-49 bomblets. Secondary explosions. "Shouts and other human sounds." Re this system [Island Tree]: "It sounds like it could be useful."

GENERAL VIEN: "We will have, probably, a big action on the B-3 Front."

ABRAMS: "When he [the enemy] reviews what happened the early part of the year, he must conclude that that came too late, the battle in the B-3 Front, because the airborne brigade, [which] had been in Lam Son 719, went to the B-3 Front and were the _stars_, the best troops involved in that situation. They're the ones that took these things and so on. And he knows all that."

ABRAMS: "In the beginning of this year, the initiative was all with you [addressing Vien]. He [the enemy] did not have the initiative. He was struggling with the problems in Cambodia and so on. And the situation in MR-3 and MR-4 was such that the entire general reserve could be taken out without placing MR-3 and MR-4 in any state of risk. . . . And so your government had the freedom at that moment to take both divisions of the general reserve and commit 'em in the north."

ABRAMS: "One thing, I think—he would not [like] to let you have that kind of freedom of action. So if he can create force in the B-3 Front and force in northern MR-1, or above Hai Van [Pass] . . . and play it so it's hard for you to make up your mind about the general reserve and whether it's in the right place and so on. This is one way that he could prevent [another] Lam Son 719, by making it uncertain in your mind about whether you should do something to help the B-3 Front or whether you can do something to go into Laos—."

ABRAMS: "We think he has his eye on the B-3 Front and northern MR-1 because those are the easiest for him to supply with adequate amounts of ammunition. He'll get all the food he needs from Cambodia for the B-3 Front. And so on. And he doesn't have any long lines [of communication] that can be threatened in South Vietnam. It's all by the base and by the border, and so it's secure for him."

ABRAMS: "For instance, if he does make some fairly substantial effort in the B-3 Front, and in the north, I think you will need both divisions of the general reserve to make sure that that doesn't become any kind of a success for him. And, as I understand it, the 3rd Division's coming along pretty good—not everything good, but it's coming and they keep working at it—and that's gonna help. But if he uses three divisions up there, they'll need some help."

ABRAMS: "So then—what to do in MR-3 and MR-4? And again, it has to be realistic. For instance, I think there's enough total force in MR-3 and MR-4 so, one, pacification does not have to go backward—I use the term pacification, I'm talking about control in the villages and hamlets, it does not have to go backward—and there's enough force that, if it can be shifted, it can contain the 5th, 7th, and 9th. Now these replacements to COSVN are not gonna get there before March. That's when they will begin to arrive. And I think they need replacements."

ABRAMS: "And then if I could suggest also, General Manh, about Krek—it looks like you should be ready, the JGS should be ready, by late January. That's when it could begin in the B-3 Front. So things should be ready by then. All right. Now, Krek is—if you're not going to have any general reserve in III and IV Corps, or if you don't want to commit and become entangled with the general reserve in III and IV Corps, then Krek needs to be examined, because it takes seven or eight battalions out there, plus the difficulty of protecting that road. If your forces were further back, it would give more flexibility. I don't mean that they have to come into South Vietnam and everybody get in a bunker—no. If you get not so much committed out there, then General Minh, or General Truong—they can run smaller operations and try to keep them [the enemy] off balance."

■ 1972

During the first six months of 1972 U.S. redeployment of 135,000 men, taken out in three increments, left 49,000 U.S. troops in Vietnam by the end of June.

Well before the year began, multiple indicators had given warning of an impending large-scale enemy attack shaping up for the following spring. That operation, which came to be known as the Easter Offensive and which commenced at the end of March and on three fronts—south of the DMZ, in the Central Highlands, and in the vicinity of An Loc northwest of Saigon—led to desperate fighting. General Abrams employed B-52s and tactical air, massively beefed up by augmentations from throughout the region and beyond, to telling effect on all three battlefields. Meanwhile North Vietnam's major ports were mined and bombing of military targets in that country resumed.

The antithesis of guerrilla warfare, this massive conventional invasion involved virtually every one of North Vietnam's divisions and a wide range of supporting units. By late June the South Vietnamese had stemmed the tide and retaken many positions lost in the early fighting, in the process inflicting—with the invaluable assistance of American airpower—such devastating losses on the enemy that it would be three years before he could mount another such major operation.

At the end of June Gen. Creighton Abrams completed five consecutive years of service in Vietnam, the last four in overall command of U.S. forces there, and returned to the United States to become Army Chief of Staff. He was succeeded in Vietnam by his deputy, Gen. Frederick C. Weyand.

4 JAN 1972: Southeast Asia Assessment

Presenting and critiquing a current assessment that General Abrams wants to present to President Thieu.

ABRAMS: "How many dry seasons now have the North Vietnamese put on their dry season offensive [in the Plaine des Jarres in Laos]?"

POTTS: "Sir, that's an annual thing, and it goes all the way back to 1962."

ABRAMS: "Why is it this year it's been so successful? What are the differences?"

POTTS: "He's started earlier to bring in more personnel, more units, and more equipment. This year he has a greater strength in the Plaine des Jarres than ever before." "He has brought in T-34 tanks—he's always used PT-76s before. He has this increased artillery. And I think, sir, he felt the time was necessary for him to make a good show of force, and that's where he had the least resistance."

BRIEFER: Significant indicators during the past two months: Movement of main force units and infiltration of personnel from North Vietnam to the south. Indicated advance preparation, planning, and thoroughly analyzed decisions. Already for 1972: 27,900 personnel in the pipeline, of which 11,700 are destined for the B-3 Front and 15,400 for COSVN. At the same time last year the total was 26,100. Then it was much less for the B-3 Front and more for COSVN. Letter suffixes indicate organized units using the infiltration system. This year 23 letter groups versus 9 for all of 1971, of which 15 (versus 3) are destined for the B-3 Front.

ABRAMS: "He's expanding his force structure in the B-3 Front," not just the number of people.

BRIEFER: Indicators reveal "the possible southward deployment of four of the five reserve divisions in North Vietnam, a commitment which occurred at Tet 1968 and during Lam Son 719 in March and April 1971."

ABRAMS (re the 304th, 308th, and 324B Divisions): "The thing we know is he's made up his mind he's willing to use them. That much is clear."

BRIEFER: Throughout the length of the panhandle (in Laos) the enemy has deployed at least 52 AAA battalions, some equipped with 100-mm guns.

ABRAMS: "In all of these, it's the growth that needs to be shown."

ABRAMS: Cites development of enemy GCI system along the border for control of his MiGs as another indicator.

■ ■ ■

ABRAMS: "The Montagnards don't regard themselves as the Highland Vietnamese. They regard themselves as <u>Montagnards</u>."

■ ■ ■

BRIEFER: The enemy has 23 battalions currently located in the DMZ area. There are already five regiments in the B-3 Front. Expect "increased main force activity in MR-1 and the B-3 Front."

ABRAMS: "One thing that he's [the enemy] been saying over and over again is to defeat Vietnamization. The effect of defeating Vietnamization, or showing that Vietnamization hasn't worked—its political impact in the United States would be fairly substantial. But we don't have to go into that. We can say that the goal of this is to show that Vietnamization hasn't worked, or to defeat Vietnamization, that sort of thing."

ABRAMS: "I want to drop 'pacification' out of this. What we're talking about now is efforts to undermine the authority, the influence, the presence of South Vietnamese government among its people, both urban and rural. And that's pretty much the way that last COSVN instruction reads—try to cope with, in whatever way they can, the effectiveness of GVN—authority, development, confidence—those terms. And that's kind of the way COSVN's saying it, too, if that instruction's authentic."

BRIEFER: "It appears that in the near future the enemy will continue the war at the current level, except for increased activity with NVA main force units in northern Laos, the B-3 Front, and northern Military Region 1."

BRIEFER: The enemy units moving south have been in North Vietnam rehabilitating and training since Lam Son 719.

ABRAMS: "I've got a—well, I say I've got—Vietnam's got a real problem. I feel <u>very</u> strongly that he's [the enemy] going to try to materialize all that we have seen here, in some way, in the course of '72. And it really will be the first six or eight months of '72—in that big gob of time."

ABRAMS: "We're in about as good a shape as we've ever been in intelligence, especially this far ahead."

ABRAMS: "Where we haven't gotten anywhere is with President Thieu." "I guess General Quang spoke to him, and he said yeah, he'd like to hear it [the assessment], after Tet sometime." "So I think I'm going to have to go and try to get to see the president, and lay this out. Somehow, out of that, in my opinion, he's got to feel some degree of urgency. It has to do with how his regular forces are handled here in MR-3 and 4, the freeing—the absolute freeing—of the general reserve, all of it, and getting it in the best of shape in the weeks that remain. He's got to move out on commanders that we know have got to be changed, and that's got to be done now. It <u>should</u> be done before the fight starts."

ABRAMS: "And incidentally, out of this, too, has got to come a more enlightened use of their air force. They've got to be able to switch the power from front to front in accordance with what the enemy's doing. And they know it."

ABRAMS: "They're doing the fighting, and they're the ones. So our advice starts about being—it's not that it's any better or any worse than it was, it's just the environment that your advice is in is [such that] it's just more suspect. And <u>you're</u> not going to do any of this, <u>they're</u> going to do it. And so <u>how</u> come you're saying all this? And then—the war has been going on a long time, and it's had its ups and downs, and they've survived it, and this is just another chapter, and why get excited about <u>this</u> one? The Americans are <u>always</u> getting excited, always want to get something done too fast and too quick and so on. Now, how do you go sailing into <u>that</u> and come out with a good result?"

ABRAMS: "Shouting's not going to do it. And throwing down the gauntlet's not going to do it. So then I was wondering—you know, we had that thing about the war going full circle, where we tried to look back several years. So maybe [provide] some feel, to start it off, in that area. We're not talking about salesmanship here, because we did take that look back to see, you know, what it kind of looked like. So maybe that would be the way to begin talking. What I'm really talking about—."

ABRAMS: "We've got to go to work here . . . [to] get me a book prepared so that I can go in the next three or four days and brief the president. And try to fit this to the history of this war."

ABRAMS: "And in there I'll want to tell him that the 22nd Division commander's just got to go. General Trien's got to be given another assignment, and General Thinh—the 22nd and the 25th. More and more the internal security thing has got to rest with the territorials and the police and the PSDF, so things like putting the regiment in Phuoc Tuy is a backward step. And maybe somewhere in there get into force structure problems. Are we going to tackle that sometime today? And manpower and these things that are going to have to be faced up to."

ABRAMS: "The only <u>possible</u> chance of this working is for me to see the president privately. You just can't talk like this to him in the presence of <u>any</u> <u>other</u> Vietnamese. It <u>rips</u> him. He's <u>president</u>. He can't. You just can't do that, not the way I want to explain it."

4 JAN 1972: Special Air Brief

ATTENDEES: Gen. Abrams, Gen. Lavelle, BG Cross, MG Carley, MG Cowles, MG Potts.

BRIEFER: Describes 1 January incident of a MiG that approached a U.S. Combat Apple RC-135 in Laotian air space (operating out of Thailand).

LAVELLE: "There's a couple of things here that bother us very much. According to the check data we have, that MiG's airborne radar has only about a 16-mile capability. Yet he said 'I had my target' at 40 clicks [kilometers], which is 24 miles. It was a bright moonlit night, and maybe he was seeing contrails in the air. But we don't want to get surprised and find out he has an airborne radar capability greater than we thought he had."

ABRAMS: "What's the pertinence of whether the B-52s go at night or in the daytime in that situation [response to Ambassador Godley's requests for strikes in the Plaine des Jarres]?"

LAVELLE: "Well, as far as I'm concerned, it's a hell of a lot easier—we can see the MiGs—to protect them in the daytime." "All those MiGs that come in up there come underneath any radar coverage that we have. And to perform an intercept on [the basis of] [***] is just about impossible. You don't know where the hell he is. We don't have the conventional radar environment. So we gotta pick them up ourselves. We're going to pick them up visually, we're going to pick them up on con trails, things we don't see at night."

LAVELLE (re reacting to these high-speed MiG runs): "What I'm trying to do temporarily is to keep the B-52s out of these high-threat areas at night" while we figure out what the hell he's trying to do.

ABRAMS: "As we go along, we've also got to be careful we don't get spooked out. It's a fine line."

ABRAMS (deciding on the B-52 employment restriction): "Jack, you're just going to have to keep going along the way you're going. And if we get into a tighter squeeze, we'll just have to talk about it some more, see what's possible."

BRIEFER: Update on Island Tree: In November 1971 "the database was sufficiently advanced to begin a test of targeting techniques." T-54, T-55, T-61, and T-62 were chosen. Leading infiltration groups were headed for the B-3 Front. First B-52 strikes were on the evening of 6 December 1971 against T-54 and T-61. On the evening of 14 December 1971 there were two B-52 strikes against T-62. Planning use of CBUs. 320th Division moving. Binh Tram 35 realigned commo-liaison system. New concept requesting target area validation instituted. Determined 18–31 December 1971 that elements of the 320th NVA Division could be passing through T-31, T-35, and T-36. Sensors placed. On morning of 23 December struck T-31 with B-52s using CBUs. Tac air was employed on the evening of 24 December. Again on the morning of 25 December B-52s with CBUs struck. T-36 was hit on the evening of 28 December. T-35 was hit on the evening of 29 December: "screams and shouts." And so on. Night of 1 January 1972: T-62 was struck in the evening with over 500 secondary explosions (much small-arms ammunition detonating).

ABRAMS: "For this group in this room it really is unnecessary to say anything, but I want this subject to be regarded as especially sensitive, and I just don't want it talked about anywhere except the fellows that have to work in it, must work in it, on a day-to-day basis. The rest of you, it's for your information, and you don't need to talk about it when you leave this room. I want him to work this out himself without having the help of an account of it in the *Stars & Stripes.*"

ABRAMS (to Lavelle): "And Jack, I think we ought to do all we can." "Incidentally, it was General Lavelle's idea to get the CBUs over at U Tapao in case something did turn up where we could use them, and it's turned out to be a very good thing. Now, Jack, I think we ought to use all of them we can in this program."

LAVELLE: Limited to three cells a day because of the loading effort. More than that means having a decrease in loading other B-52s with iron bombs. Running a total of 33 sorties (11 cells) per day.

■ ■ ■

ABRAMS (re translations of some North Vietnamese broadcasts): "We've got some very fine men in that translation business, because they do like they do in the funny papers—they just put stars and asterisks in place of some of the bad language. So it's good, clean reading."

BRIEFER (quoting a 3 January 1972 FBIS report): A Pham Van Dong 25 December 1971 speech expressed propaganda they have increasingly emphasized since Lam Son 719, that "a total Communist military victory is possible." Maintains it will be "possible to inflict a total defeat on the U.S. and to liberate the entire territory of the Indochina peninsula."

ABRAMS: "You can say it's to boost morale on high, but it's also preparing the troops for greater sacrifices."

ABRAMS: "One of Giap's great things at Dien Bien Phu was artillery, first because the French felt that they could never get it in there. And he got quite a bit in, and they just pounded and pounded and pounded those positions and the airfield and the whole thing. . . . They don't even have a devotee at Fort Sill that believes in artillery more than Giap. You reflect on all the—like the 130s over there—hell, that's just another chapter in Giap's artillery book. When he rolls out of the southern half of the DMZ, [FSB] Fuller, and Lam Son 719—first thing, moving that artillery in there."

BRIEFER: Cites 5 January 1972 Radio Hanoi statement that "the U.S. must now completely abandon its policy of Vietnamization in order to obtain the freedom of U.S. PWs."

CORDS BRIEFER: Reports only three victims of terrorist attacks in IV CTZ.

ABRAMS: "That's where it's probably a false report. That's just too good to be true. <u>Three</u> victims! That's impossible. Something's—something."

ABRAMS: "I think the answer to that is both sides are getting ready for Tet. I mean for <u>enjoying</u> Tet!"

WEYAND: "It was reported to us, and then it was confirmed yesterday by the prime minister, that Colonel Tu from Gia Dinh is going to command the 25th Division. He is a pretty good fighter."

ABRAMS: "Well, we have to be careful, but that ought to be sort of a blue ribbon thing."

■ ■ ■

BRIEFER: Puts up a chart showing six secondary explosions and no strike sorties.

ABRAMS: "That is really a very remarkable performance."

9 JAN 1972: Briefing for Lieutenant General Stilwell

Lt. Gen. Richard G. Stilwell, Army Deputy Chief of Staff for Military Operations, had earlier served in Vietnam as MACV J-3 and then MACV Chief of Staff (1963–1965) and as CG, XXIV Corps (1968–1969). Subsequently, as general, he was Commander in Chief, United Nations Command, Korea (1973–1976).

STILWELL: "When's he going to be ready in the B-3 Front?"

POTTS: "He's ready now." Lead elements of the 320th Division are also starting to come in. "He's just laying the groundwork now, and he should kick off up there sometime in January." Kontum area. "He hasn't had a division come to the B-3 Front in a long time."

BRIEFER: The last major contact in the delta was in September 1970 in the U Minh. Since then Territorial Forces, "as active as the regular forces," are conducting saturation-type operations and getting an average 80 enemy KIA per day. Cross-border operations are also being conducted out of IV CTZ.

10 JAN 1972: Secretary of the Army Froehlke Briefing

Robert F. Froehlke served as secretary of the army 1971–1973.

BRIEFER: Cites the enemy's "well planned and purposeful actions over the past seven weeks." Currently "protracted war" is being conducted. Now estimate 39,000 infiltration already. Last year 27,400 to the same date.

BRIEFER: The enemy geographic designations are: COSVN: Cambodia, MR-3, MR-4, part of MR-2. B-3 Front: Highlands area. MR-5: Three lower provinces in MR-1—Quang Nam, Quang Tin, and Quang Ngai, plus Binh Dinh, Phu Yen, etc. MR-TTH (Tri Thien Hue): All of Thua Thien and part of Quang Tri. B-5 Front: DMZ area.

BRIEFER: "During November and early December communications intelligence provided the first alert to the possible southward deployment of several NVA main force regiments. By late December, the Headquarters of the 320th and its three regiments were detected in the infiltration system, with an estimated arrival in the B-3 Front during the first two months of 1972. Also, during December intercepted messages revealed the deployment of the 24 Bravo Regiment, 304th Division, to the Laotian–Republic of Vietnam border west of Khe Sanh." The 324 Bravo Division also mentioned impending "new missions" in commo. The 308th Division also showed indications of impending movement. Thus possible southward deployment of four of the five reserve divisions in North Vietnam, "a commitment which occurred at Tet '68 and during Lam Son 719 in March and April of 1971."

■ ■ ■

FROEHLKE (looking at two photos of transporters with missiles mounted as displayed by the briefer): "Boy, you've got better eyes than I have."

ABRAMS: "One thing for sure, it's not a native on the way to market."

BRIEFER (re enemy logistics offensive that began 9 November 1971): By early January input of supplies had reached about one-half of that achieved by the same date during last year. Allied air operations interdicted the effort.

BRIEFER: Hanoi's annual offensive in the Plaine des Jarres, begun 17 December 1971, started more than a month earlier than the previous year. 130-mm artillery and T-34 tanks introduced.

BRIEFER: The enemy "has indicated that under the proper conditions he is prepared to commit the bulk of his forces to achieve an impressive advantage in Southeast Asia in 1972."

FROEHLKE: "Looking at northern Laos, the panhandle, Cambodia, and South Vietnam, and looking at our resources, it seems to me that our priorities <u>definitely</u> should be aimed at—maybe forgetting might be too harsh a word, but I'll say—forgetting northern Laos and doing <u>whatever</u> we can in the panhandle, because that's the key to Cambodia—the long-range key to Cambodia—and South Vietnam. Would you agree?"

ABRAMS: "I do think that, right now, we've spread the assets that we have too far. But I have to say, too, that what we're doing is what we've been directed to do. The priorities are in accordance with the guidance that we have."

FROEHLKE: "Are those priorities sound?"

ABRAMS: "I think very soon they're going to have to be re-sorted. And I think our <u>government's</u> going to have to do it." "Let's say Souvanna Phouma packs up his family and goes off to Paris for some kind of a—. He's stuck with it about as long as he can, and it just ain't working. And then the—and with it might go their blessing for bombing in Laos. Then the problem for our government is whether we would continue the bombing. You'd have to bite that bullet. But it's pretty clear if we don't, and if we don't focus our resources on southern Laos, particularly the air, it's going to present a very difficult problem for the South Vietnamese."

FROEHLKE: "The heat right now, from our Congress, is on the bombing, and this is where they're going to hit us. It probably would be more in terms of tonnage than it would be a dollar limit." "With that in mind, if you were given a choice to try to end run that, thinking they were going to make that decision, what is the feasible alternative if you're reassigning your priorities?"

ABRAMS: "It should be focused in that area from Mu Gia down. . . . It's really very clear."

ABRAMS: "These remaining divisions in North Vietnam—the 324B, the 304th, and the 308th—no one knows when or where they'll be committed. But the thing that <u>is</u> very clear is that he has made the decision that he will use those, even though it takes all of his reserves. The 325th I think is really a training division, anyway. That'd be the only division left in North Vietnam."

ABRAMS: "But he's made the decision that he's willing to commit all or any part of those regular forces. And he'll <u>do</u> it."

ABRAMS (re Lam Son 719): "There was always a lot of question about whether there was surprise. Well, certainly in the strategic sense there was, because he did not begin his reaction to it until <u>after</u> it got going into Laos. He was worried that—he was counting those carriers out there. He didn't know whether it was going to be an amphibious landing, whether it was going to be an airborne—. He even gave them credit for flying the troops in from the carriers at one point. I mean he was—it presented a lot of problems for him."

ABRAMS: "The initiative here was really with the South Vietnamese. And after the cross-border operations were over in '70 and that whole thing had gone on, what happened—what <u>really</u> happened—was that the situation in the COSVN area was such that the entire general reserve could be taken out of there without putting MR-3 and MR-4 in any kind of a threat position from the South Vietnamese viewpoint. The Airborne Division and the Marine Division were free, and that's what made Lam Son 719 possible. It couldn't have been attempted any other way, not with just the forces that were up here in MR-1. So the initiative then was here."

ABRAMS: "The picture—what you've got developing here, now, I think, among other things, shows the thoroughness with which he [the enemy] critiqued all of that after it was all over. And that's why the 320th is on its way down here to the B-3 Front, plus adequate individual replacements for the units already there, and for whatever losses are sustained by the 320th when it gets into it." "So sometime toward the end of this month, the beginning of next month, he can start playing this thing so that it presents the Vietnamese with a tough problem—the <u>South</u> Vietnamese—on what they can do with the general reserve."

ABRAMS: "We've been trying to make the point, now, for some time, and it's caught on to a degree, but it's kind of hard for them to—it means breaking old patterns and that sort of thing. But they've got six divisions here in MR-3 and MR-4. There're these three enemy divisions up here, and one down here—the 1st, the 5th, the 7th, and the 9th. And we feel that they should take this area here, including Cambodia, and by being able to slide those divisions, or other troops, back and forth as between corps areas and Cambodia, that basic six-division force is the way you handle these four, and the Cambodian problems. The general reserve—the two divisions in the general reserve—are available for MR-1 and MR-2. I don't mean that they have to be <u>stationed</u> there, but they should be on a more or less permanent basis available to work it."

ABRAMS: "Along with it, they've got to be able to use their air force as <u>one</u> air force. The way it <u>has</u> been—it's beginning to change—but the way it has been it's been <u>four</u> air forces, one in each military region, and the assets that are there are for the personal and private use of that military region commander. Even in the heyday of our greatest amount of helicopters and tactical air and B-52s we couldn't do it that way. <u>Nobody's</u> rich enough to have a bunch of air forces. They're easing out of it."

FROEHLKE: "If General Vien and General Lam and General Dzu were here in person and hearing you say that, would they agree in principle?"

ABRAMS: "Uh—no, no. If General Vien was here, <u>he'd</u> agree. If you got General Dzu here to talk about how to handle the B-3 Front problem, he'd agree with <u>that</u>. And then, if you got Lam in to talk about what you ought to do when <u>he</u> gets in trouble up there, he'd agree with <u>that</u>."

BRIEFER: Quotes secretary of defense guidance that "the objective of Viet-namization was to transfer progressively to the Government of Vietnam greatly increased responsibility for all aspects of the war." "One assumption with this guidance was that U.S. redeployment would continue." The RVNAF are authorized a force of 1.1 million under currently approved guidance.

BRIEFER: On 10 June 1971 the secretary of defense approved a COMUSMACV recommendation to accelerate Program 3 and reach the 1.1 million manpower ceiling by the end of FY 1972. Subsequent changes to the approved program have been dictated by several factors, including "the need for improved command and control."

BRIEFER: On 1 October 1971 the ARVN 3rd Infantry Division was formed in Quang Tri Province in northern MR-1, principally from the redesignation of existing units. Two of its three regiments are currently deployed. At about 80 percent strength. Expect it to be fully deployed by April 1972.

BRIEFER: On 1 August 1971 the 20th Tank Squadron was activated. It is stationed in Quang Tri Province and provides the only ARVN medium tank capability.

FROEHLKE: "What differentiates their marines from the army divisions?"

ABRAMS: "The big difference is they're marines and the army's army. Otherwise the equipment, mission, tactics are all the same."

BRIEFER: In RF/PF 554,000 are authorized, constituting about half the total manpower authorization.

FROEHLKE (re RVNAF Improvement & Modernization): "What concerns you, what one or two main items concern that could occur that could sort of throw this what appears to be a really good program and one that's worked out well, what could happen to really throw some sand in the gears?"

ABRAMS: "As far as this thing is concerned, I think it'll just go along. Now please understand I don't mean that this is without problems, without flaws. It's got them. But it keeps going, it keeps moving, they keep getting better and they take on more. The logistics system's coming up to snuff, and so I think it's going to be all right."

ABRAMS: "I think the thing you worry about here that would have real shock effect in it is something happening to this government, or [if] some disaster befell the economy. And that would put this under—well, the effects on the leadership. What they've had here now is almost five years of stability in government. And you go back into that period after Diem and so on—see, what that does to leadership in the army, hell, a fellow that had a division or a corps, he didn't know when he got up in the morning whether he was still going to have it. He might not have been in on something that occurred that night! So it made him a little touchy. You know, that's just a <u>bad</u> thing."

ABRAMS (responding to question about the possibility of a coup): "I just don't think that's in the cards. The military leadership that they've got here now, I don't believe could be tempted under any circumstances to touch that with a ten-foot pole. The ones that were on the periphery of that, they know that's the wrong way. They're not certain that this is the finest thing, but they know that's no good. After all, they know the Vietnamese better than we do, and they realize you can't trust any of them." [Laughter]

JACOBSON: "From my standpoint in pacification, the people in the delta, and in III Corps, have got more money than they've ever had in their lives. And, being a farmer from Minnesota, I know that if you've got a good crop and somebody that will buy it, this gives you a warm feeling toward your government like almost nothing else. Well, I've seen them walk into farm machinery shops and take out of their black pajamas a million two hundred thousand piasters and pay for a tractor, then go driving down the road with it. In fact, it isn't going to be too long before the people here are going to have to go to the zoo to see a water buffalo. They're just becoming outmoded."

FROEHLKE: "How do the Vietnamese view Vietnamization?"

ABRAMS: "I think that with two or three exceptions—I'm thinking here in terms of division commanders—the rest of the senior military feel that it is their job to do. They'll try to get all the equipment and all that sort of thing that they can from the United States, but I think—well, people like General Truong, people like General Lam—this _is_ their job. And they've been given the time, and the time's now that, the point's now arrived at, where _they_ are the ones. And they think they _should_, and they think they _can_."

JACOBSON: "I think a significant point, sir, is if you had asked that question a year and a half ago, we would have had to answer in a totally different way."

ABRAMS: "That's right."

JACOBSON: "Now they have confidence in their ability. Look at Nam in the 7th Division. He used to scream bloody murder, 'We can't get along without the Americans,' throw up his hands. Now he's confident and he's not concerned."

ABRAMS: "At the time they were considering the first withdrawal—25,000—I'll bet you, this is just guessing, but I'll bet you you couldn't have found 10 Americans in this country who would agree that that could be done safely. So they've changed, too."

FROEHLKE: "It seems to me that in the good news category we can put Vietnamization. It's working well."

ABRAMS (re General Khuyen): "This fellow _is_ one of the most capable officers they've got in their armed forces."

BRIEFER: OPLAN 208A mandates getting out of here, and getting the roll-up force out of here, by June 1st. About 9,000 people are involved in the roll-up. Going down to 60,000 left in country."

ABRAMS: "We've _got_ to continue the intelligence activity, and we've _got_ to have communications. I'm just trying to emphasize the point that this is a real tough thing that hasn't got any _real_ flexibility _left_ in it. Actually, all the actions we've taken in the headquarters for several months now have been all tuned to this . . . because we had to start a long time ago to do this if we were in fact going to be _able_ to do it."

15 JAN 1972: WIEU

ATTENDEES: Amb. Berger, Gen. Abrams, Gen. Weyand, Gen. Lavelle, LTG McCaffrey, Mr. Jacobson, MG Cowles, MG Fuson, MG Jumper, MG Potts, MG Slay, MG Adamson, MG Carley, Mr. Duval, RADM Salzer, BG Trogdon, BG Brown, BG Heiser, BG Herbert, BG Lanagan, BG Wickham, Col. Knepp, Col. Sadler, Capt. Perez, Col. Crockett, Col. Bryant.

ABRAMS: "That Island Tree is producing more than anything. We've really got to stay with it."

ABRAMS: "As far as the DMZ, the indications are that he's going to deploy his divisions to northern MR-1, and we think it could develop into some pretty heavy fighting in northern MR-1."

ABRAMS (has the map put back up): "Now, Jack [Lavelle]—say this thing gets going up here in the northern part of the country in March or April, something like that. This territory in here is all going to really be part of the battle. It'll have SAMs, you've got the Dong Hoi Airfield in here, and so on. I think we ought to be studying now the kind of authorities we want for that period, including that airfield, including their GCI, including the SAMs—the whole thing. He's got a lot in here now, and it's going to be <u>hard</u>, it's going to be hard to fight this thing, support the South Vietnamese, by having this line drawn across here. Christ, you're just going into the ring with one arm tied behind you and the other one broken and in a cast."

ABRAMS: "We'll get those things about, 'Use all your existing authorities to the fullest' and so on, but that ain't gonna work. It <u>won't</u> work. So we better start studying this now on what we're going to want and what we're going to need for that, and start working on it."

LAVELLE: "Just off the top of my head, one of the first ones we probably should get in—there are two <u>really</u> vital targets that we've got to get at up there. The Dong Hoi and Quang Khe storage areas and transshipment points."

ABRAMS: "Well, I'm not—."

LAVELLE: "What's wrong with those targets is that they're right among the damn villages and residential areas. We have to hit those on a good day [weather-wise], so we should have some standing authority that if we ever get a good day—otherwise, we can't get them because IFR they're too close to—."

ABRAMS: "I'm not talking about any one-day or 72-hour or five-day thing. This will have to go from the time it gets kind of organized, and it will have to be continuous authority. That's what I'm talking about. This battle—it will last at least 45 days, and we need the authority for the entire period. We're going to have to take losses to do it, but the kind of thing it is, that's what's going to have to be done."

ABRAMS: "Now you take the sum of what we've been looking at here and what's been happening for the last three months and—I just don't want anybody to have the feeling that this is sort of the seasonal pattern of things. You add up <u>everything</u> and this thing that we've been watching here for three months, it's no <u>damn</u> seasonal <u>pattern</u>! He's getting ready to turn on all he's got, <u>all</u> <u>he's</u> <u>got</u>! He couldn't—when this thing is over, he wouldn't have been able to do one more thing. That's what you've got coming!"

ABRAMS: "When you add what he's doing with the MiGs, what he <u>has</u> done with the MiGs, a-d-d what he's doing with the SAMs, and has done with the SAMs, and you a-d-d the possible movement of the last of all his general reserve in North Vietnam, you look at the infiltration, what you know about it at this stage of the game (and it's going up), we haven't seen the last of it. I don't want to use 'seasonal pattern' any more. That <u>ain't</u> what it is!"

■ ■ ■

BRIEFER: Describes a major reorganization of the 559th Transportation Group that is under way, involving formation of three new transportation groups: 471, 472, and 473, and several new *binh trams*. Streamlining the system, we feel.

ABRAMS: "Well, you don't streamline by adding more headquarters, I'll tell you that. This may be one of the saving graces."

ABRAMS: "I don't know, Jack, whether the time has come to think in terms of concentrating our efforts a little more. I just have a feeling we're scattering our shots a lot. Now we've got to take care of the ambassador up there in northern Laos. And, as you point out, we [get?] worried about this, too. But [Abrams is at the map as he speaks now] this part up here is very important, too. It's a real hub. In fact, one of the great things that came out of Lam Son 719—by getting in there, the use of air—B-52s and tac air, not only against the troops, but the secondaries and stuff we got out of it, when we started getting the targeting good—that was putting the <u>real</u> power on—<u>concentration</u> of air. Some of it in support of Lam Son 719 was just plain working on the peripheries of that, and did a lot of damage. And I think the presence of the SAMs in there is an indication of the importance of it to him. And I think it's something we need to think about, whether we need to spread our effort—or whether it's appropriate any longer to spread the effort. I'm not saying, one way or the other. I don't know. I think we ought to think about it."

■ ■ ■

POTTS (to Jacobson, during a break): "What do you think?"
JACOBSON: "I don't like what I'm hearing. It's too reminiscent. It doesn't look good."
POTTS (to Cowles): "What do you hear from Ambassador Colby?"
COWLES: "Well, he's back at the old store. And I'm sure he's doing the best job anybody could. He always does. I tell you, they're lucky to have him."

■ ■ ■

BRIEFER: Reports North Vietnam's reaction to "the recently increased bombing of North Vietnam," citing an 8 January 1972 report that Vo Van Sung, chief of the DRV delegation general in Paris, stated the North Vietnamese were very worried at the beginning of 26–30 December 1971 that the ports of Haiphong and three others might be destroyed. Due to the loss of Sihanoukville, the loss of these ports would have greatly complicated receipt of Soviet arms and aid shipments, and would have made the DRV almost exclusively reliant on the Chinese. Sung said "all policy for the development of the armed struggle was based upon the rhythm of resupply. Thus the destruction of the ports would quickly have become a catastrophe."

On 26 December 1971 certain bombing of North Vietnam had been resumed.

BRIEFER: In Paris this week, acting PRG chief delegate Nguyen Van Tien attended the 140th Plenary Session. RVN chief delegate Lam announced the RVN position that the withdrawal of all U.S. forces depends upon Communist willingness to negotiate the withdrawal of North Vietnamese troops, as well as on the release of prisoners of war. Ambassador Porter confirmed the U.S. position on the issue by strongly seconding the RVN position.

ABRAMS: "Yesterday morning, coincident with the president's announcement about further troop withdrawals, I just want you to know we got a message from our secretary of defense praising the magnificent leadership that had brought us so far and so on, great confidence in our—how we'll handle the future [laughter]—and I forgot to get that distributed [more laughter]. Then in the afternoon Colonel Bryant came in and said there was a report out I was being relieved [more laughter]. So every day's a little mixed—good news and bad news." [They joke about which was which, the good news and the bad, and for Weyand as well.]

WEYAND: "That's right—we were both crying." [More laughter]

SOMEONE: "I thought it was rude of you guys not to tell us of your going. We had to hear it on the radio. I thought we were more in your confidence than that."

ABRAMS: "When Colonel Bryant told me that, I said call 'em back [the press office] and find out where the hell I'm going. [Laughter] I was a little worried. My wife took off for Burma. She's visiting Burma for three or four days on one of the package deals. I didn't want to have to leave before she got back."

■ ■ ■

ABRAMS: "On B-52s, first of all we have to meet Ambassador Godley's requirements. We can't hardly get out of that and this Island Tree thing—that's a good program. Then that whole thing that's developing there in the highlands. We don't want to get tied down to some point, but that battle's coming up and we might just as well start to get to work on it. And that's basically what I think we ought to be doing with the B-52s."

ABRAMS: "We've got a message in from CINCPAC on how is all this stuff being infiltrated. It's kind of got a note or tone to it that somehow all this has snuck up on us. Somebody just hasn't been reading the traffic, because it's been marching right along."

ABRAMS: "And he wants to know which outfits these are we've been hitting in Island Tree. Well, we don't know that. And we'd better be careful about how much we start guessing." "We don't know everything yet about Island Tree—just what it is we're getting into." "We don't want to get too narrow a view of what this Island Tree program is leading to. Of course we'd all love to knock hell out of the 320th, but now it looks like there might be more involved than whatever these groups are in there. Hell, these secondaries in there—that's kind of impressive." "In other words, a fellow shouldn't be too narrow-minded about what he's willing to hit. It sounds like it's all good."

16 JAN 1972: Briefing for DEPCOMUSMACV and Lieutenant General Corcoran

WEYAND: Refers to an excellent recent J-2 JGS briefing that pointed out that for the first time the North Vietnamese are publicizing the mobilization of troops and their movement from Hanoi to "the 'front,' as they refer to it."

WEYAND: "I guess that old business of they're 'not involved' in any of this—they've given up on that."

POTTS: Have newspapers with front-page photos of troops being moved out.

■ ■ ■

SOMEONE: "All the secretary could say, when I was back for the commanders conference, was, 'Don't you let a scandal occur in a PDO [Property Disposal Office] yard.'" "They're not thinking about the security of the troops."

WEYAND: "I guess the truth of it is they don't want a scandal of any kind."

SOMEONE: "That's right—'Just don't make no mistakes.' That's what the sergeant told me when I came here in 1968: 'Sir, you'll be all right. Just don't make no mistakes.'"

■ ■ ■

BRIEFER: "During January 1971 the HES scoring system was modified to make it more sensitive to the enemy's increased political emphasis on terrorism and the work of the Viet Cong infrastructure. The major effect was to reduce the percentage of the population [judged to be] living in A or B hamlets."

BRIEFER: The 1971 Community Defense and Local Development Plan "takes into account the full spectrum of Vietnamese life."

20 JAN 1972: Special Authorities Brief: COMUS and Ambassadors Bunker and Berger

ALSO ATTENDING: Gen. Lavelle, MG Carley, MG Potts, MG Cowles.

ABRAMS: "What we thought we'd do here is just have a little summary of the assessment, and then go to this message."

BRIEFER: Begins by reading from Abrams's message to McCain and Moorer: Purpose is "to describe . . . impending enemy offensive in the Republic of Vietnam, the impact of ongoing operations on the Commando Hunt interdiction campaign, and the additional authorities that will be needed for the conduct of an effective defense in the coming period." "There is no doubt that this is to be a major campaign." Main thrust is expected to be against MR-2 from the B-3 Front and in northern MR-1. Message goes through the indicators of NVA division deployment. "We believe the enemy will be prepared to mount main force warfare in the B-3 Front, northern Military Region 1, and, to a lesser extent, in enemy Military Region 5 by late January or early February."

MESSAGE: "The [interdiction] campaign [Commando Hunt VII] has been degraded by the diversion of air effort to other missions. Last year our strike sorties in the interdiction campaign in Steel Tiger increased from 6,625 in November to 9,510 in January. During the same period this year strike sorties have declined in the area from 4,967 in November 1971 to an estimated 4,710 sorties in January 1972."

ABRAMS: "Not even half."

MESSAGE: "The forthcoming battle will probably include MiG and SAM activity in close proximity to the North Vietnam border in the vicinity of the DMZ. Effective protection of our forces will require new operating authorities which must be in hand from the outset. I therefore request that the following standby authorities be approved now for use as needed throughout the battle." Abrams requests:

■ Fighter aircraft may strike enemy MiG aircraft on the ground at Dong Hoi, Vinh, and Quan Lang.

■ Fighter aircraft, including Iron Hand, may strike active ground control intercept radars in North Vietnam below 20 degrees north. Rationale: For several years North Vietnam has had the resources and ability to integrate the GCI-fighter combination with AAA and SAMs and thereby establish a highly effective air defense system. During a MiG engagement, GCI radars perform the same function for the MiGs as do guidance radars for SAMs. Each time the MiGs have been active, the North Vietnamese radar GCI system begins to radiate as is the case in preparation for firing surface-to-air missiles. With operative GCI radar, the MiG pilots are provided with positive radar control and warning, which places them in a vastly superior position to complete their mission. It is apparent that the aggressive MiG activity is closely associated with the activation of these GCI radars, and that the enemy is training intensively toward the end of disrupting operations in Laos and destroying a B-52 or other U.S. aircraft. In addition to the use of GCI radars to control and vector attacking fighters, the enemy is using GCI radars as an integral part of the SA-2 missile fire control system. The SA-2 missiles are aimed and launched using [electronic warfare] [changed in postconference discussion among Cowles, Potts, and Carley to "early warning"] or GCI radar-derived azimuth and range information. At a predetermined time, the Fan Song radar is turned on for very short periods to provide terminal guidance information. This tactic effectively negates the protection afforded by our radar homing and warning equipment, since there is little time to evade the missile. Whether paired with missiles or MiGs, the EW-GCI radars are being utilized like any other fire control radar. Therefore the authority to strike EW-GCI radars controlling fighter aircraft and missile attacks on U.S. and allied aircraft is necessary to effectively counter the North Vietnamese air defense capability in southern Laos and northern Republic of Vietnam.

■ Fighter aircraft, including Iron Hand, may strike any occupied SAM site and associated equipment in North Vietnam that is located within 19 nautical miles, or SAM range, of the provisional military demarcation line and within 19 nautical miles of the North Vietnam–Laotian border as far north as 19 nautical miles above the Mu Gia Pass. Rationale: Immediate protective reaction strikes against SAM and AAA and associated equipment as presently authorized leaves to the enemy the initiative to contest this critical air space. The principal result to be achieved by the implementation of this proposal is to maintain control of that minimum essential air space required for the conduct of Arc Light and tac air operations in the critical infiltration passes and the anticipated battle zone in the northern Republic of Vietnam. We must not allow enemy interference with our use of air power, which may be the decisive element in the battle.

■ Sensors may be implanted throughout the DMZ.

■ Fixed- and rotary-wing aircraft may be employed for logistics support, troop lift, and medevac in support of RVNAF limited cross-border operations in Laos or the Khmer Republic when requirements exceed VNAF capabilities. Rotary-wing gunships may be employed when necessary to provide security of these operations."

MESSAGE: "The seriousness of the developing situation and the need for prior preparation demand the most urgent consideration. The stakes in this battle will be great. If it is skillfully fought by the Republic of Vietnam, supported by all available U.S. air, the outcome will be a major defeat for the enemy, leaving him in a weakened condition and gaining decisive time for the consolidation of the Vietnamization effort. When the time comes, it is imperative that the available U.S. air power be focused specifically and directly against the threat to the Republic of Vietnam, realizing that it will mean reduced support for Laos and Cambodia. As it is, we are running out of time in which to apply the full weight of air power against the buildup. The additional authorities requested . . . are urgently needed. The rate of the enemy buildup, and our uncertainty as to the exact timing of his offensive, pose a most dangerous situation in which the field commander must be accorded maximum flexibility and authority to deal with what will be probably a very rapidly developing threat of major proportions. I view the probable main battle zone as that area north and south of the DMZ in which we can expect to find the main enemy maneuver and combat support forces capable of directly influencing the course of the battle in South Vietnam. I must have the necessary authority to deal with those forces from the outset. There will be no time for reassessment of the need for additional authorities as in the past. For this reason, I am requesting the removal of those current constraints on our operating authorities which would deny necessary application of force and freedom of action within the battle zone. In the final analysis, when this is all over, specific targets hit in the southern part of North Vietnam will not be a major issue. The issue will be whether Vietnamization has been a success or a failure."

BUNKER: "Good."

ABRAMS: "At some point we're going to have to do less in Laos."

BUNKER: "Yes, yeah."

ABRAMS: "Well, hopefully it will be in hand to some degree by the time the fire breaks out in Kontum and Pleiku."

BUNKER: "Well, as I see it, the air is going to be the decisive factor in this, as it has been so often in the past in support of the ARVN. It was up there last year it turned the tide, you remember."

BUNKER: Asks whether there are any additional authorities that would be useful.

RESPONSE: We've kept it to the battle area itself. Discussion of supply storage areas, especially POL.

ABRAMS: "Let's add one thing to this—that's authority to strike his supply facilities to 18 degrees. And the rationale is these are the supply facilities that will be in direct support of the battle."

BUNKER: "If you want to add that I've seen it and concur, glad to have you do it."

■ ■ ■

BRIEFER: Comparative infiltration estimates as of this date: 1969: 26,000. 1972: 50,000.

POTTS (discussing gap groups): "If you look at all of this pattern on infiltration, and you know we have the gap groups that appear in there, and there's certain methodology. In other words, we have to get the gap groups down to where there's just four or five before we pick them up. In there right now we have some that are 11 apart. If all of those are eventually filled in, if you took all of the gap groups that surely we'll get to before long, it'll pick up 16,000 men, which would make the estimate right now what it was for all of 1971."

ABRAMS: "We consider this message to be very sensitive. I'll have the commanders in Friday evening and Saturday. I tentatively plan to let the principals read this, but I will not provide any of them with a copy. I want them to get the flavor of it. As messages go, this is probably the most unequivocal message we've ever sent—on the situation. But I think the evidence is very clear."

BUNKER: "I think it's time to be unequivocal, because there's so much at stake."

ABRAMS: "I'm in hopes that this will get all the way, or the essence of this will get all the way, to him [the president]. I don't see how they can afford not to."

BUNKER: "I can send in—I can flag it to see that he does."

22 JAN 1972: Commanders WIEU

ATTENDEES: Amb. Bunker, Amb. Berger, Gen. Abrams, Gen. Weyand, Gen. Lavelle, LTG McCaffrey, LTG Dolvin, MG Cowles, MG Bowley, MG Hollingsworth, MG Fuson, MG Jumper, MG Young, MG Clay, MG Carley, MG Watkin, Mr. Funkhouser, Mr. Vann, Mr. Duval, RADM Salzer, BG Trogdon, BG Brown, BG Heiser, BG Blazey, BG Wear, BG Bernstein, BG Herbert, BG Scott, BG Lanagan, BG Wickham, Mr. Dean, Mr. Payette, Col. Knepp, Capt. Perez, Col. Zerbe, Col. Crockett, Col. Bryant, Mr. Barnes.

BRIEFER: Infiltration Estimate for 1972 "has already reached 50,400." Of these, 21,400 (42 percent) are for the B-3 Front. 22,400 are for COSVN (44 percent). "Infiltration during the December–April period this year will far exceed that for corresponding periods in 1970 and 1971."

BRIEFER: "Letter suffixes normally indicate organized units using the infiltration system for transit to their destination." Already accepted 36 letter-suffix groups, versus only 9 for all of 1971. Of these, 20 are headed for the B-3 Front, suggesting the enemy is expanding his force structure there.

BRIEFER: "[We have a report that the] chief DRV delegate to the Paris peace conference said Communist forces in South Vietnam are about to launch a massive spring military offensive. Besides its impact upon the internal situation, the offensive is designed to accomplish major political objectives outside Vietnam. First, it will draw public attention away from President Nixon's February visit to Communist China and refocus it upon the Vietnam War. [***] said that the North Vietnamese expect that Nixon's conversations in Peking may bring new developments concerning the war, and the DRV leaders do not want to be, quote, surprised. Second, it will strengthen the DRV position at the Paris talks. Additionally, the offensive will coincide with the extensive propaganda campaign being carried out in Europe by antiwar groups which will be climaxed by an international conference on 11–13 February."

BRIEFER: Cites report of 19 January 1972 just received from the USDAO Paris quoting a source who was formerly Le Duc Tho's private secretary: The Soviets are "flooding" North Vietnam with equipment, but our stomachs are empty. Great pressure from both the Russians and the Chinese for the North Vietnamese to take sides. A new growing movement [in North Vietnam] is the "Young Guard," which is very antiforeign and nationalistic. U.S. air strikes recently added to North Vietnamese uncertainty over President Nixon's prior [sic] lack of predictability. All U.S. POWs are in Hanoi, closely guarded, but much better treated than was the case four or five months ago. North Vietnamese officials are concerned at the very heavy truck losses, and are seeking to obtain large numbers of trucks from the USSR. He stated that they have quite a large truck fleet already, but that a high percentage of the vehicles are deadlined because of repair and spare parts problems. U.S. air strikes have seriously aggravated the problem. Quoted a high-ranking DRV friend as saying, "We will make noise in Saigon next month." The North Vietnamese are very disturbed by reports that they had lost the war in the south and let Vietnamization succeed, and they were prepared to commit forces—including tanks and aircraft—in an effort to demonstrate that this allegation is untrue, quote, "even if they had to sit down to rest for a long time afterward."

BRIEFER: Quotes text of a speech given by General Vo Nguyen Giap to high-level civilian and military authorities as printed in the 19 December 1971 issue of *Nhan Dan,* the official daily publication. Theme of the speech: "We must fight with determination to win in order to ensure victory, which is near." "In order to fulfill the goals of Chairman Ho Chi Minh, all young men must fight." "A costly battle is ahead. Much sacrifice and heartache will precede our victory." "The armed forces must be increased. All youths, regardless of past deferments, must serve." "Victory is in sight."

ABRAMS: "They've got a pretty good big plan, and they're going to do a lot, but when it's all over it'll be some fraction of that. They haven't got that capability."

VANN: "We made an analysis last spring down in the delta which compared the orders that had been issued prior to Tet '68 and those that had been issued in an April 1970 high point versus what had been accomplished. We found, of course, that they had gone from somewhere around 50 percent—that is, they'd accomplished about half as much as was ordered in Tet—to far less than 10 percent of what was ordered in the spring of 1970. In the highlands a similar thing. We see the disparity over the last nine months of about 10 to 1 between what is ordered to be done and what is then subsequently accomplished."

ABRAMS: "There's no reason for the Vietnamese to be really frightened. It's good to know what he has in mind. That's how you stop it."

BRIEFER: We have various reports that the enemy offensive will begin close to Tet, "within three days" and so on.

BRIEFER: "Other agent reports in Military Region 3 have also alluded to a three-phase countrywide coordinated campaign which will be directed primarily at seizing rural areas and selected provinces in order to force the GVN into a coalition government."

BRIEFER: "In Military Region 4 a 9 January document from VC Ben Tre Province contains a special order concerning a quote, general uprising, unquote, phase to be conducted by provincial units . . . an attack to be conducted continuously until victory." "It acknowledged that, quote, almost all rural areas are pacified, unquote, but asserts that the VC must, in effect, exploit the situation before the GVN can consolidate control of the villages and hamlets."

BRIEFER: "In early January [1972] General Vien issued a directive to subordinate commanders emphasizing the need for increased security measures and preparations to be made to counter the expected enemy offensive."

VANN: "I have one observation. It's beautiful what the enemy is planning to do, because it appears in II Corps that he's going to make the same basic tactical error that he made in Tet '68, and that is fragment his forces in so many different directions that he will not put a real weight of effort on any one attack. And that loans itself very well to the way our forces are already deployed. We are making some adjustments of the forces in line with the most likely scenario so as to require a minimum of movement once the attack starts."

BRIEFER: Washington currently has General Abrams's request for additional authorities "under consideration."

ABRAMS: "Beginning Monday, we'll have 20 IG teams scouring the country to review the effectiveness with which these instructions [for an increased state of readiness] have been carried out. That'll continue until we think we've surveyed the most—. The way I look at that, I think it will be helpful to everybody. That's really the way I'm going at it. . . . There's a lot of little places all over the country, and there's always somebody who hasn't got the word."

BRIEFER: "For the first time since 1965 we face a situation in which a major enemy offensive must be defeated largely by RVNAF resources. U.S. support will consist mainly of tac air and Arc Light, with some U.S. Army combat support participation. The degree of U.S. participation will depend on the stage of redeployment during which the enemy initiates his offensive. The reduced level of U.S. force participation in comparison with prior major operations will result in a somewhat changed role for U.S. advisory elements in coordinating operational support. However, there will be an increased need to maximize the efficient employment of all available support forces, both U.S. and RVNAF."

BRIEFER: Cites MACV and JGS directives of 8 July and 14 August 1971 that provided for establishment of Operational Support Coordination Groups in each military region. "These directives were based on a study conducted in April 1971, subsequent to Lam Son 719." They've been exercised.

ABRAMS (explaining to Bunker): "What this really is all about, sir, is that air, either tac air or B-52s, or helicopters or gunships, artillery, really aren't any good unless the munitions land on the enemy. Well, even at our reduced capabilities here there's just a <u>hell</u> of a lot of it. . . . To get all that in there, where it's doing <u>good</u>, and at the right time and the right place, <u>really</u> requires some excellent coordination and understanding and all that at the field headquarters. Of course, we worry about it—you know, trying to get that going good. But when you compare what the Vietnamese are capable of doing right now in this department with <u>any</u> of these other countries around here—Laos, Thailand, Cambodia—it's really like trying to compare a kid in the first grade with a guy who's working on his doctorate. That's the difference." "The Vietnamese have come a long, long way in this whole area. That doesn't mean that anybody can be complacent about it, and that's why we're talking about it."

BUNKER: "That's very encouraging."

BRIEFER: In OSCG: Air liaison officers (VN and U.S.), army aviation elements, AF advisory team, fire support coordinator, intelligence element (including G-2 Air), G-3 element (with G-3 Air), Arc Light element, G-4 element.

BRIEFER: "Air support will play a dominant part in this campaign." Cites "the coming scarcity of U.S. helicopter assets."

■ ■ ■

VANN (re Lam Son 719): "I talked while I was on leave to Phil Brady, who was in Lam Son, in fact was shot down three times during the Lam Son operation and walked out of Laos. Phil pretty well indicated that there was a conspiracy to put the blackest possible look on it, and the operation, based upon a resentment on the part of the reporter group over the death of Larry Burroughs and others, and the refusal of the U.S. to allow them to ride on U.S. choppers, which they felt unnecessarily jeopardized their lives. What he was suggesting was that, even though it might not be cricket on their part, it was something that could be expected when there wasn't cooperation on supporting the press with transportation."

ABRAMS: "They were certainly successful in painting it as black as possible." [Laughter]

VANN: "They certainly were." "I would think that, one way or the other, they're going to get there and that, quite possibly, we should not deny them the use of U.S. space available transportation where they're going."

ABRAMS: "W-e-l-l, John, I don't know. I think the press ought to be Vietnamized as well as everybody else. And we're trying to get the senior ARVN commanders to ride in the VNAF helicopters. Interesting thing down at your residence the other evening—that damn Vietnamese publisher there, and he's bad-mouthing the VNAF, and when you get right down to it, his source is *Newsweek*. He's got reporters and—that seemed <u>incredible</u> to me, that he couldn't go out and find out for <u>himself</u>, with the resources of his newspaper, find out for himself about his military forces, the Vietnamese."

ABRAMS (re Brady): "I think it's interesting to hear his observation. I'm not at all convinced he's right. There isn't any <u>way</u> to change a skunk. I mean, he's gonna <u>stink</u> no matter <u>what</u> you <u>do</u>. You can spray him with perfume and—or anything you want to—and he's still a goddamn skunk. And I don't think you can change that."

ABRAMS: "There were a lot of other problems involved in Lam Son 719. For a long time, you know, they had a <u>real</u> effort trying to prove that we put combat troops into Laos. All <u>kinds</u> of—this was a <u>major</u> effort. <u>By</u> the <u>press</u>. To <u>prove</u> that we were doing that, and were lying about it. Remember some fellow reported that he'd gotten on the ground and he saw two Americans run and hide. And hell, that just floated right on through. . . . It was wrong, it was a lie, he didn't see any, there <u>weren't</u> any. But hell, that floated right through the whole system and back. Well, this is pretty complicated stuff."

SOMEONE: "Interesting to hear the press admit they weren't reporters, that they were slanting it."

BUNKER: "Well, in this war, my god—there's been no censorship, the first time we've ever had it like that. Fantastic."

■ ■ ■

ABRAMS: Discusses the need for a system by USAF advisors for validating the VNAF statistics reported, combat assault missions flown and so on. "How do we know that's really right? In other words, I want to know whether—you get pushing on the charts, and you like to see it come up, and it gets, goes, from 85 percent to 89, and then 92, and everybody commences to feel happy and so on. But it's a damn <u>chart</u>. That's what it is, it's a chart. It isn't any more than that. You need something <u>more</u> that would give you a feeling of confidence than what the <u>chart</u> says is what they are in fact <u>doing</u>."

ABRAMS: "So the <u>damn</u>—the <u>chart</u>—I'm mad because I've been paying attention to the chart, and I thought it <u>meant</u> something. Find out it doesn't mean a damn thing. So I just don't want any—. Have we got any bonus system in VNAF? And that other system where the gunship crew—<u>they</u> get the <u>brass</u>. Well, it's been <u>years</u> since a gunship returned up there with an unexpended round in it. Christ, you're starving your <u>kids</u> when you do that! And your poor old aunt doesn't have her <u>Honda</u>. It just knocks the <u>hell</u> out of charts!" [Laughter]

■ ■ ■

BRIEFER (re MACV redeployment plans): "The presidential announcement of 13 January 1972 requires the redeployment of 70,000 spaces, reaching a ceiling of 69,000 spaces on 1 May." "Another presidential announcement is expected before the end of April requiring further reductions. Therefore the 69,000 force on 1 May will be a transitional force."

ABRAMS: "I think what that means is that 69,000, that's a— somebody just reaches for a train that's going down the track about 80 miles an hour. And he reaches out there with a brush, and he flips it on one of those cars, and that's 69,000. And that goddamn train just keeps a-going. That's all he hit was one car! As I say, it's moving pretty fast. And there's evidence now that, even back there where the decisions are made, they haven't calculated the speed of this train very accurately. And [laughing] sacred cows down on the track, and some of them are being overrun and so on. So it's very important to understand, when he says transitional force, that's what he's talking about! It's something we'll never see. We'll pass through that damn thing so fast sometime in April that they'll forget they even had it, or forget it was even in the plan! That's what we're talking about. Transitional force means that."

BRIEFER: "In Increment 10, our current redeployment of 45,000 spaces, our flexibility is disappearing." Compares OPLAN 208A curve to that dictated by the president's announcement. 208A "provided for the orderly redeployment of forces to a balanced sustaining force on 1 July 1972." Coordinated with retrograde tonnage requirements to ensure a zero roll-up force on 1 July. Now the accelerated redeployment alters that tonnage curve. Creates a ripple throughout the entire system, including an increased roll-up force.

BRIEFER: MACV HQ to reduce from about 1,300 spaces on 1 February to about 1,000 on 1 May. "It can be anticipated that future redeployment announcements will result in a complete restructuring of the command and control arrangements." Increment 11: Out by 1 May 1972.

ABRAMS: "Maybe there comes a point, with the military, where you can't have a few military. You've got to have none." [Because not enough to sustain even themselves.] "How much of a logistics tail did Lewis and Clark have?" [Laughter]

ABRAMS: "What you all are telling me, really, is you can't do this. But we're gonna do it." [Laughter]

ABRAMS: "I want to establish that we are not going to retain Danang as a major U.S. installation. When you start going below 69,000—when you do that, we can no longer afford Danang."

ABRAMS: "It boils down to this—in the end, I think about the bluntest way to say it is that I cannot accept responsibility for the security of a major U.S. installation up there with no American infantry." "That's the kind of a thing this is. That port up there for the next several months is going to be very important. It's got a function, we've got a lot of stuff that's got to go through it, and so on. . . . If we take American casualties up there in Danang—of course I hope we don't, but if we do, command-wise we've done what we can. We've got American infantry there, they're working in the defense, and so on. You take a lot of casualties up there and no American infantry, and how are you going to answer that? What this boils down to, as I told you once before, is one of those rare opportunities for a commander where he can select the things he's going to get criticized for. And that's what I'm doing. [Laughter] And we're going to make the 69,000. And as I said in the beginning, we're going to go right through that at a speed that will be rather dazzling."

ABRAMS: "On the one hand we've got Giap's great campaign coming up. On the other hand, we've got the great redeployment thing coming up. And they tend to—there's a tendency in there for some conflict. [Laughter] But that is our problem. It's not anybody else's. We've got to take it on, and we're going to. And we're going to do it. And, like a lot of other things, it'll turn out in the end everybody'll be kind of surprised it went so well. O-o-o-h-h, the GAO, they'll show how poorly we did it, and some others."

ABRAMS: "One of the choices is abandonment. No, but it's a choice! In order to do that, I want it clearly understood what it is. But it must not be ruled out as a no choice."

ABRAMS: "The one thing I won't compromise on is having made arrangements, inadequate as they may be, but having made arrangements for the security of major concentrations of U.S. personnel. I will not back off of that. And that's why the brigade of the cav and the 196th will be there. Now the rest of it will just be administrative trials, for administrative offenses, abandoning helicopters, and F-4s—that's administrative. [Laughter] But it's a choice. I told you it's one of those rare opportunities."

LAVELLE: "God, I hope it doesn't get that rare." [Laughter]

ABRAMS: "Hell, we may straighten out this VNAF structure in ways never even dreamed of." "All right, let's go on."

BRIEFER: "Sir, in summary, accomplishment of these redeployments poses many challenges—." [Uproarious prolonged laughter]

ABRAMS: "This is one of the best briefings ever put on!" [More laughter]

BRIEFER (continuing): "No one will have all the assets he would like." [Another cascade of laughter]

ABRAMS: "I want the same thing that you do. I want to do it well so it's a credit to our country and the effort and all that."

■ ■ ■

ABRAMS: "About this coming campaign by the Communists. You know, when the crunch gets on, and some things go wrong, always there's some fellows around that want to put the old dead cat at your door, and say that you did that. I just ask all of you—when the crunch comes, let's not spend any time trying to put the dead cat at anybody's door. Let's just get the damn problems solved. That's what we've got to do, just get it solved. Don't make any difference what went wrong, or who went wrong, or if anything went wrong. Let's get on with getting the job done. Some of the Vietnamese, they're gonna cry out that we didn't do enough, or we weren't there in time or something, and so on. And it may turn out that they didn't ask, or didn't let anybody know or something. Well, there's no point in spending time arguing about who did what, or who didn't do it. Just get it done. And after it's all over we can have sort of a Fourth of July party around here, and then we can hash all that out—about who screwed it up. But while the battle's going on [laughing], let's not waste any time with that. Let's get it won and so on. And the things are here to do it with. I like that statement that fellow's supposed to have said, the ex-secretary to Xuan Thuy, he said, 'Afterwards we may have to sit down and rest for quite a while.' And by god—! And not only that, when he sits down, I want him sitting in a damn bramble patch." [Laughter]

25 JAN 1972: Semiannual Arc Light OPSEC Briefing

ATTENDEES: MG A. J. Bowley, Deputy Chief of Staff; MG J. T. Carley, J-3; BG W. F. Lanagan, Deputy J-3 (Operations). From J-2: Col. Fair, Col. Thompson, Col. Resendes, Col. Henshel, LTC Berman, LTC Hobson, Maj. Zoller. From J3-04: LTC J. Goldstein. From J3-06: Col. G. W. Aldridge, LTC J. M. Turner, LTC R. Galvin, Maj. S. E. Weary. From J-4: Col. J. T. Horrocks. From J-6: Col. H. R. Morris, Maj. E. Wittmers. From MACT: Col. L. J. Knepp. From J3-07: LTC John Herring, LTC V. B. Hildebrant. From 7AF: Col. Flowers, LTC Kannelly, Maj. Myers. From SACADVON: Col. Youree, Col. St. John, LTC J. Lawrence, Maj. Burcham, Maj. Riggs. From MACSOG: Col. F. E. Zerbe. From COMNAVFORV: Cdr. D. McCullough, LCDR M. E. Register, LT R. E. Bornman.

OPSEC Survey Results and Semiannual OPSEC Assessment

BRIEFER: Sharp increase in enemy alerting activity about [14 July?] and continuing through end of the year at a fairly high rate. About 2.5 percent of sorties alerted, vice 0.5 percent previously. Led to this survey, which began 5 January 1972.

BRIEFER: Found communications secure from brigade level on up to MACV. Only one insecure communication in 3,000 monitored. ARVN ground elements also showed significant improvement, although some weak areas remain. Good development: ARVN are processing their own targets with their own resources. Tentative conclusion: Targeting side does not explain the increase in warnings.

BRIEFER: Area of mission planning and execution: Also "a good health report," especially in the area of air strike warning (which in the past was a major source of warning) (20-minute time for passing to foreign nationals, and 5 to 7 minute broadcast warning). Looked for leaks on target location and strike timing. Enemy extremely interested in TOT.

BRIEFER: Found that bomber operations of the 307th calls the tower with bomber takeoff times as much as 12 hours in advance, and those times are posted in the tower. Those times plus two hours (+/– 10 minutes) give a pretty exact TOT. Thai operators are regularly employed in the tower. These calls are made in the clear. Other: Bus schedules for B-52 crews are provided to the motor pool, where the dispatcher is a Thai. Schedules for ground support equipment are published, and for recovery times. Gives radius of action. Pre-mission coordination between radar sites. Missions planned to run on a "bus schedule," a set pattern of actions and times, thus predictable if you know the time of any element in the sequence.

29 JAN 1972: WIEU

ATTENDEES: Amb. Bunker, Amb. Berger, Gen. Abrams, Gen. Lavelle, LTG McCaffrey, Mr. Jacobson, MG Cowles, MG Jumper, MG Potts, MG Slay, MG Adamson, MG Carley, MG Watkins, Mr. Duval, RADM Salzer, BG Trogdon, BG Heiser, BG Bernstein, BG McClellan, BG Herbert, BG Scott, BG Lanagan, BG Wickham, Col. Horrocks, Col. Sadler, Col. McDonald, Col. Crockett, Col. Stevens.

BRIEFER: 1972 MACV Infiltration Estimate: 54,700. (Last year at same date: 27,900.) Also 12,000 in gap groups. Expected in March (as part of total given above): 22,000. For 1972 already have projected 22,300 for the B-3 Front.
ABRAMS: Asks for a B-3 Front comparison with 1968, "the only other year we've ever had anything like this in the B-3 Front."
POTTS: "For all of 1968 for the B-3 Front, 22,500." [Stated later, having researched Abrams's question.]

■ ■ ■

LAVELLE: "General Surles came in to see me yesterday" with a message from Ambassador Godley saying he wanted to come down and see me re his estimate, etc. I said no, he should contact you if he wanted to come down here.
ABRAMS: "Well, I think he ought to send a message to Ambassador Bunker. If we're going to have any ambassadors going around here, they ought to contact other ambassadors." [Laughter]
LAVELLE: "I just shifted it a little higher than me." [Laughter]

■ ■ ■

BRIEFER: "In an unusual full-dress news conference in Hanoi" on 25 January, PRG representatives surfaced a policy statement calling for all South Vietnamese to overthrow the Saigon government and drive out the Americans. As part of the appeal, which was later broadcast by Radio Hanoi, the PRG reiterated a two-year-old proposal offering amnesty to any South Vietnamese soldier or civilian who would now support a general uprising." "At no time since Tet of 1968 have the Communists said for the public record that the time is right in South Vietnam for an uprising."
ABRAMS: "It's certainly the season for an amnesty program of one kind or another."
SOMEONE: "Except by the U.S. press."
ABRAMS: "No, they're taking, I would say, a sort of a favorable view of amnesty for deserters and draft dodgers. They've gone to Canada—. That's what I mean, it's the season for amnesty."
BUNKER: Mentions a *New York Times* editorial favoring amnesty.

BRIEFER: A usually reliable intelligence source who reported COSVN Directives 38 and 39 revealed some details of a new, unnumbered 1972 COSVN resolution disseminated in mid-December 1971. Cites as U.S.-GVN measures "an in-depth defense plan as the U.S. has found it impossible to win the war mili-tarily. An accelerated pacification program. An all-out effort to accomplish the Vietnamization of the war, including efforts to strengthen the government, the police, and ARVN and Territorial Forces to replace the departing U.S. troops, expansion of the war into Cambodia and Laos, aimed at destroying NVA infil-tration routes and base areas." This section admits that these measures have caused the enemy some problems, "especially during 1969 and 1970, when VC/NVA forces were driven out of some important areas."

BRIEFER: COSVN directive: "U.S. military and economic aid is diminishing and, if hit hard enough, the allies will either collapse or be forced to withdraw, enabling the revolution to regain access to the population." Calls in 1972 for "strong, determined attacks to be launched against ARVN main force units, inflicting heavy losses." "The resolution continues to call for every effort to be made against the pacification program, and for expansion of VC control of areas of South Vietnam, to include protection of base areas and supply lines." Refers to "a possible return to main force warfare." If authentic, this document signifies a departure from previous statements of strategy for 1972. Apparently it replaces Directive 01-71, a supplement to COSVN Resolution 9 that placed emphasis on protracted warfare. Directive 39, issued in November 1971, "in effect admitted to the general success of the RVN pacification program."

BRIEFER: "Our analysis of the enemy situation indicates that the enemy is in no way prepared for a major offensive campaign within the COSVN area. How-ever, he could utilize main force warfare in the B-3 Front and northern MR-1, coupled with increased activity in the rest of the country."

ABRAMS: "I think this is really a confirmation of the assessment that we've already sent in to Washington in which we said the Communists would make in South Vietnam in the first six months of 1972 the maximum military effort of which they were capable."

BUNKER: "Exactly. And very logical."

ABRAMS: The enemy's purposes—the president's visit to China, the elections, "the divisiveness—antiwar, antimilitary, and all those things that are going on in our country, those are all factors in it—which they very carefully assess, too."

WEYAND: "It's where their major successes have been."

ABRAMS: "I don't think they've followed the circle. When you take this '62, this is all a lot of very careful work going on, organizing the village and hamlet committees and that political and administrative organization [Abrams has moved to the screen where a diagram is displayed portraying a postulated circle of development of enemy activity: protracted warfare, guerrilla warfare, equilibrium stage, main force warfare stage], indoctrination and so on with hard cores that were left over from the French war and so on. A <u>careful</u> organization. And the organization of the base areas and commo-liaison routes and the whole <u>fabric</u> of the system. It establishes a government—under cover—it gives it police, and that's really kind of what the guerrillas are, it gives it an army in the form of local force and main force."

ABRAMS: "And then when they got up here, in '68, to the general offensive and general uprising, a-l-l that machinery was out there. Long An! Long An <u>really</u> belonged more to COSVN, more to the NLF, than it did to Saigon. Effectiveness of government—more effective on their part at Long An than it was from Saigon. Hau Nghia! Some districts in Gia Dinh! Binh Thuan! And that's what had been built and nourished and indoctrinated and organized and so on. And that's why they then felt that the time had come for this. Now if they want to go from here in '71 to something, this is what they're talking about. They're even talking general uprising now. The press meeting they had up there in Hanoi—want all the people to rise up and overthrow the government. This main force stuff you get now."

ABRAMS: "But what they've done, in my opinion anyway, the realities of the situation are that they've tried to jump [thumping the circle diagram] from here to here. They haven't followed this path, not the path they followed before. They haven't got that kind of organization. They admit that. They <u>want</u> to do it, first of all, because they think that the greatest weakness, the greatest weakness in the whole goddamn thing, is not here in South Vietnam—it's in the United States."

BUNKER: "Absolutely. Couldn't agree more."

ABRAMS: "That's what this is <u>aimed</u> at [pounding the circle now]! When we get to talk about the president's visit to China t-h-e-n—oh, it has something, but I think they've put the arrow on the bow and they've aimed it now at the very heart of our weakness, which is <u>the</u> United States, <u>that's</u> what it's aimed at."

BUNKER: "Right."

ABRAMS: "And that's why they're willing to skip. It's a gamble. The stakes are high. They haven't [<u>pounding</u> the board] <u>got</u> the kind of stuff for this."

ABRAMS: "And the dove movement in the States, so far as the activist groups are concerned, isn't high enough for them right now. They've got to do something to gin that up again. And we'll have a tough problem, on our side, because the press will make a hundred times more out of <u>whatever</u> they're able to do. All these things—talking to the Vietnamese, making sure they've got all the intelligence, trying to get everybody up on the step, and the Americans as well, and sending these teams out to see if everybody's got the word, and all that. It's not crying—what I want to say is it's not crying wolf. And it's not because anyone's scared. It's to understand in some depth what it is that they're trying to do, and what the problems are on our side. The helicopters that get shot down in the months of February and March [laughing] are going to be more significant in the hands of the press than the helicopters we had shot down in [Lam Son] 719. [This has now become like a revival meeting. After every sentence various people are interjecting "Yeah," "Right," "Yes," and so on.]

There's gonna be everything like that. And that's why we have to work as hard as we can. That's the <u>nature</u> of what's coming."

■　■　■

ABRAMS (re enemy attempts to boost morale): "Trying to claim that U Minh was a <u>victory</u>! I mean—I don't think even that guy <u>Hersh</u> would do that. [Laughter] He's about the worst I can think of. [More murmurs of agreement]"

■　■　■

ABRAMS: "That was a very fine message from Tom Dolvin this morning. And God bless Barnes—wow! I mean, every district in every province. It was a very heartening report. The word is clearly out, and I got a once-over lightly from Cook [Colonel Robert M. Cook, the MACV Inspector General] the other day. He has all those teams out running around, and he gives just as favorable a report on MR-1 and MR-3 as reflected in Tom Dolvin's report on MR-1. A few inadequacies in MR-3 and MR-4, but all those have been brought to the attention—. He went to one place that had been inspected three times."

SOMEONE (navy): "We're withdrawing the U.S. units that are too small to defend themselves from Vietnamese bases, and going to do so from places where the Vietnamese security continues to be unsatisfactory."

ABRAMS: "That's always a tough problem for the navy, facing up to what you have to do if you stay on shore where the enemies are."

RETORT: "Yes, sir, it's as bad as it is for the ARVN with the sappers coming after ships." [Laughter]

ABRAMS: "OK. You've got a hell of a good record here, Bob [Salzer]. No one's ever gotten on top of you." [More laughter] "That's all right."

ABRAMS: "It's always been the same way. They [the enemy] can't find a place out in this part of the world that's got as many good targets in it as South Vietnam. For someone who really loves his work, I expect he'd request a <u>transfer</u> from Cambodia or Laos to come over here where we've got 'em. All the arguments must occur on their side over which one to get."

ABRAMS: "That was a pretty good directive the JGS put out the other day. They gave the facts and details on three sapper incidents. Exactly how it happened, what the result was, and told everybody they just had to get with it."

COWLES: "They never used to do that. They would <u>never</u> put out in writing that anything had gone wrong. They might try to buck them up, but <u>never</u> with examples. It's an <u>amazing</u> thing."

BUNKER: "It's an indication of greater confidence."

OTHERS: "That's right."

■　■　■

JACOBSON: As of 31 December 1971 the percentage in A and B hamlets was 84.3 percent. In A/B/C it was 96.8 percent. The progression in upgrading B hamlets to A: "At the end of 1969 we had 599 B hamlets. At the end of 1970 we had 103. At the end of 1971—10."

ABRAMS: "See, this supports the thesis that I've just been describing, that he hasn't got that [infrastructure]. Accepting none of these figures are in fact correct—you know, whether it's ten or whether it's thirty-five, or six, is immaterial. The number was somewhere around 800 in '67. And you're talking there about what he's got control of. And he hasn't got that today."

■ ■ ■

SOMEONE (navy): "We had a navy captain, named Bill Crowe," who tested positive for drugs, "and was on orders to report within three days to the SecDef. It was on this Trust Territory thing. I know what the tests say, but at the same time I knew that he just wasn't the man. The second test came out right. A little consternation in between."

Adm. William J. Crowe Jr. later became Chief of Naval Operations and then Chairman, Joint Chiefs of Staff.

ABRAMS: "Fred Weyand volunteered over at mess night one time the information that the reason I was still here was that I was afraid to take my urinalysis."

■ ■ ■

LAVELLE (unscheduled presentation after the WIEU agenda has been completed) (putting up some kind of diagram): "This is a first attempt, going back to the GCI killing. As you know, we have a restriction that we can only hit GCI sites if MiGs are active and pose a threat. We had a long meeting with everybody involved, including Iron Hand people, our wing that does most of the air defense work up here, and our GCI sites, and we got them all coordinated so that hopefully, when the MiGs are airborne, we also have Iron Hand airborne and can strike GCI sites."

LAVELLE: "To show you how it works, last night we had a MiG CAP up in the northern Plaine des Jarres between eight o'clock in the evening and midnight. We have this up there almost every night, every night for the past month. We substituted two Iron Hand aircraft, F-105s, for two of the MiG CAP airplanes. Normally they cycle back to the tanker two at a time, the MiG CAP airplanes. On one of the cycles, we replace two of the F-4s with two F-105s and the two F-4s drop down as though they were going to return to base. But instead of returning to base, they low level, stay down in the weeds more or less, and provide protection against MiGs for the F-105s. The F-105s stay high, using F-4 call signs, MiG CAP call signs, and using their own IFF, too."

LAVELLE: "As we more or less suspected, the GCI site did come up and did illuminate. One of the F-105s expended an AIM 7E at the radar that was illuminating, which was over at [Thuong?]. The results—."

SOMEONE ELSE: "Three minutes after College Eye gave warning because an aircraft took off from Phuc Yen."

LAVELLE: "So we have to get these things all lined up. But we'll be doing this again. The results were—not a kill, sir."

■ ■ ■

BUNKER: "A very good session, especially the look ahead. My conclusion is we need all the authority we can get."

ABRAMS: "We're gonna run out of authority before we run out of enemy." [Laughter]

2 FEB 1972: COMUS and Sir Robert Thompson

ATTENDING: MG Potts, MG Carley, BG Lanagan. Possibly others.

Projected 1972 infiltration: 11,000 in gap groups, which would make 68,000 total. And for all of last year: 65,700. Nine gap groups in a block, all for the B-3 Front.

ABRAMS: "'68 is the last time he made a really significant effort in the B-3 Front." "You've got somewhere between 30 and 120 days' travel time, depending on where they're going."

POTTS: "They normally break down with a battalion per infiltration group, 450–500, something like that, and then you'll find a smaller one, which will be a headquarters unit. And it looks like the whole 320th Division is coming to the B-3 Front. That's why there're so many of those suffixes going there."

ABRAMS: "This commitment, if it turns out the way it looks, will be two or three regiments greater than Lam Son 719, and at least one regiment greater than Tet '68. They haven't come to it yet, but the 271st, which was a coastal defense regiment sort of thing, it's down there by Stung Treng in Cambodia." "He certainly has indicated that he's prepared to use all that he's got in North Vietnam."

THOMPSON: "Am I right in saying that '71 was a deployment at least in part for defensive purposes, whereas this is a deployment entirely for offensive purposes?"

ABRAMS: "Yes, yes. Yeah, that's right." "In fact you can say, certainly in '70, that the initiative was with this side—cross-border, Lam Son 719, all of those things. The initiative was here. And this is—part of this—is flipping that over so that the initiative is his."

BRIEFER: The mid-December 1971 COSVN resolution says "the U.S. has found it impossible to win the war militarily." Developments in South Vietnam, including economic, "will turn the population against the government." The Vietnamization program will fail, "and this failure will have a tremendous effect on U.S. presidential elections in 1972." Concludes that "the allies have realized that the revolution cannot be defeated militarily, ARVN forces are seriously demoralized, and their government is falling apart. U.S. military and economic aid is diminishing and, if hit hard enough, the allies will either collapse or be forced to withdraw, enabling the revolution to regain access to the population."

BRIEFER: The resolution continues to call for "every effort to be made against the pacification program." Differs from other recent resolutions and directives in reference to possible return to main force warfare, and in its treatment of the U.S. Vietnamization and RVN pacification programs. Apparently replaces COSVN Directive 01-71 as the principal Communist policy document for this year (01-71 was essentially a supplement to COSVN Resolution 9 and placed primary emphasis on protracted warfare). In November 1971, COSVN issued Directive 39 which, in effect, admitted to the general success of the pacification program. Although this new resolution assesses the problems Vietnamization and pacification have caused, it does not credit the GVN with the degree of success that appeared in Directive 39. Rather it calls Vietnamization a failure, with the VC establishing a defensive position in the counterpacification program.

BRIEFER: "Our analysis . . . indicates the enemy is in no way prepared for a major offensive campaign within the COSVN area. However, he could utilize main force warfare in the B-3 Front and northern MR-1, coupled with increased activity in the rest of the country."

BRIEFER: "If the enemy could launch an offensive at least superficially resembling the 1968 Tet Offensive, and obtain press coverage comparing the two, confidence in the RVN's ability to provide security for its people could be adversely affected. In addition, it could increase the antiwar movement in the United States, possibly even to the extent that a complete withdrawal might be forced, especially if U.S. casualties were significantly increased. World opinion could be affected as well, since the Communist press would probably exaggerate the VC/NVA accomplishments and attempt to portray the results as evidence of the popularity and strength of the VC and a failure of the U.S. to complete its policy of Vietnamization. A further propaganda advantage could be the swaying of public sentiment in the U.S. and RVN in favor of a 'peace' or coalition government, another major VC aim."

BRIEFER: "It is believed that a countrywide return to main force warfare is unlikely at this time." "Some main force warfare may possibly be employed in the Tay Ninh area." Most likely: B-3 Front, and to a lesser extent northern MR-1.

BRIEFER: The enemy appears to believe himself prepared, and the time to be right, for the general offensive and popular uprising in selected areas. This time he skips the equilibrium phase of his classic approach.

POTTS: "We think that it [the projected infiltration destined for the COSVN area] will keep the 5th, 7th, and 9th Divisions at about 80 percent strength. Then he is very low in-country—the 274th and the 33rd and all those units that are down in, well into, MR-3, they're down to practically zero strength. And the recruitment, sir, just doesn't exist hardly at all down there now. When you first made your trip over here we were up almost 5,000 a month. And it dropped down as low as 1,700, much of that forced, and we feel now may be 1,100 or 1,200 throughout the whole country."

POTTS: "And the losses down in the U Minh, even though he said in this unnumbered resolution that they were considering that a victory, the losses there have been very, very high."

THOMPSON: "Can one say that, as a result, as far as MR-3 and 4 are concerned is, if anything, better than last year because you're more solid inside. . . . In other words, his capability is no higher this year than last year?"

ABRAMS: "I think it's very clear that his capability in the delta is <u>less</u> than last year."

THOMPSON: "That's in [MR] 4. And in 3?"

ABRAMS: "In [MR] 3 it <u>certainly</u> is no better, and I would say somewhat less."

THOMPSON: "The significant factor is the missing VC, the local organization."

POTTS: "His command and control in the delta has degenerated constantly."

ABRAMS: "I've respected him for being a traditionalist as far as his doctrine is concerned. For example, when Sihanouk was thrown out and then all that started over there in Cambodia, there was a very strong feeling that he was going to march in and just topple Phnom Penh. From the very beginning I used to say, 'No! That's not his <u>way</u>! It's <u>not</u> his way!' He wants to have someday a Khmer Rouge, the true representatives of the people, the guardians of national aspirations. <u>They'll</u> be the ones marching in to Phnom Penh, and they'll be the ones that are on the TV cameras, not the good old 9th Division, none of them!"

ABRAMS: "Well, after giving him a that kind of credit, then you wonder—. See, it points to, now, that he's going to try to do something like this [a big main force offensive]. It won't be exactly like it, but it's kind of the way he's—. Now, why in the devil is he doing that? Instead of following this route, he's kind of jumping across our diagram here. He doesn't have the kind of assets to support this [thumping the chart] kind of—in a broad sense, in this country, with all of its faults and all of that. He just doesn't have it. So if he's going to try all this, then why in the devil is he doing it? We thought [laughing] the instructions in 38 and 39 fitted his book, right in the doctrine, they were based on a realistic analysis. I'm not trying to say that the South Vietnamese are all that good or anything, but it was a realistic appraisal—in his terms. Well, this thing that he's got out now is <u>not</u>—in my opinion."

■ ■ ■

ABRAMS: "They put through this pay raise for the infantry—4,500 piasters." The ARVN 51st Regiment in Quang Nam was visited by Chuck Cooper. "The regimental commander told him it has virtually stopped desertion." "It's true that the month of December was one of the two lowest months for desertion in ARVN in 1971—18 per 1,000. I'm saying this because, if it now looks like this is going to be some kind of a test period [impending enemy offensive], the timing of the 4,500 p's was pretty good."

ABRAMS: "It's going to be bloody, because for one thing we'll put all the air there is on it."

THOMPSON: "Can I make a suggestion on the last circle that's related to protracted war?"

ABRAMS: "Please do."

THOMPSON: "My view is that when you start pulling that circle out, and it starts to go round, the third circle, and will go right on—you can put it into the future, '75, wherever you like—but that on the protracted war you've got the one capability that he has, which is these NVA main force units from the north. You need a second line, as it were, to be used for psychological purposes, and the target is will. So that what one is getting is not the general offensive and popular uprising. You're getting an attack on will—American, and then a spin-off from that onto Vietnamese will and so on."

■ ■ ■

ABRAMS: We've tried to keep the Vietnamese armed forces to a 1.1 million man-power ceiling. "The JGS had tended to get that done by taking away from the territorials. I think there's now pretty good agreement that the territorial strength will not be lowered in '72. Now they've got a thing—it starts with the president, really—of taking PF out of 'A' hamlets and using those spaces in the regulars."

ABRAMS: "The reason the GVN's gotten where they've gotten, while I never deprecate the necessity for regular forces—he's going to have to have them as long as the other fellow's threatening him with regular NVA forces—but the reason the GVN's where they are is because they have built the territorials, and they have built the police, and they have got this PSDF thing going, and so on."

ABRAMS: "Now down here in the delta . . . what Truong has got working down here, and what he's trying to do, is increase the strength of his RF. He wants to move spaces from PF into RF. He agrees on 'A' hamlets. There's places down there that you don't need PF any more. The PSDF and the police can handle it as long as these other things are going—with the RF." "Truong is not interested in reducing his Territorial Forces."

ABRAMS: "I've gotten a paper now from the JGS, and they want two more regular divisions in '73. And the way you get that is take Territorial Forces. I'm kind of convinced in my mind, now, that what they ought to do is reinforce the philosophy that Truong has peddled and sold. Can you imagine province chiefs, three years ago, letting RF go out and work under the operational control of this sector commander? No, they wouldn't do that. And for this government, for these people, that is really their strength. For '72, reinforce Truong's philosophy down there. I mean back it, back it to the hilt! I believe if you do that, when December 31st of '72 comes, it will be very difficult to justify three regular divisions in the delta."

ABRAMS: "I don't want to buy in on two more divisions."

THOMPSON: "Now, if Truong goes on doing what he's doing, which I think is right . . . because the primary problem in this country, for now and in the future, is manpower, and the cost of manpower, and getting the mileage out of the manpower." "And I think Truong is right in the way he's capturing it here, to run the spaces out in the PF where they're unnecessary, put them in the RF where there's more flexibility. . . ."

THOMPSON: "The prime target for the GVN of this next 12 months, irrespective of the battles that they're going to have to face, is this manpower problem. I fully agree with you, that I would like to see the one million one hundred [thousand], if possible, <u>down</u> a bit."

ABRAMS: "<u>No</u>—I agree!"

THOMPSON: "The problem facing this government is to <u>maintain</u> the manpower that they need at a cost level that—well, they can't quite afford it—but at a cost level which the president can still help them maintain, and not just in '72, '73, but possibly right through '74 and '75."

THOMPSON: "As I said when we met last time, 'The answer to protracted warfare is stable warfare,' the definition of stable warfare being that you can indefinitely contain the threat, which to all intents and purposes is now an NVA main force threat . . . without prejudice to continued political and economic progress inside the country. Because I don't put any time limit on protracted war. It could go on for 50 years on the frontier here." South Vietnam cannot stick it out "unless the bill is one that a president can get through Congress."

■ ■ ■

ABRAMS: "Incidentally, Peter Osnos came in to see me yesterday. He's the *Washington Post* fellow, been out here a little over a year, I guess. The wicket he <u>appears</u> to be on is that, for some insidious political reason, we have created the myth of this impending campaign. . . . The thought occurred to me that he was trying that on so that I might tell him, in order to prove that it wasn't, I might tell him something that otherwise I wouldn't say. I'm sure he probably feels that I feel that he's a scurrilous <u>shit</u>. I feel that when he comes in and sits down that he feels that that's kind of the way the thing is lined up, so I'm not going to tell him very much. And of course his paper has announced a policy of not paying any attention to these 'background' rules and 'not for attribution' rules and so on, although he agreed that he would, for this occasion, abide by that. And of course I don't <u>believe</u> it."

■ ■ ■

ABRAMS: Gives Thompson a limited description of Island Tree, to include locating the T-stations, predicting within a week or two ("we're not too proud of it" with respect to how precise the prediction is) when groups will arrive, seeding with sensors, querying them, using B-52s and CBUs (44,000 per aircraft) with variable timed fuzes. Surprisingly, this "has generated a lot of secondaries. We've viewed it as sort of compartmented, where the logistics was in one parallel system, along with its storage areas, and the personnel were in another. Well, the amount of secondaries that have come out of this would cause you to wonder a little bit about that. Anyway, secondaries are a good thing, no matter how you come by them." "That's been a new wrinkle this year." "A lot of the results have actually been recorded on tape."

ABRAMS: "Binh Tram 37 had, at one time, about 12,000 in there. And of course, with that news, we tried to get in there and work with them on that. And we know they were having trouble on food, having trouble on wounded, and apparently [laughing] [***]."

POTTS: "Confusion."

POTTS: "Binh Tram 37 is the fork in the road. They take a left, they go to the B-3 Front. They go straight ahead, they go to COSVN."

POTTS: Describes confusion in Binh Tram 37: "They've even let some of the 122-mm guns that were being taken down the Trail earmarked for B-3 Front get by them, and have to call them back and send them the right way."

ABRAMS: "What we're trying to do, of course, is to strengthen Giap's hand. Now he said there was going to be great sacrifice. Well, we're giving them some sacrifice, and they'll say, 'By golly, Giap knew what he was talking about.'"

■ ■ ■

ABRAMS: "I was up in the 101st one day, about six months ago, I guess, and I visited one of the battalion setups up there, a fire support base and all that. And I'd gotten into the sapper project. Well, they were very proud. They'd had an ex-sapper down there, some fellow that had rallied, and he came down and gave them a demonstration, coming through their wire. This apparently was a very shocking experience. They saw that little character get out there and come through that damn thing like it wasn't even there [laughing], and not a sound."

ABRAMS: "So, anyhow, they got into tanglefoot then and proudly took me over and showed me some tanglefoot they'd just put in. And I reached down there and took a hold of it and, hell, it was like taking hold of a fishnet. You know, it was loose and so on. I said, 'I thought this stuff was supposed to be tight. I thought you were supposed to plunk it and it sounded like a violin string, like it's tuned up.' 'Well,' they said, 'that's right, but we just got this in. We've now got to tighten it up. That's what we're going to do.'"

ABRAMS: "Well, I got back to Saigon, and the next evening I got to thinking about that. And I said, 'I accepted that explanation, and what I really ought to do is fly back up there tomorrow, just go out there—get in a helicopter and go out to that damn thing and go right straight to that tanglefoot and look at it. And if it's tight, slap them on the back and come home. If it's loose, relieve the battalion commander.' Because I was there, I saw this, and so on."

ABRAMS: "Well, about that time I had a commanders meeting down here, so Tom Dolvin spent the night with me and I told Tom. Tom had been with me when I was up there, and I said, 'Tom, I was there and saw that, and I just now feel bad that I'm not following up.' He said, 'Don't say another word. I'll be out there myself.' The day after he got back he called me up, and he said, 'You'd be tickled to death. You can play a tune on that tanglefoot.' And that's what he did. He flew in there in a helicopter and just walked right straight to that same thing, and of course they were paddling along behind him. He reached out and grabbed a hold of it, turned around and said, 'Good job,' and got back in his helicopter and left. I mean, that's about <u>generals</u>."

■ ■ ■

ABRAMS (re the sensors): "One of the things you always worry about when you get fooling around with this gadgetry is that <u>it's</u> lying to you, it isn't functioning really quite the way it purports to be functioning, or the enthusiasm—you know, you can't get anywhere without enthusiasm. I mean, you're really stuck in the <u>mud</u> if you haven't got it. But you can also get carried away. When you get something like that [poststrike photos shown of a T-station hit with CBUs that produced 500 secondary explosions, some of which produced craters, or maybe cleared areas, 30 meters across in triple canopy], you know some of it's right, you're not being completely hoodwinked."

5 FEB 1972: WIEU

GUESTS: Amb. Berger, Adm. McCain, Mr. Jantzen, RADM Vasey, Mr. Armstrong, Capt. Quisenberry.

ATTENDEES: Gen. Abrams, Gen. Lavelle, Mr. Jacobson, MG Eckhardt, MG Cowles, MG Schweiter, MG Bowley, MG Fuson, MG Jumper, MG Potts, MG Slay, MG Adamson, MG Carley, MG Watkins, Mr. Duval, RADM Salzer, BG Trogdon, BG Brown, BG Heiser, BG Bernstein, BG McClellan, BG Herbert, BG Scott, BG Lanagan, RADM Price, BG Wickham, Capt. Perez, Col. Zerbe, Col. Crockett, Col. Stevens.

1972 Infiltration Estimate: 59,600 (22,400, or 38 percent, to B-3 Front; 27,400, or 46 percent, to COSVN). Also 12 gap groups.

POTTS: "In the area of interest, the B-3 Front, we carry 22,000 so far this year. And for all of the year 1968 the B-3 Front got 22,500. As of today, back in 1968, you would have had 2,400 only going to the B-3 Front—20,000 less than today."

■ ■ ■

ABRAMS: "Now, we've got this requirement, hooked on to authorities, about when this starts. So I want a message constructed that takes the pattern of movement—the 320th, the 308th, the 304th, the POL, the four occupied SAM sites now down there in southern Quang Binh. I <u>mean</u>, the show is <u>on</u>! The curtain's been drawn, and we're in it. And I want that to come out loud and clear, and I want the authorities. It's like one time right after the bombing halt, they had a damn rule out here you couldn't fire on anything in the southern DMZ until it fired at you. And we had FACs up there watching them set up their rockets, in the daytime, but you couldn't do anything about it until they fired. Setting up <u>mortars</u>! <u>Watching</u>! <u>FACs</u>! The kind of <u>stupid</u> situation that our government gets itself in. And all these fellows that want to talk to the press about protecting Americans. Let's dish this up as—this is the way to do it. Get the authorities, get them <u>now</u>. It's <u>all</u> there."

POTTS: "Since Giap's speech [of 19 December 1971], sir, we've continued to read every newspaper [in] North Vietnam, check every newscast, and we have a special NVA propaganda analysis."

BRIEFER: Quotes Giap's slogan: "Determined to Fight, Determined to Win." Accounts of overrunning Long Tieng in Laos. Article headlined: "Abrams Running Around." Text: "Before the defeat at Long Tieng, in the early morning hours of 7 January 1972, General Abrams flew to Bangkok to host secret talks with the Thai prime minister on the grave situation in Laos. Long Tieng was the main subject during the talks. It was agreed that Laos would be defended at any cost." Conclusion of the article: "The loss of Long Tieng is the turning point in the war." Shows cartoons denigrating American soldiers, one captioned "Hooray for whiskey! Hooray!" [Laughter]

ABRAMS: "It's safe to subscribe to that."

POTTS: "Your trip was on the sixth, sir."

ABRAMS: "I think I'll run that over to my wife, and let her know what it means when I come over there to see her. [Laughter] She doesn't realize the role she's playing." [More laughter]

■ ■ ■

ABRAMS (asking about enemy logistics movements out of Cambodia): "This mass of troops that he's getting over there in 609, somebody's got to feed them. And there isn't any food over there in <u>those</u> quantities. Either the food's coming all the way down the Trail, or it's coming out of Cambodia."

POTTS: "We have numerous reports of food coming from Cambodia, sir. It's coming, we feel, up the river there, and also by road and courier. They put them on bicycles and Hondas and carts and so forth. The sensors are lined up so they can pick up an object about the size of a truck, and if it gets down anything smaller than that we're not going to get all of them. In fact, we won't get many of those smaller vehicles."

ABRAMS: "Yeah, but the amount of force that's being assembled over there, that's going to be a tough bicycle problem."

■ ■ ■

ABRAMS (after a break, without preliminaries): "Yeah, I suppose the favorable way in which the negotiations have been going, you don't want to do anything to make them mad." "Christ, at this critical hour, to antagonize them—<u>bad</u>." To the briefer: "Let's hear the good news <u>you</u> have." [Laughter]

BRIEFER: "Sir, the analysis of the new allied eight-point peace proposal has triggered worldwide reaction pro and con." Called by New China News Agency on 30 January 1972 "a clumsy trick of the U.S. government to deceive the people and cover up its aggressive ambitions."

BRIEFER: Thursday, 3 February 1972, was the 143rd session of the Paris peace talks. Viet Cong calls for a specific terminal date for withdrawal of U.S. troops and the immediate resignation of President Thieu. In Paris, Ambassador Porter said "the United States will abide by any other political processes shaped by the South Vietnamese people themselves."

■ ■ ■

BRIEFER: "On 31 January a FAC, Covey 207, observed three trucks near the DMZ exit, loaded with supplies. He marked the target with rockets for a navy tac air strike. One rocket scored a direct hit, started numerous secondary explosions, destroying the three trucks, which were included in the truck kill totals. The tac air strike was waved off."

ABRAMS: "I guess that FAC is probably—pretty hard to hold him down."

JACOBSON: "That's like a tackle intercepting a pass and running 60 yards for a touchdown."

ABRAMS: "Well, I don't know why you picked on a tackle. How 'bout a guard? That's the one!"

Abrams had been a third-string guard on West Point's football team.

10 FEB 1972: COMUS–ROK Minister of National Defense Brief

ABRAMS: "I think what will happen over the next four or five months—the enemy will make a military effort against South Vietnam which is the greatest military effort of which he is capable. I don't know when it will begin. It could now begin any day. It could be tomorrow."

ABRAMS: "On our side, the Vietnamese armed forces and the other forces know all this, and they're in the highest state of readiness and alert in the period I've been here."

ABRAMS: "We're prepared to mass the entire air effort in the B-3 Front, in Military Region 1, wherever the difficulty may occur."

ABRAMS (re the infiltration estimate): "I have depended on this estimate, and this method, for the last four years. And, at the end of the year, when all information, and all prisoner, and all intelligence of all kinds has been in, it has never been off more than 1 percent."

ABRAMS: "It wasn't until the latter part of '68 that this method of estimating became reliable, about the summer of '68." Re forecasts of future months: "The only way it will go is up!"

ABRAMS: "What the South Vietnamese have today is really the best balanced and the strongest military force in this part of the world. Army, navy, air force, territorials, police—none of these countries have anything like it, and neither does North Vietnam. And I think when this—whatever they want to call it, an offensive, a campaign, a winter–spring or spring–summer or whatever it is—when it's all over, it will have been defeated."

ABRAMS (re question on "the pullout of U.S. troops"): "By 1 May we will have redeployed 95 percent of the maneuver battalions, 97 percent of the artillery battalions, and 91 percent of the attack aircraft squadrons."

KOREANS: Recall that three or four months before signing the Korean War armistice, the enemy launched a major assault against South Korea.

ABRAMS: I remember it, too. "Twenty divisions."

KOREANS: Want to know if he sees the coming offensive by North Vietnam as similar in intent.

ABRAMS: "I will respond to the question, but I consider it unprofessional, because it includes a lot of things which I am not responsible for, and not really the best judge of. But I will give my opinion. The Communists insist on these things: this government here must be overthrown; all troops, all aircraft, all navy belonging to the United States, and all equipment, must be withdrawn from all of Indochina; there must be no military or economic assistance by the United States to South Vietnam. That's what they insist on. So—how do you get that? You go to the weakest thing in the whole setup, the will of the American people and the will of the American government. And if they can capture Ben Het, or Kontum City, for a week, and maybe Cam Lo, and threaten Quang Tri, the press and they and all will say Vietnamization has failed. And the last few remaining members of Congress who would support economic assist—, who would support continuing economic assistance, would have lost their faith. So, I think that's what it's aimed at."

MINISTER YU (very quietly): "Thank you very much. I admire your success in Vietnam."

KOREANS: One more question, basically asking how successful the enemy offensive will be.

ABRAMS: "I would say that in the course of this our side will lose, at least temporarily, a few fire bases—two, three, four. Now he has big plans, and what's been happening for the last three years—he has repeatedly laid on big plans. Not like this, but big plans for the counterpacification, big plans for the . . . organization of . . . freedom committees. . . . I don't want to exaggerate, but in the last three years they have made many big plans, of one kind or another, and they have not been able to carry them out. In fact, there is evidence of false reporting by commanders at the bottom who have [been] urged to do this and do that, and to attack this and attack that, and they never made any attack at all. But they reported the attack was successful, and they gave the casualties on our side, and the equipment captured, and so on."

ABRAMS: "He has a big plan now, and I'm sure he intends to start it soon. And I'm sure he intends to keep it up, say through July or August, in a series of impulses. But I also think, in part, the plan is bigger than he will ever be able to carry out, or than he will ever be able to sustain, on the basis that he has planned it. It will be—you see, as the time and the hour approaches, that air, which is now the 10,000 tac air and the 1,000 B-52s that are spread from Mu Gia to Kratie, it will come like this [concentrated, apparently] overnight. And the 10,000 a month, and the 1,000 a month, will be in Base Area 609. And outside Ben Het. I know that there're going to be many casualties. The Vietnamese will have casualties, and there will be hard and bloody fighting. But he has <u>never</u> <u>yet</u> been able to stand up to that—<u>never</u> <u>yet</u>! That's what happened to him at Khe Sanh. He put <u>three</u> <u>divisions</u> at Khe Sanh, and they finally were ground to mincemeat. And when we know that he has finally got ready, that air—<u>overnight</u>—will come like that, and it will be done again.'"

ABRAMS: "He believes in firepower, <u>too</u>. He just doesn't have that much. He'll use it in this, too. That's why those 130s. So I'm sure that there will be some reverses, but I think that they will be temporary. Remember he stayed in Hue for 25 days in '68. He had, in the beginning, all but one little corner of the city of Hue, where the division headquarters was of the 1st ARVN. Everything else belonged to him. He had his own antiaircraft on the airstrip inside the walled city. And he finally was pushed out, and pushed back, and eventually—eventually, he wound up in Laos. And from there on it has <u>never</u> turned back. And that's why the Street without Joy is resettled, and the peasants are living and working there. Now he's trying to do this—this thing—without all that infrastructure and guerrillas and so on that he had in '68, so I know that will be a <u>difficult</u> time. And, you see, he is the only one left who can lie with credibility. No one else can do that. He is the only liar that is believed by the American press and so on. And even the <u>truthful</u> man on our side doesn't have a chance, because he's not believed, either."

MINISTER YU (almost in a whisper): "Thank you." "You take care of my boys. They are doing a good job."

ABRAMS: "We're all soldiers."

12 FEB 1972: Special Commanders WIEU

ATTENDEES: Amb. Berger, Gen. Abrams, Gen. Lavelle, LTG McCaffrey, LTG Dolvin, Mr. Jacobson, MG Eckhardt, MG Cowles, MG Bowley, MG Fuson, MG Hollingsworth, MG Jumper, MG Young, MG Potts, MG Tarpley, MG Slay, MG Adamson, MG Carley, MG Watkin, Mr. Vann, RADM Salzer, BG Trogdon, BG Heiser, BG Wear, BG Bernstein, BG McClellan, BG Herbert, BG Scott, BG Lanagan, BG Wickham, Mr. Ladd. Col. Sadler, Capt. Perez, Col. Houseworth, Col. Crockett, Col. Stevens.

BRIEFER: 1972 MACV Infiltration Estimate: 65,700 (26,200 for the B-3 Front, 28,900 for COSVN). With gap groups, total estimated to reach 79,300, about 2,000 more than at this time in 1968.

BRIEFER: Re "North Vietnam Propaganda Analysis" shows the center section of a North Vietnamese magazine that features a cartoon of President Nixon holding a document labeled Vietnamization report. Next to him is Mr. Laird, and next to him General Abrams, and he is saying (and pointing): "Because of you." Over there is President Thieu, saying, "Give me more," and American aid is portrayed. Also a cartoon showing three frogs all puffed up and about to explode (as in Vietnamese mythology a frog was encouraged by his friends to blow himself up as large as a cow, and got almost to that point and exploded) in 1972, sitting on three islands labeled Vietnamization program, Laoization program, and Khmerization program. President Nixon is shown swimming away, saying as he departs, "Just a little more effort and you will be as big as a cow." He is swimming in water labeled "The Nixon Doctrine."

■ ■ ■

BRIEFER: Describes recent changes in operating authorities and special action related to the enemy buildup:

■ Certain standby authorities were initially requested by COMUSMACV on 20 January.

■ On 26 January JCS granted some of these authorities for immediate execution, some for standby execution later on. Directed preparation of additional contingency plans.

■ Six specific authorities requested 20 January: (1) Strike three southernmost MiG airfields. Pending approval. (2) Strike active GCI radars in North Vietnam below 20 degrees north. Pending approval. (3) Strike any occupied SAM site within 19 nautical miles of the PMDL, or within 19 nautical miles of the North Vietnam–Laotian border as far north as the Mu Gia Pass. Pending approval. (4) Air strikes against logistics facilities below 18 degrees north. Pending approval. (5) Implant sensors in the DMZ north of the PMDL. Approved. Effective to 1 May. Sensor implants began 11 February. (6) Fixed-wing and rotary-wing support to RVNAF cross-border operations when requirements exceed RVNAF capabilities. Approved until 1 May.

■ CINCPAC asked what else was needed. "COMUSMACV has received authority to conduct intensified reconnaissance and protective reaction flights in the vicinity of Dong Hoi, Vinh, and Quang Lang. Additionally, MiGs airborne from these fields are to be considered hostile and may be engaged when south of 18 degrees north." "Iron Hand antiradiation missile strikes against GCI radars have been authorized outside Route Package 6 when MiGs are airborne and indicate hostile intent. Tac air strikes have been authorized until 1 May against enemy troop concentrations in the northern portion of the DMZ. A request for tac air, naval gunfire, and artillery strikes against North Vietnamese artillery and rocket sites within range of friendly positions is still pending approval."

■ "A subsequent request to conduct tac air strikes against 130-mm guns located north of the DMZ has been approved. This authority is to be executed during a 48-hour period at COMUSMACV's discretion, but must be completed no later than 17 February." [Nixon to China?] Awaiting a break in the weather.

■ "Authority to employ antipersonnel and antivehicle mines and persistent CS throughout the DMZ is also pending approval."

BRIEFER: Measures taken to supplement U.S. forces in Vietnam and Southeast Asia:

■ Commando Flash: On 8 February, 18 USAF F-4s arrived from Clark Air Base.

- Two carriers to be maintained on Yankee Station through 27 February. Third carrier to revert to 48-hour alert status.
- Fourth carrier, the *Kitty Hawk,* sailing from CONUS 17 February and available about 9 March.
- B-52 sortie increase from 1,000 to 1,200 a month has been authorized and is now in effect. Additional aircraft at Guam to surge at COMUSMACV discretion to 1,500 sorties per month.
- CINCPACFLT has placed four additional ships on 72-hour alert, augmenting the three destroyers normally providing naval gunfire support. A six-inch-gun cruiser, two guided missile destroyers, and an additional destroyer. To be provided when requested by COMUSMACV.
- Additional P-3 aircraft available on COMUSMACV request to augment Market Time patrols.
- Additional C-130 and C-141 aircraft on standby.
- Air force Chief of Staff has allocated worldwide stocks of CBU-24 and CBU-49 munitions to Arc Light and Seventh Air Force requirements.
- CINCPACFLT embarked marine contingent available if needed.
- Additional augmentation forces under consideration.

BRIEFER: JCS response to several additional authorities requested was tentative approval contingent on COMUSMACV declaration that the enemy offensive had in fact begun. "This decision was made by General Abrams on 5 February." "At the same time, approval of the three air strike contingency plans was recommended. Approval of this is still pending. The JCS has advised that we can anticipate authority to strike SAM sites on or about 1 March."

BRIEFER: Actions taken during the past week designed to disrupt enemy attack preparations:

- B-3 Front air strike plan developed. A 48-hour maximum effort employing virtually all B-52, tac air, and gunship assets. "Execution of this strike plan began at 0600 hours this morning."
- A similar plan has been developed for MR-1. Execution will take place after completion of the B-3 Front strikes and a 24-hour Tet cease-fire.
- Tac air strikes have been directed against 130-mm guns and other long-range artillery or rocket sites within six kilometers north of the DMZ.
- Tac air strikes on troop concentrations in the northern portion of the DMZ have been authorized and will be executed when weather conditions permit.

BRIEFER: "The Command will assume Alert Condition Gray at 1800 hours 13 February, which will continue until terminated by this headquarters." Next higher: Yellow. Expect to go to that in the next few days. "As is standard practice for alert messages, commanders will be asked to personally acknowledge receipt."

ABRAMS: "This 48-hour thing [against the B-3 Front] will end at 0600 on the 14th. Then I want to take the remaining 12 hours before the Tet stand-down and put what air we can in MR-1."

BRIEFER (Major Ross): "In response to a massive buildup of Communist forces threatening the B-3 Front and the DMZ, the JCS directed a 48-hour maximum air effort in the area of the B-3 Front. Following this operation, a second 48-hour phase was to be carried out as directed by COMUSMACV involving a shift of heavy emphasis to the Military Region 1–DMZ borders. On 6 February JCS directed a maximum effort operation, to be conducted as soon as possible, which would run continuously over a 48-hour period. The operation must be completed prior to 17 February. All available air assets in Southeast Asia, including air force and navy tac air, gunships and B-52 aircraft, are to be committed, with safety the only limitation to weight of effort." The two operations are planned to be completed prior to 24-hour Tet stand-down on 14 February.

ABRAMS: "What's been happening is Jack Lavelle and I have been meeting every day—twice. You know, trying to keep track of [word indistinct] messages coming in and the whole thing. We want to use what we've got the very best way that it can be used. And so there isn't a hell of a lot of concrete mixed into this. If there's good reason to change any of it, we'll change it!" "I've indicated to them that I probably want to surge—go to that 1,500 B-52s out here." "What's going to happen in the next two days—kind of firm on that, today and tomorrow." "I'm bound by directive on this 48 hours here, but the other 48 hours—that's just mine, so I can change that. I can't change this."

LAVELLE: "I think the important thing is we've got a 24-hour flow of aircraft now, and we can keep the flow now. It's set up, and we can keep it coming, it's scheduled, so there's something every few minutes. And we just keep it coming and change the target area, so whenever General Abrams makes a decision as to where to put the weight of effort, or where to go next, we've already got the flow of aircraft."

■ ■ ■

BRIEFER: "Effective 1 May 1972 the authorized strength of the U.S. Army element [of MACV, not USARV] will be reduced 42 percent below the 1 February level." Requires tour curtailments in substantial numbers. On 1 February 1972: 7,545 authorized (7,363 actual). Drop 3,123 authorized (982 of them officers).

ABRAMS: "Frankly, it's not democratic, and it's not equitable. We have to face that, and you have to explain it to your people. There's no way to meet these reductions, and still be able to do our job in an effective way, and handle everybody on an equal basis. It cannot be done. So you've got to tell the ones you're going to keep that you're keeping them because you need them. And as a matter of fact, once you've taken that onus on yourself, you've kind of put him in the clear. His wife can't get at him. He can say, 'It's the damn army again.' She'll write to her congressman, and then he'll write out here, and we'll have to answer and so on, but he's out in the clear as far as his family's concerned."

ABRAMS: "It's true, people are going to be able to point to what they call inequity. But there isn't any equity in the world anyway—never has been. It's a dream. What's the equity between an 11 Bravo [11B, the MOS, or military occupational specialty, of a rifleman] in a squad and another fellow the same age running a Xerox machine here in MACV Headquarters? What kind of equity is that? Both being paid the same—same grade, one out there humping around in the damn bamboo and booby traps, and—w-e-l-l, equity is a very elusive thing."

VANN: "Enlisted men, no matter how well qualified they are to advise, we do not have any Vietnamese officers qualified to receive advice from enlisted men." [Laughter]

VANN: "I hesitate to mention it in this august company, but I can't help but be concerned that the field is going to be reduced by 54 percent while MACV Headquarters is going to be reduced by only 23 percent."

ABRAMS: "Well, that's the privilege of rank. [Laughter] There's nothing new about that, John."

VANN: "You understand, sir, that's just an observation."

SOMEONE: "How much are you cutting your headquarters, John?" [Laughter]

VANN: "Exactly as directed." [More laughter]

ABRAMS: "Well, your note has been noted."

■ ■ ■

ABRAMS: "I know there's a lot of varying views on how imminent the major military effort is in this campaign, but you can see we're trying to peak the air effort, and go on this gray alert. And I think I'll put the yellow alert on, probably by the 16th. We don't _have_ any precise date that everybody will be charging forward, but I think in prudence that's what we ought to do."

ABRAMS: "You know the IG's been out looking around with a lot of teams, and I just have to say I'm quite gratified—yeah, he found some things, and of course you've all found a lot more, but _really_ the responsiveness of the chain of command I think is really quite excellent." "The total is _good_. The word got out, right down to the bottom of the thing. People knew what the hell they were doing, and they were responding. I just think that that _part_ of it is really quite healthy."

ABRAMS: "The Vietnamese—here again, as there's always been, there are deficiencies, inadequacies, inadequate performances, and so on, but the state of readiness, the alertness and activity on the part of the armed forces here in this country is the highest that I've ever seen it, even though there's some that are still asleep at the switch. You're never going to _eliminate_ it." The president has gone up to MR-1 and MR-2, where he got out and talked with his people. "And he's done that on purpose. He's not politicking, goddamn it. He's trying to take care of his country, that's what he's trying to do."

ABRAMS: "I think we're probably going to have quite a go at it here, but I'm confident that we'll work our way through—_they_ will, and _we_ will with them. And we'll try to use the air in the best and most effective way we know how. So with that I suggest we go have some lunch."

14 FEB 1972: COMUS–Ambassador Godley Brief

SOMEONE (before the briefing begins): "Kill them, that's what you're supposed to be doing, not scaring them."

■ ■ ■

ABRAMS: "You know, air is really very good if you've got a way of putting it on the enemy, and it's really always tied down to that—some guy out there that can see them, or knows where they are, and if he's got communications to a FAC, you're in business. And if you haven't got that, if you haven't got that, you're going to wind up bombing trees. It just has to be that way."

ABRAMS: "Do you have any good B-52 targets up there?"

GODLEY: "I just happen to have an envelope here." [Laughter] "No, we don't. Well, put it this way—we've got some targets north of Skyline, but we <u>don't</u> have <u>really</u> good targets. What we've got are six boxes which we think are the best boxes we can work out for the strikes before the enemy hits us." "As for the moment, we're not asking for them, because we don't think the enemy is bunched up sufficiently."

ABRAMS: "The way <u>we</u> run <u>our</u> business <u>here</u>—I'm talking about in South Vietnam and the border—this is the kind of target [enemy troop concentrations] that we value very highly. If we can get at him while he's in the preparation stage, it's a hell of a lot better than trying to deal with him after he gets going—you know, when he's on the wire."

ABRAMS: "I think probably all of us are to some degree or another parochial. Well, what we're fighting to do now is trying <u>not</u> to be. Now we've got a total effort by the enemy here that's very clear. At least as far as I'm concerned, he's making the maximum military effort in Indochina that he can make this year. Now how is the best way, with what we've got, to try to screw that up so that it doesn't get him, in the main, what he's after? He's clearly going to make an effort against South Vietnam. I'm of the view that it will begin in a few days. In a way it's already begun, coming out with his battalions and regiments. I think that ought to start before long. As I told you . . . upstairs, we don't <u>have</u> 0400 on the 19th or something like that. We haven't got that, but it's all there. We're trying not to run scared. We're just trying to work out the problem."

16 FEB 1972: DEPCOMUS Update

ATTENDEES: Gen. Weyand, MG Cowles, MG Potts, MG Carley, BG Lanagan.

BRIEFER: MACV 1972 Cambodia and RVN Infiltration Estimate: Currently stands at 67,400 (of which 27,300 to B-3 Front and 29,000 to COSVN). The total compares to 28,400 at this time in 1971. In 1968: 77,300.

POTTS: There are enough gap groups that will be picked up to run the 1972 estimate to 79,300, which will make it higher than 1968.

BRIEFER: 58,014 tons of POL were delivered by Soviet tankers to Haiphong during the month of January 1972, or 241 percent of the 24,100 tons requested by North Vietnam.

POTTS: "58,000 tons in January is the highest figure that they've ever had."

BRIEFER: Presents an analysis of North Vietnamese newspaper accounts of the war. Headline in 31 January 1972 issue of the military newspaper: "The War Is Fighting at a Fierce Level in 1971. Victory Is Near." An article describes as "the hardest problem of the war" the "mobile combat forces of the U.S." This is *The People's Army* newspaper.

BRIEFER: On 5 February 1972 a B-52 sortie increase from 1,000 to 1,200 sorties per month was authorized and is now in effect. Additional aircraft are being made available at Guam for a surge at COMUSMACV's discretion to 1,500 sorties per month. Present plans are to implement this on 17 February 1972.

BRIEFER: The higher headquarters' response to a number of the special authorities requested was a tentative approval, contingent on COMUSMACV announcing that the enemy offensive campaign had in fact commenced. This decision was made by General Abrams on 5 February 1972. "Admiral McCain was here that day, and they discussed it. All the indicators were laid out, and the decision was, 'Yes, there is plenty of evidence that the campaign is on,' and the way the message was worded was that the assault phase hasn't begun, but there's no question about it that he's under way. That triggered several of those authorities."

POTTS: "What he based that on was the appearance of the 320th NVA Division elements down in the B-3 Front. He felt they were committed adequately. And then the pushing of those 130-mm guns down in the DMZ."

SOMEONE: "We've never had so much authority as we have right this minute, and the only clear day was about two hours yesterday at noontime, right in the middle of the truce period. It's incredible." "The weather has just been zero-zero."

19 FEB 1972: WIEU

ATTENDEES: Amb. Bunker, Amb. Berger, Amb. Whitehouse, Gen. Abrams, Gen. Weyand, Gen. Lavelle, LTG McCaffrey, Mr. Jacobson, MG Eckhardt, MG Cowles, MG Bowley, MG Fuson, MG Jumper, MG Potts, MG Slay, MG Adamson, MG Carley, MG Watkin, RADM Salzer, BG Trogdon, BG Heiser, BG Bernstein, BG McClellan, BG Herbert, BG Scott, BG Lanagan, BG Wickham, Col. Sadler, Capt. Perez, Col. Houseworth, Col. Crockett, Col. Stevens.

ABRAMS (to weather briefer): "All right, let's hear the bad news first."

BRIEFER: Infiltration Estimate: 68,400 (2,700 to the DMZ/MR-TTH, 8,800 to MR-5, 27,800 to the B-3 Front, 29,100 to COSVN). There are enough gap groups, per Potts, to run the estimate up to 82,000. In 1971: 29,300. In 1968: 80,600. Both as of today's date. 205 groups in the estimate for this year (47 with suffix = organized unit).

POTTS: "The real, real difference is that this time last year, and at this time in

1968, there were only 2,800 men going to the B-3 Front. And now we carry it at 27,800, 25,000 more than for each of those two years."

BRIEFER: Soviet POL deliveries to Haiphong: Three tankers and one cargo ship during the past week bringing a total of 18,052 tons. Puts NVN POL imports for February at 42,886 tons (109 percent of request).

POTTS: "We've gone all the way back in '65, and on about five occasions have we found that two months, two consecutive months, had over a hundred percent [of POL deliveries]. But now, with February reaching it, we have five months in a row where they've gone over a hundred percent of what they had requested, with January being the all-time high."

LAVELLE: "I hope this is the result of all that POL we destroyed."

BRIEFER: Describes a series of seven articles published in Hanoi in daily newspaper in mid-December 1971 using the byline Chien Thang, "The Victor," believed to have been written by General Vo Nguyen Giap. Provides an assessment of the Vietnam War from the North Vietnamese viewpoint. Optimistic. "The more we fight, the stronger we become." "The struggle requires that we make tremendous efforts toward new victories."

ABRAMS: "Not for attribution."

■ ■ ■

LAVELLE (re the enemy logistics offensive): "The _input_ into the system, although the number of trucks that we pick up is half, the _input_ is 85 percent of last year's. But better than that, as far as _he's_ concerned, with the reduced force, and that is being used in Barrel Roll and Cambodia and B-3 and MR and everywhere else, his output—from half as much activity—is 115 percent of last year. We're not doing as good a job of stopping him, with our reduced force and then fighting in all areas and taking it out of there all the time."

ABRAMS: "We're going to have to dig into this a little bit, because we've hung a lot of hats on this system in the past. And now what's happening—just talking about the system here—we'd better get into what the enemy's doing. This can't help but sort of shake confidence in what we've been believing in the past. If now we're better at eliminating duplication, then how can we explain all the reasoning that went into our calculations in the past, which we thought were pretty good? So now we have to go back and say we were _wrong_. Instead of concluding what we concluded last year and the year before, we conclude something else. There's something about all this that, I'd say, on the intelligence side, it's a little shattering."

POTTS: "We'll pull all that together, sir, and see if we can correlate it all. Of course, we're convinced that we had the same system last year as the year before, which gave us the trend. We felt that we had correlation there."

ABRAMS: "Not only that, but every time that _I've_ raised it at this meeting what I've been informed is it's not only _equal_ to the system we had last year, but it's _better_. That's been [thumping the table] what has been said in this room! It's _always_ been, on this and other subjects, we've always talked out here to keep _ourselves_ from being misled and not accept _anything_ [thump]—. So this—and those assessments that have gone in on Commando 5 and Commando 6 and so on—."

SOMEONE: "That throughput last week was the highest ever, wasn't it?"

POTTS: "Yes, sir, that was, sir."

POTTS (displaying some bar graphs): "This is when these were started, sir, 1968 in our files. The difference between the 1969 rainy season and the 1970 rainy season, as you remember, sir, were the numbers of increased messages that they were going to try to continue during the rainy season." "And we did have indications in the rainy season of '70 that they had made an effort to keep up their [logistical] activity, based on the sensor observations."

SOMEONE: "Quite significant, then we had 24-hour sensor coverage. And we only have 18 hours now."

SOMEONE ELSE: "We had 20 last year. That's a very significant thing."

ABRAMS: "What's that?"

SOMEONE: "We had 20 hours a day coverage last year, last dry season, and we haven't had that much this time. I'm not sure at this point, though, if anyone can tell you exactly how much we have had, but it's varied by VR [?] sector."

ABRAMS: "Why has that decreased? Why has the coverage decreased?"

SOMEONE: "121s out here have reduced the orbit time, reduced it to one orbit."

ABRAMS (speaking quietly, ominously so): "My memory may be failing me on this, but I don't recall this point having been made before, that our coverage of these sensors had decreased. And at the time the 121s were withdrawn, I believe I was assured that we could continue our mission without degradation. I want this [voice rising here]—I want to get all the snakes out on the floor on this subject. There may be good reasons for everything. The only trouble is that I don't understand them right now."

LAVELLE: "After the '70 season, you no longer had the capability, because the two computers were down, and you went to a one-computer operation up there—after the '70 season. There was no way, in '71, to operate around the clock. The '71 season had a planned reduced capability."

ABRAMS: "I hear what you're saying, Jack. What [shouting] I'm saying is, I'm learning it this morning, and by god, in this position, you can't have that going on! If it's going to be bad, you've got to know it at the time! All right [to briefer], go ahead."

■ ■ ■

ABRAMS: "I really have some difficulty understanding why the 271 would be brought all the way down here [into Cambodia] to be an assault regiment, which it seems pretty clear that's what it's going to be, when they already have the 5th, 7th, and 9th down there. The 9th knows that area like the palm of their hand. So does the 7th. The 271's never been there. It was a coastal defense unit. Why? And the 9th—the 9th is one of the g-r-a-n-d old divisions of COSVN, I guess one of the first to be organized. In the vanguard of Tet '68. The greatest role in the Tet Offensive of '68 was given to the 9th Division, the honored position at the fore."

POTTS (re the 271st's lack of combat experience): On its way down "there's never been a round fired."

SOMEONE: We got "<u>fantastic</u> claims of killed by air" inflicted on the 9th Division when it moved out of its normal AO, so "if they were 50 percent right, that division isn't going to be able to operate."

ABRAMS: "But even then, you know, why not send replacements to the division? Because there's all kinds of—there's staff there, there's commanders there, you know. The expertise and the experience that must be left in that division is really tough to pass up. I guess that's why I'm not a Vietnamese—one reason."

■ ■ ■

BRIEFER: "This week in Paris the much ballyhooed World Assembly for Peace and Independence of the Peoples of Indochina took place at Versailles 11–13 February. The assembly heard totally predictable speakers and produced a totally predictable resolution condemning U.S. actions in Indochina and supporting the PRG's seven points. [Laughter] Demonstrations, tolerated by the government of France, went off calmly in the rain the afternoon of 13 February." "French TV and non-Communist press gave the conference more than usual attention because of the presence of Jane Fonda [laughter], a large American delegation, and the U.S. suspension of this week's session of the Paris meeting on Vietnam. The assembly was organized by the Stockholm Conference on Vietnam, the World Council for Peace, and 48 French Communist and associated organizations." Speeches "were of monumental dreariness."

■ ■ ■

POTTS: "Everyone agrees that tomorrow's the day."

ABRAMS: "We've almost got too <u>much</u> intelligence. But I do think that, always leaving room for the fallibility of humans, which is what this is all about, nevertheless I think the Vietnamese, the whole business, is in a state of readiness and understands, within reason, what's coming. And I'm certainly confident that, while it'll be pretty rough, it'll hold. So—have a good night's rest, and be ready for the fray."

24 FEB 1972: COMUS Briefing with Sir Robert Thompson

ATTENDEES: Gen. Abrams, Mr. Thompson, Mr. Palmer, BG Lanagan, BG Herbert, MG Potts.

ABRAMS: Recounts Vang Pao answer to a group of reporters: "Oh, yes. Americans cut off all support, we all die."

ABRAMS (continuing): "So this fellow says, 'Well, that means the North Vietnamese are better soldiers and stronger soldiers than yours.' He said, 'Oh, no. Give both sides rock, we win.'" [Laughter]

ABRAMS: "It's very clear, from all the [***] movement of artillery ammunition and artillery weapons, that when he finally gets ready to put this thing off fire-power is going to be a big factor."

POTTS: We had a large number of intelligence reports of anticipated increase in activity to begin 20–25 February, with the 20th mentioned most often. "We're working very carefully to try to see why the delay, and what would be the next period of [word indistinct]." "But there is no indication in our reports now."

ABRAMS: "I think he'd be prepared to expend 50,000–60,000 [casualties] to get what he wants." "What's he got—69,000 or something like that?—in the pipeline already for this year." "If you go back and take the replacements he furnished for '68, he had a pretty accurate picture of what it was going to cost him."

POTTS: "At this time in '68, he had 80,600 in the pipeline. Now he's got 69,800, with about 12,000 more in the gap groups that we haven't picked up as yet."

ABRAMS: "Some of these newsmen who come in and see me on a background basis, they're sort of convinced that we're putting all this out for some devious political trick. And I really enjoy it, because it looks like the war is going to finally conclude without them ever deviating from the splendid record of absolute unreliability that they've established."

■ ■ ■

THOMPSON: "I believe it was in October 1970 you told me you were trying to find out when and why the NVA inserted regular units toward the end of 1964. Do you remember that?"

POTTS: "Yes, sir."

THOMPSON: "I think I said at the time that I could think of no valid reason for inserting NVA units at that time. The VC units were doing extremely well. They'd chewed up half the national reserve, and looked like winning the war. And therefore I think the only reason for their insertion was to be in place when victory was achieved—so that the NLF didn't get away with a victory by itself, and the NVA was in a position to determine what happened afterwards. Then you had the Tet Offensive, where the NVA put the VC more or less into the front line. It was the VC that got really chewed up. It's always been my opinion that certain battalions of the VC were better than anything that the NVA had—straight infantry battalions. And they are gone now. Is there nothing that we can do to sort of bring this home to the VC, even to the villages in the country? That this is what has happened? In other words to make it absolutely clear to people that this is a straight NVA war?"

ABRAMS: "I wonder if the people in the south haven't got quite a bit of a problem with that. There are so many northerners in the south. For instance, General Giai, who commands the 3rd Division, comes from a village up there just a few kilometers south of Hanoi. You know, you've got that sort of presence here. And then—I think, for the southerners, for the southerners especially, they've had to try to be polite, if you will, so that the loyalty and sort of devotion to the cause would carry on with these fellows who came from the north. I'm just gabbing now, but in all these things there always seems to be something <u>like</u> that. You know, the Vietnamese have got sort of an internal cultural problem which they have worked around to try to do their best with."

ABRAMS: "For example, my understanding now about making General Thinh, who commanded the 25th Division—how come he was made a lieutenant general? My understanding of it now is that what the president wanted to do was to make General Minh of the air force a lieutenant general so that when Ky was out he could not go back as the commander. He would be junior in rank, and the president didn't want to be branded with having done that. So what he did was promote all major generals in the same class from the military academy to lieutenant general. And Thinh is a classmate of Minh, and was a major general, and that's how he got to be a lieutenant general. I think there were four of them."

ABRAMS: "One of us, we might never come up with a solution like that, you know. But apparently it is, as they see it, it is necessary to—. And I think when you look at the four years that President Thieu was president, all of the moves that were made in the military—Vinh Loc, Lu Lan, Khang, Thang, that whole—President Thieu has succeeded in getting all of that done. I think any unbiased outsider, coming in and looking at this thing, would have to say that the <u>quality</u> of the senior leadership that he has today is <u>far</u> superior to the quality of the senior leadership he had at the beginning of his administration."

SOMEONE: "Or at any time."

ABRAMS: "Yeah, right, right. And he's <u>done</u> all that, and he has not created some kind of a clique of out-of-office generals that would be working either with Big Minh or Ky, you know? So maybe they're not all great—maybe they're not all avid Thieu men, but they certainly are not actively and effectively working against him."

■ ■ ■

ABRAMS: "General Vang Pao says, talking about his schooling, that he went to a corporal's school, French-run, an NCO school, and a 14 months' officer school. And that is his total formal training. And he goes on to say, 'My best professors'—that's what he calls them—'my best professors have been the Viet Minh.' And that's the way he sees them today. They're Viet Minh. And he said, 'They give very tough grades, the Viet Minh. They're very stern professors. But,' he said, 'they have been my best professors.'"

ABRAMS: "For Ky, none of those fellows [the enemy] are Viet Minh. <u>He</u> represents, and the others like him, the only <u>real</u> Viet Minh. The others are bad people who were in the ranks of the Viet Minh. <u>Be</u>, down there at Vung Tao—Viet Minh."

■ ■ ■

THOMPSON: "Have you come up with any evidence of why they put them in in '64?"

POTTS: "No."

THOMPSON: "I'll tell you why. I feel that this is one of the important myths that we've got to try to deal with in this coming season and while all this is happening." "The VC side of it is over. The people have rejected the VC."

THOMPSON: "All this line they're talking in the U.S. that the NVA came in because the U.S. came in—it's just not true on the [evidence of the] <u>timing</u>."

POTTS: "The first regiment to come in-country was the 95, the one down in the U Minh now, and that was October 1964. And its first commitment was in December 1964, when it ambushed a convoy on Route 19." "That's unclassified." "It was identified at that time as the 95th," as NVA. "It came in, sir, with 2,000 strength."

THOMPSON: If they entered South Vietnam in October 1964, they must have started in August, and the <u>decision</u> must have been made about June 1964.

■ ■ ■

THOMPSON: "What this battle is we're about to have is a straight NVA invasion."

DISCUSSION: They bring back the briefer who described the Chien Thang articles, and ask him if their tone is such as to imply this is the <u>final</u> push, or just another big push. It's the final push, he says.

ABRAMS: Probably they maintained the same thing ["Victory will be ours."] in 1967.

BRIEFER: "Yes, sir, but we've never seen it this emphatic. It seems the public in North Vietnam is aware of the war and have a 'carrot in front of the donkey approach' go so long—pretty soon the people get pretty tired. I frankly feel that he feels—Chien Thang, or Giap, feels—. 'It's on the horizon' is another term he uses. They never used this before. They've always indicated long struggles ahead, much privation, and these terms. Now they say 'on the horizon,' 'near future,' things such as this."

ABRAMS: "They had a lot of wounded who went back north after Lam Son 719. I don't know, maybe they'd all go back and say 'we really licked 'em' after they'd been <u>pounded</u> for—."

26 FEB 1972: WIEU

ATTENDEES: Gen. Abrams, Gen. Weyand, Gen. Lavelle, LTG McCaffrey, Mr. Jacobson, MG Eckhardt, MG Cowles, MG Bowley, MG Fuson, MG Jumper, MG Potts, MG Slay, MG Adamson, MG Carley, MG Watkins, BG Trogdon, BG Bernstein, BG McClellan, BG Herbert, BG Lanagan, RADM Price, BG Wickham, Col. Raney, Col. Sadler, Capt. Perez, Col. Houseworth, Col. Crockett, Col. Stevens.

BRIEFER: A source stated that 1972 would be a year of liberation.

ABRAMS: "That one has all the earmarks of what happened at Tet in '68. They brought the VC province provincial committee in, and the night before they were hidden in some bunkers out in back of the province chief's headquarters. And when the thing ticked off, they were going to grab the province chief and his staff. And at sunrise there would be a flag-raising ceremony, on the one hand, for the new committee, and a hanging of the province officials to go with it. By a stroke of good fortune, they were discovered in these bunkers. And so the whole ceremony in the morning was reversed. [Laughter] But I thought it was a nice touch. They went ahead and carried out the ceremony. They raised the South Vietnamese flag, and did away with the—. [Laughing] Sort of a nice touch."

BRIEFER (re recently captured document): "COSVN warned that the National Police is a very dangerous organization because it is the key instrument with which the GVN attacks the VC infrastructure." "In short, COSVN believes all party committees . . . must devote every effort to destroy the GVN police at all costs."

JACOBSON: "That's the best news I've heard in I don't know how long."

BRIEFER: According to a prisoner, a VC military intelligence district-level section chief who had studied COSVN directives before his capture on 20 December 1971, "there is no comparison of planning between the upcoming campaign and the 1968 Tet Offensive. The 1968 attacks were designed to catch allied forces by surprise and thus achieve victory through simultaneous coordinated military attacks throughout the Republic of Vietnam. They were to be supported by an anticipated 'general uprising' of the populace. Because the 1968 plan was inflexible, with attack dates established four months in advance, when the expected uprising did not take place there was no way to change the course of the offensive. Consequently the 1968 offensive failed. The upcoming campaign has been planned to be much more flexible." Per other reports, it will be "multiphase and long term in nature."

ABRAMS (re the prisoner): "He's not really a policy maker. I'm thinking of some of those reports we get where a 'usually reliable' fellow talked with another 'usually reliable' fellow who said—."

■ ■ ■

ABRAMS: Asks Potts to read data on comparative infiltration 1968 versus 1972. In 1968: 84,000 in estimate, plus about 7,000 in gap groups, for a total of 91,000. Today: 69,800, plus 13,600 in gap groups, yielding total of 83,400. This year 25,700 more troops are going to the B-3 Front. And 2,500 more to COSVN.

POTTS (re improved collection system): "In 1968, you picked up at Binh Tram 18 and Vinh, primarily, and now we have six or seven places along the line where we can pick them up and then check them again." Using for comparisons corrected figures for prior years, yielding a valid comparison.

ABRAMS: "Well, the only thing about this is that it does seem to me that he [the enemy] does plan to do something. The precision in the figures may not always be there, but the general trend I think is pretty clear."

ABRAMS: "Everybody's got their own ideas, but I think the scenario went something like this: I think that the other side's little people have been working like hell to make good the big fight that was supposed to come up this period, right along in here. You look around, you'll find that the little guys who do this kind of thing [the CORDS briefing had been discussing terrorist incidents] for the last couple of months they've been working like beavers. They've been doing their part. Just something's gone wrong with the timing on the other side and with the big stuff, in my view, probably because of the publicity that the thing was given. I think their guerrillas are doing what they've been ordered to do. That's get ready and help out the big fight which, for some reason, has been postponed."

■ ■ ■

ABRAMS: "I'll tell you, I'm getting—. First, I guess we're pretty parochial, but I'm—. These <u>visitors</u> that come out here, especially if they've been out here before sometime, I—I haven't seen a hell of a lot of wisdom coming out of that."

JACOBSON: "Hear, hear."

ABRAMS (to Jacobson): "Your friend is an excellent example."

JACOBSON: "Mr. Komer?"

ABRAMS: "Yeah. It's very bad. On some of these things it's not so much that they, you know, matter of judgment or opinion. Goddamn it, they're <u>wrong</u>. They're just plain <u>wrong</u>! No matter what <u>way</u> you want to look at this war, they're just <u>wrong</u>! And they go back there and peddle that crap as experts, and it's really very <u>harmful</u>. It's very <u>harmful</u>. Because those people back there don't know any better. They've got no way of telling, you know, and so they believe them. And the more <u>strident</u> it is, the more believable and credible it is. And it's <u>just</u>—just <u>bad</u>. Hell, some of them are getting more damaging than the <u>press</u>! Well, I think the saving grace in all of it is that when it comes time for the critical decisions they're not in it."

JACOBSON: "I can just imagine the helpful reports we're going to get from Washington after Komer's gotten his report distributed."

ABRAMS: "Yeah, that'll <u>burn up</u> the—."

ABRAMS: "If anybody in <u>here</u> at the meeting has got any ideas of what more we ought to be doing in light of—. I sure welcome any suggestions. We've been <u>trying</u> to think of everything."

4 MAR 1972: WIEU

ATTENDEES: Amb. Bunker, Amb. Whitehouse, Gen. Abrams, Gen. Weyand, LTG McCaffrey, Mr. Jacobson, MG Eckhardt, MG Cowles, MG Marshall, MG Bowley, MG Fuson, MG Jumper, MG Potts, MG Slay, MG Adamson, MG Carley, RADM Salzer, BG Trogdon, BG Heiser, BG Bernstein, BG Scott, BG Lanagan, BG Wickham, Col. Sadler, Capt. Perez, Col. Houseworth, Col. Crockett, Col. Stevens.

Infiltration Estimate: 75,200 (31,600 to the B-3 Front, 42,000 to COSVN).

POTTS: "Fifteen thousand men are arriving in-country per month. That includes

May." Now carrying 32 gap groups out of 233 groups in the estimate. Gap groups always estimated at 570, with an arrival in-country of 485. "Out of all the groups in the estimate for 1972, 104 of them have been detected more than once as they come down the pipeline. So we feel we have a good handle on the infiltration this year." With known gap groups: 92,660. For 1968 it was 101,800.

■ ■ ■

ABRAMS: "Last night at dinner there was one of those gentlemen there who's had a lot of experience in Laos. He cited two cabinet ministers. Each had two sons, and both of them, all their sons had been killed in this war. I found that sort of a jolting thing. I haven't sort of rated the Lao very high, but those senior military officials over there—their sons are in the army, and they're getting killed. It's just a different way that they look at it. So I don't know. I haven't added all that up, but it has significance. And, you know, the Thais are that way. [Thanom's?] sons all served over here, and one of them is now commanding an infantry battalion down on the border with Burma—into combat. There's an awful lot of bad, but that's the way they are. That's what honor requires that you do."

SOMEONE (Jacobson?): "Prime Minister Kittikachorn's daughter was over here as a WAC."

ABRAMS: "I guess that won't turn anything around, but it is interesting."

BUNKER: "Yes, it is."

ABRAMS: "There are a few of the generals here who've got their sons in the armed forces. I've talked with some of them. It's not very widespread, but—. I think General Manh's one of them."

SOMEONE: "Ky's nephew died of burns about two weeks ago. Yes, sir. He was shot down up in MR-2 and brought into 24th Evac with 70 percent burns over his body. They kept him alive for about two weeks, then he succumbed."

SOMEONE ELSE: "Admiral Cang's oldest boy just went into the marines—much to his distress!"

ABRAMS: "Well, he was probably not a very talented youth." [Laughter] "All right, I take that back!" [More laughter]

■ ■ ■

ABRAMS: "We have them conducting the war at six or seven levels, and you have to work against all of those levels if you're going to succeed."

■ ■ ■

BRIEFER: A "fairly reliable" agent has reported the contents of COSVN Directive 13 dated 6 February 1972 providing indoctrination material for cadre personnel. It begins by claiming significant gains throughout Southeast Asia in 1971 that have supposedly neutralized the allied Vietnamization plan. "Military victory during Lam Son 719 completely liberated southern Laos." Says "the Republic of Vietnam is attempting to maintain too large an army for the size of their population base, and this will lead to their ultimate failure." Cites "the United States presidential election, which Nixon will lose." "The allies are seen as striving for a military victory." Cites among allied strengths vast manpower and logistics resources "and an extensive system of outposts." Closes by claiming that "the Viet Cong are enjoying great success and the situation is to their advantage in all respects."

BUNKER: "You wonder how much they <u>believe</u> of that bullshit, don't you?" [Laughter]

ABRAMS: "You wonder how the fellows down at the end of the line receive that. If they have the opportunity, of course, of seeing the thing like it is."

■ ■ ■

BRIEFER (re special film): In early February we received a request from CBS to go out and film at the 3rd Brigade, 1st Air Cavalry Division, and interview General Hamlet. "The purpose was to get the reaction of the troops to the debate about their <u>role</u> here—whether or not they were still in an active combat role or whether, as administration spokesmen have been saying, they are engaged in purely security activities. The pitfalls are obvious, but by the same token General Hamlet had enough confidence in his men that, on the basis that they'd be the primary spokesmen, he agreed to it. As you'll see in this film, the men come through in fine shape. The whole unit does."

VOICE ON FILM SOUND TRACK: "... the administration announced that American ground troops in Vietnam would no longer be used offensively in combat, that they would fight only on the defense. That, we know, hasn't always turned out to be the case. One unit that's been seeing plenty of action is the 3rd Brigade, 1st Air Cavalry Division, stationed near Saigon. Recently it's taken more casualties than almost any other unit and dished out its share. CBS News correspondent Phil Jones, after being turned down once, finally was given a rare interview with the brigade commander, General James Hamlet." [Laughter] "Here is Jones's report."

EXCERPTS: Jones: "He [Hamlet] wants the people to see that at least the men of the 1st Air Cavalry are as much in combat as they were when he first came here five long years ago. 'Come with me,' the general said, 'and I'll show you why my men are upset when the people say they aren't fighting any more. I'll show you where the war is,' he says. 'It's right down there, just a few minutes' chopper ride from my office.' [Sound of helicopter blades, someone talking on the radio.] " 'Morale is no problem out here,' says General Hamlet. 'You always hear about the protesters and the potheads who are back in the rear areas,' he says, 'but you ask <u>these</u> men how <u>they</u> feel about their mission. They have volunteered for the most dangerous job left in Vietnam, going into the bush every day, looking for the enemy.' "

SOLDIER: "Fighting dinks—exactly what we're over here for." "And we don't mind telling anybody that's what we're here for. We're here to fight dinks, and that's why we're here." "As a matter of fact, tomorrow we're gonna go out and get a couple more." [Laughter in MACV audience] "We got one yesterday. Don't mean nothing. We'll get some more tomorrow."

SOLDIER: "In the past 10 years we've lost a lot of American lives here in Vietnam, and to just toss them out the window and say 'to hell with it,' that's pretty low. And these are just a different caliber of people than what's out in the world. What you see on the streets in D.C. is pretty disgraceful. But here, I think, is what I think America should see. These are the men, not those freaks or fakes or whatever you want to call them. These are men." [Laughter at MACV]

SOLDIER: "People who went to Canada rather than coming over here getting amnesty—we don't think that's right." [Sound on sound track of others cheering in assent]

SOLDIER: "The war's not over." "Since we're here I think we have to be professional. And this company [1st Cavalry Division's Ranger Company] is the most professional company in Vietnam."

REPORTER JONES: "Do you worry about being the last casualty of the Vietnam War?"

SOLDIER: "I don't think we'll have a casualty in this [ranger] company."

JONES: "To some Washington officials, Americans left in Vietnam may be on only defensive operations. But as far as General Hamlet is concerned, it's a matter of semantics."

HAMLET: "We take the war to the enemy. We have an aggressive defense. You see our patrolling, you see our men who are prepared to go into the bush. And these men keenly resent any implication . . . that they are not out fighting the enemy." "From my point of view, the Vietnam story is the story of the American soldier who fights so well and often gets so little credit for it." [End of film]

ABRAMS: Asks if they're making 16-mm copies of the film to send out to the 1st Cav (who have small viewers for kinescopes).

JACOBSON: "It was on television."

ABRAMS: "Yeah, but you see, they don't have television sets out there." [Laughter]

SOMEONE (the Information Officer): "Jones, when he finished the film—he said to General Hamlet, he said, 'You know, I'm not so sure that—it wasn't Mudd, it was Chance—, Cronkite—he said, 'I don't think Cronkite is going to put this on.'"

SOMEONE: Points out that Cronkite was in China when this was shown.

ABRAMS: "That's what happened. Like when the UN decided to support South Korea, the Soviets were out."

11 MAR 1972: WIEU

ATTENDEES: Amb. Bunker, Amb. Whitehouse, Gen. Abrams, Gen. Weyand, Gen. Lavelle, LTG McCaffrey, Mr. Jacobson, MG Eckhardt, MG Cowles, MG

Bowley, MG Fuson, MG Jumper, MG Potts, MG Slay, MG Watkin, MG Adamson, MG Carley, Mr. Duval, RADM Salzer, BG Trogdon, BG Heiser, BG Bernstein, BG McClellan, BG Scott, BG Lanagan, BG Wickham, Col. Zerbe, Col. McDonald, Col. Crockett, Col. Stevens.

POTTS: "There's 34 possible gap groups that have not been picked up as yet. That'll run it up to 92,490." In 1968: 109,000. But a big difference: In 1968 the divisions brought into the DMZ area had infiltration group numbers, whereas this year the 304th, 308th, and 320th (or at least elements of them) do not.

POTTS: Infiltration is "still averaging about 15,000 per month for those first five months, including the month of May."

ABRAMS (re movement south of the 271st Regiment): "It's just odd—hell, you didn't even have a _patrol_ get in it. I mean, there hasn't been a firefight with it at _all_, and here it is moving _back_. It's a _little_ bit out of character."

ABRAMS: "Of course it's all COSVN, and that regiment is _pure_ NVA. They kind of know where it came from—it's a coastal defense outfit from Quang Binh Province. Thinking back to the days when I was a lieutenant down there in F Troop of the 7th Cavalry, if we'd gotten some coast artillerymen in there [laughter], I'll tell you—they wouldn't have been allowed in the mess. They'd have had to eat out on the _porch_! And that 9th _Division_, you know. That's a _VC_ division. You know, that's what that _was_, and I wouldn't be surprised if there were a couple of old hands in there, you know, that—." "And they probably think that that coastal defense regiment, well, it would be sort of an even fight between them and four brigades of Khmer."

WEYAND: "Well, the reverse of that is, if they're anything like the South Vietnamese commanders, the North Vietnamese would really shuck them right on into the battle, chogie them right on down there." [Laughter]

ABRAMS: "Well, you're right in a way. Any one of these commanders that can get some airborne or marines or rangers, they—. Well, I guess we haven't got the answer to this." [Laughter]

WEYAND: "No matter what happens, we'll have covered it." [Laughter]

BRIEFER: "Sir, if I might add one comment—." [Uproarious laughter] "Historically, the enemy has always had a regiment in the vicinity of Kim Cuong plantation to protect his LOC and his base area."

ABRAMS: "Right, plus its long history of being a very effective defensive regiment [long pause]—there's been no successful landing in North Vietnam." [Laughter]

■ ■ ■

BRIEFER: "On 7 March, according to a UPI report, Assistant Secretary of State Marshall Green delivered a letter from President Nixon to President Thieu and assured him that the United Sates had not made any secret deals with China to settle the Vietnam War." "In addition, Mr. Green assured President Thieu that there had been no secret contacts between the United States and North Vietnam under any form, and by any person, during the China visit." Meanwhile, according to a 10 March report, "Communist Chinese Premier Chou en-Lai has secretly visited Hanoi and conferred with North Vietnamese leaders in an apparent bid to explain to them the significance of his talks with President Nixon concerning Indochina." He apparently sought to assure them "that there were no secret deals concluded with President Nixon during his recent visit."

■ ■ ■

BRIEFER: Will "summarize reports received to date indicating why the increase in enemy activity expected during the latter part of February was delayed."

BRIEFER: "In northern Military Region 1, two agents indicated that the cause was ARVN's high state of combat readiness." And so on. "According to an agent, the offensive [in VC MR-5] was scheduled for 20 February." Cancelled "because of GVN preparations and a fear that its combat plans had been compromised."

DISCUSSION: An enemy message went out to all and sundry on 17 February.

POTTS: "We thought it was the 'go' signal," but now it looks as though it was the postponement.

JACOBSON: "General Dzu put out an order that everybody wear steel helmets throughout the entire corps, and you get arrested if you get caught without one. So in come these five VC, who don't have pots, but they've got uniforms—they've got everything but the pots. Jesus, the MPs grabbed them and take them in, and find out that they're just fellows from the other side without pots." [Laughter]

ABRAMS: "That gives me an idea. I think we ought to start picking up for interrogation any Americans we find wearing their uniform cap." [Raucous laughter] "I think that should be regarded as suspicious."

BRIEFER: Also "in VC Military Region 5 a recently captured document reveals that the enemy has been unable to initiate planned tactical activity due to a shortage of manpower and to the low quality of available troops. According to this report the loss of experienced local cadre has forced VC leaders to replace them with younger, less motivated recruits."

BRIEFER: "Agent reports also cite enemy reluctance to commit their forces to attacks on key ARVN installations and population centers such as Qui Nhon and Tuy Hoa City due to increased GVN security measures with the consequent probability of heavy enemy casualties." Also "shortages of food and the disruption of communications as a result of allied operations."

BRIEFER: "It appears from these reports that the allied forces' high degree of security and aggressive countermeasures have kept the enemy off balance and contributed to the postponement of the expected increase in enemy activity."

■ ■ ■

BRIEFER: "On 8 March COMUSMACV forwarded to CINCPAC and JCS a personal appraisal of the overall situation" in Southeast Asia as it now stands, "and the requirements necessary to effectively meet the situation." "Early in the enemy buildup it was felt that the enemy offensive against the B-3 Front would precede action against the DMZ area. This has not materialized, and it now appears that the enemy is capable of concurrent offensive action in all five threat areas." "Competing demands for airpower already exist as we attempt to counter enemy preparations in each threat area." "Offensive action by COSVN forces could create a threat to Military Region 3 that would complicate a JGS decision to move airborne and marine reserve forces to Military Region 1 or 2. This emphasizes the need for preemptive action against COSVN forces."

MESSAGE: "The enemy has put into position a SAM umbrella that extends as much as 16 nautical miles into northern Military Region 1, and in greater depth into the Laotian panhandle in the pass areas. He has perhaps the best integrated and most closely coordinated MiG-SAM operating environment that has yet been developed and actively exercised under combat conditions. He has driven our highly vulnerable gunships out of the pass areas in northern Military Region 1. He has made operation of fighter aircraft extremely difficult in these areas. He has kept the B-52s out of these areas, although CINCSAC has stated his willingness to fly in the SAM range when the targets justify the risk, and on 9 and 10 March B-52s did strike in the Ban Karai Pass. The enemy has developed a sustaining logistics base beneath the air umbrella. He has positioned long-range artillery just north of the DMZ, in range of friendly positions. Tank and infantry units have been positioned in the area. If he initiates his offensive at the outset of a protracted period of bad weather, we risk serious losses in northern Military Region 1."

BRIEFER: "The response to this critical situation must deal with all of the major elements of the integrated system described. . . . We must have authority to hit the MiGs, GCI, SAM sites, long-range artillery, tanks, and logistics facilities. We must have clear weather to operate effectively against this system. COMUSMACV urgently requested approval of authority to strike the enemy system above the DMZ."

BRIEFER (citing rationale in the request submitted): "The existing authority to return fire is too restrictive to be fully effective and does not adequately accommodate the fact that what we are up against is an entire system of integrated power rather than a single-weapon problem. Specific authorities needed at this time include authority to conduct tac air strikes and naval gunfire attacks against SAM sites, MiGs, GCI sites, AAA, long-range artillery, tanks, and logistics facilities in North Vietnam located below 18 degrees north. This statement of authorities needed is different from the previous request because we now know more about the highly integrated system facing us and, based upon previous attempts to attack parts of the system, realize that it must be attacked as an entity."

BUNKER: "I think that's an excellent exposition of the situation, and I certainly hope we get the authority."

ABRAMS: "He's obviously going to try to do his best, and I suppose there'll be some pretty tight moments as it all develops. . . . But, I don't know—thinking back on the tight moments there's been before, I think I view these with a little more confidence. You know, there've been those times when about all there was was faith. I really think that right now we've got a couple of pluses. You still need <u>that</u>, but I think there's just a little bit more here than there was in those other ones."

ABRAMS: "Probably the most recent was Lam Son 719. You know it got a little tight, and was hailed on <u>every</u> side as a resounding defeat and debacle of the highest order. You know, no small part of his—no small <u>part</u> of his problem here in the first couple of months in '72 is all that stuff that didn't get down in the last dry season. You see, January and February's a little too early for the logistics effort in <u>this</u> dry season to have gotten to the end of the line out in the battalions, and into the local forces and so on. So what January and February really have to live on is what came down in the <u>last</u> dry season."

ABRAMS: "And one other strategy here, Mr. Ambassador, we've got disturbed about the sensor activations and so on. Well, the real <u>truth</u> of the matter is that an awful lot, in this period, of sensor activations was the desperate effort he was making to reinforce against 719 and to <u>support</u> it. A whole lot of that sensor activation was pushing those forces—the artillery, the infantry, the supplies for them, and so on."

ABRAMS: "And then, of course, he's done a lot. He's expanded his systems. There's 40 percent more roads, kilometers of roads, up there—that we <u>know</u> about—compared to what we knew about last year. And then he's put a lot more antiaircraft. He's got the SAMs in there. And this thing up there in Quang Binh—he's running <u>10</u> occupied SAM sites between Dong Hoi and the DMZ. Last year it was 1, and this year it's 10. So if you want to go flying your Piper <u>Cub</u> up there, it's going to get noisy." [Laughter]

21 MAR 1972: COMUS Special Brief: Logistics Offensive, BDA, POW

ATTENDING: Gen. Abrams, MG Cowles, MG Carley, MG Potts.

BRIEFER: The enemy General Transportation Offensive began 1 March 1972 in the Lao panhandle. 559th Transportation Group. "Battlefield B" is the enemy cover designator for the Republic of Vietnam. The General Transportation Offensive involves all five subordinate *binh tram* groups of the 559th Transportation Group in the Lao panhandle. EXAMPLE: Shipments from Binh Tram 45 to (probably) Binh Tram 46 during the period 1–12 March 1972: Total 2,856 tons. Of that, 1,222 tons (42 percent) were weapons. 1,149 tons (40 percent) foodstuffs. 454 tons (16 percent) POL.

ABRAMS: "I talked with General Vien yesterday. I went over all those things I took over there. I told him, 'The truth is, those things that have gone well here are those things the Vietnamese thought had merit, and then the Vietnamese went ahead and did it. That's how anything that's gone well has ever happened here.' And I said, 'I know that, and I think most of my people realize it.'"

ABRAMS: "In the time I've been here, I have no evidence of General Vien <u>ever</u> lying to me. On things that he doesn't feel he is privileged to answer, he'll just say he can't answer. He won't even say, 'I don't know.' He'll say, 'I better not talk about that.' It could be I've been hoodwinked for four years, but I try not to do that." "And I used to talk to Mr. Shackley about this, too. Mr. Shackley had dealings direct with General Vien on some things, things he went to General Vien personally on—himself. And that was his evaluation of General Vien."

■ ■ ■

ABRAMS (re recent visit to II Corps): "I thought Dzu was pretty impressive up there that day. We went directly to his house. He had the maps over there, and he did all the briefing himself. The intelligence—I saw no mismatch at all with what we have here, and he was down to the detail. And no notes. Then his own forces, covered that, and where every damn one of them were. . . . And yesterday I told General Vien about my visit up there, and that I'd been quite favorably impressed. He said, 'When the commander does it himself, you know he's been in it.'"

■ ■ ■

ABRAMS (re briefing by CIA Saigon Station Chief Thomas Polgar of that morning involving some captured material about third-quarter projected enemy activity): "Kind of the way he gave it was that this replaces this stuff we've been putting out about [an] impending enemy offensive. Well, I'm going to get into that with them down there, certainly not in that way. But I'd like to know what he thinks all these regiments and battalions scattered are up to. They're not down here for the Oktoberfest."

POTTS: "He doesn't have a feel of it yet. He just doesn't know. And so many of his people. I think that's why the ambassador comes to our Saturday morning meetings. He [Polgar] just hasn't been there long enough."

25 MAR 1972: Commanders WIEU

Infiltration Estimate: 83,600 (33,400 for B-3 Front, 35,500 for COSVN).

POTTS: "March 1972 runs up to 27,200, and it's exactly the same total for August of 1968, making it the third highest month that we've ever had in the infiltration estimate."

POTTS: "'72 is beginning to look very closely like 1968." In 1968: 97,900 (including two divisions, the 304th and 308th, which are not in the infiltration estimate this year; if divisions were included, meaning for 1972 the 304th, 308th, and 324B, the total for this year would reach 111,240).

VANN: "There's also a massive change in the physical location of the VCI with respect to the population. They're now largely outside the populated areas. They _were_ largely inside the populated areas."

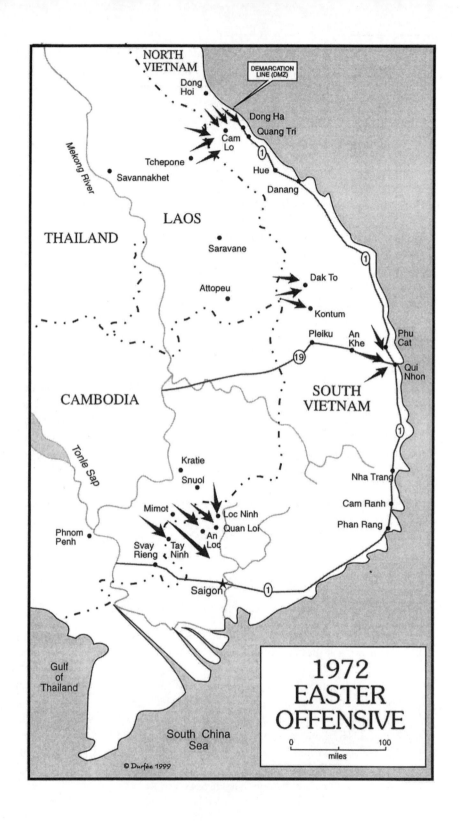

NORTH
VIETNAM

Dong
Hoi

DEMARCATION
LINE (DMZ)

Dong Ha
Quang Tri

Cam
Lo

Tchepone

Savannakhet

Hue

Danang

Mekong River

LAOS

Saravane

THAILAND

Attopeu

Dak To

Kontum

Pleiku

An
Khe

Phu
Cat

Qui
Nhon

CAMBODIA

19

SOUTH
VIETNAM

Tonle Sap

Kratie

Snuol

Nha Trang

Mimot

Loc Ninh

Cam Ranh

Quan Loi

Phan Rang

Phnom
Penh

An
Loc

Svay
Rieng

Tay
Ninh

Saigon

1

Gulf
of
Thailand

1972
EASTER
OFFENSIVE

0   100
miles

South China
Sea

© Durfée 1999

ABRAMS: "There are some pretty dramatic differences between '68 and '72, inside South Vietnam, there's no question about that. However, when you come to <u>intent</u>, the intent of Hanoi, that's where I think this is important."

BUNKER: "Absolutely right. It hasn't changed."

ABRAMS: "One of our submissions said 'Hanoi will make the greatest military effort of which it is capable in 1972.' When you take <u>this</u>—. I don't want to be leaning on 'I told you so,' that's no good. You take this, you take the artillery—122s, guns and howitzers moving down to COSVN, into the B-3 Front; 130s into the DMZ and western Quang Tri. Ten SAM sites in southern Quang Binh between Dong Hoi and the DMZ, versus <u>1</u>—<u>10</u> versus 1. MiG airfields, GCI, SAMs in Laos, tremendous increase in the antiaircraft in Laos. Put <u>all</u> of that together, and <u>Hanoi</u> <u>is</u> <u>making</u> <u>an</u> <u>all-out</u> <u>military</u> <u>effort</u> <u>in</u> <u>1972</u>. That's what the story is. That's what the <u>facts</u> are."

BUNKER: "I think it's important to keep impressing Washington, because we've <u>already</u> got amendments coming up for the appropriation bills to stop the bombing and pull out and all this sort of thing."

■ ■ ■

POTTS: "We've been carrying 70 percent of all the personnel in enemy combat units to be NVA and 30 percent VC. With all of these pure NVA units coming in now, it's going to run that up pretty high."

BUNKER: "That's another good point."

ABRAMS: "It is true that the circumstances here in South Vietnam are <u>quite</u> different in '72 than they were in '68—the effectiveness of cadre, the effectiveness of guerrillas. There's no comparison. Just take Long An out here. The way Long An was in January of '68 and the way Long An is today—it's a different province. Saigon's control and influence in Long An is, I don't know, many, many times more than it was at the same time in '68. It isn't a question of just crying wolf. But also these authorities we're after, and whether you keep more CVAs out in this part of the world, whether you keep that extra 18 F-4s down here, all of those funny things—we're still in quite a thing here. The basket of fruits of peace has not yet been delivered."

■ ■ ■

ABRAMS (re new Cambodian government organizational chart): "Now does that mean that Lon Nol holds all those positions—president, prime minister, commander in chief, chief of staff?"

BRIEFER: "Yes. He's also premier."

SOMEONE: "Facilitates coordination."

ABRAMS: "One of the things you can do with that, the president can write memos to the prime minister. The prime minister can endorse them back to the president, or send it to the commander in chief. And he in turn can send directives to the chief of staff. And the chief of staff can argue those <u>back</u>. In other words, you can have a <u>hell</u> of a lot going on there without really getting it out of the office. Get a typewriter for each position."

WEYAND: "Helps get foreign decorations, too—garner quite a few of those."

JACOBSON: "He needs those other boxes only because he's not very well."

ABRAMS: "That's right—can't do a full day's work."

2 APR 1972: COMUS Update and Ambassador Whitehouse

MACV 1972 Infiltration Estimate: 86,000 (34,900 to the B-3 Front, 35,700 to COSVN).

BRIEFER: On 29 March 1972 a SAM shot down a C-130 west of Tchepone. Three SAMs were fired.

ABRAMS: Asks whether Seventh Air Force or PACAF has a technical analysis capability to look at all aspects of SAM engagements. "I'm not saying anything that I know anything about. That's not the point. But there ought to be some technical expertise somewhere that could commence to grip this problem. Here the goddamn things, flying around up there, they got this stuff on 'em's supposed to say 'here they come.' And it doesn't work. Then there's the thing about some have pods and some don't. I don't know what pods are . . . but that has some bearing on it. They don't like to carry those 'cause it reduces the bomb load. Is there some technical way of thing to come to grips with this?"

BRIEFER: "Yes, sir, there is."

ABRAMS: "What's being done about it?"

RESPONSE: The PACOM unit people were out here. They discussed an optical device on a Fan Song radar that converts to a tracker (F Model). Trying to get one for technical analysis.

ABRAMS: "I'm not so much interested in the Intelligence Community. I'm interested in the fight that's going on and what can be done about it."

ABRAMS: "Back in the United States, I've always had a feeling, there's a great well of technical expertise. The kind of guys that land stuff on the moon and take off and all of that."

BRIEFER: The PACOM ELINT Center "cannot find any electronic difference between the Fan Song F and the Fan Song B, making it very difficult to devise countermeasures."

ABRAMS: "Well, these people that are studying it—suppose they came down here and <u>flew</u> in the gunships. Wouldn't that motivate them to study it harder?"

ABRAMS: Impressed with an SA-2 shooting down a gunship at 2:30 A.M. at a slant range of maybe 15,000 feet using an optical device. "It must look no bigger than a cigar—this cigar. That's pretty impressive."

ABRAMS: "My problem right now is that they're shooting down airplanes and we don't know how they're doing it." Asks for a message saying "the head layman out here, COMUSMACV, would like to have some technical help in trying to find out what's going on. Even if we got a couple of nuts out here it would liven it up, whether it shed any light or not."

ABRAMS: "There oughta be some better way at this than dumping your ordnance and diving for the basement. That's the only thing we've <u>got</u> now. See, there's a question about whether the Iron Hand's any good. What's happening to the Iron Hands now? In some cases they see one of those telephone poles coming [and] they drop those special things and head for the basement."

SOMEONE: "<u>Yeah</u>."

ABRAMS: "And the poor fellows they're escorting—they're dropping it and heading for the basement, too. Everybody is—the protection, the guy who's supposed to see 'em on the screen or see 'em on the scope or see 'em on the light—whatever they got there. Pods. None of that works. So everybody drops everything they got and heads for that nap of the earth stuff, afterburner on. Isn't that what's happening?"

SOMEONE: "That's about it, yes, sir."

ABRAMS: "Well, I mean—shit, they can stop <u>making</u> those things if they're not doing any more than that. See, I'm economy-minded, too—to save money. Those gunships [are] supposed to know it when it goes on, too. Well, I'd like to raise all this, some way. We'd better ask Seventh Air Force to get in on this, too."

POTTS: "I'll get with them and put together a message that lays it all out."

ABRAMS: "Let's not recommend any studies."

■ ■ ■

ABRAMS: Heard something to the effect that the C-130 that was shot down had a substitute pilot (the other guy had a pass or something) and that three other people on board were just along for the ride. "Somebody find out. It's probably just a rumor. The reason I ask about it—I've talked to C-130 crews three times over in Thailand. If I ever talked with a close-knit family—. It's kind of like some of the tanker crews. They just don't accept substitutes. Or somebody wants to borrow one of their crew members? They say, 'No, we'll take the mission.' That's the <u>impression</u> I've had. And that's a pretty complicated crew on that C-130. You know, a <u>hell</u> of a lot of teamwork's gotta go on. The gunners and the fellows that operate the radar, the low-light-level TV, and not very many of them sitting alongside each other. So I'd like to raise that question."

■ ■ ■

BRIEFER: At noon on 30 March 1972 an upsurge began in MR-1. There were widespread attacks by fire. Approximately 4,000 rounds of mixed mortar, 122-mm rocket, and 122-mm, 130-mm, and 152-mm artillery rounds had been received by 2300 hours. On 31 March there was a heavy attack at Quang Tri Combat Base. A crescent of fire support bases were abandoned (the troops withdrawn). FSB Pedro was nearly lost. Cam Lo was heavily attacked. Quang Tri Combat Base received approximately 500 rounds of artillery this morning. Reports about noon today that enemy tanks were being engaged by friendly tanks south of the Cam Lo River.

BRIEFER: A marine lieutenant colonel advisor at Quang Tri Combat Base says the situation there is desperate and has asked for a marine BLT to be landed by the navy. But General Kroesen says he has no information that the U.S. advisors are in any trouble there. He says the combat base is secure now according to his latest information. He does not think Quang Tri Combat Base needs reinforcement or evacuation at this time. He recommends no action other than planning. Kroesen says he has talked to the marine lieutenant colonel and the last he told him confirms what Kroesen reported.

This refers to Colonel G. H. Turley, USMC, and his infamous "Land the landing force" message.

ABRAMS: "Before anyone gets very wild about reinforcing with BLTs, this is a question of just fantastic proportions. And all I want to make sure is it's not done. First of all, a BLT's not going to change the course of events. Secondly, the Vietnamese have got to solve this with their own marine brigade. What's the chain of command with these advisors up there with the marines? Is it Salzer to the head advisor? Well, let's get ahold of Salzer and tell him we've just gotta stop this bullshit of some marine advisor up there requesting the landing of a BLT. My impression is that there's a hell of a lot of marijuana smoking going on. It's not in the cards! I don't know all the moves that have gotta be made to stop this crap, but it's gotta be stopped."

SOMEONE: "The navy has taken no action at all, sir, other than making plans and swapping messages."

SOMEONE ELSE: "CINCPAC has just called, sir. They've gotten copies of this traffic, and they're asking what's going on."

ABRAMS: "We'd better get ahold of Salzer and find out his understanding of whose operational control he's under. And then, from there, whose operational control are those marine advisors under. I want this shit stopped!"

■ ■ ■

SOMEONE: "General Lam called. They're going to have a meeting of their Security Council at eight o'clock tomorrow morning, and he and Phong have been told to start work on a statement their government could make about the situation in MR-1." "The thing that is fundamental and foremost in their minds is that three divisions have crossed the DMZ and violated it in that way." An invasion is under way. [Per MACV: It's the equivalent of three divisions, but not three divisions per se. The 304th is the only division thus far.]

WEYAND: "The best thing that came out of Lam Son 719 was the ARVN commanders themselves giving interviews, which they're [now] willing to do."

WEYAND: "I don't think there's a comparison between this one and Lam Son 719, because at least the press thought Lam Son 719 was fucked up because they had that moratorium on for damn near a month, which drove them right up the wall. And then, when that was released, they couldn't get into Laos. We weren't very helpful. And we stayed out of the ARVN reporting because it was partly we didn't know what was going on in Laos, and it was an ARVN show. Lam didn't want to give them any interviews. Later he changed that."

WEYAND: "The press will be getting to these advisors like Turley and others. I'm sure the security of U.S. personnel is going to be a big story. The advisors are like this, some of them up there. They want out, and they're not going to be let out—in all probability."

■ ■ ■

SOMEONE: "When it gets to be Monday morning [in] Washington, that's when the fur will start to fly."

3 APR 1972: COMUS Update (and Ambassador Whitehouse)

ATTENDEES: Tom Polgar introduced as being present.

BRIEFER: "Operational reports of yesterday and today indicate that a minimum of 24 SA-2 missiles were fired against allied aircraft operating over northern Military Region 1 and southern Laos." Six SA-2s were fired at an OV-10, bringing it down.

ABRAMS: "The cost consciousness program's gone out the window." "There's been no evidence so far that the supply [of missiles] is in any way limiting. They've been firing the damn things like they were trying to use up the inventory for a new model that's coming in. But in connection with this the heat's really on from Hanoi to carry this thing out. They've got everything that they can lay their hands on into it, and they're saving nothing for the dance. From their standpoint, there's no point in this thing winding up and them with a lot of missiles left over. They're running the course, they're not holding out reserves."

ABRAMS: "If we had just double the B-52s I think we'd be in pretty good shape—about 5,000 a month. We have 1,500. It's a very critical weapon now. It's the only thing we've got, really, that is not bothered by weather—except severe thunderstorms when they get up 40,000–50,000 feet. . . . So it's a critical thing and we're meeting somewhere around half the requirement—as stated by the various competitors for it, all of which I believe, and all of which are good. That's not the point. We have to sort it out where the shoe's pinching the worst—today."

BRIEFER: Re the Dong Ha bridge, "this was blown by a U.S. advisor, a captain, with 400 pounds of TNT that he personally put under the bridge and wired it up and blew it—uh, while waiting for clearance." [Laughter] "He was being shot at by tanks from the north side of the river at the time."

Capt. John W. Ripley, USMC, was awarded the Navy Cross for this action. In retirement Colonel Ripley is director of the Marine Corps Historical Center.

■ ■ ■

ABRAMS (to the briefer): "Say, what have you done, Major Stewart, returned?"
BRIEFER: "Yes, sir."

ABRAMS: "When did you get back?"

BRIEFER: "About a month or so ago, sir. It took about 20 days for my clearances. I've been on the job a week."

ABRAMS: "<u>Twenty</u> days for clearances?"

BRIEFER: "Yes, sir."

ABRAMS: "Gee, whiz, you're one of the <u>stalwarts</u> here. It should have been <u>automatic</u>."

SOMEONE: "He might have been contaminated back home."

ABRAMS: "That's right! What have you been doing back in the States?"

BRIEFER: "I've been a student, sir. I went to graduate school and then to the Armed Forces Staff College."

ABRAMS: "Oh, <u>yeah</u>, that's the whole problem. But anyway, <u>welcome</u> <u>back</u>."

BRIEFER: "Thank you, sir. I'm glad to be here."

ABRAMS: "And I'm glad that, in the accident of personnel administration, you wound up back here in the J-3."

BRIEFER (obviously touched): "Thank you very much, sir."

ABRAMS: "Where did you take your graduate work?"

BRIEFER: "I went to the School of Advanced International Studies at Johns Hopkins University, sir. I received a master's degree in economic development."

■ ■ ■

SOMEONE: "I talked a little while ago to the officer who is the acting senior U.S. advisor at Quang Tri Combat Base. His group has been pretty much running the 3rd Division's forward fire support coordination center. He says that <u>he</u> thinks they can hold Dong Ha. He thinks they can hold Quang Tri. He thinks they're doing all right."

ABRAMS: "Well, <u>God</u> <u>bless</u> <u>him</u>! Does he have any <u>requirements</u>?" [Laughter]

BRIEFER: Start of the enemy offensive determined to be 0600 on 31 March 1972.

4 APR 1972: COMUSMACV Update

ABRAMS: "I must say I really find that quite confusing. With the 9th, 5th, and 7th, all of whom are familiar with Tay Ninh, Binh Long, that these two strange regiments, the 271st and the 24th, would be committed in there. And even the 6th—in terms of those others the 6th is kind of a <u>green</u> regiment. It was organized last year. It never has been involved in a battle that I can remember. I realize <u>he's</u> not confused. <u>He</u> knows what he's doing. The thing I don't understand is <u>I</u> don't understand it. The confusion's not on his part."

■ ■ ■

ABRAMS: "See, one of the things that's in my mind is the time we had enemy helicopters up there in the DMZ. In the process of shooting a lot of them down we seriously damaged an Australian cruiser and sank one of our own navy boats. And then, trying to photograph some of the wreckage of the shot-down helicopters—never were able to get a picture of that, and they photographed extensively—in good weather. Then we had a helicopter problem up in Pleiku and Kontum. The enemy was bringing rockets in by helicopter. The division commander up there wanted sort of a 'guns free,' they call it, and I wouldn't do that—I had that other helicopter problem in the back of my mind—I wouldn't do that until we got some confirmation. We put a radar up there out of a Hawk thing, modified so it would track slow movers—the Hawk's built so it won't, so they can just shoot down U.S. Air Force planes and not army. Well, it's army equipment." [Laughter]

ABRAMS: "But anyway, they put that up there and, god, they had tracks and so on, more and more. We then moved to nonfiring intercepts . . . and incidentally had put all these controls on—corridors and—absolute tight control over a-l-l air traffic, so we knew who was flying, and when, and where—army, everybody. Well, we photographed Air America, army helicopters. And then, in the midst of all this, a Laotian O-1 came in and landed at the—got lost, I guess—came in and landed at the Kontum airstrip."

ABRAMS: "What we found out of that is that we really didn't have control of the air. We think we have, and we've got a lot of regulations. We've got a lot of policies, and so on, but what you have with as many aircraft as you've got over here of all kinds—there are bound to be individual pilots or crews or so on who are, oh, taking some nurse back to her billets after a party or some damn thing, you know—you don't know what it is. All kind of stuff going on that's sort of unauthorized, but [laughter] it's going on. So that's why I'm really raising this question [of potential fratricide] here, because I think there's—. I hope when we examine the wreckage of the shoot-down we'll find it is in fact an enemy aircraft, and not one of our poor fellows who is violating policy. I'm not saying that we shouldn't intercept them. But it's a tough problem."

■ ■ ■

BRIEFER: Fifty-two enemy tanks reported destroyed since the beginning of this offensive.

ABRAMS: "When we were there yesterday . . . they were planning to compose, or reconstitute, a general reserve. Then . . . by last night they figured it was possible. . . . And when the heat got turned up by the president—all ready to go! They found that worthwhile, and certainly it seems to be timely in the light of developments."

BRIEFER: "In MR-3, no significant combat activity was reported."

ABRAMS: "What we're talking about is we'll limit the B-52s escorted by 105s to 14 cells per 24 hours. Now the other three, they can go in any area where a 105 escort is not required. All right. Right now, however, this division of 14 B-52s to this situation and 3 to the B-3 Front is about—in my opinion, at this juncture—is about the minimum we can do in the B-3 Front. That thing is just gathering itself all together there, and we need to be working on that. And then, too, I want you to do the best you can on 100 strike sorties, beginning tomorrow."

ABRAMS: "There's another problem here with the B-52s. That's not going to cover all the diverts, if something goes wrong with <u>one</u> of those B-52s. And under the rules, the only thing that can go into these SAM environments are a three-plane cell. [Someone: "Giving some mutual protection with ECM."] That's right. That's right. Therefore, if something goes wrong with one of the aircraft, then the whole goddamn cell has to be diverted to a non-SAM environment. So you're not going to wind up getting 14 every day."

AIR FORCE: "SAC's been getting a little concerned about what happens if they lose one [B-52]. If they shoot one down up there, maybe it will go across the DMZ. We've been going back and forth. We say we've had the same problem with gunships. It's no different from a gunship. What they're doing back there—they're preparing a checklist for what's going to happen when that thing goes down on the other side of the border. They want to know if we were worrying about it. And I said, 'Good Lord, yes. We worry about it every damn day.' But they're worried about—what they're preparing is how they're going to respond to Washington. . . . For instance, the airplane lands on the other side of the border intact, comes in and crashes and is sitting over there. . . . The SAC people are worrying about maybe there's some equipment on board, SIOP equipment, and there isn't any. There's one piece of equipment on there that's secret, and everything else is in the confidential category. So we wouldn't ruin the SIOP if one goes down over there on the other side."

SOMEONE: "There isn't as much on them as there is on a gunship."

AIR FORCE: "That's right."

■ ■ ■

ABRAMS (re ARVN redeployments): "I really think that that's been overtaken by events. Last night they were playing with the idea of <u>withdrawing</u> the airborne from Kontum and sending the Airborne Division up to MR-1. We came down pretty hard on that. And then, as I explained yesterday, he had issued his instructions [for?] up to nine ranger battalions. Then this morning came the green light to move them. And they're moving all nine of them. So I think that has now—and he shouldn't <u>do</u> that [move the Airborne Division]. I think they're going to need that other airborne brigade in MR-2, and probably in the next couple of days. And there's no good to come of separating those airborne. The guy they've got up there is a good man—the deputy commander."

ABRAMS: "One of the characteristics of all of this is that they are capable of coming up with—you talk about imagination and initiative—they're capable of coming up with some ideas that no one ever thought of. [Laughter] Or I guess another way to put it is that these things <u>have</u> passed through more orderly minds, and then been instantly rejected. This thing last night of pulling the airborne—I can't tell you what an extraordinary scheme that is. Christ, that one outfit up there yesterday in a fight with 350 some odd enemy killed—that's one of the outfits they were talking about pulling out last night!" "Talk about taking them out—in that particular outfit they have not yet been able to get the wounded out! So—."

ABRAMS: "Now, I have talked with the chief of staff about the space problem.

We just can't <u>count</u> on this being over by the first of May. So we <u>are</u> going to have to have the things that we <u>must</u> have operationally. And we'll have to take something else. That's what it amounts to. More than that, everywhere you've got that little patch they're going to have to <u>change</u> their outlook. They're not <u>going</u> this month. And they ought to get the word. I'm talking about the <u>people</u> there. We stand fast until this battle's over, and it's probably going to last quite a while. So fasten down your seat belts and prepare for a long ride. You know, just get that psychological point."

5 APR 1972: COMUS Update

ATTENDEES: Gen. Abrams, Amb. Bunker, Amb. Whitehouse.

ABRAMS: "They claim that the 6th Regiment, down in that fighting around Veghel, they also broke and ran. They have an intercept message that the regimental commander's been relieved, and the 803rd was brought in to replace them. And the 803rd has issued orders to <u>shoot</u> and kill anybody out of the 6th Regiment that goes to the rear."

SOMEONE: "This prisoner also said that the 308th, as we thought for some time, is the strategic reserve division, and that had had to be released by High Command Hanoi to participate in this thing. It had been released, and that each of the other corps areas up there were responsible for providing a division for this operation down at Quang Tri and further south. And he said that there's also been a new division formed up there to replace the 308th as the strategic reserve. It is called the 315th Division. We have absolutely nothing on it."

ABRAMS: "I want to tell you—these North Vietnamese that are coming down there out of that DMZ, goddamn it, they're all completely—ah, number one equipment, new gas masks, new everything, new rations, every man with all these floating vests to go across the Cua Viet or the whatever, Ben Hai or any other damn stream. They're down there, and I'll tell you, they're first-class equipment, <u>every</u> <u>last</u> <u>man</u>!"

ABRAMS: "The way this thing is, if we own it somewhere, we'd better get it into the fight! There isn't anything supposed to be saved for the dance, I don't give a damn what it is. And I don't think you'll find anybody squawking back in the States about it, either. I think they all got the word, too. And they'd better, by god, be with it and not get fooling around with red tape and so on. Just get it to the front! And flying it—that's right. This battle is not going to wait for ships or any of that stuff."

■ ■ ■

WEYAND: "Hollingsworth can give a good rundown on that. While I was coming in—he is up there, Loc Ninh, and controlling everything. But I didn't butt in on him, because he is pretty busy."

■ ■ ■

BRIEFER: "And now for the <u>bloody</u> weather, sir. Today we had completely socked in, all the way up above 30,000 feet, a repeat of the same situation that happened to us on the 31st and the 1st. As a result of that we had to divert 22 Arc Lights into MR-2. The problem was that the F-105 Iron Hands can't fly up at that altitude." "Tomorrow doesn't look much better." Start improvement on the seventh, clearing by the eighth.

■ ■ ■

WEYAND: "I saw General Truong. He'd had a visitation from Colonel [Kim?] of the JGS. The requirement they put on him was moving about a division from the delta." "He's been keeping track of the situation up north through telephone calls with, he says, 'my old friends General Giai and General Phu.' But he really appreciated getting a rundown on it from our standpoint. He said that he was prepared to carry out <u>any</u> orders given to him about sending troops up there. He just wants to know where to send them—'This is the time for all Vietnamese to get in the fight.'"

ABRAMS: "There's no better team—people are always screwing around about what team to get on around here. Truong's about as good as [you could get]."

6 APR 1972: DEPCOMUS Update (General Weyand)

ATTENDEES: Gen. Weyand, Amb. Whitehouse, LTG McNickle, MG Cowles, MG Marshall, MG Fuson, Mr. Hitchcock, BG Heiser, BG Lanagan, Mr. Polgar, Col. Grego.

BRIEFER: Camp Carroll was overrun.

BRIEFER: "The apparent lull in enemy activity that we are now undergoing is believed to be only temporary. The enemy thrust appears to have been blunted for the moment; however the enemy has sufficient forces in the border area to completely tie down all friendly forces in the Tay Ninh–Binh Long Province areas and prevent reaction forces from reinforcing them. The outcome of this serious situation will depend on the ARVN's ability to outmaneuver the enemy and drive them back across the border, and the question as to whether the enemy is willing to commit more forces to this thrust."

WEYAND: "General Abrams was up there when Minh and Hollingsworth were together. Holly got a message, a note, and he turned to Minh and he says, 'Now, General, VNAF is up there in Binh Long.' And General Minh said, 'OK,' and he issued instructions to get them out of there. They were supposed to be working in Tay Ninh and somewhere else. So Abe got the impression that these two commanders, U.S. and ARVN, had divvied this thing up so VNAF took one sector and U.S. the other."

WEYAND: "If we could get that threat to Hue removed, or in hand, <u>god</u>—that would make a difference in this <u>whole</u> situation. But it's that possibility of them getting in there that really gnaws at us." "I really worry more about that than I do the B-3 Front, simply because we don't know enough. We've got the best units in Vietnam opposing the enemy there, but—."

WEYAND (re MR-3): "Check that and see what Hollingsworth's asking for, and if he's asking for something give him a thousand points just for the urgency of the thing."

WEYAND: "We've got a chance to destroy [with B-52s] the 272nd and the 6th Regiment. They can't stay dispersed. With these attacks they're making, they'll come together. And they'll be in about three gaggles out there that really would be beautiful targets. Let's not let this priority thing [in MR-1] just completely override everything. If the 1st Division commander comes in with something, or if Hollingsworth comes in with something, let's wring it out and see what you've got. And then I think we'd better talk to General Abrams, if they're coming in with targets and we're not giving it to them because of this set priority thing up in MR-1."

WEYAND: "At 1800 it will be announced that we're striking in North Vietnam." [1800 Saigon time] "The wording was given to us from Washington to be put out here, and it's very terse. It simply says it began—commenced."

7 APR 1972: COMUS Update (and Ambassador Whitehouse)

BRIEFER: As of 0800 hours this morning contact was lost with U.S. advisors on the ground, and Loc Ninh is considered under enemy control. Nine kilometers south, Fire Support Base [Tong Tam?] was being evacuated as of 1130 hours, with friendly forces withdrawing under heavy enemy pressure back across the Cam Lo Bridge, the key evacuation and entry point from the Loc Ninh area. Received reports just before the briefing from Blue Chip FACs that An Loc was under heavy attack. Tentative reports indicate by three regiments.

ABRAMS: "Now, I'd like to comment on all this. These analysts have got something about tying down this and so on. What Giap's got on here is what in basketball they call a full court press. That's what he's got on. He's committed every goddamn thing he owns! All of it has not yet been in contact. He doesn't have anything left. It's a full court press! The 7th and 9th Divisions will be in South Vietnam within the—certainly within the next week. The 5th is there now. That 24th and 271—that's just openers. Grind them up and then come in with the elite. Same thing down here, from one end of the country to the other, a full court press, saving nothing for the dance! That's what it is, and it's going to last all month."

ABRAMS: "These diaries up there in MR-1—they know. They've written it in their diaries. They know that 90 percent of them will die. They know that. They've written it in their diaries. So if only 80 percent are killed they're better off. You take 90 percent while you're winning. So just because we knock out tanks and artillery pieces and have a pretty good day—what we've got to have is 30 days of knocking the shit out of them 24 hours a day everywhere. And this is a full court press. It's from the DMZ to Ca Mau. And it's going to take everything—and all the time."

■　■　■

ABRAMS: "General Kroesen's daily report just breathed impending disaster from the southwest of Quang Tri. Are we keeping it quiet down there [i.e., no B-52 strikes] so that they'll all gather, feeling comfortable, and then one of these days we're going to unleash everything?"

SOMEONE: "We're—we're not keeping it quiet, sir. We're pushing for targets."

ABRAMS: "What'd they say, five regiments up there?"

POTTS: "Yes, sir."

ABRAMS: "I mean, I'm not trying to become a targeteer, but I was just listening to what the staff is presenting here, and what the reports say, and [laughing] I don't know why we're not trying to work the five over."

RESPONSE: They show a graphic of the cumulative B-52 strikes since the campaign began.

ABRAMS: "Incidentally, that last blob of black marks doesn't detract one iota from what I said before, because these have been assembling since those were done! So that doesn't prove I'm wrong. That's just ancient history!"

■ ■ ■

BRIEFER: This afternoon the 1st Airborne Brigade of the JGS reserve has been committed to Military Region 3. Two battalions, the 6th and 8th, left by road at 1400 hours this afternoon moving north, with the 5th Battalion to move to join tomorrow.

BRIEFER: "In Binh Long Province at 1515 hours this afternoon General Hollingsworth directed the evacuation of all U.S. personnel from Binh Long Province." At 1500, in Binh Long, Bruce Dunning of CBS News was in An Loc under incoming fire (per the MACV IO).

■ ■ ■

ABRAMS: "Fourteen is too much for the Iron Hand [F-105s], and you're losing because of SAMs—by trying to force them up into the DMZ. So what it looks like to me is that we're trying to force the thing. We're not getting maximum effectiveness, because we're trying to do more than the system is capable of doing. Therefore we're not getting them on the best targets. Talking about 14 sorties out of 51—that's what, 20 percent? Huh?"

SOMEONE: "Yes, sir."

ABRAMS: "Twenty percent? Twenty percent?! That's not good enough for government work! Now, we don't have enough stuff around here to be doing that. We're going to have to get back to work here. Everybody! I want these things on the enemy! And god knows there's enough of them out there. [Long pause] We'd do better by turning them [the B-52s] over to the FACs, the FACs with the three regiments, and another FAC with the thousand walking across the swamps down there in the Plain of Reeds."

■ ■ ■

BRIEFER: Cites reports that three SAM stations have expended all their weapons, and that they can't deal with the chaff and low-level approaches. Have 13

MiGs below the 20th parallel. Knocked out (destroyed) one SAM site and damaged another yesterday, and are hitting eight more today. Armed recce is going back and forth across the DMZ seeking targets of opportunity. Naval gunfire effort is summarized. All this in response to Abrams's questions about results obtained. The *Oklahoma City* is due to arrive on station at 1830 tonight. By tomorrow morning seven NGFS ships [and five something else unintelligible].

ABRAMS: "I think we've really got to go to work on that MR-1 situation—both B-52s and tac air. That thing's trouble up there, and it's right on us. It's coming—I don't know how long more. But it can—today—it could start tomorrow. And MR-2's just <u>got</u> to have more than that. Now I realize you've always said you can change from 1 to 2 or 3, but—. If the weather comes out like the forecaster says, the weather will be a little better in 2 than in 1, and it will be best in 3. And that should be reflected in how we use them."

SOMEONE (air force): "Sir, our chaff effort has paid off. Tonight at 0345 a 141 will land at Korat with a load of chaff for us." "This is navy experimental. It was at Homestead, Florida."

ABRAMS: "Just think of some wonderful depot guy. You know, he just had a record that it was in his warehouse. Isn't that great?"

BRIEFER: 108 confirmed + 54 possible SAM firings to date. Estimate 37 today, and 18 yesterday.

ABRAMS: "We've got to get moving divisions around here. We gonna be ready for that?"

SOMEONE: "Yes, sir. We've got the 130s ready." "Jack was in today. He's ready, too. Let him know how many 141s we want."

ABRAMS: "See, they're all meeting with the president over there this afternoon. I think it started at 1400. What I'm trying to do is get to see General Vien after they're finished with that so I can find out what the decisions are that they've made. Then I think we can take it on."

■ ■ ■

ABRAMS: "The marines will be able to fly Sunday?"

SOMEONE: "I have them in frag for Sunday noon." Two squadrons of 32 aircraft. "Most of them have never flown here."

ABRAMS: "Does anyone know—are they happy?"

SOMEONE: "I talked to them this morning, and they're happy."

ABRAMS (to air force apparently): "Have you got control of them?"

AIR FORCE: "Yes, sir."

ABRAMS: "I just wanted to know whether they're here and carved out a place of their own or are they all in the same war."

AIR FORCE: "They're all in the same war."

ABRAMS: "That's good."

■ ■ ■

ABRAMS: "Then we've got two more F-4 squadrons coming in from the States. When'll they be in?"

RESPONSE: Don't know yet. One is going to Ubon and one to Udorn or Korat.

WEYAND: "And the additional B-52 cells start—."

ABRAMS: "Tomorrow. One tomorrow, one Sunday, and one Monday. We'll be at 60 sorties on Monday."

ABRAMS: "N-o-w, I think we'd better watch this thing pretty close tomorrow. If the weather's good, if he starts down there in MR-1, then I think we're going to have to forego North Vietnam."

SOMEONE: "Easily done."

ABRAMS: "I think that's the way we have to play it—if the weather's good. In a funny sort of way, good weather's going to give us our toughest problem. I mean, I'm anxious to get those SAMs all knocked out up there, as much as you are, but if he turns on the heat on Quang Tri City and that sort of thing, well we're just going to have to get with it."

■ ■ ■

SOMEONE: "We've just been informed by CORDS that the mayor of Saigon has put a curfew on the city. He has it curfewed from 2300 to 0500. We can conform to that, of course, or go to a gray status off-duty."

ABRAMS: "What's our curfew been?" ["One o'clock in the morning, sir."] Well, let's just change the curfew [to comply with the mayor's]. Anybody see anything wrong with that? That's the minimum. The other thing would be to clamp on the gray alert, which gets everybody out of town. So let's do exactly what the Vietnamese do."

■ ■ ■

SOMEONE: "Blazey just went down in a helicopter—uninjured—down in Kien Giang. Helicopter shot down on him." [Long pause]

ABRAMS: "Why this damn thing hasn't gotten to Kroesen, and John Vann, and Wear, and Hollingsworth, I don't know. But that's where they all are."

8 APR 1972: COMUS Update

ATTENDEES: Gen. Abrams, MG Cowles, MG Carley, MG Potts, BG Heiser.

Infiltration Estimate: 88,800 (36,400 to B-3 Front, 36,300 to COSVN).

BRIEFER: Multiple MRDF on 5–6 April places the 325th NVA Division in the Vinh area, 240 kilometers south of its 30 March location in the Hanoi area.

ABRAMS: Sensors have been put in the DMZ but throughput is not being measured. "There's quite a few sensors have been put in there in the DMZ. If they weren't put in to detect throughput [speaking in measured tones], what was it that they were intended to detect?"

POTTS: "They should reflect throughput, sir. And then, of course, activity. Something may come down and then go back up and never go all the way through. Maybe there's some stockpiles in it." [Long pause]

ABRAMS: "Who, ah—who decided where the sensors would go up there?"

POTTS: "Those were decided by the Seventh Air Force, sir, as they did on the Ho Chi Minh Trail—both in numbers and in location."

ABRAMS: "Well, you've got to <u>do</u> something about <u>that</u>. They went in for a purpose, now what was the purpose and what do we <u>know</u> about it? Don't want to get too <u>complicated</u>, just want to know what they're supposed to do and what they've <u>done</u>. [Pause] And if it's been completely <u>fucked up</u> I want to know that, too! In other words, have bad schemes and bad results and wasted effort—I want to know that."

■ ■ ■

SOMEONE: Brings in a draft message for Abrams to review. Long pause while he reads through it.

ABRAMS: "Send it."

DISCUSSION: General Marshall has discussed the message with General McNichols, who is not at the meeting because he is tied up with the ambassador of New Zealand.

ABRAMS: "Well, I'm a little <u>shocked</u> that <u>anyone</u> in the command is required to waste time with the New Zealand ambassador."

SOMEONE: "Sir, he is trying <u>desperately</u> to get brought up to date. We have held him off. He's looking for J-2 and J-3 briefings here. We have not scheduled any for him at this time. If we do, it's going to be a low-level walkthrough of the command center."

ABRAMS: "That should be related to the New Zealand contribution at this time to the war effort in South Vietnam. I think a well-informed sergeant from the protocol section should be able to discharge the U.S. responsibility. We don't mind a little distraction for a minute or two, but we have got quite a thing going on here and I hope we can—it's not only B-52s and tac air and 130s and 141s and so on, but I hope the staff itself would be able to devote most of its attention, when they're not sleeping and eating, to the problem."

■ ■ ■

ABRAMS: "These aborts on B-52s—are we getting <u>all</u> of those on good targets?"

ANSWER: "Sir, every strike up in MR-1 is targeted against a target that is recommended by the FRAC commander, TRAC commander—they are not just being dumped. When the aircraft departs and goes on its mission, it has to have a secondary target. If it is diverted, it has to go to that specific secondary target."

ABRAMS: "Is that what they're doing?"

ANSWER: Yes, except in a couple of cases when they were loaded with CBUs.

ABRAMS: "We haven't got much CBU left, have we?"

ANSWER: "We've got about 44 sorties. It seems to me at this point we ought to go ahead and use it down to 15, 16, 20—somewhere around there—and then hold. If not hold, reassess."

ABRAMS: "My <u>impression</u> is that the only [true?] CBU targets in country that would be worth a goddamn would be out here in Loc Ninh. . . . There isn't that kind of intelligence up in MR-1, and recently we haven't had it in MR-2, and I think it's just wasting—. Those things [laughs] maybe never will get the kind of target—. I don't believe in losing sorties just because of CBUs. It's better to go a hundred percent iron bombs."

■ ■ ■

ABRAMS (on new topic, threat support package and avoidance): "I'm not going to get into the business of being critical, but <u>by</u> god <u>aborting</u> <u>that</u> <u>mission</u> just outside of Hue on the strength of a fucking MiG being at Dong Hoi is just— drives you up the wall! If <u>that</u> goddamn attitude prevailed throughout the armed forces I don't know how the hell you'd ever get anybody on the point or in the advance <u>guard</u>! I consider that to be <u>folly</u>! Huh! One of the bad things about war is that a lot of people get hurt. That's the way they've always run it. This newspaperman asked me yesterday why we hadn't been teaching the South Vietnamese some kind of tactics where they wouldn't shoot up things. Pretty hard to—pretty hard to hold your temper in a session like that. The guy says 'shooting up things.' I told him, I said, 'The only way you can have a war is to have two sides. There's got to be one side fighting another side. And a lot of what you do is determined by what the other fellow does.' Like General Vang Pao—he told them, 'You give both sides rocks, we win.'"

■ ■ ■

SOMEONE: "Sir, on the CBU, I really believe we ought to keep loading a cell a day. It's the only way to have it available in time to use if you <u>do</u> need it."

ABRAMS: "Yeah. If you do that, you either don't use it—keep it on the ground over there at U Tapao—or you're at a predetermined time. And it's hard to see how you're a winner."

RESPONSE: "It's hard to use. I can't explain it, sir. There's no good solution. But the only way I can reason it out is that, if we want to use CBU effectively at all, we've got to have it available when we need it, it's got to be preloaded. When we need it, and have to then load it, those targets are going to disappear."

ABRAMS: "But even then—. Let's say you load it, and you've got them sitting over there at U Tapao—. All right, you've got a target. How long does it take to have the crews briefed, the plane take off, and get on target?"

RESPONSE: "I would say six, eight hours, sir. And they have to be used in 72 hours. They can't hold on the ground longer than that."

ABRAMS: "Yeah. Kind of a tough problem."

RESPONSE: "Yes, sir, it is. We were using them on Island Tree—."

ABRAMS: "You had the best of all worlds there, the infiltration system that was more or less a continuous thing—you know, they just keep a-coming. You could listen in on there for a few days, nothing going on, then it starts picking up. So you could say, 'Get 'em ready!' And here they come, and you had half a dozen choices up there. And they could buzz those things and find out, right up to TOT."

RESPONSE: "And we knew the most profitable time of day, too."

ABRAMS: "Yeah, that's right. So it was a wired-in system. And we haven't <u>got</u> anything like that."

RESPONSE: "About the only <u>practical</u> way to do it is to go ahead and pretarget against the best targets that we can develop and let 'er go."

ABRAMS: "Yeah."

RESPONSE: "And if we get something in the meantime that's better, divert."

22 APR 1972: Commanders WIEU

ATTENDEES: Amb. Bunker, Amb. Whitehouse, Gen. Abrams, Gen. Weyand, Gen. Vogt, LTG McCaffrey, Mr. Jacobson, MG Eckhardt, MG Cowles, MG Marshall, MG Bowley, MG Hollingsworth, MG Fuson, MG Jumper, MG Potts, MG Kroesen, MG Tarpley, MG Slay, MG Watkins, MG Carley, Mr. Vann, Mr. Duval, RADM Salzer, BG Trogdon, BG Heiser, BG Wear, BG Bernstein, BG McClellan, BG Herbert, BG Scott, BG Johnson, BG Lanagan, BG Wickham, Mr. Walkinshaw, Mr. Wilson, Mr. Dean, Col. Zerbe, Col. Stevens, Mr. Barnes, LTC Baker.

General John D. Lavelle, USAF, has been charged with violating the rules of engagement and relieved of command of Seventh Air Force. He has been succeeded by General John W. Vogt Jr., USAF, who arrived just in time for the Easter Offensive.

Enemy Southeast Asia Program for 1972.

POTTS: "Sir, during the past week, based on all intelligence available and the indications, we have developed the enemy's program throughout Southeast Asia for calendar year 1972."

BRIEFER:

■ Will "comment on why he [the enemy] has been forced to modify his original plans in some areas. We believe that the enemy compiled a master plan for calendar year 1972 over a year ago. Its theme: '1972 is the year of decision.' It required VC-NVA main force units to strike hard in Laos, Cambodia, and South Vietnam to spread allied forces and emphasize U.S. and ARVN vulnerabilities. The Republic of Vietnam would be the key theater of war, and actions there would decide the fate of all Indochina."

■ "The first good indication of a marked change of strategy was the appearance of the unnumbered COSVN resolution in December of 1971. It called for a shift in the balance of power to the use of main force warfare and political initiatives. It also called for the defeat of Vietnamization and pacification programs, expansion of VC control of land areas, and protection of base areas and lines of communication. . . . Additional indications of enemy objectives have been revealed in numerous documents, agent reports, and subsequently summarized in COSVN Directive 43 dated March 1972."

■ Directive 43 reiterated the unnumbered directive and "revealed other aims, which included disrupting the . . . economy, improving the morale of the VC infrastructure, influencing U.S. and world opinion, and discrediting and removing the Thieu government." "The ultimate goal appeared to be that the enemy would demand a cease-fire in place after seizing land areas, and thus force negotiations with the objective of a favorable settlement of the war."

■ Cyclic events since 1962. Now (beginning in 1971) "he is trying to skip most of the guerrilla and equilibrium stages of protracted warfare, and is assessing himself as prepared for a general offensive."

■ North Vietnam has adopted new recruitment and training policies. The minimum draft age has been lowered from 17 to 16. The upper limit has been raised from 30 to 35. Physical requirements have also been lowered. Many who were formerly rejected are now being called, and previously exempted groups are now subject to the draft, including midlevel government managers, graduate students, industrial trainees, "and personnel classified as 'politically unreliable.'"

■ The average training time for new NVN recruits has been reduced from six to five months. We estimate that NVN is currently inducting personnel at an annual rate of 150,000 men. "In order to recover from Lam Son 719 and achieve his 1972 goals, the enemy carefully planned and coordinated his recruiting, training, and infiltration times."

■ The enemy planned to send more organized units through the infiltration system to MR-2, 3, and 4 than in previous years. We estimate infiltration as of this date to be 94,200. This compares with 109,600 at the same date in 1968. By including 15 groups expected to be accepted and included later, the current total will be raised to 101,400. At this time in 1968 there were 31 groups in the pipeline that were later accepted and included, bringing the total to 124,635. This year an additional 25,600 personnel infiltrated in main force units into northern MR-1, which were not assigned infiltration group numbers. That brings the total to 127,000. Also 6,500 for northern Laos and 2,500 for southern Laos. Grand total of personnel dispatched from North Vietnam for service in Southeast Asia is 136,000 as of this date.

■ Also enemy improvement, expansion, and protection of the LOC in the Lao panhandle. AAA (up 48 to 61 since 1971), SAMs, engineer, roads expanded, supplement of six new *binh trams,* improved command and control. Forty-nine engineer battalions, up from 39 since November 1970. Integrated air defense plan. In mid-April 1972, 56 prepared SAM sites in southern Quang Binh Province, up from 20 in mid-November 1971. SAM threat radius now extends to 6 nautical miles south of Quang Tri City and 12 nautical miles south of Tchepone. At least six AAA battalions have been noted moving elements in the DMZ and northern MR-1 region since 1 January 1972. MiGs below 20 degrees have increased from a daily average of 5 to 10. GCI site manned and activated in March 1972.

- Early October 1971: Massive enemy buildup in northern Laos. Tanks. 130-mm guns. Troops. Road building. "Has failed thus far in his attempt to overrun . . . and defeat Vang Pao's forces." "Why?" Combined effects of allied air strikes, increased number of Thai battalions committed, and Vang Pao's initiatives threatening the enemy rear and LOCs.
- Dry season logistical campaign, followed by Logistics and Transportation Offensive beginning 1 March 1972. Beginning August 1971 moved supplies south to stockpiles near the DMZ and the passes. Increased POL storage capacity south of the 18th parallel. Expanded the POL pipeline system. Also supplemented with more trawlers.
- Between October 1971 and March 1972 the USSR delivered 271,000 tons of POL (130 percent of requests) to North Vietnam.
- Propaganda and information: Prepare the North Vietnamese people for increased fighting and sacrifices in the "imminent march to final victory." Giap: "Determined to Fight, Determined to Win." Slogan for 1972.
- Deployed reserve units from North Vietnam into Laos and the Republic of Vietnam. Increased force structure in the B-3 Front by at least one division, three divisions in MR-1, one regiment in MR-3, and two regiments in northern Laos. During February–March 1972 four of the five NVA reserve divisions deployed into RVN. Only during Tet 1968 and Lam Son 719 had this previously occurred. The 320th Division went to the B-3 Front. 304th to Quang Tri. 324B to MR-TTH, west of Hue. 308th to Quang Tri. 271st Independent Regiment to Tay Ninh. 325th, the one remaining division, has moved southward from the Hanoi area, and is now in the Quang Binh border area. 141st Regiment (312th Division) and the 335th Independent Regiment are in the Plaine des Jarres.
- Enemy has also deployed the 5th, 7th, and 9th Divisions from Cambodia to MR-3, and the 2nd NVA Division from southern Laos to the B-3 Front.
- Summarizing the strategy of main force warfare for RVN, per a recent document, COSVN Directive 51: Attack in Quang Tri City, hoping to draw ARVN reinforcements north. Then attack in MR-3 to further reduce ARVN reserves. Attack Saigon with rockets and sappers. With ARVN forces widely spread and reserves reduced, demand a cease-fire in place and a coalition government.

■ ■ ■

Recap of the Easter Offensive to date.

BRIEFER:

- The enemy initiated the offensive on the night of 30 March in MR-1, on 31 March in the B-3 Front, and on 1 April in western MR-3. "We believe . . . a maximum effort has still not been attempted in the B-3 Front." "The enemy is now engaged in conventional warfare and has assumed the offensive in selected areas of the Republic of Vietnam."
- We had expected the offensive to begin around 20–25 February. Intelligence now indicates "that the earlier timetable was delayed due to B-52 and tactical

air strikes, Island Tree interdiction, allied preemptive ground operations, and the high state of alert of allied forces."

■ "Enemy planners are apparently attempting to force ARVN to accept piece-meal defeat or to withdraw to consolidated positions, thus abandoning a substantial percentage of the rural population and obviating [*sic*] previous pacification success."

■ Allied actions to counter included a dry season interdiction campaign from 1 November 1971 using tac air, B-52, gunships and continuing to the onset of the present enemy campaign, when assets had to be redirected. Heavy damage was inflicted, including 12,081 trucks damaged or destroyed during the period 1 November 1971–31 March 1972.

■ Island Tree began 6 December 1971, based on detailed analysis of the *binh tram* system and especially the location of T-stations. B-52s targeted based on sensor string activations. Both iron bombs and CBUs employed. This was also interrupted by initiation of the enemy offensive.

■ "By early March the enemy had extended the reach of his air defense system deep into MR-1 below the DMZ. He had made the operation of gunships and other slow movers impossible in the northernmost bases and had complicated operations by tac air and B-52s. Authority was granted on 4 April to strike SAMs and other military targets north to 18 degrees and later expanded to 19 degrees."

Enemy expansion of his air defense system in that manner had been possible because of the restrictions applied to U.S. forces.

ABRAMS (re shifting air effort): "This took some of the heat off his logistical effort. I don't think there was anything else to do. Nevertheless, that was the effect."

BRIEFER: Preemptive air attacks were placed on enemy units as they began arriving about four to six weeks before the offensive. Especially B-52. Included two 48-hour maximum effort tac air and B-52 operations against the B-3 Front and northwest MR-1. Also ARVN preemptive ground force operations.

BRIEFER: JGS has moved the 6th Ranger Group (three battalions) from MR-1 to MR-2, replacing the 3rd Airborne Brigade (three battalions). Airborne (and the Airborne Division Headquarters) move to Saigon to rest and refit, then reinforce An Loc.

POTTS: Points out that the infiltration estimate shows COSVN getting more men, and getting men later into the year, than in the past.

ABRAMS: "Well, all I can say about that is it's good planning, 'cause they're gonna need 'em."

BRIEFER: Last week a minimum of 270 SA-2 missiles were fired at allied aircraft operating over northern Military Region 1 and North Vietnam, resulting in the loss of three aircraft. This brings the total number of SAMs fired since 30 March to 591, and the total number of aircraft lost due to SAMs to eight since that date."

BRIEFER: "According to a recent CAS report, the decision to launch the current large-scale Communist offensive in the Republic of Vietnam may have kindled serious party dissension in North Vietnam." Quoting Politburo member and Secret Police director Tran Quoc Hoan's "stinging diatribe against counterrevolutionaries both at home and abroad," he stressed that "when the use of violence is deemed necessary to cleanse the home front, it must be used resolutely."

BRIEFER: Describes relatively restrained reactions to U.S. bombing in NVN from Moscow and Peking, suggesting they don't want to upset improving relations with the United States.

ABRAMS: "I feel urged to comment. I don't disagree that what you say—China is less abrasive, the Soviets are less abrasive, and it's because they want these things to move along on the path they're on. But if you were sitting in the jungle somewhere and a cobra looked over there, and he's coming up, not making much noise, don't want to disturb you in your sleep and all that. But it's still a cobra, and when he gets where he wants to be he knocks you off. So I don't <u>disagree</u> that they want it to be kind of smooth, but <u>there's</u> <u>damn</u> <u>little</u> <u>comfort</u> <u>in</u> <u>that</u>! There're other innings coming up."

BUNKER: "I think it's a typical Communist approach, saying one thing and doing another."

BRIEFER: According to press accounts, on 17 April Xuan Thuy said that "if the Paris negotiations were resumed in the usual manner, and if the U.S. stopped bombing North Vietnam, [Le Duc] Tho would return to Paris."

BRIEFER: Depicts North Vietnamese error in printing a photo in 6 March 1972 issues of leading North Vietnamese civilian and military newspapers showing "the bodies of South Vietnamese troops slaughtered at . . . a fire support base on Highway 9 between the Rockpile and Camp Carroll. Arms and legs of these slaughtered troops were still bound."

ABRAMS: General Lam said the Vietnamese had some trouble with the T-59 tank. One man just couldn't lift a round of the 100-mm ammunition—took two men. "And then he said it was hard to drive."

POTTS: "We'll be driving it next week, sir."

BRIEFER (on enemy equipment): "Sir, all of these items will be on display in the hallway—with the exception of the tank [laughter]—at the next break."

■ ■ ■

General Situation in RVN Briefing

BRIEFER:

■ "In northern MR-1 the 3rd Division, with its reinforcements, has stabilized the situation in eastern Quang Tri Province." Some attacks to the west. 1st Division is engaged in heavy fighting around Bastogne. 2nd Division has blocked the enemy advance in the Quang Nam area.

■ In MR-2 not yet fully coordinated offense as in MR-1 and MR-3. Pleiku City feeling the effects of QL-19 having been cut for the past 12 days. POL and ammo resupplied by air. In Binh Dinh Province, "Hoi An district town fell to an enemy attack last Wednesday when ARVN defenders panicked and fled after several days of heavy fighting and severe losses." "The situation in northern Binh Dinh remains serious."

■ In MR-3 "heavy enemy pressure on An Loc has continued for the past 10 days, with elements of 15 friendly battalions defending the city. Casualties have been heavy on both sides, but the friendly forces are holding against daily attacks by fire and tank-supported ground attacks. Heavy and sustained tac air and Arc Light strikes, many of them close in to friendly positions, have been instrumental in helping to hold the city."

■ In MR-4 "the tactical problem is different from the other military regions." Many attacks against outposts at widely scattered points. The 21st Division has been redeployed to MR-3, and the 4th Ranger Group to MR-1.

■ Getting 25 cells of B-52s a day currently. Since the start of the battle on 30 March have concentrated on four areas: Quang Tri Province, the FSBs Bastogne-Veghel area, the tri-border area of the B-3 Front, and around An Loc in MR-3. "Many strikes in close support of troops in contact." "A special targeting effort is under way here in MACV Headquarters to develop deeper targets in MR-1 and in the Steel Tiger area."

BRIEFER: On 3 April: Yankee Station from two to three carriers with the arrival of the *Kitty Hawk* from the Philippines. On 8 April: A fourth carrier added when the *Constellation* arrived from Japan to go on Dixie Station.

BRIEFER: Now 640 sorties average daily strike capability (an increase of 73 percent since January). "All of 231 aircraft [augmentation?] were deployed and in place within 17 days of the invasion, permitting a 272 scheduled sorties increase over the January figure."

■ ■ ■

ABRAMS: "I know it's bad to talk about Tet '68, because this really is quite different. One of the things reminded me of it when the CORDS briefer said the police, logistics system, and that sort of thing is functioning and so on. I remember going over to a meeting here at CMD one Sunday. And the police advisor was there—this was in the first weeks following Tet—and he got up there and described the police situation in Saigon. Coolheaded man, but he said, 'We've got a problem.' He said, 'We haven't been authorized M16s, but they've got a lot of them. And there's no way to get ammunition. Their system doesn't have it. They've got M79s. They're not authorized them. They've got PRC-25s. They're not authorized them, so you can't get batteries. And,' he said, 'they're running out. They still have the equipment, but they're running out, and there ain't no way to support it in the police system because they're not authorized it.'"

ABRAMS: "So I told, I said, 'Now I'll give you—within an hour or so after our meeting ends—I'll give a telephone number, or I'll have somebody give you a telephone number. And,' I said, 'all you'll have to do is call that telephone number and whatever it is that you need will be delivered where you want it delivered.' And I came back here and I got hold of the J-4—I guess it was Rasmussen—and I told him the story. And I said, 'I want you to designate somebody, one of your officers there, and that'll be the telephone number. I don't want any goddamn questions about paperwork or any of that. When they <u>call</u>, don't question it. Just ask them where and when they want it delivered. Then I want it <u>done</u>!' I got him in trouble with Bob Komer a few days later when he found it out [laughter], because he wasn't using the system, but it was <u>great</u>. And that's just the way I worked it."

ABRAMS: "And when this fellow said this morning that the system's working and so on, at <u>least</u> we're <u>that</u> much advanced. So I know the Tet thing, but it's unlike Tet and there may be some dangers in <u>comparing</u> it. But, psychologically, one of the things that happened in Tet was that <u>everything</u> clutched up. I've forgotten what we had in CMD in addition to the territorials and so on. About 23 battalions, something like that—<u>regular</u> battalions, U.S. and ARVN. But the great <u>trauma</u> of Tet pulled everybody to the province capitals and the big cities, to try to protect them and so on. And then, trying to push back out after the thing had finally subsided, became next to impossible."

ABRAMS: "And when they started the Accelerated Pacification plan on 1 November '68, which meant getting out, a good many didn't believe it really could be done. And finally—they'd go into some of these villages, some of these VC villages, and they'd find out there weren't any VC there at all. And, you know, PF recruiting went up and things like that. But the total thing that this government has done, since November of '68, is to involve itself with its people. That's what's happened, kind of, since November of '68, in all kinds of programs—the buildup of territorials, organization of PSDF, pushing the police out. Not all of it—well, I mean, there's been an awful lot of ineptness, but the <u>azimuth</u> of the government has been to <u>establish</u> <u>itself</u> <u>with</u> its <u>people</u>. The land reform program—hell, it's nothing but <u>people</u>. All those things down at Vung Tau—it's trying to get the representatives in there and preach to them. And get everybody involved—the self-help program, the matching funds programs, elections down in the villages and hamlets, and all that."

ABRAMS: "And we've talked the 'One War' concept, you couldn't separate it, it's all one thing. And you talk about he [the enemy] works at seven levels and the only way you can handle this kind of a war is that <u>you've</u> got to work at seven levels, the same levels he works at. And you can't get to the end of the year and say it's been a great year with five levels having gone good and two fell on their <u>ass</u>. You <u>lost</u> in those two areas, and in this kind of a thing you can't <u>afford</u> to lose in <u>any</u> of those levels. And so on."

■ ■ ■

ABRAMS: "And there's something else about this I wanted to mention. There's been some poor performances. But there <u>always</u> have been poor performances—in war or anything else. And I think that there always will be. You've got a few guys do great, few guys who are sort of satisfactory most of the time, and then you've got a few guys that are just miserable. But in this thing now, until this is over, there's no point—you've just got to accept the fact that there're going to be some poor performances. The trouble is that you're doing it with human beings. If you didn't have them, you wouldn't run into that. Some poor performances are not going to lose it. It's the good performances that are going to win it. And there's always been a mixture."

ABRAMS: "And these four corps commanders we're supporting, that's the ones we've got. There aren't going to be any others for this thing, and we've just got to get in there and back them, support them, advise them to the extent we can, and so on. And the fellows that work with you."

ABRAMS: "I remember one time in Lam Son 719, General Weyand went up there and he got in with the American staff up there. And the battle was still raging. We were getting on, and doing things, and—everybody was—doing pretty good. They'd got over some of the shocks. But what was the staff doing? Goddamn it, they were in there gathering photos and making charts and so on, all about the goddamn armor equipment that had been lost over there in Laos on Route 9! That was the thrust of the working and the thinking of the damn staff! Now—there wasn't any way to get that back. The bill had already been paid! There was [pounding the table] a fucking disaster! But there's [shouting] no point in that being the whole damn subject of conversation, the whole subject of thought, from there on! Now there's got to be some pos—. That's what will lick you. That's what will lick you. The guy that doesn't get licked is the guy that never even thinks he can be! The thought never comes to his mind! He has the patience to accept disaster and disappointment—and outrage—but he keeps after it. And that's what's got to be here. There'll be disagreements and all that, but just—. And with every one of these individuals different, I know that. Sometimes they get apprehensive. Sometimes they get excited. Sometimes they get foolhardy. And sometimes they get good."

ABRAMS: "You're on a roller coaster. But—I doubt the fabric of this thing could have been held together without U.S. air. But the thing that had to happen before that is the Vietnamese, some numbers of them, had to stand and fight. If they didn't do that, ten times the air we've got wouldn't have stopped them."

ABRAMS: "So—with all the screwups that have occurred, and with all the bad performances that have occurred—they've been there, but we wouldn't be where we are this morning if some numbers of the Vietnamese hadn't decided to stand and fight. And that's the first point. It has to be that or no amount of air will do anything. That's been a dicey thing up there in Kontum, but—and still is—but it's been enough so that that 30,000 or what has come in there has been getting banged around now for two or three months. . . . And that's something. And that's why we've had the chance to do it. And they swept through the DMZ and all over that thing. Down went the 3rd Division and all of that. But they stopped at the Cua Viet, and they haven't been able to get into Dong Ha, and they haven't been able to get into Quang Tri. And the reason, the first reason, is that the Vietnamese, including the 3rd Division, have decided by god they've gone far enough and they're going to fight if they get some kind of a chance. So that's the way I feel."

BUNKER: "When I was back in February and talked with the president, and told him what we expected, he said, 'Well, they're not going to win this one!' So you can be sure that he's going to give us all the backing he can. He's as determined as anyone."

BUNKER: "As a Vermonter, I wouldn't want to be accused of making any extravagant statements, but it looks as though we're going to be in for a fairly active period."

29 APR 1972: COMUS Special Brief for General Michaelis

Gen. John H. Michaelis was Commander in Chief, United Nations Forces, Korea; Commander, U.S. Forces, Korea; and Commanding General, Eighth U.S. Army in Korea.

ATTENDEES: Gen. Abrams, Gen. Michaelis, MG Potts, MG Herbert, MG Carley, MG Fuson.

ABRAMS: "What they've developed up there [in NVN] is quite a sophisticated system [of aircraft and air defenses], between GCI and SAMs and aircraft, and their antiaircraft. And I think the antiaircraft is largely Soviet, and its control radar and so on. It's a designed system, so I think it's probably all Soviet, and probably has had Soviet advisors in it, so the equipment's all compatible."

MICHAELIS: Asks about Chinese or Russian pilots.

POTTS: The pilots are North Vietnamese. About four years ago North Korean pilots were brought over in groups of 20, then rotated. Re the NVN pilots: "We're familiar with their numbers, we know who they are, we know their characteristics, we know their leaders. It helps us know what's going to happen when a Comrade [Thu?] moves from one field to the other."

BRIEFER: Short summary of the current situation: On 30 March the enemy began a concentrated offensive that has now spread throughout most of Vietnam. First thrust was across the DMZ in northernmost Quang Tri Province. Concurrent easterly push toward Hue. A few days later, second thrust from the Khmer Republic into Binh Long Province in northern MR-3. After these thrusts met with initial success, the enemy opened yet another front in MR-2 in Kontum Province and increased activity in Binh Dinh Province to the east. The increase in local force activity in the delta could be considered an offensive of a different nature.

BRIEFER: In MR-1: By 14 April I Corps was able to initiate a limited counterattack to the west. On 27 April the enemy resumed offensive action against Quang Tri City. Dong Ha was evacuated on 28 April. ARVN, under heavy pressure, attempting to consolidate positions around Quang Tri City. Situation serious, with enemy tanks and infantry just outside the city. Farther south, in Thua Thien Province, enemy forces attacked along critical Route 547 against determined resistance from FSB Bastogne and FSB Birmingham. FSB Bastogne was forced to evacuate under heavy enemy pressure last night.

Remainder of VNMC Marine Division moved to join the two brigades already in MR-1. Followed by three ranger groups (but the 6th has since moved to MR-2). The 18th Armored Cavalry Squadron is in Quang Tri City.

BRIEFER: In MR-3: Elements of the 5th ARVN Division at Loc Ninh were forced to withdraw south to An Loc. Since 13 April have withstood almost daily ABF and tank-supported ground attacks. City reinforced by airborne brigade from Saigon and a ranger group. Another airborne brigade in the past few days from MR-2. The 21st Infantry Division from MR-4 to deploy astride QL-13 south of An Loc. West, in Tay Ninh, ARVN consolidated positions north on high-speed approaches to the city. Airborne Division Headquarters plus one airborne brigade had been sent to MR-2, but were relieved by the 6th Ranger Group and returned to this area.

BRIEFER: In MR-2: Third enemy push began 24 April. Infantry and armor attacks forced the evacuation of Dak To II and Tan Canh. Plan all-out defense of Kontum City, the objective of current enemy drive. In Binh Dinh, three district headquarters forced to evacuate by heavy enemy pressure. Enemy succeeded in closing An Khe Pass and keeping it closed for over two weeks. Opened by ROK forces.

BRIEFER: In MR-4: Reintroduction of U.S. tac air helped replace combat power lost through force redeployments. 9th ARVN Infantry Division trying to cover the area left open when the 21st Division moved north.

BRIEFER: "Arc Light has played a key role." Seventy-five sorties (25 cells) per day currently.

BRIEFER: Naval gunfire is effective in northern MR-1, supporting the 3rd Division by eight ships (average) firing nearly 1,200 rounds per day.

BRIEFER: "Personnel losses have been heavy on both sides." Current incomplete figures: 29 U.S. KIA, 96 U.S. WIA. 3,500 ARVN KIA, 10,000 ARVN WIA, 1,000 ARVN MIA. Enemy: 18,900 KIA and 600 detained.

■ ■ ■

ABRAMS: "This all happened in April, and we had that ceiling of 69,000 to get down to by the first of May. The augmentation, including those helicopters [scheduled for redeployment but held over], amounted to about 3,000 spaces. So we had to find—in order to keep that and get to 69,000—we had to find 3,000 spaces somewhere else, which we've done."

SOMEONE: "We're under our 69[000] by a comfortable margin."

ABRAMS: "And the day of the president's announcement about the 49,000—we heard that in the morning about eleven o'clock, so that evening we sent out a message to the JCS on the moves that are going to have to be made now so that we can get to 49,000 in June. One of the big things—a lot of the air's going to have to move to Thailand. We'll retain command and control here, but they're going to have to move on that. They're going to have to open a couple of bases over there."

■ ■ ■

ABRAMS: "What you've got here is that he—the enemy—has staked all on this, and if he doesn't make it go he will have lost. And that is going to be a very difficult thing for him to accept. So you've got a thing where—let's say his battalions are reduced to 75 men—that doesn't mean they'll stop. He's prepared to fight this thing out to the last North Vietnamese that's in South Vietnam. That's the kind of a thing you're with. What you're up against is a very determined man. The first thing that'll kill him is if you can hit his logistics enough so that he's out of fuel or out of ammunition or food, or all three. The next thing is to batter up enough of the equipment, especially heavy equipment, so that he hasn't got the support. And the last thing is to batter up his men so badly that they've lost their will."

ABRAMS: "There was a report—I guess it was the first year I was over here. A Rumanian delegation was visiting in Hanoi, and one of the members of that delegation is the fellow that gave this report. They were at the museum they have up there for Dien Bien Phu, and they were briefed on the battle at Dien Bien Phu by General Giap himself. And he described the entire battle, both sides, in great detail. And he came down to the end and, in those last two or three days, he committed everything he had. There wasn't anything more— nothing! And so one of them asked a question. They said, 'Well, what would have happened if you hadn't taken the position?' He said, 'It's very simple— the French would still be here.' So you're dealing with a thing here with a 'go for broke.' There's nothing being saved for the dance."

ABRAMS (re B-52s): "The last month, I would say that somewhere around 90 percent, roughly, has been close support." Results? "It all depends on the targeting. We know that some of it's been good. Out here in this An Loc battle there's been a series of attacks during the day, and then about 4:30, or 5:00, or 5:30, something like that, and the defenders were just about exhausted, they looked out there and here was another one forming up—some tanks and infantry and stuff out there. A-n-d, while they were trying to figure out what to do about that, an Arc Light landed right on them. And that was the end of that. That was the end of the day."

ABRAMS (re ARVN morale and performance): "Well, it's a mixed bag. What I think has happened thus far is there's been enough of them with determination and will so that the thing could be held. I don't think there's any question about their capacity to do it. It's simply a question of will. And that's what this is, in his case. It's the same goddamn thing. In fact I would say, the way this thing stands right now, it's the same for both sides. It's whose will is going to be broken first. There's nothing fancy left to be done."

■ ■ ■

ABRAMS: "I'm not going to make any statements that the Americans were the [best?] here, but I'll tell you one thing—when you needed a battalion somewhere—goddamn! It could be grabbed and it went now! Now! Not this afternoon, not tomorrow, but now! And not only that, it was ready, it had its stuff, it just—it knew how to do it, it accepted it, that was a way of life. You, at one point over here, the—many people were doing it, among the Americans. They'd get—well, they'd just have a bunch of companies, or half companies, out there looking for contact, looking for the enemy. And when they got one, the reserve was all the companies that had no contact and they just started putting them right into their fight, just like that. Barsanti was great at it, the little guy, and Hank Emerson [laughs]—that brigade he had, that's the way it started every day. Every day! But his reserve was all those that weren't already in the fight. And the nature of the thing is that that's a perfectly safe—you're not overcommitted. The nature of the fighting at that time made that a very workable system. And then, in Tet of '68, it's one of the things about the Americans—hell, they could be—you could ram them all over the place, wherever trouble was the worst. Those mechanized units, moving them out on the ground; regular infantry, moving them by helicopter; artillery, and so on. Of course, I don't know if there's anybody that has more communications than the Americans have. That makes a hell of a lot of difference."

■ ■ ■

SOMEONE (after the briefing): "General Michaelis is hard to hear."

POTTS: "He had throat cancer some years ago. He whispers." "We have a tape on that, I hope."

SOMEONE: "We have a tape with not too much General Michaelis on it."

POTTS: "That's all right. The main thing we want's the COMUS. COMUS-MACV!"

SOMEONE: "We can always hear him!" "No sweat."

1 MAY 1972: WIEU

ATTENDEES: Amb. Bunker, Amb. Whitehouse, Gen. Michaelis, Gen. Abrams, Gen. Weyand, Gen. Vogt, LTG McCaffrey, Mr. Jacobson, MG Eckhardt, MG Cowles, MG Marshall, MG Bowley, MG Fuson, MG Jumper, MG Potts, MG Slay, MG Carley, Mr. McCann, Mr. Duval, RADM Salzer, BG Trogdon, BG Bernstein, BG McClellan, BG Lanagan, BG Wickham, Col. Sadler, Col. Crockett, Capt. Fluss, Col. Stevens.

BRIEFER: "In the B-3 Front, there have been no groups detected in the infiltration pipeline projected for arrival after May. This represents a steady decline from the 14,800 personnel who arrived in the B-3 Front in February." "Infiltration into COSVN has also shown a decline since the peak months of March and April." "However, except for the 100 personnel arriving in Military Region 5 in June, all infiltration projected for arrival in the Republic of Vietnam and Cambodia after May is destined for COSVN." "Countrywide, March was the month in which the maximum number of personnel arrived at their destinations."

■ ■ ■

ABRAMS: "You know, President Thieu has this July–August second effort—hangs very heavy on his mind. First he started saying that's when the offensive was going to occur. And he held onto that until it started on the 30th of March. And since then he's been saying there'll be a <u>second</u> one that'll be in July and August. And I don't know whether he has some information that would support that—."

BUNKER: "Well, I think he's changed his view a little."

ABRAMS: "Yeah, but even the other day, when we were there, he said it again."

BUNKER: "But I've seen him since then, and now he says he thinks they're going to hang in."

ABRAMS: "Well, that's what this looks like to me. This is an all-out, go-for-broke effort. And that's what that infiltration thing indicates to me."

■ ■ ■

BRIEFER: Last week a minimum of 122 SA-2 missiles were fired. Two aircraft were lost and a B-52 damaged. 745 missiles have been fired since the offensive began (836 since the first of the year), and 10 aircraft lost.

POTTS: Last year 165 missiles were fired and 10 aircraft lost. The year before, 48 were fired and no aircraft were lost.

ABRAMS: "That was the best year. That's still pretty good, don't you think, this year?"

SEVENTH AIR FORCE: "Historically, they've fired about 6,000 missiles since we got involved" and the loss rate has been less than 2 percent over a sustained period of time.

■ ■ ■

ABRAMS (re U.S. advisors): "I think the Americans have <u>really</u> performed very well. . . . There probably—I'm sure out there somewhere there are some weak sisters. You never have a thing where you're a hundred percent. But the main— somewhere over 90 percent are just working their—. And they're doing it around the clock. It's an all-out thing. In fact, the—what you've got mostly is routine performance of miracles."

SOMEONE: We're dependent on Federal Electric and PA&E for our communications and utilities, and we still have civilians in Quang Tri running those for us. Only one civilian asked out. He went to Can Tho, and a volunteer replaced him. "And these guys—we're all just amazed at them. They're sticking in there and pitching. All the way through, and they're civilians."

JACOBSON: "I lost one man that I couldn't figure out any way not to lose. That was Norm [Fernstall?], who had to go back and appear before the <u>Kennedy</u> Committee on refugees."

ABRAMS: "Yeah, well I think that's understandable. After all, our Senate has its serious business that it must continue, an august body, and functioning of government's not going to stop because of this. Yeah."

■ ■ ■

ABRAMS: "It's pretty clear that we've got a real tough situation up there in northern MR-1, and also in Kontum. That has all the potential for developing into a serious problem. The same thing in Binh Dinh. The MR-3 thing hasn't moved along probably as sharply as, well, even as it might have. But I think that they're gradually getting on top of it, and I don't think there is a crisis situation in MR-3. . . . And down there in the delta it's pretty good, what Truong and those people have been able to do so far. The American air, bringing that back in there, has been a big boost to them. . . . They really got feeling kind of lonely down there. They weren't complaining. They never said a word. But you take all those troops out of there and send them someplace else—it made them feel lonely."

ABRAMS: "I'm personally convinced that this is, from Hanoi's viewpoint, it's a make or break. They're throwing everything they've got into it, in every way they know how. And the level of brutality right now is, in my opinion, the highest it's ever been in the whole war—both ways. It's all after, in one fell swoop, to gain the whole prize. It's reflected in that COSVN letter of instruction we listened to this morning. That's what they're telling them. So it's going to go on, and we must try to get at the facts and at the truth every day to see just where we stand. But certainly we must always try, in the search for truth and the search for facts in the situation the way it is, we must strive for a balanced and considered view of it."

ABRAMS: "All through this thing, too, you know, it's meant a lot to South Vietnam that Americans—the Americans that were here and the Americans that worked here, and there's been, you know, lots and lots of them—through thick and thin they have maintained a positive attitude, a 'can do' attitude. And when it comes to winning a thing like that the influence of that kind of attitude—I'm not talking about dreaming, I'm talking about facing the facts then by god then go ahead and do something about it. The value of that attitude is worth—its effect is greater than some number of tanks, or some number of B-52s, because this is a struggle of will. That's what it's gotten into right now. And we can nurture South Vietnamese will by positive and realistic and a 'can do' attitude. And I think during this period that's going to be an important factor. I think the government itself understands the struggle in its full dimensions, so there's no problem there. And under these circumstances people get tired, and that's understandable. But you've still got to keep at it—and I think that's what's been done."

5 MAY 1972: COMUS Brief for Secretary Shillito

Barry Shillito is assistant secretary of defense for logistics.

DISCUSSION: Trawler identification and surveillance. Acquired and initially tracked covertly, then overtly. One trawler challenged by VNN "ran up a flag that was supposed to mean he was carrying fish. Damn funny fish, because when they put a round into him immediately they had four rather large explosions."

ABRAMS: "When you get in the business of 122-mm guns and howitzers, 130-mm's, tanks, and tank ammunition, you're getting into tonnage. When you try to support that kind of stuff, you're not going to do it with trawlers."

VOGT: "With all the stuff we thought we were knocking out coming down that trail, and then to wake up one morning and find out you've got a General Motors operating outside of An Loc, causes you to be a little shocked."

BRIEFER: In SVN today enemy strength is 236,000 (80 percent in combat units).

ABRAMS: "Every morning at nine o'clock we have a meeting up in my office with the [J-]3 and the [J-]2, General Vogt, General Weyand, the chief of staff, and myself, and review the intelligence and the situation. And then we review the allocation and targeting of B-52s and the weight of effort of tac air—all tac air. And at that time you review what happened in the 24 hours before. See, during that period things have happened and you've had to shift from what had been agreed upon the morning before. So you compare what you planned to do with what was actually executed, and go over what BDA there was, losses, damaged aircraft, the airlift—review that—and that sort of becomes the clincher until we meet the next morning."

POTTS: We captured an officer from the 304th NVA Division in action around northern MR-1. Said on 15 April B-52s hit his regiment and caused "very high casualties." On 29 April hit again, losing 10 tanks, plus ammunition it had taken them a long time to stockpile, plus "heavy losses of personnel." Also said a sister regiment had been almost completely wiped out. Said the third regiment had to be transferred to another division to make one division out of two.

ABRAMS: "On this question of the B-52s and the tac air, it's very clear to me that—as far as my view on this is concerned—that this government would now have fallen, and this country would now be gone, and we wouldn't be meeting here today, if it hadn't been for the B-52s and the tac air. There's absolutely no question about it."

■ ■ ■

ABRAMS: "Well, the 1st Division, and the Marine Division—the marines in this whole thing have performed well above any performance by that division, or those brigades, in the time I've been here, and yesterday was my fifth anniversary. So the Marine Division and the 1st Division are in good shape. They're stout, morale's good, and the leadership's good."

Lt. Gen. Ngo Quang Truong has been moved from CG Military Region 4 to become CG Military Region 1, replacing Lt. Gen. Hoang Xuan Lam.

ABRAMS: "The rest of those units are just going to have to have time to reorganize, refit, and so on. The change in sending General Truong up there is quite significant. He went up there and took command of the 1st Division in '66 at the time of a Buddhist uprising in which about half of that division went over on the Buddhist side against the government. In two years he transformed it into the best division, and it was up in that Hue area."

ABRAMS: "In the Tet Offensive of 1968, the night before it happened, he

[Truong] ran a surprise communications exercise, and he was dissatisfied with the results. His headquarters was up there in the corner of the Citadel in Hue. So the next night he had his staff and himself there to run another surprise communications and alert exercise with his division. And that's when it hit the fan. When the smoke cleared away the next day, the enemy had all of Hue. He [Truong] had one battalion in Hue. His regiments were outside in various other parts of Thua Thien and Quang Tri. He had that little corner over there where his headquarters was in the Citadel and the enemy had all the rest of it. And that's where he started working the problem. I was up there all that time. He's really a very cool fellow—never got excited and never panicked. And by the 25th of February he had the enemy out of Hue. It was a building by building, block by block process, the dirtiest kind of fighting. So General Truong is a symbol in that part of the country of all that's good in Vietnamese terms."

ABRAMS: "He [Truong] went up there day before yesterday to take command. And when he went to Hue the first thing he did was to get on the radio and television. He told them that they were going to defend Hue. It would not fall. And he brought with him the former province chief, who's the man who rebuilt Hue and is also quite a symbol. [Question: "Where had he been?" ABRAMS: "Down in the delta, working for General Truong."] And at the end of it he called on every soldier to report back to his unit—now. And those who failed to do it would be shot. Because part of the thing up there is to change the morale around and get the determination and the will in there to do the job. And I certainly am hopeful that that's what will happen. And he's a fellow who's very well organized in his mind and his thinking. He spent that night and the next day getting with the staff. He's got a report from Kroesen, who's the senior advisor up there. And Kroesen's been with him all day in a helicopter. He's just going to units, districts, seeing people. He said in all the time he's been up there he saw more in one day with General Truong than he did in all the rest of the time with General Lam. It's the kind of thing it's going to take to reverse the attitude up there. So I think we've got a chance. And the president went up there yesterday, he and General Vien. And so—."

■ ■ ■

ABRAMS: "What you've got here, in my opinion, is a go-for-broke thing by the North Vietnamese. And they've thrown everything they've got in it. The only thing that hasn't been committed—yet—is the 325th Division." "Every one of these regiments that are in the fight have already been engaged. It's just an all-out onslaught, and the losses on both sides—I mean, he's losing tanks like he didn't care about having any more, and people, and artillery, and equipment. The level of violence, and the level of brutality, in this whole thing right now is on a scale not before achieved in the war in Vietnam. And that's what you're in."

■ ■ ■

SHILLITO: "It seems to me there must be some area he [the enemy] wants to control, and once he's achieved that then maybe—."

ABRAMS: "I would say that what he probably would like to have had is Quang Tri and Thua Thien; Kontum, Pleiku, and Binh Dinh; Binh Long, Phuoc Long, and Tay Ninh. And maybe Chau Duc and Kien Hoa—one province in the delta. And then sit down for a settlement in Paris."

■ ■ ■

ABRAMS: "A few days ago . . . this battalion, and maybe the regimental headquarters, of the 271 separate regiment got into this little hamlet here in southwestern Tay Ninh. They came in there and started putting up flags—the people were all gone—putting up flags and that sort of thing. And this PF platoon, Vietnamese PF platoon, was still in its little outpost outside this village. So they called in and said that these fellows were in there. Then we turned loose artillery, and air, and every other damn thing on it. And they reported 200 and some odd killed—this PF platoon. You couldn't believe that, so General Weyand asked General Hollingsworth, if he had time, if he'd just drop over there and see what that all meant. Hollingsworth went over there, and the province chief and the division commander of the 25th Division were there. And Holly went around on the ground and counted himself 150, but he couldn't take time—150 enemy dead. And apparently what happened there was they were told that the thing was liberated, so they just came marching in there and started setting up for the night, or getting ready to. And the PF platoon was out there, seeing them all, and they just called in, said 'They're here,' and then all that stuff descended on them. It's the same thing that happened with a group of tanks that came into An Loc. They'd been told that An Loc was taken. So they came—I don't know, about eight or nine of them—and they came just marching right down the road in column, right into An Loc, and—well, they just knocked them all out. They [the enemy] never fired a shot. Standing up in the turret, that sort of thing."

ABRAMS (re Shillito question about tank versus tank fighting): "There was some of that in the first part of this up around Dong Ha. Apparently the 20th, which is the [M-48] A3 battalion, did very well." "Just became operational."

SOMEONE: "They were on their ATT [annual training test] when this thing started on the 30th of March."

ABRAMS: "I went up there and visited them, and there's no question but what those fellows could shoot. I saw them shoot. They're very good. Also the crews were really pretty expert in handling the tanks. They drive those things around very well. All that part I know that was in good shape. They were weak on maintenance—crew maintenance. We had a hell of a good American team in there that worked with those people. They were all handpicked—former Vilseck, Grafenwöhr, Fort Knox, all older guys and so on. It was a damn good team. But I think, after they started falling back from Dong Ha, the thing just broke down—refueling, maintenance, the whole works."

ABRAMS: "One thing I should mention that's appeared on the scene over here is this Strella heat-seeker missile. That's a bastard on helicopters and slow movers—A-1s. And it's put the FACs at 9,000 feet. That's what FACs are flying at now in that northern MR-1 where that thing has been prevalent. The only defense I know right now for helicopters is fly nap of the earth, and that puts you down in the small arms."

■ ■ ■

ABRAMS (re commanding MACV Forward during the 1968 Tet Offensive): "I was up there for the whole month of February, practically, and part of March in 1968, and I never got above 50 feet in a helicopter. You just couldn't. There was too goddamn much .50 caliber—.51 caliber—and so on. The ceiling was too low. You couldn't—the ceiling was at 400 feet, 500 feet. One day we did, we got up above it—a hole in it—we got up above it and—but hell, when we got back to Phu Bai, or where we thought it was about Phu Bai, there wasn't any hole to go down. Well—after one of those experiences you get back to that 50-foot stuff. That's better. At least you have the feeling you could jump out."

■ ■ ■

ABRAMS: "Now the artillery—that 130. They've got a thing now they think they can—the larger-caliber artillery—this C-130 gunship type of affair, they think they can pick up [locate] heavy artillery and shoot it with this thing. I guess it started last night, working up in MR-1 to see whether that will actually work out."

SOMEONE: "We heard about the M102 firing out of the aircraft, sir—howitzer. Is that just a gimmick, or is that really useful, sir?"

ABRAMS: "Ho—it's one of the best damn things, the best gunship of all! The thing is amazingly accurate. We've got two of them now. We've been keeping them . . . every night, those two, in MR-2. And that's for tanks. And we've got the TOW up there. The two helicopters with the TOW are up in MR-2. One of them is working well, and the other one there's something gummed up in it in the aiming and tracking."

6 MAY 1972: WIEU

ATTENDEES: Amb. Bunker, Amb. Whitehouse, Gen. Abrams, Gen. Weyand, Gen. Vogt, LTG McCaffrey, Mr. Jacobson, MG Eckhardt, MG Cowles, MG Marshall, MG Bowley, MG Jumper, MG Potts, MG Slay, MG Watkins, MG Carley, Mr. McCann, Mr. Duval, RADM Salzer, BG Trogdon, BG Bernstein, BG Scott, BG Lanagan, BG Wickham, Col. Knepp, Col. Sadler, Col. Norris, Col. Presson, Col. Crockett, Capt. Fluss, Col. Stevens.

MACV 1972 Infiltration Estimate: 94,900 (3,700 to DMZ/MR-TTH, 15,400 to MR-5, 33,500 to B-3 Front, 43,300 to COSVN).

BRIEFER: In 1972 (not included in the infiltration estimate) are 25,600 who entered through the DMZ/MR-TTH. These would bring the 1972 total to 120,500.

BRIEFER: During the past week the enemy expended at least 60 SA-2 missiles at friendly aircraft operating over NVN, northern Laos, and MR-1. Loss of one aircraft (an A-7). Total since 30 March: 787 SAMs. Since 1 January: 878 SAMs.

SOMEONE (re SAM sites): "We're striking every site that we get a photograph of within three to four hours of that picture coming back. Last night we had one SAM fired in the whole area despite all that air activity up there. We've had a very good, very successful, last several days destroying SAMs and SAM equipment—launchers, transporters and so forth. We have new policy now that if there's a scratching in the earth anywhere, regardless of whether there's equipment on it, we go hit it. And we seed it with mines, and with delayed action bombs. Obviously they're going to take those SAMs and start moving them south to get into the Hue area. I don't think they're going to have a chance of doing it. We're simply going to preempt. If there's a bulldozer anywhere starts scratching, we're going to work it over. We're not going to wait till the equipment's on it. I think we've got a good handle on the SAM situation right now, the best we've had in the last couple of weeks."

BRIEFER: Hanoi newspapers report that North Vietnam has now "reached a milestone in the air war against the United States. Hanoi claims that, since the war first began, they have downed a total of 3,500 American aircraft over North Vietnam. Included in this exaggerated figure is 12 B-52s." On 25 April 1972 the United States listed 944 fixed-wing aircraft and 10 helicopters as having been lost over North Vietnam since reporting began on 5 August 1964.

BRIEFER: In MR-1: Enemy forces continue their advance along Route 1. Captured Quang Tri City on 1 May. Forced evacuation of FSB Nancy on 3 May. PWs say the 304th and 308th NVA Divisions "sustained heavy losses from tac air and B-52 strikes and may have been forced to consolidate their effective forces under control of the 308th Division."

BRIEFER: On 24 April the two TOW-equipped helicopters arrived from CONUS. On 5 May 12 jeep-mounted TOW systems with trained crews arrived at Tan Son Nhut from Fort Bragg. Also six SS-11-equipped helicopters with crews arrived at Tan Son Nhut.

8 MAY 1972: COMUS Brief on Enemy Logistic Targets

BRIEFER: "Pilots reported 16 bombs out of 20 on the power plant. If there're any lights burning in Hanoi tonight, they'll be candle power."

BRIEFER: Describes enemy logistics flow from the Vinh area to Hue, then the Seventh Air Force plan for attacking it.

BRIEFER: From the Vinh area, the enemy uses three generalized routes southward: first, along the coast using the 1A route network; second, the central panhandle using the 82 route network; third, western system using rail line and Route 15 network. Western passes southward through the Mu Gia Pass into BA 604. Also feeds Ban Karai Pass. Three general corridors merge in the vicinity of Quang Khe, transversing as one corridor southward to the vicinity of Dong Hoi, where again splits into three distinct corridors. Supplies enter MR-1 along six distinct logistics corridors, the first two from Laos into western Quang Tri Province and the A Shau Valley. Third into western Quang Tri Province and south to the A Shau. Fourth into central Quang Tri. Fifth into northeast Quang Tri. Sixth into northeast Quang Tri. To Hue along four main corridors: QL-1 from the north, 77 from the northwest, 547 from the west, and along "Gorman's Road" from the southwest.

BRIEFER: There are better choke points in the north than "down below the Ban Karai and Mu Gia passes, where we've bombed those things for years and years and haven't really done much good at stopping them coming through there."

BRIEFER: "Because of our armed recce that we've been running, we have at least—you remember in the past, when we had these protective reaction missions, that those roads were loaded with all kinds of trucks, SAM equipment, and petroleum, waiting to go on down through the trails, and it's disappeared. Or maybe they've got it hidden, put away, or maybe it's been used up or destroyed. But at least it's gone, so there's another, possibly, step along the way of accomplishing this interdiction program." Route Pack 1 area.

BRIEFER: Given the additional air assets that should be available soon to be shifted here: "We ought to be able to do a real good job in that Route Pack 1 area. I don't see how they can get around it. They don't have the redundancy up there. They haven't built it like they have down in Laos, for instance."

9 MAY 1972: DEPCOMUS–General Vogt: Road Interdiction, DMZ

BRIEFER: Southwest monsoon forecast to begin about 14 May 1972. NVA has built a new road network in the central and western DMZ that will not be affected by the southwest monsoon (as the road network into the Laotian panhandle will be) (the DMZ network will be affected by the northeast monsoon in the autumn). Thus the enemy has achieved a 12-month year-round resupply capability into MR-1.

12 MAY 1972: Commanders Brief

ABRAMS: "I got you in here today—I know you're all busy—because I wanted to talk about a few things. And I want to hear from you anything that contributes to the cause."

ABRAMS: "The day started out pretty good here this morning. General Weyand,

Vogt, and myself got a chance to talk for a few minutes with some young pilots [who've] been up there shooting MiGs down. One of them got five. And I'll tell you, talking to those young fellows for a few minutes really makes you proud to be in the uniform, and proud to be an American. God they're good! They're bright, they're intelligent, they're obviously skilled. They know their business real well. They're experts in their work. And there isn't a one of them would vote for McGovern. [Laughter] I mean they're the real stuff! And it makes you feel good. So often young people, younger people, are characterized by the hippies and the dropouts and the communes and all that kind of stuff. And these are just as good as any we ever had in the whole history of our country—just as gutty and so on. That gives you a good feeling."

ABRAMS: "Now I've got a few things here I want to talk about, and for want of a better expression I'll call it operations and intelligence. I think it's about cleared up everywhere, but I still want to review it. You've got to have there at your hands—I'm talking about you commanders here—all of the intelligence. . . . And you've got to know it yourself. And right there alongside it is your operations. This means, then, that the targeting gets into things like talking with the DASC, where the FACs are going to devote a lot of their attention. It all ought to be as the intelligence picture is developing, hour by hour, day by day. And that's the only way that you can get most of the bombs on something that he owns. Yesterday's intelligence is probably not any good for today's targeting."

ABRAMS: "The intelligence officer, I think, can go only about so far. He should be accurate with you and so on, but then there's—the interpretation of all of that, I think, in the end has to be the commander. That's where the decisions are made and so on. So you need to have those things all pulled together then."

ABRAMS: "Now, I wanted to say a word about the use of air. In some places you've got a kind of a psychosis going, and in the worst cases it boils down to the ARVN commander, he's got an idea you should use the air to kill all of the enemy. When I say all, I mean the last goddamn one, and then he will advance. Now I realize that's not true everywhere, and it's only in a few cases. But the advisors and everybody [have] really got to work to get that pushed away. The air is a great thing. In fact, I think we're probably all in agreement that if we hadn't had it this would long since have been gone, the whole goddamn thing. But it just isn't going to kill all the enemy. It'll kill a lot of them, and mash up a lot of his equipment and so on. That's what we want to do with it. But they've got to maneuver, too. They've got to move."

ABRAMS: "Along with this, they've got a big thing about the enemy has got all this sophisticated equipment. And the Vietnamese love to talk about that. That sort of makes him really something, and I suppose, in a way, it explains why they were driven out of Dong Ha and Quang Tri, and why they were driven out of Dak To and Tan Canh, and why they lost at Loc Ninh."

ABRAMS: "Now, what the hell has he got that's sophisticated? What is all this? He's got the SAMs, but SAMs didn't get into the battle for Dong Ha. They're not affecting the <u>Vietnamese</u>. That's a problem for our air force. And they've got the MiGs. And that's the same thing. That's why we were talking to those fellows this morning. They're commencing to work on the inventory—<u>MiGs</u>. And they've got artillery, but they've been using—that's not new. They've got tanks, but the <u>ARVN</u> had tanks. The ARVN haven't lost their tanks because the enemy tanks knocked them out. The ARVN lost their tanks because, <u>goddamn it</u>, they abandoned them. <u>That's</u> how they lost them. And, <u>shit</u>, if they had the <u>Josef Stalin-3</u> it wouldn't have been any better!"

ABRAMS: "Over there in Lam Son 719 every time one of those crews got a little spunky he'd take that M41 and he knocked out any <u>one</u> of those tanks that <u>they</u> had. That's a good gun on there, and at the ranges that they had to work on over there—<u>shit</u>!"

ABRAMS: I don't like to—well, I must like it, because I'm always doing it, but you talk about being <u>outgunned</u> or something, <u>goddamn me</u>! Over in Europe in World War II—our light tanks had a 37-mm on them, and then we had a goddamn 75-mm on there, on our <u>biggest</u> one. That was our real <u>killer</u>. And these Germans had tanks and that damn 88-mm gun. That 88-mm gun—one of my tanks one day got hit in the front end, right where the armor plate's the thickest—that goddamn projectile went right through there, right through the transmission, right through the crew compartment, and right out through the goddamn engine! Right through the engine doors! <u>Yes</u>! And didn't even stop <u>then</u>!"

ABRAMS: "We had a lieutenant one time, and he was up on a little knoll. He looked down on an open field and there were five Panther tanks in a circle like this, all with their guns pointed out. This lieutenant was a platoon leader. So he left his platoon up there, and he took off in that M4, down that goddamn hill, got up a good speed. And he charged <u>right</u> into the <u>center</u> of those five tanks and knocked all five of them out. Now why can you do this? It took three minutes to make a 360-degree traverse of the turret on the Panther tank. And that was driven by the same engine that drove the tank, so you had to engage the engine with the turret if you'd been moving and so on. <u>Our</u> tank would make a 360-degree traverse in about 10 seconds. So he figured that thing out, that if he could get in the middle—and of course he was shooting no more than 75 yards—if he could get in the middle he could get all five of them before they could get those damn guns on him. And that's what happened."

ABRAMS: "<u>Another</u> time—got held up by German tanks, and they were all sitting down there and wondering what the hell to do about it. And all they had was <u>light</u> tanks up in the front. So we fired a lot of smoke on them, and got a pretty good cloud going down there, all over them. And then these little light tanks with the 37-mm, they ran down there and they got in back of that cloud. And pretty soon here they came, the German tanks, backing slowly so they'd get where they could see again. And they just knocked the bastards out, shooting them through the engine compartment door at about 50 yards."

ABRAMS: "<u>So</u> this stuff about the sophisticated equipment, and the goddamn tanks, and all that, and this wire-guided missile." "And in all this talk the Vietnamese don't have anything to say about the equipment they've got. So we need to push on this. I haven't heard of a <u>tank</u> being knocked out by a recoilless rifle."

ABRAMS: "Now I want to talk a little bit about VNAF. You've sent me messages, and talked to me, about VNAF. And I've talked with General Vogt. And General Vogt, in turn, with his advisors. First thing, the VNAF has taken significant casualties—not only loss of aircraft, but loss of crews. It may vary a little bit from region to region, but I'm convinced that in the <u>main</u> they're <u>trying</u>. They've suffered a lot of battle damage. I guess you're loaning them some [word indistinct] to help on that."

ABRAMS: "If you want to take it by service and compare the overall performance of ARVN with the overall performance of VNAF, I think they look pretty good. <u>But</u> the thing we want to try to get developed, I think, is where they're working closer together, the ARVN commander and the VNAF commander out there in each of the corps areas. And try to get the recrimination out of it and get into some kind of cooperation and coordination of what they do. And get it tied together. I know General Vogt will continue to work hard on this from <u>his</u> side, through his advisors and that sort of thing. But we need to get as much of the <u>friction</u> and <u>heat</u> out of the relationship and start getting more on the <u>business</u>. They really need each other, and this country needs them to work together. And that's what we've got to <u>help</u> them to do."

ABRAMS: "Now, I've been, I know, myself, I've been, for the last several years I've tried to maintain rapport with the Vietnamese that I work with. And I've tried not to do things that they would find insulting—always been kind of careful about that. And tried to get developed respect and—so you can get things done, and get them done—it ends up getting done at their speed, which—. Speed's probably the wrong word, because there isn't any in it. It's <u>movement</u>, sometimes hard to detect. But I wanted to tell you, in the last few weeks, in my conversations with General Vien, and with the president, I've said it <u>straight</u>, and called it for what it was worth."

ABRAMS: "Just the other day General Vien was telling me about some equipment they wanted, and I told him that we were doing everything we could to get this equipment to them and so on. But I then went on to tell him, I said, 'Equipment is not what you need. You need men that will <u>fight</u>. And you need <u>officers</u> that will fight, and will lead the men.' I said, 'No amount of <u>equipment</u> will change the situation. It's in the hands of <u>men</u>, and if they'll <u>fight</u>, and their officers will <u>lead</u> them, you've got—even today—you've got all the equipment you need.' I said, 'That's the trouble.' I said, "I don't think you've lost a <u>tank</u> to enemy fire. You lost all the tanks in the 20th because the men abandoned them, led by the officers. You lost most of your artillery because it was <u>abandoned</u> and people wouldn't fight.' So I think you should understand—. Now I don't want you to go back and tell your counterpart that I told the president off. That's not why I'm telling you this. I want you to know the way I'm conducting <u>my</u> business with the counterparts I have to deal with, and I think it has to be straight with them. I'm never insulting and so on, but it's a <u>fact</u>. And that's what we must talk about are the facts."

ABRAMS: "Along with this, there are <u>obviously</u> some officers out there who have done well. And I've talked with General Vien about this. They must themselves—this is a—they'll never have another experience like this to find out. They don't need any goddamn efficiency reports or high school records or <u>anything</u> to pick out now the officers they need. That's all being determined out there right now in the finest damn university you could possibly get for an army. There's no degree that will ever equal it. And this is where they should put the finger on them. And as time goes on, and <u>you</u> become aware of majors, lieutenant colonels, colonels, I'd like to have you feed them in. I don't want a report every week or—I'm not going to put it out that way. You just keep this in mind, and when they're spotted—and I don't want any iffies, just the ones that it's pretty clear that they'll fight and they know how to do it. It's not a one-time report. Just feed it in when you think you know what—you're <u>confident</u> that you know what you're talking about."

ABRAMS: "Now, I think the last thing I want to talk about are the American advisors. And I just think that their performance has been magnificent. In fact, it's probably the glue that's held this whole thing together. It's not only the heroics involved in it, but real toughness and real ability. I suppose, here and there, there have been a few that have not done well, but <u>most</u> of what I hear and see, it's really great. General Weyand had three marine advisors that were in one of those marine brigades up there—heh! Really, <u>really</u> good men. And I say the same thing for the four of <u>you</u> who are here. What you've done to hold the thing in hand has <u>also</u> been magnificent. And it applies not only to the advisors that are with the units, but to the advisors that are with the provinces, same thing there, really hanging in and tough, trying to get the things done that have to be done and stiffening the back of the whole thing. So that's what I wanted to say here."

■ ■ ■

ABRAMS: "Now I'd like to hear from each of you in turn. We'll start with you, Kroesen."

KROESEN: "Well, sir, the situation up there I think is I'd classify as hopeful. I think General Truong has moved in and done an outstanding job of recreating some kind of confidence, some kind of will to continue the resistance. I've never seen anyone quite so enthusiastically and warmly received as he was the first couple of days up there when he traveled around the districts and the regiments—particularly in the 1st Division, where they knew him, but every district. He carried with him Colonel [Thanh?], the former province chief, who was also very warmly received. You could detect a kind of a growing enthusiasm among the troops that he talked to, a reaction to his personality, as he went around. I think he's pretty much instilled in those that are now charged with the defense of the area a decision that they're going to <u>fight</u>, that they

<u>aren't</u> going to lose. They've made up their minds that they <u>can</u> do it."

KROESEN: "I think he has redisposed his forces so that he's got a reasonable defense. He's got one that everybody understands. He's got one in which each of the division commanders are aware of what the other division commanders are supposed to do. That's new. Prior to the time of his arrival we ran I Corps on the dial exchange telephone by personal calls from the corps commander to division commanders, and then never a staff follow-up to tell everybody else what was said to a particular division. He's got the staff functioning for the first time <u>ever</u> in I Corps. They have always been, prior to this time, kind of an information agency. They collected reports from the field, were then able to bring the corps commander up to date on what had been happening, but that was about their only function. I don't think they ever wrote an operations plan. They never really had a coordinated staff activity to support an operation. General Truong has got that staff working, and there's a sense of urgency in the staff that's <u>never</u> been there before. They really are trying, and I think doing a pretty good job. There are a lot of competent people among the ARVN officers on that staff. They just never were challenged and never used properly."

KROESEN: "General Truong's basic concern when he got there was the understrength of the forces that he had. The 1st Division was operating with only about 300 to 350 men per battalion in the field. They had been attrited, since the 5th of March, pretty heavily. He's started receiving replacements, he's happy with the increasing strength of the division, and so is General Phu."

KROESEN (re 1st ARVN Division): "When they've been driven off of anyplace, they've been driven off by a superior force, but they withdrew from that in order and under control." "I have a lot of confidence in the 1st Division. I think Phu is a <u>hell</u> of a good commander."

KROESEN: "The armor forces are of practically no account any more." "I think the 20th Tank Battalion is out of this war for the foreseeable future." The 18th Armored Cavalry Squadron commander "is the one guy who didn't lose everything on the way back from Quang Tri. He lost a hell of a lot of equipment, mostly from running out of gas, but he didn't lose it because his men abandoned it without reason."

KROESEN: "He's [Truong] taken great steps, <u>strong</u> steps, to keep QL-1 open." "The Thua Thien RF and PF have done a magnificent job. There has not been an interruption on QL-1 between Hue and the Hai Van Pass since this operation started—not a bridge, not a culvert, nothing."

ABRAMS: "There's a <u>fantastic</u> amount of fire support up there in northern MR-1—all those navy ships, tac air, B-52s, and all that. Have you got a good setup there—Truong, you, and so on, for really pulling that all together?"

KROESEN: "I think so. The fire support coordination center that we now have set up in I Corps Headquarters has done a very good job. And it's something that has been a revelation to the Vietnamese. Hell, they've never done anything like this before, and the corps artillery commander is just beside himself with what he's now able to do."

■ ■ ■

VANN: "The enemy is a long experience and a master at psywar, but I'm delighted he did not get together 50 tape recorders, battery-powered, of tank noises grinding and crunching, and motors going, because if he had II Corps would have solved your problems at An Loc and probably not stopped until they got to the U Minh Forest. [Laughter] I've never seen such a reaction to tanks. We've had tanks on only three occasions. We had them to come into the 22nd Division CP, with the division commander knowing they were on the way for eight hours, with the sector engaging them every step of the way and step by step telling where the tanks were, without any ground opposition to the tanks."

VANN: "We had them at Polei Kleng border ranger camp, which paid for itself in repelling infantry assaults for a period of four days, during which time it took about 3,500 rounds of mixed mortar and artillery, and held very well and killed more than the camp complement in enemy. Then three tanks showed up on the horizon, very early in the morning, and at a time when the weather was just prohibitive from getting either helicopters or tac air. They fired . . . two rounds of 106 at the three tanks and missed as the tanks came forward in trail. The defenders, who had stayed there through all these infantry assaults, broke out in the opposite direction of the camp and headed east . . . and abandoned it. Not a single M72 was fired. They didn't wait until the tanks got any closer than 500 yards. And we lost the camp."

VANN: "The third occasion was at Ben Het, where again sector gave them advanced warning, engaged and reported two of the tanks—in this case, for the first time, PT-76s—destroyed. And then subsequently we had reports of up to 10 tanks attacking the several separate portions of Ben Het ranger camp. Three positively were knocked out, two by M72s, one by direct fire 155. The three hulks are there, one at the front gate and one just coming in through half the wire on the east and another about 60 meters behind it. Reportedly there are others that are knocked out that are out in the woods."

VANN: "We have a much improved situation over the past 10 days in the Kontum area. What we have done, and it's not been an easy matter logistically, is sub-stituted the 23rd Division, which had to move there all by air, for the 22nd Division, which has become almost nonexistent."

VANN: "As of today there will be all 12 battalions of the 23rd in Kontum City. There is finally some unity of command. The decision to place all of the units up there was made by General Dzu before he was removed."

Lt. Gen. Ngo Dzu was the second ARVN corps commander to be relieved since the Easter Offensive began. He was replaced by Maj. Gen. Nguyen Van Toan.

VANN: "The 22nd Division performance has been an almost unbelievable thing, and it quite obviously reflects the years of very incompetent leadership and the defeatist attitude, particularly of General Trien, who for two and a half years made it one of his major objectives to convince all of his subordinates they could not defeat NVA. And they really took the lesson to heart. It has, between Binh Dinh and Kontum, over 2,500 men missing in action. We rate only five of the questionable number of battalions . . . as marginally effective, the other nine as ineffective because of losses of equipment."

VANN: "The only performances that we have had to crow about have been by the people at Dak Pek and Ben Het border ranger camps, where the troops are Montagnard—the officers are Vietnamese—and by the RF and PF. The RF and PF, in most places, have performed quite well and were a much more stabilizing force than the ARVN. In point of fact, both in Binh Dinh and northern Kontum it was the defeat of ARVN largely without fights that occurred before RF and PF gave up their positions."

VANN: "General Toan, 45 minutes after arrival, asked me to get him transportation and go with him to Kontum." "And yesterday [he] went down and spent the night in Kontum City." "Last evening we visited combat units until nearly midnight, and then began again at 6:30 this morning until we had visited nearly every battalion . . . in the Kontum area, where he inspected field positions and raised hell at nearly every place that he saw the field positions." "Last night he also had assembled the entire province staff, earlier in the evening, and gave them a good pep talk and told them we were going to hold Kontum City."

ABRAMS (re TOWs for ARVN): "What I did, first I had to get authority to issue these weapons from Washington. And when I had that, then I gave 20 to the marines and the 1st Division because they were the only troops I knew of that had stood and fought. I don't want these things in the hands of the enemy. And on the airborne, I told General Kroesen [that] when General Truong will give me his personal assurance that they will not be abandoned on the battlefield, then I'll consider it."

VANN: "The president has given orders to the corps commander that he will not give up Kontum, so there is no choice but to fight there."

■ ■ ■

HOLLINGSWORTH: "I don't know where in the hell to start." Sketches the situation since 4 April. "We were hit in the early morning hours of the fourth" by the 5th Division. "We fought them pretty hard the first day, and the second day we fought very hard, and on about the morning of the sixth . . . we got hit by a bunch of tanks. I counted, about six o'clock in the morning, about seven or eight tanks . . . hitting the lower compound and . . . about six hitting the north compound—attacking. We beat them out about five different times before they finally overran the two compounds and with direct fire knocked the bunkers out and completely destroyed them."

HOLLINGSWORTH: "The intensity of the indirect fire was some of the most severe I've ever seen, from 82-mm mortar and 107, 109 rockets—if we can identify the difference between the two—some 105 came in on us, our own, something heavier than that in the form of artillery that we tried to identify as 155s that they'd taken from us, and also 240-mm rockets." "This outfit here broke and ran. We got the three advisors out. As a result of that action we now know that an OH-6A can carry five Americans and take off with seven ARVN, but later on you have to drag two of the ARVN off the skids in the rubber trees in order to maintain any altitude." [Laughter] "And you finally get down in here, where it's relatively safe, and you have to stop and readjust your load."

HOLLINGSWORTH: Calls the 9th Division "the best division that's in the VC/NVA forces, and I was delighted to have them here. I couldn't think of a better goddamn outfit to give it a go." Also fighting the 275th and 141st Regiments from 7th Division, and the 203rd Tank Regiment. Think 50–52 tanks. "By documents we found that they said that they were going to destroy this thing and set up a government there." "The NVAs that we killed had in their packs freshly laundered khaki uniforms. I suppose that they were going to use those for the inaugural formation there."

HOLLINGSWORTH: "The tanks came in, as I recall, on the 13th, and we fought them very hard. Most of them were knocked out with M72 LAWs." "We think that we had about 30 tanks knocked out in town itself. There were tanks knocked out by air out on the periphery. We've had some tanks that's been counted and knocked out—one single tank been knocked out six or seven times—but this is the sort of thing you expect."

HOLLINGSWORTH: "I felt pretty good on the 19th, because we'd killed a hell of a lot of enemy and we were still holding this place. And the reason we were holding the place was not any leadership on the part of anybody, but the guts of the little bitty soldier in there. A gentleman asked me a few days ago, he said, 'Well, how can you account for this little soldier when you want to go in here and pick up their seriously wounded and the lightly wounded who's carrying him on a stretcher dumps him out and runs and grabs on the helicopter—how can you account for that versus the fact they stood up and killed these tanks in here?' And I thought a little bit about that, and I said, 'Well, you know when you look at people, you understand people, goddamn it, then you're going to go one way or the other. Goddamn it, you might as well go in there and try to kill those son of a bitches, because if you don't you've had it. And then if you get a chance to get out, by god you're probably going to take advantage of it. That's the only thing I can say except these are gutty little soldiers in here."

HOLLINGSWORTH: By 6 May we'd had 758 KIA, over 1,500 WIA, and about 1,200 MIA. With reinforcements by 10–11 April, we had roughly 5,200 ARVN and about 1,500 RF. "When the attack started yesterday morning I estimated that we had 50 percent of our ARVN and still about a thousand RF, and that would give me a strength somewhere about 3,500." "The artillery . . . we continuously took incoming. We might go for an hour where it was quite intense, and I mean in an hour's time take six or seven hundred rounds of 105, 155 equivalents, 82-mm mortars, and some 120-mm mortars." Also "severe, real severe, .51-caliber, 23-mm, and 37-mm." "We saved about 60 percent of the town. We've still got that this morning."

HOLLINGSWORTH: "These people here—the attitude of the commanders, not the soldiers, the attitude of the commanders has been, 'Well, goddamn it, we're in here and somebody's going to take care of us, so we'll just sit here on our goddamned ass and just wait'll they come.' I'm sure, and I feel strongly about this, that the little soldiers have done a magnificent job here, all on their own—for <u>survival</u>. It was a matter of either fighting or dying, and they said, 'Well, we might as well <u>fight</u>.' And they've fought. And the only reason we're still in here today is because of these little fellows keeping them [the enemy] out so we could kill them with firepower."

HOLLINGSWORTH: "The indirect fire has been rather intense early in the morning. It slacks off later in the day. Between 0035 yesterday morning through about eight o'clock the people on the ground there said that they experienced more than 7,000 rounds of indirect fire."

HOLLINGSWORTH (re An Loc): "I can't think of a better place to destroy these enemy outfits than right here, if we can maintain enough strength in there to keep them out so that they can be killed by firepower. I like to think that in this type of conflict the answer to the problem is instant decisions by the man with all the resources who is sitting looking at the battle, followed by creation of all the violence that can be created instantaneously, and maintain it continuously until the battle subsides to where you can get by with less. And this is what we have tried to do."

HOLLINGSWORTH: "If it had not been for the advisors you would have the 203rd Tank Regiment in Saigon, I do believe." "I do believe there is <u>no doubt about it</u>, that if you have an advisor with an ARVN unit, and for <u>good reason</u>, maybe being wounded, that advisor is evacuated without another one going in at the same moment, that'll be all she wrote, gentlemen."

HOLLINGSWORTH: "The FACs have just been magnificent, and so has the tac air."

HOLLINGSWORTH: "I can say that, General Abrams, on the 9th [of May 1972] I planned 17 Arc Lights, and when I got your word on the 10th, if it'd done any good to show my appreciation I'd [have] just jumped out of the damn helicopter, but I didn't think I'd do any good. [Laughter] By god, I just added eight, and it just saved us, that's all. And I'll say that your intelligence department must be awful damn good—that you know that that was the time to go. Because if we hadn't of gone, with that number of forces we've got out there now— . . . we just couldn't hit her any better on this one."

■ ■ ■

TARPLEY: "They say in vaudeville you should never follow a dog act." [Laughter]

TARPLEY: "Our war started a little later than in the other areas." Began in Kompong Trach. Truong shifted ranger and cavalry units to meet the enemy 1st NVA Division. On 6–7 April attacked by enemy 18B Regiment and D2 Regiment from the U Minh. "Overran 3 villages and 19 hamlets, and they have those to this day." Truong sought to contain the attack in areas penetrated while holding the 1st NVA Division out of South Vietnam. The battle went on for about two weeks, then "by mutual exhaustion it broke off."

When General Truong moved to Military Region 1 he was replaced in Military Region 4 by Lt. Gen. Nguyen Vinh Nghi.

TARPLEY: When General Nghi arrived he called me in. "He explained that he had never been a corps commander before. He was counting on the Americans for all the advice. He would be perfectly candid, and he expected us to be the same. He then gave me his estimate of the situation. He had been to Leavenworth, and he gave me a Leavenworth estimate. . . . He then asked what the soft spots were in the operation, which gave us a good opportunity to give it to him. The main soft spot we mentioned to him was that the 9th Division and the 7th Division were not inclined to go on the offensive. The 9th Division had contained this salient here and were content to wait and see what happened. . . . Same way with the 7th Division." "They had plenty of forces, and plenty of artillery, but were more or less interested in letting the RF and the PF fight the outpost battle, and not go to their relief."

TARPLEY: General Nghi "holds his staff meetings in the presence of Americans, and he criticizes ARVN activities in front of Americans and discusses candidly how to crack the nut he's faced with. Right now he needs all the advice he can get. I know he's strong willed. . . . Right at the moment he's buying it a hundred percent, and has disapproved Arc Lights on his own because he didn't have enough intelligence—sent them back to the drawing boards. His priorities—when he came back from the meeting last week with the president, he said that we must win this war, we must put fighters in instead of administrators in the provinces, we must put fighters in the units and get the show on the road on the offense. So that's just about what's happening here."

TARPLEY: General Nghi "has gone around and visited all the province chiefs now, and has talked to them about getting rid of district chiefs, village chiefs, and hamlet chiefs that are not supporting the war, and to put in jail any soldiers or people who are talking about losing the war." "The president told him, he told me, to engage the NVA 1st Division in Cambodia and keep it out of Vietnam."

■ ■ ■

VOGT: "As you know, we had a fairly major decision by the president the other day to mine the ports. The mines became active yesterday, as of sundown. The navy has been given the responsibility to keep all the ports mined and the ships out of it. Our responsibility in the air force will be to work the land routes portion of it, keep the railroads closed from the Chinese border on down into Hanoi. This means, unfortunately, that we have to bleed some of the air off that you've [the four corps areas] been getting."

■ ■ ■

ABRAMS: "I'll tell you about this air thing. You know, I had my fifth anniversary the other day [five years' service in Vietnam]. And this air system is now running the best, and it is the most responsive, that it has <u>ever</u> been since I've been over here. There's practically no goddarn cribbing and badgering going on in the system. It's everybody <u>with</u> it—."

ABRAMS: "Now, that president of ours has really bit the bullet on this thing. And he just isn't—<u>no one</u> is going to shove him around! That's what all that <u>means</u>, and by god he intends to solve this thing, and he'll put anything and everything he's got in it to do it! <u>So</u>, that's <u>kind of</u> why we're all meeting here today. I can't really tell you how to run your business much. I just want, in all of our work, you—if you're unhappy about something, you let [the chief of staff?] know, or call Fred or myself."

ABRAMS: "<u>And</u>, <u>wherever</u> possible, hold the Vietnamese right to it. They've <u>got</u> to do it. Be candid with them. Again, there's no point in exaggerating, <u>or</u> getting running off on a rumor or gossip. Right now there's a fellow, I would say, if he's corrupt it probably doesn't make any difference—if he's <u>fighting</u>. There will be a day when that's over, but—the honeymoon will be finished—but any man that will fight here will be supported by this government, I'm pretty sure of that, at least temporarily."

13 MAY 1972: WIEU

ATTENDEES: Amb. Bunker, Amb. Whitehouse, Gen. Abrams, Gen. Weyand, Gen. Vogt, LTG McCaffrey, Mr. Jacobson, MG Eckhardt, MG Cowles, MG Marshall, MG Bowley, MG Fuson, MG Jumper, MG Potts, MG Slay, MG Watkins, MG Carley, Mr. McCann, Mr. Duval, RADM Salzer, BG Trogdon, BG Heiser, BG Bernstein, BG McClellan, MG Scott, BG Lanagan, BG Wickham, Col. Presson, Col. Crockett, Capt. Fluss, Col. Stevens.

Infiltration Estimate: 96,400.

POTTS: "All personnel in our estimate to date will be going to COSVN after June." An infiltration group previously scheduled for COSVN in May has been diverted to the B-3 Front.

BRIEFER: "The destinations of infiltration groups are rarely changed once they have entered the infiltration pipeline."

POTTS: "You have only three groups all last year that were diverted from their original destination."

Mining the North Vietnamese ports.

COLONEL SHAW: "A week ago today we were asked to stand by and be alerted to start mining operations in the major ports in North Vietnam." Tuesday 9 May 1972 at 9:00 A.M. scheduled to start with Haiphong, putting in Mark 52s. Did so at 8:59 A.M., completed by 9:00 A.M. using 36 M52s. On 11 May at 9:00 A.M. to do the port of Hong Gai. Also Cam Pha. Mark 36s. Did it, putting in 186. All to be simultaneously activated at 9:00 A.M. on the 12th, yesterday morning, which they were. Subsequently have put in Mark 36s at Thanh Hoa and at Vinh on the 12th. At 8:30 A.M. today putting in Mark 36s at Quang Khe

(48 of them) and Dong Hoi (36). "By today all the major ports will have been mined." Re Haiphong: Navy three A-6s (at 8:59 A.M.) and six A-7s off the *Coral Sea* put in the Mark 52s (1,100 pounds, of which 625 pounds is HE). Mines set on Mod 2, or magnetic, variation. Harbor depth 25–30 feet. Mines good to approximately 100 yards. Got all 36 mines in, 33 of which "we believe are OK." Chutes tore off three, which may therefore have been damaged on impact. Put in at 400 knots at 400 feet. Follow effects by photo, visual and [***]. On the 8th, the day before the mining, total of 35 ships in harbor. On 9th rather poor weather. On 10th: 33 ships (per aerial photos). On 10th: began lightering from ships (21) moored in port (not at quays). On 13th: 27 per Buf- falo Hunter readout. 19 are en route in—don't know what they're going to do. Also Giant Scale photos. "Damn good camera." "Amazing!" Mines set for 180-day life. "No ships have been reported crossing the surveillance line" approximately 25–40 miles off Haiphong.

Enemy Transportation Offensive.

BRIEFER: All five subordinate groups of the 559th Transportation Group shipped sizable amounts of weapons and ammunition. On 29 April the 559th com- mended Group 471 for shipping the largest amount of cargo during a one-day period in its history. On 23 April Binh Tram 45 reported receiving 121 tons, shipping 165 tons, and holding 505 tons (including 66 tons of weapons). On 27 April Binh Tram 32 reported receipt of over 3,000 rounds of 130-mm ammuni- tion. [Examples] In late April and early May COMINT revealed the movement of 190 trucks, including 173 trucks loaded with weapons, from Binh Tram 45 to Binh Tram 51 in Cambodia. "At least 100 of these truckloads were specifically earmarked for COSVN." Reports of fuel shortages and bad road conditions due to weather have apparently been localized and "have not significantly hampered the enemy's overall logistics efforts to date."

VOGT (obviously irritated): "You listen to this briefing and it sounds like it's all one way and things are getting worse." "What I'm saying is that I think the rains have been having more of an impact than the briefing would indicate, General Abrams, and I've been keeping a close tab on this. There's a lot of COMINT over and above what you've discussed today which indicates they're having serious trouble, and throughout the whole area." Potts backs off, says the briefing is only intended to show what the enemy intended to do, not what he has accomplished.

Enemy attempts at seaborne infiltration.

NAVY BRIEFER: Sixteen POWs taken from Trawler 645 in the Gulf of Thailand on 24 April were from the 125th Water Transportation Group. They had a cargo of weapons, ammo, explosives, water mines, and medicine. Also on board was a cell of three sappers from the D126 Naval Sapper Regiment. The crewmen said they have made eight prior infiltration missions since late 1969. Allegedly one was successful, six aborted because of detection, and one aborted due to mechanical difficulties. Success in October 1970, when the primary landing site was not secure and they diverted to an alternate in the Dong Doi Secret Zone. Unloaded by sampans. Aborted: November 1969, April 1970, March 1971, October 1971, November 1971, and March 1972. Sunk April 1972. Have photos. In each case the ship is painted differently. Capacity about 500 tons. Group commander instructed if engaged to display CHICOM flag. Intercepted by USS *McMorris* at 2300 on 23 April. At 0745 on 24 April VNN ship (*Hai Quan 4*) intercepted the trawler and ordered it to stop. Did not comply. Warning and disabling shots fired by VNN. The trawler was self-destructed at 1019 hours by its political officer, who was killed doing so. Ship sank. "Prior to the destruction of Trawler #645, allied forces captured or destroyed 11 infiltration trawlers."

ABRAMS: "How many starts did this ship make?"

BRIEFER: "Nine that we know of, sir."

ABRAMS: "And one successful—and one <u>completely</u> unsuccessful." [Laughter]

∎ ∎ ∎

ABRAMS (re Ben Het): "They cleaned all those fellows out of there that had gotten in, and then—I think it's quite important—they were able to resupply that with helicopters, and take out the wounded, without getting any helicopters shot down. Something happened up there. . . ." "You've got to kind of pay attention to whoever's running that thing at Ben Het. Right now, just about anything he says, you've got to kind of accept it, [laughter] because they got in there with those tanks and all that other stuff, and they got organized in the morning and kicked the shit out of them—got them all out of there. Well, I don't mean they got them out—they either killed them or destroyed it. So there's something that's got a firm <u>hold</u> on <u>something</u>." "That guy at Dak Pek is the same way."

ABRAMS (re attack at An Loc): "They had the support of 72 B-52 sorties. I don't want General Vogt and Seventh Air Force to take all the credit. [Laughter] SAC got into it, too."

ABRAMS: For the 24-hour period beginning at 8:00 A.M. this morning, MR-1 is getting all the B-52 strikes, all 75 sorties, allocated to them. "That's three every 55 minutes." "They're going to have to be careful up there. I don't know what the trajectory of that 8-inch [naval gunfire] looks like at max range, but we don't want them shooting down B-52s." [Laughter]

ABRAMS: Mr. Vann has a message in requesting authority to put some TOWs in Kontum, "and I want to approve that." Going to be under command of the senior advisor to the 23rd Division, and operated by American crews. Some of the people up there are very worried about tanks. But: "My <u>real</u> reason is, as long as those advisors are going to stay there, I want to—I think it improves their situation immensely. And that's what it's for. Also they may get a chance to knock out some tanks, which will be also pretty good." "It's also reported to me that's [the TOW crews] a pretty fine bunch of men."

SOMEONE: "That's the 82nd—they're great."

ABRAMS: "And they've got that weapon that's kind of new, and they're anxious to try it out on something that's live." "I didn't feel like going the other route of training some Vietnamese crews in the 23rd. The way that thing's going up there, they haven't used what they've got—except for Ben Het."

BRIEFER (re B-52s): "Yesterday all 25 cells were scheduled to be delivered on targets in the Kontum area. However, 6 had to be diverted due to a tactical emergency in the vicinity of An Loc."

ABRAMS: "We had intended to put all 25 of them in there, but the situation just seemed to be precarious out there last night and this morning, and so 6 of them had to be taken out—I guess the last 6? ["Yes, sir."]—and put out at An Loc. That still should have been enough to do a little bit about the preparations for the attack on Kontum."

BRIEFER: "Today all 25 strikes are scheduled to be delivered on targets in Military Region 1."

SEVENTH AIR FORCE BRIEFER: In the An Loc area "in the last two days air crews are reporting the densest ground fire they have ever encountered. Seven of the 24 losses, and 15 of the 62 damaged aircraft, occurred in the An Loc area."

SEVENTH AIR FORCE BRIEFER: On first trip to Doumer Bridge some 40 SAMs fired at us, then the MiGs. "With the smart bombs we don't have any problem with the civilian population."

ABRAMS: "It looks to me like there're kind of three things, three efforts, going on. We've got this one up here, which is the B-5 and MR-TTH, and I think one of those must be in charge of it." "And then this thing in Binh Dinh, and Phu Yen, and Khanh Hoa, Quang Ngai, and Quang Thien, and Quang Nam, and the B-3 Front. It's forces out of MR-5 that are trying to cut Route 19. I think this thing is all tied together in one effort. It's MR-5 that's running it." "What is it that COSVN sees as their sort of piece of the pie?" "COSVN has a responsibility here in Cambodia." "I think that it should be examined to see whether the whole business of what he's doing in Cambodia, and what he's doing in South Vietnam, doesn't fit some kind of a picture that COSVN wanted when they finally decided to talk. And you can say, 'Well, that would sort of be good for historical work.' But it also might give us a little better feel of what we should be doing different—if anything."

ABRAMS: "You know, we started talking about this a long time ago—regard the six divisions in MR-3 and MR-4 as the forces available to counter his four divisions—the 5th, 9th, 7th, and 1st. And so the Vietnamese should . . . accept a general policy of moving forces around between here in order to meet what the enemy's doing. And I think that now the necessity for that is even more clear. And of course they have—they've moved the 21st up here, then they moved this 15th Regiment up yesterday. There's bound to be a limit, somewhere, of what you can move out of the delta in order to handle the situation in here. That's another reason why I think we ought to look at the whole."

15 MAY 1972: COMUS Brief

BRIEFER: On the situation in MR-3, especially the Saigon area, the 271st NVA Regiment tried to cross the border into South Vietnam, but suffered heavy casualties at the hands of RF and PF forces supported by VNAF and U.S. air strikes. Then on 10 May the 24th and 271st NVA Regiments attacked again, and RF and PF, plus elements of the 25th ARVN Division, supported by VNAF/U.S. air strikes, again inflicted heavy casualties.

BRIEFER: "During the entire offensive period, Saigon has been quieter than normal, with only two terrorist incidents reported in April and none to date in May. Security in and around the city is tight, and has been credited in agent reports with delaying or preventing enemy penetration of the urban area." "The enemy is not currently capable of launching a major attack on Saigon."

WEYAND: "This briefing is more optimistic, and presents a brighter picture, than I think the situation deserves."

ABRAMS: Remember several weeks ago we reviewed this whole situation, "and no province chiefs and no district chiefs in MR-3 needed to be changed. There was only one province chief in the delta, and that was that crooked bastard, although extremely competent, in Bac Lieu. There were some district chiefs that needed to be changed—three, four, or five—but nobody should mess with them because Truong and the province chiefs were changing them, one at a time, and replacing them. So keep out of that." "Now I find out the son of a bitch in Phuoc Tuy is in competition for last place as the worst goddamn province chief that Hollingsworth knows of. It's kind of between the one there and the one in Binh Duong! And you have to add in there the five up in MR-1 that he got to know pretty well while he was up there. So, of 19 province chiefs that he knows anything about, these are the 2 candidates—not only candidates to be replaced, but they're absolutely and completely unsatisfactory as far as he's concerned. . . ."

ABRAMS: "Different fellows look at it different ways. And then we have that great prophet, unfortunately dragged away from here, the former ambassador to Gabon, who said that there was very little left for advisors to do. And I want to tell you, if it wasn't for advisors, none of us would be sitting here in Saigon today. We'd either be in a PW enclosure, dead, or have managed to escape by submarine, powerboat, or some other fucking thing! To Hong Kong. That's what the advisors are."

JACOBSON: "That's right, you know."

WEYAND: "They're the only reason they're in An Loc."

ABRAMS: "That's right. They're the only reason they're in a lot of places."

JACOBSON: "The Vietnamese will admit that they get their straight information from the Americans and not from anywhere else." "It's one of the reasons they want us around, one of the prime reasons. We tell them the truth."

■ ■ ■

ABRAMS: "It's hard for me to believe that if they had the capability of rocketing

Saigon, or making sapper attacks, or even just throwing grenades around, they wouldn't have started that. Struggling as they are to get that goddamn thing cleaned up out there at Binh Long, it would just drive this government up the pole to have things going wrong in Saigon, with people scared and all of that. I just can't see—because they're so damn smart about stuff like that."

17 MAY 1972: COMUS Brief: Enemy Logistics Requirements in RVN MR-1

ATTENDEES: Amb. Bunker, Gen. Abrams, Gen. Weyand, J-2, J-3, AF.

BRIEFER: Purpose is "to review recent road construction in the DMZ area; logistics activities in southern North Vietnam, Laos, and northern MR-1; analyze indications of the displacement and organizational changes within the General Directorate of Rear Services; and to present our conclusions."

BRIEFER: At present (and until sometime in October) the Route 1039, 92 Bravo, and 9 network that runs from North Vietnam to the Lao panhandle to South Vietnam is experiencing poor trafficability. Thus the NVA has constructed Route 102, 103, and 1022 road network to the east of existing roads in Laos. Routes 103A, 102B, and 6086 run through the western DMZ. Routes 102A, 1022, and an unnumbered route run through the central DMZ to connect with the QL-9 network in three places.

ABRAMS: "Is it reaction to what's happened, or is it part of the overall plan anyway? In the overall plan, he planned to <u>have</u> these two provinces. He planned to have Hue. At one time there was an indication he wanted this by the 19th, because it's Ho's birthday and that sort of thing. . . . It doesn't <u>look</u> like that's going to transpire. It went <u>well</u> to start with, but even though there was really no necessity for the Vietnamese to pull out of here, still his follow-up on this—that went too fast for him. It really hasn't been too good. Since the fall of Quang Tri, he really hasn't been able to put anything together. Now you may say, 'Well, that's right. He didn't plan to. He's just gathering stuff together and he will eventually.' And maybe that'll happen. But we <u>do</u> know that the divisions in here—the 308th, the 304th, and the 324 Bravo—have taken really horrible losses."

ABRAMS: "A prisoner taken in here, I notice in today's report, said, 'The men are in a hell of a shape. The ARVN won't let them go forward, and the orders won't let them go back.' And all they can do is sit there and get attrited. So—it hasn't gone right, and they <u>do</u> have logistical problems."

ABRAMS: "Now looking at this situation down here in MR-3—we've had to put a lot of air effort into that thing just to hold it together. And it's <u>done</u> that, it's <u>done</u> that. But I think that that situation in a few more days is going to be such that we will not have to put the weight of air effort in there in order to keep it going. At least, at <u>least,</u> we should be—. There's no harm in looking ahead that we'd be able to gradually shift from MR-3 and MR-2 greater weight of air effort into the north."

ABRAMS: "I don't ever want to get constrained by lines that have been drawn on these charts. You go after the <u>system</u>."

ABRAMS: "This thing here is a hell of a lot more out in the open than that mess he's got over in Laos."

Apparently referring to the transportation net.

ABRAMS: "There's no failure to appreciate the importance of trying to smash his logistics system, but what we've <u>had</u> to do is use <u>most</u> of our air to keep the troops fighting. And all I'm saying this afternoon is that I see a strong possibility that we're going to be able to get by with less in the direct support of the troops, including the B-52s. And the <u>minute</u> that that's possible—. I know you've been doing a great job up here, and there've been great results out of it. <u>But</u>, I want to get it like it was in '68 where, <u>goddamn it</u>, if you were going to go through here, if a <u>crow</u> was going over this he had to carry his damn rations with him! <u>No</u>—it got <u>bad</u>! They couldn't move a damn thing in here. And that's why they had to pull all these divisions out of northern MR-1 and get them back in North Vietnam, because by god they couldn't support them down here! It's one of the best air campaigns of the war. Well—it was a <u>good</u> one, anyway."

ABRAMS: "Look at the system as a whole, and that's what we've got to work on."
"I think we ought to look at it in terms of a full month's campaign."

ABRAMS: "I think we ought to give some thought to what we try to encourage the navy to do in this part of it. I don't think we have much influence on the kinds of targets and that sort of thing they hit from day to day. And whether we want to try to get into that—. But, on the basis of explaining what we're <u>trying</u> to do here in this thing, and see if theirs can't match—. We'll probably never get in the business of specifics, but make it <u>match</u> with this. And we had the same problem, actually, in '68 as I'm now talking about, same damn thing. You had something that was well tied together in here, but the other was kind of an <u>independent</u> thing."

ABRAMS (re tac air): "The marines are <u>damn</u> good at close support. It's a game that they really play in. And it's a good airplane for that."

ABRAMS: "In the near future we should begin to be able to do more [against the enemy logistical system in northern MR-1 and southern NVN]. We need to think out . . . how we can really put together a campaign against that whole business. Then, with the mines in the harbor, keep cutting the rail lines up there and so on, we ought to be able to put the squeeze on. And we <u>need</u> to <u>do</u> it. I think there's <u>real</u> urgency in this. This fellow—what I always worry about him is that he'll get kind of desperate and he'll throw something out on the table over there in Paris that's so goddamn inviting that [Bunker: "Yes."] the fellow that turned it down would be proclaimed a public fool. So the <u>sooner</u> we can get at this the better."

ABRAMS: "I don't want anyone to get the idea that I think that he's licked, so to speak, in South Vietnam. There're going to be some <u>bad days</u>. But I don't think that we're going—." "The thing in MR-1 is better organized, it's better—it's much better in hand than it's been since the 30th of March."

ABRAMS: "In MR-2, the Kontum thing, it's hard to say anything good about that—I realize it. But nevertheless there's a different spirit up there, they're better organized, the guy that's running the show is on the ground in that thing. John Vann feels pretty confident, and they do up there." "We ought to be able to work our way out of that."

ABRAMS: "This thing down here in MR-3—I think if they ever get really going that's going to break up, too. I think the enemy's really had the hell knocked out of him out there. Even if we didn't know where he was, he's had the hell knocked out of him, because there probably—in that area out there—isn't a square foot that hasn't been blasted with something."

POTTS (re antilogistics air campaign): "J-2 and J-3, with the air force, have already done much work on this, sir. It'll come much faster than you may think."

ABRAMS: "You don't know what I think. I was thinking about tomorrow morning." [Laughter]

ABRAMS: "The way to take [reoccupy] Quang Tri City is get the marines going up to Ba Long and the 1st Division out in the A Shau, and send a platoon to Quang Tri—raise the flag. I just hope something like that—. Trying to batter your way up here, with him in the high ground, and all his supplies in here, all his goddamn artillery in here just shooting the hell out of you every step of the way—it's no way to do it! But I think all we've got to do is keep JGS out of it and let Truong develop a plan. And then it will be a good one."

■ ■ ■

BUNKER: "You know, I'd forgotten about that operation in '68. And Fred reminded me that's when Averell Harriman said they voluntarily pulled back, remember? And [asserted that] we missed a big opportunity?"

WEYAND: "To be further proof that they understood what was going to be the understanding. . . . The ambassador felt that that showed they really were going to respect the DMZ. And then they reached the so-called understanding. And now, here we are." [Laughter]

POTTS: "They had 14 battalions there on the first of November 1968. It very quickly jumped up to 22, and then up to 25 and stayed that way. . . ."

ABRAMS: "But what I was talking about was the time before this started. That's the one thing I've never forgiven Governor Harriman for, when he said that, because I really—the information was available to him for a sounder conclusion."

BUNKER: "That's right."

20 MAY 1972: WIEU

ATTENDEES: Amb. Bunker, Amb. Whitehouse, Mr. Polgar, Gen. Abrams, Gen. Weyand, Gen. Vogt, LTG McCaffrey, Mr. Jacobson, MG Eckhardt, MG Cowles, MG Woodward, MG Marshall, MG Bowley, MG Jumper, MG Potts, MG Carley, Mr. Duval, RADM Salzer, BG Trogdon, BG Hudson, BG Bernstein, BG

McClellan, BG Herbert, BG Scott, BG Johnson, BG Lanagan, BG Wickham, Col. Presson, Col. Crockett, Col. Norris, Col. Stevens.

BRIEFER: MACV 1972 Infiltration Estimate: 99,300 (33,500 to B-3 Front, 42,100 to COSVN). 23 special purpose infiltration groups now en route. 363 groups in the estimate for the year. All but 35, per Potts, have been detected in COMINT, a very good record of only 9 percent in gap groups.

BRIEFER: "27,600 personnel in the 304th, 308th, and 324B Divisions and the 101st Regiment of the 325th NVA Division have entered the RVN in 1972 but are not included in the infiltration estimate." The total would be 126,900 if they were added, or 97 percent of the 1968 estimate for the same period.

BRIEFER: During the past week 63 SA-2 missiles were fired at allied aircraft. No losses or damage resulted. This was a "relatively small number of missile expenditures" and "a significant decrease when compared with the weekly average of 165 for the first six weeks of the North Vietnamese offensive." Since 30 March at least 1,053 SA-2 missiles have been fired, downing 12 U.S. aircraft.

BRIEFER: "Two Soviet tankers which arrived at Haiphong during early May departed the harbor without unloading. Both harbor congestion during early May and the harbor mining on 9 May apparently prevented the unloading of these ships prior to their departure. The Soviet cargo ship [*Alyace?*], carrying 719 tons of POL, is the only Soviet ship known to have arrived and unloaded its POL cargo during the month of May. This total represents 2 percent of the 40,800 tons of POL Hanoi had requested for the month."

BRIEFER: VNMC airmobile operation into Quang Tri Province last Saturday. 14 May: 1st ARVN Division offensive operations vicinity FSB Birmingham/King/Bastogne. FSB Bastogne reoccupied 15 May. On Wednesday elements of the 1st ARVN Division air assaulted into two LZs overlooking the western approaches to Hue. Throughout the 1st ARVN Division AO over 36 tons of small arms, rocket, and mortar ammo has been captured or destroyed since 14 May. "General Truong has placed special emphasis on the rebuilding of the 3rd Division and the Armor Brigade. He states that he is most appreciative of the U.S. training teams and demands from the ARVN full cooperation and effort."

BRIEFER: Forty-one Arc Lights were concentrated within a 10-kilometer radius just south of An Loc. "Air target changes throughout the week in response to tactical emergencies in this area have aided the ARVN in countering repeated enemy attempts at taking An Loc."

BRIEFER: "The Hanoi highway and railroad bridge, or Paul Doumer Bridge, is a highway and rail line across the Red River into Hanoi." It was struck on 10 and 11 May by 20 F-4s "and heavily damaged." As shown, "the span and sections of the bridge are in the river."

■ ■ ■

WEYAND: "There were a couple of additional facts that we got together in case the vice president asked a question to give him kind of a ballpark idea of what this all meant. The percent of population that has come under VC control in areas like Binh Dinh and northern Quang Tri and so forth represents about 3 percent. Then if you take it by the numbers of villages and hamlets, you get— that are under VC control or have since been abandoned by the government— you come up with just a shade under 10 percent." "Trying to relate that to the HES ratings is damn near impossible because of the overwhelming impact of the security situation on the HES."

ABRAMS: "Well, to put it in perspective, that's a little better than McCloskey's doing." [Laughter]

BUNKER: "Well, I think, wherever he is, Uncle Ho didn't have a very good birthday yesterday. I think it's hot enough where he is."

ABRAMS: "Well, sir, we tried to celebrate it up there in Kontum. I think they tried to, and we decided to get with them—have a big thing."

BUNKER: "It was great."

ABRAMS: "It went right on into the night—a big celebration."

ABRAMS: "The only thing now is we've just got to stay with it." "It's going to be awfully hard for him to decide he's lost it. That's going to be a very difficult thing for him to determine—accept. Unlike some of his other offensives, you see, he's hanging in there and pushing the replacements forward. And he doesn't have any instructions out about where to withdraw to."

ABRAMS: "I think, too, this action by the 1st ARVN Division up there—pushing, pushing west and north and south and so on, it's very good. It's always the same—you can do about so much with air and then the ground people have got to move out to take advantage of it. And that's what they're doing. And in the days and weeks ahead, wherever we can, we've got to encourage the Vietnamese to do that. Some places they are. Some places the territorials—very aggressive. But more and more that's got to be everywhere."

JACOBSON: "Sir, one of the things that—for the people who claim that pacification has been set back 20 years and all that, that the people are despondent and apprehensive—we had 80,000 people, is what they figured, were ready to come south from MR-1. When Truong got up there, and Than was there, this number started going down. By the time they took back Bastogne, and had this operation in Quang Tri City, I don't have enough people from north of Dong Ha to fill up a C-46—that want to come down. They say, 'Oh, no. We want to go home first, and then we'll make up our mind.' The government had a pro-scription against anybody south of Dong Ha coming south, because obviously the ones from north of Dong Ha were the ones that ought to come south, and everybody thought they're the ones, of course, wanted to come south. They had 80,000. Now, we had to cancel the airlift. Well, Christ—. Their apprehension isn't all that bad. At least it can change awful quick."

ABRAMS: "Well, I guess the ambassador's got a farm up in Vermont. Have you got a farm, Jake?"

JACOBSON: "No, sir, but I'm working on it."

ABRAMS (to Weyand): "I guess all you've got's a condominium."

WEYAND: "Yeah—watch your language there." [Laughter]

■ ■ ■

ABRAMS (re stuff designed by R&D people without troop input): "I always remember Secretary Ailes was visiting in Europe at the time we were just getting the M-60 tank. He was sitting under a tent fly having lunch with these soldiers. And one of them, sitting across the table from him, Secretary Ailes asked him—this was a sergeant, about 25 years' service, an old tanker—asked him what he thought of the M-60. And this fellow had just speared a piece of ham off his [mess] kit, and he took that—he was waving it, and he was only about two or three feet from the secretary. He said, 'Mr. Secretary, in all the goddamn time I've been in tanks,' he says, 'this is the first time they apparently got some tanker involved in the design of the goddamn thing!' Well, you know, you can hardly get—there's no <u>way</u> to get higher praise at the using end. I think they [the enemy, with the .50-cal. gunner perched in an exposed position on the equipment just captured] suffer from the same thing."

ABRAMS: "Incidentally, you know that T-59 that was captured and driven down to Hue? The Vietnamese felt that that was a very difficult tank to drive. Now that's because they've gotten used to driving ours, where—. No power steering, and no synchromesh transmission, and so on. So it's hard to shift and it's hard to steer. You've just got to horse it."

■ ■ ■

BRIEFER: Thirteen aircraft have been lost to SA-2 SAMs since the offensive began. Estimate a minimum of 1,173 SA-2s have been fired.

VOGT (re NVN POL): "He has underground storage that we haven't been able to get to yet. He's also storing it in 55-gallon drums. Right up in the Hanoi area we found over a million gallons stored right in the outskirts of town in 55-gallon drums stacked up."

ABRAMS: "He's just built one hell of a lot of redundancy in the whole fuel distribution system—drums, tanks, pipeline—and really spread."

BRIEFER: Re South Vietnamese casualties (including territorials): Total casualties 26,000+: 5,800 KIA, 17,900 WIA, 2,800 MIA. Down from much higher MIA reported earlier. Have 34,000+ replacements programmed. "The 3rd Division, of course, is the bad one."

3 JUN 1972: WIEU

ATTENDEES: Amb. Bunker, Amb. Whitehouse, Mr. Polgar, Gen. Abrams, Gen. Weyand, Gen. Vogt, LTG McCaffrey, Mr. Jacobson, MG Woodward, MG Marshall, MG Bowley, MG Fuson, MG Jumper, MG Potts, MG Carley, RADM Salzer, BG Trogdon, BG Wolfe, BG Hudson, BG McClellan, BG Herbert, BG Scott, BG Wickham, Mr. Marlette, Col. Gentry, Col. Presson, Col. Crockett, Col. Stevens.

Infiltration Estimate: 100,400 (42 percent to COSVN).

WEYAND (re the delta): "They've had, on our side, 12,800 casualties down there in the last 60 days, of which about 4,500 were killed or missing and 8,300 wounded in action. So the Vietnamese forces that are down there are heavily engaged. And I would expect those kind of numbers indicate something of the toll that's being taken on enemy ranks. That's a real battle that's going on down there."

Presentation on all current indicators and trends.

BRIEFER: This is an update since presentation of our notional reconstruction of the enemy's program.

■ Indicator: Successful termination of resupply by sea in NVN. (Mined 9 May, mines activated 0900 hours 12 May.) At least 20 ships that were projected for arrivals in Haiphong have been diverted to other ports.

■ Indicator: Disruption of NVN's POL supply and distribution. Only 2 percent of Hanoi's May request was delivered before the mining. June request, per COMINT, is 55,000 tons, "the largest on record." Also air strikes on the major depots, to include Hanoi, Haiphong, and Vinh. Forcing use of dispersed drum storage sites.

■ Indicator: Reduced NVN ability to continue rail shipments. "The major rail lines within the DRV are being effectively interdicted." "[***] that more than 1,000 railcars loaded with war matériels were backed up at the China–North Vietnam border, unable to continue south because of damaged rail lines."

■ Indicator: Disruption of vehicular traffic on NVN's highway network. "Critical bridges on main arteries have been destroyed or damaged, and since 30 March air strikes and naval gunfire have destroyed approximately 400 trucks along roadways."

■ Indicator: Reduction in NVN's use of inland waterways. "Air operations, naval gunfire, and the mining of major river entrances between Haiphong and Vinh have almost completely halted the movement of waterborne cargo to coastal transshipment points."

■ Indicator: Disruption of the personnel infiltration system. "On 10 May a Binh Tram 18 subordinate disclosed that an infiltration group has been in its area for seven days and was unable to move. On 26 May Rear Service reports revealed that 5,500 infiltrators were backlogged near Vinh awaiting shipment to the south."

■ Indicator: Evacuation of foreign technical specialists from NVN. Seventy-four Soviet power plant and mining technicians departed Hanoi for Moscow. Twenty-one more scheduled to leave today. Others to Poland "by reason of the war situation." Included shipyard and railroad repair technicians.

■ Indicator: "North Vietnam's determined effort, but failure, to defend against U.S. air strikes." "On 10 May at least 41 MiG sorties reacted to the U.S. air raids, with 11 MiG aircraft being destroyed." Total MiG kill since 30 March "at least 30." Expended over 1,200 SAMs since 30 March, more than five times the number fired during 1970 and 1971.

■ Indicator: Late May reports suggesting lowering morale of NVN population. Report that "up to two-thirds of Hanoi's population may have been evacuated to rural areas." Increased 1972 draft is affecting agricultural workers and food production in some areas.

■ Indicator: Willingness of NVN "high command to continue the deployment of main force units to the south." On 13 May: 101st Regiment, 325th Division, detected in northern Quang Tri Province. Four days later its 95th Regiment initiated commo with the B-70 Front, thus probable deployment into northern MR-1. 18th Regiment also moving south. Recent return of two regiments of the 312th NVA Division to NVN from northern Laos provided additional reserve units.

■ Indicator: In MR-1, "reduction of enemy combat capability due to personnel and equipment losses." NVA casualties estimated at 21,000+ in this area.

■ Indicator: Enemy's continuing preparations for attack on Hue.

■ Indicator: Enemy effort to keep matériel moving for resupply in MR-1. New road construction through the DMZ. Experienced *binh trams* being shifted east into Quang Tri Province.

■ Indicator: Heavy losses of manpower and equipment in the B-3 Front, totalling 12,000 personnel to date.

■ Indicator: Enemy continuing efforts to seize Kontum City.

■ Indicator: In MR-3, enemy's determined efforts to take the provincial capital of An Loc despite heavy losses. "The enemy has lost almost 10,000 men in the heavy fighting near An Loc." Cites "devastating effects of allied air strikes on large troop formations." Mass graves found Hau Nghia and Binh Long Provinces. POW reports. Not dependent on ARVN body count reports.

■ Indicator: Enemy willingness to expend large amounts of ammunition in unsuccessful attempts to seize An Loc. During May over 47,000 rounds fired into the city.

■ Indicator: COSVN leadership discouraged.

■ Indicator: Enemy willingness to incur heavy losses in the delta in an effort to infiltrate elements of the 1st NVA Division. It is believed that the division lost 1,400 men in fighting around Kompong Trach.

■ Indicator: Enemy attempt to clear an infiltration and supply corridor into the delta.

■ Indicator: Introduction of 19 new items of matériel into RVN by the enemy. SA-7 SAM (downed seven allied aircraft). T-54 and T-63 tanks, also T-59. AT-3 Sagger wire-guided missile. 130-mm field gun first appearance in RVN.

■ Indicator: NVA counterpacification efforts.

■ Indicator: Movement of wounded north through the *binh tram* system.

BRIEFER: Analysis of these indicators reveals:

- Movement of matériel in NVN seriously disrupted.
- NVN ability to wage war in SVN reduced.
- Timetable of conquest disrupted.
- Heavy losses of men and matériel.
- Approaching (September) rainy season will adversely affect cross-DMZ operations.
- Lower intensity of attacks in Kontum reflects the impact on the enemy of losses and weather.
- Apparently withdrawing some large units from the An Loc area.

BRIEFER: Thus this forecast:

- Enemy will continue attempt to take Hue.
- Enemy will continue trying to seize control of Quang Tri and Thua Thien Provinces.
- He will continue efforts to seize Kontum City.
- He will try to consolidate northern Binh Dinh.
- He will continue to withdraw decimated units from the An Loc area and attempt to replace losses.
- He will continue to infiltrate main force units into MR-4.

■ ■ ■

BRIEFER: Four aircraft carriers are on the line. At Yankee Station: *Kitty Hawk, Saratoga,* and *Coral Sea.* At Dixie Station: *Constellation.* In port at Subic Bay: *Hancock* and *Midway.*

VOGT: Very intense MiG week. Fortunate in shooting down four without taking any losses ourselves. "Finally caught up with the navy—we now have the same number of MiGs shot down. A good week!"

8 JUN 1972: COMUS Brief: Sensors

BRIEFER: Purpose is to examine the apparent contradiction between the low level of sensor-detected enemy logistics traffic in Steel Tiger and the higher levels of infiltration and enemy activity currently experienced.

- Even though the intensity of current enemy activity "greatly exceeds that of previous campaigns," sensor string activity has not increased proportionally.
- Possible explanatory factors: Growth of the enemy's route structure, accompanying growth of the sensor field, possible transportation alternatives developed by the enemy, the marked increase in the enemy SAM/AAA threat and its effect on interdiction efforts and monitoring of sensor activations, possible greater use of daylight hours to move trucks, and the development of increased self-sufficiency.
- Try to determine why the sensor activations have failed to equal or exceed the levels reached in previous dry seasons and do not appear to correlate with recent levels of enemy activity.
- This year the enemy announced a transportation offensive commencing on

1 March, but we have no sensor-detected indications to confirm that it took place. There has been a "vast difference" in sensor activations during the heart of this (1971–1972) dry season compared with the previous year.

■ Routes increased by 40 percent last dry season, and a comparable rate of growth is suspected this year. An estimated 10 percent of the current route structure is under such heavy canopy that it prohibits the use of sensors <u>and</u> FAC observation.

■ Last year we had an average of 946 sensors in the field, configured in 123 strings. This year an average of 1,061 sensors in 152 strings. Input and throughput gates were emphasized in coverage. String life has been noticeably reduced by the change. A string is declared ineffective once reduced to fewer than three active sensors.

■ There are no indications of enemy success in neutralizing sensors. "This does not appear to be a factor."

■ From the end of the 1970 dry season to May 1972 the enemy AAA threat in Steel Tiger increased from 30 to possibly as many as 61 battalions, 13 added since November 1971. Also SAMs were introduced into the Lao panhandle and the DMZ area. This impeded daytime gunship operation, enabling the enemy to move during daylight hours. On 29 March a C-130 Specter gunship was shot down over Laos. Orbits were shifted as a result, with resultant degradation in sensor readout. Also some periods were not covered by sensor-monitoring aircraft.

■ We ran two tests on uncovered periods and found a significant amount of throughput that would have gone undetected but for the tests. Also there was some orbit downtime due to weather and other factors.

■ "An analysis performed by the Seventh Air Force has advanced the theory that input equals throughput across the DMZ and that the input into northern Steel Tiger is seven times that of the throughput from Steel Tiger into the Republic." Also developed "ratio of input versus activations of 1 to 11." Thus, every input into Laos from North Vietnam results in 11 sensor activations. Applying the Seventh Air Force methodology to the DMZ, find negligible last dry season but estimated 583 trucks this year. Using 7:1 ratio, that equates to input of 4,081 in northern Steel Tiger. If this traffic had moved through the same route as last year, it would largely make up the difference, and corresponding absence of moves in Steel Tiger area. Also waterways movement would go undetected by sensors.

■ Foodstuffs constitute approximately 80 percent of a VC/NVA battalion's estimated daily requirements for supply tonnage. Estimate 10 percent decrease in rice needed to be hauled would allow 50 percent increase in munitions hauled with no increase in trucks.

■ The computed capacity of the POL pipeline "far exceeds" the enemy's estimated daily requirements. The pipeline has been significantly extended since 1 November 1971.

■ Applying all factors, activations this dry season <u>might</u> have been approximately 7,500 more than during the same period last year.

ABRAMS: "What this briefing means to me is that it always has been an inexact sort of thing, but what's happened this year is that the level, the degree, of inexactness has now rendered it useless as intelligence."

POTTS: "Yes, sir."

ABRAMS: "Now the food thing, I never have cottoned on to that. It's been raised before. They've <u>always</u> been getting food out of Cambodia." When we've occasionally gotten a breakout of deliveries to some base area—weapons, POL, ammo, medical supplies, and so on, "I don't remember much food being there."

POTTS: "Very little."

ABRAMS: "Basically he's tried to get his food from South Vietnam and from Cambodia."

ABRAMS: "This year, with all these tanks and heavy artillery, <u>more</u> antiaircraft in South Vietnam, and more antiaircraft in Laos, his tonnage requirements—if you were his J-4—his tonnage requirements have soared <u>dramatically</u>. So, when you crank <u>that</u> factor in there, all I've got to say is this system . . . there's no point in us displaying it in the intelligence part of the briefing, because it's about the softest damn intelligence we're screwing around with. We shouldn't be afraid of soft intelligence, but somehow it ought to be off on the side where you don't really get too serious about it. Otherwise it'll mislead you. Fortunately, we had enough other intelligence so it didn't really mislead us. There weren't any bad decisions made as a result of it. In fact, you know, for <u>months</u> we've been <u>rebelling</u> [laughs] kind of. You know, there's been a lot of discussion at the WIEUs and other meetings, kind of rebelling at what this damn thing was telling us, because we <u>knew</u> better. <u>Everybody</u> did. There wasn't anybody <u>defending</u> it." "I think this system really should revert to a purely—its value should rest entirely on its aid to the interdiction and that sort."

POTTS: "In the other three years, this was one tool that was used to help us. But this year we saw that it was not a tool that helped. And that's what we were trying to figure out—what was wrong."

ABRAMS: "Actually, I consider this to be a very worthwhile briefing. It helps understand what you haven't got. That's what it does. And that's <u>good</u>. I think this is a good piece of work in the sense that it <u>shows</u> you how difficult it is to get a hold of some of these things by this means. So it's good. Thank you."

9 JUN 1972: COMUS Brief: Force Development/Force Structure

ATTENDEES: Gen. Abrams, Gen. Weyand, Mr. Jacobson, LTG McCaffrey, MG Woodward, MG Marshall, MG Bowley, MG Hollingsworth, MG Fuson, MG Cooksey, MG Potts, MG Tarpley, MG Carley, Mr. Vann, RADM Salzer, BG Trogdon, BG Wolfe, BG Moore, BG McClellan, BG Herbert, Col. Crockett.

ABRAMS: Our purpose is to go over the revised structure for 1 July, when we have to be down to 49,000. What caused us to do this: We had a structure. "While there wasn't universal happiness with it, the dissatisfaction with it had been toned down to an acceptable level for government work. Then we had this invasion and all the things that happened since the 30th of March—a lot of reinforcement out here of various kinds. We sort of took that in stride on the basis that we'd move all this air over to Thailand and so on. We're still going to do that, I'd say pretty much like we thought to begin with. But then you get into those things that are necessary to <u>handle</u> the air, like FACs and—."

ABRAMS: "We'd planned on having about 10 130s here on the first of July, and now looks like we need somewhere around 35 or 40. And can't—we've got some things here that just wouldn't be here any more if it hadn't been for the airlift, 'cause the only goddamn resupply that they've gotten, the only way they've gotten any ammunition or food, or medical supplies, by <u>air</u>. So you just got to have that, I think just got to have that. Well, anyway, there's no point in rambling on about all that. We went and looked at the thing to see what, come the first of July, we were really going to have to keep—not only keep this going, but <u>turn</u> it and start in the game of getting back—a little bit, anyway, of what's lost and so on. So we've added some stuff in and took some stuff out. I just want you to know it wasn't something we just thought it was about time to change it again or something. It was brought on because of some reasons. And it's all open—what will be presented here—it's all open for discussion." "If anyone has any ideas of how to enhance the successful outcome of the whole venture they will be gratefully received."

BRIEFER: Describes the results of a force structure review just completed. Among the tasks is orderly receipt and issue of equipment being furnished to the South Vietnamese under "Project Enhance."

BRIEFER: High priority requirements include riggers to assist in aerial resupply "in the manner that An Loc and Kontum were supported." Also recommending retention of 25 additional C-130s [for a total of 35] for that purpose and for troop movement. Assist in training two tank battalions and three new 175-mm artillery battalions, plus one ADA battalion. Retention of 39 army ARDF aircraft.

ABRAMS: Cites FACs, advisors, intelligence, naval gunfire (and ANGLICO), and airlift as key functions.

ABRAMS: Refers to action under way to combine MACV and Seventh Air Force Headquarters. "I realize you all think it's too big anyway. It's also true you're not responsible for running it. [Laughter] So—no hard feelings. That's what <u>I've</u> always done, bitched about higher headquarters being too big, sticking their nose in too many things. So there's just no ill feeling about that at all. I think you <u>should</u>. I'd feel bad if you <u>didn't</u>. But all of this packaged up, the only thing I could see to do—what it amounts to is reduce the number of infantrymen we've got here. And I thought, among the risks to be taken—going to have to take some and you take them where you think it won't hurt so much."

ABRAMS: "I think the air's just been important as <u>hell</u>. Really—even though some of it may not have landed in a good place, missed somebody or something, even <u>that</u>. Matter of fact, you can't run a lot of air without <u>some</u> of it landing in the bushes where there isn't anybody. There's no way! The intelligence isn't that good. Even when you've got everybody working good it won't do that. But I think actually it has been, overall, it's been used very well. [I'm] quite happy with the way the B-52s have been used and all that. So those things, keep it going as well as we can."

ABRAMS: "It's pretty expensive keeping these two marine squadrons out here at Bien Hoa—a thousand spaces, but that's also a good close-support outfit. Don't you think so, Holly?"

HOLLINGSWORTH: "We'd be missing the goddamn boat if we didn't hold onto them."

VANN: "In II Corps air isn't everything, it's the only thing." [Laughter]

ABRAMS: "We're going to have to be a little lenient with General Weyand today. His daughter came in from school."

HOLLINGSWORTH: "And then getting rid of the infantry, too." [Laughter]

ABRAMS: "Only an iron fellow could think of that." "You notice I saved antitank guns and no tanks. I have to take care of the internal politics of this some way."

ABRAMS: "I have been very touchy about letting the Vietnamese have this TOW, although the DA were very good about that. They came right back and said go ahead. And I put it out first I wasn't going to let anybody have it unless it was somebody that had already proved that they'd stand and fight. Actually, I didn't want them to fall into the hands of the enemy, 'cause it's a hell of a good system. But we've got to come off that now. And some of those things up there, we've got to start training the Vietnamese up there and turning them over."

■ ■ ■

ABRAMS: "In Tet of '68, you know, they got in and had seven-eighths of Hue, or nine-tenths or whatever. Anyway nothing but Truong's headquarters building over there in one corner. And that's where they were in 24 hours. And those damn fools stayed up there at Khe Sanh with something like six regiments the whole rest of the time! And what was Khe Sanh? Khe Sanh didn't even qualify as a pimple on the ass of Venus! [Laughter] That was its significance! And if they had reinforced success down there in Hue, I tell you they'd be there yet!"

ABRAMS: "You couldn't get through the Hai Van Pass on foot! Every goddamn bridge from the Hai Van Pass to Hue had been knocked out. Not only knocked out, but I mean really knocked out. Until we got going across the beach in that damn place out at Tan My—funny channel coming in there kind of crossways things, it has to be dredged—and you have to dredge it because even when it's all dredged and everything's fine, the currents are such that a ship coming through there has got to be awful careful or it's going to run aground and the whole goddamn channel's closed. We couldn't get a dredge up there and so on. So we lived on 200 tons a day coming in Phu Bai on a miserable goddamn airfield."

ABRAMS: "It got so bad I said one day, 'We're not going to be eating A rations any more in this mess. We're going to C rations. That's the way the soldiers all eat. By god, we'll set the example here.' They came back to me at night and said, 'That'll raise our tonnage in here. C rations are <u>heavier</u> than A rations.' And it's true. So I continued the A rations." [Laughter] "<u>No</u>—but that's the way the damn logistics would work. And we couldn't get another—we couldn't bring another battalion in because, by god, we couldn't feed it, we couldn't furnish it with ammunition. So I never did think he [the enemy] was too smart. He'd have whipped our ass!"

■ ■ ■

ABRAMS: "In the rainy season—September-<u>October</u>-<u>November</u>—<u>nobody</u> is going to really conduct major military operations during that period. Now I know he says he is. I mean, he's planning to. 'By golly, the rain's not going to stop him.' But they're going to have to issue a hell of a lot more life preservers than they've got now to be able to float around up there in that rain. It gets bad. So I think, in a way, <u>both</u> sides have got to get done whatever it is they want to get done in the way of a major military effort—they've got to get it done by September. So he makes this effort against Hue in the next week or two, and he gets defeated. Then I think it's realistic to feel that in July they'll be able to do something in July to get Quang Tri—the territory up here—kind of get it <u>back</u>, or get well into it."

ABRAMS: "The forces in Kontum City actually—I think, John—have done a pretty good job, certainly by comparison. It's been a bright spot."

VANN: "They're twice the division now that they were five weeks ago."

■ ■ ■

ABRAMS: "We did not have a good handhold this year on the volume of movement [of supplies] down the Ho Chi Minh Trail." "We did know that it was more than the sensors were telling us, but we had no <u>grasp</u> of how much more."

10 JUN 1972: Special Brief for Commander ROKFV

ATTENDEES: Gen. Abrams; Gen. Weyand; Gen. Vogt; LTG Sae Ho Lee, ROKFV Commander; MG Mu Hypo Han, Director of Strategic Intelligence, Korean JCS; MG Hung Jung Yun, Deputy ROKFV Commander; MG Woodward; MG Potts; MG Carley; BG McGiffert; Col. Crockett.

INTERPRETER: "Before starting the briefing, sir, General Lee would like to . . . express his feeling of regret at hearing the sad news about Mr. Vann." "It was only about two or three days ago that General Lee met him last, and now to hear that he is gone, passed away, he feels so much sorry."

John Paul Vann, director, Second Regional Assistance Group, was killed in a helicopter crash on 9 June 1972.

ABRAMS: "What's happened here is that [pause] the enemy had a good time. He got a lot of things, and he won some big fights, mostly because of poor leadership. But, as professionals, we must now look at the situation and see the way it really is. His losses have been tremendous—six regiments! You probably can't make one <u>good</u> one out of it. <u>That's</u> the <u>facts</u>. Six over <u>here</u>—you probably can't make one good one out of <u>that</u>! And he's getting pummeled every day, and it goes on and on and on, and that's the way it's going to be!"

ABRAMS: "I don't agree with what the briefer said, that he's moving his logistics in here because he's sending down the 325th, not at all. The *binh trams* are coming in here, I think, according to his original plan, because by now he expected to <u>own</u> everything north of the Hai Van Pass, and he wanted to <u>consolidate</u> it, and the <u>people</u>, and the whole thing, so that it would be <u>part</u> of North Vietnam. And he needed the *binh trams* in there to accomplish that. And it's <u>not</u> just because of the regiments of the 325th. It was part of the grand plan that this would be part of North Vietnam. And now he's not going to have it."

ABRAMS: "We've put over a thousand B-52 sorties on him in this complex, and we know a lot of it's been very good. He probably must try again at Kontum, but now I am confident he cannot take it. The troops here have defeated him. And so the 23rd Division is a <u>new</u> division—it's <u>not</u> the division it <u>was</u> last month. They have been victorious. They <u>know</u> it. And they beat the best. So he has a much more severe problem. He'll <u>try</u>, but I don't believe he can make it."

ABRAMS: "One must be very careful. One must not underestimate the enemy, but it's equally bad to overestimate him. It's like tanks. Once the enemy has showed three or four tanks, and the soldiers have seen them, then <u>every</u> night, and <u>every</u> day, it's fifty, a hundred, coming from the north, from the south, from the east, and from the west, and mostly at night."

Operational summary of the Easter Offensive.

BRIEFER:

■ "On 30 March, the initial enemy assault into Quang Tri Province pushed friendly forces back from their fire bases under intense artillery and ground attacks. By the end of the fourth day, ARVN had consolidated positions along the line from Dong Ha to Quang Tri combat base. The enemy attack then stopped, giving the ARVN time to regroup and reinforce. On 14 April the 3rd Division was able to initiate a limited counterattack to the west. This operation was designed to expand the defense westward. Combat activity continued at a low level until 28 April, when the enemy resumed his offensive and seized Dong Ha. Friendly forces fell back on Quang Tri combat base. Then, on 30 April, the decision was made to withdraw to the south and defend Quang Tri City. By that night all friendly units had moved south of the river. The next day, under threat of a major tank attack from the southwest, the forces in the city began fragmenting and withdrawing to the south. Command and control had been lost. New defensive positions were established along the southern bank of the Thach Han River, which remains the northern defensive line."

■ "The other main attack in Military Region 1 came southwest of Hue in the A

Shau Valley, along the critical Route 547 against elements of the 1st ARVN Division. Heavy fighting continued for the possession of Fire Support Base Bastogne, but it was finally evacuated, after a stubborn defense, on 29 April. ARVN defenses were reestablished at Fire Support Base Birmingham, which became the key to the southwestern defense of Hue. Pressure on Birmingham up to that time had been light—sporadic attacks by fire and small-scale ground probes."

■ "On 3 May General Truong assumed command of I Corps. Preparations for the defense of Hue continued with the reassignment of areas of operations. . . . The northern and northwestern approaches into Hue were assigned to the Marine Division. The 1st Division was assigned the southwestern and southern approaches. Command and control were improved by placing the Territorial Forces under the operational control of the ARVN sector commander."

■ "On 13 May, I Corps initiated limited offensive operations. On that date, and again on the 24th, marine forces struck north of the Thach Han River. The operations were designed to disrupt enemy offensive plans along the coast. Both operations were successful. During the last two weeks of May, enemy tank-infantry attacks along the northern front were repulsed by friendly forces, inflicting heavy enemy casualties."

■ "In the Fire Support Base King-Birmingham-Bastogne area in mid-May, two regiments of the 1st Division began offensive operations. Fire Support Base Bastogne was reoccupied after an air assault against light resistance, and a ground linkup made the following day. On 28 May elements of the 1st Division seized and occupied Fire Support Base Checkmate, located on the high ground overlooking the approaches to Fire Support Base Bastogne. 1st Division forces continue operations to clear the high ground south and southwest of Checkmate and south of Birmingham."

■ "Early in June the division areas of operations were altered. . . . The Marine Division retained responsibility for the area to the north, the Airborne Division the area to the northwest, the 1st Infantry Division to the south and southeast, and two battalions of the 3rd Division to the southeast, primarily along QL-1. The U.S. 2nd of the 1st Infantry has this area [indicating on map]. Since last Sunday combat activity has centered around Marine Corps and airborne units in the vicinity of Fire Support Base Nancy. The units have had continued light contact and moderate to heavy attacks by fire from 130-mm guns. On 8 June elements of all three Marine Corps brigades launched a limited objective offensive into Quang Tri Province."

■ "A second front began in Military Region 3 on 4 April when the enemy attacked in Binh Long Province from the Khmer Republic. His first objective was Loc Ninh. After four days of heavy fighting the friendly units were forced to evacuate their positions and withdraw to the south to An Loc, which was already under attack. The corps commander elected to stand at An Loc. His defending force then consisted of two regiments. It was later reinforced by one infantry regiment, one ranger group, and one airborne brigade. This brought the total ARVN force to the equivalent of five infantry regiments. For over two months these forces have withstood daily heavy attacks by fire and frequent tank-supported ground attacks. Initially these attacks by fire consisted of about 1,000 rounds of mixed mortar, rocket, and artillery fire daily. In late May they had diminished in intensity, and now average about 400 rounds daily. Tank-supported ground attacks were heavy for the first 17 days. Occasional ground probes against the perimeter continue. Since the end of May friendly forces have been patrolling out to two kilometers beyond their perimeter."

■ "On 9 April the Vietnamese Joint General Staff ordered the 21st Infantry Division to move from Military Region 4 to Binh Long Province. It was deployed north of Chon Thanh to prevent possible enemy drives further south. Later the division was ordered to open QL-13 north to An Loc. Movement north has been slow due to enemy pockets of resistance and accurate enemy artillery fire. In mid-May an additional infantry regiment was moved from Military Region 4 to QL-13 south of An Loc. This regiment joined the attack toward An Loc against continued heavy resistance and is currently located three kilometers south of An Loc. An Loc remains isolated and continues to be resupplied by air. Thursday lead elements of the 21st Division linked up with forces operating south of An Loc."

■ "In late April in southwestern Military Region 3, in southern Tay Ninh and northern Hau Nghia Provinces, the enemy increased pressure on Territorial Forces, who reacted well. ARVN forces were deployed to Hau Nghia Province to meet this new threat. During the month of May enemy pressure continued, and additional ARVN forces from the 25th and 18th Divisions augmented the forces already in Hau Nghia Province."

■ "In mid-May increased enemy activity in Phuoc Tuy Province threatened the district towns of Duc Thanh, Dat Do, and Xuyen Moc. The III Corps commander reacted by using one ARVN battalion and two RF companies to liberate Dat Do, which had been 40 percent enemy-controlled. Later a ranger group, plus an infantry battalion, was deployed to the area. Territorial Forces consisting of nine RF companies are primarily in a defensive posture in the district towns of Dat Do and Xuyen Moc. Isolated enemy pockets of resistance remain in the villages of Duc Thanh, Dat Do, and Xuyen Moc as clearing operations continue."

■ "In Military Region 2 at dawn on 24 April an enemy tank attack overran the 22nd Division headquarters at Tan Canh, then turned west and overran Dak To II, fragmenting friendly forces at both locations. All units withdrew toward Kontum, and an all-out defense of the city was ordered. During the same period the enemy increased his activity against lines of communications vital to the defense of key areas. On 11 April traffic on QL-19 between Qui Nhon and Pleiku was blocked at the An Khe Pass, but was later cleared by Republic of Korea forces. On 22 April the enemy blocked the Kontum Pass, isolating Kontum City."

■ "On 10 May Major General Toan, former commander of the 2nd Infantry Division, assumed command of ARVN II Corps, replacing General Dzu. Four days later the enemy attacked Kontum with tanks and infantry from the northwest, but was repulsed with heavy losses. Starting on 25 May, activity increased as ARVN units fought to maintain their defensive perimeter against the enemy attack concentrated in these areas [shown on map]. Three penetrations were made. . . . After the situation had stabilized, ARVN units with armor counterattacked to the north and contained the enemy. Currently all but a few pockets of enemy have been eliminated from the city. The airfield was closed until late Thursday night, and all supplies were being brought in by helicopter and aerial drop. The airfield is now open, but aerial resupply must be accomplished during the hours of darkness."

■ "An operation to clear the Kontum Pass began on 21 May and initially progressed slowly to the south end of the pass. Additional forces were committed along this axis [as shown on map] in order to intercept supply lines and clear the enemy from an area five to seven kilometers west of QL-14. The operation continues and the pass remains closed. Closure of the pass necessitates the resupply of Kontum City totally by air."

■ "To the east, in Binh Dinh Province, enemy activity increased significantly as troops were pulled out to reinforce the highlands. The district town of Hoai An was evacuated on 17 April, and the district town of Hoai Nhon fell 10 days later. This left only Landing Zone English and Tam Quan district town as friendly outposts in the northeastern three districts of Binh Dinh Province. Then Tam Quan was evacuated. On the second and third of May the remaining 2,000 troops at Landing Zone English were evacuated by sea to Qui Nhon."

■ "On 2 June enemy pressure increased around the Phu My District town area. Friendly forces are receiving attacks by fire, and ground contacts are increasing. Elements of two regiments of the 22nd Division, supported by air strikes, have thus far been able to keep the enemy from launching sustained operations in this area. Over 400 enemy have been killed in engagements this week."

■ "In Military Region 4 the 9th Infantry Division has been hard pressed to cope with the many widely scattered attacks by fire, ground attacks, and other harassments throughout its area of operations. This includes Chuong Thien Province, where activity was heavy and included attacks against ARVN forces. The division has been spread thin to assume the area of operations vacated by the 21st Division when that unit redeployed to Military Region 3. Reacting to the infiltration of enemy units in northern Kien Giang Province, the division imported four ranger battalions and two armored cavalry squadrons in a concerted effort to quickly drive the enemy from the coastline high ground extending from Ha Tien to Kien Luong. Additionally, five RF battalions have been conducting extensive operations since 22 May along the Kien Giang infiltration routes north of Kien Luong. ARVN and Territorial Forces have taken aggressive action against the increased enemy threat in the northern provinces of [names the three provinces]."

■ "Reintroduction of U.S. tactical air and B-52 strikes into the delta has helped to replace the combat power lost through redeployments. Along the Vietnam-Cambodian border, General Nghi currently has two ranger groups conducting daily cross-border operations along the Kampong track and the [other] enemy infiltration corridors. Their mission is to develop air targets and destroy enemy forces entering Military Region 4 from Cambodia."

■ "A dramatic increase in the Free World Military Forces' tactical air capability has been realized since the enemy offensive began. At that time forces consisted of 16 United States Air Force squadrons, 10 navy squadrons on two aircraft carriers, and 9 VNAF squadrons. Since 30 March tactical air forces of the United States Air Force, Navy, and Marine Corps have deployed to Southeast Asia from the continental United States, Hawaii, Korea, Japan, Okinawa, and the Philippines. The Seventh Fleet carrier force has been increased to six ships capable of tactical strike operations. Four are on station off the coast of Vietnam at all times. One carrier supports operations in Military Region 3 and Military Region 4, and three are dedicated to operations in North Vietnam while maintaining the capability to divert their tactical air to the Republic as the tactical situation requires. Two remain on alert in the Philippines."

■ "Our available forces now consist of 30 United States Air Force squadrons, 30 Navy squadrons, 5 Marine Corps squadrons, and 9 VNAF squadrons, an overall increase of 39 squadrons. From 30 March to 6 June tactical aircraft have flown more than 55,000 sorties. . . . The daily average has increased from 610 during the week of 29 March through 4 April to a high of 930 during the week of 17–23 May. . . ."

■ "In South Vietnam the tactical air effort has focused on two areas of operations: direct support of friendly ground operations and interdiction of enemy lines of communications and logistics facilities. Sorties are flown on both a pre-planned and immediate basis. . . . Tactical air support has been a vital factor in the success of many ARVN offensive and defensive operations. Tactical air has been very effective countering the enemy use of armor."

■ "The campaign to impede the flow of supplies through North Vietnam began in earnest with the mining of Haiphong harbor, other ports, and coastal areas on 9 May. Subsequent reduction of shipping activity in these areas has proved the effectiveness of the concept. To further isolate Hanoi and Haiphong, strikes are being conducted daily against the highways and railroads leading from Communist China south into the area. The enemy lines of communications from Hanoi to the DMZ are receiving intensive tactical air strikes. Damage to roads, railways, and—more importantly—the logistics storage areas has been impressive."

■ "The expanded use of sophisticated weaponry has increased tactical air all-weather capabilities and the accuracy of weapons delivered. The laser-guided bomb has aided the effort by reducing the number of sorties required to eliminate a particular target. The destruction of the Thanh Hoa and [Minh Ya?] bridges are examples of the effectiveness of this weapon against targets requiring precise delivery."

■ "Since the enemy offensive began there has been a total of 4,759 B-52 strike sorties in the Republic of Vietnam, North Vietnam, Laos, and Cambodia. The major weight of effort during this period has been concentrated in three areas:

the Quang Tri–Thua Thien Provinces in northern Military Region 1, the Kontum and Dak To areas of Military Region 2, and around An Loc in Military Region 3. The majority of the 279 strikes around Quang Tri City in MR-1 were employed in a defensive role, with most strikes in close support of troops in contact. The 139 strikes directed against targets in the Hue area were primarily on troop concentrations, tank and artillery locations in the A Shau Valley, and approaches to Hue City from the north and southwest. The vast majority of the 679 B-52 strikes in MR-2 were directed against large-scale troop concentrations and heavy gun positions around Kontum City. This effort resulted in heavy enemy casualties and has seriously disrupted his attempts to mount a large-scale offensive against Kontum City. The battle for An Loc came early in the offensive when, on 15 April, over 50 percent of the daily weight of effort was employed in direct defense of the city."

■ "In North Vietnam, on four different raids, a total of 70 B-52 sorties struck airfields, rail yards, warehouses, and petroleum products storage areas in the Haiphong, Bai Thuong, Vinh, and Thanh Hoa areas of North Vietnam. By 31 May the crucial situation had eased at Kontum and in the An Loc area. This provided the opportunity to implement the first phase of a planned large-scale counterlogistics campaign using B-52 and tactical air strikes against the enemy close-in supply systems in northwestern MR-1, the DMZ, and the southern portion of North Vietnam, as well as supply caches in the B-3 Front and cross-border areas in Cambodia adjacent to MR-3. This campaign will continue, consistent with the tactical situation throughout South Vietnam."

17 JUN 1972: WIEU

ATTENDEES: Amb. Bunker, Amb. Whitehouse, Mr. Polgar, Gen. Abrams, Gen. Weyand, Gen. Vogt, LTG McCaffrey, MG Woodward, MG Marshall, MG Bowley, MG Fuson, MG Jumper, MG Potts, MG Carley, RADM Salzer, BG Hudson, BG McClellan, BG Scott, BG Herbert, BG McGiffert, BG Wickham, BG Wolfe, Col. Presson, Col. Miller, Col. Stevens, Mr. Marlette, Col. Crockett.

MACV 1972 Infiltration Estimate: 100,500 (plus that direct via DMZ). 9,300 to MR-TTH. 15,600 to MR-5, 33,500 to B-3 Front, 42,100 to COSVN.

BRIEFER: 52 SA-2 SAMs were launched during the week. No losses resulted. 1,412 minimum fired since 30 March. Sixteen U.S. aircraft have been downed, an 88:1 ratio.

ABRAMS: "I always give this fellow credit, but—I don't know who's spreading it, but there's a—almost every press man that comes in to see me wants to know about this threat to Saigon. And aren't they closing in on Saigon? And why haven't they done it already, anyway? And General Vien—he wants those radars, to take them out of MR-1 and bring them down here to put them around Saigon. There's just a damn thing about Saigon. Well, I know, it's good to be concerned about it, and they should be and so on, but these fellows are really not showing up too good. <u>That's</u> what I'm getting around to. Christ, they've got to be able to at least take Moc Hoa before they start getting into the precincts of Saigon. You fire up an attack on Moc Hoa, or Tinh Bien, way the hell out there with no signs of visible support, how in the <u>hell</u> can you contemplate taking <u>Saigon</u>? Or putting it in the clutch of fear? I guess by starting <u>rumors</u>."

BRIEFER: Describes ARVN capture of 42 AT-3 Sagger wire-guided missiles in the upper delta north of Base Area 470. In boxes, scattered around. No enemy observed. Markings indicated they were manufactured in 1971. First AT-3s captured anywhere in the world by Free World Forces. Soviet manufacture.

ABRAMS: "Well, I guess what we know now is that it takes a year to get it from the factory to Kien Tuong by whatever route that it goes. And that's kind of an important thing. I noticed one of the senators think that we've got a Tonkin Gulf thing all over again, and what happened is that sometime the first part of the year we irritated them [the enemy] by bombing them without justification, and so they got mad and came down and attacked us. Well . . . in no way take those things from the factory to Kien Tuong in a couple of months."

ABRAMS: "Incidentally, you know in the long-range plan for bringing the strength of the ARVN down [reducing strength], I think our plan calls for the elimination of the Marine Division. Or the plan we worked out with JGS—I don't say it's <u>ours</u>. And I think we'd better dig into that, John. That's not <u>right</u>."

CARLEY: "We've put a note in saying this will have to be worked out later by the Vietnamese. Both the marines and the Airborne Division are performing well now. They want to trade off some of ARVN."

ABRAMS: "That's right, and they <u>should</u>. They <u>should</u>, because it's not only that they have, in this thing, have—you know, they've performed well, but both of those outfits have got that whole—they've got their own hospital, they've got their <u>families</u> in hand, they've got organizations for the widows and orphans. And I think it's one of the reasons why they perform well. Also, they've been used all over the country . . . and they've <u>designed</u> themselves to do that. The whole <u>pay</u> system. . . . That is sort of an infrastructure that you've got there that is very good. And the <u>marines</u> are going to come out of this as—well, heroes of the nation. And that's the kind of thing to build on. We ought to find something else. You could substitute, swap off, the <u>22nd</u>. [Laughter] Now it's true neither the marines or the airborne have ever been what you'd call stars at pacification. I think I said to General Weyand the other day . . . they're not as bad at that as the Koreans, but that's not saying an awful lot. But they're good fighting troops, and they'll have this all behind them."

BRIEFER: 23,073 total SVN casualties for regular forces between 1 April and 10 June. Replacements programmed: 53,000. By 1 June 39,824 in place. 1–14 June: 16,657 more put out by Training Command. Thus 55,000+ so far. Casualties: 4,400 KIA, 16,750 WIA, 1,909 MIA.

BRIEFER: RF/PF casualties: 14,000 (MR-4 the most). Programmed replacements: 33,000. As of 31 May: 23,000. About 7,000 1–14 June. Total about 30,000. Casualties: 3,668 KIA, 9,622 WIA, 1,573 MIA.

BRIEFER: Deserters: February: 12,000+ in RVNAF. March: 14,500. April: 14,000. "Just about the average that we've been running. It's not excessive, which we were afraid it was going to be." RVNAF accessions: 1 April–11 June 1972: 53,174 volunteers, 17,857 conscripts. Total: 71,000.

ABRAMS: "Well, I must say that's [manpower status as briefed] a very encouraging thing. Put a note on there—we ought to get a message in on that."

ABRAMS: "<u>Well</u>, I must say the early parts of this meeting today were a little dreary. We began to pick up speed here toward the end when we got to some of the things <u>we</u> were doing. God, I got overwhelmed with what that other fellow was doing."

ABRAMS: "The one place that looks kind of serious to me is that northern MR-1. Now General Vogt talked to me this morning . . . about the 130 [the enemy's 130-mm guns] problem. It sounds to me like they've got all the throttles open." "If we keep at it enough, we'll get there." "He's intent on staying with that thing, and so we've got to stay with it, <u>too</u>."

ABRAMS: "Now, the other one is the delta. And I must say it looked fairly ominous when you had the 5th moving over there and all that. But the other fellow didn't put that together too well. And also, General Nghi—it seems to me he reacted to that very quickly, and that meant a lot. He just didn't <u>wait</u> for them to get down into 470. And of course the territorials did very well out there. Border <u>rangers.</u> They got in some bad fights, but they've done well. So that thing—it's going to continue to be a problem, and they'll have to keep after it."

■ ■ ■

POTTS (to his officers after the WIEU, tape still running): "I'll give one bit of advice. I've found that in this political turmoil on <u>strengths</u>, throughout the United States and all of us, if there's something on strengths you don't have to send in, boy don't send it, because all you're doing is sticking your head under the buzz saw every time you do."

18 JUN 1972: Special Briefing for Sir Robert Thompson

ATTENDEES: Sir Robert Thompson, Mr. Desmond Palmer, Gen. Weyand, MG Woodward, MG Fuson, MG Potts, MG Carley, BG McClellan, BG Herbert, BG McGiffert, Col. Porta, Col. Bush, Col. Crockett.

On the agenda Thompson is identified as a White House consultant.

BRIEFER: Ammunition a problem. Authorized expenditure rate for 105-mm of 20 rounds per day, and an intensive rate of 40 rounds per day. "Immediately we began shooting 40–50 rounds per day, and certain MRs have even shot more. In MR-1, with General Truong getting ready for his counterattack, we're talking about firing for about three weeks 120 rounds per day, and then he goes to 180 rounds per day. It's very difficult to try to control ammunition expenditures. As you can imagine, cranking up the ammunition pipeline—production, moving it into country, distributing it, and so forth has been <u>a</u> chore—and a very expensive one."

BRIEFER: Re the regular force strengths on 31 March 1972: "These figures present the best personnel posture ever achieved by RVNAF up until that time. It is better today." "Actually, had not the GVN efforts to bring the RVNAF up to strength and functioning at the time the enemy offensive began, the personnel casualty loss, without an adequate pipeline for replacements, could have been disastrous."

THOMPSON: "What about the 3rd Division—have they sort of rounded them all up?"

SOMEONE: "The division is undergoing retraining now. Four battalions have been retrained and assessed as combat ready, to add to the two battalions that were considered combat ready when the breakthrough was completed." Two more in training. By 26 July all will be completed.

SOMEONE: "Even the units that have been the most badly mangled, as you will see, as you go around—the 3rd Division, the 22nd Division, the 1st Ranger Group, the 20th Tank Regiment—I don't think you detect anything <u>but</u> a highly motivated attitude to get back with it."

SOMEONE: "For General Truong to conduct a successful counteroffensive, he's going to need more than the marine and airborne divisions. Whether they'll do that I don't know, but the division's going to have to come from somewhere."

24 JUN 1972: Commanders WIEU

ATTENDEES: Amb. Bunker, Mr. Polgar, Gen. Abrams, Gen. Vogt, LTG McCaffrey, MG Woodward, MG Marshall, MG Bowley, MG Roseborough, MG Hollingsworth, MG Fuson, MG Cooksey, MG Jumper, MG Coleman, MG Potts, MG Tarpley, MG Slay, RADM Salzer, BG Cross, BG Wolfe, BG Hudson, BG Herbert, BG Scott, BG McGiffert, BG Healy, RADM Price, BG Wickham, RADM Oberg, Mr. Cruikshank, Mr. Wilson, Mr. Dean, Mr. Marlette, Mr. Barnes, Col. Presson, Col. Miller, Col. Stevens, Col. Crockett.

POTTS: "Sir, the 290th Recon Regiment provides a dual purpose up there in North Vietnam of early warning and, of course, target acquisition. And about 20 minutes ago we got a message that had been flashed by this regiment to its subordinates that perhaps is the strongest that I have ever seen concerning the conditions that they're undergoing there. We'd like to read that at this time."

BRIEFER: "From: The North Vietnamese 290th Reconnaissance Regiment. To: Unidentified regimental elements. Message No. 12. The enemy continues to strike many targets. In past times we have met with the staff of the Lao Dong Party, who are afraid that the violent sacrifices of recent weeks will scare the villagers and their families. Our forces urgently need guidance, but we have pointed out to the soldiers they are serving to hone the people to sharpness before they are completely routed. Even though they are bloody, our strength and health remain. We are still able to accomplish difficult tasks before their very eyes in order to get one last tremendous victory. We have ceaselessly met in the decided areas, and we have seriously reflected upon our losses. It is well we are side by side, even though we have been cut to ribbons. In order to analyze and talk over our problems, we must acknowledge that we cannot yet achieve our goals, and that we are slowly dying for a [word unclear] aim. We are prepared to meet the enemy, but the massive strikes by the B-52s happen outside of our influence. Detachments have risen up to accurse us and concentrate on every [word unclear] affected by the strikes. We try to slip away to the safe areas, but the air strikes also turn it into a wasteland and it continues to ebb away. Signed, [Khu Li?]."

ABRAMS: What kind of U.S. classification does that get? "I would like to have it sanitized so that every commander can take it back with him today and show his counterpart."

■ ■ ■

BRIEFER: The196th Infantry Brigade (U.S.) Headquarters stood down on 16 June. Also the 1st Battalion, 46th Infantry. The 2nd Battalion, 1st Infantry, will stand down on 25 June. That leaves one battalion task force as the only U.S. maneuver unit in MR-1.

ABRAMS: "The reporting from northern MR-1 today is far faster, far more complete, far more comprehensive, than it ever was in '67 or '68—when you had all the Americans there."

ABRAMS: "One of the reasons that General Westmoreland put that headquarters up at Phu Bai, called 'MACV Advance' [*sic:* MACV Forward], was that it took four or five days to find out what the hell happened above the Hai Van Pass. Under the circumstances it was just—you couldn't live with it. And even after we got that set up we weren't doing as good as he is today."

■ ■ ■

BRIEFER: "Losses to the SA-7 were extremely heavy this week, with 6 lost to only 14 firings. An AC-130 gunship was lost near the A Shau Valley. Two U.S. Cobras were downed at An Loc."

VOGT: "This is a very lethal weapon—no question about it. I tried to impress this on General Truong. And in that operation he'll be flying those choppers up there in that area, where there are more of them than anywhere else, he's got to be very careful. An absolutely lethal weapon, far more effective than the SA-2 in its [ratio of] successes against firings. No comparison."

■ ■ ■

ABRAMS: "Mr. Ambassador?"

BUNKER: "Yes, I'd like to say a word, General Abrams. When you and I came here, a little more than five years ago, I was hoping we would exit together. I just want to say that these five years I think have been the most rewarding of a fairly long career that began with the horse artillery in 1916. And they certainly have been fateful years, for the Republic of Vietnam and for our own country. I suppose, when the history of this war is written, it will be very clear that <u>no</u> country ever put as many restraints on itself as <u>we</u> did. And I think it's been probably the most difficult war that we've ever tried to fight. And it's been fateful for our country, because I think the question is whether we <u>have</u> the patience and the determination and the will to accept the responsibilities of power."

BUNKER: "Certainly the armed forces of the United States have shown determination and will and steadiness in a most difficult situation. I think it's clear—it's certainly clear to me—that without <u>your</u> leadership, and without what your colleagues have <u>done</u> here, there wouldn't <u>be</u> any Republic of Vietnam today. And this has been due to your leadership, to not only highest intelligence and <u>professional</u> skill, but to sensitivity, effectiveness, <u>with</u> what the Yankees call plain common sense. By <u>that</u> means you've gained the confidence and trust of the Vietnamese, which has been essential to success here. So we've all learned from <u>you</u>. I had a lot to learn, going back to the days of the horse artillery."

BUNKER: "And now that you're leaving we all take great satisfaction and pride in the fact that you're taking over as Chief of Staff, the top position in the army. And I think—you <u>know</u>, I don't have to tell you—that you leave with not only the great admiration but the greatest <u>affection</u> of all of us."

ABRAMS: "<u>Thank</u> you, Mr. Ambassador. Let's go to lunch, gentlemen."

As Chief of Staff, General Abrams set about putting the army back on its feet after the long ordeal of Vietnam. Stressing combat readiness and taking care of the soldier, he transitioned to an all-volunteer force, upgraded the educational system for noncommissioned officers, cut back headquarters and put the spaces saved into combat elements, and integrated reserve forces into the overall force more closely than ever before. Then, less than two years into the assignment, he succumbed to lung cancer, the only Army Chief of Staff ever to die in office.

Former Chairman of the Joint Chiefs of Staff Gen. John W. Vessey later summed up the Abrams legacy. "When Americans watched the stunning success of our armed forces in Desert Storm," he observed, "they were watching the Abrams vision in action. The modern equipment, the effective air support, the use of the reserve components and, most important of all, the advanced training which taught our people how to stay alive on the battlefield were all seeds planted by Abe."

During the latter half of 1972 peace negotiations continued in Paris and, in the autumn, appeared near completion. When the South Vietnamese balked at some of the provisions, especially regarding North Vietnamese forces in the south, negotiations broke down. President Nixon then ordered renewed heavy bombing of key military installations in the north, including Haiphong harbor and the Hanoi area. Soon North Vietnam agreed to return to the peace talks, and agreement was reached not long thereafter.

In January 1973 an agreement was signed in Paris ending the Vietnam War. Under its provisions the United States withdrew all forces from Vietnam by 29 March 1973 and American prisoners of war were released by North Vietnam.

Fatefully, however, North Vietnamese forces in South Vietnam were allowed to remain in place.

President Richard M. Nixon had made a number of commitments to South Vietnamese President Nguyen Van Thieu as inducements to the South Vietnamese to accede to what they viewed as a fatally flawed agreement. If the North Vietnamese failed to abide by terms of the agreement and renewed their aggression against the south, the United States would, pledged Nixon, reintroduce U.S. combat forces to punish such acts. If there were renewed fighting, the United States would, as permitted under terms of the Paris accords, replace on a one-for-one basis South Vietnamese losses of major items of combat equipment, such things as tanks and artillery pieces. And the United States would maintain a robust level of economic assistance to South Vietnam. In the event, however, the United States reneged on all three promises.

In the course of the next two years much happened to undermine those commitments. Antiwar sentiment in the U.S. Congress, and especially the Senate, led to enactment of a War Powers Resolution that sought to restrict presidential autonomy when it came to committing U.S. forces overseas. Other provisions progressively restricted use of appropriated monies for support of military forces in Southeast Asia. Yet other measures cut back the appropriations requested for support of South Vietnam militarily and economically. Meanwhile greatly inflated energy costs eroded the value of the smaller amounts that were appropriated.

Compounding these influences was a political scandal that threatened the presidency itself and eventually caused the downfall of President Nixon. Known as the Watergate affair, it involved a June 1972 burglary of the offices of the Democratic National Committee in an office building of that name by a group of people later tied to the White House. Nixon's involvement in a cover-up of the matter, revealed by tape recordings he had made in his offices, led to his impeachment and, on 9 August 1974, resignation.

Meanwhile North Vietnam, supplied and supported by its patrons the Soviet Union and China, mounted increasingly widespread military operations aimed at South Vietnam, culminating in March 1975 in a full-scale conventional invasion. America stood by. Weakened by reductions in monetary and matériel assistance, and perhaps more tellingly by loss of confidence in its ability to withstand the onslaught given abandonment by its patron, South Vietnam quickly collapsed, with enemy forces entering Saigon to take the surrender on 30 April 1975.

APPENDIX I

MEETING PARTICIPANTS

NOTES: In some cases identifications or tenures are incomplete due to lack of information or uncertainty as to the exact identity of some of those mentioned on the tapes. One-time attendees who could not be identified have been omitted. Ranks shown are those the participants held at the time they served in Vietnam and are in some cases lower than the rank eventually attained. Some served in Vietnam on earlier tours of duty before the period covered in these MACV tapes, and a few may have served in Vietnam subsequent to that time, but in most cases only their assignments during the period covered by this work are listed below. Exceptions are made for those who went on to head their services or to become Chairman of the Joint Chiefs of Staff or for comparable achievements. Officers are U.S. Army unless otherwise indicated.

Abrams, Gen. Creighton W. COMUSMACV (1968–1972). Army Chief of Staff (1972–1974).

Adamson, Maj. Gen. James B. MACV J-1 (1971–1972).

Ahern, Col. William F. Assigned to CORDS (1970–1971).

Armstrong, Mr. (1972). Not further identified.

Armstrong, Brig. Gen. DeWitt C., III. CG, Third Regional Advisory Command (1970–1971). Deputy for Military Functions, Second Regional Assistance Group (1971).

Avriett, Col. G. C. (USAF) MACV Deputy J-4 (1968–1969).

Baker, Lt. Col. Robert L. (USAF) Assigned to MACV J-3 (1971–1972).

Baker, Maj. Gen. Royal N. (USAF) MACV J-5 (1968–1969).

Baldwin, Maj. Gen. James L. Deputy CG, XXIV Corps (1970).

Barnes, Brig. Gen. John W. CG, Second Regional Assistance Command (1967–1968).

Barnes, Mr. Thomas J. Deputy for CORDS, Second Regional Assistance Group (1971–1972).

Barsanti, Maj. Gen. Olinto M. CG, 101st Airborne Division (1967–1968).

Bautz, Maj. Gen. Edward, Jr. MACV J-3 (1969–1970).

Beach, Gen. Dwight E. CINC, U.S. Army, Pacific (1966–1968).

Beckington, Col. Herbert L. (USMC) III Marine Amphibious Force G-2 (1968).

Berger, Ambassador Samuel D. Deputy U.S. Ambassador to the Republic of Vietnam (1969–1972).

Bernstein, Brig. Gen. Robert. MACV Command Surgeon (1971–1972).

Birdt, Capt. George. (USN) MACV Deputy J-5 (1971).

Bivin, Capt. Homer R. (USN) MACV Deputy Assistant Chief of Staff for Military Assistance (1971).

Black, Col. W. H. (USAF) MACV Deputy J-4 (1969–1970).

Blanchard, Brig. Gen. George S. Chief of Staff, I Field Force, Vietnam (1967–1968).

Blazey, Brig. Gen. Frank E. Deputy CG, Delta Regional Assistance Command (1971–1972).

Blessé, Brig. Gen. Frederick C. (USAF) Assistant Deputy Chief of Staff for Operations, Seventh Air Force (1971).

Bolling, Brig. Gen. Alexander R., Jr. Chief of Staff, XXIV Corps (1969).

Bolton, Brig. Gen. Donnelly P. MACV Assistant Chief of Staff for Military Assistance (1967–1968).

Bonesteel, Gen. Charles H., III. CG, Eighth Army (1966–1969).

Borders, Col. John E. (USAF) MACV Deputy J-1 (1971).

Bowley, Maj. Gen. Albert J. (USAF) MACV Deputy Chief of Staff (1971–1972).

Brown, Maj. Gen. Charles P. Deputy CG, I Field Force, Vietnam (1970–1971), and CG, Second Regional Assistance Command (1971).

Brown, Gen. George S. (USAF) Deputy COMUSMACV for Air Operations and Commander, Seventh Air Force (1968–1970).

Brown, Brig. Gen. Thomas W. MACV Assistant Chief of Staff for Military Assistance (1971) and MACV Deputy J-4 (1971–1972).

Bryan, Brig. Gen. William E., Jr. (USAF) MACV Deputy Chief of Staff (1967–1969).

Bryant, Col. Robert L. (USAF) MACV Deputy Chief of Information (1971–1972).

Buckner, Maj. Gen. John H. (USAF) Deputy Chief of Staff for Operations, Seventh Air Force (1970).

Bunker, Ambassador Ellsworth. U.S. Ambassador to the Republic of Vietnam (1967–1973).

Butts, Rear Adm. John L. (USN) Executive Assistant to CINCPACFLT (1969).

Camp, Brig. Gen. Thomas J., Jr. MACV Assistant Chief of Staff for Military Assistance (1970–1971).

Carley, Maj. Gen. John T. MACV J-3 (1971–1972).

Cavanaugh, Col. Stephen E. Chief, MACV Studies and Observations Group (1968–1970).

Chambers, Mr. Willard E. Deputy for CORDS, I Field Force, Vietnam (1970–1971), and Executive Director for Civil Operations in Office of the MACV Assistant Chief of Staff for CORDS (1971–1972).

Chapman, Gen. Leonard F., Jr. (USMC) Commandant of the Marine Corps (1968–1972).

Cheadle, Brig. Gen. Geoffrey. (USAF) MACV J-6 (1969–1971).

Chesarek, Gen. Ferdinand J. CG, U.S. Army Materiel Command (1969–1970).

Christie, Mr. Martin S. Office of the Deputy Assistant Chief of Staff for CORDS (1971).

Church, Col. E. H. Office of MACV J-1 (1969–1970).

Clay, Brig. Gen. Frank B. MACV J-1 (1968–1969).

Clay, Gen. Lucius D., Jr. (USAF) Deputy COMUSMACV for Air Operations and Commander, Seventh Air Force (1970–1971).

Clement, Brig. Gen. Wallace L. MACV Director of Training (1969–1970).

Clifford, Clark. Secretary of Defense (1968–1969).

Colby, Ambassador William E. Deputy to the COMUSMACV for CORDS (1968–1971).

Cole, Brig. Gen. Earl F. Deputy Assistant Chief of Staff for CORDS (1968).

Coleman, Brig. Gen. William S. MACV Deputy J-3 (1968) and (as major general) Chief, Army Advisory Group, MACV (1972–1973).

Collins, Lt. Gen. Arthur S., Jr. CG, I Field Force, Vietnam (1970–1971).

Conroy, Maj. Gen. Raymond C. MACV J-4 (1969–1970).

Cooksey, Maj. Gen. Howard H. CG, First Regional Assistance Command (1972–1973).

Corcoran, Lt. Gen. Charles A. MACV J-3 (1968), MACV Chief of Staff (1968–1969), and CG, I Field Force, Vietnam (1969–1970).

Cowles, Maj. Gen. Donald H. MACV J-3 (1970–1971) and MACV Chief of Staff (1971–1972).

Crego, Col. John C. Deputy MACV J-2 (1971–1972).

Critchlow, Col. D. M. (USAF) MACV Deputy Science Advisor (1968–1969).

Crockett, Col. Edward P. MACV Secretary of the Joint Staff (1971–1972).

Crooks, Col. W. M. MACV Deputy Chief of Information (1968–1969).

Cruikshank, Mr. Ralph H. Associate Deputy for CORDS, III Corps (1969–1971).

Cunningham, Col. Hubert S. Deputy MACV J-5 and MACV Director of Training (1968–1969).

Cushman, Maj. Gen. John H. CG, Delta Regional Assistance Command (1971–1972).

Cushman, Lt. Gen. Robert E., Jr. (USMC) CG, III Marine Amphibious Force (1967–1969). Commandant of the Marine Corps (1972–1975).

Cutrona, Col. Joseph F. H. MACV Chief of Information (1969–1970).

Davidson, Maj. Gen. Phillip B. MACV J-2 (1967–1969).

Davis, Col. G. W. USARV Assistant Chief of Staff G-2 (1967–1968).

Davis, Maj. Gen. Raymond G. (USMC) CG, 3d Marine Division (1968–1969).

Davison, Lt. Gen. Michael S. CG, II Field Force, Vietnam (1970–1971).

Dean, Mr. John Gunther. USAID (1970–1972).

DeBruler, Col. (1971). Not further identified.

DeFranco, Col. Theodore. Office of MACV J-2 (1971–1972).

Dessert, Col. Don M. (USAF) MACV Deputy J-2 (1969–1970).

Dettre, Maj. Gen. Rexford H. (USAF) MACV J-5 (1970–1971).

Dixon, Maj. Gen. Robert J. (USAF) Vice Commander, Seventh Air Force (1969–1970).

Doehler, Brig. Gen. W. F. (USMC) MACV Deputy J-3 for Operations (1970–1971).

Dolvin, Maj. Gen. Welborn G. MACV Chief of Staff (1970–1971) and CG, XXIV Corps (1971–1972).

Doody, Col. John J. MACV Deputy Science Advisor (1969–1970).

Duval, Mr. G. MACV Science Advisor (1971–1972).

Eason, Capt. W. R. (USN) Assistant Chief of Staff Operations, Naval Forces, Vietnam (1968).

Eckhardt, Maj. Gen. George S. CG, Delta Regional Assistance Command (1968–1969), and Special Assistant to the Deputy COMUSMACV (1971–1973).

Everett, Col. I Field Force, Vietnam, G-3. (1968).

Ewell, Lt. Gen. Julian J. CG, 9th Infantry Division (1968–1969), and CG, II Field Force, Vietnam (1969–1970).

Firfer, Mr. Alexander. Deputy for CORDS, 1st Corps Tactical Zone (1969–1970).

Flanagan, Brig. Gen. Edward M., Jr. MACV Director of Training (1967–1968).

Flanagan, Rear Adm. William R. (USN) Deputy Commander, Naval Forces, Vietnam (1969–1970).

Fluss, Capt. Richard M. (USN) Deputy Director, MACV Construction Directorate (1972).

Forrester, Brig. Gen. Eugene P. Deputy Assistant Chief of Staff for CORDS (1970–1971).

Forsythe, Maj. Gen. George I. Assistant Deputy to the COMUSMACV for CORDS (1967–1968).

Foulk, Col. J. D. Assistant Chief of Staff G-2, II Field Force, Vietnam (1968).

Franklin, Col. Louis B. (USAF) Deputy Chief, MACV Studies and Observations Group (1970).

Fritz, Mr. Carl R. Assistant Deputy for CORDS, 1st Corps Tactical Zone (1969–1970).

Frizen, Brig. Gen. John E. (USAF) MACV J-6 (1968–1969).

Fuller, Col. II Field Force, Vietnam, G-3 (1968).

Funkhouser, Mr. Richard. Deputy for CORDS, MR-3 (1970–1972).

Fuson, Maj. Gen. Jack C. MACV J-4 (1972–1973).

Galloway, Brig. Gen. James V. MACV Assistant Chief of Staff for Military Assistance (1968–1969).

Gerrity, Col. John L. Office of MACV J-5 (1969–1970).

Gettys, Maj. Gen. Charles M. USARV Chief of Staff (1970–1971).

Gibson, Col. Billy P. (USAF) Deputy Chief, MACV Studies and Observations Group (1969–1970).

Gilbert. See Gillert.

Gillert, Col. Gustav J., Jr. MACV Deputy Science Advisor (1968–1969).

Gleason, Col. Robert L. (USAF) Deputy Chief, MACV Studies and Observations Group (1968–1969).

Goodpaster, Gen. Andrew J. Deputy COMUSMACV (1968–1969).

Gorman, Col. Paul F. U.S. Negotiating Team, Paris peace talks (1968–1969).

Greene, Brig. Gen. Lawrence V. MACV J-1 (1970–1971).

Greer, Col. Howard W. MACV Headquarters Commandant (1970–1971).

Gunn, Brig. Gen. Frank L. MACV Assistant Chief of Staff for Military Assistance (1969–1970).

Haines, Gen. Ralph E., Jr. Army Vice Chief of Staff (1967–1968). CINCUSARPAC (1968–1970).

Hamlet, Brig. Gen. James F. ADC, 101st Airborne Division (1971), and CG, 3rd Brigade, 1st Cavalry Division (1971–1972).

Hanifen, Col. Thomas G. MACV Secretary of the Joint Staff (1969–1970).

Hardin, Maj. Gen. E. C. (USAF) Vice Commander, Seventh Air Force (1970–1971).

Healy, Col. Michael D. CO, 5th Special Forces Group (1969–1971).

Heiser, Brig. Gen. Joseph M., Jr. CG, 1st Logistical Command (1968–1969), and DA Deputy Chief of Staff for Logistics (1969–1972).

Heiser, Brig. Gen. Rolland V. MACV Deputy J-3 (1971–1972).

Henderson, Brig. Gen. David S. MACV Deputy Assistant Chief of Staff for CORDS (1970).

Henion, Brig. Gen. John Q. Director, MACV Training Directorate (1970–1971), and Special Assistant to the COMUSMACV (1971).

Henkin, Mr. Daniel. Assistant Secretary of Defense (Public Affairs) (1970).

Herbert, Brig. Gen. James A. Deputy Assistant Chief of Staff for CORDS (1971–1972).

Hill, Brig. Gen. L. Gordon, Jr. MACV Chief of Information (1969 and 1971).

Hinton, Col. R. J. Director, MACV Psychological Operations Directorate (1968–1969).

Hofmann, Col. Office of MACV J-3 (1969–1970).

Hollingsworth, Maj. Gen. James F. Deputy CG, XXIX Corps (1971), and CG, Third Regional Assistance Command (1971–1972).

Hollis, Maj. Gen. Harris W. Deputy CG, I Field Force, Vietnam (1968–1969).

Holt, Col. (1970). Not further identified.

Horrocks, Col. John T. (USAF) MACV Deputy J-4 (1971–1972).

Houseworth, Col. J. Edward. MACV Deputy Science Advisor (1971–1972).

Hudson, Brig. Gen. Charles F. (1972). Position not identified.

Jackson, Col. George. Office of MACV J-5 (1969).

Jacobson, Mr. George D. MACV Assistant Chief of Staff for CORDS (1969–1972) and Deputy to the COMUSMACV for CORDS (1972).

James, Mr. Hatcher M., Jr. Deputy for CORDS, MR-2 (1970–1971).

Jaskilka, Brig. Gen. Samuel. (USMC) MACV Deputy J-3 (1969–1970).

Johnson, Brig. Gen. (1972). Not further identified.

John, Brig. Gen. Ernest F. (USAF) Deputy Chief of Staff for Intelligence, Seventh Air Force (1971–1972).

Jones, Maj. Gen. (and earlier Brig. Gen.) (1969). Not further identified.

Jones, Col. John G. MACV Secretary of the Joint Staff (1970–1971).

Jumper, Maj. Gen. Jimmy J. (USAF) MACV J-5 (1971–1972).

Keegan, Brig. Gen. George J., Jr. (USAF) Deputy Chief of Staff, Intelligence, Seventh Air Force (1968–1969).

Kerwin, Col. (1969–1970). Not further identified.

Kerwin, Lt. Gen. Walter T., Jr. MACV Chief of Staff (1967–1968) and CG, II Field Force, Vietnam (1968–1969).

King, Vice Adm. J. H., Jr. (USN) Commander, Naval Forces, Vietnam (1970–1971).

Kirk, Mr. John E. MACV Science Advisor (1969–1971).

Knepp, Col. Lester J. Deputy Director, MACV Training Directorate (1971–1972).

Komer, Ambassador Robert W. Deputy to the COMUSMACV for CORDS (1967–1968).

Kraft, Brig. Gen. William R., Jr. MACV Deputy J-3 (1969–1970).

Kroesen, Maj. Gen. Frederick J., Jr. MACV J-3 (1970–1971) and Deputy CG, XXIV Corps (1971–1972).

Ladd, Mr. Jonathan F. (Fred). American Embassy, Phnom Penh (1970–1972).

Laird, Melvin R. Secretary of Defense (1969–1973).

Lanagan, Brig. Gen. W. F., Jr. (USMC) MACV Deputy J-3 (1971–1972).

Lavelle, Gen. John D. (USAF) Deputy COMUSMACV for Air Operations and CG, Seventh Air Force (1971–1972).

Lazar, Mr. David. USAID (1971). Possibly Deputy for CORDS, MR-1.

Lemos, Rear Adm. William E. Director, Policy Planning Staff, OSD.

Leonard, Col. Robert W. MACV Chief of Information (1970–1971).

Long, Mr. Edward T. Deputy for CORDS, Second Regional Assistance Group (1970–1971).

Long, Brig. Gen. Glen C. MACV Deputy Assistant Chief of Staff for CORDS (1968–1969).

Ludwig, Col. Verl E. (USMC) MACV Deputy Chief of Information (1970–1971).

Mabry, Maj. Gen. George L., Jr. Assistant Deputy CG and Chief of Staff, USARV (1969–1970).

Mahl, Col. Floyd D. (USAF) MACV Deputy J-2 (1970–1971).

Maples, Maj. Gen. Herron N. MACV J-4 (1970–1972).

Marlette, Mr. Veto J. USAID (1972). (Possible identification.)

Marshall, Lt. Col. Donald. Chief of Long-Range Planning, MACV J-5 (1968–1969).

Marshall, Maj. Gen. Winton W. (USAF) Vice Commander, Seventh Air Force (1971–1972).

Martin, Col. D. K. MACV Deputy J-6 (1970).

Matthews, Rear Adm. Herbert S., Jr. (USN) Deputy Commander, Naval Forces, Vietnam (1970–1971).

McCaffrey, Lt. Gen. William J. Deputy CG, USARV (1970–1972).

McCain, Adm. John S., Jr. (USN) CINCPAC (1968–1972).

McCann, Mr. Michael G. USAID (1972).

McClellan, Brig. Gen. Stan L. Director, MACV Training Directorate (1971–1972).

McCown, Maj. Gen. Hal D. Deputy CG, II Field Force, Vietnam (1969–1970), and CG, Delta Military Assistance Command (1970–1971).

McCutcheon, Lt. Gen. Keith B. (USMC) CG, III Marine Amphibious Force (1970).

McDaniel, Lt. Col. Albert W. Assistant Deputy Chief of Staff for Economic Affairs (1971).

McDonald, Col. (1972). Not further identified.

McGiffert, Brig. Gen. John R., II. Deputy Commander, Third Regional Assistance Command (1971–1972).

McLaughlin, Brig. Gen. J. N. (USMC) MACV Deputy J-3 and Director, Combat Operations Center (1968–1969).

McManus, Rear Adm. P. S. (USN) Commander, Naval Support Activity, Saigon (1971).

McMillan, Dr. W. G. MACV Science Advisor (1966–1969).

McNulty, Captain W. J. (USN) MACV Deputy Assistant Chief of Staff for Military Assistance (1969).

Megellas, Mr. James. Deputy for CORDS, I Field Force, Vietnam (1969–1970).

Michaelis, Gen. John H. CINC, U.S. Forces, Korea (1969–1972).

Mildren, Lt. Gen. Frank T. Deputy CG, USARV (1968–1970).

Miller, Col. Daniel L. MACV Deputy J-6 (1971).

Milloy, Maj. Gen. Albert E. Deputy CG, XXIV Corps (1970–1971).

Momyer, Gen. William W. (USAF) Deputy COMUSMACV for Air Operations and CG, Seventh Air Force (1966–1968).

Moorer, Adm. Thomas (USN) Chairman, Joint Chiefs of Staff (1970–1974).

Nazzaro, Gen. Joseph J. (USAF) CINC, Pacific Air Forces (1969–1971).

Newman, Mr. Ray D. USAID (1970). Provisional identification.

Nickerson, Lt. Gen. Herman, Jr. (USMC) CG, III Marine Amphibious Force (1969–1970).

Norris, Col. William J. Office of MACV J-4 (1972).

Nutter, G. Warren. Assistant Secretary of Defense (International Security Affairs) (1970).

Packard, David. Deputy Secretary of Defense (1969–1971).

Packer, Capt. S. H. (USN) MACV Deputy Assistant Chief of Staff for Military Assistance (1970).

Palmer, Desmond. Accompanied Sir Robert Thompson on visits to Vietnam.

Peers, Lt. Gen. William R. CG, I Field Force, Vietnam (1968–1969).

Penuel, Col. V. B., Jr. MACV Deputy J-6 (1969).

Perez, Capt. Raul B. (USN) MACV Deputy J-5 (1971) and MACV J-5 (1972).

Peterson, Maj. Gen. (1969). Not further identified.

Phillips, Col. W. E. MACV Deputy Science Advisor (1970–1971).

Pink, Col. J. T. MACV Secretary of the Joint Staff (1968).

Polgar, Thomas. CIA Chief of Station, Saigon (1972–1973).

Portaluppi, Col. Charles J. (USAF) Director, Intelligence Division, MACV Studies and Observations Group (1971).

Potts, Maj. Gen. William E. MACV J-2 (1969–1972).

Powers, Col. P. W. MACV Secretary of the Joint Staff (1969).

Presson, Col. David R. Office of MACV Studies and Observations Group (1971–1972).

Price, Rear Adm. A. W. (USN) Deputy Commander, Naval Forces, Vietnam (1971–1972).

Pursley, Brig. Gen. Robert E. (USAF) Military Assistant to the Secretary of Defense (1966–1972).

Ramsey, Col. E. L. MACV Deputy J-5 (1968–1969).

Rasmussen, Maj. Gen. Henry A. MACV J-4 (1967–1969).

Rectanus, Capt. Earl F. (USN) Assistant Chief of Staff, Intelligence, Naval Forces, Vietnam (1968–1969).

Resor, Stanley R. Secretary of the Army (1965–1971).

Richardson, Maj. Gen. Walter B. Deputy CG, II Field Force, Vietnam (1968–1969).

Roberts, Col. Sam A. (USAF) MACV Deputy J-2 (1967–1969).

Robertson, Lt. Gen. Donn J. (USMC) CG, III Marine Amphibious Force (1970–1971).

Roseborough, Maj. Gen. Morgan G. Chief of Staff, MACV/USARV Support Command (1972).

Rosson, Gen. William B. CG, I Field Force, Vietnam (1968–1969), and Deputy COMUSMACV (1969–1970).

Russ, Maj. Gen. Joseph R. Deputy CG, I Field Force, Vietnam (1969–1970).

Sadler, Col. John F. Chief, MACV Studies and Observations Group (1970–1972).

Salzer, Rear Adm. Robert S. (USN) Commander, Naval Forces, Vietnam (1971–1972).

Schweiter, Maj. Gen. Leo H. USARV Chief of Staff (1971–1972).

Scott, Brig. Gen. (1971–1972). Not further identified.

Shackley, Theodore G. CIA Chief of Station, Saigon (1970–1971).

Shaefer, Maj. Gen. Richard F. (USAF). MACV J-5 (1968–1970).

Shiflet, Col. K. E. MACV Deputy J-6 (1968).

Sidle, Maj. Gen. Winant. MACV Chief of Information (1967–1969).

Singlaub, Col. John K. Chief, MACV Studies and Observations Group (1966–1968).

Slay, Maj. Gen. Alton D. (USAF) Assistant Deputy Chief of Staff for Operations, Seventh Air Force (1971–1972).

Slusar, Lt. Col. Peter. MACV Provost Marshal (1971).

Smith, Col. (1969). Not further identified.

Smith, Brig. Gen. Albert H., Jr. MACV J-1 (1969–1970).

Starry, Col. Donn A. Office of MACV J-3 (1969) and CO, 11th Armored Cavalry Regiment (1969–1970).

Stevens, Col. Phillip H. MACV Chief of Information (1971–1972).

Stewart, Col. (1969–1970). Not further identified. Could be Stuart.

Stilwell, Lt. Gen. Richard G. CG, XXIV Corps (1968–1969).

Suerstedt, Rear Adm. Henry S., Jr. (USN) Deputy Commander, Naval Forces, Vietnam (1970).

Sutherland, Lt. Gen. James W., Jr. CG, XXIV Corps (1970–1971).

Sweat, Brig. Gen. Dale S. (USAF) Director of Combat Operations, Seventh Air Force (1968).

Sykes, Col. (and then Brig. Gen.) George K. Deputy Chief of Staff for Intelligence, Seventh Air Force (1969–1970).

Taber, Brig. Gen. Robert C. USARV Assistant Deputy CG and Chief of Staff (1968).

Tabor, Brig. Gen. Harry E. Assignment and dates not identified.

Tarpley, Maj. Gen. Thomas M. CG, Delta Regional Assistance Command (1972).

Thompson, Sir Robert. British counterinsurgency authority and consultant to President Nixon on Vietnam.

Todd, Col. W. Russell. MACV Secretary of the Joint Staff (1970).

Tompkins, Maj. Gen. Rathvon McC. (USMC) Deputy CG, III Marine Amphibious Force (1968).

Townsend, Maj. Gen. Elias C. MACV J-3 (1968–1969) and MACV Chief of Staff (1969–1970).

Trogdon, Brig. Gen. Floyd H. (USAF) MACV J-6 (1971–1972).

Vande Hey, Brig. Gen. James M. (USAF) MACV Deputy Chief of Staff (1969–1971).

Vann, Mr. John Paul. Deputy for CORDS, II Field Force, Vietnam (1968–1969). Deputy for CORDS, Delta Military Assistance

Command (1969–1971). Director, Second Regional Assistance Group (1971–1972).

Veth, Rear Adm. Kenneth L. (USN) Commander, Naval Forces, Vietnam (1967–1968).

Vogt, Gen. John W. (USAF) Deputy COMUSMACV for Air Operations (1972).

Wagstaff, Maj. Gen. Jack J. Deputy CG, Third Regional Assistance Command (1971–1972).

Watkin, Maj. Gen. William W., Jr. MACV Deputy Chief of Staff for Economic Affairs (1970–1972).

Watkins, Brig. Gen. James H. (USAF) Chief, Air Force Advisory Group (1971–1972).

Wear, Brig. Gen. George E. Deputy Senior Advisor, MR-2 (1970–1972).

Weeks, Col. (1970). Not further identified.

Wetherill, Maj. Gen. Roderick. Assistant Deputy to COMUSMACV for CORDS (1968–1969) and CG, Delta Military Assistance Command (1969–1970).

Weyand, Gen. Frederick C. CG, II Field Force, Vietnam (1967–1968). JCS Representative to the U.S. Negotiating Team, Paris peace talks (1969–1970). Deputy COMUSMACV (1970–1972). COMUSMACV (1972–1973). Army Vice Chief of Staff (1973–1974). Army Chief of Staff (1974–1976).

Wheeler, Gen. Earle G. Chairman, Joint Chiefs of Staff (1964–1970).

Wheeler, Maj. Gen. Edwin B. (USMC) Deputy CG, XXIV Corps (1969–1970).

Wheelock, Brig. Gen. John G., III. MACV Deputy J-3 (1968–1969).

Whitehouse, Mr. Charles S. Deputy for CORDS,

II Field Force, Vietnam (1969–1970). Deputy U.S. Ambassador to the Republic of Vietnam (1972–1973).

Wickham, Brig. Gen. John A., Jr. MACV Deputy Chief of Staff for Economic Affairs (1971–1972). U.S. Army Chief of Staff (1983–1987).

Wikner, Dr. N. F. MACV Science Advisor (1969).

Wilson, Maj. Gen. Joseph G. (USAF) Deputy Chief of Staff for Operations, Seventh Air Force (1971–1972).

Wilson, Mr. Wilbur. Deputy for CORDS, Delta Regional Assistance Command (1970–1972).

Wolfe, Brig. Gen. (1972). Not further identified.

Woodward, Maj. Gen. Gilbert H. MACV Chief of Staff (1972).

Worley, Maj. Gen. Robert F. (USAF) Vice Commander, Seventh Air Force (1967–1968).

Yates, Brig. Gen. Elmer P. MACV Director of Construction (1969–1970).

Young, Maj. Gen. Robert P. MACV Director of Construction (1971–1972).

Zais, Lt. Gen. Melvin. CG, XXIV Corps (1969–1970).

Zerbe, Col. Franklin E. (USAF) Deputy Chief, MACV Studies and Observations Group (1971–1972).

Zumwalt, Vice Adm. Elmo R., Jr. (USN) Commander, Naval Forces, Vietnam (1968–1970). Chief of Naval Operations (1970–1974).

APPENDIX 2

VIETNAMESE NAMED IN MEETINGS

NOTE: In some cases identifications, assignments, or tenures are tentative or incomplete due to lack of information or uncertainty as to the exact identity of some of those referred to on the tapes.

Binh, Madame Nguyen Thi. Provisional Revolutionary Government foreign minister and chief negotiator for the National Liberation Front at the Paris peace talks.

Cang, Vice Adm. Chung Tan. Republic of Vietnam Chief of Naval Operations (1959–1965 and 1975).

Canh, Brig. Gen. Vo Van. CG, 23rd ARVN Infantry Division (1968–1972).

Chau, Col. Tran Ngoc. ARVN officer and province chief who was charged with espionage because of contacts with his brother, a North Vietnamese intelligence officer.

Chinh, Truong. Democratic Republic of Vietnam official, senior member of the Politburo of the Vietnamese Communist Party.

Chon, Rear Adm. Tran Van. Republic of Vietnam Chief of Naval Operations (1957–1959 and 1966–1974).

Di, Maj. Gen. Tran Ba. CG, 9th ARVN Infantry Division (1968–1973).

Diem, Bui. Republic of Vietnam Ambassador to the United States (1967–1972).

Diem, Ngo Dinh. President of the Republic of Vietnam (1955–1963).

Diep [?], Col. [Nguyen Ngoc?]. Commandant at Con Son (1971).

Dinh, [Pham Van?]. ARVN battalion commander at Hamburger Hill.

Don, Gen. Tran Van. Republic of Vietnam senator (1967–1975) and, earlier, a senior army officer who played a leading role in the 1963 coup that overthrew President Diem.

Dong, Lt. Gen. Du Quoc. CG, ARVN Airborne Division (1964–1972), and CG, ARVN III Corps (1974–1975).

Dong, Pham Van. Democratic Republic of Vietnam premier (1950–1975).

Duan, Le. Democratic Republic of Vietnam secretary general of the Communist Party and, after the 1969 death of Ho Chi Minh, de facto leader of the DRV.

Dzu, Lt. Gen. Ngo. RVNAF JGS J-3 (1968?–1970). Later CG, ARVN IV Corps (1970) and ARVN II Corps (1970–1972).

Giai, Maj. Gen. Do Ke. CG, 18th ARVN Infantry Division (1966–1969), and CG, Ranger Command (1972–1975).

Giai, Brig. Gen. Vu Van. CG, 3rd ARVN Infantry Division (1971–1972). Earlier CO, 2nd ARVN Regiment (1966–1968).

Giap, Gen. Vo Nguyen. Democratic Republic of Vietnam minister of defense and chief military commander.

Hieu, Maj. Gen. Nguyen Van. CG, 5th ARVN Infantry Division (1969–1971). Earlier CG, 22nd ARVN Division (1966–1969).

Hoan, Tran Quoc. Democratic Republic of Vietnam director of Secret Police.

Ho Chi Minh. Democratic Republic of Vietnam president (1945–1969).

Huong, Tran Van. Republic of Vietnam premier (1968–1969), vice president (1971–1975), and acting president (briefly in April 1975).

Khang, Lt. Gen. Le Nguyen. RVNAF CG, Marine Division (1964–1972). At some times simultaneously CG, III Corps, and CG, Capital Military District.

Khiem, Tran Thien. Republic of Vietnam deputy prime minister for pacification (1969) and prime minister (1969–1975).

Khuyen, Lt. Gen. Dong Van. CG, RVNAF Central Logistics Command (1967–1975), and (concurrently) Chief of Staff, Joint General Staff (1974–1975).

Kiem, Tran Buu. National Liberation Front representative at the Paris peace talks.

Ky, Air Vice Marshal Nguyen Cao. Republic of Vietnam premier (1965–1967) and vice president (1967–1971).

La, Lt. Gen. Nguyen Van. Deputy Chairman, RVNAF Joint General Staff, for Pacification and Development (1973?–1974).

Lam, Lt. Gen. Hoang Xuan. CG, ARVN I Corps (1968–1972).

Lam, Tran Van. Republic of Vietnam foreign minister (1969–1973) and chief negotiator at Paris peace talks.

Lan, Lt. Gen. Lu Mong. CG, ARVN II Corps (1968–1970). Previously CG, 25th ARVN Infantry Division (1962–1964), CG, 23rd ARVN Division (1964–1965), and CG, 18th ARVN Infantry Division (1965–1966). Referred to as General Lu Lan.

Lien, Col. [?]. Commander, ARVN 24th Special Tactical Zone, in 1968.

Loc, Lt. Gen. Vinh. CG, ARVN II Corps (1965–1968). Subsequently Director, Training Command (1968–1970) and Commandant, National Defense College (1968?–1973?). Referred to as General Vinh Loc.

Luan, Maj. Phan Ngoc. CO, 1st Battalion, 3rd ARVN Regiment [dates?].

Lung, Col. Hoang Ngoc. RVNAF JGS J-2 (1971–1975).

Luong, Maj. Gen. Le Quang. CG, ARVN Airborne Division (1972–1975).

Manh, Maj. Gen. Nguyen Van. Chief of Staff, RVNAF Joint General Staff (1969–1974).

Minh, Gen. Duong Van. Officer who played a key role in the 1963 coup that overthrew President Diem, then was part of the triumvirate that ruled briefly until it was in turn overthrown. Served as the Republic of Vietnam's president in the final few days of April 1975. Often referred to by Americans as "Big Minh" to distinguish him from Lt. Gen. Nguyen Van Minh, or "Little Minh."

Minh, Lt. Gen. Nguyen Van. CG, 21st ARVN Infantry Division (1965–1968) and ARVN III Corps (1971–1973). Referred to by the Americans as "Little Minh."

Minh, Lt. Gen. Tran Van. Commander, South Vietnamese Air Force (1967–1975).

Nam, Maj. Gen. Nguyen Khoa. CG, 7th ARVN Infantry Division (1970–1973), and CG, ARVN IV Corps (1974–1975).

Nghi, Lt. Gen. Nguyen Vinh. CG, ARVN IV Corps (1972–1974).

Nghia, Col. Ngo Tan. ARVN Binh Thuan province chief (1969–1975).

Nhieu, Brig. Gen. Do Kien. Mayor of Saigon (1970–1975).

Phong, Lt. Gen. Tran Thanh. RVNAF JGS J-3 (1965–1967). Later JGS Chief of Staff (1967–1968), then minister of revolutionary development (1969–1971), director of the National Police (1971), and Deputy CG, ARVN II Corps (1972).

Phu, Maj. Gen. Pham Van. CO, ARVN 44th Special Tactical Zone (1968–1970), and CG, 1st ARVN Infantry Division (1970–1972) and ARVN II Corps (1974–1975).

Quang, Lt. Gen. Dang Van. Republic of Vietnam minister for planning and development (1966–1968). Special assistant to the president for military affairs and security (1968–1975). Formerly CG, ARVN IV Corps (1965–1966).

Quat, Dr. Phan Huy. Republic of Vietnam premier (1965).

Sung, Vo Van. Delegate general of the Democratic Republic of Vietnam to France.

Tam, Lt. Gen. Tran Ngoc. Chief, FWMAF Work Committee (1964–1970).

Tha, Col. [?]. Province chief. Dates include 1971.

Than, Brig. Gen. Le Van. CG, 1st ARVN Infantry Division (1972–1973).

Thang, Lt. Gen. Nguyen Duc. Republic of Vietnam minister for revolutionary development (1965–1967). Also briefly CG, ARVN IV Corps (1968).

Thanh, Maj. Gen. Nguyen Viet. CG, ARVN IV Corps (1968 until his death in a helicopter crash in May 1970).

Thiep, Col. Pham Ngoc. RVNAF J-2 (1968–1971).

Thieu, Gen. Nguyen Van. President of the Republic of Vietnam (1967–1975).

Thinh, Lt. Gen. Nguyen Xuan. CG, 25th ARVN Infantry Division (1968–1972).

Tho, Le Duc. Democratic Republic of Vietnam negotiator at Paris peace talks.

Thuan, Lt. Gen. Pham Quoc. CG, 5th ARVN Infantry Division (1965–1969), and CG, ARVN III Corps (1973–1974).

Thuy, Xuan. Democratic Republic of Vietnam chief negotiator at the Paris peace talks.

Tien, Nguyen Van. Provisional Revolutionary Government acting chief delegate to the Paris peace talks (1971).

Toan, Lt. Gen. Nguyen Van. CG, 2nd ARVN Infantry Division (1967–1972). Later CG, ARVN II Corps (1972–1974) and ARVN III Corps (1975).

Tri, Lt. Gen. Do Cao. CG, ARVN III Corps (1968 until his death in a helicopter crash in February 1971).

Trien, Maj. Gen. Le Ngoc. CG, 22nd ARVN Infantry Division (1969–1972).

Trinh, Nguyen Duy. Democratic Republic of Vietnam foreign minister.

Truong, Lt. Gen. Ngo Quang. CG successively of 1st ARVN Infantry Division (1966–1970), ARVN IV Corps (1970–1972), and ARVN I Corps (1972–1975).

Tu, Brig. Gen. Le Van. CG, 25th ARVN Infantry Division (1972–1973).

Vien, Gen. Cao Van. Chief, RVNAF Joint General Staff (1965–1975).

Vy, Lt. Gen. Nguyen Van. Republic of Vietnam minister of defense (1967–1972).

Xuyen, Gen. Nguyen Huu. Deputy Commander, NLF Liberation Army.

Yen, Col. Lu. ARVN province chief of Phuoc Long Province. (Dates include 1971.)

GLOSSARY OF SELECTED TERMS, ACRONYMS, AND ABBREVIATIONS

AA   antiaircraft
AAA   antiaircraft artillery
ABF   attack by fire
ack-ack   antiaircraft artillery
ACR   armored cavalry regiment
ADC   assistant division commander
ADM   admiral
AFB   air force base
AFN   Armed Forces Network
AFRS   Armed Forces Radio Service
AID   Agency for International Development
AIM   air intercept missile
Amb.   ambassador
AMC   Army Materiel Command
ANGLICO   air and naval gunfire liaison company
AO   area of operations
AP   Associated Press
APC   Accelerated Pacification Campaign
APC   armored personnel carrier
ARA   aerial rocket artillery
Arc Light   B-52 bomber strike
ARDF   airborne radio direction finding
ARVN   Army of the Republic of Vietnam
ASP   ammunition supply point
ASW   antisubmarine warfare
ATT   annual training test
AW   automatic weapon
AWOL   absent without leave
AX   developmental fighter aircraft

BA   base area
BAR   Browning automatic rifle
Barrel Roll   air operations in northern Laos
BDA   bomb damage assessment

BG   brigadier general
binh tram   military way station on the Ho Chi Minh Trail
BLT   battalion landing team
BT   *binh tram*

CAP   combat air patrol
CAP   combined action platoon
CAS   close air support
CAS   Controlled American Source (Central Intelligence Agency)
cav   cavalry
CBU   cluster bomb unit
C&C   command and control
C3   communications, command, and control
C3I   communications, command, control, and intelligence
CDEC   Combined Document Exploitation Center
CDLD   Community Defense and Local Development
CEP   circular error probability
CG   commanding general
Chicom   Chinese Communist
Chieu Hoi   program to induce ralliers to the GVN
CIA   Central Intelligence Agency
CICV   Combined Intelligence Center, Vietnam
CIDG   Civilian Irregular Defense Group
CINC   Commander in Chief
CINCPAC   Commander in Chief, Pacific
CINCPACAF   Commander in Chief, Pacific Air Force
CINCPACFLT   Commander in Chief, Pacific Fleet

CINCSAC   Commander in Chief, Strategic Air Command

CINCUSARPAC   Commander in Chief, U.S. Army, Pacific

CIS   CORDS Information System

CJCS   Chairman, Joint Chiefs of Staff

claymore   directional antipersonnel mine

CMAC   Capital Military Assistance Command

CMD   Capital Military District

CMEC   Combined Matériel Exploitation Center

CMIC   Combined Military Interrogation Center

CNO   Chief of Naval Operations

CO   commanding officer

COC   combat operations center

COL   colonel

College Eye   E-121 operations for detection of MiG flight activity

Combat Apple   RC-135 orbiting reconnaissance missions

COMINT   communications intelligence

Commando Hunt   annual dry season campaign of air interdiction in the Laotian panhandle

Compass Link   satellite circuit for transmission of high-resolution photography

COMSEC   communications security

COMUS   Commander, U.S. Military Assistance Command, Vietnam

COMUSMACV   Commander, U.S. Military Assistance Command, Vietnam

COMNAVFORV   Commander, Naval Forces, Vietnam

CONUS   Continental United States

CORDS   Civil Operations and Revolutionary Development Support (later Civil Operations and Rural Development Support)

COS   Chief of Station, CIA

COSVN   Central Office for South Vietnam (enemy)

CP   command post

CPX   command post exercise

CRIMP   Consolidated Republic of Vietnam Armed Forces Improvement & Modernization Program

CS   combat support

CS   type of tear gas

CSS   combat service support

CSW   crew-served weapon

CTZ   corps tactical zone

CVA   aircraft carrier

CY   calendar year

DA   Department of the Army

Daniel Boone   U.S. Special Forces cross-border operations in Cambodia

DAO   Defense Attaché Office

DASC   Direct Air Support Center

DATT   defense attaché

DCG   deputy commanding general

DCS/Ops   Deputy Chief of Staff for Operations

DEPCOMUS   Deputy Commander, U.S. Military Assistance Command, Vietnam

DEPCOMUSMACV   Deputy Commander, U.S. Military Assistance Command, Vietnam

DEPCORDS   Deputy to the Commander, U.S. Military Assistance Command, Vietnam, for Civil Operations and Revolutionary Development Support

DEROS   date eligible to return from overseas

DIA   Defense Intelligence Agency

DIOCC   District Intelligence and Operations Coordination Center

DMAC   Delta Military Assistance Command

DMZ   Demilitarized Zone

DOD   Department of Defense

DRAC   Delta Regional Assistance Command

DRV   Democratic Republic of Vietnam (North Vietnam)

DSA   district senior advisor

DSC   Distinguished Service Cross

DTA   division tactical area

DTOC   Division Tactical Operations Center

dust-off   aeromedical casualty evacuation

DZ   drop zone

ECM   electronic countermeasures

EENT   end evening nautical twilight

ELINT   electronic intelligence

EW   early warning

FAC   forward air controller

FANK   Forces Armées Nationales Khmères (Khmer National Armed Forces)

FAR   Forces Armées Royales (Royal Lao Armed Forces)

FARK   Forces Armées Royales Khmères (Royal Khmer Armed Forces)

FBIS   Foreign Broadcast Information Service

FFORCEV   Field Force, Vietnam

FFV   Field Force, Vietnam

FM   field manual

FMFPAC   Fleet Marine Force, Pacific

FRAC   First Regional Assistance Command

Freedom Deal   U.S. Air Force bombing in Cambodia

FSB   fire support base

FSCC   Fire Support Coordination Center

FWMAF Free World Military Assistance
  Forces
FY fiscal year

GAO General Accounting Office
GCI ground-controlled intercept
GDRS General Directorate of Rear Services
GEN general
GVN Government of Vietnam (South Vietnam)

H Time zone in which Vietnam is situated
  (e.g., 2015H)
HAC Headquarters Area Command
HARM high-speed antiradiation missile
HE high explosive
HES Hamlet Evaluation System
H&I harassment and interdiction (artillery fire)
Highest Authority euphemism for president of
  the United States
Hoi Chanh rallier under the Chieu Hoi pro-
  gram
HQ headquarters
HUMINT human intelligence

ICC International Control Commission
ICCS International Commission of Control and
  Supervision
ICEX Intelligence Coordination and Exploita-
  tion
ICG Intelligence Coordination Group
IFF identification, friend or foe
IFR instrument flight rules
IG inspector general
I&M improvement & modernization
IO information officer
IR improved rice
IR infrared
IR intelligence report
Iron Hand suppression of surface-to-air mis-
  siles and gun-laying radar
Island Tree program of targeting troops infil-
  trating down the Ho Chi Minh Trail (as dis-
  tinct from targeting matériel)
IW individual weapon

JCS Joint Chiefs of Staff (U.S.)
JGS Joint General Staff (RVNAF)
JUSPAO Joint U.S. Public Affairs Office

KBA killed by air
KIA killed in action

LAW light antitank weapon
LGB laser-guided bomb

LLDB Luc Luong Dac Biet (South Vietnamese
  Special Forces)
LNO liaison officer
LOC line of communications
LOH light observation helicopter
LORAN long-range electronic navigation
LRRP long-range reconnaissance patrol
LSA logistic support area
LST landing ship, tank
LTC lieutenant colonel
LTG lieutenant general
LZ landing zone

MAAG Military Assistance Advisory Group
MAC Military Airlift Command
MACCORDS Military Assistance Command
  Civil Operations and Revolutionary Develop-
  ment Support
MACEA Military Assistance Command, Eco-
  nomic Affairs
MACSOG Military Assistance Command
  Studies and Observation Group
MACTHAI Military Assistance Command,
  Thailand
MACV Military Assistance Command,
  Vietnam
MAF Marine Amphibious Force
MAJ major
MALT mobile advisory logistical team
MAP Military Assistance Program
Market Time coastline surveillance and inter-
  diction of seaborne infiltration
MARS Military Affiliate Radio System
MASF Military Assistance, Service Funded
MAT mobile advisory team
MAW marine aircraft wing
MEDCAP Medical Civic Action Program
medevac medical evacuation
MEDT Military Equipment Delivery Team
MG major general
MIA missing in action
MiG Soviet fighter aircraft
mm millimeter
MOS military occupational specialty
MP military police
MPC military payment certificate (scrip)
MR military region
MRDF medium-range direction finding
MR-TTH Military Region Tri-Thien-Hue
  (enemy)
MSTS Military Sea Transportation Service

NATO North Atlantic Treaty Organization
NAVFORV Naval Force, Vietnam (U.S.)

NCO   noncommissioned officer
NDC   National Defense Committee (NVN)
NGF   naval gunfire
NGFS   naval gunfire support
NLF   National Liberation Front (VC)
NMCC   National Military Command Center
NP   National Police
NPFF   National Police Field Force
NSA   National Security Agency
NSC   National Security Council
NSSM   National Security Study Memorandum
NVA   North Vietnamese Army
NVN   North Vietnam/North Vietnamese

O&M   operations and maintenance (budget element)
OPLAN   operations plan
OPSEC   operational security
OR   operational readiness
OSA   Office of the Special Assistant (U.S. Mission–CIA)
OSCG   Operational Support Coordination Group
OSD   Office of the Secretary of Defense

PA&E   Pacific Architects & Engineers
PACAF   Pacific Air Force
PACFLT   Pacific Fleet
PACOM   Pacific Command
Paveway   laser-guided bomb
PAVN   People's Army of Vietnam (North Vietnam)
PDJ   Plaine des Jarres (Laos)
PDO   Property Disposal Office
PERT   Program Evaluation and Review Technique
PF   Popular Forces
PFF   Police Field Forces
PFIAB   President's Foreign Intelligence Advisory Board
Phoenix   program for neutralizing VCI (U.S. term)
Phuong Hoang   program for neutralizing VCI (RVN term)
PIOCC   Province Intelligence and Operations Coordination Center
PLAF   People's Liberation Armed Forces
PMDL   Provisional Military Demarcation Line
POL   petroleum, oil, and lubricants
POW   prisoner of war
Prairie Fire   small-scale ground interdiction of the Ho Chi Minh Trail
PRC   People's Republic of China

PRG   Provisional Revolutionary Government (Viet Cong)
PROVN   Program for the Pacification and Long-Term Development of Vietnam
PRU   Provincial Reconnaissance Unit
PSA   province senior advisor
PSDF   People's Self-Defense Force (formerly Popular Self-Defense Force)
PW   prisoner of war

RADM   rear admiral
rallier   enemy who comes over to the GVN side in the Chieu Hoi program
RD   Revolutionary Development
RDC   Revolutionary Development cadre
RF   Regional Forces
RHAW   radar homing and warning
RLAF   Royal Laotian Air Force
RLG   Royal Lao Government
RLT   regimental landing team
RNO   results not observed (of air strikes)
ROE   rules of engagement
ROK   Republic of Korea (South Korea)
ROKFV   Republic of Korea Forces, Vietnam
Rolling Thunder   air operations over North Vietnam
Route Package 1   a designated area in North Vietnam for the Rolling Thunder bombing campaign (other adjacent areas were designated 2 through 5, 6A and 6B, often referred to as, for short, Route Pack 1 etc.)
RP   route package
RPG   rocket-propelled grenade
R&R   rest and recreation
RRU   Radio Research Unit
RVN   Republic of Vietnam
RVNAF   Republic of Vietnam Armed Forces

SA   senior advisor
SAC   Strategic Air Command
SACSA   Special Assistant for Counterinsurgency and Special Activities (to the Joint Chiefs of Staff)
SAM   surface-to-air missile
SAME   Senior Advisors' Monthly Evaluation
SAR   search and rescue
SASC   Senate Armed Services Committee
SEA   Southeast Asia
SEACORDS   Southeast Asia Coordinating Committee for U.S. Missions (also rendered as SEACOORDS)
SEAL   Sea, Air, Land (USN)
SEATO   Southeast Asia Treaty Organization
SECARMY   secretary of the army

SecDef   secretary of defense

sector   military equivalent of a province

SEER   System for Evaluating the Effectiveness
  of RVNAF

SF   Special Forces

SGS   Secretary of the General Staff

SIGINT   signals intelligence

SIOP   single integrated operational plan

SJS   Secretary of the Joint Staff

SKS   Communist-bloc 7.62-mm carbine

SLAR   side-looking airborne radar

SLF   Special Landing Force

SOG   Studies & Observation Group

SPECAT   special category

SR   subregion

SRAC   Second Regional Assistance Command

SRAG   Second Regional Assistance Group

SSO   special security officer

Steel Tiger   air interdiction in the Laotian panhandle

subsector   military equivalent of a district

SVN   South Vietnam

tac air   tactical air

Tally Ho   air interdiction of the area above the
  DMZ

TAOI   tactical area of interest

TAOR   tactical area of responsibility

Tet   Vietnamese Lunar New Year

TF   task force

TOC   tactical operations center

TO&E   table of organization & equipment

TOT   time on target/time over target

TOW   tube-launched, optically tracked, wire-
  guided (antitank missile)

TRAC   Third Regional Assistance Command

TSF   transitional support force

TSN   Tan Son Nhut (Air Base) (Saigon)

UI   unidentified

UN   United Nations

UPI   United Press International

U.S.   United States

USA   U.S. Army

USAF   U.S. Air Force

USAID   U.S. Agency for International Development

USARPAC   U.S. Army, Pacific

USARV   U.S. Army, Vietnam

USCG   U.S. Coast Guard

USDAO   U.S. Defense Attaché Office

USG   U.S. Government

USIA   U.S. Information Agency

USIS   U.S. Information Service

USMACV   U.S. Military Assistance Command,
  Vietnam

USMC   U.S. Marine Corps

USN   U.S. Navy

USSAG   U.S. Support Activities Group

USSR   Union of Soviet Socialist Republics

VA   Veterans Administration

VADM   vice admiral

VC   Viet Cong

VCI   Viet Cong infrastructure

VIS   Vietnamese Information Service

VN   Vietnam *or* Vietnamese

VNAF   Vietnamese Air Force

VNMC   Vietnamese Marine Corps

VNN   Vietnamese Navy

VR   visual reconnaissance

WIA   wounded in action

WIEU   Weekly Intelligence Estimate Update

INDEX

Abrams, Gen. Creighton W.
  on Accelerated Pacification
    Campaign, 49, 128, 264,
    373, 474-75
  on advice received, 339,
    349
  on advisors, 23-24, 56, 212,
    831
    improving quality, 325
    reducing number, 115
    shifting quality, 380, 393
    steadfastness needed,
      339
    training, 392-93
  on airborne capabilities,
    237, 278, 354, 396
  on air control, 267
  on air operations, 120-21,
    142, 151-52, 275, 293,
    340, 379, 384-85, 473,
    487, 499
  on allied casualties, 54
  on Alsop, 260
  on Americans, 524-25
  on ammunition expendi-
    tures, 61-62
  on antiwar movement in
    U.S., 125, 189, 210, 347,
    410
  on area security concept,
    207-208, 209
  on ARVN forces
    advising, 106-107
    casualties, 183
    confidence, 508
    deficiencies, 329

desertions, 44, 176
equipment and support,
  12, 16, 48, 56, 215
getting credit, 194-95,
  344
improving, 181
KIA sustained, 131
leadership, 106, 109,
  229, 243, 291, 294,
  371, 574-75
manpower, 176, 208,
  291, 297
operations, 21
outlook of leaders, 83-
  84, 237-38
performance, 45, 114,
  169, 180, 190, 195,
  237, 282, 291, 414
planning proficiency,
  276
Popular Forces, 126,
  224, 291-92
reorganizing, 169
roles and missions, 283
tactics, 114, 246
training, 292-93
on atrocities, 326
on Australians, 241
on authorities, 384-85
on barbed wire, 400, 774-75
on battles, unimportance of,
  252, 266, 327, 407
on B-52s, use of, 11, 16, 18,
  60, 112, 169-70, 357,
  486-87
on body count, 43, 172,

363, 382, 401
on bombing, 58-59, 133
on bombing halt effects,
  396-97
on book *Court Martial*, 571
on border camps, 386
on budget issues, 390
on Bu Prang incident, 382-
  83
on cache seizures, 162, 170,
  171, 172, 179, 190, 243,
  280
on Cambodia, 77, 442
  armed forces perform-
    ance, 472
  and ARVN after incur-
    sion, 424
  and Communist doctrine,
    430-31
  and enemy intentions,
    430
  incursion into, 429-430,
    527
  protecting civilians, 179,
    374, 382
  self-defense, 508
  vulnerability, 478
  and Washington, 489
career before Vietnam,
  xviii-xix
on casualties, avoidance of,
  175, 198, 250, 301, 566
on casualties, civilian, 213
on casualties, friendly, 399
on casualties, impact of,
  193

continued

on chain of command, 624-26, 645-47

on charts, 407

on Chieu Hoi, 351-52

on Coca-Cola, 472

on Colby, 55, 64, 233, 243

on collateral damage, reducing, 468-69, 485

on command relationships, 338, 349, 372-73

and CINCPAC, 339-41, 650-51

on Communist doctrine, 431

on Communists, 388-89

on complaints from Vietnamese, 489

on conduct toward villagers, 285-86

on C-141s, 602

on control of people, 413

on COSVN Resolution 9, 264-65, 471, 476

on cross-border operations, 161, 162

on cultural problems, 470-71

on decorating a goose, 704

on Demilitarized Zone, 56-57, 71, 104-105, 111, 189-90, 245-46, 385

on Devil the dog, 639

on Dien Bien Phu, 411

on discouragement, 201, 209, 354

on domestic U.S. politics, 39-40, 42

on disposition of allied forces, 11

on the draft, 126

on drug abuse, 499-500, 607, 623, 625

on economy measures, 35-36

on elections in RVN, 520, 524

on the enemy, 8-9, 10, 108, 359, 413, 477, 480, 487

antitank weapon, 243

attacks by fire, 75-76

base areas, 18, 153

cadre and guerrillas, 68

capabilities, 337

casualties, 214, 268

characteristics, 58, 265

communications inter-cepts, 349

dealing with Communists, 189

deficiencies, 101

dispositions, 27-28

domestic military requirements, 136

force structure, 44-46, 255-56

General Giap, 33-34, 352-53, 744

guerrillas, 120, 260, 278, 484

high points, 527

indiscipline, 44

infiltration, 57, 219, 224-25, 225-26, 249, 263, 298, 300-301, 471, 476

influence in U.S., 210, 301

intentions, 465

leadership in Hanoi, 33

logistics accomplishments, 116, 119, 159, 361

logistics "nose," 15, 62-63, 74, 111

logistics requirements, 113

manpower, 266, 300, 466, 476

NVA in South Vietnam, 68, 261, 266, 347

operating on multiple levels, 397-98

pattern analysis, 72

perseverance, 228-29, 501

planning proficiency, 84

preparations, 305

problems, 227, 240

propaganda, 55, 57, 125, 136, 176, 219

reaction to pacification, 280

sappers, 248

Sihanoukville, use of, 215, 228, 247, 285

situation, 33

staying power, 44

structure, 101, 103, 284

supply lines, 77

system, 29, 53, 56, 59, 103, 112, 152, 160-61, 211, 217, 228-29, 243, 260, 352-53,

391, 392, 394-95, 465

tactics, 41

terrorism, use of, 15, 17, 251-52, 290, 363-64, 426, 442, 471, 488, 489, 521

Viet Cong infrastructure, 46, 61, 63-64, 106, 397, 488

withdrawals from RVN, 112, 183

on equity, 782-83

on excesses, 390-91

farewell from Bunker, 877-78

on fire support bases, 279

on the French, 219, 503

on GVN effectiveness, 215-16, 268

on Hamburger Hill, 187, 194

on Harriman, 227, 246, 250-51, 389

on helicopter turned in, 179

on helping too much, 633

on herbicides, 380, 499

on inevitability of criticism, 187

on infantry manning levels, 223

on infiltration, 27, 219

on intelligence, 114, 188, 193, 242-43, 245, 263, 275, 506

on interdiction, 178, 239, 293, 356-57, 362, 371, 487, 511

on internal dissent, 378

inviting input, 49, 118, 159, 192, 362, 504, 729, 793, 842

on Khe Sanh, 129, 558

on Khiem, 158

kill ratio and firepower, 20

on Komer, 793

Korea and Vietnam compared, 339, 658

on Korean War, 26, 31-32, 62, 658

on Ky, 516

on Laird, 375

on Lam Son 719, 542, 545-46, 549, 550, 558, 562, 570, 583, 589, 657

on Lang Vei, 129

on Laos, 122, 174, 189, 239, 259, 348-49, 372,

389, 393-94, 434
on leadership, 355-56
on leaks, 378
on logistics, 35-36, 275
on MACV reorganization, 524-25
on maintaining combat readiness, 319, 369, 566, 611
on maintaining interest, 342
on maintaining secrecy, 632
on marines, 539
on McNamara, 363
on the media, 8, 13-14, 34, 57, 110, 126, 127, 128, 137, 161, 194-95, 214, 236-37, 315, 344, 358-59, 359-60, 378, 394, 428, 481-82, 484, 530-31, 536, 789
on mission as COMUS-MACV, 338
on Montagnards, 471, 520, 740
on My Lai, 347
on nature of the war, xix, 3, 57, 116–17, 127, 252, 281, 329, 343, 344, 354, 363, 382, 397-98, 477-78, 493, 497-98, 541, 561, 562
on naval operations, 275, 472
on New Zealanders, 241
on Nixon, 240, 311, 312, 329, 538, 593, 849
on the North Vietnamese, 351
"One War" concept, 19, 300, 360-61
on opportunities lost, 412
on opportunity available, 481, 489-90
on OPSEC, 346, 349, 470-71
on optimism, 214, 489-90
on order of battle, 304, 305
on organizing disaster, 298
on pacification, 16, 86, 166-67, 188, 192-93, 240, 268, 273-74, 278, 279, 281, 288, 295, 315, 327, 342-43, 345, 349-50, 352-53, 382, 489, 521, 572
on Paris peace talks, 29, 57, 214

on Patton, 292-93
on People's Self-Defense Force, 264, 290, 303, 350, 368, 398, 493, 506, 507
on perceptions, 194
on perseverance, 345
on Phoenix, 264, 353, 520
on Phong, 561
on the Pig Rule, 387, 571
on the Plaine des Jarres, 340
on police, 220, 252, 259, 350-51, 520, 521
on political leaders, 277
on political warfare, 126, 127-28
on population security, 260, 273
on preemption, 25, 27, 32-33
on press conferences, 410
on prisoner abuse, 594
on progress, 214-15, 265, 339, 475, 480, 493, 498, 520, 521, 539-40, 570, 572
on promotions, 416
on protective reaction, 277
on psychological warfare, 436, 587
on pursuit, 178
on racial disharmony, 209, 267, 355, 379-80, 499-500
on redeployment, 162, 184, 187, 210, 233, 234-35, 236, 237, 283-84, 305, 347-48, 360, 364, 379, 498, 617-18
on regroupment, possible, 388
on reinforcing disaster, 527
on relationship with ambassador, 338-39
on reporting, 26
on reserve component forces, 42-43
retrospective view, 617
on RF/PF, 69
   acknowledging accomplishments, 282, 346
   advocating, 290
   assisting, 267-68
   contributions of, 347, 471
   effectiveness, 363, 368

equipping, 252, 264, 329
expansion, 274
importance of, 350-51
and mobile advisory teams, 115
modernization, 264
performance, 172, 176, 195, 228, 247, 266, 282, 294, 345, 508, 510-11, 547
versus ARVN, 283
on retaliatory techniques, 131
on road security, 179
on ROK forces, 12, 16, 17, 241, 339, 498
on rules of engagement, 77-78, 374, 384-85
on RVNAF I&M, 186, 347, 374-75
on RVN politics, 26
on Saigon, 125, 252, 351
on security, 246, 378
on self-promotion, 344, 378
on Sergeant Greenschmidt, 322-23, 325, 327, 349, 368, 490
on service as Deputy COMUSMACV, 338
on service in horse cavalry, 276-77
on service as Vice Chief of Staff, 590-591
on service in World War II, 289-90, 840
on Shackley, 116
on shifting talent, 368, 380
on "signals," 254, 385, 502
on Sihanouk, 68, 347
on situation in 1965, 373
skepticism, 403
on soldier behavior, 285-86, 291, 300, 315-16, 355, 541, 624
on soldiers, 540
on soldiers' influence, 28-29, 35-36, 271
on the South Vietnamese, 242, 243, 276, 287, 330, 339, 347, 355, 370-71, 478, 541, 565, 620, 640-41
on spoiling attacks, 22
on standards, 625
on statistics, 127, 195
on strategic initiative, 264
on success defined, 397-98

continued
on Sullivan, 116
on supply accountability, 437
surgery, 448
on tactical air, 112, 271
on tactics, 23, 62-63, 64,
67-68, 74, 75, 83, 114,
172, 246-47, 275
tape recorded, 830
on Tchepone, 262
on Tet 1968, 55, 194, 255,
264
on Thai forces, 241-42
on Thieu, 361-62, 373, 376,
444, 493, 519, 520, 742
on Thompson, 284-85
on Thompson book, 259,
285
on Tri, 114–15
on the troops, 209-10
on Truong, 574-75, 639
on "Understandings," 104,
122, 245-46, 250-51
on unit newspapers, 327
on U.S. embassy Vientiane,
174, 175
on U.S. government, 219
on U.S. public opinion, 192,
236-37, 766
on U.S. troops, 107, 254
on Vann, 346
on VCI, 195
on veterans, 473
on Vietnamese, dealing
with, 236
on Vietnamese politics, 125
on Vietnamization, 279,
565, 568
on visiting the field, 27
on visitors, 505
on VNMC, 472-73
on warning, 23, 28
on Washington climate, 425
on Washington directives,
437–39
on Washington outlook, 435
on Weyand, 504
on WIEU coverage, 18, 19,
46-47, 67, 75, 82, 114,
128-29, 182, 253, 261,
294, 352, 386, 441, 474,
476, 479, 480, 497-98,
683
on Zumwalt, 69
Abrams, Lt. John, 179
Accelerated Pacification Campaign, 49, 177, 373, 825

per Colby, 122
described, 105-106
effects of Tet 1969 offensive, 177
enemy attacks on, 108, 120,
128, 238
enemy propaganda about,
108, 177
goals, 105-106
plan for 1969, 105-106
plans compromised, 108
status at end 1968, 96-97,
98
and Thieu, 376
per Vann, 50
Acheson, Dean, 425
Advisors, 23-24
enlisted, 618-19, 783
level of effort involved, 65
overaggressive, 238
phased reduction, 504
unsuited, 325-26
AFN (Armed Forces Network),
111
Agnew, Spiro, 469
Aiken, Sen. George, 271
Air operations
aircraft losses, 317, 837
antiaircraft forces, 317
Arc Light (B-52) strikes, 6,
11
per Abrams, 11, 16, 18,
101, 105
as Abrams's "artillery,"
59
as Abrams's "strategic
reserve," 113, 142
allocations, 151, 293
of base areas, 112
in Cambodia, 225
compromised, 180, 426,
470
Congress, U.S., and, 746
diverts, 26
effects on enemy, 19
effects of stopping, 55,
74, 76, 84, 92-93, 98,
103, 170-71, 249,
262-63
against Ho Chi Minh
Trail, 96, 103, 104,
119, 495, 581-82
intelligence, 242-43
in Laos, 157, 160, 169-
70
level of effort, 35
during mini-Tet, 39

operational security, 180,
763-64
psychological effects,
141
resumed in NVN, 751
and road watch teams,
116
per Rosson, 13
sortie rates, 242, 267,
269, 272
targeting, 379
per Weyand, 12
authorities, 384-85, 591,
637, 654
available forces, 456
avoiding civilians, 427
Barrel Roll, 317
CBUs, 157
Commando Hunt, 95, 96
Abrams's view, 112, 356
comparative assessment,
356-57
gunship effects, 356
sorties, 356
Commando Vault bomb,
508-509
C-141s, 602
contributions, 620
flying hours program, 499
gunships, 496
helicopter losses, 424
importance,613-14
Lavelle case
air power employment,
782
authorities required, 748-
49, 753-55, 780, 781,
799
Lavelle relieved, 819
MiG/SAM threat data,
742, 768-69, 799,
804-805, 807, 809-
10, 857, 873
sensor issue blowup, 787
level of effort, 534-535
MiG threat, 515-16, 680,
684
Paveway, 126
protective reaction, 384-85,
677
and redeployments, 432-33
rules of engagement, 327-
28, 364, 384-84, 591
SAM threat, 327, 337, 364,
384-85, 553, 584, 627,
675, 722, 726, 800, 822,
831, 837

smart bombs, 852
sorties available, 495
tactical air
  against Ho Chi Minh
    Trail, 103
  allocations, 151, 256
  in Laos, 259
  sortie rates, 269, 303
  target box system, 495-96,
    501, 503, 509, 524, 575-
    76, 638
  trolling, 190, 198, 328, 627
  truck kills, 523, 524, 528,
    531-32, 534, 540-41,
    561, 563, 594-95, 612,
    615, 629, 638, 641-42,
    677, 757
Alsop, Joseph
  on guerrilla forces, 254
  on forces in I Corps, 259-60
  on formality with Abrams,
    260
  revealing infiltration intelli-
    gence, 130, 214, 226,
    395
  on VNAF, 686, 701
Americal Division. See 23rd
  Infantry Division (U.S.)
Anderson, Jack, 571
ARMCO, 456
Army of the Republic of
  Vietnam (ARVN)
  capabilities, 256
  casualties sustained, 131
  combat support, 256
  compared with U.S. units,
    256
  deficiencies, 176-77, 229
  desertions, 44, 176
  effectiveness, 12-13
  expansion, 164
  helicopter support, 151
  leadership, 229, 573-74
  manpower, 176
  M-16 rifles for, 69
  mobile reserve, 82
  performance, 6, 21
  in politics, 574
  saturation operations, 524,
    562, 663, 744
  shortfalls in U.S. support of,
    12, 16, 48, 56
  tactics, 397
  unit fill, 221
Arnett, Peter, 432, 433-34
A Shau Valley, 26
  first entry since 1965, 135

forces positioned there, 240,
  246
Operation Dewey Canyon
  in, 162
Australian forces, 241
Autumn 1969 Campaign, 254

Barnes, Brig. Gen. John W.,
  300
Barsanti, Maj. Gen. Olinto M.,
  21, 511
Be, Col. Nguyen, 459, 790
Beal, Under Secy. Thaddeus
  R., 376
Beech, Keyes, 8
Berger, Samuel D.
  on cross-border operations,
    161-62
  on the French, 503
  on redeployments, 253
  on retaliatory measures, 133
Betts, Commander, 108
B-52 strikes. See Bombing,
  Arc Light
Blazey, Brig. Gen. Frank E.,
  816
Blue Ribbon Defense Panel,
  335-36, 338-41
Body count, 43, 181, 420
Bonesteel, Gen. Charles H.,
  III, 245-47
Brady, Phil, 759
Braestrup, Peter, 8
Bray, Cong. William G., 343-
  44, 432
Brown, Gen. George S.
  on BDA, 278
  on bombing halt, 85
  on bombing in Laos, 157
  on enemy vulnerabilities,
    65-66
  on interdiction, 275
  on pacification, 389
  performance per Abrams,
    275
  on reporting, 65
  on retaliation, 190
  on rules of engagement,
    190, 327-28
  on SAM threat, 327
  on sortie rates, 267, 272
  on tactics, 66
  on trolling, 190, 198, 328
  on truck interdiction, 108
  on U.S. objectives, 65-66
Brown, Harold, 109

Bruce, Amb. David K. E., 454-
  60
Bunker, Amb. Ellsworth
  on Acheson outlook, 425
  briefing for Laird, 142-48
  on cross-border operations,
    161
  on enemy negotiating
    prospects, 141
  farewell to Abrams, 877-78
  on MACV accomplish-
    ments, 100
  on the media, 564
  on Nixon, 425
  optimism, 154
  on situation in U.S., 315
  on the South Vietnamese,
    100
  sums up 1968, 97-100
  on Thieu, 97, 145
  on U.S. situation, 425
  on West Point, 425
  on Yale Class of 1916, 650
Burroughs, Larry, 759

Cache seizures, 129, 211, 248,
  263, 280, 304, 352, 387,
  414, 416, 423
  Abrams on importance,
    131, 152, 162, 170, 280
  per Bunker, 217
  in Cambodia, 447, 450,
    455-56
  near Cambodian border,
    180
  and intelligence, 243
  in Lam Son 719, 533, 535,
    539
  by marines, 153
  in Operation Dewey
    Canyon, 142, 156
  in Plaine des Jarres, 269,
    745
  in Quang Tri, 228
  Rang Rang cache, 361, 379,
    381
  rice, 170, 399, 414, 667
Cahn, Col. Vo Van, 318-19,
  354-55
Ca Lu, 110
Cambodia
  after the incursion, 424
  allied operations on border,
    78
  armed forces, 422, 436,
    451, 510

continued
    attacking Communist units, 342
    bombing in, 427, 443, 463
    border incidents, 379
    cache seizures in, 447
    and Communist claims, 360
    and Communist intentions, 460, 603
    cooperation with RVNAF, 181, 184, 187, 451
    cross-border operations in, combined, 408-409, 412, 414-15, 417, 421, 422-23, 429-30, 445-46, 447, 453, 455, 463, 527
    cross-border operations in, potential, 82-83, 131-32, 132-33, 139-40
    cross-border operations in, RVNAF, 402-403, 442-43, 464, 497, 509, 520, 523, 524, 534
    enemy casualties, 464
    enemy LOCs, 110
    enemy objectives in, 602
    and FARK operations, 342
    Hanoi's view, 400
    incursion benefits, 746
    Lon Nol heart attack, 533
    and Matak, 342, 360, 383-84, 533
    NVA in, 429
    policy change, 387
    restrictions, 461-62, 463
    situation, 364, 377-78
    supplying Communists, 105, 383-84
    and VC along border, 74
Camp Carroll, 110, 400
Cang, Vice Adm. Chung Tan, 794
Carroll, Lt. Gen. Joseph P., 37
Carter, Lt. Gen. Marshall S., 37, 188
Case, Sen. Clifford, 653
Cavanaugh, Col. Stephen E., 41, 438-39
Cease-fire, 107, 149, 216
Central Highlands, 9
Chapman, Gen. Leonard F. Jr., 244-45, 336-37
Chau case, 389-90
Chesarek, Lt. Gen. Ferdinand J., 109-115
Chieu Hoi program, 86, 135
    decline, 598, 614

goals and achievements, 97, 273, 330, 459, 540
from IV Corps, 135, 187
motivating factors, 140, 253, 304, 423-24, 474, 540
numbers, 263, 304, 351, 387
RF/PF as stimulus, 330
China, People's Republic of, 175, 538
Chinh, Truong (DRV), 51, 253-54
Chon, Commodore/Rear Admiral Tran Van, 186, 276
Civilian Irregular Defense Group (CIDG), 22
Civil Operations and Revolutionary Development Support (CORDS), 52
Clay, Brig. Gen. Frank B., 119
Clay, Gen. Lucius B. Jr., 627
Clifford, Clark, 42, 138
Colby, William E.
    on Abrams, 460
    and Accelerated Pacification Campaign, 50
    back at CIA, 751
    on changing nature of the war, 456-57, 483-84
    CORDS briefing, 52
    becoming CORDS deputy, 59
    on cross-border operations, 162
    on enemy cadre, 55
    on enemy logistics, 66
    on enemy reassessment, 80
    on enemy situation end 1968, 86
    fluency in French, 233
    on French legacy, 460
    re Fulbright Committee, 389
    on pacification plan for 1969, 62
    on Phoenix program, 381, 389
    praised by Abrams, 507
Combined Campaign Plan AB/145 for 1970, 286-87
Communist forces
    activity, level of, 522
    after 1968 bombing halt, 84, 85, 92-93

area designations, 240-41, 477, 745
artillery, 560
assessment, comprehensive, 505-506, 602-603, 604
attacks by fire, 75-76, 165, 167, 200, 450
base areas, 18-19, 135, 136, 155-56
and bombing of DRV, 117
border sanctuaries, 110
cadre, 55, 68
capabilities, 117
casualties, 79, 135, 159, 182-83, 198, 214, 221, 244, 262, 303-304, 351, 387, 454
COMINT, acquiring, 346, 469-71
cost of, 447
crossover point, 295
decline of, 656
disaggregating, 492, 495
dispositions, 135, 197, 346
expectations, 197-98
factions in Hanoi, 253-54
false reporting, 17-18, 37, 40, 138, 178, 238-39, 290-91
famine, 501
force structure, 44-46, 255-56, 258, 288
guerrillas, 260, 405
high points, 191, 200, 304, 336, 450, 495
hospitals, 119, 180, 229
indiscipline, 522
intentions assessed, 54, 56, 71, 91-94, 117, 142, 193, 219, 263, 352
leadership in Hanoi, 33
logistical accomplishments, 66, 92-93, 95-96, 103-104, 116, 119, 135, 379, 461
logistical difficulties, 58, 68, 73, 94, 121
logistics "nose," 15, 62-63, 71, 135
logistics requirements, 113, 506
lulls in offensive operations, 6, 8, 31, 38, 42
manpower resources, 65, 135, 159, 196, 220, 449-50, 453, 466, 491, 506
motivations assessed, 54

NVA in South Vietnam, 48,
68, 140, 163, 209, 258,
260, 261, 346, 347, 406,
454, 789, 791, 803
objectives, 32, 117, 133,
695
orders, 108, 405-406
perseverance, 44, 228-29
pipelines, 254, 262, 263,
427, 599, 637
in the Plaine des Jarres,
739-40
POL, 254, 262, 428, 784-
85, 786, 857, 859
politburo, 253
and popular uprising in
RVN, anticipated, 117
preemption, 62-63
prisoners held by RVN
refuse repatriation, 656
problems, 47, 303, 411
propaganda, 134, 136, 171,
298, 302, 779-80
proposed prisoner release,
86, 87
rail lines, 262
recruitment, 134, 140, 213,
466, 583, 770
rockets, accuracy of, 171
and sanctuaries, 413
sappers, 163-64, 248, 263,
557, 561
shadow supply system, 501,
530
sickness, 247
situation assessed, 10-11,
33, 266
strategy, 397, 602-603, 604-
606
strategy, change of, 110,
196-98, 216-17, 404,
405, 450, 455, 458, 477
strength. See Intelligence,
order of battle
supply lines, 92-93
supported by China and
USSR, 170, 263, 453,
483, 490
system, 29, 53, 59, 137
tactics, 41, 450, 455
targeting American will,
244
terrorism, use of, 15, 17,
135, 273, 363-64, 399,
404, 458, 464, 479, 521,
615, 660, 676
training base, 53

trucks, 254, 379, 532
unit manning, 121, 255-56,
258, 288, 455
use of Sihanoukville, 85-86,
94-95, 135-36
and U.S. public opinion,
265
U.S. withdrawal, speeding,
133-34
Viet Cong, 260, 789
Viet Cong infrastructure
(VCI), 46, 63-64
view of Nixon administra-
tion, 216
viewed by Abrams, 8-9, 10,
15
warfare at multiple levels,
794
withdrawals from South
Vietnam, 75, 92, 93, 112
See also Viet Cong infra-
structure (VCI)
Congress, U.S., 644, 803
Cook, Col. Robert M., 767
Cooper, Charles, 438
Cooper-Church amendment,
434, 445-46, 543
Conroy, Maj. Gen. Raymond
C., 158
Con Thien, 65
Conyers, 210
Corcoran, Lt. Gen. Charles A.,
22-23, 61
COSVN
characterized by Ewell,
208-209
documents analyzed, 708-
10
headquarters, 156, 416
COSVN Resolution 8, 134,
263
COSVN Resolution 9, 91
per Abrams, 264-65
briefing on, 263-64
captured lesson plan on,
263
changes from Resolution
8, 264
copy captured, 282
interpreted by Bunker,
305
per POW, 278
public release, 316-17
summarized, 268, 278-
79, 450
translating, 316, 317-1
COSVN Resolution 14,

404-405, 482
location, 136, 426
region, 336, 601
Cronkite, Walter, 795-96
Cu Chi, 74
Cunningham, Col. Hubert S.,
343
Cushman, Maj. Gen. John H.,
693, 732
Cushman, Lt. Gen. Robert E.
Jr., 50, 100, 115

Daniel Boone (operation), 78
Davidson, Maj. Gen. Phillip B.
per Abrams, 152
on Cambodian LOC, 79
on casualty reduction, 139
on cross-border operations,
139-40
departing as J-2, 187
on enemy training base, 53
on media, 79
evidence of military victory,
79
on improved intelligence,
59
on intelligence collection
conference, 69-70
on length of the war and
outcome, 139
on NVA in VC units, 163
on senior officials, 140
on strategic initiative, 139
on Westmoreland, 138
Davis, Maj. Gen. Raymond G.
aggressiveness, 111
assessed by Abrams, 111-12
artillery, use of, 110
mobility oriented, 110
tactics changed under, 111
Dawee, Air Marshal Chulalas-
apya, 217
Delta Force, 100
Demilitarized Zone (DMZ)
enemy activity near, 71
enemy violations, 100, 245-
46
fighting there, 56
retaliatory authority, 131
Democratic Republic of
Vietnam. See North
Vietnam
DePuy, Lt. Gen. William E.,
113
Devlin, 199
Dien Bien Phu, 277

Directive No. 34 (VC), 117
DMZ. *See* Demilitarized Zone
Don, Gen. Tran Van, 291
Draft (Selective Service), 126
Duc Lap, fighting at, 38, 43,
   45, 48, 53, 56
Dunning, Bruce, 814
Dzu, Lt. Gen. Ngo, 488, 574
   appointed corps com-
      mander, 493-94
   performance, 504-505, 801

Easter Offensive
   Abrams's assessment, 867-
      68
   advisors during, 831, 842,
      853 *See also*
      Hollingsworth, Kroesen,
      Vann
   air operations, 848
   air planning to repulse, 751,
      752, 772, 777, 781, 782
   alert conditions and, 781,
      783
   allied force disposition, 810
   allied losses, 812, 813, 828,
      837, 859, 860, 874
   assessment, interim, 798-
      99, 821-22, 823-24, 827-
      28, 860-62, 868-73
   attitude required, per
      Abrams, 762-63, 825-26,
      832
   authorities required, 750,
      753-55, 758, 769, 775-
      76, 780, 781, 798
   B-52 employment during,
      781, 782, 785, 807, 809-
      10, 814, 817-18, 826,
      829, 851, 852
   bombing NVN, resumption
      of, 813
   buildup of enemy prepara-
      tions for, 733, 740, 745,
      746, 750, 753, 798-99
   civilian contractors in, 831
   counterplanning for, 735,
      777
   Dzu relieved, 844
   early indicators of, 693,
      696, 725, 745, 752
   enemy atrocity, 823
   enemy expectations re, 743,
      757

enemy level of effort, 769,
   777, 803, 813, 834
enemy losses, 828, 876-77
enemy objectives in, 756-
   57, 819-21
enemy performance, 811
enemy strategy for, 747,
   765
general reserve and, 747
intelligence regarding, 741,
   758, 788, 839
Lam relieved, 833
Lavelle relieved, 819
and the media, 766-67, 779,
   789, 818
message, key, to Wash-
   ington, 753-56
Nixon per Abrams, 849
as NVA invasion, 791
offensive delayed, 789, 792-
   93, 798
ports mined in NVN, 848,
   849-50, 857
prescient Abrams observa-
   tions re, 633, 734, 741,
   777, 778-79
and redeployment, concurrent, 762, 828, 864-65,
   877
South Vietnamese perform-
   ance, 826, 829, 841-42
South Vietnamese prepara-
   tions, 758, 783
start of offensive, 781, 784,
   785, 788, 805, 808
and tanks, 835, 840
Thieu outlook on, 741
Toan in commander II
   Corps, 844
Truong to command I
   Corps, 833, 834
U.S. force augmentations,
   780-81, 815, 816, 824,
   862
and U.S. public opinion,
   766-67, 770, 778
U.S. role in, 758-59, 777,
   833
Vann killed, 867
and VNAF, 741, 747
weather, 812
Eckhardt, Maj. Gen. George
   S., 20, 25, 49, 69, 115
Edmunds, Amb., 649
18th Infantry Division
   (ARVN), 27, 45

Abrams on disbanding, 181
commanding general, 106
leadership change, 283
performance, 106, 166, 168,
   181-82, 195, 450
Elections
   assessed, 717
   "Big" Minh and, 652, 661,
      683
   per Bunker, 143, 650
   per Colby, 458-59
   Ky and, 666, 682-83
   MACV precautions, 666-67
   presidential in 1971, 515,
      524, 543, 654, 678
   reaction abroad, 682
   Thieu and, 661, 682
   validated, 682
   village and hamlet, 97, 106,
      122-23, 220, 303
Emerson, Gloria, 592
Emerson, Col. Henry E., 19
Enthoven, Alain, 59
Ewell, Lt. Gen. Julian J.
   on cease-fire possibilities,
      329
   on cross-border operations,
      161
   on permanent security, 78
   Saigon visit proposal, 396
   on tactical approach, 56
   on Vietnamese leadership
      changes, 236

FARK (Cambodian armed
   forces), 94, 95, 342
Fernandez, 591
5th Infantry Division (ARVN)
   briefing per Abrams, 299
   division commander, 106,
      299
   leadership change, 283
   performance, 106, 168,
      181-82, 251, 418, 450
   regimental commander
      (7th), 200
   and U.S. redeployments,
      232
5th Infantry Division (Mechanized) (U.S.), 25-26
Fire Support Base Ewell, 34
Fire Support Base Mary Ann,
   584
1st Cavalry Division (Airmobile) (U.S.), 18, 27
   against enemy system, 165

cache seizures, 112
fire support base, 195
and I Corps, 75
in Ia Drang, 72
moved to III Corps, 77, 78,
106, 111, 151, 153
performance, 318
tactics, 67, 78, 246-47
working with Vietnamese,
29
1st Infantry Division (ARVN),
13, 18, 27, 110, 128
against base areas, 77
commanders, 322
in Easter Offensive, 833,
858
effective population security, 75
in "One War," 117
OPSEC violations, 346
performance, 229-30, 230,
243, 294, 322, 467
prisoners (ARVN), use of,
229-30, 248
rotating through training,
292
Truong as commander, 258,
292, 467, 574-75
1st Infantry Division (U.S.), 4
and "One War," 117
supporting pacification, 166
tactics, 246-47
1st Marine Division (U.S.), 68,
70-71
Fiscal matters, 34-35, 91
Flanagan, Rear Adm. William
R., 212
Fonda, Jane, 788
4th Infantry Division (U.S.),
18, 54, 103
Abrams's counsel to, 394-
95
as contingency force, 131
deficiencies in tactics, 179,
394
small-unit operations, 101
Fraser, Hon., 396-99
French, the, 559
Fried, Joseph, 161
Friedheim, Jerry, 705
Froehlke, Robert F., 745-49
Fulbright Committee, 366, 389

Garth, Col. Marshall, 416
Gayler, Adm. Noel, 504

Gavin, James M., 139, 662
Gettys, Maj. Gen. Charles M.,
172
Giai, Maj. Gen. Do Ke, 106,
789
Giai, Col. Vu Van, 110
Giap, General Vo Nguyen
(DRV), 33-34, 51, 644
per Abrams, 352-53, 744
and artillery, 744
on Dien Bien Phu, 829
and factions in Hanoi, 253-
54
Godley, G. McMurtrie, 200,
372, 716
and bombing in Laos, 340,
676, 784
requesting B-52s, 348
speculates on enemy views,
243-44
visiting Vietnam, 240-44,
701-704, 784
Goodell, Sen. Charles, 302
Goodpaster, Gen. Andrew J.
on allied victory, 66
on B-52 effects, 60
on domestic politics, 42
endorses new tactics, 81
on enemy intentions, 34
on enemy logistics, 66
on enemy losses, 68-69
on 1st ARVN Division, 75
on infiltration intelligence,
37
on interdiction, 58
on Laos, 86
on media, 65
on negotiations, 40, 42
on Paris peace talks, 65
on Phoenix program, 66
on progress, 126
on Tet 1968, 162
rebukes Townsend, 80-81
on tactics, 64, 66-67, 68-69
on troop dispositions, 67
Graham, Billy, 107
Graham, James
allegedly convinced, 321
citing political reasons, 322
impending visit, 78
and enemy use of
Sihanoukville, 85-86,
120, 123, 168
Green, Marshall, 797-98
Gunships, 96, 109, 496, 836

Habib, Philip, 285, 288
Haig, Brig. Gen. Alexander M.
Haig Jr., 419-22
Haines, Gen. Ralph E. Jr.
charging faulty information,
420
visiting Vietnam, 30-35,
121-23, 188-91, 360-62,
460-61
Hak Ly Trucking Company,
94, 123
Hamburger Hill, 187, 194, 199
Hamlet, Brig. Gen. James F.,
795-96
Hamlet Evaluation System
(HES), 21
per Colby, 60
revised grading, 523
revised system (HES 70),
331, 407
Harriman, Averell, 40, 41-42,
107, 519
contentions disproved, 288
and infiltration "lull," 219
on Lam Son 719, 543
misrepresentation of enemy
withdrawals, 227, 246,
250-51, 856
presumed views on Laos,
214
and "Understandings"
exposed, 118, 856
Healy, Col. Michael, 533-34
Heiser, Brig. Gen. Joseph M.
Jr., 275
Helms, Richard, 493
Hemingway, [Brig.?] Gen., 552
Henkin, Daniel, 705
Herbicides, 380, 484-85, 497,
499
Hersh, Seymour, 767
Hertz, Mr., 297
HES (Hamlet Evaluation
System), 21, 60
per Colby, 367, 459, 497
beyond HES per Abrams,
698
new version (HES 70), 288,
331, 376
reaggregated, 614
running old and new in parallel, 288
validity, 177-78, 195, 366
Ho Chi Minh, 59, 253, 254
Ho Chi Minh Trail
interdiction efforts against,

continued
96, 103-104, 108
traffic flow, 92-93, 95, 103
trail loss estimated, 182
truck kills on, 104
Hoi Chanh. *See* Chieu Hoi
Hollingsworth, Maj. Gen.
James F., 731, 811, 816,
845-47
Horton, Capt. Barry, 485
Humphrey, Hubert H., 39-40
Huong, Tran Van, 145
Hurwitz (acting ambassador),
174

Ignatius, Paul R., 59-61
Infiltration, 4, 14, 17, 19, 21,
27, 41, 52-53, 61, 67, 68,
70, 91-92, 110, 128, 163,
170, 176, 197, 199, 210,
215, 258, 268, 278, 297,
302, 304, 318, 337, 358,
360, 381, 394, 395, 401,
402, 440, 460, 464, 466,
471, 476, 478, 481, 492,
494, 497, 500, 510, 516,
532, 546, 553, 576, 577,
593, 597, 627, 630, 635,
636, 650, 664, 669-70,
675, 678, 704, 707, 715,
721, 726, 733, 740, 743,
764, 775, 779, 784, 786,
793, 797, 801, 804, 816,
830, 837, 857, 860, 873
Abrams re analysis of, 219,
599-600
apparent lull in, 182, 183,
188-89, 214, 224
ARVN figures, 329
assessing, 432-33, 559
barge, 123
binh trams, 8, 218, 477,
599, 639, 667, 750, 774,
800
cadre return, 224
calculation of, 140
CINCPAC conference on,
54, 57
and collateral intelligence,
226
and COMINT, 225-26, 335-
36, 477
commo-liaison station T-10,
121
comparative figures, 223,
601

comprehensive account,
300-301
confidence in intelligence
on, 249, 320, 447, 450
cumulative, 452-53
deception operations, 342
defenses, 317, 352, 364
destinations, 454, 849
dispersion, 683
entry points, 262
and 559th Transportation
Group, 226, 247, 262,
289, 599, 750
gap groups, 30, 72, 320,
756, 794
intelligence breakthrough
on, 777
intercepts, multiple sources
of, 792
K groups, 426, 428, 441-42
through Laos, 86
letter suffix groups, 756
logistics, 376-77
loss of intercepts revealing,
36-37, 47, 187-88, 194,
196, 218, 225-26
and the media, 249, 465
numbering sequence, 696
organization for, 750
OSD figures, 328-29
pattern, 224
plan captured, 413
political significance of,
226-27
protection of, 495, 637, 800
QL prefix, 523
rail, 44
reduced, 298
reverse traffic, 218, 226,
238
resumed, 116, 188
road net, 486, 495, 800, 838
statistics, 386-87, 465
stragglers, 448
system, 129-30, 134, 155-
56, 249, 263, 495
suffix group numbers, 785
tonnage, 248
tracking, 225-26
trail losses, 214, 262, 299,
441-42, 491, 694
travel time, 298, 341, 432,
477, 583, 694, 769
trucks, 238, 248, 289, 349,
356-57, 400, 486, 502-
503, 609

validity of estimates of, 30,
777
waterborne, 387, 448, 599,
612-13, 637, 850-51
See also Island Tree
Intelligence
Abrams's use of, 69
ARDF, 462
from captured documents,
70, 239, 434
from CAS, 336
re cease-fire possibilities,
216
collection conference, 69-
70
Community in agreement,
128
coordination, 336
from defectors and ralliers,
34, 94, 289
on enemy intentions, 51
on high points, 239
order of battle
CIA estimates, 221
composition, 221
force structure, 255, 454
losses, 221, 262, 352
NVA proportion, 48, 68,
134, 140, 163, 209,
248, 251, 258, 261,
381, 405
problems, inherited, 305
strength, in-country, 134,
221, 225, 248, 251,
255, 258, 263, 303,
347, 381, 387, 583
importance of, 114, 245,
338
improvements, 59, 69-70,
263, 336
on infiltration, 36-37, 70,
129-30, 224-25
letter box number analysis,
72
from POWs, 39, 70, 94
radio intercepts, 84
responsibilities, 116
road watch, 116
sensors, 20
in DMZ, 816-17
evaluated, 862-64
along Ho Chi Minh
Trail, 96, 104, 229,
238, 356, 381, 595,
600, 609
in North Vietnam, 76
uses of, 198, 775

on Sihanoukville, 94, 120, 123-24
South Vietnam's agents, 20, 24-25, 53, 59, 70, 239
targeting, 38, 242-43, 357, 379
Thai view per Bunker, 217
at village level, 188
warming, 4, 22, 24, 28, 349, 397, 450, 455
on WIA/KIA ratio, 37, 142, 214, 220
Interdiction, 58
airpower contributions, 620
in autumn 1968, 73, 92
after 1968 bombing halt, 93, 95-96, 112, 178
assessing, 432-33
before Tet 1969 Offensive, 178, 293
before Third Offensive, 72-73
coordinated, 275
of dry season preparations, 119
effectiveness, 239, 362, 601
forcing enemy withdrawals, 112, 178, 183
frustrations, 103-104
getting Vietnamese involved, 683
impedance of flow, 73
in Laos, 76
intelligence and, 786-87
priorities, 495
at Quang Khe ferries, 118
sorties, 356, 371, 486, 492
during Summer Offensive 1969, 213
supply flow, 171
target box system, 495-96
trucks, 108, 238, 248, 289, 349, 352, 356-57, 786
waterborne, 77, 104
International Control Commission (ICC), 109
Island Tree, 688, 696, 703, 732-33, 734, 743, 749, 752, 773-74, 818-19

Jacobson, Col. George, 345-46, 376, 381
Jaffe, Dr. Jerome H., 649
Jason Group, 104
Javits, Sen. Jacob, 346-48, 363, 398

Johnson, Lyndon B., 140, 144, 145, 499
Johnson, U. Alexis, 101, 103-107
Jones, Phil, 795-96

Kahn, Herman, 207
Kalergis, Brig. Gen. James G., 18
Keegan, Brig. Gen. George J. Jr., 58, 72-73
Kennedy, Edward M., 199, 266, 614, 831
Kerwin, Lt. Gen. Walter T. Jr., 53, 64
    on Accelerated Pacification Campaign, 49-50
    and mentoring Lt. Gen. Tri, 56
    protecting RF/PF, 115
    re reducing advisors, 115
Khang, Lt. Gen. Le Nguyen, 20, 574, 790
Khe Sanh, 14-15, 17, 24, 33-34, 41, 57, 93
    and B-52 sorties, 60
    and feared loss, 65
    incoming artillery, 163
    and 304th NVA Division, 103
    slow artillery response, 129
    withdrawal from, 111
Khiem, Tran Thien, 157, 253, 274, 284
Khuyen, Lt. Gen. Dong Van, 749
Kiem, Tran Buu, 216
Kilgore, Maggie, 592-93
Kill ratios, 48
Kissinger, Henry, 132, 215
Kittihara, Mrs., 345
Kittikachorn, Prime Minister, 794
Komer, Amb. Robert W., 17, 505, 793, 825
    bafflement, 32, 48
    on bombing, 55
    on cease-fire, 40-41
    on infrastructure, 56
    mocked after departure, 108
    on pacification, 20, 21
    on press in the war,
    on strategic posture, 54
    on tactical matters, 41
    on Territorial Forces (RF/PF), 16
    on Tet 1968, 55

Kompong Son. *See* Sihanoukville
Korean War, 26, 31-32, 62
Kraft, Joseph, 100
Kroesen, Maj. Gen. Frederick J. Jr., 729, 805-806, 816, 834, 842-43
Ky, Air Vice Marshal Nguyen Cao, 373-74, 555, 717, 790, 794
Kyros, Cong. Peter, 654

La, Lt. Gen. Nguyen Van, 17, 429, 441, 507
Ladd, Jonathan F., 439-40, 449, 462
Laird, Melvin R.
    briefed by Bunker, 142-48
    first trip to Vietnam, 137, 138-39, 140-54
    need for a program, 141
    on B-52 psychological effects, 141
    problem with SFRC statement, 312-313
    statement to SFRC, 312-13
    on U.S. public's view of war, 125, 140-41
    on using available time, 141
    as viewed by Weyand, 517
    visiting Vietnam, 140-54, 365-71, 687-92
    on withdrawing troops, 138-39
Lam, Lt. Gen. Hoang Xuan, 114, 349, 429, 494, 573
    confidence, 749
    directing pacification, 157
    and President Thieu, 82
    relieved during Easter Offensive, 833, 834
Lam Son 719
    Abrams's coordination with Vien on, 554, 557, 558
    Abrams's views of, 542, 545-46, 549, 550, 558, 562, 563, 564-65, 568, 570, 583, 589, 657, 826
    aftermath of, 584, 585, 592, 608, 675, 702, 759
    air cavalry in, 567
    ARVN operations in Laos, 533, 534, 535, 539, 548, 549, 551-52, 563, 566, 567, 569-70
    ARVN withdrawals from Laos, 563, 564, 570, 575

continued

assessed by MACV, 607-608

aviation support crisis, 544-46, 562

basis for, 570, 579-80

B-52 support, 544-45, 580, 581-82, 582-83

Bunker's views of, 580, 586

caches seized, 533, 535, 539, 547, 566

calculated risk, 542

Cambodia, concurrent operations in, 534, 549

Clay views of, 585

command arrangements, 531, 552, 566-67

effects of, 600, 659, 660, 731, 800

enabled by Cambodian incursion, 724, 746

enemy antiaircraft, 543, 551

enemy anticipation of, 509, 525, 529, 530

enemy concern about NVN being attacked, 532, 547, 553, 721

enemy logistic reaction, 543, 550

enemy losses, 537, 543, 544, 550, 551, 552, 554-55, 557, 558, 563, 564, 566, 567, 568, 570, 576-77, 578, 635, 791

enemy new headquarters, 543, 547

enemy preempted by, 570-71, 637

enemy surprised by, 734

enemy troop reaction, 535-36, 538, 546, 547, 550, 552, 556, 562, 563, 567

French reaction to, 547

friendly losses, 537, 544, 551, 554, 557, 558, 563, 569

helicopter losses, 535, 537, 539, 540, 544, 549, 550, 558, 562, 566, 577, 585, 608

intelligence derived from, 583

and Khe Sanh, 531, 534, 557

Lam as commander, xx

McCaffrey, 545, 546

marines, 575

and media, 576, 586, 586-87, 759, 760, 806

objective, 537, 571

Operation Dewey Canyon II, 531

operations in RVN, complementary, 536-37

order of battle, 536, 538, 543, 547, 550, 551, 552, 553, 554, 566, 567

as part of larger scheme, 607

Phouma pro forma protest, 532-33

and pipeline, 536, 538-39, 567, 581, 599

press embargo and, 525-26, 528-29, 806

psychological impact of, 568, 569, 581

reinforcing MR-1 and, 528

Route 9 condition, 533

significance of, 537

support of South Vietnamese people for, 569, 581, 586, 598-99

surprise in, 746

Sutherland as senior advisor, 545-46

tac air support, 561, 581-82

tanks in, 547, 550, 551, 555, 559, 562, 566, 567, 577, 840

and targeting intelligence gained in, 567-568, 575, 751

and Tchepone, 563, 567, 580

Thieu's views of, 585-86

Thompson views of, 570

U.S. support, 539, 542, 568-69

Washington involvement, 542-43, 583

Weyand views of, 568, 576, 577, 578, 578-80, 581, 584, 585, 586

Lam Son 720, 587-89, 590

Lam, Tran Van, 125

Lang Vei, 129

Laos

air support in, 259, 303, 629

bombing in, 157, 174, 746

Chinese road building, 175, 320

Communist intentions in, 603-604

Communist logistics in, 175

and embassy ineptitude, 189, 239

embassy interference with bombing, 160, 169-70, 174, 199-200

enemy antiaircraft, 74

and Geneva Agreement, 389

and Godley on air support, 609-10

and Godley on enemy views, 243-44

as indefensible, 122

possible operations in, 100-101

and presidential press conference, 321

road watch teams in, 174, 200

Royal Lao Air Force, 541, 607

sons of leaders, 794

and tacit U.S.-USSR agreement, 86

temporary gains per Shackley, 280

Lavelle, Lt. Gen., 284

Lien, Col., 83-84

Lodge, Henry Cabot, 100

Logistics, xvii, 35, , 212-13

Long, Brig. Gen. Glen C., 295

Lon Nol

complicity in supplying Communists, 105, 217, 228

heart attack, 533

opposing Communists, 342

in Paris, 342

quintuple-hatted, 803-804

triple-hatted, 227-28

Lowenstein, James G., 521-22, 609

Luan, Maj. Phan Ngoc, 248-49

Lu Lan, Lt. Gen. Mong, 20, 43, 115, 573, 790

Lung, Col. Hoang Ngoc, 708

Luong, 337

Machine [Beaufea?] trucking company, 95, 123

Mahon, Cong. George, 444

Manh, Maj. Gen. Nguyen Van, 412, 794

Manpower, 115

Mansfield, Sen. Mike, 627-28, 645

Marine Corps (U.S.), 24, 111, 815
Marine Corps (Vietnamese), 833
Market Time, 76, 94, 95, 456
Marsh, Cong. John, 343
Marshall, Lt. Col. Donald, 201-209
Matak, Sirik, 342, 360, 367, 377, 384, 533
Mataxis, Brig. Gen. Theodore C., 716
McCaffrey, Lt. Gen. William J., 545, 546
McCain, Adm. John S. Jr., 44
    per Abrams, 340
    re abandoning responsibilities, 716
    advocates bending rules of engagement, 328
    on the media, 536
    re redeployment, 435-36
    on tactical nuclear weapons, 211
    visiting Vietnam, 43-44, 68-69, 77-78, 167-69, 211-12, 290-93, 327-28, 381, 418-19, 435-36l, 535-538, 613-14, 775-77
McCarthy, Sen. Eugene, 302
McCloskey, Rep. Paul, 592, 593-94
McCown, Maj. Gen. Hal D., 419, 422
McGovern, Sen. George, 302
McGovern-Goodell amendment, 445
McIntyre, Sen. Thomas, 427
McLaughlin, Brig. Gen. J. N., 78, 244-45
McMillan, W. G., 20
McNamara Line, 104, 651
McNamara, Robert S., 62, 138, 171
Media, 8, 13-14, 34, 65
    favoring amnesty, 764
    Anderson, Jack, 571
    backgrounding, 126
    per Bunker, 142, 576, 667
    CBS film, 795-96
    CBS overplaying, 127
    characterized, 460
    constrained, 475-76
    per Ewell, 266
    and GI view of Ho's successor, 254
    irresponsibility, 107

per Jacobson, 569
and Lam Son 719, 759
leaked classified information, using, 130, 214, 358-59, 395
and MACV policy, 110
misleading the enemy, 79
opposing the war, 236, 594
and statistics, 85
UPI overplaying, 127
Michaelas, Gen. John H., 293-97, 827-30
Midway meeting, 201, 215, 223-24
Mildren, Lt. Gen. Frank T., 17-18
Minh, Lt. Gen. Duong Van "Big," 291, 716-17
Minh, Lt. Gen. Nguyen Van, 319, 552-53, 544, 573
Minh, Lt. Gen. Tran Van, 790
Mini-Tet (May 1968), 31, 37-38, 43
    per Bunker, 144-45
    delayed, 110
    duration, 173
    enemy buildup for, 72
    enemy losses, 101, 110
    and the media, 127
    and 320th NVA Division, 54
Mission Council, 75-76
Mobile Advisory Teams (MAT), 115
Molinelli, Lt. Col. Robert F., 554
Montgomery, Cong. Sonny, 659
Moorer, Adm. Thomas H., 439
Moose, Richard M., 609
Moreton, Amb. J. O., 376
Morrissey, Cong., 362
M16 rifle
    for ARVN, 69, 106, 114-15, 212
    complete issue forecast, 456
    cost, 448
    decision to field, 28-29
    deliveries to Vietnam, 43
    PSDF self-equipping, 506-507
    for RF/PF, 16, 103, 115, 247, 252, 329
    ROK request for, 16
My Lai, 346-47

Nam, Maj. Gen. Nguyen Khoa, 749
National Liberation Front
    in Cambodia, 94
    GVN concern about, 98-99
    headquarters, 156
    and ICC, 109
Negotiations. See Paris peace talks
New Zealand forces, 241
Nhieu, Brig. Gen. Do Kien, 319
Nickerson, Lt. Gen. Herman Jr., 160, 380-81
9th Infantry Division (U.S.), 163
Nixon administration, 216
Nixon doctrine, 715
Nixon, Richard, 42, 240
    briefed by Abrams, 225
    changing COMUSMACV orders, 296
    and cross-border operations, 140
    election and GVN outlook, 98
    on infiltration, 296
    and Nixon Doctrine, 296
    praised by Abrams, 311, 312, 329, 538, 593
    praised by Bunker, 315, 425
    proactive on Vietnam, 132
    on redeployment, 296
    "Silent Majority" speech, 91, 295-297
    speech on Cambodian incursion, 410
    with Thieu, 240, 268
    and Thompson, 290
    on the "understandings," 297
    on U.S. casualties, 296
    on Vietnamization, 296
    visiting Vietnam, 225, 240
Noble, Frank, 275
North Vietnam
    contending leader outlooks, 51
    decision for Tet 1968, 79
    dependence on ports, 751
    intentions assessed, 79-80
    leaders characterized, 351
    reassessment in autumn 1968, 79
    and U.S. antiwar elements, 15
North Vietnamese Army, 4

NSSM-1, 118

Omega operations, 22
101st Airborne Division (U.S.)
  able assistant G-5, 326
  cache seizures, 112
  effective tactics, 67
  in "One War," 117
  performance, 652
  potential operations in
    Laos, 101
  sergeant working in village,
    322-23
  unsatisfactory briefing, 326
  working with Vietnamese,
    29, 70, 322, 471-72
173rd Airborne Brigade (U.S.),
    9, 103
  and airborne configuration,
    236
  as contingency force, 131
  and parachute operation,
    396
  supporting pacification, 260
  small-unit operations, 101
"One War" concept, 242
  per Abrams, 152-53, 168-
    69, 825
  per Bunker, 143
  per Colby, 105, 457
Ong, Ok Khiem, 217
Operation Dewey Canyon, 131,
    156, 160, 162
Operation Garrard Bay, 70-71
Operation Market Time, 76,
    94, 95
Operation Sea Lord, 77
Operations
  first combined campaign
    plan, 142
  Mobile Riverine Force, 76
  preemption, 25, 27, 32-33
  river patrol force, 76
  SLF unproductive, 71
  successes, 302
  support, 28
  against VCI, 70-71
Osnos, Peter, 773

Pacification
  per Abrams, 16, 169, 273,
    281, 562
  and advisors, 109
  per Bunker, 143
  per Colby, 60, 105, 122-23,
    149-50, 366-67, 459-60
  definitions, 177, 286-88

economic effects, 748
effects of Tet 1968 on, 60
effects per POW, 508
enemy attacks on, 108-109,
    123
enemy propaganda about,
    108
enemy reaction to, 106, 458
per Ewell, 261
and functioning govern-
    ment, 621
per Komer, 21
land reform, 303, 354, 424,
    459
  Land to the Tiller pro-
    gram, 576, 679
and lowest provinces, 681
military support for, 96-97
momentum, 235-36, 406-
    407
name change, 487-88, 496-
    97
navy support for, 212
obscure hamlets, 201
and "One War" concept,
    105
operations in IV Corps,
    186-87
organized, 220, 290
Pacification and Develop-
    ment Plan for 1970, 306
pause in, 157-58
plan for 1969, 62, 105-106
police, 367, 457, 520, 521
program renamed, 753
progress, 220, 239, 240,
    272, 273, 282, 287, 330,
    360-61, 394, 475-76,
    506, 521, 614, 620, 684,
    718, 748, 758, 767-68
priority of effort to, 281
regression, 424, 671
security for, 290, 376
in southern I Corps, 211-12,
    242
status of APC at end 1968,
    96-97
Strategic Hamlets, 117
and Thieu, 106, 122-23,
    146, 150, 273, 280, 284,
    497
top priority, 273
training village officials,
    280, 284, 303, 459
and troop behavior, 285-86
and VCI neutralization, 282
and Viet Cong, 143

Vietnamese taking lead, 497
vulnerability, 479
Packard, David, 125, 299-300
Palmer, Desmond, 284
Paris peace talks, 26, 29, 670
  allies re POW repatriation,
    751
  and battlefield events, 39,
    160
  and cease-fire possibilities,
    216
  characterized by Bunker, 99
  and design of RVNAF, 184
  enemy achievements, 134,
    722-23
  enemy objectives, 147-48,
    491
  enemy stance, 214, 216,
    518-19, 776-77
  and enemy propaganda, 57
  Le Duc Tho, absence of,
    196
  and infiltration, 224-25
  Nixon 14 May 1969 pro-
    posal, 312
  outlook of U.S. delegates,
    65
  reaction of U.S. public, 99
  RVN reluctance to partici-
    pate, 98, 146, 366
  secret sessions revealed,
    296
  Thieu expectations, 182
  U.S. commitment to mutual
    withdrawal, 510
  and U.S. domestic events,
    39-40
Paveway, 126
Peers, Lt. Gen. William R., 6,
    53, 103
  on Accelerated Pacification
    Campaign, 50
  and ammunition expendi-
    tures, 62
  on ARVN, 13
  on ARVN outlook, 83
  dispositions criticized, 67
  offering troops, 109
  operating with ARVN, 18
  on People's Self-Defense
    Force, 50
  reducing advisors, 115
People's Self-Defense Force,
    50, 91
  per Colby, 105, 366, 457,
    483
  decision to create, 457

evolution, 496
goals and achievements, 97,
98, 106, 273, 506
missions, 204
organization, 399
split into combat and support categories, 330
strength figures, 330
and Thieu, 598
training, 330, 404
per Vann, 50-51
and weapons, 105, 297,
457, 483, 506
Phoenix program, 52
capturing VCI members,
105, 261, 381
per Colby, 61, 105, 273,
381, 389, 457-58, 496
definitions, 404, 458, 496
evidence of effectiveness,
527, 692
per Ewell, 261
goals and achievements, 97,
261, 330-31, 353, 482,
496, 524
government policy for, 273
lagging, 282
and Police Field Force, 61,
792
presidential decree, 61, 105
publicity program, 331
suspect handling, 671
U.S. intelligence augmentation, 66
Phong, Lt. Gen. Tran Thanh,
273
per Abrams, 520, 561, 574
praised by Colby, 280-81
Phouma, Souvanna, 174, 210,
340, 502
Phu, Maj. Gen. Pham Van,
183-84, 575, 664-65
Phuong Hoang. See Phoenix
Pig Rule, 387, 571
Pike, Douglas, 51
Pink, Col. J. T., 76
Polgar, Thomas, 801
Political warfare, 126
Popkins, Professor, 286
Population security, 15, 16
Potts, Maj. Gen. William E.,
158, 187, , 221-22
Prairie Fire, 78, 174
President's Foreign Intelli-
gence Advisory Board
(PFIAB), 449-50
PROVN (Program for the Paci-

fication and Long-Term
Development of
Vietnam) Study, 49
Psychological operations and
warfare, 182-83, 448

Quang, Lt. Gen. Dang Van, 97
Quat, Phan Huy, 107

Rasmussen, Maj. Gen. Henry
A., 158, 825
Reagan, Gov. Ronald, 678-79
Redeployment, xix, 91, 230,
269, 365, 504
acceleration, impact of,
617-18
approaches to, 231, 634
Arc Light sortie reductions
and, 282
base camp dismantled, 618
briefing for Vy on, 222-24
budgetary impacts on, 256,
266-67, 269-72, 282,
353, 444-45, 497
capabilities, essential, to
retain, 749
ceilings, effects of, 258
combat units, role of
remaining, 611
and congressman's letter,
311
constrained by ARVN limi-
tations, 235
criteria, 231, 233, 256
and critics, 311
and cross-border operations,
162
crossover point in, 256, 257
and discussion with GVN,
223, 233-34, 464, 498
and draft calls, 444
during Easter Offensive,
864-65, 877
Easter Offensive impact on,
810-11, 828
effect of, 364, 496
"Project Enhance" han-
dling, 865
per Ewell, 265
flexibility gone, 497, 617-
18
and FWMAF redeploy-
ments, 618
GVN reaction to, 230, 232,
234, 310, 314
headquarters reductions,
504, 761, 865

and impediments, 209
impractical while NVA
remain, 283
and in-country reassign-
ments, 307
inevitability of, 234-35
initial increment, 230, 236
to MAAG level, 365, 604,
617
marine-heavy option, 306,
324, 330, 445
and Nixon, 311
and NSSM-36 planning,
306
Op Plan 208/208A, 688,
749
pace of, 445-46, 498
and Packard observations,
314-15
and parity, 269
Phase I, 256
Phase II, 256-57
Phase III, 256, 306-307,
323-24, 329-30
Phase IV, 256, 365
Phase V, 365
Phase VI, 257, 365
planning at MACV, 148-49,
231-33, 308-11
and POW issue, 616
priorities, 379
progress, 300, 306, 313
psychology of, 348
recommendations by
MACV, 283-84, 306-
308, 314, 315, 445
residual force, 148, 184,
257, 308, 330, 369, 708
risk apportionment, 231
and Rosson views, 311-12
and RVNAF I&M, 308
second increment planning,
230-31
security of remaining
forces, 642-43
sensitivity of planning data,
233
service interests, 324-25,
445
and shifting combat support
to the Vietnamese, 283
solidarity of U.S. leaders in
RVN, 235
sortie rates, 256, 258, 267,
271, 282, 307
stand-down considerations,
325

continued
  Starry briefings, 230-33,
    256-58
  structure remaining, 257
  sustaining force posture,
    688
  tactical air sortie alloca-
    tions, 256, 282
  tasks in the U.S. to receive,
    235, 310
  and Thieu reaction, 310,
    348
  and threat estimate, 308-
    309
  timing considerations, 232,
    234
  total withdrawal goal stated,
    616-17
  transitional force, 760-61
  transitional support level,
    330, 504, 617
  unilateral withdrawal, 184,
    186
  and U.S. political factors,
    445-46
  Washington outlook, 257,
    258, 310, 314-15, 444-
    46
  Wheeler views, 148-49
Refugees
  assistance to, 105, 459
  displaced by fighting, 105
  magnitude of problem, 105,
    149, 212, 313, 330, 459,
    681
  moving into secured areas,
    85
  progress in assisting, 149
  resettlement goals, 106
  returning to villages, 280
Regional Forces and Popular
    Forces (RF/PF), 91
  per Abrams, 126, 176, 347
  accomplishments, 699
  assisting, 267-68
  carrying the burden, 681
  casualties sustained as indi-
    cator, 303
  per Colby, 60, 105, 345,
    451
  compared to ARVN, 181
  per Cushman (USMC), 50
  in delta, 341
  equipment upgrading, 20-
    21, 69, 105, 172, 242,
    300

expansion, 49, 60, 105, 164,
  224, 366, 451, 457
improvement initiatives, 60
integrated into ARVN, 448
and mobile advisory teams,
  115
moonlighting, 212
night operations, 103, 403-
  404
performance, 21, 131, 181,
  228, 242, 247, 451, 457
Popular Force effectiveness,
  496, 517
Popular Force expansion,
  274, 292, 306
Popular Force missions,
  204, 399
Popular Force M-16s, 300
strength, 748
weaponry, 60
Republic of Korea (ROK)
  forces, 12, 16, 17, 62,
  241
Republic of Vietnam
  border areas, importance of,
    222-23
  Buddhist uprising, 117
  cities categorized, 75
  combating corruption, 146
  coup potential, 748
  and democratic institutions,
    146
  economy, 146
  fiscal matters, 150, 438
  flood relief, 503
  full mobilization, 98
  government characterized,
    98, 215-16
  initiative, seizing the, 397
  manpower, 143-44, 145
  near self-sustaining, 657
  police, 204, 273, 367, 404
  political considerations, 26,
    107
  situation, 143, 192
  suspicion of U.S., 117
  U.S. military and economic
    aid to, 604-605, 661,
    717, 718-19
  versus Viet Cong but not
    NVA, 150
Republic of Vietnam Armed
    Forces
  air force, 221, 295, 398
  cooperation with Cambo-
    dians, 181, 184, 187

desertions, 176, 242, 283,
  306, 671, 771
equivalencies to U.S.
  forces, 289
expansion, 185, 283, 365
general officers, 294-95
higher hurdles for RVNAF,
  308, 312, 686
I&M (improvement and
  modernization), 143, 150
  adequacy, 202-203
  army program complete,
    283
  artillery, 472
  budget shortfalls and,
    368-69, 370
  capabilities contem-
    plated, 184, 185
  completion dates, 234
  CRIMP, 442, 456, 617,
    686
  force structure, 185, 473,
    510
  objectives, 150, 184-85
  Phase III (Consolidation
    Phase), 308, 368-69
  practicality of acceler-
    ating, 186
  Rosson views, 257
  tank unit, medium, 748
  and Territorial Forces,
    283
  tracking, 177
improvements, 113, 492
leadership, 149, 283, 573,
  790
Joint General Staff, 82
manpower, 143-44, 145,
  150, 176, 185, 242, 283,
  306, 369, 619, 876
marines, 748
navy, 103, 186
new division (3rd), 717,
  730, 735, 747, 876
in pacification support, 306
percentages by component,
  347
reorganization, 448
total force, 289
two main deficiencies, 643
upgraded equipment, xix
See also Army of the
  Republic of Vietnam
  (ARVN); Regional
  Forces and Popular
  Forces (RF/PF)

Reserve components, 36, 42-43
Residual force (U.S.), 148, 184
Resor, Stanley R.
    on budget crisis, 444-45
    on the Congress, 446
    on domestic support for the war, 447
    on enemy strategy and successes, 604
    on redeployment, 445
    visiting Vietnam, 251, 444-47, 599-609
Revolutionary Development cadre
    assessed by Colby, 290
    headed by Phong, 273
    lacking M-16s, 273
    reduced emphasis on, 109
    reduced in size, 273
Rice
    per Abrams, 498
    harvest, 717
    IR-5 and IR-8 miracle rice, 103, 149-50, 303
    production goals, 303
    seized in caches, 170, 399, 414, 667
Ripley, Capt. John W., 807
Rives, Lloyd, 437, 440, 478
Rockpile, 70, 110-11
Rome plows, 20, 119-20
Rosson, Gen. William B.
    advocates bending rules of engagement, 328
    on ARVN, 13
    baffled, 461
    on B-52 use, 13
    complaints about cable reading load, 319
    on overaggressive advisors, 238
    on redeployment criteria, 257
    on RVNAF I&M, 257
Rostow, Walt W., 42, 107
Rules of engagement, 139
    for aerial retaliation, 190-91, 327-28
    along Cambodian border, 77-78
    re cross-border operations, 161
    Townsend advocates violating, 80-81
Rusk, Dean, 42, 107
Russell, Sen. Richard, 678

SAC (Strategic Air Command), 575-76, 810
Saigon
    allied forces protecting, 4, 20, 106
    appropriate forces for defense, 252
    bombing in defense of, 6
    CMD briefings attended by Abrams, 188
    comparative security of, 351
    Easter Offensive, during, 853
    enemy designs preempted, 251
    enemy outlook as assessed, 15, 53
    enemy rocketing, 132, 403
    firepower restrictions, 465-66
    first priority, 150-51
    importance per Abrams, 84
    police, 168, 220, 252
    population, 674
    protected, 199, 241
    punishing negligent defenders, 168
    rated C category, 319
    retaliation for rocketing, 133
    rocketing by enemy, 167
    terrorism in, 125, 216, 640
    wall proposed for, 351
Salzer, Rear Adm. Robert S., 806
Sanctuaries, 110
Savoeut, Lt. Col. Um (FARK), 95, 123
Scherrer, Edward, 440
Schwengel, Cong. Frederick, 431-32
2nd Infantry Division (ARVN), 29, 43, 75, 128
    commanded by Toan, 258
    on Laotian border, 176
    performance, 294, 508
SEER report, 6
Shackley, Theodore G.
    conducting "private" intelligence system, 116
    re coup potential, 127
    on Laos gains, 280
    on residual hard core enemy, 280

support provided, per Potts, 252
    on Vien per Abrams, 801
Shaplen, Robert, 569, 676
Shultz, George, 482-84
Sigma operations, 22
Signals intelligence, 4
Sihanouk, Norodom
    assessed by Abrams, 68, 347
    re bombing in Cambodia, 225
    changing outlook, 74
    character, 140, 440
    denial of complicity in supplying Communists, 252
    out of Cambodia, 342
    on Communists in Cambodia, 452
    overthrow, 400, 408
    in Peking, 395
    role in supplying Communists, 58, 105, 217
Sihanoukville (Kompong Son)
    Abrams's view, 215, 247, 285
    acknowledging VC presence, 285
    blockade, possible, 157
    Cambodian government payoff to VC, 217
    and Chinese shipments to VC, 321
    and CIA denial of enemy use, 182, 480
    closing to enemy use, 453
    deliveries gap, 216-17
    distribution from, 480
    as enemy supply port, 85-86, 94-95, 105, 120, 123-24, 135-36, 252, 364, 367-68, 453
    and Graham assessment, 168, 215, 218
    impact of closing, 635
    Kissinger interest in, 215
    McCain complaint about, 218
    and rice delivery via, 302
    Saigon Station (CIA) outlook on, 215, 218
    Washington view of, 105
SLAR imagery, 92, 121
Smith, Brig. Gen., 544
Son Tay raid, 527

South Vietnam. *See* Republic of Vietnam

Starry, Col. Donn A., 230-33, 256-58

Stars & Stripes, 22, 24, 39, 427, 464, 743

Statistics, 37, 85, 142, 195

Steel Tiger, 96

Stennis, Sen. John, 656

Stevenson, Sen. Adlai E., III, 654, 661

Stilwell, Lt. Gen. Richard G., 100-101, 171, 744

Stone, Maj. Gen. Charles, 9-10, 18, 83

Sullivan, Leonard, 703

Sullivan, William H., 86, 440
  agreement with Russians, 210
  conducting "private" intelligence system, 116
  interference with bombing, 160, 169-70, 175, 199-200
  interference with Vang Pao, 189
  views on interdiction, 104

Summer 1969 Campaign
  attacks by fire, 200, 211
  COSVN guidance, 200
  effect on pacification, 212
  high points, 200, 239, 243
  instructions, 254
  level of activity, 219
  and lull, 239-40
  resupply difficulties postulated, 211
  summarized, 211
  targets, 200-201

Sutherland, Lt. Gen. James W. Jr., 546, 628-29

Swank, Amb. Emory C., 466, 476-78, 716

Symington, Sen. Stuart, 653

Systems Analysis (OSD), 109

Tactics
  per Abrams, 23, 56, 62-63, 64, 67, 103, 246-47, 655, 829-30
  area security, 201-209
    and Colby concerns, 206-207
    defined, 203
    and destructive responses, 202

effects on enemy, 204
endorsed by Wheeler, 277
and endorsement of concept, 205-206, 207
and Ewell objections, 206, 207, 208-209
and Ewell subsequent agreement, 261
and Hau Nghia Province as test case, 205
and HES category C deficiencies, 205
in MACV Strategic Objectives Plan, 203
purpose, 330
U.S. support for, 205
zones, 203-204
artillery helilift, 242
per Corcoran, 22-23
per Ewell, 56
of Marines, 68
and PROVN implemented, 201-205
and search and destroy critiqued, 202
small-unit operations, 101
summarized, 253
per Townsend, 113
against VCI, 68, 69

Talbott, Maj. Gen. Orwin C., 137

Tam, Gen., 291

Tarpley, Maj. Gen. Thomas M., 847-48

Task Force Clearwater, 76

Task Force 117, 76

Tchepone, 104, 174-75, 262

T-Day planning, 185-86, 310

Territorial Forces. *See* Regional Forces and Popular Forces

Tet Offensive (1968)
  per Abrams, 55, 164, 308-309, 572
  per Bunker, 98, 144
  and casualty reduction, 139
  decision for, 216
  duration, 173
  effect on South Vietnamese, 14, 98
  effects in U.S., 98
  effect on VCI, 61
  enemy losses, 101, 110, 121
  and Giap per DIA, 219
  per Goodpaster, 162-63
  at Hue, 194

and Khe Sanh, 558, 778-79, 866
and MACV Forward, 836, 866-67
and pacification, 268
planning for, 72
and RVNAF performance in, 572
and U.S. performance in, 573
widespread fighting in, 255

Tet Offensive (1969), 167-68, 177
  per Abrams, 164-65, 824-25
  commencement, 133
  compared to Tet 1968, 164
  duration, 173
  enemy losses, 142, 167, 177, 198
  forecast, 124-25, 127
  intelligence, 173, 301
  outcome, 147, 216
  preemption, 168, 173
  refugees, 177
  reporting to Washington, 137
  U.S. casualties, 173
  use of B-52s, 151-52

Thai, Vu Van, 266

Thailand, 377

Thang, Maj. Gen. Nguyen Duc, 208

Thai forces, 241-42

Thanh, Maj. Gen. Nguyen Viet, 418-19

Thiep, Col. Pham Ngoc, 412

Thieu, President Nguyen Van, 519
  per Abrams, 113, 376, 444
  abilities, 106, 145
  and ARVN leaders, 574-75, 790
  Cambodians, cooperation with, 181, 184
  and flood relief, 503
  and general officer assignments, 294
  and the general reserve, 572
  leadership, 131, 133
  on negotiations, 99, 146-47
  on objectives, 201
  and pacification, 61, 62, 98, 106, 273
  and People's Self-Defense Force, 303, 376
  skill in Vann's view, 662

support by, 106, 109
and U.S. public opinion,
  147
view on negotiations, 141
view of Nixon administra-
  tion, 133
village chiefs, talking to,
  284
village elections, ordering,
  97
Thinh, Maj. Gen. Nguyen
  Xuan, 741, 790
Third Force, 125
3rd Marine Division (U.S.), 75,
  101, 117, 190
Third Offensive (1968), 31, 37-
  39
  per Bunker, 144-45
  duration, 173
  enemy losses, 101
  logistics preparation for, 72
  losses, 110
  preempted, 110
Tho, Le Duc, 196
Thompson, Sir Robert
  book, 259, 284-85
  characterized by Jacobson,
    285
  handling visit per Abrams,
    284-85
  on manpower, 772-73
  outlook on Vietnam War,
    259
  upcoming visit, 284
  on Viet Cong, 791
  visiting Vietnam, 290, 376-
    77, 471-73, 567-75, 675,
    769-75, 788-91, 875-76
Thu [?], Col., 521
Thuan, Lt. Gen. Pham Quoc,
  106
Thuy, Xuan, 40, 84
Tien, Nguyen Van, 360
Toan, Lt. Gen. Nguyen Van,
  258
Tompkins, Maj. Gen. Rathvon
  McC., 57
Tower, Sen. John, 427
Townsend, Maj. Gen. Elias C.,
  62, 65, 80-81
TRAP (Traffic Reporting and
  Analysis Program), 116
Tri, Lt. Gen. Do Cao, 43, 53
  and Accelerated Pacification
    Campaign, 50
  accomplishments, 537

health, 115
inexperience, 56
killed in action, 544
as "Patton of Parrot's
  Beak," 428-29
and President Thieu, 82, 84,
  114-15
pride, 276
tactics, 115
as trainer, 115
per Weyand, 494
Trien, Maj. Gen. Le Ngoc, 741
Trinh, Nguyen Duy (DRV), 51,
  253-54
Truong, Lt. Gen. Ngo Quang
  per Abrams, 243, 467, 574,
    639, 812
  appointed corps com-
    mander, 493-94
  as CG 1st ARVN Division,
    110, 221, 243, 258, 338,
    833
  as CG I Corps, 858
  as CG IV Corps, 812
  confident, 749
  per Stilwell, 50
  and Territorial Forces, 772
  during Tet 1968, 833-34
  per Weyand, 494, 573
Tuohy, William, 8
Turley, Col. G. H., 805-806,
  807, 808
25th Infantry Division
  (ARVN), 106, 318, 418,
  450
25th Infantry Division (U.S.), 4
  against base areas, 77
  forces in its area, 278
  in "One War," 117
  performance, 187, 318
  tactics, 246-47
  working with Vietnamese,
    471-72
21st Infantry Division
  (ARVN), 56
  operations in delta, 113-14
  performance, 237, 294
  in U Minh Forest, 571, 636
XXIV Corps, 101
22nd Infantry Division
  (ARVN), 115, 741
27th Regimental Landing
  Team (USMC), 26
23rd Infantry Division
  (ARVN), 115, 318
23rd Infantry Division (U.S.)

(Americal), 19, 29
and flawed tactics, 67, 391-
  92
ignoring "One War," 120,
  169, 326
U Minh Forest, 135
"Understandings"
  Abrams on, 122, 155, 245-
    46
  Bunker on, 148
  Davidson on, 122
  and DMZ, 104
  Ewell regarding, 227
  exposed, 118
  Goodpaster on, 122
  and Harriman misrepresen-
    tations, 227, 250-51
  and infiltration, 224-25
  violated by enemy, 132
Unger, Amb. Leonard, 377,
  716
United States
  antiwar elements, 180, 210,
    445
  Democratic convention, 39-
    40
  domestic outlook, 107
  objectives in Vietnam, 65-
    66
  political leaders, 268-69
  public opinion, 266
  questioning the war, 117
U.S. forces
  air operations from U
    Tapao, 120-21
  ammunition expenditures,
    18, 61-62
  casualties, 248, 422
  COMSEC, 349, 463
  cross-border operations
    contemplated, 159-60
  defeats, 248, 584
  dispositions, 151
  dolphins, 519
  drug abuse, 499-500, 607,
    614, 622-24, 649, 652-
    53, 705-706
  logistical excesses, 171
  mission, 139, 464
  naval gunfire support, 60
  naval operations, 76-77
  objectives, 142-43
  operations against enemy
    base areas, 18-19
  personnel, 303

continued

and political leaders, 268-
69
priorities, 150-51
public affairs guidance, 383,
462, 499
racial disharmony, 209, 267,
499-500
replacements, 298
safety, 379
size of deployed forces, 35
SOG operations, 78
spoiling attacks, 22
strategy, 509-510
strength, 298
success of, 66
supporting Phoenix pro-
gram, 66
USS *New Jersey*, 61, 173-
74
against VCI, 59
U.S. Joint Chiefs of Staff, 140
U.S. Military Assistance Command, Vietnam
(MACV), xx-xxii, 46-47,
295, 505, 619, 793
USS *Pueblo*, 132
U Tapao, 120-21

Vandegrift Combat Base, 110-
11, 160
Vang Pao, 189, 788, 790, 818
air support for, 303
on BDA per Brown, 278
praised by Abrams, 210
Vann, John Paul, 816
re Accelerated Pacification
Campaign, 50
re changing nature of the
war, 353, 406
re Easter Offensive, 844-45
on order of battle calculations, 352
re People's Self-Defense
Force, 50-51
prospects for eventual outcome, 353-54
Veth, Rear Adm. Kenneth L.,
22
Vien, Gen. Cao Van, 106, 685
on ARVN division com-
manders, 258
assessed by Abrams, 109,
800-801
briefing at MACV, 248-49,
289-90, 316-17, 346,

412, 492-93, 733-35
bypassed in chain of com-
mand, 82, 109
as Chairman, JGS, 114
and Phoenix program, 61
praised by Weyand, 491
Vien, Madame, 319
Viet Cong infrastructure (VCI)
access to the people, 478-
79, 801
attack on, 98
capabilities, 354
criteria pertaining to, 236
damaged, 191, 397
decimated in I Corps, 175-
76
definitions of, 220, 236
in delta, 279
function, 478
importance of, 46, 63-64,
106, 202, 381
measuring results of attack
on, 195, 236
neutralizing, progress in,
220-21, 236, 261
objectives, 303
persistence, 150
South Vietnamese outlook,
61
strength figures, 220, 381,
478
state of, 184, 387
Vietnamization, 91, 723
per Abrams, 568
and attitudinal surveys, 354-
55
per Bunker, 426
capabilities required, 184,
312
enemy concerns, 388
enemy parallel, 256
higher hurdles for South
Vietnamese, 256, 312
and Laird statement to
SFRC, 312-13
logistical, 608
LOC program, 498-99
navy, 608-609
objective of, 747
pace, 565
problem with Laird SFRC
statement, 312-13
rates, 234
supplemental food program,
338
as U.S. priority, 371

Vietnam War
cost of, 447
dates of key events, 708-13
interrelated aspects, 506
nature of, 397-98, 404
outcome, prospects for, 348,
353-54, 406, 426, 537,
570, 620, 679
reasons for U.S. involve-
ment, 661-662
Vinh Loc, Lt. Gen., 573, 574,
790
Vogt, Gen. John W., 848-49
Vy, Lt. Gen. Nguyen Van, 222-
24

Walker, Brig. Gen. Glenn, 394
Walsh, Lawrence E., 183-87
Warnke, Paul C., 35
Washington, D.C., 125
Wear, Brig. Gen. George E.,
730, 816
Weather
monsoons, 277, 596-97
rainfall, 67, 247, 274, 277,
484, 559
typhoon, 686
Weekly Intelligence Estimate
Updates (WIEU), xx
agenda, typical, 341
characterized by Davidson,
22
coverage directed by
Abrams, 18, 19, 46-47,
48, 75, 82, 128-29, 182,
386, 476, 479, 480, 630-
31
criticisms, 253, 294, 352,
386, 474, 683, 720
described by Abrams, 114
modifications, 22, 74
Westmoreland, Gen. William
C.
as Army Chief of Staff, 43,
221
backing Bunker on cross-
border operations, 163
as COMUSMACV, xvii-
xviii, 65, 132
confused, 450-51
and Dak To, 401
developments on his watch,
144
reassigned from Vietnam, 3
at Tet 1968, 255
unfounded theories, 138

visiting Vietnam, 450-51
West Point, 425
Wetherill, Maj. Gen. Roderick, 126
Weyand, Gen. Frederick C., 20
    on ARVN effectiveness, 12-13
    on B-52s, use of, 12
    Deputy COMUSMACV, becoming, 469
    on enemy strategy, 480
    on killing enemy, 12
    at Paris peace talks, 139, 285
    on RF/PF, 20-21
    visiting Vietnam, 288-89
    "Weydergrams" sent to him, 288
Wheeler, Gen. Earle G., 140, 219-221
    on area security, 277
    on B-52s as strategic reserve, 141-42
    bereft of ideas, 371
    on bitterness, 274
    on budget reductions, 270, 272, 274
    on cost saving measures, 270-72

on the Congress, 269, 274
on Fort Polk, 272
on Giap per DIA, 219
on the media, 269
on Nixon, 274
on oblivious political leaders, 268-69
on operating without a reserve, 141-42
on pacification, 273, 274
on potential disaster, 153-54
on progress, 274
on redeployment, 369
on RVNAF I&M, 274
on sending signals, 271
visiting Vietnam, 219-21, 268-77, 365-71
Whitehouse, Amb. Charles, 276, 804
Williams, Col. Lawrence H., 347
Wilson, Col. Wilbur, 51, 693
Wilson, Cong., 343-44
Wilton, Gen. Sir John, 284
Winter-Spring 1969-1970 Campaign, 254
Wynn, Lt. (briefer), 408, 435

Xuyen, Gen. Nguyen Huu, 197

Yen, Col. Lu, 540
Yorty, Sam, 662

Zais, Lt. Gen. Melvin, 111, 173
Zumwalt, Vice Adm. Elmo R. Jr.
    on allocation of forces, 165
    contrasting ship captains, 281
    and dealing with Vietnamese, 236
    and IV Corps operations, 69
    and pacification support, 212
    performance per Abrams, 275
    and redeployment timing, 236-37
    on Sihanoukville, 157

OTHER BOOKS IN THE MODERN SOUTHEAST ASIA SERIES

Vietnam and Beyond: A Diplomat's Cold War Education
ROBERT HOPKINS MILLER

Window on a War: An Anthropologist in the Vietnam Conflict
GERALD CANNON HICKEY

Military Medicine to Win Hearts and Minds: Aid to Civilians in the Vietnam War
ROBERT J. WILENSKY